Sir Thomas Herbert, Bart.
Travels in Africa, Persia, and Asia the Great

MEDIEVAL AND RENAISSANCE

TEXTS AND STUDIES

VOLUME 427

Sir Thomas Herbert, Bart.
Travels in Africa, Persia, and Asia the Great

Some Years Travels into Africa and Asia the Great,
especially describing the famous Empires of Persia
and Hindustan, as also divers other Kingdoms in
the oriental Indies
1627–30

The 1677 version edited with Introduction and Notes
by

John Anthony Butler

ACMRS
(Arizona Center for Medieval and Renaissance Studies)
Tempe, Arizona
2012

Published by ACMRS (Arizona Center for Medieval and Renaissance Studies),
Tempe, Arizona.
© 2012 Arizona Board of Regents for Arizona State University.
All Rights Reserved.

Library of Congress Cataloging-in-Publication Data

Herbert, Thomas, Sir, 1606-1682.
  [Relation of some yeares travaile]
  Sir Thomas Herbert, Bart. : travels in Africa, Persia, and Asia the great : some
years travels into Africa and Asia the great, especially describing the famous
empires of Persia and Hindustan, as also divers other kingdoms in the Oriental
Indies, 1627-30, the 1677 version / edited with introduction and notes by John
Anthony Butler.
       p. cm. -- (Medieval and Renaissance texts and studies ; v. 427)
  Includes bibliographical references.
  ISBN 978-0-86698-475-1 (acid-free paper)
1. Voyages and travels--History--17th century. 2. Iran--Description and
travel-- Early works to 1800. 3. India--Description and travel--Early works
to 1800. 4. Mogul Empire--Description and travel--Early works to 1800.
5. Herbert, Thomas, Sir, 1606-1682--Travel. I. Butler, John A. (John Anthony),
1950- II. Title. III. Title: Travels in Africa, Persia, and Asia the great.
  DS7.H54 2012
  910.4--dc23

                                                                    2012031582

Illustrations:
Images produced by ProQuest as part of Early English Books Online. Inquiries may be made to:
ProQuest, 789 E. Eisenhower Parkway, Box 1346, Ann Arbor, MI 48106-1346 USA
Telephone: 734-761-4700. Email: info@proquest.com. Web page: http://www.proquest.com

∞
This book is made to last. It is set in Adobe Caslon Pro,
smyth-sewn and printed on acid-free paper to library specifications.
Printed in the United States of America

This book is dedicated with much love to Sylvia Kùn,
and also to her son Gary Kozak,
both Asian travellers.

Acknowledgments

During the six years of editing this book, I have never ceased to be grateful for the co-operation of scholars in the various fields of endeavour covered by a project of this scope. No-one whose help I requested was un-cooperative or ungracious, and many went out of their way to help me track down some of the most obscure references and esoteric doctrines mentioned by Herbert. All I can do to repay them is to thank them by listing them, and hope that no-one was inadvertently omitted from the list. The best thing that the advent of e-mail has done for the scholarly world is to put us easily in touch with one another, and even though it may have taken valuable time for them to answer questions from someone they had never heard of, the response was overwhelming.

For help with India and Hinduism: Dr. Sanjay Subrahmanian; Professor Emeritus Dr. Klaus Klostermeier of the Department of Religion, University of Manitoba; Dr. Patrick Olivelle, Director of the Center for Asian Studies, University of Texas; Mr. William Dalrymple, author of many books on Mughal India, for publication suggestions and encouragement; Dr. Gavin Flood of the University of Wales, Lampeter, and Professor Ramesh Tiwari, Senior Scholar in Geography at the University of Manitoba for geographical assistance. For Persia: Dr. Mohsen Ashtiany of Columbia University and co-editor of the extremely useful *Encyclopedia Iranica*, who answered numerous requests with great patience and good humour and sent me many useful articles; John Perry, Emeritus Professor of Persian, University of Chicago; Professor Dick Davis of Ohio State University for answering questions about the *Shahnameh*, of which he is the translator; Dr. Reza Abouei of the University of Sheffield for architectural information on Shiraz; Dr. Willem Floor, an independent scholar who has written extensively on Safavid and Qajar Iran, and Elly Kluck at the Netherlands Institute of Art History for identifying Dutch artists in Persia and supplying articles as well as answering questions; Professor Bernadette Andrea of the University of Texas for sending me her article on Lady Sherley. Dr. William Poole of New College, Oxford, helped greatly in clearing up discrepancies in the footnotes on China and supplied historical information. Professor Marged Haycock of the University of Wales, Aberystwyth, patiently translated Welsh poetry for me and supplied information about the poets; Dr. Margaret Meserve helped me with some questions about the reception of Islam; Dr. Quentin Skinner, former Regius Professor of History, University of Cambridge, Dr. Jonathan Bonk, Editor of *The*

International Bulletin of Missionary Research, and Professor Jean-Paul Wiest of
the Ricci Institute, University of San Francisco all answered requests for identifications. A special thanks to Roy Rukkila and Todd Halvorsen at ACMRS for
their patience, skills, and hard work. Finally, I would like to thank Dr. Leslie
MacCoull of Arizona State University who carefully checked all the Latin quotations and much improved the translations (both mine and those of some of the
scholars I used) beyond measure, which taught me that after almost twenty years
of not looking at a Latin sentence I had no business setting about so overconfi-
dently the task of translation without getting a thorough accuracy check from an
outside source.

John Butler
University College of the North
The Pas, Manitoba, Canada

TABLE OF CONTENTS

INTRODUCTION

A good traveller has no fixed plans, and is not intent on arriving.
Lao Tzu

The Life of Sir Thomas Herbert

Thomas Herbert, the eldest son of Christopher Herbert (1577–1625) and Jane Ackroyd of Foggathorpe in the East Riding of Yorkshire, was born in a house on The Pavement, York, on 2 November 1606.[1] His immediate family were merchants and aldermen; his grandfather, another Christopher Herbert (d. 1590), Governor of the Merchant Adventurers Company (1573–1575), had also been Lord Mayor of York in 1573, and with a little imaginative genealogy Thomas could also claim as relatives William Herbert, third earl of Pembroke, his brother Philip, later the fourth earl and Philip, the fifth earl, as well as Edward, baron Herbert of Chirbury and his brother the poet George Herbert, who were actually his third cousins twice removed. Like these other Herberts, Thomas appears to have taken considerable pride in his Welsh connections, which is reflected in his book as he claims Prince Madog of Gwynedd as the first discoverer of America, quotes Welsh poetry in the original, and finds Welsh etymologies for strange and distant place-names that had absolutely no connection with Wales whatsoever other than with a little ingenious twist they might just resemble a Welsh name.

After attending St. Peter's Grammar School in York, Herbert studied at both Oxford and Cambridge; records show him as a Commoner at Jesus College, Oxford, and shortly afterwards (1621), due to the influence of his maternal uncle Dr. Ambrose Ackroyd, at Trinity College, Cambridge, of which Ackroyd was a Fellow. He may also have done a short stint at the Inns of Court. He does not appear to have matriculated, but in the seventeenth century that mattered very little as the universities and Inns of Court were often seen as finishing-schools

---

[1] This house has been beautifully restored and preserved by the York Conservation Trust. The Herberts had moved by 1618, and the house was then occupied by Sir Roger Jacques, who was successively Sheriff of York (1628), Lord Mayor (1630) and M. P. He was the great-great-grandfather of Laurence Sterne, the author of *Tristram Shandy*.

for young gentlemen rather than training for any particular profession. This is not to say that some of them did not put to use what they learned; indeed, Herbert's book is peppered with Latin tags and quotations from Ovid, Virgil, Tibullus, Tacitus, and Cicero as well as lesser-known Latin writers, some Greek ones, and a whole host of modern authorities on history, geography, religion, and travel from several countries, with some of whom he surely had become acquainted in his university years. The turning-point in Thomas Herbert's life came in 1626, the year after his father's death, for it was in that year that he was introduced by his father's younger brothers William and James to his noble cousin the earl of Pembroke, who held the post of Lord Chamberlain and was a member of His Majesty's Privy Council.

William Herbert, third earl of Pembroke (1580–1630), was a cultured, intelligent patron of arts and literature, a poet himself (he was a pupil of Samuel Daniel) and possibly the "fair youth" of Shakespeare's sonnets, a claim that is much disputed by scholars, as is a similar one that Pembroke was the "Mr. W. H." to whom the sonnets were dedicated. What is beyond dispute is that he was a good friend of Francis Bacon and the lover of Lady Mary Wroth, his cousin and the author of *The Countess of Montgomery's Urania*, by whom he had two children. He also provided an annuity for Ben Jonson. Pembroke had an interest in the wider world as well; he promoted various colonial and industrial ventures and in 1612 he invested in the Bermuda Company and contributed to the establishment of the Virginia Company. A few decades later the earl of Clarendon called Pembroke "the most universally beloved and esteemed of any man of that age," a rather hyperbolic tribute, perhaps, but not wholly undeserved. It was Pembroke who likely secured for his young relative a position in the embassy of Sir Dodmore Cotton to the Shah of Persia, but what exactly made him encourage Thomas to travel cannot be known. Perhaps the earl had simply used intuition or picked up on something the young man had said in private conversation, but whatever the reason Thomas Herbert embarked on 23 March 1627, and would not return to England until 4 April 1630. He was twenty years old, the same age the celebrated Ibn Battuta had been when he set out from Morocco in 1325 on his own extensive travels to Persia, India, Ceylon, and China.

During Herbert's years out of England, the country had been careening towards the crisis that would culminate in the Civil War. Shortly before Herbert's return, Charles I had dissolved Parliament and imposed direct rule on England, Ireland and Scotland, working with his ministers Thomas Wentworth, later earl of Strafford, and Archbishop William Laud, to consolidate secular and religious power in the king's name. The earl of Pembroke, meanwhile, did not support these actions of his master, and three years earlier he had also voiced his opposition to the Duke of Buckingham, the royal favourite whom Charles had inherited from his father and whose policies had included a disastrous defeat for England by the French at the Isle of Rhé (1627), an event chronicled and whitewashed by Lord Herbert of Chirbury. When Thomas returned from his travels he was invited by his cousin Pembroke to dine with him, but the earl died suddenly the day before and was succeeded in the title by his brother Philip (1582–1650). He was a reputedly rough-edged man but one who nonetheless may have shared his brother's interest in literature to a certain extent, as he extended patronage to the dramatist Philip Massinger. His wife, the former Lady Anne Clifford, described her husband in her *Diary* as "of a very quick apprehension, a sharp understanding, very crafty withal, and of a discerning spirit, but extremely choleric by nature."[2] Like his brother, he also had some interest in colonial and trade ventures. Philip Herbert was a supporter of the Parliamentary cause (he was made Chancellor of Oxford by the Parliamentary government), which meant that Thomas Herbert would have to make a decision about where his own loyalties lay, and he, too, elected to support Parliament when the Civil War broke out in 1640. But we are getting ahead of the story, as Herbert himself might have said; whatever anxiety he may have felt when his powerful cousin died seems to have influenced his decision to leave court life and spend a year in France (1630–1631); he did, however, dedicate his book to the new earl and maintained cordial ties with the Pembrokes throughout the next decade or so, although there is little evidence to show that Philip Herbert took much of an active interest in his young "cousin's" career after this time, although Herbert did remember to dedicate the book to him.

It was probably the Pembroke connection, nevertheless, which helped Thomas in making the acquaintance of Sir Walter Alexander, Gentleman-Usher to Charles I, whose daughter Lucy he married in 1632, and by whom he had ten children. It was almost certainly either the earl or Alexander who introduced him to the king, who offered Herbert the position of Esquire of the Body, a rather strange appointment which could be taken up only if one of the incumbents died in office, but it probably later played a part in securing Herbert the job of safeguarding the king in captivity a few years later. Herbert retired completely from court life once again, this time to his small estate at Tinterne in 1634; he published the first edition of the *Travels* the same year, and for the next few years occupied himself with business and family matters. At about this time he seems to have become acquainted with Thomas, Lord Fairfax, the grandfather of the Parliamentary general, with whom he frequently corresponded and with whose family he cultivated close ties which would later on become of benefit to him.

Upon the outbreak of the Civil War, Herbert initially chose a military career, and by 1642 was serving under Sir Thomas Fairfax, later Lord General of the Parliamentary army, with whom he remained until 1647. Herbert obviously formed a personal relationship with Fairfax, who provided a dedicatory poem to his book, and since Fairfax himself was a patron of literature as well as a poet and translator, they probably had some common interests. Fairfax also employed Andrew Marvell as a tutor to his daughter Mary, and it is tempting to think that

---

[2] Lady Anne Clifford, *The Memoir of 1603 and The Diary of 1616–1619*, ed. Katherine O. Acheson (Peterborough, Ontario: Broadview Editions, 2007), 55.

Herbert may have met Marvell, but there is no evidence. We do, however, catch a rare glimpse of Herbert during this time when he is mentioned by Thomas Daunt,[3] a fellow-member, together with Carew Ralegh, son of Sir Walter and a member of the Rump Parliament, of one of the commissions Herbert sat on, who stated in a letter to his father that "Mr. Herbert is a gentleman that understands Arabicke and Persian."[4] In May 1646 Herbert appeared as one of the Parliamentary officers arranging terms for the surrender of Oxford, which had been the king's headquarters throughout the Civil War.

In 1647 Herbert was appointed Parliamentary Commissioner and employed, together with Captains Anthony Mildmay, Silas Titus, and Robert Preston,[5] to attend the person of Charles I in captivity at Carisbrooke Castle on the Isle of Wight, a duty (he was Groom of the Bedchamber) which he faithfully carried out both there and later at Windsor until the execution of the king in 1649. This assignment probably owed something to Herbert's former employment as an Esquire of the Body, and he found himself in the position of being trusted both by Parliament and by Charles himself, who appears to have liked Herbert and who received humane treatment at his hands. Again, one is tempted to invoke the "fly on the wall" metaphor and wonder whether Herbert and Charles ever talked about travelling in exotic countries; we know that Charles had an interest in Persian art and antiquities, as he had been instrumental in sending Nicholas Wilford to Persia in 1637 to collect them and also study the silk industry and its use of colour.[6] They certainly formed a close relationship; Herbert played bowls with the king on several occasions and even mentioned a new bowling pavilion going up, "a pretty shed," Herbert wrote, "to rest in and retire when the weather

---

[3] Thomas Daunt (1619–1658) was a member of the family which owned Owlpen Manor in Gloucestershire from 1464 to 1803. The letter is written to his father, who was High Sheriff of County Cork in Ireland. The family owned extensive estates in both Ireland and Monmouthshire. This is the only direct mention I have found of Herbert's linguistic abilities; he lists words in various languages and is interested in etymology, but nowhere does he state directly that he knew both Persian and Arabic. Daunt was writing in the mid-1640s, so it is possible that after his trip Herbert may have learned these two languages, from whom we do not know, but we may suppose that his acquaintance included academics or others, such as Richard Williams the interpreter.

[4] Sir Geoffrey Mander, ed., "A Civil War Diary by Thomas Daunt of Owlpen, 1645–1650," *Owlpen Papers* 59–69, here 63. www.owlpen.com/archives.shtml.

[5] Anthony Mildmay was Gentleman-Usher and Carver. Silas Titus (1622–1704), soon to become a royalist, was equerry. He was later said to have attempted to help the king escape, and afterwards fled to Holland with other royalists. He fought with Charles II at Worcester and later wrote a pamphlet entitled *Killing no Murder* (1657) in which he advocated the assassination of Oliver Cromwell; in 1660 was appointed Groom of the Bedchamber to Charles II. Robert Preston was Sewer and Keeper of the Robes.

[6] Ian Atherton and Julie Sanders, eds., *The 1630's: Interdisciplinary Essays on Culture and Politics in the Caroline Era* (Manchester: University of Manchester Press, 2006), 114.

was unseasonable."[7] On another occasion he "blistered" John Reading, the Page of the Backstairs, for allowing Colonel Hammond, the Governor of the Carisbrooke Castle, to search the king's room (Jones, *Royal Prisoner*, 80). Herbert was present at Charles's death, although he himself later recollected in *Threnodia Carolina* that he was too emotionally overwrought to attend the king on the actual scaffold, a sad duty which was left to Bishop William Juxon. What seems in little doubt is that by this point Herbert had, at least in his heart, abandoned his support of the Parliamentary cause because of his personal contact with the captive Charles, who no longer seemed to Herbert to be the monster and "Man of Blood" represented by anti-royalist propaganda. In any event, as he stepped out of the window at Whitehall onto the scaffold Charles presented Herbert with his silver watch and cloak, as well as leaving him a number of books, amongst them a First Folio of Shakespeare.[8] Herbert, together with Anthony Mildmay, discreetly arranged with the Parliamentary authorities for the burial of Charles I at Windsor Castle. After the death of Charles I, Herbert, who still retained the good graces of Parliament, was sent to Ireland with another Parliamentary commission, and in 1651 he became its Secretary. In 1658 his daughter Elizabeth married the regicide Colonel Robert Phayre,[9] and in July of that year Herbert was knighted by the Protector's son Henry Cromwell, then Lord Lieutenant of Ireland, an honour Herbert held only until the Restoration, when all Protectoral titles were annulled.

The experience with the king must have haunted Herbert for the rest of his life, and although he wrote an account of Charles's last days, *Threnodia Carolina*,[10]

---

[7] Jack D. Jones, *The Royal Prisoner: Charles I at Carisbrooke* (London: The Trustees of Carisbrooke Castle Museum, 1978), 76.

[8] For full details, see Norman H. Mackenzie, "Sir Thomas Herbert of Tintern, a Parliamentary Royalist," *Historical Research* 29 (1956): 32–86.

[9] Robert Phayre (c. 1619–1682) came from Devonshire, where his father was a clergyman who went to Ireland and became a gentleman-farmer. In 1641 the Irish Confederates, a group of discontented Catholics, revolted against Charles I and the Phayres lost their land, at which point Robert joined the forces of the earl of Inchiquin to quell the rebellion. In 1648 Inchiquin declared his support of Charles I, but Phayre did not, instead joining the New Model Army. He was appointed, together with Colonel Hercules Huncks, to oversee the execution of the king, but both colonels refused to sign the order, notwithstanding which Phayre returned to Ireland in the service of Lord Broghill, later the earl of Orrery, brother of the chemist Robert Boyle and a well-known dramatist. Phayre was given land taken from the Confederates and was appointed Governor of Cork. In 1660 he was arrested and clapped in the Tower of London, but never tried and released two years later, staying with Herbert for "reasons of health" (*CSP Domestic Series 1661–1662*, 290). Phayre's connection with Broghill, who was a secret royalist, probably saved his skin and may also have helped Herbert.

[10] Extracts from *Threnodia Carolina* were published, apparently at Herbert's request, by Anthony à Wood in both *Athenae Oxonienses* (3: 15–41) and *Fasti Oxonienses* (2: 25,

he did not publish the work until 1678, and even then in an incomplete version. This would seem to obviate any charges that Herbert was opportunistic or self-serving; Charles II had raised Herbert to a baronetcy in 1660 not for writing *Threnodia Carolina* (although he may have known about it) but for the decency and compassion with which Herbert had carried out his duties as the king's guardian. It is likely that some of Herbert's royalist friends had made representations to the king on this matter; Sir William Dugdale, for example, referred to Herbert in 1681 as "that learned person who hath been honoured with the title of baronet in testimony of the gracious sense His Majesty hath of his dutiful demeanour and perfect fidelity in those perilous times to his dear father of blessed memory."[11] Six years after the Restoration, following the Great Plague and the Fire of London, we find Herbert back in York, where he settled for the rest of his life in Petergate House; he also had a town house in Westminster and of course retained his Tinterne estate, to which he repaired every so often, but York seems to have been his preferred place of residence. His wife Lucy died in 1671 and Herbert remarried, this time to Elizabeth Cutler, the niece of the earl of Bridgewater, who would survive him by fourteen years.[12] They had one child, Elizabeth, who died in infancy (1675).

Herbert did little further writing other than the revision of his *Travels* up to 1665 and *Threnodia Carolina*, but it was during the latter years of his life that he assisted Sir William Dugdale with his *Monasticon Anglicanum, or the History of the Ancient Abbeys, Monasteries, Hospitals, Cathedrals and Collegiate Churches with their Dependencies* (1655–1673), concentrating on the transcription of parish

---

131, 138, 143–45, 147, 150). It was published in full by Christopher Goodall in his *Tracts* (1702), as *Memoirs* by G. Nicoll (1813), and included by Allan Fea in his *Memoirs of the Martyr King* (London: John Lane, 1905). More recently, Roger Lockyer has edited Herbert's account of the trial of Charles I, together with that of John Rushworth (London: Folio Society, 1960). The story given is that Sir William Dugdale, then Garter King of Arms, had contacted Herbert in 1676 to ask him whether Charles I had ever mentioned where he wanted to be buried, and after Herbert had given a detailed reply, Dugdale requested that he "write a treatise of the actions and sayings of the king, from his first confinement to his death." The result was the basis for *Threnodia Carolina*. Nicoll also printed Herbert's letter to Dugdale (Chalmers, 382). See "Sir Thomas Herbert," in Alexander Chalmers, *General Biographical Dictionary* (1812–1817), 17: 380–82.

[11] Robert Davies, "Sir Thomas Herbert," *Yorkshire Archaeological and Topographical Journal*, Part iii (1870): 182–214, here 209.

[12] Elizabeth Cutler (d. 1696) was the daughter of Sir Gervase Cutler of Stainborough in Yorkshire, a Royalist soldier who was killed at the siege of Pontefract Castle (1645), and his second wife Lady Magdalen Egerton (1618–1664), daughter of the earl of Bridgewater, before whose brothers and sisters Milton's *Comus* had been presented in 1634. Sir Gervase Cutler was Elizabeth's second husband; the first was Henry Edmunds.

records.[13] Anthony à Wood tells us in *Athenae Oxonienses* that Herbert also, "at the proposal of [Jan] de Laet, his familiar friend living in Leyden . . . translated some books of his *India Occidentalis*, but the completion of them was hindered by some other business,"[14] and of course he found time to issue one final edition of the *Travels*.[15] These activities indicated that he, like so many other gentlemen with adequate means and leisure, not to mention a propensity for pedantry and esoteric learning, spent his retirement in antiquarian pursuits and collected oriental manuscripts which he left to various collections upon his death. Another good friend was Anthony à Wood, with whom Herbert shared his interests in historical research, and Herbert also knew Elias Ashmole,[16] who sent him books and with whom he corresponded. Herbert died at his Petergate house on 1 March 1682 and was buried in St. Crux churchyard, where his monument may still be seen. He was succeeded in the baronetcy by his only remaining son Henry (1640–1687); he was also survived by three daughters from his first marriage, Teresa, Elizabeth, and Lucy. The baronetcy itself lasted only until the death of Sir Charles Herbert (1680–1740), the sixth of the family to hold the title.

As to Herbert's personality, what can be gleaned immediately from his writings is that he was a man of wide-ranging learning who liked to display it, and that he was sometimes rather over-interested in details such as the accurate

---

[13] Sir William Dugdale (1605–1686), a Royalist in the Civil War, was a genealogist and historian in addition to being probably the best-known antiquarian in England. He occupied successively the posts of Rouge Croix Pursuivant of Arms (1639–1644), Norroy King of Arms (1660), and Garter Principal King of Arms (1673). In addition to compiling the *Monasticon Anglicanum*, Dugdale also wrote, amongst other things, *A Short View of the Late Troubles in England* (1681), *The Antiquities of Warwickshire* (1656), and *The History of St. Paul's Cathedral* (1658). Of the *Monasticon*, David Douglas stated that it "illustrated almost every phase of English social and economic history in the Middle ages" and "taught English scholars the importance of charters for history, and it published these in such numbers that a comparative study of them became for the first time possible" (Stanley Mendyk, *Speculum Britanniae: Regional Study. Antiquarianism and Science in Britain to 1700* [Toronto: University of Toronto Press, 1988], 105).

[14] Anthony à Wood, *Athenae Oxonienses*, ed. Philip Bliss (London: Rivington et al., 1815), vol. 2: 692.

[15] Two papers by Herbert on St. John's Church, Beverley, and Ripon Collegiate Church (now Ripon Cathedral) were published by the historian Francis Drake in his *Eboracum: The History and Antiquities of the City of York* (London, 1736).

[16] Elias Ashmole (1617–1692), for whom the Ashmolean Museum at Oxford is named, was a politician, antiquarian, and mathematician. A Royalist during the Civil War, he became Windsor Herald of Arms at the Restoration, and wrote several works on heraldry; he was especially knowledgeable about the Order of the Garter. His second wife was Elizabeth, daughter of Sir William Dugdale. Ashmole was also one of the founder-members of the Royal Society (1661) and helped preserve the great botanical collections of John Tradescant.

measurement of latitude and longitude, the exact dimensions of water-tanks, or how big Shah Abbas's moustache was. He was not a man for whom brevity was the soul of wit or litotes a virtue, and his digressions, most of which were added in the later editions of his book, were likely the reason that an editor like Sir William Foster exercised his privileges so broadly on Herbert's text and why Jonathan Swift later made rude remarks about it. Yet prolixity and pedantry can sometimes be part of the charm, especially if the writer is not averse to poking a little gentle fun at himself, and Herbert does this from time to time, excusing himself for getting carried off on tangents and sometimes making himself look almost foolish. It is difficult not to smile, for example, as he describes what it is like to bounce around on the back of a camel when suffering from a fever, or to chuckle at his prim but nevertheless very interested remarks about Khwaja Nazar's pornographic paintings, "Ganymede boys," and other such matters. He never misses a thing, whether it be the origins of a word, the shape of Achaemenid hats, the speculative location of Ophir, how many wives Mohammed had, which mountain Noah's ark rested upon, what dodo flesh tasted like, the exact dimensions of turbans and Parsi "towers of silence," or educated guesses about just what all those Persians sculpted on the walls of Persepolis were doing. Thomas Herbert in his book is nevertheless engaging and enterprising; his first modern editor Sir William Foster wrote that when we read his book "our sympathies go with the high-spirited and good-humoured narrator, who makes so little of the hardships he encountered and never has anything but good to say of his companions,"[17] and this is a fair assessment. Herbert was a brave man for going on this adventure, albeit one who bristled with the prejudices and shortcomings of his time and class, but withal an extremely observant man, someone who thoroughly enjoyed what he was seeing and doing, and upon whom it had such a profound effect that he felt the need to write and re-write his experiences until he had perfected what he wanted to say about them and also how he wished to be remembered by posterity. "*Si monumentum requiris,*" one might say Latinistically with Herbert, "*lege.*"

Herbert and Travel Literature

Much has been written about early travel literature, and it is not the purpose of an introduction such as this one to rehash critical assessments and theories in order to demonstrate that the editor has read some of them. However, it is certainly germane to an edition of a work like this to try and put its author into the seventeenth-century context of travelling and attitudes towards the East, which

---

[17] Sir Thomas Herbert, *Travels in Persia 1627–1629*, ed. Sir William Foster (London: Routledge, 1928), xxxvii. This will be designated as *Herbert* in future footnotes.

is what will be done here, as well as to give at least an intimation of what recent scholarship has been saying.

"Travel in the younger sort," wrote Francis Bacon in his *Essays or Counsels Civil and Moral* (1625), "is a part of education; in the elder, a part of experience."[18] This well-known phrase is particularly suited to Thomas Herbert, who was barely twenty when he embarked on his travels, but who revised and re-revised his book over several decades, almost as if he were making the journey over and over again, fleshing out his descriptions, adding information that he had gathered from voracious reading and, most likely, from talking to other travellers. Justus Lipsius, whom Herbert cites, thought that "everyone can gaze, can wander, and can wonder, but to few it is given to seek, to search, to learn, and to attain to true policy, and wisdom, which is travelling indeed,"[19] and, as Lord Fairfax wrote in his prefatory poem, Herbert "travelled not with lucre sotted, / He went for knowledge, and he got it." Bacon also noted that if a young man wanted to be a successful traveller, he should seek "acquaintance with the secretaries and employed men of ambassadors" (*Major Works*, 375), which is exactly what young Herbert did when he secured himself, with Pembroke's help, an attachment to Sir Dodmore Cotton's embassy. This, of course, would allow the traveller to make the correct observations when he travelled, which, according to Bacon, should include "the courts of princes, specially when they give audience to ambassadors . . . the courts of justice . . . the churches and monasteries, with the monuments which are therein extant," as well as "antiquities and ruins; libraries; colleges . . . houses and gardens of state and pleasure" and a whole host of other things (*Major Works*, 374), all of which Herbert diligently did in his account. Reading Herbert often makes one feel that he had a copy of Bacon's Essays in his pocket as he travelled, but of course he did not, because he had left the shores of England well behind him in his wake the year before the Essays were published.

There was, however, a great deal of literature on travelling and indeed on the art of travelling which Herbert could have read prior to embarking on what was to be the greatest adventure of his long life. "The avid European reader of the latter half of the sixteenth century, desirous of knowing the world from his or her armchair," Alam and Subrahmanyam write, "had available to him or her texts in a variety of competing genres," and by Herbert's time they note that there was a veritable "explosion" of travel-writing.[20] Many writers, and Bacon was one of them, believed that travellers had a moral obligation to inform and educate their

---

[18] Francis Bacon, *The Major Works, including New Atlantis and the Essays*, ed. Brian Vickers (Oxford: Oxford University Press, 1996), 374.

[19] *A Direction for Travailers, Taken out of Justus Lipsius, and enlarged for the behoof of the Right Honourable Lord, the yong Earle of Bedford, being now ready to travel, 1592* (Amsterdam: Theatrum Orbis Terrarum, 1979), A4.

[20] Muzaffar Alam and Sanjay Subrahmanyam, *Indo-Persian Travels in the Age of Discoveries, 1400–1800* (Cambridge: Cambridge University Press, 2007), 338, 342.

readers, and Herbert strove in his book to address this obligation, or, as Chloe Chard puts it in the current language of travel-criticism, he undertook to provide "utterances in which the subject of commentary claims to be concerned primarily with the ordering of knowledge of the world" (*Grand Tour*, 9), that is, useful information for all readers, whether they were tourists, diplomats or would-be spies. Indeed, this explains why Herbert expanded the book over the years with references to many "authors." And, in the thirteenth century, Marco Polo had observed that "all the people who wish to know the various races of men and the peculiarities of the various regions of the world" (33) should read his book. Many writers besides Bacon thought that travel would improve manners, make people worldly-wise, and help them appreciate their own countries; "Travel is a second birth / Unto the children of another Earth," wrote Lord Herbert of Chirbury in 1608 (*Poems*, 14). The diplomat Sir Thomas Palmer (1540–1625), stated that travel was "an honourable and honest action of men . . . for a private benefit and necessity."[21] Thomas Coryate, of whom more below, thought that travelling "enchanced gentility" (b.4), as did some others.[22] Non-European travel-writers agreed; the seventeenth-century Persian poet and traveller Mufid Yazdi, for example, later wrote that travel was "the court where status is gained" (Alam and Subrahmanyam, *Indo-Persian Travels*, 1).[23]

Others, however, felt that travelling was at worst a dangerous and at best a frivolous activity, or at least one which no real gentleman would engage in, and Herbert himself admitted that his trip had been undertaken "in youth and haste" (552). As eminent an educator as Roger Ascham in *The Schoolmaster* (1570) had been an early proponent of the dangers, not to mention the evils of travel; if a young man were to go to Italy, Ascham had warned, "some Circe shall make of him, a plain Englishman, a right Italian,"[24] and in any case it was much less dangerous to read translations of Italian books than to venture to their country of origin and be exposed to strange customs, immorality, or popish practices.

---

[21] Sir Thomas Palmer, *An Essay of the means to make our travels into foreign countries the more profitable and honourable* (London, 1606), 1.

[22] Michael Strachan, *The Life and Times of Thomas Coryate* (Oxford: Oxford University Press, 1962). In addition, the earl of Essex is credited with having written letters of travel-advice to his young protégé Roger Manners, fifth earl of Rutland, who was doing the Grand Tour in Europe (1595–1596). The authenticity of the Essex-Rutland correspondence has been questioned, however. For details, see Paul E. Hammer, "Letters of Travel-advice from the Earl of Essex to the Earl of Rutland: Some Comments," *Philological Quarterly* 74 (1995): 317–26.

[23] Mufid ibn Najm ud-Din Yazdi embarked from Basra and landed in Surat (1671), after which he travelled extensively in the Mughal Empire and even worked for a time at the Emperor Aurangzeb's court. He wrote the *Jami'-i Mufidi* (1679), from which this quotation is taken. For details, see Alam and Subrahmanyam, *Indo-Persian Travels* 179ff.

[24] Roger Ascham, *The Schoolmaster*, ed. Laurence. V. Ryan (Ithaca: Cornell University Press, 1967), 62.

Ascham's attitude carried on down to later writers, who felt that travel made people snobbish, affected, and unpatriotic. "An affected traveller," sniffed Sir Thomas Overbury in 1613, "is a speaking fashion. He hath taken pains to be ridiculous and hath seen more than he hath perceived." The ultimate sin for this kind of traveller, Overbury thought, was that "he disdains all things above his reach and preferreth all countries before his own."[25] Bacon also feared that his traveller might become too critical of his own country or even try and imitate the clothes and customs of foreign parts. "Let his travel appear rather rather in his discourse than in his apparel," he admonished, "and in his discourse let him be rather advised in his answers than forward to tell stories, and let it appear that he doth not change his country's manners for those of foreign parts" (*Major Works*, 275–6). This sort of traveller was mercilessly pilloried by, amongst others, Ben Jonson and Lord Herbert of Chirbury; the latter wrote in his "Satyra Secunda" (1608) of some travellers that "When they come home, like Children, yet that be / Of their own bringing-up, all they learn is / Toyes, and the Language."[26] Lord Herbert may well have known his friend Ben Jonson's *Masque of Augurs* (1622), in which an Englishman by the rather odd Dutch-sounding name of Vangoose is described as someone who "is no Dutchman, sir, he is a Briton born, but hath learned to misuse his tongue in travel, and now speaks all languages in ill English."[27]

What sort of traveller, then, was Thomas Herbert? He says little about his motivations for travel beyond what he wrote in the dedication to the first edition of his book (1634) that "my desire to see took away my sight, as it fares with those who are suddenly taken with a killing beauty or gaze upon the sun." This statement is partly echoed by a contemporary traveller, Tobias Schneebaum, who felt similarly, although he elaborates more on the reasons for his desire. "I have a need to travel to distant corners of the world," Schneebaum writes, for "at times a yearning comes over me, an urgency to rid myself of the vestments of civilisation, to find a new kind of freedom, one not found at home."[28] In Herbert's case, we also know that it was "that noble Lord William, earl of Pembroke and the Lord

---

[25] Sir Thomas Overbury (and Others), *Characters*, ed. Donald Beecher (Ottawa: Dovehouse Editions, 2003), 209, 275–76.

[26] G. C. Moore Smith, ed., *The Poems English and Latin of Edward Lord Herbert of Cherbury* (Oxford: Oxford University Press, 1923; repr. New York: AMS Reprints, 1976), 14. Herbert wrote the satire whilst he himself was sojourning in France.

[27] Ben Jonson, *The Works of Ben Jonson*, ed. William Gifford (London: Camden Hotten; New York: Kessinger Reprints, n. d.), vol. 3: 163. Vangoose is said by some scholars to be a caricature of Inigo Jones, Jonson's collaborator in the masque, on the grounds that his strange English looks a bit like Welsh-inflected, hence Jonson's use of the word "Briton" rather than "Englishman."

[28] W. Zinsser, ed., *They Went: The Art and Craft of Travel Writing* (Boston: Houghton Mifflin, 1991), 157.

Powys who gave me my first encouragement to travel," as he tells us at the end of his book and that he wrote it for the "private" use of the earl (552). In the first edition of the book Herbert stated that he hoped "that these relations might find acceptance from that most noble Lord the earl of Pembroke, Lord Steward (now with God) & my Lord of Powys, from whose encouragements I affected travel" (225). It seems that all we can say is that Thomas Herbert, like Schneebaum, obviously had "a need to travel," and that he used his connections with Pembroke to realise his dream. His decision to ask Pembroke for help was also a practical one; without considerable means Herbert could never have embarked on his journey and he would have needed permission to go abroad as well as documents, which would have included a license from the king or the Privy Council, of which latter Pembroke was a member. As for money, Sir Robert Dallington had stated in his *Method for Travel* (1606) that "an English gentleman travelling on the Continent required eighty pounds a year to cover his living and travelling expenses," and even as far back as 1470 Afanasy Nikitin[29] had noted that "living in India is very expensive."[30] Herbert would have required at least eighty pounds for a three-year journey which took him to India, Africa, and Persia. As an attendant on Sir Dodmore Cotton he might have been paid something, but the likelihood is that his family, perhaps with Pembroke's help, also put up some funds for Thomas's travels or that the Earl himself provided an allowance. Wood tells us that Pembroke "sent [Herbert] to travel . . . with allowance to defray his charges." (*Athenae* 3: 182). Thomas Herbert, then, fitted roughly into that category of traveller Palmer called the "voluntary regular" traveller, one who was "neither too young nor too old," and who set out on travels "that afterwards [he] may lead a more quiet and contented life, to the glory of God" (1 B).

It must also be remembered that Thomas Herbert was very much a pre-colonial traveller, and that his book cannot be read within the same context as can standard colonial or post-colonial narratives and the discourse of orientalism, defined by Edward Said as "a Western style for dominating, restructuring

---

[29] Afanasy Nikitin, *Voyage to India*, ed. and trans. Count M. Wielhorsky [Vyelgorsky] (Cambridge, Ontario: In Parentheses, 2000), 18. Afanasy Nikitin (d. 1472), a Russian merchant born in Tver, was one of the first Europeans to travel to India and Persia (1466–1472). He died in Smolensk on his way home to Tver. He wrote an account of his experiences, which included the story of his conversion to Islam (and repeatedly expressed regrets for having converted).

[30] Michael Strachan, *The Life and Adventures of Thomas Coryate* (Oxford: Oxford University Press, 1962), 16. Sir Robert Dallington (1561–1637) was a courtier and traveller perhaps best-known in his time as the translator of Francesco Colonna's *Hypnerotomachia* (1592). He also wrote two guide-books, the *View of France* (1604) and the *Survey of Tuscany* (1605). For details, see K. J. Holtgen, "Sir Robert Dallington (1561–1637), Author, Traveller and Pioneer of Taste," *Huntington Library Quarterly*, 47. 3 (1984): 147–77.

and having authority over the Orient."[31] Matar states that "In America, discourse went hand in hand with colonization," and calls Hakluyt's work a "prose epic," thus placing it along with Camoens's *Lusiads*, which he calls "one of the most anti-Muslim epics in the national history of Renaissance Europe" (Nabil Matar, *Turks*, 164) as a quasi-colonialist discourse, although he insists that unlike Said's characterisation of eighteenth century orientalism as colonialist discourse which led to actual occupation and exploitation, "what Renaissance English writers produced was merely a discourse — without colonialism — that was generated by superimposing the discourse about the conquest of America on Islam" (Matar, *Turks*, 17). Furthermore, Matar earlier on makes the point that "critics . . . have projected the military and industrial decline of Muslim countries in the modern period on English drama and travelogue" (Matar, *Turks*, 8). Jyotsna Singh, moreover, argues that pre-colonial travel literature cannot be cited as "foundational in a discourse of colonialism,"[32] which makes perfect sense when readers consider what the discourse actually was. To explain what exactly the discourse might have been if it were not colonialist, Pramod Nayar, for example, believes

---

[31] E. Said, *Orientalism* (New York: Vintage Books, 1979), 3.

[32] Jyotsna G. Singh, *Colonial Narratives / Cultural Dialogues: "Discoveries" of India in the Language of Colonialism* (London: Routledge, 1996), 2. It has to be pointed out, however, that some pre-colonial travel literature gives a rather different impression. George Best, for example, known mostly for having travelled in the Arctic, wrote a preface to Frobisher's account of his travels in that region (1576) that "Whole worldes offer and reach out themselves to them that will first vouchsafe to possess, inhabit, and till them" (Giles Milton, *Samurai William* [London: Hodder and Stoughton], 5), but he probably considered those worlds "uninhabited." And then of course there is John Donne, exulting in the metaphorical possession of a woman's body as "my America, my new-found-land / My kingdom, safeliest when with one man manned." However, these attitudes did not make much sense when applied to the Mughal Empire, China, Japan, or Persia. They did, however, apply to North Africa, at least for Henry Roberts, a former English agent in Morocco (1585–1589), who wrote to James I in 1603 that there were "new lands of Barbary that needed to be conquered for king and Christ," which would also, he said, being "profite and increase of your Mties demynions, trafique or merchants." Roberts had kept his ideas secret, he told the king, until Queen Elizabeth had passed from the scene (Nabil Matar, *Britain and Barbary, 1589–1689* [Gainesville: University Press of Florida, 2005], 40). He seems to have forgotten that it was a Moroccan sultan who had defeated and killed King Sebastian of Portugal in 1578, not thirty years before Roberts wrote to James I. Camoens had believed in an imperialism of a similar kind; he wanted King Sebastian to conquer foreign lands for Christ first, and then perhaps for trade. In the case of Roberts, as his letter was private, "at no point did King James respond to such a colonial discourse in regard to Muslim territory" (Matar, *Turks*, 10). Given the fate of King Sebastian, this was probably a wise move. A similar plea was also made by John Harrison, the English agent in Morocco, to Charles I in 1630, who wrote about settling "a Christian plantation" in Morocco, but abandoned it in favour of containing the expansion of Muslim naval power in the area (for details see Matar, *Turks*, 10–11).

that in the case of India (and by extension Persia, for Herbert) "English travellers were confronted with a radically different topography, climate, animal and plant life, and diseases." This meant that in their observations they would have been "informed, and in many ways facilitated, by the aesthetics of the marvellous . . . with its dual emphases on variety and otherness"[33] rather than with any desire to colonise or even indulge in what Said called "an exercise of cultural strength" (*Orientalism*, 40). The discourse, then, was one of wonderment and discovery, not of possession or desire to control or exploit; Matar would add "fear, anxiety and awe" (*Turks*, 9). Moreover, it appears that the "otherness" is often defined in terms of religious beliefs and customs, a fact which Nayar does not fully address. I respectfully submit that whilst topography, climate, and the rest are certainly differences, writers took pains also to point out similarities, and that the real "otherness" of the "degenerate / Lands of Africa and Asia," as Camoens, writing in 1572, termed them in the *Lusiads* (1. 3) was not strange-looking animals so much as strange-looking gods and what might be entailed in their worship, and it was here that the discourse of control or conversion sometimes made its appearance. The word "degenerate" speaks volumes: it applies to non-European religious beliefs, an arrogant (to our eyes now) dismissal of the great systems of Hinduism, Buddhism, and Islam, but not racial prejudice in the modern sense of the word. For Herbert, too, the Angolans were "black-skinned wretches" not because they were inferior as human beings but because they were "miserable in demonomy," which included belief in the power of witches and a propensity for cannibalism (77–8).

Even when observers were more positive they would return to religion to point out where the West was superior; Giles Milton, for example, cites an early Portuguese visitor to Japan as writing "You should not think that [the Japanese] are barbarians, for apart from our religion, we are greatly inferior to them" (*Samurai William*, 19). Camoens, as we have seen, took a more sanguine view; he wrote that he hoped King Sebastian would "yoke and humble / Arabia's wild horsemen, infidel / Turks, and India's sons and daughters / Who yet drink the Ganges' sacred waters" (1. 8), thus opening the way for Christian missionaries to eradicate Hinduism and Islam, lines which bear out Matar's censure cited previously. And that is why there is so much emphasis on the "idolatry" and "superstition" which Christian writers found amongst the followers of two of the world's other great religions, Buddhism and Hinduism; Islam, of course, they had known about since the Crusades, and their attitudes were relatively unchanged since those times, even though some knowledge had been gained. For most medieval Christian writers (Mandeville being a possible exception), Islam was often denigrated as a degenerate monotheism, with its Prophet usually de-

---

[33] Pramod K. Nayar, "Marvellous Excesses: English Travel Writing and India, 1608–1727," *Journal of British Studies* 44 (2005): 213–38, at 214.

scribed as a fraud or impostor, and the other religions simply as gross idolatry or superstition. This will be discussed in more detail below.

Marvels there certainly were, though, and readers wanted to know about them, but they also wanted material which was arranged systematically and perhaps more "scientifically," which is why writers like Bacon emphasised the comparison not so much with the unknown but with the known. It was a way of understanding, not of controlling or possessing; there was so much in the world that was not known and it gripped the imagination by its sheer volume. Wonder and amazement certainly played a great part in the observations of early travellers, and it would have been very difficult for the twenty-year-old Thomas Herbert not to have given in to his sense of the marvellous; indeed, had he not, the book would not have been as interesting.[34] As Ian Frazier remarked in our own times, "most places have a double existence: one in reality and another in the imagination of people" (Zinssner, *They Went*, 25), a point which may explain Herbert's uncritical use of sources such as Mandeville (who says, for example, that he had seen sciapods, people with one enormous foot which shaded their heads from the sun),[35] his acceptance of accounts of Prester John and of various

---

[34] The editor very much regrets that at the time he wrote this introduction he did not know that someone had finally written a book on the subject of travel-writing rhetoric. From what I have seen of this book, although it ends just before Herbert's time it takes a thorough look at the language of travel-writers and the tropes employed by them to register their sense of wonder and sometimes bewilderment. See Jonathan Sell, *Rhetoric and Wonder in English Travel Writing, 1560–1613* (Aldershot: Ashgate Publishing, 2006). It is also worth noting Stephen Greenblatt's contention in *Marvellous Possessions* (Chicago: University of Chicago Press, 1992) that a sense of wonder indicates toleration and acceptance of "the other" in the eyes of European explorers; Greenblatt concentrates on North America, but the argument could easily be applied to other "new" worlds.

[35] See Sir John Mandeville, *Travels*, trans. C. R. D. Moseley (Harmondsworth: Penguin Books, 1984), 119, 137. In all fairness, people in the East had some rather odd ideas about Westerners, too. Hendrik Hamel, a Dutchman who had been shipwrecked and stranded in Korea for a number of years (1653–1668), noted that the common people had heard all sorts of peculiar tales and half-truths about Westerners, believing, for example that "in order to drink something we had to place our noses behind our ears," and for them, blonde hair did not make the Dutch look attractive, but rather "more like underwater creatures than humans" (15). Misconceptions about Westerners were prevalent in Japan until the nineteenth century; Emperor Komei (1846–1867), from all accounts an otherwise intelligent man, was convinced that they had horns. And then there was the unfortunate Joseph Pitts, captured at the age of fifteen by Algerian pirates off Spain, whose account (after fifteen years of captivity from 1678 to 1692) informs us that people who lived inland thought that all Christians looked like pigs (Vitkus, *Piracy, Slavery and Redemption*, 240). For more on Pitts and more extensive extracts, see Michael Wolfe, ed., *One Thousand Roads to Mecca: Ten Centuries of Travelers Writing about the Muslim Pilgrimage* (New York: Grove Press, 1997), 102–26. Pitts's book is entitled *A True and Faithful Account of the Religion and Manners of the Mahometans* (1704).

unfounded stories, rumours, and fabrications from a motley number of historians. This kind of exaggeration and flights of imagination, not to mention outright lying and reporting of rumour as truth, had been going on for a long time; Marco Polo, for example, who never went to Japan, had told his readers that "You may take it for a fact that [the Emperor] has a very large palace entirely roofed with fine gold" (*Travels*, 244). James I himself, in a sonnet addressed to Lady Cicely Wemyss, began by idealistically invoking "oriental Indus' crystal streams,"[36] which he would never see and which, in any case, hardly fit that description. Some travel-writers liked to emphasise the danger and even horror that could be evoked in foreign lands and by the customs of strange peoples; Jan Janszoon Struys, a Dutchman who travelled to Persia and other places east (1678), provided a lurid account (with an equally lurid illustration) of a Persian nobleman who was said to have flayed his Polish wife alive when she tried to get away from him with help from the Polish ambassador in Isfahan,[37] and of course most travellers who wrote of India could not forbear descriptions of sati. Others larded their accounts with tales of human sacrifice, polygamy, torture, or unusual sexual practices. Marco Polo, for example, has quite a good description of cannibalism and another of tantric sex,[38] and Mandeville, too, wrote of cannibalism in "Lamory" or Sumatra (*Travels*, 117). Some of these things were true, others not, but all were described with relish and often in great detail.

If Herbert had any "methodology" at all in writing his book it was based on comparison and contrast, because there was really no other way to give readers an understanding of what he had seen and experienced. This is markedly different in the seventeenth century from what post-colonial writers term "Eurocentrism" or from Edward Said's rather extreme extrapolation that *any* attempt to explain the foreign by analogy with the domestic is in some way a subversive attempt to control or dominate whatever is unfamiliar. It is simply using the familiar to explain the unfamiliar, argument by analogy with no colonialising agenda or assumptions. A river in India, for example, might be compared in size or depth to one in England, the huge (to a European) size of an Asian town's population might be best seen by a comparison with that of Paris or London. Furthermore, as Kate Teltscher, in her analysis of earlier travel-writing, suggests, referring to Samuel Purchas's compilation of travels, "order" was all-important not just to editors and collectors of travel-accounts like Hakluyt or Purchas but to individual writers like Herbert, and the method of comparing and contrasting things was a part of this ordering principle. Travel-accounts were seen, particularly by writers like

---

[36] Alastair Fowler, ed., *The Oxford Book of Seventeenth-Century Verse* (Oxford: Oxford University Press, 2001), 66.

[37] See Elio Brancaforte, *Visions of Persia: Mapping the Travels of Adam Olearius* (Cambridge, MA: Harvard University Press, 2003), 102–7.

[38] Marco Polo, *Travels*, trans. Ronald Latham (Harmondsworth: Penguin Books, 2004), 110, 231, 281.

Bacon, as being part of the discipline of 'cosmography,' a mixture of history, sociology, geography, natural history and other things. A travel-writer, according to this view, "must find a way of marrying 'cosmographic' observations with personal narrative,"[39] which produces the needed order. It could certainly be argued that ordering is in some sense a form of control, but an ordering principle of one kind or another is simply the way thought-processes work, and need not imply a desire to own, dominate, or colonise.

Thus Herbert seems to have decided, as he grew older, that there was something missing in his account, namely some of the cosmographical material which was thought essential to such a work as his. He wanted to change the nature of the book from a mere "travel account" to something more learned, something in which he could demonstrate to readers that he had been more than a mere tourist; he wanted, in short, to turn his book into a chorography, a work in which he explored all kinds of subjects and relationships in the context of or arising from the simple account of his travels. This means all the revisions that Herbert made, his extensive additions to the narrative over the years of historical background, and his expansion of the sections describing Hinduism, Islam, and Zoroastrianism, gleaned from his reading of Henry Lord, Edward Brerewood, and others, not to mention the comparative linguistic tables and the splendid description of Persepolis accompanied by a specially-commissioned engraving by Wenceslas Hollar, were part of his desire to 'order' his text in chorographical form, although the autobiographical elements remained (more or less) at the core. Herbert invited the readers in the final edition to make comparisons; how was the government of the Mughal or Persian Empire like that of England? What was the state of the common people, and how did they live? Did Persians write poetry? How do orientals dress differently from us, or how do they dress the same? What do they know about us? What sort of things do they eat and drink? What are the women like? What do other authors, ancient and contemporary, have to say about them? These kinds of questions were all asked and answered by Herbert, who makes comparative observations on all of them. The lengthiest discussions and the most comparisons are in the area of religion, because that was where, at least for Herbert, as for so many Christian travellers, the real "otherness" lay, almost as if what was really important was, as to the Christian, the kind of hereafter the orientals might expect, given their benighted state. All these subjects were discussed with reference to what Herbert had been reading and learning over the years of revision. From a relatively short book with a few commonplace Latin tags and references, Herbert eventually created his chorographical panorama, placing it in the company of works such as John Norden's *Chorographical Description of Middlesex, Essex, Sussex, Surrey, Hampshire, Wight, Guernsey and Jersey* (1595), John Stow's *Survey of London* (1598) or William Burton's *Description of Leicestershire* (1622),

[39] Kate Teltscher, *India Described: European and British Writing on India 1600–1800* (New Delhi: Oxford University Press, 1995), 14–15.

all of which start out on a geographical base and branch out into all kinds of wonderful linkages and extrapolations.[40]

The enthusiastic young traveller does not quite get lost in the succession of editions, but the retired gentleman-antiquarian, with his sometimes prolix and pedantic mind, increasingly makes his presence felt, as if Herbert had a desire to satisfy older and more experienced readers who wanted more than exuberant reactions to the wonders of the Orient. First-time travellers, overwhelmed with difference, record anything and everything they see, often in no particular order, and by and large Herbert retains the spontaneity which his initial experiences afforded him. However, in the later editions Herbert wanted to relive his experiences, look back on them with the eyes of an experienced man of the world, to, as it were, detach himself from himself, put some order in his universe and in his text. To quote Tobias Schneebaum once again, "Scenes from my past sometimes cry out for description. They come back to me time and time again, demanding to be put on the printed page, as if the experiences return to my conscious mind solely to be recorded," he writes; "I relive them to the full, sometimes taking myself deeper into the event than I had originally gone" (Zinsser, *They Went*, 143). That, essentially, is what led Herbert to revise his text over and over again, and by enlarging it (occasionally verbatim) with what he had read in others' texts, until he had gone as deeply into the events as he could.

Herbert's Sources on India

The main source of historical information used in this edition of his book by Herbert for Indian history was his Dutch friend Jan or Joannes de Laet's *De imperio Magni Mogolis, sive India vera, commentarius ex variis auctoribus congestus* (1631). De Laet (1593–1649) was a man of wide-ranging interests; he was a naturalist, philologist, and geographer as well as being one of the directors of the Dutch East India Company. De Laet had spent four years in England (1603–

---

[40] William Burton of Lindley Hall (1575–1645), elder brother of Robert Burton, was an antiquarian whose book on Leicestershire contained "matters of antiquitye, historye, armorye and genealogy" in addition to his topographical descriptions. For details, see Daniel Williams, "William Burton's 1642 Revised Edition of the *Description of Leicestershire*," *Transactions of the Leicestershire Archaeological and Historical Society* 50 (1974–1975): 30–36; Mendyk, *Speculum*, 88–9. John Norden (1548–1623), the Surveyor of the Duchy of Cornwall, also wrote *Speculum Britanniae* (1593) and produced magnificent maps of London and Westminster. For details see Heather Lawrence, "John Norden and his Colleagues: Surveyors of Crown Lands," *The Cartographic Journal* 22 (1985): 54–56; Mendyk, *Speculum*, 57–74. Apart from his well-known *Survey of London*, John Stow (1525–1605) edited Chaucer and wrote another chorographical work, the *Annales, or a General Chronicle of England from Brute until the present yeare of Christ 1580*.

1607) and married an Englishwoman; after he returned to Leyden he kept up a correspondence with, amongst others, Sir Thomas Roe and the scholar John Morris, and he certainly knew Herbert, who offered to translate one of his books for him.[41] De Laet did not travel much himself (as far as we know), but he was a voracious reader and his book is, as its title says, a commentary drawn together from a number of authors. It is in two parts: the first part deals with geography, government, and an assessment of Mughal wealth and military strength, and the second, which he calls "A Fragment of the History of India," gives an account of the Mughal emperors from Humayun's defeat by the Afghan usurper Sher Shah Suri (1540) to the death of Jahangir (1627) as well as a detailed history of the reigns of Akbar and Jahangir. This "fragment" was actually edited in large part by Pieter van den Broecke, President of the Dutch factory at Surat, from a manuscript known as the *Remonstrantie* by Frans Pelsaert, who was in charge of the Dutch factory at Agra. S. N. Banerjee states that "while the Fragment is associated with the name of van den Broecke, it appears to be primarily the work of Pelsaert, who is said to have mastered the language of the country and studied its history. . . . De Laet's part was merely that of a translator and compiler, with the exception of a sprinkling of information concerning events that happened after 1627."[42] De Laet himself, as Banerjee points out, used many sources in his compilation, including English ones such as Sir Thomas Roe, William Hawkins, Nicholas Withington, Edward Terry,[43] and William Finch, "making the *De imperio Magni Mogolis* a monument of painstaking industry and a storehouse of varied information" (De Laet, v). The fact that he did this means that De Laet inherited some of the inaccuracies in his source-material; nevertheless it is obvious that Herbert found De Laet's work very useful indeed, and that it provided him with references to other possible source material. Banerjee calls it "a faithful and reliable compilation," whose defects and inaccuracies "are more than offset by the large amount of acknowledged fact which it records" (vi). Herbert did, of course, have other sources of information about India at his disposal. "The avid

---

[41] See Rolf H. Bremmer, "The Correspondence of Johannes de Laet (1581–1649) as a Mirror of his Life," *LIAS* 25 (1998): 139–64.

[42] Joannes de Laet, *The Empire of the Great Mogol* (1631), trans. J. S. Hoyland, annot. S. N. Banerjee (Delhi: Oriental Books Reprint Corporation, 1974), v.

[43] Edward Terry (1590–1660), an eccentric clergyman, was Sir Thomas Roe's chaplain and the author of *A Voyage to India* (1655). He had been formerly a chaplain with the East India Company (1616), but transferred his services to Roe, whose own chaplain had died, and whom he served until 1619. Terry returned to England as Vicar of Great Greenford and revised his book in retirement, having published a short version in 1622. Oaten comments that "the worthy divine grafts some very excellent moral discourses on the depravity and wickedness which he met in India" (R. F. Oaten, *Early Travellers in India during the Fifteenth, Sixteenth, and Seventeenth Centuries* [Madras: Asian Educational Series Reprints, 1991], 165.)

European reader of the latter half of the sixteenth century, desirious of knowing the world from his or her armchair," Alam and Subramanyam remark, "had
available to him or her texts available in a variety of competing genres" (*Indo-Persian Travellers*, 338), and by Herbert's time there were hundreds of them,
many available in English translation. Indeed, Alam and Subrahmanyam speak
of "the seventeenth-century 'explosion' of travel-writing" (*Indo-Persian Travellers*, 342).

No account of Indian travellers would be complete without a mention of the
wonderful Thomas Coryate, "England's first modern tourist,"[44] who travelled
all over the sub-continent and whose grave Herbert reported seeing near Surat.
Coryate's preferred mode of travel was walking; having made a pilgrimage to the
Holy Land, he then walked the entire distance from Aleppo to Ajmer in Eastern Rajasthan and went on walking to attend the court of Jahangir in Agra, after
which he then set out on his final journey, still on foot, intending, as he wrote
to his mother, "to see in Asia, where I now am, namely ancient Babilon and
Nymrod's Tower, some few miles from Ninive, and . . . Caire in Egypt, heretofore Memphis, upon the famous river Nilus" (Strachan, *Coryate*, 254). He never
made it: after staying with Sir Thomas Roe, then the English ambassador to the
Mughal court, he set out for Surat, where he died in December, 1617. Herbert
may well have read Coryate's *Crudities* (1611), the account of his travels in Europe, but of more interest to him would have been a pamphlet which appeared
in 1616 entitled *Thomas Coriate, Traveller for the English Wits: Greeting from the
Court of the Great Mogul.* This publication contained letters purporting to be from
Coryate, and quickly went into a second printing (Strachan, *Life and Adventures*,
295); parts of these letters, together with fragments and notes written by Coryate in India, appeared in Samuel Purchas's *Pilgrims* (1625).[45] The enthusiasm for
Coryate and his adventures was not shared by everyone; James I, for example,
remarked when hearing about Coryate's doings in India, "Is that fool yet living?"
(Oaten, *Early Travellers*, 163). Edward Terry was kinder; he wrote cheerfully of
Coryate's death that "if one should go to the extreme part of the world, East,
another West, another North, and another South, they must all meet at last together in the Field of Bones, wherein our traveller hath now taken up his Lodging" (Oaten, *Early Travellers*, 163–64).

Sir Thomas Roe's embassy (1615–1619) marked the first formal diplomatic
contact at the governmental level between England and the Mughal Empire,

---

[44] Richmond Barbour, *Before Orientalism: London's Theatre of the East, 1576–1626*
(Cambridge: Cambridge University Press, 2003), 8.

[45] In connection with Purchas, who printed some of them, it is possible that Herbert also read some "captivity accounts," of which there were quite a number by the time
he was an adult. For a list of these, see Matar, *Turks*, Appendix A, 181–83. For a detailed
study of them see Daniel Vitkus, *Piracy, Slavery and Redemption: Barbary Captivity Narratives from Early Modern England* (New York: Columbia University Press, 2001).

indeed "England's first attempt to assert its dignity as a country of consequence in India" (Barbour, *Before Orientalism* 146). Herbert very probably had read his account of the Mughal court, which contains a detailed description of the Emperor Jahangir, whom Herbert himself did not get to meet. He had certainly read Richard Hakluyt's *Principal Navigations, Voyages and Discoveries of the English Nations* (1582; 1598/99–1600) and Samuel Purchas's *Hakluytus Posthumus or Purchas his Pilgrims, containing a History of the World in Sea voyages and land travels by Englishmen and others* (1610–1626); other available works on India included Thomas Mun's *Discourse of Trade to the East Indies* (1621), Roe's chaplain Edward Terry's *Voyage to East India* (1655), and William Bruton's *News from the East Indies* (1638), the last two appearing during the time in which Herbert was rewriting and expanding his own book. Herbert may have known the merchant Joseph Salbancke's *Voyage of Master Joseph Salbancke through India, Persia, part of Turkie, the Persian Gulf and Arabia, 1609* (1610), an account written for Sir Thomas Smythe[46] and excerpted by Purchas, or a longer one by Sir Henry Middleton, *An Account of the Sixth Voyage set forth by the East India Company in three Ships.*[47] Finally, there was also Robert Coverte's *True and almost Incredible Report of an Englishman, that (being Cast Away in the Good Ship Called the Ascension in Cambaya, the Farthest Part of the East Indies, Travelled by Land through many Unknown Kingdoms and Great Cities* (1612).[48] There were many others, of course, in Purchas and elsewhere, too many to be discussed here.[49]

---

[46] Sir Thomas Smythe (c. 1558–1625) was one of the great merchant-princes of his time. His early career was with the Virginia Company, and he went on to become an MP (1597), Governor of the Muscovy Company (1600), and Governor of the East India Company (1600–1601; 1603–1605; 1607–1621). Smythe also served as a soldier in Ireland with the Earl of Essex, a connection which nearly destroyed him, but in 1603 he was knighted by James I. Smythe served as James's ambassador to Russia (1604) and retired a very rich man.

[47] For Salbancke, see Purchas 3: 82–89; for Middleton, 3: 115–194. Sir Henry Middleton (d. 1613), himself a director of the East India Company, made six notable voyages, including one to the Moluccas (1604–1606), of which he wrote an account, and the Red Sea (1612). In 1609 he was appointed to lead a group of three ships by the East India company, and was given the right to defend himself, which he interpreted to mean plundering and attacking wherever he felt like it. He died of a fever in Java.

[48] Robert Coverte was the steward on the *Ascension*, although his modern editor gives him the rank of captain. He sailed to Surat in 1607 and then journeyed to Agra, where he met Jahangir, travelling with Salbancke and some others. He left India in 1610, and was one of two remaining members of his group to get home the next year. The dates of his birth and death are unknown. See Oaten, *Early Travellers*, 158–9, and Boies Penrose, ed., *The Travels of Captain Richard Coverte.* (Philadelphia: W. Fell, 1931).

[49] For a comprehensive list with short discussions, see, for example, Beni Prasad, *History of Jahangir* (Allahabad: Indian Press, 1962), 426–41.

Herbert does not stop with English narratives, drawing for his sources from both Hakluyt and the earlier collections of Giovanni Battista Ramusio; there are, for example, several references to the remarkable Ludovico Varthema from Bologna, who was "the earliest non-commercial, non-missionary traveller to reach India," and who "apparently followed along Marco Polo's route between 1501 and 1508" (Singh, *Discoveries of India*, 5); his account was published in translation by Richard Eden in his *History of Travel in the East and West Indies* (1577). Varthema also went to Mecca and may have converted to Islam; we know that he was taken for a Mameluke and hired to guard pilgrims, which certainly seems to suggest conversion. There was also Don Garcia de Silva Figueroa's *Comentarios de Don Garcia de Silva, que contienen su viaje a la India y de ella a Persia* (1624), which were available to Herbert in a French version by Herbert's own translator de Wicqfort (1668), and whose author Herbert mentions twice. Herbert also cites Jan Huyghen van Linschoten (1563–1611), whose *Discourse of Voyages into the East and West Indies*, which van Linschoten had published after a six-year sojourn in Goa, was available in an English translation made through the efforts of Hakluyt (1598). And there was Gasparo Balbi, who was distinguished as the first European to visit Burma and whose account of India and Burma was included by Purchas in his *Pilgrims*. Finally, we should mention Johann Albrecht von Mandeslo (d. 1644), who travelled with the embassy of Duke Friedrich III of Holstein to Persia (1635), but then split from the group and went to India, where he visited Surat, Agra, and Ahmedabad. Mandeslo left Surat in rather a hurry because of a chance meeting with relatives of someone he was supposed to have killed in Persia, after which he journeyed to Lahore and points beyond in the Far East. In 1639 he returned to Holstein after a trip to England with William Methold, the English agent in Surat and author of *Relations of the kingdom of Golconda*, whom he had befriended. His account was printed by his friend Adam Olearius and was included in Davies's translation of Olearius (1668). There were still others whose later accounts Herbert may have read but does not mention, such as that of the French jeweller-merchant Jean-Baptiste Tavernier (1605–1689), who travelled to India in 1648 and produced a lengthy account of his experiences, *Six Voyages* (1676), a work "which enjoyed immense success, success so great that it roused the jealousy of other travellers" (Oaten, *Early Travellers*, 189). His countryman and (for a while) fellow-traveller François Bernier (1625–1688), an associate of the philosopher Pierre Gassendi, actually stayed in India for a number of years (1656–1668), during which time he became the personal physician to the emperor Aurangzeb, Shah Jahan's successor, and wrote his *Histoire de la derniere Revolution des Etats du Grand Mogul* (1670). It would also be interesting to know whether Herbert had read Sir Richard Fanshawe's translation of Camoens's *Lusiads* (1655); he could have used it not just for information about the Portuguese in India, but in Africa and other places as well.[50] Herbert lived long enough to have also known an English translation of the Dutch missionary Philip Baldaeus's *True and Exact Description of the Most Celebrated East-India Coasts of Malabar and Coromandel, as also of the Isle of Ceylon* (1672).

Mughals and English: The Background

Historians seem to be in agreement that when Jahangir succeeded his father Akbar I in 1605, the Mughal Empire was approaching its most powerful and most impressive phase. The reign of Akbar (1556–1605), usually surnamed "the Great," had led to a great consolidation of central power in the hands of the emperor and a turning away from the more strictly Islamic principles that had guided the administrations of his predecessors. Akbar, whom his biographer called a man whose "knowledge shed a peculiar light on the jewel of his wisdom,"[51] made Persian the language of the court, understanding that linguistic differences could be a source of internecine strife in a kingdom. He was personally tolerant in matters of faith, had even created one of his own which recognised the truths in all religions, and he had removed Islam from its primacy as the state religion of the empire. He even organised interviews with Portuguese Jesuits so that he could learn about Christianity by himself questioning them. Later, however, he seems to have turned more and more to the mystic teachings of the Sufis, although he never lost his latitudinarian outlook. Akbar was a great patron of art and literature, in spite of the fact that he found writing difficult (scholars dispute Akbar's standard of literacy) and had a close confidant, Abu'l Fazl, compile the memoirs of his reign, the *Akbarnama* and the *Ain-i-Akbari*, a major part of which was dictated by the emperor himself.[52] "He was a great man," Philip Mason writes, "great in his bodily vigour and his passions, in the spiritual restlessness that led

---

[50] Another non-English account of India with which Herbert might have been familiar was Pierre du Jarric's *Histoire des choses plus memorables . . . en l'establissement et progrez de la foi Chrestienne et Catholique . . .*, which appeared in three parts (1611–1614) as well as a Latin version (1616), and contains information on Akbar and Jahangir (see B. Prasad, 428). Fanshawe's translation of Camoens has been edited by Geoffrey Bullough (Carbondale: Southern Illinois University Press, 1963).

[51] Abu'l Fazl, *The Akbarnama*, trans. H. Beveridge (Delhi: Low Price Publications, 1993), 1: 237.

[52] There is a dispute amongst scholars about the extent of Akbar's literacy. Eraly writes, rather oddly, that Akbar was "formally illiterate," but that he "had a library of 24,000 volumes," as well as having "a large translation department" at his disposal (*Mughal World*, 333). As his grandfather Babur wrote not only his own memoirs, the *Baburnama*, but poetry and religious works, and Akbar's father Humayun had given his son "a solid education" (V. Berinstain, *India and the Mughal Dynasty*, trans. Paul G. Bahn [New York: Abrams, 1998], 38), it seems unlikely that he was illiterate. He may simply

him all his life to seek truth, in his occasional cruelties, in his startling and far more frequent humanity, in his wide tolerance."[53] Herbert himself used the adjective "restless" to describe Akbar (149) and speaks of his "endless" ambition more than once.

Akbar was also a great builder, starting with the beautiful tomb he erected for his father Humayun in 1562–1570, in which he employed a synthesis of Persian and Indian styles, and of course his ill-fated new capital which took shape at Fatehpur Sikri. He was, too, a great conciliator; there are numerous accounts in the *Akbarnama* and elsewhere of his diplomacy and of his attempts to solve potentially volatile problems by negotiation, several of which are narrated by Herbert, who seems to have been an admirer of the great emperor. Not least of Akbar's problems was his family; several of his sons revolted against him, including Prince Salim, who later became the emperor Jahangir. Herbert gives a very full account of this event which came at the end of Akbar's reign, but it is often inaccurate, as his sources make claims, for example, that Akbar was poisoned by his own doctor with Salim's knowledge, but he in fact died of dysentery shortly after Prince Salim had proclaimed himself emperor at Allahabad and arranged the ambush and death of the loyal and faithful Abu'l Fazl. Jahangir inherited a stable, well-administered, and extremely wealthy empire, whose splendours would dazzle the world for years to come, until the inevitable decline set in and the sun finally went down when the last Mughal, Bahadur Shah II, reduced to the title of "King of Delhi," an ill old man of nearly eighty and (as Zafar) a distinguished Urdu poet, was deposed and exiled by the British in 1857 as a result of the Indian Mutiny.

The very first Englishman to land on Indian soil was Thomas Stevens (1548–1619), who sailed there as a Jesuit missionary in 1579, remaining in India as Rector of the Jesuit College in Salsette until his death forty years later. Stevens was based in Goa, but he appears never to have travelled outside its boundaries. However, "he was the first Englishman," Sir William Foster tells us, "to make a study of the Konkani language, and wrote two religious works, one of which, a long epic in Marathi, is still quite popular in Portuguese India."[54] Foster relates that Richard Hakluyt passed on a letter from Stevens to a merchant called John Newbery, who wanted to see whether it might be possible to establish trading relations with the Middle East and eventually places even further afield. Newbery himself was determined to go to India, and he even obtained a letter of recommendation to Akbar from Elizabeth I which he presented in person to the emperor at Fatehpur Sikri "in August or September 1584" (Foster, *England's Quest*,

---

not have had the time to sit down and write his own book; dictation can be done in any spare hour.

[53] Philip Mason, *The Men who Ruled India* (New York: Norton, 1985), 9.

[54] Sir William Foster, *England's Quest of Eastern Trade* (London: A. C. Black, 1933), 91 n. 2.

92). He travelled in the company of Ralph Fitch, who is several times mentioned by Herbert and whose own account of his journey was printed by Hakluyt. It was through the efforts of Newbery and some others that the [British] East India Company was founded in 1599, originally to make sure that England got its share of the Portuguese spice trade after Portugal became part of Spain.[55] Its charter was drawn up and approved by Her Majesty's Privy Council in December 1600. In 1601 its first merchant fleet left England, commanded by Sir James Lancaster, and the stage was finally set for an English presence in the subcontinent. Ominously, the next year saw the foundation of the Dutch East India Company, which meant competition for English traders, and therefore it was imperative that England make formal contact with Mughal rulers to ensure that the East India Company got its share of the Indian market and that there was some check to the expansion of Portuguese trading power. As Richard Hakluyt had observed, "Our chief desire is to find out ample vent for our woollen cloth, the natural commodity of our realm,"[56] and there were vast markets to be opened from Aleppo to Persia, to China, Pegu, Siam, and Japan.

It was to this end that the East India Company sent William Hawkins to India, where he arrived in 1608 at Jahangir's court suitably dressed for the occasion, for the Company appears to have done its homework and realised that a first impression must be memorable. "His apparel," Prasad tells us, "was to be of scarlet and violet, his cloak lined with taffeta and embroidered with silver lace, befitting his dignity,"[57] designed, no doubt, to compete with the best of Mughal finery. Appearances were not all; Hawkins could speak Turkish, which probably impressed Jahangir even more than his rich clothing, and he was a sociable man who enjoyed drinking, which was another point in his favour, although some people who met him found him "arrogant and tactless" (Foster, *England's Quest*, 193). Jahangir, on the other hand, actually liked Hawkins so much that he "pressed him to remain at court as a resident ambassador, and promised that he would grant all his requests for trading concessions" (Foster, *England's Quest*, 188). In spite of continued feuding and difficulties with Muqarrab Khan, the man in charge of ports in Gujarat, not to mention with the Portuguese in Goa, Hawkins retained Jahangir's good opinion, although from time to time the Emperor listened to his minister and Hawkins had to indulge in fancy footwork to get back in Jahangir's good graces. Hawkins adapted Mughal clothes and, at the

---

[55] Newbery's later career is obscure; Fitch states that he intended to go overland to Persia, but Oaten cites Sir George Birdwood's *Report on the Old Records of the India Office* (1891) as stating that he "settled down as a shopkeeper in Goa" (108), although there is no evidence cited for Birdwood's speculation.

[56] Richard Hakluyt, *Voyages and Discoveries*, ed. Jack Beeching (Harmondsworth: Penguin, 1972), 38.

[57] Ram Chandra Prasad, *Early English Travellers in India, 1583–1619* (Oxford: Oxford University Press, 1921), 201.

Emperor's hint, married the daughter of one Mubarak Shah, although Foster mistakenly stated that Hawkins had an Armenian wife (*England's Quest*, 192). Eventually things became difficult for him; he never quite understood Mughal politics and the constant changing of the Emperor's mind as well as being "continually frustrated by Portuguese influence"[58] at Jahangir's court. He finally left India in 1612 with Sir Henry Middleton's East India Company fleet, which had docked at Suwali. Poor Hawkins never made it home; sailing from Bantam with his wife, he died of fever in Ireland before reaching England (1613),[59] which by then must have seemed to him, as it did for Herbert later on, "not unlike that long-looked-for Ithaca."

Other English travellers, apart from the redoubtable Coryate, included Nicholas Withington, who was in Agra buying indigo for the East India Company (1614) and served as factor at Surat from 1613 (Foster, *England's Quest*, 201), William Finch,[60] whom Hawkins had left in Surat and who later joined him in Agra (1610), and John Mildenhall, whom Foster calls 'Midnall,' reflecting the pronunciation of his name. He was a rather shady character who had left England in 1599 to travel to Persia, but took three years to get to Agra, remaining there until 1606 and passing himself off to both Akbar and then Jahangir as an English ambassador. He departed for Persia, where he tried to get the East India Company to pay him for his services. When they refused, he returned to England, but was back again by 1609 with an appointment as a factor. He then returned to Persia, where, according to Purchas, he was reputed to have poisoned two people and stolen their property. Mildenhall even married an Indian woman, whom he un-chivalrously left in Persia when he fled precipitately to India to avoid prosecution for his alleged crimes. Mildenhall died at Ajmer in 1614, leaving an account of his experiences, the *Travailes into the Indies*, which Purchas published, and having the dubious privilege of being the first Englishman to be buried in India.

The most important diplomatic event before Herbert's arrival with the embassy of Sir Dodmore Cotton was James I's dispatching of Sir Thomas Roe to India, this time as the king's envoy. Roe succeeded William Edwards, "a well-meaning

---

[58] Kenneth R. Andrews, *Trade, Plunder and Settlement: Maritime Enterprise and the Genesis of the British Empire, 1480–1630* (Cambridge: Cambridge University Press, 1984), 271.

[59] See Hawkins's account of his experiences, *Captain William Hawkins his relations of the occurrents which happened in the time of his residence in India, in the countrie of the Great Mogoll*, in Purchas 3: 1–50.

[60] Nicholas Withington sailed under Captain Best, travelling from Surat to Agra in 1614; his account occurs in Purchas as *Extract of a Tractate . . . left in the Mogul's Country by Capt. Best* (4: 519). Purchas printed the *Observations of William Finch, merchant, taken out of his large Journall* (4: 1–77). Finch arrived in India with Hawkins but died in Baghdad (1608) as he was returning overland to England.

man but one who had suffered all sorts of indignities without complaint,"[61] who seems to have been held in rather low esteem by the Indians partially because of his compliant character and partially because of his lack of anything resembling flamboyance or self-confidence. What was needed to remedy the situation was a man of substance and determination, at least according to Sir Thomas Smythe, Governor of the East India Company, someone who could earn the trust and respect of the Mughals. Roe was probably the best choice that was available at the time; he was a Londoner who came, like Herbert, from a family of merchants and aldermen. Roe's father had been knighted during the reign of Elizabeth I and held considerable estates in Bedfordshire at the time of his death. An introduction to court circles during the latter years of the reign of Elizabeth was effected by Roe's connections with the Berkeley family[62] and his own wealthy relatives, and by 1603 Roe had done well; he had made friends at court, including Prince Henry, James I's eldest son, his daughter Elizabeth of Bohemia, and Shakespeare's patron the Earl of Southampton. He also knew some eminent literary figures such as John Donne, who was very interested in exploration and with whom he corresponded for years, as well as Ben Jonson (Brown, *Itinerant Ambassador*, 7–8). Compared with Roe, Philip Mason rather unfairly remarks, even Hawkins was "a mere trader bearing letters" (*Men who Ruled India*, 6).

James's commission to Roe talks of "offices of Frendshippe with the said Great Monarch [Jahangir]," but does not fail also to mention "the Entercourse and Traffique which hath so happylie been begun . . . or the better supporting of our said Subjects in their Trade,"[63] and therefore Roe kept closely in touch with Sir Thomas Smythe, his personal friend, who had recommended that Roe be sent to India. But was this mission more than simply trade and friendship? Can we raise once again the spectre of colonial discourse? Edward Oaten, writing in 1909, for example, had noted that Roe "left behind him a new aspect of the English character, an aspect which India was destined to know better in the coming years," although he admitted that "It was but slowly that India learnt that the British were an imperial, as well as commercial, race" (*Early Travellers*, 154). According to M. G. Aune, however, when modern scholars consider early contacts with the Mughal Empire, the emphasis is no longer on the idea that these trade contacts formed any kind of design for "an originary point for an

---

[61] Michael J. Brown, *Itinerant Ambassador: The Life of Sir Thomas Roe* (Lexington: University Press of Kentucky, 1970), 42.

[62] On the death of Roe's father (1588), his mother had married Sir Richard Berkeley, Lieutenant of the Tower of London, and through him Roe had been introduced to the Queen, who appointed him an Esquire of the Body, the same position which Thomas Herbert would later enjoy under Charles I.

[63] *The Embassy of Sir Thomas Roe to the Court of the Great Mogul, 1615–1619*, ed. William Foster, 2 vols. (New York: Kessinger Reprints, n.d.), 2: 550.

inevitable British domination of the subcontinent,"[64] although this misconception is echoed by writers as recent (1970) as Michael Brown, biographer of Sir Thomas Roe, who stated that from Roe's trade mission "ultimately flowered the astounding British Raj in India" (*Itinerant Ambassador*, vii).

However, in the minds of diplomats like Roe and travellers like Herbert there were no such notions, because by the time Englishmen reached the dominions of a ruler like Jahangir, it did not take them long to find out that they were dealing with a powerful and sophisticated civilisation, one that could raise armies larger than any European ruler could have dreamt of, one whose wealth far surpassed the imagination of the richest monarchs, and with whom, in the end, they could hardly treat on an equal basis or by handing them a few shiny trinkets or interesting mechanical devices. And in any case, England in the first half of the seventeenth century "possessed neither a working knowledge of nor a collective will for imperial sway in India" (Barbour, *Before Orientalism*, 6). Thus it really makes no sense any more to speak of these early relations between England and the Mughal Empire in terms of "proto-colonialism" or "proto-imperial discourse" (Aune, "Elephants," 3), and it would have made no sense to Sir Thomas Roe, either. In the seventeenth century, at any rate, nearly all significant intercultural contacts (Nabil Matar makes an exception for North America, as we have seen, and Edward Said, of course, sees colonialists and imperialists lurking behind the most innocent travellers' words or actions) were not determined by colonial aspirations, but by mercantile interests, political reasons or alliances, and a genuine desire to expand cultural, not imperial horizons.

Richmond Barbour, writing about Roe's letters and reports to his employers and friends in England, observed that Roe catalogued in his letters home both the power and wealth of the Mughal Empire and the abject poverty of many of its poorer inhabitants, not to mention the corruption of many of its officials,[65] although in view of what was going on at James I's court at the time, such as the Overbury scandal in 1612–1613 and the subsequent trial of the countess of Somerset for poisoning him, the observations about Mughal corruption and vice may sometimes ring a little hollow. Indeed George, Lord Carew,[66] replying to a

---

[64] M. G. Aune, "Elephants, Englishmen and India: Early Modern Travel and the Pre-Colonial Movement," *Early Modern Literary Studies* 11 (2005): 1–35, here 3.

[65] Richmond Barbour, "Power and Distant Display: Early English 'Ambassadors' in Moghul India," *Harvard Library Quarterly* 61 (2000): 342–68, here 342.

[66] George, Lord Carew and Earl of Totnes (1557–1629), held a number of offices under Elizabeth I and James I, including that of Chamberlain to the Prince of Wales after the death of Queen Anne of Denmark (1619), whom he had also served in that capacity. Like Herbert after him, Carew was an antiquarian and a friend of William Camden, whom he assisted in research for the Britannia. Maclean calls Carew "a man of learning and ability" (ix). His letters kept Roe up-to-date with what was happening in Europe and England.

letter from Roe in 1617, said of the Great Mughal "I do nott a little admyre of the greatnes of thatt monarque; the description you make of the riches you saw when he left Adsmere [Ajmer] exceeds all the reports thatt ever I read of, and yet I observe (in your discourse) more basenes in thatt prince and people than canne be imagined where suche abundance of earthlye treasures are found."[67] Did Lord Carew really mean to suggest that "abundance of earthlye treasures" necessarily corresponded to an equal abundance of virtue? As Philip Mason puts it, "It is not easy for honesty or pity to flourish at the court of absolutism anywhere" (*Men who Ruled India*, 12). However, John Maclean, the editor of Carew's letters to Roe, also made the claim in 1860 that "Our Indian empire owes much to the treaties which [Roe] established" (*Letters*, x), but he, too, did not understand that initially trade and economic matters did not actually register very high on the scale with Jahangir, and that purely commercial interests, such as those represented by Hawkins in 1608, were really rather beneath his imperial consideration.

Thus it would be first naval and then military strength (particularly against the Portuguese, whose fleet the English defeated off Surat in 1612) which would make the English a power to be reckoned with, and that the Mughals would see them as an ally against the Portuguese, as the Persians would a few years later. As far as trade was concerned, Barbour notes that the Mughals "had small need of English goods . . . the English were tolerated rather than welcomed" ("Power and Distant Display," 343). This is echoed by Simkin, who writes that "the Mughals, notwithstanding their fondness for luxuries and novelties, were indifferent to foreign trade."[68] As an example of this, we find Roe rather amusingly recording how Jahangir took a fancy to some hats that he noticed the English had, "for that his women liked them." He asked Roe to give them to him, but Roe explained that one of them was his own, at which the emperor graciously said "I like them, and yours I will returne if you need it, and will not bestow that on me" (*Embassy*, 2: 386), but fancy hats did not a treaty make.

When Roe went to Jahangir's court, he expected that he would get some kind of written permission from the Emperor which would clearly spell out his trading rights, and he was frustrated when Jahangir did so only to countermand it later. "A procedure of this nature," Sir William Foster stated, "was entirely foreign to the ideas of the emperor and his advisers . . . the Emperor was a personage far too exalted to enter into engagements with the monarch of a distant kingdom, especially on such despised topics as the trade of merchants" (*England's Quest*, 283), a view echoed later by Mason, who states that "it did not seem fitting that [Jahangir] should bind himself, as though dealing with an equal, to any man, and certainly not to the king of an obscure and distant island of fishermen and

---

[67] John Maclean, ed., *Letters of George, Lord Carew to Sir Thomas Roe, Ambassador to the Court of the Great Mogul 1615–1617* (London: Camden Society, 1860), ix.

[68] C. G. F. Simkin, *The Traditional Trade of Asia* (New York: Oxford University Press, 1968), 174.

wool merchants" (*Men who Ruled India*, 8). Thus Roe was told that he would have
to deal with Prince Khurram (later emperor Shah Jahan) rather than attempt any
more to approach the emperor himself. Khurram was Governor of the province
where the port of Surat was located, and his position was that if the English were
to be allowed trading privileges there, so should the Portuguese, which immediately put him at loggerheads with Roe, who was actually in his bad books already
because of his earlier disagreements with Zulfikar Khan, the Governor of Surat and hence Khurram's subordinate. If this was not bad enough, Roe had also
to contend with Asaf Khan, brother of Jahangir's favourite wife Nur Jahan, an
"avaricious and rascally arch-plotter,"[69] who was a man of considerable power in
Jahangir's court. Unfortunately, Asaf Khan, with whom Roe had many dealings,
did not favour the English, and when Jahangir died he would become the chief
minister to his successor Shah Jahan, whom as Prince Khurram he had always
supported. In fact, in Herbert's first edition of his book he suggests that Asaf
Khan may have murdered Jahangir: "and (if the vulgar sort may be believed),"
he reported, "[Jahangir] was poisoned, and that by his only friend and chiefest
favourite, his brother-in-law Asaf Khan" (30). He did not repeat this passage in
later versions, perhaps because de Laet stated only that "the king fell sick in Cas-
simere. He returned to Lahor [*sic*] by easy stages; but the disease becoming more
serious, he passed away at [Bhimbar] in the year of our era 1627" (237). Western views of Mughal "politics of poison" seem to have been prevalent in Herbert,
who had already subscribed, as we have seen above, to the view that Akbar had
met a similar fate.

King James, meanwhile, was sent a letter in which Jahangir wrote, with
typical Mughal diplomatic hyperbole but also with a certain charm in the phras-
ing, as Roe recorded: "When your Majestie shall open this letter lett your royal
heart bee as fresh as a sweete garden. Lett all people make reverence at your gate;
lett your throne be advanced higher; amongst the greatnes of the kynges of the
prophett Jesus let your Majestie bee the greatest."[70] What Jahangir really seemed
interested in, however, was the presents which had accompanied Roe's embassy, "upon which myne eyes were so fixed." He told Roe, "that I could not easily
remoove them to any other object" (2: 558). In the end, Roe decided that in spite

---

[69] J. Charpentier, review of *Embassy*, ed. Foster, *Bulletin of the School of Oriental Studies* 4 (1928): 862–64, here 863.

[70] In 1599 Sultan Ahmed al-Mansur of Morocco (r. 1578–1603), the victor over King Sebastian of Portugal, had sent his ambassadors to England with a letter in which he addressed Queen Elizabeth in similar language as a ruler "who has status and majestic glory, firmness and stability, a rank which all her co-religionists, far and near, recognise, the Sultana Isabel whose status among the Christian peoples continues to be mighty and elevated" (Matar, *Britain and Barbary, 1589–1689*, 25). Elizabeth had sent an envoy, Ralph Skidmore, to al-Mansur (1579), but he was unfortunately murdered six years later by an English merchant, who was later extradited (Matar, *Turks*, 63–4).

of the flowery language from the Emperor and Jahangir's almost childish delight in getting a lot of presents he was not going to get what he wanted; "Yow can never," he wrote testily to the East India Company office, "expect to trade here upon capitulations that shalbe permanent. Wee must serve the time . . . all the government depends upon the present will, where only appetite governs the lords of the kingdom" (Foster, *England's Quest*, 286). As for Jahangir's blandishments, Roe wrote to King James on 15 February 1618 that "He hath written your Majestie a lettre full of good woordes, but barren of all true effect" (2: 495).

Roe's view of the Mughal government, then, seems to have been based on his observation that it was somehow "degenerate," that it ran on the whim of the Emperor and the lust for power and influence of his ministers and courtiers. His private feelings, as he wrote to Sir Thomas Smythe, were that "My employment is nothing but vexation and trouble; little honor, lesse Profitt" (2: 498). Part of the problem was that Roe, albeit "a shrewd, careful, accurate if somewhat aloof and aristocratic man" (B. Prasad, *History of Jahangir* 130), knew very little about India and the Mughals before he got there, although it would not do justice to him to claim that he never learned anything as he interacted with the Mughal court. However, especially in the early weeks and months of his mission, Roe sometimes misunderstood the complexity of Jahangir's character and the way he reacted to these visitors from a faraway land. Initially, Roe described Jahangir as "gentle, soft and good of disposition" (2: 310), and somewhat later praises his "wisdome and goodnesse above the malice of others" (2: 363). However, "the kinge hath no content," Roe told Sir Thomas Smythe, "who expectes great Presentes and Jewelles, and reguardes no trade but what feedes his unsatiable appetite after stones, rich and rare Pieces of any kind of arte" (2: 498). Roe, like other observers, also noted that the Emperor could be cruel (2: 228), for he was "feared for his rages and terrible acts of revenge. The Europeans at his court were struck by the cruelty of the punishments he inflicted on his enemies" (Berinstain, *India*, 74), and he even ordered his rebellious son Khusrau blinded, only to order the wounds tended when the punishment was botched and his temper subsided, as Herbert narrates. Edward Terry, Roe's chaplain, observed of Jahangir's character that "it ever seemed unto me to be compared of extremes, for sometimes he was barbarously cruel, and at other times he would seem to be exceeding fair and gentle."[71] Mandeslo, too, credited Shah Jahan's occasional cruelty to his having inherited "his father's passionate temper and lust for blood" (Oaten, *Early Travellers*, 180).

Jahangir, from a reading of his memoirs, known as the *Tuzuk-i Jahangiri*, seems on the whole to have been an intelligent man of refined, sensitive, and cultured tastes, including an interest in European art, some of which appears to have been hanging in Jahangir's throne-room, as a painting done somewhat later

---

[71] Edward Terry, *A Voyage to East India* (London, 1655), 386.

(1650) by Payag (c. 1590–1655) shows.[72] King James himself, carefully copied from his portrait by an English artist, appears in another marvellous painting by Bichitr (fl. 1615–1650) which shows an ageing Jahangir, sitting on an hourglass symbolising the passing of his life and reign, accepting a book from a Sufi rather than spending time with either King James or the Ottoman sultan, who is also depicted. This is not meant as a snub to his fellow-monarchs, but as an observation that at his time of life Jahangir's mind was perhaps engaged, or at least Bichitr may have thought it should be engaged, with non-material matters. Following Jahangir's rather odd religious syncretism, two plump and very Western-looking cherubs are shown hovering on either side of the Emperor's golden halo (possibly borrowed from pictures of saints that the Jesuits had shown him or his father), one of whom is covering his eyes in an amusing gesture that was perhaps designed to lighten the serious symbolism in the painting.

Jahangir was not by temperament a warrior; indeed, as Berinstain notes, "his attachment to protocol and the heavy organization of his days prevented him from taking an active part in the command of his armies" (*India*, 74). De Laet added that the Mughals under Jahangir were "pronounced by almost everyone to be poor fighters, and by many to be unwarlike and effeminate . . . enervated by Asiatic luxury" (*Empire*, 244). Hawkins earlier had noticed the emphasis on ritual at the Mughal court, which consisted of such things as "a very elaborate and rather humiliating series of salaams expected of a nobleman returning to court after a long absence" (Gascoigne, *Moghuls*, 144); Jahangir's schedule was very rigorously defined, following the rules set down by Akbar, who had "instituted a very precise court ritual" (Berinstain, *India*, 54). Like many of his family, Jahangir enjoyed a drink, and in later years progressed to near-alcoholism, but not nearly to the extent that that disorder was manifested in his offspring and in some of his ancestors such as Akbar's son Prince Murad, whose "venerous and drunken disposition" is described by Herbert (150), or Jahangir's own son Prince Parvez, to whom Roe presented a case of wine, which by the evening had rendered the prince completely unable to grant Roe a personal audience. Yet Jahangir himself was much more than "a drunken despot subject to outbursts of fiendish cruelty," as C. C. Davies described him in the *Encyclopedia Britannica* (R. Prasad, *Early English Travellers*, 54), "a wild uncontrolled cruel man" in von Garbe's opinion,[73] or, as Mason states, "a drunkard . . . debauched by power as well as by wine and opium" (*Men who Ruled India*, 6). As Roe noted, however, Jahangir was also a discerning art connoisseur; he described in detail the Emperor's reaction to some portraits he had brought with him, asking questions and "requiring many judgments of them" (2: 386) and he dearly loved gardens full of roses, which would explain the imagery in his letter to James I. Jahangir also

---

[72] Bamber Gascoigne, *The Great Moghuls* (London: Jonathan Cape, 1971), 149.

[73] Richard von Garbe, *Akbar, Emperor of India* (New York: Kessinger Reprints, n. d.), 39.

had, as Bamber Gascoigne puts it in his discussion of the *Tuzuk i-Jahangiri*, "an almost ecstatic response to simple facts of nature, as when he marvels at a tree in blossom and then, as he looks more closely, marvels "equally" at a single blossom on that tree" (*Great Moghuls*, 34). In addition, Jahangir was a great lover of Persian poetry, and his passion for the beautiful extended even to producing his own designs for such objects as swords and daggers (Berinstain, *India*, 83)

Jahangir also deeply loved his beautiful and intelligent wife, the Persian-born and devoutly Muslim Mehr un-Nisa, otherwise known as first Nur Mahal, or "Light of the Palace," then Nur Jahan, "Light of the World," and she had a great influence over him; de Laet, for one, noted that Jahangir "loved her so deeply that he set her above all his other wives" (*Empire*, 182). More recently, von Garbe even rather hyperbolically credits her "wisdom and determination" (*Akbar*, 39) with saving Jahangir from his own vices of drunkenness and cruelty. Her portrait even appeared on the reverse of some of Jahangir's coins, a doubly unorthodox move because Islam frowned on images and disapproved of female power, at least the public kind; what influence women had behind the scenes was quite another matter. Roe underestimated Nur Mahal's power at first, but he has not been in India long before we find him writing to the Surat factor Thomas Kerridge in 1616 that he should make sure Nur Mahal's present gets to her soon; "The neglect of her last yeare," Roe complained, "I have felt heavyly" (2: 290 n. 1). Later Roe wrote that "a woman is not only alwayes an ingredient, but commonly a Principall drugg and of most vertue;" he also judged Nur Mahal "not incapable of conducting business nor herself voyd of witt and subtiltye" (2: 364). Peter Mundy, on the other hand, described Nur Mahal as "haughty and stomachful" (2: 205), but he likely had never had any dealings with her and was probably reporting hearsay.[74] Nur Mahal was the daughter of Itimad ud-dowlah, Jahangir's chief minister, the man of whom the Emperor himself wrote that he was "a wise and perfect Vizier" (TJ II, 222), but her brother was the devious and duplicitous Asaf Khan, who, as we have seen, was no friend to the English. Roe was aware fairly early on that he would have to deal with Nur Jahan and her "powerful faction" (1: 118), but it was a difficult situation and he did not like to give offence by going over her (or Asaf Khan's) head to the Emperor. All this was made considerably worse because in his relationships with his sons Jahangir was not fortunate; Herbert gives full accounts of the rebellions of Prince Khusrau and of Prince Khurram, and it was this last which hurt Jahangir most, which is evident when Jahangir renamed him in the *Tuzuk i-Jahangiri* "Bi-daulat," meaning "the

---

[74] Peter Mundy (c. 1596–1667) was an employee of the East India Company. He was travelling in India for a number of years (1629–1634). B. Prasad calls his account of Nur Jahan "nasty" and "gossiping" (*History of Jahangir*, 166 n.6). In 1627 Mundy was appointed factor at Surat, arriving in September 1628, after which he travelled in other areas of India for the Company.

wretch,"[75] as opposed to Prince Parvez, whom he calls "my fortunate son" from the time of Khurram's revolt.

As far as the Emperor's religious beliefs were concerned, Roe thought that Jahangir was an "atheist" who had been "brought up in no religion at all" (2: 314); at first glance this might look strange, but, as Prasad notes, "his religious views perplexed his contemporaries and posterity alike. There were those that regarded him as an atheist or an eclectic, a devout Muslim or a Christian at heart, sunk in superstition or a scoffer at all faiths" (*History*, 405). In fact Jahangir was at least a nominal Muslim, but a tolerant one like his father, "too enlightened to be satisfied with mere dogma or superstition" (Prasad, *History*, 400), and he had confirmed the policies of Akbar regarding the state religion. "Sometimes he will make profession of a Moore," wrote Roe, "but alway observe the hollidayes, and doe all Ceremonyes with the Gentilles too" (2: 314). He recorded Jahangir's respect for the Christian religion; "Of Christ he never utters any woord unreverently" (2: 315) Roe stated,[76] but went on to describe what he saw as Jahangir's easygoing tolerance towards Christians in his dominions in a backhanded way, following it with the words "he loves to heare, and hath so little religion yet, that he can well abyde to have any decided" (2: 316). Roe sometimes mistook the Emperor's tolerance for indifference and intellectual laziness, but Jahangir was a man who "combined a strong aesthetic response to life with an obsessive desire to dissect, analyse and record what he saw" (Gascoigne, *Great Moghuls*, 131), which was quite the opposite, and this included an attempt to understand religions other than his own. Jahangir seems to have been sceptical about the miraculous, but inclined to Sufism and interested rather in "meditation on the one God, in reverence for saints, in the society of ascetics and in the observance of religious ceremonies" (Prasad, *History*, 407).[77] What is more, like Akbar before him, Jahangir understood, which perhaps Roe and other Europeans sometimes did not (although James I in his religious policies came closer than most), that toleration makes for better unification than division; Akbar himself thought that "there was some truth in every religion, and that his role consisted in gathering them together into just one, but in such a way that they be one and all at the same time" (Berinstain, *India*, 68). It is not surprising that even intelligent observers like Roe found this odd; whilst Roe was in India the catastrophic Thirty Years War began with a Protestant-Catholic dispute over Bohemia (1618), and there had been religious strife in France all through the sixteenth century, not to

---

[75] *The Tuzuk-i-Jahangiri, or Memoirs of Jahangir*, trans. A. Rogers (1914) (Delhi: Munshiram Manoharlal, 1968), 2: 222.

[76] Coryate also noted this about Jahangir (Purchas 4: 474) but Edward Terry observed that in spite of his respect for Christ, the Emperor (quite sensibly, some might argue) could not make sense of stories about the virgin birth or the resurrection (389).

[77] For a more detailed discussion of Jahangir's religious beliefs, see Prasad, *History of Jahangir*, 405–10.

mention tensions between the Church of England and the Puritans with which James I was struggling at the time of the embassy.

Roe's mission did not end with any great trading undertakings or treaties, but he did get another flattering letter from Jahangir to King James and a *firman* from the Emperor backing up the assurances he had given in his letter that the English would at least get a fair deal. "How gratious is your Majestie," wrote Jahangir this time, "whose greatnes God preserve. As upon a rose in a garden are myne eyes fixed upon you. . . . And the same Honor which God hath given unto Moses and to Jesus, the same God give to you." More to the point, he told the king that "I have given my command to all my kyngdomes, subjects and vassalls, as well to the greatest as to the least, and to all my Sea ports, that it is my pleasure and I doe command there bee given freedome and residence." Further, the Emperor went on, "I have confirmed my woord that no subject of my kyngdomes shall bee so bould to doe any Injurie or molestation to the sayd English" (*Memoirs* 2: 559–60).

Roe had managed to change Indian attitudes towards English merchants, and Foster was probably right when he claimed that "his high character, energy and skill had made a deep impression at court, and had much enchanced the prestige of his nation" (*England's Quest*, 287). Sir Thomas Smythe had been very perceptive recommending Roe for the ambassador's job, for he was indeed "well-spoken, learned, industrious and of a comelie personage" (R. Prasad, *Early English Travellers*, 130). Roe's recent biographer concurs with Foster, adding only that his assessment of Roe's accomplishments in India "is surely just" (Brown, *Itinerant Ambassador*, 107), although it could be argued that what Roe actually got was a *firman* (decree or declaration) from Jahangir, not any kind of real, formal treaty. Yet by 1623 the English had, apart from the main factory at Surat, smaller outlets at Burhanpur, Broach, Ahmedabad, Masulipatam, and Agra itself, and by 1647 they had "twenty-three factories and settlements in India" (Mason, *Men who Ruled India*, 15). Something, at any rate, had started, and Roe, looking back on his experiences in India from his posting in Constantinople, praised Jahangir as "an affable and courteous prince . . . a man that lives humanely with men," as opposed to Sultan Osman II, whom he described as "a dumb image" (Roe, *Negotiations*, 37–38, cited by Barbour, *Before Orientalism*, 196), although he was, apparently, "received with great courtesy" by the Sultan (Brown, *Itinerant Ambassador*, 124).[78] As Richmond Barbour puts it, looking back on his Turkish experiences, "he loved India as never before. He envisions the Moghul court as a magnificent, generously inhabited world where an English aristocrat might feel at home" (*Before Orientalism*, 196).

---

[78] Brown states that this was "hardly a fair comparison to make, for the Turkish prince was but a boy of eighteen," and had just got back from a disastrous campaign against Poland (*Itinerant Ambassador*, 125–26).

India in 1626

When Charles I decided to send an embassy under Sir Dodmore Cotton to Persia via India it was the first purely diplomatic contact to be made with the Mughal Empire. Cotton, from an old and distinguished Cambridge family, was the son of Robert Cotton and Elizabeth Dodmore or Dormer. We know little about his early life save that he was born around 1585, matriculated from King's College, Cambridge (1607), and that the next year he was attending Lincoln's Inn. Cotton was a Gentleman of the king's Privy Chamber, but what special qualifications he had to lead an embassy to the East is not clear, and he had only been created a knight a short time before his mission was to set out for Persia. The fact that he had, at least at first, no direct connections with the East India Company might have weighed in his favour, but too little about the exact circumstances of his appointment is known, and there were, as we shall see, some problems between Cotton and the Company. Herbert states merely that he was a "religious gentleman" and wrote a poem extolling "His country's love and duty to his King" (328–29) and in the 1634 edition expressed regret that "though his memory and virtue cannot die, yet I would he had a monument, a more eminent memorial" (126). Dr. Henry Gooch, Cotton's chaplain and executor, called him "a most noble friend,"[79] and his communications with the East India Company as well as his dealings with Emamqoli Khan later on in Persia indicate that he must have been a person of some grit and determination who had a healthy sense of his own dignity, both of which were good characteristics for an ambassador.

Cotton's mission was, in fact, primarily with Shah Abbas I of Persia rather than with the Great Mughal, but since both monarchs had quarrels from time to time with the Ottoman Empire (and indeed with each other) and might quite possibly want alliances or assistance, a visit to the court of Jahangir was an obvious stop on the way. Charles had instructed Cotton to clear Sir Robert Sherley from the imputations of the Persian envoy Naqd Ali Beg (which will be discussed in full below) and to offer royal friendship to both Shah Abbas and Jahangir. Cotton's relationship with the East India Company, as we have seen, was ambiguous. "The king and the Lords have resolved that Sir Dodmore Cotton should in no sort intermeddle with the Company's servants or goods or have any power over them, and that they do not employ him in anything for the Company," the Company's minutes read. However, following this declaration came the words "yet not wilfully to reject any good office for the advancement of trade if he should voluntarily undertake the same" (*CSP Colonial* 2–5 March, 1627). In other words, although Cotton was not officially working for the Company, no-one would object if he "voluntarily" helped them out by making favourable deals with the Mughals or Persians if the opportunity presented itself. In fact,

---

[79] *The Journal of Robert Stodart*, ed. Sir E. Denison Ross (London: Luzac, 1935), 32.

it appears that Cotton had initially wanted to work with the Company when he was made an ambassador; Foster cites a letter from Sir Morris Abbot[80] (28 March 1626), who had succeeded Smythe as Governor, as stating that "so long as he had hopes to be employed by the Company into Persia as an ambassador, he had a stomach to the journey, but being rejected he is not so forward to undertake so long and tedious a voyage" (*Early Travels*, xx). This may well account for the testiness with the Company which Cotton later displayed prior to the departure of his embassy.

Cotton's embassy arrived in India at a time when Jahangir's power was waning and his sons were squabbling over the possibility of succession. Nur Mahal wished to secure the throne for her son Shahriyar, the product of her first marriage, but her brother Asaf Khan had attached himself to the ascending star of Prince Khurram. In 1622 Shah Abbas of Persia had invested Kandahar, a city which had always been a site for dispute between the Mughals and the Persians because it effectively controlled the caravan route between Persia and India. Jahangir, by now in failing health, had ordered Prince Khurram, who was in Mandu, to stop the Shah, whilst he himself would come up with another army, but the prince had decided to delay his march because he did not want to be too far away if his father died, especially since he was well-informed about the activities of Nur Jahan and Prince Shahriyar. Khurram gave as a reason that it was the monsoon season and even after it was over he would bring his army only if he himself were named commander-in-chief of the Kandahar operation. Jahangir, prompted by Nur Jahan, saw this as open rebellion; he told Khurram that he must send his soldiers at once to Agra, but that he must not accompany them himself, as his father did not want to see his rebellious face; he then sternly rejected an overture from his son. Hearing that Khurram and his army were marching towards Agra anyway, Jahangir led his own forces south to meet his son's army; this family feud was fortunate for Shah Abbas, who promptly occupied Kandahar. Jahangir dispatched Prince Parvez against Khurram, together with Mahabat Khan, whose military experience was greater than that of Parvez and who up until now had been a reliable supporter and friend to the Emperor. They spent the better part of three years chasing Khurram up and down India, and it was into this maelstrom of rebellion, ill-health and political crisis that Sir Dodmore Cotton and his embassy found themselves thrown. As Herbert put it at the time, "the affairs of Industan, by this variety, possess all men's minds with astonishment" (187).

One can hardly wonder that the English envoys and matters of trade were not on Jahangir's priority list by the time Cotton's delegation arrived in India,

---

[80] Sir Morris or Maurice Abbot (1565–1642) of Guildford was a merchant who rose to become Lord Mayor of London, an MP (1621), and was one of the original Directors of the East India Company. He became Governor of the Company in 1624. Abbot was also active in the Virginia Company. He was knighted by Charles I in 1625.

and there seems to have been no direct contact with the Great Mughal, although Herbert was certainly in both Fatehpur Sikri, Akbar's new capital, and Agra, which of course he saw some years before its principal monument, the Taj Mahal, had been erected.[81] The closest they got to a Mughal Emperor was when Prince Khurram "came within two day's journey of Surat," at which "the English ships thundered out his approach and welcome by two hundred great shot, which he afterwards thankfully accepted of" (194). Herbert also visited some other major cities, including Lahore, Burhanpur, Delhi, Broach, and Kabul. He spends much of his time detailing the history of the Mughals from their origins to the time of Shah Jahan, who was of course the Emperor when Herbert augmented the information in his later editions. He draws heavily on De Laet for his information, but often adds his own commentary to the events described; he seems to find the family and internecine strife that often flared up in the Mughal Empire very fascinating. Herbert admires Akbar, although he more than once uses the terms "restless" and "ambitious" to describe him, and when he comes to Jahangir, words like "credulous" are frequent, because he sympathises with the ageing Emperor in his troubles with Khusrau and Khurram. Prince Khurram, or Shah Jahan as we should call him, does not fare very well in Herbert's estimation. Herbert brands him "that fratricide" for the killing of Princes Hoshang and Tahmuraz, the sons of his uncle Prince Daniyal, and after the murder of Emperor Dawar Bakhsh (Sultan Bulaqi), whose character he praises, he refers to Shah Jahan as a man with "infernal ambition." He records with some satisfaction how after Khurram seized power with the help of Asaf Khan his "sins" had "drawn down the heavy judgment of God Almighty, both in taking his beloved wife away" and that "this year his Empire was so wounded with God's arrows of plague, pestilence and famine as this thousand years before was never so terrible." He is delighted that the Persians have captured Kandahar and the Tartars Kabul; "the event is in the hands of God," Herbert rather sanctimoniously remarks. "who even in an infidel hates the sins of blood, incest and dissimulation."

Persia and Europe before Herbert

The history of European contact with Persia is perhaps not so well known as that with India, but in the sixteenth and seventeenth centuries Persia under the Safavid shahs was a country almost as powerful as the Mughal Empire or the

---

[81] Of course, the Taj Mahal was built during Herbert's lifetime; Shah Jahan began its construction in about 1632 and it was completed in 1653. It is possible that Herbert might have read about it in, for example, Francois Bernier's book (1668), which contains a detailed description (293–98) concluding that "I understand that nothing can be conceived more rich and magnificent" (298) than the interior tomb, which unfortunately, as a non-Muslim, he could not view.

Ottoman Empire and equally important in terms of trade and commerce. More-over, as Margaret Meserve has shown,[82] Persia occupied a rather special place in the minds of Europeans and had done so since the second half of the fifteenth century; it was "a genuinely exotic country, not a malign and unknowable neigh-bour but a fabulous resource . . . arguably it was during the early modern period a positive alternative to views of Asia as either as the home of barbarous hordes or of the hellish doctrine of Islam" (which was curious since it was an Islamic country). However, Persia was also a country that the West could, in modern parlance, "do business with" because it was seen, despite its Muslim faith, as a bulwark of resistance to the expanding power of the Turks, whom the West now regarded, amongst other epithets, as "cannibalistic wild men" (Meserve, *Empires* 218), whose Sultan was almost synonymous with Satan, and of course whose scourge would soon be felt all the way to the gates of Vienna. By 1601 James VI of Scotland, who had himself written a youthful epic poem on the battle of Lepanto (1590), was writing to Shah Abbas that he hoped to see "the hateful en-signs of the Turks" brought low, and he regretted that he could not do more to fight the Turks until he becomes king of England and will have a larger navy.[83] And a few years later, Thomas Sherley, Sir Robert's brother, described the Turks in his *Discourse of the Turks* (1607) as "all pagans and infidells, Sodomites, liars and drunkardes" (Matar, *Turks*, 124–25). Even in 1668, the diplomat and his-torian Sir Paul Rycaut was referring to the Turks as "that formidable enemy and scourge of Christianity."[84]

Three "Persian" rulers, Timur, Uzun Hassan, and Ismail I, became very fa-miliar names in the West. When Timur, usually known in England as Tamer-lane or Tamburlaine, defeated Sultan Bayezid I in 1402, his reputation in Europe was mixed; people "vacillated between admiration for his victories . . . and horror at the cruelty with which he pursued them," but after Mehmet II captured Con-stantinople in 1453 Timur, decades dead, became "a sympathetic hero, a warrior with Christian Europe's best interests at heart" (Meserve, *Empires*, 204). He en-tered European literature: the Italian humanist Beltramo de' Mignanelli wrote a biography of him, and later on in England Christopher Marlowe produced a

---

[82] The account given here owes much to Margaret Meserve's book *Empires of Islam in Renaissance Historical Thought,* especially to Chapter 5, "Wise Men in the East," 203–37, which is, of course, much more detailed and concentrates on the reaction of Italian humanists to Timur, Uzun Hassan, and the rise of Ismail I in 1501. Herbert himself gives a full summary of the history, concentrating on Ismail and the Safavids and going on into the reign of Abbas I, beyond the scope of Professor Meserve's study. In later editions he describes Abbas's death, the reign of Safi, and the accession of Abbas II.

[83] *Letters of King James I and VI,* ed. J. P. Akrigg (Berkeley: University of California Press, 1984), 491.

[84] Sir Paul Rycaut, *History of the Present State of the Ottoman Empire* (London, 1668), 398.

two-part drama about him, *Tamburlaine the Great* (1589–1591).[85] For Marlowe, however, Tamburlaine was a morally ambiguous figure who stood for greatness, certainly, but also for incredible cruelty and overweening pride, definitely a man to be admired, but also one to be feared and as an example of a ruler probably one to be avoided. In the plays Marlowe depicted Asia as a location "at once exoticist and cautionary, consumable and ominous," but "for the most part, Tamburlaine's enemies are Christendom's enemies" (Barbour, *Before Orientalism*, 16), just as they had always been. By the 1460s, as Meserve tells us, influential figures like Cardinal Aeneas Sylvius Piccolomini, later Pope Pius II (cited more than once by Herbert), had come to regard Persia as "not a barbarous place but in fact a rather civilized and possibly even Christian dominion" (Meserve, *Empires*, 221). Herbert himself wrote favourably about Timur, referring to him as "that noble Prince" and praising him for acting "in commiseration to . . . distressed Christians." He further commended Timur for bringing Sultan Bayezid's "insolence" to heel and placing the Ottoman ruler "in an iron cage as accustomed to wild beasts" (405), a story which Herbert had probably read in Pius II's fifteenth-century treatise *Asiae Europaeque elegantissima descriptio* (1534), but which is historically inaccurate, as Bayezid simply died in captivity.

In the next decade Western admiration would light upon Uzun Hassan, Sultan of the White Sheep Turkmen, who, like Timur before him, became almost a kind of saviour-figure in the eyes and writings of some Europeans. He had married the daughter of Emperor John IV of Trebizond,[86] and on the strength of this

---

[85] Some other "Persian" plays which Herbert might have known included Thomas Preston, *King Cambyses, a Lamentable Tragedy mixed ful of pleasant Mirth* (1569); John Day / William Rowley / George Wilkins, *Travels of the Three English Brothers* (1607), based on Anthony Nixon's prose account of the Sherleys; Sir John Suckling, *Aglaura* (1637/8); William Cartwright, *The Royal Slave* (1639); Sir John Denham, *The Sophy* (1642); Robert Baron, *Mirza* (1655); and Elkanah Settle, *Cambyses, King of Persia* (1671). Cambyses was a favourite because of his supposed mental instability. For an excellent discussion of Baron's *Mirza*, which claimed Herbert as its source, see Birchwood, *Staging Islam*, 86–91. Another work drawing at least partially on Persian antecedents was Sir Thomas North's translation of *The Moral Philosophy of Doni*, known more familiarly as *The Fables of Bidpai* (1570). It contains the story of the Persian physician Burzoe, who was sent to look for this great book of wisdom by Chosroes II Anushirvan as well as other Persian elements. It has been edited by D. Beecher, J. Butler, and C. Di Biase (Ottawa: Dovehouse Editions, 2001).

[86] A rather curious double standard exists here; of two Ottoman sultans, Selim II (1566–1574) actually appointed Nurbanu Sultana, the former Cecilia Venier-Baffo, as *Valide Sultan*, although there is debate about their actual marriage, and his son Murad III (1574–1595) had a very serious relationship with Safiye, who may have been an Albanian. By a mix-up between numbers (Selim I for II) there was a story that Selim I (1512–1521) had been in love with an Italian woman, and Suleyman the Magnificent married his Roxolana, known as Hürrem in Turkish. None of this helped their reputations: Turks

Christian alliance he could seek alliances with Western countries to curb Ottoman power; as it turned out, some Western powers began to court him. Pius II's predecessor Calixtus III (1455–1458) had been the first to contact Uzun Hassan after the fall of Constantinople, and a year later Pius II himself sent Ludovico da Bologna "to try to find Uzun Hassan" (Meserve, *Empires*, 225). Diplomatic exchanges went back and forth over the next few years, and a treaty with Uzun Hassan, now identified in the West as "King of Persia," was brokered by the Venetian emissary Caterino Zeno (1472).[87] In 1474 Uzun Hassan sent Ambrosio Contarini on a mission to Casimir IV of Poland, "for centuries being perceived as a potential ally in the fight against the Turkish domination," to whom the Persian ruler offered friendship and asked for military help against the Turks, an offer which the Polish king rejected because he did not want to cause trouble with Mehmet II or offend the Tartars of the Crimea, with whom he was already allied.[88] Herbert, who called Uzun Hassan "the famous Armenian Prince" (229), described him later on as a "great Prince" to whom "many Christian Princes despatched their messengers," and mentions that "amongst others Zeno came ambassador from the Venetians to engage him against the Turk" (407). Uzun Hassan did not disappoint his admirers; he routed the Turks at the battle of Erzincan (1473), and even when he was defeated equally heavily a few weeks later and then proved rather chary about more European alliances, "his image in the West was hardly tarnished" (Meserve, *Empires*, 230). His praises were duly sung by such writers as Barbaro, Contarini, Zeno, and Angiolello, to name four travellers mentioned by Herbert.

The third great Persian "champion" was Shah Ismail I, the founder of the Safavid dynasty and grandson of Uzun Hassan. Like Timur, Ismail was seen both as a great and magnanimous warrior and a man who could inflict astonishing cruelty on his enemies. Because there had been a war between Venice and the Turks (1499–1503) in which the Venetians were getting the worst of it, "it was not hard for Venetians both in the Levant and at home to imagine that providence had sent them a savior from the East, one endowed, moreover, with all the best qualities of a prince of the West" (Meserve, *Empires*, 232). Herbert

---

were Turks, it seemed. Even the Prophet Mohammed was rumoured to have once married a Greek wife, which of course was not counted in his favour. For further details see Leslie P. Peirce, *The Imperial Harem: Women and Sovereignty in the Ottoman Empire* (Oxford: Oxford University Press, 1993), 92–95.

[87] Zeno was also "elected," as he tells us himself, "with a commission . . . our government offering to arm one hundred galleys and many other small and large ships, and with them to attack the empire of the Turk from the sea, if he from the East would not fail to press them with all his forces" (Barbaro, *Travels*, 12).

[88] Lech Alex Bajan, "Polish-Persian Diplomatic Relations during the Safavid Period," *Poland-Iran* (2008): 2. http://polandiranblogspot.com/2008/05/polish-persian-diplomatic-relations.html

tells us how the Persians, "perceiving in [Ismail] an extraordinary ingenuity as well as courage, wished for him to advance higher," and goes on to relate how Ismail defeated all his enemies and took power, at the same time explaining how the Shah of Persia came to be known as the "Sophy," which name, he writes, "was not more ancient than Ismail at his coronation." Herbert went on to explain that it derived from Ismail's ancestor Sheikh Safi ed-din al-Ishaq, and then digresses into a long etymology which includes a speculation that as the "Armenian idiom *sophy*" means 'wool,' and the Persians wore woollen headgear, it might be from that word, or from the word *shoff*, which, Herbert says, "I find the shash in ancient times was termed." Herbert does not stop there, but treats readers to a further disquisition on Scythian words, Greek ones, and a comparison with the title of "Great Mughal." Meserve tells us that an Italian writer, Marino Sanudo, came up with the name "Ismail Sophy" in around 1502, "a title derived either from his family name," as Herbert also thought, "or from his religious role as head of a powerful Sufi order of mystics" (*Empires*, 232), both of which make sense. The name "Sophy" became synonymous with any Persian ruler after Ismail. Like Uzun Hassan and Timur before him, Ismail was seen as being "enormously sympathetic to Christians and might even secretly harbour Christian beliefs" (Meserve, *Empires*, 233). He was, like them, a great fighter; Herbert tells us how Fernão Gomes de Lemos, a Portuguese commander, was cordially received by Ismail at Kashan in 1515 and allowed to inspect the Shah's army, after which he returned to Goa where he reported to Governor Albuquerque "that he verily thought Ismail had not fewer than fifty thousand tents in which were lodged a hundred and thirty thousand men." A short time later Ismail engaged Sultan Selim I's forces at Chaldiran and was defeated, due as much to Selim's overwhelming superiority in artillery as to his numbers, because the Persians fought furiously "with such resolution," as Herbert says, "that the Turkish annals call the battle 'the day of doom'," and he praises Ismail's "singular personal valour" (414).

Thus it was that in the sixteenth and early seventeenth century the idea that the Persians might just be the allies needed to counteract the Ottomans still prevailed. Ogier de Busbecq, the Imperial ambassador to the Ottoman court in 1554 and 1556, thought that "Persia alone interposes in our favour" against the Turks.[89] There appears to have been some scepticism. ambiguity, and apprehension as the years went on, although we still find Herbert referring to "the cruel and inexorable Turks" (361) and at the same time praising Prince Hamza's noble efforts to defeat them. According to Herbert, when Sir Dodmore Cotton came before Shah Abbas he told him that "he had undertaken a very great journey to congratulate his success against their common enemy the Turk," and the Shah replied, "raising his body," that in his opinion "the Turks were a mean people compared with the generous Persian," and that "than the Turks no people in the

[89] Bernard Lewis, *What Went Wrong? Western Impact and Eastern Response* (New York: Oxford University Press, 2002), 9.

world were more inconsiderable" (282). Yet even Persian rulers were, in the last analysis, oriental despots, and in spite of all the attempts to tie them in with a heroic past or look for instances when they appeared to tolerate or protect Christians, misgivings began to surface in the minds of Western observers, who had always been aware of the cruelty and "corruption," as they saw it, of Eastern rulers. Trade, of course, was quite another thing, and its prospects and possibilities, then as now, could transcend moral considerations if they were once allowed into play, or so the Europeans believed, for the Persians, like the Mughals, were immensely wealthy. Herbert reported that in 1560 Shah Tahmasp I "received eight millions of crowns gathered from fifty sultans who farmed his income" (459). Perhaps the Shah might be persuaded to part with a few of them when he saw what the English had to offer.

Persia and England

The Russia or Muscovy Company, through which trade with Persia should have been established, had been founded in 1555, but it was the newly-founded Levant Company which in 1581 attempted to develop a Persian trade involving the exchange of cloth for silk. During the interim the first Englishman to actually succeed in making contact with the Persian court was Anthony Jenkinson, who was received by Shah Tahmasp in 1561. Jenkinson was actually employed by the Russia Company; a Russian envoy from Tsar Ivan IV, Osip Nepeia,[90] had arrived in England (1557) and had been received by Mary I, and it was he with whom Jenkinson sailed, "not so much to supervise [English] trade in Russia," as Foster states, ". . . but evidently he was engaged for the express purpose of pushing east from Moscow" (*England's Quest*, 17). It was not until 1561 that Jenkinson, after two false starts, finally set out for Persia, this time carrying letters from Elizabeth I to Shah Tahmasp as well as to Tsar Ivan, through whose territories Jenkinson needed to pass to reach Persia. The Tsar at first refused Jenkinson's request to go to Persia, but after Nepeia interceded for him Ivan relented and even authorised Jenkinson to make purchases of "silk and gems" for him whilst he was there (*England's Quest*, 25).

---

[90] Osip Grigorievich Nepeia was the first Russian ambassador to be sent to England (1556). He almost never got there; on the way over his ship was wrecked off the coast of Scotland before he was sent on to England. After being received by Queen Mary I he returned to Russia, taking with him an English physician, Richard Standish, who was received by Ivan IV. For details, see Samuel H. Baron, "Osip Nepea [*sic*] and the Opening of Anglo-Russian Commercial Relations," *Oxford Slavonic Papers*, New Series 11 (1978): 42–63. A second Russian expedition departed for Persia under Stepan Tverdikov some ten years later (1567).

Jenkinson was duly presented to Shah Tahmasp at Qazvin on 20 November 1561, but got off on the wrong foot when he explained, politely enough, that he was "neither an unbeliever nor Mahometan, but a Christian." The Shah asked the king of Georgia's son, who was at that time an exile in the Persian court, to explain what Jenkinson meant, but that did the Englishman little good, as Tahmasp then told him: "Oh thou unbeliever . . . we have no need to have friendship with the unbelievers," at which Jenkinson was abruptly dismissed, and as he left "after me followed a man with a bassinet of sand, sifting all the way that I had gone," presumably to prevent further contamination of the Shah's palace floors by the feet of the unbeliever (Hakluyt, *Voyages*, 99–100)![91] However, after further consideration and consultation, the Shah relented and sent Jenkinson "a rich garment of cloth of gold" (Hakluyt, *Voyages*, 101), although he still did not grant the English any trading rights. However, the English had made a favourable impression on Abdullah Khan, the semi-independent ruler of Bokhara, and it was due to his good offices that Tahmasp's attitude had become more friendly, which also encouraged Jenkinson to make arrangements for another Persian venture in 1564, resulting in Thomas Alcock travelling to Shemakha in Azerbaijan, where he was cordially treated by Abdullah Khan (Foster, *England's Quest*, 31). From this time for a number of years various attempts were made to establish trading relations with Persia through Russia, with varying success, the most significant being that of Arthur Edwards, who was received by Shah Tahmasp in 1566, who this time "offered a flattering welcome to his English visitor" and even gave him permission to import woollen goods (Foster, *England's Quest*, 32), although when Edwards reappeared a year later the Shah "had evidently forgotten the Englishman's previous visit, and Edwards had some difficulty in making the monarch understand his nationality" (37).

Shah Tahmasp I, who succeeded his father Ismail at the age of ten, was far from being the rather vague-minded and somewhat bigoted ruler that Jenkinson's and Edwards's experiences might have led them to believe. In fact, Tahmasp, whom the English dubbed "Shaw Thomas," was an extremely talented and cultivated man who wrote poetry and painted; in addition, he was a skilled calligrapher, an art much in demand in Muslim countries where it adorned so many paintings and books as ornament in addition to communication. In spite of this, some European writers did not think much of him; Vincentio d'Alessandri, for example, whom Herbert cites, stated that Tahmasp was "of a melancholy disposition," that he was "a man of very little courage," and that his greatest enjoyments were "women and money" (216–17). Although Tahmasp was also a great patron of artists, there came a time when his "guilt-inspired dreams and unsettling

---

[91] Ambrosio Contarini did rather better in 1474 when he met Usun Hassan, who feasted Contarini's delegation in Isfahan and otherwise entertained him royally. "The Persians," Contarini wrote, "are well-behaved and of gentle manners . . . While in Persia we did not suffer a single outrage" (Barbaro, *Travels*, 131).

feelings of political responsibility,"[92] which led the Shah in the late 1540s, under the influence of a newly-acquired mystical religious fervour, to forsake the arts as frivolous, and some of the artists to leave the court for greener pastures, including the court of the Mughal Emperor Humayun, Akbar's father, although some of his sons and nephews continued their patronage. Herbert gives a detailed and fairly accurate account of Persian history from ancient times to the accession of Tahmasp, so there is little need to repeat it here.

The next English visitor of note to Persia was the merchant John Newbery, who seems to have had no particular object in mind other than to see interesting parts of the world, although Foster believes that "he was probably moved by a desire to see what the conditions of trade were in the Levant, with a view to later on venturing farther afield" (*England's Quest*, 80). He arrived in Hormuz on 22 June 1581, where he found that trade was controlled by the Portuguese and the Venetians; Newbery, however, had no goods with him, and it seems that the authorities regarded him simply as a tourist, although he naturally came under suspicion by the traders. Newbery then proceeded to visit most of the important towns in Persia, stopping at Gamrun, Lar, Isfahan, Kashan, Qum, and, finally, Tabriz. He stayed in Tabriz until December 1581, after which he journeyed on to Constantinople. Newbery had been the first Englishman to visit Hormuz, but, unlike Jenkinson before him, he does not seem to have been granted an audience with the Shah, who by 1581 was now Mohammed Khodabanda, after the brief reign of Ismail II (1576–1578), a vicious drunkard who contrived to massacre several of his own brothers. Mohammed Khodabanda, however, had somehow managed to survive his brother's murderous rampage, and when Ismail died in "an unexpected and mysterious fashion" (Jackson and Lockhart, *History*, 253), he had been proclaimed Shah. During his reign, as Herbert relates in detail, there was much fighting between Persians and Turks, during which Mohammed's son Prince Hamza showed his mettle as a general and won several important victories over the Ottoman forces, only to be murdered by his own barber. Shortly after this Sultan Murad III, "the better to prosecute his intended war in Europe," as Herbert writes, "by his ambassador desired a cessation of arms with the Persian" (430), but in 1586 Shah Mohammed decided to abdicate, perhaps under duress. He was succeeded by his son Abbas I, one of whose first acts was to order the Turkish ambassador to be "chabuched . . . upon the soles of his feet," as Herbert tells us, after which the Shah "posted him out of the country miserably disgraced" (431).

---

[92] Stuart Cary Welch, *Persian Painting* (New York: Braziller, 1976), 23.

The Sherley Affair

The purpose of Sir Dodmore Cotton's embassy to Persia was partly (if unofficially) commercial, but the interesting aspect is the diplomatic wrinkles which Cotton was supposed to iron out when he came before Shah Abbas. These largely concerned the status and treatment of Sir Robert Sherley, who had been in Persia since 1599, and whose exploits need some retelling here to put them in context. In 1599 Sir Anthony Sherley, Robert's elder brother, who previously had been in the service of the earl of Essex on an expedition to Cape Verde and the West Indies, had embarked for Persia, Foster tells us, "for the double purpose of inducing the Shah to join the princes of Europe in attacking the Turks, and promoting commercial intercourse between England and Persia." However, as Foster also points out, it is quite likely that Sherley's "real aim was to push his own fortunes by courting the favour of the Persian monarch" (*England's Quest*, 296). Shah Abbas welcomed both the Sherleys and English proposals for an alliance against the Ottomans, and appointed Anthony, whom he made a *mirza* (Prince), as Persian ambassador to Europe. Robert Sherley was left behind as a hostage, and for nine years he served the Shah in various capacities, being especially esteemed for his military skills, which he displayed by accompanying Abbas on his Turkish campaigns.

Prince Anthony, meanwhile, did not do very well in his mission to European rulers, possibly because he was "an irascible man, opinionated, truculent and turbulent,"[93] and did not return to Persia because he was afraid that the Shah would punish him for lack of success. In fact, he was imprisoned in 1605, but afterwards went to Prague, where his luck changed and Rudolph II appointed him Imperial ambassador to Morocco. What Abbas might do in the meantime to his hostage brother does not seem to have concerned him very much; however, Robert continued to thrive, became a Catholic, and married (1607) a Circassian woman, Teresa Sampsonia. The year after his marriage Robert, like his brother before him, found himself appointed Persian ambassador to Europe, because Abbas was still quite keen on an alliance with any European states who would help him fight the Turks or who might be persuaded to buy Persian goods, particularly raw silk. Robert, together with a Persian colleague, Ali Quli Beg Mardan, went to Poland, Germany, Spain, and Italy. Ali Quli Beg went with Sherley as far as Rome, after which Robert, now ennobled as a Count of the Lateran by Pope Paul V (Chew, *Crescent*, 306), went on alone to England via Barcelona and Madrid. He arrived back home in 1611 and was received by James I and Prince Henry, James's eldest son, who, with Queen Anne, stood as a godparent to Robert and Teresa's boy Henry, born that year. As far as his mission was concerned, however, Robert, like his brother, did not succeed in making any

---

[93] Samuel C. Chew, *The Crescent and the Rose: Islam and England during the Renaissance* (New York: Oxford University Press, 1937), 271.

alliances; Emperor Rudolph II was now an ally of the Turks, and no-one seemed that interested in the silk trade, although Sherley was well received by everyone and royally entertained wherever he went.

With all the favour being lavished on him in England and the friendship of Prince Henry, Robert Sherley must have thought that he would have little difficulty persuading English merchants to buy Persian silk, but they apparently balked at the conditions; as Foster put it, "the Shah's terms required the purchase of a very large quantity of silk and the payment in ready money of at least half the price" (*England's Quest*, 298), and as for Sherley himself, some people, including Sir Thomas Roe (Foster, *England's Quest*, 298; Brown, *Itinerant Ambassador* 83–84), were suspicious of his motives.[94] Sherley decided to return to Persia in 1612, but wandered around India for two years on the way there, finally reaching Isfahan in 1615, only to have to make an about-turn almost immediately when Shah Abbas decided that he would like an alliance with Spain. Sherley arrived there in 1617 and stayed until 1622, "during which time," according to Stodart's modern editor Denison Ross, "he seems to have achieved nothing of diplomatic importance" (Stodart, *Journal*, 12).[95] In spite of this, the ever-watchful Roe was alarmed that Sherley might have some success with Philip III and recommended that the English ambassador in Madrid run interference, as Sherley had "apparently . . . given the Shah a hopeful account of his negotiations with the Spanish monarch" (Foster, *England's Quest*, 298).

During the years that Sherley had been having his adventures, trade with Persia had continued rather sporadically. In 1615 Richard Steel, "an enterprising person with an eye for the quick chance,"[96] and John Crowther[97] were given

---

[94] Some scholars have claimed that Roe himself went to Persia in 1618–1619 to "settle the trade in silkes," as Sir William Smith told the Secretary of State, Sir Dudley Carleton, in January 1619 (Brown, *Itinerant Ambassador*, 97, n. 83). However, Brown concurs with Foster that Roe never went to Persia and "at no time . . . did he ever refer to any personal effort in Persia" (98).

[95] Robert Stodart is a rather obscure figure. He came from Caernavon, but, as Sir E. Denison Ross tells us, we know little else about him "beyond what he himself tells us" (*Journal*, 10). Herbert mentions him only twice, and all we know is that he attended Cotton in Shiraz and was present at the ambassador's funeral. His journal starts in April 1626, but goes on for only a few days before stopping until April 1628, so we know nothing about his movements in between those dates.

[96] R. W. Ferrier, "An English View of Persian Trade in 1619: Reports from the Merchants Edward Pettus and Thomas Barker," *Journal of the Economic and Social History of the Orient* 19 (1976): 182–214, here 182.

[97] Richard Steel was to become the father of the first English boy born in India (Ferrier, "English View," 182). The *Journal of a Journey from Azmere in India to Spahan in Persia* was printed by Purchas (4: 266–79) and is available online. John Crowther (or Crowder) was a factor for the East India Company. They travelled from Ajmer to Isfahan in 1615.

privileges to trade there, and just two years later Edward Connock,[98] the first English agent appointed in Persia, managed to negotiate a formal treaty with Abbas, which was confirmed after Connock's death that year by his successor (and ill-wisher) Thomas Barker in 1618.[99] Here again we find Sir Thomas Roe, who did not trust Connock or Barker any more than he had Sherley, airing his misgivings about Persia; he was always worried that the Persians and Turks would make peace with one another and would therefore not be as favourably disposed towards the English, and he feared that as the two nations were currently at war, the Turks would in any case seek to prevent English trade with Persia from going anywhere (Ferrier, "English View," 182). For Roe, it was really a lose-lose situation.

Sherley then journeyed to Rome, where the new Pope, Gregory XV, received him courteously, and the next year we find him again in England, where he again met with James I, whom he persuaded to think seriously about "a project for sending out shipping to Persia independently of the [East India] Company to bring back silk on freight terms" (Stodart, *Journal*, 12). Whilst Sherley had been negotiating with Philip III, Shah Abbas, as Herbert tells us, captured Hormuz from the Portuguese with English help. This, more than anything else, probably put a stop to any hopes of success that Sherley might have in Spain, for Philip was also king of Portugal, and in spite of a treaty between Spain and England, Philip's Portuguese subjects were always at loggerheads and sometimes at blows with the East India Company, and it was partly with the Company's help that the Persians were able to control Hormuz, in return for which they allowed trading concessions to the English. When James I died (1625) no formal negotiations with the Shah had yet taken place with reference to the "project" that had interested the English king, but Charles I decided to pursue the possibilities and send an English ambassador back to Persia with Sherley.[100]

It was at that point (February 1626) that one Naqd Ali Beg turned up in England claiming status as official Persian ambassador, and one of his first

---

[98] Edward Connock (d. 1617) arrived in Jask on the *James* in 1616. In a short time he had managed to get an audience with Abbas, who treated him "with marked cordiality" (Foster, *England's Quest*, 302) and secure an agreement by which the English were, amongst other things, allowed to build their own churches and cemeteries. For further details of Connock, see Foster, *England's Quest*, 299–303.

[99] Barker was described in 1618 as "graced much by the Emperor of Persia" in the minutes of the East India Company (*CSP Colonial*, Volume III, 6–10 November 1618).

[100] Another reason might have been that the Dutch East India Company had established a trading station in Isfahan under the merchant Huybert Visnich in 1623. Moreover, Charles likely knew that Abbas had also sent Musa Beg as ambassador to Holland; he arrived at the same time as Naqd Ali Beg in England, and seems to have caused a great deal of trouble; Blow notes that he "drank a lot, importuned women and resorted frequently to insults" (*Shah Abbas*, 137). cf below, n. 112.

actions was to denounce Sir Robert Sherley as an "impostor." Naqd Ali, whom Henry Gooch later described as "a man of no great quality" (Stodart, *Journal*, 39) was nevertheless given every consideration as an ambassador when he arrived, but shortly before he was to have an audience with Charles I Sir Robert Sherley called on him to deliver his letters of credence and prove that he was no impostor, at which point the real trouble began. The king's Master of the Ceremonies, Sir John Finnett,[101] witnessed the meeting and described how Naqd Ali, "suddenly rising out of his chair" when Sir Robert presented his credentials, "stepped to Sir Robert Sherley, snatched his letters from him, tore them, and gave him a blow on the face with his fist." The Earl of Cleveland stepped between them to break it up, at which point Naqd Ali's son then got into the act, knocked Sherley down and tried to kick him, "while we of the company laid hands on our swords, but not drawing them, because not any one sword or dagger was drawn by the Persians." Naqd Ali backed down, but not before accusing Sherley of forging the Shah's signature, which he said was always "set on the top of his letters, when these letters he had shewed had it on the back side." He also shouted that Sherley had lied when he said he had married "the king's niece," and that he was a "mean" person as well as a fake. Sherley, angry and insulted, protested that he had never claimed that his wife was Abbas's niece but that she was, in fact, "the Queen's kinswoman," which was true. He then told Naqd Ali that when Abbas "employed a stranger" to be an emissary, he would sign the back of the letters "that before their opening they might shew who sent them" (Stodart, 15–16). This, at least, seems to have convinced the English that Sherley's pretensions were genuine, and temporarily silenced Naqd Ali, who made his apologies.

Charles I, when told of this disgraceful incident, "demanded what satisfaction should be given to Sir Robert," but was told that "the Persian did not acknowledge [Sherley] to be an ambassador, and would not yield [him] to be an ambassador, and affirmed that if he should have done less he should have been cut in pieces joint by joint at his return into Persia." The king then decided that at some point he would grant Naqd Ali an audience, but nevertheless "declared his intention of sending Sir Robert as a private gentleman into Persia to justify himself, and one with him of His Majesty's own servants," an arrangement which apparently satisfied Naqd Ali for the time being (*CSP Colonial*, VI, April 1626). Charles seems to have put off the reception of Naqd Ali Beg and instead spoken privately to Sherley "in his withdrawing-chamber" (Stodart, *Journal*, 16). It was as a result of this meeting that a decision was made to send Sherley with Sir Dodmore Cotton's embassy, together with Naqd Ali Beg, back to Persia, where,

---

[101] Sir John Finnett or Finet (1570–1641) served as Master of Ceremonies to both James I and Charles I. He was the author of *Finnetti Philoxenos. Some choice observations of Sir John Finnett, Kt. and Master of the Ceremonies to the two last Kings* (1656). His *Ceremonies of Charles I: The Notebooks of John Finet 1628–1641* have been edited by Albert J. Loomie (New York: Fordham University Press, 1987).

amongst his other tasks, Cotton was to try and get Sherley's name cleared; as Charles had intimated, Sherley was not being sent in any official capacity. We have seen above that as far as Cotton's mission was concerned, he was not specifically working for the East India Company but for the Government of Charles I, and his instructions came from the king's Privy Council. In addition to clearing Sherley's name and reputation with the Shah, Cotton was to "represent unto ye King ye Propositions made unto us by Sir Robert Sherley," and that he was "to comply with ye King as farre as may stand with Reason & ye condition of our affaires in whatsoever shall be found behoveful for confirmation of our friendship & ye Commodity of Our Kingdome and people." Cotton was further told that he should not "take upon you any title, power or employment of a Consull, Nor yt to intermeddle with ye Good of our Merchants trading to Persia" (Stodart, *Journal*, 20–21). The *Court Minutes of the East India Company* further stated that whilst "the king did intend to send Mr. Cotton as an ambassador to the king of Persia, but that the Company had no intention to use or employ him." The man who had authority from the Company to conduct business was not Cotton but William Burt, "to whom they had given very large and ample authority" (*CSP Colonial*, VI, 10 April 1626). On 5 April 1626 it was observed that "the Persian ambassador had had audience of the king, whereat they stood looking upon one another, neither as it seemed being prepared for the meeting, but at last they had spoken together and the ambassador took his leave" (*CSP Colonial*, VI, 5 April 1626).

Sir E. Denison Ross, the editor of Robert Stodart's Journal, believed that "it is more than probable that the conduct of this Persian and the charges he brought against Robert Sherley were instigated by the East India Company" because they feared that Sherley might start his own company (17), and it seems that "the East India merchants exerted themselves to do signal honour to [Naqd Ali Beg]" (Chew, *Crescent*, 327). It was certainly true, as Foster noted, that Sherley's proposals had "failed to elicit any support from the East India Company" (*England's Quest*, 306 n. 1), but it seems possible that the Company might have behaved this way because they had known of Sir Thomas Roe's reservations about Sherley's trustworthiness. Chew suggests that "they feared lest Sherley turn pirate en route and ruin their commerce or might confiscate their goods stored in their factories on the Persian Gulf in revenge for their rejection of his proposals" (*Crescent*, 332). Furthermore, suspicion and mistrust might well have been aroused in their minds by the sight of an exotic Englishman who dressed like a Persian (he and his wife were subjects of two spectacular portraits in full Persian costume which Vandyke painted in 1622), had married one, spoke the language, and was in the service of a Muslim monarch.[102] Sherley had clearly, in the language of

---

[102] There is, apparently, a portrait of Herbert himself in Persian dress, but its whereabouts are not known. Foster cites an article in the *Evening News* (11 February 1927) as stating that "a painting representing Herbert as a young man wearing a Persian dress was seen in a shop-window in Holywell Street just prior to the destruction of that

the nineteenth century, "gone native," which may not have endeared him to the merchants and governors of the East India Company; indeed, as Thomas Fuller rather cattily remarked, Sherley "much affected to appear in foreign vests" and "accounted himself never ready till he had something of the Persian habit about him."[103] As Nabil Matar has pointed out, "Englishmen and other Europeans in the Islamic world lived by Muslim rules," and he noted that James I had not much liked Sherley's Persian attire (*Britain and Barbary*, 107).[104]

In any event, the Governor told Secretary of State Lord Conway and the Lord Treasurer on 8 April that not only would they refuse to lend Sherley any money "on his jewels," which he had requested and which they had been told that the king "expected" them to redeem (*CSP Colonial*,VI, 5 April 1626) but "the truth was they desired to have nothing to do with him" (*CSP Colonial*, VI, 8 April). In any event, Sherley and Naqd Ali would be sent to Persia in the same fleet, perhaps even in the same ship; Sir Dodmore Cotton was none too happy with this arrangement and told Lord Conway that "it might cause mischief" (*CSP Colonial*, VI, 30 April). The Court Minutes of the East India Company tell us of delay after delay in the embarkation of the ambassador's ships, arguments about when certain ships should sail and further dithering about who was to sail with whom and what they should take. At one point Sir Dodmore Cotton himself wrote angrily to the East India Company and told them bluntly "you will perform the duties of obedient subjects, lose no more time in such unnecessary delays," to which the Company replied testily that they did not like the tone of Cotton's letter, which they found "written in a more lofty style than they are accustomed to receive from personages of the highest degree in this kingdom," and protested that they were doing everything they could (*CSP Colonial* VI, 6 May 1626).

---

thoroughfare early in the present century, but the writer could give no information as to what had become of it," nor could Foster himself track it down (Foster, *Herbert*, xiii).

[103] Thomas Fuller, *The Worthies of England* (London: P. A. Nuttall, 1840), 2: 393.

[104] When Sherley was in Rome (1609), the diplomat Sir Henry Wotton had written to Secretary Cecil describing Sherley's Persian clothes, which at that time had included a turban to which he had fixed a large gold cross, a gift from Pope Paul III. Chew tells us that when King James heard about this, doubtless from Cecil, he "remarked bluntly that Sir Robert Sherley was a humbug" (*Crescent*, 306). He later changed his mind when the ever-persuasive Sherley told him in 1611 that he had served the Shah at Abbas's "express command" and "could not disobey." When Sherley left the king "commended his prudence, eloquence and modesty" and his strange attire was evidently forgiven (311). In 1624, however, "Robert's turban again caused trouble" at court; "to remove his turban would be an offence to the Shah; not to remove it would be an offence to King James." Sir John Finnett solved the problem by suggesting Sherley remove the turban and put it on the floor, after which he could put it back on again, a compromise which satisfied King James, who had been, one presumes, forewarned (325).

By January 1627 the arrangements had still not been finalised; an angry Cotton, accompanied by Endymion Porter[105] as Charles I's representative, showed up at East India House "with a message from the king that he expected the Company to make the necessary arrangements as far as Cotton and Sherley were concerned," which the Company, after petitioning the king, finally did (Foster, *Herbert*, xxiii). Shortly before the final departure, Lady Teresia Sherley, who was returning to Persia with her husband, was so appalled at the possibility of the trouble which might ensue if Naqd Ali and Sir Robert disembarked anywhere together during any stopovers on the voyage that she requested the Privy Council that after what she termed "the brutish disgrace done . . . by that barbarous heathen who styles himself likewise Ambassador" a "mandamus" be "directed to the captains of every ship not to suffer the said two Ambassadors to go on shore together until they arrived in Persia" (*CSP Colonial*, VI, February 1627), a request which Secretary Conway granted. Sir Robert and Lady Sherley would sail with Sir Dodmore Cotton in the *Star*, and Naqd Ali Beg would be aboard the *Hart*. The other ships on the expedition were the *Mary*, under Captain John Hall, together with the *Hopewell*, the *William*, the *Exchange*, the *Jonas*, the *Scout*, and the *Refuge*. Sir Dodmore Cotton was not best pleased, however, to discover that Naqd Ali had been given pleasant quarters by the Company aboard the *Mary*, a brand-new ship, rather than the *Hart*; moreover, he described those on the *Star* as "kennels," and complained bitterly that the Company had given Naqd Ali a large wine allowance whilst he and Sherley got none (*CSP Colonial* VI, 18 March 1627). These slights Cotton and Sherley attributed, perhaps correctly, to the animosity of the bureaucrats at the East India Company offices.

Nevertheless, compared to that of the Company, the king's attitude towards Sherley was more positive, which suggests that Atherton and Sanders are correct in stating that Charles "frequently attempted to circumvent the monopoly privileges of the Company" (*Interdisciplinary Essays*, 115), and might have had some interest in detaching Cotton and Sherley from its grasp. Cotton's instructions from Charles I not only recognised Sherley as the Shah's ambassador, but deplored Naqd Ali Beg's behaviour in no uncertain terms. "He did teare ye Commission & stroake Sir Robert Sherley," the instructions read; "which demeanours of his to a person of a noble family of this Kingdome & allyed to many principall & chief persons here could not have been passed over in a Government where Justice and Civility are executed" (Stodart, *Journal*, 18).[106] In the end, however, as we know from Herbert's account, Naqd Ali, apparently sensing that condign punishment awaited him if

---

[105] Sir Endymion Porter (1587–1649) was Groom of the Bedchamber to Charles I from 1622. He had been born in Spain, spoke several European languages, and served as a diplomat in Spain and The Netherlands. Porter was also a noted art-collector, and had worked as an art-agent for Charles I, acquiring several important collections.

[106] Ross quotes from the Owen Wynne MSS., Vol. XII, 144 (the original) and Vol. XXII, 84 (an official copy of the original). See his note in Stodart, *Journal*, 17, n. 1.

Sherley could persuade the Shah that he had done wrong, committed suicide in Suwali by overdosing himself with opium. In spite of this, as Herbert tells us, the reception of the English embassy was lukewarm at best in the end, and the unfortunate deaths of both Sherley and Cotton himself concluded the business. Herbert, who seems to have admired and respected both Cotton and Sherley, also greatly sympathised with Lady Teresia and devoted considerable space in his account to the telling of her story; he evidently kept himself up-to-date with her fortunes, mentioning that she was still living in Rome at the time he made the last revision to his book. Of Sherley himself Herbert wrote in the 1638 edition that "He was the greatest traveller in his time, and no man had eaten more salt then he. . . . He had a heart as free as any man" (203).

A Failed Mission

Why did the Cotton mission fail? Was it simply because, as John Cartwright had observed a few years earlier, that the Persians were "full of crafty stratagems and are breakers of their promise,"[107] or was there more to it? Cotton and Sherley both died before anything concrete had taken place, but Herbert, as well as other witnesses such as Stodart and Dr. Henry Gooch, were convinced that failure was largely due to the machinations of Mohammed Ali Beg, whom they called the "the king's great favourite" (Stodart, *Journal*, 24).[108] He was a man "discovered" by the Shah, who had been impressed with his intelligent conversation and had raised him from obscurity to the rank of Intendant of the Household. The story of his rise makes an interesting parallel with that of the duke of Buckingham under James I and Charles I, something which likely escaped English observers at the time. Stodart calls him "a merchant" (49), and Gooch states that Mohammed Ali Beg was "at first was taken from the shop and now advanced unto the supreme managing of the greatest affairs of state" (Stodart, *Journal*, 29). Just who this man was is not completely clear (Iskandar Beg Monshi does not mention him at all), but his rank of Intendant of the Household placed him in a powerful position when it came to granting access to the Shah. Denison Ross believes that he was also possibly the person of that name who was sent by Abbas as an ambassador to India (Stodart, *Journal*, 86, n.1; Foster, *England's Quest*, 197), although this seems unlikely. Stodart further recounts how Mohammed Ali denied the validity of Sherley's credentials; after the latter's death he told Dr. Gooch that

---

[107] John Cartwright, *The Preacher's Travels* (London, 1611), 63.

[108] Mohammed Ali Beg is also a major character in Robert Baron's play *Mirza* (1655), where he leads a conspiracy against the Prince and is punished in a horrible way at the end. Baron, incidentally, cites Herbert as the source for his plot as well as claiming the use of a letter written by Sir Dodmore Cotton to a friend. Needless to say, the plot is a fiction.

"the kinge tore them," and that if Sherley really had been the Shah's ambassador "why should the king have soe much neglected him as to lett him dye in disgrace and never looke after him" (63)? Herbert himself included a whole section on Mohammed Ali Beg's "undue practices," as he termed them, and noted that Mohammed's conduct was typical of a man with his lack of education and venality, going on to say that the minister was obviously bribed and probably linked to Naqd Ali Beg, who still had his supporters at court. Herbert also had a low opinion of the way the Persians treated people who gave them loyal service, such as Sir Robert Sherley, a practice which he traced back to ancient times as proof that things had not changed that much in Persia. Sir Dodmore Cotton himself, on the other hand, at least according to the report sent by William Burt to the East India Company, had, shortly before his own death, blamed "Sir Robert Sherley and his own unadvisedness" for the failure and "the extreme wants in things exteriorly befitting so high a minister," which had "caused him much disrespect, of which he was very sensible" (*CSP Colonial*, VI, 22 October).

Another reason for the failure of Cotton's mission may have been the machinations of the East India Company, although there is little evidence other than that which is purely circumstantial to support such a contention. However, the limitations which the Company put on Cotton and the complete lack of support they gave him, not to mention their mercenary hint that he could engage in actions which might do them good if he wished, makes it seem quite likely that they had a hand in it. Perhaps they had even bribed Mohammed Ali Beg to make sure that he placed every obstacle in the embassy's way; Chew, for example, states that Mohammed Ali was "an old enemy of Robert's" (*Crescent*, 334), but he does not give any reference for making this assumption. One might hazard a guess that William Burt's report, cited above and coming from a Company man as it did, might have been exactly what the Company wanted to hear, but it would be no more than a guess.

Apart from corrupt ministers and quarrels over the legitimacy of ambassadors, it may be noted here that apart from the fact that the English had been useful to the Persians in the capture of Hormuz, the attitude of the Shah was not that much different from that of Jahangir towards them, although Abbas seems to have been shrewder than Jahangir when it came to the possibilities of profit to himself from trade, since raw silk was a royal monopoly.[109] We find no mention either of the Sherley brothers or of Cotton's embassy in Iskandar Monshi's long

---

[109] The monopoly lasted only until 1634, when Shah Safi lifted it. He wrote to Charles I to explain that he had done so "that middlemen in my country might reape the benefit thereof: and that those who are the owners of the Silke might sell it to whom they would" (*P. R. O. S. P.* 102:40, pt. 1, fol. 190, cited by R. W. Ferrier, "The Armenians and the East India Company in Persia in the Seventeenth and Early Eighteenth Centuries," *Economic History Review*, n. s. 26 [1973]: 38–62, here 45).

and detailed "official" account of the reign of Abbas I,[110] although he does mention the siege of Hormuz and the part played by the English soldiers who helped Emamqoli Khan capture the city from the Portuguese. Relations with the Mughal Empire and difficulties with the Turks naturally overshadowed any dealings with the representatives of a distant European sovereign, and the English simply weren't much of a priority for Abbas in 1627 any more than they had been with Jahangir. They were probably lucky, in fact, to have been granted an audience with the Shah at all; one positive outcome was that Abbas himself seemed, at least according to Herbert's account, apparently sympathetic towards Sir Robert Sherley and spoke well of him at first, but, as Ross observed, "from that time onwards they received nothing but discourtesy from the Persian officials of the court" (Stodart, *Journal*, 21), and when first Sherley and then Cotton himself died (23 July 1628), there was scarcely a need for pretence any more and the Persian officials provided the bare minimum in both provisions and courtesy.

However, Dr. Gooch, who appears to have taken charge after Cotton's death and wrote of how the Persians "play fast and loose in their treaties" and were otherwise dishonest and difficult to deal with (Stodart, *Journal*, 41), nevertheless partly blamed Sherley for the mission's lack of success. "The Lord Sherley," Gooch wrote, "was a stranger, and therefore naturally envied of all, and hated especially by the friends of [Naqd Ali Beg]." This being said, Gooch went on to note that "by his far too liberal speech he exasperated the minds of all against him," although at first even Abbas himself had found that quality refreshing. As the Shah aged, Gooch continued, "that nature changed, so his affection also towards the Lord Sherley cooled, as in reason needs it must," and when Sherley was away from Persia he did not inquire after Abbas's health or "solicit his remembrance" (39), a tactless omission which likely contributed substantially to his loss of favour. Herbert himself had noted in 1634 that Sherley's "condition was free, noble, but inconstant" (125). On the other hand, it should be remembered that Gooch had been a close personal friend of Cotton's, seems to have disapproved of Sherley, and himself was not entirely free of tactlessness; William Burt reported that Gooch had displayed an "uncivil demeanour" towards one of Abbas's messengers who had presented him with a vest, which Gooch, who for some reason didn't like the royal gift, "threw at the bringer's feet" a gesture which looked like a calculated insult and caused the Shah to pack the English "very meanly" off to Gamrun (*CSP Colonial*, VI, 22 October 1628).

Herbert provided a physical description of the Shah; he says Abbas was "of stature low, of a quick aspect, his eyes small and flaming, without any palpebrae or hair over them . . . his moutachios were exceeding long and thick, and turned downwards." John Cartwright, similarly, had noted a few years earlier that Abbas's face was "very sterne, his eyes fierce and piercing, his colour swaffy [*sic*], his

---

[110] Iskandar Beg Monshi, *History of Shah Abbas the Great*, trans. R. M. Savory, 2 vols. (Boulder: Westview Press, 1978).

mustachees on his upper lip long" (72). Cartwright had found the Shah "courteous and affable, easie to be seene and spoken withall" (*Preacher*, 73), which is
borne out by Herbert's recording how Abbas "seated [Sir Dodmore Cotton] by
his side, smiling that he could not sit cross-legged" and then "lifted up his turban" when the ambassador proposed a toast to the king of England." Sir John
Chardin called Abbas, whom he of course had never met, "a Just and equitable
Prince," and went on to note that "all his Endeavours had this one Tendency, to
render his Kingdom flourishing, and his People happy" but he was writing some
decades later with the benefit of hindsight (1673), and under Shah Suleiman, Abbas II's son, says Chardin, perhaps a little disappointed with what he saw, "their
Wealth and their Plenty were found to be excessively diminished."[111]

Herbert's assessment of Shah Abbas is similar to that he made of Jahangir;
there is the obligatory section on Abbas's cruelty, which Herbert, like other western writers, believed to be a given ingredient in the rule of oriental despots, and
in the 1634 edition he went so far as to call the Shah a tyrant (127). Iskandar
Beg Monshi, however, saw Abbas's actions differently. "Reports of his severity,"
he wrote, "had a restraining influence on those who oppressed their subordinates" (*Abbas the Great*, I, 525), and Abbas's biographer David Blow agrees, noting that "Abbas had to be ruthless to create , as he did, a well-ordered state out
of the chaos he inherited."[112] Herbert, like other Europeans, repeats anecdotes
of Abbas's cruel deeds and dilates conventionally on the death that must inevi-
tably overtake all tyrants, however powerful they might have been in life. At the
same time, he stresses Abbas's greatness amongst Persian rulers and applauds his
victories over the Turks. English and European observers professed themselves
shocked at the absolutism exercised by the Shah, on whose word everything depended, and whose favour, like that of Jahangir, was needed in order to get the
slightest headway in diplomacy as in anything else. They also, like the Carmelite
friar Paul Simon, who was in Persia twenty years earlier than Herbert, credited
the Shah's autocratic rule with making the country safe; Simon spent, he tells us,
four months in Isfahan, during which time there were no murders at all (Blow,
Shah Abbas, 159).

Herbert was impressed by the Shah's great wealth, but does not fail to notice the abject poverty of many of his subjects, and more than once compares the
Persian mode of government unfavourably with that of England, where, Herbert
firmly believes, people are not slaves subject to the whims of their overlords as
are the modern Persians; "heathen potentates, swerving from the divine rule of
justice, pamper the corrupt habit of their minds out of a monstrous opinion that
they may every way inebriate their lust without control" (285). He noticed that

---

[111] Sir John Chardin, *Travels in Persia 1673–1677*, pref. N. M. Penzer, intro. P. Sykes
(New York: Dover, 1987), 139.

[112] David Blow, *Shah Abbas: The Ruthless King who Became an Iranian Legend* (London: I. B. Tauris, 2009), 158.

like Jahangir's, "the king's goodwill became soon diverted," and that "whom he loves the king honours, such as he hates the king crushes all to pieces" (283). This bears out what Roe had observed a few years earlier; Abbas, he wrote to Edward Connock in 1617, might well be "affable and Courteous to strangers," but "will eate upon any man" (*Embassy*, 2: 433). Stodart's account also notes the cruelty of which Abbas was capable; he relates how two men delivered a petition to the Shah but that Abbas "did not like the maner of writeing of it," so one man "he caused to be drubed soe that within a while after he died," and the man who had actually written it "he caused . . . to have his hand cutt in the middle, the two fingers and thum up to the wriste" (*Journal*, 51). Dr. Gooch called Abbas "extremely covetous" (Stodart, *Journal*, 38), and Herbert more than once mentions the Shah's love of *pishkash*, the Persian word for presents, a trait which Abbas shared with Jahangir. Roe, too, had noticed that Abbas was "very familiar with strangers if they bee in Cash. In hope to gett, no man can escape him; when hee hath suckt them hee will not know them" (2: 419). Like most other European writers, Herbert failed to mention the Shah's appreciation of literature, his extensive patronage of the arts in general, and his love of building. However, as Sir John Chardin later noted, Abbas "was very well inform'd of what passed among the Europeans" (*Travels*, 100), and perhaps it was this shrewdness which made him play his hand close to his chest. Abbas was also inclined to parsimony when it came to other peoples' needs; Gooch noted with indignation that the allowance paid to maintain the English embassy after Cotton's death "did not come unto 6s. 8d. the day, which is not so much as, in England, we allow the poorest, vilest labourer; or, scarcely, as they themselves in Persia, their basest slaves—such is the magnificence of the Persian court!" (Stodart, *Journal*, 41).

Herbert took leave of Persia by writing a poem in which he decried the vanity of earthly power and glory, but nonetheless noted that Abbas's death came "after he had attained to a higher elevation of glory then any of his race," and he made some complimentary remarks about Abbas II, who had succeeded Shah Safi, the grandson of Abbas I, in 1642. There would be no further formal contact with the Persian court until the embassy of Sir Gore Ouseley to Fath Ali Shah in 1810–1814.

Herbert's Sources on Persia

For his account of recent Persian history Herbert had a number of sources at his disposal. One of the most interesting is Don Juan de Persia, or John of Persia, who as Uruch Beg had been on the staff of Abbas I's first embassy to Europe in 1599, and, as Bernadette Andrea observes, is an interesting example of a reverse process of "going native," a kind of parallel to Sir Robert Sherley from the Persian side.[113] In 1604 he published a book of *Relaciones* in Spanish, which he had managed to learn in a remarkably short time. Don Juan was well-travelled, having been not only to Spain but to France, Russia, and Italy, where he was received in audience by Pope Clement VIII. He was converted to Christianity (some accounts state that Philip III of Spain sponsored him, others that the Pope himself had converted him) and settled in Spain, but unfortunately died in a violent altercation on the streets of Valladolid (1605) at the age of forty-five. Herbert relied on Don Juan for his account of the Sassanid era of Persian history, as well as some of his geographical information for places he himself had not visited, and mentions him by name (229) as a source, which means that Herbert had a reading knowledge of Spanish, because Don Juan's book was not available in English until the twentieth century. Thus, as had been the case with his Indian sources, Herbert reproduces errors and confusions from Don Juan; examples are Herbert's muddling Ali Qoli Khan, beglerbeg of Fars, with Allah Verdi Khan, father of Emamqoli Khan, the "Duke of Shiraz" (233), or his inaccurate dating of the Daylamid rulers of Fars (238). Then there is the account of the mysterious "Deli Mohammed," whom Juan de Persia says defeated the Turks "near Bitlis" and captured Suleiman the Magnificent's harem (416–17); no such person was mentioned by Iskandar Monshi in his account of the Safavids, and more modern authorities such as Le Strange believe that he was, in the latter's words, "a patriotic invention"[114] (Juan de Persia, 323, n. 12). Errors on a larger scale which cannot be attributed to any particular sources are also present, such as a repeat of the account of Prince Hamza's victory over the Turks with its date moved forward. Herbert also used Pedro de Texeira's *History of the kings of Hormuz*, a useful but often inaccurate work. There were also two more historians whom Herbert could have read. Barnabé Brisson, whom he does not mention, was a jurist and politician who had served as Advocate-General of France, but had unfortunately been hanged for treason by order of Henri IV in 1591; he had never been to Persia, but his posthumously-published *De regio Persarum principatu* (1606) seems to have been well received, as was Pietro Bizzari's *Rerum Persicarum historia*, which came out the same year (Brancaforte, *Visions of Persia*, 5). Bizzari, whom Herbert does mention once, was, like Brisson, better known for something other than Persian history as well as also having never visited Persia; he was a distinguished Latin poet who had lived in England for a while, where he got to know Queen Elizabeth I and her spymaster Sir Francis Walsingham.[115]

---

[113] Bernadette Andrea, "Lady Sherley: The First Persian in England?" *The Muslim World* 95 (2005): 274–95.

[114] *Don Juan of Persia, a Shi'ah Catholic*, ed. and trans. Guy Le Strange (New York: Harper and Partners, 1926), 323 n. 12.

[115] When Bizarri returned to Italy he seems to have functioned as an agent for Walsingham in Venice, keeping him abreast of Venetian affairs whilst there were no official

For his account of ancient Persia Herbert used the standard classical sources, Herodotus, Xenophon, Pliny, Ptolemy, and Strabo (for geography and anecdotal information), as well as Arrian and Quintus Curtius Rufus, who supplied him with a great deal of information on Alexander the Great, much of which found its way unnecessarily into the later editions of Herbert's book. A great deal of Herbert's sometimes inaccurate information about the Achaemenids comes from the Bible, particularly the books of Daniel and Esther, now both known to be ahistorical. Non-biblical authorities include Jordanes and Diodorus Siculus for accounts of dubious historical value such as the story of Sardanapalus and the reigns of quasi-legendary figures such as Belochus. In the case of his sources for Sassanid history, Herbert used Byzantine writers such as Theophylact Simocatta and Sebeos's *History of Heraclius*, both of which reinforce the Christian bias of Herbert's account of the Persian-Byzantine wars in the seventh century. Inaccurate information abounds in this section of the work, although it is attributable to Herbert's sources rather than to his own ignorance; the story of the baptism of the Sassanian ruler Khusrau II, for example, is pure fiction and comes from Baronius's *Annales ecclesiastici* (1599–1607), and when Herbert follows Baronius's chronology for the dates (and names) of later Sassanian rulers he becomes completely confused (396–98).

For the later, post-Sassanian legendary history of Persia it would be tempting to think that perhaps Herbert somehow knew of Ferdowsi's great epic poem the *Shahnameh*, because much of the information he gives on this topic may be found in it, but this seems highly unlikely as there would be no available translation until the nineteenth century. Unfortunately, Herbert never mentions Ferdowsi, although he was certainly aware of other eminent Persian men of letters such as Sa'adi, whose *Gulistan* or *Rose-Garden* had been translated into French by André de Ryer (1634), into German by Adam Olearius (1654),[116] and into Latin by Georg Gentius (1651), the latter being Herbert's translation of choice (227).[117] Herbert also writes of the Sufi poet Hafiz, whose poems also remained

---

relations between London and Venice due to Pope Sixtus V's having excommunicated the queen.

[116] Olearius was lucky in that he had some very skilled help; when Shah Safi sent an embassy to Duke Frederick of Holstein its secretary, a distinguished scholar named Haq Verdi, had defected and remained behind in Holstein for the rest of his life. He lived with Olearius for some years and became a Christian. For details, see Brancaforte, *Visions of Persia*, 70–72. André, Sieur du Ryer (c. 1580–1660) had been the French consul-general in Alexandria and had traded for some years in the Levant.

[117] Sa'adi was well served in the seventeenth century. There was another German translation by Johann Friedrich Ochsenbach, *Gulistan. Das ist, königliche Rosengart: Des persischen Poeten Sa'adi* (1636) and some selections from the *Gulistan* together with the Persian text appeared in Levin Warner, *Proverbiorum et sententiarum Persicarum* (1644). George Strachan (see below) owned a manuscript of the *Gulistan*.

un-translated until the nineteenth century (231). On the other hand, it is quite possible that Herbert became acquainted with people amongst the East India Company officials who knew Persian (Steel, for example, had spoken Persian, and of course there was the interpreter Richard Williams, not to mention Sir Robert Sherley himself) and may have discussed literary matters with them. There was also George Strachan, who had arrived in Persia a few years earlier than Herbert (1619) and was still there in 1634; he was a collector of Persian manuscripts and a translator of poetry from both Persian and Arabic. Again, one may wonder whether Herbert met him, but there is no mention of him. [118] By the time Herbert was revising his text Abraham Wheelock, the Professor of Arabic at Cambridge, had produced an edition of the Gospels in Persian (1653). [119] It is a pity that we do not have more information on Herbert's acquaintances and friends in the later part of his life, although it might not be too far-fetched to suggest that as he was intimately acquainted with Sir William Dugdale and Elias Ashmole it is not unlikely that he would have met other antiquarians and schol- ars, particularly at Oxford.

Probably Herbert drew mostly on travel-accounts for historical information; the ones he cites by name include, besides Marco Polo (or M. Paulus Venetus, as Herbert rather confusedly calls him), Friar Odoric of Pordenone, who travelled to Persia sometime after 1318 and whose *Relatio* was printed by Hakluyt (335– 36); Pietro della Valle; Iosafà Barbaro, who had visited Persia in 1471, a Venetian nobleman and ambassador; Ambrosio Contarini, who was there in 1473–1475; Vincentio d'Alessandri, secretary to the Doge of Venice (1571); and the enig- matic John Cartwright, cited above, who was the first English traveller to visit ancient sites such as Nineveh, Babylon, Persepolis, and Susa. Cartwright trav- elled in the company of John Mildenhall, whom we have mentioned above, and although Foster calls him "the Reverend" and Cartwright's account is called *The Preacher's Travels* (1611), he never once mentions doing any preaching and there is no evidence anywhere that he was ever ordained. Herbert calls him "a merchant," and he seems to have been well acquainted with Anthony and Robert Sherley.

There were a few other writers and travellers in Herbert's own time whose books he might have known, although there is no evidence in his text. Given the

---

[118] George Strachan (d. after 1634) was a Scot who, after travelling around Europe for ten years (1599–1609), decided to venture further. In 1615 he was living at Aleppo, and during the next years travelled to Persia, where he visited Baghdad, Gamrun, and Isfahan. He settled in Isfahan (1619) and took up employment with the East India Company, which valued his language skills. He became an intimate friend to Pietro della Valle, who men- tions him several times and corresponded with him (Bosworth, n.p.n.). Strachan left no accounts of either his life or travels. For details, see G. Levi Della Vida, *George Strachan: Memorials of a Wandering Scottish Scholar.* (Aberdeen: Aberdeen University Press, 1956).

[119] See G. A. Russell, *The 'Arabick' Interest of the Natural Philosophers in Seventeenth- Century England* (Leiden: Brill, 1974).

fact that he knew the author, it is strange that he did not mention Adam Olearius's very important account of his travels in Russia and Persia, which appeared in several German editions from 1647 to 1656, but which he could have read in English by the time the final edition of his book came out; it was translated by Dr. John Davies of Kidwelly as *The Voyages and Travels of the Ambassadors* (1662). It is not known whether Herbert read German (he certainly cited a number of German authorities), but if he did he may have known of an early account of Persia written by Hans Schiltberger (printed in 1473), a soldier from Bavaria who spent some time there as a prisoner of war and wrote of his experiences.[120] Schiltberger's book, according to Elio Brancaforte, was "very straightforward, and reflected his background and lack of education" (*Visions of Persia*, 7), but its observations are no less meaningful for that, and apart from Afanasy Nikitin's account, which Herbert certainly could not have known (and in any case it was in Russian) and missionary writings,[121] Schiltberger's was the earliest. Another traveller was an Austrian nobleman who rejoiced in the name of Hans Christoph von Teufel (Devil); he went to Persia in 1589 and was "one of the few travellers to find the country ugly and inhospitable, in contrast to the prevailing view that considered the land to be green, fruitful, and blessed with mineral wealth" (Brancaforte, *Visions of Persia*, 7).[122] Herbert's good friend Jan de Laet also produced a history, *Persia, seu regni Persici status* (1633), which was published a year before the first edition of Herbert's book, and may have been initially helpful to him with historical background, although this is greatly expanded in subsequent editions. Herbert even lived long enough to have read Sir John Chardin's *Travels in Persia 1673–1677*; Chardin, another French jeweller, had visited India and

---

[120] Hans Schiltberger (1381–c. 1440) entered the service of Bayezid I in 1396 after being captured in battle during the Nicopolis Crusade. In 1402 he found himself working for Timur after the latter had conquered the Turks. His *Reisebuch* first appeared in Augsburg (1460), and was printed several times in the fifteenth and sixteenth centuries. It is a mixture of fact (as he had actually been to the places he talks about) and fiction; C. W. Moseley found that he "demonstrably borrowed freely from Mandeville" (Mandeville, *Travels*, 12).

[121] A later missionary with whose work Herbert could have been familiar was Jacques Dutertre, known better as Raphaël du Mans (1613–1696), a Capuchin monk who wrote an account entitled *Estat de la Perse* en 1660. Brancaforte notes that du Mans "was firmly convinced of the superiority of Western thought and was in general unimpressed by the achievements of Persian civilization" (*Visions of Persia*, 8). Du Mans arrived in Persia in 1647 and spent the rest of his life there running a convent. His book was edited by Charles Scheffer (Paris: E. Leroux, 1890).

[122] For details, see Alfons Gabriel, *Die Erforschung Persiens: Die Entwicklung der abendländischen Kenntnis der Geographie Persiens* (Vienna: A. Holzhausen, 1952). Also see Brancaforte, *Visions of Persia*, 5–8. Teufel (1567–1624), after completing his studies in Italy, immediately (1587) embarked from Venice for travels which led him to Turkey, Egypt, Syria, Mesopotamia, and Persia.

Persia in 1665, returning to Persia in 1671 for four years and later settling in England (1677) to avoid persecution as a Protestant. It would be tempting to suggest that the two men met but there is no evidence that they did.

This representative list, which is of course not comprehensive, shows that Herbert did the best he could with what he had at hand, and his reading is quite impressive. There was no way, apart from personal observations he made, for him to have known about or checked up on the accuracy of his information about either Persia or India, and in terms of English authorities there was little for him to go on. This is why when Sir William Foster decided to edit part of Herbert's book in 1923 he chose the Persian section, because it is here that Herbert makes most of his original observations, and Persia was, after all, the final destination of Sir Dodmore Cotton's embassy. Herbert's is simply the best English account of Persia to date; it includes, for example, a detailed description of the ruins of Persepolis, which was accompanied in the 1677 edition by a specially-commissioned engraving by Wenceslas Hollar, and within that description Herbert transcribed the cuneiform inscriptions there, although he did not know what they meant, as well as accounts of major cities such as Isfahan and Shiraz. A description of Persepolis could have been found in both Della Valle and Olearius, whose account of the inscriptions (1662) came in turn from that of his friend Mandelslo, who had, as we have seen, been in Persia some years earlier, but Herbert wanted to be the first Englishman to describe them, and his choice of Wenceslas Hollar to engrave them was inspired. His almost cinematographic description of the reception of the English ambassadors by Shah Abbas contains some of Herbert's best writing, and so does his account of Emamqoli Khan's banquet; these are best left to the reader's judgment and will not be paraphrased here.

However, for the historical information Herbert presents he had to rely on outside help for the details; we may assume that apart from a knowledge of Herodotus and standard historians of Alexander the Great, Herbert's knowledge of Persia before he went there was probably mostly biblically-based, and contained information that we now know to be ahistorical, such as the entire books of Esther and Daniel and the stories of such rulers as Belshazzar and "Sardanapalus." Many sources he cites were added as he augmented the book over the years, which shows that Herbert kept up with his reading; this is one of the advantages of the later edition, as it indicates a mind which continued to update knowledge for many years to make the account more informative and to fill out the background. The other side of the coin is that Herbert tends towards prolixity when describing, for example, the history of Alexander, which must have been well known to his readers, and when he gets sidetracked into long and often boring disquisitions about such topics as which cities are the biggest and the minutiae of Persian clothing.

Herbert and Oriental Religion: Hinduism

For many seventeenth-century travellers and scholars, what set the Orient apart was its religious beliefs, and most of them spent considerable time attempting to explain Indian and other religions to their readers, sometimes with bewilderingly contradictory results. Many of them did it in terms of biblical analogy, yet in spite of this most of them were convinced Indians were not "unfallen angels of an imaginary earthly paradise," but "matter-of-fact members of the human race whose only differences are due to their strange religious practices" (Prasad, *Early English Travellers*, 345). With the Hindus, it was their belief in reincarnation or "the great veneration they show for cows" (de Laet, *Empire*, 85). The only "otherness," to use the literary-critical term, was religion—otherwise "they" were like the rest of us. William Bruton,[123] for example, in his *News from the East Indies* (1638), several times refers to the Bengalis as "barbarous," but this negative characteristic is attributed to their religious beliefs, which are non-Christian, and Bruton also praises their honesty and integrity. Nicholas Withington's account of Hinduism is cited by Prasad as being completely free from prejudice (259). Herbert also, as he describes Hindus and Parsis, emphasises their good qualities far more than those he does not like; that he would condemn suttee, for example, is predictable and understandable, but he, like Bruton and others, finds many good things to say about other Hindu beliefs and practices, although he more than once deplores their "idolatry" and "superstition." Pietro della Valle liked the fact that Hindus "do what they can to preserve the life of all inferior creatures,"[124] which was also noted later (1689) by John Ovington,[125] but at the same time he could, incredibly, claim that even with so many different sects "they have no learning"! On the other side, there is James Howell,[126] who stated unequivocally

---

[123] William Bruton, an ordinary sailor, made a seven-year voyage around India starting in 1633 at Orissa. His rather short (35 pages) book is generally positive about the country; Oaten cites him as stating that the people of Bengal, for example, were "notable, ingenious men, let it be in what art or science whatever, and they will imitate any workmanship that shall be brought before them" (Oaten, *Early Travellers* 175). For details see Lach and Van Kley, *India* 3: 672–78; Oaten, *Early Travellers* 173–76.

[124] *The Travels of Pietro della Valle in India*, trans. E. Grey (London: Hakluyt Society, 1892), 437.

[125] John Ovington (1657–1731) wrote *A Voyage to Surat in the Year 1689* (1696). It has been edited by Sir Henry Rawlinson (Oxford: Oxford University Press, 1929). He went out to India as a chaplain, and later wrote *An Essay upon the Nature and Qualities of Tea* (1699), an early examination of the wonderful properties of that beverage. Ovington, it seems, travelled only to Bombay and Surat, and because of its limitations, his book on India "met . . . with not a little ridicule" (Oaten, *Early Travellers*, 248).

[126] James Howell, *Instructions for Foreign Travellers* (London, 1642), 8. Howell (c. 1594–1666), an Oxford graduate. was a traveller, diplomat, and factory agent as well as a distinguished linguist and grammarian. He travelled in Europe on commercial business

(1642) that "arts and sciences and all moral endowments as well as intellectual
. . . budded first amongst the Brachmans and gymnosophists in India." Camoens
wrote that the Hindus "are disciples of Pythagoras / Who gave philosophy its
name" (*Lusiads* 7. 40) and de Laet, who states that in India "almost all the Heathens follow the sect of Pythagoras" (*Empire*, 85), also mentions that Hindus
"refrain from slaughtering any animals," but ascribes it to their belief in transmigration of souls, which he terms a "superstition" (88). To modern readers, it is unfortunate that early writers were so completely persuaded that Christianity held
the absolute truth and that no religion which did not recognise Christ as the Saviour could be wholly valid, but in the seventeenth century that bias was a given,
and was also the reason why travellers made every attempt to find parallels with
Christianity in order to convey a favourable impression of what they found. It is
something with which modern post-Christian era readers simply have to live.

In the 1634 edition of his book Herbert gave a short description of Hindu
religion followed by a slightly longer one of the Parsi faith which included an
illustration of a "Tower of Silence," where the Parsis lay out their dead for the
vultures and kites to devour. However, by the time he finished the final version
he had read Henry Lord's pioneering study of Indian religions, *A display of two
foreign sects in the East Indies, viz. the sect of the Banians . . . and the sect of the Parsis* (1630), and his descriptions are much more detailed. Herbert may have read
Lord by 1634, as he does list the four Hindu castes and provides details of the
Parsis which he repeats in later editions. However, he seems to have felt that he
needed a much fuller description of both religions in his final version, and he relied heavily on Lord for the information. Henry Lord, recruited by the factor of
Surat, Thomas Kerridge, had lived in India for a number of years as a chaplain
with the East India Company, and whilst there he had made a study of Hinduism and Zoroastrianism. He claimed to have "essayed to fetch material out of
their manuscripts and by renewed access, with the help of interpreters, made my
collections out of a book of theirs called the Shaster" (*Display*, 7). What he ended
up with was a hodge-podge of Hinduism, Jainism, and Zoroastrianism, but Herbert, who had himself actually conversed with Lord, evidently decided that he
was as reliable an authority as he was likely to get, and indeed Lord should get
some credit for having been the first Englishman to attempt a systematic theology of the two Indian religions, even though it may have been based on "scattered

---

and learned several languages, and, like Herbert, could trace a relationship with Wales
and the Pembroke family. Howell was also fluent in Welsh. He is remembered for the
posthumously-published *Epistolae Ho-Elianae*, a series of familiar letters, some of which
are addressed to Pembroke. Amongst many other books Howell also wrote a study of
Louis XIII and his reign (1646); he was the first author to actually earn his living by
writing in English.

bits of information that managed to pass through the filter of his interpreters."[127] Herbert may also have found some information in De Laet, who discusses the "Baneans," the "Rasboots," and the "Hendowines" with varying degrees of inaccuracy, but even his information is second-hand, as he cites Pedro Texeira's *Travels* as his source (*Empire*, 86–88). Another possible source for Herbert, although he did not cite him, may have been Roberto de Nobili, an Italian Jesuit who spent half a century in India (1605–1656) and who learned several Indian languages, including Telugu, Tamil, and Sanskrit, the last of which he may have been the first European to master.[128]

Henry Lord's work is regarded with some caution by most scholars today, and perhaps does not get the serious attention it deserves. Lorenzen, for example, states that he was "less well-informed" than de Nobili ("Who," 644), and it is certainly true that Lord did not have de Nobili's language skills, nor did he have fifty years in India to develop them. One example which may serve to illustrate the problems is Lord's account of Purusha and Prakriti, whom he (and Herbert) term "Porous" and "Parcouty," based on the *Purusa-Sukta*, or *Hymn of Man*, as it is usually known in English (*Rig Veda* 10.90). What happens in the *Rig Veda* is that Purusha, a cosmic giant, is dismembered by the gods as a Vedic sacrifice to create the world. Part of him becomes Viraj, whom Wendy O'Flaherty defines as "the active female creative principle" who was "later replaced by Prakriti or material nature, the mate of Purusa in Sankhya philosophy."[129] Lord goes on to state that from Purusha and Prakriti were born the four castes, and that each representative of the caste took a wife; this is all faithfully recorded by Herbert. Lorenzen calls this "a confused account based on the sacrifice of Purusa" ("Who," 645), whilst Lach and van Kley see it as "a romantic and fanciful description of how the four brothers met their wives;"[130] where Lord got it from can only be guessed, and this editor, certainly, was unable to find the exact origins of the story. Furthermore, there really is no one Shaster, as Lord terms it, but many

---

[127] David Lorenzen, "Who Invented Hinduism?" *Comparative Studies in Society and History* 41 (1999): 630–59, here 643.

[128] Roberto de Nobili (1577–1656), "a lean, handsome man, with large pensive eyes, a sweeping brow and aristocratic features" (Eraly, *Mughal World*, 335), became, to all intents and purposes, a Brahmin, whilst remaining a Jesuit! De Nobili "kept his distance from native inferiors," Robert Birn writes; "He proffered them Communion on the end of a long stick or left the wafer at their door" (239). This syncretic outlook and his demonstrations of compliance with Brahmin customs made de Nobili highly-respected amongst Indians; he wrote twenty-one religious works in Sanskrit and Tamil.

[129] *The Rig Veda*, trans. Wendy O'Flaherty (Harmondsworth: Penguin, 1981), 31 n. 5.

[130] Donald Lach and Edwin Van Kley, *Asia in the Making of Europe* (Chicago: University of Chicago Press, 1994), 647.

sastras, which may be defined as "authoritative teaching,"[131] and it is by no means clear to just which sastras Lord had access. He actually seems to think of these teachings as if they were the Bible, and indeed he follows the biblical order in his explanations, starting with the creation and moving onwards therough the flood and other events as if the two religions were somehow cognates, or perhaps should have been.

Lach and van Kley, too, believe that Lord's sources could not have been wholly accurate; as he was in Gujarat he may well have consulted Nagar brahmans, who were regarded as skilled religious interpreters, but their transmission of knowledge about the Vedas, Puranas, and Brahmanas may have been confused by inadequate translations into English by Lord's own interpreters, which of course was hardly Lord's fault, as scholars are only as accurate as their sources. Prasad is more generous; having pointed out that if Lord "resorted to his own individual judgment," he concedes that he "intelligently wove a fabric, partly authentic, partly fanciful, to explain the Hindu view of creation," and that since he collected information "from every man, from every merchant, and from every relevant book" . . . "It is therefore sometimes extremely difficult to locate exact Indian sources for the numerous passages." Finally, as Prasad says, Lord's informants "appear generally to have been local and regional" (*Early English Travellers*, 316). Yet in spite of the confusion, even Lorenzen admits that Lord gives "a confused but recognizable account" of such Hindu principles as the transmigration of souls, the trio of gods, and the four *yugas* ("Who," 645), and Lord did, in the end, give his English readers probably the earliest extended European description of Hinduism. Herbert's book, in which the description of both Hinduism and Zoroastrianism relied so heavily on Lord, may well have helped spread the knowledge of Indian religions to a larger audience.[132]

---

[131] Klaus K. Klostermeier, *Hinduism: A Short History* (Oxford: One World, 2000), 303.

[132] Another very important early study of Hinduism was that of the Dutch Reformed minister Abraham Roger, *De open deure tot hed verborgen Heydendom* [*The Open Door to Occult Paganism*] (1651). Lach and van Kley call this "the most complete discussion" of the subject and claim that it "really opened the door in Europe for an understanding of the Brahmanical faith" (*Asia*, 478–9). It contains a great deal of information about castes, sects, and social mores. An English translation appeared in 1670, so it is possible that Herbert made use of it in his last revision. Herbert probably knew François Bernier's extended account of Hinduism, in which the author stated that he had consulted a learned pandit as well as his own *agah*, but at the same time admitted "I regret that I cannot bear my testimony to the truth of all that people report" (320). For details, see Bernier, *Travels*, 318–49. There is also a shorter account in Tavernier (Jean-Baptiste Tavernier, *Travels in India*, vol. 2 [New York: General Books, 2001], 105–9).

Zoroastrianism

As far as Zoroastrianism was concerned, there had been knowledge of it and some attempts to make sense of it from the time of Eusebius and Augustine; besides them, a brief list of the writers who mentioned it and whom Herbert cites would include Isidore of Seville, St. Jerome, Jean Bodin, Rabanus Maurus, Sir Walter Ralegh, and Marsilio Ficino, who found connections between Zoroastrianism and his own brand of Christian Neo-Platonism. Ficino, indeed, named Zoroaster as one of six ancient theologians and cited him as an authority on the immortality of the soul.[133] Theories about Zoroastrianism included the idea that its founder was a descendent of Noah, possibly identifiable with Nimrod, although both Noah's son Ham and grandson Cush were suggested. Lord, for his part, claimed that he had received his information directly from the *Zend-Avesta*; indeed, Mary Boyce states that "in 1620 a Parsi clerk at the English factory in Surat interpreted between a priest of his own faith and" . . . "Henry Lord" (*Zoroastrians*, 183),[134] but some scholars have again pointed out that Lord may have employed an interpreter who either had a less than perfect understanding of the *Zend-Avesta* and other holy books or whose interpretative skills were not up to the transmission of its rather (to a Western reader) esoteric and complex doctrines. Boyce notes further in her study of Zoroastrianism that it is "the most difficult of living faiths to study, because of its antiquity, the vicissitudes which it has undergone, and the loss, through them, of many of its holy texts" (xvii), which must have been just as true in Herbert's time as it is now and would have proved an obstacle to the faith's own adherents as well as to those outsiders who wished to learn about it. Christian writers of the seventeenth century, firmly convinced of the truth of their own faith and of its biblical revelation, tended not to cope very well with religions which were infinitely older than their own, and certainly these two are prime examples of such religions.

Lord wrote his book not simply to explain Hinduism and Zoroastrianism, but to condemn them and "to beget in good Christians the greater detestation of these Heresies, and the more abundant thanksgiving for our Calling" (*Display*, 53). His conclusion was that the Parsis, with their worship of the sacred

---

[133] For details, see Michael Allen, ed. and trans. *Marsilio Ficino: The Philebus Commentary* (Berkeley: University of California Press, 1975).

[134] Europeans trading in the Mughal Empire had no trouble employing both Parsis and Hindus, who themselves seem to have got along with each other quite well. As usual, the toleration extended towards the Parsis was due to Akbar, who actually asked to hear more about their religion and cordially received a priest, Meherji Rana from Navsari, in 1573. Five years later he granted them freedom of religion, and later on asked Shah Abbas to send him someone "to help in compiling a Persian dictionary." Dastur Ardashir Noshiravan came to the Mughal court in 1597 (Mary Boyce, *Zoroastrians* [London: Routledge, 2001], 182–83).

fire, are actually sowing the seeds of their own destruction, namely preparing themselves rather for the fire of the Christian hell rather than the purifying fire of Zoroaster's teachings. Lord was by no means wholly negative in his handling of what must have seemed a very strange religion indeed; he lists the precepts of the faith and does not condemn every aspect of it, especially if he can find some correlation with his own faith, which, for him, partly legitimises it. Herbert cannot forbear, however, in his discussion of Zoroastrianism, to call its practitioners "heathen idolators" (71), although he too does not omit to mention points of agreement, as his description is so close to Lord's. However, Lord's attitude towards religions other than his own must not be allowed to detract from the valuable service he performs in elucidating these two religions, and his description of Zoroastrianism, which Herbert largely adapts and paraphrases in his book, seems to be the earliest one available in English from the pen of someone who was actually on the spot, knew some Parsis, and had taken the trouble to talk to them. Lord's account was quite influential outside Herbert's own use of it; it was cited, for example, by Thomas Hyde (1636–1703), the eminent Oriental scholar whose *Historia religionis veterum Persarum* (1700) was a landmark in early comparative religious studies, and who saw Zoroaster as a man who had carried out a significant reform of Persian religious practices.

The Parsis were seen by Westerners as generally prosperous, peace-loving and law-abiding; many travellers remarked on these aspects. They were also hard-working, and we find John Ovington commending them as "very industrious and diligent" (*Voyage*, 219); della Valle also referred to them as "very industrious people" (*Travels*, 443). Of course, some of their religious customs were bizarre; Sir Streynsham Master,[135] for example, noted that if Parsi houses caught on fire, they would not use water to put it out, "rather choosing to load them with dust or sand" (2: 315). It might also be worth pointing out that whilst the Parsis were generally friendly towards strangers, they were also, as Tavernier discovered a few years later, "scrupulous in discovering the mysteries of their religion" (Tavernier, *Travels*, 163). Herbert noted that the Parsis, whom he found "living peaceably," were themselves friendly enough, although he too observed that they did not like to go too deeply into their religious beliefs; this might well have been because by Jahangir's time the Mughals had become somewhat less tolerant, and they may have feared that the foreigners' tongues might become too loose. Herbert himself found that "they seldom feed together, lest they might participate one another's impurity," a comment also found in della Valle, who stated that "they will not eat with any mixt company" (443). The Parsis did not like talking

---

[135] Sir Streynsham Master, *Diaries 1675–1681*, ed. Sir Richard Carnac Temple, 2 vols. (London: John Murray, 1911), 2: 315. Master (1640–1724) was the East India Company agent, later Governor, in Madras (1678–1681). He is known for having made significant administrative reforms in Madras and for having successfully defended Surat against the Marathas.

about the "towers of silence," as their *dakhmas* were termed; "they do not delight," Herbert wrote, "that it [the *dakhma*] should be seen of strangers," and he remarks on the putrid smell of the decomposing corpses which he could see from where he stood. However, he made a drawing of a tower of silence, which is prominently displayed in the book.

Buddhism

The existence of Buddhism had been known to the West since Hellenic times, when Greek kings in the region of Bactria had adapted it. Furthermore, as Audrius Beinorius writes, "information about Buddhism had filtered through to the early Christian world . . . most notably from Clement of Alexandria"[136] in about 200 C. E., and missionaries had made contacts in subsequent centuries, as did Marco Polo and other secular medieval travellers. Marco Polo mentioned "Sakyamuni Burkhan" (Buddha) in his discussion of idolatry in Ceylon; he was, people told Polo, "the best man who had ever lived among them, and the first they revered as a saint and in whose name they made idols" (*Travels*, 282–83). Polo gives a reasonably accurate account of Buddha's childhood and upbringing, stating in conclusion that "assuredly, had he been a Christian, he would have been a great saint with our Lord Jesus Christ" (283); however, he habitually refers to Buddhists as "idolaters," reflecting the orthodox view of Christians of the time towards people of other faiths. When Francis Xavier was in Japan, he received information about Buddhism from one Anjiro, the first Japanese convert, but Anjiro could only explain his former beliefs in Christian terminology, and the results were, to say the least, mixed, as the bewildered Francis Xavier heard about the Buddhist "Supreme God" and a kind of "trinity" of Buddhist deities. What is more, as Anjiro was not a well-educated man, his conception of Buddhism was, as a result, less scholarly than based on popular beliefs.

Herbert, on the other hand, writes only indirectly of Buddhism, which he sometimes conflates or confuses with Hinduism or Shintoism and which he usually dismisses as idolatry. The likely reason is that by the time Herbert was in Asia, Islam and Hinduism had practically suppressed Buddhism in India, and there were no really sustained accounts of the religion available to him outside Marco Polo and Francis Xavier. When Herbert writes of Buddhism at all, he usually repeats second-hand information about temples or monuments in places he himself has not visited, such as Burma, Siam, Pegu, and Japan. Here he relied on the accounts of travellers such as Ralph Fitch, who certainly visited Pegu and Burma, or John Saris, whose journals supply much of what Herbert had to say about Japan, including a description of the *daibutsu* at Kamakura, various

---

[136] Audrius Beinorius, "Buddhism in the Early European Imagination: A Historical Perspective," *Acta Orientalia Vilnensia* 6 (2005): 7–22, here 8.

fotiques (as he calls images of Buddha), and possibly the Sanjusangendo temple in Kyoto with its Kannon statues and huge Buddhas. Herbert might have known something of the writings of Matteo Ricci or of Francis Xavier on the subject; the latter was, according to Beinorius, "shocked by the morals of the Japanese Buddhist monks and lay people" ("Buddhism," 12).[137] Herbert also gives some flavour of the antagonism of Christianity towards Buddhism in his account of Dom Constantino de Bragança's pillaging of and the subsequent destruction of Buddha's tooth in Ceylon (1560), where it had been taken from its home in the temple at Kandy and publicly burned by the Archbishop of Goa.[138] As Beinorius states, "for Christians, there could be no question of any dialogue with Buddhists as equals, for the simple reason that truth could never be balanced against error" ("Buddhism," 13).

Herbert drew most of his information on Buddhism from the accounts of John Saris, Francis Xavier, Marco Polo, and one or two others. He does not seem to have known either François Caron and Joost Schouten's *True Description of the Mighty Kingdoms of Japan and Siam* (1671), perhaps the most accurate description of those countries, or the account of Jorge Àlvares, which Sindemann describes as "neutral," and which, she noted, "contained neither discriminating statements about the foreign rituals or religious practices."[139] When he discusses its Japanese manifestation Herbert confuses Buddhism with Shintoism, and the result is sometimes bewildering, but the Japanese section contains most of what Herbert has to say about his conception of Buddhist religious practices. "At that time," Sindemann explains, "Buddhism had many close ties to native Shintoism so that different religious teachings were often confused in an illogical manner" (126). Herbert usually conflates the two religions, as his source, more often than not John Saris, also did; for example, Herbert writes of "fotics," which is his word for a shrine or temple (he does not distinguish between the two), not realising that the very word is a corruption of the Japanese *hotoke*, which means either Buddha himself or refers to religious objects within a Buddhist temple. He then describes a "fotic" at a place he calls *Tencheday*, which turns out to be Tensho Daijin, another name for the sun-goddess Amaterasu, not a place at all. This is a mistake not even Saris made, and Herbert must have misread the latter. Saris got it from Will Adams of future

---

[137] It is also possible that Herbert knew Daniello Bartoli's biography of Francis Xavier, *De vita et gestis S, Francisci Xavieri libri quatuor* (1666). For details, see Beinorius, "Buddhism," 12. Until the nineteenth century, there was little scholarly information on Buddhism available. For details, see Philip Almond, *The British Discovery of Buddhism* (Cambridge: Cambridge University Press, 1988).

[138] Charles Allen, *The Search for the Buddha: The Men who Discovered India's Lost Religion* (New York: Carroll and Graf, 2002), 31–32.

[139] Kerstin-Katja Sindemann, "Japanese Buddhism in the 16th Century: Letters of the Jesuit Missionaries," *Bulletin of Portuguese/Japanese Studies*, 2 (2001): 111–33, here 119.

Shogun fame, who told him that he had seen "the fotoqui dedicated to Tencheday, to which image they make devout pilgrimage," and that Tencheday "is thought to be the Devil."[140] A further error occurs when Herbert, following Saris once more, writes of a place known as *Dabys*, which is evidently the Daibutsu at Kamakura! To cap off this litany of misattribution, Herbert wrote in the 1638 edition that "at solemn times" the Daibutsu "was enflamed within, and sacrificed unto by offering him a child, which in his embraces is fried to death in an infernal torture" (335), a passage which was subsequently expunged.

Islam

For many people in the Renaissance and seventeenth century, when they thought of Muslims they thought of the Turks,[141] and whenever Western scholars wrote about Islam their writings, as we have already seen, more often than not tell us more about their attitudes towards the religion than they do about the religion itself. Because the subject is so large and because there are many available books about the relationship between Islam and Christianity, this section will concentrate on Herbert and his source material rather than discussing the whole vexed question in detail.

Herbert's attitude towards Islam is that of a typical Protestant Christian; he is an inheritor, to a great extent, of all the prejudices and misconceptions about Islam and its prophet which had been expounded in the writings of Europeans since medieval times. The attitude in the Middle Ages had been either that Islam was just another "pagan" religion, or that it was some kind of perversion of Christianity and that Mohammed was a heresiarch of the most diabolical kind. Dante, for example, had placed both Mohammed and Ali in hell with other

---

[140] Sir Ernest Satow, ed., *The Voyage of Captain John Saris to Japan, 1613* (London: Hakluyt Society, 1900), 133.

[141] Herbert almost certainly knew Richard Knolles's *General History of the Turks* (1603), which "framed Ottoman history for Stuart England." Knolles (c. 1550–1610) was a schoolmaster in Kent who had neither travelled to Turkey nor understood Turkish, but "derived his narratives from Greek, Latin, French, German and Italian — not from English — sources" (Barbour, *Before Orientalism*, 16–17). Later editions contained material contributed by Sir Thomas Roe based on his own experiences in Turkey, and Herbert may have also known the continuation by the diplomat Sir Paul Rycaut, author of *The Present State of the Ottoman Empire* (1668). He may also have known some of the "slave-narratives" of people who had endured years of Turkish captivity; some of these are discussed by Bernard Lewis, notably Georgius de Hungaria (c. 1422–1502) who was captured in 1438 and escaped only after twenty years to write his memoirs, *Tractatus de moribus, condicionibus et nequicia Turcorum* (printed 1576) and Giovanantonio Menavino, seized as a child and brought up in the Sultan's court, escaping in 1513 and the author (1548) of *Della legge, religione et vita de'Turchi* (Lewis, *Islam and the West*, 75–77).

schismatics; "See how mangled Mahomet is," he wrote, "In front of me, Ali goes weeping / His face split open from his chin to his forehead" (*Inferno* XXVIII, 31).[142] A second random example[143] of what this entailed may be found in the writings of Riccoldo de Monte Cruso (c. 1243–1320), a peripatetic Dominican who spent a number of years wandering around western Asia and the Middle East doing missionary work. Whilst in Baghdad he had produced his most admired and influential work, *Contra legem Saracenorum*, which appeared in print in 1550 but had actually been translated a few years earlier by none other than Martin Luther (1542), in whose favour it must be said that he admitted that Muslims "were better at charity, fasting, devotions and prayers" than Catholics.[144] This book was, according to Kurt Jensen in his introduction to Ricoldo's *Libellus ad nationes orientales*, another anti-Islamic polemic, "an elaborate refutation of Islam divided into seventeen chapters which are mainly concerned with the content of the Quran and claim that it is contradictory, not confirmed by miracles, irrational and violent" (n.p.n.). However, as Birchwood and Dimmock observe: "most of these Christian writers of the Middle Ages who write anti-Muslim polemics do so from the position of . . . subjected minorities desperately . . . seeking to instill disdain for Islam in their flock to sustain the tide of apostasy" (*Culturaal Encounters*, 15). One of Herbert's authorities, Edward Brerewood, noted in his *Inquiries Touching the Diversity of Languages and Religions* (1614) that "it hath ever been the condition of the conquered, to follow for the most part the Religion of the Conquerors" (103). This is an interesting comment if one remembers that Afanasy Nikitin, the Russian merchant, had actually converted to Islam in the 1470s.[145]

---

[142] Dante Alighieri, *The Divine Comedy*, trans. C. H. Sisson (London: Pan Classics, 1981).

[143] Ramon Llull, for example, whom Herbert cites in his book, also had some favourable things to say about Islam, and in fact argued that Islam should be formally studied, if only because so many people had embraced it and therefore could not be saved. Mandeville, whom Herbert cites more than once, also showed tolerance towards Islam; "his summary of Muslim attitudes to Jesus and Mohammed," says Moseley, "is fair, sensible, and detailed" (Mandeville, *Travels*, 27). In Herbert's own time Edward Brerewood admitted that the Muslims were tolerant towards Christians in Constantinople and elsewhere (*Inquiries*, 2–3).

[144] M. Birchwood and M. Dimmock, *Cultural Encounters between East and West, 1453–1699* (Cambridge: Cambridge Scholars Press, 2005), 14.

[145] Nikitin's conversion may well have been an early example of "conversions of convenience." Nabil Matar, for example, points out that by the sixteenth century "Christians, seeking to improve their fortunes or end their enslavement, converted to Islam and joined Muslim society and enterprise" (*Turks*, 9), a theme taken up by dramatists (see below).

As the centuries wore on, the attitudes often remained the same.[146] Samuel Chew cites lines from a play by John Mason, *The Turk* (1610), in which the evil Muleasses addresses Mohammed as "Eternal substitute to the first that mov'd / And gave the Chaos forme," and calls Islam "the fooles Philosophy" (396).[147] Robert Daborne's play *A Christian Turned Turk* ends with a tirade against Islam uttered by the real-life pirate John Ward in which he gleefully imagines a new crusade under a united Christianity and a slaughter of Muslims, "Beating out a path to Jerusalem / Over the bleeding breasts of you and yours"[148] (Vitkus, *Plays*, 230). Herbert, like George Sandys, the poet-traveller whose *Paraphrases of the Psalms* (1636) he cited more than once and whose *Relation of a Journey begun An. Dom. 1610* he probably read, certainly had "the Protestant spirit . . . very much alive in him" (Haynes, *Humanist as Travellers*, 91); in the latter work Sandys refers to Mohammed as "the Impostor" (Purchas 6: 217). Thomas Newton, a schoolmaster and Latin poet whose *Notable History of the Saracens* (1576) Herbert probably consulted, called the Quran a work of "pestilent doctrine and gross opinions,"[149] and for Herbert in the seventeenth century as much as for Riccoldo in the thirteenth, Islam was a dreadful perversion of Christianity, "a confused hodgepodge or mass of superstition" (459), as he puts it. Chew observed very aptly that "the Renaissance inherited a confused and contradictory mass of grotesque notions" (*Crescent*, 387) about Islam, and Herbert, together with some of his contemporaries, seems to have "inherited" a fair number of them, too. Even whilst admitting, for instance, that Jesus and Mary are admired and respected by Muslims, Herbert essentially saw the Quran as a devil-inspired parody of the Bible and believed that the false prophet Mohammed's sole purpose in writing it had been to undermine the true faith and proceed towards world-domination. André du Ryer, the translator of the Quran, also called Mohammed "ce faux Prophète" and warned his reader "tu seras estonné que ces absurditez ayent

---

[146] To be fair, this is not always quite the case, even with some of Herbert's contemporaries. Tavernier, for example, calls Hindus "idolators," but does not apply the term to Muslims, whom he refers to only as having a "false religion" (*Travels*, 97), and refrains from diatribe.

[147] Mason's play was performed in 1607 by the king's Revels Children. There is a modern edition by F. Lagarde (Salzburg: Institut für Anglistik und Amerikanistik, 1979). Other plays with Turkish themes which Herbert may have known include Thomas Kyd's *Soliman and Perseda* (1588), Robert Greene's *Tragedy of Selimus, Emperor of the Turks* (1594), Robert Daborne's *A Christian Turned Turk* (1612), and Philip Massinger's *The Renegado* (1623). Daborne's play, which has been edited by Daniel Vitkus together with those of Massinger and Greene, is also discussed in Part II of Gerald Maclean, *Looking East: English Writing and the Ottoman Empire Before 1800* (London: Palgrave Macmillan, 2007).

[148] Daniel Vitkus, ed., *Three Turk Plays from Early Modern England* (New York: Columbia University Press, 2000), 230.

[149] Thomas Newton, *A Notable History of the Saracens* (London, 1576), 133.

infecté la meilleure parti du Monde" (Chew, *Crescent*, 449). Edward Brerewood wrote that "Arabia was indeed the nest that bred and fostered that unclean bird . . . from Arabia that poyson hath in such sort dispersed it self through the veins of Asia, that neer the one half is at this day corrupted by it" (*Inquiries*, 100); della Valle thought that "because [Islam] contains much in it very pleasing to flesh and blood . . . and complies exceedingly with corrupt Nature," that "like a Gangrene, it spread it self into many parts of Asia and hath enlarged itself like Hell" (*Travels*, 419) and he worried about the fact that there were more Muslims than Christians in the world. Islam was also seen by some as a kind of proxy for Satan; Camoens, for example, wrote of "a priest, / A devoted follower of the law of Mohammed" who was "allied" with the Devil, and to whom Bacchus appeared, disguised as Mohammed (*Lusiads* 8. 47–48), whilst Islamic angels such as Munkir and Nasir are recast as "devils." Herbert himself characterised the Quran towards the end of his discussion as "the way to Acheron" (477), and in the 1634 edition referred to Mohammed's "lying miracles" (153).

Islam was, moreover, Herbert wrote, "mixed with so many fantasies and inventions as renders the whole full of absurdities and contradictions and forced with such trash as may powerfully provoke any sober student to height of laughter." He also saw Islam as an enslaving creed, a characteristic reflected in the fact that Muslim governments were absolutist and autocratic in nature, whilst Christian governments (who only enslaved people who were not Christian) were motivated by a liberating creed. He concluded his lengthy and highly fanciful exposition of Islam by calling its beliefs "fanatic dogmas" and Mohammed, whose name, Herbert incorrectly states, "Arabically signifies 'deceit'," a "more crafty then learned lawgiver" who enforced Quranic rules "by commanding that none upon pain of damnation presume to question a syllable of it," echoing what he had found in Brerewood, who writes of the "peremptory restraint (even on the pain of death) to all Disputation touching their Religion" (*Inquiries*, 103) and della Valle, who calls Mohammed "a man fill'd with all Subtlety and Craft" (*Travels*, 419). Even Adam Olearius in his translation of Sa'adi warned readers that the great Persian poet "was raised like his compatriots in the seductive belief of Mohammed and the sect of Ali," and that the reader must treat "Mohammedan concepts" in the same way that Virgil sifted the writings of Ennius "when he picked beautiful pearls out of the dirt" (Brancaforte, *Visions of Persia*, 69).

Herbert lived long enough, however, to have seen the rise of genuine oriental scholarship (as opposed to Said's "orientalism") at the universities, with the establishment of chairs of Arabic and other signs that attitudes towards Islamic cultures might be changing, although as Daniel Vitkus points out in connection with, for example, William Bedwell's book discussed later on,[150] "Islam was nar-

---

[150] William Bedwell (1562–1632) is often called "the father of English oriental studies." He published an Arabic edition of the Gospel of John (1612) in addition to this work on Islam; his interest in Arabic works was connected with his study of mathemat-

rowly defined and caricatured as a religion of violence and lust that advocated *jihad* in this world and sensual pleasures in the next" (*Plays*, 11). That Bedwell and many of his contemporaries still did not seem to grant Islam some of the respect it deserved, and which it seemed to be getting by the last quarter of the seventeenth century, is unfortunate, but the attitudes of scholars like Olearius in his edition of Sa'adi surely reflect that some change was in the offing.[151] For example, Ros Ballaster, whose study of "fictions of the East" begins in 1662, notes that "Attempts were made in the seventeenth and eighteenth centuries to correct errors about Muhammad and Islam," but even she qualifies this by stating that they were made "largely . . . to protect the Christian case against it [Islam] from counter-charges of imposture."[152]

However, we can still see in Herbert illustrations of the most basic of difficulties between East and West, namely the West's persistent misunderstanding of Islam, a situation which, as Margaret Meserve states, "is a story that has yet to find an ending" (*Empires*, 245), and which for Herbert is evident in the attitude he takes towards Islam, as we shall see below.[153] It is perhaps telling that there was no Latin translation of the Quran in the Renaissance until a medieval one from about 1143 appeared in print (1543), and although this was made available in other European languages, there was no English one until that usually

---

ics, a science in which Arabs excelled. The work mentioned here was actually "an English translation of an anonymous Arabic original," and "consists of three dialogues between two pilgrims returning from Mecca," one of whom is a Christian and converts the other to the "true faith" (Chew, *Crescent*, 436).

[151] It might be germane to note here that in Herbert's lifetime Abraham Wheelock (c. 1593–1653), Professor of Arabic at Cambridge, had produced an edition of the Gospels in Persian (1653) and that the *Polyglot Bible* (1652–1657) of Bishop Brian Walton (1600–1661) had included Persian as one of its languages. See Russell, *'Arabick' Interest*.

[152] Ros Ballaster, *Fabulous Orients: Fictions of the East in England 1662–1785* (Oxford: Oxford University Press, 2005), 50.

[153] In all fairness, it should be noted that for many centuries Muslims thought equally badly of Christians. Mandeville, for example, has a chapter where he claims to have spoken with "the Sultan," who told him that "Christians are so proud, so envious, such great gluttons, so lecherous and moreover so full of covetousness that for a little silver they will sell their daughters, their sisters, even their own wives to men who want to lie with them" (*Travels*, 107–8). Of course, the writer of this passage may simply be indulging in satire and rating his own countrymen's hypocrisies. Bernard Lewis cites one Sa'id ibn Ahmed of Toledo writing in 1068 about the "northern and southern barbarians" (Europeans), who "lack keenness of understanding and clarity of intelligence, and are overcome by ignorance and apathy, lack of discernment and stupidity" (Bernard Lewis, *The Muslim Discovery of Europe* [New York: Norton, 2001], 68). However, by the fourteenth century the eminent Tunisian historian Ibn Khaldun was praising the development of philosophy and science in "the lands of the Franks," where, he says, "the philosophic sciences are thriving, their sessions of study increasing" (149).

ascribed to Alexander Ross (1649), and it was made not from the Arabic which had been edited by Hinkelmann the same year, but from André du Ryer's French version, which had appeared two years earlier. On his title-page the translator said that his English version would satisfy "all that desire to look into the Turkish vanities," not a particularly good start for tolerance and understanding, and he follows up with an introduction in which he refers to the Quran as an "Ignis Fatuus" (A4v)[154] and goes on to state that in fact he had produced the work so that Christians might know their enemies better. Yet, in spite of the negativity of views expressed, Arabic scholars in the seventeenth century, not to mention Herbert himself, evidently felt that there was nevertheless a need to make this material available to a wider public, and posterity should be grateful to them for doing so, as should those who feel that the relationship between East and West is rarely a matter of black-and-white. Samuel Chew, writing specifically about du Ryer's translation of the Quran, thought rather charitably that condemnation of Islam by those who at the same time sought to make it known "was necessary . . . in order to obtain permission to issue [their] work" (*Crescent*, 449). Two good examples from different parts of the seventeenth century may be found in *Mohammedis imposturae* (1615) and *The Confusion of Muhamet's Sect, or a Confutation of the Turkish Alcoran* (1652). The first is a treatise by William Bedwell, in which he stated, in spite of his book's title, that "in the Alkoran" . . . "there is no one opinion so impious & wicked, which may not be found in the bookes of" . . . "Irenaeus, Tertullian, the Ecclesiastical historians, Epiphanius, Philastrius and Augustine" (A3r; cited in Birchwood, *Staging Islam*, 28). The second, a translation by Joshua Nostock of a Spanish work by Johannes Andreas 'Maurus', a converted Moor, "is at pains to dismiss Islam as an insubstantial chimera, and yet such bluff

---

[154] Alexander Ross's authorship of the English translation of the Quran has recently been under debate; see, for example, Alastair Hamilton and Francis Richard, *André du Ryer and Oriental Studies in Seventeenth-Century France* (Oxford: Oxford University Press, 2004). This is a distinct possibility, as Birchwood points out; "in contrast to the defiant tone of the preface," he writes, "Ross strikes a scholarly rather than doctrinaire attitude, explicitly referring to a discrete 'Translator' in the course of his defence" (M. Birchwood, *Staging Islam in England: Drama and Culture, 1640–1685* [Woodbridge: D. S. Brewer, 2007], 67). Ross's "Needful caveat," which is included as an appendix to the translation, demonstrates what Birchwood calls "cultural mediation" as opposed to the author of the preface's polemic stance (68). Chew believed that Ross was responsible for the "doctrinaire attitude" noticed by Birchwood, although he does call the translator "anonymous" and asks "was he Ross himself?" (*Crescent*, 450). Ross did write a work entitled *PANSEBIA: or, a View of all Religions of the World* (1653), in which he called Islam "a mere hodge-podge of fooleries and impieties" (144; cited in Chew, *Crescent*, 450), the word "hodge-podge" echoing (or copied by) Herbert.

confidence belies the threat such writers obviously felt was posed by this rival, and increasingly ubiquitous, ideology" (Birchwood, *Staging Islam*, 88).[155]

One subject which Herbert focuses on is oriental sex practices, beginning, of course, with polygamy, which he understands as originating with the insatiable lust of Mohammed for a younger woman. After recounting how Mohammed met and married his first wife Khadijah, who was older than him, Herbert says that "his stomach growing weak, one sort of meat began to loathe him, for Khadijah was stale and others better fancied him," so he contracted to marry the six-year old Aisha. Mohammed, Herbert continues, "was so insatiably libidinous that he was not ashamed to become a precedent and countenance his incontinency by a law" allowing him to marry Aisha, and he adds for good measure that the prophet had more than a hundred wives (462).[156] This and similar passages are fairly typical of the horror which the Muslim custom of allowing more than one wife aroused in Christians, particularly in Protestants with Puritan leanings like Herbert. Herbert also noticed paintings depicting sexual acts on the wall of Khwaja Nazar's house in New Julfa and some more (together with strategically-placed mirrors) in Shah Abbas's palace at Farahabad which reminded him of Aretino's postures, something one would not have expected him to know much about, until we remember that he was twenty-one when he saw them! At the Shah's entertainment, Herbert describes "the Ganymede boys, in vests of cloth of gold, rich bespangled turbans and embroidered sandals, curled hairs dangling about their shoulders, with rolling eyes and vermillion cheeks," who "carried in their hands flagons of best metal and went up and down proffering the delight of Bacchus," a nice example of juxtaposing the oriental and the classical in order to explain an unfamiliar scene to his educated English readers and hint at the homosexual practices of Muslim despots. As Nabil Matar points out, "Just as sodomy had functioned ideologically in the conflict with the [American] Indians, it was also made to function in the conflict with the Muslims . . . The alleged prevalence of sodomy among the Indians and Muslims presaged their moral and subsequently military decline before the sinless Christians of England" (*Turks*, 127). In the case of Shah Abbas and his court, however, Herbert's observations may not have been so ill-founded; David Blow notes that "Abbas seems to have been bisexual," and adds that "bisexuality and pederasty were not uncommon amongst the Iranian elite in Safavid times — as indeed they were not in Elizabethan and Jacobean England" (*Shah Abbas*, 172). As Herbert says, when Islam broke up under what he calls "schisms," the result was that Muslims in Persia became "exceeding voluptuous," and "lascivious poems" replaced any good doc-

---

[155] Andreas's book was *The Confusion of Muhamed's Sect, or a Confutation of the Turkish Alcoran* (1652).

[156] This is nonsense; after Khadijah's death Mohammed had thirteen wives. Herbert is simply repeating rumours and speculations recorded by numerous other Christian writers determined to misrepresent Islam and its prophet.

trine until the number of "sects" was reduced; "Mohammed's Paradise," Herbert states, "was then in being" (478), founded, of course, on decadence and unnatural sexual practices.

Herbert liked also to comment rather pruriently from time to time on other "lewd" customs of the people he encounters; the "lustful Turk," for which read "Muslim," was already becoming a stock literary figure, and those who had never seen either were already having visions of harems dancing in their heads and fantasising what it might be like to be waited on by girls in diaphanous clothes bearing sherbet and other "oriental" delicacies. Thomas Dekker's play *Lust's Dominion* (1600) had a Turkish setting, and even John Donne, the future Dean of St. Paul's, in his well-known "Elegy XIX: On his Mistress Going to Bed," imagined "Mahomet's Paradise" as an afterlife where men get to make love to beautiful girls whose virginity is renewed every day. Multiple wives, and their corollary the "seraglio," "harem," or "serail" become rooted in the minds of male travellers as "a locus for an entire range of preconceived notions about . . . decadence and deviance" (Birchwood, *Staging Islam* 122), which observers like Herbert were apt to ground in the Muslim religion.[157] These notions survived well into the nineteenth century, and may be found in writers as diverse as Montesquieu, Lady Mary Wortley Montagu and Daniel Defoe, to name three in the century immediately succeeding Herbert's.

Herbert's summation of Islam, then, is based on a fairly typical outlook shared by many writers of the time. He will allow that there are some good things in it, but essentially the faith is dismissed as being hostile to Christianity, based on fabricated revelations, and presided over by a false prophet, whose followers, especially the Turks, are greedy for conquest and the spreading of their faith to all quarters of the world. The Quran, he states puritanically, looks "more like ordinances of war then instructions to conquer lust." When Mohammed needed miracles, Herbert tells us, "some of those his bosom friends and others his familiars taught doves to feed out of his ear and camels to expect their food of him, which blazoned his holiness"; perhaps a Muslim commentator would have similarly mocked the credulity of a man who believed that someone could walk on water or raise the dead, but the irony did not occur to Herbert. Recent history, which featured Ottoman expansion, would have proved to Herbert that Muslims in general but Turks in particular were not to be trusted; rather, they were to be feared and guarded against because they wanted to spread their religion all over the known world. The Persians, however, still retain some of the standing they had in previous centuries, but only because and as long as they are enemies of the Turks; for Herbert, the gallant Prince Hamza, at whose death "all

---

[157] For details on this subject, see for example Dror Ze'evi, *Producing Desire: Changing Sexual Discourse in the Ottoman Middle East, 1500–1900* (Berkeley: University of California Press, 2006), esp. Chapter 6, 149–67.

Persia mourns," is almost as much a hero as Don John of Austria had been for the Christian victory at Lepanto.

Other Lands

Herbert did not confine his observations to Persia and India, although the earlier editions of the book certainly do just that. Essentially, when he came to expand his book Herbert added sections about places he had not visited, such as Burma, China, Siam, Japan, and Pegu, as well as writing about Madagascar, Ceylon, the Comoros Islands, and parts of Africa and Arabia where he did at least touch down, even if the stays were not very long. In some of these places he made quite detailed observations, often including some of his own drawings (including the one of the dodo) and giving information on some of the languages he encountered there. His tone is curiously ambiguous; he never quite states that he was in the places that he did not visit, but he never explicitly says that he wasn't, either. For example, he describes Osaka Castle and the Daibutsu at Kamakura in some detail, but both descriptions were modified from those given by Captain John Saris in his account of Japan. Herbert is well acquainted with all the major accounts of Portuguese, Spanish, and Italian travellers who ever set foot in these places, and freely lifts chunks of their accounts; in all fairness he usually mentions his sources, but it seems sometimes as if he would almost like the reader to assume that he had in fact been to places where he hadn't, because he does not directly cite or refer to any authorities. Why would he, otherwise, have devoted space to accounts of warring factions in Siam or Pegu, conflicts between the Siamese and Burmese, and speculations about Chinese religion? The answer is, of course, that as he grew older and realised that his great adventure would never be repeated, Herbert did the next best thing and became an armchair traveller, "living" the experiences of his reading, perhaps letting his imagination meld with memories and wishful thinking, without directly making claims that were patently untrue. The only give-away is the fact that descriptions of places Herbert had never travelled to are in third-person narrative. The immediacy is gone, and what emerges is Herbert the reader of travel-accounts taking the place of Herbert the actual traveller, visiting those places in spirit which his body had not experienced and, by 1677, would never experience.

The Edition

Herbert's book first appeared in a folio edition (1634); every subsequent edition and impression (1638, 1639, 1662, 1665) was also printed as a folio, up to and including the last one in 1677. In the first edition we find two separate title-pages, one of which is engraved and has the short title *A Description of the Persian*

Monarchy and the second, which is printed, has *A Relation of Some Yeares Travaile.* Herbert dropped the separate Persian title-page after 1634, but expanded the first to include the Mughal Empire and Africa, as well as "other Parts of Asia," most of which he had not visited. The title-page of the 1677 edition reads *Some Yeares Travels into Africa and Asia the Great, Especially describing the Famous Empires of Persia and Industant, As also Divers other Kingdoms in the Orientall Indies and The Adjacent.* This gave him the opportunity to display his learning (and reading) about China, Japan, Burma, and other places, and "describing" was a suitably ambiguous word. In the final revision of his book Herbert presented his readers with his last word on his experiences. He added a wealth of historical information and demonstrated that he had kept himself up-to-date with new works in the area. It was as much a tribute to his scholarship (or pedantry, as some might believe) as it was a travel-account, and it represents a man looking back on a part of his life which was obviously very important to him, or he would not have continued to expand it. Some might argue that there is a loss in the "freshness" of a young man's wonderment which was present in the 1634 edition, but Herbert has kept nearly all the text in his expanded versions, and the additions to the work place what he had experienced in historical and intellectual context. For example, Herbert wished, it appears, to be the first Englishman to fully describe the cuneiform inscriptions at Persepolis, and indeed this ancient city was so important to him that he included the Hollar engraving, which appears only in the present edition. His long description of the monument reflects his later serious interest in antiquarianism; the young traveller has now become the historical scholar, yet the words he uses in his description retain all the traces of his former enthusiasm and sense of awe, and are heightened by the quality of Hollar's illustration. In fact, in many places the 1634 edition is rather sketchy and lacks continuity; Herbert often simply lists places he travelled through without providing any descriptions, and the text jumps from one subject to the next without much transition. These characteristics are part of the spontaneous style and give the book the impression of being written in haste whilst the author was travelling, but apart from some interesting passages, which I have reproduced in the appendices, it reads rather jerkily and is, of course, written without the benefit of hindsight, the elaboration of memory, and the erudition of the scholar-antiquarian (or pedant, depending on the reader's own preference).

In the prefatory note to the 1634 edition Herbert apologises to the reader for the fact that he has not packed his book with references; "More authors I might have used," he writes in a note that does not appear in the last edition, "and rendered myself more useful in that way" (1). If we look again at what Bacon wrote about travel, however, we can understand both why Herbert said that in 1634 and why he decided to contradict it with constant editing, updating, and expanding in the ensuing years. As a young man, Herbert would, according to Bacon, be getting an education by travelling, but as an older man, travelling would be "a part of experience." Herbert, who did not literally travel as an older man, did it vicariously by reading other people's accounts; in his older age he became an arm-chair traveller, but one who had his own experiences to compare with those of the people he was reading. Herbert thus became what Bacon called a "tutor," the ideal kind who "hath the language, and hath been in the country before, whereby he may be able to tell [readers] what things are worthy to be seen in the country" (*Major Works*, 374). In the 1634 edition Herbert was a young man who had "put his travel into a little room," as Bacon says (375); in subsequent editions, starting with the "revised and enlarged" 1638 edition and following with the 1665 edition, where he says on the title page that the book is "much enlarged, with many additions, nigh a third part more then in any of the former impressions," he was the reflective scholar looking back on what was in that little room, re-arranging the furniture, adding a picture here and there, laying down new carpets, and filling up the cabinets with ornaments,[158] in short, turning his travel-narrative into a chorography, as we have earlier discussed. The final revision, with its "many additions throughout the whole work," as Herbert stated on the half-title page, presents us with the room completely furnished, a lot larger, and ready for visitors to enter. Later readers have sometimes proved reluctant to enter; Jonathan Swift, who usually enjoyed reading travel-books, was not too happy about what Herbert had done, and must have had the 1677 edition before him. "If this Book were stript of its Impertinence, Conceitedness and tedious Digressions," he harrumphed, "it would be almost worth reading, and would then be two-thirds smaller than it is."[159]

The room, of course, was a common memory-device from at least the time of Matteo Ricci's famous Chinese "memory palace," but in this case Herbert was able to embellish it and expand its contents with the "authors" who could not be fitted in when he had so little time on his hands and was actually travelling. Their writings would give his own observations the weight of scholarship he evidently thought he needed. In 1634 Herbert had written that "all travellers are subject to untruths," an ambiguous statement which might mean either that

---

[158] In the 1638 edition's dedication Herbert had promised the Earl of Pembroke that "my hand shall not be guilty of more intrusion," a promise he managed to keep until 1665, but he retained the same sentence verbatim in the preface to the present edition, in which nonetheless "are added (by the author now living) as well many additions throughout the whole work, as also several sculptures, never before printed." Foster thought that the hiatus in editions might have been because Herbert may have felt that "the troublous times of the Civil War and the Commonwealth were unpropitious for the issue of travel literature" (Foster, *Herbert*, xi). It seems more likely that Herbert was just too busy.

[159] J. A. Downe, *Jonathan Swift: Political Writer* (London: Routledge, 1984), 266. There have been various attempts to ascertain the influence of Herbert's book on *Gulliver's Travels*, and it is known that Swift owned a copy of Herbert's book. Downe gives the date of Swift's copy as 1634, but this edition is, in fact, "two-thirds smaller" than the 1677 one, so it seems more likely that Swift had the latest edition. Some readers might, moreover, argue that *Gulliver's Travels* is a better read without Book III.

travellers themselves are prone to telling lies, or that they are open to believing lies from other people, or perhaps both. Adding authorities to back up what he was saying might have been Herbert's way of avoiding this double trap, or at least of convincing his readers that he was trying to avoid it. If readers were to ask "was it really like that?," Herbert could say that it was, and they did not have to take his word alone for it. Thus we find that in the second edition (1638), Herbert added historical information gleaned from the vast amount of reading he must have been doing between 1629 and 1638. More was added in 1665, with Herbert claiming the book had been "much enlarged," and in 1677 he wrote of "many additions," which by now included some new illustrations.

We thus end up here with a book which not only records the young man's travels and retains most of the freshness of the descriptions (we remain "in his pocket" throughout), but also shows a mind trying to contextualise in later years what he saw in the light of his own earlier experiences. Herbert's book is not just a travel-book, but history as well, history which he himself partook of, albeit in a minor way, but he had been there, done those things, and he had done them against the background of what for many fascinated readers must have been utterly unfamiliar, a saga of participation in the unknown, the exotic, and the incredible. And Herbert's book was read; apart from its several editions it is not surprising to find that there were two translations made in Herbert's own lifetime, one in Dutch by Lambert van den Bosch (Dordrecht, 1658)[160] and another in French by Abraham de Wicquefort (Paris, 1663),[161] and that at least one dramatist acknowledged him as a source. Andrew Marvell might have imagined the lover in "To His Coy Mistress" finding rubies by "Ganges' side," but Herbert had actually been by Ganges's side whilst Marvell remained in spirit always complaining "by the tide of Humber." Herbert probably didn't find any rubies either, but what he did find was himself, and the way he put this book together in its

---

[160] Lambert van den Bosch (1610–1698) from Amsterdam was a distinguished translator of Greek plays and of a variety of other material, including Castiglione's *Courtier*. He also had an interest in things English; amongst his own works we find a *History of Charles II* (1660) and *Florus Anglicus* (1651). His translation, entitled *Th. Herberts Zee en Lant Reyse na verscheyde Deelen van Asia en Africa* is available online. Foster noted that van den Bosch "made considerable omissions, yet his version contained over 90,000 words" (*Herbert*, xi).

[161] Abraham de Wicquefort (c. 1598–1682), son of a Dutch diplomat, emigrated to France and followed his father's profession. He represented the Elector of Brandenburg at Louis XIII's court, but after getting into some political trouble found himself in England (1658), then Holland (1659). He went on to become one of the best-known diplomats of his time and wrote a book on the subject, *L'ambassadeur et ses fonctions* (1682), which became a classic in its field. Wicquefort also translated Olearius (1656), Mandelslo, and Garcia de Silva Figueroa (1667). His translation of Herbert is entitled *Relation du voyage de Perse et des Indes orientales, traduite de l'Anglois de T. H.* It was even longer than the Dutch translation, "filling 567 quarto pages" (Foster, *Herbert*, xi).

successive manifestations shows us how he did it and indicates his changing self-perception and his desire to become an "expert" by reading as much as he could. "When a traveller returneth home," Bacon wrote, "let him not leave the countries where he hath travelled altogether behind him" (*Major Works*, 375); for the rest of his life, Sir Thomas Herbert never did.

A Note on the Illustrations

Herbert states in several places that the illustrations are, for the most part, engravings based on his own drawings, which makes his book a rare example of a self-illustrated account, although Herbert is consistently modest about his own "poor skills," as he says in more than one place. Sir William Foster believed that William Marshall, who engraved the 1634 title-page, was likely responsible for the "thirty-five copper-plate engravings which are scattered throughout the volume" (*Herbert*, ix). Marshall (fl. 1617–49), about whom relatively little is known, had made the engravings for, amongst other works, the poet George Wither's *Collection of Emblems* (1635), as well as the symbolically-charged portrait of King Charles the Martyr for *Eikon basilike* (1649), a book now usually attributed to William Gauden but probably based on writings of Charles I and a major example of royalist propaganda. Marshall had also engraved a portrait of John Milton for the 1645 edition of his poems, but Milton was not happy with Marshall's efforts, stating that he had been "clumsily engraved by an unskilful engraver . . . because there was not another in the city in that time of war."[162] Viewing such efforts as the engraving of the dodo and the perspective skills displayed in such plates as the one illustrating the Parsi *dakhma*, one cannot but conclude that Milton was quite right.

The splendid engraving of Persepolis by Wenceslas Hollar, which Herbert commissioned, first appeared in the 1665 edition. Hollar, who had left Prague for England in 1627, was one of the most famous engravers of his time, and too well-known to need much introduction here. Since he was also the engraver for Sir William Dugdale's *Monasticon Anglicanum*, which started to appear in 1655 and for which Herbert did research, it could have been Dugdale who introduced Hollar to Herbert. However, a letter from Herbert to Elias Ashmole written in 1680 on the subject of the latter's *Institutions, Laws, and Ceremonies of the Most Noble Order of the Garter* (1672), in which Herbert writes about "the variety of incomparable sculptures" and says that "Mr. Hollar's death is much-lamented" (Van Erde, *Hollar*, 95) suggests that it might well have been Ashmole who made the introduction. On the subject of the Persepolis engraving Katherine Van Erde states that "the aerial view conveys a sense of the magnificence and grandeur, in

---

[162] Katherine Van Erde, *Wenceslaus Hollar, Delineator of his Time* (Charlottesville: University of Virginia Press, 1970), 16, n. 26.

spite of considerable decay, that the text describes." Hollar even clearly shows the cuneiform tablet, and with the aid of a magnifying glance the reader could also see "the processional figures . . . each drawn minutely and exactly yet in no way distracting from the baroque sweep of space and the play of light and shadow" (*Hollar*, 79). Foster is probably correct when he states that the attribution to Hollar of other illustrations is incorrect, his reason being that they are not signed (*Herbert*, x). The Dutch translation of Herbert's book was also illustrated, but evidently Lambert van den Bosch felt that Herbert's own drawings, engraved by Marshall, were not quite good enough, and he had them "replaced by nine engravings of some merit, specially drawn to elucidate the narrative." Abraham de Wicquefort's French translation, however, contained no illustrations at all (xi). In this edition, it was decided that only a selection of illustrations would be reproduced, partly due to the quality of the original printing, and partly to obviate the length of the book. The introductory sentences to the illustrations have been retained so that interested readers can look them up.

Editorial Practice

A brief word on editorial practice. The objective here was to produce a readable and accessible edition in modernised English of Herbert's 1677 text, something which might appeal to a general audience but with enough of a scholarly apparatus to give some satisfaction to more specialised tastes. The edition used was also the text chosen by Sir William Foster for his abridgement of Herbert's book which appeared as *Travels in Persia 1627–1629* (1928), and which Foster claimed left "only what the author actually saw or might reasonably be supposed to have gleaned at first hand."[163] He, too, believed that the 1677 text, being "the author's final revision," was the appropriate one to use. What the present editor has done, in essence, is put back all the material that Foster subjected to what he called "an unsparing use of the pruning-knife" (xii), as well as noting some significant textual differences in footnotes and providing an appendix of one or two interesting passages from other editions, such as the detailed account of Queen Ketevan's death given in the 1634 edition but omitted from later ones. Sometimes bushes should be allowed to grow wild, and Foster's rather excessive pruning of Herbert's digressions, language-lists, dilations on historical and theological material

---

[163] Foster's abridgement is the only modern edition of Herbert's book apart from a few extracts here and there. He mentions that "condensed versions have appeared in some collections of travels, such as Harris's (1705) and Moore's (1785)" (xi–xii). Foster's edition contains detailed notes, and it is a tribute to his scholarship that the present editor, with all the electronic and other resources at his disposal, still found a wealth of useful information in Foster, particularly his identification of some places and things which had completely eluded his own research skills.

such as the location of Noah's ark, the Garden of Eden, and the exact geographical site of Ophir, let alone his claims that the Welsh discovered practically every unknown continent and his deleting of several illustrations, deprives the book of much of its charm and some of its whimsical pedantry, although some readers, like Swift, might yet complain about prolixity. The later editions (1662–1677) show the mind of a seventeenth-century gentleman-antiquarian and armchair traveller at work, but one who had actually done some real travelling as well. An abridgement, sensitive or not (and Foster was not always sensitive), deprives readers of the opportunity to see Herbert's mind working over a number of decades as well as eliminating the important chorographical aspects of the work.

Because of the great interest today in the Islamic world through which Herbert travelled, the editor felt that curious readers might be interested in discovering that many of the difficulties we associate with that geographical area were also perceived as such in the seventeenth century. An example of this is the development of Western misunderstanding of Islam, as discussed earlier in this introduction; of particular interest might be Herbert's handling of Sunnis, Shi'as, and other Muslim sects as he writes about "schismatics" like Ali and his Shi'ite followers in Persia. Another might be the political relationship between the West and countries like Iran and the Ottoman Empire, which has almost undergone a complete about-face since Herbert's time; for Herbert the dire threat to world peace was thought to be the Ottoman Empire, whilst for the United States government in 2010, for example, it is Iran, with the Turks, presumably as secular Muslims, being almost acceptable, an interesting reversal. Then, as now, many who did not think too deeply into the situation saw Islam as the enemy of Christianity, whilst at the same time allowing that some Islamic nations (Persia for Herbert) could be political as well as mercantile allies, and played off against others (the Turks), an attitude which no-one seemed to find contradictory, because by the seventeenth century politics was becoming just as important as trade. For these and other reasons it seemed imperative to the editor that an accessible text should be the prime objective rather than one designed to be read by only scholars and specialists.

As Herbert revised his book, he added a great deal of supplementary material from outside sources, but comparatively few major changes were made to his description of the actual events apart from some fleshing-out. Some notable exceptions and variations in editions have been explained in footnotes and some have been cited, especially when Foster found it necessary to note them, although this applies only in the Persian section; a good example in the Indian material is the way Herbert altered the discussion of *sati* from the first to the second edition, tempering his harsh claims about the wife's immorality and replacing them with a more generalised and sympathetic description, and the editor has taken pains to examine the various editions for other such examples. Furthermore, the editor has reproduced the Preface to the 1634 edition so that Herbert's original feelings about his book may be compared to what he wrote in 1677. It seemed to the editor that outside the scope of such examples a collation of all the editions and a huge list of word-variations (many of which would be trivial), apart from serving little purpose for readers, would not repay the vast amount of extra time which would need to be spent on it, especially given the fact that the 1677 edition was the one which Herbert himself wanted to be the final version of what he had to say, the result of many years thinking, reading and revision. The editor can only hope that modern readers will not react to it the way Swift did.

Secondly, although the editor has attempted to identify all the anonymous quotations from classical poets with which Herbert liberally sprinkled his text, the task has proved impossible, and some had to be simply left with his ascription to "a poet," "a noble poet," or someone similarly unnamed. Unless an editor of this text had a brain literally filled with Latin poetry and unlimited time in which to exercise it, which this one has not, it simply could not be done, especially in the case of citations which bear no clues as to where they might be found. At the same time, if an identification comes to mind or can be fairly readily traced, it is noted. I have done some of the translations from Latin myself, but for most passages I have used good modern translations (whenever I could find them) in preference to my own, and I have also accepted the improvements and corrections of my editor, whose meticulous care with the translations showed me just how rusty one's Latin can get after fifteen or so years of disuse. In the end, however, I was able to identify more of them than I had believed possible, due to the fact that many of them were commonplaces or tags which anyone with an education similar to Herbert's would probably have recognised.

Thirdly, there may be some personages or geographical locations on which a note or identification has not been supplied; the reason for this is either that they probably could not be found outside un-translated Persian, Arabic, or Hindi sources, in which the editor has no linguistic competence, or that version (spelling) of the name Herbert gives did not yield the desired results from the available works of reference or online resources, even when recognised scholars in these fields were consulted; Herbert's erratic transcription of names proved too much even for some of them. Every effort has been made to check the accuracy of the notes, which have been reviewed by scholars in the relevant fields, and any mistakes are mine, not theirs. Herbert's book contains many references to people and authors who may be unfamiliar to modern readers; this has necessitated a great number of footnotes, because without some background information the names are meaningless and the events lack context, but it also necessitates an apology to those who are well-versed in Mughal or Safavid history. I have tried to keep them fairly short, but sometimes this is not possible, and I have checked the accuracy of every single identification; when it cannot be found, I have said so.

Fourthly, I have modernised the spelling and punctuation and have modified sentence-structure without changing any words; Herbert, a man of his times, often writes immensely long sentences, some of which occasionally go out of control and sometimes lack main verbs or proper subordination. These I have broken up, but the ones which are grammatically coherent I have tried to leave relatively unscathed. Some peculiarities of style, such as "then" for "than," I have retained, as well as some inconsistencies such as "contemn" and "condemn," which Herbert uses interchangeably. I have glossed unfamiliar words and translated Latin quotations; however, when Herbert himself supplies a translation as well as the Latin I have omitted the Latin. I have also tried in my footnotes to point out modern editions of the works Herbert used, in case readers wish to look further into them, as well as articles or books written by modern scholars which effect the same end.

Fifthly, the editor makes no apology for including some contemporary descriptions of places mentioned by Herbert; it is interesting to compare what he saw in 1627 with what a tourist armed with a *Lonely Planet* or *Rough Guide* might see in 2010. Very often these were the only descriptions available of some of the locations visited by Herbert; now some of the sights he saw are gone, others have fallen into ruin, and some have changed beyond recognition. Herbert was in Agra before the Taj Mahal was built, but even by his time Fatehpur Sikri was a ghost town, and he passed through many towns which have radically changed in nearly four hundred years or have even disappeared from the map altogether. Modern travel guides are accurate and informative, and they also help alleviate the constant stream of references and footnotes to obscure foreign potentates and equally-obscure Latin authors who all appear so frequently without contextualisation.

EUROPA

SOME YEARES

TRAVELS
Into
AFRICA & ASIA
the Great.
Especially Describing the
Famous Empires of
PERSIA and INDUSTANT.
As also
Divers other Kingdoms in the
Orientall INDIES,
and
I'les Adjacent.
The third Edition further inlarged.
By S.r Tho: Herbert Bar.t

LONDON
Printed in the yeare 1677

Pawb yn y Arver.

PAR MER.   PAR TERR.

[DEDICATION TO THE 1634 EDITION]

TO
THE RIGHT
HONOURABLE
PHILIP
Earl of Pembroke and Montgomery, Baron
Herbert of Cardiff and Sherland, Lord Parr
and Ross of Kendall, Fitzhugh, Marmion
and Saint Quentin, Lord Lieutenant
of Kent &c.
Lord Warden of the Stanneries in Cornwall
And Devonshire, Lord Chamberlain of
His Majesty's House, Knight of the
Most Noble Order of the Garter and one
Of His Majesty's most honourable
Privy Council

My Lord,

Good wine needs no bush, but this traveller wants a guide, and as under age, a guardian too. In the wars a beard becomes a captain, and in travel years do well, at least some years of discretion, to enable the looker-on to mark the most remarkable things and those only.

My desire to see took away my sight, as it fares with those who are suddenly taken with a killing beauty or gaze upon the sun. Yet some glimmerings I have observed, like an ill-sighted man who sees with spectacles or perspectives, the rather that Your Lordship's protection may have the same operation on me the sun hath upon barren ground, to call out some useful herb and by virtue only of your own influences.

At tennis he that takes not the first bound loseth the rest, but in a second or third place a man may be the instrument of good, and I care not what room I fill up nor what posture I stand in, so my company be good and the action noble.

This casts me still upon Your Honour's goodness as the patron of virtue and my safeguard both from the ignorance of those who can find fault at home and the malice of such as carp at any rate and condemn before the book be printed, it may be before 'tis ended, who antedate their exceptions and like merchants with their goods enter them before they ship them. Such impressed money I do not like, but protest against it and the paymaster. Yet, why should I fear haste or detraction when Your Honour's favour is my pilot?

To believe myself safe is to be so, since opinion strikes a great stroke in the judgments and affairs of men, and that it is impossible in any subject to find more safety or calmness before this poor barque, which, I assure Your Lordship, hath endured many tosses at sea and is now tossed on land to be ploughed up in long furrows and to bear the brunt of the coldest and hottest air summer and winter censures, which by the just temper of Your Lordship's good name, made surer by that descending interest, you being our chief, shall be thawed and made gentle unto me, who have nothing more to boast of then your nobleness and the title of

Your Lordship's
humblest servant,
Th. Herbert.

Preface
[the Proem to the 1634 Edition]

This journal was taken in danger, which admits of no curiosity and craves but the same favourable light for approbation it was drawn by. Many storms it has endured for company, but more hot days, which have sunburned my lines as well as face, and though I am on shore, yet I fear the sea is not yet calm, for each book sent into the world is like a barque put to sea, and as liable to censures as the barque is to foul weather.

When I landed, I thought to have hoist sail no more, but friends, whose breath is powerful, have once more launched me into the deep (and may it prove a fair gale) by commanding these rude and indigested notions from me, which being accompanied with truth and simplicity, the soul of history, are then like the elements, in most splendour when least mixed and troubles with quotations or observations of other men.

I challenge no thanks for what I publish nor reward, because I plead guilty to unworthiness and all the imperfections you can throw upon youth or haste. None can think so ill of me as I do myself, the rather that your pardon may flow freely and work a kind of miracle upon me in raising my dead thoughts to life, and that my well-wishers, who have offered a civil violence to friendship in forcing my private satisfactions into public shame, may own my faults, which must reflect upon them, since in my obedience I have made all my errors theirs.

More authors I might have used, and rendered myself more useful in this way, but I was on my way to many countries, and travellers have enough to do with variety in men and manners, which make up a library in themselves, besides the situations and present beings of cities and territories seeming better then to labour in uncertain stories which not only perplex the hearers but beget incredulity oftentimes amongst the credulous. My other travails into some parts of Europe I could have troubled you withal, but I love not repetitions nor to entertain you with that from myself I hate in others. Besides, since all travellers are subject to imputations of untruths, I had rather go far to fetch it and send you far off to disprove it then give you the liberty of condemning me at home.

If my thoughts have wandered, I must entreat the well-bred Reader to remember I have wandered through many deserts as to afford me his help to call home by itinerant notions, to fix them, by his favour, upon the Island of Isles,

Great Britain, which like a real map of the whole world, contains the sum and abridge of all sorts of excellencies met here like parallels in the proper centre.

At sea I learned to pray, though I was taught it from my cradle, and he that is more given to swearing then praying may see the wonders of the deep for his recovery, and take the receipt from me with a *probatum est.*[1]

This will serve for induction, that the Reader dwell not upon impertinencies.

---

[1] It has been proved.

To the Right Honourable
PHILIP[2]

Earl of Pembroke and Montgomery, Baron Herbert of Cardiff and Sherland, Lord Parr and Ross of Kendal, Lord Fitz-Hugh, Marmion, and St. Quentin, Lord Chamberlain of His Majesty's most honourable Household, Lord Lieutenant of Kent, Wilts., etc., Lord Warden of the Stanneries in Cornwall and Devon, Knight of the Most Noble Order of the Garter, and one of His Majesty's most Honourable Privy Council.

MY LORD,

Having passed the pikes, I take new courage to come on again. One blow more and I have done; ten to one it lights on my own pate, but if my head stand free, my hand shall not be guilty of more intrusion. No more pressure to the press; the crowd is too strong already, and I will get out by head and shoulders rather then fail.

Your Lordship's word may pass for me, and I dare not break it. Greatness hath a great stroke over men, but goodness a greater, men choosing to obey for love rather then fear; in both you have a strong interest, and in both sorts of men they have taken possession, and like twins grow up together, "*Quam bene conveniunt!*"[3] And may their residence be as immovable as your constancy to God, yea, may the title of plain-dealing and honest man be the worst reproach malice or double-dealing can fix upon your name and memory, who have gained much honour, and ease too, in court and country, by that excellent dialect and general belief.

The Dedication, like a fair frontispiece to a mean house or a beautiful sign to an ill lodging, hath tempted travellers to look in and make some stay, but I fear to have used my readers as my host the guests, that set a mark on the door to pass by and came in no more. 'Tis my fear only, which, being begot of modesty, may serve to invite the best and most ingenious company.

To please most is my desire, but my choice a few, taking the bigger number to be the less in virtue, and swollen only by a timpani of wind and water.

The boat is in Your Lordship's hand, which steers as you direct. Yours is the greatest interest, you are our chief, yours is the leading judgment. Do but approve, the mark is hit and you make many followers, which is the request of
Your Lordship's
humble servant,
THO. HERBERT.

---

[2] Philip, fourth earl of Pembroke (1583–1650), Parliamentary supporter and Chancellor of Oxford University, brother of William, third earl of Pembroke (1580–1631), the man who had helped Herbert get his place in Sir Dodmore Cotton's embassy. Herbert leaves this dedication in all the editions of the book.

[3] "How well they consort together" (Ovid, *Heroides* 7. 187)

To my honoured cousin Sir Thomas Herbert

What! Is't the love thou bear'st the southern clime,
Or care to instruct us, that the second time
Thou engagest fame, or is't thy love to pay
Thanks to mild censures, or thy friends to obey,
Or to enlarge, or deck thy maiden lines
Like to a nurse whose eyes on th'infant shines?
Which of them all, or all it be? 'Tis well;
Who threats goodwill imparts a part of Hell.
CH. HERBERT[4]

Appulit eois Herbertus sospes ab oris,
*   Vicit et immensi mille pericla maris.*
Non tulit hinc secum piper, aurum, balsama, gemmas,
*   Costum, aloen, myrrham, cinnama, thura, crocum.*
Rettulit hic mores hominumque, viator et urbes,
*   Regna, habitus, linguas, praelia, jura, deos.*
Divite ne posthac quaeras e Perside gazas,
*   Anglia nunc Anglis Persia tota domi est.*
AR. JOHNSTONUS Med. Reg.[5]

Descriptio decoris reciproci inter arborem no-
bilem seu familiam de Herbert, & authorem
vere ramum ejusdem arboris seu familiae.

---

[4] Charles Herbert (1603–?), successively Vicar of Abergavenny (1632) and Rector of Ystradgunlais (1634), is a probable candidate. He may have been another one of Herbert's ubiquitous "cousins," but he is certainly not the Charles Herbert who was brother to Lord Herbert of Chirbury and George Herbert; this Charles Herbert died in 1617. A much longer English poem appears in the 1634 edition, togther with a Latin poem and a verse-address to the reader. The longer English poem refers to Thomas Herbert as "Cousin," but is not signed; the shorter "To the Reader" is signed "C. H." The Latin poem is prefaced "To his worthy cousin, Thomas Herbert Esquire" and immediately follows the long English one, which indicates that Charles Herbert wrote all three of them. The poem which appears here is also in the 1662 printing, but not in the 1634 edition.

[5] Arthur Johnstone. Unidentified, except by his title, which describes him as a registered physician. His poem is not in the 1634 edition. Translation: "Brought safely back from eastern shores, Herbert / Had overcome the thousand perils of the sea. / He did not bring back pepper with him, gold, gums, gems, / Aromatic plants, aloes, myrrh, cinnamon, frankincense or saffron./ A traveller, he brought back here customs of men and cities, / Kingdoms, habits, languages, battles, laws and gods. / He did not become wealthy afterwards with Persian royal treasure; / Now, all Persia is here at home in England through an Englishman."

Nil tantum decorat ramum quam nobilis arbor,
   Florentem ramum sic decus arbor habet.
MAR. BELWOOD Dr. Med.[6]

Urbes quod varias solers vidisset Ulysses
   Et mores hominum, clarus honore fuit.
Soler inter Phrygiam licet errans Hesperiamque
   Littora lustrasset per duo lustra maris.
Tu spatia ut saperes immensae mensus es orbis
   Herberte, inque salo graviter inque solo.
Comperta unde tibi mova multa & mira Britannis
   Candidus impertis veridicusque tuis.
Fallacem hoc Ithacum superasque peritia rerum,
   Quod tua candori sit fideque comes.
                    WALT. O.QUIN. Armig.[7]

---

[6] Mark Bellwood (1586–?) is listed as a graduate of University College, Oxford and is here described as a physician; whether this is the same person cannot be determined. No further information about him is available; these lines do not appear in the 1634 edition. Translation: "A description of the proper relationship between the noble family of Herbert and the author, a true branch of the same family tree. Nothing so much adorns a branch than a noble tree; / Thus this tree has a blossoming branch as an ornament."

[7] Walter O'Quinn. Unidentified; the title "armiger" simply denotes his status as an arms-bearer, hence a gentleman, and the verse is not in the 1634 edition. Translation: "The artful Ulysses saw the various cities / And customs of men; he was covered in honour; / Skilfully wandering between Phrygia and the Western land. / You graced the shores with two crossings of the sea, / You traversed the huge tracts and measures of the world, / Herbert, and with dignity on the open seas and land / You imparted many wonderful events / Candidly and truthfully to Englishmen. / You rose above the deceit of Ithaca in your experience of things / Because honesty was your faithful companion."

To the READER
Here thou, at greater ease then he,
Mayst behold what he did see;
Thou participates his gains,
But he alone reserves the pains.
He travelled not with lucre sotted:
He went for knowledge, and he got it.
Then thank the author; thanks is right
Who hath presented to thy sight
Seas, lands, men, beasts, fishes, and birds,
The rarest that the world affords.
THO. Lord FAIRFAX[8]
            Baron of Cameron

---

[8] Sir Thomas Fairfax, third baron Fairfax of Cameron (1612–1671), Lord General of the Parliamentary Army during the Civil War and under whom Herbert served. He defeated the King's army in many battles, but refused to sit in the court that tried Charles I, and retired from public life. Fairfax was also an MP, poet, scholar, and translator, as well as the friend and employer of Andrew Marvell. He did not write a prefatory poem to the first edition, but it appears in all the subsequent ones.

TRAVELS

Begun *Anno* 1626[1]
DESCRIBING
Divers parts of Africa and Asia the Great:
But principally the two famous Monarchies,
The Mughal and Persian.

[Part I: Africa and Arabia]

Upon Good Friday in the year 1626[2] we took shipping at Deal near Dover, having six[3] great and well-manned ships in company, all which were bound for the East Indies. In a few hours, coasting close by the Isle of Wight (called so from *gwydib*, a British word signifying "cut off," or "seen from a distance;" *Vectis*[4] in Pliny, *Vecta* in Eutropius),[5] a sudden borasque[6] or gust assaulted us, which, after an hour's rage, spent itself, and blew us the third day (double-solemnised that year by being the Feast of Mother and Son), upon The Lizard's Point, the utmost

---

[1] Originally "Begun Anno 1616," which has been silently emended.

[2] Herbert is using Old Style dating. It was actually March 1627.

[3] See Introduction. Herbert does not count the *Refuge* and the *Scout*, which were smaller vessels.

[4] Vectis appears to have been the name given in 43 C. E. to the island after Claudius's conquest. It was settled by the Jutes in the fifth century, and seems to have been known as Wiht. It is indeed mentioned by Pliny, but also by Ptolemy (II. 2). The Welsh connection seems ahistorical, and is the first of many attempts by Herbert to prove that the Welsh discovered everything. For details, see Henry H. Howorth, "The Beginnings of Wessex," *English Historical Review* 13 (1898): 667–71.

[5] Flavius Eutropius (fl. 350–370) was a Roman soldier and historian. He served the emperor Julian as his secretary and was with him on the Persian campaign which led to the emperor's death. He wrote the *Breviarium historiae Romanae*, which he dedicated to the Eastern Roman emperor Valens. His book was continued by Paul the Deacon (later cited by Herbert) and Landolphus Sagax. It was first edited by Henricus Glareanus (1561).

[6] This word is a corruption of the French *bourrasque*, a squall.

promontory of Cornwall, from whence to the extremest Cape of Africa. In this voyage we compute our longitude, and not from the Azores, albeit the first meridian.

The wind blew fair, so as the seven and twentieth day falling by Bilbao[7] in Galicia, which is that called *Terraconensis*,[8] of old a colony of the Persians, we launched into the Spanish Ocean, which we no sooner entered but that we descried seven tall ships, whom, reputing enemies, we bore up to speak with them, howbeit they proved friends, Hollanders out of the Levant, who drank our healths and saluted us as they passed with a roaring culverin,[9] and we in turn vomited out a like grateful echo. Thus, ploughing the liquid seas in merriness till the nine and twentieth day made us the sport of danger, struggling with such mighty waves and deep seas as oftimes made us seem to climb up mountains of salt water, [we] were straightway precipitated headlong as it were 'twixt cloven seas, a good while Heaven and sea seeming undivided. This put me in mind of the third Ode in the First *Lib.* of Horace, where 'tis said:

> A heart of brass that man had sure,
> Who in a barque durst first endure
> The raging waves, not valuing life
> Midst fierce South-West and North winds' strife.
> The Hyads (whom clouds seldom want)
> Not blustering South his sp' rit could daunt.[10]

Howbeit, after thirty hours the quarrel 'twixt wind and sea ended, for then a serene sky re-animated us, so as we finished March in the chase of a Turkish pirate, whom with topgallant sails and a soft wind we pursued six hours, but being as well-fitted for flight as fight, he out-sailed us. So, returning to our course, the first of April we cut our passage through the Atlantic Ocean, by Arabs called

---

[7] Foster noted that "they certainly passed the coast of Galicia; but Bilboa [*sic*] (if that is intended) was far away to the eastwards" (*Herbert*, 299). Bilbao, of course, is located near the Bay of Biscay.

[8] Hispania Terraconensis (or Tarraconensis) extended along the east coast of Spain and included the north and central parts of the country. There is no Persian connection.

[9] A culverin is a small cannon with a long barrel, often mounted on ships.

[10] Horace, *Odes* 1.3. 9–16. The first line, however, should read (in W. G. Shepherd's translation) "Oak, and triple bronze/ were about his breast" Herbert sometimes takes rather gross liberties with translations, but he could have availed himself of translations of Horace's *Odes* by Francis Beaumont (1629) or Sir Richard Fanshawe (1652). He does not quote this verse in the 1634 edition.

Magribana,[11] saith Marmolius[12] from *Atlas Mauriae*, Japhet's son and brother to the star-gazer Prometheus, a contemporary with Moses, from whom two famous mountains, one in Mauretania,[13] the other in Libya, are denominate. Long we had not been in these seas but another barbarian Sally man-of-war[14] came up, skulking all night in hope to board the first he saw divided. At daybreak we descried the pirate, who, loath to parley in fire and shot, fled amain, and left us, who swum so well that the third of April, at Titan's first light, we got sight of Porto Santo,[15] a holy port, in thirty-three degrees (called *Cerne* in Ptolemy), commanded by the Spaniard, and also of Madeira (i.e. Isle of Wood), 12 leagues south-west from Porto Santo, from the Canaries distant 70 leagues, the first of which isles was discovered by Perestrellus[16] an. 1419, and given him upon condition that he would people it, which he found difficult, the conies in such number resisted by undermining him. The other was found out the same year by Gonsalvo Zareo,[17] from the encouragement of Henry,[18] son to John I, King of

---

[11] The modern term "Maghreb," meaning "place of the setting sun," usually denotes Morocco, Algeria, and Tunisia. Here, it refers to the part of the Atlantic Ocean off the coastal areas of those countries between the Atlas Mountains and the Mediterranean.

[12] André Marmolius was a name used by the French traveller André Thevet (c. 1516–1592), author of *La cosmographie universelle* (1575) and other works. He was one of the most widely-travelled Frenchmen of his time, visiting, amongst other places, Brazil and the Levant as well as North America. R. Schlesinger and A. Stabler have recently edited *André Thevet's North America: A Sixteenth-Century View* (Montreal: McGill-Queen's University Press, 2005). Sometimes Herbert does not seem to remember (or know) that Thévet and Marmolius are one and the same person!

[13] *Mauretania* often denotes modern-day Morocco in Pliny.

[14] This refers to pirates from the Moroccan port of Sallee near Rabat (Foster, *Herbert*, 299).

[15] Porto Santo is an island 50 km north-east of Madeira.

[16] Bartolomeu Perestrelo (c. 1395–1457) was a Portuguese explorer of Italian ancestry. He discovered Madeira (1419) and was granted the island of Porto Santo, from which headquarters he moved to the conquest of other adjacent islands. His daughter married Christopher Columbus.

[17] João Gonçalves Zaréo (c. 1390–1470), together with Tristão Vaz Teixera, was sent to Africa (1418) by Prince Henry the Navigator. They discovered Madeira (1420), where Zaréo was granted a fiefdom of half the island by Prince Henry. Together with Teixera and Perestrelo, he started the colonization process of Madeira.

[18] Prince Henry "the Navigator" (1394–1460), son of João I of Portugal, planned and financed many explorations, although he never himself took part in any of them. He was a generous and intelligent patron to many of the great Portuguese discoverers who opened up new worlds. In 1419 João I appointed him Governor of the Algarve, and it was there that he built an observatory at Sagres in northwest Portugal and invited geographers, mathematicians, and others to come together in a common interest. "Henry's fame is justified," Sir John Hale writes, " as the first rational organizer of exploration based on co-operation between pilots at sea and experts at headquarters" (J. R. Hale, *Renaissance*

Portugal, taken and sacked *an.* 1596 by Sir Amyas Preston[19] our countryman, as some 'tis presumed yet living there have cause to remember. The holy port has five and twenty miles compass, fruitful as it is in wheat, rye, rice, oxen, sheep, boars, conies,[20] *sanguis draconum,*[21] fruits, flowers, and grapes. At eight leagues distance it thus respected us.

Porto Santo [illustration not shown]

The Canaries

The sixth of April by observation we had 27 degrees and a half latit[ude], at that distance descrying the Canary Isles, so-called *a multitudine magnarum canum,*[22] saith Pliny, by some taken for the Fortunate Islands,[23] about which has been no small difference amongst writers, some placing them at the Azores, at the Hesperides others,[24] some in our Britain, others at or near Rhodes, but the commentator upon Horace near the Ultima Thule,[25] where Tzetzes[26] as truly finds the Elysian Fields. But certain it is that they were undiscovered, but more certain

---

Exploration [New York: W. W. Norton, 1968], 29.) However, recent scholarship has tended to suggest that Prince Henry's role was less than had been previously thought.

[19] Sir Amyas Preston (d. 1617) was a wealthy landowner and soldier turned privateer; he was one of the sponsors of the Roanoke colony (1585). In the same year that he launched a raid on Spanish treasure-ships off the coast of Newfoundland, Preston served in the fight against the Spanish Armada (1588), where he was wounded, and a few years later we find him attacking Spanish settlements in what is now Venezuela. He raided Madeira and Cadiz (1596), and in 1599 he saw action in the Azores. Luis Britto-Garcia, a Venezuelan historian, calls Preston "el piromaniaco corsario" (see L. Britto-Garcia, "Filosofia del botin," *El Nacional,* 4 April 1999).

[20] Rabbits.

[21] "Dragon's blood" is a red resin from the *Croton* plant family. It had various uses, such as varnish, incense, and a medicine for stopping bleeding.

[22] Pliny, *Natural History,* 6.205. The name comes from the Latin *canis,* because early explorers thought there was a great number of "dogs" there, which scholars suspect were actually monk seals. It has nothing to do with canaries. The early Portuguese discovery is sometimes dated to 1336, but has not been substantiated, and Luis de Cardozo is unidentified. In any case, the name has nothing to do with canaries.

[23] Other candidates included Madeira and Cape Verde. The Fortunate Isles, or Isles of the Blessed in Greek mythology, were thought to be in the Western Ocean. Camoens identified the Canary Islands as the Fortunate Isles (*Lusiads* 5. 8).

[24] Camoens, however, identified Cape Verde as the Hesperides (*Lusiads* 2. 103).

[25] A name commonly used to denote any remote northern island, but sometimes applied to Iceland, Greenland, and other places.

[26] Joannes Tzetzes (c. 1110–1180), Byzantine grammarian, chronicler, commentator, and poet, author of the *Book of Histories* or *Chiliads,* a verse compilation in over 12,000 lines of miscellaneous information on history and mythology masquerading as a political treatise and bursting with ostentatious learning. It was first edited by N. Gerbel

uninhabited till the year 1328, by one Machant,[27] an Englishman, whose relation Luis de Cardozo two years after sailed thither, and by commission from Pedro, King of Aragon,[28] had liberty of conquest and command, but long enjoyed neither, for John II, the Castilian King, an. 1405 (which some would have to be the first discovery), displacing him. Ventacourt[29] snatcheth them from the Castilians but by John de Betancourt,[30] a well-descended gentleman kinsman to Bracomonte the French admiral,[31] Ventacourt is likewise disposessed, an. 1417, shipping 10,000 volunteers, by whose valour he subdued five of the isles, namely La Palma, La Gomera, Lanzerote, El Hierro, and Fuerteventura, an achievement very honourable. Yet such vexation possessed the ambitious Gaul that Canary mastered him as made him entertain death with a useless complement, his

---

(1546), who coined the title *Chiliads* from the book's being roughly divided into one-thousand-line sections.

[27] Herbert probably got this (and much more information) via Richard Hakluyt's translation (London, 1601) of Antonio Galvano's *Summary of the Discoveries of the World, from their first Original to the year 1555*. The author had served as Governor of Ternate in the Moluccas (1538–1539). Galvano writes that in about 1344 an Englishman named "Macham" was blown off-course and landed in Madeira with some of his men. He had been on his way to Spain with his fiancée, who also disembarked with him. Whilst they were still on the island, their comrades set sail without them, for what reason we are not told. The woman died of grief, and Macham erected a chapel in her memory, after which he and his surviving sailors built a boat and reached the coast of Africa, where a kindly ruler rescued them and finally repatriated them. Jack Beeching states that the "traditonal" names for the castaways were "Robert Machim or à Machim or Macham, and his mistress was called Anna d'Arfet" (Hakluyt, *Voyages*, 435 n. 13).

[28] Probably Pedro IV, who ruled 1336–1387.

[29] There is no-one of this name mentioned in any of the numerous accounts of these events. Herbert may have confused the name with that of Betancourt (Béthencourt).

[30] Jean de Béthencourt (c. 1360–1422/25) was a Norman nobleman who colonised the Canary Islands and received the title of king at the hands of Enrique III of Castile (1390–1406) and whose conquest was recognised by the Avignon pope Benedict XIII (1394–1423). His colleague Gadifer de La Salle, who had conquered Lanzarote, El Hierro, La Gomera, and Fuerteventura, did not take kindly to Béthencourt's elevation to royal rank, quarrelled with him, and returned to France. In 1406 Béthencourt himself returned to Normandy. Today there are many families in South America who claim descent from him: the spelling is now changed to Betancourt.

[31] Rubén de Bracamonte is probably Robert de Braquemont, Admiral of France and Lieutenant-General of Rouen and Honfleur from 1417. According to Galvano, he "craved grant of the Canary Islands for his kinsman John de Betancourt" and "caused the conquest of the islands of the Canaries with the title to be king of them" (*Summary*, 61–2). He had emigrated from France to fight in the dynastic wars of Enrique III of Castile to whose court he had been ambassador, and defeated the English at La Rochelle (1420). He was said to have discovered Madeira.

nephew Menaldus[32] being left heir to what Betancourt had got, and has added his misfortunes. For Myndus,[33] a haughty Bishop, incensing the Castilian king through his power, Menaldus was soon forced thence, glad of a small compensation paid him by Don Barba, the bishop's kinsman. Barba repents the purchase, and for a little profit assigns his property to Don Fernando Perazzo, whose brain taking like infection, grows weary of command, and for other employment confers this upon the Prince of Castile, from whom it was soon after torn by Don Enrico, Infante of Spain, remaining this day fixed under Spanish servitude.[34]

These isles, perhaps the same Ptolemy and Mela[35] mistakenly called *Deorum Currus*, by Plato, Aristotle and Plutarch the *Atlantiades*, by Pliny the *Hesperidae* are from the Morocco or Libyan continent 20 leagues, from Spain 200. Seven commonly they be numbered (Cadamastus[36] imagines ten) by old authors as Ptolemy, Strabo[37] and others called *Canaria, Capraria, Nivaria, Junonia, Ombrian* or

[32] Actually Maciot de Béthencourt (c. 1390–1458), who was Jean's cousin, not nephew, and the second king of the Canary Islands. He had been left as governor in 1406, and he later married the daughter of King Guardafia of Lanzerote. He ruled the island until 1447 and established Villa Real, which served as the capital of Lanzarote until 1852.

[33] Mendo de Viedma (d. 1431), a Franciscan, was made Bishop of San Marcial de Rubicon in 1406. Pope Martin V appointed him Bishop of Lanzarote in 1417. Viedma had also been with Bracamonte when the latter had landed in Madeira. He intrigued against Maciot de Béthencourt at the court of Castile and forced him to retire.

[34] Herbert's account is rather simplified. Maciot actually sold the island to three people. Don Pedro Barba de Campos, the first, was an admiral working for Queen Catalina of Portugal, mother of King João III, who succeeded Maciot as king of the Canary Islands (1415–1418). Prince Henry the Navigator was the second purchaser, and Don Fernando Perez de Sevilla the third. Don Fernando sold his bit to Enrique de Guzman, conde de Niebla, who had taken over the royal title from Don Pedro in 1418. Niebla in turn sold his lands in 1433 to Don Guillen de las Casas in 1445, who sold them to Hernan Peraza, conde de Valdeflores (d. 1452), after which King Enrique IV of Castile (1454–1474) granted the islands to Don Martin de Atayde Gonzales. In 1477 the territory was taken over by Ferdinand V and Isabella II. From 1448 to 1459 there was a dispute over the ownership of the islands between Portugal and Spain.

[35] Pomponius Mela (fl. 37–50), Roman geographer and epigone of Strabo, whose principal work is *De chorographia*, In this book Mela divided the known world into zones and continents, and commented extensively on the lives and customs of the peoples in them. His first modern editor was Schott (1579).

[36] Alvise Cadamosto (1432–1511) was a Venetian explorer in Prince Henry's service who discovered Guinea and became probably the first European to get to Cape Verde Island. He also explored the Gambia River and travelled up the Atlantic coast of Africa. He visited Madeira and the Canary Islands. His *Voyages* (1507) have been published by the Hakluyt Society (Series II, Volume 80).

[37] Strabo of Amasia (c. 63 B. C. E.–19 C. E.) wrote a geography of the Roman Empire in 17 books, most of which are still extant. He also compiled a continuation of the historical works of Polybius. He was one of the first geographers to suggest that

Pluvialia, Aprosita or *Stella Lancea* , and, as Martian[38] adds, Casperia or Fortunata, but at this day Canaria, La Palma, Tenerife, Lanzerote, Hierro, La Gomera and Fuerteventura. They knew no God but Nature, were ignorant of the use of fire, they shaved with flintstones, gave their children to be nursed by goats, cultured the earth with horns of oxen, abominated the slaughter of beasts, "for how can they be good / Who dare each day imbrue their hands in blood?," used women in common, no *meum* and *tuum*,[39] lust and carelessness so availing them that little difference was 'twixt them and their other animals. "The woods their dwelling was, the herbs their diet, / And on the leaves and boughs they sleep in quiet."

Gran Canaria [illustration not shown]

Some glimmering nevertheless one would think they had of the immortality of the soul, for the dead they washed and kept erected in a cave, a staff in one hand and a pail of milk and wine set near him to support and comfort him in his pilgrimage to Elysium.

At this day they are Spanish Christians. The Inquisition affrights those of the reformed persuasion to come among them. Grand Canary is almost as broad as long, the diameter being about fifty miles. Usually it is the residence of the Inquisitor, whether all the other isles repair for justice. It abounds with many good things as goats, beeves, asses, hogs, barley, rye, rice, variety of flowers, grapes and other excellent fruits, as also with *ingenios* or sugar-houses, wherein they grind their canes and boil the juice to make it sugar. This isle is from Santa Cruz in Tenerife 13 leagues, from Fuerteventura 20, from Lanzerote 18; at the south end is a large bay called Maspalomba, where fresh water is afforded. The isle, as I took it, thus seems at eight leagues distance.

---

circumnavigation of Africa might be possible. A Latin translation was made as early as 1472, and the first Greek edition was printed by the Aldine Press in 1516. Herbert probably used Isaac Casaubon's Latin translation (1620). There is an English translation in 8 volumes by H. L. Jones (Cambridge, MA.: Harvard University Press, 1917–1932), which is available online in its entirety. References to Jones's edition are to his (not Strabo's) volume and page numbers.

[38] Martianus Felix Capella (fl. 410–425) was the author of the *Liber de nuptiis Mercurii et Philologiae*, an allegorical work on the subject of education and learning which attained its greatest level of popularity in the Middle Ages and early Renaissance. It appeared in many editions, and was first (1499) printed in Vienna; Guillaume Budé edited it (1514). There is a modern translation by W. H. Stahl, *Martianus Capella and the Seven Liberal Arts: The Marriage of Philology and Mercury* (New York: Columbia University Press, 1977).

[39] Mine and yours: a legal truism or set phrase.

Tenerife

Tenerife is 50 English miles long, and for multitude of inhabitants compares with Great Canary; her chief towns be Santa Cruz and Anagona or Laguna, exceeds it in grapes, yielding yearly, as some say, eight and twenty thousand butts of sack, and outbraves not only the rest of the circumadjacent isles, but all the earth for supereminence. Her high peak Teide[40] towering so loftily into the air as seems not only to penetrate the middle region but to peep into Heaven, from whence Lerius[41] metaphorically calls it Atlas and Olympus, and I may more fitly apply that of Lucian in his *lib*. 2: "Then which no earthly part doth tower more high / In any place, nor nearer joins the sky." 'Tis accounted 15 miles high; one Nichols,[42] our countryman who lived there, affirms it to be 47 miles high, the top belched out flames of old, yet unable to melt the girdle of snow which is in the middle. And this height I all the more admire, seeing geog[raphers] attribute a far less height to the highest hill in the world, some not allowing above 4 miles in a perpendicular, others but 15 furlongs; nevertheless Thevet makes the height 54, Sanuto[43] 60 miles in the ascending. Seen it is (in fair weather) sixscore (some say 300) English miles, serving as an excellent Pharos, exceeding those at Cairo on the side of Nilus. The shape I present there as it appeared to us sailing by it:

Tenerife [illustration not shown]

---

[40] Teide [*Teyda*] is in the central part of the island; it is the world's third-largest volcano, and is presently dormant. The references to Atlas and Olympus are not that far-fetched, as it was a native place of worship for centuries. It is 12,188 feet high.

[41] Jean de Léry (1536–1613) was a French Protestant minister and explorer. He is chiefly remembered for his voyage to Brazil and the account he wrote of it, *Histoire d'un voyage faict en la terre du Brésil* (1578). There is a good modern translation of this interesting book by Janet Whately (Berkeley: University of California Press, 1993).

[42] Thomas Nichols (1532-after 1583) was born in Gloucester and first went to Tenerife in 1556 for only three months, but the next year returned as the representative of a commercial venture. The book to which Herbert alludes is *A Pleasant Description of the Fortunate Islands, called the Isles of Canaria, with their strange Fruits and Commodities* (1583). Nichols also translated Francisco de Gómara's *History of the Conquest of the West Indies* (1578) and other works. For details, see Francisco Javier Castillo, "The English Renaissance and the Canary Islands: Thomas Nichols and Edmund Scory," in *Proceedings of the II Conference of SEDERI*, ed. S. G. Fernández-Corugedo (Oviedo: Oviedo University Press, 1992), 57–71.

[43] Marino Sanuto (c. 1260–1338) was a Venetian traveller and avid propagandist for a renewal of the Crusades. He is remembered for the *Liber secretorum fidelium crucis* (1307) in which he elaborated on his plans for an all-out war against the infidels, and included a number of helpful maps and charts, to which Herbert refers here. Amongst other places Sanuto travelled to Cyprus, Cilicia, Egypt, and Constantinople.

This Tenerife is about 13 leagues west from Gran Canaria, from La Palma 20, from Gomera 5, from Africa 75 leagues, to Madeira 70. Hierro or Ferrum gave itself very high land as we sailed by it, and bears from Grand Canary south and by west; such time as Phoebus is to us vernal, it grows insufferably scorching. As yet woody and full of springs, the middle of the hill is cold, but the top very hot, scarce to be endured after sunrise. Some presume to say that there is neither rain nor wind there. Between the town called Santa Cruz is good riding, in about 27 degrees 30. Gomera is 6 leagues from Tenerife and above 8 leagues long; Palma is about 12 leagues from Gomera and in circuit towards 20. Hierro is 10 leagues from La Palma and not above 6 leagues in compass. Famous is Hierro in one tree, for it has but one such, which, like the miraculous rock in the desert,[44] affords fresh water to all the inhabitants. Sylvester[45] gives it this true and vive[46] description:

> In th'Isle of Iron (one of those same seven
> Whereto our elders happy name have given),
> The savage people never drink the streams
> Of wells and rivers, as in other realms.
> Their drink is in the air! Their gushing spring
> A weeping tree out of itself doth wring,
> A tree whose tender bearded root being spread
> In dryest sand, his sweating leaf doth shed
> A most sweet liquor, and, like as the vine
> Untimely cut weeps at her wound, the wine
> In pearled tears incessantly distils
> A royal stream, which all their cisterns fills
> Throughout the island, for all thither hie,
> And all their vessels cannot draw it dry!

which is very rare. Howbeit, in St. Thomas, an isle under the line, most of the trees there have the like property. La Palma is very high and woody. Fuerteventura is 15 leagues long and 8 broad, and near to Lanzarote. Lanzarote is less then Tenerife; it was taken by that English Leonidas the earl of Cumberland[47]

---

[44] The account of this "miraculous rock" may be read in Numbers 20: 2–11.

[45] Joshua Sylvester (1543–1618), English poet and translator of du Bartas (1598, 1604). He served as Groom of the Chamber to Prince Henry of Wales, for whom he wrote an extravagant elegy (1612), and was highly-esteemed as a translator by James I. His poems appeared in anthologies such as *England's Parnassus* (1600). Sylvester was also Secretary to the Merchant Adventurers Company and has business interests in England and Holland.

[46] Lifelike, lively.

[47] George Clifford, third earl of Cumberland (1558–1605) was actually more of a buccaneer than an emulator of the heroic Spartan King Leonidas II, who died at Thermopylae defending Greece against Xerxes' Persian army. He fought against Spain in the

Anno 1596, and Tenerife 4 years after by the Dutch, the first pillaged, the other burned, since when both are better fortified. 'Twixt Lanzerote and Fuerteventura is another little isle called Lobos; also there are two small isles near Lanzarote called Gratiosa and Alagrania in 28 d[egrees] 30. To the east of these isles be Fez and Morocco, which are part of Mauretania Tingitana, so-called from Tangier, a strong and considerable town upon the African coast opposite to Gibraltar in Spain, which resemble Dover and Calais and have like influence upon that narrow strait.

Tropicus Cancri

The ninth of April we crossed the Tropic of Cancer, of like distance from the Equator the utmost limit of the temperate zone is from the Pole, called Cancer from Apollo's crab-like retrogradation, moving back in June from that sign in the Zodiac. The 12 day we had the wind high but large, so that in two days' sail we made the sun our zenith or vertical point, his declination then being 14 degrees north, where note that only then, when we are nadir to the sun, we have no shadow, as also, whereas to all in the temperate zone, in the sun's meridian their shadows cast north, having past the zenith, the umbra becomes quite contrary. Lucan[48] in his 10 *lib.* observes, saying: "Those whom the burning zone / Divides from us, their shadows ever be / Southward, as ours we northward always see,"[49] forcing wonder from the sunburned Arabians upon their descent into Thessaly. As noted by the same poet, "An unknown world, Arabians, you invade, / Wond'-ring to see the groves yield right-hand shade."

And because we have *nil nisi pontus*,[50] which nevertheless Virgil,[51] Horace and others call the Father of Gods, men all other things, and air to observe upon,

---

Caribbean, and captured the citadel of Puerto Rico in 1598. He was a great gambler and seems to have lost quite often, which is perhaps why he needed to capture Spanish treasure-ships (see for example Foster, *England's Quest*, 138–39).

[48] Marcus Annaeus Lucanus (39–65), poet, was the nephew of Seneca. His masterpiece, the *Pharsalia*, is an epic poem about the rivalry between Caesar and Pompey, which ended with the latter's death after his defeat at Pharsalus. There were several translations available to Herbert if he had wanted them. Nero ordered Lucan's suicide. His poem was very popular in the seventeenth century, and was translated several times; Thomas May's translation (1631–1633) was probably the best-known English one. There is an excellent modern translation by Susan Braund (Oxford: Oxford University Press, 1992, repr. 1999).

[49] Lucan, *Civil War* 10. 290–291; 3. 247-248.

[50] "Nothing except the sea" (Ovid, *Heroides* 13. 22).

[51] As this is the first mention of Virgil, and given that Herbert often cites English versions, the following list gives available translations. The *Aeneid*, in part or whole, was translated by Gavin Douglas (1513; published 1553), Henry Howard, Earl of Surrey (before 1547; published 1557), Thomas Phaer (1558–1562), and John Vicars (1632); the *Ec-*

we have the more liberty to theorise a little upon that subject. The inhabitants within this zone (the torrid) we are now in are called *Amphiscii*, in respect they cast their shadows both ways according as the sun is in his declination, and *Ascii* or shadowless, when Sol is zenith, from which point when it fleers either north or south the shadow ever darts contrarily, as falls out ever when the gnomon or coelated body is interposed. But the *Persicii* have their shadow circulating, their meridional shadow having no existence from the vertice, but oblique and extended to the plane of the terrestrial horizon, glomerulating[52] the gnomon[53] or body opaceous. These sorts of people, freezing within the polar circles (of like distance from the Pole the tropics are from the Equinoctial), the Pole is their vertex and the Equator, being 90 degrees distance, is their direct horizon. The *Heteroscii* are such as live in the temperate zone, whose shadows at noonday turn but one way. The mathematics also teach us that the Heteroscii comprehend 41 parallels, the Amphioscii seven, the Persicii (those in the frozen zone) half the year. With these go others as they stand comparatively, the *Perieci, Antaei, Anticthones*.[54] The first be such as dwell in two opposite points of a like circle, distant one from the other a semi-circle or 180 degrees, so they be numbered after lesser parallels. The Antaei are also opposite, but vary neither in meridian nor equidistance from the horizon, respecting either hemisphere.

Antipodes

The Antipodes are such as be feet to feet, a precise straight line passing through the centre from one side to the other; these differ from the *Perieci* by degrees of a smaller circle, whence we observe that such as be to us *Perieci*, be *Antaei* to our *Anticthones*, each being inverted to other in a perfect contrary. Nor doubt we that there be Antipodes, the veil of ignorance being rent away, the sphericity of the world and that every place in the earth, though opposite, is habitable, being now so well-known as nothing seems more familiar. Notwithstanding, it was not so of old, when Boniface, Bishop of Mentz,[55] a clerk well-learned in that blockish age, was excommunicated by Pope Zachary,[56] *Anno* 745, for maintaining what

---

logues or *Bucolics* and *Georgics* were translated together by Abraham Fleming (1589) and John Ogilby (1649).

[52] Clustering together,

[53] The *gnomon* ('indicator' in Greek) is that part on a sundial which casts the shadow.

[54] An *anticthone* is an opposite earth, belief in which was prevalent in the Middle Ages.

[55] St. Boniface of Mentz (680–755), "the Apostle of Germany," began life as an Englishman called Wynfrid, born in what is now Devonshire. He held various offices in the Church and was martyred by the Frisians, after achieving great success in the conversion of large tracts of what is now modern Germany.

[56] Pope St. Zachary reigned 741–752. Of Greek origin, he was a reforming pope, who actually encouraged (at least at first) the activities of Boniface of Mentz, whom he

was then a paradox, yea, was sentenced to be burnt for a heretic, except he had recanted in his opinion, the Pope bringing in St. Augustine against him in his 16 book *De civitatie Dei*, "*qui Antipodas esse fabulantur etc., nullo modo credendum est*,"[57] and Lactantius,[58] another great scholar, deriding it in his third book of *Institutions*.[59] Very strange such learned men should be so ill-read in chorography,[60] especially since such a tenet was acknowledged before them by many, as by Euclid, by Cicero in his 4 *lib. De Academ. question.*, by Tiberianus,[61] who records an old letter beginning "*superi inferis, salutem*,"[62] by Strabo, and of all others most ingeniously by Lucretius[63] in his first book:

> When they see Sun, we see the lamps of night,
>   And with alternal courses times do change,
>   Dividing equal dark with equal light,
> But error vain in fools makes these seem strange.[64]

---

appointed as Papal Legate to the Frankish Church, an action which led to the downfall of the enfeebled Merovingian monarchy of Childeric III.

[57] "That the Antipodes are fables" . . . "[their existence] not to be believed in at all" (Augustine, *City of God* 16).

[58] Caecilius Firmianus Lactantius (250–317), philosopher and mythographer. Amongst his many works are found *De opificio dei*, a discussion of the body/soul dichotomy, and the *Divinae institutiones*, the work mentioned by Herbert here. It is a comprehensive survey of religious beliefs and contains the famous assertion that the gods of the ancient world were simply people whom idolatry had raised to immortal status. There were numerous editions of Lactantius starting from 1465; Herbert may have used Jean de Tournes' edition of the *Opera omnia* (1613). Professor Jackson Bryce of Carleton College has prepared a complete list of all editions, available online.

[59] *Institutiones*, Cap. 19 (Mountain 29).

[60] Chorography is a term used frequently by Ptolemy and other early geographers to denote the study of smaller areas such as provinces, cities, or regions.

[61] Tiberianus (fl. 335), a late Roman poet who may have been the author of the famous *Pervigilium Veneris*. He was also the author, according to the grammarian Servius, of a fictional "letter" from the Antipodes to "our Hemisphere," the work Herbert cites here. See A. Hiatt, "Petrarch's Antipodes," *Parergon* 22.2 (2005): 1–30.

[62] "The higher ones greet the lower ones" (fragment quoted by Servius, *Commentary on Book 6 of Virgil's Aeneid*, 532).

[63] Titus Lucretius Carus (c. 99–55 B. C. E.) is, of course, the Roman poet and Epicurean philosopher who wrote *De rerum natura*. There were many editions of this work going back to 1497; there is a good possibility that Herbert used the edition of David Paré (1631) and made his own English translation. There was no English translation until that of Thomas Creech in the year Herbert died (1682).

[64] This quote appears to be a paraphrase of several passages in Lucretius, *On the Nature of the Universe* 1. 63–65. Without the Latin, I could not match the exact places.

To return: in changing so many parallels, the weather increased from temperate to warm to raging hot, the sun flaming all the day so as it would have been intolerable had it not been compensated by the nights being of equal length, insomuch that calentures began to vex us. A sailor also by accident falling from the shrouds into the tempestuous waves aggravated our extremity, increased by a sudden and violent gust and storm of wind and rain, which in 6 degrees affrighted us; our skiff, which was fastened to the upper deck, in less then two hours being filled with nasty rain, which ended in thunder and flash mingling, and a great while the tornado in that manner amazing us. Weather so variable as was admirable, now blowing fresh and fair, and forthwith storming outrageously, the wind in one hour's space veering about every point of the compass, not unlike that of the poet: "The winds from East, West, North and South advance/ Their force, and urge the frothy waves to dance."

Now albeit these airy contests were not a little frightful to us passengers, who had never seen the like, yet the infectious rains that usually accompany the tornadoes were what most damnified the sailors, who in those storms are necessitated to be upon the decks to haul in their sails and to abide the brunt, and, which is worse, commonly get forthwith into their beds or hammocks, resting their wearied bodies in wet, nasty clothes, thereby breed many diseases as fevers, calentures, fluxes, aches, scurvy and the like, which, doubtless, did they moderate their bibbing strong waters, might in great measure be prevented. Other unlucky accidents oftimes happen in these seas, as when, especially in becalmings, men swim in the bearing ocean; the greedy hayen called tuberon[65] or shark, armed with a double row of venomous teeth, pursue them, directed by a little rhombus[66] or musculus,[67] variously-streaked and coloured with blue and white, that scuds to and fro to bring the shark intelligence, which pilot fish, as one describes: "His body is right fair, though seeming small, / And fitly him by name of guide men call," the shark, for his service, suffering him to suck when he pleaseth. In the history of Tobit 'tis writ that as he washed himself in the River Tigris a great fish leaped at him with an intent to have devoured him,[68] which, though it have no name, is like enough to have been a shark, for save that and the crocodile, what other fish are so bold as to dare living men and to devour them? Now that this fish was capable of such a feat we have for witness A[ulus] Gellius,[69] who reports

---

[65] Foster informs us that 'hayen' comes from the Dutch *haai* and 'tuberon' from the Portuguese *tuberao*, both of which mean 'shark' (*Herbert*, 299).

[66] Turbot.

[67] Pilot-fish. Herbert likely found this word in Pliny.

[68] Tobit 6:1–5.

[69] Aulus Gellius (c. 125-after 180), Roman poet, author of the *Noctes Atticae*. A version of this work was made by the Spanish humanist scholar Pedro Mexìa under the title *Silva de varia lecion* (1543). The *Noctes Atticae* is a vast compilation of 20 books containing miscellaneous information on philosophy, history, grammar, and all kinds of

that the Nicaeans took a shark that weighed 400 pound in which they found
a whole man coffined, and thence some think Jonas was in a shark's belly. But
this we may affirm, that many have been devoured by this ravenous fish and that
more have suffered in their members, whose shape, mistaken in the posture by
the engraver,[70] take thus resembled:

A Sharke Fish [illustration not shown]

Mauritania

By this, under 13 degrees north we were parallel with Sierra Leone, a cape island
upon the Libyan shore, by old geographers called *Deorum Currus, Frons Africae,
Tagazza* and *Zanguebai* in Thévet and Marmolius, strengthened by a castle built
by the Spaniard, famoused for refreshing our English Neptune, Drake, at his
return from circumnavigating the body of the whole earth,[71] and that thence to
Bab-mandal, the entrance to the Red Sea, Africa is nowhere broader. This cape is
from Cape Verde distant about 100 leagues, from Rio de Gambia.

The inhabitants here along the golden coast of Guinea and Benin bounded with Tombulo, Gualata and Melli[l]a and watered by the great river Niger, Cape[s] Palmas, Lopez Gonsalvo etc.,[72] but especially in the Mediterranean parts, know no God nor are willing to be instructed by Nature; "*Scire
nihil, jucundissimum.*"[73] Howbeit the Devil, who will not want his ceremonies,
has infused prodigious idolatry into their hearts, enough to relish his palate and

---

miscellaneous knowledge, written in no particular order. Gellius was an avid observer of
life around him, and the work might be termed a "commonplace book." There is a modern translation by J. C. Rolfe (Cambridge, MA: Harvard University Press, 1927) and a
modern edition, complete with notes and preface in Latin, by R. K. Marshall (Oxford:
Oxford University Press, 1990). Also see L. Holford-Strevens, *Aulus Gellius* (Oxford:
Oxford University Press, 2003).

[70] For William Marshall, the engraver, see Introduction.

[71] Sir Francis Drake sailed around the world in 1577–1580.

[72] Tombulo, Gaulata, and Melilla were all parts of the old Kingdom of Fez, now in
Morocco, which flourished 1472–1554. Melilla was conquered by the Spaniards in 1497,
and remains an autonomous city within Spain. Cape Palmas is on the south-eastern coast
of modern Liberia at the furthest south-western corner of Africa; Cape Lopez, between
the Gulf of Guinea and the Atlantic Ocean, is a peninsula on the west coast of what is
now Gabon.

[73] To know nothing is to be happiest, or "ignorance is bliss." The origin of this tag
is obscure, but the latter version of the quote seems was first used by Thomas Gray in his
"Ode on a Distant Prospect of Eton College" (1742). Herbert's entire paragraph, incidentally, complete with the Latin tag, was cited by one John Fletcher of Louisiana in his book
Studies on Slavery, in Easy Lessons (Natchez: Jackson Warner, 1852), 148.

aggrandise their tortures when he gets power to fry their souls as the raging Sun
has scorched their coal-black carcases.

A ship of ours, of late years coasting along and landing for discovery, was
so admired by the salvages as if they had never seen men nor ship before. Two
of ours adventuring the shore, some hostages being kept in the boat till they
returned, were welcomed by thousands of naked black-skinned Ethiopians,[74]
who were so far from doing them any injury that they presented them with flowers, fruits, toddy,[75] and what else they judged acceptable, after extraordinary ad-
mirations returning them safe aboard all contented, but since then have been
found more savage.

April the 18 we had 15 degrees, and before the next morn were in height
of Cape Verde in 14 degr[ees], so-named by Florian[76] *Hesperion Cornu*, or *Hes-
peri ceras* by Pliny, *Lybia interioria & Africae extremum cornu & promontorium* by
Strabo, of old called *Surentium* & *Arsinarium*, this day by the Ethiopians *Bisecar*
and *Mandangar*, *Hacdar* by al-Farabi,[77] that which strictly is called Mauretania,
here being terminated to the south, adjoins to Gambia. Discovered these were by
Dio[g]o Fernandoso or Antonio de Noli[78] a Genoan, *Anno* 1445, at the charge
of King Alfonso V,[79] famoused especially in the Hesperian Garden, which was
enriched with golden apples, conquered by Alcides his club, in despite of that
hundred-headed dragon that was engendered by Typhon or Echidna. A Greek
fable, thereby intending to set forth Paradise, the moral was this: the garden was
a pleasant field, the golden apples were sheep worth gold, such sheep and fleece

---

[74] "Ethiopians" denoted any Africans who lived south of the Sahara Desert. It was
first used by Herodotus, who was followed by Pliny the Elder.

[75] A drink made from fermented sap of various palm trees. Yule derives it from *tari*,
the "palmyra," and traces the description of it back to Megasthenes (320 B.C.E.), as cited
by Arrian (*HJ* 927).

[76] Joannes Florianus (d. 1586), a scholar from Antwerp, produced and printed a version of Leo Africanus's *De totius Africae descriptione lib. IX* (1556).

[77] Abu Nasr Mohammed al-Farabi (870–951) was a Persian scientist, philosopher,
mathematician, and musician. His most noted philosophical work was *On the Intellect*.
He founded a school of philosophy which was not based on Plato and Aristotle, and developed a non-Aristotelian system of logic. In addition he wrote works on physics, music,
and psychology. Latin versions of al-Farabi's work had been available since 1140.

[78] Antonio di Noli (1418–1491), the discoverer, together with the Portuguese navigator Diogo Gomes, of the Cape Verde Islands. Herbert probably refers also to Gomes by
citing "Dio. Fernandoso" as di Noli's co-discoverer.

[79] Alfonso V, king of Portugal 1438–1481, was known as Alfonso the African, because he took great interest in the exploration and colonisation of that continent. During
his reign the Portuguese seized Tangier. He should not be confused with Alfonso V of
Castile (see below).

as Jason had, the error partly arising from the word *melon*,[80] admitting a double construction. The club was philosophy, the dragon concupiscence or a flux of the sea in form of a dragon environing it, branching into 100 fluxes, which Hercules, to enrich Spain, passed over and exported. These, and not our Serlings or Isles of Scilly,[81] as Dionysius of Alexandria[82] supposes, were called the *Hesperidae*, so-named from Hesperus, whose 3 daughters, signifying anger, voluptuousness, and avarice, were Aegle, Arethusa, and Hesperia, now Mayo, Sal, and Bonavista. There be three other islands neighbouring them, the Atlantiades, which we will but name, the magnificent fabric of Antaeus calling us away to look upon, but alas, find nothing extant save memory, a palace albeit once so brave and capacious as to entertain the lord of it, who is by poets said to be 70 cubits high, a dozen ordinary men's proportion, an excellent log for Hercules to smite at. Yet, the Greeks persuade us, his club could not conquer, nor was he overcome when by prodigious force Jove's son threw him thrice upon the ground, the Earth his mother still re-animating him, till, being perceived, he strangled him in the helpless air. But passing by the Greekish fable, for, as one says well, "*Dicuntur Hesperidae hortum, propter eximiam loci amoenitatem.*"[83]

Tornados

It is more worthy of our observation that the omnipotency of God is most apparent in extremes, seeing that by inanimate things as heat, storms, and rain, he is more formidable then all the puissance of man put together can make, as these parts very notably make out unto us. For example, April 21: not one breath of air comforted us, the sun over-topping and darting out such fiery beams that, the air inflamed, the seas seemed to burn, our ship became sulphurous, no docks, no awnings nor invention possible to refresh us, so that for 7 days (70 better-endured in a zone more temperate), we sweat and broiled, unable to sleep, rest, eat, or

---

[80] The word is in Greek script in the text. In the seventeenth century "melon" usually meant "apple," as in Marvell's poem "The Garden," in which he writes "I stumble on melons."

[81] These may be found off the southwestern tip of Cornwall.

[82] Dionysius of Halicarnassus (first century B. C. E.), Greek rhetorician and historian, author of the *Antiquitates Romanae* which traces the history of Rome from its foundation to the First Punic War. He is often cited as an authority on religious customs. A French translation was made by Robert Estienne (1546), and Herbert could also have used the Latin version of Gelenius (1549).

[83] "They are called the Garden of the Hesperides because of the uncommon beauty of the place" (source unknown). Camoens uses this comparison, calling the islands "the Kingdom of the Hesperides" (*Lusiads* 2, 103, 45), and see also, for example, Milton: "There I suck the liquid air/ All amidst the gardens fair / Of Hesperus and his daughters three" (*Comus* 980–982). Aegle means 'dazzling light." There is sometimes a fourth nymph, Erytheia, 'the Red One.'

drink without much faintness, in which space our ship made no way, no current being felt in the ocean, till the first day the billows began to roll and the air to be troubled (for the wind, expiring from under the sea, first causes the waves to rise and the sea to bubble, the wind not being perceived by sense, till there be eruption of a great quantity and from thence gets into a body), and then, travelling with an abortive cloud, which suddenly fell down in the form of an inverted pyramid it became equally wonderful and dangerous. A cloud exhaled by the sun, a powerful magnet, not agitated by the wind but missing the retentive property in the lower region, distils not in moderate and condensed drops, but diffuses or falls hideously, the whole cloud or lump downright together, so impetuously into the ocean that many ships have been dashed and sunk past recovery. Lucan in his 4. *lib.* alludes to it:

> The fogs which India and Arabia make
> Exhal'd under the sun a place do take,
> But being so huge, those clouds can hardly be
> Involv'd in such strait room 'twixt earth and sky,
> For, being so crushed together, not in vain
> Contrasted in the air, they roll amain
> In fearful gushing showers.[84]

And, what's little less formidable, the stinking rain is no sooner in the sea but, as a churlish farewell, a whirlwind usually circles with such violence as helps the cloud lash the murmuring seas so outrageously that oftimes the waves rebound topgallant height, as if it meant to retaliate the air in another region. Pliny, *lib.* 2, *c.* 49, treating of prodigious kinds of tempests, thus describes it: "*Ex eodem genere & in longam veluti fistulam nubes aquam trahit,*"[85] and Olympiodorus,[86] commenting upon Aristotle's meteors, thus: "*Aristotelis Typhonem vocat typonem, quod valide verberet frangatque solida corpora, nautae Syphonem vocant quia in modum fistulae trahat aquam e mari.*" God be praised, we missed the rage of rain,

---

[84] Lucan, *Civil War* 4. 61–66.

[85] This kind [of tempest] draws up the clouds into a long siphon of water.

[86] Olympiodorus of Thebes (c. 375–430) was a historian of the late Roman Empire as well as a commentator on other historians. His *Historikoi logoi*, now mostly lost, contained a great deal of information about places within the Empire, and the surviving fragments suggest a moral interpretation of history and wide travelling experience. The quotation reads: "In Aristotle, a typhoon is called *typon,* which powerfully strikes and breaks solid objects; sailors call it *syphon,* because in the same way it draws water up from the sea." His works were known through Photius's *Bibliotheca*, a compilation of classical learning, which was in print from 1585.

albeit the gust somewhat endangered us, but it contraried Seneca's philosophy, *"Finis alterius mali, gradus est futuri."*[87]

A pleasant breeze first, increasing into a prosperous gale, cooled the air and posted us out of those exuberances of nature, so that on May Day we crossed under the Equinoctial, a circle imagined to divide the world into two equals, from either pole removed ninety degrees, where we lost sight of the *Sidus salutare*,[88] the Pole-star, a star of a third magnitude fixed in the tip of the Little Bear's tail, the sun's path this time being in the 19 degree of Taurus, in Arctic declination 17 degrees 31 minutes, and here we may observe that by reason of so long a calm, the heat became outrageous. Nevertheless, experience assured us that the heat is not so insufferable under the Equator as where more remote, with good reason, too, seeing that the breezes be more constant towards sunset, and greater where the motion of the air has greatest circles. The nights also are equal there in length to the day, and ordinarily dewy, which refrigerates and compensates the heat of the day. Besides, the heat is much abated by the two winters there, and, as a learned and noble person conceives, the extreme heat within the Zodiac attracts such streams of cold air or atoms from each pole into the Torrid Zone as exceedingly qualifies the burning heat, and may peradventure cause the constant breezes, which at 9 and 4 seldom fail, as do the rains which ordinarily fall at noon when the beams are hottest.

Monsoon

May 6. We had some thunder and lightning, or *corpo sanctos*, such as seem good omens to the superstitious. At night we passed by Sainte Croix,[89] the holy cross, every hour expecting the monsoon, an anniversary wind that from one rhomb constantly blows one way for six months, beginning exactly from the sun's entrance into a sign of the Zodiac, and the other half-year the contrary way, till the sun enters into the opposite degree, which, if seamen neglect, they go near to lose their passage into India. Now, how preposterous the year and wind proved elsewhere I know not. Doubtless it is the emblem of inconstancy; experience taught it us, but the weather so long time proved our antagonist that our passage to the Cape of Good Hope became five weeks longer then we looked for, so that we were forced to run into much more longitude then we desired.

---

[87] "The end of one evil is a step towards the next one" (Seneca, *Hercules furens* 208–209).

[88] The star of safety.

[89] Unidentified. Foster, too, was unable to locate it (*Herbert*, 299).

Angola

May 8. We had 8 degrees 10 minutes Antarctic latitude, the Monomatapan on our one side, the Brazilian coast on the other siding us. The Africa shore runs on in divers names, Congo[90] in 4 degrees, much of which was taught Christianity by Gonsalvo de Sosa[91] at the command of John II, Angola in 9, Manikongo, Loanga, Monomotapa, Benomotapa and Cassaria,[92] an Arabic word signifying men without law and religion, full of black-skinned wretches, rich in earth, abounding with the best minerals and with elephants but miserable in demonony. The discovery of these parts is attributed to sundry men, the first not agreed upon, some to Petrus Cavillanius,[93] others to Jacobus Canus,[94] Bartolomeo de Diaz,[95]

---

[90] This is the old kingdom of Congo in what is now northern Angola. It was converted to Christianity in the sixteenth century.

[91] Gonçalvo de Sosa (d. 1491) was sent by João II to Congo in 1490, and was supposed to return to Portugal with an ambassador from one of the Congolese rulers. Unfortunately, de Sosa died on the voyage home.

[92] Manikongo was not a place, but the title of the ruler of the Kongo Empire, which covered Angola and part of the modern Democratic Republic of Congo; in 1483 Manikongo Nzinga was persuaded by Diogo Cão (see below) to open trade with Portugal, after which a protectorate was established and the rulers converted to Christianity, taking Portuguese names. The kings at this time were Garcia I (1624–1636) and Ambrosio (1626–1630). Loanga, also known as Brama, was a kingdom situated along the coast of what used to be Congo-Brazzaville in French Equatorial Africa and is now in the Democratic Republic of Congo. Monomatapa is another Portuguese corruption. It refers to Mwene Mutapa of the Karanga Kingdom, the ruler of the Rozvi Empire, which lated c. 1450–1798. Camoens wrote of "the empire of Monomotapa / With its forest peoples, black and naked" (*Lusiads* 10. 93). Benomatapa was a south Zambezian state, also part of the Rozvi Empire, and now in Zimbabwe. Cassaria is marked on a 1509 map of Angola.

[93] Pêro da Covilhan (fl. 1487–1515), an Arabic speaker, was first sent out from Portugal with Afonso de Paiva to search for the legendary ruler Prester John and to increase trading possibilities for João II. Posing as a merchant, he went to Goa (Paiva set out for Ethiopia), the east coast of Africa, and Mozambique. Hale calls him "a state-sponsored Marco Polo" (*Renaissance Exploration*, 35). Count Francesco de Ficalho has edited the *Viagens de Pedro da Covilhan* (Lisbon: A. Pereira, 1898). After Paiva's death Covilhan also travelled to Ethiopia where he spent forty years, never returning to Portugal.

[94] Diogo Cão or Cam (c. 1450–?1489) was a Portuguese explorer and squire to Joao II who discovered the mouth of the Congo river (1482), sailed about 100 miles up it, and, with the German Martin Behaim von Schwarzbach (c. 1458–1507), revisited the area two years later. Cão is sometimes credited with having discovered America (1483), but this claim is much-disputed by scholars. Cão also reached Cape Cross (1485). His voyages were described by João de Barros, *Decadas da Asia* I, iii, Chapter 3.

[95] Bartolomeu Dias (c. 1450–1500) was the Portuguese discoverer of the Gold Coast, now Ghana. He also navigated the Cape of Good Hope (1488) and rounded the southern tip of Africa. He called the Cape the Cape of Storms, but, as Herbert relates, João II changed its name. Together with Covilhan, Dias executed what Hale called a

Vasco da Gama,[96] and such as John II, King of Portugal,[97] employed about it *Anno* 1497 or thereabouts, which Diaz, in a fight he had with the Angolans, took so many prisoners as, having cut off their noses, he filled 2 butts and presented them to the King of Portugal, unlike Hannibal's present after Varro's overthrow at Cannae.[98] Let one character serve for all. For colour, they resemble chimney-sweepers; unlike them in this, they are of no profession, except rapine and villainy make one, for here *demonia omnia plena*,[99] *mokisses*,[100] fetishes or deformed idols being endeared amongst them, the Red Dragon usurping worship in a dragon's shape, goat, owl, bat, snake, cat, dog, or what the witches (*Acheronta movebunt*[101]) urge them to, and to adore in an infernal posture, gaping, whooping, soiling and discolouring their carcasses with juice of herbs, rice, roots, or what the old impostor[102] infatuates them with. And here the female sex each new Moon defy pale Cynthia, imagining her the cause of their distempers, which, to comply with the weaker sex, the men threaten with their shafts, as if they could reach that planet albeit distant from them no less then one hundred and twenty thousand miles, the space between the earth and the Moon being seventeen times the diameter of the earth, if we can credit Ptolemy and other astronomers. A dog was of that value here that 20 salvages[103] have been exchanged for one of

---

"pincer-movement" which helped "to identify, in a reasonably practical manner, [almost] the whole African coastline" (*Renaissance Exploration*, 35).

[96] Vasco da Gama (1460–1524) was the great Portuguese explorer who journeyed to India via the southern part of Africa (1497–1498). On his way around the African coast da Gama came into contact with the people in what is now Mozambique and then went on to Calicut (Calcutta). Da Gama was in India (1502–1504) and became Viceroy, dying in India. His story is a central theme in Camoens's *Os Lusiadas* (1572). Camoens himself went to India (1553), the first European literary figure to do so.

[97] João (John) II "the Perfect," was king of Portugal 1481–1495. Hale states that if he wasn't actually perfect, "certainly he was a perfectionist" (*Renaissance Exploration*, 33); he had a great ability to pick the right men to to claim land for Portugal and find gold (33–34).

[98] Gaius Terentius Varro was one of the Roman consuls defeated by Hannibal at the battle of Cannae (216 B.C.E.).

[99] Everything [is] full of devilry.

[100] Albinos. The word appears to be still used in Jamaica, and is synonymous with *dundus*. See F. G. Cassidy and R. B. Le Page, *Dictionary of Jamaican English* (Cambridge: Cambridge University Press, 1980), 164, who cite a 1774 usage, but this is much earlier.

[101] "They shall move Hell." This seems to be quoted not from Virgil (*Aeneid*, 7. 312), original "*Flectere si nequeo superos, Acheronta movebo*," i.e. "If I cannot move Heaven, I will move Hell," but from Robert Burton, who pluralises the quote. See Robert Burton, *Anatomy of Melancholy* (London: N. Hailes, 1854), 239.

[102] The Devil.

[103] Savages, i.e. natives or slaves. Note that Herbert is more worried about "damage to the purchaser" of slaves than whether they can be "saved" or not.

them, but of late years the exchange here made for negros into the Caribbean Isles and continent of America is become a considerable trade, which, seeing the gain by their slavery is more aimed at then the conversion of their souls to Christ, I fear the end proves rather damage then advantage to the purchaser. Their coin are a sort of wampum[104] or shells, glass, beads, stones or like trash. They marry not, bury thus: the dead are washed, painted, apparelled, and laid to sleep in a spacious dormitory. His armlets, bracelets and voluntary shackles accompany him; they circle the grave with mimic gestures and ejaculations, concluding with the sacrifice of a lusty goat.

An Inhabitant of Angola [illustration not shown]

Loanga

But in Loanga, which some put to the north of Congo but under the Equator, and the Anzigui, near which Nilus draws his origin even from Zaire, a lake near the Mountains of the Moon in 12 degrees south, the people (if Gonsalvo Sosa say true) are little other then devils incarnate. Not satisfied with nature's treasures as gold, precious stones, flesh in variety and the like, the destruction of men and women neighbouring better contenting them, whose dead carcasses they devour with a vulture's appetite, whom, if they miss, they serve to their friends (so they mis-call them) such scurvy sauce, butchering them and thinking they excuse all in a compliment, that they know no better way to express love then in making not two souls, [but] two bodies one by an inseparable union, yea, as some report, worn by age or worm-eaten by the pox, proffering themselves to the shambles, accordingly are disjointed and set to sail upon the stalls. Juvenal,[105] it seems, met with the relation of such monsters, for, says he, "The slaughter of a man doth not suffice / Those cannibals we see, but breasts, arms, eyes/ Like dainty meat they eat," and by which we see that these barbarians, by this lewd and detestable custom, to the infamy rather then honour of religion, make man's flesh a common sacrifice or offering. Nothing so commendable in them as their archery, in which they excel, shooting, if true that some report, a dozen shafts ere the first touch ground, their Amazonian neighbours forcing their diligence. The only ornament

---

[104] Sacred beads made out of shells, usually associated with native North Americans.

[105] Juvenal, *Satires* 15. 169–71. Decimus Iunius Iuvenalis (c. 55–140), the pre-eminent Roman satirist. Between 110 and 130 he produced five books of satires, which were much admired, translated, and imitated from medieval times through the sixteenth and seventeenth centuries. The earliest printed edition was that of Badius (1498), and there were many subsequent ones. In England, one of the best-known editors of Juvenal was A. E. Housman. Herbert may have known the English translations by Sir John Stapleton (1644) or Barten Holyday (1673). Other contemporary poets, such as Jonson and Dryden, translated individual satires.

they have is flashing and pinking their skin and faces. The sun and moon are reputed man and wife, the stars their children in their religion; the Devil is their oracle. Those parts have store of gold and yet use shells for coin as do the Americans.

May 24. We had 19 degrees and a half, from whence to the thirtieth degrees the wind was large and prosperous. Nothing in that great distance observable, save that on the 26 day our admiral the *Mary*, in which Capt. Hall[106] commanded, early descried a sail, which he made after with his barge and long-boat manned with 80 men. At two leagues distance they perceived her a carrack of 1500 ton, who, not daring to adventure her hulk against our shot, therefore made all her sails draw, so that at night she escaped. To recover her, our fleet divided all night, yet saw her not till the 27 day, and but saw her, her velocity so much excelled ours, till the 7 of June she again deluded us after two hours' chase, as a phantasm vanishing from our sight, steering towards Goa.[107]

Tropic of Capricorn

Upon May Day we crossed the line, and on the last of May the Tropic of Capricorn, the utmost limit of Apollo's progress towards the Antarctic, so as 53 days we sweat within the burning zone ere we passed under both the tropics. The first of June our observation was 24 degrees 42 minutes south latitude, the sun then being in 23 degrees 8 north, in the 20 degree of Gemini. In which height we had many sudden gusts and storms contrary to our desires, as unable thereby to direct our course as should have been, being driven to leeward 100 degrees upon the coast of Brazil, to 25 degrees latitude and 27 of longitude from The Lizard. Howbeit, *post multos sequitur una serena dies*,[108] for on the 13 day, in the first watch, our long looked-for Favonius[109] blew sweetly upon us. "The west wind, most men know,/ From the vast sea is ever felt to blow," at which time some boobies[110] perched upon the yard-arm of our ship and suffered our men to take them, an animal so very simple as becomes a proverb.

A Booby [illustration not shown]

---

[106] Captain James Hall of the *Mary* had formerly been employed by Christian IV of Denmark, and had named Cape Sophia (now in Canada) for the king's mother (1605). He was also with William Baffin in 1622. He is not to be confused with the Captain John Hall mentioned by Herbert later on.

[107] 1638: Herbert states that the carrack arrived the previous month.

[108] "After all these events a calm day followed" (Tibullus, *Elegies* 3. 32).

[109] The west wind.

[110] A large seabird whose name derives from the Spanish *bobo*, meaning silly or stupid, so-named because they are very tame and were easily caught by sailors when they landed on ships' decks.

A Great Storm

Long it is not since I told you how favourably the wind had been unto us, but ere long found that his other adjunct is inconstancy, for after a short time we observed the ocean to wrinkle her smooth face and, veering into a contrary rhomb, to puff and bluster, and next day to storm so outrageously that the seamen themselves, to my apprehension, had some fear, and not without reason, the Capeland being thought, (not near enough and yet in this condition), too near. For four days and nights we were forced to hull, not the least rag of sail out, but driving whither wind and tide, being near the shore, compelled, during which we were now tossed as it were into the air and then thrown down into an abyss, dancing upon the ridge of dreadful waves, others at a greater distance threatening to swallow us, the air and ocean contending who should make the greater noise, that it was not possible to behold a fiercer conflict 'twixt those elements. Nevertheless, hoping in the Lord, and being six ships, through good providence after sixteen days longer sail, by this storm having been put forth farther to sea, our fleet, which were all dispersed, met joyfully together at the Cape, where I had better leisure to contemplate that ironic satire of Juvenal, saying "Go now, and to the winds thy life commit, / Trust the smooth wood four or seven fingers set / From death, the broadest heart of pine admit."[111]

Nevertheless, albeit the waves were extreme high in this late storm, they were withal extraordinary long, and experience taught us that in the narrow seas, as 'twixt England and France, or Wales and Ireland, where the sea is shallower the waves are much shorter and break more, whereby they become much more dangerous, for where the ocean is vast and deep, there it rolls in long waves and has the slower motion. It may also be remembered that during this late tusson, lightening was seen to fall and hang like fire, sometimes to skip to and fro about the yards and tackling of our ships. In old times the Greeks called them Castor and Pollux, whom they feign'd to be Leda's twins. The Portugal term them *corpo santos*, withal believing that when two are seen they foretell halcyon weather and safety; if one, it imports danger, but three threaten storms and shipwrack. *Sed non ego credulus illis,*[112] well-knowing that these meteors are no other then natural exhalations.

June 24. We raised the Pole Antarctic six and thirty degrees, at which time our longitude from the meridian of The Lizard was 25 degrees wanting three minutes, variation three degrees, course ESE, Sun's declination 22 degrees, 26 minutes, and as many seconds north, in the 17 degree of Gemini, where note, that the same time being midsummer in England it was midwinter with us in this south climate, being near the Antipodes.

---

[111] Juvenal, *Satires* 12. 57–59.
[112] "But I'm not credulous about those things" (Virgil, *Eclogues* 9. 34).

July 7.[113] Betimes in the morning by the sargasso or seaweeds we saw floating upon the sea, the seamen knew they were near the Cape, and accordingly
we descried land betimes next morning, which, though threescore miles distant,
being so high it seemed to be nigh unto us, the wind and tide not favouring, we
could not reach the continent, but dropped our anchor 14 leagues short of Souldania Bay,[114] afore a small isle called Coney Isle[115] through corruption of speech,
the proper name being *Coin-yne* in Welsh of that isle. The said isle is three
miles about, in which we saw abundance of penguins, in Welsh "white-heads,"
agreeable to their collars, a bird of all others that goes most erect and upright in
its motion, the wings or fins hanging down like sleeves. A degenerate duck I take
it, for using both sea and shore, feeding in the one, breeding in the other, very
fat and oily, yet some adventure to eat them. Curiosity may indeed invite, seeing
jejunus raro stomachus vulgaris temnit,[116] but to make a meal, I cannot advise other
then as the distich directs: "Divide the duck; only the neck and breast / They favour well; the cook may take the rest."

A Penguin [illustration not shown]

Here we found also abundance of conies, who resemble our cats, great and ram-
mish, as they report that eat such dainties. Indeed, such food require good stomachs and hot water to help digestion ere it turn into a reasonable chylus.[117] Here
were also great number of seals or sea-calves, or that some call *piscis marinus*, as
big as the greatest sort of mastiffs, something like them in visage, and in voice
out-bark them, but the comfort is rather like the bellowing of bulls. These also
are amphibii, equally using land and water, and albeit easily destroyed if one interpose between them and the sea, yet being past have so good a faculty in striking the loose stones with their hinder feet or fins that the pursuer is thereby endangered. Those are not food, they are so oily, but their skins being tanned are
converted into many uses.

---

[113] Herbert says in the 1638 edition that they actually saw land on the seventh.

[114] Souldania Bay, now known as Table Bay, was originally named by a corrupt form
of the Portuguese explorer Antonio de Saldanha's surname. The English established a
trading station there in 1591. There is also a Saldanha Bay, "some distance to the northwards," which "was the one really discovered by Antonio de Saldanha" (Foster, *Herbert*,
300), who was there in 1503.

[115] Named by Sir Edward Michelburne, whose ship the *Tiger* sailed by it in 1605.
Curiously enough, Herbert does not seem to have known this, and decides, quite arbi-
trarily, that its name shall be a Welsh derivative.

[116] "A hungry stomach will eat anything" (Horace, *Satires* 2. 2).

[117] Fatty lymph formed in the digestive tract.

Ethiopia

Weighing anchor, we next came to Penguin Island,[118] so named from that abundance of those birds we found there. This isle is about 6 leagues NNW from Souldania, and albeit this is so near the mainland, yet well I remember that all the way we sailed 'twixt the last isle and the bay we anchored at, we were disported by whales, who in wantonness fuzzing the briny ocean out of those pipes or vents Nature has placed upon their shoulders, like so many floating islands accompanied us, and after their guise thundering out our welcome into Ethiopia. These leviathans are indeed the largest, not only of all the fish in the sea, but, as I think, of all other bodied creatures. Pliny,[119] Massarius[120] and Nearchus[121] report that some whales in the Indian Ocean have been found to be four hundred cubits long; I am even ashamed to say how many. Those we saw, as we conjecture, could not be less then threescore foot from head to tail, the head being well-nigh a fourth, the mouth little less then ten foot wide, the tongue proportionable, but the eyes no bigger then an apple. The body is thick and round; the savages eat them, but merchants covet them rather for profit, one usually giving 12 ton of oil. Engendering, belly touches belly; in bringing forth they have but one at a time, therein like that behemoth the elephant.

July the first, we came to anchor in Souldania Bay, 12 leagues short of that great Cape which is meritoriously called Good Hope, the former name *Tormentozo* imposed by [da] Gama[122] being wisely rejected by King John II of Portugal from this consideration, that in prosecuting those Indian voyages, having attained this place the half-way and greatest danger is overcome. This bay is of a semi-lunary form, both safe and large, and affording good anchorage; towards the shore the land is low and fruitful, but 5 miles from the bay appears high, for in a perpendicular, as we observed, the mountain which from its resemblance is called the Table is no less then eleven thousand eight hundred and sixty feet, near which is

---

[118] This became the infamous Robben Island; that name was derived from the Dutch word for 'seal,' *rob* (Foster, *Herbert* 300).

[119] Pliny, *Natural History* 9. 12–18.

[120] Francesco Massari (?1507–1538), a Venetian doctor, was known for one single work, *In nonum Plinii De naturali historia librum castigationes et Annotationes* (Basel, 1537). According to Gesner, whom Herbert also quotes, Massari died young and was a great loss to scholarship. He was one of the earliest naturalists to study fish, particularly those in the Mediterranean areas, and there is evidence that he himself was quite widely travelled.

[121] Nearchus (c. 360–300 B.C.E.) was one of Alexander the Great's generals. He wrote a report (now lost) of a voyage he made up the coast of Persia, which contained much historical information and served as the primary source for Arrian in his own book, the *Indica*. Parts of it are cited in several ancient authors.

[122] It was not da Gama but Dias who initially named the cape.

another pyramidal hill called Herbert's Mount, from the top of any of which we plainly see the utmost promontory or Cape of Good Hope.

Cape of Good Hope[123]

Cabo de buona Speranza the Portugal calls it, which is about 12 leagues SSW thence, also S[outh] and by E[ast] ten leagues thence we see Cape Falso and Cape de Aguillas, which three promontories are separated from each other by large bays, but the 2 last are found inconvenient to anchor in. Distant they be from one another 10 miles N[orth] and S[outh] on all sides save to the sea, environed with mountains which surge so high as they penetrate the middle region. To the Table lately mentioned seamen for their recreation ordinarily climb up, the ascent (the height considered) not being uneasy. But the prospect, being once up, fully compensates the labour, for from thence into that country, where higher hills do not anticipate, is a very noble view and pleasant, and into the ocean we could see 100 miles and upwards. Into Souldania Bay a small, but most sweet and wholesome water streams from the Table Mountain, to the north of which Rio Dolce,[124] 'twixt which and two pretty rising hills, by Capt. Fitzherbert[125] called King James's and King Charles's Mounts, and in whose behalf he laid claim to that country, such as land here for refreshment usually pitch their tents. About half a league thence is a broader stream, but so shallow near the bay as is not navigable; the Portuguese call it Rio de Jacquelina,[126] which, when I tasted, was brackish and insalubrious, but 'twixt the two other capes is a larger stream which springs, as some say, from the Mountains of the Moon which are under the South Tropic, how truly I know not.

Africa, of which this is part, is a peninsula, where that isthmus of 20 leagues divides the Red from the midland sea. This great continent, which the

---

[123] A. Wilmot, who quotes a long passage from it, writes that Herbert's description of the Cape of Good Hope and its inhabitants is one of the earliest. Herbert, he continues, "descants in the most profound manner upon the ancient circumnavigation of Africa" (*History of the Colony of the Cape of Good Hope* [Cape Town: Juta, 1869], 28).

[124] The Rio Dulce, or Sweet River. Foster notes that it comes down from the north face of Table Mountain and flows into Cape Town (*Herbert*, 300).

[125] Humphrey Fitzherbert made the first English voyage to Java (1620) on behalf of the East India Company in a ship called *The Royal Exchange*, where he landed at Nailaka and forced an agreement with the Dutch (Foster, *England's Quest*, 276). He briefly landed on the Cape of Good Hope, and erected a stone cairn there, claiming the land for England and naming the place King James's Mount, as Herbert states. What he does not say is that the King did not recognise the claim. Fitzherbert wrote a journal of his voyages. The two hills are identified by Foster as the Lion's Rump or Signal Hill (King Charles's Mount) and King James's Mount as "the step on the North side of the Rump" (*Herbert*, 300).

[126] Now known as the Salt River.

Equinoctial parts in two, and by Homer well-distinguished by *intra* & *extra*, is
by others into Major and Minor, either of which is well-nigh as big as Europe. In
length it runs north and south from Tangier, a city in the mouth of the Straits of
Gibraltar, heretofore called *Julia Traducta* and *Tingia Cesaria*, whence that part
of Mauritania is called *Tingitana*. To this promontory De Bona Speranza, the
first being in 35 d[egrees] 50 min[utes] north, the other in 34 degr[ees] south
latitude, is computed 4200 English miles, and the greatest breadth is from Cape
Verde upon the Atlantic to Cape Guardafui,[127] *Aromata* of old, in Ethiopia near
the Red Sea, being about 2000. Leo[128] divides all into four, viz. Barbary,[129] Numidia, Libya and *Negritarum Terra*, most of which is comprehended within the
Tropics. Howbeit, in old times the whole world was divided but into two, viz.
Asia and Europe, in which last Africa was comprised, for proof whereof we have
Philostratus[130] in *Vita Isocratis*, Lucan I, 9, and Virgil, *Aeneid l.* 7: "In which how
fates contrive,/ To make both worlds, Europe and Asia, strive," as also in his 10
lib.: "In which alarums,/ Europe and Asia both were forc'd to arms."[131] Ovid
likewise, in that 12 *Eleg. de arte amandi*: "But for which Queen / Europe and
Asia in firm peace had been," by which no doubt the whole world was intended,
those quarrels drawing all parts into their engagements, after which it was called
Libya, *per synecdochem*[132] *Lucan l.* 6 "Of Europe, Libya, Asia stand in fear," which
few instances may serve for many, but since America is the fourth, Africa for
grandeur has the second place.[133] The name Africa is, as some pretend, from
Epher, one descended out of the loins of Abraham by Keturah,[134] who, having

---

[127] Cape Guardafui, now known as Asir, is the headland which forms the apex of
the Horn of Africa. It is located in modern-day Somalia. "Now see Cape Guardafui, once
known / By its inhabitants as Aromata," Camoens wrote, "Guarding the entrance to the
famous / Red Sea, so named for its coloured sands" (*Lusiads* 10. 97).

[128] Leo Africanus was the baptismal name of Al-Hassan ibn Mohammed al-Waz-
zan (c. 1483–1554), a great Arab traveller and explorer who was the principal source of
the West's knowledge of Islam in the sixteenth and seventeenth centuries. Captured by
pirates and presented to Pope Leo X, who had him baptised, Leo learned Italian and
wrote his *Descrittione dell' Africa* (1550; English translation, 1600).

[129] Present-day Mauretania.

[130] Flavius Philostratus (c. 170–244/49) was probably born in Lemnos, and taught
philosophy in Athens before going to Rome, where he moved in the circle of Empress
Julia Domna, wife of Septimius Severus. He wrote the *Life of Apollonius*, which was a
work about the sophist Apollonius of Tyana, and the *Lives of the Sophists*. Charles Blount
made a partial translation of *Apollonius* (1680); a Latin translation was made by Rinuccini
(1501) and an edition by Beroaldus, whom Herbert cites, in 1504.

[131] Virgil, *Aeneid* 7. 297–298; 10. 123–124.

[132] As a synecdoche, i.e. substituting a part for the whole.

[133] Lucan, *Civil War* 6. 816.

[134] Keturah was Abraham's second wife, although some Jewish authorities call her
a "concubine." She had six sons, who founded the Arab tribes in the south and east of

first conquered Libya, there exercised regal power; others from the Greek word
ἀδίκη, which signifies "without cold," agreeable to which is the etym of Ethiopia, αἰθίοψ, which is "to scorch the face." Albeit, some others feign from Aethi-
ops, son of Vulcan, whom some think Cam the rather, for that by the Hebrew 'tis
called *Cham* and *Chu*, which gives the Nigro its name, and *Phutt*. *Ifrichia* by Leo,
Besecath by the Indians, Atlantia *per synecdochem* and *Aetheria* by the poets, for the
two last properly comprised, and *Aethiopia sub Aegypto*, and by Thévet *Alkebulan*.
Howbeit, Pliny saith that *"Graecis tota Africa dicta est Lybia."*[135]

Ethiopia

But concerning Ethiopia, albeit Laudivius[136] will not grant that it anywhere
exceeds the Tropics, geographers no less accurate allow it a much larger extent, for that which is superior stretcheth from the Equator and is confined by
Egypt to the north, the Red Sea to the east and by Libya to the west. The inferior thrusts itself from the Equinoctial southerly to this very Cape of Good
Hope, being to the west and east circumscribed with the great Ocean. *"Aethi-
opes Aetherii & Machrobii qui Africam ad australe mare habitant,"* saith Herodotus
l. 3,[137] admitting which it needs must transcend the Tropics, with which agrees
one of the most ancient poets, *Od[yssey]* 13: "The utmost sort of people known to
man / Is the divided Ethiopian." And, albeit the expression in Lucan, *lib*. 4, "The
Ethiopian land sees not at all, / The signs north from the Equinoctial, / Excepting Taurus . . ."[138] probably grounded Laudivius in his opinion. To him I oppose
that of the Prince of Poets, *lib*. 4 *Aen[eid]*, ". . . the Ethiopian ground / Which

---

Palestine. Their names were Zimran, Jokhshan, Medan, Midian, Ishbak and Shua (Genesis 25:1). Afer or Efer was the son of Shua, and therefore Keturah's grandson.

[135] For the Greeks, all of northern Africa west of Egypt was known as Libya. The
etymology of the name "Africa" is disputed, as Herbert notes. Josephus is responsible for
the Epher story; he was the son of Abraham whose descendents overran Libya (see Genesis 25:4). The Latin word *aprica* does mean 'sunny,' and the Greek *aphrike* 'not cold;' the
latter originated with Leo Africanus. The Romans were the first to use the name Africa,
to denote modern north Africa (Pliny, *Natural History* 5,. 1).

[136] Laudivius [Hierosolymitanus] or Laudivio Zacchia de Vezzano was a Knight of
Jerusalem and humanist. He compiled or wrote "a spurious collection of letters addressed
from and to Mehmet II" (Meserve, *Empires*, 228), the *Epistolae Magni Turci* (1473). It
consisted of letters supposed to have passed between Sultan Mehmet II and rulers such as
Uzun Hassan. This was reprinted in Leipzig (1488) and Herbert could have availed himself of an English translation (1607). Laudivius may also have been the author of a drama,
De captivitate ducis Jacobi; otherwise little is known about him. There was a seventeenth-
century cardinal of the same name.

[137] The Ethiopians, Aetherii and Macrobii inhabit Africa down to the southern sea.

[138] Lucan, *Civil War* 3. 253–255.

by the world's utmost extent is bound,"[139] and may serve to prove that Ethiopia exceeds the Tropics. I am not ignorant that the 3 Arabias also call Ethiopia Asia, to which we refer that in Genesis, but not being under that dominion I need not speak further of it, yet some there be that will not have it to exceed the countries possessed by Prester John.[140]

To return, this famous Cape elevates the Antarctic Pole four and thirty degrees and three minutes latitude, has longitude from the meridian of The Lizard 28 degr[ees]; the variation is westerly but one degree and 40 minutes, but at Cape de Aguilas[141] little or no variation at all is of the needle, the best reason being that the ocean is on both sides alike and the land in equidistance from the Land's End of Cornwall six thousand six hundred miles English, from the greater Java 5550, from Surat 5400, and from St. Helena, which is south-east 1800, the furthest part south of the known world according to that of Homer lately mentioned. *Extremos hominum* etc., and agreeable to what is mentioned in this distich, "By salt sea limited the world's end we / Inhabit. None with us to trade agree," so that all that can be objected is that seeing this Cape or more southerly parts of Africa then to 12 degr[ees] south were unknown to Ptolemy. How came the other by the discovery? That is not in this place pertinent for inquiry, albeit

---

[139] Virgil, *Aeneid* 4. 664–665.

[140] Prester John's name has been immortalised by John Buchan in his novel of that name, which seems to have been the last in a long line of literary re-tellings of the story. The earliest mention seems to date from the twelfth century, when Prester John was believed to rule over a Christian realm in "India." During the reign of Pope Calixtus II (1119–1124) an "archbishop" and a "patriarch" purporting to be from India were in Rome, and in about 1165 a mysterious "Letter of Prester John," written to the Emperor Manuel II Comnenus, was circulated, translated into many languages, and finally made its way into print in the fifteenth century. Literary mentions go back as early as Wolfram von Eschenbach's epic poem *Parzifal* (13th century) and are liberally sprinkled in Sir John Mandeville's *Travels*. In 1177 Pope Alexander III sent his physician, one Philip, to find Prester John, but this story may be apocryphal. Prester John's name then became attached to the Emperor of Ethiopia, although never by Ethiopians; when Emperor Zara Yaqub (1434–1468) sent delegates to the Council of Florence they had never heard of anyone called Prester John, but that did not stop the Europeans from insisting that the delegates were his! The Ethiopians have had four emperors named John (Yohannes), but that seems to be as far as it goes. "Prester" may be derived from "presbyter" or priest, and it is true that for centuries the existence of an ancient Christian kingdom was suspected, sometimes in India, then in Africa. In Herbert's own time the emperor was Susenyos (1606–1632) and Ethiopia, which had declined from its imperial power, was in the process of recovery. For the later editions of his book, Herbert could have used William Lithgow's *Discourse of rare Adventures and painfull Peregrinations of long nineteen years Travels, from Scotland to the most famous Kingdoms in Europe, Asia and Africa* (1632), which contained an account of Abyssinia. For further details see Robert Silverberg, *The Realm of Prester John* (Cincinnati: Ohio University Press, 1996).

[141] The southernmost cape of South Africa.

this little I may say for satisfaction, that Herodotus *lib.* 4, by what I have cited, is positive. Somewhat also can be gathered from that report he makes how that Pharaoh Necho,[142] after that loss of a million of men he suffered by his vain attempt in cutting off that narrow neck which interposes betwixt the Red and Midland Seas.[143] The Phoenicians, at that time the most expert in navigation, receiving encouragement from that Egyptian prince to discover southward, are said in three years space from the Red Sea to surround Africa. Pomponius Mela has the like tradition of two Carthaginians, who at their return, reported they sailed from some part of India into the Atlantic sea, Strabo the like of one Eudoxus Cyzicenus,[144] who in the reign of Euergetes the Egyptian king[145] doubled this great Cape. Relation is also made to another Eudoxus, who upon some offence committed, to avoid the punishment designed by Ptolemy Lathyr[us],[146] another Egyptian prince, embarks himself in the Arabian Gulf and, compassing south Africa, came ashore at Gibraltar in Spain. Pliny reports the like of Hanno the Carthaginian,[147] who, taking ship at Cadiz in Spain, passed through the Atlantic and thence brought his vessel into Arabia, the credit of which I shall not enforce nor say more herein save that *Melpomene*, supposed to be writ 2000 years hence by Herodotus,[148] makes Africa on all sides to be compassed with the sea except where that isthmus divides the Red Sea from the Mediterranean. Albeit, Ptolemy after him gives no further extendure of land south then 12 degr[ees], affirming also that the two oceans had no conjuncture. But leaving this to better inquiry, more certain it is that the Portuguese first doubled this cape these last centuries, divers years before Columbus made his expedition into the West Indies. *"Lusitani mare Atlanticum navigantes cunctam Mauretaniae & Aethiopiae*

---

[142] Necho II was king of Egypt c. 610–595 B.C.E. He defeated Josiah of Judah (609) but was himself defeated by the Babylonians six years later. The "million of men" is an exaggeration, typical of the inflated numbers often cited by Herodotus.

[143] The Mediterranean.

[144] Eudoxus of Cyzicus (fl. 240 B.C.E.) was a Greek traveller mentioned by Pliny (6, 198). He is mentioned several times by Strabo (1.337–338; 1.381, 383, 389). Strabo states that Eudoxus "was convinced that the circumnavigation of Libya was possible" (1.381). The other Eudoxus mentioned numerous times by Strabo is Eudoxus of Cnidus, a Greek astronomer and mathematician who spent some years amongst the priests of Heliopolis in Egypt.

[145] Ptolemy III Euergetes reigned 246–221 B.C.E.

[146] Ptolemy VIII [Soter II] Lathyros reigned 116–107 and 88–81 B.C.E.

[147] Hanno (? fifth century B.C.E.) was a Carthaginian navigator who sailed beyond the Pillars of Hercules into what were then termed "Libyan" regions of Africa, voyaging at least some distance south of the Equator. Scholars place the date at about 465 B.C.E. Hanno's account of the trip is extant in a Greek version probably copied from an earlier Greek version, itself a copy of the original Punic. For details see David Soren, A. ben Khader, and H. Slim, *Carthage* (New York: Simon and Schuster, 1990), 66–67.

[148] *Melpomene* is the title given to Book 4 of Herodotus's *Histories*.

oram usque ad magnum illud & vastum promontorium Bonae Spei antiquis geographis ignoratam &c. Plurimis annis antiquam Chr. Columbus Ligur occidentalem oceanum perlustrasset,[149] says a late good author. The first we can therefore honour for the first discoverer of this cape is Vasco da Gama or Bartolomeo Diaz, both of them eminent Portugals, who in the year 1497, says Osorius,[150] by instructions they received from King John II coasted round about this cape-land and so opened the first way by sea into the Orient.

The soil here is exceeding good, the earth being at all times covered with grass and drapered with flowers and herbs in great variety. I well remember that by accident I digged up the root of one that came up like a big parsnip, which for many days sweat a gum or clammy juice that had a very aromatic smell, and though few roots save orris[151] are odoriferous, which, having a tender dainty heat vanishes in the sun and air, yet this, when dry, kept its perfume a month together. The leaf was broad and prickly, and something resembling the holy thistle, and grew close to the ground. I also observed there stores of agrimony, betony, mint, calamint, sorrel, scabious, spinach, thyme, carduus benedictus, and coloquintida,[152] with which and several other beneficial flowers which the skillful might have better distinguished, nature all the year long robes the fruitful earth with tapestry. The Hebrews have a proverb, "there is not a herb upon the earth but that has his *mazal*,[153] or star answering it, and saying 'grow'." I know not how true that is, but here they prosper, all of which is summed up by another as follows:

*Quamvis enim mentosa appareat, & collibus multis
distincta et interim tamen multis vallibus, silvis, pratis-*

---

[149] The Portuguese navigated the Atlantic Ocean all along the coast of Mauretania and Ethiopia to the vast promontory of the Cape of Good Hope, unknown to the ancient geographers, many years before the Italian Christopher Columbus passed through the western ocean. Who the "late good author" was remains a mystery.

[150] Jeronimo Osorio (1506–1580) was known as "the Portuguese Cicero." He taught at the University of Coimbra and was a scholar of Greek, law, and philosophy. Amongst his works are *De vita Emmanuelis*, a biography of King Manoel I "the Fortunate", and a posthumously-published treatise on politics and government, *De regis institutione et disciplina* (1582). His sermons were collected under the title *Concionum* (1607).

[151] Orris-root, a relative of the iris, smells a bit like violets when it is dried; it is used to clear sinuses, and, more lately, as an ingredient in gin.

[152] Calamint or calaminth is a mint-like herb of which there are over thirty different species. Scabious is a white daisy-like flower which is related to the teasel; *carduus benedictus*, otherwise known as the "blessed thistle," was thought to be an antidote to some poisons; coloquintida, now known as colocynth, is the fruit of the bitter gourd, and is shaped like white balls.

[153] A Hebrew word meaning 'spiritual pathway,' which comes down to earth from the stars.

que decorata est, gramina & flores suavissime olentes
magna copia producit. Cervosque & feras & leones multo
numero nutrit, quae omnia visu & aspectu longe iucun-
dissime existunt: praeterea, lymphidissimis fontibus
scatet quam plurimis, qui non sine gratissimo susurro,
de montibus altis prorumpentes fluminibus esse passim
insinuans,& cum eis postmodum in mare exonerantur.[154]

The rivers yield no less variety, as trouts, pike, pickerel, tench, eel, and of shell-fish crab, lobster, rockfish, crayfish, cockle, mussel, limpets, tortoises, which be very small and curiously-coloured, and oysters, which though have no discriminate sex are as good as can be. We see also gudgeon and other sea fish, which sometime are taken in the *aestuarium* of the fresh water. The mountains are not without marcasite and minerals, which but by search are not to be discerned. The country affords withal plenty of beasts of sundry sorts, as buffalos and cows, which are large, but lean and bunch-backed, sheep with long ears like hounds, much unlike those in Europe, red deer, antelopes as large as stags and delight-fully-headed, apes and baboons of extraordinary size and colour, lions, panthers, pards, jackals, wolves, dogs, cats, hares, and zebras or pied horses, as also elephants and camels, which 3 last we saw not, and Garcia de Orta,[155] physician to the Viceroy of Goa, reports that he saw unicorns here headed like a horse, if the zebras deceive him not. And for birds the change and store is no less, as hens, geese, turkeys, penguins, crows, gulls, thrushes, pheasants, storks, pelicans, ostrich, pintados,[156] albatrosses, vultures, eagles, cranes and cormorants, which last upon the sea, when without ken of land we saw so numerous as, if related, will scarce be credited, this bird having a smell equal to the vulture, after battles have been noted to fly some hundred of miles by scent to prey upon the carcases. Here also are store of those beautiful birds called passe-flamingoes, whose feathers are

---

[154] "This may appear exaggerated, but it is distinguished by being decorated with many hills, valleys, woods and fields, grass and beautifully-scented flowers, which it produces in great numbers. It nurtures stags, wild beasts and many lions, a most pleasant sight to see. Moreover, there are many of the clearest springs, which, not without a pleasing murmur, break forth from the high mountains to become rivers, which are presently released into the sea."

[155] Garcia de Orta (c. 1500–1568) was a Portuguese doctor and botanist from a Jewish convert family. He became Physician to João III (1525) and Professor of Natural History at the University of Lisbon (1530). He accompanied Martim de Sousa to the Indies (1534) and set up a medical practice in Goa. After his death his sister was burned as a suspected Jew (1569) and he himself was denounced to the Inquisition; in 1580 his body was exhumed and burned. He wrote the first treatise on tropical medicine, *Coloquios dos simples e drogas e cousas medicinais da India* (1563).

[156] The Cape petrel, so-called because of its contrasted black-and-white colour pattern. The word means "painted" in Spanish.

crimson and white, as pure as can be imagined, so far above the rest it enticed my pen to give you its figure:

Flamingo [illustration not shown]

The Savages Described

The natives[157] being propagated from Shem, both in their visages and natures seem to inherit his malediction. Their stature is but indifferent, their colour olevaster, or that sort of black we see the Americans that live under the Equator. Their faces be very thin, their body as to limbs well-proportioned, but by way of ornament so pinked and cut in several shapes as fancy guides them. Their heads are commonly long, about which they place their greatest bravery, for though their hair, after the African mode, be woolly and crisped, nevertheless by way of dress some shave all their skull, some half, othersome only leave a tuft atop. Some, instead of shaving, have several other dresses for their head, as spur-rowels, brass buttons, pieces of pewter, beads of many sorts, which the mirthful sailor exchanges for mutton, beef herbs, ostrich eggshells, tortoises or the like. Their ears are extended by links of brass, stones, broken oyster-shells and the like ponderous baubles; their arms and legs be loaden with voluntary shackles of copper, brass, iron and ivory. About their necks, either in imitation of the Dutch commanders' chains, or those worn by coxswains and boatswains, they wear the raw guts of beasts, which serve as well for food as complement, usually eating and speaking both together. The rest of their body is naked, save that about the waist they have a thong of leather which, like the back of a glove, serves to cover their pudenda, which without doubt they imagine a dress both rich and an ingenious sort of ornament. The natural and first garment Adam used was long before the art of weaving was invented, according to which the better sort here wear a lion or panther-skin or like that the leopard and the baboon, also a calf or sheep, the hair inverted, elsewhere their body being naked. Only upon their feet they have a sole or a piece of leather tied with a little strap resembling the Roman *crepidula*,[158] which, while they were in our company, their hands held, their feet having thereby the greater liberty to steal, which with their toes

---

[157] The natives Herbert describes here are the Khoikhoi, cousins to the Bushmen and formerly known as Hottentots. Their name, given to them by the Dutch, who established a colony in Table Bay a little later then Herbert's visit (1652), refers to "stuttering," because their language appeared to contain a series of "clicks." Their language, which Herbert alludes to later, is known as Nama, and is now spoken in the southern part of Namibia. Their name actually means "people," *khoi* meaning "person," and doubled meaning "people." They have been in the area for about thirty thousand years, and have an extensive folklore tradition.

[158] A small sandal.

they can do exactly, all the while looking one in the face the better to deceive, which vice, how criminal soever it be in most places, was nevertheless among the Lacedaemonians,[159] a reputable practice at first, though after held ignominious and punished severely. Theft not being punished, but rather such as could not filch neatly. What the generality of the natives are I cannot say, but some we saw were semi-eunuchs and some of the women use excision[160] through custom rather then religion. Their habitations are usually in caves, so as these are the proper troglodytes. Democritus[161] persuades us that knowledge concerning nature lies hid in certain deep mines or caves of the earth; these, living constantly in the entrails of the earth, have good opportunity to gain that perfection, did not their brutish disposition avoid it. Now, concerning their diet, former time spoke modestly of them. Solinus[162] calls them *agriophagi* and *ichthyophagi* from their food; *acridophagi* I might add, seeing they have plenty of locusts brought thither by wind, which, being sprinkled with salt, they eat greedily, but more properly *anthropophagi*,[163] for the truth is they would commonly violate the graves of those dead men we buried and feed upon their carcases, the greatest piece of barbarity within the compass of expression, one would think, for in humanity men naturally abhor it. And herein they are more savage then lions, who *cadavera mortuum non gustant; enim vero, quod vivit corripiunt et ex eo comedunt*,[164] in that being more physical then those barbarians, who, it seems, are ignorant that no creature that dies of itself is good to eat, nor considering that there is a disparity 'twixt the

---

[159] The Spartans.

[160] Female circumcision.

[161] Democritus of Abdera (c. 470–360 B.C.E.), a Greek atomist philosopher, much admired and cited by Aristotle. He held that the world is made up of invisible atoms of infinite shape and number which exist in infinite space. There are hundreds of fragmentary atomist writings attributed to Democritus (many quoted by Aristotle), and he also wrote on ethics. His work survives in fragments, for which see Kathleen Freeman, *Ancilla to the Pre-Socratic Philosophers* (Cambridge, MA: Harvard University Press, 1983).

[162] Caius Julius Solinus "Polyhistor" (third century C.E.) was a geographer and botanist, famous for his *Collectanea rerum memorabilium*. This work, which cribs mercilessly from Pliny the Elder's *Historia naturalis* and, to a lesser extent, from Pomponius Mela, was nevertheless one of the first Latin books to be printed (Venice, 1473). In 1629 Salmasius prepared a modern edition, to which Herbert is referring here. Solinus (or his book) is often referred to as "Polyhistor" by later scholars. It is part geography, part ethnography, with a fair amount of botany and mythography thrown in for good measure; medieval and Renaissance readers alike were fascinated by its description of monsters and marvels.

[163] Wild animal-eaters, fish eaters, eaters of bitter things, cannibals.

[164] "Have no taste for dead flesh; it is true that they violently seize and eat what lives." The source was untraceable.

nourishment and the thing nourished, albeit Ficino[165] is of the opinion that in deep consumptions no such cure as by sucking human blood in its best constitution. I suppose he means when the physician gives orders for the opening a vein. But among these brutes, albeit they have plenty of dead whales, seals, penguins, grouse and raw-puddings, which we saw them tear and eat as dainties, for they neither roast nor boil, yet do they no less covet to destroy such as through old age or sickness are not able to provide for themselves, leaving them upon such mountains destitute of help, where, if famine and cold destroy them not, the wild beasts put a period to their languishing conditions, a barbarism scarce to be paralleled save by the Caspii[166] in Margiana, who had the like base custom, as we read in the 11 *lib.* of Strabo, for, being superannuated, *parentes decripitos angusto loco includentes, fame enecare dicuntur.*[167] "With such, no violent death nor 'stroying rage / Of lust is half so dreadful as old age." The women give suck, the uberous[168] dug being stretched over their naked shoulder, whose portraits, with a landscape of the Table and other neighbouring mountains, I present the reader so well as I was able to draw them:

A Man and Woman at the Cape of Good Hope [illustration not shown]

Their language is rather apishly then articulately founded, with whom 'tis thought they have unnatural mixture, so as what the commentator upon Ptolemy observed long since, saying "*humana voce fere carent, ut stridere potius quam loqui videantur,*"[169] having a voice 'twixt human and beast, makes that supposition to be of more credit that they have a beastly copulation or conjuncture, so, as considering the resemblance they bear with baboons, which I could observe kept frequent company with the women, their speech, not unlike the Semicani[170]

---

[165] Marsilio Ficino (1433–1499), the great Italian humanist, Neoplatonist philosopher, and translator who headed the Accademia Fiorentina and served Lorenzo de' Medici, to whom he dedicated *De religione Christiana* (1475–1476). His principal work is the *Theologica Platonica de immortalitate animae* (1488). His translation of Plato appeared in 1484, and *De vita libri tres* (1489) is another well-known philosophical treatise, and appears to be the one mentioned here. See *Three Books on Life*, ed. and trans. C. V. Koske and J. R. Clark, MRTS 57 (Binghamton: CMERS, 1989).

[166] A Scythian tribe who inhabited the western side of the Caspian Sea, which is named for them.

[167] "They are said to put their aged parents to death by means of hunger, confining them to a narrow space " (5.283). Later on he states that the Caspians "starve to death those who are over seventy years of age and place their bodies out in the desert" (5.293).

[168] Fruitful.

[169] "They almost lack a human voice, so appear to grate rather than speak." See Ptolemy, 4.6.

[170] Literally "Half-dogs."

neighbouring the Massagetes[171] mentioned by Apollonius[172] in his *Argonauts* rather agreeing with beasts then men. Their savage life, diet, exercise and the like, these may be said to be the descent of satyrs, if any such ever were, and probably 'twas one of these that appeared to Anthony the hermit in his life mentioned.[173] Now what the philosophers allege concerning the function of the soul may be applicable to these animals, saying that the soul of man is gradually rather then specifically differenced from the souls of beasts no otherwise then the sun is amongst stars, or gold amongst metals, upon which account the Spaniard of late years made it the subject of their dispute whether the Indians were of descent from Adam or no, or whether they were not rather a middle species of men and apes. Had it been a *quaere* concerning this people, [it] might have carried with it greater probability. Boterus[174] also, treating of monstrous births in Peru, says that it proceeds from a copulation of women with monkeys, which, as repugnant to the due course of nature is not to be maintained, though these are subject for that dispute as much as any. Aristotle, albeit a heathen, *l.* 1 *De Caelo* hath this position: "*Omnes homines notionem deorum habent*,"[175] and another, "*Universum gentis humanorum ubique terrarum colit deum verum vel falsum.*"[176] Nevertheless, if that maxim fail everywhere, here it may, for during the time I stayed amongst them, I saw no signs of any knowledge of God, the laws of nature scarce being observed, no spark of devotion, no symptoms of Heaven or Hell, no place set apart for worship, no sabbath for rest.

And as to their language, something I writ from one that I selected as the most sober in the company, for through the frequency of ships that anchor there for refreshment some of them are a little civilised, from what Herodotus *lib.* 4 writes of their progenitors the Garamants, "*qui fugiunt aspectum commerciumque*

---

[171] The Massagetes, who lived north of the Oxus river, were a Central Asian tribe related to the Scythians.

[172] Apollonius Rhodius (c. 270–after 245 B.C.E.), Greek epic poet and scholar, was also Chief Librarian in Alexandria. The *Argonautica* was first printed in Florence, edited by Lascaris (1496), and a Latin version was printed in the edition by J. Hölzlin (1641). There is a modern translation by Richard Hunter (Harmondsworth: Penguin Books, 1982).

[173] This story is told by Jerome in his life of Paul the Hermit, PL 23. 23–24.

[174] Giovanni Botero (1544–1617) was an Italian poet, diplomat, and priest whose main distinction is that he attacked the theory of Machiavelli in *The Reason of State* (1589). He was in the service of Cardinal Federico Borromeo to 1599. His treatise was translated into English and has a modern edition by P. J. Waley and D. P. Waley (New Haven: Yale University Press, 1956). His *Travellers breviat, or an historicall description of the most famous kingdomes of the world* was translated into English by Robert Johnson (1601).

[175] Every human being has an idea of the gods.

[176] All over the world the human race worships either a true or false god.

hominum,"[177] and indeed Pliny in the Proem of his 5 *lib. Nat. Hist.* says, in his time their names and places were inexpressible to him: *"anonimi sunt in Africa propriis nominibus carentes."*[178] The words are as follows: one, *istwee*; two, *istum*; three, *tstgwunny*; four, *hacky*; five, *croe*; six, *istgunny*; seven, *chowhawgh*; eight, *kishow*; nine, *cusho*; ten, *gheshy*, and further they could not number. Aristotle, not without good reason, admired that both Greeks and barbarians used a like numeration unto ten, which, seeing it was so universal, could not rationally be concluded accidental, but rather a number that had its foundation in nature. They call a knife *droaf*, a quill *guasaco*, a hat *twubba*, a nose *tweam*, a sword *dushingro*, a book *bueem*, a ship *chicunny*, water *chtammey*, brass *hadderchereef*, a skin *gwummey*, a bracelet *whohoap*, eggshells *sann*, seals *harkash*, a woman *traqueosh*, bread *bara*, give me *quoy*, the yard *gwammey*, stones *wchraef*, womb *wchieep*, paps *semigwe*, genitor *istcoom*.[179] To draw towards an end, lest Myndus's gates[180] be opened, here in exchange for trifles we got cattle and salads for refreshment. *Anno* 1600 Sir James Lancaster,[181] landing here, had 1000 sheep and 50 oxen for bables, and might have had more plenty, had not our emulous neighbour the Dutch, after some disgust given the natives, rode with our collars out, which made them the less amicable to us, who have at all times expressed kindness to them, and not in vain, seeing *nomen amicitiae barbara corda movet*,[182] and is the more prudential, seeing jealousy so possesses them. An example we have in Cory, a savage brought thence into England in the year 1614, where, being civilised, he returned in a few years after to his country, where, to express how nobly he had been treated, entering the woods in a copper-guilt armour, whether in revenge of his departure

---

[177] The Garamantes were the indigenous people of Libya. Herodotus noted that "they shun all intercourse and contact" with others and that "they have no weapons of war" (4. 174–175).

[178] In Africa they are anonymous, without proper names.

[179] Foster notes that these words come from "the now extinct Cape Hottentot language" (*Herbert*, 301). See, for example, R. M. Beach, *The Phonetics of the Hottentot Language* (Cambridge: W. Heffer, 1938).

[180] Myndus was a town in Caria, now Turkey, near Halicarnassus; its ruins are to be found in the modern town of Gümüslük. It was famous for its strong walls and outsized gates and is mentioned by several Greek historians including Herodotus, Arrian, and Dionysius. Alexander the Great was driven away from it.

[181] Sir James Lancaster of Basingstoke (1554–1618) undertook the first voyage to the East Indies (1591–1594) and in 1600 commanded the first fleet belonging to the East India Company, which sailed to Aceh, Indonesia. In 1603 he was knighted, and subsequently became one of the Directors of the Company. He established the British factory in Bantam. See Sir Clements Markham, ed., *The Voyages of Sir James Lancaster* (London: Hakluyt Society, 1877), and Sir William Foster, ed., *The Voyages of Sir James Lancaster to Brazil and the East Indies 1591–1603* (London: Hakluyt Society, 1940).

[182] "Friendship's name moves barbaric hearts" (Ovid, *Tristia* 3. 2. 100).

or to be possessed of so great a treasure is not known, but instead of a kind reception which he thought he should have had, they butchered him.[183]

The cattle they sold us, had they not been secured by tying their heads to some stakes, usually would break after the savages upon one man's whistle, which was so full of discord as if five men had whistled together, not to be counterfeited. They differ not now from what the Garamants their ancestors were, "*qui matrimoniarum expertes passim cum femina degunt, cibus caro ferina, & lanis pabulum uti pecoribus. Qui neque moribus, neque legibus, neque imperio habent. Nullas certas sedes habentes, vagi palantes, semper quos nox coegerat,*"[184] pretty well resembled by Havillan[185] in his *Architrenius*:

> Their garments are raw hides of beasts, whose blood
> They drink, in spacious cups of hollow wood.
> Their caves their lodgings are, bushes their beds,
> Rocks serve for tables, and by prey are fed.
> Theft, slaughter, rapine, and what bad we call,
> These monsters act, though the earth do groan withal.

---

[183] Cory was actually Xhory, a Khoikoi tribesmen more or less kidnapped by Sir Thomas Smythe, the first Governor of the East India Company (1613) and brought to England together with a companion, who died on board ship. Xhory became quite well known in England, and was presented to James I. He was well-treated and dressed like a gentleman, but appeared incapable of learning English. Seeing him depressed, Smythe attempted to comfort him, and was astonished when Xhory, in perfectly-articulated English, told him how homesick he was and offered information about his homeland. In 1614 he returned home; the accounts I have found mention the armour, but there is nothing about him being killed by his own people, although apparently they were so impressed with him that they made him a leader. He then took control of the bartering system and raised the price of meat, which may have angered some of his fellow-tribesmen. For further details, see K. Parker, "Telling Tales: Early Modern English Voyagers and the Cape of Good Hope," *Seventeenth Century* 10:1 (1995): 141–44.

[184] "Who do not use marriage but pass time with women [i.e. are not monogamous], whose food is the delicate flesh of wild animals, who use sheep for wool and nourishment, who have no morals, laws, or government, and no settled homes, wandering the plains, often by night." The source was untraceable.

[185] Johannes de Hauvila or Jean de Hauteville (c. 1150–after 1200) wrote the *Architrenius*, an allegorical poetic satire (1184) which was very popular in the Renaissance because it contained graphic descriptions of the physical characteristics of women. Its hero, known as "The Prince of Lamentations," travels to Ultima Thule. There is a modern translation by Winthrop Wetherbee (Cambridge: Cambridge University Press, 1994). It was first printed in Paris (1517).

They have little art in war, their weapon commonly an assegai[186] or javelin headed with iron, directed by some feathers which they take off and on at pleasure. Some quarrels happened by some indiscretion 'twixt us and them, and in the skirmish found that a dozen muskets will chase 1000, at every discharge falling down as thunder-struck. Yet let me advise our men to avoid needless bravados, and not condemn them from their indefensive nakedness. Here is an example: Almeida,[187] one of the bravest captains the Portugals ever had, after many gallant achievements in Asia and Africa, returning *Anno* 1510 out of India, he, with eleven experienced captains and other gallants, upon a small affront putting some of the savages to death, were unexpectedly set upon by these naked barbarians, who had the arma antiqua, i.e. manus, ungues, dentes,[188] and slain were every man of them. "*Qui*," saith Osorius,

> *cum per medios flammas, per pilis innumerabilis, per tela,*
> *per gladios, sine ulla formidinis significatione ruentes,*
> *maximum terrorem hastibus intulissent & insignes*
> *victorias contra innumerabiles inimicos adepsi fuissent,*
> *tunc a paucis hominibus inermibus atque nudis*
> *interfecti et spoliati fuerunt.*[189]

I will sum up the character of this *agreste hominum genus*[190] with that which Salvian[191] *Libro de vero judicio* gives of other the Africans:

---

[186] The word is derived from the Arabic *az-zagayah*, a throwing-spear.

[187] Francisco de Almeida (c. 1450–1509), Portuguese soldier and statesman "whose fame," Camoens wrote, "Fortune will beacon to the heavens" (5. 45). Counsellor to Joao II and Manoel I (1495–1521), he became the first Viceroy of India (1503), and the first Portuguese to travel to Bombay. Almeida was also the conqueror of Mombasa and Zanzibar, and defeated a combined army of Egyptians and Indians at the battle of Diu (1509). He was killed by the Khoikhoi at Table Bay, after his men had attacked them and killed some children, hardly "some small affront." The number of Portuguese killed is given in most accounts as sixty-four, including twelve captains.

[188] Old-fashioned weapons, such as hands, nails, and teeth.

[189] Who, rushing amidst the firing [of guns], innumerable spears, javelins, and swords without any indication of fear, inflicted a great deal of damage with their blows and obtained a remarkable victory against a large number of enemies, who were killed and despoiled by a few unarmed, naked men.

[190] Wild species of human beings.

[191] Salvian (c. 400–496) was a Roman jurist who became a monk and retired to the monastery of Lerins. There he wrote his best-known work, *De gubernatione Dei*, in which he asserted that the Roman world was in decline because people had rejected God's commandments. This work ranged all over the empire in its scope, and was first printed in 1530. Salvian's *Ad ecclesiam* was printed in 1526, and selections of his letters appeared in 1580 and 1611. His *De vero judicio* was printed together with other works in 1580.

Omnes quippe gentes habent sicut peculiaria mala,
ita etiam quaedam bona; in Afris pene omnibus
insunt omnia mala, inhumani, impuri, ebriosi, falsissimi,
fraudulentissimi, cupidissimi, perfidissimi, & obscenis
libidinum omnium impuritati & blasphemiis addictissimi, [192]

and for a farewell take that which Leo [Africanus] gives the Libyans, "They have no letters, faith, nor law, living, if it be a life, like wild beasts for ignorance, like devils for mischief, and like dogs for poverty."

Having bid this *terrarum ultima* [193] farewell, upon the 19 of July we weighed anchor, heading our course towards Madagascar. The wind was favourable till such time as, doubling Cape Falso, being off at sea we perceived a storm intended us, happy in the sight of a small black bird, long-winged, injustly by seamen called the Devil's Bird, an *antimilago*, [194] a kind of natural astrologer by sense discovering the least alteration of air, and seldom seen but against stormy weather, doubtless a warning from God, as be the pintado birds, like jays in colours, who about these remote seas are constantly flying, whereby they give seamen an infallible knowledge that, when neither sounding nor observations from Sun, Moon or planets for many days are had, they are upon this coast; these birds and sargasso or rockweed, and *trumbaes*, eradicated by storms, being never seen in such quantity in any other part of the universe, upon these for 50 leagues into the sea never failing our intelligence.

The three and twentieth day of July the wind got up, enraging the ocean; one surging wave, I well remember, struck us so pat upon our broadside as forced the ship, in despite of her helm, then close by the lee, to turn about above 5 points of the compass, with a noise little inferior to a cannon, insomuch as our captain cried out we had struck upon a rock, but his error soon appeared after so great a thunder, the wave splashing upon our decks so salt a shower as soundly washed us all. The storm continued until the eight and twentieth day, when, veering into a milder quarter, our course east north-east, it grew calm and moderate. The storm was not greater then we expected, for it is a general observation that very seldom any ship doubles this great cape without a storm or extreme high sea, from whence it was called Cape Tormentoso [195] at first. Now the reason of those usual blustering of winds and rough seas is obvious, for that being the utmost promontory of Africa towards the south, the two great seas running on either

---

[192] "Indeed, all the natives have their own brand of evil besides a certain good; amongst the Africans almost all are in the power of every kind of evil. They are very cruel, drunken, mendacious, untrustworthy, greedy and faithless, addicted to all the sexual vices and to blasphemy." The quote is actually from Salvian, *De gubernatione Dei* 7.15, PL 53. 142.

[193] Most distant of lands.

[194] Foster identifies this as the stormy petrel (*Herbert*, 301).

[195] By Bartolemeu Dias.

side the Africa[an] continent here meet in their current, and the wind, being commonly loud, makes them struggle the more violently against each other, to the hazard of such ships that sail there.

And now the seas are peaceable, the air calm and the sky serene. Let us look about for some isle or other, that we may discover, if possible, that which Venetus,[196] probably from an optic glass upon a terrace beyond Tartary, descried about this place. He not only assures us of an isle, but saw a bird there (if his multiplying glass deceived him not) so big as a ship, and so strong as in her talons could easily grip and truss up an elephant. Take his phantasma in his own explanation, *nam falsa est veris affinia multa locutus*:[197]

> *In quadam insula versus meridiem prope Madagascar*
> *certo anni tempore apparet mirabilis species avis, qua*
> *ruc*[198] *appellatur, aquilae quidem habens effigiem, sed*
> *immensae magnitudinis: plerasque alarum pennas habet,*
> *in longitudine continentes duodecim passus, spissitudinem*
> *vero eius proportionem tenere longitudinis, & totum avis*
> *corpus pennis proportione respondet. Est etiam tante*
> *fortitudinis, ut sola sine aliquo adminiculo elephantem*
> *capiat & in sublime sustollit, atque iterum ad terram*
> *cadere finat, quo carnibus eius vesci posset.*[199]

A bird worthy of Gesner's[200] knowledge, which we may rank with those gryphons that guard the Ophyrian mounts of gold against the Arimaspi, who, from winking

---

[196] Marco Polo (1254–1324). His *Marci Pauli de Venetiis de consuetudinibus et conditionibus Orientalium regionum*, edited by Pepuro di Bononia, appeared in 1485. There was an English translation made as early as 1579; Herbert could also have used a more recent printed edition of 1671. Herbert is, of course, mocking Polo's claims here.

[197] For in many cases truth and falsehood are close to one another.

[198] This is the Roc, or Rukh, which makes an appearance in the story of Sinbad in *The Arabian Nights*.

[199] In this island, towards the south of Madagascar, a wondrous species of bird, called the Roc, appears at a certain time of the year. It is like an eagle in appearance, but of an enormous size; it has a great many feathers on its wings, which stretch out for nearly twelve [Roman] paces [about sixty feet, Ed.], and in thickness are proportional to its length. It is so strong that alone, without any assistance, it can seize an elephant, bear it up on high, then let it fall to the ground, where it can feed on the flesh.

[200] Conrad Gesner (1516–1565), a Swiss scholar who taught philosophy at the universities of Basel and Zurich. Gesner wrote mainly on biology and medicine, but also was interested in theology and ancient philosophy, particularly that of the Stoic emperor Marcus Aurelius. Herbert is probably referring to Gesner's monumental five-volume treatise *Historiae animalium* (1551–1558; 1587); he was also the editor of Aelian (1556), whom Herbert quotes several times.

when they shoot, are said to be *monoculi*,[201] not seldom from their Scythic holes attempting the conquest of Mammon enclosed in the Riphean Hills,[202] as Tostatus[203] in Rabanus,[204] Aeschylus, Dionysius and Herodotus would persuade us. Aristaeus,[205] a Greek poet, was the first that discovered them, sufficiently derided by Michovius.[206] Those north parts having neither gold nor gryphon, "*Gryphus in illa septentr. nec in illis orbis partibus invenire affirmarem*,"[207] let us rest awhile upon Madagascar, the empress, some think, of all the islands in the universe.

Madagascar

Madagascar, as called by the natives, is by Ptolemy *Menuthyai*, by M. Paulus Venetus *Magaster*, by Thévet *Albagra*, by Mercator[208] *Do Cerne* and *Insula Sancti Georgii*, which he takes from Pliny, *lib. 6 cap.* 31, another bearing that name being in the Atlantic opposite to Mount Atlas, and by some reputed Madeira, by

---

[201] One-eyed. The Arimaspi were actually a legendary, rather than actual tribe.

[202] The Riphean Hills are situated to the east of the Adriatic Gulf.

[203] Alonzo Tostado (1400–1455) was Bishop of Avila and a commentator on Eusebius. He studied Greek and Hebrew at the University of Salamanca, and wrote also on the historical books of the Old Testament. His *Works* were published in Venice (1507 and 1547).

[204] Rabanus Maurus (fl. 842–46) wrote *De rerum naturis*, also known as *De universo*. It was published and edited by Adolf Rausch (1466), and translated into English, together with his other works, by George Colvener (1627). There is a modern (on-line) edition of the Latin text prepared by W. Schipper from MSS Augiensis 68 and 96. See PL 111. 9–614.

[205] Aristaeus of Proconnesus (c. 700 B.C.E.?) was a semi-mythical poet to whom was ascribed the *Arimaspeia*, a lost work about the Arimaspi. He is mentioned by Pindar, Theopompus, and other authorities, but his existence is questioned. For details, see Cordelia M. Birch, "Lives and Work of Aristeias," *Classical Journal* 46 (1950): 79–111.

[206] Maciej Miechowita (1450–1523), rector of the University of Cracow, wrote *Librorum 2 de Sarmatia europaea & Asiatica* (1532), a treatise on the history of Europe and Asia. He was cited by Sir Thomas Browne in *Pseudodoxia Epidemica or Vulgar Errors* (1646) as an expert on griffins, of whose existence he was evidently sceptical (III. xi. 142) and from which work Herbert probably cited Michovius.

[207] "I cannot affirm that the gryphon is found either in the north or in any other part of the world." For an interesting view of gryphons see Adrienne Mayer, *The First Fossil Hunters* (Princeton: Princeton University Press, 2000), 15–53.

[208] Gerardus Mercator, or Gerhard Kremer (1512–1594), was a map-maker, mathematician, and philosopher trained at the University of Louvain (Leuven), and, apparently, self-taught in astronomy. He was, of course, also the man who produced the great atlas of the world, the *Theatrum orbis terrarum* (1570) and gave us "Mercator's Projection" of the world. He was also the first cosmographer to employ both latitude and longitude as a tool for sailors. There is a recent biography of him by N. Crane, *Mercator: The Man who Mapped the Planet* (New York: Holt, 2002).

others Gratiosa, one of the Azores, and by Tristan da Cunha,[209] the Portuguese who discovered it *Anno Domini* 1508, Saint Lawrence, being that saint's day he first viewed it. Great difference is in Spanish writers about the first that landed here;[210] Manuel Teleso de Meneses[211] anchored here, say some, two years before da Cunha. Osorius, in his 4 *Lib. de vita Emanuelis reg. Port.*, fol. 140, says that Fernando Suares and Roderigo Freire, mariners, in two ships returning from India to Lisbon, *Anno* 1506, accidentally fell upon this isle and suffered from the treachery of the savage inhabitants. But, in honour of Lourenço, son of Almeida, the admiral and commander of all the forts in India from his name so named it, forgetting that in his 5 book, fol. 162, da Cunha formerly so named it.

Madagascar (that name sounds best), is, questionless, the greatest island in the world, for, accounting its extent from Cape Roma in the south to the north point called St. Sebastian, which is from sixteen to six and twenty degrees Antarctic latitude, it is not less then 1000 miles. The north end parallels Cuama in Quilos, a famous part of Africa. South, the great river of Magnice, the reputed breadth in some part 230 [miles]; Osorius says 400, but more certain that it is 100 where it is narrowest. The air is temperate, save when the sun is in or near the zenith. The soil in most places is luxuriant, fitted both for seed and fruit; in the Mediterranean parts 'tis thought gold may be found, but much wood there is, amongst which store of ebony. The rivers abound with fish, and it wants not reasonable good roads and harbours for ships to ride in. Pity that so noble and place and so populous should continue so long uncivilised and corrupted by Mahometanism and Gentilism,[212] which, as with an impure breath, has infected the whole island.

Map of Madagascar [illustration not shown]

Maritime towns and ports known to us are Roma, Augustine, Antabusta, St. Jacob's, Matatana, Angoda, Ferendo, Fermoso, Antongill and Jungomar; the two last are wellnigh opposite to each other. Augustine Bay, under our Winter

---

[209] Tristan [Tristão] da Cunha (c. 1460–1540) was a Portuguese explorer who was appointed as the first Viceroy of Portuguese India (1504), but was prevented from taking up the position by a temporary fit of blindness. In 1506 he discovered Madagascar, then went on to occupy Mozambique and the island of Socotra.

[210] According to Pedro Alvares Cabral, who was there, it was Diogo Dias who first discovered Madagascar (10 August 1500), when his ship drifted apart from the others in the area. See Pedro Alvares Cabral, *The Voyage of Pedro Alvares Cabral to Brazil and India*, trans. W. B. Greenlee (Waterloo, Ontario: Laurier Books, 1995), lxvii–viii. Dias named the island after St. Lawrence, not for the younger Almeida.

[211] Manoel Tellez de Meneses is difficult to locate. He may be the sixth Senhor de Unhao, who died around 1536, but this identification is tentative.

[212] Paganism.

Tropic, and Antongill, upon the east side, afford best anchoring.[213] The first we usually ride at in passing to Bantam or southward, the other home-bound is best, as Sir James Lancaster *Anno* 1600 made proof of, who rode in 8 fathom water in the bottom of the bay, a small isle being behind them to sea, oozy ground; the place was good for victualling, the ice quick, and the natives well-conditioned. Howbeit the Dutch, at this place two months formerly, through distempers lost 200 men of agues and fluxes, which has made some to report it for an unhealthy place. At Augustine Bay the variation is 16 degrees.

The whole isle was lately tetrarchical, four several Kings swaying their ebony sceptres in each toparchy, jealous of one another's greatness. The maritime towns and places are infected with Mahometanism, brought thither with the little trade they have from Arabia not long since; the mediterran[214] with Gentilism. Nature, abhorring cruelty, instructs them to punish murder with death, adultery with public shame, theft with banishment. Fishing delights those that live near the sea more then tillage, Thetis[215] being better accounted of then Ceres, if their ignorance in agriculture do not rather so dispose it. The natives are generally strong, active and courageous; the male sort from their infancy practice the rude postures of Mars, covering their naked bodies with massy targets, their right hand brandishing a long but small assegai or lance of ebony barbed with iron kept bright, which by exercise they know how to jaculate as well as any people in the universe, discommendable only in their being empoisoned according to the Ethiopian custom. *"Aethiopum geminata venenis vulnera,"* in Claudian,[216] and

---

[213] The most important of these places was St. Augustine Bay, which apart from being a pirate hideout from the early eighteenth century was also the site of a very short-lived English colony (1645–46). People had been enticed there with great expectations; Walter Hammond, an East India Company employee, wrote a book called *Madagascar, the Richest and Most Fruitful Island in the World* (1643), which may have encouraged settlers to try their fortunes there. For details see W. Foster, "An English Settlement in Madagascar 1645–46," *English Historical Review* 27 (1912): 239–50. Jungomar is a bit of a puzzle; in most accounts it is on the north-west corner of the island, but in modern maps (as Vinganora) it appears to be on the western side. Antongill Bay is situated on the north-east coast of Madagascar, north of St. Mary Island.

[214] The middle part of the country, i.e. the interior.

[215] Thetis was a sea-goddess and the mother of Achilles.

[216] Claudius Claudianus (c. 355–408), the official poet of the Emperor Honorius, composed, in addition to panegyrics on the imperial family, the mythological epic *De raptu Proserpinae*. Claudian was an elaborately ornamental, sometimes convoluted poet, but he was admired nonetheless for his skill with allegory. The quotation refers to the "doubly-poisoned wound of the Ethiopians." Printed editions of Claudian existed from 1482; Herbert may have known those of Bentinus (1534) or Stephanus Claverius (1602). A rather free English translation of *De raptu Proserpinae* was made by Leonard Digges (1617).

"sagittas inungunt radix quaedam mortifera est," Theophrastus.[217] They are black, at no time shading their bodies from the parching Sun, but rather delighting to rub and anoint themselves all over with grease and tallow, being proud to see their flesh shine, the stink never offending them. Their hair is black, and, contrary to the Africans, long yet curled; the length is held an ornament. They have a few leaves plaited about the waist, elsewhere go naked; their ears are bored and wide enough. Pinking[218] and cutting the flesh is here in fashion. Whiles the better sex seek prey abroad, the women, therein like themselves, keep home and spin. Bigamy is tolerated; copulation they effect very early, the youth scarce knowing 12, the maiden 10 years in the world the name of virginity. Delighted with sports and novelties, hunting, hawking, fishing (of which the isle affords variety) and dancing, in meanders winding, beating and clapping their breasts and hands, their feet spurning the native sands, forcing the spectators further off, during which the women, with a savage harmony, modulating with hands and eyes observing measure, equal if not exceed the men in their laborious treadings.

Till of late they knew not letters, art being burdensome to savages. They complete that jeer of Sophocles, *"nil scire, nihil jucundus,"*[219] howbeit necessity has taught them part of the rudiment of arithmetic, when the number ten limited their invention for passing the Mexicans, who number but to six. *Isso*, 1; *tone*, 2; *tello*, 3; *effad*, 4; *fruto*, 5; *woubla*, 6; *sidda*, 7; *fonlo*, 8; *malo*, 9; *nel*, 10. And albeit this character renders these people no other then savage, let us not condemn them overmuch, seeing that the most civilised nations amongst us have in their infancy been no less incultured, as some render our ancestors the Britons, and what the Saxons were, observe out of Tacitus describing the Fenni, then inhabiting part of Germany:

> *Populi sunt, quorum mira erat feritas et foeda paupertas;*
> *non arma equi nec penates; victui herba, vestitui pellis,*
> *cubile humus; sola in sagittis spes, quae feri inopia ossi-*
> *bus sperans. Venatus viros pariter ac feminas alebant.*

---

[217] "They anoint their arrows with a deadly root." Theophrastus (372–287 B.C.E.) was Aristotle's successor as head of the Peripatetic School in Athens. His most enduring work was his *Characters*, a book much admired in England and imitated in the seventeenth century by writers such as Joseph Hall and Sir Thomas Overbury. However, Theophrastus was also a botanist, and Herbert may have got this quote from one of his treatises on botany, which were available in Latin as *De causis plantarum* or *De historia plantarum*, translated by T. Gaza (Treviso, 1483) at the special request of Pope Nicholas V. For details, see Costas A. Thanos, "The Geography of Theophrastus' Life and of his Botanical Writings," www.biology.uoa.gr/cthanos

[218] Making perforations [in their skin] as ornaments.

[219] To know nothing is to take pleasure in nothing.

Vivebant in sylvis, quod beatius arbitrabantur quam
ingemere agris vel illaborare domibus . . . .[220]

Rich in minerals and marcasite,[221] gold, silver, and, as Edoardo Lopez, iron and
copper, the beams or influences of the Heavens, chiefly of the sun, operating so
as not only the surface, but the inward bowels of the earth, as Sir Francis Bacon
observes, when turned up appear impregnate with a masculine spirit of the celestial influences. For which cause, observing the avarice of the Portugal, they prohibit the use and digging up the earth, contenting themselves rather with useful
herbs and grain, of which they have store, then by the magic of gold and pearl to
allure the hearts of greedy men to afford them disturbance, a quality which the
Portugal is as liable to as any other nation, against which one well inveighs, saying "Not Crassus's wealth, nor Babel's vast command, / India, Arabia, nor the
Taeres land / Can speak not rich nor happy; if with them / I throw away my more
price, worthy fame."

But if you would buy anything the isle affords, peradventure the isle itself,
you must furnish you with agates, heliotropes, jasper, and, which they value more
then all the diamonds and pearls in India, long red carnelian beads, of which
they put so high a value that one string is enough to put them all into a combustion. And of no small esteem are bracelets, copper chains or manellios, bells
and bables, triangular glasses or fool's paradise, and for which, or one carnelian,
you have in exchange sheep, big-tailed like those in Syria, buffalos[222] big-boned,
fat and camel-backed, antelopes, red deer, leopards, pards,[223] goats, mink, hens,
eggs, wheat, barley, rice and couscous, with what fruit you like, oranges, lemons,
limes, pomcitrons,[224] plantains, sugar-canes, ginger, toddy, cocos etc. Here also

---

[220] The full passage reads: "[The Fenni] are astonishingly savage and disgustingly
poor. They have no proper weapons, no horses, no homes. They eat wild herbs, dress in
skins, and sleep on the ground. Their only hope of getting better fare lies in their arrows,
which, for lack of iron, they tip with bone. The women support themselves by hunting,
exactly like the men; they accompany them everywhere and insist on taking their share
in bringing down the game. They live in the woods and count their lot happier than that
of others who groan over field-labour" (Tacitus, *Germania* 46).

[221] A kind of brittle white iron sulphide; the term 'marcasite' is improperly used to
describe jewellery made of white iron pyrite.

[222] Herbert probably means 'water-buffalos'; he certainly does not mean wisents or
bisons.

[223] An animal with a spotted coat; it was believed that leopards were the result of
cross-breeding between pards and lions.

[224] An apple grafted on to a lemon-tree. For details, see G. B. della Porta, *Magica
naturalis* (1558; English translation 1658), III, Chapter VII. There is an on-line version
of the 1658 English translation edited by Scott Davis. Herbert could have used a French
or Italian translation if he did not have the original Latin.

are lizards and chameleons, which Isidore[225] derives from a camel and a lion, but in the Greek it is "a little lion," which it resembles not so much in shape, for it is a very lean, deformed beast, as condition. It is an old and vulgar opinion that it feeds upon the air, for what we be fed by must be subject to touch, which air is not. Chameleons will lick up flies, beetles and the like, and that very dexterously. Nevertheless the chameleon, the hieroglyphic of a dissembler, takes thus from Alciati: "She always gapes, she eats the slender air, / Changing her looks, she varies colours rare; / Even so the flatterer applauding feeds, / Clawing his Prince's most opprobrious deeds,"[226] with which Seneca agrees, "*Contra morsum sycophanti, nullum est remedium.*"[227] Salamanders there be here also, a sort of lizard extreme cold by nature, whence, like ice, for some time they endure the fire, yea, a little extinguish it, as Aristotle affirms, yet by trying all, we find that they will quickly be burnt if the fire be powerful. Howbeit, the proverb is that "the salamander endures fire without danger," commonly they obscure themselves in moist and umbrageous places, so as when they appear they are sure presages of a storm approaching. Their teeth and tongues are venomous, but the other parts may be eaten without danger. The French have this proverb, nevertheless, that "If ere the salamander hap to bite thee, / Thy coffin and thy winding-sheet invite thee."[228]

---

[225] St. Isidore of Seville (c. 560–636), Bishop of Seville from 602, was the author of the very popular *Etymologiae, sive origines*. This book was not only a compendium of word-origins, from which Herbert gets the rather odd derivation of the word "chameleon" (17.9. 70), but also contained a great deal of information on current knowledge in all areas. The *Etymologies* was first printed by G. Zainer (Augsburg, 1472) with ten editions between this date and 1530.

[226] Andrea Alciati (1492–1550), Italian jurist famous more for his *Emblemata* (Augsburg, 1531) than for his works on law (6 volumes; 1571) or his posthumously-published *Historia Mediolanensis* (Milan, 1625). The best-known edition of Alciati's book on emblems was probably that of Tozzi (Padua, 1622), which featured commentaries by Claude Mignault. It is likely that Herbert used this version.

[227] "There's no remedy against the bite of a flatterer." This, and similar ones from Seneca, was a favourite maxim of many authors; Jonson cites it in *Timber*, and the Puritan minister Thomas Brooks in *Apples of Gold for Young Men and a Crown of Honour for Old Men* (1660) says that the Emperor Anastasius I (491–518) used it as a motto in the form "Smooth talk proves often sweet poison" (Chapter 6, Direction 3, n. p. n.). Also see Robert Burton, *Anatomy of Melancholy* 2. 3.

[228] Herbert had recourse to many authors on the subject of salamanders, which are mentioned by Pliny (*Natural History* 10. 86) and several others, including Paracelsus. Perhaps he also knew Conrad Wolffhart (Lycosthenes)'s *Prodigiorum ac ostentorum chronicon* (1557), which was translated and updated by Stephen Batman as *The Doom, Warning to all Men* (1581) and in which there is a discussion of the animal's "fire-proof" nature. Lycosthenes connects it with basilisks and dragons. Salamanders apparently like to live in

My *valedictum* shall be this: the land seems to mourn to see itself trod upon by a people so much estranged from God and virtue, in discontent as it were, concealing like useful treasures, making unuseful so many ports, obscured so far beyond her merit, albeit seated so advantageously for traffic with all the world, as both the Indies seem possible to be awed by her and to command those golden countries of Mozambique, Quiloa,[229] Soffala,[230] Mombasa,[231] Magadoxa,[232] Zimba,[233] Malindi,[234] proffering also many other pretty islands under her as those of Comoro,[235] Primero, Mascarenhas, Assada, Castle Isle, Mauritius, Digarrois and England's Forest,[236] which, as it were environ, and in a sort defend her upon occasion, so as she seems to fit as Empress amongst them.

Shoals of Judaea

Nine leagues from Madagascar, being upon a north-east course, we had well-nigh, for want of heed, run upon the Shoals of Judaea,[237] sands memorably dangerous since Annius, a Frenchman, here perished. Our variation was 13 degrees

---

rotting wood, which is often used as kindling, and so they sensibly evacuate when someone sets it alight, thus their reputation.

[229] Modern-day Kilwa, a town on the east coast of Africa. It was occupied by Almeida (1507), who built a fort there, but abandoned it in 1509.

[230] Sofala is south of modern-day Beira in Mozambique. The Portuguese built a fort here in 1505. The area is now in ruins. It is described by Camoens as "ancient Sofala, where the gold comes down" (*Lusiads* 5. 73).

[231] Mombasa, on the Indian Ocean, is now Kenya's major port city. It has a long history, being founded well before the twelfth century C.E. and famous as a centre for gold and spices. Vasco da Gama was there in 1498, and the Portuguese, who were not exactly welcomed by the Mombasans, sacked the city in 1500, although it did not become a Portuguese possession until 1638.

[232] Modern-day Mogador on the Atlantic coast of Morocco.

[233] Zimba may refer either to a people who inhabited the southern end of Lake Nyasa, or perhaps the area including modern-day Zimbabwe.

[234] Malindi or Melinde is a large town on Malindi Bay, which is on the Indian Ocean coast of modern-day Kenya. It was once as important a city as Mombasa. Vasco da Gama was there in 1498 and signed a trade treaty, which led to the establishment of a Portuguese trading post the following year.

[235] The Comoros Islands.

[236] All these places will be discussed in more detail as Herbert comes to the end of his voyage.

[237] Foster notes that the name of this atoll was actually (in Portuguese) *Baixos da Judia*, which means 'the Flats of the Jewess,' but that they show up on English maps as 'Bassas da India,' also known as the Europa Rocks, "from a vessel which sighted them in 1774" (*Herbert* 301). Apparently the *Judia* was a Portuguese ship which ran aground here, not actually the name of a person. "Annius" has not been identified. The place is uninhabitable.

18 minutes from the Cape; hence we steered north-east and by east, aiming at Mohelia. By the way, one of our men took a shark, a man-eating fish who seldom miss the hook out of too much greediness; 9 foot she was in length and a half by the rule. I speak it by this respect; we found in her paunch five and fifty young ones, every fish a foot long. 100 in our ship saw it. This ravenous fish, 'tis credibly reported, spawn not like other fishes but whelp like bitches, and, as Richard Hawkins[238] witnesses, in storms or dark nights receive their young ones, though each one be a foot long, into their belly for security.

That night we sailed merrily by the Mascarenas, a Charybdis in 21 degrees, variants 13 and 17 minutes, where, suspecting no danger, and the wind favouring, we were at ten at night thrown by the force of an insensible current upon the shoals of Monambi, so as, sounding where we thought we had 1000 fathoms, the lead found barely eight. The wind was high, the sea rough; *cumulusque immanis aquarum in [montis] speciem [curvari]*[239] was here true. The Moon was also clouded; it stood our captain upon to give speedy notice, for that night he bore the light in her main top, which was successfully done by the echo of two roaring culverins, which warned our fleet, guided by our lantern, to tack about so that all the fleet lowered their topsails, hovering until daylight might help us by discovery. At our second sounding we had 14 fathoms, but 15 and 14 after that, then we had 27, 24, 33, 35 and 40 fathoms upon our further sounding, by which we saw the Lord in mercy had, as by a thread, directed our course from out of those dreadful flats of death, where, notwithstanding our hydrographic cards, if His Providence, which let us ever magnify, had not prevented, in half an hour's sail further we had doubtless been cast away most miserably. For future caution, accept this distich: "From us learn to avoid that deadly sand, / Where Neptune cannot lend a helping hand." Captain Saris[240] found the current here much more to his disadvantage, for, notwithstanding a fair gale filled all this sails and that his course afore the wind, the current here so strong as in 24 hours it forced the ship 70 miles back, withal being so dreadful that the sea raged and seemed disturbed,

---

[238] Sir Richard Hawkins (c. 1562–1622) was the son of Sir John Hawkins, one of the most illustrious of the Elizabethen "sea-dogs." He sailed to the West Indies (1582) and served against the Spanish Armada (1588), after which he embarked on a career of exploration and privateering. He voyaged to Brazil and raided Valparaiso (1593–1594), was subsequently captured and imprisoned, returning to England in 1603 when he was knighted by James I. Hawkins's *Observations on his Voyage into the South Sea* appeared in print the year of his death.

[239] "A huge mass of water shaped itself into a mountain" (Ovid, *Metamorphoses* 15. 508–509). I have supplied the rest of the passage.

[240] John Saris (c. 1580–1643) was the captain of the first English expedition to Japan (1613), and ran the East India Company factory in Java. His *Voyage to Japan* was published by the Hakluyt Society and edited by Sir Ernest Satow (1900). Saris's full account of his voyages appears in Takanobu Otusuka, *The First Voyage of the English to Japan by John Saris* (Tokyo, 1941). For further details see Milton, *Samurai William*, Chaps. 7–9.

as it is under London Bridge. The froth made him doubt it was shoal-water, but sounding he found 100 fathom; experience teaches that from that Cape de Buona Speranza the current sets strongly westward. From Cape de Corrientes[241] to the Equinoctial line the Africa shore is for the most part called Malindi, a country abounding in fruits, corn and minerals As we passed along, Juan de Nova,[242] Primero and other dangerous isles environed us. Under 17 degr. 37 min. lat. 20 degr. 20 min. long. cape ver. 13 deg. 52 min. the current sets south-west.

At daybreak we were close by the peninsula Mozambique, part of the great Kingdom of Zanzibar, in which also is Mombasa and Quiloa, not far distant from that cape or promontory which Ptolemy calls *Prasum*,[243] 'twixt which and the other cape-land called *Raptum*.[244] The people in his time were men-eaters, and at this the negroes are little better. Heretofore, and as yet I think, abounding with the best of merchandise, as gold, silver, elephant-teeth and ambergris. A fort of good strength was here raised by the Portugal *Anno* 1560, soon after the conquest thereof, who both along this south African and the east Indian coast have towns and fortified places, where they have several colonies for their better plantation.

Mozambique [illustration not shown]

Dolphins

At a small distance Mozambique appeared in this shape unto us as we passed, which we scarce lost sight of when an armado of dolphins compassed us, a fish incredible for celerity and quickness of sight but unlike the porpoise, which some nevertheless take for the true dolphins. Such we salted as we could entice to taste our hooks or fizzgigs.[245] It is no bigger then a salmon; it glitters in the ocean with variety of beautiful colours, has few scales, from its swiftness and spirit metonymically surnamed the Prince and Arrow of the Sea, celebrated by many learned pens in sundry epithets: *philanthropoi* for affecting men; *monogamoi* for their subtle constancy. Generated they be of sperm, nourished like men, embrace, join, and go great 10 months, a careful husband over his gravid associate, detesting incest, abhorring bigamy, tenderly affecting parents, whom, when 300

---

[241] Cape Corrientes is on the south-east coast of modern Mozambique in Inhambane province. Vasco da Gama was there in 1498, and a fort was erected to mark the boundary of Portuguese territory.

[242] An island in the Mozambique Channel, now usually known as St. Christophe.

[243] Probably Cape Delgado on the modern Mozambique-Tanzania border.

[244] Ptolemy located the Promontary of Raptum on the Ethiopian coast (*Geography* 4. 8); he believed it to be the limit of what he called "Barbaria." It is not mentioned by Strabo, but Roman geographers pair it with the Promontary of Prasum.

[245] Harpoons. See George Sandys, "Cans't thou with fisgigs pierce him [the whale, Ed.] to the quick" ("Paraphrase on Job 41," l. 13).

years old, they defend against hungry fishes, and when dead, to avoid the shark and like marine tyrants, carry them ashore and thence, if Aristotle, Aelian[246] and Pliny err not, inhume and bedew their sepulchres. They were glad of our company, as it were affecting the sight and society of men, many hundred miles in an eager and unwearied pursuit frisking about us, and, as a poet observed: "On every side they leap and dew their fin, / Advance from sea and bathe again therein; / In sport and measured dances, nimbly fling / Themselves, whilst seas do from their nostrils spring."

Dolphin [illustration not shown]

Mayotte

Six leagues north-east from the last land we descried another isle, full of palmetto trees. The current here see[s] us 20 leagues forward in 24 hours; the latitude of this isle was 16 degrees and a half, longitude 21 degrees and 28 min., thus shaped as we sailed by it:

The 7 of September we descried more land; it proved Mayotte, one of the Isles of Comoro, seated to the north of Madagascar. To the east it rose very high as we sailed by it, where it mounts into a pyramid which doubtless has a large aspect into the ocean. Its latitude is 12 degrees 56 minutes south, and longitude 23 degrees 59 minutes, in this shape proffering itself unto my table-book as we passed by it.

Mayotte [illustration not shown]

Isles of Comoro

These isles are five in number, called the Isles of Comoro, either because *Chumro* or *Cumr-yne* the Welshman's Isle[247] is greater then the rest or that it was the first discovered, named *Cumro, Meottia, Joanna, Mohelia* and *Ganidia*; by others *Juan de Castro, Spirito Sancto, Sancto Cristoffero, Anguzezia* and *Mayotto*, each of them praiseworthy for refreshing passengers in that they abound with delicate fruit, and such cattle as are commended and had at easy prices. None of these isles be above a hundred miles about. Comoro is the highest and best land but branded

---

[246] Claudius Aelianus (c. 170–235), a Stoic, was a priest at Praeneste who wrote a treatise on animals and the *Varia historia*, a work on human history and mythography. He believed that reason demonstrated itself in the creation of the animal world. The *Varia historia* was first printed in 1545 and subsequently edited by Conrad Gesner (1556); Herbert could have used Abraham Fleming's English translation (1576), which was supplanted in Herbert's lifetime by that of Thomas Stanley (1665).

[247] There is no Welsh connection here outside Herbert's fervid etymological imaginings.

with the most perfidious people, and good reason I have to say so, for an. 1591, thirty of our men, being amicably invited ashore out of the *Penelope* for water and other refreshment, were treacherously slain by the inhabitants, since which they are justly suspected and seldom trafficked with but in case of necessity. Joanna is inhabited by a better people, and to be confided.[248] Here was buried Galvano,[249] a gentleman that was dispatched by Dom Alfonso [V], King of Portugal, for the discovery of Prester John's country, as Friar Francisco Alvarez[250] writes, who but improperly makes this to be an isle belonging to the Red Sea. It lately obeyed a queen, but now submits to a King, who, though tyrannical, yet better so, as Tacitus[251] says, then where it is anarchical. To these isles we sent our boats ashore, which returned laden with buffalos, geese and a variety of fruits, in that exigent very heartily welcomed.

And though our rendezvous be now in sight, suffer me, whiles in memory, to tell you of a fish or two which in these seas were obvious. The sea-tortoise is one, a fish not much differing from those at land, her shell only being something flatter. By overturning they are easily taken; some we took for pastime more then food, and upon trial we found that they taste waterish and dispose to fluxes. They have neither tongue nor teeth, superabound in eggs; in those we took, some having near 2000, pale and round, and not easily made hard though extremely boiled. They cover their eggs with sand and are hatched by the heat of the sun, as some affirm; such as have strong appetites eat them, and the flesh, or fish as

---

[248] The *Penelope* was part of Sir James Lancaster's fleet. It later sank with all hands off the Cape of Good Hope.

[249] Herbert seems confused here. Alfonso V of Aragon (1416–1458), not Portugal, had sent some artisans to Ethiopia at the request of Emperor Yeshaq I (1428), who proposed an anti-Muslim alliance and suggested that his daughter marry Alfonso's son Pedro. They all died en route. Galvano was a member of Covilhan and Paiva's expedition, sent by Joao II; he survived this but died in the Comoros Islands (1520).

[250] Francisco Alvares (1465–1541) was a Portuguese priest and missionary. He visited Abyssinia and wrote an account of his experiences there (1525); Alvarez was the first European to see and describe the ancient churches at Lalibela, which date from the twelfth century. His *Viaggio fatto nella Etiopia per Don Francesco Alvarez* was printed by Ramusio. There is an English translation by G. W. Huntingford (London: Hakluyt Society, 1961). "It is known," R. A. Skelton writes, "that Alvares wrote, or planned to write, a longer work on Ethiopia" (G. B. Ramusio, *Navigatione e viaggi*, ed. R. A. Skelton and G. B. Parkes [Amsterdam: Theatrum Orbis Terrarum, 1967–1970], 1: 10).

[251] Publius Cornelius Tacitus (c. 55–120), the eminent Roman administrator, senator, and historian. Several of his works survive; Herbert cites the *Germania*, an ethnographical study, the *Agricola*, a biography of the general of that name, and the *Annals of Imperial Rome*. Herbert probably knew Sir Henry Savile's translation of the *Annals* (1591); there was an edition of Tacitus's *Works* by Lipsius (1600), and the *Germania* had been available since 1519. After that time there were numerous other editions which Herbert could have used here.

you please to call it, but by the Levitical law it was forbidden. And though our religion consists not in ceremonies ending in the prototype, yet except famine or novelty invite, with such cates my palate craves not to be refreshed.

The manatee is the other fish being good meat, and from their using the shore have a fleshy taste resembling veal both in show and eating; the entrails differ little from that of a cow, from whom, in respect of physiognomy, some so name her. Her face is like a shrivelled buffalo or cow, her eyes small and round, gums hard instead of teeth. The stone that is generated in her head is most valuable, being sovereign, as some report, against cholera-dust,[252] stone-colic[253] and dysentery, so it be beat small, infused in wine and drunk fasting. The body of this fish is oftimes three yards long and one yard broad, thick skinned, without scales, narrow towards the tail, which is nervous, slow in swimming, wanting fins, in place whereof she is aided with two paps which are not only suckles, but serve for stilts to creep ashore upon when she grazes, where she sleeps long, delighted to suck the cool air, unable (contrary to the other watery inhabitants) to be half an hour under water. A docile fish and apt to be made tame, famoused like lizards for their love to man, whose face they delight to look upon and in weakness have refreshed them, though most unhappy to our captain Andrew Evans, who, striking one at the Mauritius with his harping-iron, and leaping into the sea to make short work with his stiletto, was so crushed by the manatee who circled him that he died shortly after, as in our description of St. Helena, where we entombed him, will in due place be remembered.[254]

The carvel[255] is a sea-foam, floating upon the surface of the ocean, of a globous form, like so many lines throwing abroad her strings, which she can spread at pleasure, angling for small fishes, which by that artifice she captivates. A sea-spider she may properly be called, for when she sees her web too weak, she blows an infectious breath and seems armed with such a sting as if she had borrowed it from the scorpion.

Mohelia

September 11: we rode in 25 fathoms. The ensuing morn, wafting nearer shore, we dropped it again in 17 and so came to an anchor at the west side of Mohelia, a bowshot from a small village of straw, unworthy the notice, though by the

---

[252] It was believed that cholera was spread through airborne particles or 'cholera-dust.'

[253] Black bile and "colic attributed to stone in the kidneys" (Foster, *Herbert*, 302).

[254] Captain Andrew Evans commanded the *Hart*. Stodart says that he did indeed catch a "cowfish" (*Journals*, 90), but that he died in January 1629 of "consumption" (102) rather than by poison from the manatee. Herbert repeats the story later on and mentions that Evans was "spitting blood."

[255] Portuguese Man-of-War, from 'caravel,' a Portuguese ship.

inhabitants called Maringa,[256] governed by a *shabunder*,[257] Alicussary by name, a black big-boned man but a Mahometan by profession, sly and crafty in bartering his victuals and fruit for commodities.

Mohelia [illustration not shown]

Mohelia elevates the Pole Antarctic 12 degrees 15 minutes, has longitude from the meridian of the Cape of Good Hope 24 degr., variation of the compass 26 degrees 20 minutes and is about 60 miles in circuit, distant from Comoro southeast 14 leagues, from Joanna east and by south 10. The maritime parts of the isle rise gently, the inland parts mount high and appear woody. A little village here and there we saw scattered; the houses are of reeds and straw, fitted to such a torrid climate. Moella some pronounce this isle, and Mal-Ilha or "Bad-Isle," a countryman of ours[258] fancied, an incongruity that from a Spanish resemblance so sweet a place should be disparaged. From Madagascar Mohelia is removed about 50 leagues towards the south-east, from Kilwa in the Africa continent under 10 degrees 60. The inhabitants are a mixture of Mahometans and Gentiles, to whom the sun is a principal deity. The sun, saith Solomon (Ecclesiastes 11:7), is a pleasant thing to behold,[259] but not to worship; howbeit the Portugal has of late preached Christ here but have few proselytes. Some fragments of their language I took, so well as I could read them from their own idiom: a King, *sultan*; bracelets, *arembo*; a hen, *coquo*; an ox, *gumbey*; coconuts, *sejavoye*; plantains, *figo*; a goat, *buze*; an orange, *tudah*; a lemon, *demon*; water, *mage*; paper, *cartassa*; a needle, *sinzamo*, which is a mishmash of Arabic and Portuguese.[260]

---

[256] The road of Maringa [*Meriangwy*] is on the western side of the island. Foster, citing Captain Pashley's log, notes that "the *Mary* and the *Hart* anchored off the King's town (now Fumboni) on the N. E. side of Mohilla, while the *Star* went round the south of the island to the road of Maringa" (*Herbert*, 302).

[257] The *shabunder* is actually a harbour-master, "the title of an officer at native ports all over the Indian seas, who was the chief authority with whom foreign traders and shipmasters had to transact" (*Hobson-Jobson*, 816) (hereafter *HJ*). Foster guesses that his name was probably Ali Kusari (*Herbert*, 302).

[258] Foster identifies him as Captain Best (*Herbert* 302).

[259] "Truly the light is sweet, and a pleasant thing it is for the eyes to behold the sun."

[260] Foster believes that Herbert lifted his list of words from "the vocabulary given by Peyton" in Purchas (*Herbert*, 302). This would be Captain Walter Peyton in 1615, whose account is printed by Purchas (1: 528).

A Mohelian [illustration shown above]

The people are black, the sun drawing the blood to the outward parts, whereas we observe the extreme heat of fire makes pale only by licking the spirits up, and yet negroes may be reputed sanguine and ruddy, if so be their jetty skin would but suffer the discovery. To our eyes we may say with the Spaniard "*Son endos mos negros como couros*," they are black as ravens. This extreme blackness, some say, proceeds not much from the soil or heat of the sun as it does from the seed extracted from accursed Shem, but 'tis not so; naturalists can best determine. These Mohelians have big lips, flat noses, sharp chins, large limbs, in mode affecting Adam's garb, a few plantain leaves circling their waists veiling their modest parts, nevertheless cut and pinked in several works upon their duretto[261] skins, faces, arms and thighs, striving to exceed each other in variety. The Meccan zealists have here

---

[261] Somewhat hard.

a few poor mosques of coarse materials, being no better then straw and bamboo without, but matted neatly within, admitting no entrance with shoes on. Some of the natives are doubtless magical: this reason I give for it. Another gentleman and myself one evening sitting under a tree to avoid a storm, for at that time it thundered and rained excessively, a negro stood by us trembling, whom we could see now and then to lift up his hands and eyes muttering his black art, as we apprehended, to some hobgoblin, but, when we least suspected, skipped out, and in a lymphatic rapture unsheathed a long skean[262] or knife which he brandished about his head seven or eight times, and after as many muttering spells put it up again, then kissed the earth three times. Which done, he rose, and upon a sudden the sky cleared and no more noise affrighted us.

Two kings of late commanded these people, *Phaneomal* and *Synal-beg* by name; the one was a native, the other an Arabian. Both were made great by their wives, the daughters of Sultan Sharif [Abu Bakr], Bibi Sharif and Nannan-galla, who were alive about 20 years since.[263] The two Kings, envious of one another's greatness, live at defiance, the poor savages paying dearly for their ambition; the sisters, whom nature has united, burn in envy against each other and exasperate their husbands so 'tis thought that one of them will down the stream ere long, seeing the proverb holds that "Love and sceptres ill agree/ To admit society."

Tobacco here is in plenty and good account, not strong or rolled but weak and leafy, sucked out of long canes called hubble-bubbles. Sneezing-powder is not more frequent with the Irish or Spaniard then areca,[264] by Arab and Indians called *tauffet* and *suparee*, is with these savages. Areca, resembling the nutmeg, the tree the toddy, is not used alone, for they usually add to it betel, which, like ivy, involves the areca, that hath neither flower nor juice, and burnt oyster-shells, whereby it becomes a chalky substance found good in the operative property, for it discolours their white teeth to a pure crimson, perfumes the breath, kills worms, intoxicates the brain, dries rheums, helps nature, and begets an appetite. I am no physician; therefore, if I err, blame the interpreter.

---

[262] A Scottish or Irish dagger, a dirk.

[263] By *Phaneomal* Herbert probably means the *Phany*, or King of Mwali (Mohelia); it is not, as Foster thought, a name. The "Arabian" refers to the fact that the Comoros were ruled by Shirazi Arabs who had arrived there in the fifteenth and sixteenth centuries. They had set up trade in such commodities as ambergris, rice, and slaves, the latter becoming the chief export by the seventeenth century. Lists of the names of Comoran rulers are notoriously inaccurate until about 1786; however, Sultan Sharif Abu Bakr bin Said was ruling the Ndzuwani Sultanate (Anjouan) c. 1610, and the ruler of Moheli (Mwali) was subject to him. The Ndzuwani Sultanate was founded in 1500. "Sharif" means that a person is a descendent of Mohammed. As Foster notes, Herbert may have got these names from John Saris's journal, but Saris states that "Managalla [*sic*] was the mother, not the wife, of Booboocarree," whom Foster identifies as possibly Sultan Sharif Abu Bukhari, or Abu Bakr, as I have stated above (*Herbert*, 302).

[264] The areca is a kind of palm-tree whose nut is used for chewing.

The isle accommodated us with many useful things as buffalos, goats, turtles, hens, huge bats, chameleons, rice, peas, couscous, honey, and the sea with breams, cavallos,[265] oysters, mother of pearl, and good pearl too 'tis probable, if dived for. We had also toddy, cocos, plantains, oranges, lemons, limes, pomcitrons, ananas,[266] cucumbers, tamarind and sugar-canes; an isle so verdant all the year long, few days but a gentle breeze or shower of rain to bedew the earth and leni-fy[267] the flaming Sun, attired in Flora's summer livery, yea, robed with Nature's best arras and silver-purling streams, making it so pleasant as many may parallel it with that proud paradise of Alcinoe[268] poets have so liberally commended, this having *"campos ubi sol totumque per annum durat, aprica dies."*[269]

Of fruits we will select but three for description, yet such as may merit your acceptance. The plantain, for taste and odour second to none, is a fruit so good and veiled with so broad a leaf that Goropius[270] persuades us Adam offended in eating it, and with those leaves made his transgression manifest, being the same sort were by the discoverers brought Moses out of Canaan, says he, but that they were grapes we are assured in Numbers 13:23.[271] By the Arabians it is called *musca-mawm*, and *pican* by the Indians.[272] They hang in clusters like beans upon a branch or stalk; their shape is long and round, not unlike a sausage. If they

---

[265] Probably a horsefish (from Spanish *caballo*), a silvery fish with a flat body, of which there are several species.

[266] Pineapples.

[267] Make more favourable.

[268] This reference is a little obscure. There are two mythical Alcinoes; one was a sea-nymph and the other a woman who (to make a long myth shorter) cast herself into the sea after being cursed by a weaver whom she had refused to pay and who sought revenge from Athenc. Their "paradise" seems to mean the sea.

[269] "Fields where the sun's bright day lasts all year long" (Valerius Flaccus, *Argonautica* 1. 844–845).

[270] Jan Gerartsen van Gorp (1519–1572) was a Dutch doctor and linguist who served as personal physician to the sisters of the emperor Charles V but refused a similar appointment offered by his son, Philip II of Spain. He was also an antiquarian, and seems to have had a rather mixed reputation. He advanced a theory in his *Hieroglyphics* that the language of ancient Egypt was essentially a dialect of the language spoken in Brabant (now part of Belgium), a claim which prompted Joseph Scaliger to state "Never have I read such nonsense!" His admirers included Hakluyt and Ortelius, but later readers, including Hugo Grotius and Leibniz, echoed Scaliger. His *Collected Works* appeared in 1580.

[271] "And they came unto the brook of Eshcol, and cut down from thence a branch with a cluster of grapes."

[272] Herbert got this information from van Linschoten, *Voyage*, 2: 40–41 (Foster, *Herbert* 302). The "fruit" is the pecan. For details, see Jan Huyghen van Linschoten, *The Voyage to the East Indies, from the English Translation of 1582*, ed. A. C. Burnell and P. A. Tiele, 2 vols. (London: Hakluyt Society, 1885).

peel off the rind, the fruit appears of a gold-yellow and is relished like a Windsor pear,[273] and so delicious that it melts ill humours, leaving a delightful gust, good for urine but bad for fluxes, meeting with crude stomachs, and, if too liberally used, disposes to dysenteries.

The coco, another excellent fruit, is covered with a thick rind, equal in bigness to a cabbage; some resemble the shell to the skull of a man or rather a death's head-like eyes, nose and mouth being easily discerned. Within we find better then the outside promised, yielding a quart of ambrosia coloured like new white wine but far more aromatic. The meat or kernel, like other nuts, cleaves to the shell and is not easily pared; the pith or meat is above an inch thick and is better relished then our filberts, enough to satiate the appetite of two reasonable men. The tree, which is straight and lofty, not branching save at the very top, where it spreads in a beautifying plume, or palm rather, the nuts like pendants adorning them, is good for timber and from which they make canoes, masts and anchors. The rind is dressed like flax and serves for sails, mattresses, cables and linens, the shell for furniture, the meat for victuals, the leaves for tents or thatching: rare dwellings! And take them contracted in that excellent poem of my cousin Herbert, late Cambridge Orator:[274] "The Indian nut alone / Is clothing, meat and trencher, drink and can ,/ Boat, cable, sail, mast, needle, all in one."[275]

The toddy-tree is not unlike the date or palm; the wine is got by wounding or piercing the tree and putting a jar or pitcher under, so as the liquor may distill into it. At the very top it has a pulp or marrow which, being boiled, eats like a cauliflower, but being cropped, the tree dies, the soul or life consisting in it. These, as the dates, thrive not except at some certain time the flowering male and female united. Toddy for colour resembles whey, but tastes like Rhenish;[276] at first draught it is uncouth, but every draught tastes better then other. A little makes men merry, much inebriates; in the morning 'tis found laxative, in the evening costive,[277] at midnight dangerous. Of this, as of the coco, Herodotus and Pliny give this eulogy, "*Ex quibus panem, mel, vinum, acetum et vestitum*

---

[273] According to the botanist John Parkinson's *Paradisi in sole paradisus terrestris* (1629), the Windsor pear is "an excellent good peare [that] will beare fruit sometimes twice in a yeare, and (as it is said) three times in some places" (Cited in Robert Hogg, *The Fruit Manual* [New York: Kessinger Reprints, 2007], 150).

[274] George Herbert (1593–1633), brother of Lord Herbert of Chirbury, Rector of Bemerton (1630) and metaphysical poet. His principal works included *The Temple, or Sacred Poems and Private Ejaculations* and *The Country Parson*, both published just before his death. He was Public Orator at Trinity College, Cambridge (1619–1627). His *Poetical Works* have been edited by F. E. Hutchinson (Oxford: Oxford University Press, 1961) and more recently by John Wall (New York: Paulist Press, 1981). See also H. Wilcox, "Herbert, George," *ODNB* 26: 677–685.

[275] George Herbert, "Providence," 126–128.

[276] Dry white wine from the Rhineland.

[277] Sluggish.

conficiunt.[278] To conclude, these are bought with little charge; thirty oranges or lemons the blacks exchange for a sheet of paper, for two sheets ten coconuts, an ox for a piece of eight, a goat for sixpence. Ships they have none, nor boats, save what are hewed out of one stump, yet capable to receive three men. If they sink, their swimming helps them, and though of little use with us, yet for rarity sake accept what by this draft may better be apprehended.

A Canoe [illustration not shown]

White Sea

The 15 of September we bade farewell to Mohelia by benefit of a fair gale that filled all our sails, ploughing up the yielding ocean. The long billows made us dance apace, yet without dread, seeing the mariners made so good use of this advantage as in four days more, by observation we found ourselves but for degrees from the Equinoctial. I may not forget how this night, being the 19 of September, the ocean, for about ten leagues space through which we sailed, was white as snow, contrary to the usual colour, which resembled a serene or azure firmament. How this came to pass I inquired of the Master of the ship, but little to satisfaction, for all he could say for solution was that in this latitude others sailing upon that point of the compass had observed the like. What other cause there was he could not tell, seeing the sea was exceeding deep and smooth and no disturbance by wind to curl the waves or make it frothy. The sea-water, when it rests, is black, white when it moves, because when the beams of light pass not straight 'tis dark, but when smooth pass straight. Seeing splendour hath a degree of whiteness, the Lord Verulam[279] tells us; howbeit, this whiteness may rather happen through a subtle intermixture of air with water, seeing that two diaphanous bodies intermixed, their optic portions in a simple order equally placed, do constitute whiteness. For proof whereof, some examples we have: the water near Glauca in Misana is reported to be white; in Idumaea[280] also is a fountain that at some time of the year is white. Gaspar Balbi[281] the Venetian, sailing through the Persian Gulf, reports that betwixt Ormuz and Diu he found the sea milk-white,

---

[278] From these they produce bread, honey, wine, vinegar, and clothing.

[279] Sir Francis Bacon.

[280] A region in Palestine bordering on Judaea and Arabia Petraea.

[281] Gasparo Balbi (c. 1550–after 1590) was an enterprising Italian jeweller who set out on travels (1579–1588) which took him to Asia, where he was the first European to visit Burma and describe the great Shwedagon pagoda. Balbi also journeyed up the Arabian coast from present-day Qatar to Ras al-Khaimah, now one of the United Arab Emirates. He wrote an account, *Viaggio dell' Indie Orientale* (1591). Only the Burmese part of his travels has been translated into English. See Olga Pinto, ed., *Viaggi di C. Federici e G. Balbi* (Rome: Istituto Poligrafico dello Stato, 1962).

which we did not. Andreas Corsalius[282] informs that in some parts of the East Indian Ocean the water for 100 leagues is white. Peter Martyr[283] affirms the like concerning the West Indian seas. Now seas there are, I acknowledge, which have their names from divers colours, as *Mare Rubrum*, the Red Sea, the name rather then the colour giving the denomination, *Mare Nigrum*, the Black Sea, so the Euxine. *Mare Album* or White Sea, so the archipelago is called; the ocean is ceruleum or blue, yellow Eridanus.[284] The colour is green in the narrow seas, but Virgil tells us of a *Mare Purpureum*, for so he terms the Adriatic, *1. 4 Georgics*,[285] which is rarest. But concerning this white sea, Capt. Saris gives a pretty conjecture. Sailing between Madagascar and Zeybon, at or near this place in a dark night, suddenly there appeared a gleam of light so bright that he could easily read by it. Amazed he was at this alteration, but at length perceived it was occasioned by a number of fish whose glistering shells made that artificial light in the night and gave the sea a white repercussion. This was accidental; now, seeing those watery citizens are seldom resident in one place, it may be presumed that the discolouring of the water upon this occasion will hardly appear so in that degree to other passengers unless they should encounter the like accident, or, why do not the like gleam happen elsewhere, considering their motion? But, seeing 'tis found that about this very latitude and place the sea is constant to this whiteness, it cannot be referred to that cause. But, as it is occult, I leave the further scrutiny to such as are curious in nature's occurrences.

Having a fair gale still, next day we made the sun our zenith, in which latitude and position we coasted along that rich and famous part of South Africa now called Soffala, part of Aegisymba[286] of old, where the Portugal has a considerable castle and fort that sufficiently awes the negroes, and with good reason, seeing

---

[282] Andrea Corsali (1487–?) was a Florentine geographer and traveller. He went to Asia on a Portuguese ship in about 1516. His epistolary account of his travels, *Lettera d'Andrea Corsali Fiorentino . . . della navigazione del Mar Rosso et Sino Persico fino a Cochin citta a nella India* (1516–1517) was published by Ramusio in his collection (*Navigazione*, 1: 191–92; 192–203). Very little else is known about him, except that he may have been the first person to describe New Guinea and that he may have died during a visit to Abyssinia. The letters were written to Giuliano and Lorenzo de' Medici.

[283] Peter Martyr d'Anghiera (1457–1526) was a historian and traveller. He journeyed to Egypt (1501) and served as chronicler to the State Council of [Portuguese] India (1511). He was probably the first scholar to note the significance of the Gulf Stream. In 1524 he was appointed Abbot of Jamaica, although he never went there. Some of his important writings include *Legatio Babylonica, Oceanidae, Poemata epigrammata* (Seville, 1511), which was a historical account of Spanish exploration, and *De orbe novo decades* (1516).

[284] The Latinised version of the Greek name for the River Po.

[285] "And pours itself [the Po / Eridanus, Ed.] into the purple sea" (Virgil, *Georgics* 4. 171).

[286] Another name for the Kingdom of Monomatapa.

that land has a store of gold. From whence Vertomannus,[287] Volaterranus,[288] and from them Ortelius[289] labour to persuade the world how that this was Ophir.[290] Yea, David Kimchi,[291] a learned rabbi, albeit he name not Soffala, nevertheless he places Ophir in South Africa, to oppose whom I bring Josephus,[292] as well-read as himself, who is of opinion that Ophir was part of the East Indies,[293] of which

---

[287] Ludovico Varthema (fl. 1502–1510) travelled from Venice to Egypt, Tripoli, and Damascus (1503). He joined the Mameluke sultan's army in Egypt and became a Muslim, after which he went on a pilgrimage to Mecca and Medina. His account, *Itinerario de Ludovico de Varthema Bolognese* (1510), was translated into English by Richard Eden (1576) and can also be found in Ramusio (*Navigazione*, 1: 159–88). J. W. Jones translated the work for the Hakluyt Society (London, 1863).

[288] Raffaello Maffei (1451–1522) compiled an encyclopaedia entitled *Commentarium urbanorum* (1506) which contained information on geography, science, medicine and history, as well as biographies of famous people such as popes and kings. It was divided into three sections: *Geographia*, *Anthropologia*, and *Philologia*; its items were alphabetically arranged, a very unusual procedure at such an early date. His Latin name derives from his place of birth, Volterra.

[289] Abraham Ortelius (1527–1598), the great Belgian cartographer, was born in Antwerp. He travelled extensively in Europe, and also visited England. His *Theatrum orbis terrarum* (1570) is considered the first modern atlas. A supplement was added in 1573. For a recent study, see Paul Binding, *Imagined Corners: Exploring the World's First Atlas* (London: Review Books, 2003).

[290] Herbert provides readers with a much more detailed discussion of this vexed question, which he evidently felt was very important (or he had forgotten he had written about it already), in Part VI, where an explanatory note will be provided.

[291] Rabbi David Kimchi (1160–1235) was born in Narbonne and was known as a great exegete; his commentaries range into such subjects as geography. His commentary on the Torah criticised Christian interpretations of the Bible, and his Hebrew grammar, the *Michlol*, became the standard book of its kind for many years. His works were available in print from 1488 onwards, but there is no evidence that Herbert could read Hebrew. However, Hans Wecker had translated parts of Kimchi's writings into Latin (1560) and the *Michlol* seems to have been available in English from the 1530s.

[292] Flavius Titus Josephus (c. 37–after 100), a Jewish soldier, scholar, and priest, wrote *The Antiquities of the Jews* and *The Jewish War*, for a long time considered the authentic histories of the Jewish people, although many people deplored what was perceived as his pro-Roman attitude. Josephus has been translated many times; in his own century Herbert could have availed himself of Genebrand's French translation (1609), Pierre de la Rouière's Greek/ Latin text (1611), or a hybrid translation culled from several others by Peter Morwing, *A compendious and moste marveylous history of the latter times of the Jewes commune weale* (1561). The earliest printing dates from 1470, and there was a magnificent edition by Arlenius and Gelenius (1544) which set the standard for later Latin editions. For Ophir, see Josephus, *The Complete Works*, trans. William Whiston (1737) (Grand Rapids: Kegel Publications, 1981), 32.

[293] Josephus, *Works* 32.

judgment are St. Jerome, Philo Judaeus,[294] Agricola and many more. And theirs is best, as I suppose, for if Soffala were the place, its being so near a neighbour to Ezion-geber, the port in Edom[295] where Solomon's Ophirian fleet used to ride, we can see no reason, notwithstanding the use of the compass was not then known, why they should make it a three years' voyage, our ships with a fair wind usually reaching it within one month, which, if they should be bound to ride within ken of land all the way, little longer time would compass it. Nor are there peacocks and such other rarities there as be mentioned in the *Paralip[omena]*;[296] moreover, albeit there were two Havilas in scripture, the one grandson of Ham, the other a descendent of Shem, yet was there but one Ophir, who with Havila, all authors do agree, planted themselves in the East Indies soon after the confusion of Babel, which place, from its distance and plenty of gold there had best excuse so long a voyage. Neighbouring that is Mombasa, a small isle under 3 degrees 50 south, subdued to the Crown of Portugal by Almeida in the year of Our Lord 1505, to which joins Magadoxo,[297] which has 3 degrees, and to it Zanzibar, Pata,[298] and Brava,[299] places very hot sometimes, in regard the Equinoctial cuts them. The shore thence trends towards Barnagasso,[300] a port once under the great Negus, who till of late held all that long tract of land in subjection which runs from Cape Guardafui to Suaebom.

That all those maritime countries which verge upon the ocean have been (especially since Vasco da Gama's times, which was *Anno* 1500) discovered and traded to, both along the west and south sides of Africa is unquestionable, but the mediterranean parts are not under that capacity. Ptolemy, as accurate in geography as any of the ancients, was totally ignorant of the utmost extent of Africa to the south beyond the Garamantes, as he draws his *terra firma* only to 10 degrees south from the Equator, unable to penetrate so far southwards as his own

---

[294] Philo of Byblos (c. 47–after 120) was a grammarian who also wrote on rhetoric and Jewish history. The reference to Ophir may be found in his translation of the quasi-historical Phoenician writer Sanchuniathon. He is mentioned also by Eusebius and Porphyry and by Suidas, who says that he wrote a work on cities and their famous men. Philo's *Works* were edited by Adrian Turnebus (1552) and Gelenius (1613).

[295] A country south of the Judaean border on the Sinai peninsula, traditionally the land settled by the descendents of Esau. In Roman times it was known as Idumea.

[296] Literally, a "supplement." The term was frequently used to refer to the Books of Chronicles, which were seen as a supplement to the Books of Kings in the Old Testament.

[297] The Portuguese name for Makdashau or Mogadishu, then "the name of a town and state on the Somali coast" (*HJ* 533). Some early explorers, including Marco Polo, confused it with Madagascar.

[298] A town in the central African kingdom of Kabu.

[299] A port town on the south-east coast of modern-day Somalia.

[300] Barnagasso, now known as Bahr Nagash, is the name both of a province on the Ethiopian borderlands and of its ruler.

country river Nilus brings, albeit suppositiously he gives it from the *Lunae montes* under 15 degrees south, which has passed for current with succeeding ages. But that any have valleys answering to their height, "*tam immensa profunditatis ut illic centrum terrae videatur,*"[301] or that any hitherto ever saw those Mountains of the Moon, or Zembre or Zaire, supposed to be a lake in circuit equal to Palus Meotis,[302] I have not yet met with, albeit enough have taken it for granted that such there are, but with the same *historica fides* I fear we believe the imaginary lines and signs in the globe celestial.

Prester John

But to come nearer to our station: under little more certainty do I reckon those formal descriptions of the territories of this supposed mighty potentate Prester John, concerning whom the Romish emissaries have spoken liberally, and though I am as free as any to allow them their due reward for the infinite toil and hazard they have undergone *sub specie fidei propaganda,*[303] as in story they give abundant testimony, both in Africa and Asia the Great, nevertheless I dare not say 'tis *pia fraudes,*[304] but, both by what I have observed and learned, found that they have assumed too great a liberty in blazoning the success of their labours and withal of invention. But, leaving everyone to his own credulity, I shall only, but with submission, give my present apprehension of this Abyssinian emperor, who like himself is too much veiled and obscured. For notwithstanding that he is exhibited to the world under several appellations, as Prester John (that being their usual name since they deserted the other of Philip),[305] he is called *Asiel, Abassi* by the Moors, of his own people *Acegus* and *Negus,*[306] and for power supposed not inferior to the great princes of the world, able "*decies centum millia hominum ad bellum instruere,*"[307] saith Maginus,[308] and of such worth as appears by offering the Portugal a million of gold to aid him against his adversaries, or for extent of

---

[301] So deep that the centre of the earth may be seen there.

[302] The Sea of Azov.

[303] Under the pretext of spreading the faith.

[304] "Pious fraud" (Ovid, *Metamorphoses* 9. 711). The complete passage reads *pia mendacia fraude latebant.*

[305] Why Prester John should be called "Philip" is unknown, unless it is a confusion with Pope Alexander III's emissary of that name who was sent to find Prester John in 1177.

[306] The usual title of the ruler of Abyssinia, meaning 'King' in Amharic.

[307] Able to draw up two hundred thousand men for war.

[308] Giovanni Antonio Magini (1555–1617), the Italian astronomer, cartographer, and mathematician who championed the geocentric view of the cosmos against Galileo. The work Herbert refers to here is probably Magini's famous atlas, the *Atlante geografica d'Italia* (1620), posthumously published by his son, a work which supplied a good deal of comparative geographical information.

dominion, northward stretching as far as Nubia and the confines of Egypt, east-
ward to the Red Sea and the Barbary Gulf as far as Ajanam and Dogali,[309] kingdoms within the Ethiopian exterior. Southward as far as the Luna Mounts,[310]
and west as far as Nilus, Niger, the two greatest rivers in Africa, so as his empire,
consisting of 70 kingdoms tributary and subordinate, in a sort extends to either
tropic, divided by the Equinoctial, under or near which is Asmara, his chief fort,
and comprehended totally within the burning zone. That vast tract or scope of
land, commonly comprising those parts which Ptolemy and other ancient cosmographers termed *Aethiopia sub Aegypto*, the *Trogloditae* and *Cinnamomifera*, regions now known by the name of Cassaria, Gojjam, Begemder, Trigemahon,
Barnagasso etc.,[311] and said to descend from Maqueda,[312] the Sabaean queen that
gave Solomon an affectionate visit which made her people Jewish proselytes after
converted unto Christ by Candace's eunuch,[313] or by St. Thomas the Apostle of
the Orient,[314] which profession they have ever since continued.

I must nevertheless adhere to my former profession as to the description we
have of those several Kingdoms and provinces usually attributed to him in his
titles; not that I deny there is such a Christian prince in that part of Africa, albeit
the epithet we give more properly belongs to another Nestorian prince of Tenduc,

---

[309] Dogali is near Massawa, now in modern-day Eritrea. Ajanam is unidentified,
but it may be Gojjam.

[310] The Mountains of the Moon, whose location is still uncertain, were thought to be
in central Africa, and were claimed, by the authority of one Diogenes, a Greek merchant
who claimed to have been there, to be the source of the Nile, a notion accepted by Ptolemy in his *Geography*. In more modern times they have been identified as the Ruwenzori
range (since Grant and Speke's expedition in 1862), but the Mount Abuna Yosef range in
Ethiopia has also been asserted as a candidate.

[311] Begemder [*Bagamidra*] in Tigré province and Trigemahon [*Tigremahon*] were
southern Ethiopian kingdoms. Cassaria or Gasaria was a northern province; Gojjam
[*Goyame*] was another independent kingdom, this time in the north-west.

[312] Maqueda is another name for Balkis or Nikaule, the famous and probably legendary Queen of Saba or Sheba, who is supposed to have visited Solomon in about 1050
B. C. E. Saba is located either in central Ethiopia or Arabia, depending upon which
scholars are consulted.

[313] See Acts 8: 27–38.

[314] St. Thomas (Didymus) was the disciple famous for doubting Jesus (John 20: 24–
29). Origen, Eusebius, and others credit him with being the apostle of the Parthians, and
in the apocryphal *Acts of Thomas* (c. 200 C.E.) it is related that he went to India, where he
landed in Maliankara in about 52 C.E. He was also said to have visited the North Indian
court of King Gondophares (reigned c. 21–after 50 C.E.). There is a St. Thomas's Mount
near Chennai (Madras) where Thomas is thought to have been martyred in 78. In 1523
his remains were transferred to the São Tomé Cathedral in Chennai. Herbert returns to
this in Part VI. For a contemporary account of St. Thomas in India, see Edward Brerewood, *Inquiries touching the Diversity of Languages and Religions through the chief parts of the
World* (1614), especially Chapter XX, 177–84. Herbert refers directly to this work later.

being part of Cathay or Scythia extra Imasum, but have some doubt, and "*qui dubitat, neganti est proximus*,"[315] of the considerableness of his power as well as of the description made by Friar Alvarez, who, *Anno* 1520, having buried his comrade Galvano at Comoros, travelled to most parts of this empire, a story so well-credited by Ramusius as induced him to illustrate his relation with cuts in brass. For were he a prince of that force and extent of dominion as I have above mentioned, is it probable he would suffer himself to be shut up and confined to the most scorching and unpleasant parts of Africa where the greater part is rolling sands, which permit no foundation of towns nor long stations for his vagrant course of life and inhabiting in tents after the old Numidian manner will partly excuse that. But to be pent in, without any intercourse with the Red Sea or Aegisimban Ocean, which would render him a more puissant prince, give him the advantage of trade and access to his country and better associate him with Christian Kings and states, make his supposed greatness very dubious. For if what we read be true, of late years the naked unwarlike savages, whom the Portugals make little account of, have totally forced him from the ports and commands he had upon the Aegisimban coast in Ethiopia Inferior, from the Kingdom of Adell, which stretches to Cape Guardafui (*Aromata* in Ptolemy) in which the city Zeyla[316] stands, near unto that bay called *Sinus Avalites*[317] we find expressed in Ptol. l. 4 table of Africa, to Magadoxo, Mombasa and places near Mozambique, which doubtless were of greatest value to him both in reference to the sea and gold those parts afford abundantly. But also Sultan Suleiman the Turkish emperor[318] *Anno* 1558 expelled him out of Arqiqo and Suakin,[319] the only ports he had upon the Red Sea, and the King of Dallaqua,[320] the like of what other territories he had which gave him any passage thither, so as I fear his power and extent of empire is of like certainty with the library some friars found in the castle of Amara,[321] where among the rest are some manuscripts of Enoch and Livy.

But I have said too much of this Abassin, a name either given him in relation to his pontifical habit and as the Hebrew and *Vox Persica*[322] signify "father,"

---

[315] "Whoever doubts it is close to denying it" (Seneca, *De beneficiis* 2).

[316] Captured by the Portuguese under Lopes Soares de Albergaria (1507), who was Viceroy 1515–1518.

[317] *Avalites* was an old name for the present-day Eritrean port city of Assab in the southern Red Sea. The *Sinus Avalites* is also known as the Bay of Zeyla.

[318] Suleiman II, "the Magnificent," was Ottoman Emperor 1522–1566.

[319] Arqiqo [*Ercocco*] is a port on the northern Red Sea, now in modern Eritrea; it was famous for its connection with the ivory trade. Suakin [*Suachen*], now an extensive area of ruins, is not far from Port Sudan. In the fifteenth and sixteenth centuries it used to be the most important port on the Red Sea.

[320] The Dhalak Islands near Massawa, Eritrea.

[321] There is a town of this name in southeastern Iraq on the Tigris river.

[322] The Persian language.

or flowing from *abrech*, with which title and ceremony Joseph was honoured amongst the Egyptians, or otherwise taken from the principal river of the country Abas,[323] *Astabas* of old, springing from the Lake Barenna, albeit some derive it from a Coptic word which signifies a scattered generation. And assuredly under no less ignorance are we of all that great space of ground which lies between the southernmost part of Prester John's country and the Cape of Good Hope, which is not all discovered, partly by reason of the great and uninhabitable deserts those parts without doubt afford, excessive heat and other distemperatures of weather when the sun approaches the Equinoctial, penury of the soil, rolling sands, noisome serpents and wild beasts of all sorts, but principally by the truculence and perfidious disposition of the inhabitants, renders the enterprise, any considerable distance from the shore, scarce possible. So that 'tis no wonder if, as to the true knowledge of those savage parts, we are still under an invincible ignorance, which would not be, had those Abassin Christians, who are reported to be an ingenious and civil people, that voisinage[324] with the Lunae Montes, Zembre[325] etc., is commonly credited. Nay more, I may say the like concerning much of that part of the world which had neighbourhood with the first seminary after that universal deluge wherein Noah was preserved, we now call *Scythia extra Imasum*. For albeit it is true that Vertomannus, [John of] Plan Carpino[326] and his fellow-monk M. Paulus Venetus and some others have presumed to give us a plenary manifestation of *Serica regio*,[327] the mighty city Cambalu,[328] i.e. the Great Cham's[329] place of residence, and other parts of Cathay far beyond the deserts

---

[323] Probably the Awash river, which is Ethiopia's one navigable river.

[324] Are situated close to.

[325] Lake Zaire-Zembre was a mythical lake in central Africa, thought to be one of the sources of the Nile.

[326] Giovanni da Pian Carpino (c. 1180–1252) was sent by Pope Innocent IV as an emissary to the Great Khan Kuyuk (r. 1246–1248) at his capital Karakorum. In addition to founding some Franciscan monasteries in China, he wrote an account of his experiences which was the first European account of Mongolia, *Liber Tartarorum*. There is a modern translation with the Latin text, *The Long and Wonderful Voyage of Friar John de Plano Carpino* (Adelaide: University of Adelaide eBooks, 2004). The earliest printed version seems to have been issued in 1497.

[327] The Seres were people of eastern Asia, renowned for silks. The Latin word *serica* denotes silken garments. They are, of course, the modern Chinese. Pliny noted also that "they are well-known for a woollen substance obtained from their forests" (*Nat. Hist.* 6. 54), which was probably calico.

[328] Cambaluc is the city we know now as Beijing.

[329] The Great Khan, sometimes called the Emperor of Mongolia.

of Lop[330] and Mount Beligian[331] of which Haython the Georgian[332] speaks by hearsay, and of the extreme parts of Tartary towards that from which Pliny we call *Tabyn* and the Straits of Anian,[333] where near unto Arsaret and Argon some pretend to find the transplanted tribes of Dan and Napthali, the rather for that the name is found mentioned in the I Esdras 13: 40,[334] albeit most take Ararat to be signified by it and thence deduce their Gog and Magog, Ung and Mongul.[335] I much suspect the truth of those peregrinations and relations, but, rather as our Mandeville,[336] those aforenamed had fame only for their authority, *"quia multoties*

---

[330] This desert is in China, extending east to the Tarin river basin in the Xinjiang Uygur Autonomous Region.

[331] Mount Bel[i]gian is identified by Glenn Burger (see below) as "Burqan Qaldun, ?i.e. Kentei Khan, a peak in the Great Kentai Mountains (south-west of Lake Baikal)" (Hetoum, 136). It is mentioned in Book III, 3 (26).

[332] Prince Antonius Haitho of Korikos [*Hetoum* or *Curchinus*] (c. 1235–1314) was not a Georgian, but an Armenian historian who worked in Cyprus and Poitiers. He wrote the first systematic geographical study of Asia, *Histoire merveilleuse, plaisante et recréative du Grand Empereur de Tartarie*. It was highly influential on European conceptions of the East (see Meserve, *Empires*, 178–79), being translated into Latin and printed (Hagenau, 1529) and used as a reference by Ortelius in his atlas. Ramusio included some of it in his collection (*Navigazione* 2: 61–66). In England it was translated by Richard Pynson as *A Lytell Cronycle* (c. 1521). There is a modern edition of Pynson's version by Glenn Burger (Toronto: University of Toronto Press, 1988).

[333] The mythical Straits of Anian were thought to separate Asia from America, and they were part of the legendary North-West Passage. Their origin is in Marco Polo, and they were first marked on a map by Gastaldi, one of Herbert's sources, in 1561. Juan de Fuca later claimed (1592) that he had sailed through them. The name may be taken from the Chinese province of Ania. For details, see G. Sykes, "The Mythical Straits of Anian," *Bulletin of the American Geographical Society* 17. 3 (1915): 161–72. More recently, there is a long and detailed account of the Straits of Anian in Samuel Bawlf, *The Secret Voyage of Sir Francis Drake 1577–1580* (New York: Walker, 2003), 275–91; esp. 287ff.

[334] Herbert (or his printer) is mistaken; the reference, which concerns the deportation of the tribes of Israel, is actually in 2 Esdras 13: 39–47.

[335] These names often refer to two legendary giants, but here they are places. Marco Polo located them in the realm of Prester John, and says that the Gog tribe lived in Ung, the Magog (Mongul) tribe in Tartary.

[336] Sir John Mandeville (?fl. 1320–1330) was the reputed English author of an Anglo-Norman compilation of travels, many of which appear to be fictitious. He claims to have travelled to Turkey (1322) and then to the Middle East, Egypt, Ethiopia, and other places. Some believed him to be an English knight from St. Albans, but there are no records of his existence, and his book may be the work of one Jean de Bourgogne (d. 1372), a doctor from Liege who claimed to have written it. Printed editions have existed since 1482; there is a good modern translation by C. W. Moseley (Harmondsworth: Penguin Books, 2005), and see also Giles Milton, *The Riddle and the Knight: In Search of Sir John Mandeville* (London: Allison and Busby, 2003).

dicendo mendacia sese delectat.[337] And concerning Essedon, a great city discovered by Pius II,[338] in 42 degrees east from the Emodian and Auxatian and abutting upon the Asmerians[339] (Asmeer we find in Hindustan). They are but ideas, and seeing Ptolemy, notwithstanding his utmost scrutiny, acknowledges that Scythia *extra Imasum* both to the north and east "*habet terras incognitas,*"[340] give me leave to say that we remain still under the same ignorance, for albeit a Great Cham we find mentioned in the life of Tamurlane[341] and elsewhere, without opposing that there is a principal Horde, of which Genghis Cham,[342] predecessor to Tamurlane, had the title, albeit "Cham," which we should pronounce "Chan" or "Kawn" in our dialect, is the same that "count" is with us, and prefixed usually to persons of honour in Persia, Industan and Tartary, as with us Count Mansfeld, Count Harcourt etc. That he is such as M. Paulus Venetus describes, among other epithets, being styled "the Shadow of Spirits," "Monarch of the Whole World" and "Son of the Immortal God," an historical faith will not easily embrace such a tradition. Yet, as counterfeit as they be, we must accept of them until we can make a better discovery.

Fearing I have made too great a digression, I proceed. All this while having propitious winds, upon the 23. day we the second time crossed under the Equinoctial line, once more bidding farewell to those Antarctic constellations the

---

[337] Because by often speaking lies he pleased himself.

[338] Pope Pius II [Enea Silvio Piccolomini] (1405–1464), reigned 1458–1464. He wrote, amongst other things, novels and plays, as well as the posthumously-published *Historia rerum ubique gestarum, cum locorum descriptione non finita Asia Minor* (1477), containing geographical and biographical information, which appears to be the work Herbert is citing, although of course Pius II himself did not "discover" anything. This work is described by Rubiés as "an ambitious historical-geographical work motivated by the desire to prepare the crusade against the Turks on a more empirical basis" (Joan-Pau Rubiés, *Travel and Ethnology in the Renaissance: South India through European Eyes 1250–1625* [Cambridge: Cambridge University Press, 2000], 91). His *Opera omnia* were published in 1551. Margaret Meserve discusses his work in great detail (*Empires*, 79–80, 113–15, 197–202 and *passim*) and has edited his *Commentaries* (Cambridge, MA: Harvard University Press, 2007).

[339] Inhabitants of Asmara, now in modern Eritrea.

[340] Has unknown territories.

[341] Timur "the Lame," Tamerlane or Tamburlaine (c. 1336–1405), who did indeed claim descent from Genghis Khan, was the Mongol Emperor from 1369, establishing his capital at Samarkand. He conquered the sultanate of Delhi and defeated the Ottoman Emperor Bayezid I. Christopher Marlowe wrote a two-part play about him, *Tamburlaine the Great* (1590), and Justin Marozzi has recently published *Tamerlane: Sword of Islam, Conqueror of the World* (New York: Harper, Collins, 2006).

[342] Genghis Khan [*Cingis*] (1165–1227) became the first Mongol Emperor in 1206. His exploits need not be rehashed here as he is too well known.

Crosiers,[343] 4 stars of a second magnitude resembling a cross, distant from the South Pole 17 degrees 20 minutes, Noah's Dove,[344] Magellan's Cloud, a constellation of such small stars as be scarce visible other then that the sky is discoloured, Polophilax[345] and others, the two Bears, which were depressed, now reappearing again in our hemisphere. Under 8 degrees north the wind, weary, it seems, of too much constancy, veered into east north-east, so as the monsoon became averse to us upon that course, for we could come no nearer then south-east, at which time many of our ship's company died of calentures or sea-fevers, fluxes, scurvy, aches and such distempers as usually attend seamen in those fiery climes.

Nevertheless, this mortality was not more to be imputed to the extremity of the heat, albeit thereby our biscuit, meat, and water became so putrid and so stinking that, save necessity enforced it, would not have been tolerable, which, as the zone became more temperate, beef, pork and water recovered their sweetness, then indeed might be to their intemperate eating and overcharging their stomachs with fresh meat got at Mohelia, which was crude, little salted and rudely-dressed, as also by quaffing toddy too exorbitantly, a liquor though wholesome enough if moderately drunk, yet excess disposes the body to dangerous fluxes. Our admiral out of his ship threw five and thirty dead men overboard, the Hopewell eleven, the Star five; every ship lost some, too many, if God had otherwise pleased. This was aggravated by the death of Harvey Keynell,[346] an expert and ingenious seaman; master's mate he was in the *Star*. Captain Goodall[347] died then also, one whose disposition was so civil and obliging that indeed his name and nature were harmonious. Their bodies being committed to the ocean, a spacious grave, a volley of small shot and two and twenty great guns from our ship proclaimed their farewell to the watery citizens, inviting them to safeguard such a treasure, Heaven itself also seeming to bear a part in that threnody, at that very instant distilling so abundantly that, to the best of my remembrance, I never saw a sadder and suddener shower of rain then that was or of less continuance, which indeed made me take the greater notice of it. By this failure the master of our ship had a remove into the vice-admiral, and into the rear-admiral Captain

---

[343] The Southern Cross.

[344] A group of stars in Canis Major, named by the Dutch astronomer Petrus Plancius (Pieter Platevoet) in his *Nova et exacta terrarum tabula geographica et hydrographica* (1592).

[345] The name means "Guardian of the Pole"; this constellation, also named by Plancius, is in the southern hemisphere in the shape of a man. Herbert may have known Plancius's map from Linschoten, who reproduced it.

[346] Harvey Keynell or Kennell is otherwise unknown, but is also mentioned by Stodart as a "mate" to Captain Evans of the *Star* (*Journal*, 111). A Captain Harvey Keynell, perhaps a descendant, appears in the *CSP Colonial* (1679).

[347] Captain Bartholomew Goodall was appointed master of the *Jonas* in 1626. Stodart does not mention him.

Malim[348] was translated from the *Hopewell*, who lived but a few days to joy his advancement, a person so civil in his nature and so careful in his charge, so expert in his vocation and so valiant in fight, as well witnesses that memorable conflict he maintained against the Turk in the Levant, which honours him to posterity, that in his behalf I may properly attribute that out of the Prince of Poets: "The heroic deeds of all/ Brave men are written in Fame's glorious roll."[349]

Socotra

The wind here added to our affliction, for, growing high and contrary to our course, the waves broke boisterously upon our broadsides, but being close-hauled, were patient in all those checks, so as though the ships cut their way slowly, they passed securely, and at length passing by the cape called Bab el-Mandub,[350] brought us near the isle Socotra into the *ostium*[351] of the Red Sea, where let us repose a while till the wind be more favourable. Socotra is an isle well-known to former ages, to some by the name of Dioscorida, of Succaba to others, and, as othersome conjecture, is the same isle Pliny in his 6. *Lib.* Nat. Hist. calls *Topazo*, deriving its name from the plenty of those precious stones found there, like as the neighbouring isle Saphyrina upon the like occasion. The Turks call it *Katuchomar*, the Persians *Cabar*; by the Spaniard 'tis called *Acebar*, and by others *Aceur*. It elevates the Arctic pole 13 degrees, is near 15 leagues long and 10 broad, about a hundred of our miles about, and though in its position seems more neighbour to Africa then Asia, yet is challenged and recorded reputedly an appendix to Ajman[352] or Arabia the Happy. It affords sufficient for supply of the inhabitants as corn, fruit, and cattle, and for olives, cocos, dates, pistachios, pomegranates, pomcitrons, melons, sugar-canes and like fruit, as also aloes, which it has with an emphasis *"sempervivum et sanguis draconum"*[353] has to spare for strangers, civet cats also, which enrich the owners though sold at easy prices.

---

[348] For Captain Richard Malim of the *Hopewell*, see the *Journal* of Abraham Sayers, 24 February 1627–12 December 1629, *East India Company Ships' Logs, Ledgers and Receipt-Books 1605–1701*, British Library Microform No. XLVI. Capt. Malim had been "specially recommended by Capt.[James] Hall to go master in the *Hart*," and then as "Vice-Admiral" (*CSP Colonial*, VI, 11 December 1626 and 2 January 1627) He was replaced by Capt. John Pashley, who had been mate in the *Palsgrave* and the *Charles*.

[349] For many, the "prince of poets" would have been Virgil; for many Englishmen, he was Spenser. The quote is not possible to track down.

[350] Bab-el-Mandub, "the Gate of Weeping," is the entry to the Red Sea.

[351] Mouth.

[352] One of the emirates now known as the Gulf States.

[353] "Houseleek and dragon's blood." The *sempervivum* or houseleek is a plant of the *Crassulaceae* or orpine family; some readers may be familiar with the Jade plant, which is in the same group. It is found in an area ranging from Morocco to Iran and is believed to have medicinal uses.

The inhabitants are a mixture of Christians and Mahometans, their complexions black, the sun twice every year darting his fiery rays perpendicular amongst them, and then no place is hotter in the world. Their natures be reasonably civil; 2000 years ago the Greeks planted this place, if *Geographica Nubica* say true, for he reports, by what authority I know not, that Alexander the Great, returning by sea from India, made his way to Babylon, and being here met by Aristotle, according to his Master's advice planted a colony of Greeks there, who afterwards, some say by the preaching of St. Thomas the Apostle of the Orient, others say Bartholomew, and some the Ethiopian eunuch mentioned in the 8 and 27 of the Acts of the Apostles, the third year after Our Saviour's death were converted unto the Christian profession, and how dubious soever the convertor be, that they were Christians is evident in ecclesiastic stories.[354] Their churches express no less, being built in the form of a cross; a Patriarch or Primate thay had till of late there resident and other clergy whom they reverence, to whom they cheerfully pay their tithes and by whom they are instructed in the worship of God and how to observe both fasts and festivals. Elders they highly regard; humility is both commanded and commended. Second marriages, except where issue is wanting, they approve not of. In baptism they use the sign of the cross, partake of both sacraments; the dead they wash, and, being bound in clean linen, they bury with their heads towards Jerusalem but express little mourning. Of late years they were subjected by Emir bin Said, King or rather governor of Fartak,[355] but expulsed by de Cunha the Portugal, whose firelocks[356] made the Snake (so is the Prince styled) fly to Caeshem, where at a safe distance he dare hiss at the victor, who, in the first place restored the Christians their liberty both of body and conscience, and then, by their help, built a castle for their defence and planted a

---

[354] There is a great deal of speculation about the Christians in Socotra, but recent archaeological excavations seem to confirm an early date for them. See Stephen Missick, "Socotra: The Mysterious Island of the Assyrian Church of the East," www.Soqotra.info/history.

[355] Modern Ras Fartak. However, the term in Herbert's time denoted a sultanate in the west part of Hadhramaut (Yemen). Herbert's description probably comes from Barbosa (Duarte Barbosa, *An Account of the Countries Bordering on the Indian Ocean and their Inhabitants* (1518), trans. M. L. Dawes [London: Hakluyt Society, 1812; repr. New Delhi: Vedams, 2002], 1: 58–60). Mulay Emir bin Said was actually the Sultan of Socotra or Mahra, ruled by the Banu Afrar dynasty, which lasted until 1967. The capital was at Qishn (see below).

[356] An alternative name for a flintlock musket.

colony.[357] But about five years after, Albuquerque[358] the admiral slighted it, pretending that the merchandise of the place proved not equivalent to the charge incumbent, which reduced the poor indefensive natives to fresh thralldom. Joao de Castro[359] for many days found it high water here at the Moon's rising, and, as the Moon ascended, the tide decreased; so as it was low water when the Moon was highest, contrary to what we observe in most other places.

Red Sea. Arabia

Aden, a town upon the Arabian continent from whose *cabobarra* Socotra may be seen, has 12 degrees 35 minutes north latitude; the variation is 19 degrees west. Of old known by the name *Madena*, of *Madoga* to Joao de Castro, called *Adana* by Calistus,[360] *Achania* by Eupolemus,[361] not unlike to be that Eden which is enumerated with other Arabian cities in Ezekiel 27:23[362] opposite to Azana, snatched by the Turks out of Arabian power *Anno Domini* 1458. Solyman Bassa[363] and a

---

[357] This is not quite accurate. Da Cunha landed in 1507 at the port of Suq and proceeded to "liberate" local Christians. However, his reception by them was less than enthusiastic and by 1511 the Portuguese had abandoned Socotra, which then passed to the control of the Mahra Sultanate of Yemen (see above). The remains of a Portuguese fort may still be seen there.

[358] Afonso de Albuquerque (1453–1515), Portuguese soldier and explorer, was Viceroy of the Indies (1509–1513). He conquered Ormuz (1507) and Goa (1509–1510), after which he consolidated Portuguese hegemony in the Indian Ocean. In 1511 he attacked and conquered Malacca, which gave Portugal control of the spice-routes. He attacked Aden (1513) on his way to Jeddah. He died at sea. T. F. Earle has edited a volume of his writings, *Albuquerque: Caesar of the East. Selected Texts by Afonso de Albuquerque and his Son* (London: Aris and Phillips, 1990).

[359] João de Castro (1500–1548), Portuguese explorer and fourth Viceroy of the Portuguese Indies (1547–1548). He distinguished himself at the siege of Tunis (1535) and in India, where he defeated Sultan Mahmud Bagada of Gujarat (1547). He died in the arms of his friend St. Francis Xavier, and was buried in Goa.

[360] Calistus (Kallistos), properly Nicephorus Xanthopoulos (c. 1256–1335), was a Byzantine historian. He wrote the *Historia ecclesiastica*, a 23-volume work (18 now survive) containing many anecdotes and fables about people and places, many of which were based on spurious authority. It was printed in 1553 and was used as a source by Ortelius.

[361] Eupolemus (fl. 158/57 B. C. E.) was a Jewish historian who is quoted in fragments by Eusebius. There are also fragments known as the *Pseudo-Eupolemus*. For details see J. H. Charlesworth, ed., *Old Testament Pseudepigrapha* (New York: Doubleday, 1985), 2.

[362] "Haran, and Canneh, and Eden, the merchants of Sheba, Asshur and Chilmal were thy merchants."

[363] Suleiman Pasha al-Khadim (d. 1541), Ottoman Governor of Egypt. His troops looted Aden (1538) when they landed there for provisions, and he had a varied career which included a massacre of rebels in South Yemen and false reports to the Sultan that

regiment of obscure people who, like locusts, about that time swarmed thither out of Trebizond. This, though it be a much-frequented road, is none of the best, for at the change it flows not above 8 foot water, where a south-east and north-west Moon make a full sea. From Bab el-Mandub, which Ptolemy *Lib. 4, Cap.* 1 and Arrian[364] in *Periplo*[365] some think called *Diodori insula*,[366] though I rather think Socotra to be it, is distant 18 leagues from Moeho, which some call *Moha*, others *Moscha*,[367] a town low in its situation and sulphuriously shaded by the high and barren mountain Cabobarra, whose brazen front so scorches this miserable place that it gives a lively character or representation of Turkish baseness. The sea so circles there that it becomes a chersonese, and, as it were for breath thrusts its head a good way into the blushing sea. The circuit is large enough, but sparingly-built; those that are by their outsides discovering an inward discontent by outward slavery, so as 'tis much changed since those were there who gave Osorius and Münster[368] occasion to blaze it for a city of great commerce and magnificence. Of most note is the castle, built near the sea to command the road, which is strong in its situation, but more by those many pieces of cannon which are planted upon the bulwarks, having withal a large graft and counter-scarp not to be entered save by a long and narrow path, so as one would think it prepared to

---

he had defeated European armies. Suleiman II had him executed when the Portuguese and their allies invested Suez, thus showing up his lies.

[364] Flavius Arrianus Xenophon (c. 95–180), a Greek from Nicomedia, studied Stoic philosophy under Epictetus and became a general in the Roman army. Hadrian appointed him Governor of Cappadocia in about 135, and when the emperor died Arrian returned to Greece. His most famous work is his *Life of Alexander the Great*, which appeared in a Latin translation by Bartolomeo Fazio (1508) and was also edited by Matthias Apiarius (1554). There is a good modern translation by A. de Sélincourt (Harmondsworth: Penguin Books, 1958). "He wrote," Chugg says, "to rescue the king's reputation as a general and conqueror from a morass of misconceptions and inaccuracies" (A. M. Chugg, *The Lost Tomb of Alexander the Great* [London: Periplus, 2005], xiv). There are also some extant fragments of a lost *History of Events after Alexander*.

[365] Arrian was not the author of the *Periplus of the Erythraean Sea*, which was an anonymous work on navigation and trade-routes around Egypt, East Africa, and India. It is now thought by scholars to date from the first century C.E. It was edited by Sigismund Gelenius (1553); there are moderns translation by Lionel Casson (Princeton: Princeton University Press, 1989). and G. W. Huntingford (London: Hakluyt Society, 1980).

[366] This is actually Perim, a rocky and almost uninhabitable island now controlled by Yemen. The Portuguese occupied it in 1513, but were driven out by the Turks. It came under British control in 1799, after long occupation by France.

[367] All these are names for Mocha, then an important Yemeni port on the Red Sea, but now largely displaced by Aden.

[368] Sebastian Münster (1488–1552), the great German cartographer, scholar, and cosmographer, was Professor of Hebrew at the University of Basel from 1527. His *Cosmographia* (1544), which contained illustrations by Holbein, was the earliest description of the world by a German scholar. He also made a Latin translation of Ptolemy (1540).

safeguard the whole treasure of Arabia, whereas within are only store of iron bullets, arms, and a company of miserable ragamuffins who both secure the Turkish interest in that place and extort contribution from all that south part of Ajman.

And being now in the Red Sea, by the colour it bears greater credit may be given to those who say the name was mistaken, for it is *verbum aequivocum*,[369] and although 'tis true that as it is called *Mare Idumeum* or the Sea of Edom, and *Mare Erythraeum*, the Septuagint might warrantably translate it *Rubrum* or Red, although indeed the Sea rather took its denomination from the country of Edom upon which it verges, or from King Erythraeus, both which signify "red," a King whose tomb, albeit erected at the other end of the Happy Arabia near Ormuz, son, as say the fictitious Greeks, to Perseus and Andromeda, and from whose name this, as the Aegean and Icarian, took its denominate, yet reigned and had his longest residence here. And though with us it has but one name, most memorable through that miracle the Almighty by Moses expressed in preserving the Israelites when pursued by the Pharaoh Cenchres,[370] who with his whole army here perished, in authors we have nevertheless that is has many other, for the Hebrews call it *Zuph* and *Saph* , the Arabians of old *Mare Aelaniticum* from *Aelana*, now Toro,[371] a port at the end of this gulf distant from Mount Sinai in Arabia 20 leagues, or Melanis, where David built ships for the gold of Urphe, as Eusebius[372] *l. 9 De praeparat. Evang.* out of Eupolemus reporteth; the Turks the Gulf of Mecca, near which at Medina Mohammed was entombed; the Gulf of Arabia [in] Strabo *Lib.* 6, Ptolemy, and Arrian *Lib.* 8 *Vita Alex. Bobar Colzun*, or

---

[369] A questionable, or perhaps "loaded" word.

[370] Herbert could have found Cenchres in many sources, including Ralegh, Archbishop Ussher, Berossos, and Eusebius, to name four. He was thought to have been the "Pharaoh of the Exodus," although Strabo, amongst others, says he did not exist. Cenchres has been identified with an "Amenophis" who succeeded Ramesses II (who was actually succeeded by Mer-en-Ptah, sometimes suggested by scholars as the Pharaoh of the Exodus, although he did not drown) and as the successor of "Achoris" (Eusebius and Berossos).

[371] *Aelana* was the Roman name for the port of Aqaba, so-called from the ancient city of Ayla, which was nearby. It is the Edomite settlement of Elath.

[372] Eusebius, bishop of Caesarea (c. 260–340), was the author of *The History of the Church* (first printed by Erhard Ratdolt in 1483) and of a brief chronicle of universal history down to the time of Constantine I, where he advanced the claim that the Bible was superior to all pagan philosophy and theology. His *Praeparatio evangelica*, first printed by Robert Estienne in 1544 and cited here by Herbert, is essentially an introduction for pagans who wish to convert, but it also contains a great deal of interesting information on history and philosophy which cannot be found anywhere else. There is a translation of *The History* in 2 volumes by R. J. Deferrari (Washington: Catholic University of America Press, 1955) and a shorter version by G. A. Williamson (Harmondsworth: Penguin Books, 1965).

rather *Kalzem*[373] the Ethiop and some, *Zabara* and *Brachia*; from some principal port of old, others from the seaweeds or sargassos floating there, *Mare Algosum* and *Carectosum*.[374] Yet the name Red is not without some colour or show of reason, seeing that the sand, especially when the sun begins his visit towards the Antipodes gives a ruddy reflection; besides, it is observed that from Suschen, a noted place upon the Ethiopic side, to Alcozar,[375] which is 100 leagues, the water is shoal, and by reason of the plenty of red coral found there, seems to have a reddish tincture. But let the controversy and uncertainty be what it will as to the colour. This is certain, that albeit the length of this sea be near a 1000 English miles, for no less is accounted from Cape Guardafui, a promontory now so-called upon the Ethiopian shore near Dice in Ptolemy and to former ages known by the name of *Aromata*, to Suez at the very bottom of the Gulf, by some thought *Arsinoe*, *Heroum Civitas* and *Danao* in Pliny, and 80 miles broad from Cape Guardafui to Fartak, formerly *Ziagrum*. Nevertheless, 'twixt Aden near *Possidium*[376] of old in Arabia, and Zeyla[377] upon the Africa coast where 'tis narrowest, the fretum[378] which the Arabs call *Albatto*, and under 12 degrees 15 minutes, is not above 18 miles English. A shoal and dangerous water 'tis found, except in the middle of the channel, where greatest vessels in fair weather sail boldly.

Now, though heretofore upon the Ethiopic or Troglodytic shore, especially towards the northwest end which properly we call *Aethiopia sub Aegypto*, there have been sundry sea-towns and ports of note much frequented, as *Zybit*, *Sabat*, in Ptolemy *Alcozar*, Suakin, Massawa, Dallaqua, old Phileteras[379] in 27 degrees, Theram, and Zeyla, which last is in the Kingdom of Awdal near the Sinus Avalites, which joins to the territory of Abex, the original seat of the Abassines[380] and on the opposite or Arabian coast Toro, Elana or Eloth, Petra, Ezion-geber and others. Yet at this day Mocha upon the Arabian side is most traded to, which though I think too much south, by some is thought the relic of Ezion-geber, the port from whence Solomon's fleet usually set out for Ophir.[381] At *Pihahiroth*[382] of old, which is betwixt Toro and the Suez, is yet shown the place where Moses first

---

[373] The Sea of Kolzum or Calzem is another name for the Arabian Gulf.

[374] *Mare Algosum* means 'Sea of Reeds' or 'Sea-weed.' *Carectosum* is from *carectum*, meaning 'sedge.'

[375] A city in what is now Syria.

[376] Posidium in the ancient kingdom of Coele-Syria has been identified as the modern town of al-Basit, near Latakia.

[377] Zeyla, now in northern Somalia, was, as Herbert states, the capital of the Awdal Sultanate, which extended into southern Djibouti and parts of Ethiopia from about 1415 to 1555. Its last ruler requested Portuguese help against the Ethiopians.

[378] Estuary, strait.

[379] This is another name for the island of Santorini in the Aegean Sea.

[380] Abyssinians.

[381] Ezion-geber is described as being near modern Eilat (see 1 Kings 9:26); cf. above.

[382] The Hebrews camped there just before crossing the Red Sea.

entered the Red Sea; Petra, under 30 degrees, which the Hebrews call *Jachshut*, now Arach, the place where Ruth was born,[383] is branded for the base ingratitude to their Princess Cleopatra, setting fire upon those vessels which she had with marvellous labour hailed to the Suez from the Nilus over that isthmus of land which divides Asia from Africa about 300 furlongs, designing her flight with M. Antony through the Red Sea to some remote part of India after that overthrow Augustus Caesar gave them at the battle of Actium or Naupactum near the Gulf of Lepanto.[384]

From Suez to the Nile is not more then 25 leagues. From Grand Cairo to Toro by land is about five days' travel, but from Pelusium[385] or Damiata[386] upon Nilus to Suez, which I suppose de Castro mistakes Strabo *lib.* 17 to make it 900 furlongs, albeit without doubt the place where several attempts have been made to cut such a slice as should give ships a free passage from the Mediterranean thither, which was thought might have been effected. The isthmus exceeds not 80 miles, the country being flat and fit for cutting, but where God sets the terminus, for 'tis he that laid the foundations of the earth, gives the sea its bounds, and weighs the earth as in a balance.[387] We see the power and wit of man may not contradict or alter, so as in vain Sesostris first, after him Darius, and then some of the Ptolemies endeavoured to make those seas communicable, albeit the last in greatest part effected it by a sluice of 100 foot broad and 30 deep, discouraged when he perceived strange diseases sweep most of the pioneers away, hideous noises, if the report be true, affrighting others. But what most discouraged the prosecution was the fear they had that level-country of Egypt might, especially when land-floods and spring-tides met, be overthrown, and that the salt water of the Red Sea would alter the sweet taste of the River Nile, so as upon mature deliberation it was found the most prudential course to desist. And such a vain attempt might have been presidential to Nero in that successless enterprise of transecting the isthmus in that narrow neck of land near Corinth which links the peninsula of Peloponessus to the main of Greece, to Seleucus,[388] labouring to unite the Black Sea with the Caspian, to Trajan, the like with Tigris and Euphrates, and to the Great Turk of late, endeavouring to force Volga into Tanais.[389] Pliny, who like other historians took much upon trust, relates how that

---

[383] Ruth was from Moab, which is in modern-day Jordan.

[384] Augustus (Octavian) defeated the forces of Cleopatra VII and Antony at Actium in 31 B. C.

[385] Now Tel el-Farama, east of Port Said.

[386] Now Damietta, a Red Sea port in Egypt.

[387] Herbert is citing biblical references without noting them; they are, respectively, Job 38: 4, Job 26: 10, and Isaiah 40: 12.

[388] Seleucus I was king of Coele-Syria 311–282 B.C.E.

[389] "A site now under water near Taganrog (in the province of Rostov, southern Russia), on the gulf of that name in the northern part of Lake Maeotis (the Sea of Azov) west

in Augustus Caesar's time, which was 200 years before his, certain Spanish ships suffered shipwrack in this sea, but how they came there he resolves not.

We do not read that the Cape de Bona Speranza was known in 1300 years after those voyages of Hanno, Iamblichus[390] and some others being not to be credited. And yet Sir Walter Ralegh inclines to believe that the Phoenicians, when subjects to the Egyptian sceptre and the most expert in navigation, in that time when Pharaoh Necho, by whose hand good Josiah[391] fell, having in vain attempted to cut a sluice 80 miles long and broad enough for two galleys to row abreast 'twixt the Red Sea and the Nile, with the fleet that he had built encouraged them to discovery. Herodotus *l.* 4 reports that they compassed Africa, and after three years' voyage returned into Nile through the Straits of Gibraltar, which, if it were so, was quite forgot when Vasco da Gama made his passage. When the Portuguese had settled his plantations in Socotra and such other maritime places as best pleased him upon those Africa and Arabian coasts, and soon after in India and the Persian shore, for so propitious was the time, or so little was the resistance he found, as he had the liberty to pick and choose, that *Anno* 1520 Albuquerque, having taken Aden, then persuaded himself the Empire of the Indies was perpetuated to the Crown of Portugal, "*Qua victa,*" saith Osorius, "*putabat India Imperium fore sempiternum.*"[392] But it proved otherwise, for not long after many of his plantations were destroyed through their own luxury, but most through the treachery of the negroes, albeit sufficient remains yet under obedience.

This warm part of the Interior Ethiopia being the northernmost of the Troglodytes' country, by most called *Aethiopia sub Aegypto*, bounded to the east by the Red Sea, was, say some, first planted by Chus the son of Shem after his departure out of Arabia, or as others by Sheba the son of Rhegma. The *caelum* and *solum*,[393] such as the first being extreme in heat during those months the sun is vertical, the country extending equally on both sides the Equinoctial beginning from 20 degrees north, necessarily instructs the inhabitants for the most part to seek shade and other refreshing in subterranean habitations, and the rather for that

---

of the mouth of the river Tanais (Don)" (Michael Grant, *A Guide to the Ancient World* [New York: Barnes and Noble, 1986], 621).

[390] Iamblichus of Chalcis (c. 245–325) was a Syrian Neoplatonic philosopher and founder of a Pythagorean school at Apamea. Many of his works, such as his *Collection of Pythagorean Doctrines*, survive only in fragments. However, an edition of his treatise *Theurgia, or On the Mysteries of Egypt*, would have been available to Herbert in an edition by Ficino (printed 1552) or a Latin translation (1607). There is a modern translation by Emma Clarke and John Dillon (London: Society of Biblical Literature, 2003).

[391] Josiah was king of Judah 640–609 B.C.E. He was killed at the battle of Megiddo. See 2 Chronicles 20–35.

[392] By which conquest he thought that the empire in India would last forever.

[393] The topmost / lowest parts.

the country is observed to be full of hills 600 miles from the Red Sea and more towards the west, sterile towards the east, and the Mediterranean so covered with loose sands as renders it impassable. Upon the western banks of the Mare Rubrum there have been port towns such as Zeyla, Suakin, Massawa,[394] Theran, with some others that of late years have been resorted to not only by the Egyptian but by other merchants of most countries. Howbeit, since the principal marts were translated to Goa and Hormuz, Mocha and Aden on the opposite coast are most frequented. Moreover, albeit the Egyptian princes of old have been of great power for many ages, yet such was the poverty or rather natural defence this country was provided with against the invasion of any numerous party, it continued ever independent without being subdued or harassed by any of the four monarchies who, unless in an auxiliary way if they be the Sukkiims that assisted Shishak[395] mentioned in II Chronicles 12:2 from hence never exacted tribute; all that Cambyses the son of the great Cyrus aimed at after subjecting Egypt to the Persian Empire, about the year from the creation of the world 3400,[396] revolting under Darius Nothus and reduced by Ochus,[397] being for their returning him by his ambassadors some of their earth and water, their usual symbols of subjection, which they nevertheless scornfully refused.

Now concerning the commerce this Red Sea has afforded, the first I find story takes notice of is the trade which King Solomon from hence engrossed for gold of Ophir. The port from where his fleet usually set sail was Ezion-geber, a convenient riding-place for ships near the city of Eloth, which is also called *Elanon* in the land of Edom, part of Arabia Petraea, named so either from the stoniness thereof or from Petra, now Roth-Halala, the capital city, situate upon the brink of that sea, a town famoused by being the birthplace of Ruth[398] and for the defence it made against Severus[399] and Trajan the Roman emperors, but infamous for their ingratitude to Cleopatra their princess in her distress. For that the Kings of Judaea extended their empire from the Euphrates to the Red Sea or confines of Egypt is evident by what is recorded in I Kings 4: 21, where 'tis expressed

---

[394] Massawa is a very ancient Ethiopian port-city with a large Arab population.

[395] Shishak or Sheshank I was king of Egypt 945–924 B.C.E. The passage noted reads "And it came to pass, that in the twelfth year of king Rehoboam that Shishak king of Egypt came up against Jerusalem" The "Sukkiims" are the Sukkites, and Herbert's reference is quite correct.

[396] Cambyses II [Kambuya] was king of Persia 529–521 B.C.E. He conquered Egypt in 525 B.C.E.

[397] Darius II Nothus was king of Persia 423–404 B.C.E. Artaxerxes III Ochus was king of Persia 358–338 B.C.E.

[398] Ruth was actually born in Moab, not Petra (see above, for another claim of her birth).

[399] Publius Septimius Severus was Roman emperor 198–217. M. Ulpius Traianus (Trajan) reigned 98–117.

that Solomon "reigned over all the Kingdoms from the river Euphrates . . . unto the border of Egypt," who brought Solomon presents and served him all the days of his life. This port of Ezion-geber and the rest of Edom were formerly conquered by David, II Samuel 8: 14, where 'tis said that "he put garrisons in Edom;" throughout all which country he put soldiers, so as all they of Edom became David's subjects. Hadad,[400] one of the Princes of Edom, flying for succour to Pharaoh King of Egypt, so insinuated himself into the favour of the Egyptian king that that he not only gave the Edomite his wife's sister in marriage, but hearing that David and his general Joab were dead, seemed little importunate for his stay. Solomon by his gross idolatry having so provoked the Almighty that He not only permitted the revolt of divers, amongst others of Hadad, but albeit Solomon made a nearer alliance with the Egyptian King. Yet so jealous was he of the Jews' extended empire that probably he gave Hadad the readier leave to depart, and so envious at his wealth that the ten tribes no sooner revolted under Jeroboam but that the Egyptian king, by that weakening, or rather as a further chastisement from the Lord for the apostasy of the land, overrun Rehoboam's Kingdom and despoiled Jerusalem of all the treasure it had, and carried thence all Solomon's shields of gold.[401] Notwithstanding which it was reduced by Jehoshaphat,[402] in whose reign "there was no king in Edom, a deputy being king" (I Kings 22:47), the deputy or *prorex* 'tis likely being substituted by the Judaean king, whose navy, prepared to go for Ophir, was broken in pieces for associating with Ahaziah, King of Israel.[403] But in his son Jehoram's time Edom rebelled and appointed themselves a King whom albeit he beat afterward in the field, and that Amaziah also gave them a notable defeat in the Valley of Salt,[404] and that Uzziah (who is also called Azariah), succeeding his father Amaziah, built Eloth "and restored it to Judah" (II Kings 14:22).[405] It appears not in story either sacred or profane that any of their ships continued their voyage to Ophir or that any commerce was from this sea in the succeeding ages.

---

[400] Ben-Hadad I (d. 851/845 B.C.E.) was King of Syria. He revolted against Shalmaneser III of Assyria and was defeated, having previously threatened Baasha of Israel, who also defeated him.

[401] Jeroboam I became the first King of Israel (933–911 B.C.E.) when the kingdom split, with Rehoboam (933–916 B.C.E.) ruling the new kingdom of Judah. Sheshank I attacked the two Kingdoms in about 928 B.C.E. Rehoboam may have given up the treasure to keep his throne (see F. Castel, *The History of Israel and Judah*, trans. M. J. O'Connell [New York: Paulist Press, 1973], 101–2; I Kings 14: 25–28).

[402] Jehoshaphat was king of Judah 870–846 B.C.E.

[403] Ahaziah was king of Israel 853–852 B.C.E.

[404] Now the Arabah Valley on the south side of the Dead Sea.

[405] Jehoram was king of Judah 846–841 B. C.E.; Amaziah was king of Judah 796–781 B. C.E.; Uzziah or Azariah was king of Judah 781–747 B.C.E.

It appears that about 300 years after Jehoshaphat Egypt was by Cambyses subjected under the Persian yoke, and so continued till the time of Darius Nothus, at which time the Egyptians broke the Persian yoke but were subdued 50 years after by Ochus, the eighth monarch of Persia, during which the Persians intermitted that commerce, having nevertheless, besides the earth and water they required, a yearly revenue of 6000 talents, which was accordingly paid Alexander. Ptolemy surnamed Philadelphus,[406] the second of the Lagi, about 270 years before the nativity of Christ, was the first that revived the Ophirian trade after Jehoshaphat; his navy set sail usually from Alcozar (*Nichosea* in Ptolemy under 36 degrees wellnigh parallel to Coptos[407] upon the Nile, so as it cannot be Berenice,[408] which exceeds not 24 degrees) and continued by the Egyptian kings till the time of Alexander. The fleet that went was usually not less then 120 vessels great and small, the space upwards of two years coasting all the way, 'tis presumed, and the return very advantageous, for every crown increasing not less then 100, as Pliny reports, so that *communibus annis*[409] twelve million crowns came into his exchequer. In Ptolemy Auletes's[410] reign the cargo amounted to seven millions of gold, and little less was paid to Cleopatra his daughter, which raised the greater force against his rival Augustus. The gold and other rich lading was from Chozar conveyed by sledge and camels, sometime from Chozar[411] to Coptos, the usual emporium, and otherwhile from the Suez to Pelusium[412] or Damiata, and thence after Alexander's time by boat to Alexandria, which after Coptos for a long time was the common emporium ot place for trade. But when Julius Caesar and after him Augustus reduced Egypt to a province, the former tax was doubled; the Ophyrion, or at least the golden trade thither or to Sofala[413]

---

[406] Ptolemy II Philadelphus was king of Egypt 281–246 B.C.E.

[407] Coptos is north-east of Thebes. It was the starting-point for roads to the Red Sea, but its importance as a trading-town was eclipsed by Berenice. It recovered, and flourished again until its destruction by Diocletian (292), after which a Christian settlement grew up. Today it is only a village, but has a famous temple of the fish-god Min.

[408] Berenice is a Red Sea port on the western coast of the sea, now known as Madinet al-Haras. It was founded by Ptolemy II, who named it after his mother. It was "the principal Egyptian landing place for goods from Arabia, India and East Africa" (Grant, *Guide* 107).

[409] Over a number of years.

[410] Ptolemy XII Neos Dionysos, surnamed "Auletes" (the Flute-player), was king of Egypt 80–58 and 55–51 B.C.E. He was the father of Cleopatra VII.

[411] Chozar is now Alalakh in modern Syria. It was also known as Gozan, and is the place to where the Israelites were deported during the Babylonian captivity.

[412] Pelusium, which was the site of Cambyses's victory over the Egyptians, is a city "on the easternmost (Pelusiac) mouth of the Nile" (Grant, *Guide*, 482).

[413] Sofala, once a gold-trading centre, was located south of modern-day Beira in central Mozambique. "Sofala lyeth between Cuama and Magnice, two rivers" (Purchas 4: 284). These rivers were located in Monomatapa, now Zimbabwe.

being to that time probably continued, but when the Arabians and Goths from adverse quarters like inundations overflowed most part of the universe, in which storm the Roman majesty was eclipsed, the Indian trade ceased, so as the Red Sea voyages were but little prosecuted by the Constantinopolitan emperor, from whom Omar, the third caliph[414] of Baghdad, wrested it, and from whom the Saracen who preceded Saladin, when the Indian commerce by merchants was brought to Samarkand and thence by caravan with extreme charge, toil and hazard removed to Trebizond upon the Euxine, whence being conveyed to Damascus and Aleppo. The Venetians monopolised it for some time to the great enriching of their Seigneury, but after Vasco da Gama *Anno* 1497 discovered the way into the East Indies by compassing Africa, the Venetians, though unwillingly, gave place to the English, Dutch and others who now share with the Portugal in that navigation. But to return.

A Persian Convert

October 18, the wind being fair, at sea our observation was 17 degrees north, our longitude 19 from Mohelia. Soon after we were becalmed, then we had such hot weather as made us fry, and the sweat dropped from us no otherwise then if we had been stewed on stoves or hot baths, which put some into calentures, but all grew exceeding faint, notwithstanding our best provision to abate it. Indeed, I think there are not hotter places in the world then the Red Sea and Persian Gulf about Ormuz when the sun displays his beams during the summer solstice, for then the earth inflames equally with the air. And experience teaches us that the heat, not only under the equinox, but the tropics when the sun comes to the vertex, is much more intense and violent, notwithstanding the long nights, then it is about the polar circles, albeit for near six months together the sun sets not, but constantly keeps his circuit above the horizon.

In this distemperature of heat Mohammed, a Persian merchant returning for Persia in our ship, died of a burning fever, his father Hajji Shahsavar[415] having paid nature her last tribute in London the year before. "*Nemo ante obitum beatus*"[416] was verified in this person, for a happy man we hope this Mohammed died, if throwing away the rags of Mawmetry[417] he clothed his soul with the

---

[414] Omar I was the second, not third caliph. He reigned 634–644. He was based in Damascus, not Baghdad, which was not founded until after 750 C.E.

[415] Hajji or Khwaja Mahmud Shahsavar [*Hodge Suar*] (d. 1626) was the Persian ambassador to Venice in 1613 and 1621. He eventually settled in London, where he appears to have set up as a merchant. He had accompanied Naqd Ali Beg to London in 1626. When he died the East India Company arranged his funeral, and there is an account of him in Anthony Munday's continuation of Stow's *Survey of London*. For details see Chew, *Crescent*, 328–30.

[416] "Nobody is blessed before death" (Ovid, *Metamorphoses* 3. 136).

[417] Mohammedanism.

robes of true faith in Christ, whom, we are told, a little before he left the world, he called upon as the only efficacious means of his salvation. Again I say happy, if unfeignedly. At his putting into the sea the captain of our ship honoured his funeral with the rending clamour of four culverins, his carcase at that instant being committed to the mercy of the sea, no less sure a treasury then the earth, till the resurrection.

Flying Fishes [illustration not shown]

Flying Fishes.

The 26 of October. By observation we found that we were got north from the Equator 19 degrees 40 minutes, longitude from Mohelia 20 degrees, our steerage at that time being south-east, when again the wind abating the sea calmed and was as smooth as glass, not the least curl or wrinkle discernible. This increased our heat, and only refreshed our memory with the zone we were in, properly called "torrid." The greatest recreation we had was the view of such large shoals of flying fishes as by their interposing multitude for some time darkened the body of the sun, a fish beautiful in its eye, the body though no larger then a small herring, yet big enough for those complemental fins which, so long as moist, serve as wings for 200 paces or more and 40 foot high, helping them to avoid the pursuit which sharks, dolphins, eonates, albacores and other sea-tyrants make, and causes them for preservation to forsake their proper element, where usually birds of prey upon the wing hover to question them for invading their habitation, by this pitiful evasion becoming the true emblems of misery, no sooner having escaped one danger but encountering another equally destructive. During the night season here we saw a perfect rainbow, which was extraordinary, for albeit rainbows be formed of a dewy cloud in the air above, and usually appear in a beautiful arch while the sun is above the horizon, the Moon we seldom see to have this operation.

[Part II: East India]

Goa. East India.

The 17 of November we descried that *terra exoptata*,[1] the coast of India, land in 15 degrees latitude and 32 of longitude, ill weather having formerly driven us to leeward many degrees. This is that very place where Goa, Barigaza of old, the bravest and best-defended city in the Orient is seated, the magazine, refuge, and seat of justice of the victorious Portugal.

The city is not visible to such as sail along the coast, being three hours journey within land. Of old the seat of the Canarins[2] in an isle called Tilsoar 30 miles in circuit, a sweet place it is, surrounded by a fresh river streaming from the mighty mountain Bellaguate, encompassed with a strong and beautiful wall, which glories in her aspiring turrets and is not a little dreadful in many sorts of roaring cannon. Her strength and beauty took rise from the Deccan Kings Zabaym and Idalcan,[3] from whom *anno* 1509 Albuquerque the victorious Portugal conquered and after that defended it against 70,000 foot and 3500 horse which Idalcan brought to reduce it with, but it was aggrandized by the Lusitanian. The

---

[1] Longed-for land.

[2] The Portuguese applied this term to specifically to "the Konkani people of Goa" (*HJ* 154). However, "throughout the sixteenth century the term [Canara] was applies to the country above the Ghauts, sometimes to the whole kingdom of Narsinga or Vijayanagar" (*HJ* 152). Gradually the term narrowed to the Goan version, which seems to be what Herbert uses here.

[3] These "Kings" were actually the rulers of Bijapur and Calicut, who had been independent since 1490. The sultans of Bijapur had formerly been vassals of the Bahmani sultans of the Deccan. "Idalcan," which is actually a title used by the Portuguese to denote the rulers of Bijapur (see *HJ* 431) is probably Sultan Yusuf Adil Shah, who reigned 1490–1510. His successor Mahmud Begara fought the Portuguese for twenty years, until 1530. "Zamayn" is not a name at all, but a title of the Raja of Kozhikode (Calicut), variously rendered as "Zamorin," "Samoothin," or "Samoothiripaddu." The use of this title goes back to Ibn Battuta, writing in about 1343, and is used by Varthema, one of Herbert's sources (see *HJ* 977). The man in question is Raja Manavikram, who received da Gama in 1498, but expelled the Portuguese two years later. As Herbert relates, he joined up with the Sultan of Gujarat against the Portuguese and fought them at the battle of Diu (1509).

great bazaar or market, being in the centre of the town, is gallantly and regularly built. Many other streets there are, but after the Indian mode, narrow if not sufficiently nasty; the buildings generally are spacious and not uncomely, thick and dark within, terraced above, and made suitable to that hot climate. Watered it is with a delicious stream, which, by benevolence of the air, refreshes the fields, forcing Flora to dismantle. The gardens also be filled with variety of sweet and eye-pleasing flowers, the whole isle so abounding with with grass, groves, corn, cattle, fruits and such sense-ravishing delights as a reasonable man can well require. Above 20 little towns, all planted with Portugals, are seen in this 30-mile compass, as also the ruins of 200 idol-temples which the Viceroy Antonio Noronha[4] totally demolished so that no memory might remain or monuments of such gross idolatry.

In Goa nothing is more observable then the fortifications, the Viceroy's and the Archbishop's palaces and the churches. Field-pieces here are numbered above 300, the palaces are very strong, built of good stone, furnished and adorned with rich arras and painting. The churches of best rank are that dedicated to the Blessed Virgin Mother of God, in which is kept the bones and skull of St. Thomas the Apostle, whose relics were brought 150 years ago from Meliapore by Manoel Frias[5] at the command of Don John,[6] successor to Emmanuel, Kings of Portugal, St. Paul, St. Dominic, St. Katharine and St. Saviour, in which last are laid the bones of the great and valiant Albuquerque who died here and was buried in the year 1516, da Cunha, Don Francisco, and that late canonised China saint, Francis Xavier the Navarrean Jesuit, who died 4 December 1552 aged 55 and rubricated by Pope Gregory XV[7] the 12 of March 1622, when many more were sainted.

Hence we hasted towards Suwali[8] Road, judging the worst past, the Indian shore all the way being in view of us and the sea everywhere 20 leagues from land was anchorable. But upon a sudden the scene was quickly changed, for the

---

[4] Dom Antonio Garcia de Noronha (c. 1520–1569) was Captain-General of Malacca and Viceroy of Portuguese India (1564–1568). He pursued an aggressive policy against the Moors and Gujaratis. "After will come Noronha, destined / To repulse from Diu the Turkish siege" (Camoens, *Lusiads* 10. 62).

[5] Manoel de Frias was appointed by the Viceroy Dom Duarte de Meneses to the post of Captain of the Coromandel and Fishing Coasts in 1521. He was given jurisdiction over all the Portuguese settlers on the coast and had a small fleet to ensure that proper passes were issued to any ships trading in the Coromandel area. He was at Meliapore in 1524; the year before an investigation about the authenticity of St. Thomas's body was carried out and its report dedicated to him.

[6] João III "the Pious" reigned 1521–1557.

[7] Pope Gregory XV (Alessandro Ludovisi) reigned 1621–1623. He also canonised, amongst others, Ignatius Loyola and Teresa of Avila. To "rubricate" means to colour or illuminate a letter in a manuscript red.

[8] Modern-day Suvali, near Surat on the Arabian Sea.

elements grew dreadful, the wind roaring and the sea so sublime and wrathful, and for three days' space raging with such fury that we verily believed a hurricane was begun, which is a vast or unwonted tumour in the air called Euroclydon[9] in The Acts 2, a tempest so terrible that houses and trees are like dust before it, many ships by its violence having been blown ashore and shattered. Olaus Magnus lib. 1 cap. 4 and lib. 7 cap. 3 *Sept. Histor.*[10] gives some memorable examples of it; once in nine years it uses to thunder among them, and is presaged by birds and beasts, who three or four days before it come give notice by their noise and hiding themselves underground as if an overture of the world were ensuing. And as in these, so in most other parts of the world there are certain times for stormy weather. In the West Indies every September the north winds bring dreadful storms, so as during that month none put to see unless necessity enforce them. But this and other our water-scapes made that saying of Bias[11] come to mind: *"Navigantes, nec inter vivos nec inter mortuus esse numerandos,"*[12] agreeable to which is Anacharsis[13] his ironic question *"Quae naves essent tutissimae quae in siccum pertractae sunt?"* And Callimachus[14] also, no less wittily: *"Iucundissimum esse mare sed si quis de terra illud contempletur."* Praised be God, we missed a typhoon, but not a second disadventure, this storm forcing a Malabar junk, a pirate, in view of us, whom our ordnance could not reach, though the longest saker we had vomited

---

[9] Euroclydon winds are very strong cyclonic winds which blow in the Mediterranean. Cf. Acts 27: 14.

[10] Olaus Magnus (1490–1557) was a Swedish cleric and scholar based in Rome. His *Historia de gentibus septentrionalibus* (1555), cited here, was a great classic in its day. It contained a great deal of information on the history and folklore of Nordic people, and was translated into English (1658). Olaus also produced a marine map with commentary (1539).

[11] Bias of Priene (fl. sixth century B.C.E.), a philosopher, was one of the Seven Sages. Most of our information about him comes from Diogenes Laertius's *Lives of the Philosophers,*

[12] Those who sail are accounted neither amongst the living nor the dead.

[13] Anacharsis (sixth century B.C.E.) was a Scythian philosopher and another one of the Seven Sages of Athens. Diogenese Laertius relates that Anacharsis was murdered by his own brother for becoming too "Greek." He advocated moderation in everything; his nautical connection comes from Strabo, who credited him with inventing the double-fluke anchor (7.35). The quote reads: "Which ships are the safest? Those which are hauled up on dry land."

[14] Callimachus of Alexandria (c. 305–240 B.C.E.), librarian and poet. Announcing that epic poetry was now passé, he promptly wrote the epic poem *Aetia*, which ran to over 3000 lines. He was an outstanding writer of shorter, witty lyrics, however, and on these his fame rests. Early editions include those of Gelenius (1513) and Hieronymus Froben (1532). An excellent modern translation is that by Stanley Lombardo and Diane Raynor (Baltimore: Johns Hopkins University Press, 1988). The quote reads "The most pleasant seas are those one looks out over from ashore."

fire of defiance after him, so as we were forced to chase her with two barges each manned with fifty musketeers, and *"vela damus, quamvis remige navis eat."*[15] But it appeared that we made too much haste in boarding her, our men being entertained with such store of fireworks and a sort of hand-grenado, with a volley of invenomous shafts, and, which was worse, with such desperate courage, that after small hurt done them we were constrained to retreat with loss, one-half being slain, hurt, and scalded, our ships all the while being made an unwilling theatre of this affront and the wind bidding us to retaliate.

Dabul,[16] St. John, Choul, Daman.[17]

The 22 of November, the wind abating, sounding we found ground at forty fathoms, and saw many snakes swimming about our ships, which, with the waters changing colour, assured us we were near the shore, the last storm having driven us out of sight of land and somewhat puzzled us as to our way, and soon after descried land in 19 degrees 35 minutes latitude and 29 in longitude, which by its height we knew to be Dabul, called *Dunga* by Castaldus,[18] and soon after we had sight of St. Joao de Vacas, a town likewise subject to Portugal, the south end of which place mounts in a pyramid of Nature's work named St. Valentine's Peak,[19] the land continuing high from thence to Gandavi, a hill six leagues short of Suwali Road. This is a round hillock and bay of importance unto mariners.

St. John [illustration not shown]

The 27 of November we hailed an Indian *piscadoro*[20] aboard us. Never was antic so better habited; he told us that many enemies were at hand, but we feared them not. After a long toil tiding with upstream anchors, every six hours weighing and dropping, in short time we got to Choul. Then we came to Daman, a lovely town inhabited by Portugals and conspicuous to passengers, in this most memorable that, as some conjecture, it was the *ne plus* or furthest place which the great

---

[15] A slight misquotation. The text should read *"vela damus, quamvis remige puppis eat,"* which means "I'm raising sail on a ship that's already under oars" (Ovid, *Tristia* 5. 14).

[16] Modern-day Dabhol in the Konkan region of Maharashtra. It was the capital of Bijapur.

[17] A town in the southern part of Gujarat, captured by the Portuguese in 1531. Its surrounding area was granted to the Portuguese by Sultan Bahadur Shah of Gujarat in 1559.

[18] Giacomo Gastaldi (1505–1566), an Italian cartographer from Piedmont who worked in Venice and who was cited by Ortelius for his maps of Asia and Africa. He worked closely with Ramusio (see previous pages).

[19] Now known as Mahalakshmi (Foster, *Herbert*, 302).

[20] A fisherman.

Macedonian monarch with his army marched unto in India. Some authors nevertheless say that after the defeat he gave King Porus he passed his army as far as Ganges, mistaken for Indus, down which river he sent vessels for discovery. At the north end Daman has a castle which we could well perceive was large and strong, the material good white chalky stone, flanked with ordnance and mounted to play at advantage. At the south end we perceived a fair church with white battlements atop; the houses were some of like stone, others unburnt brick, three other temples there affording pleasure to the heart and eye.

The 29 day we got near the bar at Suwali, where we cast anchor because we perceived 13 sail of great ships riding there and knew not whether they were friends or foes. The last day of November we ventured over the bar 'twixt two buoys in four fathoms water, a hundred paces asunder, set there to direct the passage either side without the marks, being shoal water and dangerous. The ships at anchor proved our friends, six English and seven Dutch, most of which were ships of 1000 ton. Those of our nation were the *Palsgrave*,[21] the *Exchange*, the *William*, the *Blessing* etc., each of which entertained our ambassadors with hearty welcome. We rode in five fathom, others in nine, 'twixt the shoals and continent.

Tom Coryate's Grave.[22]

The same day we came to anchor in Suwali Road, Naqd Ali Beg the Persian ambassador,[23] Sir Robert Sherley's antagonist, died, having, as we were credibly informed, poisoned himself, for four days eating only opium. The *Mary*,[24] where

---

[21] This ship was named after Frederick V, elector of the Palatinate, who married James I's daughter Elizabeth, and whose appointment as king of Bohemia had sparked the outbreak of the Thirty Years War in 1618.

[22] Thomas Coryate (1577–1617), for whom see the Introduction, was an English eccentric and traveller. He gained fame first with his account of his European travels, *Coryate's Crudities* (1611). As a member of the Prince of Wales's household, he knew many literary men, including John Donne, Ben Jonson, and, more pertinent here, Sir Thomas Roe, the first English ambassador to the Mughal Empire. Coryate became "the first Englishman ever to visit India purely out of curiosity" (Strachan, *Life*, 1). He actually walked from the eastern Mediterranean to Persia, Afghanistan, and the Mughal Empire. He learned Persian and conversed with Emperor Jahangir. He died in India and was buried near the town of Suvali, where (if it is authentic) his grave can be seen to this day.

[23] Naqd Ali Beg (d. 1626) had attempted to discredit Sir Robert Sherley in London (see Introduction). In 1675 Dr. John Fryer reported that he was shown Naqd Ali's tomb, "not far from whence, on a small hill on the left had of the road, lies Tom Coriat, our English fakier (as they name him) together with an Armenian Christian" (Strachan, *Life*, 267). For details, see Strachan, *Life* 266–69, and the Introduction.

[24] Foster says that Naqd Ali died in the *Hart*, (*Herbert*, 303), which is incorrect, because he was in fact in the *Mary*, the new ship to which he had been assigned by the East

he died, gave him eleven great ordnance at his carrying ashore; his son Ibrahim
Khan conveyed him to Surat, 10 miles thence, where they entombed him not a
stone's cast from Tom Coryate's grave, known but by two poor stones that speak
his name, there resting till the resurrection. Now this tragic end of Naqd Beg was
not without cause, for it seems, despairing of his master's favour and conscious to
himself of his abusive carriage in England both to Sir Robert Sherley and some
other misdemeanours of his which begot a complaint against him to Shah Abbas and made known by way of Aleppo after his departure out of England, he
gave himself this desperate exit, well knowing that his master was at no time to
be jested with in money matters or business relating to honour and reputation,
so as neither his past service against the Turks, his alliance at court or what else
he could think upon could animate his defence, other men's sufferings upon his
account making his seem less pardonable. For in the year 1612, a Persian ambassador at Constantinople assenting to such articles 'twixt his master and the
Grand Seigneur as seemed advantageous to him, but otherwise to the Persian
and eccentric to his instructions, was upon his return beheaded at Qazvin. The
conditions were indeed dishonourable, as: that the Prince of Persia should assume to himself no other title but Pasha of Tabriz, that the Persians should pay
as a yearly tribute for Gilan 400 bales of silk, that the kadi of Tauris should be
of the Turk's election etc., which demands Abbas spurned back to Ahmet[25] with
indignation. Tahmasp Quli Beg also, it may be, came into his mind, who died
miserably, though once second in Persia, upon spleen ill-grounded by the King,
and of Turkish barbarism not a few examples. That ambassador probably was
first in his memory whom Abbas beheaded at his return from Constantinople for
no other crime then for expressing too humble and submissive behaviour to the
Grand Seigneur, which the Persian thought was an abatement to his grandeur.
The like we have in the Athenians who put Timagoras their ambassador to death
only for reverencing Darius according to the customs of the Persians. Ibrahim
Pasha, Cycalu, Sinon Pasha[26] and Nassus,[27] each of them in their times sitting at
the stern, guiding as they listed the Turkish greatness, yet ere death summoned
them came to miserable ends such as made the remembrance of their past glory

---

India Company. 1638: "the ship he died in."

[25] Ahmet I was Ottoman sultan 1603–1617 and 1622–1623.

[26] Sinan Pasha (d. 1596), governor of Egypt (1569), conquered Yemen (1571) and
defeated Spain at the siege of Tunis the same year. He campaigned against Persia (1580)
and was appointed Grand Vizier by the Ottoman Sultan Murad III (1589). In and out of
office, he was finally disgraced when he suffered defeat in Wallachia.

[27] Herbert is probably referring to the eunuch Narses (478–573), Justinian I's great
general. He defeated the Ostrogoths and the Franks but was dismissed by Justin II under
a cloud of suspicion. In 568 the Lombards invaded the Byzantine Empire and Narses,
then ninety years old, volunteered his services, but they were refused. He was suspected,
probably unjustly, of having encouraged the invasion to get his reputation cleared.

relish the sourer. And as for Naqd Beg, as we after heard the King protest, if he had not thus prevented it, at his coming to court his body should first have been hacked in pieces, and then in the open market-place burnt with dog-turds, such a ceremony as brands the delinquent with shame to posterity, and none more infamous then that mentioned [in] 2 Maccabees 13: 5.[28]

Suwali Road. Surat.

Suwali road is from the Equator 20 degrees and 56 minutes north, has westerly variation 16 degrees and a half, longitude from Mohelia 28 degrees. At a low ebb it resembles an isle beyond the sands of Goga, called Biballa formerly, being easily discovered. The first of December with some *peunes*,[29] or olive-coloured Indian foot-boys who can very prettily speak English, we rode to Surat. Our chariot was drawn by two buffaloes, who by practice are nimble in their trot and well-managed. We passed first through Suwali, then through Batwa,[30] famous for good toddy, and Damka, all which are villages, and after to Surat, the chief factory of the East India merchants, whose President[31] has there his usual residence. At that time one Master Wilde[32] was in that office, an ingenious and civil merchant to whose kind respect I owe acknowledgment, and in whose house ('tis called the English House) we had tidings at that time of Sultan Khurram's[33] coronation at Agra, as I shall speak at large of after we have viewed the town, which challenges a description.

---

[28] 2 Maccabees 13: 4–8 describes the fate of one Menelaus, who urged Antiochus Eupator to attack Judaea (149 B.C.E.), but who was found to be "responsible for all Antiochus's troubles." Menelaus was thrown down the shaft of a tower which was filled with ashes and then refused burial.

[29] Herbert's version of *peon*, a Portuguese word meaning "footman." It came to mean, in India, a messenger, orderly, or even a foot-soldier. *Hobson-Jobson* says that an explanation of it first appeared in a commentary on the *Lusiads* by Manoel Correa, written before 1613, proving that it was already obsolete in Portugal by then (*HJ* 696).

[30] Batwa [*Batty*], now a suburb of Ahmedabad.

[31] Actually, when Herbert arrived, Thomas Kerridge was still the President; Wilde did not succeed him until April 1628.

[32] Richard Wilde or Wylde went to India in 1624 as a factor and served as President at Surat (1628–1630). He seems to have returned home under a cloud, for he was not re-appointed due to possible corruption. In 1655 we find him petitioning Secretary of State Thurloe for a new appointment, which was not granted because of the twenty-year old suspicions. For details see Philip Aubrey, *Mr. Secretary Thurloe, Cromwell's Secretary of State 1652–60* (Athlone: Continuum Books, 1989).

[33] The name of Shah Jahan before he became Mughal Emperor. He was crowned in February 1628; Herbert seems to be confusing Khurram's actual coronation with the proclamation of his accession issued in January. Herbert is still referring to him as Prince Khurram in December 1627 (see below).

Surat is that old *Muniria* in Ptolemy,[34] if my judgment deceive me not, nor am I ignorant that Choul[35] and Onor are imagined it by Moletius[36] and Ramusius;[37] it is a city at this day no less great and rich then populous and famous, albeit neither the air nor soil agree well with strangers, the one being inflamed through the torridness of the zone, the other being sandy and sulphurous. The arctic pole is here elevated 21 degrees, 3 minutes, subject in June to become nadir to the sun; thence to September the clouds shower there continually. An insalubrious moisture, whether occasioned from the Aselli and Prasepe, two stars in Cancer, who have their influence here as noted by Pliny *Lib.* 16 *Cap.* 35, or from some other occult cause, others may enquire into. Yet observed it is that wind and thunder so commix that no place in the world during these months seems more unhealthy, the other eight months either parching or freezing.

Surat is accounted the third best town in the Gujarat Kingdom, Ahmedabad and Cambay having the precedency. From the first she is removed four, from the other, two days' journey, all adding lustre to the Mughal's diadem. Whether Gujarat take name from the Sura,[38] whom Pliny places here, or that it comply with the Greek idiom or be denominate from *gezurat*, which in the Arabic signifies an isle, I question not, but this without doubt, that a province it is so useful to the Mughal as that his annual tribute here amounts, as merchants say, to 150 tons of gold at this day. 'Tis a town of the greatest note and trade in India, which it has

---

[34] The modern city of Surat appears to have been founded, at least according to legend, by a brahmin named Gopi, who built the so-called Gopi Tank in 1516 and called the city Suryapur, which means "City of the Sun," a name which lasted only until 1520, when it became Surat.

[35] Modern-day Chaul, a Konkan seaport mentioned by Ptolemy, who often replaced "ch" in Indian names with "ti" and calls it Timoula. It was under siege twice (1571–1572 and 1594).

[36] Giuseppe Moletti (1531–1588) was an Italian scientist, mapmaker, and mathematician from Messina. He is perhaps best-known for his *Dialogue on Mechanics* (1576), but he also produced an atlas, the *Africa Minor nuova tavola* (1562).

[37] Giambattista Ramusio (1485–1557), a Venetian politician, editor, and diplomat. He was the Italian equivalent of Richard Hakluyt (although not as patriotic), his *Delle navigationi e viaggi* (1550–1556 and reprints to 1613) containing many important accounts of exploration including those of Marco Polo, Magellan, and many other Portuguese navigators, some for the first time appearing in print, covering Africa, America, and Asia. Indeed, Ramusio's work provided "a template that is drawn upon by later creators of compendia such as Richard Hakluyt or Samuel Purchas" (Alam and Subrahmanyam, *Indo-Persian Travels*, 333). Hakluyt himself noted that "John Baptist Ramusius, hee gathered many notable things" (Ramusio, *Navigazioni*, 1: xiv).

[38] The name Gujarat comes from *Gujjar Rashtra*, which means "Gujjar Nation." The origins of the people is obscure and uncertain, with various theories about nomadic tribes and possible Georgian connections amongst them.

acquired but of late, for scarce 100 years ago Antonio de Silveira,[39] a Portuguese, with 200 men entered and burnt it, since when this town is so increased both with building and inhabitants that a far greater force would find it a hard enterprise. After that, *anno Domini* 1566, which is of the Hegira 946, by valour of Azam Khan, who defeated the confederacy of Mirza Khan, Hussein, Mirza Mohammed, Koka Khan and other conspirators, it was made subject to Akbar, the Great Mughal.[40] Now 'tis under a quiet government, watered with a sweet river called Tapti or Tindy,[41] as broad as the Thames at Windsor, which, arising out of the Deccan Mountains, glides through Burhanpur[42] 420 miles distant hence, and in meanders runs by the walls of Surat, and after 20 little miles circumgyring or playing to and fro, a league from Suwali road discharges itself into the ocean. 'Tis circled with a mud wall, and hath a large castle of stone built at the southwest side,[43] the river washing it; planted with great ordnance and awed by a garrison, who make dainty to admit strangers to see their fortifications. The west opens into the bazaar through a fair gate of stone, where toll-gatherers are every day ready to search and exact a customary tribute for the Mughal their master. The *maidan*[44] is of no great beauty, nor do the shops give more then common splendour, the Banian[45] desiring rather to be rich indeed then so accounted. The houses are indifferent beautiful; some, as to the outside, are of carved wood, others of bricks dyed in the sun. The English and Dutch houses at the north end excel all the other for space and furniture. The suburbs have three posterns pointing out three several ways, one to Varia and Cambay,[46] a second to Burhanpur, the

---

[39] Antonio de Silveira also burnt down the city of Bassein (Wasdi) in the Maharashtra area, crossed the river and attacked Bombay (1530). He defended Diu when it was besieged by Turkish forces: "Diu, defended by the strategy / And courage of Antonio de Silveira" (Camoens, *Lusiads* 10. 62).

[40] The city was captured by Akbar's forces in 1573 after a very long siege.

[41] The Tapti [*Tuppee*] river is one of three Indian rivers which run from east to west. It goes from the southern part of what is now Madhya Pradesh to the Gulf of Cambay, about 700 km.

[42] Burhanpur [*Brampore*] was founded in 1400 by the rulers of Khandesh. It was named after the religious leader Hazrat Shah Burhan-ed-din. When Akbar annexed it (1601) it became the administrative centre of the Deccan under Mughal rule until 1635, when Shah Jahan moved the capital to Aurangabad. Akbar erected the Lal Kila Palace there and there is a fine Jami Masjid (Great Mosque) built by Sultan Ali Khan in 1588.

[43] Built by the Portuguese in 1546, the castle is now used for government offices.

[44] Open area or square.

[45] "A Hindu trader, and especially of the province of Gujarat" (*HJ* 63).

[46] Varia or Baria is a city and former princely state in eastern Gujarat. Cambay [*Khambat*]. In Herbert's time this name applied to the whole region as well as to the city, but now denotes the old sea-port of Ahmedabad. Marco Polo mentioned it in 1294, and it may be the place called "Camanes" by Ptolemy. Singh notes that the region was of such

third to Nagsari,[47] ten courses thence, whence is the road to Gandavi, Balsac and Daman upon the ocean.

The town affords no monuments, no mosques worth taking notice of. The English garden without the town has pretty walks and [is] adorned with variety of sweet flowers, but inferior to another I saw there, which, besides the trees and flowers that adorned it, had a delightful prospect. Adjoining Naneery Gate I saw a tank or magazine of water, a very stately work indeed and worthy noting; it is of good free-stone, circling in above 100 sides and angles, 28 ells[48] 'twixt every angle, in compass very near 1000 paces. It diminishes its largeness *gradatim* by 16 degrees or steps towards the bottom, [and] is useful to receive a very great quantity of rain-waters, which many times is of use to quench the flagrant thirst of the sunburned Indians. The river by this seems somewhat unwholesome; if neither good for drink nor navigation, what serves it for save to inundate the idolatrous Banian, who we could observe in great numbers to the waist in water and with lifted-up hands and eyes to attend the sun rising? *"Plures adorant Solem orientem quam occidentem,"*[49] could Tiberius say to Macro, and truly many Sun-idolaters have I seen, all which worship his rise, but none his setting, a form of worship long and much-used in these oriental parts which also crept in amongst the Jews, for we find it reproved by the prophet Ezekiel, Ch. 8 verse 16.[50] Now, saith Lactantius, could but these idolaters fix their mind upon heaven by following the guide of the celestial light which is much more glorious then that of the sun, it would convince them of their fault and without error direct them to the port of everlasting happiness.[51] *"Bonus quidem est Sol in ministerio, non in imperio,"*[52] the sun, saith Ambrose,[53] is a good servant, not a minister.

---

importance that when Elizabeth I sent an embassy to Akbar in 1583 she addressed him as "the King of Cambay" (*Colonial Narratives*, 427).

[47] Nagsari [*Nansacy*], a port on the Arabian Sea.

[48] An English ell was 45 inches.

[49] "More people worship the rising sun rather than the setting sun" (Erasmus, *Adages* 3. 3. 15).

[50] ". . . their backs toward the temple of the Lord, and their faces toward the east, and they worshipped the sun toward the east."

[51] Lactantius, *Institutiones* 6. 8, PL 6. 660.

[52] St. Ambrose, *Hexaemeron* 4. 3. Herbert likely got his quotation from Sir Walter Ralegh, *History of the World* I. 30.

[53] St. Ambrose of Trèves (c. 340–397) was bishop of Milan and the greatest opponent of the Arians, as well as a proponent of the superiority of the ecclesiastical over temporal authority. "He was," Attwater writes, "the first teacher in the West to make extensive use of hymns as a popular means of divine praise and of fostering right belief," and he perhaps wrote the Athanasian Creed (D. Attwater, *The Penguin Dictionary of Saints* [Harmondsworth: Penguin Books, 1984], 41). Ambrose wrote extensively on church doctrine in works such as *De mysteriis*, and his letters are also extant. The *Hexaemeron* deals with the six days of Creation. He also wrote a commentary on *The Song of*

Hindustan, as it is a fruitful soil, so it abounds with people, and that of divers nations and languages, who also in habit, manners and religion differ much. For besides the aborigines of the land, there we find Jews, Persians, Arabians, Armenians, Christians of St. Thomas; Tartarians are now lords, and others, of which the Banians are the greatest for numbers, but the Moors command. They have a peculiar language of their own, but the Persian tongue is understood by those of best rank and is accepted as the most courtly. The Indian Mahometans are a people not less crafty then valiant; those who are swordsmen by profession are most either *Bashoots*[54] or Persians, and delight to go abroad with sword, buckler, bow, arrows and dagger. Their habit is a quilted coat of calico cloth under the left arm, a small shash, small in comparison to that worn by Turks, a turban upon their head, large stockings and sometimes sandals, in an ordinary and effeminate garb thus resembled:

A man and a woman of Industan [illustration not shown]

The other sort of people are merchants, brahmins, gentiles and Parsis, which are the original inhabitants, with whom in order suffer me to tempt your patience. This first remembered, that when any ships ride at Suwali, which is from September to March commonly, the banians all along the seaside pitch their booths and tents and huts of straw in great numbers, resembling a country fair or market, for there they sell calicos, China satin, porcelain-ware, escritoires or cabinets of mother-of-pearl, ebony, ivory, agates, turquoises, heliotropes, carnelians, as also rice, sugar, plantains, arrack etc. There are withal many little boys or peons who, for four pice[55] a day (2 pence of our money) are ready to serve you, either to interpret, run, go errands or the like. These will not eat and drink with a Christian, nor out of the same leaf they drink their toddy. The Banian and other Indian females, after the oriental mode, are seldom visible, for their jealous husbands mew them up, but here we see elephants and horses, but 'twixt Batty and Surat oxen do most labour, for 'twixt towns men usually travel in chariots drawn by oxen, but in towns upon palanquins, and with *sombreros de sol*[56] over them.

The current coins here are *pardaos, mahmoudies, rupees* and *dinars*,[57] heavy round pieces of brass, 30 make our shilling; the mahmoudy and rupee are good

---

Songs in which he argued that this erotic poem was actually an allegory symbolising the union between Christ and the Church, a notion gratefully taken up by many of his successors in theology.

[54] *Bashoots* is a corruption of *bashaw*, itself an Anglicisation of "pasha."

[55] A small copper coin.

[56] Parasols.

[57] *Pardao* was "the popular name among the Portuguese of a gold coin from the native mints of Western India" (*HJ* 672). Its name is a corruption of *varaha*; it was also known as the *pagoda*, which name appears in Varthema and Barbosa. For details see

silver,[58] round, thick and after the Saracen sort, who allow no images, stamped with Arabic letters. A mahmoudy is our shilling, a rupee two shillings and three pence, a partlow four shillings; the dinar is a piece of gold worth 30 shillings, but Spanish reales, pistoles and Persian larrees, abbassis and English gold (each twenty shilling piece in Persia going for twenty-six shillings) are here current. Again, as I have been told by merchants, a hundred thousand rupees makes one lakh, a hundred lakh make one crore, ten crores one areb. Again, in silver, fourteen rupees make a *masse*, 1150 masse make a hundred *toles*,[59] ten toles of silver value one of gold. In brass, thirty *tacks* or *pice* make one rupee in weight, the *batman*[60] is eighty-two pounds English, but fifty-five of their pounds. The *maund* is as much; howbeit, as in Persia, the *man shahi* and *tabriz* differ,[61] as our Troy and Avoirdupois, so in all parts of the world where wealth and traffic is are such distinguishments.

Banians.

In a word the Banians, as crafty, the proverb goes, as the devil, by a moderate outside and excess in superstition make many simple men lose themselves, when by a heedless admiration of their hypocrisy they entangle themselves by crediting their figured words in way of trade or compliment, baits pleasingly swallowed when one contemplates their moral temperance. They are generally good arithmeticians, till of late have little else then number of the mathematics save in the

---

H. W. Codrington, *Ceylon Coins and Currency* (New Delhi: Asia Educational Services, 1994), 91–93. The *mahmoudy* is a coin worth ½ rupee, named for Mahmoud Shah III, ruler of Gujarat 1536–1553. In 1612 it was worth 9d. and by Herbert's time its worth had climbed to 1/-. By *dinar*, according to Foster, "Herbert means . . . the gold mohur" (*Herbert* 304), a coin introduced by Sher Shah Suri (1540–1545) and weighing 169 grains. See also *HJ* 672–78.

[58] "Good silver." A rupee of Akbar contained 174.5 grains of pure silver, divided into 40 dams or pusas of 191.5 grains of copper each. A shilling of Elizabeth I contained 88.8 grains of pure silver. For details see Count Wielhorski's note in his translation of Afanasy Nikitin's voyage to India (*Voyage*, 14, n. 40).

[59] Actually, 12 *mashas* (Herbert's *masse*) make one *tola* (Herbert's *toll*). For further details and definitions, see *HJ* 928. Foster says that Herbert "has here been misled by de Laet" (*Herbert*, 304), who in Chapter VI discusses money, weights and measures. Banerjee concludes his lengthy note (*Empire*, 104–6) by stating that he does not know "what De Laet means when he says . . . that a *masha* was 14 rupees" (106).

[60] The *batman* was "a Turkish weight, often employed by writers of the time as another name for the Indian maund" (Foster, *Herbert*, 304).

[61] The *maund*, modern *man*, varies in its weight depending on the area where it is used. The "*tabrizi man*" is "a little less than 7 lbs" (*HJ* 564). All the details on this measure may be found in *HJ* 563–65 and Banerjee's note (*Empire*, 105). The *man shahi* is the King's maund or royal maund (Foster, *Herbert*, 304).

art of dialling, concerning which some report that the Banians here had a clock that struck 64 times in 24 hours. The day and night they divide into 4 and subdivide that into 8, and some little skill they have in navigation. And, saith Seneca, *"quid enim aliud est Natura quam Deus,"*[62] reason to the natural man being the face of God, as was the law unto the Jews and gospel to the Christians.

The Banians or Vanyans are alabaster, or of a tawny complexion, for the most part spare of body. They let their hair grow long and yet, according to the country mode, their head is wreathed with a full sash, which usually is white. Their habit is a long coat commonly of white quilted calico of the Dalmatic sort, their shoes various in colour and fashion, some being checkered and ingraled in elegant order, wrought according to each man's ingenious fancy, without latchets, sharp and turning up at the toe, thin-soled, high-heeled, surrounded with steel, fast and durable. The women are of a whiter colour then the men, not exposing themselves to the sun, yet want the sanguine mixture to adorn them, which they nevertheless supply by art, there being found the best vermilion. They likewise wear their hair long and dishevelled, albeit part be obscured by a fine thin lawn through whose transparency it seems more lovely. Their ears, noses, arms, and legs are loaden with many *manilios*[63] or voluntary rings and fetters of brass, gold, and ivory. Their behaviour is silently modest, but full-gorged, as some say, with libidinous fantasies. Marriage here is so honoured that most times they contract at seven, and at ten years old are often parents, which puts me in mind of that which Pliny in his 6 and 8 *Lib*. Ch. 17 and 14 writes concerning the Kalinga,[64] whom he places hereabouts and would have us believe that the women are pregnant at five and seldom live above eight. But this is certain, that if an infant dies ere he be married, his parents procure a virgin, to whom they they give some dinars of gold, to be his bed-fellow or wife for one night, to avoid this reproachful proverb, "that he died unmarried."

---

[62] "For what is Nature, if not God?" (Seneca, *De beneficiis* 4. 7).

[63] A Portuguese word meaning 'bracelet.'

[64] Kalinga was "a very ancient name for the region known as the Northern Circars, i.e. the Telugu coast of the Bay of Bengal . . . The Kalingas also appear frequently, after the Puranic fashion, as an ethnic name in the old Sanskrit list of races" (*HJ* 486). Herbert's reference to Pliny is partly correct; the word (Pliny writes *Calingae*) may be found in *Natural History* 6. 18, 19, 20.

An Indyan Marchant or Bannyan:

An Indian merchant [illustration above]

Polygamy here is odious, in which respect they cease not to vilify the Mahometans as people of an impure soul. In this they parallel the antique Romans
who, as Tacitus, Marcellinus[65] and Tertullian tell us, so hated digamy[66] (both
in enjoying two wives at one time and being twice-married) as no holocaust[67]
was ever offered, no holy fire looked into by such, nor such as issued from such

---

[65] Ammianus Marcellinus (c. 330–400), a soldier, was the last great pagan historian. He was a partisan of the Emperor Julian, whom he accompanied on his campaign
against the Persians. His book was first printed in 1474, and there was a distinguished
English translation by Philemon Holland (1609) available to Herbert. Modern scholars
state that early editions of Ammianus were based on corrupt manuscript sources. His
Later Roman Empire has been edited and translated by Walter Hamilton (Harmondsworth: Penguin Books, 1986).

[66] Remarriage after death or divorce.

[67] Here, an offering of fire.

parents. Their funerals are of the old stamp, recorded by Curtius,[68] sacring the corpse to ashes in a holy fire compounded of all sorts of costly woods and aromatic spices; the wife also, in expectation to enjoy her husband 'mongst incomparable pleasures, envelops her dainty body with the merciless flames, for which affection she obtains a living memory.

Banians' Religion. [69]

Their priests, called *Bramyni* or *Brachmani*,[70] are such as in old times were named *gymnosophi*, as saith Porphyry the great Platonist[71] in his 4 Lib. *De abstinentia ab esu carnium*, and Tertullian *Adversus gentes*, "*Neque enim Brachmanae, aut Indorum*

---

[68] Quintus Curtius Rufus (d. 53), Roman soldier, historian, and proconsul of Africa. He wrote *The History of Alexander*, which contains information not found in Arrian and others. His propensity for drawing morals and including impressive speeches makes him sometimes comparable to Livy. Tacitus wrote about him in the *Annals* (11.21). The *History* was first edited by Vindalinus (1471); Herbert may have known the edition of Johann Freinsheim (1640), which he probably used here; Michel Le Tellier's 1678 edition is too late. A good modern translation is that of John Yardley (Harmondsworth: Penguin Books, 1984).

[69] Herbert's knowledge of this, as he acknowledges later on, owes much to Henry Lord's account of Hinduism, *A display of two foreign Sects in the East Indies.* Lord's account is riddled with inaccuracies, and he often mixes Hinduism with Jainism, an observation made by Dr. Klaus Klostermaier, Emeritus Professor of Religion at the University of Manitoba, Winnipeg, Canada. Insofar as I can, I have attempted to sort some of this out, but even with expert assistance it was not possible, and rather than cause more confusion I have decided to leave some of the material as I found it. Further details of Lord's book may be found in the Introduction. From what I can understand, much of Lord's and Herbert's knowledge is based on an account which they received of the *Puranas*, "a vast body of complex narratives which contains genealogies of deities and kings up to the Guptas, cosmologies, law-codes and descriptions of ritual and pilgrimages to holy places" (Flood, *Introduction*, 109).

[70] "Brachman" was the acceptable form of "Brahmin" until at least the eighteenth century (for details see *HJ* 111–12), derived from the Greek found in writers like Strabo, who frequently quotes older authorities. As Herbert's source for this information is Henry Lord (see above), the particular brahmins consulted here were, as Lach and Van Kley suggest, probably Nagars (3: 645). They sometimes claim Aryan or even Greek origins (which no doubt appealed to Westerners) and had come to Gujarat from Sind in the early fifth century C.E. Nagar brahmins are supposed to be exceptionally well versed in the interpretation of the Vedas, Puranas, and Brahmanas, although modern scholars have questioned both the accuracy of the information they gave Lord and his interpretation of what they told him.

[71] Porphyry (c. 232–305) is known mainly as a disciple of Plotinus and the editor of the latter's great Neo-Platonist treatise the *Enneads*. He himself wrote a work on theurgic practices, which Herbert cites here, but only fragments survive. His first Renaissance editor was Marsilio Ficino.

gymnosophistae sumus silvicolae,"[72] a name given them from their going naked, for *gymno* is "naked."[73] Now if by descent he continued constant to his contemplation he then attained to the degree or title of a Brachman; if he sought this degree by election he was for seven years, says Bardesanes of Babylon,[74] styled *kalyana* and *samana*,[75] and after that by other attribute Brachman, who with the Stoics held that God is *Anima mundi*, albeit Plato and Socrates could have taught them that "*Deus non solum est mens mundi*," but that "*Deus universa complet*,"[76] and Virgil that "*Deum ire per omnes terrasque tractusque maris caelumque profundum*."[77] Of all sorts of philosophers they were held the most learned and contemplative. Tertullian calls them "*gloriae animalia*;"[78] Apollonius supposes they were and were not earthly, their thoughts being so transcendent as if they were ravished by the sweetness of that harmony the rolling orbs in an exact diapason send forth by their forced motion. Their imagination flew beyond nature, believing that this fabric of the inferior world was created of nothing, made spherical, yet subject to dissolution; that it had an efficient cause, being unable to form itself, and that that cause is the commander of nature; that number is the first and most essential element in the constitution of all creatures, our birth to be no other then a quick conception perfected by death, which is the true nativity of the soul and entrance to immortality, a tenet, however, opposed by the Stoics, yet by these banians from the tradition of the phoenix, observation of corn, and the like, so resolutely maintained that from hence arose the magnanimity of Calanus the Brahmin,[79]

---

[72] This quote from Tertullian should read: "*neque enim brachmanae aut Indorum gymnosophistae sumus silvicolae et exsules vitae*," which means "We are neither brahmins nor gymnosophists of India, who live in the woods cut off from life" (Tertullian, *Adversus gentes* 429).

[73] Herbert has mixed up the brahmins with the "sky-clad" Jains, whose ascetics often dispensed with clothing.

[74] Bardesanes, actually Bar Daisan (154–222) was a Syrian poet, historian, and astronomer. In addition to a number of Gnostic hymns, he wrote a history of Armenia and the *Book of the Laws of the Countries* (modern edition by T. Krannich and P. Stein [Berlin: De Gruyter, 1979]). He was quoted by Eusebius, Stobaeus, and Porphyry.

[75] The word *kalyana* means 'beautiful'; it was also an epithet applied to some of the disciples of Buddha. A *samana* is an itinerant ascetic; the most famous one was Buddha himself. Herbert seems to be confusing Hinduism and Buddhism at this point. For the brahman called Kalyana, see note below.

[76] God is not just the mind of the universe; he fills all things.

[77] God permeates through all lands, all the extent of the sea, and the highest heaven.

[78] Creatures of glory.

[79] Kalyana of Taxila [*Calanus*] (c. 408–334 B.C.E.) was a gymnosophist who attached himself to Alexander the Great and committed suicide when he became critically ill. He is mentioned by several of Herbert's sources, including Onesicritus, Arrian, and Megasthenes in his *Indica*. See J. W. McCrindle, *Ancient India as Described by Megasthenes*

who at Pasagardae[80] in Alexander's sight voluntarily committed himself to the fire to become immortal, as Lucan *Lib.* 3, "Who whiles alive, their funeral piles erect,/And leap into the fire helping death to effect / The close of life."[81] These, from the adoration they at the least pretended to make, would with fixed and unwearied eyes all the day gaze upon the sun, during which they would with their naked feet endure the scalding sands, the like of which I beheld at Surat, neither extreme heat nor cold amazing them. Alexander, visiting Calanus, the brahmin who burnt himself in the monarch's view in token his contempt of death and certainly a transmigration or shadowed immortality, and telling him and others of his opinion that he would grant them whatever they crave, they answered "Give us immortality, for of all things 'tis that we covet most." "How can I," replied Alexander, "do that, who am mortal?" "Seeing thou acknowledgest thyself to be a man," say they, "why dost thou not then rather choose to live contentedly at home then by an unbounded avarice thus to put the whole world into a combustion?" But to return.

The banian religion at this day hath these tenets: the whole frame or body of the world had a beginning, created by a God of immense power, eternal and provident; after he had made man, to associate him he created woman to to sympathise in similitude of body and disposition. These he named Purusha and Prakriti,[82] a couple so innocent that they reputed it a crime to cut anything that had a sensitive life, feeding only upon herbs and fruits and the like vegetables, therein agreeing with those who imagine Adam having the liberty to live upon herbs and fruit. The killing of any creature for food was not used till after the flood; Noah indeed was in express terms not only licensed herbs and fruit, but everything that moveth and liveth was allowed him for food, Genesis 1: 20 and 9: 3.

---

and Arrian (Bombay: Thacker and Spink, 1877) or, more recently, Richard Stoneman, "The Brahmans in the Alexander Historians and the Alexander Romance," *Journal of Hellenic Studies* 115 (1995): 99–114.

[80] For Pasagardae, see Arrian, 3.18.10; Q. Curtius Rufus, 5.6.10; 10.1.22. It was a city founded by Cyrus the Great and surrendered to Alexander. Herbert will describe it in more detail later.

[81] Lucan, *Civil War* 3.240–241.

[82] Purusha and Prakriti [*Porous* and *Parcouty*]. In the *Rig-Veda* (10.90; 10, 129–30) Purusha is "cosmic man," with a thousand heads, eyes, and feet. He generated a female principle, Viraj (later replaced by Prakriti, see below), from which he was reborn when he was sacrificed by the gods, after which the world is made out of his parts. The castes or varna are part of this creation. Purusha became one of the names of Brahma. However, Herbert, following Lord, conflates this version with that given in the Sankhya system of Hinduism, founded by the semi-legendary Kapila but articulated by Ishvara Krishna in the *Sankhya Karika* (c. 200 B.C.E.). Here Purusha (Shiva), the male principle, represents pure consciousness and is eternal and unchanging; Prakriti (Shakti), the female principle, is primal nature and the material world. In Vaisnavism (worship of Vishnu) Purusha is an emanation of Vishnu-Narayana (Klostermeier, *Hinduism*, 90).

From this abstemious couple sprang two couples of boys, the emblems of the four complexions: *Brammon, Kshatriya, Sudra* and *Wise,*[83] of different constitutions, for Brahman was melancholy, Kshatriya choleric, Sudra phlegmatic and Vaisya sanguine, each of which affected a several calling, the first being a priest, the second a warrior, the third a merchant, the last a peasant.[84]

Brahman the priest, from whom the Brahmin have their title,[85] and not from Abram who taught astronomy and from Keturah, as Postellius[86] thinketh, was directed, says their *Shastra*[87] or book of laws, to travel east to find a wife, it being revealed to him that God had formed four women for him and his brethren on whom to propagate, for the reason they had no sisters to generate upon was because so holy a race should not descend from incest. After a long pilgrimage and prayer he espies his long looked-for virgin, clothed with naked innocence; her face was yellow like gold, her hair and eyes black. Of a complete nature she was, and whom without much courting Brahman wooed and married; this Lady

---

[83] The four castes (in Herbert's incorrect order) are: *brahmins* (priests), *kshatriyas* (soldiers, rulers), *sudras* (labourers, servants, farm-workers or serfs), and *vaisyas* (traders, shopkeepers, craftsmen, common people). Herbert does not mention the "casteless caste" or untouchables. The castes sprang from the dismemberment of Purusha; the brahmins from his mouth, the kshatriyas from his arms, the vaisyas from his thighs, and the sudras from his feet. The banians, of course, are vaisyas, the third caste, not the lowest. The spelling will be normalised from now on. The stories about how the four brothers met their wives are described by Lach and Van Kley as "romantic and fanciful" (3: 647), and are lifted here from Henry Lord's book (see below). They, and many other passages from Lord (or perhaps from Herbert as well as others), show up in Richard Head's satirical work *The English Rogue Described in the Life of Meriton Latroon, a Witty Extravagant, being a Complete History of the Most Eminent Cheats of Both Sexes* (1665). Head (c. 1637–1686) was a dramatist and hack poet who managed to get himself out of debt with this book, which reads like a seventeenth-century version of Mandeville, only much funnier. See Head, *English Rogue*, 278–281.

[84] Herbert has the order of the last two castes reversed, and appears to keep it that way in his discussion of them later on.

[85] Herbert is too quick to collate etymologies; he may be confusing Brahma (the creator-god) with Brahman (the soul of the universe, also personified as Ishvara or Bhagavan) and Brahmin (the priestly class). They are related, but they are not quite the same. Brahma is in every being, but at the same time he is every being.

[86] Guilaume Postel (1510–1581) was a French diplomat, astronomer, and linguist. He believed that all the major religions stemmed from the same foundation, but that Christianity contained the best parts of them all, so it would be rational if everyone became Christian. His translations of the seminal Hebrew texts, the *Zohar* and the *Kabbalah* (1552), actually predated their first appearance in Hebrew!

[87] The Hindu laws or scriptures are known as *shastra*. The word means "doctrine, treatise, authoritative teaching" (Klostermeier, *Hinduism*, 303). It is a shortened form of *Dharmashastra*, also known as the *Dharmasutras*. The other famous book of laws is the *Laws of Manu*.

Savitri[88] proved the mother of a holy generation. Kshatriya went west to find his mate, his sword in his hand, habited after his nature, all the while fretting for want of resistance and that his patience was so long trod upon. At length he espies afar off one coming towards him equally inflamed with impatience. Without compliment they forthwith assailed each other with such fury and so much bravery that the first day's fight the victory was not to be decided. Next day they renew their courage, giving and receiving wounds insensibly, till in conclusion Kshatriya grappled and seized Toddicastree by the tresses of her hair, but instead of subjecting her is, by the fresh outbreak of her beauty, captivated. Yet, after submission and repentance for his rage against such an earthly angel, she is reconciled, and from them the west swarmed with a generation of radies or soldiers.

Sudra, the third son of Porous and Parcouty, travels north, in equal hope to find his mistress. Far he went, and many strange adventures passed through and saw, witness that rock of diamonds he light on, many of which, as any other merchant would, he carried along with him, till at last he met with Visagundah, whom he won, being of a tractable sweet nature and condition, and on her begat so many sons that the north quickly became pregnant and inhabited.

Now Vaisya, the simplest of Purusha's sons, a man of much plain honesty and comportment, goes southward, having strange intelligence that his female was thereabouts, whom, after he had passed seven seas (the breadth and way is concealed in the *Shastra*) and built him a fair mansion, whither Jejunnogundah came to admire so rare a structure. Whom he soon saw, but not knowing how to court her, is o'ercome with Love's passion, so as long time he is rejected till, by providence, she is mollified and made to yield, upon condition that he should build many pagodas or idols for worship, and adore pictures under green trees and arbours, which to this day his posterity observe ceremoniously. Thus from these two the south was filled with mechanic men and such as practice husbandry.

When these four youths had consumed some years in these contrary quarters of the world whither Fate had directed them, all four became equally mindful of their first home and desirous to visit their parents, not only to propagate there also and furnish that meditullium[89] of the earth but to recount their memorable fortunes and adventures. After much circumstance and toil, they arrived at the place from whence they came, each of them attended by a troop of their own offspring. 'Tis too great a labour to decipher the joy and mutual embraces that passed 'twixt them and their aged parents, revived by this good hap from the benumbing frost of old age, as also the reciprocal kindness and love that was amongst the four travellers; a dull sense may easily comprehend it was without the least mixture of discontent or malady.

---

[88] Savitri [*Savatree*], the daughter of the sun, who represents the sun at dawn or sunset (Flood, *Introduction*, 47).

[89] Pith or matrix.

Notwithstanding, to show no *summum bonum* can be had in this life, in process of time the issue of these four multiplying, the world began to lose her virgin purity, discord, pride, and rapine mingling amongst them so as brotherly love was laid aside, no appearance now but of violence and voluptuousness. For Brahman grows idle and careless in his devotion, Kshatriya becomes insolent and aspiring, regarding neither the venerable admonition of his parents nor the dignity of Brahman, his eldest brother. Sudra also invents deceit, not regarding justice and equity but delights in cheating his either brethren. Vaisya also grows unthrift, in a good conscience banishing his innate honesty to entertain riot, for which his cruel brother Kshatriya dominates, imposing such burthens upon the countryman that Vaisya is now the object of cashiered riot and the abject of his lordly brother, who also picks a quarrel with Sudra and admits not of any reconciliation till the poor merchant had satisfied his avarice with half his store, so that such hate and fear grew amongst 'em that all their designs were involved in dark confusion.

Now though deceit, riot and tyranny sway awhile, an all-seeing Majesty sits above, who in his own time retaliates in the extremity of justice. So it now happened, for upon a sudden, when they were most exercised in villainy and least dream of an account, God robes himself with clouds and flashes terror, whereat the seas multiply their noise and swell so formidably that they threaten an universal deluge. In the interim, the people were amazed with horrible cracks of thunder and such thick flashes of lightning that the entrails of the earth seem to gasp and quake with terror, which done, in a moment the sea breaks o'er her bounds and in silence sweeps away all creatures upon the earth, purging thereby the nasty smell of their pollution. But God,[90] who delights in mercy, his great attribute, repenting him of his severity, resolves again to furnish the earth with a new generation replete with more purity and perfection. To which end he descends, and upon the high mountains called Meropurbates[91] he commands Brahma to rise up, who, though till then uncreated, obeyed, and forthwith worshipped his Maker. In like sort, at two other calls, came up[92] who performed their obeisance.

---

[90] It is not clear which deity Herbert means here; perhaps it is Indra, who has sometimes been identified by scholars with Zeus or Jupiter because his origins are so ancient and he was associated with the sky. Herbert's attempts to make Hindu mythology intelligible to his readers often results in a confusion of Hindu sources.

[91] This is Mount Meru, "the golden mountain, the great central mountain of the world, the navel of the earth, adorned by three luminous peaks" (J. Knappen, *Indian Mythology* [London: Diamond Books, 1995], 171). It is the Hindu equivalent of Mount Olympus, where the gods live, and their abode was established there by Indra. In Puranic cosmology, the universe spreads out from it in "an array of concentric circles . . . enclosed within the vast 'world-egg'" (Flood, *Introduction*, 112).

[92] Brahma [*Bremaw*] and Vishnu [*Vistney*] are familiar, but Rudra [*Ruddery*] is usually replaced by Shiva. However, Rudra was originally "the howling, roaring one," the

Brahma had power given him to create other creatures, Vishnu had order to preserve them, and Rudra strength to massacre and be God's executioner by inflicting death, plague, famine, war, diseases and the like mischiefs.

According to this appointment these three new-created lords manage their particular employment, to each of them a set time being allotted to live upon earth, for Brahma at the end of the second age in a fiery chariot was translated, Vishnu continues double his time and then dies, leaving the issue to Rudra, at the end of three times so long commonance to destroy the world and to translate the souls of good men into a garden of ravishing delights, an Elysium. But ere this was accomplished, it is fit to acquaint you how Brahma came to furnish the earth with more inhabitants. The *Shastra* tells us that as Brahma was ruminating how to act, suddenly he fell into a deep sleep or trance, and upon recovery felt his body troubled beyond measure, purporting some immediate alteration. Nor did his apprehension deceive him, for lo, forthwith his body began to swell, yea, so great anguish to afflict him that in all points resembled a woman's travail. His bowels began to extend more and more and his dolour to increase, till after great toil the second swelling found vent, broke, and delivered their burthen, being two twins of each sex, whom he needed not give suck to in that by like miracle they immediately grew up to a perfect stature and were miraculously furnished with language and education. Brahma the parent named them Manu[93] and Satarupa[94] whom, after he had blessed, he sent east to the great mountain Mounderpurvool, where straightway Satarupa brought forth three more sons and as many daughters. The boys she called Priya-Vrata, Utanappada, and Soomeraus, the girls Kamya, Sandhya and Shambu.[95] The eldest son went west to a mountain called Segun, the two seconds north to Bipola, the two last of each sex to Supar,

---

Lord of Time and Death. Sometimes his name is joined with that of Shiva, "a name which originally meant 'friendly'" so that they balance out and they are "often invoked jointly as Rudra-Shiva" (Knappert, *Mythology*, 210). In the *Dharmasutras* he is a storm-god, his usual function in Hindu mythology.

[93] Manu [*Manaw*], the name of seven "patriarchs" who ruled the earth during periods called manavantaras. This first Manu, who came out of Brahma, was also known as Svayam-bhuva, which means "he who exists out of his own power." Manu is also the name of the first man "who plays a central role in the Indian myth of the flood" (P. Olivelle, trans. *The Dharmasutras* [Oxford: Oxford University Press, 1999], 345).

[94] Satarupa or Shata-Rupa [*Ceteroupa*]. Brahma made her from himself and then fell in love with her. She hid from Brahma behind his elbow, behind his back, and then behind his right side, but he grew extra heads so he could find her. When she tried flying to heaven he grew a head that pointed upwards. His persistence paid off and she married him. If Herbert had known the full story, he would not have claimed that Brahma wooed her without any trouble! Later she became identified with Saraswati.

[95] Shambu may refer to either Shiva or Parvati, depending on whether the *u* is long or short, but the context certainly suggests Parvati. I am indebted to Dr. Klaus Klostermaier for this observation.

where they so generated that they quickly peopled each their quarter. Which done, God, perceiving the hearts of men inclined to all sorts of vileness, to give them directions how to live virtuously and avoid temptation, he left heaven for a while, and, alighting on the high Mount Meru, thither he called Brahma, to whom he spoke many things out of a dusky dark cloud, now and then flashing glimpses of his majesty, acquainting him why he destroyed the first world, their sins provoking him, and how desirous he was never to do so again, and to that end delivered Brahma a book, the *Shastra* by name, divided into three tracts dedicated to the great castes, the first containing moral precepts, the second the ceremonies of worship, the third a division of them into three, with peculiar instructions to each caste or tribe.

Their moral law, read and taught them by Brahma out of the *Shastra*, has eight commandments, most of which agree with the seven which Rabbi Solomon[96] says Noah taught the world in his time, called the Noahide.[97]

1. Thou shalt not destroy any living creature, for thou and it are both my creatures.[98]

2. Thou shalt not sin in any of thy five senses, thy eyes not beholding vanity, thy ears to be stopped in hearing evil, thy tongue not to utter any filthiness, thy palate hating wine, flesh and other vile things, thy hands abhorring things defiled.

3. Thou shalt duly perform set times of devotion, as praying, washing, elevating, prostrating etc.

4. Thou shalt not lie or dissemble.

5. Thou shalt not be hard-hearted, but helpful unto others.

6. Thou shalt not oppress or tyrannise.

7. Thou shalt observe certain festivals and fasting-days.

8. Thou shalt not steal.

These eight principles are divided into four, each of the four old castes retaining them. Brahman and Kshatriya, i.e. the brahmins and banians, are tied to a most severe and strict observance in the decorum of their worship. Sudra and

---

[96] Rabbi Solomon Luria (1510–1574) was known as the Maharshal, after the initials of his full name, which was Morenu ha-Rav Shlomo Luria. He was the author of two celebrated works on the Talmud, the *Yam Shel Shlomo* and the *Chochmot Shlomo*, a gloss that is printed with most editions of the Talmud.

[97] The Noahide Laws [*Noaheady*] were seven laws which the Talmud says were handed down by God to Noah. They prohibit idolatry, murder, theft, promiscuity, blasphemy, cruelty to animals, and unjust laws. Their present-day adherents are known as the B'nai Noah.

[98] This is an example of a Jain or even a Buddhist belief rather than a Hindu one; it is the doctrine of *ahimsa*, respect for all living creatures.

Vaisya, i.e. the justice and labourer, agree in theirs, from whence it comes to pass that the priests and merchants, appropriating the first and second to themselves, are more superstitious then the castes of soldiers and mechanics, who assume a liberty of meats and wine in variety. Notwithstanding, all of them believe the metempsychosis of Pythagoras, whose conceits we will parallel by and by with these banians, in this place drawing your judgment to a remembrance of what is already related, wherein we may perceive the delusion Satan charms them with, whose custom it hath ever been to erect to himself worship and idolatry, in some things to make them more authentical cohering with the story of our Bible and in imitation of the Jews. Now that this *Shastra* of the banians is a depraved story of the Bible, either introduced by some Jews [at] such time as Solomon traded to Ophir, near these parts, or from the Father of Lies, who usually dictates to his servants, is plain. For, speaking of the creation of the world out of a chaos and forming of Purusha and Prakriti successively, who sees not the alluding to Adam and Eve in this resemblance, like Ovid and Plato, borrowed from the first book of Moses his Pentateuch, which sacred penman lived *anno mundi* 2430 before the Incarnation about 1490 years, and is found to be more ancient in time then the very first of any of the heathen deities. The other of the creation, delivered by Moses, shadowed in it, the universal deluge and destruction of mankind pointing out that of Noah, by Brahma's receiving the law from God in a dark cloud and lightning upon the high Mount Meru, Moses his being on Mount Sinai where the Decalogue was given, and in Brahma's departure from earth to heaven the translation of Elias.[99]

The banians are commanded, as in most hot countries in all other pagan religions is observed, to wash often, first daubing their naked bodies with dirt and mud, the emblem of sin, the, diving three times in the water, their faces turned to the east, shaking a few grains of rice as a thanksgiving to that element for purging them. "*Baniani e lecto surgentes ad orientalem solem se convertunt et iunctis manibus orent,*"[100] is observed by Pope Pius II. A threefold ducking and tripartite thread is hung at three holes in a stone about the neck, the rice fixed each morn in an unguent of red paint, besmearing the forehead with a little white or yellow sauders tempered with water, which probably was an old practice amongst the heathen, and is with them a symbol of baptism and signifies fruitfulness. Their turning to the east in memory of judgment and creation and to adore the sun and Moon, in that they take them to be God's eyes, "*Sol omnia videns oculis delectabilis,*"[101] is full of purity, heat, and nurture. But this their attending the

---

[99] Elijah. The account may be read in 2 Kings 2: 8–12. Note how Herbert (and Lord, his source) go to great pains to derive Hindu theology from Judaism and hence, like the Quran later on, turn it into a "corrupted" version.

[100] When the banians get out of bed they turn themselves to the east and pray with joined hands.

[101] The beloved sun, seeing everything with its eyes.

blushing Sun at his arising, the elevation of their hands, murmurs, plashing the water in magic order, diving, writhing and acting other fopperies, albeit we can with Solomon say "It is a pleasant thing to behold the sun,"[102] yet in this their view, hear them condemned by a neighbour of theirs, Job the patient Edomite: "If I beheld the sun when it shined, or the Moon walking in brightness, and my heart hath been secretly enticed or my mouth hath kissed my hand, this also were an iniquity to be punished by the Judge, for I should thereby have denied the God which is above."[103] And by the Psalmist: "if we have forgotten the name of our God and holden up our hands to any strange god, shall not God, who knows the secrets of the heart, search it out?"[104] And by Ezekiel, Chap. 8 verse 20, "The House of Judah for this kind of idolatry was reproved."

Above all, their idolatry to pagodas[105] or images of deformed demons is observable; placed these idols are in chapels commonly-built under the banyan trees, or that which Linschoten[106] called *arbor de rayes*, or tree of roots, Sir Walter Ralegh *ficus indicus*,[107] like that which Cardano[108] calls *ceiba* growing in the West Indies, or that the Spaniards call *gorda*, a tree of such repute amongst 'em that they hold it impiety to abuse it either in breaking a branch or otherwise defacing it, but contrarily they adorn it with streamers of silk and ribbons of all sorts

---

[102] Ecclesiastes 11: 7.

[103] Job 31: 26–28.

[104] Psalms 44: 20–21.

[105] According to *Hobson-Jobson*, the word "pagoda" can mean not simply the place where images are kept, but the image itself (654). Yule and Burnell derive the term from *bhagavat*, "holy," and cite Linschoten (see below) as calling pagodas "houses of divels" in 1598 (*HJ* 656). Ralph Fitch mentions them in his *Voyage to Goa and Siam* (1591) [see Hakluyt, *Voyages*, 259]. Herbert uses the word in both senses.

[106] Jan Huyghen van Linschoten (1563–1611), a Dutch merchant and explorer, arrived in Goa (1583). When he returned to Holland in 1592, having been attacked by English pirates and shipwrecked, he "devoted himself to the task of persuading his fellow-countrymen to send ships to the East, particularly to those regions such as the Malay Archipelago, where the position of the Portuguese was weak" (Foster, *England's Quest* 143). He was one of the first Europeans to go to Laos. His *Itinerarie Voyage after Schipvaert van Jan Huyghen van Linschoten* (1598) appeared in English the same year as *John Hvighen van Linschoten, his Discourse of Voyages into ye Easte and Weste Indies*. A. C. Burnell and P. Tiele edited it for the Hakluyt Society (London, 1885).

[107] Now usually known as *ficus bengalensis*, the Bengal fig-tree.

[108] Girolamo Cardano (1501–1576), doctor, mathematician, psychologist, and gambler, was one of the great Renaissance eccentrics, a man who (usually on purpose) managed to annoy practically everyone he knew. His *Ars magna* (1545) was a treatise on mathematics, and he wrote several works on natural history, including *De varietate rerum* (1559), to which Herbert is probably alluding here. Cardano is now known for his *Liber de ludo aleae*, a work on chance and gambling, but this was not published until 1663. His autobiography *De vita propria* (1576) is also well known. See N. Siraisi, *The Clock and the Mirror: Cardano and Renaissance Medicine* (Princeton: Princeton University Press, 2005).

of colours. The pagodas are of sundry resemblances, in such shape as Satan visibly appears unto them, as Sedulius,[109] Lib. 4 *Carm.* says well, *". . . imagina falsa / Visibus humanis magicas tribuere figuras."* Ugly-faced they are, with long black hair, goggle-eyes, wide-mouthed with forked beards, every way so misshapen and horrible as somewhat resembles the old obscene forms of Pan and Priapus.

Under these trees they actuate their idolatrous devotions; there they pay their tithes and offerings, receive the unction and sprinklings of sundry-coloured powders. There they perform their ceremonies, notice being given by the sound of a little bell. There they repeat their orisons, make processions, sing and perform many mysteries; yea, so numerous grew their idol-temples that, till the Mussulman mixed among them each village had its several pagodas, many of which to this day are standing. One of the chief in Industan was that at Varia near Surat, another at Nigracut, where the Dewry[110] is sealed and paved with gold, yearly visited by many thousands of banians, who in way of devotion have used to cut out part of their tongues as a sacrifice, and whereby to speak the sibboleth better thereafter. Others of repute were at Benares upon Ganges, at Echapore,[111] at Javalmukhi,[112] Elabas, Sibah[113] and other places. Part of their religion consists in invoking holy men famoused for virtue; howbeit the cow is not of least esteem with them, if not worshipped. They have the Cyrenian or Egyptian goddess for an example, the image of a cow, and signified the tillage that preserved them by Serapis, i.e. Joseph's prudence, from that memorable famine mentioned in Genesis. In wars the kshatriyas or *radhyas*[114] call only on Bhagavan,[115] the rich upon Maheshvara,[116] the poor upon Syer, the labourers upon Gunner,[117] the

---

[109] Caelius Sedulius (fifth century C.E.) was a Christian poet whose origins are sometimes thought to have been Irish. He wrote the *Carmen paschale*, which is the work cited here. It is a meditation on sacred writings, Book 1 on the Old Testament, Books 2–5 on the New Testament. Sedulius was an imitator of Virgil, employing a great deal of allegory and symbolism (see R. P. H. Green, *Latin Epics of the New Testament* [Oxford: Oxford University Press, 2006], 135–250). The *Carmen paschale* was first printed in 1499. The quotation reads "by false representation / To human faces and forms they attribute magical appearances."

[110] Devi [*Dewry*], a goddess; the word is the feminine form of *deva*.

[111] Perhaps Ishapur, a village just outside modern-day Calcutta.

[112] Jvalamukhi [*Jallamexa*] is "a renowned place of pilgrimage, north of the Punjab, where fire issues from the earth. It is the fire in which Sati, consort of Siva, is said to have burnt herself" (Banerji, 480).

[113] Sipra, a river in Gwalior. "Every mile of it is marked by holy spots" (Banerji 495).

[114] The road-guardians.

[115] Bhagavan [*Bemohan*], the Lord, a general term for God.

[116] Maheshvara [*Mycassar*], a name for Shiva.

[117] *Syer* is probably *Seyyon*, which means "red" and denotes Shiva; *Gunner* may be *Kannan*, which means "black" and denotes Krishna. These are South Indian names. I am indebted once again to Dr. Klaus Klostermaier for this information.

married upon Hanuman[118] etc. Moreover, they effect pilgrimages to rivers, especially Ganga or Ganges, which is more venerable then any other in that (they say) Brahma frequented it and that it has at Sipra, where it springs out of a rock, a head in the form of a cow, which they little less then worship not only in respect of her fruitfulness but in imitation, it may be, of the Egyptian Apis, which was a pied ox, idolatry so notorious that it seems strange to me what Eusebius in his 6 *lib.* of *Evang. prop. cap.* 9 affirms, that the Seres by their laws prohibit murder, adultery and adoration of idols.

The brahmans eat not anything animate, drink no strong liquor, are free from passion, employ their whole time in service of the great God,[119] avoiding the adoration of idols. Albeit, there are Indians in the same region who defile themselves with idolatry and such vices as most nations punish; yea, the Persians by a law did allow of incestuous marriages, which was so loathsome to the neighbour nations as they branded them with the name of *magussees*, then which a more odious name could not be given to any. But how much now those places are altered from those customs will appear by the observation we shall make in travelling amongst those nations. But to return: these banians wash oft, and thereby suppose themselves purified from sin and dirt, in requital enriching her womb with gold and jewels, hoping to thrive the better, especially when they die, thirsting to have their mouths moistened with a drop of that holy water, which is no less valuable then if it immediately flowed out of Paradise.

In baptism the priests' children and merchants, that is to say brahmins and banians, anoint with oil and cleanse by water. The other profaner sort, as they call men of war and manufacturers, have only water with the point of a pen opposed to their forehead as wishing that God would write good things there, to which the company say amen. Their marriages are sometimes at seven years old, but cohabit not until ten, and if any die unmarried they conclude him unhappy, so that oftimes they marry them dead, afore they be buried. The marriage-ceremonies are not many nor frivolous; the boy rides about the town attended with such little ones as can ride, robed with jewels, scarves etc. one day, the maiden bride the next with a like train of virgins, no less richly attired. He bride and bridegroom are known and distinguished from the rest by their coronets, and the ceremonies celebrated by many kettledrums, trumpets, pageants and the like. The bride has no money-portion, for they hold it contemptible, only some jewels and dinars of gold such as they that day are attired with; I dare not say those *ednas* or marriage-gifts mentioned by Homer, 9 *Iliad*, Suidas[120] and others. The wedding

---

[118] Hanuman [*Hurmount*], a general of the monkey-kingdom who helped Rama overcome the evil Ravana.

[119] Another Jain precept; *satya* is renunciation of the secular world.

[120] Suidas. He was thought to have been a mid-tenth-century Byzantine historian and philologist, but the name applies to the book which bears it, the *Suda*, rather than to an actual person. It contains an enormous amount of lexicographical and other infor-

is thus: a fire is interposed, intimating the purity and heat of their affections, a silken string circles both their bodies as the hieroglyphic of wedlock, then a linen cloth is out betwixt them in token that till then they were unknown to each other in nakedness. This done, the brahmin blesses them, prays that she may prove as gentle and fruitful as a cow. The cloth is torn away, the string untied, and they are one another's ever after. These never marry out of their own castes; brahmins marry the daughters of brahmins, kshatriyas the daughters of kshatriyas, sudras sudras and vaisyas not only so, but also compare in their own trades, as tailors the daughters of tailors, barbers, barbers' daughters etc., and, contrary to the custom of Mahometans, their wives live not under much subjection.

In sickness they call upon *Marraren*, an epithet of God expressing mercy; if they perceive he is going the way of all flesh then they expand his hand and moisten it with holy water, water of Ganges. When he is dead, they wash the carcase and carry it silently to the waterside, where they utter two or three words to that element, then burn his body in sweet wood or spices, which as earth mixes with the corpse, and throwing the ashes into the river, they think they have given every element his peculiar due, and so depart well-satisfied. The priest presents his son the roll of his deceased forefathers and bids him fulfil the ceremonial law of deploring for ten days, neither using his wife, laughing, eating opium nor betel, putting on no clean clothes nor oil on one's head, but that day month yearly ever after make a feast and pay a comp[lemental visit to that river which drunk his father's ashes. Oftimes the wife, to express her love, incinerates herself at that time her husband's body is burned. They effect no scond marriages, the rajahs and vaisyas excepted. Now the reason they burn their dead is either in imitation of those recorded by the prophet Amos 6: 10,[121] or in way of pity lest the enemy should offer it some villainy, or, if buried, it would stink and so putrefy the grass and make kine unhealthy. Besides, out of their carcases would issue worms, who, for ought they know, may starve when the dead body is consumed, and that should prove a sin inexpiable.

The brahmins are of 82 castes or tribes; the Vratyas[122] are of a higher degree but fewer in number. Their habit is a girdle of an antelope's skin tied about their middle, a thong of the same hide reaching from the neck to the left arm, being

---

mation, much of derived from other sources. It was very popular, and appeared early on in print, edited by Demetrios Chalcondylas (Milan, 1499). Herbert probably knew the Latin translation by H. Wolf (Basle, 1546), and there were numerous later versions. A complete English translation is available on-line.

[121] "And a man's uncle shall take him up, and he that burneth him, to bring out the bones out of the house . . . ."

[122] Vratyas [*Vertaes*] are defined in the *Dharmasutras* as "sons fathered by an uninitiated man" (Baudhayana 1.16.16). However, Lach and Van Kley identify them as Svetambara or "white-clad" sect of Jains (3: 647), which may fit better with Herbert's mixing Jainism and Hinduism.

elsewhere naked. Some of them wear a threefold thread reaching from the right shoulder to the left arm, which serves as a badge of their profession and in memory of the three sons of the second creation.

The kshatriyas assume a greater liberty, for being men of war they scruple not to shed blood, eat flesh, and to appear libidinous. They are for the most part called Rajahs or great men, have six and thirty castes, from some of which none of them is but descended. Of these are the tribes of Dodepuchaes, some being *Chawah*, some *Solenkees*, some *Vaggelaes*, some *Figlitters*, and some *Paramores*.[123] Of long times they have been owners of Industan, the last of which by Ala-uddin,[124] a Pathen King of Delhi, had wrested from him Gujarat, since when most of remainder is taken away from them by the issue of Timur. At this day they call themselves Rajputs, or sons of Kings, and live lawless to the Moors, the chief of which at this day are Rana Raji Mardout, Rajah Surmalji, Raja Berumshaw, Mahobet Chan, Rajah Barmulgee, Rajah Joob, Jessingh, Tzettersing and Mansingh.[125] And these value neither the Porans nor the Baluchis, which be the fighting-men among the Mahometans.

The sudras or banians are merchants, and contrary to their name, which signifies "harmless," are the most crafty people throughout India. Full of phlegmatic fear they be and superstition; they are indeed merciful, grieving to see other people so hard-hearted as to feed on fish, flesh, radish, and such things as have either life or resemblance. They for their parts will not kill so much as

---

[123] *Chawah* are Chauhans, *Solenkees* are Solankhis, *Vaggelaes* are Vaghelas, and *Paramores* are Paramaras. The Chauhans, Solankhis, and Paramaras were three of the Rajput kshatriya clans "who sprang into existence from the sacred Agni-kunda or firepit on the summit of Mount Abu" (*HJ* 754). The Vaghelas are a sub-clan of the Gujars. Herbert is correct about the number of clans. The others I have not been able to identify. The *Figlitters* are a problem; they may be the Fagana, another sub-clan of the Gujars.

[124] Ala ud-din Khilji was sultan of Delhi 1294–1316. In 1297 he send his general Ulugh Khan to attack and plunder Gujarat, but the latter was defeated by Kanhad Sangara of Jalore in Rajasthen (1299). Kanhad then allied himself with another one of Khilji's generals, Mohammed Shah, after which they both joined Raja Hamir of Ranthambore to once again defeat Ulugh Khan. Ala ud-din attacked Ranthambore and finally took it (1300). "Pathen" signifies a "Pushtun," an ethnic group which includes many people in Afghanistan.

[125] Some of these Rajput rulers may be identified as: Raja Surmalji of Rajpipla (late sixteenth century); Rana Bharmalji I of Kutch (1585–1631); the raja of Prant Ramnagarh (now Dharampur), who in Herbert's time was either Ramdevi I (1600–1635) or Somdevi (1635–1670); "Berumshaw" is probably Rana Kalyan Singh of Banswara (1620s); Man Singh could be Raja Man Singh of Amber (1590–1614); "Jessingh" is likely one of the maharawals of Jaisalmer, Kalyan Das (1624–1634), Manohar Das (1634–1648), or Ramchandra (1648–1651); "Joob" is one of the rajas of Jubbal, probably Bhag Chand (1629–1676). Which ones they were exactly depends on whether Herbert was thinking of the date of revision (1664) or his original book (1634).

a louse, a flea or a cockroach or the like: "*Non usus erat carnium ante diluvium,*" saith Comestor,[126] but contrarily Vaisya buy their liberty of such sailors and others as of necessity must crush them, yea, they have hospitals for old, lame, sick, or starved creatures, birds, beasts, cats, rats or the like, and have no worse men to oversee them then the Pushelans,[127] the best-respected sorts of brahmins whatsoever. These are of Pythagoras his doctrinating, believing the metempsychosis or trans-animation or passage of souls into beasts, as for example the souls of drunkards or epicures into swine, the lustful and incestuous into goats and dogs, the dissemblers into apes, crocodiles and foxes, the lazy into bears, the wrathful into tigers, the proud into lions, the bloodthirsty into wolves, ounces, snakes; the perjured into toads and the like, but the souls of good men, abstemious, pitiful and courteous into kine, buffalos, sheep, storks, doves, turtles etc., an opinion mentioned by Ovid, 15 *Metamorph.*:

> Flesh fed with flesh; oh, what impiety
> Thy greedy corpse with corpse to fat thereby!
> One living thing to live by other's death
> Oh spare! I warn you, to disturb the breath
> Of kinsmen by fool slaughter, for your blood
> With others' blood to feed is no ways good.[128]

And in justification of this opinion they have the best-learned amongst the heathens, no less then Plato himself for their instructor, who, to persuade men that the soul was immortal and that there was *poena* and *praemium*[129] after this life, feigns the metempsychosis of the souls of men into bees and ants if good, into wolves and dogs if bad etc., which nevertheless, he professes he neither believes for truth himself nor takes for any other then a fiction.

The last sect or caste of gentiles are the vaisyas, a name albeit derived from Vaisya, the youngest son of Purusha and Prakriti, yet in their tongue properly signifying a labouring man. These be of two sorts, the vaisya and coolie,[130] the

---

[126] Peter Comestor (d. 1178), French theologian and Chancellor of Notre-Dame de Paris. He wrote commentaries on St. Paul and the gospels as well as many sermons, all of which are still unpublished. His principal work was the *Historia scholastica*, which went into many editions from 1469 onwards. For details see Saralyn Daly, "Peter Comestor: Master of Histories," *Speculum* 32 (1957): 62–73. The quote may be translated as "there was no use of meat before the flood."

[127] The Pushelans are the followers of Pushan, "god of food and nourishment" . . . "guardian of living creatures" (Knappert, *Mythology*, 200).

[128] Ovid, *Metamorphoses* 15.86–91.

[129] Punishment and reward.

[130] The word "coolie" is derived from Koli, "the name of a race or caste in Western India who have long performed such offices (hired labourer, burden-carrier) as have been

first agreeing with the banian in abstinence, the other of late years not forbearing to eat any manducable creature. The purer sort are divided into 36 castes.

The result of all is that these four castes grew in time so impious that God required Rudra to command a blast of wind to sweep away that generation, which accordingly he did. That tempest raged so violently that the mountains and the rocks were hurled and tossed to and fro like dust or tennis-balls, for the seas were turned out of their course, yea, holy Ganges out of her channel, wherein all, save a few honest men and women which were spared and left to replenish, in that tempest perished. This was the second confusion. Soon after, God gave them a King propagated from the seed of the brahmins called Dasharatha,[131] who begat Rama,[132] so famous for piety and high attempts that to this day his name is honoured, insomuch that when they say *"Ram, Ram,"* 'tis as if they should say "All good betide you."[133]

Now, to show the imbecility of man's nature, in process of time the world again grew abominable, so that Rudra commands the earth to open and swallow down quick those ungodly wretches, a few excepted, who the third time people the earth with human inhabitants. Then, as Brahma had formerly, Vishnu, the mediator of mercy, ascended into heaven, leaving Rudra to over-rule this Age of Iron, at the end of which he also will be wrapped into paradise. These four ages they call Krita-Yuga, Dvapara-Yuga, Treta-Yuga and Kali-Yuga.[134]

Touching the Last Judgment, they hold it shall be more dreadful then the other. The Moon will look as red as blood, the sun will shed his light like purling brimstone, after which will follow an universal flashing of fire with loud thunders, then a flamy redness will o'erspread the heavens, and the four elements of which the world consists shall maintain a dreadful fight so long and so fiercely one against the other that at last it will be resolved into a dark confusion. The souls of such as were good men Rudra is to transport into heaven; the wicked must perish, but the bodies of both rise no more, being too incredulous of the resurrection.

Now, albeit these people believe in a continued series of ignorance that their Shastra was immediately from God, yet that it is grounded upon tradition and patched out of histories Jewish and gentile, I have already showed, both what is

---

mentioned, and whose savagery, filth and general degradation attracted much attention in former times" (*HJ* 249).

[131] King Dasharatha [*Ducerat*], father of Rama and King of Ayodhya.

[132] This is of course Rama, who is the seventh incarnation of Vishnu. His story is recounted in the great epic the *Ramayana*, written by Valmiki in the third century C.E.

[133] Herbert is wrong. The words mean simply "God, God," and have nothing to do with Rama.

[134] The four periods are: Krita-Yuga (Golden Age); Dvapara-Yuga (Second Age); Treta-Yuga (Third Age); Kali-Yuga (Age of Strife). Herbert calls them *Curtain, Duauper, Tetrajoo* and *Kolee.*

in imitation of the Holy Scripture and from the rule and practice of other nations, and we may add that their burning the dead is borrowed from Amos 6:
10,[135] their marriage after death from Cerinthus and Marcion,[136] old heretics
who used to baptise after death in case they were not pre-baptised. The thread
tripartite hung about their neck is a mysterious denotation of the Trinity; rice
and painting in their forehead not only a symbol of baptism but in imitation of
the star Remphan[137] fixed in the brow of the idol Moloch or of Julius Caesar as
an emblem of immortality. See also in how many things they concur with Pythagoras, to this day famous among them. These brahmins in most places affect
silence; for five years they are not suffered to speak in the schools, but understand one another very much by dumb signs. They adore toward the sun, honour
angels, observe a Monday sabbath, abstain from second marriages (some from
the first), affect white garments, loathe coughing, spitting and the like, forbear
swearing and blasphemy, shun pleasure, drink water, believe the transmigration
of men's souls into beasts, offer inanimate sacrifices, deny the body's resurrection, hate to touch a pot or cup with their mouths but rather pour the liquor at a
distance, reverence elders, eat nor drink with men of other religions, use washings much, touch no unclean thing, and many others, in little of nothing differing with the Pythagoreans, as may be gathered out of Josephus, Suidas, Philo,
[Diogenes] Laertius and others.

Religion of the Parsis in East India

For variety's sake, turn we now to another sort of gentiles in Surat and Gujarat
called Parsis, who are a people descended out of Persia, banished hither to avoid
Mahometry and circumcision upon the death of valiant Yazdegerd [III][138] the
Persian King, who died *Anno Dom.* 635 or thereabouts, whose life and doctrine,

---

[135] "And a man's uncle shall take him up, and he that burneth him, to bring out the
bones out of the house . . . ." Herbert's citation is correct. Cf. above, n. 121.

[136] Cerinthus (first to second centuries C.E.) was the leader of a sect whose beliefs
were similar to those of the Gnostics. A contemporary of the evangelist John, he claimed
angelic inspiration and was attacked by the author of 1–2 John. Marcion of Sinope (c.
110–160) was a theologian and the founder of the Marcionites, who created a church
parallel to that which became the Roman Catholic church, for which they were branded
heretics, and attacked by such famous fathers as Irenaeus and Tertullian.

[137] The Star of Remphan is the six-pointed star. The reference to Moloch comes
from the Old Testament: "ye have borne the tabernacle of your Moloch and Chiun"
(Amos 5: 26–27). "Remphan" is taken as a synonym of Chiun.

[138] Yazdegerd III (632–51), the last of the Sassanian monarchs of Persia. The Arabs
took Ctesiphon in 637 after defeating him at the battle of al-Qadisiyyah and ended the
Sassanian dynasty. Yazdegerd fought on for a number of years but was eventually killed.

as it is gathered from the *daroo* or priests of this sect by Mr. Lord,[139] a minister for some years resident in the Factory of Surat, with what I gathered there myself, take briefly as follows.

Into India these Parsis came such time as Omar, the second caliph[140] after Mahomet, subjected Persia, in five junks from Jask sailing to Surat, where after treaty with the Rajas and banians they got leave to plant, and, living peaceably. to exercise of their religion, a religion, if I may so call it, deduced from the reign of Vishtaspa, who was King of Persia *anno mundi* 3500,[141] before our Saviour's incarnation 500 years, written in their *Zend-Avesta* to this purpose.[142]

---

[139] Henry Lord (1563–c. 1641) was a chaplain employed in Surat by the East India Company (1624–1629). At the request of Thomas Kerridge, senior factor at Surat, he studied the Banians and the Parsis, and published a work on their religions, *A Display of two foreign sects in the East Indies* (1630), which is heavily drawn on by Herbert in his account, here of course augmented from its original version and supplemented by a reading of Lord's book. It is highly likely that Herbert met Lord during his stay in Surat. Will Sweetman has edited Lord's book (Lewiston: Edwin Mellen, 1999). Herbert could also have found some of the information on Parsis in Della Valle, *Travels*, 443–46, who would have been helpful in the earlier editions of this book. For more details see Introduction.

[140] Herbert got Omar's succession from Mohammed correct this time around.

[141] Herbert accepts Archbishop James Ussher's calculation in *Annales veteris testamenti, a prima mundi origine deducti* (1650) placing the Creation in 4004 B.C.E. Vishtaspa [*Gustasp*] was a ruler (likely a satrap, not a real king) named Kavi Vishtaspa, who may have reigned over the region of Chorasmia in central Persia about 750 B.C.E. (some scholars date his reign as late as 588 B.C.E.), and was said to have received Zoroaster at his court. This may be because the father of Darius I was also called Vishtaspa (Greek version Hystaspes), and Darius would claim that his father had personally known Zoroaster, a manifestly blatant piece of propaganda for the official religion. Darius and his successor Xerxes I are the only Persian rulers whose monuments actually make mention of Zoroastrianism.

[142] Joseph Campbell called the origins of Zoroastrianism "an obscure and as yet completely unsolved problem" (*The Masks of God* [New York: Viking Press, 1962]), 243. R. C. Zaehner, for example, in *The Dawn and Twilight of Zoroastrianism* (1961), put the dates of Zoroaster at about 628–551 B.C.E. Some modern scholars have determined that Zoroastrianism was actually founded much earlier than the date Herbert gives and the one accepted until quite recently; Puhvel, for example, says that "a sixth century B.C.E. date is too late" (J. Puhvel, *Comparative Mythology* [Baltimore: Johns Hopkins University Press, 1988], 96.) They cite internal and linguistic evidence from the *Zend-Avesta* which suggests that the religion was founded around 1500–1000 B.C.E., and that it was already well-established by the time of Cyrus I, the founder of the Achaemenid dynasty in Persia. Mary Boyce gives the dates "between 1700 and 1500 B.C." as "a reasonable conjecture" (*Zoroastrians*, 18). Herbert's (incorrect) date of 500 B.C.E. places Zoroaster in the reign of Darius I, who did indeed make the religion the official creed of the Persian Empire. "By the grace of Ahura-Mazda I am King," he proclaimed in an inscription (Campbell, *Masks*, 246). The *Zend-Avesta*, whose origins were much older, was put together in Dar-

Such time as Vishtaspa, the 14th King of Persia from Kayumars,[143] by some thought Noah, swayed the imperial sceptre, it chanced that [Purushta] Spitama and Dughdova,[144] two poor people, man and wife, Chinese by extraction, lived long together in good repute but without Fortune's blessings either as to estate or children. Howbeit, upon Dughdova's prayer, a son was given her, who in his conception promised, by some rare and fearful dreams the mother hatched, great matters, not only to the astonishment of his parents but amazement of the China King, who out of jealousy and disposition to credit any report, sought to prevent all danger by killing or poisoning him. But, to show a superior power sways and never misses to accomplish its designs, though by man never so much oppugned, nothing could do him harm, yet, fearing his parents' ruin and to ease the King of his fear they consent to give China a farewell, and seek a securer abode in a region more remote where they might more freely live and meditate.

Far they travelled, many rare things they saw, passed over many great rivers on foot, for Zoroaster,[145] so was this young prophet named, turned them into solid ice and thawed them at his pleasure, and many rare adventures found, all of which are here omitted in that religion is the mark we shoot at, not staying long in any place till they arrived in Persia, where they rested and intended to settle. Zoroaster, as good men used, spent most of his time in meditation, but observing the disorder of men's living, sorrow overcame him, and, finding the place he was in not fit for revelation, away he goes, without resting till he came into a dark valley which was obscured by two lofty mountains, a solitary and fit place for meditation. There he ingeminates his murmurs with dejected eyes, erected

---

ius's reign from a variety of sources, many of them of considerable antiquity. The Zoroastrians moved from Persia to northern India (Gujarat) in the tenth century C.E. The *Zend-Avesta* itself contains the *Gathas*, which are "the only remaining fragments of the actual teachings of the sage Zoroaster" (C. F. Horne, trans. *The Zend-Avesta* [New York: Kessinger Reprints, 2001], 11). There was no European translation of the *Zend-Avesta* until that of Anquetil du Perron (Paris, 1771).

[143] Kayumars [*Kayumarraz*] was the legendary first King of Persia. Ferdowsi writes that he was "the first man to be king, and to establish the ceremonies associated with the crown and throne" (*Shahnameh: The Persian Book of Kings*, trans. Dick Davis [Harmondsworth: Penguin Books, 2007], 1).

[144] Pourushaspa Spitama and Dughdova [*Espintaman* and *Dodoo*]. There is no evidence that they originally came from China; the prophet seems likely to have been born in Rhages, which is near present-day Teheran, and his parents were said to have been "a family of poor warriors" (Niels C. Nielsen et al., eds., *Religions of the World* [New York: St. Martin's Press, 1983], 374).

[145] Herbert, together with other English writers, spells the name *Zertoost*. An alternative version of his name is, in fact, *Zartosht*, which is closer to Herbert's spelling of the name. As noted above, his dates are conjectural, as are his origins; Puhvel tells us that "scholars have seen in him everything from a hashish-using witch doctor of the shamanistic east to a polished courtier of the Achaemenian west" (*Mythologies*, 96).

hands and knees bended, when lo, an angel, whose face was more coruscent then the Sun, in this manner salutes him: "Hail Zoroaster, man of God, what wouldst thou?" Who straight replies, "The presence of God, and that I may receive his will and directions how to instruct my nation." His prayer was granted, his body purged, his eyes sealed and wrapped up. Being passed the element of fire and the higher orbs, as saith their *Zend-Avesta*, he was prostrated before a Supreme, who was arrayed with such refulgent glory that till he had angel's eyes put into his head he could not gaze upon such a dazzling majesty. There he received his laws, (no place but heaven will serve to teach philosophy from to converse with men, Laertius writes to Socrates), uttered by the Almighty, whose words were encompassed with flames of fire, such laws, such secrets as some of them are not to be promulgated. Zoroaster before his return makes this request, that he might live so long as the world endured, in that protract of time the easier to make all the people of the earth to embrace his doctrine. But his simplicity being pitied, and in a mirror the reflex of time, Lucifer's craft, man's misery and other mysteries being revealed, soon altered his vain desire, so that, having taken the *Zend-Avesta* in his left hand and some celestial fire in his right, by Vohu Manah[146] his good angel, who cleft the air with his golden wings, he was in a trice set down in that same valley where the spirit formerly found him.

Zoroaster, having armed himself against all temptations, bidding his hermitage farewell, travels homeward to publish his law. Satan, who all the while looked asquint upon Zoroaster, labours to seduce him, and after a short excuse for his rude intrusion, professes himself his unfeigned friend, assuring him the other angel had deluded him, that God, in no wise delighted with Zoroaster's design, sufficiently expressed as much by suffering him to withdraw so quickly. The denying of his request argued God's neglect of him, his travel to reclaim the world was vain, men's minds so doted upon pleasure; his book was stuffed with lies, and that in publishing it shame would be his reward. His fire was a merciless element, useless in those hot regions, concluding that if Zoroaster would depend upon him, he would furnish him with all delights, honours and pleasures imaginable, give him power to do miracles so that he would be worshipped as a god, which, if he refused, he was but simple and in no wise worthy his charity.

Zoroaster, perceiving the tempter was no better then Lucifer, bade him avoid, and to his addition of terror call to mind how by his impiety he lost heaven, and how malice made him desirous to draw others into like damnation; the book he so scoffed at should condemn him, that fire torture him and all such black-mouthed detractors as himself. Whereupon the fiend vanished, and Zoroaster at length arrived where he found his parents, who received him with inexpressible gladness, to whom he imparted his past fortunes and intentions. Dughdova his mother, imagining it a crime inexplicable that so excellent a prophet

---

[146] Vohu Manah (Good Thought or Mind), "an archangel nine times larger then a human being" (Nielsen et al., *Religions*, 374). Herbert has Babaman Vrashauspan.

should be longer concealed, grew so transported that without longer circumstance she blazons abroad the story of her dreams, and his conception, enthusiasms, visions, the excellency of his book and the authority he had to publish it. The people admire what they heard, so as Vishtaspa the Persian King, having notice thereof and desiring to see the man and inquire into the truth, sends for him, and, after some discourse, is so well-satisfied that forthwith wavering in his former religion, he judges Zoroaster's better, which sudden persuasion so dejected the arch-flamen[147] that he forthwith invents all ways possible to reclaim the King. To effect it, first he bribes Zoroaster's servants to convey under his bed the bones of dead carcases, things hateful to the Persian, and then possess the King that this stranger was a banished man of an impure conversation, witness the stuffing the bed he slept upon. The King, hereupon being brought to view that nasty deceit and finding the report true, first abominates him and then shuts him into a loathsome dungeon. But this misery of his endured not, for the King, having a horse of great account deadly ill, proposes great rewards to any could recover him. None durst undertake it, fearing the penalty, till Zoroaster, giving him a drink, recovers him, an act so acceptable to Vishtaspa that the prophet was received into grace again, whereby he had the readier way to discover the flamen's knavery, and having thus vindicated his own integrity, had the opportunity to publish his doctrine, which, by some miracles intermixed, was, especially by the vulgar sort, credited.

It chances that the King, either stimulated by his churchmen or judging Zoroaster able to do anything, calls for him, professing his propensity to be of his religion. Conditionally, he would grant him four things: first, that he might never die; secondly, that he might ascend heaven and descend as often as he listed; thirdly, that he might know what God had done and intended; fourthly, that his body might be invulnerable.

Zoroaster, amazed at these unreasonable demands and perceiving it otherwise impossible to have his dogma received, tells the King that for one man to have all those properties was to be god more then man, that the King should have the liberty to choose any one for himself and the other three should be distributed to any other three he should he should please to nominate. Which being accepted, Vishtaspa makes the second his choice, that he might ascend and descend at pleasure. To know the secrets of heaven was granted to the King's churchman; to live forever was conferred upon Pischiton, the King's eldest son, who, they say, lives yet upon Damoan's high mountain guarded by thirty spirits to forbid others the entrance. To be free from hurt was granted to Esfandiyar,[148] the

---

[147] High Priest. In the *Zend-Avesta*, the priests who opposed Zoroaster are known as *karpans*. A *flamen* in Roman times was a priest who served important state deities. Herbert uses the word frequently to denote priests of "official" religions.

[148] Herbert is mistaken; Esfandiyar was actually the eldest son of Vishtaspa and father of Bahman, who fought against Rostam and was killed (see *Shahnameh* 371–422).

King's youngest son, after which the *Zend-Avesta* was opened, the new-broached doctrine read and universally accepted of. The *Zend-Avesta*, then, has a three-fold division. The first, treating of judicial astrology, is called *Astoodeger*,[149] and committed to the care of those they call *jessops*, i.e. sages; the second, of natural philosophy,[150] is studied by the *hakims*, i.e. physicians; the last is a compound of religion, named, from the inventor, Zoroaster,[151] kept by the *daroos*,[152] i.e. predicants,[153] each of which three contains seven chapters. The Zoroaster also consists of three parts pointing at three several sorts of men: laymen, clergy and archbishop. To every one of them it enjoins an increase of commandments: to the first sort five, to the second eleven, to the third thirteen.

The *behedins*[154] or laymen's precepts are five, viz.:

1. To cherish shamefacedness, a virtue deterring all sorts of ugly vices as pride, revenge, theft, adultery, drunkenness and perfidy. 2. To cherish fear. 3. To premeditate what they are to do, that if bad they may reject, if good observe it. 4. Each day's first object is to be a memento of God's love to urge their gratitude. 5. To pray daily to the sun and nightly to the Moon as the two great lamps and witnesses which be most opposite to the Devil, who delights in darkness.

The eleven given to the *herbuds*,[155] daroos or priests to practice are these; the others also of the behedin they observe. 1. To be constant to that form of worship in the Zend-Avesta mentioned. 2. Not to covet what belongs to another. 3. To abhor lies. 4. Not to be worldly-minded. 5. To learn the *Zend-Avesta* by rote. 6. To keep themselves free from pollution. 7. To forgive injuries. 8. To teach the laity how to comport themselves in adoration. 9. To license matrimony. 10. To be

---

[149] *Astoodeger* probably refers to the *Ahuna-Vaiti Gatha* (Chapters 28–34), part of the *Yasna* (Sacred Liturgy) of the *Zend-Avesta*.

[150] Herbert is probably referring to the *Bundahisn* or *Zend-agahih*, a compilation of sacred writings in Old Persian dating from the ninth to the eleventh centuries and dealing with such subjects as creation and the nature of life on earth. It is not a division of the *Zend-Avesta*, as Herbert believed, but one of many other works which make up the scriptures of Zoroastrianism.

[151] Again, Herbert may be inaccurate here. I am not certain, but this may allude to the *Hymns of Zoroaster*, which is a section of the *Zend-Avesta* but is not called simply the *Zoroaster*. These have been edited with an English translation by J. M. Chatterji (Calcutta: Parsee Zoroastrian Association, 1967).

[152] *Daroo* is an honorific title applied to some of the *mobeds* (priests) who perform certain ceremonies.

[153] 'Predicant' usually refers to a member of a religious order which was founded through preaching, such as the Franciscans in the Christian church.

[154] Herbert is correct, including the spelling. The word translates as "members of the good religion."

[155] A *herbud* is a man of the priestly order who is still studying to become a *mobed* (a priest who tends the sacred fire), but he can officiate at rituals and ceremonies.

frequent at church. 11. Upon pain of fire eternal to believe in no other law, which they are neither to add unto nor to diminish.

The *dastur*[156] or Pope, but one at once, has thirteen, and, as he precedes the rest in dignity so is his life most strict, for he is obliged to observe not only his own, but also the two former tables. 1. He must not touch any profane thing, no, not the laymen or daroos of his own belief, without washing or purifying after. 2. He must do everything having relation to himself with his own hands, as planting, sowing, cooking etc. 3. He is duly to receive the tenth of what the laity possess. 4. He is to avoid vainglory, and with his great income to exercise acts of charity. 5. His house is to adjoin to the church, so as he may be oft there and go and come without being taken notice of. 6. His washings are to be more frequent then others, his food purer, and he is to refrain his wife's company during her pollution. 7. He is not only to be perfect in the Zoroaster, but of greatest knowledge in judicial and natural philosophy. 8. That his diet be moderate. 9. That he fear none but God. 10. That he tell every man his offences. 11. That in visions he distinguish 'twixt good and counterfeit, and give right judgment. 12. That whensoever God communicates his goodness to him by nightly vision, he is to admire his mercy and to keep them secret. 13. That the pyre be ever kindled till fire destroy the universe, and that he pray over it. This is the sum and substance of the *Zend-Avesta* which Zoroaster brought from heaven.

A word of their feasts, fasts, weddings and burials. They are tolerated most sorts of meat; nevertheless, in obedience to the Mahometan and banian amongst whom they live, they refrain beef and hog-flesh, howbeit the Rajputs eat the last. They seldom feed together lest they might participate one another's impurity; each has his own cup, so as if any of his own caste chance to use it, the other washes it three times and forbears it a while after. Six solemn festivals they yearly observe. The first, called *Maidyhoi-zaremaya*, is kept the 15 of Fere or February. 2. *Paitishahya*, on the 26 of Sheruar or April. 3. *Ayathrima*, on the 16 of Mahar or May. 4. *Maidhyairya*, on the 16 of Deb or August. 5. *Hamaspathmaedaya*, on the 30 of Spindamud or October. 6. *Maidhyoi-shema*, on the 11 of Adeboso or December.[157] After each of these feats they eat but one small meal a day for five

---

[156] There is not one dastur, but several. He is a High Priest, and the word means literally "one who wields power." However, Herbert may be stating that there is only one in each separate Parsee community.

[157] Herbert has the names approximately correct (I follow Boyce in the modernisation), but the months and dates are inaccurate. He names the obligation festivals, known as *Gahambars*, as follows, in the order given above: *Meduserum, Petusahan, Tatrum, Medearum, Homespetamadum,* and *Medusan.* The correct dates of the festivals, together with the names of the Persian months, are as follows: 2–6 October (Ardibehesht); 14–18 February (Shehrevar); 15–19 March (Meher); 1–5 December (Tir); 12–21 August (Aspandarmad); 3–7 June (Dae). They are successively the Mid-spring festival (Maidhyoi-zaremaya), Mid-summer festival (Maidhyoi-shema), Feast of bringing in the corn

days after, and whatsoever that laymen eat any flesh, they bring part to their *atash-zohr*[158] or temple to pacify the Lord, in that for their sustenance the lives of those good creatures are annihilated.

Now concerning the fire[159] they adore, 'tis in memory of that which Zoroaster brought from heaven, wherein they memorise the Vestals or rather apishly imitate the Jewish law, (the Devil as near as may be desiring to counterfeit the best), in Leviticus 6:13, where 'tis commanded that the fire that came from heaven should be ever burning upon the altar and never go out.[160] And as to this fire-worship, we find in story that it has been more anciently used in Persia then what is here ascribed by the *Zend-Avesta* to Zoroaster's time, being probable that as the Grecians borrowed that idolatry from the Persians, so from the Greeks was it borrowed by the Vestal Romans. In Persia they had many pyres; most of them were destroyed by Heraclius the Roman emperor during his wars with Chosroes,[161] at which time Mahomet served in his army. Some to this day are remaining, having, as they report, the idolatrous fire from 1000 years unextinguished. In India also the banished Parsis have their *atashkadas*, one of which is at Navsari,[162] whose fire has continued this 200 years, if report say true. Where note, that this their god-fire is not composed of common combustibles as wood, straw, coals, slates etc., nor blown by any bellows, breath of man, wafting, or like profane things, but compounded of sparks flying from a hot-burning tempered steel, and kindled either by lightning from heaven or by beams from a burning-glass or the like, for such only is proper for their *antishebarann* or idol-fire.

But if by chance the fire have need of cherishing, the dastur and other laymen at twelve foot distance surround their deity, and after some mimic gestures

---

(Paitishshaya), Feast of the home-coming (Ayathrima), Mid-winter (Maidhyairya), and Hamaspathmaedya, "the feast of *fravashis*, which was celebrated on the last night of the year, before the spring equinox" (Boyce, *Zoroastrians*, 33).

[158] The Classical Persian word for "house of fire." Herbert calls them *eggarees*. Lord uses the term *agiary* (*Display*, 40), which Boyce states "is clearly a reference to the 'atash-zohr'" (185).

[159] Parsis do not worship fire; rather "they regard it, like water and air, as a purifying element" (Nielsen and Hein, *Religions*, 382). In short, it is a symbol of God, not God himself, what Lord Herbert of Chirbury called a *cultus symbolicus*.

[160] "The fire shall ever be burning upon the altar; it shall never go out."

[161] Flavius Heraclius was Byzantine emperor 610–641; during his reign there was a protracted war with Chosroes (Khusrau) II Anushirvan, Sassanid emperor of Persia 590–628, discussed later on by Herbert. For details, see Walter Kaegi, *Heraclius, Emperor of Byzantium* (Cambridge: Cambridge University Press, 2003).

[162] Navsari [*Nancery*] has been "the headquarters for the Parsi community since their early days in India." The oldest fire, however, is at Udvada, quite near Navsari (N. Crowther and P. Raj, *India: A Travel Survival Kit* [South Yarra: Lonely Planet, 1981], 432). Boyce also notes other traditional centres in Vankaner, Broach, Variav, Anklesar, and Cambay (*Zoroastrians*, 167).

the priests add some sort of fuel, and, returning to the other people, fall to their worship, beseeching that they may not only give it due reverence, but honour solemnly all things that resemble it, as Sun, Moon and stars, yea, and common fire, which also they so divinely esteem that they hold it an impious thing to spit upon it, throw water into it, or put it to any vile or unnecessary use, but give a more then common respect to wood and such things as it receives life and vigour from. Now albeit these people say their ancestors first practised this form of worship, we find in story that the fire was in divine esteem with the Chaldaeans such time as Abram dwelt at Ur,[163] and then in equal veneration with the Persians. This holy fire was carried by the flamens in the van of the army when Darius [III] fought at Arbela against Alexander,[164] and continued un-put out for many generations.

The baptism of these heathen idolaters is of this nature: so soon as one is born, the daroo is called upon, who delays not, but being instructed in the precise time of his nativity, calculates his fortune. The daroo gives the name, the mother assenting to it. This done, they together haste to the atashkada, where the priest puts a little water into the bark of a tree, the name of which is holm,[165] the place it grows in Yazd, a city in Persia not far [from] Isfahan, a tree Zoroaster blessed, and in this very memorable, if we may believe these people, that it never admits of any shadow. The water out of this hallowed rind being poured out upon the infant, a prayer is then made that it may be cleansed from impurity. At seven years of age the child is confirmed by the daroo, and taught to say his prayers over the fire, but with a cloth fastened over his head which covers his mouth and nostrils lest his sinful breath might offend their deity, after which he drinks a little cold water, chaws a pomegranate leaf, washes in a tank, clothes his body with a fine *chudder*[166] reaching to his waist, ties a zone of *cushee*[167] about his loins woven with *inkle*[168] of the herbud's making, which he wears ever after, and after a short prayer that he may never prove an apostate but continue a fire-worshipper, that he may eat no man's meat nor drink any man's drink but his own, he is ever after reputed a true professor.

---

[163] Abraham's date is usually placed at about 2900 B.C.E. The Chaldaeans settled in Ur in about 900 B.C.E.

[164] This battle (331 B.C.E.) ended the Achaemenid Empire and also saw the destruction of many Zoroastrian records when Alexander burned Persepolis.

[165] The holm is a kind of evergreen oak tree which also grows in southern Europe. It has leaves like holly and very hard wood.

[166] "A sheet, or square piece of cloth of any kind" (*HJ* 217). Herbert spells it *shudderoo*.

[167] Any soft and comfortable material.

[168] A linen braid or tape.

Their marriages are distinguished into five orders. 1. *Shaulan*, which is a marrying of two young children[169] agreed upon by the parents unknown to the children, the virtue being that if either die, they go to heaven. 2. *Chockersan*, which is a second marriage. 3. *Codesherabasan*, when the woman is her own chooser. 4. *Ecksan*, when a dead body, not being married before, is to one alive married. 5. *Cetersan*, when having no sons he adopts his daughter's son etc. The ceremony is this. At midnight the daroo or priest enters the house, for they wed not in churches, and finds the bride and bridegroom placed upon a bed together. Opposite to each two churchmen stand with rice in their hands, the emblem of fruitfulness, when first one lays his forefinger on the bride's forehead and asks if she be willing to take that man to be her husband, who, saying yea, the like rite and question is by the other priest made to the man, who, after like answer, makes a promise to enfeoff[170] her in a certain number of dinars, to which in a grateful manner the bride replies, she and all she has are his. The priests thereupon throw rice upon their heads, praying that they may multiply as rice. The woman's parents give the dowry, and eight days are usually spent in jovial merriment.

Their funerals are these. They neither burn nor bury their dead, but having first put the body into a winding-sheet, all the way as they pass towards the grave his kindred beat their breasts, but with little noise until they come within 50 or 100 paces of the burial-place, where the herbud meets them, usually attired in a yellow scarf, and on his head wearing a thin turban. The *nessalars* or bearers carry the corpse upon an iron bier, for wood is forbidden in that it is dedicated to the fire, to a little shed, where, so soon as some mystiques are acted, they hoist it up to the top of a round building, some of which are twelve foot high and eighty in circuit. The entrance is most part at the north-east side, where, through a small grate, they convey the carcase into a monument, good men into one, bad into another. 'Tis flat above, open to the air, plastered with white loam, hard and smooth like that of Paris. In the midst thereof is a hole descending to the bottom, made to let in the putrefaction issuing from the melted bodies, which are thereupon laid naked in two rows or ranks, exposed to the sun's rage and [the] appetite of ravening birds who spare not to devour the flesh of these carcasses, tearing asunder and deforming them in an ugly sort so that the abominable stink of those unburied bodies, in some places 300, is so loathsome that, did not a desire to see strange sights allure a traveller, they would prove much worse seen then spoken of. The dislike the Parsis expressed at my taking a view of this Golgotha made it appear that they do not delight that it should be seen of strangers. A rare, yet no new way of burial, for I find the like mentioned by Strabo in his 15 *Lib.* saying

---

[169] J. Modi states that there were no marriages in the Parsee religion until the age of 15 for either boys or girls, and that since there are many records of women praying for suitable husbands, it is unlikely that "children" married ("The Marriage Ceremony of the Parsis" [Bombay: privately printed, 1921], 17.)

[170] Endow.

of the brahmins, "The brahmins, being an incestuous race, being dead, desire to be exposed to the birds as the noblest sort of burial."[171] Nor is it otherwise now then it was in ancient times, most nations using several sort of burial, for Lucian in his discourse *De luctu* hath this observation: "The Greeks burn, the Persians bury, the Indians besmear with hog's grease, the Scythians eat, the Egyptians powder, the Romans embalm, the Gangestics drown, the Narsingans[172] immure, the brahmins expose to birds, the Bactrians to dogs." This figure I took may give the better resemblance:

The burial-place of the Parsis [illustration not shown]

---

[171] For Strabo's discussion of the brahmins, see 7.99–103 and *passim*.

[172] Narsinga was "the name most frequently applied in the sixteenth and seventeenth centuries to the kingdom in Southern India otherwise named Vijayanagara" (*HJ* 619). It seems to have been used first by the Portuguese.

Part III: The Mughal Empire

And seeing we are now by Providence brought into so noble a Kingdom as at this day is extant in the universe, give me leave to digress awhile, that I may the better present you, but in a summary way, the topographic description of this mighty Empire of Hindustan, which I shall mix with a narrative of such remarkable occurrences as have happened there within these last fifty years, which, though it may appear too great an interposition to our travel, will nevertheless I hope find acceptance.

India then, which takes its name from the River Indus that bounds it to the west, is part, but the greater part, of the greater Asia, and by some reputed a third part of the Old World; so Strabo, *Lib.* 55, in whose age it was much more flourishing then at present, who reports that it had then not fewer then 50,000 towns, none inferior to Co, which was considerable, in Egypt. Ganges divides it into two, Intra and Extra, nevertheless there be [those] that subdivide it into three, viz. Major, Minor, and Inter-media. The soil for the most part is very good except where the sun rages, yet there too, by reason of the long night's breezes and showers it has for three months every year, the trees, especially to the southern parts, are ever verdant and abounding with fruit which twice-yearly comes to maturity. And for minerals of the best sort, gems of richest lustre, silks and spices of most value and use, no part of the world yields greater plenty. It abounds with inhabitants and cattle of most kinds. Arts also, especially in Hindustan and China, are in perfection. It has excellent horse, and elephants of greater size and more docile then those of Africa, [and] so numerous in islands as they are scarce numerable.

And concerning the Emperor of Hindustan, can you lend your eyes to any nobler part of the world, which for spaciousness, abundance of fair towns, numberless inhabitants, infinite treasure, mines and all sorts of merchandise, equals if not exceeds, any other Kingdom or potentate in either Asia, his vast but well-compacted monarchy extending from 20 to 43 degrees of north latitude, east and west from the Bengal Gulf unto the Indian Ocean, south to the Deccan and Malabar, north and north-west to Canosia and Transoxiana Tartar and Persian; 2600 miles some ways, 5000 in circuit, in which are 38 large provinces (petty Kingdoms of old). The most considerable are Gujarat, where we now are,

Malwa,[1] Punjab, Bengal and part of Deccan (*Ariacae* in Ptolemy), together comprehending 30 large cities, 3000 walled towns and castles for natural defence, seeming impregnable. And well may be, seeing this country, 'tis probable, was the first seminary or station of Noah or Noachus after his descent from Ararat, not far distant hence, and afterwards the delight of Bacchus or Boacchus, from which some imagine him to be Noah, the wonderful increase appearing by that huge army Staurobates[2] drew out in his defence against Semiramis the Assyrian empress, both armies making three millions. And so answerably builded and planted was this part of India that when Alexander by the overthrow of Porus[3] near the River Hydaspes entered India, Curtius and Herodotus[4] report that Alexander should say he found greater cities and more sumptuous buildings in King Porus his dominions then he had observed in all the world beside.

But to return. His yearly revenue is ordinarily accounted 50 crore of rupees; each crore is a hundred *lakh*, a *lakh* a hundred thousand rupees, a rupee two shillings three pence, sometimes two shillings six pence. And indeed, both what wealth and power this emperor is of may be conjectured by that one province called Cambay, wherein Surat stands, the annual customs and other revenues of which, as merchants report, is £200,000 sterling, and for power appears by that army which Bahadur[5] who only ruled over this province, fought with against the Tartar Mahmud, whom the King of Mandu invited to his assistance, being no less then 130,000 horse and 400,000 foot, 200 elephants, 500 waggons, and as

---

[1] Malwa is in west-central northern India. Its sultanate was established by Dilawar Khan (1401–1405), who declared it independent from the sultanate of Delhi. From 1434 to 1562 it was ruled by the Khalij sultans, and was then conquered by Akbar I. Its capital was Mandu, which had been abandoned by the seventeenth century.

[2] Staurobates is probably Sthvarapati, who is mentioned in the *Puranas*, the sacred Sanskrit text which relate the exploits of the various gods. He is said to have fought with and defeated "Semiramis," whom some scholars have identified with Shammuramat, the wife and then widow of Shamshi-Adad V of Assyria (824–811 B.C.E.), thus dating her at about 800 B.C.E. The battle described here is likely fictional. Semiramis has also been identified with the mother of Adad-nirari III (811–783 B.C.E.), for whom she acted as regent until he came of age; her story has been greatly embellished by writers such as Herodotus, Diodorus Siculus, and Quintus Curtius Rufus.

[3] Usually identified with Puru or Pururava (d. 317 B.C.E.), king of Paurava in the Punjab. His capital was probably modern-day Lahore. Alexander defeated him at the Hydaspes (Jhelum) River in 326, but later reconciled with him. Porus was later assassinated by Eudemus, a Thracian, one of Alexander's generals.

[4] See Q. Curtius Rufus, *History of Alexander* 8.12.13ff; since Herodotus lived more than a hundred years before Alexander, Herbert must have had a chronological lapse.

[5] Bahadur Shah was sultan of Gujarat 1526–1536. He captured Mandu in 1526. Mahmud Shah II was Sultan of Mandu 1510–1526. Herbert seems to be a little confused with names, which he got mostly from de Laet. Mandu was also known as Mandavgarh or Shadiabad, "City of Joy" (Crowther and Raj, *India*, 477).

many chests full of treasure for pay of his forces. Howbeit, out of this prodigious income issues many great and surable payments to his Lieutenants of Provinces and *umrahs*[6] of towns and forts, having also in continual pay three hundred thousand horse and two thousand elephants fed with *donna* or pulse[7] boiled with butter and unrefined sugar, to those only his fiscal or treasurer yearly giving out above forty millions of crowns, and his continual wars with his emulous neighbours are no less chargeable.

The Mughal's Pedigree.

The descent or pedigree of these Mughals or Magors, whither so-named from the *Mogli* whence they descend, or by possessing the brahmins' country, of old called *Gens Magorum*, I know not. We find stamped upon their seals thus: 1. Alamir Timur Saheb, i.e. Timur, prince of the four quarters of the world; 2. Miran Shah; 3. Mirza[8] Sultan Mohammed; 4. Sultan Abu Said; 5. Umar Sheikh Mirza; 6. Babur Padishah; 7. Humayun Padishah; 8. Akbar, called also Abu Fatta Jalaleddin Mohammed Akbar; 9. Shah Salim or Jahangir Padishah Ghazi; 10. Sultan Khurram, or Shah Jahan. Their genealogy is by some deduced from Genghis Khan, a prince of Tartary, son of Babur, son of Portan, of Philcan, of Bizan Beg, of Shah Dubkhan, of Tuman Khan, of Bubu Khan, son of Buzamer, all of them men of note, as stories speak romance-like in their generations.[9]

Genghis Khan, as Haithon and others his contemporaries say, was at first by profession a blacksmith, but the influence of Heaven now moulding him, in little time instead of his hammer he took into his hands a regal sceptre. His ambition took rise from the encouragements a man in white armour mounted upon a white phantasma gave him, promising his help and stimulating his courage, so as communicating the vision to some chief hordes, they give credit to his destiny and make him their general. He quickly shows how his metal was refined, for with a troop of Mongols, one of the seven hordes, marching due south he subdues the

---

[6] *Umrah* is a general term for a Mughal nobleman (William Dalrymple, *The Last Mughal: The Fall of a Dynasty, Delhi, 1857* [London: Bloomsbury, 2000], 495). *Hobson-Jobson* confirms this, but designates it a term which "should be applied collectively to the highest officials at a Mahommedan court, especially that of the Great Moghul." It is a plural word, but "in old European narratives it is used as a singular for a lord or grandee in that court" (637).

[7] Here, any kind of beans.

[8] "A prince or gentleman" (Dalrymple, *Last Mughal*, 491).

[9] These Timurid rulers are: Sultan Mohammed Miranshah of Samarkand (1405–1408); Mohammed Mirza, his son; Sultan Abusaid Mirza of Samarkand and Herat (1451–1469); Umar Sheikh Mirza (1456–1493), ruler of Afghanistan and father of Zahiruddin Mohammed Babur, the first Mughal Emperor. For details see Babur, *Baburnama*, trans. W. M. Thackston (New York: Modern Library, 2002), 7–10; translator's preface, xxxvi–xxxix.

countries as far as Mount Beligian, part of Imaus, at this day called Nigracot and Copizat by the Indians. There the sea stopped his career, but, prostrating himself and nine times fumbling out his prayers, the effect followed, for, as the chronicle relates, the hill clove asunder, the sea parted in two and yielded nine foot broad a safe passage. He was no sooner upon the continent but that he hammers out his way with rusty iron, first against Unc Khan, King of Tenduc,[10] and after that doing such marvellous feats of arms as requires a strong faith to give credit to.

Genghis Khan, King of the South-East Tatars, after other victories against the Russians and Tatars, died at Karakorum, An. 1228; some say 60 years sooner, of the Hegira 608, having divided amongst his four sons what was his by conquest. To Jochi Khan he gave Dast-i-Kipchak, Russia, and Bulgaria; to Chagatai Khan Transoxiana, Aygot and Khorasan; to Ogadai part of Bactria and Caucasus; to Tolui Khan his jewels and treasures. Jochi died two years after his father, Chagatai died in the year 1242, both of them without issue, whereby their seigneuries descended upon Ogadai Khan, who at home and abroad expressed himself the son of Genghis Khan, compelling the Persian monarchy as far as Babylon to acknowledge him sovereign.[11] But in the year 1252, conquered by death, followed the fate of his predecessors, having nominated for his successor his infant son Güyük Khan[12] under the tuition of Töregene[13] his wife, but in the third year death called him also away, and gave Mangu Khan,[14] son to Tolui Khan the youngest tetrarch, advantage to claim the sovereignty by right of survivorship.

This young prince, thus mounted to the imperial greatness, perceives the eyes of all about him inflamed with envy and threatening his expulsion, enraged by the villainy of some that whispered out his guilt in the last infant's death, so that, albeit he was armed with integrity and a just title, he contracts for his defence with some neighbouring princes, to whom he entrusted the command

---

[10] "Unc Khan" is a corruption or the Chinese Wang Khan, and refers not to a person but to the ruler of Tenduc, which was part of the Chinese Empire. Marco Polo calls it "a province which lies towards the east" (*Travels*, 375).

[11] The sons of Genghis Khan were: 1. Jochi or Tushi [*Tusha-chan*] (c. 1185–1227) who died in February 1227, two months before his father, not two years later. He was assigned territory north of the Aral and Caspian Seas, which comprised Dast-i-Kipchak [*D'hast*], Russia [*Roz*] and Bulgaria [*Abulgharr*]. After his death his two sons Batu and Orda divided his territory and became founders of the Blue Horde and the White Horde. 2. Ogadai [*Ogg* or *Ogtay-chawn*] (1186–1241) reigned as Great Khan (1227–1241) over areas of East Asia, including China; 3. Tolui Khan [*Tuli-chan*] (1190–1232) ruled over Mongolia and Karakorum (1227–1232); 4. Chagatai Khan (1194–1241) ruled northern Iran and central Asia. Much of this information comes from de Laet (*Empire*, 122–25).

[12] Guyuk Khan [*Gayuk-chan*], who was young, but not an "infant," reigned as Great Khan 1246–1248.

[13] Toregene Khanum [*Minnehonna*], widow of Ogadai Khan, was Regent 1241–1246. De Laet calls her *Turakina* (*Empire*, 123).

[14] Mangu or Mongke Khan ruled as Great Khan 1251–1259.

of several provinces of his empire, upon condition they would hold him in chief and be ready upon occasion to defend him. To Kublai Khan he gave Ketoachatan and the royal city Kambalek, peradventure that which some call Cambalu[15] upon Polisanga, a river streaming through China to the ocean. To Hulagu Khan[16] his brother, Persia, Chusistan and Cherman, and to Chun Khan Ghaznavan, but ere he had occasion to experience the inconstancy of his men, death summoned him away *Anno* 1259, but not before he had nominated Hulagu Khan his successor, who proved of another spirit, his delight being to dance in armour to Bellona's[17] trump, first quieting his domestic broils at home, and then adding to the lustre of his diadem Babylon, a great part of Arabia, and in Syria Aleppo and Damascus, which places he kept in life under subjection and governed the people with great prudence to the year 1265, when, by the extremity of his disease finding death at hand, he calls his three sons before him, exhorts them to unity, divides his lands among them, and dies at Meragab, five farsangs from Tauris, with all solemnity buried. Abaqa Khan[18] the eldest had for his share the provinces of Hyerac, Mazenderam and Khorasan, comprising Media, Parthia, Hyrcania, Bactria and Sogdiana. *Hyashamet* had Aro and Adarbayon, part of Armenia and Iberia comprising Salmas, Coy, Nazivan, Maraga and Merent, cities of note. To *Tawdon Khan* were bequeathed the seigneuries of Dyarbee and Rabaion or Mesopotamia, part of Syria and what was made fruitful by Tigris and Euphrates. And to his sons by another venter, *Tekuder-Oglan* and *Targabe* Khan he gave money-portions. Abaqa Khan died that year (1282) in Persia and made protector to his son Tekuder-Oglan,[19] who by devilish art would have sent him to an untimely grave, but saving himself by flight. Tekuder re-establishes himself by the name of Ahmed, whose reign was so pursued by divine vengeance that in the year 1275 he dies mad and was buried at Casban. In his place Arghun Khan[20] the right heir returns from banishment, by the people joyfully welcomed, and at his coronation assumes the name of Tangador Aqaba Arghun, i.e. son to Abaqa Khan. This man swayed the sceptre five years tyrannically, not only massacring Tekuder's son and alliances, but spares not to bathe his sword in the blood of innocents, so that he became hateful to his own and stimulated the Parthian to revenge, by whom in a set battle he was overcome and by the name of Arghun Khan upbraided with cruelty, yea, to compensate the like measure he was cruelly tormented, his belly

---

[15] Now known as Beijing.

[16] Hulagu Khan [*Vlakuk*] was the founder of the Ilkhan Dynasty of Persia. He ruled 1256–1265.

[17] The Roman goddess of war. Perhaps of Etruscan origin, Bellona was sometimes identified as the sister of Mars.

[18] Abaqa Khan [*Habkay-cawn*] was Ilkhan of Persia 1265–1282.

[19] The dates are wrong. Ahmed Tekuder Khan reigned as Ilkhan 1282–1284.

[20] Arghun Khan [*Argon-cawn*] was Ilkhan 1284–1291. Herbert only gives him five years.

ripped open and his guts were given to the dogs. To Arghun succeeds his brother
Gaikhatu,[21] who in the fourth year of his reign perished by Baidu Khan[22] his
uncle, who after five years' rule died issueless. Batu, son of Targabe, youngest son
of Hulagu, by assent of all the nation mounts the throne, whose affections he so
well answered that never any before him was more beloved or honoured. Howbeit, so soon as he declared himself to his people that he was a Christian his subjects' love grew cold and many treasons fomented by Satan were hatched against
him so that at last he was slain, or rather martyred, by Ghazan Khan, cousin to
Arghun, who had small cause to brag of that his treachery, for by the permis-
sive hand of God, when he least suspected treason, he was wounded to death in
Carbin by his own household-servants, not any cause assigned in history for their
so doing, but say that his body lay for a long time unburied. This happened *An.
Dom.* 1304, *Heg.* 685.

His brother Oljeitu,[23] or Mohammed bin Arghun, by his valour purchased
the diadem, to whom followed Abu Said Bahadur Khan,[24] who consumed his life
in venereous exercises, so that for want of issue this Kingdom became a theatre of
much trouble, no less than thirty at one time contesting for the sovereignty. The
people thereby were compelled to look for help from home, and none more safe
to trust then the Lord of Samarkand, Timur, a prince famoused for his justice
and success against the Sarmatic Tartar, Praecopenses and Chinese. Him they
invocate by many presents of their love and a letter filled with hideous complaints
describing their misery through the division in their Kingdom and pride of thirty competitors. The Scythic prince promises them speedy aid, and accordingly
with fifty thousand horse enters Persia without doing any hurt save against the
tyrants, whom he so prosecuted and with such speed that within three months
they were all taken and made to quaff their farewell in the bitter cup of death.
Hereupon the people urged Timur to accept the crown, who after seven and
twenty years honourable government, in that time captivating the Great Turk
Bajazet, whom he brought home in an iron cage, subduing all Asia, yea, in eight
years conquering more Kingdoms and provinces then the Romans did in eight
hundred, and 'tis noteworthy that as Alexander from Thrace was terminated in
the advance of his conquest by Samarkand, Timur, after his victorious march

---

[21] Gaikhatu Khan [*Giviatoc-cawn*] was Ilkhan 1291–1295.
[22] There are some chronology problems here. Baidu Khan [*Balduc*] ruled for a few
months in 1295; de Laet states that he was the son of Torgahe Khan, the son of Hulagu
(*Empire*, 124). It was Ghazan Khan [*Gazun-chawn*] whose reign lasted nearly ten years
(1295–1304). As for Batu Khan, Herbert seems to be confusing him with the grandson of
Genghis Khan, who ruled the Blue Horde 1227–1255 and the Golden Horde 1242–1255.
There was no Ilkhan ruler called Batu, and nothing to indicate that Baidu Khan was a
Christian. De Laet does not mention Batu Khan at all.
[23] Oljeitu Khan [*Aliaptu Abusaid*] was Ilkhan 1304–1316.
[24] Abu Said Bahadur Khan [*Abusaid Babador-chan*] was Ilkhan 1316–1335.

through both the Asias was limited by Thrace. Such were the contrary race[s] of these two conquerors; this monarch of the Asiatic world was nevertheless subjected by imperious Death, and entombed *Anno* 1405, of the Hegira 785, at Anzar in Cathay, leaving his sons and grandsons to inherit, viz. Jahangir, Ahmed, Miran Shah[25] and Shah Rukh,[26] of which Jahangir died, some say three years before, some, after his father, in Palestine, leaving his two sons Mohammed Sultan[27] and Pir Mohammed,[28] which Pir Mohammed was by his grandsire placed in Ghazneben and Hindustan, where he ruled till Pir Ali slew him treacherously. Ahmed Khan was slain in Lorestan, some say in his father's last combat with Bayezid. Miran Shah, the third son, was slain in battle *Anno* 1408 by Kara Yusuf the Turkoman[29] in Azerbaijan, but left issue, Sultan Mohammed, father of Sultan Abu Said,[30] from whom the present great Mughal is lineally descended, and Mirza Shah Rukh, the youngest of Timur's sons, surviving the other[s], held most parts of the empire till dying in the year 1447. He left Azerbaijan or part of Media to Jahan Shah,[31] son of Kara Yusuf of the Turks, who was new-entered Persia, whiles Miran Shah's issue to this day preserve the splendour of the Tartarian Emperor.

Miran Shah left issue; Mohammed, called Mirza Sultan Mohammed,[32] who died *Anno* 1451, leaving to his son Barkhan, at his coronation new-named Mirza Sultan Abu Said, many spacious provinces as Badaskhan, Ghazna, Kabul, Sistan, Kerman, Khorasan and Hormuz, all of which were not of force to secure him against the Persian, who, having endured much affliction for trial of conquest, at last Jahan Shah with Asen Ali his son, grandson to Kara Yusuf, were beaten down, by which victory Usun Hassan,[33] Lord of the White Sheep, took upon him the government. Under this Usun Hassan, an Armenian, the Persians invade Sultan Abu Said, who in a pitched field was vanquished and eighty thousand men, he himself also slain, three hundred elephants taken and all his country harassed by the Persian horde. Yet, by reason of discords reviving among the Persians, they set Abu Said's son upon the throne, by name Mirza Sheikh Ahmed, whose four and twenty years were spent in ease and peace.

---

[25] Jalal ud-din Miran Shah [*Myramsha*] reigned as sultan in what is now Azerbaijan (1405–1408). He was killed at the battle of Sandrud by Kara Yusuf (see below).

[26] Shah Rukh [*Mirza Sharoc*] reigned in Samarkand 1405–1447.

[27] Sultan Mohammed ruled in Samarkand 1447–1451.

[28] Pir Mohammed was a Timurid sultan who ruled in Fars 1405–1407.

[29] Kara Yusuf was Sultan of the Black Sheep Turkmen in Khorasan 1388–1400 and 1406–1420.

[30] Sultan Abu Said reigned in Transoxiana and Samarkand 1451–1469.

[31] Jahan Shah [*Joansha*] ruled the Black Sheep Turkmen 1457–1458.

[32] Sultan Ahmed Mirza, son of Abu Said, ruled in Samarkand 1469–1494.

[33] Sultan Usun Hassan (see Introduction) ruled the White Sheep Turkmen (1453–1478) in what is now western Iran, Iraq, and parts of Turkey.

At his death his empire descends *Anno* 1493 upon his brother's son Babur Mirza, named upon his access to the crown entitled Prince of Transoxiana, Balkh,[34] and Samarkand, but in the seventh year of his reign he was expelled his Kingdom by conspiracy of Mahmud Shah, called also Shah Beg Khan, who claimed the crown, pretending he was son and heir to Ahmed Mirza the late emperor, being (as he said) by craft stolen from his nurse and conveyed amongst the Uzbek Tartars, whence, for some offence he had made, he fled with his lawless troops, enters India, and attempts the conquest, where, after he had tyrannised a long time, he was in the year 1532, of the Mahometan account 912, sore against his will sent to an untimely grave, leaving no issue, so the crown descended by right of inheritance upon the eldest son of Babur, Humayun by name, who was sadly prosecuted through the power and malice of Mirza Kamran,[35] his younger brother that confederated with Sikandar [Lodi],[36] at length forced him into Persia, where he was entertained, and after three months returned back in the head of an army.

This also is remarkable, the story whereof we see painted in Lahore Palace, that King Babur, thirsting after the conquest of India, disguised himself with thirty noblemen in his company in the habit of kalenders or friars as if they were on a rummery or pilgrimage, the better by this craft to espy their advantage, but being in Delhi, the greatest city of the Pathan king, could not so conceal themselves but that Sikandar discovered them and pardoned them upon condition they would swear never to attempt the conquest during either of their lives. But when both were dead, Humayun, Babur's son, entered and dispossessed Ibrahim and Selim Shah, Sikandar's sons, of the crown.[37] Howbeit, Sher Shah,[38] a brave

---

[34] Balkh [*Balke*] is an important city in Transoxiana. See *Baburnama* 32–36 *passim*.

[35] Prince Kamran Mirza (1509–1557) was the second son of Emperor Babur and Humayun's half-brother. In 1530 Humayun appointed him ruler over Kabul and the Punjab. He was also Governor of Lahore, where he "sternly reporved the timidity and cowardice of his brother" (De Laet, *Empire*, 135) when Sher Shah deposed him in 1545. Humayun and Kamran were never easy with each other, and in 1552 they fought in Afghanistan. From 1543 onwards Kamran was in and out of rebellion, and at one point fled to Persia and tried to enlist Shah Tahmasp's support against his brother. After a defeat Kamran was turned over to Humayun, who had him blinded (1553) and then sent him to Mecca, where he died.

[36] Sikander Lodi was Sultan of Delhi 1489–1517.

[37] Ibrahim Lodi succeeded his father as Sultan in 1517, and fought against both Babur and Humayun. Babur defeated him at the battle of Panipat (1526) and entered Delhi. For Babur's account of this, see *Baburnama* 266b–267b and *passim*.

[38] Sher Shah Suri [*Tzerchan*] was an Afghan, not a Bengali, although his centre of power was in Bengal and Bihar. He drove out Humayun (not Babur) in 1540 and ruled as Mughal Emperor (although he did not use the title officially) 1540–1545. He was a great warrior and builder as well as an extremely able administrator. Herbert's account of Humayun's flight is correct, although he did not return to Delhi after Sher Shah's death.

Bengali prince, fights against this new-come Tartar, and defeats his army near Ganges, forcing him into Persia where he married the King's sister, and with her and Bairam Khan in the head of twenty thousand horse returns, and, being re-seated in Delhi, is acknowledged King.

Sudden Death of the Mughal

Humayun, son of Babur, great-grandson of Timur, being re-invested with the imperial diadem of Hindustan by the means of Tahmasp the Persian King, and returned triumphant by the overthrow of Sher Shah the intruding King, who *Anno* Dom. 1550 and of the Hegira or Mahometan account 960, died disconsolate.[39] Humayun, I say, after he had committed his eldest son Abdul Fattah Jalal ed-din Mohammed, a while after surnamed Akbar, to the trust and care of Bairam Khan, a discreet and valiant man, being in Delhi, one evening chewed too much opium. Hasting to his orisons upon the watchword usually given from a high tower, suddenly slipped down forty steps, which so bruised him that after three days' torment he deceased, and was with much solemnity put into his grave, here called an eternal habitation, leaving Akbar his son inheritor to his greatness and miseries.

[The Reign of Akbar the Great]

Akbar, by the help of Bairam Khan and Abdu'r Rahim Khan[40] his son, having first disappointed some plots designed by Abdul Khan to disturb the public peace of that Kingdom, was with all due ceremony crowned King or Great Mughal in Delhi, after which he bent his endeavour to enlarge his territories and make known that he was verily the great-grandson of victorious Timur. In

---

[39] Sher Shah was not overthrown, and (see above) he had several successors before Humayun was able to return to his kingdom. They were Islam Shah (1545–1553), Firuz Shah (1553), Mohammed Shah Adil (1553–1555), Ibrahim Shah Suri (1555), Sikander Shah Suri (1555), and Adil Shah Suri (1555–1556). When the last was expelled, Humayun finally regained the throne. De Laet, however, does mention the successors to Sher Shah, or at least Firuz and Adil Shah (*Empire*, 139–40), but he states that Sher Shah died in Gwalior, which is in fact where Islam Shah died in 1553 (138), and he mentions the defeat of Sikandar Shah at Sihrind by Humayun's forces (139). Herbert supplies none of these details.

[40] Mirza Abdu'r-Rahim Khan, known as the Khan-i-Khanan [*Ganganna*] (1556–1627), was a scholar, poet, general, and astrologer. He translated the *Baburnama* from Turkish into Persian, and wrote several books on astrology. He is probably best known for his poetry. He was the stepson of Akbar. He will play a prominent part in events from this point onwards.

the first place he takes revenge of Hemu,[41] who had formerly chased Tardi Beg Khan,[42] whose head three months after by mischance of war coming under command of Bahadur Khan[43] was cut off and set up in Delhi, which province thereby was for some time quieted. Then by Ali Quli Khan[44] he subdues Dosh, by some called Sanbal,[45] a province surrounded by Yamuna[46] and Ganges, the noblest river in India, which springs from Shiva out of a rock near Hardwar,[47] resembling the head of a cow, say the banians, and in four months empties itself, running through Bengal into the ocean. "*Sibae*," saith Stephanus,[48] "*populi sunt Indiae, qui cum Coriade pugnaverunt contra Bacchum.*"

At that time Bairam Khan, otherwise called Bairam Khan the Persian, aging fast and tired with the fopperies of this world, having well-discharged the

---

[41] Hemu or Hemuchandra [*Hemaw*], "a Hindu general . . . who had gone over to the service of the Afghans and dreamed of overturning the Mughal ruler" (Berinstain, *India*, 38) attacked Delhi and Agra, captured both of them, and proclaimed himself Raja Vikramaditya, "The King Whose Effulgence is Equal to the sun's" (Stanley Wolpert, *A New History of India* [New York: Oxford University Press, 1989], 126). He was defeated at the second battle of Panipat and executed by Bairam Khan, after Akbar had spared him (1556). See Abu'l-Fazl, *The Akbarnama*, trans. H. Beveridge (Delhi: Low Price Publications, 1993), 2, 9–11; De Laet, *Empire*, 140–42.

[42] Tardi Beg Khan [*Turdichan*] (d. 1556) was a general who served both Humayun and Akbar.

[43] The brother of Ali Quli Khan (see below). He was put to death after the brothers were defeated in 1567.

[44] Ali Quli Khan, also known as Zaman Khan (d. 1567), an Uzbek leader "of perverse sexual morals and overweening conceit" (A. L. Srivastava, *Akbar the Great*, 1: *Political History 1542–1605* [Agra: Shiva Lal Agarwala, 1962], 100), was Governor of Jaunpur (now in Uttar Pradesh). He defeated the Afghans (1564) but then rose against Akbar (1565–1567). After Akbar captured Jaunpur he was captured and pardoned. In 1567 Akbar defeated him at a battle near Fatehpur Parsaki; it was in this engagement that he was trampled to death. Herbert appears to think that Ali Quli and Zaman are different people.

[45] Sambhal [*Sanbal*] is a city about 100 km east of Delhi.

[46] The west bank of the river Yamuna [*Jeminy*] is the site of Agra, Akbar's capital to 1570 and again in 1599–1605.

[47] Hardwar is in modern-day Uttar Pradesh; the exact spot is the Har-ki-pairi ghat.

[48] Hieronimo di Santo Stefano from Genoa travelled from Cairo to Calicut and wrote a letter from Tripoli (1499) describing his experiences which was printed with the Portuguese edition of Marco Polo (1502). Ramusio translated it back into Italian (*Navigazione*, 1: 372–73). Stefano was also in Pegu (1495–1496), and his letter includes an early account of *sati*. R. H. Major included an English translation in his *India in the Fifteenth Century, being a Collection of Narratives of Voyages to India* (London, 1857). The quote states "The Sibae were a people of India who with Corias (?) fought against Bacchus." The source was probably Arrian, *Anabasis 8. 10*.

trust reposed in him by his old master and not a little to his comfort observing in his pupil a spirit fitted for the government of that monarchy, obtains leave to spend the residue of his time at Mahomet's sepulchre in contemplation. But in his roomery on the way to Medina, at Patan[49] in Cambay he was wounded to death by an obscure slave of his whose father he had formerly slain,[50] so that by Abdu'r Rahim his son, then not fourteen years old, and much-afflicted company this great captain was brought back to Agra and there honourably buried.[51] Akbar laments his death, though by some, how truly I know not, thought an agent,[52] but nothing can recover him, and the better to forget his death he spends some time building a castle at Agra[53] which was formerly of mud, but by him pulled down and so altered for the better that now it scarce admits a comparison through all Asia, for 'tis of durable stone, well-polished and so spacious that it comprehends three miles' circuit of grounds built upon the pleasant banks of Yamuna, compassed with a stone wall, moated, and to be entered by many draw-bridges, having four strong gates, some bulwarks and counter-scarps without to make it more defensive.

Agra Described

Agra, east from Surat seven hundred and seventy miles English, the navel of the Mughal's territories and empress of cities in Hindustan, has 28 degrees 38 minutes north latitude, and is watered by Yamuna, *Iomanes* in Pliny and *Hynamanes*

---

[49] Patan is about 120 km north-west of Ahmedabad (Gujarat).

[50] Bairam Khan was assassinated by one Mubarak Khan Lohani, an Afghan "whose father had been killed in the battle of Machhiwara in 1555" (Srivastava, *Akbar*, 1: 49; De Laet, *Empire*, 143 and n. 23). He was not "an obscure slave." De Laet calls Bairam Khan "the good old man," although he was actually about thirty-seven when he was killed (143).

[51] Abdu'r Rahim was actually four, not fourteen; De Laet gives his age as twelve (144). After his father was murdered, he was rescued from the hands of those who killed Bairam Khan and brought with his family to Ahmedabad. He would become the Khan-i-Khanan and commander-in-chief of the Imperial army (see later on *passim*).

[52] The assassination may have been engineered by Maham Anaga, Akbar's former nurse, under whose influence the young emperor fell in the early years of his reign. She wanted to further the cause of her son, who was Akbar's foster-brother (for details see Berinstain, *India*, 39). Banerjee gives another version, namely that "the Kashmiri wife of Islam Shah [successor to Sher Shah] with her daughter had attached herself to Bairam's suite and it had been arranged that the daughter was to marry Abdu'r Rahim, Bairam's son. This is said to have annoyed the Afghans" (De Laet, *Empire*, 143–44 n. 23).

[53] Akbar began the construction of this fort in 1565, and by the time of his grandson Shah Jahan (1627–1658) it had become more of a palace-complex. See De Laet, *Empire*, 144.

in Polyaenus his 8 *Lib. Semiramidis*,[54] which from Delhi glides hither, and commixing with Ganges, flows into the Bengal Sea. Agra was of old, some say without good authority, called Nagra, and ere that Dionysia, whence some imagine
'twas founded by Bacchus, Dionysia being a compound word taken from Dios Jupiter his supposed father and Nysa his nurse. Others call him Janus, which causes
some to imagine he was Noah looking into the old and new world, and so-called
by reason of his vine-planting, in Hebrew jain signifying wine. But when this
Bacchus lived will be difficult to know, seeing *"multos fuisse Lyberos,"* said Diodorus Siculus.[55] Howbeit, Fatehpur[56] till of late, no longer then fifty years ago bore
away the same. But some there be that imagine it took its name from the conquering Agradarus, as Cyrus was first called, who from his own name gave several denominations. Others there be that derive it from the river Agranis, which
from hence streams pleasantly into Ganges, as Arrian, *Liber de Indicis*[57] called
it. Nevertheless in respect it's new-built since the race of Timur came hither; it
may most probably take its name from agara, which in the Tartar tongue signifies a town of carts new-built, or of wood, as Hakluyt *fol.* 489 observes concerning it, and agreeable to the Scythic towns who, having no fixed station, want not
a decorum in ranking their carts so as they resemble streets orderly-disposed.

---

[54] Polyaenus (fl. 160–170) was a Hellenistic historian from Macedonia who served
as a general under the Emperor Lucius Verus. His principal work is the *Strategemata*
or *Strategita*, which appeared in a Latin translation by Isaac Casaubon (1589). Book 8,
Chapter 26 contains the discussion of Semiramis.

[55] Diodorus Siculus (c. 90–30 B.C.E.) was a Greek historian born in Sicily. His
chief work is the *Bibliotheca historia*, a forty-book encyclopaedia of world history. Book II
is dedicated to Mesopotamia, Arabia, and India. There was a Latin translation of Books
I–V by Poggio Bracciolini (1472), but Herbert was likely using the complete (minus some
of the later books, which are lost) version published by H. Stephanus (1559). C. H. Oldfa-
ther edited and translated it for the Loeb Classical Library (London: Heinemann, 1935).
The quote translates "there were many Libers (Bacchuses)."

[56] Fatehpur Sikri was the capital of the Mughal Empire from 1570–1586, Akbar
having decided to move the court from Delhi and build a new city, which was abandoned
some years later because of problems with the water-supply. It remains to this day a won-
derfully-preserved Mughal ghost city. For details see Crowther and Raj, *India*, 250–525;
C. Ross Smith, *In Search of India* (Philadelphia: Clutton, 1980), 89–93. The latter states
that "What you will see today is almost exactly what you would have seen three hundred
and fifty years ago . . . it is no Rome, which, changing with the centuries, is manifestly
modern. It is wholly and beautifully what it was" (89). Singh notes that Fatehpur "is at its
most atmospheric at sunset or first thing in the morning" (Sarina Singh, *India* [Victoria:
Lonely Planet, 2008], 342).

[57] Arrian's *Indica* is really an appendage to his major work on Alexander the Great,
the *Anabasis Alexandri* (see above, n. 48). It deals with Nearchus's voyage after the king's
death but also gives much information about the geography, history, and culture of India.
The modern translation is that of P. A. Brunt (Cambridge, MA: Harvard University
Press, 1983).

Whatever the name was, the shape is semi-lunary like London; the streets are many and long and narrow but nasty. The city is seven miles in circuit, in part walled about; the ditch fences the remainder. From Agra to Lahore, most of the way being through a shade of trees, are five hundred miles, to Bharampur are reckoned one thousand, to Ajmer[58] two hundred, to Surat seven hundred and seventy or thereabouts.

[Maharana Udai Singh],[59] the most potent and noble prince of India, whose progenitor was Porus of the old race of Indians, at this time lost his strong castle of Chittor,[60] upon this occasion, having entrusted that important garrison with Sain Das,[61] a captain of Akbar's army formerly, but fled to the rana upon discontent. Sain makes many inroads into Gujarat, to let Akbar know how little he valued his forces in those quarters. Akbar, glad of the occasion, hastens with fifty thousand horse against him. Some months he spent in besieging this place, but so fruitlessly that he rather attempts the conquest in an unusual way, undermining the fort, and, to the terror of the besieged, blows the trains up with powder, causing such a breach as himself and twenty thousand men immediately entered pell-mell with such haste that Sain the rebel, perceiving treaty of no value, gathering in one his family, consumed himself and them in flames, to prevent the tortures provided for him by Akbar and [the] Maharana, his enraged master. In this sort this famous fort was taken, which Ala-ud-din[62] by twelve years' siege could not do, a victory so great that Akbar causes it to be expressed in sculpture at Agra. He had no time to surfeit of this victory, receiving letters from Rajah Bhagwant [Das],[63] Viceroy of Lahore, that Mirza Mohammed with thirty thousand horse out of Kabul had attempted to prey upon Lahore. Akbar delays no time, but with

---

[58] Ajmer in Eastern Rajasthan was one of the residences of the Mughal Emperor; Akbar built a palace there in 1570. In 1616 Sir Thomas Roe was received there by Emperor Jahangir. Crowther and Raj call it "a green oasis on the shore of the Ana Sagar lake" (*India*, 380).

[59] Maharana Udai Singh II (1537–1572) [*Radgee Rana*] of Mewar (now Udaipur) was the most powerful Rajput prince, whose family had been leading resistance to the Mughals for decades. As Herbert notes, he was overcome at the siege of Chitor (1568). After the siege he moved the capital to Udaipur.

[60] Chittor or Chittogarh was the former capital of Mewar. When it fell to Akbar in 1568 Maharana Udai Singh II moved the capital to Udaipur. De Laet gives a full account of the siege (*Empire*, 144–46).

[61] Sain Das [*Zimet*] was the Rawat of Salumbar. His heroic defence of the east gate of Chittorgarh is still celebrated today. He fell fighting on 25 February 1568.

[62] Probably Ala-ud-din Khilji. Sultan of Delhi 1294–1316.

[63] Rajah Bhagwan Das [*Radgee B'han*] was the ruler of Amber 1574–1589. Akbar appointed him Governor of Punjab and invested him with the title of Amir al-Amara. In 1562 Akbar had married his sister, "the start of four generations of loyal service by that Rajput house in the Mughal army" (Wolpert, *New History*, 127).

his army presents himself so suddenly to the enemy that without any resistance Mohammed flies away, leaving his camp to the mercy of Akbar's army.

This occasion drew the King to view other places of defence, which he both bettered by his eye and gave in charge to such as he could trust. He also takes a survey of Punjab, out of which he is soon called by letters from his mother then in Agra, acquainting him with the rebellion of Bahadur Khan and Ali Quli Khan, who were sent that spring against the Pathans, whom in Doab they put to flight; at Sambel also and at Lucknow[64] got a greater victory, and three weeks after at Jaunpore utterly defeated them, subduing to the Mughal all such provinces as lie engirt 'twixt Ganges and Tsatsa, conquests of so great note that they grew inflated beyond measure, conceiting all Hindustan under like possibility, and which they resolved to make trial of. But the reward and destiny due to traitors overtakes them, for Akbar by swift marches, long before the rebels expected him, pitches his tents on the east of Yamuna, the river at Agra, which struck the adverse part with such amazement that as men struck with guilt, forfeiting the memory of their past victories, they betook themselves to a speedy and shameful flight, after whom Akbar eagerly pursues, and after long pursuit the heads are taken. Ali Quli Khan was trodden underfoot by the horse, and Bahadur Khan, by Akbar's command and in his sight, was strangled.

The Mughal's Pilgrimage

This done, Abdu'r Rahim is sent to Jaunpore against Mirza Suleiman[65] and the King retreats to Agra, where he fancies a pilgrimage to Ajmer, albeit a hundred and thirty course or two hundred English miles distant thence, fancying that by invocation of Mandi,[66] a reverend hajji or disciple of Mahomet, he should obtain some issue masculine. Accordingly, after much foot-toil, at every mile's end a fair stone being pitched to rest upon, which as yet remain, he gets thither, where barefoot very devoutly he entreats dead Mandi for children. This is a prophet of great fame in those parts, and through the liberality of some devoted princes is there entombed in a stately monument graced with three fair courts, each of which is paved with stone, the outside fabric after the Persian mode being pargetted or plastered and polished in mosaic order.

Ajmer is under 25 degrees 15 minutes north latitude, seated upon a high mount, the greater part of the city being below, much after the similitude of

---

[64] Lucknow eventually became the capital of the Nawabs (later Kings) of Oudh or Awadh.

[65] Sultan Suleiman II Karanani of Bengal (1565–1572). After his defeat by Akbar, he continued the struggle until his death in 1574.

[66] Mandi was a Sufi holy man who came to Ajmer in 1192. His tomb is known as the Dargah, and there is also a shrine built by Humayun. Akbar made yearly pilgrimages there (for details see Crowther and Raj, *India*, 380–81).

Dover, the houses being well-built but of small strength, albeit moated with a dry grass and walled about with solid stone, not far from which place is Kotah, once the seat of the valiant Rajput princes.

Fatehpur Sikri

The country is champagne and fruitful, in many places affording the ruins of antique magnificence, which by time and war are exceedingly obscured; these Akbar coupled to the rest of his empire, and by this, having made an end of his oblations, in his return he visits a holy dervish, Said Salim[67] by name, of great repute amongst the people, who took it for so great a favour that (by what skill I know not) he foretold the Mughal how that ere long he should be father of three men-children, which proved so, and upon which account his first-born was called Salim, he who afterwards was Jahangir the Great Mughal, when Sir Thomas Roe had audience at Agra in the quality of an ambassador. The other two were named Murad Shah and Daniyal,[68] a prophecy so grateful to Akbar that in gratitude there he erected a very magnificent mosque walled in the old town, Zikerin or Sikri, as some pronounce, and from this occasion new-named it Fatehpur, which signifies a place of pleasure, yea, grew so affected to it that he adorned it with a palace for himself and a bazaar for trade scarce out-vied by any other in the orient, and had made it the metropolis and usual residence of the court, had the river affected him, by whose unwholesomeness he forsook it, from whence ruin and neglect have so moth-eaten her as at this day she lies prostrate and become the object of contempt and pity, from Agra being distant eighteen miles English.[69]

Whilst things were in this sort digesting, news comes to King Akbar, then in Fatehpur, that another rebellion was begun in Gujarat by Ibrahim Husain, Mirza Khan, Mohammed Hassan and Jun Khan,[70] who had foraged as far as

---

[67] Salim Chisti (1478–1572), the Sufi "sayed," or saint, was indeed a historical figure, and the legend Herbert relates is still told today. His tomb, surrounded by elaborate marble lace, is in the mosque, and childless women still visit it. For further details, see Crowther and Raj, *India*, 250–52; Singh, *India*, 343.

[68] Prince Murad Shah [*Amurath*] (1570–1599) became a soldier; he besieged Ahmednagar on his father's behalf in 1595. His brother Prince Daniyal [*D'han Shah* or *Daniel*] (1572–1604), a competent army commander who fought successfully against the Rajputs, was appointed Viceroy of Deccan. Both died from alcoholism.

[69] According to Crowther and Raj, Herbert is correct; Akbar had to abandon the city because of "difficulties with the water-supply" (*India*, 250). In 1583 the population exceeded that of London.

[70] Ibrahim Hussein Mirza and his two brothers Mohammed Hussein and Mirza Shah rebelled on more than one occasion against Akbar. They were defeated at the battle of Sarnal (16 January 1573) and Ibrahim was killed later at the battle of Talumba (May 1573). In September of the same year Mohammed and Mirza Shah were defeated at

Baroda and were marching to Ahmedabad, hoping with their troops of thieves and coolies to make a prey of the wealthy city.

Ahmedabad

Ahmedabad seems to me to be that city which is called *Amacastis* in Ptolemy, *Amadovastis* in Arrian. Howbeit, some say it takes denomination from King Ahmed,[71] who in the Year of Mahomet 375 made it large and beautiful. The Pole Arctic is there elevated 23 degrees 18 minutes; 'tis at this present the megapolis of Cambay or Gujarat, watered by a sweet river and circled by a strong wall of four miles' compass, well and orderly, advanced with many pretty towers and a dozen pasterns out of which few pass or re-pass without a pass, fearing treason from Prince Bahadur,[72] who in our times with a hundred thousand horse ransacked Cambay thirty-seven courses thence, (a course is equal to a large English mile or somewhat more), and daily threatens this fair city. The streets are many, pretty large and comely; most shops be redundant with aromatic gums, perfumes and spices, silks, cotton, calicos and choice of India or China rarities owned and sold by the ambitious banians, who here surpass for number other inhabitants. Of most note is the bazaar, which is rich and uniform; the castle is strong, large, moated, and the receiving palace of the Cambayan governor. The houses in general are of sunburnt bricks, low but large and terraced. Adjoining is seen the monument of a certain pedagogue who was so dearly-beloved by Shahriyar the King that by a stately mausoleum he strove to make him seem immortal.[73] The building, which is arched, and pavement are of well-polished marble; it hath three fair courts, one of them fastidious in four hundred porphyrian pillars framed in Corinthiac architecture. Joining to it is a tank of water compassed

---

Ahmedabad; Mirza was killed and Mohammed captured. He was executed a short time later. "*Jun Khan*" is not identified, but there were other leaders with the Mirzas (see De Laet, *Empire*, 148–50). The Mirzas, Banerjee explains, "belonged to that dangerous class of 'royal cousins' who committed so much mischief in medieval England." They were descended from the royal ine of Timur; and their title "Mirza" is "a shortened form of Amir Zada. Originally it was applied to kings and princes" (De Laet, *Empire*, 148, n.28).

[71] This was Ahmed Shah (1411–1442), who founded the city in 1411.

[72] Prince Bahadur (d. 1615) was the son of Muzaffar III of Gujarat. In 1606 he sacked and occupied Cambay for a fortnight.

[73] This is probably a reference to one Shah Alam (d. 1475), who became "one of the most revered of Musulman religious teachers" (De Laet, *Empire*, 22, n. 34). Crowther and Raj think it is a description of the tomb of Ahmed Khattu Gaj Buksh (d. 1445), "a renowned Moslem saint," near to which is actually a "tank" (*India*, 426), but this is in Sarkej (see below), not in the main city.

with cloisters, adorned with spacious windows, most of which give the observer a delicate horizon.[74]

At Sarkhej,[75] one hour's riding hence, are seen the dormitories of many Cambayan princes, being Rajputs and the ancient nobility before the Tartars, from whom the present Mughals descend, were propagated, lodged in a princely temple which is much resorted-to by the banians, who branch from the same root as the Rajputs. And two miles nearer the city, we behold the curious gardens and palace of Mirza Abdu'r Rahim Khan, who was the son of the great Bairam Khan the Persian, an *umrah* by whose valour of late years the last of the Cambayan Kings in that very place, by loss of his life gave conquest to that warrior and dominion to Akbar his master, and in memory whereof he built that stately house and made those spacious gardens, the view whereof worthily attracts a traveller.

But return we to Akbar, who no sooner received intelligence of Husain's rebellion but with incredible haste he gets thither, each twenty-four hours posting seventy, in seven days four hundred courses, and gives those rebels battle at the sun's first uprising, and with their noise and clamour so terrify them that after small resistance their whole army broke into disorder. Many were slain in the pursuit, and by a fresh supply of horse led by Koka Khan,[76] an expert soldier, after a small skirmish they are further chased and in the flight Ibrahim Husain and Mirza Khan were slain, and Mohammed Hassan himself taken prisoner and forthwith beheaded. By this advantage not only Ahmedabad was recovered and better fortified, but Surat also was conquered and most of Gujarat made subject to Akbar.

This done, Akbar returns crowned with victory, and as the product of peace begins the castle in Agra, which is built of such good stone and the building so large that it deservedly challenges the title of Princess of Agra. Twelve years scarce finished it, though twelve hundred labourers at some time were employed about it; there he expended fifty thousand crore of tucka.[77] A crore is a hundred lakhs, each lakh a hundred thousand; thirty, sometime twenty tucka make one

---

[74] Perhaps Herbert was describing it from memory. A tank is not a water-tank, but "a reservoir, an artificial pond or lake" (*HJ* 898).

[75] Sarkej is now a suburb of Ahmedabad, about 8 km from the centre of town. The "dormitories" Herbert mentions are probably the mausolea of Sultan Mahmud Begara, his wife Rajahbai (1460) and others. For details see Crowther and Raj, *India* 426. S. N. Banerjee notes that "the place was famous for its indigo; the Dutch established a factory there in 1620" (De Laet, *Empire*, 22, n.35).

[76] Zein Koka Khan [*Goga-cawn*] was the foster-brother of Akbar. A commander of Akbar's army, he was appointed successively Governor of Kabul (1587) and Punjab (1600), and in both posts he distinguished himself for mild and benevolent administration. His daughter married Prince Salim, later Emperor Jahangir.

[77] Stamped silver money; "this is the word commonly used among Bengalis for a rupee" (*HJ* 940). However, given Herbert's figures, the value had obviously changed by the time Yule and Burnell were writing. Their earliest citation is from 1809.

rupee. A rupee is two shillings three pence, so that accounting but twenty tucka to a rupee the total he disbursed amounts to two millions and five hundred thousand rupees. At Fatehpore at that time also he spent about the wall and palace a million and five hundred thousand rupees, in all four millions.

Burial-Place of the Mughal

At *Tzekander* or *Secandra*, as some pronounce it likewise, three course or five miles from Agra as we go to Lahore is the mausoleum or burial-place of the Great Mughals, the foundation of which was begun by Akbar, the superstructure continued by Jahangir his son and is yet scarce finished, albeit they have already consumed 14 millions of rupees in that wonder of India. It well merits a little more in that description; it is called Sikandra,[78] i.e. Alexander, a place where the greatest of Grecian Kings made his *ne plus*, when he made his utmost progress or march into India, which place Akbar, the most magnificent prince of Timur's race, selected as the noblest place of burial. 'Tis a mausoleum of four large squares; each side has about three hundred paces. The material is freestone[79] well-polished; at each angle is raised a small tower of parti-coloured or chequered marble. Ten foot higher then that is another tower, on every side beautified with three towers. The third gallery has two on each side, the fourth, one, the fifth, half, and a small square gallery or terrace about, mounting in the whole to a royal pyre resembling not a little that famous Septizonium[80] of [Septimius] Severus the emperor in ancient Rome which you have represented in sculpture by Laurus, or, but in far less proportion, that famous tower which Semiramis built in Babylon and dedicated to the memory of Jupiter Belus, her husband's great ancestor. In this, at the very top, within is the mummy of Akbar bedded in a coffin of gold. The whole structure is built in the midst of a spacious garden which is surrounded with a wall of red-coloured stone, and in that is a rail mounted by six stairs which discoveres a little garden, but exquisitely beautiful and delightful, so that of this noble fabric I may say "Such a monument/ The sun through all the world sees none more great."

While these vast buildings were erecting, Abdu'r Rahim prosecutes Mirza Suleiman [Kharani], but, whether of grief or age is doubted, died suddenly,

---

[78] Actually it is named after Sultan Sikandar Lodi of Delhi (1488–1517), who also built the Baradi Palace in the gardens, and has nothing whatever to do with Alexander the Great. However, Herbert's description is accurate in all its details (see Crowther and Raj, *India*, 245–47). Sikandra is 10 km north of Agra.

[79] Sandstone.

[80] The Septizonium was built in 203 C.E., but no-one knows exactly what it was for. Some scholars believe that it may have been a temple to the seven planetary gods, others that it was just an ornamental building. It decayed over the centuries, and the final remnant was demolished by order of Pope Sixtus V in 1588.

leaving the prosecution thereof to Iskandar his son, who in short time was made away by some conspirators. In his place Daud, Bayezid Khan's son,[81] a man both effeminate and hated, succeeded him, so that now occasion presented itself most seasonably to Akbar to link Bengal to his crown imperial, a design so worthy his enterprise that with an army of fifty thousand horse, two hundred thousand foot and six hundred elephants he advanced against the Pathan prince and passed over Ganges ere Daoud Shah had notice of his coming, which when he was assured of, he [Akbar] dispatched Rajah Bhagwant [Das] with twenty thousand horse to encounter them. 'Twixt Ziotsa and Mahabalipur they affronted one another and for three hours' space skirmish gallantly, but Akbar, overpowering them with his numbers, at length has the mastery and courageously pursues them to Patan, which King Daoud had fortified. Akbar by no means could provoke them to battle nor in three months' siege enter the city, for Patan is a town both great and well-fortified. Yet in the fourth he forces it, giving it as a prey to his men, who used all sorts of hostile violence. The unlucky King was buried in drink all that time, senseless of loss till too late to repent it, so that he was conveyed away in a boat and at three days' end made headless and sent to Akbar as a symbol of their submission and vanity.

The King, having thus fortunately proceeded in Bengal, goes back to Fatehpur, where whiles he oversees his buildings he is nevertheless mindful to increase his empire, which was then but in the adolescency, and to that end by the valour and vigilancy of Rustum Khan and Sadiq Khan[82] the strong castle Ranthambore[83] in Malwa was soon after taken from the Rajahs who of many hundred

---

[81] Suleiman II Kharani of Bengal was briefly succeeded by his son Bayezid Khan [*Bazat-cawn*] (1572). Daoud Shah [*Dowett*] reigned 1572–1576. Herbert's relation of the events is not quite accurate; in her list of rulers of Bengal, Mabel Duff does not mention an "Iskandar" at all (*The Chronicles of Indian History* [Delhi: Cosmo Press, 1972], 314), nor does Srivastava (*Akbar*, 1: 155). When Daoud succeeded, Akbar sent an emissary to treat with him, and Daoud's prime minister advised compromise, at which Daoud had him killed, provoking Akbar's wrath. The victory over Daoud was won in 1574 and Bengal became part of the Empire (for details see Berinstain, *India*, 42–43). Daoud finally surrendered to Akbar in 1576.

[82] Sadiq Khan was one of Akbar's most trusted generals. After the capture of Ranthambore he went on to quell a rebellion in Bihar (1580) and conducted an unsuccessful campaign in Lahore, where he failed to capture Nasirpur (1587).

[83] Ranthambore [*Rantipur*] is now in ruins, but was (from 944 onwards) a significant fortress near the modern town of Sawai Madhopur. Before Akbar captured it (1559) it was actually in the hands of the Haras from Bundi. In the seventeenth century it passed to the maharajas of Jaipur, who owned it until 1947, when it became part of the Ranthambore National Park.

years had owned it, after which the castle Rota, *Oreophanta*[84] of old, in Berar[85] in Bengal was taken by a merry sleight. This castle for many ages acknowledged the Rajah her governor, her building both from nature and art being impregnable; 'tis seated upon a perpendicular hill, the ascent cut oblique out of the rock for three miles compass. The rest of the rock is round about and precipitous; the top is a plain of eight miles every way, the circuit twenty-four, healthy and abounding with all good things necessary, as water, corn, fruits, wood and sixteen villages included by the castle wall, which gives the defence twofold wonderful. In a word, not any fort or castle in Asia or, it may be, in the universe, is more delightful or of greater strength as those that see it have imagined.

This the Great Mughal looks upon with a lustful eye, immeasurably thirsting, but knows neither by bribe nor valour how to compass it, and though he comprehends no way, yet ceases not to torture his invention till the enterprise was undertaken by Muhib Ali Khan,[86] a Vaisya and daring captain, who, having leave, without acquainting Akbar or any other with his design, attempts it with four hundred young men who were privately-armed with *krisses*[87] as a common guard to his seraglio, which were in two hundred *dhoolies*[88] or *cadjowas*,[89] as if he were going upon a journey into Bengal. In this order passing on, when he came within view of the castle he shows a Rajah his concubines and bribes him to procure leave of the lord above that in regard of his haste he might with safety leave his seraglio there till his return. This message being delivered, the Rajah,[90] who loved women well, entertains the notion, and Ali Khan, imparting the secret to a prudent eunuch, disrobes the women and with their apparel clothes himself and the four hundred youths, commanding the women to put on their masculine attire and to continue the journey to Orissa, and accordingly the eunuchs, twelve in number, with bows and arrows guard the seraglio and by the Rajah's command are received, but like Sinon's horse into wretched Troy, for, Ali Khan giving the

---

[84] Oreophanta is located "between Celydna and Aganagora" on the Ganges (William Hazlitt, *A Dictionary of Ancient Geography* [London, 1851], 253).

[85] Berar had been part of the Deccan sultanate until the beginning of the sixteenth century, when the sultanate split into five Kingdoms, one of which was Berar. In the twentieth century the title "Prince of Berar" was revived for the son of the Nizam of Hyderabad.

[86] Muhib Ali Khan was the son of Mir Khalifa, who had been Babur's prime minister. He conquered Thatta (1571) and defeated the rebel Arab Bahadur (1579).

[87] A kind of dagger usually associated with Malays, but "often applied to analogous weapons of other nations" (*HJ* 274). Herbert spells it *cryze*, and it also appears spelled crease.

[88] Covered litters. A dhooly "consists of a cot or frame suspended by the four corners from a bamboo pole and is carried by four men" (*HJ* 313).

[89] "A kind of frame or pannier, of which a pair are slung across a camel, sometimes made like litters to carry women" (*HJ* 140).

[90] Burhan Imad Shah was the Sultan, not Rajah, of Berar 1562–1568.

word, the *dhoolies* were no sooner dismounted but that thereout issued the Amazons. In the first place they secure the porters of the castle gate, then with incredible speed assail the astonished inhabitants, whom without much resistance they took prisoners, and in the end the Rajah himself, whom, to prevent excuse, they beheaded. Thus is the castle Rota won, which, but by stratagem, was not to be taken by all the hostile force of India.

Akbar entertains the news and manner of surprise with incredible delight, and joys the more in his belief when he views that mass of treasure which was sent him thence by Ali Khan to confirm the truth of that conquest, after which the invincible castle Jalalabad was by Ghiyath ud-din Shah, an apostate Mahometan, also betrayed to the Mughal, although to his own brother's confusion, the fame whereof afflicts many princes of the Rajputs, each of them labouring to conserve their own against this overspreading Tartar, to which purpose some courageously defy his greatness, of which Roopmati,[91] a lady both fair and valiant, who albeit her beauty was more forcible to subdue then any arms she could manage, nevertheless she confides more in her lance then beauty, so that animating her party she vigorously falls into the Mughal's dominions. But in the midst of her career she was encountered by Adham Khan,[92] an expert soldier, who with his body of horse so furiously opposed her that most of her Pathans in that skirmish were cut off, no quarter being given any but herself, who rather then endure the shame of her imprisonment, the assault of her chastity or those scoffs they probably would have entertained her with, put a period to her life by poison.

---

[91] Rani Roopmati (d. 1561) was a former singer and dancer who married Baz Bahadur, Sultan of Malwa (1555–1562). She committed suicide after Baz Bahadur's defeat and flight rather than fall into Mughal hands, as Herbert relates. Her husband built the Roopmati Mahal in Malwa for her and also an aqueduct so that she could always have fresh water. It is said that Adham Khan (see below) was in love with her, which was his pretext for attacking Malwa. For details of Roopmati's heroic and tragic end, which does not seem to have included fighting, see Srivastava, *Akbar*, 54–56 and De Laet, *Empire* 153. A film of her life has been made (1959) and her poems are still read. Banerjee notes that De Laet "emphasises the influence of [Roopmati] over the king," but cautions that "as a piece of historical information we may not be disposed to attach importance to it" (De Laet, *Empire*, 153, n. 34).

[92] Adham Khan (d. 1562) was the son of Akbar's nurse Mahum Anaga, and is described by Srivastava, together with his comrade Pir Mohammed Khan as a "heartless tyrant" (*Akbar*, 55). After his victory Adham plundered Malwa's treasury and stole the Sultan's art works. He also seized all of the Sultan's concubines who were left alive after Baz Bahadur's flight and had not been killed on the Sultan's orders. He promised to return the wounded Roopmati to her husband, but went back on his promise. In 1562 Adham murdered Akbar's vizier, and the Emperor ordered him killed; when this proved difficult, Akbar had him thrown several times off the palace terrace until he expired.

Muzaffar Khan[93] in the meantime, this year 1583 being in Gujarat, hatches a conspiracy against Akbar, and in the first place strangles Qutb ud-din Mohammed Khan,[94] the King's viceroy in Ahmedabad and some *umrah*; he then siezes upon all the advantageous places for the strengthening his rebellion, but by Abdu'r Rahman, Bairam Khan's son, is no sooner opposed then vanquished, and, fearing to obtain pardon, destroyed himself in like sort as did the late-named Amazon,[95] the report of whose death was no sooner bruited but the same also of Mirza Mohammed Hakim,[96] brother to Akbar. His death occasions Akbar to assure himself of Kabul, which during Hakim's life was impossible to be compassed, but using with all kind respect his wives and children, he confirmed upon Qaiqubad Khan, Hamid Beg and Masum Khan[97] both large stipends and commands in Masulipatam, Orissa[98] and other places suitable to their merit.

---

[93] Muzaffar Shah III (d. 1592) was sultan of Gujarat 1561–1573 and 1583. Srivastava describes him initially as a "puppet" (*Akbar*, 130) who was controlled by Aitimad Khan, a powerful nobleman. He submitted to Akbar in 1573 and was replaced by a Governor. His rebellion in 1583, in which he demonstrated some military skill and bravery, was a serious one, and he nearly took Ahmedabad.

[94] Qutb ud-din Mohammed Khan (d. 1583) [*Gotobdas Mamet-cawn*] was the *faujdar* [sub-governor] of Broach, not a viceroy. When Muzaffar III rebelled (1583) he moved against him and sent him fleeing to Junagarh. There is no evidence that he was killed by Muzaffar himself, although on 2 November he was "defeated and treacherously killed by the rebels near the town of Sarnal" (Srivastava, *Akbar*, 321).

[95] Herbert is wrong. After his defeat Muzaffar went to Kathiawar; when Abdu'r Rahim left Gujarat on leave he reappeared, and he continued to be a nuisance for another ten years. It is true that he killed himself, but this was in 1592 after his final defeat and capture at Dhrol.

[96] Prince Mirza Mohammed Hakim (1553–1585) was actually Akbar's step-brother and governor of Kabul. "A drunkard of mediocre talent and devoid of resolution and foresight" (Srivastava, *Akbar*, 295), he rebelled against his brother and set up his own quasi-Kingdom in Kabul; Akbar only moved against him in 1581 after he had been formally proclaimed ruler by Bihari rebels. He invaded India and attacked Lahore. Failing to get support he returned to Kabul where Akbar defeated him, pardoned him and reinstated him as Governor. A reassessment of him may be read in Munis D. Faruqui, "The Forgotten Prince: Mirza Hakim and the Formation of the Mughal Empire in India," *Journal of the Economic History of the Orient* 48 (2005): 487–523.

[97] Qaiqubad Khan [*Chabec-chawn*] (b. 1570) was Hakim's eldest son; his second son was named Afrasiab (b. 1571), but is not mentioned by Herbert. Masum Khan Kabuli [*Maxuen-cawn*] (d. 1599) was a leader of the rebels and became Hakim's "Prime Minister". Mohammed Beg Qaqshal [*Hamet Beg*] was a rebel leader in Bengal.

[98] Orissa is in eastern India, and was once a thriving centre of Buddhism.

At the same time Shahbaz Khan,[99] late President of Kabul and famoused for his victory that year against Masum Khan, Baba Khan[100] and other rebels in Bengal was made Viceroy of that province and Rajah Todar Mal[101] called to Fatehpur, such as time as Rajah Ram Chand, Lord of Bhatha,[102] a province adjoining Agra, redundant only in sand and stones, by persuasion of Rajah Bharmal[103] presents himself to Akbar at Fatehpur and enrols his country as a member of appendix of the Mughal's great seigneury, by whose example sundry other petty gentile Kings submitted themselves unto Akbar, and yearly, as a symbol of their subjection, present him besides earth and water their daughters to be his concubines, and for their better satisfaction to court them in, at Prayag,[104] an hundred and ten course from Agra, Chrysobarca in Pliny, by some Nitaea, raises a triumphant palace upon a promontory where Yamuna empties herself into Ganges. The material thereof is hard stone artistically-polished and calls it Allahabad, in nothing more observable then a deep dark cave in which are preserved as relics divers deformed pagodas, ridiculously by them supposed to be Baba Adam, Mamma Evah, Seth, Enos and Methuselah, whom they affirm lived here and to whom, from most parts of India, resort innumerable banians for benediction, first purifying themselves in Ganges, reputed holy and no doubt

---

[99] Shahbaz Khan [*Zebber-cawn*] (d. 1599) was the general who defeated Masum Khan, as Herbert states. Akbar put him in charge of the expedition against Bengal and in 1583 was made commander of the Imperial army. He also led armies in the Deccan and Punjab.

[100] Baba Khan Qaqshal [*Bama-cawn*] was one of the leaders of the rebel forces in Bihar and Bengal. He defeated Muzaffar Khan, Akbar's governor in Tanda, and took the city (1580), ordering the governor to be tortured to death,

[101] Rajah Todar Mal [*Radzia Thormiel*] (1515–1589) was one of Akbar's ablest advisers. A more than competent general, he is best remembered, however, for his land reforms and his complete overhaul of the Imperial revenue system (1560) rather than for any military exploits. In fact, as the man responsible for much of the central administration he could be said to have been a prime minister. Todar Mal also required that officials be competent in Persian, a move which led to the establishment of Urdu as an "official" language for the Mughal Empire.

[102] Rajah Ram Chandra Baghela of Bhatha [*Radgee Ramgien*] had fought against Akbar's general Asaf Khan (1563) and had been defeated and then pardoned by Akbar, who let him continue to rule his state.

[103] Rajah Bharmal Singh of Amber [*Radgee Bhyrmiel*] (r. 1548–1573) married his daughter Maryam Zamani (mother of Jahangir) to Akbar (1562) and became one of the emperor's staunchest allies and friends. In 1573 Akbar left him in charge of Agra whilst he was attacking Surat, and Bharmal foiled a sneak attack on the city by an Afghan force. The same year Bharmal also sent an army to help defend Delhi against Ibrahim Husain Mirza.

[104] Allahabad [*Elabassa*] is at the junction of the Yamuna and Ganges rivers, but Herbert gives the old name, Prayag [*Praije*] (Crowther and Raj, *India*, 260). Akbar changed the name in 1584 and built a fort here, not a palace.

excellent, for we find that a pint of Ganges water weighs less by an ounce then other water thereabouts, and, shaving off their hair as an unclean excrement, suppose that thereby they have merited. The whole is surrounded with a triple wall, the first being of square red stones and highest raised; the inmost is of white stone, retaining an obelisk which is fifty cubits high, little less under ground, as they say, to make it more firm and durable, probably fixed there for ostentation by Alexander or Bacchus, Ovid *Lib.* 4 *Met.* "Whose conquests through the orient are renown'd, / Where tawny India is by Ganges bound."[105] In this, which many Pathan kings formerly in vain attempted by reason of the overflowing rivers, the King spent a myriad and two hundred thousand rupees. Here also they have a tree which many Pathan Kings have sought to eradicate and destroy, but as report goes, could never effect, so as 'tis little less then adored.[106] Near Allahabad also is worth seeing the stately tomb which Jahangir built for his first wife, Rajah Man Singh's[107] sister, who poisoned herself as soon as she received the report of her son Khusrau's rebellion.[108]

The Mughal's affairs succeeding thus fortunately, no clouds appearing, Akbar broaches new chimaeras and fancies the entire conquest of Furop, Patan, Coromandel,[109] yea, of all Bengal to the south, and to stretch his empire north as far as Tartary, to further which he hears that Abdul Khan,[110] son and heir to Sikandar Khan, King of Turan, part of Tartary,[111] was coming to Fatehpur to give him a friendly visit. He prevents part of his journey and meets him at Lahore, where there wasted no ceremony to content the Tartarian prince, who after a short stay returned home with satisfaction.

News at this time being brought to King Akbar that Mirza Shahrukh[112] in Badakhshan had been injured by the Uzbek Tartar, the King resolves to vindicate

---

[105] Ovid, *Metamorphoses* 10. 21–22.

[106] The tree, a banian, is still there today, and is known as Akshai Veta. "This tree is mentioned by Hiuen Tsang who tells of pilgrims sacrificing their lives by leaping to their deaths from the tree in order to seek salvation" (Crowther and Raj, *India*, 262).

[107] Singh was rajah of Amber 1590–1614. He was also one of Akbar's generals.

[108] Man Bhai (d. 1606) married Jahangir, then Prince Khurram, in 1585. Her father rajah Bhagwan Das (r. 1574–1589) was the brother of Akbar's wife Jodhabhai. Man Bhai's tomb is in a garden now called the Khusrau Bagh, named for Jahangir's son Khusrau, for whom see below.

[109] Coromandel was "a name which has long been applied by Europeans to the Northern Tamil Country or (more comprehensively) to the eastern coast of the Peninsula of India from Pt. Calimere northward to the mouth of the Kistna, sometimes to Orissa" (*HJ* 256).

[110] Sikandar Khan, king of Transoxiana (Bokhara), died in 1583. He was succeeded by his son Abdullah Khan II.

[111] Turan, which Herbert calls Maurenabar, is in Transoxiana.

[112] Abdullah Khan II attacked Badakhshan (1584) and drove out the ruler, Suleiman Mirza, who, together with his grandson Mirza Shahrukh, escaped to Kabul. The

him, but first, as more considerable, bends his march towards Orissa that he might once command entirely over Ganges. At Atak[113] he musters and orders his army; to Rajah Bharmal he disposes one part, to Ganesh Bahadur[114] another, and to himself the third. Bharmal leads the van, and outstripping the army, falls furiously upon the Pathans, who by their lieutenant-general Zel Ali are received with no less bravery but answer blow for blow, so long and with such success that Bharmal was forced to retreat with loss, so as Akbar, by such as fled having quick notice of it, at first the news puts him into a rage, but reason having got the mastery of his passion, he rallies his men and with fresh supplies makes a quick return, and, having received a sharp charge by Zel Ali and his late victorious party, after some hours close fight Akbar, having far the greater army, had the day; Zel Ali first and then Turcoft the lieutenant-general being slain, and fifteen thousand of the army left dead upon the place, by which overthrow the rich and noble province of Bengal was totally subjected and to this day remains a member of the Mughal's large empire.

This happily effected, the conquest of Kandahar is next designed, to which end Akbar, hearing of a variance at that time happening 'twixt the two princes Husain and Rostam,[115] sons of Sultan Husain Mirza the Kandahar governor and a Persian; he confederates with the two young men and sends [the]

---

ruler of Kabul, Mirza Hakim (Akbar's half-brother), was afraid that Abdullah would attack him as well, and appealed to Akbar for help. He was told that if he remained loyal he would be protected (for details see Srivastava, *Akbar*, 331). Mirza Shahrukh later married Akbar's daughter Shakar-un-Nisa and became Governor of Malwa (*Tuzuk-i Jahangiri* 1. 27; see also De Laet, *Empire*, 156 and n.44). References to the *Tuzuk i-Jahangiri* will be cited hereafter as *TJ*. Badakhshan, now a province in Afghanistan, used to include northeast Afghanistan and south-east Tajikistan. In 1623 we find James I writing to Buckingham about "a carcanet or collar of thirteen great Balas [Badakhshan] rubies" to give his wife (Akrigg, *Letters*, 399).

[113] This is Atak Banaras, a fort on the east bank of the Indus river. However, there is more confusion here. Janesh Bahadur [*Jehan-cawn*] was the name of one of Akbar's generals, but in December 1585 Akbar was encamped at Hasan Abdal, not Atak, and the army was under the nominal command of Shahrukh (Srivastava, *Akbar*, 336).

[114] Rajah Ganesh [*Janesh*] of Nandun in the Punjab had been defeated by Akbar in 1562. He subsequently held various posts in Akbar's service through the good offices of Todar Mal.

[115] Muzaffar Husain Mirza and Rostam Husain Mirza were two of the sons of Sultan Husain Mirza (whom Herbert mistakenly calls Mirza Beyram), who was supposed to be governing Kandahar for the Shah of Persia. Father and sons were now rebelling against the Shah, however, and Akbar seems to have been able to deal with them through diplomacy because the sons were quarrelling (see Srivasatava, *Akbar*, 367–68). Mirza Bahram was actually the eldest son of Muzaffar Mirza, and he was sent by his father to treat with Akbar.

Khan-i-Khanan[116] with five thousand horse thither, who at midnight were let into the town by the two brethren and the city made a vassal of Akbar's empire.[117] But Abbas the Persian King,[118] not liking his enlargement that way, soon recovered it from the Indian.[119]

Conquest of Kashmir

Akbar's ambition nevertheless grows endless; so he can overcome he cares not how now where he conquers, for, hearing of the old King of Turan's death, he sends Shahbaz Khan and Hakim Khan[120] his ambassadors, who under an amicable colour of condoling and comforting Abdullah for his father's death at the year's end return well-instructed. But the Great Mughal reserves the practic part to himself, for, perceiving Kashmir interposing, and at that instant not under his power, he sends Ali Mirza[121] in embassy to Yusuf Khan,[122] a fearful King, with this message: that if he with his sons would come to Lahore and do him homage he should have his seigneury established and by that alliance his power at all times would be ready to defend him. If otherwise he would refer it to the chance of war, he must expect a perpetual slavery. The Kashmiri King, affrighted at this threat and doubting his power, hastens to Akbar and becomes his vassal, howbeit Yakub Khan[123] his son, being of more spirit and not able longer to dissemble, without leave returns home followed by such as loved him so that he quickly

---

[116] Abdu'r Rahman Khan. He will subsequently be referred to as the Khan-i-Khanan.

[117] Herbert's information is mistaken. Muzaffar surrendered Kandahar to Akbar's commander Shah Beg; Rostam had been besieging Muzaffar Husain but had made peace and gone to Herat. Akbar received Rostam's surrender in October 1593.

[118] Abbas I had succeeded his father Shah Tahmasp in 1576.

[119] Not true. Abbas had sent an envoy to Akbar in 1591 so that Kandahar would not be taken by the Mughals, but the Persians made no move against Akbar once the occupation of Kandahar was a *fait accompli*.

[120] Hakim Humam (d. 1595), "a shrewd diplomat" (Srivastava, *Akbar*, 345) and one of Akbar's intimate friends, was one of the "nine jewels" of his court. His official post was Superintendant of the Royal Kitchens, but he served as a provincial governor and part-time general as well. The condolences he brought to Abdullah II were a few years late.

[121] Akbar actually sent Mirza Shahrukh and Rajah Bhagwant Das to Kashmir to get the ruler, Yusuf Khan, to render homage in 1585. This did not work and they fought with the Kashmiris at Buliyas Pass (1586). Peace was in fact made in February 1586. Srivastava mentions "other commanders," and perhaps Ali Mirza was one of them. Herbert also has Ali Mirza leading the army against Yakub Khan (see below). However, it may be a mistake for Mirza Shahrukh.

[122] Yusuf Khan [*Justoff-cawn*] succeeded to the Kashmiri throne in 1580. He did come to Akbar's court in 1586, but Akbar disapproved of the treaty that had been made, detained him in Lahore and ordered the invasion of Kashmir anyway.

[123] Yakub Khan [*Jacob-cawn*] thought that his father was not coming back from Lahore, as Akbar had placed him under watch. Yakub declared himself ruler as "Shah

expels the Indians out of the city and is acknowledged King, but his halcyon days were of small continuance, for Akbar orders Ali Mirza and Qasim Khan[124] with thirty thousand horse to hasten after him, so as the young King, not daring upon equal terms to adventure battle, flies to the high mountains of Bhimbhar,[125] whither also Qasim Khan, directed by some native, so hotly pursues that they become masters of those hills, whence Yakub flies to Srinagar in Kashmir, but there also they follow him, where neither strength in men nor walls were sufficient to repel, but in despite of both he is taken and forced to bend under the yoke of slavish bondage.[126]

Kashmir is part of that part of Asia which of old was called Sogdiana, being part of Scythia *intra Imaum*. The North Pole is there raised 41 degrees 9 minutes. This city from Agra three hundred, from Surat about a thousand English miles distant. The province generally is mountainous, barren, cold and windy; her metropolis Srinagar, which some call Syrenabar, is three miles in compass, watered by Behat or Phat, a river some think Acesines, which from Caucasus after many glomerating dances increases Indus, in nothing more observable then a lake eight leagues hence which is fifteen miles about, in center whereof is an isle in which is built a palace, out of which is seen a variety of sports as fishing, hawking, rowing etc.[127] Now whether this was that Cyropolis which the great Cyrus raised to keep out the threatened invasion of the Tartar, as some surmise, I cannot tell, seeing another of that name was where Sbyras now stands.

Ismail" and prepared a defence against the Mughals. Later on he led a guerilla war. He was not in Lahore with Yusuf Khan, as Herbert appears to believe.

[124] Qasim Khan [*Cassem-chawn*] had served Akbar well at Chittorgarh, Rathambore and Surat. He was by profession an engineer, and had been in charge of the construction of Akbar's fort at Atak.

[125] Bhimbhar is a mountain and a town in the Swat area of Kashmir.

[126] In fact, after Qasim Khan entered Srinagar he became repressive and rebellions continued sporadically; Yakub himself was not captured and made a slave as Herbert says, but kept up the fight against the Mughals for some years more. He finally submitted in July 1589, and was pardoned by Akbar, although he was kept under loose arrest. After an attempt as escape, Akbar sent him to Bihar and granted him a jagir in 1590 (Srivastava, *Akbar*, 352).

[127] The river at Srinagar [*Shrynakar*] is the Jhelum. Crowther and Raj do not mention a palace on an island lake, although there are certainly Mughal buildings present in Srinagar. The lake is known as the Dal Lake, and it is actually a series of three linked lakes rather than one body of water. For details see Crowther and Raj, *India*, 210–14.

Thatta

This done, restless Akbar, while deferring the conquest of Bactria, aims at Thatta[128] and all those territories that abut upon the east side of Indus, a notable enterprise, but being a very prudent prince, well understood the strength and condition
of every principality and how the rulers were reputed of. Well-knowing therefore
how odious Mirza Jani Beg[129] was by reason of his tyranny, and especially to his
inferiors, he sends the Khan-i-Khanan, Akbar's favourite, with twelve thousand
men to surprise that place, who, to make the quicker march and less noise, by boat
sailing down Ravi into Indus, arrived at Thatta, which nevertheless having intelligence so provided that for six months it held out, but in the seventh the tyrant was
necessitated to yield it up, and upon conditions having surrendered the fort, was
entertained friendly, but by this acquisition all Sindh even to Loore Bander upon
the ocean came to acknowledge Akbar their sovereign.

Thatta, till of late commanded by the Rajputs, is east from the city Jaisalmer
and west from Bikaner, and is reputed one of the most celebrated marts of India,
so circled by a branch of Indus that it is a peninsula. From Lahore it is about thirty
days' journey, but by Indus is in less time attained. Upon the ocean she has Loore
Bandar, which is three easy days' travel thence, observable in this, that such ships
as ride at anchor there are not so gnawed and spoiled with worms as usually they be
at Suwali, Choul, Dabhol, Daman, Goa, and other adjacent places.

Prince Murad's Death

About this time Murtaza Nizam Shah the old King of Deccan,[130] paid nature her
last tribute, and [Ismail] his son was stated in his throne. Akbar, whose disease
was ambition, is sick till he attempts the conquest of that also, which he resolves
neither cost nor toil should hinder. The enterprise was more hopeful, seeing a
woman was at that time rectrix of the Marches. The Khan-i-Khanan being chosen general, having received his instructions, with thirty thousand horse marches

---

[128] Thatta [*Tutta*] is in Sindh, now part of Jammu and Kashmir.

[129] Mirza Jani Beg (d. 1601) [*Mirza Jehan*] sent an envoy to Akbar in November
1586 (for details see Srivastava, *Akbar*, 1: 358). He fought against Sadiq Khan (1587) and
against the Khan-i-Khanan, but Thatta was captured in October 1593 and Jani Beg was
appointed Governor of Multan by Akbar. His daughter married the Khan-i-Khanan's
son and Akbar returned Thatta to him. He was commanding a battery at the siege of
Asirgarh (1600) and died shortly thereafter. There is no evidence that Jani Beg was a tyrant, at least not from Srivastava.

[130] Murtaza Nizam Shah I was sultan of Ahmednagar 1565–1588. His "debt to nature" consisted of being boiled to death by order of his son Husain Shah II, whom in a fit
of insanity he had tried to kill by setting his bed on fire (Srivasata, *Akbar*, 421)! Husain
himself was murdered in 1589 and his cousin Ismail became sultan, until he was deposed
by his own father Burhan ed-din II, Nizam Shah's brother, with some help from Akbar
(1591). He reigned until 1595.

from Lahore to Bahrampur, where Rajah Ali Khan[131] the governor meets him with five thousand more, and after some months' greater preparation set forward towards Deccan, the army being provided of all things necessary both for fight and sieges. Chand Bibi,[132] daughter to the last King, hearing of the Mughals' approach, in the first place fortifies Ahmadnagar, a frontier town, and having from the Kings of Bijapur and Golconda received an auxiliary force of forty thousand horse, the command of which she commits to her field-marshal eunuch Suhail Khan.[133] He attends the enemy upon the confines, first skirmishing with Ali Khan, Mirza Qasim and half the army, and soon after the pagans enter pell-mell, guided only by courage and desire of conquest, so as on both sides many were slain. Now one then the other part seeming victorious, so long, so courageously the battle continuing that when the sun, weary of so much bloodshed, had hid his face in the west, they ceased not, but by moonlight continued the fight with that equal resolution as for many years a more memorable battle hath not been with more courage, in eighteen hours none knowing to whom the victory inclined, till such time as the sun, sparkling his beams again in that horizon, the Khan-i-Khanan, who was their reserve, fell in with his brigade and in so good order that after three hours more dispute the Deccans very unwillingly give back, leaving their heroic captain honourably slain in the field.[134] The Mughals follow the chase fifteen miles, but the Princess [Chand] Bibi gallantly interposes them with fresh horse, forcing the Mughal to a retreat to Burhanpur, which recovered the Deccan some reputation. Akbar, having notice of what had passed, entreats Shah Murad his beloved son to reinforce his army by a new levy of fifteen thousand horse, and from Burhanpur with the other forces quartered

---

[131] Rajah Ali Khan was the ruler of Khandesh 1576–1597. In 1577 he had submitted to Akbar and had become one of his most distinguished generals. He died fighting for Akbar at the battle of Ashti.

[132] Chand Bibi or Chand Sultana (d. 1600) [*Tzeiend Bieby*], wife of the late sultan of Bijapur, Ali Adil Shah (d. 1580), was the sister (not daughter) of Burhan ed-din Shah II and his suspected murderer. As Regent of Ahmadnagar for the young Sultan Bahadur (son of Ibrahim Beg, who had ruled briefly in 1595) from 1595, she proved one of Akbar's most determined foes, personally directing the defence of Ahmadnagar and forcing Prince Murad to raise the siege. In 1600 she wanted to negotiate a surrender to Prince Daniyal, but she was murdered by those who opposed peace with Akbar. Ahmadnagar fell anyway and King Bahadur was captured.

[133] Suhail Khan [*Godgee Shuhel*] was actually a general from Bijapur appointed by Ibrahim Adil Shah II, Sultan of Bijapur (1580–1627), Chand Bibi's son. At the battle of Ashti (see above and below) he was forced to retreat. Herbert's *Godgee* is probably the title *khwaja*. This is used mostly in Kashmir by Mussulman landowners, but also by Persians in Punjab, Gujarat, Maharashtra, and Rajasthan.

[134] This is Herbert's version of the battle of Ashti, which lasted from 9 a.m. on 6 February and went on all day, resuming the next morning. Suhail Khan was not killed, but "beat a retreat to Shah Durg" (for details of the battle see Srivastava, *Akbar*, 432–33).

thereabouts to make a fresh invasion into those meridional provinces. Merrily
the youthful prince advances thitherward, but during his stay in Burhanapore
gave such liberty to his venerious and drunken disposition that his radical vigour
soon became spent, his lungs consumed, and death gave the period to his consumption.[135]

This sudden farewell struck the army with such amazement that many *umrah*, to avoid the suspicion of his father, fled, not caring to inhume the carcase.
Akbar, having quick intelligence of this sad accident, though he was pretty well-
acquainted with his son's debauchery, yet will not be persuaded but that they had
poisoned him, and for his better information his Chancellor, the Prince's schoolmaster Abu'l Fazl[136] is despatched, who, finding the dead prince his own con-
sumer, prudently assembles the Khan-i-Khanan, Yusuf Khan, Mohammed Khan,
Mirza Shahrukh and such other *umrah* as were at hand, He calls back such as had
fled for fear and then satisfies Akbar where the fault was, and, being commissioned
by the King, undertakes the Prince's charge, having first sent the dead body to
Delhi to be buried. In small time he subdues the provinces of Chand, Berar and
many other wealthy places, and by letter he acquaints the King with his success,
desiring him to forsake Lahore a while, having spent twelve winters and summers
there, and remove his court to the city of Agra which so long languished by his absence, further putting him in good hopes in small time to add Deccan, Golconda
(by the Persians called Hyderaban), Bijapur and other parts of India to his empire.
Akbar in the interim orders Shah Salim his son, afterwards called Jahangir, with
fifteen thousand horse to fall upon Rajah Amar Singh,[137] the only successor to Porus, and of all the rajahs the most powerful and eminent. Shahbaz Khan follows

---

[135] The verdict is mixed on Prince Murad. Srivastava calls him "a very intelligent
and active prince" and claims, citing the *Akbarnama* (3. 753), that his death was due to
"violent fits near Dihari" (*Akbar*, 437). Other historians agree that he was a drunkard and
a difficult man to deal with at the best of times. De Laet says that "in spite of his former
prudence and courage he gave himself up to drunkenness in such a way as to bring on a
serious illness" (*Empire*, 161).

[136] Ab'ul Fazl ibn Mubarak (1550–1602) is, of course, the great statesman and the
author of the *Akbarnama*, in which he gives a detailed account not only of Akbar's life, but
records much of what he said as well. He stated that Murad's "excessive drinking brought
on epilepsy" (*Akbarnama* 3. 753). Ab' ul Fazl sent Murad's body to Shahpur (not Delhi,
as Herbert states) for burial and made sure that the siege of Ahmadnagar went forward.
Akbar had sent him on 5 January to bring Murad back to Agra, but he was too late. Ab'-
ul Fazl opposed the succession of Jahangir, a move for which he paid with his life.

[137] Rana Amar Singh I of Mewar succeeded his father Pratap Singh in 1597. Herbert's description of him is more apt for Pratap Singh, a great warrior who had been
Akbar's implacable foe for twenty-five years. Since 1585 Akbar had left him alone and
Pratap had recovered most of his lost territory in west Mewar. Rana Amar Singh proved
to be almost as difficult to deal with as his father had been (see Srivastava; Salim was sent
on two occasions against him (1599, 1603) and returned without result, as did several

the Prince with five thousand horse, Shah Quli Marham[138] with three thousand, Rajah --------, favourite afterwards to Jahangir, with three thousand more, and many *umrah* and *munsubdars*[139] of note attended him with what forces they could, which, being brought into a body, the Mughal bids Lahore farewell for some time, and, according to Ab'ul Fazl's advice, removes both court and lascar[140] unto Agra, into which he was received with all demonstration of joy that could possibly be expressed, the citizens supposing he came by his residence to enrich the town, whenas indeed his aim was to gain there the better intelligence from the army and that he might prosecute his intended war the better against the King of Deccan. Lahore in the meantime sorrows for his departure.

Lahore described

Lahore, a city both great and famous, is competitor for the title of metropolis with Agra. The Pole Arctic is there advanced 32 degrees 15 minutes. The air for eight months is very pure and restorative, the streets graceful and well-paved, most of them being cleansed and served by the river Ravi, a branch of Indus, which from Punjab and the Kashmiri mountains streams pleasantly near this city, and after a flux of three thousand English miles, the channel all the way being deep enough for junks of threescore ton, at Thatta in one broad stream near Diu at 23 degrees and 15 minutes it empties itself into the ocean. In Lahore are many things observable, as the castle, palaces, mosques, *hamams*,[141] tanks, gardens etc. The castle is large, uniform, and nobly-seated, the material stone, white, and polished, entered by twelve pasterns, three of which respect the town, the rest the country, the last of which points out two ways, one to the King's durbar and jarneo, where according to custom he daily shows himself to the people, the other to the divan[142] where every evening from eight to eleven he discourses with his *umrah*.[143] On the wall are pictured sundry stories and pastimes, viz. Jahangir, otherwise called Shah Salim, cross-legged upon a carpet under a state,

---

other Mughal commanders. He died in 1620. It is curious that Herbert does not mention Pratap Singh at all in his account.

[138] Shah Quli Marham served Akbar as Governor of Punjab (1575) and against the rebels in Bengal (1582). In 1585 he was campaigning in Kashmir.

[139] The *munsubdars* were "quasi-feudal dependents of the Mogul Government who had territory assigned to them on condition of their supplying a certain number of horse" (*HJ* 598).

[140] The camp (for details of this word's derivation, see *HJ* 507–8).

[141] A *hamam* is a bath-house, popularly known as a Turkish bath.

[142] This is the *diwan-i-am*, or "hall of public audience," as opposed to the *diwan-i-khas*, the "hall of private audience" (Crowther and Raj, *India*, 777).

[143] The *durbar* is "the court or levée" (*HJ* 331); the *diwan* "a council or tribunal" (*HJ* 309). The term came to mean the actual place or meeting which the ruler held on a regular basis.

his son Parvez[144] being on the right hand with Khurram and Timur, his brothers Daniyal Shah and Murad. About him are Amir Sharif Khan Alam's elder brother, of such wealth and pride that, having above an hundred concubines, he new-clad them every day, and every night tearing their apparel off, buried them in the ground; Mirza Rostam,[145] once King of Kandahar, the Khan-i-Khanan, Qutbuddin Khan, Rajah Man Singh [of Amber], Asaf Khan,[146] and Rajah Jagan Nath,[147] the Crassus of India, for at his death he left Jahangir a legacy sixty maunds of pure gold, each maund being five and twenty pounds' weight, which in ours amounts to near sixty thousand pound sterling, and three hundred elephants richly covered, and other things, at whose death his wives, sister, nephew and seven other friends burnt themselves, for compliment's sake, in his fire. And on the left hand are Rajah Bhuj Singh, fly-scarer, Rai Ram Das,[148] sword-bearer, Magrebh Khan a jester, Rai Durga,[149] as also the Rajahs Ram Singh, Man Singh, Bir Singh and Basu etc., and in another *goozul-khana*[150] near the former is painted the Mughal under a cloth of state cross-legged upon carpets, upon the doors of which are the images of the crucifix and of the Blessed Virgin Mother. In another, the King's progenitors, amongst whom is Babur with thirty nobles in the habit of pilgrim kalendars etc. This was a noted city in Porus's time; upon the banks of this where it meets Hydaspes the victorious Greek Bucephala in memory of his horse that died there. Here it is thought that the patriarch Noah seated

---

[144] Prince Parvez (1590–1626) was Jahangir's second son; like his brother Khusrau he died in mysterious circumstances, possibly "orchestrated by Khurram, whose ambition knew no bounds" (Berinstain, *India*, 81). More from him will be heard later as he assumes military commands under Jahangir.

[145] Mirza Rostam Kandahari was the son of Mirza Bairam, a governor (not king) of Kandahar. See De Laet, *Empire*, 115, 157.

[146] Qutbuddin Mohammed Khan Koka was described by Jahangir as being "in the place of a dear son, a kind brother, and a congenial friend" (*TJ* 1. 115). Asaf Khan [*Assaph Can*] was the brother of Mihr un-Nisa, Jahangir's favourite wife. His daughter Arjumand Banu married Prince Khurram, later Shah Jahan. In 1627 he put down a rebellion by Prince Shahriyar, Shah Jahan's brother. In 1631 he was defeated by the forces of Bijapur.

[147] Rajah Jagan Nath [*Jugonath*], the nephew of Bharmal Singh, was a successful military commander. He fought at the battle of Haldighati against Pratap Singh (1576), and against Mirza Hakim, and was one of Akbar's generals at the fall of Ahmadnagar (1600).

[148] Rai Ram Das [*Rajea Randas*] was appointed deputy *diwan* (Prime Minister) by Akbar (1574) to assist Rajah Todar Mal in his reforms. As "a partisan of Salim" (Srivastava, *Ackbar*, 487) he was repaid by being in this picture with other loyal friends, servants and family of Jahangir.

[149] Rai Durga [*Rajea Rodorow*] was another administrator and military man; in 1581 he fought against Mirza Hakim, and in 1583 became one of Todar Mal's assistants. He was appointed joint Governor of Lahore by Akbar in 1586.

[150] This word literally means "bath-room," but was actually an "apartment . . . used by some of the Great Moghuls as a place of private audience" (*HJ* 388).

himself after leaving his ark, and hence Ophir and Havilah, sons of Joktam, re-moved towards Ganges and Malacca. The province wherein Lahore is seated is Paigah, west from Jenba, or rather from the Persian word *panch-ob* or five wa-ters or rivers, which are now called Ravi, Jhelum, Chenab, Beas and Sutlej, in-creased by *Padder* and *Damiadee*, but by Ptolemy and old hydrographers *Acesines*, *Cophys*, *Hydaspes*, *Zaradras* and *Rhuadeb* or *Hispalis*. In a word, no province of India out-vies it for pleasure and trade, nor any part of the East for a continued shade of ash, elm, and mulberry trees, which reach from here to Agra more then three hundred miles, whose spreading and verdure lenify the sun's heat, and for whose further accommodation each eight miles there is a convenient serai[151] bilt for travellers to repose in gratis. Lahore is from Ispahan four months' travel by caravan. Asafoetida abounds here. But to return.

Akbar, now at Agra, resolves in person to prosecute the wars in Deccan, so that *Anno* 1597, of the Hegira 977, having made preparations for that expedi-tion, he sets out towards Burhanpur mounted upon a horse, where note that the custom was when they issue out of their palace on horseback it signifies war, if peace, then with a palanquin or litter, or upon an elephant, but, contrary to ex-pectations, so soon as he had passed the river Narmada he had news that Baha-dur Shah,[152] a courageous rajah, had fortified Asir, a very strong castle, against him. The Mughal likes not to leave so considerable a place and enemy behind him and therefore sits down there and resolves to take it by force or famine. Asir is three castles in one, called Chotzan and Kamargarh;[153] the last is mounted high and so well defended by Nature as seems impregnable. Therefore Akbar re-solves to famish it, and half a year to that end he blocks it up, at which the Rajah within seeing, and not knowing of any that would either raise the siege or relieve the garrison with provisions which they then stood in need of, he thought it his best way to treat betimes that he might expect the better conditions, and accord-ingly he beat a parley, and, upon treating with Akbar, upon articles had his life and goods granted, which upon rendition of the castle were performed, and such quarter kept as induced the Rajah to accept of a command in the army, and so he

---

[151] Originally a word for palace or royal residence, it came to mean "a building for the accommodation of travellers with their pack-animals, consisting of an enclosed yard with chambers round it" (*HJ* 811).

[152] Bahadur Shah of Khandesh [*Badursha*] was in trouble already because he "had not shown due regard to [Prince] Daniyal" (Srivastava, *Akbar*, 444), who was thinking about attacking Burhanpur. It was galling to Akbar as Bahadur's father, Rajah Ali Khan, had been an ally. Akbar decided to give him a chance to come and pay homage, but Ba-hadur holed up in Asirgarh, also known as Asir. Herbert's date is mistaken; these events took place from the end of 1599 to February 1600, not in 1597.

[153] By *Chotza* Herbert might mean Korhi, a hill south of the fortress, but there is no fort of this name. The forts were Mali, Antari or Juna Mali, Kamagarh [*Cummergbar*] and Maligarh (Srivastava, *Akbar*, 445–46).

followed the lascar, which upon this success marches more cheerfully, till such
time as news was brought how that Shah Salim and Shahbaz Khan, with the
residue aforenamed going against Rana Amar, in Ajmer Shahbaz Khan departed
this life,[154] of poison as some thought, which for some time alters the Prince's
progress. For forthwith seizing on Shahbaz's treasure, amounting to a crore or
ten lakh of rupees, therewith he purchases the mercenary affection of so many
of his soldiers that to Agra he returns, unnaturally resolved to thrust his father
out of his throne, which Akbar was so amazed at, and with this unexpected rebellion that what with fear of his son's popularity and what with grief to leave
Deccan unconquered, his heart droops and a deep melancholy seizes his spirit,
until Abu'l Fazl rouses him, and, by the reasonable encouragement he gave, not
only revives but exasperates. Whereupon, turning his back of Asirgarh with half
his army, leaving his son Shah Daniyal with Abu'l Fazl, the Khan-i-Khanan,
Bahadur Shah and other *umrah* to prosecute the war of Deccan, he speeds towards Agra, whither Shah Salim had got before him in hope to secure the treasury, but missing his aim he marches back by Ranveri and Anawal,[155] and after
twelve days march came to Allahabad, having forced his passage through Berar,
Shyampur, Kalpi[156] (not that which some think Tarsis), Lucknow, [Kora] Manikpur, [Kora] Ghatimpur,[157] Kanauj,[158] Chausa,[159] Bihar and other towns and
provinces which seemingly acknowledged him, and in which he put garrisons
of his own choosing. The King now returned to Agra, being sensible of his son's
conspiracy, wishes all were well again, by kind letters first attempting it by discovering the shame and danger he was in, the curse of Mahomet and deprivation
of his birthright. So he persisted, but promising pardon if he would submit and
come in. Howbeit, such persuasions were of small power with Shah Salim, who,

---

[154] Shahbaz Khan died on 11 November 1599. Herbert is correct about the treasure; Salim then went towards Agra, on the way failing to visit his grandmother (serious
breach of etiquette), and marched to Allahabad, where he stole more treasure from local
landowners and declared himself Emperor. "Akbar feigned not to believe all this," writes
Srivastava, "and so did the nobles and officers of the empire" (*Akbar*, 465).

[155] Ranveri and Anawal are cities in Gujarat.

[156] Kalpi was an important town in the Ganga-Yamuna area which was taken by the
rebel Hemu without a fight in 1556. Salim appointed one of his own supporters there as
governor in 1600.

[157] Herbert mistakenly thinks that "Kora" is a separate town. Kora Manikpur was
one of the towns held by Uzbek rebels, which Akbar subdued in 1567. It was another
town which came under Salim's control. Kora Ghatimpur was the third town to come
under Salim's rule in 1600.

[158] "Only a few dismal ruins indicate that this was once a mighty Hindu town"
(Crowther and Raj, *India*, 255). It was also the site of Humayun's defeat by Sher Shah
in 1540.

[159] Chausa was part of the territory held by Bahadur Khan; it is located to the east
of Benares.

to assure his father of his constancy in that course first derides the messenger and then o' er-runs the Empire as far as Bengal, hoping (but in vain) the Viceroy there, Rajah Man Singh [of Amber] would side with him.

Nevetherless, what made some amends was the good fortune his other son Prince Daniyal had in his march towards Deccan, for he, having entered the country, in the first place besieged Gandetzin,[160] one of the most considerable castles for strength and situation in the whole kingdom. Herein the distressed lady with many of her nobles had pent themselves, stored with victuals for two years' siege and provided with all sorts of warlike instruments, notwithstanding all which, the dice of war so ordering it, in the seventh month the enemy took it by storm, many of the defendants losing their lives but all their wealth and liberty. [Chand] Bibi only, rather than suffer imprisonment, made herself away by poison and so put an end to her misery. But her treasure of gold and silver came to the conqueror's hands, who, giving it in charge to Abu'l Fazl and the Khan-i-Khanan, the castle he trusted to Shahrukh Mirza, and without any further resistance marched his whole army through the counties Berar and Kandesh, receiving some acknowledgement from the faint-hearted kings of Golconda and Bijapur, and so, loaden with triumph and treasure, returns to Burhanpur victorious.

Burhanpur Described

Burhanpur, *Baramatis* in Ptolemy, or Brahmanpur as my notion prompts me, of old and at this day a seminary of brahmins, yogis, coolins or gymnosophs,[161] whose academy about this place is recorded by Porphyry and Ptolemy, is in Arctic elevation twenty-eight degrees three minutes, from Surat east two hundred and twenty miles, from Ajmer four hundred and twenty, and from Agra not much less than one thousand. The province is called Khandesh or Sanda, where being watered by Tapti, the river at Surat, it becomes fruitful and pleasant, but elsewhere is barren and sandy. The city is built upon low ground, in an unhealthy but spacious vale, and by banians most inhabited. The streets are many but narrow, the houses not high and but meanly beautiful. At the north-east end it has a castle upon the flood, which is large, and in the river we see an artificial elephant so skilfully shaped that by the banians 'tis of some veneration, and by others admired. In times past here resided the Deccan kings who by the Mughal now are

---

[160] This location remains unidentified. It is possible that Herbert meant Gandevi, a town in Gujarat. However, Herbert is wrong about what happened. Chand Bibi did not poison herself, but was put to death by Jita Khan, "an influential eunuch," acting on orders from "a powerful clique" which opposed her desire to negotiate with the Mughals. Her death took place on 3 July 1600 in Ahmadnagar (Srivastava, *Akbar*, 442–43).

[161] A yogi [*jogee*] is "a Hindu ascetic . . . who practices yoga" (*HJ* 461); a *coolin* is "a class of Brahmans of Bengal Proper who make extraordinary claims to purity" (*HJ* 249); "gymnosophs" are ascetics or sadhus.

beaten from it, and near this is the Khan-i-Khanan's house and gardens at Lal-bat, adorned with a delightful prospect of several trees, which for the fruit and shade and for variety of flowers of all sorts, express the ingenuity as well as the greatness of that noble person, as also the water-works two courses thence, are well worthy the view. But to return.

Abu'l Fazl the Chancellor Slain

Akbar no sooner understood how fortunately his son Daniyal had proceeded southward, the news whereof 'tis likely came to Shah Salim's ear, but Rajah Ja-han presents him with a penitential letter from Shah Salim his rebellious son to the contrary quarter. After a little stay Jahan returns with the Mughal's prom-ised pardon, provided he would dismiss his army and make speedy submission. His ungracious son, repeating his former impiety, returns this for an answer: that having an army of seventy thousand horse and many brave men upon most of which he had conferred some command, it was evident he needed not to submit, nevertheless he would submit provided an amnesty were forthwith given him and those that were in this conspiracy, their lives and well-being being equally valuable with his own, which if his father would not grant he was resolved to de-fend himself and to continue his army in their former courses.[162] Akbar, having ruminated a while, returns him a tart answer such as incensed the Prince, who, having advised with his Council of War, forthwith dislodged and in good order marched speedily to Allahabad, where he commands all sorts of coin of gold, of silver, to be stamped with his own name and mottoes. Yea, to vex his father more he dishonestly courts Anarkali,[163] his father's wife, which names signifies

---

[162] Herbert is vague about dates, and perhaps not quite accurate in some other de-tails. According to Srivastava, Salim asked to go and see Akbar in March 1602, but he was turned down. He then appears to have begun a march towards Agra with thirty (not seventy) thousand horse. Akbar responded by telling Salim he must dismiss the army and come with a reasonable escort. In May Akbar made Salim Governor of Bengal and Oris-sa, apparently trying out "reverse psychology" by giving the Prince some real responsibil-ity. Salim refused, "and continued to act as an independent king at Allahabad" (Srivas-tava, *Akbar* 466; *Akbarnama* 3. 806). A "course" is Herbert's rendering of the Mughal *kos*, which is just over 2 1/4 miles.

[163] Anarkali [*Anarkala*] (d. 1599/1600) is not described by Srivastava as Akbar's wife, although some historians call her a "concubine." It may be," he writes, "that the story . . . of Anarkali [was] not without substance" (*Akbar*, 462–63), but historians are divided about whether she even existed (Jahangir never mentions her in the *Jahangirna-ma*) or is a folkloric character. A famous and widely-popular Indian film was made about her (1953). The story is that she was a dancing-girl named Nadira or Sharf-un-Nisa with whom Prince Salim fell in love; Akbar forbade the relationship, and the unfortunate woman ended up being immured alive on Akbar's orders. There is a tomb in Lahore in the grounds of what is now the Punjab Civil Secretariat, with inscriptions saying "I would

"pomegranate," and withal sent him some of his new-stamped money, a crime of so high a stain that the enraged father first curses him and then acquaints his chancellor Abu'l Fazl with his condition, who, having laboured he could to moderate his master's passion, with all convenient haste, accompanied with three thousand horse he follows the post to do his master service. But Shah Salim, having intelligence how all past, writes to Rajah Bir Singh,[164] Lord of Orchha, through whose country he must go, to lie in wait for Abdul's passage and, promising him gratuity with command of five thousand horse so he would send him Abdul's head. The Rajah promises his best and with a thousand horse and three hundred foot ambushes near Gwalior, and, such time as poor Abu'l Fazl passed by suspectless of any enemy, [the] Rajah fell upon him, and, notwithstanding the advantage he had, for three hours the fight continued, but o'erpressing them with men and troops, in the end Abu'l's company were most part slain and himself, after twelve wounds which he received in fight, was at length taken and beheaded.[165] Salim receives the present joyfully, but Akbar, who loved him dearly, becomes so passionate that for three days he withdrew from all manner of company and for some time refused to be comforted. But, like waves, see another horror afflicting him: news was brought him of his other son Shah Daniyal his death,[166] killed in the same city and by the same disease Murad was formerly, which was by intemperance. Hereat the old man afflicts his decaying body immeasurably, cries and sighs and vows revenge upon the Khan-i-Khanan for no better regarding him, who so soon as the Prince was dead made what haste he could to court to purge himself, but was not admitted to Akbar's presence, till by mediation of others being brought into His Majesty's presence, he gave so good an account that the Mughal was pacified and with new instructions hastens him back to the army in Deccan.

---

give thanks to God to the day of resurrection / Could I behold the face of my beloved once more," and "the profoundly enamoured Salim." Her name actually means "pomegranate flower." Also see *Akbarnama* 2. 1155.

[164] Bir Singh Deva Bundela [*Radgee Beresingh*] was Rajah of Orchha [Soor]. His brother Rajah Madhukar had rebelled against Akbar earlier (1577) but had submitted, although he rebelled again and was a nuisance until his death in 1593 (see Srivastava, *Akbar*, 230–31). When Bir Singh succeeded he continued to be hostile to Akbar, hence his support of Salim.

[165] According to Srivastava, Bir Singh himself killed Abu'l Fazl with a spear-thrust to the breast. He then cut off his head and sent it to Salim in Allahabad (*Akbar* 467–68). There is no doubt of Salim's involvement in the murder (see also Berinstain, *India*, 71). In March 1605 Rajah Rai Singh of Bikaner defeated Bir Singh, but unfortunately failed to capture or kill him. See also De Laet, *Empire*, 168–69 for an account of the murder.

[166] Daniyal died of alcoholism on 11 March 1605. De Laet states that he "died of over-drinking at Brampore" (168). Jahangir himself gives the details of his brother's death in his autobiography (*TJ* 1. 35).

Nevertheless, the vexation he endures by the continued rebellion of his son Salim takes from him all comfort, and, seeing him hardened in his exorbitancies, is at his wits' end how to reduce him. Therefore first, as a king, he marches against him with thirty thousand horse, but by his mother's sudden death was recalled,[167] whose body, when he had sumptuously interred [it] in Delhi in King Humayun her husband's sepulchre, then as father he tries once more what fair persuasion could operate, to which end he dictates a pathetic letter mixed with love and anger, reproving, persuading, dissuading, promising and putting him in mind he was or at least should be his joy and comfort and that he had no more sons living. Miran Sadr,[168] once the Prince's tutor, was thought the fittest person to carry it, who so forcibly penetrates the yielding or rather convinced nature of Shah Salim, that forthwith taking Parvez his little son along with him he leaves Allahabad, passes Yamuna, and after two days, the wizard allowing the day fortunate, with all his *umrah* he arrives at Agra and by Murtaza Khan[169] was brought to Akbar, then in the goozul-khana, who, blushing to eye him, leads him into the Mahal or private lodging where, forgetting his promise and remembering the dances Salim led him, into such a rage that rapt him that after he had flashed terror into his heart by the fury of his eyes and thunderstruck him with a storm of words, with his fist he struck him so hard upon the mouth that Salim, throwing himself down, requests his father to destroy him, to which end he shows him his breast, the sword and hand ready to it. But Akbar, by this abating his choler, intends no such sacrifice, but, commanding him to arise, dissembles his affection and terms him ass and fool that, commanding seventy thousand men, would forsake them to trust the sugared promises of any. That said, he brings him forth again and sends him back to prison, giving all the principal *umrah* his associates like

---

[167] Begum Hamida Banu or Mariam Makani (1526–1604) was a Persian girl of fourteen when Humayun fell in love with her just at the time he was ousted by Sher Shah. She shared his triumphs, tragedy, and exile, and her advice, though not always taken, was valued by Akbar. She was "loved and respected by the emperor, and held in the highest esteem by the nobles and the common people" (Srivastava, *Akbar*, 477). She had been distressed by Akbar's decision to attack Salim, whose rebellion and its aftermath probably hastened her death. She died on 29 August 1604. Herbert's chronology is a little confusing.

[168] Herbert, following De Laet (*Empire*, 168) gives the name *Myrad Zedda* as Salim's "tutor," but he was actually Miran Sadr Jahan, "Akbar's agent at the court of Salim and a great favourite of the prince, who regarded Sadr as his sp[iritual preceptor" (De Laet, *Empire*, 168, n. 59). Maulana Mir Kalan Haravi had been appointed as Salim's tutor by Akbar in 1573.

[169] Murtaza Khan (d. 1617), also known as Shaykh Farid, was one of Akbar's principal generals. In 1599 he served with Prince Murad and besieged the fortress of Gawil and was also with Prince Daniyal at the fall of Ahmadnagar. He was given the title of Shaikh Farid Bokhari (Srivastava, *Akbar*, 487) and supported Prince Salim, under whose rule he rose to high position.

welcome, Rajah Basu[170] excepted, who, wiser then the rest, escaped. By this imprisonment Shah Salim, contrary to his custom, abstains four and twenty hours
from opium, which next day Akbar, fearing that in a passion he would make
himself away, comes in person and persuades him to take. The third day, by intercession of his ladies and concubines, Salim was freed and sent to his own house,
where he behaved himself orderly, in a dutiful manner each day visiting his father, till upon some old men's malicious surmises or his father's new jealousy he
was restrained again and the Mughal de novo exasperated against him.[171]

Akbar the Great Mughal poisoned by mistake

But this ill-grounded rancour had little effect, for Akbar, taking distaste against
Mirza Ghazi, the Viceroy of Thatta's son and one formerly high in his favour,
for speaking one word which Akbar ill-interpreted, no submission will serve his
turn, no less then his life must pay for it, to which end the King's physician was
directed to prepare two pills of like shape but contrary operation. Ghazi must be
trusted with them and bring them to Akbar, who, imagining by a private mark
he knew the right, bids Gashaw swallow the other. Ghazi, ignorant of the deceit, by chance light upon the best, so as Akbar by mistake was poisoned.[172] Too

---

[170] Rajah Basu of Mau and Pathankot (d. 1613) [*Radgee Batso*] had initially submitted to Akbar (1590), but revolted in 1600, As Herbert notes, he joined Salim's rebellion,
but managed to escape punishment by getting out of Agra quickly after discovering that
Akbar had ordered his arrest and returning to his realm. Mau was a small state in the
Punjab. The others were actually pardoned by Akbar, not imprisoned. Salim made him a
military commander upon his accession. For details of Salim's submission to Akbar, see
De Laet, *Empire*, 168–69.

[171] Herbert's account is not accurate, at least according to Srivastava. Akbar did indeed imprison Salim, but not in a gaol; he was confined to a "bathroom," where he was
put "under the custody of a noted physician named Raja Sali-Vahan." Here Salim was
"deprived" not of opium, but of wine, "which," Srivastava remarks, "was the hardest of
punishments for a confirmed drunkard" (*Akbar*, 473). Herbert was correct about the ladies' intervention (after ten days) and Salim's confinement to his house.

[172] Akbar was not poisoned, either by design or mistake. Mirza Ghazi Beg [*Mirza
Gashaw*] (d. 1612) was the son of Jani Beg and a distinguished poet, although Banerjee
calls him "a dissolute scamp" (De Laet, *Empire*, 170, n.63). As Jahangir speaks highly of
him and records the details of his death (*TJ* I, 223–34), the story about the pills is probably apocryphal. Herbert got it from De Laet (*Empire*, 170–71). Srivastava relates how
Akbar became upset after "an open rupture between Salim and the latter's son Khusrau."
This was occasioned by an elephant-fight in which Salim's elephant defeated Khusrau's,
and a dispute erupted when a reserve elephant was brought in to save Khusrau's beast.
Father and son quarrelled, and Akbar was upset. He later became feverish and developed
dysentery, which the doctor cured. He spent fifteen days in bed, and then found that he
could not get up. He died on October 15 (O. S.) 1605 (for details, see Srivastava, *Akbar*,
484–88); the *Akbarnama* states that he "withdrew the shade of his Heavenly self from the

soon the miserable Mughal perceives his error and too late repents his choler, but for shame concealing the cause, after fourteen days' torment and successless trial to expel the poison yields up the ghost in the 73 year of his age and 52 of his reign,[173] and with all possible solemnity in Sikandra, three courses from Agra, in a monument which he had prepared, that great monarch was buried, and Shah Salim, though a while resisted by Rajah Man Singh and Aziz Koka,[174] who in vain endeavoured to make his son Khusrau[175] Mughal, nominated by Akbar as they alleged, with such ceremony as was requisite was crowned at Agra by name of Jahangir, king, in the year of Our Lord 1605, and of Mahomet 984.[176]

---

heads of mortals and spread out the shadow of his beneficence over the heads of the celestials." According to the *Akbarnama*, the emperor became ill on 22 September, and his doctor, Hakim Ali, did nothing for eight days. When Akbar insisted he do his duty, Hakim Ali treated him for ten days, during which time Akbar got worse, at which point the doctor "ran away." The *Akbarnama* states that Hakim Ali did not know what to do "from want of knowledge" (3. 157), but does not accuse him of murder. Some accounts mention "slow poisoning," but there is no hard evidence. When Hakim Ali died (1609), Jahangir called him "an unrivalled physician" (*TJ* 1. 154).

[173] Herbert is wrong here. Akbar was sixty-three years old, not seventy-three. His reign had lasted precisely "forty-nine years, eight months and three days" (Srivastava, *Ackbar*, 1. 488). De Laet is even more inaccurate, giving Akbar a reign of sixty years (*Empire*, 171).

[174] Mirza Aziz Koka [*Azam Chan*] was the ruler of Dipalpur in the Punjab. In 1572 Akbar appointed him Governor of Eastern Gujarat (which included Ahmedabad). He was in and out of favour with Akbar and was even arrested once, but finally regained the Emperor's trust and held various appointments. He was instrumental in foiling Prince Salim's attempt to seize power, as Herbert relates.

[175] Prince Khusrau [*Sultan Gushroes*] (1587–1622) rebelled against his father in 1606, and appears to have died in mysterious circumstances (Berinstain, *India*, 79). However, some historians report that Jahangir had him blinded (as Herbert relates below) and then regretted his actions, at which point he found a doctor who managed to restore Prince Khusrau's sight in one eye. It was Khusrau's brother Prince Khurram (Shah Jahan) who is said to have had him murdered in 1622 to ensure that he would not stand in the way his accession, but more likely because of "his open political attitudes" (Berinstain, *India*, 79). Herbert's version of the story is partly accurate, based on that of De Laet (*Empire*, 173–77).

[176] Jahangir succeeded Akbar after the failure of a plot, which had started before Akbar's death, to place Prince Khusrau on the throne. It had been engineered by Man Singh and Aziz Koka, now "acting as the Prime Minister (*wakil*) of the empire" (Srivastava, *Akbar*, 486). The court supported Salim, Aziz Koka submitted to Jahangir, and Man Singh decamped. Salim, for the moment, forgave Khusrau.

[Part IV: The Reign of Jahangir]

Give me leave now to present you various scenes composed of a miscellany of subjects happening in Hindustan during Jahangir's reign.

Prince Khusrau beaten

Jahangir, so now we call him, by the mediation of Murtaza Khan, Mohammed Quli Khan[1] and others of his council, receives his son Sultan Khusrau his late competitor into favour, and, to lay the foundations of his greatness in the good-will of his people he freely receives Aziz Koka and Rajah [Man Singh] into grace again. But Khusrau, struck by his own guilt, suspecting his pardon counterfeit, by letter desires Hassan Beg,[2] Viceroy of Kabul, his old friend, to meet him near Fatehpur with some horse that he might fly away, being assured that if he stayed long at court he should be put to death. By his zantel the letter is speedily delivered, who as readily obeys the disconsolate prince, and with three thousand horse hastes to Akbarpur, which is from Agra four and twenty courses, whither the Prince, escaping about twilight from court, comes followed by five hundred gallants who altogether hasten to Lahore. Jahangir, having immediate notice of his son's flight and resenting how dangerous it might prove, charges Malik Ali Beg, Captain of the Guard, with such force as he then had to pursue Khusrau and bring him back again. The Cotwal[3] with three hundred horse and Murtaza Khan with fifteen hundred horse more all night post after [Malik Ali Beg]; yea, after both but more leisurely, Jahangir himself, persuaded to it by [the] Amir al-*Umrah*, with fifty elephants and eight thousand men, so that the poor prince, every way pursued, feared to be made prisoner again.

---

[1] Mohammed Quli Khan, who had fought as a general in Akbar's army since 1567, had been governor of Kashmir in 1604 when the Chak tribe rebelled against Akbar. He defeated them and forced their submission (see *Akbarnama* 3. 835–36).

[2] Husain [Hassan] Beg Badakhshi (d. 1606), commanded troops against rebels in Afghanistan (1597) and had been appointed governor of Kabul by Akbar in 1601. As Herbert relates, he did indeed support Khusrau's attempt to rebel against his father. Jahangir had him sewn up alive in an animal skin and paraded through the streets of Lahore together with Abdul Rahim, a former diwan of Lahore (see also below). Hassan Beg died, but Abdul Rahim survived and was later tortured to death.

[3] A *cotwal* or *cutwaul* is "a police-officer; superintendent of police" (*HJ* 265).

Yet such was the haste Hassan Beg made afore them that none of the three came near him by fifteen courses; yea, all the way they plundered villages and made havoc of what they could, so that on the ninth day the Prince made Lahore. But, intending to enter the castle, they were, contrary to expectation, kept out by Ibrahim Khan[4] the Governor, premonished of the Prince's flight, and, which was worse, by Said Khan[5] (three courses from the city and in his way to Bengal, the place of his government) making as if he would join with him. Upon the river the poor prince is imprisoned, but by virtue of a bribe escaping, he returns to Hassan, where he was endangered by another bait, for Salah-ed-din Husain presents himself unto the Prince assuring him that his father, out of his abundant love, had passed by his offences and has assigned his true friend Hassan Beg the additional command of the provinces of Kabul and Banafoed, with which seeming not contented, he desires the addition of Zerbind, all this being but to dally and allure his stay till Jahangir came to catch him. The Prince, nevertheless, was not so simple but that he easily discovers his father's drift, so that after three weeks' fruitless attempt to take the castle in Lahore, he forsakes the city and with twenty thousand horse in a quick march moves back again witj a full determination to bid Jahangir battle nearer home.

It happened that he pitched one night where Murtaza Khan with six hundred horse, hearing of Khusrau's coming, was ambushed; Murtaza falls upon him, but such was the premeditated care Hassan had of the place that in two hours' skirmish their enemies were beaten and Sha-Chelya the captain slain, so that had not Godgee Meleck with the King's standard entered proclaiming with great outcries that the Mughal was at hand, the King's party had been wholly routed. But of such terror was the King's approach, then past Sultanpore, that Abdul Rahim, who bore the Prince's colours, most cowardly threw it away and fled. By his dastardly example the rest of the army did the like, most of them by the rustic time-serving people being chased and knocked down and all the baggage seized upon by the country people. The King is so sensible of this good hap that in memory of this deliverance he erects at Sikri, i.e. "a place of hunting," a stately castle, and names the place Fatehpur, which signifies "paradise" or "place of delight."

---

[4] Ibrahim Khan Fath Jang (d. 1627) [*Ebrahem-cawn*] was made joint paymaster of the Imperial Household (1614), which Jahangir described as an "exalted dignity" (*TJ* 1.260). He was also a competent military commander. He fought in Bihar and conquered Khokhara. He later became Governor of Bengal and Viceroy of Deccan (1617–1623). He died fighting against Prince Khurram.

[5] Said Khan [*Sayet-chan*] was one of Akbar's generals. Jahangir sent him to Kashmir and he advanced on Lahore. Jahangir writes that Said "sent word to the garrison of the fort that he came with a loyal intention and that they should admit him" (*Jahangirnama* I, n.p.n.). In the event, he did not capture Prince Khusrau, as Herbert claims.

Fatehpur described

Fatehpur, if the water had been good, by this time had triumphed over all the cities of India, for 'tis walled about, and to the NNW discovers a lake five miles over. The NE has a fair bazaar five hundred paces long, neatly-paved and well-built on both sides. At one end is the Mughal's house[6] and a mahal[7] curiously-built; on the other side is a mosque[8] which is ascended by thirty steps barred with a gate, in all so observable that it is scarce equalled throughout India. The top is full of little pyramids; the court within is six times bigger then the Royal Exchange in London, neatly-paved with free-stone, the aisles large and paved, the columns all out of stone, beautiful. And affronting this gate is a sumptuous monument, the parget whereof is covered with paint and oyster-pearl shells, but proudest in the Kalender[9] who lies there buried.

[Prince Khusrau's Revolt, continued]

To return. The miserable Prince, after this defeat, accompanied with Husain Beg, Abdul Rahim and Badakhshi Khan,[10] scarce looks behind him til they had attained Lahore, where Rahim stays, but Sultan Khusrau and Badakshi cross the Ravi and labour to arrive with safety at Rantas, a castle by some reputed impregnable. Bad fortune, it seems, follows them everywhere, for, passing the river Zenab, by the treacherous watermen they are kept between deck and brought into the power of Qasim Khan's sons, then besieging the castle, who without delay convey them to Jahangir, by that time past Latur,[11] a flood seven days' travel thence. The King, overjoyed with this good hap, returns to Lahore, and by the way put to death many *umrah* who were the Prince's followers, and the Prince

---

[6] It is unclear which building Herbert refers to here. There are several palaces in the neighbourhood, including "Mariam's House," used by Jahangir's mother and also known as the Golden House, as well as the audience halls used by Akbar (Crowther and Raj, *India*, 252).

[7] House or palace. The one Herbert mentions is probably the Jodh Bai ka Mahal, "named after Jahangir's wife, although it was probably more used by Akbar's wife, who was a Hindu" (Crowther and Raj, *India*, 252).

[8] This is almost certainly the Jami Masjid or Dargah Mosque, "said to be a copy of the mosque at Mecca and is a very beautiful building containing elements of Persian and Hindu design . . . . The impressive gateway is reached by an equally impressive flight of steps" (Crowther and Raj, *India*, 251),

[9] This is the tomb of Sheikh Salim Chisti, who predicted the birth of Akbar's son. His grandson Islam Khan is also buried there (Crowther and Raj, *India*, 251–52).

[10] Herbert mistakenly thinks that Badakhshi is a third person; it is Husain Beg's surname.

[11] There is a city, Latur, now in Maharashtra, but the main river is the Manjara.

was committed to the custody of Zaman Beg,[12] called after Mahabat Khan, a beloved lord, of which Mahabat Khan I may say as Livy speaks of Cato: in this man were such abilities of mind and such heroic virtues that into what climate soever his nativity had cast him, he seemed to be able to command a fortune. Husain Beg and Abdul Rahim, being first publicly disgraced, [were] then made close prisoners;[13] such was the conclusion of the Prince's first outbreaking.

Whether some noblemen reputed Jahangir tyrannical[14] or that they thought Khusrau had better title to the Empire or that envy was the cause is uncertain, but some of these so wrought that one night, when but few men watched the Prince, some malcontents conspired to take away the Mughal's life upon the high moutains as he passed over thence to Kabul, and to place Khusrau in his room. The traitors were of no mean rank, being Mirza [Mohammed] Sherif, brother to Asaf Khan,[15] Mirza Nur-ed-din[16] his cousin, Mirza Fatullah,[17] Mirza Chaffen Beg, Lotta Beg and Murdoph Khan, Jahangir having no notice thereof and suspecting no treachery passes on, but by good fortune was so well-attended that they durst not attempt their villainous intent. Howbeit, in the interim Itimad ud-Daulah[18] the Treasurer was accused by one of his slaves to have converted to his own use and for the encouragement of traitors 500,000 rupees out of the

---

[12] Mahabat Khan (d. 1634) had been one of Akbar's generals and continued to serve Jahangir. In 1608–1609 he fought against Amar Singh of Amber. He defeated a rebel army in Deccan (1623) but later supported Jahangir's son Prince Parvez against the empress Nur Jahan. He also joined Prince Khurram (later Shah Jahan) in his rebellion against Jahangir and helped seize Jahangir and Nur Jahan, who were later freed. He was made governor of Ajmer in 1628.

[13] For details, see above. It is odd that Herbert did not seem to know about their gruesome end.

[14] For an interesting view of this subject see Ellison S. Findly, "Jahangir's Vow of Non-Violence," *Journal of the American Oriental Society* 107 (1987): 245–56.

[15] Mohammed Sherif (d. 1607) was the younger brother of Asaf Khan (d. 1641), himself the elder brother of Nur Jahan and the father of Mumtaz Mahal, for whom Shah Jahan built the Taj Mahal. In spite of his brother's treachery, Asaf Khan became governor of Lahore (1625) and Prime Minister (*Wazir*) to both Jahangir and Shah Jahan.

[16] Mirza Nur ed-din (d. 1607) was the son of Ghias ud-din Ali Asaf Khan, whom Jahangir made Grand Vizier (1606). He was put to death. See *TJ* 1. 122–123.

[17] Mirza Fatullah was the son of Hakim Abu'l Fath of Bijapur, one of the sardars of the Deccan. Jahangir had him imprisoned (1607) for his complicity in the Prince Khusrau affair. See *TJ* 1. 123.

[18] Ghias ud-din Beg, known as Itimad ud-Daulah (c. 1549–1622), a Persian, was the father of Nur Jahan and her brothers (see above). In spite of his son Sharif's treason, he became one of Jahangir's closest friends and advisers. He served Jahangir as Treasurer and subsequently Prime Minister, and as a mark of esteem Jahangir presented him with one of the Imperial turbans (*TJ* 1. 378). His tomb at Agra, built 1626–1628, "was the first Moghul structure totally constructed of marble" (Crowther and Raj, *India*, 244).

Mughal's treasury. That, and the news of Asaf Khan, Itimad ud-Daulah's son-in-law his treacherous murder of Qutb ed-din Mohammed Khan Koka,[19] Lieutenant of Bengal, near Rajo Mahal, albeit Azam Khan the Turk upon that score was also soon after slain by Ghias ud-din and Kishwar Khan,[20] brother and son to the Lieutenant, and his mother and wife oft basely abused, were imputations reflecting so much upon ud-Daulah that he was not only discharged of his place and himself imprisoned in Dayanat Khan's[21] house during His Majesty's pleasure, to his own grief and the astonishment of all Industan, who ever reputed him an honest officer and counsellor to the Mughal.

But greater was Jahangir's fear when by Khwaja Wais he was at length acquainted with the conspiracy intended against him by men of power such as he never provoked and yet as were nearly-related, but by [the] Amir al-Umara's advice throws off all abject fear, and, having discovered and apprehended the conspirators, without delay he commands them to execution, Itimad ud-Daulah only excepted, who at the request of his keeper was pardoned upon payment of 200,000 rupees to the King and him for his life, after which the King returns unto Lahore and by the way remembering the danger he had escaped and deeply-grounding his jealousy that Khusrau his son was partly causer of it, he commands his son's eyes by juice of Aeck to be made blind, but the poison was more merciful, leaving one eye a little sight. Azam Khan also, Khusrau's father-in-law, was clad in loathsome rags and brought into the goozul-khana where every *umrah* was ordered to spit upon his beard, after which he was manacled and led to prison, where two full years he lay close, till by the prevalent importunity of his wives he was set at liberty.

This year *Anno* 1609 Khurram, another of Jahangir's sons, and other of his friends, to make his way easier to the crown prevailed with Jahangir that his kinsman Shah Salim's brother's sons might be christened, which accordingly was done in Agra. The Jesuits that baptised the young princes named them Filippo, Carlo and Enrico. That year also they baptised another grandson of Akbar's by the name of Don Edoardo.

This year 1019, of our account 1609, [the] Amir al-Umara being apoplectic thereby became incapable of the further execution of his office. Salim Khan also, in Qutb ed-din's place, was made Viceroy of Bengal and commanded to send up as prisoners Azam Khan's family, which he did accordingly. In this way the

---

[19] Qutb ed-din Mohammed Koka (c. 1570–1606) was one of Akbar's generals.

[20] Kishwar Khan [*Kisweer-chan*] (d. 1612) was the son of Jahangir's foster-brother Qutb ed-din. He was killed in battle against the Afghans. See *TJ* 1. 211.

[21] Dayanat Khan [*Dianet-cawn*] was the title given to Qasim Ali, "one of the servants of the late King Akbar" (*TJ* 1. 123) whom Jahangir promoted. He is recorded as having insulted Itimad ud-Daulah and being punished for it (*TJ* 1. 278–279), released from prison and pardoned. He was subsequently restored to his rank. Jahangir does not mention him as one of the custodians of Prince Khusrau.

young widow Mehr un-Nisa,[22] Itimad ud-Daulah's daughter and sister to Asaf Khan, was met by a wizard orfortune-teller who told her many stories of that her ensuing greatness, which soon after happened, for they were no sooner arrived at Agra, whither Jahangir was by that time come, but were kindly welcomed by Ruqayya Sultana the Mother-Queen.[23] It happened that one day, being led into the Mahal with her little girl, Jahangir being there accidentally, in merriment lifting up her veil he discovers so rare and forcible a beauty that thenceforward he became her prisoner and the sum of all he contemplates. Now he is no longer Itimad ud-Daulah's foe, but to ingratiate himself into the free affection of his goddess rather studies how to advance Daulah her dejected father. In this passionate dotage he forgets his state and the power he had to command and privately passes by boat to Itimad ud-Daulah's house and all night consumes himself and his precious time in amorous dalliance, for seeing beauty is a beam of divine refulgency; no wonder then if an inamorado neglect all other things to enjoy his beloved, without whom there seems nothing but darkness. To enjoy her the more and better, at length he commands Rajah Abdul Husain to ask Daulah's goodwill for his daughter, which Husain admires, and laying before him the indignity he offers to so great a majesty, Jahangir, now Cupid's slave, is both deaf and blind, so as in choler he bids him go or stay eternally. Husain replies no more, but speeds away and uses small persuasions, for Itimad ud-Daulah, rapt from his discontented orb, after some professions of his baseness returns Jahangir his humble and thankful condescension, so that Mehr un-Nisa is forthwith espoused with all solemnity to the King and her name changed into Nur Shah Begum or Nur Mahal, i.e. "Light or Glory of the Court," her father upon this affinity being advanced before all other *umrah*, her brother Asaf Khan and most of her kindred smiled upon with the addition of honours, wealth and command. And in this sunshine of content Jahangir spends some years with his lovely queen, without regarding ought save Cupid's corantos.

---

[22] Mehr un-Nisa, better known as Nur Jahan (1577–1645), was the widow of Sher Afghan Ali Quli Khan Istalju (d. 1607). She was of Persian birth, but born in Kandahar, and married Jahangir as his twentieth wife in 1611. Jahangir had known her since they had both been young, and when her husband conveniently expired he married her quickly, naming her first "Nur Mahal," which means "Light of the Palace," and then "Nur Jahan," which means "Light of the World." She and her family became very influential at Jahangir's court and she was instrumental in upholding Islam at court. "Everybody agreed that she was beautiful and intelligent," states Berinstain, and in his later years "Jahangir relied on the decisions of this wife, who directed the empire with competence" (*India*, 78–79).

[23] Ruqayya Sultan Begum was the daughter of Prince Hindal, Humayun's brother. She became Akbar's first wife in 1551. She was not a "Mother Queen," but Jahangir's grandmother-by-marriage, She was entrusted with the upbringing of Prince Khurram, later Shah Jahan. See De Laet, *Empire*, 180–83.

Anno 1610, of the Hegira 990, and in the fifth year of his reign, Sultan Shah-riyar[24] the prince, under the tutorship of Murtaza Khan, was sent Viceroy to Gu-jarat, at which time Jahan Khan[25] was sent to Burhanpur and Mahabat Khan appointed general, and ordered with an army against [the] Rajah Rana [of Mewar], who that instant was broken out into rebellion. The county also of [the] Rajah of Kotah, a branch of Bengal, was that year subjected under the Imperial Crown of Industan by the valour and conduct of Salam Khan,[26] during which Mahabat Khan, by that time in [the] Rana's provinces, goes on victoriously, forcing many holds and castles from those indomitable Indians, but, by envy of some at court in this his prosperous proceeding, Mahabat was recalled back to court and Abdullah Khan made general in his place.[27] This alteration did not much alter the state of the army, as some thought, for Abdullah prosecutes [the] Rana with no less vigour and success, urging him to a set battle at Sismer, where Abdullah got the better, chasing [the] Rana to Udaipur and Porbandar, killing many of his men, enriching themselves with abundance of spoil and captives, and after much toil and some loss he sacks Chavand,[28] [the] Rana's strongest castle, till then judged impregnable, wherein they had store of warlike provision and many pagodas which for above 1000 years had stood there surreptitiously adored. These the Mahometans burned, and in place of them reared a stupendous mosque for Mahometan devotion.

---

[24] Prince Shahriyar (1605–1628) was the youngest son of Jahangir by a slave-girl. In 1621 he was married to Nur Jahan's daughter. He became a zealous Sunni Muslim, and was supported by more orthodox Muslims who did not approve of his brother Khusrau's liberal outlook; he was also backed by Nur Jahan when in 1627 he declared himself emperor in opposition to Prince Khurram (later Shah Jahan), but was defeated by Asaf Khan. He was blinded and later executed by order of Shah Jahan.

[25] Jahan Khan Lodi (d. 1631), who ably served Jahangir as a general and administrator, eventually became Viceroy of the Deccan. In 1628, however, he revolted against Shah Jahan, whose armies defeated him without much trouble and consolidated Shah Jahan's power in the Deccan.

[26] Salam-ullah "the Arab" [*Tzalam-cawn*], later called Shaja'at Khan (d. 1624), was sent to Deccan (1609). Jahangir records giving him a promotion in 1615 (*TJ* 1. 285) and the title (1616), as well as becoming "one of the royal servants," an honour which required him to have his ears pierced like Jahangir (*TJ* 1. 320 and n. 1).

[27] This is the campaign against Amar Singh I of Mewar. Mahabat Khan's campaign lasted from 1608 to 1609, and Abdullah Khan continued the fight until 1611. The struggle continued until 1614, after three more generals had failed; Prince Khurram took charge in 1614 and recommended that Jahangir make peace, which he did, to everyone's mutual satisfaction.

[28] Chavand [*Syavend*], also known as Prassanagad, is in the Pune district. Amar Singh was crowned there in 1597; it was, as de Laet states, "the capital of the rana's ancestors" (*Empire*, 183).

The Coolies destroyed; War in Deccan

Abdullah Khan so fortunately managed this war against [the] Rana that Jahangir the Great Mughal sends him thanks and orders him to live awhile in Gujarat, not only to curb but to extirpate that rascal-race of Kolis[29] that so thievishly robbed the castles and lived upon the spoil of peaceful passengers. Abdullah fails not in that command, for with fifteen thousand horse which he sent out in several parties he ferrets and pursues them in all places where he knew they lurked, and after many petty encounters took Idar,[30] their retreating-place, seventy course from Ahmedabad, yea, happily fell upon them one time when they were together, and, having with ease put them to flight, in the chase he slew half their rabble together with Lal Koli, their ringleader, whose head he sent to Ahmedabad and, as a memorial of his victory, commanded that it should be set upon a pinnacle.

But Jahan Khan, during these broils, waiting all occasions of conquest in Deccan, through discord and envy of some *umrah* in the army, finds his success to grow worse and worse against Malik Ambar,[31] and knows no remedy without acquainting the Mughal therewith, and as an expedient entreats that one of his sons might come thither to command, by whose greatness the army might be better ordered. After consideration the King sends Sultan Parvez his son and with him Raja Ram Das, who from Burhanpore sends Jahan Khan and Man Singh with an army to Bellaguate, where they send defiance to Malik. But Jahangir, better knowing the prudence of Malik Ambar and his power, speeds Azam Khan after them with four thousand men more to reinforce his army, which done he removes his lascar to Ajmer, a place convenient for hunting. Azam Khan was no sooner come to Burhanpur but he entreats the Khan-i-Khanan to

---

[29] Herbert has *Coolis*. They are not labourers this time, but a collective term for "hill-people" (*HJ* 250). The term also refers more particularly to a fishing people in the coastal regions of Maharashtra, Gujarat, and Goa, who still live on islands near Mumbai.

[30] Idar [*Eder*], a city and former princely state in Gujarat, 25 km from the Rajasthan border. De Laet writes of the raja of Idar allying himself with Lal Koli, and that "after an obstinate battle lasting some hours," Abdul Khan defeated the raja's forces (*Empire* 185).

[31] Malik Ambar (1550–1626) was one of the most remarkable men of his time. An Ethiopian by birth, he was enslaved by Arabs and ended up in India, where he somehow managed to gather an army of about 1500 men which was so effective that various local rulers in Deccan hired it, and it was never defeated. After Akbar's capture of Ahmadnagar (1600), Malik Ambar fled, and by 1610 he was acting as Regent and Prime Minister for the young Sultan Murtaza Nizam Shah II, whom he had restored to the throne of Baz Bahadur. Jahangir called him "Ambar, that black wretch." He founded a city on the site of Khadke (see above) which was later named Aurangabad after Emperor Aurangzeb, and after his death his son Fateh Khan killed Murtaza Shah and became king himself (1631). He later submitted to the Mughal Emperor. For details see B. N. Goswamy, "Malik Ambar: A Remarkable Life," *The Tribune* (13 August 2006).

join with him and so hastens towards Bellaguate[32] with an army of 100,000 men, 600 elephants, of which huge creatures this Empire is thought to have 40,000 and 12,000 camels; yea, of such fame grew this expedition that ere they departed Cuncam they were horse and foo no less than 600,000. Abdullah Khan penetrates into the very heart of Deccan, no resistance being made either in field, town or garrison, so that through all Bidar, Ahmadnagar, Gentfro and as far as Khadke, the seat royal, they marched without resistance, burning and plundering as they listed, sparing neither villages, temples nor inhabitants to be counted. The Deccan king, astonished at the numbers and unable to resist this torrent flies to and fro, not resting anywhere till he came to Daulatabad,[33] ten miles from Khadke, a castle of great strength. For, having made some small skirmishes and ambuscados, they appeared to so little purpose that Malik Ambar, albeit Mohammed Lary and [the] wakil Adil Khan were new come to his aid with above twenty thousand horses and some infantry, he devises rather to quit his kingdom of them by stratagem then to hazard it by chance of war, to which end he cunningly writes counterfeit letters directed from some rajahs about Jahangir's court containing a private advertisement of the Mughal's death and of Khurram's advancement to the crown. These he gives in charge to a crafty banian who, circling about as if he came from Agra, was taken as a spy, and, his counterfeit letters being read, their lying contents so astonished the general that without one more consultation they presently divide the army, quit such places as they had placed garrisons in, and each captain to his former quarter. Sultan Parvez he marches to Burhanpur, Abdul Khan to Surat, and Azam Khan towards Agra, giving Ambar re-admittance to his towns and castles, which otherwise in all probability would hardly at least not speedily have been recovered.

But so soon as Jahangir had intelligence of that deceit, he becomes enraged at their simple credulity, threatening their punishment and then entreating Mahabat Khan to go Governor to Burhanpur, who, having received his commission, repairs thither, where he was with joyful acclamations received. And such was Mahabat's discretion that from thence he employs what force he had in short space subduing Berar, after which he enters Deccan without any considerable loss as far as Khirki,[34] where Abdullah Khan's army had been the year before, by that second inroad making Deccan a most miserable country and, loaden with

---

[32] As Herbert mentions later on, this city was identified with Hippocura in Ptolemy, *Geography* 3. 23. 30. It is the capital of South Ariaca, north-east of Sarimagula, now in modern-day Hyderabad. Some writers identify it with Visapur, a fort near the famed Karla Caves in Maharashtra (Crowther and Raj, *India*, 536).

[33] A "magnificent hilltop fortress" whose name means "city of fortune" (Crowther and Raj, *India*, 548).

[34] Khirki, whose name means "perforated window," was founded by Malik Ambar as the capital on the site of a village of that name in 1610. It was later called Aurangabad.

abundant spoils, returns to Burhanpur with victory, which good success, when it came to Jahangir's ears, it made amends for his last year's failings. And further, when by Khurram's mediation, having first by many battles and pursuits tired him, Rana [Amar Singh] presents himself, his son and many gifts unto the King, amongst which an elephant valued at 100,000 rupees, submitting all he had to Jahangir to be disposed of, who, heartily forgiving, embraces him with affection, offers his son his daughter in marriage, and returns him to the government of Pormandel, Porus his country, Udaipur and other places, but soon after, whether for grief he had submitted, for which he suffered reproach sufficient, or some other cause, died, and with much ceremony and hymns in a doleful manner sung to his memory, in a sepulchre amongst his noble progenitors this great prince was at Chittor buried.[35]

Jahangir, having in the meantime consumed eighteen months in pleasure at Mandu, sixty courses from Burhanpur and above twice as much from Ahmedabad, departs, and in progress comes to Ahmedabad, where he discharged Abdullah Khan from that command and ordains him Viceroy of Kalpa and Kinnaur,[36] and after twelve months pastime there returns to Agra, *Anno* 994 and of our account 1614. That year Shah Beg,[37] Governor of Kandahar, was displaced by reason of his age and Bahadur Khan made commander there. Shaja'at Khan also was sent to succeed Zalim Khan in Bengal, but at that time Uthman Khan,[38] a Pathan with a numerous army besieging Dacca, the metropolis, he and Itimad [ud-Daulah] with fifteen thousand men gave Uthman battle, which was bravely-fought on both sides, but by reason of a mad elephant on which Uthman sat, Shaja'at Khan was unhorsed and maimed; yea, the Mughal's forces discomfited, but by strange chance a wounded man seeing Uthman pass by, transfixes him with his lance, and by that mischance the Pathans retreat and at length fly,[39]

---

[35] Amar Singh did not die until 1620. In spite of the fact that Jahangir had returned Chittor to his rule (1616), the capital remained at Udaipur. "Today the fort of Chittor is a virtually deserted ruin," Crowther and Raj write, "but impressive reminders of its heyday still stand" (*India*, 388). The events Herbert describes seem to have been compressed; they run from 1615 to 1620.

[36] Kinnaur [*Kheer*] is a region in the Sutlej valley almost bordering on Tibet and now in Himachal Pradesh; Kalpa [*Kalpi*] is the largest town in the area, "the legendary winter home of Lord Shiva" (Crowther and Raj, *India*, 203).

[37] Akbar had appointed Shah Beg to Kandahar in March 1594

[38] Uthman Khan [*Ozman-chan*] (d. 1612), an Afghan *zamindar* (chief), attacked the Mughals first in 1601, but had been defeated by Man Singh, who had secured Dacca at that time. The date of these events is 1612, not 1614 as Herbert states; Jahangir noted that in April of that year "through the blessing of Allah's favour and through the benign influence of royal grace, Bengal had been freed from the disturbance of Uthman the Afghan" (*TJ* 1. 207).

[39] Jahangir has a different version of Uthman's death; according to him Sha'ajat Khan was in trouble after a rather one-sided battle with Usman, who was on an elephant.

the Mughals not only recovering Dacca, but piercing into the very hearts of the gentiles' country, they captivate his wife and children, foraging at pleasure and making all his wealth, which was very great and sent to Agra, a testimony of their valour as well as victory. That year the Mughal journeyed to Lahore with his lascar.

An Embassy into Persia. Kabul described.

Abdul Khan after seven weeks arrives at Kalpa where, and of Kinnaur, he was to receive the government. He straightway executed his commission in small time, quieting and destroying those swarms of rebellious Rajputs which still there remained; he levelled also the most defensive places with the ground and made sale of so many of the inhabitants as paid the charges of war, amounting to 200,000 rupees and upwards. Alam Khan[40] also at about this time went ambassador from Jahangir to Abbas the Persian; not any ambassador in man's memory went more richly-despatched with presents or more bravely-attended than he did. He presented the King, then at Isfahan, with twelve chests of choice linen, two other chests filled with sashes woven with gold and silk and silver, many daggers whose halts were set with stones of value estimated at 70, 000 rupees, and for discharge of his own port and travel he had an allowance out of the Mughal's exchequer of sixty thousand rupees, the better to represent the majesty of so great an Emperor. Abbas entertains the ambassador nobly, cloys him with invitations, shows, sports and other pastimes, and at his departure makes five hundred qizlbashes[41] with Ali Quli Khan, Rostam Beg and other noblemen to attend him two days' journey on his way towards Kandahar, recommending his well-wishes to the Mughal in a princely return of five hundred swift coursers, twenty mules and five hundred asses of great value, one hundred and fifty dromedaries or *qizlbash* camels,

---

As he was looking around for another mount, an unknown Imperial soldier mortally wounded Uthman with a gunshot. "However much they enquired for the man who fired it," Jahangir related, "he could not be found." Uthman did not die right away; "two watches of the night had passed," the Emperor wrote, "when Usman [sic] went to Hell" (*TJ* 1. 211–12). De Laet says that Uthman was killed by a wounded soldier who "chanced to shoot him in the eye as he was riding past on his elephant" (*Empire*, 190).

    [40] Khan-i-Alam [*Chan Assem*] was the title given by Jahangir to Mirza Barkhurdar (1609), one of the Khan-i-Khanan's sons. Jahangir appointed him ambassador to Persia in 1618, and relates how the Shah graciously relaxed the no-smoking rule of the Persian court for him (*TJ* 1. 371). His visit is described from the Persian side by Eskandar Beg Monshi in his *Life of Abbas the Great* (3: 159–60). The embassy was returned in 1622.

    [41] *Qizlbash* means "red-head." It was a name originally given to those Turkmen tribes who supported the Safavids in Persia when they took over in 1501, and refers to the red caps they wore. It was also a name used to denote Persian-speaking Turkmen in Kabul. Herbert seems to be using it in both senses in this section.

eighteen chests or sandoughs of choice carpets and bezoars,[42] twenty camels' load of Shiraz wine, and eight of conserved dates, pistachios etc., all of which were acceptably received by Jahangir, who that year took his progress to participate the pleasures of Kashmir, having first removed Mahabat Khan from Burhanpur to the command of Kabul and Banges.[43]

Kabul, by Ptolemy in his sixth book and 18 chapter called *Chabura*, by some supposed that *Alexandria Arachosiae* which the Macedonian built near the mountain Caucasus, on the north is confined by Caucasus, south with Multan, on the east with Kashmir and Chari [Sharif],[44] west with Indus, is now subject to the Mughal, but not many years since to the Tartar and Persian. The name from the Syriac signifies "sterile," and agrees with the nature of the country, which is cold and windy, being not over-fruitful save where the Nilab[45] fattens her, a river by Ptolemy called Choa, Coat and Cophia by others, which, not far hence arising, streams south into Indus and is one of those five which empty themselves into that princely river and then in one stream near to Diu disembogue themselves into the ocean. The city Kabul is north from Lahore eight days' journey, the way hilly and dangerous albeit the inhabitants be most part banians. The houses are low; nothing more observable in the town than the serais and two great and well-built forts or castles, in one of which was King Babur born, from whom in three descents Jahangir is descended.

Prosecution of the wars in Deccan.

Sultan Khusrau, upon his father's removal to Kashmir, was taken from the custody of Asaf Khan and given to Jahan Khan to secure. Sheikh Qasim[46] was also made Lieutenant of Bengal in his brother Islam Khan's[47] stead. Islam Khan's

---

[42] A bezoar-stone was made of "hard concretions found in the bodies of animals to which antidotal virtues were ascribed, and especially one obtained from the stomach of a wild goat in the Persian province of Lar" (*HJ* 90).

[43] The River Bangi.

[44] Chari Sharif is south of Srinagar "on the road to Yusmarg, and has the shrine of Kashmir's ziarat or patron saint" (Crowther and Raj, *India*, 223).

[45] Nilab [*Nylob*]. Another name for the Indus.

[46] Qasim Khan [*Cheq'-Kassem*], the son-in-law of Itimad ud-Daulah and husband of Manija, sister of Nur Jahan, was sent by Jahangir in 1610 to support his brother Islam Khan, with whom he had been earlier quarrelling (*TJ* 1. 147). He received the appointment as subadar as Herbert describes, but some years later, so Jahangir related, "as for a long time no good had been heard of the affairs of Bengal and of the conduct of Qasim Khan." . . . "I sent for Qasim Khan to Court" (*TJ* 1. 373). This was in April 1617; he does not mention the elephant story, nor the horrible events which followed. Jahangir later made him Governor of Lahore and of Punjab (see *TJ* 2. 182, 230).

[47] Islam Khan [*Tzalam-cawn*] (d. 1613) was originally called Ala-ud-din. In 1608 Jahangir sent him to Bengal as Viceroy with orders to "consider that province his jagir"

son, hearing of his uncle's coming that way and ever hating him, from Dacca he travels towards Agra with all his father's wealth to be disposed of by the Mughal. But in the way, near Rajmahal,[48] Qasim Khan met him and takes violently away from him his best elephants and some other things of value, which, being by his nephew to the full related at court, Qasim was immediately displaced, and Ibrahim Khan,[49] Queen Nur Mahal's cousin, put in his place, who meeting at Rajkot with Qasim Khan, at that time with all his goods and people packing away, Ibrahim demands restitution of the elephants he took from [Islam Khan's son]. But Qasim was so enraged at these successive indignities that after some words they fall to blows, and in the skirmish Qasim, finding his party weakest, retires to his harem, where most inhumanly he murders his concubines then flies away, leaving Ibrahim possessor of his treasure, who by the assent of some *umrah* and most of the vulgar sort, was admitted their Governor, after which he falls upon *Moeckham*[50] the rebel and defeats him and his forces, killing some and selling others as slaves, yea, enriches himself with so much spoil as puffs him up with pride and made him so reputable at court that Jahangir, in token of thanks, send him a horse, a battleaxe and a dagger, and as an ornamentation of honour changes his name to Firuz Jahan Khan. The same time Murtaza Khan was sent by the King to besiege Kangra,[51] a castle so fenced by both art and nature as made many judge it invincible, and the rather for it had contemned the best and worst the kings of Delhi could do against it. Notwithstanding which Murtaza, after some danger of ambushments in that thick wood being seventy miles broad and no less trouble in passing his men over high rocks, and eight months siege, in despite of their best defence by scalado[52] entered and subjected it to the Mughal, though Murtaza lived not three months after to ruminate his victory, which

---

despite objections from advisers about his youth. The Emperor had a high regard for "the excellence of his disposition and natural quality," (*TJ* 1. 208) and he was not disappointed, as Islam Khan crushed all resistance to the Mughal rule. He moved the capital from Rajmahal to Dacca. It was Islam Khan who led the fight against Uthman. "If death had not overtaken him," Jahangir wrote, "he would have done perfect service" (*TJ* 1. 257).

[48] Rajmahal was the name given to the city of Agmahal by Rajah Man Singh in 1592 when it became the new capital of Bengal. Three years later the name was changed again, this time to Akbarnagar.

[49] For Ibrahim Khan Fath Jang [*Ebrahem-cawn*], who "had carried on successfully the affairs of the Subah of Behar and had brought a diamond mine into the possession of the state" (*TJ* 1. 373), see n.177.

[50] This name is lifted from de Laet (*Empire* 194). It actually refers to one Durjan Sal, the *zamindar* (landowner) of Khokhara, which, Banerjee tells us, "was annexed in 1615" (De Laet, *Empire*, 194, n.110).

[51] Kangra is a town in modern-day Himachal Pradesh, which "in Jahangir's reign was paved in plates of pure silver." The fort Herbert mentions is now "much ruined . . . on a bridge overlooking the Baner and Manjhi Rivers" (Crowther and Raj, *India*, 183).

[52] an escalade, i.e. a device to scale walls.

when Jahangir heard, with a mixture of joy and sorrow he leaves Kashmir and removes his court to Lahore, where Sultan Khusrau, the true idea of misery, by persuasion of the Queen and Asaf Khan, was taken from Jahan Khan and put to Khurram, his emulous brother, to be his keeper. At that time Jahangir affected his son Khurram beyond measure, imagining no honour too much, no command too great for so spriteful a prince, so that little-knowing what would follow, he gives him the command of forty thousand horse, and attended by Rajah Abdul Hassan[53] and other *umrah*, hastens him to the conquest of Deccan with order to subdue or spoil the kingdoms of Golconda[54] and Bijapur for omitting their annual tribute of three pound weight of diamonds.

This year 1619, of Mahomet 1029, Abdul Aziz Khan succeeding Bahadur Khan the Uzbek in his command of Kandahar, Jahan Khan was Lieutenant of Multan through which Indus runs, Sultan Parvez of Pathan and Rajah Bir Singh Bundela and Abdul Khan Governors of Kalpa were commanded to raise some forces and jointly to march unto Sultan Khurram into Deccan to rescue his army.

Sultan Khurram, by this time having levied his forces and made all things ready for this new war upon Deccan, first commands all men to entitle him Shah Jahan, i.e. King of Hearts,[55] then with his whole army in goodly equipage he travels to Burhanpur, which was the rendezvous whither Abdullah Khan and Rajah Bir Singh, according to command, come and wait upon him with Tbedder-cawn his cousin and many other Rajputs of quality. Khurram (for by that name we can best remember him) now swells beyond measure to see himself general and in the head of so brave an army, and, loath to spend the least time in vain, with all speed he gives order to Abdullah Khan, Rajah Bir Singh, Abdul Hassan and many other *umrah* to begin the war with Malik Ambar, and that he and his residue would follow them. Mirza Mukarram [Khan][56] and Shadur-cawn in the interim march to Golconda against Qutb-ul-mulk,[57] and Mohammed Taqi[58] to Bijapur against

---

[53] Abu'l Hassan Khwaja was sent to Deccan in December 1620 (*TJ* 2. 193). He later (1622) became Vizier after the death of Itimad ud-Daulah.

[54] Golconda was the seat of the Qutb Shahi kings until 1590, when Hyderabad, then a new city, replaced it as the capital. In 1600 Akbar forced the ruler to pay tribute, but the fort of Golconda itself was only captured in 1687 by Aurangzeb.

[55] Actually it means "Ruler of the world."

[56] Mukarram Khan [*Mirza Mackry*] was another of Jahangir's "houseborn" retainers (*TJ* 1. 433) and the son of Mu' azzam Khan, Governor of Orissa. He conquered the territory of Khurda, which was between Orissa and Golconda (1617), and threatened the ruler of Golconda (see below).

[57] Qutb-ul-Mulk Abdullah [*Cotabul Melek*] was the Sultan of Golconda 1611–1672.

[58] Mohammed Taqi Khwaja [*Ma'met Tacky*] was Jahangir's "diwan of buildings" (*TJ* 1. 258). Jahangir later made him diwan of Deccan and gave him the title of Mutaqid Khan (*TJ* 2. 126).

Adil Khan[59] either to receive by force or fair means the accustomed tribute of diamonds due to the diadem of Industan. Abdul Khan in the first place, pursuant to his commission, passes without any opposition to Bellaguate, (a fastidious mountain 'twixt Cunca and Deccan and, as some think, that which is called *Hippocura* in Ptolemy, but more probably that Gates which is mentioned in those old writers who affirm that, as the Apennines in Italy, this runs in a continued ledge from Caucasus as far as Cape Comry, the utmost promontory of Malabar,[60] penetrating from north to south through the heart of many kingdoms), Khurram, bringing up the other parts of the army at fifteen miles distance to succour the van upon all occasions. The King of Deccan at all advantages interposes and opposes them in many petty skirmishes, but Abdul Khan, formerly acquainted with his rodomontades,[61] passes on, burning and spoiling what they met with, not resting till they came to Kerki, the King's best house, which they levelled with the ground, enriching themselves with store of booty and treasure, reducing also Berar and Khandesh, forcing composition from all the country as far as Ahmadnagar and tribute from the kings of Golconda and Bijapur, whither Mukarram and Shadur-cawn were sent to quicken it.

Prince Khusrau murdered.

Jahangir, overjoyed with such good fortune, to relish it better solaces himself in his son Parvez's gardens beyond the river. Itimad ud-Daulah, Queen Nur Mahal's father, dying at that time,[62] his great estate was by the King divided 'twixt his daughter and Asaf Khan, but his office of Treasurer was conferred upon Khwaja Ab'ul Hassan. Khurram also, who sat as Emperor in his own opinion, with a greedy eye respects the diadem, but perceiving his imprisoned brother interposing, such is the magic of his ambition that it runs on not caring how, though masked with never so much deformity, so that feigning himself sick (his disease was horrible), nothing can recover him but his eldest brother's death. The Khan-i-Khanan, one of his infernal council, presently acquaints some munsubdars with the remedy, of which rascal troop Reza or Raja Bandar, a most notorious villain, being quickest of apprehension makes no scruple to act it. In the meantime Khurram, as if he knew nothing of the plot, conveys himself out of Burhanpur

---

[59] Ibrahim Adil Khan II was the ruler of Bijapur 1579–1626. In 1610 he offered his loyalty to Jahangir, and the latter recorded a diamond "valued at 40,000 rupees" being sent to him in 1617 (*TJ* 1. 400), as well as his own gift to Adil Shah of his portrait in 1624 (*TJ* 2. 86).

[60] Malabar was "the ancient Kerala of the Hindus" derived from the Dravidian term for "mountain" (*HJ* 539).

[61] Boasting, blustering.

[62] Itimad ud-Daulah died at the end of January 1622. "What shall I say about my feelings through this terrible event?" wrote the grieving Jahangir; "He was a wise and perfect Vizier, and a learned and affectionate companion" (*TJ* 2. 222).

upon pretence to better his health, whilst that incarnate devil at an unseasonable hour in the night knocks at Khusrau's chamber door, who, awakened out
of a fearful dream starts up and demands his errand. The villain replies he came
from the Mughal his father about his delivery. The miserable prince, affrighted
and suspecting treason, desires him to stay till the morning, but the villain, perceiving no entrance by entreaty, breaks in, grapples with the amazed prince, and
having got him down, strangles him; that done, lays him in his bed, locks the
door, and sneaks away as if the prince had died of some imposthume,[63] by which
we see that *"nulla fata loco possis excludere / cum mors venerit."*[64] This damnable villainy being bruited, Khurram, you may believe, has quick news of his brother's
death, and albeit he outwardly expresses some sorrow, inwardly rejoices. But ere
sunrise Khusrau's afflicted wife, Azam Khan's daughter, going to visit him, finding him speechless and, by his contorted face perceiving that he was murdered,
never did poor wretch pour out greater abundance of tears or express more passion. First tearing her hair, she then deforms her beautiful face, mixed with such
loud cries and symptoms of distraction that her father and all his family both
hear and see it, to their grief and admiration. But when they see the cause also,
they wonder not at her complaint, none of them forbearing to express their sorrow after several modes without moderation. Not only the prince's house but all
Burhanpur rings with the horridness of this treason; they suspect the author and
curse him, but Khurram, clothed with hypocrisy, comes dejectedly thither, falls
upon the murdered corpse, and expresses so much sorrow as many were induced
to believe that he was innocent. After two days they bury the murdered prince,
and Khurram writes his father word of his brother's sudden death, concealing the
cause. Jahangir, who had a fatherly affection, first weeps, and afterwards grows
mad with rage, suspecting that he was treacherously made away, but not knowing upon the sudden how to discover it, feeds upon discontent, writes back a letter of reproof and threats to Khurram and his *umrah* vowing a strict *inquisition*
into the cause of his death, and if any treason appeared that he would revenge it

---

[63] The accuracy of Herbert's account may be questioned, as some historians seem to
think that Prince Khusrau's death may have looked suspicious, but that responsibility for
it may not unquestionably be laid at Khurram's door. However, Berinstain calls it "mysterious and opportune" and says that it and the death of Prince Parvez (1626) "seem to have
been orchestrated by Khurram, whose ambition knew no bounds" (*India*, 79). Ja-hangir
himself recorded rather laconically that "a report came from Khurram that Khusrau . . .
had died of the disease of colic pains and gone to the mercy of God" (*TJ* 2. 228). He died
either at Burhanpur or Asir in the Deccan; Rogers and Beveridge give the date as 29 January 1622 O.S. (*TJ* 2. 228 n.). Jahangir, if he had any suspicions, did not mention them in
his account. The question is of Martial, *Epigrams* 4. 60. 5-6, meaning "Nowhere can you
keep the Fates out when death comes."
[64] "You cannot shut out fate from any place / when death comes" (Martial, *Epigrams*
IV, 60).

when they least suspected it. He withal commands the body to be digged up and brought with solemn state to Elabas, which was done, and there he inters him in his mother's monument. Then he sends for Azam Khan and his afflicted daughter, comforts them and takes them for his constant companions, from whom, being truly informed of Khurram's accessoriness, he forthwith upon Sultan Bulaqi his grandson, son to Prince Khusrau, entails the Imperial Crown, gives him the command of ten thousand horse and commits him to the tuition of Azam Khan his grandsire of the blood royal of Tartary, by him to be educated.

Khurram, perceiving that the murder was discovered and that by the love his father expressed to Sultan Bulaqi he was disregarded, thenceforth not caring to please, in a discontented humour he forsakes the court and desperately flies out into rebellion.[65] Abdullah Khan, having notice of his intent, without leave-taking forsakes the army and hastens towards Kalpa to his government, but by the Mughal (who was still desirous to continue the Deccan war) he is rebuked and made to return. Yet ere long he was revoked thence, for at that time Abbas King of Persia with thirty thousand men had laid close siege to Kandahar, pretending it was a member of his Empire.[66] The city was defended by Aziz Khan [Naqshbandi],[67] a captain of valour and honesty, who for sixteen days kept in despite of the Persian, but perceiving his garrison too weak if they intended to storm, he acquaints Jahangir with his condition and the time he could probably maintain the place, by which if he had not relief he should be forced to surrender.

Jahangir, having notice thereof, sends word back that within that space he would not fail to succour him, either by relieving the garrison or raising the siege, so that posting to Lahore and having advised his Council of War, first he commands Jahan Khan [Lodi], then Lieutenant of Multan, which adjoins Kandahar, with such force as he had in readiness to haste thither whilst the enemy in the interim attempt day and night the entrance and Jahangir ruminates whom to appoint for general; at last fixes upon Abdullah Khan, who by that time and by Khurram's leave was again returned. This famous captain readily accepts the charge, speeds to Lahore, and is embraced with such joy by the Mughal that he presently contracts his fair granddaughter to Mirza Khan, Abdullah Khan's

---

[65] From this point on Jahangir refers to Khurram by the name "Bi-daulat," which means "the wretch" (*TJ* 2. 248) and commanded that he be henceforth known by it.

[66] According to a letter from Shah Abbas which Jahangir included in his memoirs, the Shah claimed that he had "set off without apparatus for taking [Kandahar]," and that he went there "to see the place and hunt there." Because the Mughal authorities "did not receive the conciliatory order and message in the proper way but showed obstinacy and a rebellious spirit," Abbas felt "there was nothing more to be done," so he ordered the attack! (*TJ* 2. 241).

[67] Abdul Aziz Naqshbandi was one of Jahangir's generals. He took Kangra fort (1619) and was promoted to *faujdar* of the district of Kangra (1620). By December of the same year he was made Governor of Kandahar.

eldest son. And so, with a hundred elephants and fifteen thousand horse, five thousand of which he brought along with him, he makes haste to give the Persian battle, but ere he could attain thither Jahangir, having notice that the Persians were exceeding strong and no less resolute, by letters commands Aziz Khan to surrender the place unto the enemy, but the valiant governor, doubting they were counterfeit, holds out, till by mine a great part of the wall was blown up, and, as Abbas was entering the breach, he sounds a parley, and after a short treaty agrees upon articles for the yielding it up, on condition that they might depart safely with their lives and baggage.[68] Abbas, who only aimed at the conquest of the city, condescends and has it given up, wherein he places Ali Quli Khan and returns to Isfahan, whilst Asaf and Abdullah Khan by easy marches retire back to Lahore, where, notwithstanding the loss, by Jahangir they are welcomed.

Kandahar and Mandu described.

Kandahar has Arctic elevation four and thirty degree and longitude from the first meridian ninety-eight. There be that repute it to be in Parapamisa, which some call Sablestan;[69] to the west it hath Aria, Arachosia to the south,[70] and adjoins that part of Sogdiana which of old was called Bactria to the north, or rather Margiana, which some call Jesselbash. The country, especially towards the south, is reasonable fruitful and redundant in most necessary things, yet by reason of the many caravans passing and re-passing from Lahore to Persia, all sort of provision is dear and the passage, in regard of many rascal troops of Pathans, Afghans and Coolies, which like the inhospitable Arabs prey upon cassilaes, it is found both chargeable and dangerous travelling. The city is not so spacious as 'tis strong, made defensive as well by help of nature as industry; to the south and east it is surrounded with a thick wall, to the west and north with hills. The suburbs also, though not well-defended, are large, adding to the city beauty and wealth, nothing wanting save good water, which there and all the way to Isfahan is brackish, through the distemperature of the earth which is for the most part barren and uncomfortable.

Jahangir, infatuated by the crafty persuasion of Asaf Khan, sends him with a peremptory order to the Treasurer and Castle-keeper of Agra that without delay

---

[68] Kandahar fell to the Persians on 11 June 1622 and Shah Abbas's letter was presented to Jahangir early in November. Haidar Beg Qurbashi, "one of the sincere Sufis," as Abbas called him (*TJ* 2. 242), delivered the letter and was accompanied by the commanders of the Mughal garrison.

[69] Parapamisa was a former Indo-Greek kingdom in North India bordering on modern Afghanistan.

[70] Aria is the modern city of Herat and also a province in Western Afghanistan. Arachosia was an old province of the Achaemenid Empire of Persia, covering South Afghanistan and parts of modern Pakistan. In 329 B.C.E. Alexander the Great founded the city of Alexandria Arachosia there.

he should remove the public treasure thence to Lahore, where the court was then and for some time he had intended to settle.[71] This was a message of so much astonishment to Itibar Khan[72] both from the consideration of the length and danger of the way, trouble of carriage and his own integrity, which the King had no reason to distrust, as also the extraordinary strength of the exchequer where the treasure was then hoarded that at first he could hardly credit his master's letter, but at length he fell to dissuade Asaf Khan, though in vain, had his arguments been trebled, so that on the one side haste and the Mughal's command is urged, on the other delay and diverting Jahangir's meaning to another sense, on either part with that eagerness that from words blows became their uncivil moderators. But in that excess Asaf Khan, for all his greatness, found himself too weak; the eunuch's guard was so strong and Itibar Khan, Provost of Agra, so near at hand to second him. Nevertheless, the eunuch abates of his pertinacity, and Asaf Khan at length prevails for the remove of the treasure. But whiles the eunuchs were preparing for the journey, this deceitful man posts away a swift zantel to his son-in-law Khurram, then upon the confines of Deccan, advertising him what had passed, advising his speed to ambush betwixt Agra and Delhi if he had any desire to intercept his father's treasure. The prince receives the letter with joy, and without any check of conscience or respect of loyalty, immediately commands all his officers out of such provinces as his father had assigned him from Burhanpur to Surat, and all Cambay to Ahmedabad, the Governors of Broach, Jaunbasser, Madhapur, and of the maritime coast, Goga, Diu, Nagsari, Mangalpur and Unarpur, as also out of Mandu, Gandevi, Udaipur, Berar, Ahmednagar etc.[73] in an enterprise so full of peril, desirous to engage and bring them under like hazard and the better to oblige their future dependence upon his fortunes. And so with no less than seventy thousand horse he marches towards Mandu as if he intended a contrary progress.

Mandu, threescore courses from Burhanpur, is seated on the side of a declining hill in which both for ornament and defence is a castle[74] which is strong by

---

[71] Jahangir merely states that "Asaf K. was sent to Agra to bring to court the whole of the treasure in muhrs and rupees which had accumulated from the beginning of the reign of my father" (*TJ* 2. 245).

[72] Itibar Khan [*Ethabar-chan*], a faithful courtier, was given land in Gwalior by Jahangir in 1607, and promoted to a higher rank with more property in 1617. In 1622, "as he was an old servant and had become very weak and old," Jahangir related, "I promoted him to the [Governorship] of Agra and entrusted to him the defence of the fort and treasury" (*TJ* 2. 231–32).

[73] Broach [*Baroch*] is in Gujarat; Madhapur [*Medapore*] is in Hyderabad; Nagsari is a port on the Arabian Sea; Mangalpore [*Mangarelpore*] is in Orissa; Unarpur [*Onnepore*] is in the Thatta area; Gandevi [*Gandersee*] is in Gujarat. The other locations have already been noted elsewhere.

[74] Crowther and Raj note that "the extensive, and now mainly deserted, hilltop fort of Mandu is one of the most interesting sights in central India" (*India*, 476).

being encompassed with a defensive wall of near five mile. The whole heretofore had fifteen miles circuit, but the city later-built is of less assize yet fresher beauty, whether you behold the temples, in one of which is entombed four kings, palaces or fortresses, especially that tower which is elevated one hundred and seventy steps, supported by massy pillars and adorned with gates and windows very observable.[75] It was built by Jahan Khan, who there lies buried, and was lately owned by the kings of Delhi till such time as Humayun the Mughal ravished it from Sher Shah, King of Delhi, at his return from Persia whither Sher [Shah] forced him. From Broach 'tis distant an hundred and fifty English miles.

Battle between Sultan Khurram and his Father

Khurram, after two days' rest in Tattapani,[76] advances with such haste that his army, ignorant of his intent, thought he had been half-frantic, every day marching above forty miles so that in thirteen days he attained Fatehpur, which is from Burhanpur near five hundred miles, yes, ere Itibar Khan knew of his being in that country. But as it fell out, he made more haste then good speed; for long he could not lurk with such a numerous company without the knowledge of Itibar Khan the careful Treasurer, who, as if all the enemies in the world were approaching, unloads the camels of their precious burthens, conveys it in again, fortifies the castle and sends quick notice to Jahangir of his son's traitorous intention, who at this report was astonished above all measure so that presently he sends every way for assistance, for Sultan Parvez out of Pauben, Jahan Shah out of Multan, and for Mahabat Khan out of Kabul. Whilst Khurram, perceiving he was discovered, with his whole army divided amongst several great officers, by name [the] Khan-i-Khanan, Rostam Khan,[77] Rajah Bikramajit,[78] Mirza

---

[75] Herbert may be describing the Jami Masjid mosque (1454), begun by Sultan Hoshang Shah (1405–1435) and continued by Mahmud Shah (1436–1469). It is "claimed to be the finest and largest example of Afghan architecture in India" (Crowther and Raj, *India*, 479).

[76] Tattapani is a small spa town in Himachal Pradesh.

[77] Rostam Khan was the son of Mirza Sultan Hussain. He had been sent at the death of his father to the Deccan, where, Jahangir tells us, "he had a small jagir." Jahangir sent for him in 1614 "with the intention of showing him favour" (*TJ* 1. 262).

[78] Rajah Bikramajit Baghela (d. 1623), whose real name was Sundar Das, "Sundar of evil deeds," as Jahangir later called him (*TJ* 2. 254) ably served Shah Jahan in Cutch and at the siege of Kangra (1618), for which he was rewarded with a jagir in Barhana (*TJ* 2. 26). He went on to conquer Mau later in the same year. When Khurram was defeated he was killed. "On the next day they brought me the head of Sundar," Jahangir recorded; "It appeared that when the ball struck him he gave up his soul to the lords of Hell" (*TJ* 2. 256).

Darab,[79] Sayed Khan, Mohammed Tajiq and others appear and show themselves in the very face of Agra, making a bravado as if the conquest were easy and in no way to be doubted of. But the two eunuchs keep close to their charge in the castle, while Rajah Bikramajit, at Khurram's appointment, begins the churlish play, followed by Bairam Beg,[80] Rostam Khan, Wazir Khan[81] and Darab, whose assault was full of bravery. Yet Itibar Khan, desirous to sacrifice his best endeavours to express his loyalty to the King, retaliates him such an entertainment that after three hours dispute, having lost five hundred men and being without hopes of attacking the place, they were forced to retreat well-beaten and no less ashamed, so that Khurram, now letting loose the reins of discipline, falls upon a more pleasing but less honourable design, for after a retreat they fall to plundering the houses of such *umrah* as were likely to have booty in them. Bairam Beg begins with the house of Mirza Abdullah, Azam Khan's son, which was of some strength but where, contrary to expectations, he finds hot welcome. Howbeit, Rajah Bikramajit entered with better fortune Asaf Khan's, which in this confusion found no exception, out of which they draw twenty lakh of rupees, Rostam Khan out of Lashkar Khan's[82] sixteen lakh, and Darab from Nur-ed-din Quli's[83] ten, in all above threescore lakh of rupees, after which, as if they had effected wonders, they returned triumphantly to Fatehpur.

Khurram, after three weeks' stay at Fatehpur, remembering that he who attempts any great business with small means at least fancies to himself the advantage of opportunity that he may not despair, albeit he found it above his reach either by force or subtlety to obtain that treasure, resolves nevertheless to march back and give his father battle, whom by intelligence from Asaf Khan he heard was coming towards him. To this end, after double allowance given to each soldier, with protestations of some extraordinary reward he retreats towards Delhi, in five days attaining Faridabad,[84] ten courses from Delhi, such time as Jahangir,

[79] Mirza Darab, "the wretch Darab" (*TJ* 2. 254) was the son of the Khan-i-Khanan. In 1620 he had defeated rebels in Afghanistan, but now fought with his father against Jahangir.
[80] Bairam Beg served as Prince Khurram's *bakhshi*. He was also a military commander.
[81] The only Wazir Khan mentioned by Jahangir is Muqim Khan, who was styled Wazir Khan. He initially served Prince Parvez as diwan of Bengal, but was dismissed from his post by Jahangir in 1608.
[82] Lashkar Khan, also known as Mutaqid, had been a former Governor of Agra (1619). Jahangir says that Rajah Bikramajit (not Rostam Khan), "the ringleader of the people of error and the chief of the seditious" took "Rs. 900,000" from his house (*TJ* 2. 249–50). He later commanded troops against the rebels.
[83] Nur-ed-din Quli was the *kotwal* or Chief of Police in Agra.
[84] This city was founded by Baba Farid, Jahangir's treasurer, in 1607. It is now in modern-day Haryana state.

having made all possible speed, with his army pitched three courses from the town and not above seven from Khurram's quarter.

Khurram beaten.

Early the next morn Khurram, seeing it was now no time to dally, commands Rajah Bikramajit with eight thousand horse to engage his father, against whom Jahangir, though in person there, constitutes Mahabat Khan his Lieutenant-General and under him Abdullah Khan, Itibar Khan, Asaf Khan, Rajah Abdul Hassan, Sadiq Khan,[85] Mirza Mohammed, Rajah Bir Singh, Zabardast Khan[86] and other principal *umrah* had command, and by Mahabat Khan's advice the whole was divided into three brigades, one part himself and Rajah Bir Singh's command, the second Sultan Shahriyar his youngest son and Mahabat Khan, the third Abdullah Khan and Sadiq Khan, of whose loyalty and experience he so little doubted that he needed not to use more argument then Khurram's late cruelty to his elder brother and that his further aim was through his father's blood to step into the Empire. Nevertheless, to each commander, as they were entering the field, he sent some token of his respect to wear that day for their better encouragement. But Zabardast Khan in the first place, carrying Abdullah Khan his master's present, for want of good scouts falls into a forlorn of five hundred horse of Khurram's and perishes. Bikramajit, pursuant to Khurram's orders, with a smart body of horse charges Bir Singh and the Mughal's wing so furiously that many parted with their lives to express their loyalty, whiles [the] Khan-i-Khanan and Khurram with the main body enter pell-mell upon that part of the Mughals that was commanded by Mahabat Khan, Rostam Khan with *Tsossally* doing the like upon Abdullah Khan, so that for three hours the battle was continued with equal hopes, each part fighting so resolutely that no advantage for some hours could be discovered, till victory at last inclines to Khurram. For Rajah Bikramajit, after a terrible slaughter of that party the Mughal commanded, in despite of his guard entering sternly, dyed in blood, Jahangir's royal tent, arrested him as his prisoner, which he had scarcely done when the battleaxe of a *munsubdar* then in presence gave him such a blow that down the rajah fell, with a curse breathing out his unwilling soul, and such terror into the hearts of his followers that without considering how much they had the better of the fight they fled, and gave the

---

[85] Sadiq Khan was appointed Governor of the Punjab(1623) and also served as Jahangir's *bakhshi*.

[86] Zabardast Khan (d. 1623) was appointed as Jahangir's *Mir Tuzuk*, or Master of Ceremonies, in 1620. Two years later Jahangir honoured him with his own standard (*TJ* 2. 252).

Mughalthe opportunity to rally his scattered men and after a little more dispute to have the chase of the enemy.[87]

Khurram was in some amazement at this unexpected change, yet like a courageous captain does all he can to embody his army. He persuades, threats, opposes and cries aloud that Bikramajit was slain yet he was living, yea, that many as good officers as Bikramajit were in the army, but in vain, for such was their disorder and panic fear that it was impossible to revoke them, so that, volleying out a thousand imprecations, expressing all symptoms of frenzy, he rides to and fro, not knowing whether he had better here put a period (by his death) to future misfortune, or to fly and hope for better afterwards. At last, by the Khan-i-Khanan's advice secretly sent, he hastes away, leaving his treasure and baggage to the will of his enemies, so that with some few of his friends he attains the desolate mountains of Mewar, in whose solitary rocks he ruminates his misery and the justice of God upon his unnatural practices and rebellion.

Sultan Parvez[88] with a glad heart meets his victorious father at Balasore,[89] after which the seraglios are freed and the castle gates opened, fearless of any further opposal. And now the old Mughal again begins to cheer up his drooping spirits and to solace himself with Nur Mahal, the light of his eyes if not the best object of his devotion. His delights and caresses give a fair occasion to Asaf Khan to mediate a reconciliation for Khurram, which the old man, desirous of one, inclined to, so that from Ajmer letters of love and forgiveness are once more despatched unto the prince, who reads them with no small-seeming joy and prepares for his submission. With the Khan-i-Khanan, Abdullah Khan, Darab Khan, Bairam Beg and other *umrah* he descends the mountains of Mewar, and through Vasravi,[90] Amber and Lalsot,[91] unable to forbear pilfering by the way, he came to Ajmer where he throws himself at' s father's feet and upon his repentance vows never more to fly out, is pardoned.

But his submission appeared counterfeit, for so soon as Rajah Bikramajit was slain, Khurram in his place constituted Abdullah Khan[92] Governor of Gujarat,

---

[87] This story is not recorded in the *TJ*. It has already been noted that Rajah Bikramajit was killed by a gunshot and was afterwards beheaded.

[88] It is interesting to note that Jahangir refers to Parvez as "my fortunate son" from the time of Khurram's rebellion.

[89] Balasore [*Balzol*] is in northern Orissa. "It was once an important trading centre for Dutch, Danish, English and French factories" (Crowther and Raj, *India*, 507). In Herbert's own times (1634) it became the first factory in Bengal for the British East India Company.

[90] Vasravi [*Bassawer*] was a small town near Broach in Gujarat, now little more than a village.

[91] Lalsot is a town about 120 miles south-east of Agra,

[92] This is the same Abdullah Khan who had previously served Akbar and Jahangir so well; Jahangir noted how in the battle against Khurram and Rajah Bikramajit he "threw 10,000 cavalry into confusion and joined the enemy." It was at this point that Ja-

Ahmedabad, Surat and Cambay. Abdullah Khan, though glad of so considerable a command, delays his repair thither both in regard of his desire to see Khurram freed from his troubles and to enjoy the gain he every day got by Khurram's depredations, so that obtaining leave to say a while, he sends his eunuch Wafadar Khan[93] as his deputy to prepare business the better against his coming. The eunuch in good equipage travels thitherward, and by the inhabitants of Ahmedabad was received with due ceremony, but not being able to bear with modesty the greatness of that command was so puffed up with simple apprehensions of his high station that he looks upon all others within the circle of his government as abject persons, which pride in the end rendered him ridiculous and made him the contempt of divers, amongst which was Safi Khan,[94] an eminent officer, being no less then Chancellor to the Mughal in those provinces, who in an amicable way having in vain laboured to make him understand himself, in plain expressions told him the people were so dissatisfied with his behaviour that they would no longer endure his command over them, which sober advice the eunuch took in such ill part that instead of thanks he threatens punishment, not content with which he so disgusts the Chancellor that unable to bear more, he flies for safety. He therefore with what force he had takes his way to Nahir Khan,[95] Viceroy of Patan and Baba Khan of Kapadwunj,[96] whom by his complaint and the affront offered he so inflames that hearing the eunuch had not above five hundred horse under command, they presently advance to Ahmedabad with a thousand horse and five elephants, enter the city, and, forcing the castle, imprison Wafadar Khan the eunuch with his associates Mirza Madari, Motnah-cawn and Mohammed

---

hangir re-named him Lanatullah, "God's curse," adding "as he had received this name from the hidden world I also called him by it" (*TJ* 2. 255).

[93] Wafadar Khan [*Bassadur-cawn*], wrote Jahangir, "with a few ragamuffins entered Ahmadabad and took possession of the city" (*TJ* 2. 262). When Jahangir's forces entered Ahmadabad, Wafadar "took refuge in the house of Shaikh Haidar." The latter turned him in, and "they tied his hands to his neck and brought him," at which point the unfortunate Wafadar disappears from history (*TJ* 2. 264). The Emperor does not give any details which correspond to Herbert's account.

[94] Safi Khan [*Saffichan*] was made *bakhshi* of Gujarat (1617), and Jahangir wrote praising him for his skill in creating a garden in Ahmadabad (*TJ* 1. 420). He played a significant part in the final defeat of Khurram and his rebellious army, as both Herbert and Jahangir himself relate; the latter says "I honoured him with the title of Saif Khan Jahangir-shahi and conferred on him a standard and drums" (*TJ* 2. 264–67).

[95] Nahir Khan [*Nazor-cawn*] was given the title of Shir Khan by Jahangir in 1623. He was not "Viceroy" of anything, but his great-uncle Puran Mal had been Governor of Raysin and Chandheri and was killed by Sher Shah Suri in 1545. Akbar gave Nahir the *pargana* of Mohammedpur in Malwa. "In my service he advanced more and more," Jahangir wrote; ". . . he has found the advantage of doing what was right" (*TJ* 2. 268),

[96] Kapadwunj [*Chapperbenita*]. Now in Kheda district, Gujarat, it is known for its wealth of historical buildings.

Hassan the Cambayan *podesta*,[97] whom after they had disgraced they left the city satisfied, but the country full of astonishment. Khurram, having quickly taken notice of this passage, seeing it a plot merely to dishonour him, after he had given vent to his passion he straightway breaks out into fresh rebellion, albeit Abdullah Khan made sport with it as unworthy Khurram's impatience, their antagonists being but three, one of them a lawyer and the other two were merchants, none of them of any influence in the army. Nevertheless, knowing satisfaction would not be without blows, and that Safi Khan might not insult longer, Abdullah congregates his *umrah* Ahmad Khan, Governor of Baroda, Ali Beg, Rostam Bahadur [Khan], Mohammed Hassan, Mercan-beg, Zerdzie-cawn, Maizael-cawn and others, to whom he relates the prince's dishonour and his own vexations; not that he either feared or valued such enemies but that he saw the fire of discord a-kindling, which by the constancy of his friends he doubted not to extinguish. They hear him, and unanimously with seven thousand horse haste to chastise Safi Khan and his associates. Fourteen hundred thousand rupees were distributed by Abdullah Khan upon this preparation and to increase his army with ten thousand infantry, so that now he makes sure to punish, yea, to extirpate the memory of his enemies. Indeed, many swell themselves with empty fancies and by a foolish admiration of their own power think meanly of other men's abilities; we see it so in Abdullah Khan, a man of great power and experience, yet at this time so efflated with pride and scorn that by too much contempt of those he was to grapple with he prepares his own ruin. For from Mandu with his army he marches to Baroda, and thence to Wasai,[98] judging all Gujarat affrighted at his coming.

But Safi Khan and his were nothing troubled at it, no, although Sultan Bulaqi and Azam Khan their supplies were then at Seroy, a good way distant. Not that he wanted the nerves of war, money, and that the people were, though his was the Mughal's cause, indifferent, but rather throws off all apparition of fear and, to add something to his treasury, forages such towns as refused to contribute, forces the exchequer and spoils that rich throne or state which Sultan Khurram had lately set up in Ahmedabad as a monument of his glory. With this and other helps he makes shift to pay an army of twenty thousand horse, five hundred musketeers and thirty elephants for war, and by proclamation acquainting the country with the occasion of his making that preparation, being to defend the King's right against rebels, above twenty *umrah* of quality, Mirza Qasim, Mirza Makam, Rajah Quli Khan, Rajah Daula, Kamal Khan, Parvez Khan, Sadeq Khan, Saad Yakub and others repair unto him at Kankrej where he was encamped, and marched with him to Assampur, where, hearing of Abdullah Khan's

---

[97] I have not been able to identify these men.

[98] Wasai [*Wasset*], a small town in Gujarat (see Habib, *Atlas*, 7A, 23+ 72+). These references are the co-ordinates in Irfan Habib's *Atlas of the Mughal Empire* (Delhi: Oxford University Press, 1982), and are supplied when little or no other information about the place is available.

coming, he arose and came to Baola (?), six course from Ahmedabad, where very courageously he attended the coming of his enemies.

Abdullah Khan at *Anamogery* having received intelligence of their encamping, in scornful manner acquaints him with his coming, at that instant looking upon his own company so merrily that the wiser sort could not choose but condemn him of too much confidence. Yet, loath he should perceive any want of will in them, they equal his haste and march through Nadiad to Mahmudabad, which was but six course from the enemy. There Abdullah Khan, by sober advice of his *umrah*, commands Matzaheyl Khan to prison and shackles him, having received some intelligence that he had correspondence with the enemy, and the next day sends him with his son Raja Sultan upon an elephant to Mandu to receive their trial. The ensuing day his army moves towards Kanisa, and there hearing how strong the enemy was, which a little startled him, he wheeled about to Broach, thinking to assail Safi Khan in the rear, but in vain, for they disocvered him. The next day he resolved to fight, and accordingly divides his army into three; one part he assigns to Himat Khan and Salih Beg, another to Sharza Khan, Masud Beg and Mohammed Quli, and the last unto himself, in which equipage the whole camp moved to Jaitalpur and Fathbagh, where Nahir Khan, his five sons, two sons-in-law Kara Mohammed Khan and Khan Mohammed Khan with three thousand more begin the fight, and charge so hotly upon Abdullah Khan that they forced him to retire. Besides, the infantry played so fiercely with their muskets that they disordered Abdullah Khan's cavalry and, by wounding their best elephant, constrained him to turn and execute his wrath upon his own company.

Khurram's chief captain sees the peril, but knows no way for prevention save by challenging to a single combat Nahir Khan that was so valiant. The old man was so full of youthful heat that he accepts it, and with his lance wounds Abdullah Khan in the arm, but the old man, being hurt in the head, had perished had not his sons then made proof of their valour. Howbeit, in the rescue three of them were sore wounded, Khan Mohammed was slain and the residue so discouraged that but for Dilawar Khan, who animated them, they had fled and left Abdullah Khan victorious.

While they were thus bandying in the Field of Mars, Sayed Khan and Sayed Yakub gave a charge upon Salih Beg and Ahmed Khan, where after mutual giving and receiving blows, Aziz Beg was first unhorsed by his adversary's elephant and then by Sayed Khan slain. Ahmed Khan also, advancing further then discretion warranted, was taken prisoner by Raja Daula and beheaded (which two had the command of one-third part of Abdullah Khan's army), so was Salih Beg, and both sent to Safi Khan as a trophy of their loyalty. The death of these great men struck such terroe into Abdullah's army that each man fled which way his fancy directed him, Ahmed Khan the Governor of Baroda only excepted, who thought it too great a blemish for him to turn tail, having five hundred horse and three elephants as yet lusty and courageous. But what could his opposition do when Safi Khan in person came to charge him? To contend were madness, and thereupon on good terms yields and had fair quarter afforded him, but his example could work but little with Mohammed Quli his son, for he, imagining his father had acted dishonourably, with forty horse and one elephant flies to Abdullah Khan, who though welcome, received little joy in such an inconsiderable addition, so as observing that Safi Khan the Chancellor was master of the field, he advises Mohammed Quli to shift for himself, and so did he, with what force he could secure from the pursuit of the enemy. In the flight Mutasib Khan was taken and brought back to Safi Khan, and Abdullah Khan, by unexpected onsets of the coolies and highway rogues, as also by intolerable tempests amazed, beaten and discouraged, hastens to Broach, next day to Surat, and after eight days' refreshment and some recruits, to Burhanpur, where he attends Khurram's command and makes provision to repair his honour, which till then was never so notoriously blemished.

[Part V: Mahabat Khan's Rebellion and the Accession of Sultan Khurram]

Broach described

Broach, where the pole septentrional is elevated twenty-one degrees fifty-five minutes, is a town of note in the Gujarat province. Distant from Variao[1] four and thirty English miles, from Cambay fifty-four, from Ahmedabad an hundred and twenty-four, from Burhanpur two hundred and eleven or thereabouts, it is seated in a beneficial soil and watered by Narmada, a delightful river which from Deccan mountains mixing with the Tapti, flows through Burhanpur hither, and at Hansot, a village eight course lower, making a pretty isle a small hour's travel thence, in two streams four miles asunder incorporates with the ocean. Broach is visible, by way of her high standing, a good way distant, built upon the best advantages of Nature and Art, both so excellently contending as makes it at first view seem impregnable. She is well-peopled, and with such industrious inhabitants as extract wealth both by land and water. The buildings are generally low, especially those below the mountain. In quondam times the royalties were spacious, as sovreigning over many towns and and provinces of note a great way distant as Mednipur,[2] seventy miles thence, Rajapur or Baroda, eighty. Jhanjmer[3] thirty, and Jambusar[4] in Surat, each of which enjoy peculiar podestates.[5] Howbeit, the Mughal has received hereout as an annual tax or tribute no less than one million two hundred thousand mahmoudies (or shillings in our money), which revenue from one province shows what a vast exchequer all his empire yearly

---

[1] Variao [*Parli*], which de Laet calls *Periaw* (*Empire*, 24) is a village on the road from Surat to Broach.

[2] Mednipur is a town in the modern state of Bihar.

[3] Jhanjmer is a fortress near Gopnath Beach in Gujarat; it is 275 km from Ahmedabad.

[4] Jambusar [*Jawnhasser*] "is a large village, nine or ten Dutch miles distant from Brochia [Broach]" (De Laet, *Empire*, 25).

[5] Herbert uses the Italian word derived from *podesta*, which means an administrator. He is suggesting that the three larger centres were independently administered.

contributes. 'Twixt Broach and Ahmedabad is entombed Pali Medina,[6] a Mahometan saint highly-regarded by the people, who in a way of meritorious pilgrimage repair thither loaden with cains or stones and locking up their mouths from speaking vanity, by such penance expecting to obtain children, health, wealth or what else they may lust after. But to return to our story. Jahangir during these last broils was resident at Fatehpur when he heard of Abdullah Khan's pranks and Khurram's fresh rebellion, which makes him sleep unquietly till both of them receive due punishment. To which end he calls Sultan Parvez his son, and, acquainting him with his design, gives him order to levy new forces wherewith to prosecute his brother and those outlawed *umrah* that accompanied him.

Parvez, prevailing with Mahabat Khan to associate him, with fifty thousand horse moves against Khurram, by the way imprisoning Mirza Khan, Abdullah Khan's son, who but lately was married to Jahangir's grandchild, and by his order he is sent manacled to Itibar Khan, in Agra castle to be confined, whiles Abdul Aziz Khan, who by Abdullah Khan's persuasion was brought to Khurram's party, escapes, and upon submission to the Mughal is pardoned. Khurram has early notice both of the levies that were made to reduce him and of the approach of his enemies, and from Ajmer hastes to Mandu to recruit his army, with a full determination to bid them battle. Parvez follows his motion, and after a long and speedy march pitches ten English miles from his brother's camp with a resolution to engage him speedily, and accordingly the next morning, drawing out his men, he assails him, who at the first shock, by mishap of Rostam Khan[7] and Barqandaz Khan,[8] gave ground and let the enemy possess his trenches. In a word, after a short dispute Parvez has the day and Khurram flies to Burhanpur, his old receptacle. The Khan-i-Khanan, in the interim, noting Khurram's sadness, takes advantage of it and persuades the Prince to send him to treat with Parvez for an accommodation, intending indeed to betray and deliver him into

---

[6] De Laet calls this saint "Polle Nedonii" (*Empire*, 25). S. N. Banerjee, following Sir Roper Lethbridge's article in the *Calcutta Review* 51 (1870), identifies him as Pir Ali Medinai, who originated in Medina "and settled near Ahmedabad." The name is a corruption of Boulee Muduni, "the name of one of the most celebrated saints of Islam" (De Laet, *Empire* 25 n. 38).

[7] Rostam Khan Kandahari is described by De Laet as "king of Kandahar" (*Empire*, 115) in 1609, and as one of the sons of Mirza Bairam, a governor of Kandahar who had "defected" to Akbar "on account of injuries received by [Shah Abbas]" (De Laet, *Empire*, 157). B. Prasad mentions him, with Barqandaz Khan (see below), as one of "ablest and most powerful supporters of Shah Jahan" who was won over to the Imperial side by Mahabat Khan's diplomacy (*History*, 334).

[8] Barqandaz Khan [*Berkender-cawn*], formerly known as Baha-ud-din, was a gunner who commanded a detachment of musketeers. He "made an agreement with Mahabat Khan," Jahangir recorded; "When the armies were ranged opposite to each other, he got his opportunity and attacked with a body of musketeers and joined the royal army, crying out 'Success to King Jahangir!'" (*TJ* 2. 272).

Parvez his hands, having pre-contracted with Bairam Beg and Darab Khan to secure him, who to that end had ambushed near the river Narmada twenty thousand horse. But Abdullah Khan dissuades Khurram, distrusting the Khan-i-Khanan's villainy, which could not be so secretly apprehended but that by some means or other the Khan-i-Khanan had notice given him, which gave him a reasonable opportunity to escape the Prince's fury, so that as soon as his intended treachery was made public, Bairam Beg with his associate were loaden with irons and placed on an elephant, and with some select troops Khurram leaves Burhanpur and flies into Deccan, where by Malik Ambar, glad of such confusion, he was welcomed and feasted in Nasik Trimbak,[9] where he dictates patience. His elephants and men in the meantime are sent to Daulatabad, to be there quartered till he had further use of them.

Sultan Parvez and Mahabat Khan after this rout enter Burhanpur, where they had intelligence whither Khurram was retreated. They presently give Jahangir notice of their good success which he entertains with no less joy then as if he had triumphed over a dangerous enemy. But behold, this fair sunshine of content was enveloped with an unexpected cloud of danger, for Ilangtosh,[10] an Uzbeg Tartar, of long time watching a fit occasion to forage the Mughal's territories and taking the opportunity of Khurram's outbreaking, with thirty thousand horse overruns Kabul, plundering the country and doing all the spoil and mischief he was able, which known to Jahangir, so soon as he had given vent to his passion he sends post to Khan Zad Khan, son to Mahabat Khan,[11] at that time Viceroy of Banges, to advance with what force he could against that invading Tartar. This young gallant delays not, but with twenty thousand horse hastens to find the enemy, and sooner then the Tartar expected entered his quarters and gave him so furious a charge that Ilangtosh, after short trial, found his men better at plundering then fighting, for after a short engagement they betook themselves to flight, which, by reason of the spoil they were loaden and loath to part with, gave the Indians the better opportunity of overtaking them, by which mishap the Tartar lost half his men besides such rich bag and booty as gave Zad Khan the occasion of encouraging his men beyond their expectations. And to requite the Tartars they delayed not to prosecute their victory by following the dismayed Tartars into their own country, and as far as Cassanien burn, spoil and

---

[9] Nasik Trimbak [*Nassier-Throm*] is an "interesting little town with . . . picturesque bathing ghats" on the Godavari River, "one of the holiest rivers of the Deccan" (Crowther and Raj, *India*, 543–44).

[10] Ilangtosh [*J'hen Thouz*] was an Uzbeg fighting for Nazar Mohammed Khan, the ruler of Balkh (De Laet, *Empire*, 214 n. 137). Herbert even duplicates the number of his army from De Laet's account.

[11] Khan Zad Khan [*Ganna-zied-cawn*], as Herbert states, was the son of Mahabat Khan and held the posts successively of governor of Banges Province (not viceroy, as Herbert states) of Kabul (1623) and governor of Bengal later in the same year.

make havoc of what they could meet with, marching back with great wealth and many elephants to Kabul, where with acclamations of joy they are welcomed, and Jahangir so much pleased that Zad Khan had thanks and addition of five hundred horse to his former number.

Khurram's success in Bengal.

This cloud over-blown, the horizon now appears serene, and Jahangir afresh contemplates in what part he may enjoy his beloved Nur Mahal with most pleasure and least interruption, whose equal care it was to captivate him with charms of love. Kashmir at length is the place he pitches upon; it abounds with variety of choice sports, but, what was most in objection, the progress was long, and Kashmir remote from most places where whence in those active times he was to expect intelligence. Howeit, delight swayed him again against reason, giving Khurram by that distance so fair an advantage that with speed, sending his *umrah* word to follow him, he forsakes Deccan and through Golconda and Orissa advances into Bengal, yea, with four thousand horse and three hundred elephants passes through the solitary deserts, and so suddenly presents his force before Debikot[12] that Ibrahim Khan,[13] governing that province, in this surprise flies away first to Benares and then to Patna, then to Masulipatam, not knowing where indeed to rest securely, whiles Khurram smiles at his fear and without scruple or let seizes upon his treasure, which with his fair words so bewitch most of the *umrah* of that fruitful country that they immediately came to serve him with unexpected recruits of horse, money and arms.

Overjoyed with which good hap, this daring Prince forthwith breaks into Puri,[14] flashing so much terror into the eyes and heart of Mukhlis Khan the Governor[15] that without any show of manhood he posts towards Allahabad to acquaint Rostam [Khan] the captain with his danger, by whom instead of thanks he was first soundly rated and then for his cowardice imprisoned. Khurram hears

---

[12] Debikot [*Debaka*] is a small city in Bengal. See Habib, *Atlas*, 11A, 25+ 88+.

[13] Ibrahim Khan Fath Jang (d. 1624) was the governor of Bengal (1617–1624) and brother to Nur Mahal. According to Jahangir's somewhat cryptic account, "a notice came to him from Bi-daulat that by the decree of God and the ordinances of Heaven what was not suitable to him had appeared from the womb of non-existence." Khurram then informed Ibrahim that he could either safely leave with his family and go to Jahangir's court, or stay, in which case Khurram would "bestow upon him any corner of the country he might ask for" (*TJ* 2. 299). As this is the last entry made by Jahangir in the book, we are not told by him what happened next. Ibrahim was succeeded in Bengal by Mahabat Khan.

[14] Puri [*Purop*] in Orissa is one of the four holiest cities of India, as it was supposed to have been once a hiding-place for Buddha's tooth (Crowther and Raj, *India*, 499).

[15] Mukhlis Khan [*Makolidischan*] had served in Bengal since 1618, and in 1619 was appointed *diwan* to Prince Parvez (*TJ* 2. 107).

of that passage also, but so long as he continues prosperous regards no man's misery, but rather passing his army over Ganges, aims at Kheri,[16] not doubting of the conquest. Howbeit, by the way at Rajmahal he was with such fury assaulted by Ibrahim Khan, by this time re-encouraged and here ambuscadoed with six thousand horse, that little wanted of putting him to the rout, had not Abdullah Khan, who brought up with him the best part of the army, interposed and after three hours' sharp skirmish recovered him. In this smart conflict three thousand were slain of Khurram's party and four thousand of Ibrahim's, who also lost his life by too much avarice amongst his men, but chiefly out of too eager an appetite to regain that honour which was so lately blemished. Khurram rubricates this in the calendar of his greatest deliverances; it teaches him how to travel with more vigilancy, but dissuades not from the prosecuting his unjust design spoiling and robbing all that wealthy province, passing over Ganges and entering as conqueror Tanda, Gaur, Benares, Chatgaon, Sujapur, Satgaon, Bakla[17] and other such towns upon Ganges or in Orissa and Bengal as resisted him, preying upon their gold and jewels, acting unchastities, and forcing oaths and hostages from the inhabitants to become his subjects. Thence he marches to Patan, whither [the] Rajah [of] Ujaina[18] with five thousand horse and twenty thousand foot came to offer him their service.

Parvez hears of his brother Khurram's extravagancy and supplies, and intends to find him out. He therefore commits Burhanpur to Rostam Khan and Lashkar Khan's charge, and with fifty thousand horse comes with long toil to Allahabad, and, entering Lala Bir Singh's territories, Lala meets him with seven thousand horse and offers him a present of three lakh of rupees.

Jahangir, lest he should surfeit of delight, at Kashmir entertains news of his son Khurram's fresh outbreaking, as also of Ibrahim's death and disomfiture, and fearing his vagrant son might grow too popular and potent, he rouses himself, and after advice with his council forthwith commands Jahan Khan out of Multan and Bokhara, countries adjoining to Kabul, to raise a considerable force to hasten into Gujarat with the tribute of those provinces to advance a new army and join with Parvez, that he might be the better able to march against the rebels. Jahan Khan, being come to Fatehpur, there loiters, and as long at Agra wraps himself

---

[16] Kheri or Qutab Kheri [*Kerry*] is near Fatehpur, now in Uttar Pradesh State.

[17] The following towns were located in Habib, *Atlas*: Tanda [*Tando*], 11A, 24+ 88+; Chatgaon [*Chatighan*], 11A, 22+ 91+; Sujapur [*Serrapore*], 11A, 26+ 88+; Satgaon [*Satigan*], 11A, 22+ 88+; Bakla or Ismailpur [*Bacola*], 11A, 22+ 90+; Gaur [*Gouro*], 11A, 24+ 88+. Chatgaon is now Chittagong in Bangladesh, described by Huen Zhang, a Chinese traveller in the seventh century C.E. as "a sleeping beauty emerging from mists and water." It was known as Porto Grande by the Portuguese.

[18] Following De Laet, Herbert assumes that Ujaina [*Usiem*] is the ruler's name. Ujaina is a small city in the Province of Malwa (see De Laet, *Empire*, 34). The "rajah" was actually a zamindar, a large-scale landowner with hereditary rights.

in idleness, forgetful of the Mughal's command, the Prince's need and his own honour. But Rostam, captain of Allahabad, shows himself more considerate, for having imprisoned Mukhlis Khan for his fear and flight he then fortifies his castle and stores it with men, money and provision, which when Khurram heard, he alters his intent of beleaguering that place and draws his force against Rantas, a strong castle which nevertheless by Sayed Mubarak[19] was yielded upon treaty. After that he assaults Chunar, which though awhile defended by Hasti Beg, was in the end delivered up, after which Abdullah Khan forces Jahangir Quli Khan,[20] captain of Benares, into Allahabad, and Wazir Khan into Jaunpur and other towns, out of which quarters they drew abundance of treasure. And hearing of his brother's approach with Mahabat Khan, he appoints Abdullah Khan, Rajah Bhim[21] and Bairam Khan to try their fortunes against Allahabad, which by Rostam Khan was so resolutely defended. They obey, and with all haste besiege that place, next day assaulting it with utmost fury, but by Rostam were beat off and forced to retreat with loss, in which action the seed of so much emulation was sowed betwixt Abdullah and Rajah Bhim as was not quenched (as soon appeared) without either of their destructions. Sultan Parvez and Mahabat Khan hasten, if possible to be at Allahabad to relieve the garrison ere the rebels rose from before it, to which purpose they pass Buckery[22] and Manikpur,[23] but Abdullah Khan, hearing of their advance and disheartened by the late storm, arises and hies thence over Ganges, and at Benares joins with Khurram's army.

The Khan-i-Khanan's family sent prisoners to Agra.

The Khan-i-Khanan, bankrupt in credit with with Khurram and Abdullah Khan, had not been long in Parvez's army but by Mahabat Khan's command for some unworthy prank there also was imprisoned. A servant of his, Miyan

---

[19] Probably Mubarak Khan Sazawal [*Munbark*], who was promoted by Jahangir in 1615, and was later sent by him to accompany Prince Khurram on his expedition to the Deccan (*TJ* 1. 289).

[20] Jahangir Quli Khan was the son of Aziz Koka Khan. Jahangir dismissed him from the Governorship of Bihar (1618), but later rewarded him with a "dress of honour" when he left for Deccan (*TJ* 2. 117).

[21] Rajah Bhim (d. 1624) [*Radgee Rhiem*] was the son of Rana Karan of Mewar. He helped Khurram defeat Ibrahim Khan and fought valiantly in many encounters with Imperial armies. He was sent to attack Patna, which he captured, and overran Bihar in December 1623. He was killed in action at Kampat near Jhansi. See Herbert's description below and also B. Prasad, *History*, 352.

[22] De Laet has "Backery," but Banerjee is unable to identify it (De Laet, *Empire*, 217 n. 143).

[23] Manikpur is a town in modern West Bengal.

Fahim,[24] took this indignity so impatiently that with five hundred men he ambushes 'twixt their passage to Kalpi and Lala's country and by force attempts his lord's delivery. His goodwill was much but his success unanswerable, for Mahabat Khan, then none was more vigilant, fearless of such a scarecrow disovered the plot and in small space slew him and cut in pieces most of his rash society. The Khan-i-Khanan was thenceforth more strictly looked-to and his estate seized upon; his wife, son and family upon elephants were sent slaves to Agra,[25] whiles Parvez, Mahabat and the army, after a long and swift march, arrive at Allahabad, where by valiant and faithful Rostam Khan they were welcomed and lodged in the castle with entertainments suitable to such high guests.

Mahabat Khan's victory. The Khan-i-Khanan's misery.

Mahabat Khan, now impatient of stay till he could engage Sultan Khurram's army, who by that time had recruited and drawn into the field a great force of horse assured by the magic of his gold and language, prepares for fight. Near [the river] Tons,[26] fifteen miles from Benares, the two armies pitched their camps in view of one another, either side resolved with the utmost of valour to purchase victory. Ganges, that great and deified river, a while forbade them, restraining either's fury save what volleyed from the arquebuses. Howbeit Bairam Beg began the play with four thousand horse and foraged the country towards Allahabad, but by Mohammed was met upon Chaunsa's[27] banks, where his men were discomfited, Bairam Beg slain and his head severed. Mahabat Khan, interpreting this as a good omen, draws out his forlorn, but knows not how without peril to pass his men over Ganges, till by a native he is directed to a ford, where with a party of horse he got over luckily, and then having secured the pass, he quickly marches his men through the river.

Having now nothing to interpose, Mahabat Khan faces Khurram's army. Khurram, being of too high a spirit to be thus braved, specially by Mahabat, whom though for his gallantry he needs must honour, yet contemned as being his adversary, straightway prepares for fight, and, having disposed his battle into the best posture he could, he first orders Rajah Bhim with his elephants to charge Mahabat. This courageous officer very gladly undertakes it and gives Mahabat so

---

[24] Miyan Fahim [*M'hia Fehiem*] (d. 1624), was, according to Banerjee, "the great favourite of the Khan Khanan. People said he was his son by a slave girl, but he appears to have been Rajput. He died in a fight with Mahabat Khan. The Khan Khanan built him a tomb known as Nilah Burj near Humayun's tomb" (De Laet, *Empire*, 217 n. 145).

[25] Actually his daughter Jana Khanum, the widow of Prince Daniyal, was kept with two younger sons in custody with their father (De Laet, *Empire*, 217).

[26] Tons [*Thonec*] is identified by Banerjee as indicating "the battle of the Tons" (De Laet, *Empire*, 218 n. 147). The rebels, B. Prasad writes, "fortified themselves in Kampat on the bank of the river Tons" (*History*, 351).

[27] The Chaunsa [*Shahwezi*] river is named "Ziauzia" by De Laet (*Empire*, 218).

hot a charge, yea, with his warlike elephants so disordered his party that had Abdullah Khan or Darab Khan seconded him, as was appointed, Khurram had, 'tis thought, obtained the victory. But Abdullah Khan, swelling with envy against Rajah Bhim ever since their attempt at Allahabad, not only delayed to second him but rather seemed pleased when Mahabat Khan's company recovered, and Rajah's elephants, wounded and maddened with rage, execute their wrath upon their own party. In the end Rajah [Bhim], after as much proof of courage and skill as could be in man, was slain, and his whole body disordered. In this miserable sort perished one of the best soldiers in all India, and Abdullah Khan basely accessory to his death. But revenge, or rather justice, pursues him, for finding it high time to give over looking on, he sees Parvez entering with Rajah Jai Singh, Rajah Shyam Singh,[28] Rajah Bir Singh and their whole army. Khurram also falls on, doing what lay in the power of man, the battle now pell-mell enduring for five hours, wherein was expressed a great deal of bravery on both sides. Khurram was hurt in the arm; Parvez, though upon his elephant, by Darab Khan was wounded in the side, and but for the excellency of his mail had there breathed his last.[29] In the end the King's army, by the excellent conduct and unusual valour which Mahabat afresh had afforded them, have the victory. The rebels, pusillanimously opposing that new torrent of destruction, gaze awhile, and then remembering the injustice of their side make a slow retreat and in the end fly amain, resolving not in haste to remunerate such a business. Khurram, not able to alter his destiny, striking the ground with his lance leaves the field, and with four thousand horse flies away to the inexpugnable castle of Rantas, which was yielded by Mubarak and wherein he had placed Rajah Ghulam,[30] one of the murderers of Prince Khusrau, leaving the residue of the army to sip the bitter cup of death, the honour of the field to his brother and Mahabat Khan, who of gold, silver, precious gems, elephants, camels, horses and slaves of both sexes found there a great abundance.

Sultan Khurram, now in his strong castle and at such a distance, has time to ruminate his misery, and accordingly with a discontented mind sees how insensibly he precipitates his hopes, at that instant fixed in the centre of melancholy, and

---

[28] Maharaja Shyam Singh [*Radgee Ziand*] was the ruler of Garhwal 1611–1622. He was honoured with more territory and the gift of an elephant by Jahangir in 1615 (*TJ* 1. 281).

[29] Herbert does not always paraphrase or rephrase De Laet; the latter merely mentions that Prince Parvez "incurred considerable danger" (*Empire*, 219). In any case, both accounts give the lie to those writers who state that Parvez had no flair for military command or was ineffectual.

[30] This name is out of place, as we know from various sources that Raza Bahadur was the killer. De Laet has "Radia Gholam" (*Empire*, 219); Banerjee thinks that he is probably the same as Raza Bahadur, whose name also appears in De Laet as the assassin. "Probably his full name was Raza Ghulam or Ghulam Raza," Banerjee suggests (De Laet, *Empire*, 219 n. 148).

as an aggravation flies thence to Patan with Asaf Khan's lovely daughter only in his company, who had lately brought him a young princess, and by a zantel dispatches letters to Darab Khan, then in Bengal, to levy more force, and appoints the rendezvous at Rajmahal, where he would expect him.

Mahabat Khan and Prince Parvez in the meantime pursue Khurram, carrying [the] false Khan-i-Khanan in company but under a guard, scarce resting day or night till they came to Rantas, where, hearing which way he took, they chase him to Patan, but there they breathe awhile, and hearing of Darab's obsequiousness to Khurram they prevail with his aged father [the] Khan-i-Khanan by letters to dissuade him and to promise him the King's thanks if he would join with them. Darab, incensed by Mahabat Khan's severity to his father and supposing his persuasions counterfeit, goes on to levy men for support of the rebellion. Prince Parvez hereupon proclaims him traitor and allots four thousand rupees to any that would bring him to his camp alive or dead. The time-serving multitude, knowing that Khurram was fled, not only bring Darab Khan but his children and kinsman Murad, who was son to Shahnawaz Khan, all whose heads were immediately struck off and sent to Parvez, and by Mahabat Khan's permission presented to [the] Khan-i-Khanan, by that made a wretched father, and thence as a trophy of their care and to the terror of others dispatched to Agra to be set up on poles, the report of which sad action was no sooner known to Khurram but that it struck him into a fright, so that bidding farewell to [Mumtaz] Mahal, he flies to Mednipur and thence to Ayutthaya,[31] but is quested after by Mahabat to Mednipur, where missing him he hales to Prince Parvez and sends Baqir Khan[32] and eight thousand horse in pursuit after Khurram. At this Ayutthaya, a city in Bengal watered by Ganges,[33] are many antique monuments. Especially memorable is the old castle Ranichand, built by a banian pagod of that name about 994,500 years ago after their accompt, from which time to this the banians customarily have repaired to offer and to wash away their sins in Ganges, each of which is recorded by the Brahmins, who, as they believe, acquaint this pagod with their offerings.

---

[31] Ayutthaya [*Odjea, Oudee*] is a very ancient Buddhist city, formerly the capital of the Kosala kingdom which is described in the *Ramayana*. It was also the seat of government for the rulers of Oudh until Lucknow became the capital in 1722. Its principal monument is the Masjid-i-Janmasthan, the "Mosque of the Birthplace," so-called because it was thought to have been Rama's birthplace. It was erected by Babur in about 1528. In the *Puranas* Ayutthaya is described as one of the six holy cities of India, and the city in Thailand of the same name was named after it.

[32] Baqir Khan [*Baker-chan*] was successively *faujdar* of Multan (1618) and Governor of Oudh (1621). "Having exalted Baqir Khan to the duty of the Subah of Oudh," Jahangir recorded, "I dismissed him" (*TJ* 2.217).

[33] The river on which Ayutthaya is situated is actually the Gogra or Ghaghara, not the Ganges.

During these intestine broils Malik Ambar, perceiving the season advantageous to recover what he had lost, advances fifty thousand men and so unexpectedly charges Lashkar Khan, Mirza Sher Mohammed and Ibrahim Hassan that as men surprised they render up their forts and suffer the Deccan to repossess his former castles and garrisons, in which attempt 15,000 of the Mughal's men were slain and as many expelled the Deccan's country. The three *umrah* were also sent prisoners to Daulatabad to attend the pleasure of their conqueror. Baqir Khan, also having commission to prosecute Khurram, procrastinates not but in a few weeks attains Ayutthaya, where the Prince, though he had five thousand horse and three hundred elephants, durst not abide him battle, and so terrified with his late bad success as that he flies into Golconda contrary to Baqir Khan's advice, who rather desired battle.

The King of Golconda,[34] having notice of his strength and the danger of his diamond-mines, had some cause to remember what Tigranes the great Armenian king said, going against the Romans with 400,000 men and seeing the Roman army not above 14,000, who for all this got the victory. "There be too many," quoth he, "for an embassy, and too few for fight," Khurram having surreptitiously got from him a diamond as big as a hen's egg, (as credibly reported weighing 98 mangelins, every mangelin being five grains),[35] which the Great Mughal soon after bought for a million of rupees, considerations that made him to receive Khurram with counterfeit kindness and to attend him with twelve thousand horse, and for his further security doubled his guards in Cuada-ver and Chuda-poly, two of his most defensive castles wherein he commonly put his diamonds with much other treasure, also knowing full well that Khurram, not considering the annual tribute thence presented to the Mughal, had a vehement desire to visit and search the intrinsic of that precious piece of earth which report had so sufficiently blazoned, as he was assured it would abundantly compensate his pains and hazard.

The diamond-mine in Golconda described.

This famous diamond-mine is distant from Masulipatam about fourscore and ten English miles; the nearest village is called Mercanda.[36] The mine itself is a large rock under part of that mountain which extends towards Bellaguate, the Alps of those parts, at the foot whereof runs a quick stream our European merchants name

---

[34] The King of Golconda was Abdullah Quli Shah, who reigned 1611–1672. For a detailed description of Golconda Fort see Crowther and Raj, *India*, 647–48. The names of the "castles" given here by Herbert are indecipherable.

[35] A mangelin is "a small weight, corresponding in a general way to a carat . . . used in the S. of India and Ceylon for weighing precious stones" (*HJ*, 553).

[36] Markanda [*Mercanda*] is in Maharashtra near Nagpur (Habib, *Atlas* 15A, 16+ 81+).

Christena, which after forty miles' flux increases another river, and in the latitude of about eighteen degrees north in one channel empty themselves into the Gulf of Bengal. The soil for many miles round by reason of the extreme heat is barren and sandy, but near the mine the earth appears to be of a ruddy colour, albeit the vein itself is of a pale yellow. No part of the world for such a scope of ground affords greater plenty of diamonds than this or of a better water, those of Soaodania in Borneo not excepted, although many be yellow. The quarry also has several other translucent stones which want neither beauty nor esteem, namely topazes, amethysts, spinels, heliotropes and other sorts of agates, garnets, crystals and the like. The distribution of the ground when the mine is exposed resembles a lottery, some for their adventure happening to find much to their advantage, others to loss; in digging, if a diamond exceed twenty carats (a carat is four grains),[37] such by the law of that place are reserved for the King, but under that weight for the adventurer. When the mine is open, as the number is great of those that from most parts resort hither, so the guard increases answerably, thereby to give the better security. Howbeit, the danger is greatest in travelling, the mountaineers supposing that few come or go empty, and therefore for the most part merchants consort in caravans, and for their money are sufficiently guarded.

Malik Ambar, with less suspicion but more subtlety, heartily glad of this fresh rebellion, the Mughal's troubles bringing peace to his empire, sends an ambassador to Khurram, well-attended, with letters of affection and a large sum of money and other necessaries with an invitation into Deccan (if need were) where at all assays he should command his utmost. Khurram, perceiving his design about the diamond-mine frustrate, very heartily accepts this invitation, but after three months' stay in that country, aweary of idleness, he projects the recovery of his old eparchy[38] of Burhanpur, and so, without long advice bids Ambar farewell and with ten thousand horse divided amongst Abdullah Khan, Mohammed Taqi[39] and Yakub Khan,[40] shows himself again before Burhanpur but was forbade entrance by Rostam Khan, appointed Governor there by Sultan Parvez, which so enrages Khurram that after he had breathed out a thousand fruitless threats he assaults the walls with violence, but by Rostam as churlishly

---

[37] *Hobson-Jobson* notes that a carat "is also used as a weight for diamonds. As 1/124 of an ounce troy this ought to make it 3½ grains" (161).

[38] administrative district.

[39] Mohammed Taqi [*Tazkjeck*] (d. 1626), also known as Shah Quli Khan, was a military commander under Prince Khurram in 1614 against Mewar, where he served with distinction. He was seized along with Wafadar Khan (see above) and imprisoned. He was rewarded by Shah Jahan for his loyalty by being made his *bakhshi* (paymaster) in 1623. He was executed by order of Mahabat Khan for supporting Asaf Khan (see below).

[40] Yakub Khan [*Jacob-cawn*], like his master Malik Ambar, was an Abyssinian. Upon Malik Ambar's death in 1626 and the accession of Fateh Khan he became commander-in-chief of the army.

answered, and with great loss he is compelled to retreat to the Khan-i-Khanan's curious gardens, there to ruminate. Howbeit, Abdullah Khan is so transported that he mounts again and advances his standards, yet was also forced to march away, being well-beaten by Rostam, who filled the ditch with the carcases of Abdullah's followers. Mohammed Taqi at twilight tries his destiny, that in despite he mounts the wall and was bravely followed, that in small time he enters the citadel and on many parts of the wall flourished his colours in sign of victory and as a call to Abdullah Khan to second him, but Abdullah, poisoned with envy to see a merchant's son possessor of so much glory, forbears to succour him, so that this heroic captain, too far engaged, was assailed by Rostam and Asad Khan with such eagerness that his company were cut in pieces and Mohammed struck dangerously in his eye, yea, after as much proof of valour as was possible, was taken and imprisoned.

In this sort the second time has Abdullah Khan forfeited Khurram the victory, yet conceals the reason in his breast and goes unpunished, whiles Sultan Parvez and Mahabat Khan continue their quest, and, receiving notice of the siege of Burhanpur, haste thither with Alam Khan,[41] Rajah Sher Singh and a great army of Rajputs, but Khurram, premonished, seeing no good likely to be done, arises with his army and falls towards Bellaguate, in the way attempting Asirgarh, but missing it redelivers Rantas into his enemies' hands and once more returns to Malik Ambar, then at Kerki in Deccan, which now seems to be the receptacle of his misfortunes.

Asirgarh described.

Asirgarh,[42] five courses from Burhanpur as you pass to Agra, the strongest and in all advantages the best-defended castle through Khandesh, is built upon the top of a precipitous mountain, walled by nature and by its largeness capable to feed and lodge forty thousand horse, for within are springs of wholesome water, the earth also so fruitful in herbs, corn and what else is requirable for defence or pleasure, and upon all sides six hundred great ordinance of brass mounted, here placed by the last king of Gujarat, that it is as royal a fort as any in India. Howbeit, one discommodity it hath, making all the other relish badly: worms engendering in the legs and thighs of such as drink the water, oft proving mortal, and which only gave Akbar the conquest of this castle, which otherwise was accounted inexpugnable.

---

[41] This is the same Alam Khan who had served as Jahangir's ambassador to Persia.

[42] Asirgarh or Asir [*Hasser*], whose fort was "one of the strongest in the world" (B. Prasad, *History* 335) was besieged by Akbar in 1572 (*TJ* 1. 34–35) and was a stronghold for Prince Salim's rebellion. As Emperor Jahangir, Salim in turn had to face its surrender to his own rebellious son (B. Prasad, *History*, 335–36).

Jahangir, further rejoicing at the victories his son Parvez and Mahabat Khan had obtained, to express how well he took it, taking special notice of the sprightly valour of Khan Zad Khan, lately made Viceroy of Kabul. He calls him to court and expresses good affection to him, and more then so adds five thousand horse to his command, and under his seal of commission makes him Governor of Bengal, of all the provinces of Industan the most rich and honourable, of late years reduced under the Mughal's diadem, of old named Barleura and Gandarida, into whose gulf the great and noble river Ganges, by Ptolemy called Sinus Agaricus, a province for number of inhabitants in towns and plenty of all things requisite not inferior to any other throughout the Orient.

Nur Mahal contrives Mahabat Khan's ruin.

Nur Mahal and Asaf Khan both of them cast a squint eye upon the new favourite Khan Zad Khan, and for no other cause then that he was the son to Mahabat. No other known reason caused it, and being no idiots in the school of mischief (virtue ever being persecuted by envy), in the first place to better affront Mahabat, whose vexations are now broaching, they prevail with the old Mughal to command Mahabat without delay to send [the] imprisoned Khan-i-Khanan unto Agra. Mirza Arab Dast Ghaib,[43] one of Nur Mahal's creatures, is sent with this message, and Mahabat, loath to show any example of disobedience, although he knew Jahangir abused and that this was a mere plot to work his confusion, lets him go, who forthwith begins to chatter and spill his utmost malice against Mahabat, exhibiting many unjust complaints and incensing as much as he possibly could the old Mughal against his champion, and principally that he had put to death his son with others of his kindred, yea, after he had voluntarily left Khurram to serve in the King's army.

These accusations wrought somewhat with the credulous Mughal, but more when from the seeds of distrust sown by the Khan-i-Khanan in the heart of Parvez. In his letter to Jahangir he gives Mahabat the character of a vainglorious man, one that delighted to eclipse his splendour and that it was probable his ambition might have a dangerous influence in the army, with other such glances as quickly took impression on the Mughal's weak fancy, so that without further consideration or memory of Mahabat's former service, the Khan-i-Khanan's reports are esteemed no longer mendacious, so as without advising with his own reason or Mahabat's friends at court, he unadvisedly condemns him unheard, disposes of his command in the army to Jahan Khan (forgetful of his loitering at Fatehpur), and having nulled

---

[43] Arab Dast Ghaib [*Arabdesta-cawn*] is described by B. Prasad as "an Imperial agent" (*History*, 367). Later on, when Mahabat Khan captured Jahangir, he was amongst the attendants who were imprisoned by Mahabat's Rajputs.

Mahabat's commission, revokes him home where he should be better-acquainted with the reason of his proceeding. Thus *fraude perit virtus*.[44]

Mahabat admires the villainy of the Khan-i-Khanan and Nur Mahal's envy, and thinks by the candour of his own innocence it is impossible his master should believe such imputations, till, remembering his dotage upon Nur Mahal and her inveterate spleen, he grants it, resolving nevertheless to take another course till time might better evince his innocence. Therefore, as love and duty bound him, he first goes to Prince Parvez to bid him farewell, whom he finds so strangely altered, so coy and stately, it struck him with amazement, an excellent sympathy and union till the Khan-i-Khanan dissolved it having been betwixt them, so that with a sad look he leaves the camp but carries along with him the hearts of all the army. From Burhanpur he goes; many guess but none, no, not himself, knows whither Fortune led him. At length, by the advice of some friends who assured him that if he went to court he should at least be branded with the name of traitor, he secured himself in his castle of Ranthambhore, resolving first to vindicate his honour by letter to Jahangir or otherwise safeguard himself from Nur Mahal's spite and other his court enemies.

This discord between Parvez, Mahabat and Nur Mahal sounds sweetly in Khurram's ears, hoping by their divisions to advance his own ambition, and perceiving his old father senselessly nuzzled in apparitions of love, he resolves to exercise his craft and in the Mughal's weakness to fix the strength of his conspiracy, so that first he presents him by Khwaja Jahan,[45] tutor to his two sons, a letter neatly-penned but dictating nothing save hypocrisy. He knew also the appetite of his father after gold and rarities, and therefore adds a pishkash of rare coins, a hundred choice elephants and some portraits which he borrowed or rather bought from the Portugals. The old King, desirous of ease, and as an indulgent father glad of his seeming submission, accepts his present and invites him home, assuring his pardon. Accordingly, Asaf Khan by the Mughal's directions gives him notice and adds his secret advice to return to court whiles his father was in this good humour. In the meantime, Muzaffar Khan at Lahore receives the government or provostship of Agra, Qasim Khan[46] being displaced. He attained that command upon his marriage with Manija Begum, sister to the

---

[44] "By fraud virtue is destroyed" (Ovid, *Fasti* 2. 227).

[45] Khwaja Jahan [*Gadgee Jehan*], whose name was originally Dost Mohammed, was also governor of Agra (1612). An engineer by trade, he had laid out the Imperial Gardens in Agra (1619).

[46] Qasim Khan Juvaini [*Cassem-cawn*], governor of Lahore, was the husband of Nur Jahan's sister Manija, as Herbert states. Promoted by Jahangir in 1611, he was also "a poet of very high order" and "a master of extempore verse" (E. B. Findly, *Nur Jahan: Empress of Mughal India* [Delhi: Oxford University Press, 1993], 226) in addition to being a capable administrator.

Queen, and this disgrace was so impatiently digested by that ambitious woman that she ceased not till she got him re-established.[47]

Two young princes baptised in India.

Six years past, viz. 1618, I told you how Jahangir, at the request of Asaf Khan, took his eldest son Khusrau from Ani Rai Singh Dalan[48] and Jahan Khan, delivering him to Khurram, who, finding him a stumbling-block to the Imperial crown, by Raza Bahadur[49] got him made away. At that same time were committed to that fratricide Shah Hoshang and Tahmuraz,[50] sons to Daniyal Shah his brother (who died from distempered drinking at Burhanpur), who because he saw towardly young princes and apt to avenge their father's death he was the more free to send them through that bloody bath to destruction, but durst not perpetrate such apparent butchery, perceiving all men's eyes and expectations upon them and the deaths of their father and uncle yet recent and not a little murmured-at, so that he had no other way to anticipate their claim unto the Empire but by having them instructed in the faith of our Blessed Saviour Christ and to be baptised, by which profession of faith he well knew they would be made incapable of that great earthly monarchy, albeit heirs of a better, for *virtus locum habet inter astra*.[51] After this he ever led them with him to keep them strictly, till such time as being vanquished at Allahabad by Rostam Khan, Tahmuraz escaped to Parvez and thence to Lahore, where his uncle entertains and marries him to Bihar Banu Begum,[52] his daughter. At Khurram's next flight from

---

[47] Manija Begum [*Monissan-begem*] was, as Herbert states, a formidable character in her own right. Not wishing to leave Agra, she first approached her sister and then Mahabat Khan on behalf of her husband, and within three days Qasim Khan got his job back. For details see Findly, *Nur Jahan*, 270.

[48] Ani Rai Singh Dalan [*Anna-Rha-Rhadja*] was the commander of the fortress-prison at Gwalior and one of the guardians of Prince Khusrau. In 1627 he had been sent to seize Mahabat Khan's treasure.

[49] Raza Bahadur [*Radgee Bandar*] was the slave usually believed to have killed Khusrau, but there are several versions of the story. For details see Findly, *Nur Jahan*, 169–72.

[50] Prince Hoshang [*Sha Hossen*] (1605–1628) and Prince Tahmuraz [*Ethymore*] (1607–1628) were both murdered on 23 January 1628, probably on the orders of Shah Jahan. "Shah Jahan's atrocious order was duly carried out," Beni Prasad writes (*History*, 402); they perished along with Prince Gahrasp (1609–1628), another brother (who is never mentioned by Herbert), as well as Prince Shahriyar and the unfortunate Dawar Bakhsh, who had been briefly Mughal Emperor. All three princes had been baptised (1610), probably for the reason Herbert states. Tahmuraz was named Don Philippe, Hoshang became Don Henrico, and Gahrasp Don Carlo (Findly, *Nur Jahan*, 201).

[51] "Virtue has its place among the stars" (Seneca, *Hercules Oetaeus* 1564).

[52] Bihar Banu [*Bhar banoo*] (1590–c. 1665) was "one of two known surviving daughters of Jahangir" (Findly, *Nur Jahan*, 126). She married Tahmuraz when he was twenty.

Burhanpur, Hoshang also escaped and fled to Rajah Rostam and thence to his brother, where he lived with more safety.

Mahabat Khan's son-in-law disgraced.

Mahabat Khan, at his castle in Ranthambhore, practising to digest his affront with patience, receives a peremptory command from Jahangir (Nur Mahal, I might say) to deliver up his castle to the Queen, who had given the keeping of it to Baqir Khan (no friend to Mahabat) and that he should forthwith remove into Orissa to his son, who was the King's lieutenant there. The message was tart, but being sent to one impatient of affronts and albeit divided in himself 'twixt the necessity of self-preservation and offending his master, at length resolves upon this answer. that he was very ready to manifest himself a dutiful subject and therein to spend life and goods to do him service, but to stoop to the lure of his malicious adversary could not condescend. He was ready in person to give him the reason, provided he might repair to court and return to Ranthambhore in safety. With this ill-digested message the post returns, with news also that Abdullah Khan, either weary of his vagaries or that he saw the wind of Khurram's good fortune still averse, or doubting his former clashes with Rajah Bhim and [Mohammed] Taqi might undo him, for some or all of these he deserts Khurram and flies to Jahan Khan at Burhanpur, where Prince Parvez then also was, by both whom Abdullah was seemingly welcomed.

Jahangir, having received Mahabat Khan's letter, as it is true that *nemo amat quam metuit*[53] so he throws off his wonted love and not a little wonders at his presumption. But Mahabat no less admires his misapprehension, so that after the earnest persuasion of his kindred and friends about him, he assumes fresh courage, and, attended by five thousand voluntary Rajputs, Mahabat issues from his castle and through Rassanwer journeys to Lahore, at that time resolving to make his defence in person to Jahangir, who was then removing to Kabul, or was resolved to die in doing it. The Queen and Asaf Khan, having notice of his intent but fearing his force, and that if he were admitted to any private discourse with Jahangir probably he would re-ingratiate himself, they prevail with the Mughal to set his seal to their dictate, the substance being that Mahabat should come in person attended only with a few of his confidants to answer what should be objected against him. But Mahabat, contrary to his former resolution, being not inexperienced in Nur Mahal's deceits, rather then adventure his person, chose by his son-in-law[54] to present his excuses, which with a willing heart this gallant

---

"In God's mercy," Jahangir recorded, "a daughter was born of Karamsi, who belonged to the Rathore clan, and the child received the name of Bihar Banu Begum" (*TJ* 1. 19).

[53] "No-one loves what he fears" (Augustine, *De divisione quaestiones* 33, PL 40.23).

[54] This was Barkhudar Khan, son of Khwaja Umar Naqshbandi, and he was actually only a fiancé, as the marriage had not yet taken place. Herbert's description of his punish-

undertakes, who, being arrived at court, at his entrance into the lascar found it true that *non est ira super iram mulieris*,[55] for he was no sooner dismounted from his elephant but by the Queen's order was disrobed of his bravery, and being being clad in rags was chawbucked[56] upon the soles of his feet with rattans, and bareheaded, the greatest shame, set backward upon a jade, with kettledrums led through the army, and made a scoff to all the multitude; overjoyed she had this occasion to manifest her hate upon the idea of Mahabat, and withal to let him see how much she despised his interest.

Mahabat Khan had quick intelligence what uncomely entertainment his son-in-law had for his sake received, but assuring himself it proceeded not from his master he the better digested it, and the rather, being informed the whole country blamed Nur Mahal and the Khan-i-Khanan for such barbarism. In it he sees their hate and his own misery if he had rendered himself, so as now more then ever discovering the Queen's ambition to advance her son and Asaf Khan. Khurram, to that end guarding themselves with an army of thirty thousand horse, violently seizing the public treasure and in many transactions of state abusing the Mughal's authority. These things being duly pondered by Mahabat, and convinced of his loyalty to his master and zeal to Bulaqi, right heir unto the crown, Mahabat puts on a resolution to bid Nur Mahal defiance. Nevertheless, expressing his zeal to his old master, to whom in a brief manifesto he enumerates Nur Mahal's and the Khan-i-Khanan's abuses to the Crown, and then portrays the late indignity offered his son, which, as he alleged, was an unparalleled act of barbarity. This done, he acquaints his friends and fellow-soldiers both what he had published and what he resolved to enterprise. Having their faithful assurance to live and die with him, he forthwith surveys his army, gives strict command to offer no violence to Jahangir or his tent, and with twenty thousand valiant Rajputs, his countrymen, advances to find out Nur Mahal's army and the lascar, at that time consisting of above fifty thousand men. By accident part of the army at that instant marched by led by Iradat Khan,[57] the residue being passed over the River Bihat [Jhelum], conducted by Khwaja Abu'l Hassan, intending to beat up Mahabat's quarters. But that experienced warrior had his scouts abroad, and

---

ment is more graphic than B. Prasad's who states that he was "severely bastinadoed, had his hands bound to his neck, and thus, bareheaded, was remanded to prison. Mahabat Khan's dowry was forfeited to the state" (*History*, 369).

[55] "There's no anger worse than the anger of a woman" (Ecclesiasticus 25:13).

[56] *Hobson-Jobson* defines "chawbuck" as "an obsolete vulgarism from P(ersian) *chabuk*, 'alert;' in H(indi) 'a horsewhip" (185).

[57] Iradat Khan [*Eradet-cawn*] had been Governor of Kashmir since 1622. He was placed in charge of Dawar Bakhsh (Bulaqi) by Jahangir, created Khan Azam (1627), and supported Dawar Bakhsh as emperor against the claims of Prince Shahriyar. He later supported Shah Jahan and was rewarded by him for services rendered, as Herbert later notes.

having the eyes of prevention always open, finding the advantage his he gives the word unto his party and with gallant resolution charges Iradat with such good order that in less then two hours, ere Ab' ul Hassan could come unto his rescue, he not only disordered but slew above six thousand of them, filling the rest with such fear that each man fled away for his own safety, but unluckily, for the flood without mercy swallowed most of them, both dangers equally so assailing them that with ghastly looks and outcries such as escaped made known the horror of this conflict.[58]

The other part of Nur Mahal's army stood still, till by Asaf Khan, Abu'l Hassan and other *umrah* they were cheered up and prepared to encounter the rebels, who with Mahabat their general were come into view, and with victory in their foreheads, regarding neither their greatness nor their multitude, so courageously charge their adversaries that for five hours there was giving and receiving blows, each side equally heated with rage and inflamed with desire of conquest. The Queen's army were fresh and excellently-armed, but by the overthrow of Iradat not a little disheartened. Mahabat's men, though come from afar, yet of a more warlike constitution, were hopeful of booty, so that in the end Nur Mahal's party gave back, well-beaten and unable any longer to abide the strokes of their adversaries. Asaf Khan in the meantime rides up and down like a distracted person, now upbraiding, then entreating and using all possible means to rally, but fear and the Rajputs' swords had flashed too much terror amongst them to fight again, so that with a sad heart upon an Arabian courser Asaf Khan flies away with Mirza Abu Talib[59] his son to a castle of good defence not far distant thence, but by accident espied, are chased by Mirza Bihroz,[60] Mahabat's third son, and being taken, are shackled in silver fetters and in that posture brought to Attock, are there safely guarded, whiles Mahabat Khan and his army, galloping in the air of good fortune, beat down the Queen's forces, at that time more willing to die then fight, so that without more let they proclaim themselves lords of India, and prey upon infinite riches of all sorts which they found in the lascar.

---

[58] Herbert's chronology is seriously inaccurate. Mahabat Khan had *already* secured the person of Jahangir by the time the battle with Nur Jahan's army took place. The Emperor's attendants and much of the army, with the treasure, had crossed the Jhelum and Jahangir was due to follow the next morning. At that point, B. Prasad writes, "Mahabat Khan formed the bold design of taking the emperor captive," because he realised that "the power of the ruling faction rested primarily on their control of the emperor" (*History*, 370).

[59] Mirza Abu Talib [*Mirza Abontila*] was later known as Shaista Khan. He was freed when his father submitted to Mahabat Khan. He married the Khan-i-Khanan's grand-daughter. When Dawar Bakhsh was proclaimed emperor after Jahangir's death, Abu Talib was one of the people who found and arrested Prince Shahriyar. For details see Findly, *Nur Jahan*, 282.

[60] Mirza Bihroz [*Mirza Byrewer*] was, as Herbert states, the third son of Mahabat Khan. He later rebelled against his father's authority (see below).

The aged Mughal was found sleeping, lulled in Morpheus's golden bed, till by Mahabat Khan he was gently awaked and assured of his welfare.[61] Upon a stately elephant they conveyed him to Attock, a strong castle to the east of Indus, leaving slain behind him twelve thousand men and many *umrah* of note, as Mirza Qasim, Rajah Daulah, Abdul Khaliq,[62] and taken prisoners Jahangir the Great Mughal, Queen Nur Mahal, Asaf Khan, Mirza Abu Talib his son, Sultan Bulaqi, Sultan Shahriyar, Shah Tahmuraz, Shah Hoshang, Iradat Khan and Mullah Mohammed Tathi,[63] all which are led prisoners to Kabul to expect the pleasure of their conqueror. Now is Mahabat elevated upon the majestic chariot of command, resolving nevertheless to detract as little as might be from the splendour of his master, his only aim being to clear his honour from an unjust imputation and to retaliate his enemies what in his friends he had formerly suffered. Nur Mahal, now clouded with shame, was brought forth, so that by the advice of Mahabat's Council of War the poor Queen was condemned to lose her head. Not till then did she perceive the thorny path she had walked in nor meditated upon the mutability of fortune, nor till then could she frame her ambitious heart to fear or servitude, but seeing no remedy arms herself with patience and craves a farewell of her lord, to whom after much entreaty she is admitted, where

---

[61] This is not what happened at all, at least according to Mutamid Khan, who was there, although Findly agrees that Jahangir was asleep (*Nur Jahan*, 268). The whole incident was reported by Mutamid Khan in his *Iqbal-nama-i Jahangiri*, the author being attendant on Jahangir and therefore an eye-witness to the events. "For these last three years of Jahangir's life," Findly states, "it is one of the best of the Persian sources available" (*Nur Jahan*, 373). Mahabat Khan and some of his Rajputs went to Jahangir's camp and were accosted by Mutamid Khan at the entrance to the imperial tent. They elbowed Mutamid Khan aside after he attempted to get them to wait, but just then Jahangir himself came out and simply went to the palanquin which was to carry him across the Jhelum. Mahabat Khan "approached the emperor—not audaciously but deferentially," and tried to plead with him, asking Jahangir to protect him from Asaf Khan. As they spoke the conversation became heated; Jahangir, wrote Mutamid Khan, reached for his sword and twice "seemed intent on cutting off Mahabat Khan's head, but was restrained by Mansur Bhakhshi, an aide, who told Jahangir in Turkish (so that Mahabat Khan couldn't understand) not to get violent and to "leave the punishment of this wicked faithless fellow to a just God," at which point things calmed down and Jahangir condescended to ride out with Mahabat Khan (For details see Mutamid Khan, *Ikbal-nama-i Jahangiri*, 400–38; quoted by Abraham Eraly *The Mughal Throne: The Saga of India's Great Emperors* [London: Weidenfeld and Nicolson, 2003], 289–90; also see B. Prasad, *History*, 370–73).

[62] Abdul Khaliq [*Abdul-Gallec*] was the nephew of Khwaja Shams-ud-din. He was executed by order of Mahabat Khan, not killed in action (B. Prasad, *History*, 380).

[63] Mullah Mohammed Tathi [*Molena Mahomet*] was the "spiritual preceptor of Asaf Khan." Citing the *Iqbalnama*, B. Prasad states that he was "accused of invoking supernatural punishment on Mahabat Khan" because his chains, not secured properly, fell off when he moved, and at the same time he was heard muttering verses from the *Quran*, "the whole of which he knew by heart" (*History*, 380). He was beheaded.

she prostrates herself clothed with so much sorrow that Jahangir melts into compassion and entreats Mahabat for her freedom. Mahabat, loath in anything to discontent his master, condescends, so that contrary to the advice of his confederates Nur Mahal was set at liberty, but to show that none is more thirsty after revenge then that sex, she becomes more enraged by this lenity and speedily put it in practice. The residue of the royal prisoners were used with due respect, Iradat and Mullah Mohammed excepted, who by too much rigour were so enraged that [the] Mullah died. Sadiq Khan sped best, for before the fight, upon some occasion jarring with his brother Asaf Khan, he fled to Mahabat and for that service was made Governor of Lahore, and Qasim Khan, by mediation of Monisa Begum his wife, sister to the Queen, is restored to his government of Agra and Muzaffar Khan displaced, so that now Mahabat sways Industan, till by vicissitude of time he falls from his meridian and as well as others experiments the mutability of Fortune.

Khurram beaten.

Khurram was all this time in Deccan, lurking till he might espy some advantage to recover his lost credit and once more shake off the title of a rebellious exile, but when news was brought him from Asaf Khan of the almost incredible change the Empire had and with what a dismal veil it was then enveloped, his father and father-in-law being in subjection, Sultan Bulaqi and Prince Daniyal's sons imprisoned and his own sons with Khwaja Jahan their governor brought to Mahabat by time-serving Muzaffar Khan to abide his mercy. He disputes not what Mahabat means, but what had happened, so that, exasperated with a thousand fancies he gives Malik Ambar many thanks, and with Rajah Bhim's son and twelve thousand horse passes, under leave, through [the] Rana's territories and at last comes to Ajmer, intending suddenly to surprise Agra and proclaim himself king. But his desire was by Rajah [Kishan Singh's] sudden desertion prevented, half his company upon that occasion forsaking him,[64] whereat, doubting some treachery in the Ajmerians, into such hate his robbing and other disorders had brought him, and that Mahabat Khan had sent some force against him and Sultan Parvez also had ambushed for him, he hastens to Thatta, hoping by conquest thereof to command Indus and Cambay, so as at his encamping

---

[64] Herbert's account is a little confusing here. He does not specify which "Rajah" deserted him, but it appears that it may refer to Kishan Singh, the son of Rajah Bhim and a supporter of Mahabat Khan who had "highly distinguished himself and inflicted a severe defeat on the Rajputs" in 1612 (B. Prasad, *History*, 211). He was also a supporter of Prince Khurram, but, according to B. Prasad, he died (rather than deserted) in June 1626, at which point Khurram "had the mortification to see . . . his [Kishan's] 500 retainers disperse forthwith" (391). This explanation seems the more likely because both Herbert and B. Prasad mention his departure for Thatta.

before it he sends the Governor[65] a summons to deliver it, but the captain, Sharif al-Mulk, sends him word he had particular order to keep him out, and that if he attempted it he should receive the entertainment of an enemy. Khurram returns him back again that he was son unto the King; al-Mulk confesses it, but withal a rebellious one. Khurram re-greets him that he came to defy Mahabat Khan and to bring deliverance to his father; al-Mulk answers, rather by all their confusions to grasp the diadem. Khurram, enraged by these retorts and heightened in his hope by Darya Khan,[66] prepares for an assault, and accordingly at one and the same time storms the city walls in several places, but al-Mulk the Governor so well defends the butt-works and walls that the assailants were forced to draw off with loss, the besieged the next day sallying out and with such gallantry falling into Khurram's camp that in the skirmish Darya Khan and 300 of his men were killed, and Khurram himself forced (his old shift) to fly to Delhi, where finding no welcome he hastes with his chafed troops to Bakar, a fort 'twixt Lahore and the sea, to breathe awhile.

Ganges and Delhi described.

Delhi is the name of a city and province which of late belonged to the Pathan kings, the originary inhabitants, but at this day is reduced under the crown of Industan.[67] The city is ancient, large and pretty beautiful, such appearing in the variety of ancient monuments and tombs of above twenty kings and other great

---

[65] Sharif al-Mulk [*Xeriff Melek*], the Governor of Thatta, was "a devoted adherent of Nur Jahan, impervious to any entreaties, promises of threats which the prince could hold out" (B. Prasad, *History*, 391). He was also "a devoted supporter of Shahriyar through Nur Jahan" (Findly, *Nur Jahan*, 276).

[66] Darya Khan [*Derra-chan*] (d. 1626) was an Afghan officer in Prince Khurram's service. He had fought at Dholpur (1622) whilst Sharif al-Mulk had been *faujdar* there, and had been beaten by him.

[67] As Crowther and Raj state, "there have been at least eight cities around modern Delhi" (*India*, 131), the first one believed to have been near the old fort, named Purana Qila, which may be the word from which Herbert derived "Poran" kings, which is what he calls "Pathan kings." Mention of the city goes back to the period of the *Mahabarata*, but today architectural interest is aroused by buildings which date back to the Early Pathan Period (1193–1320). Before that the city was the centre of a kingdom under the Tomar and Chauthan dynasties. There are traces of monuments dating from the time of the Mauryan Empire, which succeeded Greek rule under Alexander the Great in 321 B.C.E. and whose greatest ruler was Ashoka (263–232 B.C.E.). The "new" Delhi Herbert writes about was actually the sixth city, founded by Sher Shah when he ousted Humayun in 1540. Humayun's tomb, built by his widow Haji Begum, is an example of early Mughal architecture, with "red sandstone and marble details" (Crowther and Raj, *India*, 136). "Old" Delhi, now "in beautiful ruins and . . . peopled by many of modern Delhi's destitute," was, writes C. Ross Smith, "one of the East's major cities in prestige and beauty," but now "what remains of this fabled beauty is pathetically small" (*In Search*, 76).

persons who lie there entombed, so as it is a place no little visited by travellers
and by infinite numbers of banians, who for some superstitious end resort thither,
little less then adored. Not a little famous also by reason of that pyramid which
is from old Delhi, three miles distant, where lies buried King Humayun who
was grandfather to Jahangir, by frame and inscription supposed to be erected by
Alexander, at which time Delhi was the mausoleum of sundry potentates. New
Delhi is walled about, watered by parts of Jumna, over which we must enter on
a twelve-arched bridge of stone, which river, arising from a little spring in the
mountains of Jammu,[68] drifts to Agra, and after a great increase of her channel at
Peage flows into Ganges, and with her in two huge wide mouths near 100 miles
asunder empties her watery stomach into the Bengalan Gulf in about twenty-
two degrees of north latitude and then mixes with the salt ocean.

Ganges by cosmographers is reputed one of the noblest rivers in the world.
It arises, some say, out of Nigracus, part of Caucasus, others say from Syba, supposed Sephar mentioned in Genesis 10:30,[69] and after 1000 miles flux loses itself in the Gulf of Bengal, as lately spoken. It has many rivers streaming into it,
which swells her channel, especially after Jumna at Praej mixes with her. The
banians esteem it sacred, and from the cow they so much reverence give out that
the rock from whence it first springs has the resemblance of a cow's head, no new
fancy, for Virgil in his *Georgics* [4. 371-372], describing the River Po in Italy, says
"Golden Eridanus with a double horn, fac'd like a bull, etc."

Asaf Khan released.

Malik Ambar, so soon as Khurram was marched out of his country, to procure
protection from Parvez also gave liberty without treaty of ransom to Lashkar
Khan, Ibrahim Husain and Mirza Manu-Chehr,[70] and with a safe convoy sends
them to Burhanpur. The same month Mahabat Khan received 26 lakh of rupees
from Khan Zad Khan his son, at that time Viceroy of Bengal, which he extracted
as an annual rent out of Patan, Benares, Sujapur, Tanda, Bakla and Chatgaon,
rich and well-peopled towns upon Ganges, as also out of Sanjan, an isle twenty
leagues from Chatgaon, then which is none more fruitful in India. Jahangir also,
removing his court from Kabul to Lahore by Nur Mahal's rash persuasion, condescends to the slaughter of such Rajputs as Mahabat had mixed with his own
guard, and after that openly declared that he could not be satisfied without the
destruction of Mahabat ere he received any supply from his kinsmen Alam Khan

[68] Jammu [*Jenba*] is the most likely identification, because it is a mountainous hill-
state in Punjab. See Banerjee's note in De Laet (*Empire*, 8 n. 11*a*).
[69] "And their dwelling was from Mesha, as thou goest, unto Sephar, a mount of the
east."
[70] Unidentified. De Laet has "Mirza Manoutzier" (*Empire*, 220); Banerjee does not
attempt to identify him.

and Rajah Rostam, who were then advancing up towards him. And for her part, to leave nothing unattempted that might conduce to the execution thereof, she empties all her husband's coffers and hires men from all places to serve her, so that Hushiar Khan,[71] Viceroy of Bajwara, brings her 5000 horse, Khwaja Sher 3000, Muzaffar Khan 12,000, and of her own she had 19,000 more, hoping also that Fidai Khan,[72] fled from the battle at Attock into the deserts of Tulamba[73] to [the] Rajah of Kumaon, would associate her, but he was so afraid of Mahabat's good fortune that he would not appear against him, but went to Prince Parvez, then at Burhanpur, to whom by a commendatory letter from Rajah Bir Singh he was very welcome.

Mahabat Khan has notice of the Queen's project and new preparation, but not any whit discouraged draws all his horse and foot into a body and presently advances towards the Queen's army. In the way, at his master's request, he uses Asaf Khan and his son with more respect then formerly. Nur Mahal also hastens towards him, having sent her son Shahriyar to Lahore with 8000 horse to secure that imperial city against Mahabat. In his passage by good hap he chances upon Sultan Bulaqi and the two christened princes, whom he rescued, with whom he got so privately and with such haste into Lahore that without resistance most of the Rajputs were cut off and the castle manned with the Queen's army. Jahangir also, roused out of his long sleep, now plays his part, for being come within eight miles of Nur Mahal and her army, and having at all times the freedom of hunting, hawking and such like pastime, he makes it his advantage, escapes, and is joyfully welcomed by the Queen, who, crying out "Mubarak!,"[74] impales him in her arms and cries for joy; then, as one assured of the victory, gives present order to march on to assail the traitors.[75]

---

[71] Hushiar Khan [*Ouripargan*] was one of Nur Jahan's eunuchs who collected men for her in Lahore (B. Prasad, *History*, 385).

[72] Fidai Khan, "by all accounts one of the most impressive personalities in Nur Jahan's camp," actually made several attempts to rescue Jahangir (B. Prasad, *History*, 377–78), but eventually "went up the river to his sons at Rohtas" (Findly, *Nur Jahan*, 268). Fidai Khan, formerly Suleiman Beg, was promoted by Jahangir in 1619 and 1620. In 1627 he was appointed Viceroy of Bengal. On two occasions Jahangir commends his skill in hunting.

[73] The Desert of Thar [*Thombal*] is near Jaisalmer.

[74] Herbert probably means *mabrouk*, which signifies "Well done!"

[75] Herbert's account differs from that given either by the *Iqbalnama* or by Pieter van den Broecke's *Chronicle* (1627). Both Jahangir and Nur Jahan were captured by Mahabat Khan, but at different times; however, there is no evidence in these accounts, or in that of Findly, who has read most available sources, that they escaped at different times. In fact, as the *Ma'asir-i Jahangiri* relates, after Mahabat Khan had secured Jahangir, he "realised his mistake in not taking Nur Jahan into custody" (Khwaja Kamgar Husaini, *Ma'asir-i-Jahangiri*, ed. Azra Alavi [Aligarh: Asia Publishing House, 1978], 49). However, Nur Jahan surrendered herself to Mahabat Khan after Asaf Khan had fled to At-

Mahabat Khan, like all other occasions when at highest, descend, quickly knows of Jahangir's flight, and is not so grieved at his being gone as at the manner, intending never to have withheld him longer then he fancied, yet the revolt of 5000 of his men did trouble him. Howbeit, perceiving his enemies were approaching and that it was no fit time to discover his discontent, he apparels himself in a rich and tried coat of mail, and with his shield and spear spurs up in the front of the Mughal's lascar, where by all signs he perceives the Mughal's affections estranged. He sighs at it and returns, and after a short oration to encourage his men orders his forces, but ere the battle begun, Buland Khan[76] brings him a peremptory message from the King to this effect: that if he desired to be accounted loyal he should express it by releasing Asaf Khan and other *umrah* he kept imprisoned, by whose mediation probably he might obtain pardon. Mahabat Khan knows it was Nur Mahal's device, yet loath in anything to disobey the King, sends him a protest of his loyalty and that so soon as he came to the river Behat his commands should be accomplished. So he arises, and at the place presigned calls for Asaf Khan and his son, shows him he had power to destroy him, but his virtue swayed him to another end. Which said, he not only pulls away his marks of servitude but vests him with princely robes, mounts him upon his best courser, girds him with a precious blade, and with a convoy of eight hundred horse sends him to court, his farewell only pointing to remember him. Jahangir receives him with tears of love, but Nur Mahal with words of disdain, upbraiding him with cowardice that durst not attend her time or depend upon her power to force him from a rebel he both feared and hated. Asaf Khan laments her lunacy but is afraid to vex her, yet both in goodwill publicly and in private discourse at any time with the King he speaks well of Mahabat, and as an honourable person labours his reconciliation, whereby we see that valour gains praise even in an enemy.[77]

The affairs of Industan, by this variety, possess all men's minds with astonishment; whiles Jahangir and his beloved Amazon with the lascar pass on to Lahore to advise with Sultan Shahriyar her son how to reduce the King's power

tock (B. Prasad, *History*, 378). They appear to have plotted their escape together, with Jahangir "softening up" Mahabat Khan by promising to keep him informed of what Nur Jahan was saying to him in private, thus making him drop his guard, whilst Nur Jahan planned their escape and secured allies. Once they were safe, Nur Jahan then demanded the release of her brother Asaf Khan, which Mahabat Khan agreed to do. For details, see Findly, *Nur Jahan*, 271–73.

[76] Buland Khan [*Balant-chan*] was one of Jahangir's attendants (De Laet, *Empire*, 231; B. Prasad, *History*, 381).

[77] According to Findly, this is not quite what happened. Jahangir did indeed welcome Asaf Khan and even rewarded him by making him Governor of the Punjab, and Asaf Khan did get told off by his sister for not waiting for her to rescue him. However, "when Jahangir asked him if he realized how obligated he now was to Mahabat Khan, Asaf Khan duplicitously replied that he would forget what he owed or repay it benignly" (*Nur Jahan*, 273). Both Asaf and Mahabat would flourish under Shah Jahan.

to his proper channel. But what pleasure can the contemplation of her reviving glory afford her so long as Mahabat lives unpunished? She knows not why she is entitled sole Empress of the best parts of Asia, commandress of so much men and treasure, so long as Mahabat, an obscure Rajput (as she called him) dares eclipse her splendour and travel to and fro unresisted, guarded with such applause and popularity. She ruminates a thousand several sorts of revenge, but by too much choice knows not which to fasten on. The surest and most honourable is by war, and thereupon [she] calls Ahmed Khan,[78] Siphadar Khan,[79] Nur ed-din Quli,[80] Ani Rai Singh, Mirza Rostam and other nobles, desiring them to hasten Mahabat's destruction. Each man promises his best, and with fifteen thousand horse go joyously on to attempt it. In the first place, hearing of some treasure his son Zad Khan had sent him out of Bengal, they ambushed near Shahabad, a castle of strength, and break out on the Rajputs that then were no more then eight hundred valiant men who sold their money at a dear rate, two thousand of Nur Mahal's men giving their lives for it and her ambition, but by their multitude were at last defeated and most of them slaughtered, leaving twenty-six lakh or 2,600,000 rupees to their avarice, which was brought to Lahore and there some part distributed for pay. The rest was coffered.

The Khan-i-Khanan, by this time recovered, was notwithstanding his dotage made general of Nur Mahal's forces. Mahabat Khan was not troubled by it, but the revolt of his wild son Bihroz afflicts him sadly. This young gallant had no sooner triumphed over Asaf Khan, whom he delivered to his father, as it is spoken, but with a brigade of three thousand horse his father had made him commander of being ordered to assail Rajah Chhatr Singh at Narnol,[81] not regarding his father's instructions wheels by Bargant, the contrary way, to force his father's castle of Ranthambhor, albeit in vain, for Musawi Khan[82] the captain, suspecting him, fools him with fair words and by like art divides his forces, so that Bihroz,

---

[78] Ahmed Beg Khan Kabuli [*Amet-cawn*], nephew of Ibrahim Khan Fath Jang (see n. 7 above), had been appointed governor of Kashmir (1616), where he had shown himself both cowardly and incompetent.

[79] Siphadar Khan [*Zeffer-cawn*] was the Mughal general who served as Commandant of Agra.

[80] Nur ed-din Quli [*Nouradom-cooly*] was one of the leaders of the Ahadis, mortal enemies of the Rajputs and therefore very hostile to Mahabat Khan. According to B. Prasad, these men only commanded a thousand, not fifteen thousand Ahadis when they seized Mahabat Khan's treasure as it neared Delhi (*History*, 394–95). The larger army was sent by Nur Mahal to get Mahabat Khan as soon as he had released his imperial hostages, not to seize Zad Khan's money.

[81] Chattr Singh [*Tzetterisngh*] and Narnol [*Nurnal*] are identified by Banerjee (De Laet, *Empire*, 235 n. 178), but no details are given.

[82] Musawi Khan [*Motzaib-chan*] is probably the same man who was sent by Jahangir to negotiate with Shah Jahan during his 1623 rebellion (B. Prasad, *History*, 330).

making an escape, flying hence to Rao Ratan[83] at Bundi, a place to the west of Agra, was unexpectedly taken and imprisoned.

Death of Prince Parvez. Mahabat Khan turns eremite.

Jahangir, finding his thoughts free and refreshed by the new delights his youthful Queen each day invented for his recreation, labours only to forget the rebellion of Khurram and his late adversity, yea, gives his lascivious mind full scope, covering himself with the effeminate robes of sloth and wantonness. But in the plenitude of those his joys the glory of his estate grows cloudy and his motion whirls into a malignant orb by the disconsolate news he receives from Burhanpur of his beloved son's unexpected death,[84] at which report his eyes grow dim, his heart fails, and all apprehensions of pleasure relish unsavoury when the sad departure of Parvez presents itself and those hopes and comforts he had now seem fantastical, so that he recounts his loss, sadly crying out "Khusrau and Shah Daniyal are dead, Parvez is now no more, Shah Tahmuraz and Hoshang my grandchildren have turned Christians; Bulaqi, is he not a child, Shahriyar a fool[85] and Khurram the eyesore of my conceptions, a rebel, wild, proud, greedy, treacherous and deceitful? Can I deny that I am old, and at my death, which cannot be avoided, how subject will my empire be to innovation?" In these and suchlike dolorous exclamations Jahangir sighs out the few remaining minutes of his life, Death (*ultima poena*[86] as some call it) summoning him a few months after to the resignation of both life and empire, whiles Mahabat Khan in the meantime chews the afflicting news of Prince Parvez his death, 'twixt whom, forgetting the Khan-i-Khanan's treachery, an entire friendship was revived. He sees in him the privation of

---

[83] Rao Ratan [*Ray Ruttang*] was the "valiant prince of Bundi" (B. Prasad, *History*, 357) who had successfully defended Burhanpur against Shah Jahan (1623) and his army of rebels.

[84] Prince Parvez died "a victim to alcohol like so many members of the Imperial house and court" on 28 October 1626 (B. Prasad, *History*, 393). This is corroborated by I. Prasad, who states that the Prince, who "became a hopeless decrepit at the early age of 37, had died of excessive drink in October 1626" (*Humayum*, 453). Eraly states that Parvez was "a frivolous alcoholic" (*Mughal Throne*, 301). However, Findly quotes van den Broecke as stating that Jahangir loved Parvez deeply because "he was more gentle and obedient than the other sons" (*Nur Jahan*, 276; see also De Laet, *Empire*, 233–34). The usual rumours about Shah Jahan being involved in his brother's death surfaced, but there is no foundation for them at all this time.

[85] Again, this harsh judgment seems to be corroborated by modern scholars. Eraly calls Shahriyar "an imbecile" (*Mughal Throne*, 301). B. Prasad merely noted that he was a "coward" (*History*, 401). However, since in March 1627 he had contracted what Findly identifies as Fox's Disease, a form of leprosy which made his hair and beard fall out, he should perhaps be pitied rather than despised (for details, see Findly, *Nur Jahan*, 276–8).

[86] The last punishment.

all his joy, the hopes he had in his succession annihilated, and the ambition of Nur Mahal and Asaf Khan, suspected to have poisoned him, engendering to a monstrous height, so that bidding farewell to the world, he contracts himself to privacy, feeding upon the contemplation of what had passed and the lubricity of terrestrial pleasures.[87] For certain it is that life and death are but indifferent things and of themselves not to be shunned or sought save for the good or ill that either brings. He forsakes his strong and delightful castle Ranthambhor, through Zialor comes to [the] Rajah of Jaisalmer and under license fixes himself at Jaisalmer, where he turns anchorite.

Howbeit, Khurram's air swells with chimaeras now more than ever affecting the Empire, none but children interposing him. He knew his father's affection was easily recovered and Asaf Khan restless to state him in the chair of majesty, so that armed with confidence and accompanied with forty elephants and sixteen hundred horse he leaves Bhakkar, Chittor, Thatta, and through Thasra,[88] Sholapur and Akluj,[89] comes to Nasik Trimbak in Deccan, where Malik receives him with joy and to his party adds four thousand horse, with promise of forty thousand to assist him if he had occasion.[90]

Chittor described.

Chittor, in mid-way 'twixt Burhanpur and Ajmer, is a city upon a high rock claiming precedence for antiquity amongst all the cities of India.[91] It was formerly called Taxila and is supposed to be that metropolis whence King Porus issued against great Alexander. Rana Amar Singh, lineally descended from him, (of late years and title by entreaty of Sultan Khurram *Anno* 1614, he came to Agra and in slight sort did some obeyance), here sovereignated, and in Udaipur. The city in former ages was so great and nobly built that it was termed the umbrella of the

---

[87] Mahabat Khan "at first took the route toward Thatta, but before he got there he went off into Hindustan. There he 'concealed himself for some time in the hills of the Rana's country,' waiting apparently for the final events of Jahangir's reign to unfold" (Findly, *Nur Jahan*, 273). After a short stay in Mewar, Mahabat then made overtures to Shah Jahan and joined him, helping him secure the throne. Shah Jahan made him Governor of Ajmer and promoted him. He never "turned anchorite," as Herbert believed, but merely lay low, waiting to see what would happen. He died in 1634.

[88] Thasra [*Tessel*]. This is a tentative identification. See Habib, *Atlas*, 7A, 22+ 73+.

[89] Akluj [*Ecclisser*]. Another tentative identification. It is a town in Bijapur; see Habib, *Atlas*, 14A, 17+ 75+.

[90] Malik Ambar died in May 1626. The "Malik" with whom Shah Jahan was apparently so friendly would have been Malik Ambar's son Fateh Khan, who succeeded his father as Regent.

[91] Legend has it that the fort at Chittor was built by Bhim, one of Pandava warriors from the *Mahabarata*. For detailed information on the city, see Crowther and Raj, *India*, 386–90.

world, but at this day is but meanly beautiful and albeit about 3 miles in compass
not a third part of what is was formerly. Time, war and weather have furrowed
her, not only disrobing her of her bravery in buildings where men inhabited, but
in temples and monuments of antiquity, for of this place it might be said "*Tot templa deum quot in urbe sepulcrae heroum, innumerate licet*,"[92] so many temples here
were built and so many princes buried. The ruins nevertheless, of above an hundred to this day remaining of stone, white and well-polished, albeit now inhabited by storks, owls, bats and like birds, of whom the superstitious people have an
esteem little short of veneration. The North Pole is elevated in this place twenty-
five degrees. The province is bound by Cambay on the south, by Kandesh on the
north, by Berar on the east, and on the west the ocean.

The Khan-i-Khanan dies.

The Khan-i-Khanan, not a little blown up by his late honour and employment
against Mahabat Khan, whom he verily thought had left the society of men for
fear of him, in the midst of his bravado is arrested by death, and his carcase conveyed to Delhi to be entombed amongst his great ancestors.[93] At that time Yakub
Khan, an *umrah* of great wealth and experience commanding eight thousand
men under Khurram, by reason of some affronts which were without cause put
upon him by Malik Ambar's son, was so exasperated that without more ado he
revolts from Khurram and flies to Jahan Khan [Lodi], general of Prince Parvez
his army then at Burhanpur, who receives him with joy and togther with four
hundred elephants and forty thousand horse marches in haste to Bellaguate, the
widow and child of Sultan Parvez in the meantime being committed to the care
of Lashkar Khan, where they practice all the extremities of war as plundering,
burning and captivating all they had a mind unto.

Abdullah Khan disgraced.

By rare chance intercepting some letters from Hishar Khan[94] they discover Abdullah Khan, the now weathercock of those times, whose intention was to turn
from the King's party and return to Khurram, for which he is convicted, his estate confiscated, his honour reversed, himself manacled and upon an elephant
in disgraceful sort sent to Burhanpur, where by Lashkar Khan he is imprisoned.
This done, they enter Deccan and pierce fortunately into the very midst of Malik Ambar's kingdom, doing what they pleased without opposition, so that after

---

[92] Variant text of Prudentius, *Ad symmachum* 1.1
[93] The Khan-i-Khanan died in the winter of 1627 in Delhi, without carrying out his
mission to pursue Mahabat Khan.
[94] Hishar or Hizbar Khan [*Gadgee Hessary*], the *faujdar* of Mewat, was one of the officers initially involved in hunting down Shah Jahan.

six weeks' hostility they return loaden with abundance of wealth, overjoyed with their easy victory. But when they thought themselves most sure, Malik[95] presents himself with eighty thousand men, encircling them on the one side as the hills did on the other, so that surrounded also with amazement they encamp, not daring to hazard the fight or force their passage, but in that miserable sort are blocked up, the Deccan at no time offending them, till by famine finding no pleasure in their riches, where no meat on safe terms was to be purchased, they were constrained to parley, and the issue thereof, according to articles, was to march undisturbed without their arms or baggage, having only their lives and some unserviceable horse allowed to return upon, a disgrace utterly defacing the memory of their past triumphs in the country.

The Tartarian ambassador's rich presents.

Jahangir the Great Mughal has quick advertisement of this bad success but knows not how to amend it, nor cares he much, the memory of Prince Parvez's death so afflicteth him. Nevertheless, Nur Mahal ceases not to pursue her revenge against Mahabat Khan, and finding him hard to be dealt with, she begins with Khan Zad Khan his valiant son, whom first she recalls home and places Muqarrab Khan[96] in his command over five thousand horse and twelve thousand men, but Muqarrab had small joy in his advance, for in less than three weeks, sailing over Ganges by accident the boat was overturned, whereby he was drowned and Fidai Khan by commission from Jahangir made Viceroy of Bengal and the territories near Malacca in his place, during which, Jahangir being at Lahore, a Tartarian ambassador, Ziet Berke by name,[97] arrives with presents and commends from the King of Turan, accompanied by the only oracle and wonder of

---

[95] It was not Malik Ambar (since he was dead) but Hamid Khan, "another Abyssinian . . . able and unscrupulous" (B. Prasad, *History*, 389) who now, after the fall of Fateh Khan, held the supreme command of the army. His authority was greater than that of either Sultan Nizam al-Mulk or of the Regent, Fateh Khan. Furthermore, Hamid Khan actually bribed Jahan Khan to turn over the whole area as far as Ahmednagar, and to get Mughal commanders to surrender their forts to Nizam al-Mulk (B. Prasad, *History*, 390).

[96] Muqarrab Khan [*Mocrib-cawn*] (d. 1626) had served Jahangir first as ambassador to Goa (1607), then as governor of Surat, where in 1613 he got compensation from the Portuguese, who had seized Mughal ships (B. Prasad, *History*, 187). It was reported that he became a Christian and took the name John (Findly, *Nur Jahan*, 201). He supported Jahangir against Mahabat Khan, and then became governor of Bihar before his fatal transfer to Bengal.

[97] The particulars of this visit are mentioned by De Laet. See also Findly, *Nur Jahan* 277. Banerjee does not give any explanation about the two holy men, "held in such high honour . . . for their supposed sanctity" (De Laet, *Empire*, 235–36). The name may be Sayed Barkhan, whom De Laet calls "Ziedborchan" (*Empire*, 235).

his time, Kadi Abdul Rahim, brother to Kadi Kallaun, one admired by most and resorted to by many sorts of Tartars from Bokhara, Tashkent, Balkh, Samarkand, Ghazni and many other parts, none of which came empty-handed, so that in small time this santoon became comparable with most potentates in Asia. He was brought into Lahore with no small joy and admiration, all the *umrah* of the court, Abdullah Khan excepted, attending him, and he was no sooner lodged but that he was presented from the Queen with a goblet of pure gold, massy and of curious work, with so many jewels as out-valued a lakh of rupees. These he accepts cheerfully, but scorning to be behind in courtesy returns her and her lord five hundred dromedaries swift and beautiful, some precious sword-blades and other gifts of value so great that, the report went, never any ambassador came so richly-furnished, was better-entertained, or went away more rewarded. Nor let any ambassador think himself welcome to any Asiatic prince that brings nothing for a present save only compliment, for the very natives seldom make addresses to any great one without a present.

Yet is not Nur Mahal suited with content so long as Mahabat makes frustrate her vows to have him ruined. Her power seems small, her endeavours idle, seeing, as she thought, his ease was in contempt of her, so that her thoughts project several ways for his destruction. The indignity offered his son-in-law gladded her in part, and much more to see his son Zad Khan by her means cashiered from his employment and at court affronted. Howbeit, by Asaf's means Jahangir himself countenances him, yea, Nur Mahal, had not the overflowing hate she bore his father hindered her, had doubtless become amorous of this accomplished young gallant and made him in Cupid's court Jahangir's competitor. But spite so o'ersways her that forthwith she calls unto her Ahmed [Beg Khan], Nur-ed-din Quli and Amira Beg,[98] her minions, to whom she discovers her enmity and entreats their diligence. They obey, and accordingly with fifteen thousand horse advance to fight with him, whiles Nur Mahal and the King journey to Kashmir,[99] his ne plus ultra, and Asaf Khan, mindful of Mahabat's kindness to him, loath so brave a man should perish through the malice of a woman and especially by his civilities to engage him to Khurram, by a swift and trusty messenger sends him a letter discovering his sister's resolution and solicits [the] young Rana to preserve him.

---

[98] Unidentified. De Laet has "Ametbeeck Chan" (*Empire*, 236). This could be Ahmed Beg Khan, a former governor of Orissa and the nephew of Ibrahim Khan (De Laet, *Empire*, 214), but it is uncertain. He also mentions "Amira," who is Herbert's *Hemyr Beg*, an unidentified nobleman. It might mean simply "other nobles" (*umrah*).

[99] They left for Kashmir in March 1627. With the emperor and Nur Mahal went Asaf Khan, Prince Shahriyar and Prince Dawar Bakhsh. Jahangir was now in poor health; "every day saw him weaker," B. Prasad writes (*History*, 396). By this time Asaf Khan was probably also in touch with Shah Jahan as well.

Mahabat, upon receipt of Asaf Khan's letter, after some sorrowful expressions forsakes his cell, flies to Jaisalmer and thence to [the] Rana,[100] who ever loved him. Nur Mahal's army has notice of his flight, but dare not enter [the] Rana's country in a hostile way, and therefore they post intelligence to Nur Mahal, who writes to [the] Rana mixing entreaties with threats, making Jahangir sign what after long and swift running is delivered him. [The] Rana at first contemns her bravados, but upon better consideration assures her he is not willing to give the Mughal or her any just cause of offence, which answer being returned, he forthwith assures Mahabat that his heart was true towards him and that if he would have it so was ready to engage in his defence against all the power of India. Yet in prudence he thought it more adviseable for him to withdraw to exiled Khurram, who, as he was Nur Mahal's antagonist, would without doubt entertain him gladly. Mahabat Khan, by the circumstances of his speech judging him fearful, tells him he intended not to be any occasion of loss to him, and so mounts to be gone, but [the] Rana will not let him go till he promise him a delivery of a packet which he had written and directed to Khurram. After much persuasion he condescends, and with five hundred Rajputs and one thousand other men led by Wazir Khan, he speeds into [northern] Deccan, where at Junnair upon the limits of Nizam Shah's kingdom he finds Khurram, who was so amazed at his sudden coming that he instantly sounds an alarm, but when he had read [the] Rana's packet, after some astonishment he embraces Mahabat with unspeakable joy, by protestation forms a perpetual friendship with him, and gives him the command of that castle and other forces. India admires this agreement, and Nur Mahal, now too late, repents her folly, for "The mind oft in remorse / May with the thing undone, rage did enforce."

Jahangir the Great Mughal dies.

Jahangir also blames her inconsiderate wrath and grows so afflicted at this conjunction that in a deep melancholy he forsakes his pleasures at Kashmir, removes towards Lahore, and calls for the *Chronicles* for his recreation. Scarce anything is done or said by these monarchs which is not registered, nor is it a new custom, for Plutarch [in] Symposium I reports that when Alexander chanced but to sleep at table it was registered, and Esther 6,[101] when Ahaseurus King of Persia could not rest in his bed, the *Chronicles* were called for and the eunuch's treason remembered that was discovered by Mordecai the Jew. But to our story. Upon the high mountains of Bhimbhi he falls sick and at three days' end, after three and twenty years' reign, to the astonishment of the lascar, Nur Mahal's endless sorrow and

---

[100] The Rana of Mewar was Karan Singh, son of Amar Singh I. He reigned 1620–1628. The ruler of Jaisalmer was Maharawal Kalyan Das (1624–1634).

[101] On that night could not the king sleep, and he commanded to bring the book of the records of the chronicles, and they were read before the king (Esther 6:1).

the grief of the whole Empire, Jahangir dies, suspected of poison, the twelfth of
October or Ardabehish, in the year of our accompt 1627 and of the Hegira 1007,
nominating upon his death-bed his grandson Bulaqi, son of Sultan Khusrau his
eldest son, his successor, also ordains that Khurram should have no portion of
favour save what he might merit from Bulaqi by his submission. Accordingly they
conveyed the old Mughal's dead body to Lahore, where they prepared for his
funeral, and after with all due solemnity carry it to Sikandra, three course from
Agra, where they entombed him in King Akbar's monument, and at Delhi they
crown Sultan Bulaqi, aged thirteen years,[102] king with all royal accustomed state,
and unanimously cry out "*Padshah salaam*," that is, "God save the King."[103]

Bulaqi the Great Mughal murdered.

Nur Mahal in Jahangir's end fears the beginning of her miseries, but being of an
active spirit she instantly conceives and swells with the ambition of that Empire.
Her pregnancy was bettered by having the whole treasure in her hands, also animated in that Bulaqi was too young to nourish opposition, his council careless
and Khurram a great way absent thence, so that taking occasion by the forehead,
she arms herself with confidence and a pretended title and resolves to name her
son Shahriyar to the supreme ascent of majesty, or in the attempt to set all India
on fire and to consume herself as a sacrifice in that great action. In this resolve
she lets her treasure fly, hires fifteen thousand horse, and sends in post-haste to
her son in Jaunpur,[104] a pretty town in Punjab, to levy as many more, which done,
he intends to strangle her brother Asaf Khan and Bulaqi the King, who at that
time were advancing towards her, but so soon as they had understanding of her
meaning, they leave Chotelen and with thirty thousand horse haste to Lahore
to apprehend Shahriyar, whom they heard was lately baffled by Rajah Abdul

---

[102] Bulaqi was actually twenty-four in 1627.

[103] Jahangir died on 28 October 1627 N.S. (Herbert was, presumably, using Old
Style dating). He was on his way to Chinghiz Hatli which is close to Bhimbhar, but he
never got there. He did not himself nominate Bulaqi, although some contemporary writers claimed that he had (Findly, *Nur Jahan*, 280); it was Asaf Khan who proclaimed Bulaqi emperor, but not before he had sent his signet ring to Shah Jahan to show that Bulaqi
was "a mere sacrificial lamb," as B. Prasad put it (*History*, 399) to ensure that there was no
gap in the succession and be used as a stopgap until Shah Jahan arrived. Jahangir's body
was not entombed with Akbar, but buried in Nur Jahan's garden at Dilkusha, where Nur
Jahan afterwards built a mausoleum. Asaf Khan put Nur Jahan under "house arrest," and
she then acted against him by sending a message to her son Shahriyar, who declared himself emperor in Lahore (For details, see B. Prasad, *History*, 400–2)

[104] Shahriyar was actually in Lahore, not Jaunpur, when he received Nur Jahan's
message; "this message," Findly states, "was to be her last-known political act" (*Nur Jahan*, 281). He seized the royal treasure and proclaimed himself Emperor (B. Prasad, *History*, 400–1).

Hassan, once his stipendiary, and then encamped only with four thousand horse. But in the way, to prevent Nur Mahal's pursuit after them, they block up the narrow passage that is upon the mountains through which her army needs must pass, so as ere the Queen could come to join with Shahriyar, Asaf Khan, Iradat Khan and other *umrah*, with the young Mughal in company, arrive at Lahore, where they find Shahriyar's army, by the expense of ninety thousand lakh of rupees, trebled. They delay not, but with extremity of rage assail him, and in two hours, by the villainy of Ahmed Beg and Sher Khwaja,[105] two of his chief captains who most basely betrayed him, get the victory, forcing him into the castle, which for two days was defended against Sultan Bulaqi and all his army, but in the third was treacherously yielded, many of his men slain, much treasure taken as also Shahriyar himself, who, to make him incapable of future government, had his eyes put out, Sultan Bulaqi in pity not suffering him to be killed.[106]

That done, they again proclaim Sultan Bulaqi emperor, and send Iradat Khan with twenty thousand horse against the virago Queen, who, hearing how ill her son had sped, and doubting treason in her army lets fall the majesty of her spirit, sighs at the perfidy of her brother, grieving that she slew him not when she had him in her powers, complains of her own weakness in continuing so long so needlessly enraged against Mahabat Khan, deplores her abusing his valiant son, and with a dejected eye beholding the sudden eclipse of her glory and the inconstancy of her friends, wraps all up in dismissing her guard, and thus disrobed of bravery she submits to Bulaqi's mercy, who like a noble Prince forgives and consoles her, gives her his oath for safety, and during his reign affords her all respect and freedom becoming her quality.

This noble Prince shows himself in the darbar to the people not so oft as was expected, nor long enjoys his sovereignty, for Asaf Khan, seeing all he desired, speeds away in a post with letters to Khurram, who made such haste that in fourteen days (as they report) he ran two thousand of our miles as far as Datta in Deccan, eight courses from Nakur and from Rajapur one hundred and twenty to the east. Overjoyed with the intelligence and sending his excuse to the Deccan king for not taking leave in a more ceremonious manner, he sets forward with Mahabat Khan, Zulfikar Khan and seven thousand Rajputs and munsubdars, passing through Gujarat to Ahmedabad, where by Safi Khan he was welcomed. There he slept not long, for making Agra the object of his race he bids farewell to Safi Khan, and with a great recruit, feeding them greater promises when he

---

[105] Sher Khwaja [*Sheirgadgee*] was, according to Banerjee, "one of the commanders of the *altamish* (troops between the vanguard and the centre) of Asaf Khan's army. Shahriyar sent his troops under the command of Baisanghar, to fight Asaf Khan" (De Laet, *Empire*, 239 n. 183). Baisanghar was Prince Daniyal's son (baptised as Don Carlos).

[106] Shahriyar, "who had hid [*sic*] himself in the harem, was brought out by a eunuch and made to pay homage to Dawar Bakhsh. He was then thrown into prison and blinded" (Eraly, *Mughal Throne*, 295).

had the crown. After three weeks' march he comes to Agra, the object of his race, where he claims the Imperial title, and by the kotwal and his favourites was proclaimed King by name of Padshah Shah Jahan. Then, giving notice from the goozul-khana to Asaf Khan how far and with what success he had travelled, as also that so long as Sultan Bulaqi was living his greatness was but counterfeit. Asaf Khan, fleshed in former homicides and not caring how, so he could fix the diadem upon Khurram, at that time tottering, he makes Raza Bahadur of his counsel, who forthwith without examination of right or wrong posts to Lahore and with Asaf Khan's keys enters the hamam where the innocent princes were, suspectless of danger, and with horrid speed and infernal cruelty strangles them all to lead Khurram through a bloody path to the Crown.[107]

> Such is th' insacred famine of a Crown,
>   That is to satisfy before men fail;
> What in their way doth stand all must go down,
>   Seeing bonds of blood and friendship nought avail.

In this lamentable manner died young Bulaqi, after he had been but three months Emperor of Industan.[108] Others were forced to taste of that bitter cup, for in that massacre there accompanied him Sultan Shahriyar, Shah Tahmuraz and Shah Hoshang (the baptised sons of Prince Daniyal), the two sons also of Sultan Parvez, and the two sons of Sultan Murad, all whose carcases were without ceremony buried in a garden in Lahore near to the entrails of Jahangir,[109] but their

---

[107] According to Findly, it was Shah Jahan who, "certain now that his benefactor Asaf Khan was in the ascendant," gave the order that "it would be well if Dawar Bakhsh the son, and (Shahriyar) the useless brother of Khusrau, and the sons of Prince Daniyal, were all sent out of the world" (*Nur Jahan*, 283). This was done on 23 January 1628. Her account is confirmed by B. Prasad (*History*, 402). Mohammed Salih Kambu, whose *Amal-i Salih* gives an account of Shah Jahan's reign, wrote that this action was "conducive to the common good" and "entirely lawful" (cited by Eraly, *Mughal Throne*, 296).

[108] There were rumours that Dawar Bakhsh survived, and a for number of years afterwards pretenders surfaced. De Laet and other contemporary writers appear to confirm Herbert's account, but at least one modern writer accepts that Dawar Bakhsh somehow escaped the assassin. "When Shah Jahan returned from the Deccan," S. M. Jaffar writes, "Dawar Bakhsh, the emperor stop-gap, was allowed to escape to Persia" (*The Mughal Empire from Babur to Aurangzeb* [Delhi: Ess Ess Publications, 1974], 222). Adam Olearius claimed that he had seen Bulaqi alive after 1628, and later writers such as Elphinstone in his *History of India* take it up; Beni Prasad dismisses these accounts as "wholly unreliable, being opposed to a mass of clear Persian evidence" (*History*, 402, n.12). The "Persian evidence" is found in Monshi: "The five princes thus done to death were Sultan Shahriyar, who had been blinded; Davar Bakhsh" . . . "known as Sultan Bolagi and entitled Sir Shah" (*Shah Abbas*, 3: 1293).

[109] Herbert's account is derived from that of De Laet (*Empire*, 240), who is his source for stating that Raza Bahadur carried out the murders at Shah Jahan's behest. The *firman*

heads, as an undoubted testimony of their death, were sent to Khurram, therewith to glut his infernal ambition.

Khurram proclaimed Great Mughal.

The murder of the royal blood of Industan, quickly spreading itself, affrights the whole realm, and being known to Jahan Khan, Sayid Khan and other *umrah*, they were overcharged with fearful apprehensions, for albeit they see Asaf Khan was guilty, nevertheless they want power to question him, especially for that they knew very well it was acted by Khurram's approbation if not procuration, so as all the remedy that was left was only to heap a thousand maledictions on their heads and the crave vengeance from above to compensate this villainy. Khurram sees the Empire storming at him, but his incantations quickly quiet them, so as after long turmoil, having through the Ocean of Inconstancy arrived at the port of greatness and ease as he thought, with great pomp he made his intrado into Agra, and forthwith gave orders for his coronation, which accordingly by a general assembly of the *umrah* and nobles of his Empire was performed. Then by a proclamation he assumes the name Sultan Shahbeddin Mohammed, for albeit we give him the name of Mughal, they call him Padshah, that is *rex magum*, concerning which word I have formerly given my apprehensions, and may add that as Moghul in Arabic signifies "unknown" or "a stranger," the same probably was first imposed by the Arab stipendiaries upon the Tartars' first invasion or when Tamerlane's race made it the principal seat of their Empire; upon the like occasion the word Welsh was here imposed by the Saxon, after which, A.D. 1628, A.H. 1008, he orders the affairs of his monarchy, placing and displacing at his pleasure. His father's seraglio was by his appointment shut up, Queen Nur Mahal and her three daughters confined,[110] Asaf Khan nevertheless made second in the Empire. Next him, Mahabat Khan was advanced, Abdullah Khan released, and Khan Zad Khan re-established in the Viceroyalty of Bengal. Ambassadors from Persia, Arabia, Tartary and Deccan repair with presents to the court and to congratulate his access to the crown. Divers rajahs, as Rajah Kishan Singh from Nagor,[111] Azam Khan from Ajmer, the

---

ordering the princes' deaths was received by Asaf Khan on 21 January, and it was he, according to modern scholars, who carried it out (Findly, *Nur Jahan*, 284).

[110] De Laet thought that Nur Jahan went with Asaf Khan to Agra "and personally handed over the royal treasure to Shah Jahan" (Findly, *Nur Jahan*, 284). However, it appears that she was made prisoner by her brother and then taken to Lahore, where she lived in retirement until her death (1645) with an allowance from Shah Jahan.

[111] Kishan Singh [*Radgee Kessingh*] was the son of Bhim Singh.

puissant Rajah Man Singh, Jagat Singh[112] and Gaj Singh[113] from Fatehpur with
fifty thousand horse move in solemn state to Agra, whither after six weeks repaired
also Asaf Khan, Sadiq Khan, Iradat Khan, Rostam Khan, Safi Khan, Mir Jumla[114]
and other principal *umrah*, whom he affectionately received, remitting and putting
in perpetual oblivion all offences whatsoever committed during his rebellion, after
which he proclaims a jubilee which was celebrated with all manner of sports and
pleasures imaginable.

Khurram in this manner attained the highest dignity of the Eastern
world, guarded by a power in his opinion irresistible. Howbeit, these sins have
apparently, even in our own times, drawn down the heavy judgment of God Almighty, both in taking his beloved wife away, since when he made his daughter
by that dead lady his wife,[115] incest of so high a nature that this year his Empire
was so wounded with God's arrows of plague, pestilence and famine as this thousand years before was never so terrible. The sword also seems to threaten him,
the Persians having snatched from him Karman and Kandahar, the Tartar Kabul, Sharif al-Mulk[116] endangers Thatta, Rajah Jajhar [Singh][117] with his Koolis
troubles Burhanpur, and two counterfeit Bulaqis have lately sown the seeds of an
universal rebellion. The event is in the hands of God, who even in an infidel hates
the sins of blood, incest and dissimulation. We will close therefore with a caveat
to Khurram from a heathen, but of more reason and temperance:

What? That great Jupiter the world that shakes,
When Aetna's thunderbolts in hands he takes,

---

[112] Jagat Singh [*Tzettersingh*], rajah of Kangra, was the son of Rajah Basu. He had
supported Shah Jahan during his rebellion (B. Prasad, *History*, 332), but was pardoned
through the intercession of Nur Jahan. "In order to satisfy her," Jahangir wrote, "the pen
of pardon was drawn through the record of his faults" (*TJ* 2. 289).

[113] Gaj Singh I [*Ghessingh*] was the maharajah of Jodhpur. In 1623 he had been part
of the Imperial army sent against Khurram (B. Prasad, *History* 333). In 1624 his sister
had married Prince Parvez, as Jahangir noted, "according to my order" (*TJ* 2. 295).

[114] Mir Jumla [*Mirgomlay*], whose real name was Mohammed Amin, was a Persian,
who, Jahangir tells us, after good service with the Shah, "set the face of loyalty towards
this Court. . . . As he had come with devotion and sincerity I conferred favours and kindness on him" (*TJ* 2. 2–4). Jahangir appointed him Examiner of Petitions and promoted
him further, making him a *Khansama* (steward) and finally he achieved the rank of *diwan*. See also B. Prasad, *History*, 386.

[115] Mumtaz Mahal died at Burhanpur on 7 June 1631. Shah Jahan, far from marrying his own daughter, "went into seclusion for two years, reappearing, according to legend, with eyeglasses and hair now completely grey" (Findly, *Nur Jahan*, 51).

[116] This is the same Sharif al-Mulk who held Thatta for Prince Shahriyar. He apparently wanted to "make himself independent in the kingdom of Tatta," at least according
to De Laet (*Empire*, 240).

[117] Jajhar Singh [*Radgee Joogh*] was the son of Bir Singh Bundela.

Think'st thou from him who all the world doth see,
In acting those deep crimes conceal'd to be?

To conclude, at our being in this country Khurram came within two days' journey of Surat, and in ceremony the English ships thundered out his approach and
welcome by two hundred great shot, which he afterwards thankfully accepted of.
And being that we are now leaving the Mughal's kingdom, accept in good part
that little gleaning I made of the language there spoken, which by commerce and
near neighbourhood I find hath mixed with it much of the Persian.

God,	*Allough,* and *Choddaw.*	Merchant,	*Souldager.*
King,	*Patchaw.*	A great man,	*Buddye-murd,*
Queen,	*Begun.*	A poor man,	*Fouckeire.*
Nobleman,	*Nobobb.*	A good man,	*Coob Adam.*
Military Officer,	*Umbrau.*	A bad man,	*Badd Adam.*
Souldier,	*Suppya,* and *Haddee.*	A Christian,	*Fringy.*
Gentleman,	*Beg.*	A Mahometan,	*Muſſalmone.*
A Priest,	*Moolae.*	Sea,	*Deriaw.*
A Judge,	*Hackame.*	Fire,	*Augi.*
A City,	*Sheer.*	Devil,	*Shytan.*
A Village,	*Gome.*	Clouds,	*Boddily.*
A Castle,	*Chute.*	A Captain,	*Cappitain* or *Umbrau.*
A Prison,	*Bande Chonna.*	Pylot,	*Noccadame* or *Mollym.*
A House,	*Gur.*	Storm,	*Budde Cane.*
A Fort,	*Nunne.*	A Taylor,	*Durge.*
A Rogue,	*Haram zedda.*	Shooe-maker,	*Mouche.*
A Slave,	*Golum.*	Barber,	*Hajame.*
Thief,	*Chure.*	Gold,	*Fawcha.*
Dead,	*Murda.*	Silver,	*Tuppa.*
Alive.	*Cutea.*	A Book,	*Catob.*
Earth,	*Zemme.*	Table,	*Meaſe.*

A Cheſt,	*Sanduck.*	Bread,	*Rute.*
Light,	*Noor.*	Butter,	*Gee,* or *Moccon.*
A Cup,	*Peola.*	Roſe-water,	*Gulob.*
Towel,	*Rumale.*	Lemons,	*Limboo.*
The Court,	*Mahal.*	Orenges,	*Orenge.*
Knife,	*Churre.*	Pepper,	*Merchy.*
Spoon,	*Chimchaw.*	Sugar-candy,	*Sucher-miſſery.*
A Pomgranade,	*Anarkala.*	Cinamon,	*Dolchiny.*
Candle,	*Mumbatee.*	Ginger,	*Sunte.*
Trencher,	*Racheeby.*	Nutmeg,	*Joyfull.*
Carpet,	*Delicha.*	Mace,	*Contry.*
Baſon,	*Goula,* or *Baſea.*	Cloves,	*Clofar.*
Servant,	*Nuſler.*	Dates,	*Cohugure.*
Meat,	*Conna.*	A League,	*Teane curſe.*
Drink,	*Panne.*	A Mile,	*Yeck curſe.*
Cheeſe,	*Panier,* or *Panulo.*		

List of Urdu words [illustration shown above]

Diu. The River Indus.

Not many leagues from Surat, and near the Cambayan Gulf, Gedrosia[118] of old,
is Diu or Dew, in former times called Delta from a resemblance it has with that in
Egypt; *Patala*, *Patalena*, and *Hidaspa* as Arrian, Pliny and Strabo have pleased to
call it. Seated it is at the entrance into the Persian Gulf, in the latitude of twenty-
two degrees eighteen minutes north, confined by Gedrosia, distant from Hormuz due south sixty leagues, and from Cape Comorin[119] two hundred; a stream
encompasses her so that she becomes a peninsula. The haven before the town is
landlocked and so good for anchorage that then at Suwali, Choul, Rajpura and
other havens thereabouts is no better riding, whether you respect the ground or
fort safeguarding them. Alexander, after his victory over Porus returning, upon
the banks of Hydaspes, a branch of Indus, built Bucephala[120] in memory of his
horse that was killed in that great battle, after which he spent six months in easy
marches, till coming to this place he took ship and sailed into Cambay, which
some authors call *Psituleia*. At Alexander's command Nearchus his admiral from
this place began his voyage when he sailed to Hormuz, where he was necessitated
to repair his weather-beaten navy.

The city itself was large, yet by reason of the Portugals' lofty disposition
and humours Christians, it is observed, are less-beloved here then in many other
places. 'Twas a town of good trade when it afforded opium, asafoetida (most of
which is from Lahore), *puccio*,[121] cotton, indigo, myrabolum, sugar, arrack, agates, carnelians, diaspries,[122] chalcedony, haematites, pearl and elephants' teeth
in great quantities, but since Surat and Cambay, her neighbours, have attracted
the English and Dutch thither, her traffic is become small and her other allure-
ments inconsiderable. What she now most boasts of is a castle which was built
after long fight and much bloodshed by Albuquerque the famous Portugal *Anno*
1515, through whose cost and care it was so much bettered that at this day it
may compare with any other, either fort or maritime town in that part of the
Orient. Nor could it ever have succeeded had not bribes, threats and other devices drawn belief into the pagans that their desire to have so many castles and
maritime forts was only to defend themselves in parts where they were altogether
strangers, but it appeared afterwards that avarice, rapine and lust rather allured

---

[118] Gedrosia corresponds to the modern-day Baluchistan Province in south-west
Pakistan. It stretches from the Indus river to the south-eastern border of Iran. For Diu,
see Singh, *India*, 662–64.

[119] Known now as Kanyakumari, this is in Travancore at the southernmost point of
the Indian sub-continent, where the waters of the Bay of Bengal, the Indian Ocean and
the Arabian Sea meet. It is also the name of the town there.

[120] For Bucephala, see Q. Curtius Rufus 9.3.23. The town was on the west bank of
the Hydaspes (Jhelum) river, which was the site of Bucephalus's death.

[121] Marble (Italian).

[122] Mod. *Diaspore*. It is a transparent, pearly mineral.

them, even as Osorius their bishop in *Vita Emmanuelis* 11 *libro. Fol.* 347 spares not to speak concerning them: "*Etsi Lusitani imprimis acer cupiebant ad se defend- endas; postea tamen visum est, perspeciem foederiae & amicitiae, dominationem queri & tyrannidem agitari . . .,*"[123] which caused such turmoils that in no other part of India they found so long or such considerable resistance, partly from their own valour, but chiefly by help of *Mirbocem*[124] and those Mamelukes which Qansuh al-Ghuri,[125] the then great Sultan of Egypt, sent thither to quell their insolen- cies. Notwithstanding, by the downfall of that great Sultan, which was not long after by Selim the First[126] about the year 1516, the Portugals by little and little grew victorious, though to obtain it Lourenço de Almeida, the son to their Vice- roy, the most excellent of all their captains, at that time in the achievement per- ished. Upon the banks of Indus and in this Gedrosian territory it was where Al- exander left the memorials of his Indian conquests to amuse future ages, making his camp, cabins, mangers, horses' bits and armour of a more than ordinary size, a mean to make the truth of his conquests suspicable.

The River Indus, by Pliny called *Sandus, Sinthbus* by Arrian, is now named *Scynd* or *Sinde*, and in twenty-three degrees fifteen minutes latitude (some ob- serve twenty-four degrees forty minutes) and west variation sixteen degrees thirty minutes, commixes in two great ostiums (Thévet imagines seven, one of which is called *Sagappa* in Ptolemy) with the oceans, for after three thousand miles flux from the Kashmirian, or as Mela in his third book, the Parapamis- sian mountains, part of Caucasus, which some call *Naucracos* or *Nagracus*, being in the Scythian language the same which *Moschici* and *Nyphatis* are in the Ar- menian, *viz.* mountains covered with snow, like to the Alps and our Snowdon, in her descent receiving growth from many notable rivers which from that and other hills derive their origin, mellow India, and at last exonrate themselves into the Indus, from whose name the most noble part of the universe in termed. The rivers are Behat, Ravi, *Damiadee, Ob-chan*, Vehat etc., of old named Hydaspes[127]

---

[123] Although the Portuguese sincerely desired to defend themselves, it was seen af- terwards that what looked like alliance and friendship was a plan for domination and the imposition of tyranny.

[124] Unidentified. It may refer to Barakat II ibn Mohammed, Emir of Mecca (1497– 1525), an ally of Qansuh al-Ghuri who also fought against the Portuguese.

[125] Sultan al-Ashraf Qansuh al-Ghuri [*Campson Gaurus*], the Mameluke ruler of Egypt 1500–1516, was killed in the battle described below. Details of the battle and its aftermath, including the capture of Cairo, are reported by Don Juan of Persia (*Relaciones*, 121–23). His beautiful mosque, intended as a tomb, is one of Cairo's great landmarks.

[126] Selim I "the Grim" was Ottoman sultan 1512–1520. He invaded Western Persia and occupied Tabriz (1514). After that he evacuated Tabriz, invaded Syria and defeated the Egyptians, who were allies of the Persians, near Aleppo (1516), the battle to which Herbert refers here.

[127] Hydaspes is the Jhelum; its Sanskrit name was *Vitasta* and the Mughals called it *Behat*. However, Banerjee notes that "The Nilab . . . is the upper Indus and not the

from which Hydaspes took his name who was King of Media, Chenab, Beas,
'twixt which and Hydaspes is the kingdom of Aria, now Khorasan, of old inhabited by the Astaceni, Massani,[128] Prasii[129] etc., Adris, Obitarmis, Coas, Suastes,
Bibasis, Melzidus, Hirotas, Sutlej, Ravi etc. Let it not be improper to tell you
that Scaliger has it from some that at the estuarium or mouth of Indus the new
moon increases the sea, which at Calicut is at the full and at Socotra found to be
very different.

Behat or the Kabul river, as De Laet and other European writers wrongly suppose." He
also explains that further confusion is caused by the fact that "even in the 16th century a
city named Nilab stood on the east bank of the Indus at a small distance below its con-
flux with the Kabul river" (De Laet, *Empire*, 5 n. 5). De Laet himself noted that "all the
geographers who up to the present have drawn maps have made a great error in locating
the mouth of this river Indus" (*Empire*, 3). Herbert seems to be confusing Behat with Vehat (the Punjabi name), which he calls *Wiby*. The connection with the King of Media is
ahistorical.

[128] The Massani are mentioned by Diodorus Siculus (17.102.4) and are identified by
Heckel as the Ossadians (Curtius 296 n. 48).

[129] The Prasii [*Pissei*] are mentioned by Q. Curtius Rufus as living "on the far bank
of the Ganges" (9.2.3).

[PART VI: ARABIA AND PERSIA]

Arabia the Happy.

On the other side the gulf in Arabia the Happy is Muscat or Mascat-Saif, not far from that promontary which is now named Ras al-Hadd,[1] formerly *Corodamum* and *Maces* in Ammianus *Lib.* 23, almost nadir to the Tropic of Cancer. I dare not conclude that this was that *Raamah* which took name from Raoma son of Chuch son of Cham, by Ptolemy called *Rhaguma* and *Rhegma* in Ezekiel 27: 22: "The merchants of Sheba," a city in South Arabia whence came the Queen of Sheba, and not from Ethiopia, "Kush" being misinterpreted, to visit Solomon, "and Raamah were thy merchants, etc."[2] Howbeit, 'tis certain it has been more populous and noted then at this present, though now she begins, since Hormuz was lost, to revive, being the port, haven and defence for frigates, junks[3] and other vessels of war and trade belonging in these parts to the Portugal, who first conquered the isle *Anno Domini* 1507, and after the adjacent towns, Kalhat, Karyat, Suhar, *Orfaza* and other places which till then were under the Hormuzian Empire.[4] About which time Saif ud-din[5] was king, and, being in nonage, unhappily ruled over

---

[1] Ras al-Hadd [*Rozelgate*] is "the most easterly point of the coast of Arabia" (*HJ* 769). Herbert uses the Portuguese corruption of the Arab name.

[2] Herbert is not quite accurate; the text reads: "The merchants of Sheba and Raamah, they were thy merchants."

[3] Nowadays usually applied to Chinese ships, this word referred in Herbert's time to "a large Eastern ship" (*HJ* 472). The word was used by Odoric of Pordenone several times, by Purchas (1. 2, 43) and many other writers.

[4] Karyat [*Curiate*] and Suhar [*Soar*] are towns adjacent to Muscat. Kalhat [*Calajate*] is a port city on the coast of Oman. See Serjeant, Map 2 (between 64–65), "The littoral of the Indian Ocean." All these places were subject to the king of Hormuz, whose governor resided in Kalhat (R. B. Serjeant, *The Portuguese Off the South Arabian Coast: Hadrami Chronicles with Yemeni and European Accounts of Dutch Pirates Off Mocha in the Seventeenth Century* [Oxford: Oxford University Press, 1963], 11). The Portuguese first showed up in 1529. *Orfaza* has not been identified.

[5] King (actually Emir) Saif ed-din III was about thirteen at the time. In 1507 Albuquerque, after capturing the city, had restored the deposed ruler, Saif ed-din's father, and then forced a treaty on Hormuz in return for his assistance. The city was burned after a revolt against the Portuguese (1515), but in 1523 Saif ed-din signed another treaty with

by Azar, a spiteful eunuch who for no occasion that is known but from the perverseness of his nature, not only put this town to flames but had wellnigh ruined his master's whole empire. Torus, the King's brother, after that commanded here with Mahmoud, the King's son, who was poisoned by Nur ed-din, the second officer in degree, after which it was betrayed to the Turks by Jacquez, a Portugal, but soon after recovered. Howbeit, next year by bribery the Turks re-entered, and so soon as Piri Beg the Pasha[6] had planted a colony there he returned, but ere he got home hears of its revolt and the slaughter of his men in garrison, which news so amazed him that he went to Mecca as a pilgrim, but by command of Suleiman the Great, who would not pardon him that mishap, was forced thence and for a reward of his fifty years' service beheaded and his great estate forfeited, notwithstanding all which it now obeys the Portugal. The town is seated in a plain 'twixt two rising mountains; a ditch and parapet drawn from one hill to the other so environ her that to some she seems inacessible. The castle is large, well-manned and stored with great ordinance.

The seventeenth of December we took ship in the *William* for Gamrun in Persia; the *Exchange*, the *Hart* and other gallant ships went along with us and above three hundred slaves were put aboard whom the Persians had bought in India, *viz.* Parsis, Hindus, Bandaris[7] and others, whence it is true what one says, that ships are a noble advantage, for besides the transporting of riches and rarities from place to place, they consociate the most remote regions of the earth by participation of commodities and other excellencies to each other, which, besides the ease we have (especially in hot zones) by that kind of accommodations in travel, now having coasted India and Arabia where the sweetest spices and gums do grow, some have found that the spirits issuing from their flowers have so perfumed the air when gently blowing towards passengers as they have discovered whereabouts they were even when no land was in sight of them. The eighteenth day we crossed the Tropic, and the next day elevated the North Pole twenty-four

---

them. The Turks sent a fleet against the Portuguese in 1546, and in 1552 Piri Ra'is (see below) tried to capture Hormuz and Bahrain. For details see Abdul Aziz Awad, "The Gulf in the Seventeenth Century," *Bulletin of the British Society for Middle Eastern Studies* 12 (1985): 123–34.

   [6] Piri Ra'is, or Muhiddin Piri ibn Mehmet [*Peri Beg*] (c. 1465–1554), was a Turkish admiral (*ra' is*). He captured Aden (1547) and Muscat (1551). He then unsuccessfully attacked Hormuz (1552) after which his fleet was scattered by mist and bad weather (Serjeant, *Portuguese*, 179). He was executed at the age of eighty-nine by order of Suleiman I for his failure to support the Ottoman Governor of Basra against the Portuguese in the Persian Gulf. Piri Rais is well-known for having produced an early Turkish world-map (1513) and for writing *The Book of Navigation*, or *Kitab-i Bahriye* (1521–1525). For details, see Gregory McIntosh, *The Piri Rais Map of 1513* (Athens, GA: Georgia University Press, 2000).

   [7] Bandaris [*Bannaras*] are "the class of people (of a low caste) who tend to the cocopalm gardens [in Bombay]" (*HJ* 57).

degrees odd minutes. The Gulf in this place was straitened, the shores of Carmania[8] and Arabia in this form appearing to us.

The Persian Gulf [illustration not shown]

Arabia.

Arabia, denominated from Arabus,[9] son of Apollo and Babylonia, at this day is more obscured then it was in ancient times, such time as it was the seminary of sundry famous men. No part bred better physicians, mathematicians or philosophers; Galen, Hippocrates, Avicenna, Algazalus, Albumazar, Abubir, Alfarabi, Mohammed bin Isa, bin Abdollah, Said Jub[ayr], bin Kassim, bin Sidi Ali[10] and others, all which were here born or sprung or hence educated, the Arabic tongue having so enchanted these men that it is a common hyperbole the saints in Heaven and those in Paradise speak it. Albeit, as in it the holy Decalogue was given, so also there was hatched the delusive al-Quran, but if gums aromatic, succulent fruits, fragrant flowers and such delicacies that can captivate thy sense, say then Arabia is the Phoenix of the East, with Danaeus[11] the epitome of delight,

---

[8] Carmania is modern-day Kerman Province in Iran, which stretches from Azerbaijan to Baluchistan.

[9] See Pliny, *Natural History* 7. 197.

[10] Hippocrates of Cos (c. 460–375 B.C.E.) was the great physician of the ancient world. Unfortunately the so-called *Corpus Hippocraticum*, a collection of writings ascribed to him, is of a later date. G. E. R. Lloyd has translated it (Harmondsworth: Penguin Books, 1978). Avicenna is Ibn Sina (980–1037), the eminent Persian physician, astronomer, and commentator on Aristotle; Algazalus is Abu Hamid Mohammed al-Ghazzali (1058–1111), Persian philosopher, theologian, and Sufi mystic. He attacked Aristotle in a work entitled *The Incoherence of Philosophers* and wrote *The Alchemy of Happiness* in Persian. Albumazar is Abu Maskar Ja' afar ibn Mohammed (c. 800–885), the great Persian astronomer. Abubir may refer to Abu Bakr ibn Tufail (c. 1105–1185), a philosopher and scientist born in Granada and died in Morocco; Mohammed bin Isa is probably Ali bin Isa, a ninth-century astronomer who measured the earth's circumference. Said Joob is probably Ibn Jubayr (1145–1217), an Arab astronomer, geographer, traveller, and poet who died in Egypt, but may possibly be the Persian theologian Abu Ali al-Jubbai (c. 849–916); Bin Kassim is Abu al-Qasim al-Zahravi (936–1013), an Arab philosopher, doctor, and scientist from Andalusia. The others have not been identified. For Mfarabi see above 000.

[11] Lambert Dané (1530–1595), a French Protestant lawyer, theologian, and epitomiser of Calvin, was Professor of Theology at the Universities of Geneva, Leiden, and Ghent. His books include *Ethica Christianae libri tres* (1577), translated by Thomas Twyne as *Discourse of Christian Natural Philosophy* (1578) and *Examen libri de duabus in Christi natalis* (1581). He attacked witches in *Les sorciers, dialogue très utile et très necessaire pour ce temps* (1564), which was translated into English as *A Dialogue of Witches* (1575). He also edited Tertullian (1565).

and with St. Augustine paradise, *"ex propter aurum, thus & myrrham."*[12] By the ancients it was termed *Eudemonia*, also *Panchaya, Terra Beatissima*, and with the poet, as India sends ivory, so Sabaea gums.

'Tis usually divided into three: *Deserta, Petraea* and *Felix*. Deserta is also called *humilis, profunda* and *aspera* by Servius, Lucian and Aristides,[13] Petraea from Petra, the metropolis built by Petrusius, the fifth son of Mizraim the Egyptian, Genesis 9:14,[14] for indeed this part of Arabia is more sandy than stony, so as 'tis more properly called *Inferior* by Strabo, *Nabataea* by Ptolemy, *Barrha* by Castoldus,[15] *Razbal al-Baga* by the inhabitants and *Bengacalla* by Zeiglerus.[16] Felix[17] has like variation; by Pliny it is called *Sabaea, Mamotta* by Solinus, *Ajman* and *Jaman* by bin Ali, which comprehends only the south part or Hadhramaut,[18] and Nabataea, so named from Naboth the first-born son of Ishmael.[19] This, with the other two Arabias, was first called Ethiopia, to which was added *Asiatica* to distinguish it from that in Africa; the name it took from Cush, was watered by Gibon, a branch of Euphrates, which empties itself with Pison, that runs

---

[12] Because of the gold, frankincense and myrrh.

[13] Marius (or Maurus) Servius Honoratus (fourth century C.E.), Roman grammarian who wrote the commentaries on Virgil which plagued many generations of schoolboys; Lucian of Samosata (c. 114–200) was a Greek barrister and satirist who wrote, amongst his more amusing works, *De dea Syria*, a very serious treatise on the goddess Astarte; Aristides of Miletus (fl. c. 100 B.C.E.) was the author of a collection of obscene stories, the *Milesiaka*, quoted by Lucian and Petronius, but he was also the reputed compiler of collections of historical anecdotes.

[14] Herbert's biblical reference is mistaken by one chapter. Genesis 10:13–14 reads "And Mizraim begat Ludim, and Anamim, and Lehabim, and Naphtahim. And Pathrusim, and Casluhim (out of whom came Philistim), and Caphtorim." Mizraim was the son of Ham. By "Petrusius" Herbert means Pathrusim.

[15] Giacomo Gastaldi [*Castoldus*] (1505–1566) was an Italian map-maker who worked with Ramusio. He designed over one hundred maps, many of which were used by Ortelius for his atlas, including the ones of India and Persia. His most famous production was the posthumously-printed *Asiae novae descriptio* (1574).

[16] Jakob Ziegler [*Zeiglerus*] (1471–1549) was a Bavarian humanist, geographer, and map-maker who worked at Ingolstadt. His most significant contributions to cartography included a map of Scandinavia (1532) and one of Palestine, presumably the one Herbert is referring to here.

[17] Minucius Felix (fl. 200–400) was a Roman lawyer who wrote *Octavius*, a dialogue between a Christian and a pagan on the various religious subjects. There was an edition by Balduinus (Heidelberg, 1560) and a more modern translation by R. E. Wallace is available (New York: Kessinger Reprints, 2004).

[18] Hadhramaut or Hadramawt is the eastern part of modern-day Yemen.

[19] Ishmael was Abraham's son by Hagar. The Muslims venerate him as the ancestor of all Arabs and consider him a prophet. His progeny of twelve sons is mentioned in Genesis 25:2 and is reiterated in the Quran.

through part of Susiana,[20] into the Persian Gulf. Herodotus distinguishes these from the African Ethiopians by their hair, which may be combed, the other not, and accordingly were differenced in Xerxes's army, which was a world of men not less than five millions.

In the first is Kedar, oft named in the Psalmist; in the second the mounts Horeb and Sinai, as also Jathrib and Medina, places of account among the Saracens. The Happy is now called *Mamuta*, is unhappy in the *Medina Telnabi*, but otherwise in being Job's birthplace. It has also Saba, by Ptolemy called *Save*, now named *Samiscashac*, and many other towns of note as *Adedi*, *Neopolis*, *Phocidis*, *Abissa*, *Teredon*, *Areopolis*, *Acadra*, Jathrib,[21] *Alata*, *Acyna*, *Munichiates*, Amba, and, more near the Persian Gulf, *Ocetis* and *Cana*, with others converted at this day into other names, as Aden, Mocha, *Zieth*, Mecca, *Zidim*, *Jemina-babrim*, *Huguer*, Medina, *Zarval*, Oran, *Synon*, Merbat, Mareb, *Danchally*, Muscat, *Imbum*, Zama, *Moffa*, *Lazzach*, *Gubelcama*, Meshed Ali, *Cusa* or *Cusace*, *Damarchana*, *Barag*, Al-Tawr,[22] some of which places are by authors placed in the stony Arabia, and many more now under the Ajamites or Saracens, but in old time these were distinguished into the *Sabaei*, whence Guilandinus[23] says was the queen

---

[20] Susiana or Sosiana is the region of Persia named for the old capital of the Persian Empire, Susa.

[21] Jathrib or Yathrib is the old name for Medina, the burial-place of Mohammed and the second holiest city in Islam; Ptolemy called it *Lathrippa* (*Geography* 6. 7. 139). It was the main city of Agra, a district in what is now called Saudi Arabia.

[22] Many of these place-names are little more than locations in Ptolemy's *Geography* and are difficult to match with modern towns. *Neopolis* is Nablus, now on the West Bank, which was ancient Shechem and was re-established by Vespasian in 72 C. E. *Teredon* is a Gulf coastal city near modern Basra where Nebuchadnezzar may have built a hanging garden; it is about 200 miles from Babylon. *Areopolis* is now Rabbath-Moab in Israel. Amba [*Ambe*] is located by Ptolemy in Arabia Felix (*Geography* 6. 7. 137); Merbat may refer to Ras Merbat in modern Oman; Zama is in Numidia (North Africa, modern Tunisia), in the vicinity of which Scipio Africanus defeated Hannibal; *Mareb* was the capital of the ancient Kingdom of Sabaea from the fifth century B.C.E. and is now in Yemen. Meshed Ali [*Massad*] on the Euphrates is the holy city of the Shi'a Muslims which contains the shrine of the Imam Reza and which grew up after the decline of Tus, the birthplace of the poet Ferdowsi, author of the *Shahnameh* (for details see Robert Byron, *The Road to Oxiana* [Harmondsworth: Penguin Books, 1992], 83–85). *Lazzach* may refer to the old Sultanate of Lahej, which included Aden and is now part of Yemen. Al-Tawr [*Eltarch*] is at the entrance to the Gulf of Suez (see Serjeant, *Portuguese*, 99–100). *Jashrip* could be the "Djasariyah" mentioned in a Hadrami chronicle of 1538–1539, but of whose exact identity Serjeant is uncertain; he suggests it might be "Khwar Maksar" (*Portuguese*, 95 n. 3) near Aden. It could be just as misprint for *Jathrip* (Medina).

[23] Melchior Wieland [*Guilandinus*] (c. 1520–1589) was a German botanist, natural historian, and pharmacologist who taught at the University of Padua. In 1561 he became the Director of the Botanical Gardens at Padua. He also travelled extensively, visiting Syria, Palestine, and Egypt, and at one point was captured by Barbary pirates and held by

that came to hear Solomon's wisdom, and the three Magi who had the honour
of presenting their offerings unto Christ. And 'tis not without reason that this
part of Arabia abutting upon the Persian Gulf from against the island *Babrim*
mentioned by Eratosthenes,[24] where the city Calah was (now called *Obollach*),[25]
as far as Muscat was the Sabaean land, which from the abundance of gold there
found was reputed Ophir, though indeed both Sabaea and Ophir are near Ganges. From the plenty of myrrh and frankincense it was called *Thusifera Regio*,
most abounding near the hilly country of *Merbat* and *Segar*, neighbouring the
land of Hadhramaut or *Atramit*, as Pliny. And Pomponius Mela thus *Lib.* 3, *c.* 18:
"*Sabei Arabiae Felicis tenent partem ostio maris Persici proximi Carmaniae* (meaning
opposite to it) *ubi montes Arabi sunt;*"[26] albeit many suppose that Saba or Sheba,
which Strabo *Lib.* 16 calls *Metroba*, was in the western part of Arabia near to the
Red Sea, in regard Mocha is reputed to be "*portus Adramisicum, Sachaliti & Ziagri
promontorio proximum*," by some called *Atomum*.

I take leave to digress a little farther. After the constitution of tongues,
which was about 120 years after the Flood, when such as were of one language
separated from the rest and planted by themselves, the earth being waste before
them, Nimrod sovereigning at Babylon, his brother Havilah seated his colony in
Susiana. Seba, Raamah, Sabbata and Sabbatheca (his other brethren), doing the
like in Arabia, so 'tis conjectured that Seba or Sheba sat down in that part which
extends from Ezion-geber in the stony Arabia to Aden along the west banks of
the Red Sea, where he built a city after his own name from whence 'tis supposed
the Queen came that visited Solomon. Sabbata planted the south of Arabia and
Raamah or Rhegma that north part which neighbours Basra over against the
Kingdom of Luristan[27] where they built cities after their own names, mentioned
in the 27 of Ezekiel.

Also, I cannot but note how that the Hebrew (Chaldaic, Arabic and Syriac drill from the Hebrew, which is the mother-tongue to all others), Greek and
Latin, which in their times were epidemic, are not now anywhere spoken save by

---

them for some years. After his return he took up his university work once again. He also
wrote a treatise on Pliny's *Natural History* (1575).

[24] Eratosthenes (c. 276–194 B.C.E.), Greek mathematician, geographer, and astronomer who invented a system of latitude and longitude and was the first to make a
map of the earth and calculate its circumference. He is cited as an authority by Ptolemy,
Strabo, and Pliny, but his works are now known only in an epitome by Cleomedes, a later
Greek astronomer of uncertain date.

[25] Calah [*Calach*] was "an important city of Assyria" (Charles F. Pfeiffer and Howard De Vos, *Historical Geography of Bible Lands* [New York: Moody Publishers, 1967],
3).

[26] The Sabaeans of Arabia Felix live in the part of the coastal area of the Persian Sea
which is next to Carmania, where the Arabian mountains are.

[27] Luristan is the area of Persia extending from Meshed Ali to Fars.

derivative, and that the heathen gods and goddesses Jove, Saturn, Mars, Apollo, Juno, Diana, Venus and thirty thousand more, as Varro says, once idolised the earth over, are now nowhere invocated, for indeed oracles ceased at the Passion of our Saviour. The Arabic nevertheless at this day is of as large extent as where Mohammed is professed, so as the habitable part of the world being divided into three equal parts hardly one can be found without it; part of Europe, most of Africa and well-nigh whole Asia in their *al-fatahs*[28] accept of it. Howbeit, 'tis no original but a derivative from the Hebrew, with which it has the same congruity the Italian, French and Spanish have with the Latin; *"Arabica, Hebraica lingua adeo est affinis, ut siquis sit diligenter versatus in Hebraismo possit ante biennium bonam partem illius linguae intelligere,"* saith Postel, "a good Hebrician may in less than two years' study gain the Arabic language," which is the easier to be attained in that, as one observes, *"Unum idemque verbum ita variat, ut multa in paucis comprehendunt."*[29] A little of what we found of most use I shall only insert here.

Comparative word-list [illustration not shown]

Gulf of Persia.

Leaving Arabia, crossed we the Gulf of Persia, which by Plutarch in the "Life of Lucullus"[30] is called the Babylonian Sea, by the Syrians *Yowmacbana*, *Mesendin* and *Deriah Farsistan* by the Persians, *Behar al-Naharim* by the Arabians and by the Turks *Elcatiph*. We sailed also near Cape Gwadar (*Dendrobosa* of old) within view of that other promontary we call Cape Goadel,[31] which is in twenty-five degrees north, where we found the compass to vary seventeen degrees fifteen minutes. An infamous port it is, according to the report which that noble knight Sir Robert Sherley made thereof as we passed by, for he and his lady, travelling that way in the year 1613, they with one Newport[32] their captain were allured by the townspeople to go ashore for refreshment, where but for the honesty of a *haji* or

---

[28] *Al-fatah* is the Arabic word for 'victory.'

[29] Thus [whilst] the same word may vary, a lot may be understood from a little.

[30] Lucius Licinius Lucullus (c. 118–56 B.C.E.) was a Roman statesman, soldier and epicure with a particular interest in gastronomy, for which latter his name became a by-word. He fought successfully against both Mithridates VI of Pontus and Tigranes II of Parthia, defeating both of them at the Battle of Artaxata (68 B.C.E.) before retiring to pursue his more peaceful hobby, which included giving dinners that bore the name "Lucullan" as they were so opulent and delicious. We will hear more of him later.

[31] Foster believed, probably correctly, that Herbert had simply given two variants of the same name. There are not two separate promontories (*Herbert*, 305).

[32] Captain Christopher Newport (d. 1617), an East India Company sailor and privateer who "probably knew the Caribbean better than any other Englishman at that time" (Andrews, *Trade*, 314), is best-known as one of the founders of Jamestown in North

Mohammedan priest then in town who gave Sir Robert timely notice, their lives as well as their goods had been hazarded, so perfidious and covetous were those wretches to possess that little money they carried about with them, which is remembered only for caution.

Jask.

The next place of note we saw upon the Carmanian coast was Jask,[33] where the Arctic pole is elevated twenty-five degrees fifty-eight minutes, from Hormuz distant about forty leagues. Pliny calls it *Carpella*, so does Ptolemy, but under twenty-three degrees, another author *Cassandra*, and other some judge it to be that *Thapsacus* where Alexander the Great built vessels for the recruit of his navy. Nevertheless the name it now bears 'tis thought was inspired by that Yazdegerd[34] who was son to Shapur or Sapor once King of Carmania and at that place buried. Albuquerque, having reduced this place under the Crown of Portugal, built a large castle here and strengthened it with seventeen pieces of brass cannons, which when our countrymen took it from them in the year 1623, thereto provoked by the death of Captain Shilling,[35] who was unhappily slain there, then was found besides the other a cannon-petro, two whole culverins, two demi-culverins, four sakers of brass[36] and one thousand muskets unadvisedly put into the hands of the Persian soon after the destruction of Hormuz, both which he

---

America (1606). He later operated in the West Indies and died of fever at Bantam. For more details, see Foster, *England's Quest*, 230–31.

   [33] Herbert always uses the Portuguese form of the name, *Jasques*. It is now known as Ras Jashak or Jask, and is situated on the eastern side of modern-day Oman near the entrance to the Persian Gulf. English goods first landed there on the *James*, an East India Company ship (1614), and Thomas Baker was appointed English agent there. He later made a treaty with Persia.

   [34] Herbert must mean Yazdegerd I, who reigned 399–420.

   [35] Captain Andrew Shilling (d. 1621) worked for the East India Company. He sailed to Surat and Mocha on the *Anne Royal* (1617–1618), a voyage now remembered because William Baffin was his surveyor and Master's Mate, although it was also the ship in which Sir Thomas Roe returned to England. Shilling was again in Surat commanding the *London* (1620), but was mortally-wounded in a fight with Dutch ships in the Persian Gulf. Baffin himself was killed in the engagement on Kish Island against Ruy Freire d'Andrade the next year. Foster says that the castle and its capture "appear to be mythical" (*Herbert*, 305).

   [36] A *cannon-petro*, usually known in England as a cannon-perier, was a short-barrelled 6" calibre gun similar to a mortar. It fired medium-sized stone shot. The name was a corruption of the Spanish *pedrero*, and in fact Herbert calls it a *pedro*. A culverin was a 5.2" calibre gun firing an 18 lb shot; the demi-culverin a 4" calibre gun firing a 9 lb shot. The saker, a 3.65 calibre weapon named after a kind of hawk, fired a solid iron shot weighing 4–6 lb.

now posesseth. They usually fire as many guns as they see ships under sail to give warning to Hormuz and the adjacent towns upon that coast.

Carmania.

Carmania is twofold, *Major* and *Deserta*. The desert along the shore extends from this place to Aria towards the N. E. The greater is contained by Gedrosia to the N. W. and the Parchoatran Hills. Near this is a small isle called *Aphrodisia* by the Greeks, in regard Venus had her shrine there erected, a country in Alexander's time famoused for sword-blades, which were so excellently-tempered that they were preferred before those of Damascus, memorable likewise in that famous march the victorious Greek made (after he had rigged and victualled his navy) through the country of the Oritae into Gedrosia, which did comprehend Cambay, and then into Carmania, where albeit he buried a great part of his army; he nevertheless solemnised the orgies after the wildest manner that was possible. Here we entered the Hormuzian Strait, called the umbrella of the Gulf, which in length stretches from Balsora[37] to Cape Ras al-Hadd. This *fretum*[38] is about nineteen leagues at the most from thence to that promontory Ptolemy calls *Asaborum*. Next day we came in view of Qishm,[39] which by the latitude seems that *Carpella* above-named, where the Portuguese had another fort, whence we heard the pieces giving warning to Larak, an isle formerly called *Aratbos* and upon the opposite coast, of our approach that way, not above four leagues from Hormuz, near which we passed and then came to an anchor before Gamrun,[40] the best port the Persian is master of.

Hormuz.

Hormuz is a kingdom in that part of Carmania Major which Ptolemy calls *Armucum extremum sub 23 deg, 30 min*, where Arabia may be seen, also an isle in the Persian Gulf where the North Pole is elevated by 27 degrees. 'Tis about one league from the continent and in compass about fifteen miles, so as the diameter

---

[37] Modern-day Basra in Iraq. It is sometimes called *Basorah*.

[38] Strait or estuary.

[39] Qishm Island, now part of Iran (as Gheshm), was of strategic importance because it commanded the Indian Ocean entrance to the Persian Gulf. The Portuguese captured it (1507), but Shah Abbas recovered it (1622) with English help, although William Baffin was killed in the fight. It was variously occupied by the Dutch and others afterwards until 1918. For details and a map, see Paul Greenway and David St. Vincent, *Iran* (Hawthorn: Lonely Planet Publications, 1998), 275–78. It should not be confused with Kish Island.

[40] Gamrun [*Gombrawn*] is "the old name in European documents of the place on the Persian Gulf now known as Bandar Abbas." It took its name from Shah Abbas, who captured it from the Portuguese (1614); the original name of the town there had been Gamrun (*HJ* 284). In the same year Edward Connock was appointed the first English Agent

may be five, and, as then the city Hormuz none was more flourishing,[41] so also then the isle Hormuz none was more barren, the isle, which is compared to a ring serving as a foil unto the diamond, agreeable to the poet: "If all the world were made into a ring, / Hormuz the gem and grace should be therein."

For from the year of Our Lord 1507, when it was reduced under the Crown of Portugal by that great captain Alfonso d'Albuquerque, Saif ud-din Shah who was at that time King and rather by reason then force induced to enrol himself a tributary to Manoel [I], remaining still a *titulado*[42] with a yearly pension of 1500 crowns *per mensem* unto the year 1622, such time as Emamqoli Khan, Duke of Shiraz[43] by help of the English commanded by Captain Weddell[44] and other subjected it to the Persian. It was a city for building so elegant, for inhabitants so populous and for trade so singular that it sat as empress, not only alluring merchants and travellers from all parts of the world, but by reason of its marine power derived from Goa the metropolis of the Portuguese in India, gave laws to all the neighbouring potentates, so that simply considered, the isle had nothing; the city nevertheless, being furnished from most parts of the Orient, abounded with all things and was capacitated to supply those other parts with what was desirable or requisite either for the belly or eye. Such was the excellency of the situation of the place for commerce, such the industry and commendable ingenuity of the Portugal who, without ostentation might say *"Qua regio in terris nostri non plena*

---

[41] Hormuz is now a "pleasant little village. . . . Sadly, little of the great medieval settlement remains" (Greenway and St. Vincent, *Iran*, 275). It became legendary for its luxurious life and great wealth.

[42] A person who is entitled to or qualified for something (Spanish).

[43] Emamqoli Khan (d. 1632) [*Emangoly-chawn*], a Georgian whose family name was Undiladze, an emir of the *divan*, was the son of Allah Verdi Khan (see below). He was made Governor of Lar (1610) and Viceregent of Southern Iran by Shah Abbas I in 1613. He was also in charge of blasting operations to improve the water-supply of Isfahan (1619). In 1621, after stout resistance, he captured Qishn from the Portuguese, whose garrison he then massacred (Monshi, *History*, 3: 1202), and in 1628 he was appointed to lead an expedition to Basra, but postponed it because of the death of Shah Abbas (Monshi III, 1299). He was executed by order of Shah Safi (1628–1642), who took over all his lands in an attempt to strengthen his imperial authority. For further details, see V. N. Gabashvili, "The Undiladze Feudal House in Sixteenth to Seventeenth Century Iran According to Georgian Sources," *Iranian Studies* 40 (2007): 37–58.

[44] Captain John Weddell (d. 1639) worked initially for the East India Company. In September 1621 he came with six ships to Suwali, from which location he sailed to Jask and then on to the siege of Hormuz (Foster, *England's Quest*, 309–10). In 1635 he was granted a charter to trade from Africa to the Far East, and later, branching out on his own, became involved in the slave trade. He died in the service of Courteen's Association, which had a charter to trade in India, fighting the Chinese near Macao (Foster, *England's Quest*, 327–28). Weddell was probably the first Englishman to visit China.

laboris?"[45] And, to give them their due, from whose achievements what civilised people are there that have not derived some advantage?

The city itself was compact and yet large enough, though the streets were narrow, the better to evade the heat, which in summer season by being so near the perpendicular glances of the sun and inflamed by the salt and sulphur of the earth which is the main composition of the isle, renders this place as torrid and intolerable to live in as any other part of the universe, which occasioned the inhabitants to sit and sleep in troughs filled with rainwater preserved in jars and tanks, usually falling in June, July and August, the whole isle not affording one spring of sweet water, salt so predominates, which I have seen resembling crystal. And seeing salt, as philosophy teaches, is the first rudiment of life and *omnia sapit*,[46] it needs must here as elsewhere valuable, so as beside silver-shining sand and a little mountain, one half being a mineral of sulphur and the other of salt, both which are esteemed of, it has nothing else worth the consideration, and yet from the advantageous situation thereof the laborious Portugal made it the staple and glory of the world, secured indeed by many natural props, on all sides commanding isles and towns to furnish her, as Basra, Larac (*Azgillia* of old), Qishm (by some called *Quexome* or *Broict*), Kish or Quiago Isle (*Gulsan* in Ptolemy),[47] Angen, Abyan, Heber, Andreve (or De las Pasaros), Kargh or *Carichi*, Babarem (*Ioara* in Pliny), Dozaro, Jask, Kostack and others;[48] "*in initio Persica est insula in qua multi et pretiosi uniones gignuntur*,"[49] in Ptolemy called *Apphana*. So as to the eye of man no place could be more offensive or defensive, several garrisons of the Portugals being constantly maintained in these islands, and yet when the god of nature had decreed a ruin, it could not be withstood but was in some degree miraculously effected, yet at such a time when they least of all suspected it. The houses within were exceeding neatly-furnished with gilded leather and with Indian and Chinese rarities; the bazaar was rich and beautiful, the churches splendid both within and without, the castle so regularly-built and so well-fortified with deep trenches, counterscarp and great ordinance commanding both city and haven that none exceeded it through all the Orient.

---

[45] "What region of the earth is not full of our labour?" (Virgil, *Aeneid* 1. 460).

[46] Gives taste to everything.

[47] Kish or Qais Island [*Keys*] is situated between India and Basra. It is known for pearl-fishing. Marco Polo noted some pearls worn by an Imperial Concubine in China was was told they came from Kish; Greenway and St. Vincent note that it is now "a bizarre place," and call it "a quasi-Disneyland" and "a poor man's California" (*Iran*, 279). They give a detailed map (280); the old cities of Harireh and Saffein were located there.

[48] Abyan [*Abron*], a district rather than a town near Kish; *Dozaro* is al-Djuzur Island in the Husn al-Ghurab group (Serjeant, *Portuguese*, 105 n.4). Kargh is an island on the western edge of the Persian Gulf, now a major oil pumping station.

[49] From the beginning it was a Persian island from which many precious pearls were brought forth.

And for the name, albeit by that it now bears it has been known these 900 years, nevertheless I find it has several other names well-known to antiquity as that of *Organa* and *Gera* to Varrerius,[50] of *Neokrokin* to ben Jonah,[51] *Zarurbi* to the Tartar and *Vorella* to Niger,[52] yet the present name without much variation was known unto Josephus, who in his 1 *lib. De Jud.* calls it *Hormuzia, Omiza* to Pliny, and *Armozon* to Ptolemy, for in the degree of 24 he places the town *Armuza* upon the continent. But by what I find in Curtius, and Curtius out of Dionysius[53] it is the same isle where, when called *Ogyria*, Prince Erythrus (from whom the *Mare rubrum* had its denomination) was buried, agreeable to this tetrastich:

Ogyria looks into the sea, from whence
Carmania lies, and place of residence
Where Princely Erythraeus liv'd, whose fate
This tomb contains, in mountains desolate.

About which Erythrus give me leave to say that as he was a victorious Prince by land, so by some he is reputed to be the great master of marine arts and navigation, by the Greeks especially, by whom he is supposed to be Janus and

---

[50] Gaspar Barreiros (d. 1574) was a Portuguese scholar and geographer from Viseu. His most significant works are *Censura in quendam auctorem, qui sub falsa inscriptione Berosi Chaldei circumsertur* (printed 1598), a study of the authenticity of works ascribed to Berossos (see below, n. 54) and *Commentarius de Orphyria regione* (1561), a treatise on early America.

[51] Ben Jonah, or Benjamin of Tudela (twelfth century), was a Navarrese rabbi and explorer. He travelled in Asia, Africa, and the Middle East as far as Baghdad. He wrote the *Masa'ot Binyamin* (*Voyages of Benjamin*) or *Sefer ha-Masa'ot* (*The Book of Travels*). Arias Montanus issued a Latin translation (1575) which was itself translated into English and made available by Purchas. Marcus Nathan Adler's translation (1907) is available online at *Project Gutenberg*; there is also a recent English version by Joseph Simon (Malibu: Pangloss Press, 1993). See also S. Benjamin, *The World of Benjamin of Tudela* (Madison, NJ: Fairleigh Dickinson University Press, 1995).

[52] L. Calpurnius Piso Niger (d. after 120 B.C.E.), Roman statesman and historian. His only extant work is the *Annales*, a history of Rome from its foundation until his own day. Cicero, Varro, and others cite him as an authority on mythology, although no book of his on that subject is known today.

[53] Dionysius of Halicarnassus (1st cent. B.C.E.) was a rhetorician and historian who worked in Rome. His *Antiquitates Romanae* traced the history of Rome down to the time of the First Punic War. He was highly-regarded in the Renaissance, although not by modern scholars; Robert Estienne edited the Greek text (Paris, 1546) and Herbert could have availed himself of a good Latin translation by Gelenius (Paris, 1549).

Saturnus mentioned in Berossos,[54] from whose example Sesostris[55] first taught it the Egyptians as Bhagavat[56] did the Indians, notwithstanding which we may not conclude that Erythrus gave the first, seeing Noah was the former practitioner in that art, for which we have the best authority, and that it was long before the birth either of Danaus or Neptune, who by reason thereof and their antiquity were ranked in the catalogue of the heathen gods. And without controversy, it was from them that the Phoenicians derived their skill and from them the Egyptians, who instructed the Greeks, (amongst whom the Cretans excelled even to a proverb, *"Cretensis nescit pelagus?*, Is there a Cretan that cannot sail?"), from whom the Romans had their sea-knowledge, and of whom Venice and Genoa were the leaders.

But to return to Erythrus; for proof hereof observe what Pliny *l.* 30, c. 50 records concerning him. *"Inventis ratibus, in Mari Rubro inter insulae ab Erythraeo rege ceptum est navigare etc."*[57] Moreover, so intricate is what we find in reference to these two gulfs, the Arabian and the Persian, and so equivocal the word *Erythraeum* seems, that I cannot refrain from giving you a glance thereof, to the end you may better help in this dilemma. I Kings 9:26 we read that Hiram,[58] King of Tyre, furnished King Solomon with ships and mariners for his voyage to Ophir. Now that Tyre was a city in Phoenicia, part of Syria and frequently mentioned in Holy Writ, is evident, albeit in the original 'tis *Zor*, as we see in the margent of I Kings 9:11, and having the cedars of Libanus at command, [Hiram] permitted Solomon to cut what he pleased towards the building of the temple, so as 'tis undeniable that Tyre was part of Syria, whose chief city was Damascus.[59] Nevertheless, seing Hiram furnished Solomon with wood for his ships that were bound for India, it could not otherwise be then that the place or dock to build

---

[54] Berossos (fl. 290 B.C.E.) was a priest of Bel and the author of a history of Babylon which contains a famous description in Book I of the Babylonian flood-story, and whose work was drawn upon by many historians. He is mentioned several times in Pliny, e.g. *Natural History* 7. 123. 95. His remaining fragments may be found collected in G. B. Verbrugghe and J. M. Wickersham, trans., *Berossos and Manetho: Native Traditions in Ancient Mesopotamia and Egypt* (Jackson: Michigan University Press, 2001).

[55] Sesostris was a semi-legendary Egyptian king who is conjectured to have ruled, if he existed at all, in the 2nd millenium B.C.E. See Pliny. *Natural History* 23. 52, 294 and Herodotus 2. 102–11.

[56] The supreme personality of the godhead.

[57] "After rafts had been invented, people since king Erythraeus began to sail amongst the islands in the Red Sea" (variant text of Pliny, *Natural History* 7.206).

[58] Hiram I reigned 979/8–945 B.C.E.

[59] The city of Tyre is, of course, now in Lebanon and is known as Sur. I Kings 9:11 reads "Now Hiram the king of Tyre had furnished Solomon with cedar trees and fir trees . . ." Tourists are shown "Qabr Hiram," the tomb of Hiram, but scholars now date it to the later Persian period (525–332 B.C.E.). For details, see T. Carter and L. Dunston, *Syria and Lebanon* (Victoria: Lonely Planet Publications, 2004), 345–52.

was at Ezion-geber upon the Red Sea,[60] so that if oaks or other wood fit for ships was cut in Phoenicia or any other part of Syria, then 'tis probable that from Pelusium it was by sledge or camels brought thence to the Red Sea, albeit Solomon's extent of jurisdiction then stretching into that part of Arabia could as well command their wood as haven, for that he had the freedom of those parts and countries appears both by his fleet that rode there and his personal being there, as in [II] Chronicles 8:17.[61] Solomon went to Ezion-geber and to Elat, which was near it, and Hiram sent him ships and servants that were expert in sea-affairs and they accompanied Solomon's servants to Ophir, whence they brought four hundred and fifty talents of gold.

Yet that there was a *Tyrus* also in this sea we learn from Ptolemy and Strabo, who testify that "*Tyrus est insula in alto mari versus austrum, duobus mille stadiis a Carmania distans, in quae Erythrei regis sepulchrum ostenditur, ingens sane tumulus est et sylvestribus plamia consitus; hic Erythraeus his in locis regnavit,*"[62] concerning which Tyre Stephanus agreeth: "*est et Tyrus insula in mare Erythraeo, quam Artemidorus Tylon vocat,*"[63] by which directions it is of some difficulty to find the direct place, seeing the one says this Isle of Tyre is within the Red Sea, the other in the Persian Gulf, which is implied by its vicinity to Carmania. In Ptolemy's sixth geographic table of Asia Major, it is also termed *Tylus*, which, with the neighbouring island *Arathos*[64] was placed under the latitude of twenty-five degrees, but how the ancients distinguished these two gulfs, the Arabian and Persian, is no less abstruse, they seem so confusedly related by authors. For Nearchus, Alexander's admiral in these Arabian seas, giving his master an accompt of the voyage, amongst other observations relates that being by storm driven into the Red Sea, there he had the sight of King Erythrus his tomb, who though he lived in Carmania, died in an island two thousand furlongs from that mainland, which isle Strabo called *Tirnia*,[65] where he was buried. Now, albeit the Red Sea be mentioned in this story, we well know that most writers agree that Nearchus sailed only from Diu or some other part of the River Indus up to Balsora, which is at

---

[60] I Kings 9:26 reads: "And king Solomon made a navy of ships in Ezion-geber, which is beside Elioth, on the shore of the Red Sea, in the land of Edom."

[61] "Then went Solomon to Ezion-geber, and to Elioth, at the sea side in the land of Edom." Herbert paraphrases the next verse, where Hiram meets Solomon with "servants that had knowledge of the sea," who accompany Solomon's servants to Ophir.

[62] Tyre is an island in the deep sea towards the south, two thousand miles distant from Carmania, where the tomb of King Erythraeus is shown; it is a huge mound placed on a flat plain amidst woodlands; here Erythraeus reigned.

[63] "[Tyre] is an island in the Red Sea, which Artemidorus calls 'Tylon.'" Artemidorus of Ephesus (fl. c. 100 B.C.E.) was a geographer whom Strabo often cited, but whose works only exist now in small fragments.

[64] Probably Arad or Arwad, which is actually a group of islands. Some scholars say the name means "shelter" in Phoenician.

[65] Possibly Tiran Island in the Gulf of Aqaba.

the bottom of the gulf, for, as concerning Alexander's sailing from Indus to Socotra where he met his master Aristotle and at his persuasion planted the isle
with a colony of Greeks, little credit is given. Quintus Curtius acknowledges
that the Red Sea took its name from Erythrus the king: "*nomen est inditum ab
Erythraeo rege; propter quod ignari rubere aquas credebant,*" whence it was the ignorant gave out that the water was red.[66] But Pomponius Mela labours hours
to solve it by this distinction: "*Mare Rubrum in duos sinus dividitur, Arabicum &
Persicum, in quos varii fluunt omnes.*"[67] Pliny, the like: "*Mare Rubrum in duos sinus
divisum est; is qui ab oriente est, Persicus appellatur. Ex adverso unde est Arabia, vo-
catur Arabicus,*"[68] from which amphibology[69] it doubtless is that Suidas, Solinus
and others thus report, that Tigris and Euphrates empty themselves at Balsora
into the Red Sea, being well-known that they run into the Persian Gulf, called
Elcatiph and *Mesenden* by some, which to the Red Sea has Arabia Felix and part
of Petraea interposing, so that by what I have said it may appear these two great
gulfs in their terms were convertible.

Tigris and Euphrates.

These two famous rivers are in name the most ancient we have in any story; Divine Writ instructs us that they streamed through Paradise, both of them arising
out of Taurus[70] where called *Periarda*. In their flux through Assyria, which towards Armenia was called *Arrapachisa*, towards Susiana Sittacene[71] from the city

---

[66] "Its name derives from King Erythrus, and for this reason people who know no
better think its waters are red" (Curtius Rufus, *History of Alexander* 8. 9 & 14). Erythraeus's name actually means "red" in Greek.

[67] The Red Sea is divided into two gulfs, the Arabian and Persian, into which all
the various rivers flow.

[68] "The Red Sea is divided into two gulfs; that in the east is called the Persian, and
from the opposite one, whence is Arabia, the Arabian" (variant text of Pliny, *Natural History* 6. 108).

[69] An amphibology is a statement made ambiguous because of grammar. Herbert is
suggesting that later writers like Suidas and Solinus were confused by Pliny and Pomponius Mela, thus mislocating the mouths of the Tigris and Euphrates and confusing the
Persian and Arabian gulfs.

[70] The Taurus Mountains (mod. Toros), "regarded by the ancients as the backbone of
Asia" (Grant, *Guide*, 630), stretch along the southwestern peninsula of Asia Minor. The
range should not be confused with Mount Taurus, which is in Sicily. The Tigris rises in
eastern Turkey (Armenia) and moves through Babylon to the Persian Gulf. Herbert will
discuss them later in considerable detail.

[71] Susiana is in south-west Iran. It was also known as Elymais or Elam. The capital city was Susa, which of course was the centre of Achaemenid Persian power from the
time of Darius I to the conquest by Alexander the Great.

Sittace, and Adiabene[72] 'twixt Apamea[73] and the Altars of Hercules near which
Babylon was situate, constituting that region which by the Greeks was thence
called Mesopotamia, now *Diarhee* by the Persian, and after six days' passage
by boat from Baghdad, where the stream is not broader then the Thames 'twixt
Greenwich and Gravesend; mixing again at Gurnah,[74] the channel becomes four
miles broad, whence in a friendly and uninterrupted course they flow to Meshed
Ali where, as it were by consent, they compass that isle we now call Balsora (*Teredon* in Ptolemy), which was mastered by the overspreading Turk about an hundred years since, at the end of which isle under 30 degrees 30 minutes in two
wide mouths they empty themselves into the Persian Gulf and under 24 degrees
endlessly wander by, being swallowed up in the vast Indian Ocean.

Hormuz.

Having sufficiently strayed, return we now to Hormuz, which albeit by the
Greeks signifies *portus*, a haven, "*unde nauta dicantur horomuzare, i.e. navem an-
choris instructere,*[75] I presume was so-named by Shah Mohammed Dram Ku,[76] an
Arabian dynast that A. D. 700 crossed over from Mergastan to Jask in Carmania, a place hateful to Mirza Babadin, the fourteenth king after, who for most
quiet removed A. D. 1312,[77] of the *Hegira* 692, to this isle and from that *Har-
muz*, part of *Macela*, which is twelve leagues from Kostack where his predecessors dwelt, so named it, from which time to this it has been disturbed, first by
Jahan Shah, the Persian king who was slain by Uzun Hassan,[78] who for pearls

---

[72] Adiabene was an area of Assyria near the two Zab rivers which became a kingdom under the Seleucids and the Parthians. The Emperor Trajan conquered it and made
it a Roman province in 116. Adiabene also means Azerbaijan, but this name is "strictly
applicable to a more northern region" (Grant, *Guide*, 78).

[73] There are two Apameas in Asia Minor, both named for Apama, the Persian wife
of Seleucus I Nicator (312–281 B.C.E.). Herbert is probably referring here to Apamea
Cibotus, "a town in southern Phrygia (west-central Asia Minor)" (Grant, *Guide*, 45).

[74] Gurnah is a town in Zanzibar.

[75] From which sailors take [the verb] *hormozare*, that is, "to draw up a ship at anchor."

[76] Mohammed Dram Ku [*Mohammed Dramki*] was probably from Oman. No dates
are given by Teixeira (or anyone else) for the first eleven rulers of Hormuz. Sinclair states
that the date of 700 is far too early, and that 1100 is a more accurate date for the founding
of Hormuz (Pedro Teixeira, *Travels and The History of the Kings of Hormuz*, trans. W. F.
Sinclair [London: Hakluyt Society, 1902], 155).

[77] Bahadin [*Babadin*] Ayaz ruled 1294–1312. According to Sinclair, he made a move
to Gerun in 1302, where he spent the rest of his reign (Teixeira, *Travels*, 179).

[78] Uzun Hassan [*Usun Cassan*] was the Sultan of the White Sheep Turkmen 1453–
1478, and probably their greatest ruler, "a distinguished Prince, a friend of Christians,"
as Pope Sixtus IV called him (Meserve, *Empires*, 226). As Herbert tells us later, he mar-

broke through Lar and forced Malik Nazam-ed-din into Arabia, and again it was recovered by Mirza Qutb ed-din five years after, *viz. An.* 1488, but long slept not so, for Alfonso [de] Albuquerque the valiant Portuguese subjected it to Manoel his master, only suffering Saif ed-din the titular Prince to enjoy the title and a small pension.

Yet, to do her all the right I can, I shall remember such Princes as have ruled here. Shah Mohammed Dramki is the first I find, who in the 80 year of the Hegira, of Christ 700, left his seat at Oman in Arabia and sat down at *Calcias* upon the shore, but disliking it, moved to Kostack in *Mogestan*, six and twenty leagues from Jask, and there built a city which he called Hormuz, from whence part of Arabia took name. To him succeeded Suleiman, to him Isa Khan, to whom Mahmoud, Sharan Shah who bequeathed the crown to his nephew Shabadin Molongh whose daughter and heir married Saif-ed-din ibn Ezer, son to Ali Shah, Lord of Kish Island.[79] The crown, they wanting issue, then came to Shah-bedin Mohammed his cousin, to whom followed Ruqn-ed-din Mohammed, Mohammed's son, who, dying 1278, left the rule to his infant son Saif-ed-din Nusrat, who was slain by his brother Murad eleven years after, he being forced to fly into Kerman, not able to withstand his brother's servant Mir Babadin. Mir Babadin is in like manner forced to fly, as unable to resist the Turks which Murad brought against him, so that with many of his friends, such as especially hated the tyrant, he removed to Kish, but not well liking the place he rose thence and sits down at this isle Gerun, or wood (*Vorolla* some name it), fortified, and from the other named it Hormuz, in the year 1312, of the Hegira 692, to whom succeeds a man of noble extraction, Gordun Shah; to him his son Turan Shah [I], a brave Prince, yet fell by the axe of treachery which Mir Shahbeddin Isa struck him with, who had like retaliation by the late Prince's youngest brother Mirza Qutb ed-din, banished by his cousin Malik Nizam ed-din, at whose death Qutb ed-din returned and swayed the Hormuzian sceptre and at his death left all to Turan Shah [II], a victorious Prince, yet by death conquered *An.* 1488, to

---

ried the daughter of the Emperor of Trebizond and became almost lionised in the West because of his opposition to the power of the Ottoman Turks, whom he defeated at Erzincan (1473), only to suffer defeat himself at Bashkent a week later. Pope Calixtus III sent a delegation to him (1457) as did Pius II the next year, and his emissary Ludovico da Bologna returned with "a delegation of Asistic ambassadors, including one purporting to represent Uzun Hassan" (Meserve, *Empires*, 225). Western rulers believed him to be the "King of Persia." For full details of this, see Meserve, *Empires*, 223–31.

[79] The rulers are as follows: Mohammed Dram Ku, Suleiman, Isa I, Lashkari, Kai Kobad, Isa II, Mahmud I, Shahshanshah, Shahbadin I Molongh, Saif ed-din I, Mahmud II. Herbert omits some of them. Scholars have not been able to establish dates for these rulers, although it is known that Mahmud II died in 1243. Sinclair confirms that the daughter of Shahbedin Molongh married Saif ed-din Azar, King of Kish, who then succeeded to the throne.

whom succeeded Masud [II], Salgor Shah [I], Shah Wais and lastly Saif ed-din
[III], subdued by Albuquerque *An.* 1507, who caused him to be strangled.[80] After which Nur ed-din, Khaja Shah and Dalam Shah severally attempted the sovereignty, but Mohammed, the right heir, was in despite of them crowned king,
to whom succeeded his son Said Mohammed Shah, *An.* 1622[81] subdued by the
English and Persians, whom at my being at Shiraz I saw prisoner, but honourably used, at the entertainment which the Duke of Shiraz gave our ambassador
as we passed towards the Court of Persia. The Persian now commands there,
thank the English.

Hormuz taken and ruined.

The particular acts and passages in taking this famous city is thus in brief remembered. By command of Shah Abbas, Emamqoli Khan, Governor of those territories that extend from Shiraz unto the Gulf of Persia, advances towards Gamrun with nine thousand horse and foot, such a time as he expected to meet the
English fleet there. Being met, the conditions betwixt them under hand and seal
were these: 1. That the castle of Hormuz, in case it were won, with all the ordinance and ammunition should belong to the English; 2. That the Persians might
build another castle in the isle at their own cost when and where they pleased;
3. That the spoil should be equally divided; 4. That the Christian prisoners be
disposed by the English, the pagans by the Persians; 5. That the Persians should

---

[80] The names and dates of these rulers are: Ruqn ed-din (1243–1278), Saif ed-din II
Nusrat [*Nocerat*] (1278–1291), Masud I (1291–1294), Bahadin I Ayaz (1294–1312); Gordun Shah [*Azadin-gourdan-Shah*] (1312–1318), Turan Shah I [*Mabaraz-ed-din Bahram
Shah*] (1318–1319), Mohammed Shah I (1319–1320), not mentioned by Herbert, Qutb
ed-din (1320–1347), Turan Shah II (1347–1378). At this point, Sinclair states, the chronology again becomes confusing, because it appears that Teixeira and other authorities
have missed out some of the rulers who followed Turan Shah II (Sinclair, in Teixeira,
Travels, 188 n. 3). No actual dates are now given by Teixeira until 1507, but the reigns can
be dated with some accuracy, as follows: Fakhr ed-din Turan Shah III [*Paca-Turcansha*]
(d. 1455), Masud II [*Mozad-sha Bedin*] (1455–1465), Shahbadin II (1465–1476); Herbert appears to have conflated these two. Then Salgor Shah I [*Salger-sha*] (1476–1487),
Shah Wais [*Shawez*] (1487–1507), and finally Saif ed-din III (1507–1514). For details,
see Teixeira, *Travels*, 186–89. Herbert's chronology is sometimes inaccurate, and I follow Sinclair.

[81] The later rulers of Hormuz are: Turan Shah IV (1514–1521); Mohammed Shah
II (1521–1534); [Muizz ed-din] Salgor Shah II (1534–1543); [Fakhr-ed-din] Turan Shah
V (1443–1464); Mohammed Shah III (1564–1565); Farrokh Shah I (1565–1602) who
shared his throne with Turan Shah VI (?1585–1597) and Farrokh Shah II (1597–1602);
Firuz Shah (1602–1609) and finally, after a struggle with other claimants, Mohammed
Shah IV (1609–1621), whose son Herbert saw at Emamqoli Khan's banquet. See also
Monshi, *History*, 3: 1201, for some details about these rulers.

allow for half-charge of victuals, wages, shot, powder etc.; 6. That the English should be custom-free in Bandar Gamrun for ever. These articles being signed, each party prepare for fight. Captains of note in the pagan army under the Duke of Shiraz were Ali Quli Beg,[82] Pulat Beg,[83] Shah Quli Beg, Shahriyar, Mohammed Sultan and Ali Beg, King (*shabander* they call him) of the Port. These, with the army, first encamped before Bandar Gamrun, and two days after, *viz.* the twentieth of January 1622, with small difficulty became masters of the port, for at that time it had in it but a small garrison of Portugals in an inconsiderable fort, after which success the Duke and English captains played upon the castle with a dozen pieces of cannon for five hours, but to little purpose. The ninth of February the English transported some three thousand Persians in two frigates which they had lately taken and two hundred Persian boats which were good for little other service; these, so soon as they had landed, having formerly made sconces for their men and raised bulwarks to plant great ordinance upon, made towards Hormuz. But the Portugal, though they let them land, stopped the current of their fury; at first encounter from their barricadoes [they] defended, with shot and pike slaying over three hundred, and with their ordinance beat them back with more haste and amazedness then their approach had courage. In this disorder a flanker by mischance was blown up, but the siege continued.

Little hurt was done on either side till the 24 of February, when the English advanced towards the castle, under which was riding the Portugal armado, and in despite of the castle and fleet (being then five galleons and twenty frigates), set fire on their admiral the *San Pedro*, a ship of one thousand five hundred ton, which mischance observed, the rest of the Spanish fleet, to prevent more danger cut her cables, and in that flaming posture let her drive whither wind and tide would. The English were well-pleased with that sad sight, and though a prize rich enough, nevertheless thought it not safe to adventure boarding, so down she drove towards Lar, in the way a rabble of Arabians and Persians boarding her, and like jackals with hunger-starved fury and avarice tearing her asunder.

The seventeenth of March the Persians, to show they were not idle, gave fire to a mine stuffed with forty barrels of powder, which blew up a great part of the wall, doing some harm to the enemy, through which breach the Portugals immediately sallied and maintained a fight above one hour against the Persians, who had drawn out all their body, and when the trumpets sounded the besieged went on so courageously that the hindmost discovered plainly a contempt of death. After nine hours the defendants were forced to retreat, and the heated Persians

<hr>

[82] Ali Quli Beg Garamillu Samlu (d. 1624), "an old retainer who had served the Shah since the latter's childhood" (Monshi *History*, 3: 1261) was one of the principal officers of state under Abbas I. He held the position of *Esiq-aqasibasi* of the Supreme Divan as well as high civil office.

[83] Pulat Beg [*Pollotbeg*] was a chief minister of Emamqoli Khan. See also Stodart, *Journal*, 68.

began to mount and enter the city in many quarters, at which the Portugals were glad, for they entertained them with so many hand-grenados, powder-pots and scalding lead that the assailants were forced to fall back, a thousand of their men perishing, which when Shah Quli Beg had viewed, with a party of two hundred men he passed through those affrighting fires and after a short storm scaled one of their flankers, which he held not above half an hour, they were so tormented with small shot and flames of lead and sulphur, and in descending were beaten off by fifty *hidalgos*,[84] who for three hours maintained their ground and retreated gallantly. This entertainment so cooled the Persians' courage that for five days they did nothing but ruminate upon the valour of their adversaries. The three and twentieth day our cannon from the shore played so hotly and battered their fortifications so to purpose that at length, making the ships their object, they sank the vice- and rear-admirals of Ruy Freire's[85] fleet. March the twenty-eight necessity humbled them, plague, famine and fluxes raging in the city, so as five days after two gentlemen in a fair equipage first made towards the enemy's camp, who were ushered by some qizilbashes of Shah Quli Beg's regiment into his tent, and after a short complement moved for a cessation of arms, which if the Duke would agree to, they were ready to present him with two hundred thousand tomans[86] in hand and an annual tribute of an hundred and forty thousand rials.

Shah Quli Beg, having dismissed the *hidalgo*, not till next day acquaints the general, who, wanting money, agrees both to a cessation and lasting peace, so they would deposit five hundred thousand tomans (amounting with us almost to two millions of pounds) and pay as a tribute yearly to the King of Persia two hundred thousand more. The Portugals returned him this answer: they were in no such distress as to purchase peace at so dishonourable a rate, after which a final cessation followed, for they began a treaty with the English, putting them in mind both where and what they were, and of the amity that had been betwixt those two nations of old. If they had injured them, they were ready to make satisfaction. Their kings were at that instant good friends, and how could hostility betwixt them be defended either by the Law of Nations or religion? These and the like were sent, but whether or not the behaviour of the *fidalgo* displeased our

---

[84] Spanish nobleman or gentleman. Herbert should have used (and later does use) the Portuguese version, *fidalgo*.

[85] Ruy Freire d'Andrade (d. 1633) was sent with a fleet from Lisbon in 1619, and arrived at Hormuz in June 1620. When the English attacked Kish in 1621 as part of their deal with the Persians to help subdue Hormuz, Freire, after conducting a gallant defence, was captured, but he later escaped and continued to fight the English. For details, see Foster, *England's Quest*, 309–10. C. R. Boxer has edited the *Comentarios do Grande Capitao Ruy Freire d'Andrade* (Lisbon, 1647) (London: Routledge, 2004).

[86] The toman was the standard Persian unit of currency. *Hobson-Jobson* cites Pietro della Valle's value of it (1617) as about £3 10/- but Herbert, also cited in *Hobson-Jobson*, gives it as 5 × 13/8d. (928–29).

men or that they understood themselves so far engaged that with reputation they could not forsake the Persian, I know not, but the messenger departed not well-satisfied. Two days after a hideous noise of thunder amazed them, the English giving fire to several mines so as the breach gave an open prospect unto the city, but the banners of their assailants durst not travel with their fight, their senses the last time were so confounded that they only became spectators and gave new courage to the Portugals, most of which were half-dead with flux and thirst (the three great reservoirs of the city being exhausted), famine and pestilence. The fourteenth day a ship's load of mulattoes from Kish arrived at Hormuz to help the Portugals, but perceiving it impossible to approach with safety, they turned back, thinking to land at some better quarter, but the Persian general, assuring them they should receive no threat from his army, they foolishly gave credit to it, till fourscore of their heads being struck off and the rest in chains made the survivors see their folly.

The Hormuzians, languishing thus under many afflictions, every hour hoped for Ruy Freire to raise the siege, but he failed their expectation. The seventeenth day another breach was made by giving fire to sixty barrels of powder, which took such effect that the Moors entered in swarms, who yet were beaten back by eighteen gentlemen from the bulwark; howbeit, next day the infidels re-entered and possessed it. The eighteenth of April two famished renegados stole into the Persian camp and discovered to the Duke the sickly condition of the city and the little defence the besieged were able to make; that gave the Persian fresh encouragement upon the next opportunity to make a general storm, which the Portuguese, wisely forseeing and well-knowing the treacherous and faithless disposition of the infidels, especially towards Christians, they without further procrastination sent unto the English captains who were aboard, letting them know their willingness to render the castle unto them and to submit themselves and what they had to their mercy, which upon the three and twentieth day they performed, only craving that they might have their lives and a safe envoy to Markat in Arabia. The English, according to promise, transported three thousand of them as they desired, intending like favour to the rest, but the Persians intercepted above three hundred Arabs, amongst which were many Portugals, which contrary to their oath they barbarously slew and sent their heads to Gamrun as a signal of their conquest, which done, the magazine of arms, victuals and treasure were sealed up with the signets of both nations. The interim, contrary to agreement, was employed by the Persian in massacring of more then half-dead men, violating women, polluting temples and defacing houses, during which an Englishman, contrary to order, breaks into a monastery, but in his return is descried by the rattling of his burthensome sacrilege, at which the Persians, judging the agreement broken, fell to plundering everything that was valuable. The English, dreaming of no such accident, charge the infidels with breach of articles, but got no other answer then that the English made the first breach, so that for all this service our men got no more then twenty thousand pounds. The brass ordinance

in the castle and rampires[87] were divided betwixt them; some say they were three
hundred, others as many more, howbeit our men acknowledge but fifty-three
great brass pieces which were mounted: four brass cannon, six brass demi-can-
non, sixteen cannon-petros of brass, three of iron, ten brass bases, seven brass
sakers, some basilisks[88] of two and twenty foot long and ninety-two brass pieces
that were unmounted, which I rather name in that the Portuguese allege they
had small defence. Those belonging to the Persian were transported to Gamrun,
Lar, Shiraz, Isfahan and Babylon. The King of Hormuz, Sayed Mahmud Shah,
was made prisoner to the Persian, being at this day in Shiraz under an allowance
of five marks *per diem* in lieu of a former pension which, during his prosperity,
was paid him by the Portugal, amounting yearly to an hundred and forty thousand rials, so that Hormuz, which of late was the glory of the East, is now become the most disconsolate, and, agreeable to her condition, she may well change
that name to *ormah*, which signifies "destruction."[89]

After the sack of this city, the seamen found enough to throw away, by that
little they got showing their luxury, nothing but *alea, vino, Venus*[90] appearing in
the ascendant of their devotions. Captain Woodcock's[91] luck was best and worst,
for by chance he lighted on a frigate that was stealing away laden with above a
million of rials (as some say if their multiplication deceive them not), the most
of which he presumed came to his own share. But alas, what joy had he in that
fading pelf, for whether Woodcock minded more his Mammon then the steerage
of his ship, who can tell? But many by sad experience found that the *Whale* sank
close by Suwali Bar, the name neither of bird nor fish availing against that merciless element, which is a good servant but a bad master, and then yielded neither safety nor comfort. Such was the exit of this famous city after the Portugals
had been master of it six score years or thereabouts, and but for too much pride,
the Portugals upon needless occasions irritating the English, probably Hormuz
had stood, and but for too much avarice who knows but the *Whale* might have
swam still in its proper element the ocean. Such was the sad and miserable effect of avarice and animosity, the more to be lamented seeing so considerable a
place for trade and strength was thereby forced from one Christian by another to

---

[87] Ramparts.

[88] A basilisk was a 5" calibre gun firing a 14 lb shot.

[89] A Persian account of the attack on Hormuz may be read in Monshi, *History*, 3:
1202–04. He mentions the agreements with the English and the cannon, "cunningly-
wrought by skilled Portuguese craftsmen" and notes that Emamqoli Khan "took steps to
conciliate the townspeople" (1204) .

[90] Gambling, booze and sex (to put it colloquially). It is a Latin proverb.

[91] Captain Nicholas Woodcock, described as "late Master of the *Whale*," is noted
as presenting a petition to the Court of the East India Company in 1624 (*CSP Colonial*,
VI, 17 November 1624). In 1623 della Valle wrote of a ship at Hormuz he called "the
Whalem" as "the command-ship on which I had embarked" (*Travels*, 1: 130).

the weakening of both their interests and prostituted under the arbitrariness of a thankless Mohammedan. And yet the cause may not be concealed, insomuch as the excessive pride and luxury of the place no doubt hastened this fatal revolution. Nevertheless, that reciprocal and inordinate desire of revenge and gain is justly taxed and not improperly made applicable to this place by an ancient poet, who says "Pray girds fiercer armies oft with ireful swords, / Whence blood, whence slaughter hasty death affords; / Pray doubles danger in th' inconstant deep, / Whiles warlike beaks danger-fraught ships do keep."

The English Ambassador's landing in Persia.

The tenth of January, 1627. Sir Robert Sherley, at the desire of Sir Dodmore Cotton our Lord Ambassador, went ashore, and being in Gamrun, acquainted the Sultan and *Shabander*, the one the principal officer in military, the other in civil affairs in the town, with the Ambassador's arrival, and according to the custom of nations demanded such civility and necessaries as the Ambassador should need for his accommodation and travel to the Persian Court. At first the message relished not so well as Sir Robert expected; nevertheless, producing his *firman*, the Sultan disenabled his humour, protesting that he was transported with joy in that he had so good an opportunity of expressing himself an obedient slave to Shah Abbas his master and that the town should be honoured by so noble a stranger, sorry only he was so surprised and badly-provided that his unexpected landing prevented the ceremony intended him. Sir Robert, having returned his compliment, forthwith invited our Ambassador ashore, at whose issuing from the ship Captain Brown thundered out his farewell in a hundred great shot, whose echo not only made Gamrun tremble but seemed to rend the highest regions with their bellowings. Wrapped in smoke and flames we landed safely, though Neptune made us first dance upon his liquid billows and with his salt breath festooned the epicinia. At His Lordship's landing the cannons also from the castle and citadel vomited out their choler, ten times roaring out their wrathful clamours to our delight but terror of the pagans, who of all noise most hate artificial thunder. The Sultan and Shabander handed him out of his barge and mounted him upon a stately Arabian horse whose saddle, being of the Morocco sort, was richly-embroidered with silver and seed-pearl and the stirrups of gold. All the Ambassador's gentlemen and followers were also well-mounted. In this equipage, attended by his followers and servants, the sea-captains, the English agent Master Burt[92] and two hundred qizilbashes, the Ambassador moved slowly towards the Sultan's palace, which was in the bazaar, all the way passing between a double guard of archers and musketoons, and being alighted were ushered into

---

[92] William Burt (d. 1630) was the chief factor of the East India Company in Persia. He left England in April 1626 and was in Persia by January 1627. He died on 24 November 1630 (Stodart, *Journal*, 49, n. 1).

a delightful chamber, the floor of which was spread with a rich Persian carpet altogether as large as the chamber itself. And albeit the invitation was only to take his bread and salt, the Ambassador nevertheless found those words to be of a larger comprehension, for they were entertained with a very neat collection of sweetmeats and pelo, choice Shiraz wine and music both of that country and from our ships, the whole resembling another old reception near this place, which had *"Persica peristromata, vina, fidicina, tibicina etc.,"*[93] and with the Sultan's often repeating the Persian compliment *"khosh amadid, safa awardid"*[94] i.e. "Welcome, heartily welcome," assured us either we were welcome indeed or that it was to remove a complaint he feared would otherwise have been made unto his master the great Duke of Shiraz for neglecting that ceremony which *secundum ius gentium*[95] he would know was due to such eminent persons and passengers.

Gamrun.

Gamrun, by the Persians called Bandar, i.e. the port town, and not unaptly, this being more valuable than then all the rest the King of Persia hath, is situate upon a level ground close by the sea, the country almost round about rising for some miles very insensibly without any hill of note save to the north, which though seeming near is said to be fifteen miles distant. Near this place the gulf is narrowest, Arabia the Happy opposing it to the west towards ten leagues, but so visible that it seemed no more then Dover does from Calais. The city stands in Carmania and not Gedrosia, as some have said; the Persians call it *Kermoen*, albeit some erroneously suppose it *Khuzistan*. Some call it *Gamrou* and *Gomrou*, others *Gamroon* and *Cammeroon*, for so I find it variously pronounced. And albeit the town be but of small antiquity, taking its rise from the fall of Hormuz, nevertheless one Newbury,[96] an English merchant, reports that at his being here about the year 1581 it was then a town, though I believe a very small one, since which the Portugals have built two castelettes or forts, the first by Albuquerque *Anno* 1523, under whose power it rested until the year 1612, at which time by Allah Verdi Khan[97] it was wrested from them to the Persian, but upon the destruction of Hormuz which was in the year 1622, by removal of much of the inhabitants

---

[93] Persian curtains, wines, lutenists and flute-players.

[94] Herbert's version is *hashomody suffowardy*.

[95] According to the law of nations. The phrase could have originated with any number of writers from Aquinas to Grotius.

[96] This is John Newbery (d. 1584), for whom see the Introduction. For further details, see his letters in Hakluyt, 8: 449–81; his career is described in detail by Foster, *England's Quest*, 79–100 *passim*.

[97] Allah Verdi Khan (d. 1613) was the father of Emanqoli Khan. A distinguished military commander, he annexed Lar (1602), conquered Bahrain (1603), and served respectively as Governor of Fars and Governor of Kuh Giluya. He was made Commander-in-Chief of the Army and raised to the dignity of Khan (from Beg) by Shah Abbas in

this village so increased the buildings that for grandeur it is now ranked with towns of best note in Persia, so as through the access of merchants from most parts, namely English, Dutch, Dane, Portuguese, Armenians, Georgians, Muscovites, Turks, Indians, Arabians, Jews and banians this Gamrun is become a city of great commerce by reason of that notable concourse which in the winter season usually both by land and sea from the most remote places of the world resort thither, raw silks, carpets, cotton and other inland commodities being thither brought by caravan against that time, and by ship merchandises of all sorts, so as trade here during these months appears quick, both as to the enriching of the natives and exotics in such a degree as verifies that maxim of Plato his *Republic*: "*Civitas vix potest subsistere sine commerciis.*"[98] Parallel to which is that out of Flores's *Historia*,[99] referring to Lorenzo de Medici, the great Tuscan duke: "*Qui dicit mercatorum esse caput, unde robur et parus, manet in Rempublicam,*"[100] appearing also in the Persian exchequer, which acknowledges that it has no suchlike custom and other advantage from any other city within that Empire. Now, albeit Gamrun be but newly-advanced, nevertheless I meet with an ancient author that seems to point at it by this expression: "*Baraomati sunt populi qui Indum versus accolunt, Gumbroto proximi,*"[101] which how applicable it be to this place I leave to better judgments then my own, contenting myself with such other observations as I made during our fourteen days' stay there.

And first, concerning the buildings. They are for the most part of brick, not burned with fire but hardened by the sun, which makes them so hard that they appear no less solid and useful then those the fire obdures. They are low-built and most with small Courts and with balconies, all terraced or flat at top, pargetted with plaster in hardness not inferior to that of Paris, for indeed, such is the distemperature of heat sometimes that to live there is scarce tolerable, but when the air becomes more moderate, which is when the sun is furthest, to have more breath they use to sleep upon their terraces, to which end they spread carpets aloft

---

1598. He enjoyed a close personal relationship with the Shah, who attended his funeral (Monshi, *History*, 3: 1083–84).

[98] A state can hardly exist without business.

[99] Juan de Flores was a Spanish writer and historian best known for his two sentimental novels, *Historia de Grisel y Mirabella* (1485) and *Grimalte y Gradissa* (1488). Both works are about the debate between men and women on relations between the sexes. Herbert is referring to the first one (in which Lorenzo de Medici is quoted), which was better-known and also had an adaptation, the *Historia de Aurelio y Isabella* (1526) which was very popular. Not much is known about the author, except that he was probably a nobleman attached to the Court of Juan II of Aragon (1458–1479) and his successor Ferdinand V (1479–1516). Flores also wrote, but did not finish, a *Chronicle of Catholic Monarchs*.

[100] Whoever says that he is chief of the merchants, from whom comes strength and sufficiency, let him remain in the republic.

[101] The Baraomati were a people who lived in the vicinity of the Indus, near Gamrun.

for their better accommodation. This kind of building is common in all these hot places; that the Jews had their building such appears by what we frequently read in Scripture, as in Deuteronomy 22:8, Joshua 2:6; I Samuel 9:25; Jeremiah 19:13; Acts 10:9.[102] The windows are not glazed but wooden-trellised, made to shut and open as they see cause, to welcome the breeze when it murmurs. The mountain, which they say is six leagues thence but by its heighth seems not half so much, by anticipating the cool north winds makes this place much the hotter, so hot as in the summer season enforces the inhabitants to move to Lar and other neighbouring villages where cool streams, rocks and trees give shade and cool the air that at Gamrun is insufferable, so as some, according to what was practised in Hormuz, use to lie naked in troughs filled with water, which nevertheless so parboils their flesh as makes it both exceeding smooth and apt to take the least cold when any winterly weather succeeds the heat, which by that becomes little less offensive. Now their summer being no less then nine months, during all that time it is rare if one cloud be visible in the skies, whereby the air, in the daytime especially, is not to be endured, for by a reverberated heat which the sunbeams strike forcibly from the ground both earth and air become intolerable to man and beast by reason of the inflammation.

Howbeit, of late they have raised a bazaar, which in some places by its narrowness and most by being arched and close at top, checks the sun's heat when the beams dart perpendicular, in the sides attracting what air there is to refresh such as either sit in shops for sale of wares or those other that keep taverns, here being plenty of Shiraz wines brought in long-necked glasses and jars that contain some gallons, the best wine indeed in all Persia. Here be coffee-houses which also are much resorted to, especially in the evening; the coffee or *coho* is a black drink or rather broth, seeing they sip it as hot as their mouth can well suffer out of small china cups. 'Tis made of the flower of the bunny or choava-berry, steeped and well-boiled in water, much drunk though it please neither the eye nor taste, being black and somewhat bitter, or rather relished like burnt crusts, more wholesome then toothsome, and, if it be true as they say, comforts raw stomachs, helps digestion, expels wind and dispels drowsiness, but of a greater repute from a tradition they have that it was prepared by Gabriel as a cordial for Mussulmans.[103] Also sherbet-houses, a drink that quenches thirst and tastes

---

[102] "When thou buildest a new house, then thou shalt make a battlement for thy roof" (Deuteronomy 22:8); "But she had brought them up to the roof of the house and hid them with the stalks of flax, which she had laid in order upon the roof; Samuel communed with Saul upon the top of the house" (Joshua 2:6); "And the houses of Jerusalem and the houses of the kings of Judah shall be defiled . . . because of all the houses upon whose roofs they have burned incense" (I Samuel 9:25); "Peter went up upon the housetop to pray" (Acts 10:9).

[103] Herbert may have been one of the first Englishmen to try coffee; it was first exported from the Middle East to England in 1657. It later became a favourite drink of

deliciously; the composition is cool water into which they infuse syrup of lemons and rose-water, in these torrid countries being the most refreshing sort of liquor that can be invented, albeit the wine there was so good we refused not to drink it with moderation. *Arrack* or strong water here is plenty of, which qualified with sugar is cordial, and much drunk at sea and land in the hottest seasons especially where the diet is coarse and stomachs crude and weak through the diffusion of heat, which in cold seasons is contracted. Howbeit, for our better entertainment we had variety of fruits, some growing here but most imported from places more remote, some of which were oranges, lemons, pomegranates, pomcitrons, figs, dates, currants, myrobalanes,[104] apricocks, almonds, pistachios, apples, pears, quinces, sugar; also flowers and nuts in great quantity as well as variety, which with that plenty we had of *cabritos*[105] and mutton, hens, eggs and rice bought very cheap, made this place much more delectable, and for oysters and many sorts of fish, the sea being so near furnishes them abundantly and would do more were the people more industrious. The best houses in the town are the Sultan's, the Shabander's, the English and Dutch agents' houses, ours in memory of the good service they did the Persians at the taking Hormuz being privileged to wear their flags displayed at the top of their public houses, and for some time the English had half the imported customs according to articles.

At the north and south ends of the city are two castles in which are planted fourscore pieces of brass ordinance, part of the spoils or trophies of ransacked Hormuz. Two hundred other, great and small, were sent to Lar, Shiraz, Isfahan and other places. The gunners here were not very expert, for when they had occasion to give fire, I could perceive them to stand on one side of the piece, and in a fearful manner, though with a linstock as long as a half-pike, which had a lighted match, to touch the powder, which was a bad way to take aim by. The

---

Richard Cromwell (1626–1712), the former Lord Protector, who during his last years in England was frequently spotted in a coffee-house. It was during his Protectorate that a pamphlet appeared entitled *The Nature of the drink Kauhi or Coffe, and the Berry of which it is made* (1659). Edward Pocock, Professor of Arabic at Oxford, had translated it from the Arabic of "an Arabian Physitian." Chew states that coffee was first mentioned by Gianfrancesco Morosini, a Venetian agent in Constantinople, in a letter to the Senate in 1585, and in English the credit must go to William Parry and George Manwaring, who had been with Sir Anthony Sherley in Persia, who mention it in their accounts of Sherley's travels (1601–1602). William Lithgow, who wrote about the drink in 1612, "has often been accredited, incorrectly," Chew says , and it also makes an appearance in George Sandys's *Relation*, which Herbert certainly knew and in Robert Burton's *Anatomy of Malancholy*. Chew also tells us that the East India Company first offered coffee for sale in 1660 (*Crescent*, 183–84).

[104] "A name applied to certain dried fruits and kernels of astringent flowers, but of several species . . . which were from an early date exported from India, and had a high reputation in the medieval pharmacopoeia" (*HJ* 606).

[105] A *cabrito* is three-month old goat (Spanish).

mosques for the Mohammedans and synagogues for the Jews here are few and inconsiderable in their structure, but the *hamams* or stoves are more conspicuous, no less resorted to and with small expense. The streets are narrow, the town badly served with fresh water and without wall or graff to make it defensive.

Now, albeit here we have abundance of camels, horses from Arabia and Persia of the best sort, and mules and asinagos in great numbers, which were worthy the view, yet we were not more pleased with them then offended by those troops of jackals which here more than elsewhere nightly invaded the town and for prey violated the graves by tearing out the dead, all the while ululating in offensive noises and echoing out their sacrilege. They are the lions' informers and for reward always have something of the prey left them to pick, as at the Cape of Good Hope we observed. Some sport we had in hunting them with swords, lances and dogs, but we found them too many to be conquered, too unruly to be banished. These animals the Greeks called *allopecidae*, an unnatural mixture of fox and bitch, the Romans *crocutae* and *lyciscae*,[106] according to that of the poet, "*multum latrante lycisca*,"[107] an epithet from the quality not improperly attributed to Messalina's[108] wanton chambermaid, and if not that which Lucan speaks of, "That bark'd like dogs, and like to wolves did howl," yet doubtless the same that Virgil, *lib.* 1 *Georgics* points at, "Some cities did resound / With howling wolves that walk their nightly round,"[109] and the same that historians of old termed *canes sepulchrales*[110] with the unnatural Bactrians,[111] who used to throw unto them the bodies of their aged or impotent friends and parents, being one of their more then brutish kind of burial.

These wild dogs either by diversity of air or soil vary their species, as exemplarily we see in the Indian ounce,[112] which is the product of an European cat, wolves in New Spain from Castilian dogs[113] and the like, or from what other mixture I shall not examine. But with these 'tis no great injury to couple those filthy prostitutes ancient times properly termed wolves, that infect this town in

---

[106] *Crocutae* are hyaenas; a *lycisca* is a cross between a wolf and a dog.

[107] Virgil, *Eclogues* 3. 18.

[108] Empress Valeria Messalina (d. 53) was the wife of Claudius I (41–54), known for her immorality and vicious habits, at least according to the account in Suetonius. She was put to death the year before her husband was poisoned.

[109] Virgil, *Georgics* 1. 48.

[110] Bishop Joseph Hall (1574–1656) spoke in his "Sermon XXXI" (1637) of the "*canes sepulchres*, that care not to violate the tombs of the dead" (Joseph Hall, *Works* [Oxford: D. A. Talboys, 1837], 5. 440).

[111] Bactria (*Bakhtrish* in Persian) is "the most eastern of the truly Iranian lands" (Olmstead, *History*, 48). It is "a flat territory situated between the Paropamisus (Hindu Kush) mountains and the river Oxus (Amu Darya); now part of northern Afghanistan" (Grant, *Guide*, 97).

[112] Lynx.

[113] Wild dogs from the plains of Castile.

seasonable weather, which is November, December and January, and makes it the rendezvous for merchants and travellers from most places; women, I mean, who as to their bodies are comely, but as to their dress and disposition loathsome and abominable. For albeit their hair be neatly-plaited and perfumed, and about their cheeks are hung ropes of orient pearls, about their necks carcanets of stones, in their ears many rings, some of which are beaded with ragged pearl, one by another in their noses, a brooch or piece of gold three inches or more in length and half an inch in breadth, embellished with turquoises, rubies, spinels and sapphires and like stones of value, which for all their lustre athwarting the face, makes that which is an ornament to them to us seem very deformed. And as a supplement to all the rest, want no *fucus*[114] for complexion, which save for the desire they have to please white people agrees not with colours olivaster,[115] and that their arms and legs are chained with *manilios* and armlets of silver, brass, ivory and the like, the rest be veiled with a thin *shuddero*[116] of lawn and upon their feet wear sandals, though others go barefoot.

A Persian man and woman near the Gulf [illustration not shown]

Yet this morisco dress, together with their intolerable impudence, rendered them, at least to my view, no other than Ovid's remedy of love, so as pity it is that the Persians have not such as the *gynaecocosmi*[117] which were amongst the Athenians, whose care it was to see that women in their attire and behaviour carried themselves modestly. And yet albeit as bad as bad can be, they make me call to mind a Rabbi's doctrine which maintains that such as be desperately naught do not so corrupt good manners or be so great enemies to good life as those hypocrites who are but half-evil or corrupted in part, persuading others that they have some seeming goodness in them by a dissembled sanctity, no less well-observed by Jean de Léry that the naked American women do not so much incite to wantonness or appear so libidinous as European women do by the magic of their eyes, mimic dress, painting, patching and gestures of several immodest fashions and loose inventions. Howbeit, the better sort wear linen drawers or calzoons[118] of pantado and want not jewels and bracelets for further ornament, but when they go abroad they are covered with a white sheet from top to toe so as they are not easily known to any.

---

[114] Literally a red or purple dye; here Herbert means make-up.

[115] Olive-coloured; some dictionaries credit Herbert with inventing this word.

[116] From *chudder*, "a sheet or square piece of cloth of any kind" (*HJ* 217).

[117] Herbert is correct, although exactly what these magistrates did is uncertain.

[118] Italian breeches, fashionable in seventeenth-century England, and known in Italy as *calzoni*.

Banians.

The men are of the same dusky complexion; upon their head they wear sashes, about their waists girdles of many ells of linen-cloth, are elsewhere naked, and to express Cupid's vagaries have the impression of round circles and pink their skins in way of bravery. Mela also has this description, "*Carmani sunt sine vestre, fruge et pecore; sedibus piscium se cure velunt*,"[119] which last expression puts me in mind of another sort of people that *non vescuntur carne*,[120] who, being the aborigines of these parts, swarm throughout the Orient, the banians I mean, who are here pursuing trade in infinite numbers, concerning whom I have little more to say, seeing they were so unsociable that with us they would neither eat flesh, eggs, radish or any other root that had a red colour nor drink wine, for that it resembled what it is called, the blood of the grape. They believe the transanimation of souls into beasts and vegetables, and as the Lord Verulam notes, have this objection, that man's body is found to be most variously compounded, seeing herbs and plants are nourished by water, beasts by herbs and fruits, but man by beasts, birds, fish, herbs, fruits, grains, juice and other things which, they say, both alters and weakens his primitive nature. For before the Flood, when men were longest-lived and had most experience, 'tis thought they lived upon the same abstemious diet these banians now do, without destroying for food the life of any creature. But on the contrary we find that mediocrity in diet usually enervates nature, and albeit a temperate diet, in hot countries especially, preserves health, yet I observed that the banians, though healthy, are but of weak bodies and small courage, yet well enough agreeing with their condition. And indeed, how universally soever the contrary is practised, yet besides Pythagoras, Empedocles,[121] Lucretius and others who were earnest advocates for the preservation of the lives of innocent creatures, give me leave to present you with what Tibullus[122] elegantly did unto his mistress, hinting therein somewhat of this persuasion:

---

[119] The Carmanians are without clothes, fruit and cattle; they nourish themselves from fishes' dwellings.

[120] Do not eat meat.

[121] Empedocles of Agrigentum (c. 490–430 B.C.E.) was a pre-Socratic philosopher whose writings, in verse, survive only in fragments. Like Pythagoras he believed in reincarnation, and advocated a cosmogenic philosophy centred around the four elements, which were controlled by the forces of Love and Strife.

[122] Tibullus, *Elegies* 3. 7. 205–212. Albius Tibullus (c. 60–19 B.C.E.), the Roman elegiac poet, was celebrated for his restrained, elegant, and tender poems about love, peace and the charms of life in the country. His poems were often printed together with those of Catullus, Propertius, and sometimes Statius; Sir Aston Cokayne (1608–1684) wrote that "Whilst they did live they often were together / And now th'are dead th'are bound up so in leather." The first separate edition of his poems was that of Florentius (1472), and there was another edition by Scaliger (1577). There is an excellent modern translation by Philip Dunlop (Harmondsworth: Penguin Books, 1972).

When furthermore the grave my bones shall hide,
Or ripened days to swift-foot Death shall glide,
Or lengthened life remains in shape exchang'd,
Making me horse, well-managed to range
The field, or bull, the glory of the herd,
Or through the liquid air I fly, a bird,
Into what man so'er long Time me makes,
These works, begun of thee, fresh verses takes.

The banian tree near Gamrun.

About three miles from Gamrun I rode to see a tree we commonly call the banian tree. 'Tis not far from that fort called the great *mastanga*, opposite to Hormuz; a tree well worth the view, for spreading its boughs, which by their weight fall, root and rise again, they do so circle the bole or trunk that it resembles an arch'd circumference, affording umbrage and refreshment to some hundred men, that without crowding may well fit under it. I measured, and found it to be two hundred and nine paces. The arched fig-tree some, *arbor de rais* or tree of roots others call it, othersome the Indian and *de Goa*, but we the banian, by reason that they adorn it according to fancy, sometimes with ribbons, othersometimes with streamers of varicoloured taffeta, which how strange soever it appear to novices, such a dress we read of in Ovid, *l. 8 Metamorphoses*, in the story of Baucis and Philemon,[123] where "He saw the boughs with ribbons neatly hung," and in Virgil, *l. 2 Georgics* not unlike the *aesculus*,[124] whom "Tall branches guard and whose vast boughs display'd / Protect her round, with her excessive shade." For indeed, these boughs are so neatly-trimmed within that without interruption one may toss a pike in it; within these is built a pagoda in which, for I adventured in, I beheld, but notwithout amazement, three images whose visages were so grim, lineaments of body so distorted and misshapen and postures so uncouth that invention could not well represent demons more deformed, yet in memory of their forefathers Sudra, Kshatriya and Vaisya by these gross idolators they are formally invocated. Of these Pliny reports that "*hac fuere numinum templa, priscesque ritu; etiam nunc, simplicia rura deo praecellentem arborem dicant*,"[125] to which tree-worship the banians are not singular, for the Persians themselves in old times adored the tree they called *patalanga*, under which like these idols were erected called *bluime*. And of what repute the idol oak has been, witness our Druids who derive their name from thence, and our neighbours the Celts, who by it represented no

---

[123] Ovid, *Metamorphoses* 8.632–724.

[124] The Italian oak, also known as the "winter oak." Virgil mentions the oak twice in *Georgics* 2, but the lines Herbert cites are not a translation of "*nemorumque Iovi quae maxima frondet / aesculus*" (46), which is the only mention of this particular oak in the book.

[125] "Trees were temples of the gods, and, following old established ritual, country places even now dedicate an outstandingly tall tree to a god" (Pliny, *Natural History* 12. 3).

less then Jupiter. In Ovid, *quercus oracula prima*[126] is acknowledged. Also Gildas[127] our countryman, the better to engage us to the Lord for his distinguishing mercy, spares not to acquaint us with the ignorance of our forefathers the Britons, who attributed divine honour to groves, rivers and fountains, for indeed such was the miserable blindness of those ancient times that as every tree had its peculiar Genius, groves being commonly consecrated to some deity, so scarce was there any tree that by one or other was not dedicated to some *numen* or other, and little less then adored. Virgil, 7 *Eclogue*: "Herc'les the poplar, Bacchus the vine embraces, / Venus the myrtle, Phoebus the laurel graces,"[128] so that so great was the superstitious custom of devoting trees that, as Claudian observes, "there was scarce any tree that had not its veneration."[129] And in opinion, little was the difference between the Druids, the Magi and the Brahmins, all defending the immortality of the soul and the translocation from one into the another after death, was accounted good philosophy until it was discountenanced by Augustus Caesar such time as true light coming into the world dispelled error and darkness, and under Claudius was so persecuted that it then seemed extinguished, as we find by Suetonius.

Fourteen days we tarried in Bandar Gamrun, which albeit the view and other accommodations, the sea and proximity to Happy Arabia contribute, such time especially as the temperate months make it habitable, might have allured our longer stay had pleasure been our object. Our ambassadors, thinking the time long, used the best persuasions they could with the Sultan to hasten their provisions for the journey, and albeit horses for our own riding and camels for the caravan were ready, nevertheless such was his superstition that go we must not until upon his calling the dice the chance proved to his satisfaction. The four and twentieth day, the die it seems happening right, the kettledrums gave us warning to prepare to horse, for those there serve instead of trumpets, and little time served to make us ready. The ambassadors' caravan consisted of twelve horse and twenty-nine camels; the horses were such as were not liable to exception, the camels of those better sort they call *qizilbash* camels, a beast abounding in Persia and of great use, esteem and value in those oriental parts. Long-lived they are, oftimes exceeding threescore years, of disposition very gentle, patient in travel and of great strength, well enduring a burthen of towards a thousand

[126] "Oaks, the first oracles" (Ovid, *Amores* 3. 10. 9).

[127] St. Gildas (c. 516–570), sometimes surnamed Bandonicus or Sapiens, was a British priest and chronicler who was probably born in Strathclyde. His *De excidio et conquestu Britanniae* consisted of a number of sermons in which he excoriated his contemporaries for their misdeeds. It also contains a fair amount of history from the Roman Conquest down to Gildas's own times. It was first edited by Polydore Virgil (1525), and in England by John Josseline (1568).

[128] Virgil, *Eclogues* 7. 41–45.

[129] Claudian, *De raptu Proserpinae* 3. 344.

pounds weight, content with little food and that of the meanest sort, as tops of trees, thistles, weeds and the like, and less drink, in those dry countries usually abstaining little less than four days, which is of extraordinary advantage, seeing that oftimes they are necessitated to pass through desert places.

The first day Mr. Burt, the English agent, a civil and ingenious merchant and of high repute at the Persian Court, with several other English and Dutch factors then in town accompanied our Lord Ambassador three miles upon his way until the Sultan (the Shabander and other of the natives having fetched a compass about) met us, and, well-pleased with the present the Ambassador had gratified him with, returned His Lordship a hundred *salaams* and *taslims*,[130] elevating his eyes to Heaven, his hands to his breast, and declining his head wellnigh as low as the Ambassador's stirrup, bade also the rest of his train farewell, and having ordered us a convoy retired with his troop of qizilbashes, all the way disporting themselves with the *giochi di canni*,[131] darting at one another so dexterously as sufficiently expressed their skill and well deserved our commendation.

Bandar-é Lengeh.[132]

Here our Ambassador met with intelligence that Shah Abbas was that time in Astarabad,[133] a city upon the Caspian seashore, where he presumed the King intended audience. Therefore setting forwards, our first day's journey was to Bandar-é Lengeh, most part of the way being near the seashore; that village was sixteen miles from Gamrun, or five *farsangs* and a half. The word *farsang* is ancient, and to this day continued over all the Persian dominions; it is derived from *persa*, and appropriated to the dialect yet used in Persia, which is more likely from the Hebrew and Arabic, where the word *persa* signifies three miles, three of which the Jews might travel without breach of the Sabbath. Pliny calls it *parasanga*, and makes it to be four Italian miles, which, if so, it equals the German. Xenophon phrases it *pharasanga*, and computes it thirty furlongs or *stadia*, every furlong being twenty-five paces, so that accounting eight furlongs to an English mile, a *farsang* is three miles and a half English, and two furlongs over.

At Bandar-é Lengeh our tents, which the Ambassador bought at Surat and was advised to carry along, afforded us our best accommodation; howbeit, to give

---

[130] The *taslim* is usually "a benediction at the close of the usual form of prayer" (T. P. Hughes, *Dictionary of Islam* [Chicago: Kazi Publications, 1994], 628).

[131] "The exercise of throwing pointless spears," an Italian phrase. The Persians call it *jarid* (Foster, *Herbert*, 307).

[132] Bandar-é-Lengeh or Lingeh [*Bandar-ally*], a small city west of Bandar Abbas, is now a major port.

[133] Astarabad [*Asharaph*] is an important coastal town north-east of Teheran on the Caspian Sea. Herbert will describe it later on, when he attends the Court of Shah Abbas there.

that place its due, we found there a very neat caravan *serai*,[134] a building resembling an empty college. The Greeks call them *pandochia*, the Turk *imarets*, the Indians *serais*; buildings they be, erected by well-minded Mohammedans as works of charity and in which they express their magnificence more then in any other sort of building. Of great use they be, seeing these parts have no inns for the reception of travellers, but here *en passant* may rest sweetly and securely *gratis*, for they are set apart for public use and preserved from violence of thieves, wild beasts and intemperate weather. At the gate is sometimes a bazaar or tent that, like sutlers in armies for money furnish passengers with provision, yet seldom is it but that travellers, not daring to depend upon uncertainties, rather choose to provide and carry their necessaries along with them.

The people inhabiting hereabout fetch their water usually from a great large cistern which they call a "tank," rather resembling a vault or cellar underground more then a spear deep, sometimes made round but for the most part oval. The arch that covers it is wellnigh equal to the depth, and so well-plastered that when filled by the beneficial rains it preserves it sweet to the last bucket, which is strange, considering how long 'tis kept and without motion, save what it has when the water is drawn out by *hussinees* or bags of leather and other vessels that are not more cleanly then needs. The plaster is white and hard, comparable to that of Paris, so as were not this provision made for travellers and caravans it would necessitate them to provide in great leather bags for common use, as they are forced to do travelling over deserts, especially those of Arabia. Now, these tanks or conservatories are so ordered that when any rains fall, which is but seldom, perhaps one month in twelve at most, and when it comes distils not as with us, but falls or pours down in great drops, if I may properly so call them, the ground is so disposed that it quickly fills their spacious cisterns.

Tang-é Dalen

The second night we came to a small village called Gachin, five farsangs from the last, the next night to Kuristan, being seven *farsangs* from Gachin and next to Tang-é Dalen,[135] i.e. a strait or narrow way, as indeed it was, being pent in betwixt two hills, where the *caravanserai* was very neatly-built, adorned with

---

[134] "The usual modern meaning in Persia . . . is that of a building for the accommodation of travellers and their pack-animals, consisting of an enclosed yard with chambers around it" (*HJ* 811). 1627: Herbert added that it gives "all civil passengers a resting-place *gratis*, to keep them from the injury of thieves, beasts, weather etc." (124).

[135] Gachin [*Gacheen*] and Kuristan [*Couriatan*] are identified by E. Denison Ross in Stodart, who calls them *Gochine* and *Cauristan* respectively. Gachin is in modern Kerman province and the site of a nuclear station. Kuristan is the same as Laristan. Stodart calls Tang-é Dalen *Tangettelon*. The name means "the defile of Dalen, from a neighbouring town of that name" (Foster, *Herbert* 307).

cupolas at top. The water also was sweet and plentiful, not springing there but flowing from a high mountain that was three miles distant thence, by pipes conveyed thither through the bottom of an intersected hill near the lodge, and so streaming into the tank gave both delight to the eye and refreshment to weary and thirsty travellers. From the hilltop we beheld the valley below, which was very level, large and marvellous pleasant, by reason the spring-water runs in meanders and mellows it in all places, so that it brings forth grass and fruit in abundance; still, being compared with hills of equal heighth give it a more elegant fence then art could have done for the greater security and satisfaction of the villagers, who have but one common way for entrance, so as it resembled that which the poet speaks of Tempe for delight, and no less fortified by its situation. But what set this vale the better-off was the circumadjacent country, which for the most part was barren and sandy, producing indeed plenty of dates, which are more valuable for their fruit then shade. That day's journey was four *farsangs*.

Our next was eleven to Hormuz, which in the Persian tongue signifies "dates."[136] Upon the way near the town we passed by a small black pavilion in which upon the ground we could perceive sat cross-legged three ancient grey-bearded Arabians, who out of the al-Quran ingeminated a doleful requiem to their brother's carcase, intending, according to the Jewish custom of *septem ad luctum* mentioned in Ecclesiasticus 22:12, where 'tis said "*luctus mortui septem dies*,"[137] practised as we find it in Genesis 50:10, II Samuel 12:18[138] and accustomed by many others, full seven days to perform that ceremonial farewell, singing, sighing, weeping, and not in vain, seeing that "In tears we find content, / For grief would break the heart without a vent," without which expression of love they imagine the soul rests under an everlasting mourning. And, that want of sepulture was a grievous punishment, Homer in his *Odyssey* [11. 72-73], speaking of Ulysses and Elpenor his fellow traveller being dead, gives us this authority: "Do not depart from hence, letting me be / Unmoan'd, unburied, lest neglecting me/ Th' offended gods entail a curse on thee."

Nigh Hormuz are Duzgun,[139] Laztan-dé and other towns, where is got the best asafoetida through all the Orient. The tree exceeds not our briar in heighth, but the leaves resemble rose-leaves, the root the radish; the virtue need be much, it smells so sweetly,[140] but though the savour be so offensive to most, the sapor is so good that no meat, no sauce, no vessel pleases some of the Gujaratis' palates

---

[136] Herbert is wrong here. The Persian word for 'dates' is *khurma* (Foster, *Herbert*, 307).

[137] The rite for the dead is seven days.

[138] ". . . and he made a mourning for his father seven days" (Genesis 50:10); "And it came to pass on the seventh day the child died" (2 Samuel 12:18).

[139] Modern-day Dasgar.

[140] Herbert seems here to be attempting some humour, as in 1638 he had written "it stinks so odiously."

save what relishes of it, and how ingrate soever it may seem at first, yet by use
it becomes sufficiently pleasant, for what pleases quickly cloys the stomach and
satiates. Next night we got to Ourmangel, five *farsangs*, and the next day to Lar.
Two miles short of the city the *Cuway*,[141] the *Kalantar*[142] with other of the prime
citizens welcomed us with wine and other adjuncts of compliment. We had not
rode above half a mile further when lo, a Persian, anticky-habited, out of a poetic
rapture (for the Persians are for the most part poets), sung our welcome. The epi-
logue was resounded upon kettledrums, timbrels and other barbarous jangling
unmusical instruments, some being shaped like to a large gourd, having but three
strings; Terpander of Lacademon his being punished for adding a string to his
harp without leave of the state, though more musical, might be their example.[143]
A homely Venus, attired like a Bacchanal, attended by morris-dancers, began to
caper and frisk their best lavoltas, so as every limb strove to exceed each other,
the bells, cymbals, kettle-music and whistles storming such a Phrygic discord
that to comfort we might have squeaked out "Your rustic pipes do jar/ With
notes that horrid are," so that had it been night it would have resembled an orgy
to Bacchus, for glass-bottles being emptied of wine clashing one against another,
the loud braying of above two hundred asses and mules (the last is a compound
between a mare and an ass, for mules do not generate) and continual shouting
and whooping of above two thousand plebeians all the way, so amazed us that
albeit they no doubt thought the entertainment was noble, never any strangers
were bombasted with such a triumph. But *his quoque finem!*[144] With much ado we
reached our lodging, infinitely wearied; for my own part I was somewhat deaf
for three days after.

After a little repose our Ambassador and Sir Robert Sherley were invited by
Ibrahim, the Magistrate of the city, to eat of his bread and salt, which he presented them at his own house with a better collation. The room they seated in
was large and beautiful; the floor was covered with a rich silk carpet as large as
the floor. The sides of the room were gilded and painted delightfully; the roof
was arched in mosaic sort and embossed with stones of several colours. The light
was at one end through a window that was large, the frame neatly-carved and the
glass no less-curiously painted with such knots and devices as the Jews usually
make for ornament. In a word, it was a very noble room such as I admired to find

[141] Herbert may mean the *katib*, who is "the official charged with delivering the *kot-
ba*, or formal address, on Fridays in the mosque" (Savory, in Monshi, *History*, 2,: 1389).

[142] The Mayor (Savory, in Monshi *History*, 2: 1388).

[143] Terpander (seventh century B.C.E.) was actually from Lesbos, but he settled in
Sparta. Herbert is alluding to a story repeated by Strabo about an improvement the poet
made to the lyre (6.145). He was also believed to have been the father of Greek lyric poetry.

[144] "[God will put] an end to these things," from "*dabit deus his quoque finem*" (Virgil, *Aeneid* 1. 199).

in that country, but what made it more delectable was the garden that wellnigh encompassed it, which was stored with as large succulent and fragrant pomegranates, pomcitrons, oranges, lemons and like fruit as any I sver saw elsewhere, replenished also with trees for shade, amongst which I observed the cypress to be exceeding large, a tree the more valuable for that it is ever verdant, sweet and lasting. Some think the gopher-wood of which the Ark was built was of this timber. "*Perpetua moritura cupressus,*"[145] a poet tells us.

Lar.

A word of Lar. Lar is both a city and province so-called within three days' journey of some part of the Persian Gulf and part of that we strictly call Persia. It has Kerman to the east, Khuzistan[146] to the east, Ayrac or Farsistan[147] to the north, and to the south the Gulf of Persia. The diameter of this province is about an hundred *farsangs* or three hundred miles English, by old authors reported to be full of springs, grass and fruit, but length of time has, it seems, much altered it, for in crossing the country we found the greatest part barren, having only date-trees or palms which grow where the earth is sandy, but where rivulets or springs appear there the people live, thrive, improve and have oranges, lemons, pomegranates, figs and fruits, as also grain in variety. Yet though the ground be bad, nevertheless 'tis thought here are mines of sundry sorts and sulphur, which makes some amends but for want of art remain undiscovered.

The city of Lar is in the centre of the province, elevates the Arctic pole 27 degrees 40 minutes and has about 90 degrees longitude from the meridian on Cape Bona Speranza, a city that pleads antiquity, especially if it be that which Ptolemy calls *Corrha*, as some think; albeit I am not of that opinion, seeing that he places *Corrha* under 31 degrees. But *Laodicea* it was called by Antiochus, as du Pinet[148] guesses, and 'tis no better then a guess, seeing that towns of the same

---

[145] "The ever-dying cypress" (Martial, *Epigrams* 6. 73.7). The exact passage says "*perpetua numquam moritura cupresso,*" which of course means "the *never*-dying cypress." As for the exact identity of 'gopher-wood' (left untranslated in the King James Bible), scholars are still at a loss. Pine has also been suggested.

[146] Khuzistan is modern-day Khuzestan, a province of Iran which stretches from the Zagros Mountains to the east bank of the Tigris. Its capital is Ahraz, which seems to be the city Herbert calls *Ayrac* and which he locates in Farsistan.

[147] Farsistan is South Central Iran, once the heart of the Achaemenid Empire and, according to modern scholars, also known as Persis (see below). It is now known as Fars.

[148] Antoine du Pinet, sieur de Noroy [*Pynetus*] (d. 1584) was a French scholar and publisher bestknown for his *Historia plantarum* (1561). However, he also wrote a commentary on Pliny's *Natural History* (1542) and a work about the cities and fortresses in Europe, Africa, Asia and the New World (1564).

name are also built in Phrygia and Coele-Syria,[149] as we find in Ptolemy. Appian
calls it *"Seleucia Elymaidis, urbs Persica, a Seleuco filio Antiochi condita, qui novem
civitates sui nominis struxit."*[150] Pliny calls a town in Arabia opposite to this by
that name, but whether some transplanted thence and in memory of their former habitation gave it that name is but conjectural. Heylyn[151] calls it *Lara*, which
comes near the name it now bears, and ranks it with Isfahan, which he makes
the same with Qazvin[152] and others in Persis, but how Persis and Persia are different, though he makes them so, I oppose not so learned a geographer, though
I meet not with his authority for that distinction. But sure, to make *Hispian*, for
so he calls Isfahan, the same with Qazvin is a great mistake, seeing they are two
hundred miles asunder, and no less erroneous in the position, seeing that Lar is
in Persia, Isfahan in Parthia, and Qazvin in Media, so that to reduce them to
Persis is incongruous. His placing *Sava* also in Persis is likewise mistaken, as is
Ctesiphon, which he makes a city in Parthia, being in Susiana.[153] *"Vicus maximus
prope Seleucium,"* saith Strabo, *"ubi regis Partharum ----- solebant,"* for I presume
he means *Saway*,[154] which we travelled through and found to be a great town in
Media. Gasparo Balbi gives its right name, Lar, but his making it an isle is mis-
reported. Paulus Venetus calls it *Laar*, which may be granted, for I apprehend it

---

[149] Coele-Syria, now Lebanon, was the area ruled by the Antiochid kings. Its most
famous landmark is the city of Baalbek or Heliopolis. It is the hinterland of Phoenicia.
Seleucia was its capital, also known as Elymais. There is a Laodicea "on the Lycus" in
Phrygia, now called Eski Hisar, near Denizli, Turkey (Grant, *Guide* 328), and Laodicea
"on the Sea," which may be found on the Syrian coast, "occupying a rocky cape flanked
on its west and south sides by the Mediterranean" (Grant, *Guide*, 329).

[150] Appian of Alexandria (2nd century C.E.) was the author of an ethnographic
history of Rome in 25 books. Some time after 117 he moved permanently to Rome and
became a knight, surviving until the reign of Antoninus Pius (138–61). The quote reads
"Seleucia Elymaidis, a Persian city founded by Seleucus the son of Antiochus, who built
nine cities named after himself."

[151] Peter Heylyn (1600–1662), a Royalist theologian and historian, wrote a history
of the Reformation and a biography of Archbishop Laud, *Cyprianus Anglicanus* (1668).
The work which Herbert refers to is the *Cosmography* (1652), in which Heylyn attempted
to cover every part of the known world. It is memorable because it contained what was
probably the first printed description of Australia.

[152] Qazvin [*Casbyn*] is a city east of Teheran. It served as the Safavid capital from
1548. Herbert describes it in some detail later.

[153] Persis, as we have seen above (n. 67), is now known as Fars. It was named for
the Persai, which was the Ionian Greek version of Parsa, and this form became common
use under Timurid rule. The province of Persis, strictly-speaking, is east of Elam or Susiana.

[154] There is a town in Afghanistan of this name, but *Saway* is otherwise unidentified.

was founded or increased by *Laar-gebeg*,[155] son of *Phyroe* and grandson to *Pyloes*, who was succeeded by Girgin Milad,[156] of whom their histories report wonders. After him followed eighteen Princes, Ibrahim Khan [II][157] being the last, who was subjected *Anno Hegira* 985, of ours 1605, by Emanqoli Khan, Duke of Shiraz, to satiate the avarice and ambition of Abbas his great master, and, which is rare considering the penury of this country, for the King's part only he loaded away with treasure seven hundred camels. The captived King Ibrahim had his life and a pension promised him, which he enjoyed but a while, an unexpected sword of death betraying his hopes, without which the diadem, as was pretended, could not sit right upon the head of Abbas the Persian King.[158]

Nine days we stayed in Lar; shame it were if in so long time that we had gathered nothing. Lar, then, is from Gamrun seven small days' riding, from Shiraz fourteen, from Babylon twenty, a town parched with the scalding sun, in which respect they have devioces like turrets upon the tops of their chimneys to suck in the air for refreshment, defaced by rage of war and overturned by many dreadful earthquakes. *Anno Domini* 1400 it shook terribly, when five hundred houses tumbled down; *Anno* 1593, of their account 973, she boasted of five thousand houses, but that very year the earth swelled with such a tympany that in venting itself all Lar was forced to quake, and would not be suppressed but by the weight of three thousand houses turning topsy-turvy, with the death of three thousand of the inhabitants. The old castle on the east side of the town,

---

[155] Herbert might be referring to Lahak, the brother of Piran, who features in the *Shahnameh*. However, Lar is also said to have been Girgin's son (John Malcolm, *History of Persia* [London: John Murray, 1815] 1: 348).

[156] Gorgin or Girgin Milad [*Gorgion Melek*]. According to Iskandar Monshi, "the Governors of Lar are descended from a certain Gorgin Milad, who was appointed Governor of Lar in the time of the Kayanid monarchs" by the legendary ruler Kai-Khusrau (see Ferdowsi, *Shahnameh*, 306–66). Monshi writes that this was "four thousand years" ago (*History*, 3: 807–8). In the *Shahnameh* Girgin is a *pehlwan* (wrestler) at the Court of Kai-Kavus who turns traitor, gets defeated by Rostam and pardoned. Foster identifies him as Ala al-Mulk Gurgin Shah, who ruled Lar in 1420 (*Herbert*, 307), but this is probably a mistake, as the context implies someone legendary.

[157] Ibrahim Khan II (r. 1575–1605) came in for trouble because at Shah Abbas's succession he failed to pledge allegiance, and when he started "levying extraordinary taxes on merchants and travellers," Iskandar Monshi tells us, that "gave the Shah the excuse he needed" and, when after a threat had secured a few months of good behaviour Ibrahim began all over again with his taxes, the Shah decided it was time to deal with him (Monshi, *History*, 3: 805–07).

[158] According to Iskandar Monshi, Ibrahim Khan "died of a sickness than affected many of the troops. He was an able youth of simple habits, a lover of poetry, well-versed in all the customary sciences, an expert musician, but he lacked statecraft. In his early adolescence he became an opium addict. He was thirty-five years old when he died" (*History*, 3: 808).

which owes its foundation to Girgin Milad, though built upon the top of a solid rock, groaned in a like affrighting downfall. And to me it seemed strange a city so strongly, so surely founded should be subject to such commotions. Now whether it be, as Democritus dreamt, from the gaping sun-torn earth quaffing in too much water, and (like a glutted drunkard) overcharging her caverns, vomits it up in a forcible and discontented motion, or whether, as Aristotle teaches, it be from vapours engendered in the bowels of the earth, which, loath to be imprisoned in a wrong orb, rends its passage by a viperous motion, or whether from subterranean fires, the air being inflamed upon sulphur or other like exuberances of nature, I leave the scrutiny thereof to those that study the causes of meteors. Howbeit, this being in Asia puts me in mind that no part of the world is so subject to earthquakes as Asia is, for in Tiberius Caesar's time twelve cities in one night were overturned by earthquakes, and in Trajan's time the like in and near Antioch.[159] And indeed, this country hath had many trials of that kind, as in our travel we could both see and hear of.

Lar, the metropolis of the province, is now an unwalled town, as most Asiatic towns be, art being needless, seeing the lofty rocks which are to the east and north so naturally defend her, for a brave and stately castle at the north quarter, mounted upon an overlooking hill, not only threatens an enemy but awes the town in a threatening posture. The ascent thereto is narrow and steep; the castle itself of good stone, the walls well-furnished and beautified with battlements and platforms whereon are mounted twelve brass cannon-pedros and two basilisks, the spoils of Hormuz. Within the fort are many small houses or huts which lodge the soldiers, who have sometimes there an armoury sufficient to furnish with lance, bow and gun three thousand men. Howbeit, the walls are weak, not flanked nor so regularly built but that the situation and art rather seems to make it defensive, though large in compass, usually well-victualled, armed and manned, as serves not only to command the city but country also and to secure them against foreign invasion. The bazaar is also a very elegant and noble fabric; the material is of good chalky stone. The building is long and beautiful; a quadrant 'tis like, though I cannot call it such, the sides are so unequal. 'Tis covered at top, arched and coupled after the mode of those oriental countries, and within, burse-like, is furnished with shops and trades of several sorts. The alley or aisle, which extends from north to south, is one hundred and seventy of my paces; from east to west it is an hundred and sixty, the circumference of the oval in centre is about an hundred and ninety, a building in some hundreds of miles not be paralleled. Near this bazaar the larins[160] are coined, a famous sort of money being pure

---

[159] Tiberius [I] reigned 14–37; Trajan (M. Ulpius Traianus) reigned 98–117.

[160] A larin [*larree*] is "a peculiar kind of money formerly in use on the Persian Gulf." *Hobson-Jobson* confirms that it "originated in the territory of Lar" (506). In 1622 Pietro delle Valle described it as "most eccentric in form, for it is nothing but a little rod of silver

silver, but shaped like a date-stone, the king's name or some sentence out of the al-Quran being stamped upon it. In our money it values tenpence.

The mosques here are not many. One more remarkable then the rest it has, which is round, either shadowing out eternity or from that pattern of the *al-kaaba* in Mecca, whose shape they say Abraham had from Heaven, imitated by the Jews. In some part this is varnished with Arabic letters, and upon the parget painted knots, beautified in other places with counterfeit mosaic but low and without glass, wooden trellisses artificially-cut after their invention supplying them. The entrance is through a brazen gate near which is hung a mirror or steel glass; divers lamps it also has for use and ornament. Some of their prophets rest their bones there: Imam Ali Zadeh Amir,[161] a long-named, long-boned (if his grave be of right dimension), long-since rotten prophet is there interred. The older prophet, the fresher profit, zeal and charity oftimes cherishing antiquity; but how can I credit what they report, that he was a Mohammedan, since they say he died a thousand five hundred years ago, which is six hundred years before Mohammed, and yet a Mussulman? But leaving that tradition, more certain 'tis this place affords variety of fruits, as dates (*dactiles*, from the finger-like shape, the Romans called them), a tree distinguished into male and female, so that unless the female have yearly a flowered bough of the male engrafted, she pines away and becomes lean and fruitless. Here also were oranges, lemons, melons, pomegranates and pomcitrons most excellent, and of flowers jessamines, roses, tulips, July-flowers[162] etc. Here also at easy rates we bought goats, hens, rice, barley, *arak*[163] *and aqua vitae.*[164]

Howbeit, the mosquitos or gnats pestered us extremely, but of more vexation was the water we drank, and in these torrid places thirst after, nay, were necessitated to dress our meat withal, and is the best the people have to drink out of the large tanks they keep it in. They call it *ab-baran,* which in the language of Persia signifies "rainwater," but with far more reason may I call it *aqua mortis,* death seeming to bubble in it. A base-qualified water it is, whether in regard their tanks are ill-made or nastily-kept, whereby the water corrupts, or whether the rain itself is insalubrious or other hidden cause in nature there may be, I cannot tell, but this I can, that it is unsapory, so ill to the gust, as worse water for taste and specially for property can scarce be relished. As little of it came in my belly as could be borrowed from extremity of thirst, for, as experience teaches, it

---

of a fixed weight, and bent double unequally. On the bend it is marked with some small stamp or other" (*Travels,* 2: 434).

[161] I have not been able to identify Ali Amir but "Imam Zadeh" is a Shi'a title for a saint, and there are many "Imam Zadeh" tombs in Iran. Foster guesses Ali Zaydi Amir (*Herbert,* 68), but this is incorrect.

[162] The gillyflower, a kind of carnation.

[163] Palm-wine or liquor.

[164] "Water of life," that is, any distilled alcoholic drink.

causes catarrhs, breeds sore eyes, ulcerates the guts, and, which is more terrible then the rest, engenders small long worms in the legs, a sort of nasty vermin not more loathsome to look upon then dangerous to the itching disease in them that breed them, by no potion, no unguent to be remedied. Nor is there any other way known to destroy them save by rolling them about a pin, which, if in screwing the worm chance to break, it gives them very doleful music, for it makes the leg apt to gangrene and by lancing hardly curable. The water, doubtless being the natural cause of this malady, seems to me to bring its venom from the region where it is generated, either for that the springs are vitiate or that the rainwater is corrupt. For albeit clouds are seldom seen there, yet sometimes they are, but undigested and unagitated by the wind, nor do they at all times distil their rain moderately in drops, as is usual in colder climates, but in violent eruptions, dangerous both in the fall and no less noxious in the drinking. Now the reason (as I apprehend) that they have few clouds is because the country is desert and sandy, and wants rivers and other moist places to occasion exhalations, which begets rain. Howbeit, at our being here it rained a great shower, which made our company the more acceptable, and we could observe that the soil, not only here but in most of the province as we travelled, is either stony or a slate sort of mould, yielding little grass or grain of any sort or fruit, save what was forced in gardens, unless it be dates, which here are exceeding good and plentiful. But in valleys and where springs meliorate the earth, it produces rice, barley and like grain, as also fruits in variety.

The inhabitants are a mixture of Jews and Mohammedans. Most of those I saw were blear-eyed, rotten-toothed and mangy-legged; the violent heat and unwholesome water doubtless causes it. The habit of the greater part of them is only a wreath of calico tied about their heads, their mid-parts circled with a zone of varicoloured plaid, with sandals on their feet, and are elsewhere naked. Some, nevertheless, though but few, have sashes of silk and gold tulipanted about their heads, and robe themselves in *cabayas*[165] of satin, their fingers being adorned with rings of silver set with turquoises, that being the stone they most affect in Persia, in which they have engraven their name or some selected posy out of the Talmud or al-Quran. The Mohammedans delight much in archery, and on their thumb commonly wear a ring of horn which makes the arrow go off both strongly and easily. Their swords afford them no small delight, the blades being exceeding good, and the hilts no less valuable for with the better sort usually they are of gold. Here are some, nevertheless, that are proficients in philosophy and the mathematics, the principal delight they take being in astrology, but in the mechanic and other curious arts, it gives place to few in Persia. In this city should be a river, and that not a small one if our geographic maps were true, but therein they err, for here could I see no river, nor any in near an hundred miles' travel

---

[165] A *cabaya* is a "surcoat or long tunic of muslin." The word is a Portuguese corruption of the Arabic *kaba* or *kabaya* (*HJ* 137).

northward, for both by enquiring of some Persians and our own further travel, I could neither hear nor see any nearer then Tabb, a river famous in separating Susiana from Carmania, and from Lar westward about five small days' journey, or that other side of Chur, over which we rode 'twixt Shiraz and Persepolis. Some brooks indeed we passed over, so small that they had no name, but rivers no man calls them, since none of them in breadth or depth exceed three foot, rivulets worth little more then the noting.

Jarri.

West of Lar is a town called Jarri[166] about twenty *farsangs*, which is sixty English miles from Lar. Most of the inhabitants are Jews, by some reputed little less then a thousand, much less then what ben Jonas numbered in the year 1100, for at his being in Ja'aria, which is presumed to be this place, it had then twenty-five thousand Jews inhabitants. Some make this their road from Lar to Shiraz, but the way we took was more to the east and more frequented, being neither so hilly as the other nor so stony.

Transmigration of the Ten Tribes.

Concerning the name [Jarri]; whence it is derived I suppose it is either, for that these are the descendants of that Kiriath-jearim we find mentioned mentioned in I Chronicles 2:50,[167] i.e. plenty of wood, which grew there as we find mentioned in I Samuel 7:1,[168] which probably the transplanted Jews might commemorate. Also, when out of these captives Cyrus gave leave for the re-edifying the Temple, we find in Ezra 2:7 and Nehemiah 7:12 that from Elam and Kiriath-jearim several of the Jews returned, where in the 24 verse, the other Elam is recorded, or else from Jare or Joarab, Joktan's fourth son, Genesis 10:26,[169] whose brethren Ophir and Havilah, travelling from Babel to plant about Ganges, 'tis likely they left him by the way to increase their cousin Elam's plantation.[170] But seeing these are the offspring of those the Assyrian Prince Shalmaneser [V] (called Enemessar[os] in Tobit 1:2),[171] forced out of Samaria as we find recorded in II

---

[166] Jarri or Ja'aria [*Jaarown*] is a small city in Fars province; it is now known as Agha-Jari.

[167] "These were the sons of Caleb the son of Hur, the firstborn of Ephratah: Shobal the father of Kiriath-jearim."

[168] "And the men of Kiriath-jearim came and fetched up the ark of the Lord."

[169] "And Joktan begat Almodad, and Sheleph, and Hazarmaveth, and Jerah." It is 10:29 which mentions Ophir and Havilah.

[170] "The children of Elam, a thousand two hundred fifty and four" (Ezra 2:7); the words are identical in Nehemiah 7:12.

[171] Shalmaneser V was King of Assyria 727–722 B.C.E. He attacked the Kingdom of Israel and captured King Hoshea "in unknown circumstances" (François Castel, *The*

Kings 17:6.[172] A.M. 3220[173] — the name from then has more probability, for in Scripture we read that he "placed them in Halah and Habor," Median cities near unto the River Gozan, the finding of which river has been not a little controverted, and the quest continues yet obscure, for some would have it to be a river in Bactria, not far from Oxus,[174] and to have the like vent into the Caspian, which, being so remote from Media, cannot be approved of. Others place it near the Araxes, which has the greater semblance of truth, Araxes flowing through that part of the Medes' country which about Alexander's time was re-named *Atropatia*, notwithstanding which ben Jonas in his *Itinerary* finds Gozan hereabouts and reports that it empties its fresh streams into the Persian Gulf. Yet to close with this Jew in his Kabbala is not safe, seeing he finds not only infinite numbers of Jews all along from hence to *Nisibor* (or rather *Nisipor*, i.e. *Bacchi civitas*)[175] in Sogdiana, which Ptolemy places in Aria under 35 degrees 20 minutes, but several Gozans also, which brings it under such confusion as none indeed can tell where to find it. And concerning that *Gozania*,[176] I find it in Ptolemy's tables to be 40 degrees, 40 minutes, and by being in Media it has affinity with the name, but in the map not being taken notice of, cannot tell where properly to place it. Moreover, albeit the way these banished tribes took from their own into the Median territories was in probability the usual or nearest way, which was to pass betwixt Babylon and Nineveh, yet their progress is so mysteriously described in the

---

History of Israel and Judah, trans. M. J. O'Connell [New York: Paulist Press, 1973], 123). Tobit, as he tells us himself, "was taken captive in the time of Enemessaros, king of Assyria" (1:2). He uses the Greek form of Shalmaneser, which the ever-pedantic Herbert also cites.

[172] The verse reads: "In the ninth year of Hoshea the king of Assyria took Samaria and carried Israel away into Assyria, and placed them in Halah and Habor by the river of Gozan, and in the cities of the Medes." Hoshea was King of Israel 732–724 B.C.E. Castel states that Samaria was taken by Shalmaneser V's successor Sargon II in 722 B.C.E. "Sargon II," he writes, "claimed to have deported 29, 290 inhabitants" and sent people from other conquered cities to replace them (*History*, 123).

[173] Herbert sometimes uses the chronology developed by Archbishop James Ussher (1581–1656) in his *Annals of the World* (1650–1654), in which he posited, using mathematical calculations based on Old Testament chronology, the date of the Creation as 23rd October, 4004 B.C.E. 'A. M.' stands for *Anno Mundi*. Ussher's book has been newly-edited by Larry and Marion Pierce (Green Forest: Master Books, 2003), and the text may be read online at www.revelationwebsite.co.uk./index/ussher/ussher 5.htm

[174] Now the Amu-Darya River.

[175] This is moden Nishapur, the birthplace of the poet Omar Khayyam. It is in Sogdiana.

[176] A region in Mesopotamia where the Israelites were in captivity. There is a Gozan river, which flows through Gozan, now known as Kizzel-Ozan, and an ancient city in Syria. The river is mentioned in 1 Chronicles 5:26.

Apocrypha, II Esdras 13:40, that some think they went through Palmyrina in Syria and the south part of Armenia the Great into the Persian dominions:

> These are the ten tribes which were carried captive by
> Shalmaneser in the time of King Hoshea, beyond the
> River Euphrates, who, resolving amongst themselves to
> leave the multitude of the heathen and to sequester
> themselves into a country where never mankind dwells,
> they entered in at the narrow passage of Arsareth,
> the springs being by miracle dried up until they had
> passed over, and after a year and a half's journey from
> Arsareth they sat down, where they inhabited until
> the later times.

by which relation, notwithstanding Paulus Venetus and others find this Arsareth in the most easterly part of Scythia *extra Imaus*, albeit some think they passed through the Arabian deserts to Babylon, others nevertheless suppose that their way was through that part of Syria which is called *Palmyrina regio* to Armenia, 'twixt those parts where Euphrates and Tigris have their springs, and so through the Iberian Straits called *Portae Caucasiae* struck into Mazanderan and thence to Bactria. But that Bactria was the country they rested in cannot be imagined, seeing that was not remote enough for eighteen months' travel from Arsareth,[177] if we should grant Arsareth strictly to be in Armenia, being indeed not above two months' journey thence, but more specially, seeing that Bactria was so far from being uninhabited as the place should be they designed to withdraw themselves thereunto, Bactria at that time flourishing so excedingly that it had no less than a thousand cities, so as it may rationally be concluded, albeit in that dejected and depolorable condition these exiled Jews were desirous to find out such as desert country as Esdras speaks of, it was doubtless an enterprise very difficult in case they had the liberty to be their own choosers, which too rarely happens unto captives. For in those days, through Noah's originary and after by Shem's posterity successively, the oriental countries were better-planted then Japhet's was, for in Alexander's time, after subverting the Persian monarchy, invading India and part of Scythia *intra Imaum*, he reported that there he found more people and consequently more opposition and greater and wealthier cities then he had done in his conquest of all other that were under the stroke of the Persian sceptre, even from Indus beyond the Hellespont.

Therefore into what part of the world these poor Jews were sent is not so easily to be discerned, though I imagine they were not permitted to cohabit together, for then their increasing generations would here, as formerly in Egypt, have

---

[177] Arsareth is probably Arsharunik', a province in northern Armenia. However, it has been located in Syria, Romania, and the Ukraine, to mention a few; Columbus located it in America.

rendered them formidable, but rather were separated and made to plant in several colonies. Howbeit, the cause of their banishment appears in the prophecy of Jeremiah 24:9, where 'tis recorded that by reason of their propensity to idolatry they should be removed into all the kingdoms of the earth and become a reproach and a curse in all places whither the Lord would drive them, which was fulfilled, for transplanted we see they were into the East, and seeing the Scripture declares not the place, 'tis of no avail more then to their separation afterwards to make a more curious inquiry concerning it, albeit Jovius,[178] Leunclavius[179] in his *Pandects to Genebrard* and some others from the word *tattar*, in the Hebrew and Syriac denoting a remnant, *Giog-chan, Gioc-Elp* and other proper names there used, circumcision and other Jewish rites there practised, fancy to themselves that into those then uninhabited parts the Jews withdrew, which if so, was in all likelihood to the N. E. of the Mare Caspium, beyond Oxus and Jaxartes,[180] rivers now called *Nycaphrac* and *Chesel*, albeit Abu'l Fida[181] and Rabbi Moshe ben Nachman[182] in his paraphrase upon the Pentateuch conjecture that Gog and Magog, Meshach's progeny, is not so much a general as a particular name of Princes and persons of command in those Scythic provinces, howbeit frequently mentioned in the Prophets and especially in Ezekiel 38 etc.,[183] so as that supposition

---

[178] Paolo Giovio, Bishop of Nocera (1483–1552), was a historian and antiquarian, one of the first people to collect paintings from the New World. His works include a biography of his patron Pope Leo X (1521), *Historiarum sui temporis, vitae virorum illustrium* (1549) and *Eligium virorum bellica virtute illustrium*, a posthumous publication (1554). His *Elogium doctorum virorum*, also posthumously-published (1557) is available in a modern translation by Florence Gregg (Boston: Chapman and Grimes, 1935).

[179] Johann Löwenklau (1541–1594) was a humanist, scholar of Greek, and historian from Westphalia. His most notable works are *Annales sultanorum Othmanidarum* (1588) and *Historiae Musselmanae Turcorum*. The *Pandects* mentioned by Herbert were commentaries on Byzantine and Turkish history, which were later cited by Gibbon in his *Decline and Fall of the Roman Empire*.

[180] The Jaxartes or Orexartes River borders Sogdiana on one side, with the Oxus on the other. It is also known as the Chesel or Qizil Uzum River.

[181] Prince Abu'l Fida ibn Alf'Imad-ed-din (1273–1331) was a geographer, scientist, theologian, and soldier from Damascus, who ruled as sultan over Hamah (1320–1331) under the Mameluke Sultan Malik an-Nasir. His work *An Abridgment of the History of the Human Race* was translated into Latin (1610) by Dobelius, Professor of Arabic at the University of Palermo, and included in Muratori's compilation *Rerum Italicarum scriptores*.

[182] Rabbi Moshe ben Nachman, known as the Ramban (1194–1270), was a Talmud scholar, poet, and expert on Jewish law. He wrote a *Commentary on the Chumash* (the five books of Moses) in 1263, including interpretations of the Kabbala, to which Herbert here makes reference. A printed edition of the work appeared in Basle (1580). Rabbi Charles B. Chavel has recently translated the *Commentaries on the Torah* (New York: Shilo Publishing House, 2005).

[183] For example, "Son of man, set thy face against Gog, the land of Magog, the chief Prince of Meshech, and Tubal, and prophesy against him" (Ezekiel 38:2).

is but weakly-founded, at least in my apprehension. For of equal force is that tradition the Jews here residing as yet retain, that the offspring of Dan, Zebulon,
Asher and Naphtali being planted near Damavand[184] under Mount Taurus, but
themselves the issue of Reuben, Gad and half Manasses, were by Tiglath-pileser
[III][185] removed to this Jarri and parts about Lar. The same time, the inhabitants
of Damascus were by that Prince removed into Kir in Media, II Kings 16:9.[186]
But that they should sequester themselves from the rest of the world was not
without reason, for though the meaning thereof no doubt was to express their
sorrow and desire to avoid the temptations of the heathen, yet seeing in those
times of all sorts of men they were the least sociable, as Ovid says, having as
Tacitus *l.* 5, "*hostile odium contra omnes alios*,"[187] and in requital thereof were styled
by heathen "men-haters," "of all nations the worst," and other like epithets, yet
doubtless have inherited that voluntary execration they entailed unto their posterity at the contemnation of Our Saviour, living ever since, to our sorrow, we
see in an obdurate and wretched condition all the world over, and is thought will
continue until by miracle they be converted as the Almighty shall think fit or at
the personal return of Christ to judgment, or of Elijah, which is thought will be
a little before the world's consummation, albeit as that great scholar Mr. Fulke[188]
observes from Matthew 11:13, in John the Baptist Elijah is already come,[189] the
translation of the Septuagint which to Elijah adds "the Tishbite," being what
doubtless in that text misled St. Chrysostom.[190] Moreover, these Jews, notwithstanding their itch after idol-worship is over, and that in the synagogue they have
a formal way of singing service expressing very little reverence and differing from

---

[184] Damavand [*Damoan*] is a town on the Havir River about 30 km. from the mountain of the same name. Traditionally, the tribe of Dan settled in Tel al-Qadi, now in
northern Palestine.

[185] Tiglath-pileser III, King of Assyria (745–727 B. C. E.) annexed southern Ar-
menia and exiled most of the populace; in 738 B. C. E. he forced tribute from Tyre and
Israel, and in 732 he annexed Galilee and Gilead from King Pekah (for details see Castel,
History, 120–21).

[186] ". . . the king of Assyria went up against Damascus and took it, and carried the
people captive to Kir."

[187] "With hostile dislike towards all others" (Tacitus, *Histories* 5. 1).

[188] William Fulke (1538–1589) was a Puritan divine and Professor of Hebrew at St.
John's College, Cambridge, then Master of Pembroke Hall (1578). His principal work,
and the one alluded to here by Herbert, was *A Defence of the sincere true translations of the
Holy Scriptures into the English tongue* (1583).

[189] "For all the prophets and the law prophesied until John."

[190] John Chrysostom, *Homilies on Matthew* 10. 4. St. John Chrysostom (c. 347–407),
Archbishop of Constantinople (398), a post from which he was deposed through political machinations, and eminent theologian, one of the "four great Greek doctors of the
church" (Attwater, *Dictionary*, 194). He wrote many exegetical works and homilies as
well as the *Baptismal Instructions*, one of his best-known books.

that which Ezra appointed, yet have they no sacrificing priest, holding no place proper save Jerusalem, where the Christians would oppose it as well as Turks. The five books of Moses they have agreeable to ours, and though they have no *tirshatha* or civil Magistrate of their own, or dare not break the peace where they live under Christian, Mohammedan or Gentile government, yet are not without separation amongst themselves, the five great points betwixt the great families of Shammai and Hillel[191] still spreading like a gangrene so irreconcilably that till the Tishbite come, as one says, none else will be able to agree them, not Rabbi Elias,[192] who from the first verse of the first chapter of Genesis, where the letter *aleph* is six times found, kabbalistically concludes that the world shall endure for six thousand years, *aleph* in the computation standing for a thousand, albeit he should enter the lists to vanquish either party.

But to return. In or near this place is a precious liquor or mummy growing, *mumnaky-koobas*[193] they call it, which none presumes to take, it being carefully-preserved for the King's sole use. In June only it distils from the top of those stupendous mountains every year about five ounces. A most redolent gum it is, sovereign against poison, and, if we may believe them, a catholicon for all sorts of wounds whatsoever, so as when other Princes send Shah Abbas gold, pearl or like costly presents, he returns them a little of this balsam as a suitable requital. After Alexander had prayed and sacrificed in Susa (betrayed by Abulites,[194] a time-serving satrap), he led his wanton army towards Persepolis; his nearest passage was over this hills of Jarri, in those days by authors called *Pilae Persidis* and *Susaidae*, where to his amazement he was so well-beaten by Ariobazarnes,[195] a

---

[191] Herbert is referring here to controversies in Jewish law on points laid down by the Mishnah scholar Rabbi Hillel (d. c. 10 C.E.), who founded a dynasty ("family") of sages that would provide leaders for the Jews until the fifth century. Rabbi Shammai (50 B.C.E.–30 C.E.) and his group represented the opposition to Hillel.

[192] Rabbi Elijah Levita (1469–1549), poet, Talmud scholar, Kabbalist, and grammarian, was from Neustadt, Bavaria. He led a varied life, living in Venice to avoid persecution in Bavaria (1500–1504; 1527–1549), Padua (1504–1509), and Rome (1509–1527), where he ended up staying in the residence of Cardinal Egidio of Viterbo. He even set up a printing-press for his own works with the blessing of Pope Leo X. His works include a commentary on Rabbi Moshe Kimchi's (brother of David Kimchi, whom Herbert cites) *Journey on the Path of Knowledge* and a Hebrew grammar which was a model of its kind.

[193] Foster defines this as "a kind of bitumen that exudes from the rocks and is much prized for its supposed healing qualities" (*Herbert*, 308).

[194] Abulites (d. 324 B.C.E.) had been appointed satrap of Susa by Darius III, and surrendered it to Alexander in 331 B.C.E. He retained authority there until he was executed for bad government (see Q. Curtius 5.2.8 and 5.2.17).

[195] Ariobazarnes had been a commanding general when the Persians were defeated at Gaugamela, but his resistance to the Macedonians at the Persian Gates (*Pilae Persidis*) was one of Alexander's few setbacks. His "little army," at least according to Quintus Curtius, was in fact "25,000 infantry" who bombarded the enemy with everything from small

valiant Persian and his little army, that contrary to the accustomed pace of the world's monarch he was constrained to retreat gladly, and found another way to avoid the storms of stones and arrows which that noble Persian freely sent him.

The eleventh of February we left Lar, *Cadgea-Obdruzy* the Governor[196] having furnished us with mules, emblems of sobriety. Our harbinger, or *mammandor* as called in Persia, was an old *qizilbash* who would be sure, hopeful of some reward, at every place where we made our *manzil*[197] to provide us with good quarter and such meat as the places could afford, by virtue nevertheless of force rather of his authority domineering over the wretched rustics, more then pleased us, for he would proffer them a little money for what he liked, which if they refused, then *nolens volens* he would have it, and *alla soldado*[198] paid them with big words and bastinados, so as we saw that in miserable slavery these peasants live, contented to submit to the arbitrary will of the soldier. The first night we pitched our tents not far from Lar, but were stopped next day by an immoderate flood of rain, which though it was very welcome, yet made the earth so slippery as our camels' glib hooves could not foot it. The rain falls seldom here, but when it comes they both feel and hear it; sometimes it raises such a deluge as sweeps men and houses away, for, as we were told, six years ago in this very place a caravan of two thousand camels in part perished by the fury of it.

The fourteenth day we rode to Dihkuh or Techoo,[199] which signifies "a town under a hill," where we saw many pretty tombs, few without a gravestone and an Arabic memorial. The Alkoran commands that none be buried in cities, for fear the dead infect the living; this *ius sepulchri* was according to the ancients, Silius Italicus *lib.* 1, "that no grave should be made in the place where any other had formerly been buried."[200] And by the Law of the Twelve Tables[201] burials were prohibited and not permitted to be within any city but rather in cemeteries

---

stones to huge boulders, resulting in Alexander suffering "agonies, as much of shame as despondency" (3.5.17–21).

[196] Possibly Qazi Abu'l Qasem, who had been appointed Governor of Lar in 1602 when Allah Verdi Khan captured the city. Foster identifies him as possibly Khwaja Abdurriza (*Herbert*, 62).

[197] A *manzil* is a place where travellers stop; the word means "descending or alighting" in Arabic (*HJ* 599).

[198] Like a soldier.

[199] Dihkuh [*De-schow* or *Techoo*]. Stodart calls it *Dehcohibibia*.

[200] Titus Catius Asconius Silius Italicus (c. 25–101) was a Roman politician and historian, consul in 68 under the Emperor Nero. He wrote the *Punica*, a 12,000-line poem about the war with Carthage, which has the distinction of being the longest epic poem in Latin. The scholar Daniel Heinsius edited it in 1600. J. D. Duff edited and translated the work (London: Heinemann, 1934) and the full Latin text may be found online.

[201] The Law of the Twelve Tables or *Lex duodecim tabularum* was an ancient Roman legal code dating from about 450 B.C.E. Details of it and the story of its origins may be found in Livy, *Rise of Rome* 3.57.

without the city, or nigh the public highway, that by viewing the sepulchres of
the dead (according to the customs of the Romans and of the Egyptians, who had
them in their banqueting-houses), they might the better contemplate their mortality. A mile from this town we viewed about threescore long black pavilions,
which were black without but within they had female beauties; the Persians call
them *vlachs*, the Arabs *kabila*, the Turkestanis and Armenians *ta'ipha*, the Tartars *urdu*, the ancients *nomades* made from the Numidians, concerning whom the
poet says truly that "Their carts their houses are, their sole delight / To wander
with their house-gods day and night."[202]

Suffer me to wander a little with such novel company. Seeing that virtue, the
trophy of a refined ambition, is purchased by embracing the wholesome notions
of a humble soul, of a well-tempered spirit, that Heavenly radiance respects no
other object with delight save virtue, from which pure streams flows moderation,
to whose excellency, next to spiritual sacrifice, we may safely devote our best endeavours, howbeit, so apt to every immodest act is man's corrupt disposition that
to enjoy sensuality he conceits virtue (though never so gorgeously-arrayed) foul
and deformed, till moderation force him to a strict account and discover how
much he erred in preserving intemperance before the transcendent qualities of a
virtuous life. From whence, when we contemplate the contented life and poverty
of these *uloches*, needs must we contemn ourselves of loathsome riot, for how free
from unseasonable care, pale envy, affrighting tumult and nasty surfeit do these
enjoy themselves? Happy conquerors! How mutually do they accord, how joyfully satiate nature in what is requireable? Hear Lucan in its commendation: "Base
luxury! Wherein so much is spent,/ Learn with how little Nature is content./ In
gold and myrrh these drink not, but are best/ In health when bread and water are
their feast." [Civil War 4. 373-374, 376-377, 380-381].

Biriz.

To return. So soon Phoebus had run thrice fifteen degrees in our hemisphere, we
mounted our melancholy mules and made our next *manzil* at Biriz. Nothing observable in the way except a thick wall of great length and heighth cut by extraordinary toil out of the rock as a boundary and to safeguard the Larians from the
Shirazians, the Kingdom of Lar in that place terminating. Biriz is a village which
promises much at a distance, but when there deludes the expectation, howbeit
not a little famous through the Persian territories, both from the immunities
which an ancient learned *sayed* endued it with, confirmed by successive Princes,
and from an Arabic school which is there kept and distinguished into several
classes of civil law, astrology, physic and what leads to Mecca, commendable

---

[202] Herbert seems to be referring to gypsies; the word *vlach* denotes people from
Wallachia (Romania), *taifa* is an Arabic (not Armenian) word meaning 'tribe' or 'people,'
and sometimes refers to Bulgarian gypsies.

in their Pythagorean silence, practising to discourse by winks, nods and dumb signs, for babbling and noise in all Arabic schools is detested. They observe two rules especially: obedience and moving the body toward [Mecca] whiles they be reading. Adjoining this school is a *jama masjed* or mosque of great veneration, by being the dormitory of that great doctor Imam Zadeh Amir Ahmed Ali,[203] who was a prophet's son and allied to their great Ali,[204] in this grave enjoying, say they, eight hundred years' rest. His tomb raises four foot from the pavement, is longer and larger then the included carcase, for it is eight foot long and covered with a white fine linen cloth. The tombstones are carved and painted with knots and poesies of Arabic; near him are fixed two lances to memorise his *quondam* profession, and some ensigns not of ordinary invention. Upon his coffin lies a set of beads, which, if you will credit them, to this day retain their master's virtue in working miracles. Within the coffin in his body, a mummy that has continued long; the brains and entrails are taken out, for they corrupt the soonest, and the carcase, as they say, is embalmed in wax or such gums as both smell delicately and are of longest continuance. At the top of the chapel is a steel mirror wherein these lynx-eyed people view the deformity of their sins.[205] They also showed us a square stone which was pierced and hung near the wall, a rare stone, a relic most notorious, for the prophet used to burthen the backs of impenitent sinners with it, telling them that their impiety made it seem heavy, a weight so ponderous as made them take the right path to be quit of it. A little pot they also showed us, holding a sovereign unguent made eight hundred years since, oft-used, and, which is a miracle, never exhaused; 'tis not only good to help sore eyes, but a panacea, as they would have us believe, against all diseases. To crown all, a book, no Alcoran of devotion, was laid upon his coffin; anybody may be suffered to see it afar off, but to touch it was presumption. In storms and crosses, they say, they find remedy with only naming it. The church was neatly-matted; a mosque it is of so great veneration that none enters with boots or shoes on. Such as want issues

---

[203] Probably Pir Ahmed Ali (d. 840), an Ismaili leader who preached in Iran. He was not related to Ali, although the Ismailis are a Shi'a sect. They believe that the true Imam was Ismail ibn Ja'afar as-Sadiq (Hughes, *Dictionary*, 220).

[204] Ali (601–660) was the son of Abu Talib, the Prophet Mohammed's uncle. He ruled as the fourth Caliph from 655–60 and was assassinated. By the Shi'as he is considered the legitimate Caliph, who as the Prophet's grandson should have succeeded Mohammed in 632, because Mohammed had adopted him as his own son and married him to his daughter Fatima. The Persians, who revere him, call him "*Sher-i-kuda*, i.e. 'the Lion of God'" (Hughes, *Dictionary*, 13). Herbert (and other Western writers) refers to him as *Mortis-Ally*, by which he means "Murtaza,"a title of respect. There is a recent study of him by Mohammed Abdul Rauf and Seyyed Hossein Nasr, *Imam 'Ali ibn Abi Talib: The First Intellectual Muslim Thinker*, (Alexandria: Al Saadawi Publications, 1996).

[205] 1638: Atop of the chapel hangs a globe to express his power and greatness; in the wall are round glasses such as are in dove-houses, in which these people see representations of their sins.

(in legs I mean not), health, wealth, friends or the like, according as their offering is, have satisfaction. The oracle (the priest) they say never deceives them, *sed non ego credulus illis*,[206] and with that I bid farewell to Biriz, which some make to be the first town in that which strictly may be called Persia, howbeit we usually extend it south as far as the Gulf of Persia, having Media to the north, east the two Carmanias and west Susiana, according to the 5 book of Ptolemy.

Binaru. Goyn.

Next night we got to Binaru. The last town feasted us with traditions, this with good cheer, music, kettledrums and six dumb muskets. The ruins of an ancient castle demolished by the Persian here shows its ribs, through which the cool air blows, seldom failing from the top of that mountain. One side of the castle wall is anatomised to the town, the other to the stony desert. Next night we lay in Goyn,[207] bragging that it has a thousand but ordinary houses. After we had reposed an hour, a hocus-pocus for the Ambassador's better repast performed rare tricks of activity. Some of them I remember: he trod upon two sharp-edged scimitars with his bare feet then laid his naked back upon them, suffering a heavy anvil to be set on his belly and two men to hammer out four horseshoes upon it as forcibly as they could bear. That trick ended, he throust his arms and thighs through with many arrows and lances, then, by sheer strength of his head and agility of body lift up no less then a yard from the ground a great stone weighing six hundred pound, and then, as if he had done nothing, knit his hair to an old goat's head and with a scornful pull tore it asunder, at that crying out *"alhamdolel-lah"* i.e. God be thanked, the standers-by with a loud yell applauding him. This was notable, but what was he to speak of Marius, one of the Thirty Tyrants,[208] who with one of his fingers could overthrow a loaded wain?[209] Or of Polydamas, who with one hand would hold a wild bull by his hinder leg, as Caelius Rhodigi-

---

[206] "But I'm not credulous about such matters" (Virgil, *Eclogues* 9. 34).

[207] Binaru [*Bannarow*] and Goyn [*Goyome*] are small towns now in Kerman province. Stodart mentions neither of them.

[208] During the reign of Gallienus (253–68), the Roman Empire was in near-anarchy at times. The "Thirty Tyrants" was a collective name for the number of usurpers to the Roman throne who sprang up during that time and to about 275. M. Aurelius Marius was emperor in Britain and Gaul for a few months in 268–69. Of him the *Augustan History* says that there was "no-one whose hands were stronger". . . "he is said to have thrust back oncoming waggons by means of his forefinger" (*Lives of the Later Caesars: The First Part of the Augustan History, with Lives of Nerva and Trajan,* trans. Anthony Birley [Harmondsworth: Penguin Books, 1976], 81).

[209] A farm-waggon.

nus[210] and Trebellius Pollio[211] report? But in remembering these I had almost forgot how that in Goyn is entombed Malik Mohammed, who in these parts is not a little famous for fomenting the authority of his master Mohammed, when the Saracens, not liking the innovation, first began to canvass it.

Next night we lost one another by a careless associating, whereby we procured to ourselves a miserable lodging in that solitary wilderness, having neither grass nor trees nor water, but stones which gave no refreshment, and sand in abundance, nor beheld we other than ostriches, storks and pelicans for companions. The earth has heretofore worn Flora's livery, but by the rage of war and continued ardor of the sun becomes miserably desert, or rather from the wrath of the almighty God, who, as the kingly Prophet sings, "makes a fruitful land barren for the ungodliness of them that dwell therein" [Psalm 107: 34]. Next day we quested in search of our caravan, and after some pain recovered it. That night we again pitched in the desert, and were entertained by such a sudden storm of rain, thunder and lightning as made our cheer very wretched, imprisoning us also in our tents. Next day we had the weather more comfortable, the sight of a few date and mastic trees exceedingly refreshing us; Coryate's report that mastic is found nowhere but in *Syo* was here confuted.

An antic tomb.

By the way we took notice of an odd-conceited tomb which inhumed a harmless shepherd. Hung it was to and fro with threads tripartite (peradventure shadowing out a trinity), each thread being trimmed with particoloured wool, at each end of which was placed a puppet to protect it and some cypress-branches stuck about to revive, as I apprehended, an antiquated ceremony mentioned in Virgil *lib.* 3, which then was to erect ". . . altars their ghosts to please, / Trimm'd with blue fillets and black cypresses."[212] And in the 6 *Aeneid*, "About the sides they mournful cypress place."[213] And that it was an ancient custom to adorn the sep-

---

[210] Ludovico Ricchieri (1450–1520), Italian humanist and scholar, was the author of *Lectionum antiquorum libri XXX* (1516). This was an extensive study of the mystic and symbolic interpretation of the pagan gods, old pagan vestiges of the Trinity, and speculations on Egyptian hieroglyphics.

[211] Trebellius Pollio, who may or may not have been a pseudonym for someone else, was one of the biographers in the *Augustan History*. He probably lived during the reign of Constantine I (306–37), and wrote the biographies of Valerian, Gallienus, Claudius II, and the British usurper Postumus, who was one of the "Thirty Tyrants." The *Historiae Augustae* was edited by Isaac Casaubon (1613), who gave it the name.

[212] By 1677 Herbert had four verse-translations of the *Aeneid* at his disposal: Thomas May and Gavin Douglas (1553), Thomas Phaer and Thomas Twyne (1573), John Vicars (1632), and John Ogilby (1649).

[213] Virgil, *Aeneid* 3. 90–1; 6. 305.

ulchres of the dead with fillets, Statius[214] *lib.* 4 *Silvarum* saith: "*Pande fores supe-rum vitrataque templa Sabaei / Nubibus et pecudum fibris spirantibus imple.*"[215] ". . . *Et ab arbore casta / Nectent purpureas niveo discrimine vitras*," saith another poet, and Valerius Flaccus[216] *lib.* 8 to the same purpose: "*Ultima virgineis tum flens dedit oscula vitris.*"[217]

The next being the two and twentieth of February, by the way we had some sport in dislodging a wild boar whom we pursued, but neither shot nor dogs could reach him. That night we made Qutbabad our *manzil*, Mochak[218] our next, in which are buried Mohammed, Hajji, Ismail and Ali, four Musselmanish doctors intombed here four hundred years ago and resorted to with no small reverence. Next day to *Coughton,*[219] where the people in few years before before suffered in a high measure by locusts, which these parts are sometimes infected with, yet not so much as the more south and easterly parts of the world, where as God's revengeful armies they are observed to fly in numbers infinite and in order admirable, devouring the fruits of the earth so exceedingly that famine commonly ensueth. Howbeit, in some places the inhabitants in requital devour them again, esteeming them both savoury meat and easy of digestion. The next day we got to Unghea, the day following to Moyechaw, next to Pol-é Padishah, leaving Baba Hajji[220] on our left hand, and the next night pitched a *farsang* short of Shiraz. According to custom we expected a ceremonious entrance, but seeing none came out to that purpose, our Ambassador, who was ever-sensible of his master's honour, send his *mehmandar*[221] to the Governor to demand fresh horses and

---

[214] Publius Papinius Statius (c. 45–96), the Roman epic poet whose career was cut short by order of Emperor Domitian. Statius's most famous poem is the *Thebaid*, but Herbert quotes here from the *Silvae*. Statius also wrote another epic, the *Achilleis*. There were many editions of the *Silvae* available to Herbert, dating from its first printing (1483) to Gronovius's edition of 1637.

[215] "Fling wide the doors of the High Ones and fill the garlanded temple with Sabaean / Clouds and the breathing entrails of beasts" (Statius, *Silvae* 4. 8, 1–2).

[216] Gaius Valerius Flaccus (d. c. 93) was the author of an unfinished epic poem, the *Argonautica*, which he dedicated to Emperor Vespasian. This poem owes a great deal to Apollonius Rhodius, but has its own individualism, and has lately seen a revival of interest amongst classical scholars. It was first printed in 1474, and there is a modern translation by David Slavitt (Baltimore: Johns Hopkins University Press, 1999).

[217] "Then, weeping, she kissed her virgin fillets for the last time" (Valerius Flaccus, *Argonautica* 8. 6).

[218] Qotbabad [*Cut-bobbo*] is not mentioned by Stodart; it is in modern Hormozghan province.

[219] Foster tentatively identifies this place as Kuiduna (*Herbert*, 66).

[220] Baba Hajji [*Babbaw-hodgee*] is called *Bobeohogi* by Stodart. It is probably modern-day Hajjiabad. Pol-é Padishah [*Pully-potshaw*] means "the Emperor's bridge."

[221] The *mehmandar* is "an officer appointed to attend on ambassadors" (Foster, *Herbert*, 308).

fitting accommodation. The *daruga*[222] in person came to dissemble his neglect, first excusing the Duke's absence, whose displeasure he feared, for not acquainting him with this excellent advantage to manifest his integrity unto our nation, in comparison to whom all other in that part of the world were contemptible. In a word, perceiving our haste, he prayed His Lordship to exercise but three days' patience till the great Duke came purposely to honour his entrance, a favour of a double reflex in that it would infinitely content the Governor and citizens and accumulate an incomparable splendour to his entrance, closing his compliment with an if not, he was ready to usher His Lordship to his lodging. The Ambassador, though he well descried his hypocrisy, yet thought it best to dissemble his discontent, perceiving no remedy. We jogged leisurely on upon our mules and asinagos, who, so soon as they winded the air of this great city, spared the Persians the labour of their kettledrums, timbrels, oboes and such Phrygic music, sometimes braying out, at other times echoing to one another in their Myrmillonian[223] cornets as if some orgy to Liber Pater[224] had been solemnizing, insomuch as many ran out of doors, others fired their flambeaux to know the cause and glut their wonder. After long circling we alighted at the house of Shaikh Ali Beg, the Duke's deputy, where our Ambassador, after a prolix apology from the Governor, was entertained with a short banquet and then conveyed to [the] Alikhan, a house at the east end of the city belonging to the King, encompassed with curious gardens and as spacious as most in Persia. And now we have overcome the trouble of our passage into the city, albeit we entered not in the daytime to see and be seen, do not think it novelty or that it was without reputation, or as if nocturnal entries had not equal lustre with the day, seeing that Holofernes chose the night to make his triumphant entry into Damascus, Antiochus also took some time to enter into Jerusalem, Augustulus into Rome, and haughty Shapur into this city.[225]

---

[222] The *daruga* is the town governor (Savory, in Monshi, *History*, 1387).

[223] A *myrmillo* was a Roman gladiator who was armed with sword and shield.

[224] Liber Pater is another name for Bacchus.

[225] Holofernes was the Babylonian general slain by Judith; Antiochus IV Epiphanes (175–164 B.C.E.) was the Seleucid king who captured Jerusalem and rededicated the Temple to Zeus (170 B.C.E.); Romulus Augustulus (r. 475–76) was the last Emperor of Rome, deposed by Odoacer the Visigoth; Shapur I (r. 241–72) was the great Sassanid ruler of Persia who defeated and captured the Emperor Valerian (260).

Shiraz.

Shiraz, for so they pronounce it, the pleasantest of Asiatic cities, is removed from the Equator 29 degrees 20 minutes north, its longitude 88 degrees, by Phil[ippus] Ferrarius[226] and some others supposed to be the relics of Persepolis,[227] which I no ways allow of, not only from the difference of situation and distance of place from *Chilamor* being no less then thirty English miles and without all peradventure part of it, but principally in regard to many rising and rough grounds and some considerable hills are interposing. For ben Jonah, a Jew travelling these parts about 500 years ago found *Syaphaz* hereabouts, which doubtless was this city. By Cornelius de Judeis[228] 'tis named *Sytas*, a mistake probably in the transcript, seeing that *Sivas* another author likewise miscalls it. Don Garcia[229] calls it *Xirias*, Paulus Venetus *Zyraz*, Sir Walter Ralegh *Siras*, Osorius *Xiras*, Stephanus *Cirecatha* and *Cirec-batha*, borrowed, as I suppose, from Caelius [Rhodiginus], who does the like from Muslih ed-din Saadi,[230] the philosopher and traveller, whose native

[226] Filippo Ferrari (d. 1626), an Italian monk, was the compiler of several geographical dictionaries such as the *Epitome geographicum* (1605). He also wrote *Tabula longitudinis ac latitudinis urbium et oppidorum per totum terrarum orbem* (1627), which was translated by William Dillingham and published in London as *Lexicon geographicum* (1657). It is to this work which Herbert refers.

[227] Don Juan of Persia, for one, says that Shiraz "was in ancient days called Persepolis" (*Don Juan*, 38).

[228] Cornelis de Jode (1568–1600) was a Flemish geographer who produced a map of the world, *Totius orbis cogniti universalis descriptio* (1593). It is remarkable because it includes a map of Australia and makes the claim that the Portuguese discovered Antarctica.

[229] Don Garcia de Silva y Figueroa (1550–1624) travelled extensively in Persia, visiting Shiraz, Isfahan, and Qum amongst other places. In 1614 Philip III had appointed him ambassador to Persia, where he finally arrived in 1617, and upon his return to Spain he wrote *Totius legationis suae et Indicarum rerum Persidisque commentarii* (1620) and *Comentarios de Don Garcia de Silva, que contien su viaje a la India y de ella a Persia* (1624). He was probably the first European to describe Zoroastrian funeral rites, which may have prompted Herbert to go into more details about the religion. There was a French translation of his work by Abraham de Wicquefort (1667), who was also Herbert's translator.

[230] Muslih ed-din Mushrif ibn Abdollah (c. 1184–1283) known as Sa'adi, the great Persian poet, traveller and philosopher, born in Shiraz as Herbert states. He travelled in Anatolia, Syria, Egypt, and Iraq, and may have gone as far as India and Central Asia. His best-known work is the *Gulistan* or *Rose-Garden* (1258), a work of great beauty and tasteful eroticism in mostly prose but with some poetry as well. It influenced the work of Goethe in his *West-Ostliche Diwan* and was translated by several distinguished westerners, including Emerson. Georg Gentius's Latin translation, *Rosarium politicum*, appeared in 1651; there was an earlier French version by André de Ryer (1634), not to mention another Latin one by Olearius (1654), any of which Herbert could have known. There is a good modern English translation by Omar Ali-Shah (Reno: Tractus Books, 1997). He also wrote the *Bostan* or *Orchard* (1257), which was translated by Olearius (1671).

place this was and is by him called *Ciropolis*, alluding rather to its ancient Greek name, if right translated, then to the name it then bore, seeing authors more ancient then himself call it by name of *Syros*, as the Jew I lately mentioned and others. This Saadi lived A. D. 1200, Heg. 600, at which time ruled there Muzaffar ed-din Abubakr, son to Saad, son to Zangi,[231] as appears by that learned treatise of Saadi called *Rosarium politicum*, in our time translated by Gentius. The name Ciropolis, as the word imports, we may suppose assumed from Cyrus that noble river, which also gave name to that magnificent Prince who was formerly called Agradatus,[232] albeit we have a clearer authority for it, seeing God, by the prophet Isaiah 44 and 45 calls him by that name an hundred years before his birth, being anointed to be the deliverer of his people from the Babylonian bondage.[233] The river, whether it be that springing from the Coraxian Hills in thirty-eight degrees, empties itself into the Mare Caspium and has neighbouring it the two other rivers, Cambyses and Araxes,[234] for that in Sogdiana near Jaxartes mentioned by Quintus Curtius, and that other in India spoken of by Aelian are not it, is evident, or that it be this which streams in the mid-way 'twixt Shiraz and Chilmanor. Being unsatisfied myself, I leave it unto others better to consider of, and shall only give my apprehension concerning the etymology.

Shiraz, then, probably derives itself either from *sherab*, which in the Persian tongue signifies a grape, here abounding and then which no part of the East has more generous nor any climate more benevolent, or else from *sheer*, which in the Persian signifies milk, and the rather, seeing several other towns

---

[231] These are Salgharid sultans of Fars. Saadi was born during the reign of Muzaffar ed-din Takla bin Zangi (r. 1175–1195). Abu Bakr bin Saad bin Zangi (r. 1226–1260) became Saadi's patron. Herbert (or possibly Gentius) seems to have inverted the two sultans and conflated their names into the bargain.

[232] Herbert's source for the name-change is Strabo (*Geography* 7. 165).

[233] Cyrus II became King of the Persians and Medes in 549 B.C.E. and a few years later began his war on Babylon, whose King Nabonidus he defeated in 539 and founded the Persian Empire. He allowed the Jews to return to Judaea, which many did, and Cyrus became for them a liberator. The Isaiah who prophesied the coming of Cyrus we now know to be the "Second Isaiah," who flourished from about 550–539 (Castel, *History*, 147–48), which means that he lived during the time that Cyrus was consolidating his rule and moving against Babylon. Isaiah 44:24–28 reads "I am the Lord . . . that saith of Cyrus, He is my shepherd and shall perform all my pleasure." In 45:1 the Lord speaks to Cyrus, whom he calls "his anointed . . . whose right hand I have holden." The River Cyrus , with "its waters, pure and gold from its source in nearby rocky heighths" is southeast of Parsagada (A. T. Olmstead, *History of the Persian Empire* [Chicago: University of Chicago Press, 1959], 61).

[234] The Araxes river is on the north-west border of Persia, and formed the boundary of the Achaemenid Empire. Also known as Astarachay or Araz, it flows 1072 km through parts of Turkey, Armenia, Iran and Azerbaijan; The Cambyses River is now known as the Iori; it is a tributary of the Kur (Cyrus) River.

have their denominations accordingly, namely Aleppo from *halip*, i.e. milk, albeit some would have it from Alypius, Julian's[235] lieutenant, and several Persian towns have the like, as *Hormont*, a town of dates, *De-achow*, a town upon a hill, *De-gardow*, a walnut-town, *Bazabachow*, Firuzkuh, *Cut-babbaw*. Or otherwise, passing by the Greek synonyms, i.e. *per astum*, and that of Strabo *l.* 9, "*a Minerva, quae dicta est Sheraz*,"[236] which signifies a lion, or from the *Syrases* as the aborigines or *incolae*[237] of old hereabouts were termed, and appears by Polyaenus *l.* 8 *De Semiramide*, or else "*a Schyris Arabiae populis*," who, to give Pliny's expression, *lib.* 6 *cap.* 13, "*Indorum vel potius Persacum lingua loquentes ibi sunt remeantes.*" Nor was this city less ancient then great if the report be true which the inhabitants make that Jemshid, the fifth King of Persia and predecessor of Chedor-Laomer,[238] laid its first foundation. For Boterus affirms for truth that "*Quando Syras erat Syros (i.e. civitas), tunc Cairus erat ejus pagus*," which proverb notwithstanding he borrows from Muslih ed-din Saadi, who has this hyperbolising question: "*Quid est Cairum? Quid Damascus? Quid terra? Quid ipsum mare? Omnes enim urbes pagi sunt, & sola Schyras urbs est*," rendering thereby Shiraz only worthy to be named a city, in comparison of which Cairo, Damascus and all others extant upon the continent or isles were but villages, Saadi also in this taking his pattern from Rome, "*quae sola per excellentiam urbs vocabatur.*"[239] But that it was a very great city long ago is indubitable, and for proof I give you these few instances. Ulugh Beg,[240] a learned geographer and nephew to Tamerlane, in his time finds her to

---

[235] Flavius Claudius Julianus, "Julian the Apostate," was Roman Emperor 361–63. He perished from wounds sustained during a campaign against the Persians. He was also a noted philosopher and satirist. Alypius of Antioch, a geographer whose works are no longer extant, was appointed prefect of Britain by Julian and commissioned to rebuild the temple in Jerusalem.

[236] From Minerva, which is called Shiraz.

[237] Inhabitants.

[238] Chedor-Laomer was a king of Elam, whose name in Elamite would have been Kudur-Lagamar, "servant of the deity Lagamar." He is mentioned in Genesis 14:9. Historians date him between the eighteenth and twelfth centuries B. C. E. In the *Shahnameh* Jamshid is actually the fourth, not fifth king, and his predecessor is Tahumeres, who is obviously (for Herbert) the equivalent of Chedor-Laomer (Ferdowsi, *Shahnameh*, 4–6).

[239] Which only because of its excellence was called a city.

[240] Ulugh Beg or Chagatai Khan (c. 1393–1449), born Mirza Mohammed Taragai bin Shahrukh, was Timur's grandson, not nephew. Born in Sultaniyeh, Iran, he was Khan of the Mavrannahan Khanate in Transoxiana. He was an eminent scholar, being a scientist, poet, mathematician, soldier, and theologian of the highest order. In 1428 he built an observatory at the University of Samarkand, and wrote the *Zij-i-Sultani* (1437), the greatest star-catalogue between the times of Ptolemy and Tycho Brahe. It was translated into Latin by Thomas Hyde, Professor of Arabic at Cambridge, as *Tabulae longitudinis et latitudinis stellarum fixarum ex observatione Ulughbeighi* (1665). Robert Byron

have fifteen miles' compass; Contarini[241] after him the like, and eighty thousand houses. Barbaro[242] eightscore years ago reports her to be twenty, Cluverius[243] the like, Teixera after him to have six hundred and thirty miles circuit, Schickhard[244] upon the *Tarikh*[245] the like circumference, a circuit very large but occasioned by the many and spacious gardens this as most other Asian cities have, rather then

---

calls Ulugh Beg "the most amiable of all his family, and the only scientist among them" (*Oxiana*, 257).

[241] Ambrogio Contarini (fl. 1474–1499) was a Venetian nobleman and diplomat. He travelled to Persia in 1473–1475 and wrote an account, *Il Viaggio dell'Ambrosio Contarini, ambasciatore della Signoria di Venetia, al Uxan Cassan, Re de Persia*, later published in Venice (1543) and again by Ramusio. He was reputedly also the first European traveller to describe Moscow, as he also visited Russia (1476–1478). His *Travels to Tana and Persia* was translated by William Thomas (see above), later edited by Lord Stanley of Alderley (London: Hakluyt Society, 1873). Foster notes that "no reference to the population of Shiraz" may be found in Contarini (*Herbert*, 310).

[242] Iosafà Barbaro (1413–1494), another Venetian nobleman, travelled to Persia, India, and other places in 1471–1479, following Caterino Zeno to Persia. His account of his travels, *Viaggi del Magnifico Messer Josaphet Barbaro*, which he wrote in 1487, was edited by A. Manuzio in his compilation of Venetian travel-accounts, *Viaggi fatti da Vinetia alla Tana, in Persia, in India et in Constantinopole* (1545). Barbaro is cited several times by Juan of Persia, and is reprinted in all editions of Ramusio. William Thomas, Clerk of the Council to Edward VI, made an English translation in about 1550, but it was not published.

[243] Philipp Clüver[ius] (1580–1623) was a geographer and antiquarian from Gdansk, highly-regarded as the founder of modern historical geography. He visited Norway, England, France, and Italy, and wrote the *Introductio in universam geographiam* (published 1624). For an appraisal, see H. A. M. van der Heijden, "Philipp Cluverius and Dutch Cartography: An Introduction," *Quaerendo* 32 (2002): 222–44.

[244] Wilhelm Schickhardt (1592–1635), a Lutheran minister and polymath, was simultaneously Professor of Astronomy and Professor of Eastern Languages at the University of Tübingen from 1631. In addition to writing on these subjects, he also produced works on optics, mechanics, and cartography, as well as being an engraver, teacher of Biblical languages, and the inventor of what may have been the first calculating machine. He produced the *Hebraische Rad* (1621), a textbook of Hebrew, and *Der Hebraische Trichter* (1627), both of which were likely of use to Herbert. He was a friend of Kepler's. His family suffered greatly during the Thirty Years War; his mother was shot by soldiers and he himself, as well as his daughter and sister, died of plague.

[245] Abi Ja'afar Mohammed al-Tabari [*Mironda Tarikh*] (838–923), born in Amol, was the earliest and one of the most eminent Persian historians and theologians. He travelled to Spain, Palestine, and Egypt, and wrote the *Tarikh al-Taban* or *History of the Prophets and Kings*, which covered the period from the Creation to 915 C.E. Herbert sometimes confuses part of his name with the title of his book. M. J. de Goeje edited the work in 15 volumes (Leiden, 1879–1901); there is a modern edition with translation by E. K. Rowson et al. in 40 volumes (Albany: SUNY Press, 2007).

from the numerous buildings. John of Persia[246] in his time numbered her inhabitants eighty thousand, bin Ali three hundred thousand; I dare not gaisay their reports because no present inquiry can well disprove them. Let us therefore rest contented in her description as I could observe her to be at present.

Shiraz is distant from Hormuz one hundred and eight *farsangs* or three hundred and four and twenty miles, from Lar one hundred eighty-six, from Babylon three hundred, from Isfahan two hundred and two and twenty, from the Caspian Sea six hundred, from Qazvin four hundred and eighty-six, from Firuzkuh[247] four hundred and forty, from Kandahar six hundred and sixty, from Yezd two hundred and nineteen, from Firozabad sixty English miles or thereabouts. The ancient inhabitants were the Artiatae, Tapiri, Cartii and Orchatii, now converted into Pars, Furs, Fares and Farsistan.

Shiraz at this day is the second city for magnificence in the monarchy of Persia, watered by Byndamir, as Ferrarius calls it, though indeed it is the bridge, the water being called Kur,[248] formerly either *Orontis* as in Ptolemy *l. 6 c. 3*, another of the like name being in Coelo-Syria, or else that *Rhogomana* in Ptolemy, a river that draws her descent from the Tapirian,[249] as some say, but rather from the Parchoatrian Mountains,[250] and after above 200 miles circling in meanders commixing with Choaspes[251] (now Tabb) and Ulay,[252] not far from Valdac (old

---

[246] John of Persia or Don Juan de Persia (1560–1605) was originally named Uruch Beg and had been one of the secretaries to Shah Abbas's embassy to Europe in 1599. He travelled to Russia and most major European countries, including Italy (where he met Pope Clement VIII), France, and Spain. He wrote his *Relaciones* (1604) in Spanish, converted to Christianity, and was killed in a streetfight in Valladolid, where his book was published. "It has never been reprinted, nor has it ever been translated from the Castilian into any other language," writes its modern translator, G. Le Strange (v). Cf. above, 000.

[247] Firuzkuh [*Periscow*] is a city west of Teheran.

[248] Byndamir or Bendameer was "a popular name, at least among foreigners, of the River Kur (Araxes) . . . Properly speaking, the word is the name of a dam constructed across the river by the Amir Fana Khusrau, otherwise called Aded-ud-daulah, a prince of the Buweih family (A.D. 965), which was thence known in later days as *Band-i-Amir*, "The Princes's Dam" (*HJ* 83).

[249] Tapiria is a name for Tabaristan, better-known as Mazanderan, in northern Iran.

[250] The central mountain range in Persia.

[251] The Choaspes, also known to the Greeks as the Eulaeus, is at the foot of the Zagros Mountains. "Precise identification with the courses of the modern rivers Karkheh [or Kerka, *see* Charax], Ab-i-Diz, Khersan and Karun is impossible owing to hydrographic changes" (Grant, *Guide*, 610).

[252] The Ulay river in Susiana may be an eastern branch of the Choaspes, but some scholars identify it as the Rud-é Karun or Karoun, Iran's one navigable river, which rises in the Zagros mountains and runs to Khuzestan. It is mentioned in Daniel 8:2 and 16.

Susa now called),[253] lose themselves into the gulf and promiscuously thence disgorge themselves into the Indian Ocean.

Some walls it shows which were raised by Uzun Hassan the famous Armenian Prince who lived *Anno* 1470, but seems to scorn a limited bondage, for now it stretches from the south-east to the north-west well-near three miles and not much less the other way, the compass being seven miles or thereabouts. It is very pleasantly-seated at the north-west end of a spacious plain twenty miles long and six broad, circumvolved with lofty hills, under one of which this town is seated. Defended by nature, enriched by trade and by art made lovely; the vineyards, gardens, cypresses, sudatories[254] and temples ravishing the eye and smell, so as in every part she appears sweet and delightful. Here art-magic was first hatched, here Nimrod for some time lived; here Cyrus, the most excellent of heathen Princes, was born and here all but his head, which was sent to Pasagardae,[255] entombed. Here the great Macedonian glutted his avarice and bacchism, here the first Sybilla sung our Saviour's incarnation, hence the Magi are thought to have set forth towards Bethlehem, and here a series of two hundred kings have swayed their sceptres.

The houses are of sunburnt bricks, hard and durable; the building not very lofty, seldom exceeding two storeys, flat and terraced above, having balconies and windows curiously-trellised. Within they are spread with carpets; little other furniture otherwise is noted. Sultan Sheykh Ali Beg's[256] house, where the first night we were banqueted, is inferior to few, for his dining-room was high and round and spacious; the roof was arched, the walls well-embossed with

---

[253] Susa, now known as Shush, is in Khuzestan province. As an inhabited place it goes back to pre-history, but is primarily known as first a large Elamite city and then the capital of the Sassanian Empire. By Herbert's time it was no longer important (John of Persia, for example, does not even mention it), and did not receive much attention until British archaeologists went there in 1852. For details of Susa see Greenway and St. Vincent, *Iran*, 312–13; Grant, *Guide*, 610–11.

[254] A sudatory is a medicine which makes one sweat; here, Herbert seems to mean plants or trees.

[255] (Pasagardae), located "on the great north-south road of the plateau on its way from Ecbatana to the Persian Gulf" (Olmstead, *History*, 60) was the old capital of Persia. Its monuments include remains of the palace of Cyrus I, who was buried there in 529 B. C.E. "Pasagardae," Olmstead writes, "although terribly ruined, is superior to the more grandiose Persepolis" (*History*, 67). Greenway and St. Vincent, however, whilst admiring the tomb of Cyrus, nonetheless think that Pasagardae is "nowhere near as visually stimulating as Persepolis, and what remains is fairly scattered" (*Iran*, 302).

[256] Sultan Sheykh Ali Beg had been the governor of Herat and *amir al-omara* (military governor) of Khorasan under Shah Ismail I (see Monshi, 1. 303–4). In the 1638 edition Herbert added "the Sultan had been twelve times in battle against the Turks and most times a victor, and in a single combat with Ali Pasha, whom he slew, received a lameness" (62).

gold and wrought into imagery, so shadowed that it was hard to judge whether embossed, ensculpted or painted. The windows were of painted glass, the floor spread with curious carpets. Few here are without their gardens, forests rather, of high *cheuers*,[257] resembling our elms, and cypresses, so as indeed a more delightful object can hardly be then what this city yields the eye from the neighbouring mountain; the palaces rise so amiably and the mosques and hamams with their ceruleal tiles and gilded vanes amongst the cypresses so glitter by reflecting the sun-beams in a curious splendour.

Fifteen mosques[258] express their bravery here, which in shape are round, after the *al-Kaaba* in Mecca,[259] tiled with a plaster made of limestone burnt, which so soon as it is dry becomes so exceeding hard that it rather resembles true stone then mortar, with which they not only parget the outside of their houses and trim it with paint after the Morisco[260] manner, but also spread the floors and arches of their rooms. But on the top and outside these are pargetted with azure stones resembling turquoises, lined most parts within with black and well-polished marble, and the tops are beautified by many double-gilded crescents or spires which reverberate the sun's yellow flames most delightfully. Two are especially noteworthy in their steeples (so some call them), being small but exceedingly high towers; the one is square, above fifty foot high in the body, leaded in some part, in other part discoloured with gold and blue, the outside varnished and wrought with knots and poesies, vast and unfurnished, or rather unfinished within, and above, spiring in two slender but aspiring *alkirans*[261] of wood, being round and

---

[257] Probably the Kurdish elm, known as *qara-ayaj*, 'the black tree.'

[258] The most significant mosques are the Masjed-é Shihada, or Martyrs' Mosque, built at the end of the twelfth century by Sultan Sa'ad ibn Zangi, and the Masjed-é Atigh, or Old Friday Mosque, built in 894 but mostly destroyed by an earthquake and rebuilt during the seventeenth century. It might be germane to mention here that another building of significance is the Madrasseh-ye Khan, a religious school founded in 1615 by Emamqoli Khan.

[259] Herbert had obviously (like most non-Muslims) not seen the Kaaba, as its name means "cube," the shape of the building "which contains the Hajaru 'l-Aswad, or black stone" venerated by Mussulmans when they make their pilgrimage to Mecca. (Hughes, *Dictionary*, 256). In fairness, it should be noted that the stone itself is actually round.

[260] Moriscos (Moors) were Muslims who converted to Christianity after being conquered by Spain or Portugal; Herbert is referring here to "moorish" architecture and decorative style.

[261] *Hobson-Jobson* has a special entry for Herbert's use of this word [*alkoran* in Herbert], which I quote in full. "What word does Herbert aim at in the following? [The *Stanford Dictionary* regards this as quite distinct from *Alcoran*, the Koran or sacred book of the Mohammedans, and suggests *al-qorun*, 'the horns,' or *al-qiran*, 'the vertices']" (11). Foster, on the other hand, believed that Herbert found the term in Garcia de Silva's account (in Purchas 2: 1533), where he calls the pillars of Persepolis "Alcoranes, for so they call those high, narrow, round steeples which the Arabians have in their mesquites" (*Herbert*, 310).

coupled at the top, garnished with great art and cost, very near as high as Paul's in London, from whose top the clear-voiced boys sing thrice every twenty-four hours to their prophets Ali and Mohammed, for bells are nowhere tolerated in Mohammedans' temples. The other, rather resembling a caravanserai, is quadrangular, the superficies[262] of it Arabic invention embossed with gold, painted with azure, flagged with porphyry, garnished in several forms or mazes, and made resplendent at some solemnities by many lamps and torches.

Other mosques within this city are not so remarkable and yet no so mean as not to invite the observation, for what they want in architecture they supply in relics, venerably accounted of for entombing the carcases of some Alcoranish doctors, whose seeming sanctity hath got such repute amongst those superstitious people, their tombs being enriched by the superfluity of zeal, as no cost nor pains is thought too much to evidence the reality of their devotion. Some sepulchres are of well-polished marble, others of wood cut into an antic kind of carving; others express the painter's art and some the sculptor's skill in brass and other metal, so that where art is defective, Nature out of the treasures of darkness has supplied them. In one place Amir Ali Hamza,[263] a prophetic Mohammedan, rests his bones, seven hundred years since, some merrily say, ferried by Charon into Acheron for doting upon his Alcoran. The mosque is square, for threescore paces long I found the structure he is buried in to be, and in breadth just so many. In another sleeps Sa'ad ibn Mu'adh,[264] contemporary (as tradition gives) with Mohammed, and many more, whose dust rests until the Trumpet dispose them to a resurrection. A little out of the town is interred that learned poet and philosopher Muslih ed-din Saadi, who wrote the *Rosarium* which is lately translated into Latin by Gentius, and near him his brother poet Hajji Hafiz,[265] whose

---

[262] Surface or external features.

[263] Hamza (d. 625) was Mohammed's uncle. "The warlike deeds of Hamza," Hughes states, "are recorded in Persian poetry, in which he is celebrated as Amir Hamzah" (*Dictionary.* 160–61). Hamza "was always a conspicuous figure," writes Rogerson, "whether out hunting or as a boisterous drinker" (*Muhammad*, 156). He was killed during the war with Mecca.

[264] Sa'ad ibn Mu'adh (d. 625) [*Sandant-emyr-amabow*] was "one of the companions [of Mohammed] and an Ansari of great reputation" (Hughes, *Dictionary*, 554). The term *ansar* means "helper," and refers to people who were early converts to Islam and assisted Mohammed in his ministry; he was also killed in the war against the Meccans whilst defending Medina (Rogerson, *Muhammad*, 166). Foster notes that the term *sandant* probably means *santon*, "a European designation for a kind of Muhammedan monk or hermit. Herbert frequently uses the term in that sense" (*Herbert* 310–11).

[265] Shams ed-din Mohammed, known as Hafiz (c. 1320–1389) [*Hodgee Haier*], was a poet and Sufi master born in Shiraz. His great collection of poems, which actually represents less than a fifth of his output, is known as the *Diwan*, and he, like Saadi, became famous in Europe through the efforts of Goethe. The majority of his poems, according to his modern translator Daniel Ladinsky, "is said to have been destroyed by clerics and

poems are of great esteem in Persia. And indeed Shiraz has a college wherein is read philosophy, astrology, physic, chemistry and the mathematics, so as 'tis the more famoused throughout Persia. Upon many of these mosques the travelling storks have piled their nests, a bird as of the Egyptians, so of these people divinely-estimated:

> The famous stork, which buildeth in the air,
> Fosters her naked young with tender care,
> And by what love their duty doth engage,
> When need requires, to help her feeble age;
> Nor fail her hopes, for when she cannot stir,
> The pious brood both feed and carry her.

The gardens here are many, and those both large and beautiful, so as I may truly say of this, what the Syrians attribute to those of Damascus, *"operatissimi sunt in hortis."*[266] Many of them, as I paced, are eight hundred paces long and four hundred broad; *Hony-shaw,*[267] which is the King's, challenges superiority over the rest, being square every way two thousand paces. Most of them be safeguarded with walls fourteen foot high and four foot thick. The gardens, from their spaciousness and plenty of trees, rather resemble groves or wilderness, but by that name (the Persian word is *bagh*) are called; abounding in lofty pyramidical cypresses, broad-spreading chenaers,[268] tough elm, straight ash, knotty pines, fragrant mastics, kingly oaks, sweet myrtles, useful maple and of fruit-trees also, as grapes whose wood, though little worth, some say never rots, pomegranates, pomcitrons, oranges, lemons, pistachios, apples, pears, peaches, chestnuts, cherries, quinces, walnuts, apricots, plums, almonds, figs, dates and melons of both sorts, exceeding fair and of incomparable sweetness, also flowers rare to the eye, sweet to the smell and useful in physic. The earth here is dry but green, the air salubrious though sharp a little while, yea, such as may make good Tibullus his fancies of Elysium, for "Here songs and dances have esteem, and small / Sweet-chirping birds with music comfort all./ Th' uncultured ground sweet shrubs doth freely bring; / Sense-sweet' ning roses without art do spring."[269]

Amongst other pastimes there used, I remember I saw ropes or cords stretched from tree to tree in several gardens, boys and girls and sometimes those

---

rulers who disapproved of the content." His admirers included Nietzsche, Lorca, Pushkin, Carlyle, Emerson, and even Queen Victoria, "who used to consult Hafiz" as a "living oracle" (2).

[266] They are very experienced with gardens.

[267] Unidentified. Foster suggests that "it is perhaps the garden now known as the Bagh-i Takht" (*Herbert* 312).

[268] Unidentified.

[269] Tibullus, *Elegies* 3. 59–62.

of riper years swinging upon them, the Turks especially during the Bairam[270] time using that recreation, a pastime first practised by the Athenians. I may confine my commendations to a small compass, places more remote being at this day sterile, mountainous and unable, if then as now, to make Alexander an epicure, the wine excepted, which is indeed the most generous wine of Persia and famoused all over the Orient. Nothing is more complained-of by the inhabitants then want of water, yet a pretty shallow rivulet it has, and might have more were the citizens more industrious, a gallant river, Cyrus of old, streaming not fifteen miles thence in the way to old Persepolis, which by pipes and like other aqueducts might be drawn hither.

The Cyrenians[271] and Epicureans place their *summum bonum* or chief felicity in pleasure and make virtue to be the handmaid, without which felicity cannot be well-attended. Diogenes Laertius tells us that felicity is only a serenity and tranquility of the mind, free to delight and void of all sadness or purturbation, whence I may conclude these Shirazians to be of that sect. For at the Nau Roz[272] or spring they not only send vests and other presents to one another, a ceremony no less ancient then Cyrus, as Xenophon has it. Also Plutarch in *Vita Alexandri* notes that Artaxerxes the Great gave Mitradates, that unhappy captain who suffered a miserable death by the cruelty of Parysatis[273] the Queen Mother for vainboasting that he slew Cyrus her son when in rebellion, a gown or vest of gold which he wore during a royal banquet,[274] practiced also by Alexander, who having put on his head the royal diadem of Persia, vested divers of the Macedonian

[270] Ramadan Bairam, the festival after the period of fasting.

[271] The ancient inhabitants of Cyrene, a Greek colony, which is now in Libya. Herbert may be alluding indirectly to the philosopher Aristippus of Cyrene (c. 435–356 B.C.E.) who taught that one could seek pleasure in life by adapting any circumstances to oneself, which gave one control over both happiness and unhappiness, a philosophy which Herbert links here with that of Epicurus. Aristippus was known for his luxurious lifestyle and for consorting with the famous prostitute Laïs. For details, see Diogenes Laertius, *Lives of Eminent Philosophers,* trans. R. D. Hicks (Cambridge, MA: Harvard University Press, 1925), 1: 192–231.

[272] Nau Roz "is a day of great festivity. It is observed the first day after the sun has crossed the vernal equinox, and the festivities last for a week or more" (Hughes, *Dictionary*, 431).

[273] Parysatis was the daughter of Artaxerxes I and wife of Darius II. She was half-Babylonian (her mother was Andia of Babylon), and exercised great influence over her husband, whom Olmstead calls "the real master" of the two (*History* 357). She favoured her son Prince Cyrus as heir to the throne, which led to the war between him and Artaxerxes II.

[274] Artaxerxes II ruled 404–358 B.C.E. When Cyrus, the younger brother of Artaxerxes, rebelled, he was defeated and killed at Cunaxa (401 B.C.E.). Mitradates, "in his cups" (Olmstead, *History*, 375) claimed that he had killed the rebel, but this was a lie, and Queen Parysatis had him cruelly put to death.

officers with robes of gold. "*Longe vests auratas sumere jubet*," saith Justin *l*. 12.[275]
Then also the gardens are opened for all to walk in; the women likewise for fourteen days have liberty to appear in public, and when loose, like birds enfranchised
lose themselves in a labyrinth of wanton sports. The men also, some riding, some
sitting, some walking, are all in one tune, drinking, singing, playing till the
bottles prove empty, songs be spent, or that Morpheus[276] lay his caduceus[277] over
them. In all my life I never saw people more jocund and less quarrelsome. "They
revel all the night and drink the round / Till wine and sleep their giddy brains
confound." 'Tis to be feared chastity is no virtue here, an unseen martyrdom, for
heat makes lust so outrageous that they make little defence against it, thinking
pleasure to be a delightful conqueror. Now how far such liberty coheres with that
tenet of the Epicures mentioned by Kedrenos,[278] "*voluptatem esse finem sapientum
et bonorum*,"[279] I determine not, seeing that Epicurus his *summum bonum* "*consta-
bat voluptate, non corporis sed animi*."[280] This feast of Nau Roz was begun by King
Jalal ed-din, son of Alp Arslan,[281] and is commonly celebrated when the sun enters into Aries; for then this they celebrate no feast more solemnly.

---

[275] "He told them to put on long golden garments." M. Junianus Justinus (3rd century C. E.), the Roman historian and Christian gnostic, is often mixed up with Justin
Martyr (as Herbert does here), the second-century Christian historian and apologist. He
wrote, or rather compiled, the *Historiarum Philippicarum*, a collection of passages from
Pompeius Trogus's *Historiae Philippicae et totius mundi origines et terrae situs*, a lost work
on world history. There were two translations available to Herbert, that of Arthur Gold-
ing (1564) and a more recent one by Robert Codrington (1654). The J. S. Watson translation (1853) may be read on the *Corpus scriptorum latinorum* website, and there is a modern
edition by M.-P. Arnaud-Lindot (Paris, 2003).

[276] The god of sleep.

[277] A wand with wings at the top and two snakes entwined around it.

[278] Giorgios Kedrenos [*Cedrinus*] was a Byzantine monk and historian whose *Compendium historiarum ab orbe condita ad Isaacum Comnenum* epitomised world history down
to the year 1057. A Latin version, which is the title given here, was published by Xylander
(Basle, 1566) but a better translation, perhaps the one used by Herbert in later editions of
his book, was that issued by Goar and Fabrot (Paris, 1647). Smith remarks that Kedrenos
"must be perused with great caution" (W. Smith, *Dictionary of Christian Antiquities* [Lon-
don: John Murray, 1875–1880], 1, 658). See *ODB* 2: 1118.

[279] "Pleasure is the goal of the wise and the good" (Cicero, *Academica* 2. 45); Kedrenos quotes Cicero rather than Epicurus directly.

[280] Consists of pleasure, not of the body but of the mind.

[281] Alp Arslan was sultan of the Seljuk Empire or Great Seljuk 1064–1072. He conquered Armenia and Georgia, and his greatest triumph was the defeat of the Byzantine
emperor Romanus IV at the Battle of Manzikert (1070). His son Jalal ed-din, usually
known as Malik Shah I, reigned 1072–1092 and made more expansions to the Seljuk
territory, enlarging it to border on China in the east and on the Byzantine Empire in the
west as well as controlling Anatolia, Central Asia and Afghanistan.

The Ambassador feasted.

Somewhat of Emamqoli Khan, the great Duke, and his banquet. This man is a Georgian by descent, a Mussulman by profession, and one of those tetrarchs that under Abbas rule the Empire. His territories reach every way wellnigh four hundred miles, and afford him the titles of Archduke of Shiraz, Sultan of Lar and Jarri, Lord of Hormuz, Maqueron, Kerman, Khuzistan, Sigestan and Farsistan, Prince of the Gulf of Persia and isles there, the great Beglerbeg,[282] Commander of Twelve Sultans,[283] fifty thousand horse, slave to Shah Abbas, Protector of Mussulmen, Nutmeg of Comfort and Rose of Delight. He is of an extraordinary descent for nobility as honour goes in these parts, his father and grandfather having been Dukes before him, but, which is no less strange, privileged from degradation by Abbas his oath upon a good occasion, Ali Quli Khan[284] his father having been victorious in some engagements against both Turk and Tartar. It added no small lustre to Mohammed Khodabanda's[285] diadem, most memorably when by command of Murad, the saucy Pasha of Erevan,[286] with fifteen hundred muskets breathed defiance against Murad the Julfa Governor for presuming to take part with Ismail in that famous overthrow they gave the Turks on the Calderan Plain in the year 1514, as they arrogate to themselves, albeit the Turks say otherwise.[287] Murad, being thus unexpectedly assaulted, sends a timorous excuse,

---

[282] "Military governor-general of a major province" (Savory in Monshi, *History*, 1387).

[283] A Sultan in the Persian Empire was an "officer of the rank below Khan" (Savory in Monshi, *History*, 1391).

[284] Herbert seems to be getting muddled here; he writes *"Aliculican"* and calls him Emamqoli Khan's "father," which is wrong. Ali Quli Khan was the Beglarbeg of Fars, dismissed by Mohammed Shah (see below) in 1582 for "failing to send his quota of men to take part in the operations in Azerbaijan during the last two or three years" (Monshi, *History*, 1: 411). However, Herbert mixes him up with Allah Verdi Khan all through this very confused account.

[285] Shah Mohammed Khodabanda (c. 1523–1595), usually designated Mohammed Shah, was the father of Abbas I. He reigned 1578–1587; a half-blind, peaceful and ascetic man who was having more trouble with the Turks than he could handle, he decided to abdicate and turn over the throne to his son Abbas. For full details of his reign, see Monshi, *History*, 1: 331–502. Herbert discusses his reign in some detail later on.

[286] Murad Pasha [*Amurath*] (d. 1611) was the Ottoman Beglerbeg of Qaraman. He was taken prisoner in the ensuing battle. I have left his name as Herbert spells it to distinguish him from the other Murad. He became Grand Vizier under Sultan Ahmed I in 1606, and was nicknamed "the Well-Digger" because when he crushed the Jelali revolts he threw the bodies of rebels down wells.

[287] Shah Ismail I reigned 1499–1523. It was actually Sultan Selim I (not Sultan Amurath or Murad) who sent troops against Persia and the Murad mentioned by Herbert is the nephew of Selim I, whose brother Ahmed had been proclaimed Sultan but had been killed by Selim. Murad fled to Shah Ismail for protection, which is why Selim

which rather enraged the Pasha, who was not to be pacified until Murad had
glutted his appetite with a present of two thousand pound in gold, commanding him thence to Nashivan (old *Artaxata*)²⁸⁸ and by that time hungry again. Ali
Quli Khan, Shah Mohammed's lieutenant in Georgia, expressing his displeasure
against Murad, undertakes to make the Turk eat cold iron, meat the Pasha cared
not for, but by Ali Quli Khan's fierce charge with six thousand horse made him
return his bribe back, so as after a small dispute the Turk was forced to a speedy
retreat over Anti-Taurus (now Mezis Taur)²⁸⁹ and gave the valiant Georgian the
liberty to extract a treble contribution from Murad for his compliance with the
Turk, and, when returning victor to the Court, was for that service recompensed
with the Shiraz dukedom, and his son after him no less fortunate in Shah Abbas
his field-service, having quieted Georgia, subdued Lar and Hormuz and made
tribute parts of Arabia and Diyarbakir.²⁹⁰

Some days after our being here the great Duke absented himself merely to
please his humour, for albeit Sir Robert Sherley took the pains to ride unto him
and to tell him how acceptable his being in town would be at the Ambassador's
entrance, he answered it was no dishonour for any man, his master excepted, to
stay his leisure, not knowing or not considering that the persons of ambassadors
are sacred and challenge high respect in all places according to the custom and
consent of all nations, both from the representation they make and the nature
of their employment, so that this would not have been endured had our Ambassador been provided with a convoy and necessary for travel, which wanting,
constrained him to practice patience. After six days' attendance, His Eminency
made his entrance into Shiraz attended with 2000 horse, where he took his ease
for two days without the least notice of our Ambassador. At length, finding that
our Ambassador would not make application to him, he sent a gentleman to invite him to his palace, who returned with this answer, that he was weary, having
come a great journey, and that his journey was to see his master. The Duke, not
pleased with that message, thought it best nevertheless to dissemble it, knowing
the King had given express command that in his passage he should everywhere
receive honour and hearty welcome, so after some pause the Duke sent word he

---

attacked Persia. The Turks are right; even Iskandar Monshi admits that Selim's forces
won the battle at Calderan (see *History*, 1. 68–70 for a detailed description).

²⁸⁸ Artaxata in Armenia is modern-day Artashat. It was founded by Artashes I in
about 188 B.C.E. as the new capital. The Romans burned it down in 58 C. E. but rebuilt
in 114 (Grant, *Guide*, 70),

²⁸⁹ That part of the Taurus mountains in Cappadocia and Armenia. Strabo seems to
have coined the name.

²⁹⁰ Diyarbakir or Diar Bakr [*Diabec*] is in south-eastern Turkey on the right-hand
bank of the Tigris, and was known as Amida (for details and history, see Grant, *Guide*,
30–31).

proposed next day to visit him, yet failed in his promise, but his son the Begler-beg, eighteen year old, came in person to execute[291] him.

Next day our Ambassador sent word by Sheykh Ali Beg to the Duke's son that his visit be retaliated. Emamqoli Khan the father seems to be displeased that he had not the honour of the first visit and marvelled what kind of people we were, since his own little less then adored him, nevertheless made use of it to his own satisfaction, for he was no sooner alighted near the Duke's palace when by Sheykh Ali Beg he was ushered into a long gallery rich in common beauties, plate, carpets and other furniture, where, contrary to expectation the Duke himself, like a statue at the end of the room sat cross-legged, not moving one jot till the Ambassador was almost upon him, and then, as one affrighted, skipped up, embraced and bade him welcome, vouchsafing also (upon knowledge that his attendants were gentlemen) to give us the *khosh amadid* and to entertain us with a banquet. So after two hours' merriment we departed, invited to return next day to a more solemn welcome. The entertainment our Ambassador had was wine and sweetmeats which were of variety, and then, *inter pocula*[292] but according to the common mode of these Eastern parts, the dancing-wenches went to work, who first throwing off their loose garments or vests, the other was close to their body resembling trousers, but of several pieces of sateen of sundry colours (as there much used). Their hair was long and dangling in curls; about their faces were hung ropes of pearl, carcanets set with stones about their necks, and about their wrists and legs were wreathed golden bracelets with bells which with the cymbals and timbrels in their hands made the best consort. Their dancing was not after the usual manner, for each of them kept within a small circle and made, as it were, every limb dance in order after each other, even to admiration. These are they whom I may say "*convivia laeta frequentant. Tibia demulcent sonitus & fistula ubique cantus & saltus & grata licentia vulgi, quales esse solers epulis vinoque madentes.*"[293]

Next day being come, we were conducted by a sultan through two fair courts, whence on foot we were ushered into a stately banqueting-house, which was a large room opene at the sides supported with twenty gilded pillars, the roof

---

[291] Represent.

[292] Between cups.

[293] "They celebrate at parties. They caress their pipes, they sing and dance all around with free and vulgar abandon, skilfully pouring the wine for the banquet" (Quintus Smyrnaeus, *Posthomerica* 13. 1–4 [Aldine Latin version, 1504]).

embossed with gold and so exquisitely-painted as if Ersenge,[294] the Apelles[295] of Persia, had pencilled it. The ground was spread with extraordinary rich carpets of silk and gold; a state at one end of crimson satin was erected, embroidered with pearl and gold, under which the Duke was to enthrone himself. Upon one side thereof was painted his Hormuz trophies, no cost to art being left out to do it to the life, for it expressed their encamping upon the shore, their assaults, storms, batteries and entrance, plunder of the city, massacre of the Hormuzians, some beheaded, some chained, some their heads serving for girdles, as also the English ships, sea fights and the like, but so to life ". . . As seem' d indeed / Men arm'd to fight, march, strike, till each man bleed." And when the green and crimson curtains or scenes of silk were drawn, there was a lively prospect into a great square Court, which upon this occasion, to aggrandise the invitation was round set with the prime men of the city, as also into another adjacent Court where I think I told near five hundred plebeians, who, Moscow-like, were invited to illustrate the Duke's magnificence.

Before this great Duke meant to display his radiance, for as yet he was not entered, Sir Dodmore Cotton was seated on the left hand of the state, where note that all Asia over the left, being the sword hand, is most honourable. Upon the other side sat the discontented Prince of Tartary. At the Ambassador's left hand was seated the Beglerbeg, the Duke's eldest son, and next him the captive King of Hormuz. Next to the Tartar Prince sat Teimuraz Khan,[296] a disconsolate Prince of Georgia, a gallant person, expert in arms and a constant Christian. Opposite to the state Sir Robert Sherley seated himself, and in the same room with such gentlemen as attended the Ambassador were placed the two Princes of Hormuz, some sultans and other great officers. The rest of the banqueting-room was filled with persons of note, as sultans, merchants and qizilbashes, during

---

[294] *Ersenge* refers not to a person but to the *Arzang*, a now-lost holy book of the Manicheans. It was illustrated with drawings and paintings, and was supposed to have been produced by Mani himself, who was "known in late Islamic tradition as . . . an artist." It was mentioned in 1700 by the oriental scholar Thomas Hyde (see Introduction). For details, see J. P. Asmussen's article "Arzang" in *Encyclopedia Iranica Online*, n.p.n. I am indebted to Dr. Willem Floor for making this identification and for the reference.

[295] Apelles of Cos (fourth century B. C. E.) was the most famous of all classical painters, whose work survives only by virtue of Roman copies. Herbert could have read stories about him in Pliny's *Natural History* (Bk. 35), and he was imitated during the Renaissance by many who never saw his work. For details see, for example, E. H. Gombrich, *The Heritage of Apelles: Studies in the Art of the Renaissance* (Ithaca: Cornell University Press, 1976), esp. 3–18.

[296] King Teimuraz I (Dadiani) of Kakhetia (1589–1663) was a warrior and poet. He fought against Abbas I (1614–1617), a terrible war which ended when Kakhetia was devastated by the Persians and Teimuraz's mother killed because she would not convert to Islam. It was not until 1625, however, that the Georgians were finally defeated. After his return to Kahkhetia Teimuraz continued the struggle against Persia until his death.

which entertainment young Ganymedes, arrayed in cloth of gold with long crisp locks of hairs resembling those *"pueri calamistrati pulchre indusiati"*[297] mentioned in Apuleius his banquet, went up and down bearing flagons of gold filled with choice wine, which they proffered to all the company one by one so long as the feast endured. Upon the carpets were spread fine-coloured pintado tablecloths forty ells long at least; broad thin pancakes six one upon another served for trenchers, near which were scattered wooden spoons whose handles were almost a yard long, and the spoons so thick and wide as required right spacious mouths to render them serviceable. The feast was compounded of several sorts of pilaf of various colours and store of candied dried fruit and meats, variety also of dates, pears and peaches curiously conserved. Such I took notice of, I mean as pleased me best, were jacks,[298] myrobalans, durians,[299] pistachios, almonds, apricots, quinces, cherries and the like. The Duke is not yet taken notice of; the truth is His Eminency was not yet entered, nor were we sorry that when our bellies were full our eyes might have the better leisure to survey his greatness. Howbeit, the feast was no sooner ended but the vulgar strove to rend the sky with *"Tough Ally-Whaddaw-Bashat,"*[300] i.e. Ali and God be thanked, expressing by voice and music their joy, and then like that in Ovid, *"Phoebus adest, sonuere lyrae, sonuere pharetrae; / Signa deum nosco per sua, Phoebus adest,"*[301] the echo being as the signal for that great Duke to enter.

His entrance was ushered by thirty comely youths who were vested in crimson satin coats, their tulipants were silk and silver wreathed above with small links of gold; some had also pearl, rubies, turquoises and emeralds, for I do not remember that I saw one diamond. They were girded with rich-hilted swords in embroidered scabbards; they had hawks upon their fists, each hood set with stones of value. After them the Duke followed; his coat was of blue satin, very richly-embroidered with silver, upon which he wore a robe of extraordinary length, glorious to the eye, for it was so thick-powdered with great oriental pearl and glittering gems as made the ground of it imperspicable, not less rich, I thought, then

---

[297] "Curly-haired boys in fine underwear" (Apuleius, *The Golden Ass* 2. 19).

[298] Jacks are the fruit of the tree "called by botanists *Artocarpus integrifolia*," and its name is derived from a Portuguese corruption of its Malayalam name *chakka* (*HJ* 440). It is mentioned by Pliny (*Natural History* 12. 12) and is highly-complimented by early European writers for its succulent sweetness. In the West Indies it is known as "jackfruit."

[299] Durians are a large spiky fruit (often found today in the Asian areas of supermarkets) which have a particularly horrible smell when opened, but are absolutely delicious inside. In fact, people in Asia often open them outside before eating them. In a Bangkok hotel the editor saw a sign at the desk forbidding people to bring durians into the premises!

[300] Possibly a corruption of *"Yaa 'Ali madad,"* meaning "with Ali's help," still a common saying in Iran.

[301] "Apollo's here, lyre sounding, quiver rattling; / I know him by his signs: Apollo's here" (Ovid, *Remediae amoris* 705–6).

the Empress Agrippina when clothed in a robe of woven burnished gold. His turban or *mandil* was of finest white silk interwoven with gold, bestudded with pearl and carbuncles; his scabbard was set all over with rubies, pearls and emeralds, such as that which Pompey found worn by Mithridates,[302] which was valued at four hundred talents, as Plutarch *Vita Pompeii* mentions. His sandals had the like embroidery, so as he seemed that day to resemble Artaxerxes, whose apparel was commonly valued at ten tousand talents, as Plutarch relateth. To this glorious idol the people offered their devotion in many *tessalaams*, bowing and knocking their foreheads *à la mode* against the ground. Sir Robert Sherley, constantly wearing the Persian habit, also sizaeded very formally, and after that in a cup of pure gold drank His Eminency's health and then, knowing it would please the Duke, put it in his pocket with this merry compliment, that after so unworthy a person had breathed in it, it was some indignity to return it, which the Duke amiably accepts as good satisfaction, but perceiving our Ambassador was not very merry, darted him a smile and then drank the King his master's health, and exceeding civilly bade him and his company heartily welcome, and so withdrew. The truth is our Ambassador was scarce well-pleased at the Duke's long absence and proud carriage, but prudently dissembled it, so as after reciprocal salaams, some qizilbashes attended him to his horse, and so returned to his lodging.

Capable is this Archduke to purchase his renown at those high rates, his yearly revenue being bruited excessive great, for, say merchants, he has towards four hundred thousand tomans *per annum* (a toman is five marks sterling), out of which he pays fifty thousand horse upon muster. His plate and jewels are commonly estimated, how certainly I cannot tell, at three hundred thousand *mahmoudies*. A scantling of his great wealth may be taken by that memorable present or New Year's gift he sent the King upon the fiscal's secret advice three years hence, *viz.* fifty flagons of gold, seventy-two of silver, and in *larrins* four hundred and sixty-five thousand florins, the whole being three hundred and fifty *qizilbash* camels load, a royal present, beside wines, and for which the King, as a symbol of his acceptance and gratitude, remunerates the Duke with fifty Arabian coursers, six change of rich garments, a sword he wore himself and his word that he should continue in that command, which to the Duke was most significant.

This Duke here and in other seraglios (*harems* the Persians call them) has above three hundred concubines, no surer way in these pagan countries to distinguish one man's greatness from another then by exceeding in that sort of voluptuousness, albeit he hunts elsewhere, other sports serving but as a provocation. Nor do they refrain more manly exercises as chasing the lion, hunting the tiger,

---

[302] Mithradates VI Eupator (r.120–63 B.C.E.) conquered Colchis and made his son Governor, soon after executing him for treason (D. M. Lang, *The Georgians* [London: Thames & Hudson, 1966], 81). He was supposed to have been the master of twenty-two (not twenty-six, as Herbert later on tells us) languages, at least according to Pliny. He fought many wars with the Romans.

dislodging the boar, unkennelling the jackal and the like, at which sports he first raises whole countries, not less then twenty thousand men serving to rouse that kind of savage game, for when the whole herd are embattled upon some mountain they impale it with a huge toil of wire and cords supported with stakes, six hundred camels' load, and so either dart them from without the rail or venture in and, by drawing a cross line, single what beast they please to combat with. Philotas[303] in all Alexander's marches had ever ready 13,000 fathoms of net and toil to impale mountains, the better to hunt wild beasts, as Pompeius Trogus[304] reports, so that it seems in that country this is no new invention.

Two days after this feast the Duke, with a train of thirty sultans and qizilbashes came galloping to Alikhan (so the house was called we lodged at), and albeit he endeavoured to surprise Sir Dodmore Cotton with a sudden visit, yet such was the seasonable intelligence he then had that at his alighting he found a choice shade as the first part of his entertainment and then chambers neatly-furnished, from the balcony looking into a pleasant garden where large cypresses and other trees appeared in their best apparel for his better welcome. Here the facetious Duke encamped with all his company, resolved to encounter the fury of his own wine and our English chymic-waters, for 'tis their belief that ". . . *corpora magna virorum / Dulcia vina levant, animisque et viribus augent.*"[305] And indeed, no part of the world has wine more or better than Shiraz, so that for three hours the skirmish continued, charging one another with equal resolution. Many bottles and flagons were emptied, but by strategem from the Duke's quarters revived afresh, thundering such an alarm in the Duke's brains that at his mounting his horse he fell back, and had not our Ambassador, who as he was very abstemious so was he most civil, by chance upheld him, he had been dismounted. Mr.

---

[303] Philotas was one of Alexander's generals who was left in charge of Tyre and its surrounding areas when Alexander moved on Egypt in 332 B. C. E. It should be pointed out, however, that this identification is a guess, as there were no fewer than five people called Philotas mentioned by Q. Curtius Rufus.

[304] Pompeius Trogus (1st century C. E.) was a zoologist and botanist, the author of the *Historiae Philippicae*, a digest of universal history written in a leaden style and with an unfortunate propensity for moralising and, as A. M. Chugg points out, "was a dedicated Republican and therefore highly antagonistic to absolute monarchy" (*The Lost Tomb of Alexander the Great* [London: Periplus, 2005], xvi). However, Pompeius makes many interesting observations in his digressions on customs, beliefs and religions in places like Parthia and other eastern realms which are valuable. Most of our knowledge of his work comes from M. Junianus Justinus. There was an edition of Justin by Bongarsius (1581) containing Trogus's surviving writings. J. C. Yardley has translated Justin's epitome of Trogus (Oxford: Oxford University Press, 1997).

[305] Sweet wines stimulate men's strong bodies; both their spirits and their strength are increased (variant from Eobanus Hessug's Latin verse translations from *The Iliad*, 6. 261-262).

Stodart[306] of Caernavon and Mr. Emery,[307] two gentlemen attending the Ambassador in his chamber, helped them homewards. Next day the Duke, sensible of his civil treatment, returned his thanks in a present of twelve good horses with bridles and rich saddles suiting them, by which it appeared that all were pleased, and the Ambassador, who without such an entertainment had never satisfied them, acquired the epithet of a generous and well-bred person. After other ceremonies of welcome in which *pishkashes* and gifts were not left out, we had leave to prosecute our travel towards the Court; I call it "leave," the Duke now seemed so unwilling to part with us. The Ambassador's attendants also, pursuant to the Duke's directions, were very well-mounted and furnished with fresh camels and asinagos for our sumpters,[308] able beasts capable to endure the brunt of travel.

Great is the difference between the Turks and Persians, for the Turks, being by law prohibited, abstain from wine yet drink it covertly, but the Persians now, as of old, drink openly and with excess. It was so of old, for Plutarch in the *Life of Artaxerxes* reports that the Persians were liberal wine-bibbers and lovers of magic. Cyrus, craftily endeavouring to supplant his brother Artaxerxes in the crown before the battle of Cunaxa, being his lieutenant in the Lesser Asia, the better to ingratiate himself with the Lacedaemonians writ unto them and among other virtues boasted that he was fitter to rule then Artaxerxes, and the reason he gave was this, that he could drink more wine and better understood natural Magic[309] then his brother did. Peradventure this same Genius was in this great Duke we are now speaking of.

To proceed. Six and twenty days we consumed in Shiraz, forced to so long commorance by the merry Duke, so as on Lady-Day in Lent we departed thence towards Isfahan, the Persian metropolis. But I cannot willingly part without first celebrating our *vale dictum* in this charistery:[310]

> Why should our wits dispute where Eden stood,
> If in the earth, or air, or if the Flood
> Did spoil the surface? Thus we fall from thence,
> And too much knowledge lost the residence.
> Yes, if that place remain, for us to guess
> By outward attributes of happiness,
> Why should thy plains, Shiraz, give place to those

---

[306] This is the only mention Herbert makes Robert Stodart. For details, see Introduction.

[307] James Emery was Cotton's secretary. Stodart called him "my adopted brother . . . a gentleman whom I dearly loved and wished well unto" (*Journal*, 99).

[308] Pack-animals. The term is also used for their drivers.

[309] Giambattista della Porta defined this in *Natural Magick* (1581; English translation 1658) as the "perfect knowledge of natural things . . . which all excellent wise men do admit and embrace and worship with great applause" (1. 1–2).

[310] Song of praise or thanksgiving.

Where fruitful Nile and Ganges overflow?
Thy curious prospect, lodges, soil, the rich
Variety of pleasures that bewitch
Each gazing eye, would make the looker-on
Think Paradise had no destruction,
Or else replanted there. For there the grape
In dangling clusters tempts another rape
To taste the relish as the apple did,
And some would touch thy fruit, although forbid.
Thy towers, baths, gardens, temples make thee seem
Like Memphis, Troy, Thebes or Jerusalem;
Thy natives, Nature's models, to compose
Inferior beauty by the looks of those.
    Farewell, sweet place, for as from thee I went,
    My thoughts did run on Adam's banishment.

Yet ere we go farther, let me give you a brief account of such potentates (to let pass Solomon whom they derive themselves from) as had their seat-royal in Shiraz, begun seven hundred years ago and but lately ended, the first of which was Daylam Shah, by some said to descend literally from Ardashir, the last King of Persia and the hundredth in descent from Adam, as they pedagorise, and from his name and the delight he took in fishing and navigation is injuriously-termed a fisherman. No otherwise then Tamerlane was a shepherd, from the manner of living which is usual amongst most hordes or septs in Tartary. Daylam Shah, surnamed *Boia* or *Mobeia* rather, which signifies a fish, had three sons: Ali, Hassan and Ahmed. Ali, surnamed Ibn Hassan, had no issue; his father and he were both buried in Shiraz *Anno Dom.* 940, *Heg.* 320. Hassan, by the death of his elder brother became Lord of Fars, Rayy[311] and Khurasan, and Ahmed had assigned Kerman and *Macron*. To Hassan succeeded a stranger, *Zedda-Mobee* by name, brought in by Mustapha the Babylonian Caliph, to whom succeeded Ain ud-Daula, who had no issue. Ruqn ud-Daula, Hassan's son, being possessed of his father's seigneuries, died peaceably *Anno Dom.* 980, *Heg.* 360, dividing first his territories amongst his three sons Sharaf ud-Daula, Samsam ud-Daula and Baha ud-Daula. The eldest had Shirazstan, Larestan and Kerman, the second Iraq and Diyarbakir, the youngest had *Gerinom* and Tabrizstan. Sharaf ud-Daula died issueless *Anno Dom.* 990, *Heg.* 370, so that the seigneury descended upon Baha ud-Daula, youngest son of King Ruqn ud-Daula. Baha ud-Daula ruled twelve years, at his death commanding that his eldest son Sultan ud-Daula should succeed him. This Prince, being trained up in field-exercises from his cradle, albeit by his valour he enlarged his Empire, yet could not defend himself from Husain Musharrif his restless brother till by agreement the Kingdom was divided

---

[311] Rayy [*Reig*], made into a caravanserai by Abbas I, is now part of Tehran. Settlement there dates back to at least Median times.

between them. To Sultan ud-Daula was allotted Farsistan and Aywaz, to Husain [Musharrif] Iraq. At that time Jalal ud-Daula their brother was invested with the Caliphship of Baghdad, *Anno Dom.* 1021, *Heg.* 401, and Sultan ud-Daula was, dying *Anno Dom.* 1025, buried in Shiraz with great solemnity. Abu Kalijar his son reigned after him, but perceiving the crown to totter by the unnatural practices of Saif ud-Daula his traitorous uncle, he was forced to fly to Jalal ud-Daula his other uncle, the late-made Caliph, who was glad of the occasion, having long looked with a squint eye upon his nephew's diadem, but dissembling it, with a great army he descends from Bandar and with ease expels Saif ud-Daula and then mounts himself into the throne to Abu Kalijar's amazement, who to save his life flies into Arabia, whilst Mahmoud of Ghazna[312] from Hindustan enters forcibly into Ayrac and Shervan but was quickly forced to retreat into Sablestan. Saif ud-Daula by that time got so highly into the Caliph's favour that he was restored to the crown, but death cut off his hopes, leaving Abu Kalijar the banished Prince his right, who upon this advantage returns and is by his subjects joyfully welcomed. But he also, surfeiting of too much joy, lived not long after it, for seeing no way but one he commends his body to the earth and bequeathed the royalty to Ibn Malik Rahim, or the Merciful, who died *Anno Dom.* 1054, *Heg.* 434 without issue, in whom after a series of fifteen kings took end the Mobeyan race or family.[313]

To Malik Rahim succeeded Abu Mansur, who pretended himself to be the legitimate son of Jalal ud-Din the above-mentioned Caliph. Abu Mansur took

[312] Mahmoud, Sultan of Ghazna (971–1030), ruled over an empire which eventually stretched from the borders of Fars and Kerman to the River Indus and to Khurasan and parts of the Hindu Kush. He reigned from 998 to 1030. Much of his reign was spent at war, but he has a reputation as a greatly-skilled administrator and reformer. Muhammad Nazim has written a biography, *The Life and Times of Sultan Mahmud of Ghazna* (New Delhi: Munshiram Manoharlal, 1971; orginally published by Cambridge University Press, 1931).

[313] Herbert's information is largely accurate, but his dates are sometimes wrong. These rulers are generally known as the Daylamids of Fars; they ruled in Rayy and Iraq as well, sometimes at different times, so I here append a list of them. 1. Daylam Shah (d. 940); 2. Ruqn ud-Daula [*Rocknadaule*] (935–976 in Rayy); 3. Sharaf ud-Daula [*Sherfadaule*] (983–989 in Fars; 987–989 in Iraq); 4. Samsam ud-Daula [*Shamsdaule*] (989–998 in Fars; 983–987 in Iraq); 5. Baha ud-Daula [*Bahadaule*] (998–1012 in Fars; 989–1012 in Iraq); 6. Sultan ud-Daula [*Sultandaule*] (1012–1024 in Fars; 1012–1021 in Iraq); 7. Musharraf ud-Daula [*Hocem Masharafdaule*] (1021–1025 in Iraq only); 8. Jalal ud-Daula [*Geladaule*] (1025–1044 in Iraq only; Herbert mistakenly calls him a "caliph," but the Caliph of Baghdad at that time was al-Qa' im); 9. Abu Kalijar [*Abdul-cawn*] (1024–1048 in Fars; 1044–1048 in Iraq); 10. Malik Rahim [*Aben Melec-Rahim*] (1048–1055 in Iraq only). Herbert does not mention Fakhr ud-Daula, who ruled in Rayy 976–980 and 984–997. Saif ud-Daula's usurpation lasted for only a very short time in 1044. In any case, the number of kings does not add up to fifteen.

to wife Dauta, daughter of Toshal Beg, and after five years died in Kerman and lies buried at *Hurkawn* not far from Jask. He had five sons by that lady, viz. Abu Mansur Fulad Sutun, Chosroes Firoz,[314] Abubir, Abu Zaid and Abu Ali Kai Chosroes.[315] Abu Mansur enlarged Shiraz and spared no cost to make it beautiful, but while he busied his fancy at home his ambitious brother Chosroes Feroz unexpectedly took possession of his territories. Revenge pursues, for travelling to Baghdad to see his sick grandsire Toshal Beg, his cruelty to his brother being there called in question and proved, he was forthwith committed to a loathsome prison where famine and stench quickly made an end of him. This sharp discipline could not terrify Abu Zaid the fourth brother from intruding into Abu Mansur's right, albeit his injured brother, having escaped, had gathered an army who so stood to him that Zaid in the conflict was slain with most of his associates. Abu Mansur, one would think, was born to an iron destiny, being unable at his second return to safeguard himself from Fazl his lieutenant, who unawares seized upon him and secured him in a noisome prison, adorning his base brows with his master's diadem, which treachery Abu Ali the youngest brother could not resent, for he, taking a happy advantage, pulls it from Fazl, and crowns him with one better becoming traitors, of flaming iron. Abu Ali, after he had sovereignised seven years, was arrested by death *Anno Dom.* 1100, *Heg.* 480, and for scant of issue after the sceptre falls to Mohammed Abu Talib Toghrul Beg[316] son of Mikail, son of Seljuk, son of Duqaq, a Turkman.

---

[314] Khusrau Firoz was the ruler of Alamut, now little more than a ruined fortress in Zanjan province, where it is known for its association with the Assassins (for details see Greenway and St. Vincent, *Iran*, 338–39). He and his brother Ali, the Governor of Ray, were Justanids, an offspring of the Daylamids. Rayy, "one of the most historical places in Tehran province," is now "sadly swallowed up by the urban sprawl of Tehran" (Greenway and St. Vincent, *Iran*, 185). The origins of the Justanids are not known, and their authority was centred in a town called Rudbar "in a side valley of the Shahrud basin" (R. N. Frye, *The Golden Age of Persia* [London: Phoenix Books, 2000], 208). The same name was also borne by Abu Mansur Fulad Sutun (see below), which is confusing.

[315] Herbert's information is very confusing here. It appears that Herbert's "Abu Mansur" and Abu Mansur Fulad Sutun are the same person; he ruled in succession to Malik Rahim from 1048 to 1055. Abu Mansur Abdul Rashid was a Ghaznavid who ruled 1049–1052. and may be the cause of Herbert's evident confusion, especially since he was succeeded by Abu Fazl Farrokhzad (1052–1059). What *is* certain is that the Seljuk ruler Toghrul Beg bin Mikail (see below) conquered Shiraz and ruled 1055–1063. Where Herbert got the date 1100 from I do not know.

[316] Toghrul Beg [*Tangrolipix*] was Sultan of the Seljuk Turks 1037–1063. He married a daughter of Abu Kalijar and went on to capture Baghdad (twice) and subsequently overran most of Persia, including Khurasan and Khwarazm. In Baghdad he claimed to the the "Protector" of the Caliph al-Qaim (1031–1075), For details of his ancestry see J. A. Boyle, *The Cambridge History of Iran* (Cambridge: Cambridge University Press, 1968), 5: 17–18. Herbert's peculiar spelling of the name probably came from Thomas Newton's

In the Seljukian family it continued until Mohammed Abdul Kassem[317] died *Anno Dom.* 1220, *Heg.* 600 without issue. For then a race of Tartars followed, successfully conducted by Genghis Khan, Lord of Maurenabar and Ghazna, al-Mustansir then being Caliph of Mecca and.[318] To Genghis Khan, who died *Anno Dom.* 1228, followed Tolui Khan and Chagatai Khan; from Chagatai descended Tamerlane whose issue now rules India *intra Gangem.* After the Tartar the Turks fresh-planted here led by Qara Mohammed,[319] *Anno Dom.* 1415, *Heg.* 795, original of the *Karakula Guspan* or Black Sheep [Turkmen] as they style themselves, banished *Anno Dom.* 1470, *Heg.* 850 by Asen Beg, otherwise called Uzun Hassan,[320] an Armenian whose grandson Alwand was the last of the White Sheep [Turkmen] or *Acorlu Guspan*, thorn to the very bone of Ismail-Sophy[321] his ambitious kinsman, *Anno Dom.* 1504, *Heg.* 884. Ismail [I] was great-grandfather to Abbas, the Persian king who now reigns, and is of the bin-Alian or Safian stem or pedigree.

Persepolis.

From Shiraz we travelled to Persepolis,[322] which is thirty English miles to the north-east of Shiraz. First we passed that noted aquaduct resembling that at Tang-é dalen, the pipes by supporters reaching from mountain to mountain, so

---

Notable History of the Saracens (1575). This book was in part translated from a work of the same title by Celio Augustino Curione (1538–1567), but also contains material from "sundry other good authors."

[317] Sultan Ala al-din Mohammed was a Khwarazmid ruler who reigned in Eastern Iran 1199–1220.

[318] Al-Mustansir was the Abbasid caliph of Baghdad 1226–1242. The Mongol invasion of Syria actually began in 1258 with the death of the Caliph al-Mutasin Billah, his successor. Herbert seems to have conflated the two caliphs.

[319] Qara Mohammed Turmush (1378–1388) founded the dynasty which ruled the Black Sheep Turkmen until 1468. Herbert's date is inaccurate.

[320] Alwand [*Alvan*] was ruler of the White Sheep Turkmen 1500–1501, after which the kingdom split. Shah Ismail deposed the last ruler, Murad (1498–1500; 1502–1508).

[321] The name derives from Sheykh Safi al-din (see below) and the Safaviyya order of Sufis. According to *Hobson-Jobson*, the term appeared in English accounts in 1561, when Anthony Jenkinson took Elizabeth I's letters addressed to "the Great Sophy of Persia" (Hakluyt, 1: 381). In literature, it appears, for example, in Shakespeare (*Twelfth Night*, III, iv) and Milton (*Paradise Lost* X, 431) as well as in several plays, including Sir John Denham's *The Sophy* (1642).

[322] For a good account by a modern scholar of what Persepolis might have looked like in its heyday, together with a detailed description of some of the rituals and events which took place there, see Olmstead, *History*, 172–84. Greenway and St. Vincent have a special section on Persepolis, with some good photographs (*Iran*, 296–301). More recently than Olmstead, D. N. Wilber has written an account of the city, *Persepolis: The Archaeology of Parsa, Seat of the Persian Kings* (Princeton: Darwin Press, 1989).

as by the Indians 'tis called *Akbar Tangby*, by the Persians *Tengbe-buzergh*, signifying the same thing, that is "the great strait," from whence water is conveyed
into most pleasant gardens full of flowers and fruit, and on each side visible. It
also serves the Duke's great pond, stored with fish and fowl so as it affords him
great delight and no less pleasure unto weary travellers. The rest of the way was
somewhat sandy and about the mid-way hilly from whence to Chehel-minar[323]
are about ten miles, in which mid-way runs the River Cyr or Cyrus, over which
is a well-built bridge of stone called Band-Emir. And, being come to Persepolis, first suffer me to present you in little with revival of the palace as it stood in
perfection.

Persepolis was the metropolis of the world such time as the monarchic sceptre was swayed by Cyrus and succeeding kings until the subversion of that Empire by great Alexander. By that name it is usually called in all Greek and Latin
authors, for so we find in II Maccabees 9:2,[324] which St. Jerome[325] reports was
writ in Greek, where 'tis called Persepolis, but by the Persians and other oriental
nations was named *Elymais*, as in the I Maccabees 6:1,[326] which book was writ
in Hebrew, those various originals occasioning that difference of names, but by
comparing those two the story, for matter of fact, appears to be the same, so it
is evident that Elymais and Persepolis were one same city, which being so, that
supposition which Postel and others have that Susa and Elymais was one is of no
more weight in my opinion than that of Ferrarius, who in his *Epitome urbium* erroneously makes Shiraz to be situate in that place. Moreover, as the name Persepolis is derivative from "Persia," so was Elymais from "Elam," by which last that

---

[323] Chehel-minar [*Chilmanor*], a name originating in the thirteenth century, means
"forty columns or minarets." At the present day Persepolis is known locally as Takht-é-
Jamshid, after the legendary king of that name. Ferdowsi tells us in the *Shahnameh* that
he "had his demons raise him aloft from the earth into the heavens, and he sat on his
throne like the sun shining in the sky," and that he celebrated the first Nau Roz festival
there (7).

[324] [Antiochus IV] "had entered the city of Persepolis and attempted to plunder its
temples and assume control."

[325] St. Jerome or Eusebius Hieronymus (342–420) was one of the great early Latin
fathers of the church. He held various offices, such as Secretary to Pope Damasus II
(382–385), who asked him to produce a revised Latin version of the New Testament, and
he ended up translating most of the Bible by 404; it became known as the Vulgate Bible. In addition Jerome wrote many exegetical works and letters. Nowadays he is better-
known for his misogyny than for his scholarship, which is a pity.

[326] "As King Antiochus marched through the upper provinces he heard that there
was a city in Persia called Elymais, famed for its wealth in silver and gold." Elymais was
a term used to denote the inhabitants of the Susiana region, sometimes called Elam, as
Herbert states.

country was denominate until Daniel's time, albeit in Acts 2:9 [327] we find the Persians called Elamites by the Jews who then spake the Syrian tongue.

Now albeit the first founder of this city is thought to be Sosarmus, third in succession from Arbaces, who, conspiring with Belochus the Babylonian governor against Sardanapalus [328] *Anno Mundi* 3150, put a period to the Assyrian Empire after it had continued under eight and thirty great kings. [329] Nevertheless, the city was enlarged and beautified by Cyrus and Cambyses [II] [330] his son, and made the royal seat upwards of two hundred years during the reign of thirteen kings, the last of whom was Darius [III], [331] who unwillingly gave place to the Greeks. In its flourishing condition it was, saith Q. Curtius and D. Siculus, the richest, the noblest and the loveliest city under the sun, so rich as invited Antiochus [IV] Epiphanes [332] (for his frantic humour surnamed Epimanes) to march

---

[327] Parthians and Medes, and Elamites, and the dwellers in Mesopotamia . . .

[328] The Greek name for Shamash-shum-ukin, King of Babylon (not Assyria) 668–648 B.C.E. However, the mixture of history and legend here is very confusing. Arbaces, one of the generals of "Sardanapalus," is said to have destroyed Nineveh in collusion with one Belesis or Belochus. Herbert's source here is Diodorus Siculus (2. 32), who is actually citing the historian Ctesias of Cnidus (fourth century B.C.E.), who accompanied Artaxerxes II on his expedition against his brother Prince Cyrus. According to Ctesias Arbaces then became king and ruled for 28 years. Scholars are very sceptical about Ctesias; R. W. Rogers (*A History of Babylonia and Assyria* [New York: Abingdon Press, 1915] 1, n.p.n.) notes that he "disguised the real names" of the people involved, who were actually Cyaxares (Uvakhshatra), King of Media and King Nabopolassar of Babylon (626–605 B.C.E.), father of Nebuchadnezzar. Nineveh fell in 612 B.C.E; when in 610 Nabopolassar finally defeated King Asshur-uballit II (612–609 B.C.E.), Cyaxares, having first made peace with Nabopolassar, "destroyed the last pretense of Assyrian rule and won all northern Mesopotamia" (Olmstead, *History*, 32). As for Sosarmus, he is also listed by Diodorus and Ctesias with a 30-year reign, the intervening king being one Mandauces or Mandanes, who reigned 50 years. Sardanapalus will feature again in Herbert's narrative.

[329] According to Olmstead, "Darius laid down the general plan of the Persepolis buildings, but the Persepolis we know is the work of Xerxes" (*History*, 272). Earlier Achaemenid kings had used Parsagarda as their capital, but "Parsagarda spoke too eloquently of the supplanted dynasty," Olmstead states; "Darius sought a new site for his capital" (*History* 172). Darius, as the son of Hystaspes, was technically a usurper.

[330] Cambyses II ruled Persia 529–522 B.C.E. He is known for his belligerence and cruelty, possibly due to mental instability, and renowned for his conquest of Egypt. Herbert discusses his reign in more detail later.

[331] Darius III Codomanus reigned 336–330 B.C.E. After his defeat by Alexander the Great in several battles, he lost his kingdom to the Macedonians and was murdered.

[332] Antiochus IV reigned 175–164 B.C.E. and was given, or gave himself the surname "Epiphanes" (the Glorious), but his subjects generally called him "Epimanes" (the Crazy) instead, as Herbert tells us. A cruel, megalomaniacal, and warlike king, he captured Jerusalem and destroyed the Temple.

thither with a considerable army in hope of mastering the greatest exchequer in the world with like success he had at Jerusalem, whence but a little before he had sacrilegiously ravished ten ton of gold, but hence by the cititzens and Diana's priests that avaricious Syrian was repulsed with shame. Justin calls it "the capital kingdom stuffed with no less then the spoils of the universe," so that Sir Walter Ralegh observes "there was no place in the whole world which, being laid in the balance with Persepolis, would have outweighed it." For although Babylon and Susa were very rich, the one furnishing the Macedonian victor with fifty thousand talents, the other with nine millions of gold and fifty thousand talents in bullion, in Persepolis the main bulk of Darius his vast treasure lay as in a hoard, there being found upwards of a hundred and twenty thousand talents, or, according to Strabo, two and thirty millions seven hundred and fifty thousand pounds, all which came to Alexander's own share after he had allowed the soldiers three days' free plunder of the town.[333] So beautiful also and so stately in its structure, the timber being most of cedar and cypress wood, and the elegancy of building so curious and regular as in that age it was accounted and styled the glory of the world, and may therefore justly challenge this inscription:

>PERSEPOLIS, *Totius orbis splendor vere fuit.*[334]

Now albeit the city was such, yet it cannot be denied but that her greatest lustre was borrowed from the lofty palace of the Persian emperors, which both for situation, prospect, richness in material and curiosity of art rendered it incomparable. Plutarch in *Vita Alexandris* calls it "the proud and stately palace of the Great Kings;" of that majesty it was as put the Macedonian victor into amazement at his entrance thereinto, for in the presence was a state of pure gold, thick-powdered with sparkling stones, in which Alexander was enthroned. In the bed-chamber amongst other curiosities an artificial vine, presented by Pythias, the stalk of which was burnished with gold, the clusters of orient pearl mixed with rubies of great price, and no less rich the bed. The bedstead also was gold and thick-set with gems, the bolster was estimated worth five thousand talents and the footstool at three thousand talents of gold; the Hebrew talent is four thousand five hundred pounds, so you may well wonder at the sum.[335]

Give me leave now to describe a part of this structure, by which the whole may be imagined. It was built at the east end of a spacious vale upon a rock or rising ground four hundred paces from the city, the plat containing fifty acres of ground or thereabouts. The walls on either side were elaborately-carved with figures of men and beasts. The second storey was of porphyry mixed with marble

---

[333] Strabo 7.159.

[334] Persepolis was truly the splendour of the entire world.

[335] The gold talent is worth today about £7400 or $US 15000; the silver one-tenth as much. We may still "wonder at the sum."

of other several colours, embellished with costly stones in mosaic sort, but the
architrave, freize and most part of the arches were studded with gold, being flat
and terraced at the top. Towards the east it had a high and stately tower or keep
circled with a triple wall each higher then other and at such a distance as gave
a pleasant walk between. The first was sixteen cubits high, the second was double as much, the last threescore, all three of marble well-polished, battlemented
above and below to be entered by seven gates of burnished brass. From the summit of this tower the kings had not only a delightful prospect over all the city
spread itself below, but (notwithstanding the hills that surround the plain) as it
were an unlimited horizon uncircumcribed save by Heaven itself. Adjoining this
was a mount which contained about four acres of ground and was built after the
noblest manner; it was the mausoleum in which, and in the contiguous hills,
were entombed several of the old Persian kings.[336] The roof and casements, says
an old author, were of gold, silver, amber and ivory, and the walls were polished
marbles of several colours. Adjoining that was the temple dedicated to *Anaia*,
so Diana is there called; *Anaia* in Diodorus Siculus, *Nanaea* in II Maccabees
1:13,[337] equal to that at Ecbatana, which in those times, as Josephus and others write, was so exsquisitely built and with such extraordinary cost that it excelled any other then extant in the world, for the materials were of the best sort
or marble of several colours intermixed with precious stones. And no less admirable was the art, of that kind the Arabs called marquetry but the Jews mosaic,
a composition of many small pieces of marble variously-coloured or otherwise
gilt and disposed agreeable to the figure or place they assume in the pavement or
other part of the structure, which, set together, look as if they were embossed,
and represent men, beasts, flowers or other fancies, exhibiting an unexpressible
pleasure and stateliness to the eye, a sort of work those of old much gloried in.
For the temple at Delphi, Artemisia's[338] tomb and that erected by Alexander for

---

[336] Most of the tombs are in "the contiguous hills" at Nagsh-é-Rostam, although
Artaxerxes II (404–359 B.C.E.) is actually buried in Persepolis itself. The kings buried
here are probably Darius I, Artaxerxes I, Xerxes I (486–465) and Darius II (423–404),
from left to right,"though this is subject to intense debate among historians" (Greenway
and St. Vincent, *Iran* 301). There is also an unfinished tomb which may belong to either
Arses (338–336) or to Darius III (336–330). See also below, for Arses.

[337] "For when the king [Antiochus IV] went into Persia with an army that seemed
invincible, they were cut to pieces in the temple of Nanaea through a stratagem employed
by Nanaea's priests."

[338] Artemisia (d. 351 B.C.E.) was the wife and sister of King Mausolus of Caria (r.
377–353 B.C.E.). The original "mausoleum" was built for them at Halicarnassus [modern
Bodrum in Turkey] and was, of course, one of the ancient Seven Wonders of the World.
Herbert probably knew that Mausolus was also the satrap of Caria under the Achaemenids, because his country was in the Persian Empire.

his dear Hephaestion[339] were such, yea, many relics and broken pieces of such we find as yet remaining in old monuments through several parts of Asia and in Europe also, as at Constantinople the roof of Santa Sophia, at Rome the temple of Bacchus now dedicated to St. Agnes, in Venice that to St. Mark, in Florence that to Cosimo, the first of the Medicis,[340] and towards the east end of the abbey in Westminster the imitation of mosaic may be observed in the pavement and in Edward the Confessor's tomb.

Wenceslas Hollar's engraving of Persepolis [illustration shown on pp. 324–25]

This rich and lovely city, yea, the palace itself, albeit they forced admiration and deserved commendation from the Greeks, nevertheless at a drunken feast, in a debauched humour by the instigation of Thaïs, that infamous strumpet then following the camp, to retaliate what Xerxes had in a hostile way perpetrated whilst he was at Athens, Alexander commanded, nay helped, to set all on fire, an act so unbecoming that great Prince as when he more considerately viewed the flame made him repent, yea, so repent that if possible he would have quenched it with his tears.[341] Howbeit, this sad execution rendered that famous city "*polis apolis*,"[342] as one says of another place, so that nothing now remains save what the merciless fire could not devour; I mean the walls and pavements, which, being of marble and by expert masons hewn out of the main rock and by rare artificers carved into story and *grotesco* work, have hitherto also resisted air and weather, so as if not defaced by barbarous hammers and hands it probably will remain to express the old Persian magnificence unto all succeeding generations.

---

[339] Hephaestion (c. 356–324 B.C.E.) was one of Alexander's generals and a very close personal companion of the King. In 324 Alexander appointed him *chiliarch*, which was the second-highest office in the kingdom. "When Alexander had mourned the death of his friend Hephaestion for a long time," wrote Herbert's "cousin" Lord Herbert of Chirbury in *De religione gentilium* (1645), "he erected a tomb for him that cost twelve thousand talents" (*Pagan Religion*, ed. and trans. John A. Butler, MRTS 152. [Ottawa: Dovehouse Editions; Binghamton, NY: MRTS, 1995], 199).

[340] Cosimo I de' Medici was Duke of Florence 1537–1574.

[341] In all fairness to Alexander, scholars today are not quite sure whether the fire was a deliberate act or if it was an accident. In Herbert's time there was little doubt about what happened, and an account of it, including the role of Thaïs, may be found in Q. Curtius Curtius (5.7.3); "The Macedonians were ashamed," Curtius wrote, "that a city of such distinction had been destoyed by their king in a drunken orgy" (5.7.10). Herbert usually relies on Curtius's account, but it is Arrian who states that Alexander did it because "he wished to punish the Persians for their invasion of Greece" (3.19). Significantly, Arrian mentions neither Thaïs nor any drunken party. John Dryden wrote his splendid poem "Alexander's Feast" (1673) based on these accounts, which provided the words for Handel's dramatic cantata of the same name.

[342] A city but not a city (the pun does not work very well in English).

RVINES of

PERSÆPOLIS

The Valley

At this day 'tis called Chehel-minar, as the Persians pronounce, which in their tongue signifieth "forty towers." The palace, whose ruins I shall now describe, was, as I lately mentioned, built upon part of a mountain of dark-coloured marble which the great architect Nature has placed at the north-east end of that large plain where the city of Persepolis once stood, the middle of which was watered by the River Araxes, which Q. Curtius *lib.* 4[343] and Strabo *lib.* 15[344] say streamed about twenty furlongs from Persepolis, although others of equal authority name it Cyrus, which I rather approve, seeing the modern name it bears is Kur and al-Kur as some Persians called it, albeit others call it Pulwar,[345] over which is that notable stone bridge which was built over two hundred years ago by Emir Hamza Daylami[346] or a Persian Prince of the Seljukian race in whose memory 'tis called *Bind-Emir*, i.e. "the Prince's bridge." The circumference of the plain, surrounded with rising hills, is near forty English miles. About threescore acres of this mount, which Diodorus Siculus *1.* 17 calls "the Royal Hill" but by the modern Persians Shah-é Kuh, and Kuh-é Rahmet, i.e. "the Mountain of Mercy," by extraordinary toil and art was dissected and designed for the foundation and other accommodations of this marvellous structure, which both for perpetuity and elegancy in sculpture was in several places sunk and polished for lasting walls and pavements. The ascent into this palace is at the west side of the hill by ninety-five steps, every step being twenty inches broad and three inches high one above another; the staircase, that is to say from one side of the stair unto the other, is in breadth six and thirty foot, but so contrived that it gives a double passage leading two several ways, one towards the north, the other south, each stair also in the half-way having a pause or half-pace which is very large and square, flagged with porphyry and lined at the sides with a brighter-coloured marble then the rock, which divides the double stair and above the half-pace winds the contrary way to what it is below, both being so easy that I very well remember we saw a dozen Persians ride up abreast without crowding. The other part of the hill adjoining this stair is precipitous, its heighth being two and twenty foot as I guessed, for I had no certain measure, seeming of old to have been slightly damasked or wrought into grotesque, and runs due north and south above five hundred paces, not unlike the view we have of Windsor Castle from Eton.

---

[343] Q. Curtius Rufus 4.5.4.

[344] Strabo 5.135.

[345] A small river which flows into the Kur (Cyrus). Herbert calls it the *Poully-Gourck*.

[346] Herbert is wrong. The bridge was built by Adud ud-daula or Azod od-daula Fana Khusrau, the Buyid (not Daylamid) emir of Fars (948–983) and of Iraq (973–983). He was a great patron of literature and learning as well as the founder of the Al-Adudi hospital, which employed the great Arab physician Rhazes or al-Razi. Foster dates the bridge to c. 970 and says this date is "generally accepted" (*Herbert*, 312).

At the stair-head there is some remains of the gate or place of entrance into the Court, being about twenty foot wide so well as my uncertain way of measuring by paces would ascertain, but the heighth of the gate and what superstructure it had is not now demonstrable. The prospect we have from thence towards the left hand is a large empty piece of ground, by gentle hills bounded both to north and east, seeming to have been some garden-plat or like place of recreation, but eastwards more near the stair are the figures of four strange beasts carved in stone, not such beasts as we see in nature, but rather as issue from the poets' or fictors' brains.[347] At first view I thought they had some resemblances with those four monsters the prophet Daniel in his nocturnal vision saw rising out of the sea, alluding to the four supreme monarchies, but by comparison found myself mistaken. These quadrupeds stand two and two, the first two being about twenty feet from each other in breadth, but are thrice that space in length from the two former and have their faces turned towards the hill, which is the contrary way, so 'tis probable these four beasts, together with the four interposing pillars, of which two are fallen and two remain, served, as one may imagine, to support some gallery or terrace that had its prospect north towards the garden, under which a piazza was where attendants might walk, and south towards the palace. The main structure ranges all along towards the south from the top of the stair, the prospect being most part to the west, the hill towards the east interposing. One of the four beasts, to give it the nearest resemblance I can, is like an elephant, and the second, being nearest to it, is somewhat like his opposite, a rhinoceros; the third is like unto a Pegasus, or rather that violent griffin Ariosto[348] describes in his *Orlando furioso*,[349] but the fourth is so disfigured that it cannot be described. Howbeit, herein these beasts differ, for two of them have visages with beards and long hair like men, agreeable to that fourth beast which Daniel 7:7[350] looked upon as the most dreadful, prefiguring the Roman Empire. Their heads are armed with helmets or caps of defence, upon the necks of which are great round globes of like material, and the Pegasus is trapped with warlike mail so studded that it seems

---

[347] These are the *lamassus*; two of them (at the western end) are actually bulls with bearded heads; the other two (at the eastern end) have wings and heads of a Persian man. They were erected by Xerxes I.

[348] Ludovico Ariosto (1474–1533), the great Italian epic poet and dramatist, best known for *Orlando furioso* (1516–1532). Herbert would have used Sir John Harington's translation (1591); there are two excellent modern translations by Guido Waldman (Oxford: Oxford University Press, 1999) and Barbara Reynolds (Harmondsworth: Penguin Books, 1975).

[349] Ariosto introduces "hippogriffs" (half-horse, half-griffin) in several episodes of *Orlando furioso*. Astolfo uses one to run away to the land of Prester John and search for Orlando's lost wits (Book XXIII, 14–16), and they also appear in Books IV and VII.

[350] "After this I saw in the night visions, and behold a fourth beast, dreadful and terrible, and strong exceedingly; and it had great iron teeth; it devoured and brake in pieces and stamped the residue with the feet of it."

a sort of mosaic work, and in such lively and permanent colours as if it had been embossed or wrought but very lately.

A few paces thence is a large square stone cistern or laver[351] twelve foot in diameter and twelve inches thick, supported by stones of a large size, near which, still towards the south, are the fractures of some pillars, but of what use, seeing they are demolished, cannot well be ascertained. Flanking this is a wall that runs from east to west, which I suppose is part of the mountain, and terminates that room to the southward; it is marble, about nine foot thick and thirty foot high. Near the middle there is another double stair of thirty or forty steps, as also a half-pace in the half-way, flagged with a large square marble and faced at the side with figures embellished and carved by no rude hand. This brought us to a large square room which I shall anon speak of.

In the first place, therefore, I return to the foot of this stair to take a view of the wall or frontispiece, which on either side the stair has engraven *in relievo* several figures and in several rows over each other, resembling some memorable procession. The images on either side have their faces towards the stair as if they were to march that way; those that be figured in the lowest rank by their habit and posture seem to be of inferior quality, for the *aljoba*, or garment most of them wear, reaches scarce to the knee and is somewhat strait near the waist, where 'tis girt about, but toward the skirt more large and circular according to the form we see the Moors wear at this day in Hindustan. Some are naked downward, others have *calzoons* reaching to the calf of the legs, some are barefoot and others wear sandals. Howbeit, these seem to be of the military profession, for in one hand they hold a spear upright in the same posture a pike is ordered, but in the other hand there is a variety, for one carries somewhat that is of a circular form, others baskets with fruit, others some chests with boxes not unlike the *sanduks*[352] now used in Persia, wherein they carry preserves and dates, pots for perfume and the like. Some also lead a horse, others an elephant and some a camel, othersome a mule and some lead oxen and sheep with long ears, high noses and horns very oddly-distorted. This solemnity induces some to think it is the representation of some remarkable sacrifice, and the rather for that not far from thence and in like sculpture several figures of their priests or Magi are carved, amongst which is an arch-flamen. Now, whereas there is a horse led with the rest and peradventure for sacrifice, Diodorus Siculus, Xenophon and other historians acquaint us that in old time it was commonly practiced by the Persians. And concerning the dedicating a horse to the sun their deity, represented by the Mithra, we have something typified in that famous election of Darius Hystaspes, as also in that memorable march of the last Darius against Alexander before the engagement at Issus, where Quintus Curtius relates how that the horse dedicated to the sun followed the chariot of Jupiter, after which went the archflamen that carried the Holy

---

[351] A large basin, often used for ritual or ceremonial washing.
[352] A Turkish word meaning 'chest' or even 'coffin.'

Fire, as the Persians esteemed it. This gross idolatry spread itself also amongst the kings of Judah, who in II Kings 23:11[353] are reproved, in that after the manner of the gentiles they had devoted horses to the sun. Sundry other figures are engraven here in garb little differing from the former, but in their weapons they do, for some are armed with lance and shield and some have short clubs with thick round branches at the end like that I have seen used by the savage Floridans in war, and others carry *borricos*.[354] Amongst the rest there is a chariot which has two wheels, drawn by a single horse, the charioteer going by it, which sort of chariot is not unlike that the Roman dictators and other generals sat in triumph as represented by Laurus,[355] so that this without doubt was either appropriate to the King's own use, according to the relation Xenophon and others give concerning Darius his march, or, which is more probable, was sacred to the sun.

In the upper rank the images are more large and majestical, by their habit and manner of session seeming to represent some sovereign Princes, as may be presumed by the tiaras or high sharp-pointed caps that are upon their heads, which none in those days durst cover with but Princes of the blood, and they only by permission. They have also chains of gold about their necks, as some prime satraps had the privilege to wear. Those of the upper rank wear long robes or garments, the Persians thereby appearing to be *gens togata* before the Romans, and indeed we may observe that from Poland that garb continues in use amongst all the oriental nations. But the greatest variety is in the attire or dress of their heads, for besides the tiara which was worn by *serenissimos*,[356] the *cidaris* was worn by several sorts such as king, priests and people.

Now, as I find occasion, give me leave to make a few cursory observations, and first concerning long hair. Albeit in these modern times I find it is the common mode of the Eastern people to shave the head, all save a long lock which superstitiously they leave at the very top, such especially as wear turbans, mandils, dustars and puggarees,[357] in ancient times, nevertheless, it is apparent (witness these images) that the nobler sort of men wore their hair very long. Herodotus *l.* 6 and Athenaeus *l.* 4[358] afford us some examples: "*Persae a prosipia et speciosa*

---

[353] "And he [King Josiah] took away the horses that the kings of Judah had given to the sun . . . and burned the chariots of the sun with fire."

[354] The editor could not find this form of the word. Foster's guess that Herbert meant the Portuguese word *barricas*, 'casks,' seems acceptable (*Herbert*, 312).

[355] Giacomo Lauro (fl. 1584–1637) was an engraver, printer, and antiquarian. He wrote a guide to all the principal monuments and buildings in Rome entitled *Splendore dell'antica e moderna Roma* (1612–1615, expanded editions 1628 and 1641), to which he supplied many superb illustrations.

[356] The highest nobility, i.e. "Serene Highnesses."

[357] These are terms for various kinds of turbans.

[358] Athenaeus of Naucratis (fl. 200 C.E.) wrote a witty dialogue entitled *Deipnosophistae* (*The Learned Feast*). Smith describes it as "a work illustrative of ancient manners, a

coma quae capillati sunt, comatos dicuntur,[359] whence a part of Gaul had its denomination, short hair in those days being regarded a mark of servitude. Likewise, in that sharp and memorable contest betwixt the two brothers Cyrus and Artaxerxes for the crown, Cyrus, being slain and stripped amongst many other dead corpses, could not, save by his long hair, be discovered. And as to chains of gold, they were accustomed to be worn by favourites and persons in principal trust amongst those nations, as recorded in sacred writ concerning Joseph, Genesis 41:42,[360] Daniel 5:29,[361] and in profane stories many examples, as of Astyages the Median king contemporary with Nebuchadnezzar,[362] whose exterior vest or garment was long and richly-embroidered; his hair also was of great length and crisped, his face was also sanguined with vermilion. Under his eyes was drawn a small black stroke like that the women now use to paint with in Turkey, and about his neck a rope or carcanet[363] of great oriental pearl, as Xenophon describes him. Over their heads an officer holds a mace or other like ensign of majesty, another an umbrella. In the one hand the King holds a short spear, which I apprehend was the sceptre of old, and by the Persians had in veneration. *"Venerantur sceptrum,"* saith Justin *lib.* 43, *"etenim ab origine, reges hastas pro diademata habebant."*[364] And, saith Spondanus,[365] *"hasta nihil aliud est quam sceptrum; ut Achilles hastam tenens, iuravit per sceptrum,"* the spear was none other than a sceptre, as for example Achilles, holding a spear in his hand, swore by that sceptre, which nevertheless was soon after converted into gold, as we have authority in Esther 5:2,[366] where Ahasuerus the Persian King held out the golden sceptre

collection of curious facts . . . As a body of amusing antiquarian research it would be difficult to praise it too highly" (*Dictionary*, 1. 401). The work was first printed by the Aldine Press (1524) and there was a later edition by Isaac Casaubon (1600).

[359] The Persians are called 'long-haired' from the abundant, beautiful hair they have.

[360] "And Pharaoh took off his ring from his hand and put it upon Joseph's hand, and arrayed him in vestures of fine linen, and put a gold chain about his neck."

[361] "Then commanded Belshazzar, and they clothed Daniel with scarlet and put a chain of gold about his neck . . ."

[362] Astyages was king of Media 585–550 B.C.E. Nebuchadnezzar was king of Babylon 605–562 B.C.E.

[363] A jewelled necklace or collar.

[364] From the very beginning the kings had spears even before they had diadems, so they venrate the sceotre..

[365] Henri de Sponde (1568–1643) was a French Protestant scholar who converted to Catholicism and became Bishop of Pamiers. He was a prolific writer, and Herbert may have found some use for his *Annales sacri a mundi creatione ad eiusdem redemptionem* (1637) or his continuation of Baronius, *Annalium Baronii continuatio de Anno 1127 an ann. 1622* (1639). Herbert translates the Latin after the quote.

[366] ". . . and the king held out to Esther the golden sceptre that was in his hand. So Esther drew near, and touched the top of the sceptre." Ahasuerus is the Biblical name for Artaxerxes. The Book of Esther is not historical; "scarcely any scholar would now argue

in his hand for the Queen to touch in sign of favour, and probably it was enriched with precious stones, with which this great Prince was so delighted that the jewels he usually wore were estimated at ten thousand talents. In the other he holds a mound or round ball signifying sovereignty. Some others seem to be of principal note, for they have round folded caps a span long and flat at the top not unlike to Caps of State or Maintenance,[367] with long vests in large plaits and folds, and ample sleeves like unto the ancient maunch[368] or surplice,[369] and armed with short crooked scimitars stuck athwart their breast into a girdle. And other some, according to the mode now used there, wear high-peaked caps such as I found in Mazanderan,[370] and in the right hand they hold a short staff or baton such as in pictures are given generals or those that have eminent command in armies. Others resemble soldiers in pay, and are armed with sword and dagger, half-pike and bow with very large arrows, but their quivers are of an antique shape different from those which are at this day used. There are also the figures of lions contending for prey, tigers, goats and other beasts, and in vacant places betwixt the images the wall is damasked *a la grotesco* or adorned with trees and landskip, which though not drawn by Lysippus,[371] nevertheless for the great antiquity they bear may worthily receive attention from any traveller.

---

for the historical character of the work . . . the story as it now exists is a fictional narrative, told with more or less religious purposes and expressing well-known OT themes," writes Raymond Brown in his introduction to *The New Jerome Biblical Commentary* (Englewood Cliffs: Prentice-Hall, 1988, 576). My thanks to Fr. John Perry of St. Paul's College, University of Manitoba, for this information and reference.

[367] Herbert refers here either to the crimson velvet ceremonial cap lined with ermine fur which was carried in front of the monarch on state occasions by the marquess of Winchester, who bore it on a white staff (the Cap of Maintenance), or to the cap worn by peers under their coronets. It was also worn by Lord Mayors of various cities (Cap of State or Estate).

[368] A maunch is actually a lady's sleeve, often used in courtly love as a token, which also appears as a heraldic device denoting a man who is dedicated to the pursuit of love.

[369] Usually worn by priests in Western countries, a surplice is a tunic made of linen or cotton which reaches half-way down the body. It usually has big, wide sleeves.

[370] Mazanderan, also known as Tabaristan, is a northern provice of Iran which borders the Caspian Sea. Under the Achaemenids it was part of Hyrcania, and its capital was Sari. It figures prominently in the *Shahnameh*, when Rostam rescues the captive Shah Kai-Kavus from the clutches of the King of Mazanderan, thus enabling the Shah to march in and capture the city (Ferdowsi, *Shahnameh* 142–52).

[371] Lysippus (fourth century B.C.E.) was a Greek sculptor from Sicyon who worked in bronze. His fame rested on his connection with Alexander the Great, whose portrait he made, of which a Roman copy may be seen in the Tivoli Museum. There are other Roman copies of his work in the British Museum, but no originals appear to have survived. These include a statue of Heracles. Lysippus was known for his realism as a portrait-maker.

Adjoining these towards the west is a jasper or marble table about twenty feet from the pavement, wherein are inscribed about twenty lines of characters, every line being a yard and a half broad or thereabout, all of them very perfect to the eye and the stone so well-polished that it reserves its lustre. The characters are of a strange and unusual shape neither like letters nor hieroglyphics, yea, so far from our deciphering that we could not make any positive judgment whether they were words or characters, albeit I rather incline to the first, and that they comprehended words or syllables as in brachiography[372] or short-writing we familiarly practice. Nor indeed could we judge whether the writing were from the right hand to the left, according to the Chaldee and usual manner of these oriental countries, or from the left hand to the right, as the Greeks, Romans and other nations imitating their alphabets have accustomed. Nevertheless, by the posture and tendency of some of the characters, which consist of several magnitudes, it may be supposed that this writing was rather from the left hand to the right as the Armenian and the Indian do at this day. And concerning the characters, albeit I have since compared them with the twelve alphabets in Postellus, and after that with those eight and fifty different alphabets I find in Purchas, most of which are borrowed from that learned scholar Gramaye,[373] which indeed comprehend all of most of the various forms of letters that either now or at any time have been in use through the greatest part of the universe, I could not perceive that these had the least resemblance or coherence with any one of them, which is very strange, and certainly renders it the greater curiosity, and therefore well worthy the scrutiny of some ingenious persons that delight themselves in this dark and difficult art or exercise of deciphering.[374] For how obscure soever these seemed to us, without doubt they were at one time understood, and peradventure by Daniel, who probably might be the surveyor and instruct the architector of this palace as he was of those memorable buildings at Susa and Ecbatana, for it is very likely that this structure was raised by Astyages or his grandson Cyrus, and [it] is acknowledged that this great prophet, who likewise was a civil officer in

---

[372] The modern term is "brachygraphy." The meaning remains the same.

[373] Jean-Baptiste Gramaye (1579–1635) was a Belgian scholar and traveller who held a professorship at the University of Louvain. In 1619 he was captured by Barbary pirates and spent some time imprisoned in Algiers; during this time he kept a journal and when he returned home he wrote *Africae illustratae libri decem* (1622) and the *Specimentes litterarum et linguarum orbis* (1622) as well as a *History of Asia* which was cited by Ralegh (II, 88). Herbert's reference is to the work on language. Gramaye's journal is available in a modern edition by Hadi ben Mansour (Paris: Editions du Cerf, 1998). Gramaye also wrote about the history of the Low Countries; his *Antiquitates Belgicae* appeared posthumously in 1708.

[374] The inscription was finally deciphered by Sir Henry Rawlinson in the nineteenth century: see R. W. Ferrier and S. Dalley, "Rawlinson, Sir Henry Creswicke (1810–1895)," *ODNB* 46: 156–57.

highest trust and repute during those great revolutions of state under the mighty monarchs Nebuchadnezzar, Belshazzar,[375] Astyages, Darius and Cyrus, had his mysterious characters, so as how incommunicable soever these characters be to us, for they bear the resemblance of pyramids inverted or with bases upwards, triangles or deltas, or, if I may compare them, with the *lamed* in the Samaritan alphabet, which is writ the contrary way to the same letter in the Chaldee or Hebrew. Yet doubtless in the age these were engraven they were both legible and intelligible, and not to be imagined that they were there placed either to amuse or to delude the spectators, for it cannot be denied but that the Persians in those primitive times had letters peculiar to themselves which differed from all those of other nations, according to the testimony of a learned author, "*Persae proprias habebant characteres, qui hodie in vestigiis antiquorum monumentorum vix invenientur.*"[376] However, I have thought fit to insert a few of these for better demonstration,[377] which nevertheless, whiles they cannot be read, will in all probability, like the *mene tekel*[378] without the help of a Daniel, hardly be interpreted.

Cuneiform inscription [illustration not shown]

---

[375] Belshazzar was not techically one of the "mighty monarchs," but the regent; he was the son of King Nabonidus (556–539 B.C.E.), the last ruler of Babylon. However, "for eight years [Nabonidus] had withdrawn to a distant oasis," Castel relates, "and entrusted the government of his kingdom to his son Belshazzar" (*History*, 146–47). Nabonidus returned just in time to lose his kingdom to Cyrus. Herbert, following the biblical error originating in Daniel, confuses Nabonidus with Nebuchadnezzar and elevates Belshazzar to the rank of "king" rather than of regent.

[376] "The Persians had their own characters, which may be with some effort found in the remains of ancient monuments." There is no way to identify the author of this quote.

[377] Prior to the later editions of his book, Herbert did not insert the illustration of what we now know as cuneiform writing, but he added various details to his description over the years, presumably working from notes. However, as Rogers suggests, he may have included it because he wanted to make sure that he was known as the first Englishman to transcribe the inscriptions (some of which had been noted by Della Valle earlier). He likely read Mandelslo's description of them in his account of the Duke of Holstein's embassy to Persia, which was written down by Olearius, to whom Herbert refers several times, and which was translated into English in 1662. However, according to Rogers and others, Herbert actually transcribes two lines from one inscription and one line from another, which means that they make no sense. Interestingly enough, most of them come from an inscription confirming the involvement of King Arses in the building at Persepolis, for it reads "Arses, [son] of Artaxerxes, King of Provinces, the Achaemenian, made this."

[378] Part of the "writing on the wall" which Daniel deciphered for Belshazzar. He told Belshazzar that *mene* meant "God hath numbered thy kingdom and finished it," and *tekel* "Thou art weighed in the balances, and found wanting" (Daniel 5:26–7).

Adjoining these is a spacious room best resembling a hall, albeit some think it was a temple; the dimensions, by the ruinous walls that compass it, may well be disocerned. In it there are nineteen columns or pillars, most of which are perfect, albeit some have their capitals either broken or defaced, and upon those the storks build their nests, whom winter weather offends more then do the people, who have them in little less then veneration. Those that remain, each are, contrary to usual form, sharp towards the summit or top, so that it is not easy to guess what manner of arch or superstructure is supported save what I have described concerning Persepolis, or of what kind of structure the whole was, whether agreeing with the Doric, Ionic or Corinthiac.[379] In heighth these pillars are about twenty cubits, which at the least makes thirty foot, and in compass near three yards and fluted, every pillar having forty flutes and every flute three full inches as I measured and distant from each other about nine yards. The capitals have their buildings enriched; the pedestals also were wrought into grotesque with figures, and both pillars, capitals and pedestals are all of the best sort of white marble and ranked in perfect order or rows such as we see in cathedrals or in the halls of illustrious Princes. Now, albeit there be but nineteen pillars at this day extant, yet the fractures and bases of other one and twenty more are perspicable, from whence, and from the resemblance they bear with the *al-qirans*, i.e. high slender turrets which the Mohammedans usually erect for use and ornament near their mosques. They term these minarets, or towers, so as 'tis probable that forty of these pillars were standing such time as the Persians gave this place that new denomination, but how long it has been imposed those I asked the question of could not satisfy, the precedent name being utterly forgotten. Notwithstanding this limitation, it is evident that there were in all a hundred pillars when the place was in perfection, as appears by the vacant spaces and also by the bases or foundations of several rows of columns which are yet visible, in the whole amounting to that number.

Hence, ascending a few marble steps, we entered into another large square chamber which might be a room of presence. I paced every side, an uncertain but the best way of measuring I could then make, and found them fourscore and ten paces, the four sides making three hundred and threescore paces. Into this large room are eight several doors but unequal places of entrance, for I found four of them have six, the other two, four paces. Each door is composed of seven well-polished black marble stones close-laid one upon another; every stone was about twelve foot in length and four foot in heighth, which, as also the walls and broken arches, were wrought or portrayed with figures resembling some great persons on horseback, after whom proceed several others in sacerdotal habits bearing branches in their hands, followed by sundry others that lead along with

---

[379] Doric columns have no base, have twenty concave grooves and a smooth capital. They may be seen in the Parthenon; Ionic columns have a base, and their capitals are decorated with scrolls; Corinthian columns are slender and fluted, with ornate capitals.

them beasts of several species, but whether by way of triumph or for sacrifice I know not.

Out of this we passed into another room contiguous to the former, which some Persians in company persuaded us had been a nursery, othersome that it was part of a seraglio. The room is large, though unequal in the sides, for I found two were threescore and the other two threescore and ten of my largest paces. It had seven doors for entrance, probably typifying their Mithras or the sun[380] with seven gates which the Persians had in divine adoration, mysteriously representing the seven planets. Adjoining this was another, which in pacing I found how two sides thereof were twenty, the other two thirty of my largest paces. The walls here, as of the rest, were of black marble, but so incomparably polished and glazed that we beheld it with admiration, for several parts of it was as bright and splendent as touch[381] or steel mirror, so as we could very perfectly see the reflex of our faces and bodies when we stood before it. In other some places the gold also that was laid upon the freize and cornice as also upon the trim of vests was also in as perfect lustre as if it had been but newly-done, which is to be wondered at, the violence of the weather to which 'tis exposed and length of time, being upwards of two thousand years, duly considered, an art of great value with the ancients and longest-preserved amongst the monastics, as we find upon figures and capital letters in old vellum manuscripts and bibles, but since well-nigh lost or by our painters nowadays but meanly imitated.

The sculpture upon both sides the wall has variety of figures somewhat larger than the life, unless that men in those times were greater then now they are, some of which represent sovereign Princes, as by their sitting, habit and ornaments may be imagined, for they are seated in antique chairs of state, the hair upon their heads being very long and crisp, and about it some wear high-peaked tiaras which the Venetian ducal cap most resembles, and in little, the tag or sharp point the Mazanderan coolies have that are lined with curious wool, or that you see worn by the old inhabitants of Persia in my following description of Isfahan. Others have caps that be flat and round, and other some more high and folding like Caps of State, which together with the long robes or upper vests they wear is resembled by those our Knights of the Garter use at St. George's Feast or Installation of that most honourable Order, differing only in the sleeve, which is more large and purfling,[382] like those we see worn by bishops, save that these

---

[380] "The Persians," Lord Herbert of Chirbury wrote in 1645, "also worshipped the sun under the name of Mithras," and he cites evidence from Hesychius, Ovid, and Herodotus to prove it (*Pagan Religion*, 92).

[381] Alternate form of "touchstone," which is a shiny black marble or basalt used often in the building of stately homes. Ben Jonson commanded the Sidneys for not using it at Penshurst. "Thou art not, Penshurst, built to envious show/ Of touch or marble," he wrote in "To Penshurst." Some considered it ostentatious and ultra-fashionable.

[382] Having ornamental edges.

be wider and looser at the band. In their hand one holds a half-pike, another a pastoral staff, others short thick truncheons or staffs of command, and in the other hand round balls or mounds signifying, as I suppose, sovereign dominions. Amongst other attendants two officers of state are most remarkable, for one of them holds a sombrero over his head, which in those primitive times and after was used; the other erects a mace or like ensign of honour crooking towards the end, in those days doubtless reckoned among the regalia.

Upon the frieze or architrave[383] over the heads of the images are some characters inscribed which differ from those I lately mentioned, bearing (so well as the distance would suffer me to judge) a little resemblance with the letters anciently of use amongst the Georgians, which were corrupted from the Greek, and if so, it cannot be withstood that as to most nations the Syrians have given language, so unto the Greeks arts and sciences of most sorts owe their original, and concerning whom in travel, so to speak the truth, we meet with more remarkable memorials of antiquity then we find extant of succeeding Romans or indeed of any other nations. In lesser figures are represented the *satrapae* or Persian nobility, who with their arms stand on the one side of those majestic figures, and on the other side the Magi or archflamens, some of which hold lamps, other censers or perfuming-pots in their hands. I questioned some of the best sort of Persians then in company whom they thought these Princes did represent; one said he supposed Kayumars, another Jemshid, a third Aaron or Samson, a fourth Astchar, i.e. Ardashir,[384] the last of the Persian kings in the hundredth descent from Adam, though I think it means Ahasuerus, whom some make the founder of this palace, which I cannot think was a temple, both from the variety of rooms and ascents as also from the nature of the story portrayed in sculptures, and another Suleiman, as they call Solomon, whereas I expected that in these various conjectures Rostam their great champion would have had mention, concerning whom I have formerly given my apprehension.

Now forasmuch as the remaining figures or images are many and different and so many as in the two days' stay I was there it was impossible I could take the full of what I am assured an expert limner may very well spend twice two months in ere he can make a perfect draft, for to say truth this is a work much fitter for the pencil then the pen, the rather for that I observe how that travellers, taking a view of some rare piece together, from the variety of their fancy they usually differ in their observations, so that when they think their notes are exact they shall pretermit[385] something that a third will light upon, a defect the painter can best supply. And seeing I did not take them in order as I went from place to place, I shall nevertheless from the idea and mixed notes I then took enumerate

---

[383] The door-frame or epistyle.

[384] Ardashir III (628–630) was not the last king of the Sassanian line, that being Yazdegerd III, who has already been mentioned.

[385] Let something go by without noting it.

particulars, so as upon the whole I shall leave little unspoken that is remarkable. These walls in their perfection doubtless expressed an unspeakable majesty and an unparallelled, howbeit through length of time and barbarousness of people they are in some parts broken and demolished, although the arches and square fragments yet remain, so as the story that is engraven upon the marble, which is high and thick, continues to this day in many places unblemished.

Upon the wall in like sculpture is figured a person of quality, as his habit declares, contending with a lion, whom with his right hand he grasps by the leg to prevent this outrage, and thereby seems to have the victory, the contest with lions being no unusual practice with the Persians. Near them are two more inferior or servile persons, one of which holds, as it were, a flaming torch in his hand, then which lions fear nothing more, the other a basket full of provision, but the basket for shape differs from any I have seen in other stories.

Near this is a square of five broken pieces resembling arches and windows, 'twixt which upon both sides are the figures of some great Princes, most of which as to their habits are little differing from those I lately described, albeit their postures vary, for some of them are wrestling with lions. Betwixt the arches are flat pieces of walls lower then the arches, embroidered with several sorts of antique work with figures intermixed and characters writ upon the top, difficult to our understanding. Adjoining that is the figure of a monarch whose right hand grasps a sceptre of unusual length, for part of it seems to be underground, and behind him but in less proportion attend divers of his servants, one of which advances something towards his head which I took for some kind of mace, though much differing from those great maces we use in England. Others bear lighted torches or flambeaux, for they are large, nigh whom is an image of monstrous shape, for albeit the body be like a man he has dragon's claws instead of hands and in other parts is deformed, so that doubtless it was an idol, and not unlike some pagodas I have seen amongst the Brahmans in the Mughal's country, all of which are as ugly in shape as can be imagined. There are also several armed men which hold pikes in their hands erected.

Thence ascending four easy steps, upon the walls we see cut the effigies several persons in pontifical habits, most of them following as in a file each other. In their hands they carry several things, some of which resemble dishes and censers. Near forty paces thence in another large square room is the portrait of some great person, for he has the regal robe upon his shoulders and the tiara upon his head, and is followed by sundry petitioners, but in several habits as men of several nations, and may be presumed such both by their different habits and for that they have scripts in their hands which they seem to present the King in the nature of suppliants. In the rear march the guard, some armed with spears and swords and some with bows, who also by the long crisped hair they wear seem to be of more then ordinary quality, for even in those times that gave some distinction. Upon another part of the wall is the like figure of another great man over whose head one officer holds a parasol, another a lamp, near whom stands a flamen, as by the vesture may be conjectured, and his sleeve is either carelessly or modishly thrown over his arm, after whom follows a marshal, for in one hand he holds fetters and with the other leads a prisoner, who as in an afflicted state seems to supplicate. After him proceed several others all in order, one of which leads a ram, and sundry flamens follow with censers in their hands, as in those times was accustomed in preparatory sacrifice.

Near this, towards the centre of a large square room there is a hole which gives way into a vault through an entry that is about seven foot high and five foot broad, first leading towards the north and after bending towards the east. 'Tis flagged at the bottom with square marble stones of extraordinary size, arched above and broad enough for three abreast, leading into a fair room or chapel which is also arched and supported with four pillars four yards about, eight in heighth and four yards in distance from each other, and through which is a a passage by another entry towards the mount, upon the wall whereof is engraven their grand pagod. The sides of these two entries, in like sculpture and matter cut, have been carved with figures of several men, by their habit seeming to be priests, orderly following one another with their hands held up and joined together, as in those oriental parts was usually acted when they would express triumphs or other causes of rejoicing. The front is artificially engraven into the similitude of men and beasts in various postures, as men combatting with lions and other wild beasts of sundry shapes and beasts against one another. Amongst the rest is the figure of a horse preparing to defend himself against a lion, but so rarely-fancied as gains the sculptor praise sufficient, the posture is so natural, such as when that art was more in perfection would hardly have been bettered. Over and on each side the door through which we entered are carved in the marble some men armed with sword and pike and some with targets, over whose heads upon the architrave are characters engraven, which like the rest proved adverse to our intellect.

Near that is a second subterranean passage into another square chapel, strongly-arched and supported with four white well-wrought marble pillars, each about seven yards high, (for 'tis presumed that the greatest part of this pile was vaulted under ground), near which is a fair arch of like stone whereupon is engraven a man of extraordinary size wearing his hair extraordinary long and curled both upon head and beard, the last of which is cut square after the mode of the aged devout Arabians. His head is covered with a flat round cap and at his feet, in sign of eminency or conquest, a lion couchant is placed. Another man a few steps thence holds a crooking-staff, mace or other ensign of Magistracy in one hand and a lamp in the other; several pikemen also seem to guard the place, who appear only from the waist upwards. Nigh these is another sovereign Prince (in these particulars I repeat not, seeing they are several figures), royally-seated in a chair of state; in his right hand he holds a long sceptre such as I have formerly mentioned. On the one side an officer of state advances his mace or suchlike ensign towards the Prince's head; a little higher a man is placed upon one knee, and by his bowing posture, albeit his face is turned towards the north-west, seems to supplicate some deity. On either side the Prince in two several ranks stand many flamens, whose heads are filletted (for 'tis that gave them their names) and in their sacerdotal garments holding up their hands and joining them together, dancing and rejoicing as in old times was used in paeans to the sun, their Apollo. Not far thence is the like story, in this only differing: here the prisoner, being upon his feet, makes his prospect towards the east with his finger either saluting the rising sun or seeming to contemplate Heaven.

A few paces thence are figured two great giants who by pure force subject two lions whom they hold down by their hands fastened within their hair. Nigh them are placed another guard of foot armed with spear and sword. as it were safeguarding some notable prisoner. Adjoining that is the image of another sovereign Prince, in habit and posture little differing from the former, only the sceptre here rather resembles a bishop's or pastoral staff, which he holds erect in his right hand. At first view I imagined it was the image of an arch-flamen, but more deliberately that it rather represents some sovereign Prince. Now, albeit of late times kings amongst the infidels in some parts imitate our European monarchs not only in state but also in their regal ornaments of crown and sceptre, nevertheless of old the variety was far more in those distinctions. For that I may not exceed my bounds, in Persia the tiara, the *mithra*,[386] the *cydaris* or diadem, which was a fillet or wreath of blue and white silk embroidered with precious stones which the Surena[387] crowned Cyrus with (and some say not till then invented), the wreath or chaplet were the regalia, as now the *mandil* is with which the Shah, and with the *puggaree* the Mughal's head is adorned. Amongst these the *mithra*, which some make one with the *cydaris*, as in Zechariah 3:5,[388] where after the vulgar Latin *cydaris* is translated "mitre," was not least in esteem with kings, seeing it gave the *agnomen*[389] to the Persian king Chedor-Laomer, albeit the priests of Jupiter and the sun were in solemnities and noted sacrifices also permitted to wear it, so that as that attire became undistinguishable, in like sort was the pastoral staff which, albeit properly attributed to the flamen or principal Magus, kings nevertheless sometimes used to hold it. Now, albeit they were

---

[386] Mitre.

[387] As Herbert states here, "Surena" is not a name but a title. It was hereditary, and is usually associated with the famous Parthian general Rustahan Suren-Pahlav (84–52 B.C.E.) who defeated the Romans under Crassus at Carrhae. The hereditary title "Suren" appears also in the *Shahnameh* in connection with Kai-Kavus, who is sometimes identified with Cyrus. The name "Rustahan" became associated also with the hero Rostam, who figures prominently in that legendary king's reign (Ferdowsi, *Shahnameh*, 104–441).

[388] "And I said, Let them set a fair mitre upon his head. So they set a fair mitre on his head and clothed him with garments . . ."

[389] Surname. This was often given to someone as a recognition of military conquest, service, or a character-trait, such as Antoninus "Pius" or Edward "the Confessor."

never convertible terms, the *pontifex* usually deriving his civil power from the regal, yet in regard kings, whose charge it is both in spirituals and temporals to take care of the people, even amongst the gentiles have oftimes exercised the sacerdotal function, which amongst the Jews after the law was in some cases sharply reproved, as I Samuel 13:13 and II Chronicles 26:19.[390] Give me leave therefore to quote Virgil. 3 *lib. Aeneid*, concerning Aeneas, who sacrificed a white bull unto Jupiter,[391] upon which the commentator[392] observes "*tunc erat hic mos ut reges essent sacerdotes vel pontifices*," that Princes in old times have sundry times executed the priestly office, and concerning which I might instance several examples besides that in sacred writ of Melchizedek,[393] who was both king and priest. But in profane, take that of Annius,[394] who (Virgil *lib.* 3) was "*rex idem hominum Phoebique sacerdos*," whence probably it is out of Cicero and others our Rider[395] in his dictionary notes that "*Episcopi sunt aliquando monarchae appellantur*," which the Babylonian caliph and Roman *pontifices*, by reason of their mixed power and usurpation over the just rights of sovereign kings and other potentates, according to my apprehension most resemble, albeit the pastoral staff in this figure, as I fancy, is

---

[390] These verses read, respectively: "And Samuel said to Saul, Thou hast done foolishly; thou hast not kept the commandment of the Lord thy God which he commanded me . . .;" "And they withstood Uzziah the king, and said unto him, It appertaineth not unto thee, Uzziah, to burn incense unto the Lord, but to the priests, the sons of Aaron . . ."

[391] Virgil, *Aeneid* 3. 165–67. However, the bulls are sacrificed to Neptune and Apollo, not to Jupiter.

[392] By "the commentator" Herbert is referring to Servius (fourth century C. E.), a Roman grammarian whose *Commentarii in Bucolica, Georgica et Aeneidem Virgilii* first appeared in Venice (1471). See *Commentarii*, ed. G. Thelo and H. Hagen (Leipzig: Teubner, 1881–1900, repr. Hildesheim: Olms, 1961)

[393] Melchizedek was the king of Salem. He "brought forth bread and wine, and he was the priest of the most high God" (Genesis 14:18).

[394] "King Anius, / Both king of Delos and priest of Phoebus, / Garlanded in snowy wool and laurel, / Came to meet us" (Virgil, *Aeneid* 3. 110–13).

[395] Virgil, *Aeneid* 3.80. John Rider (1562–1632) was a lexicographer and theologian. He was Bishop of Killaloe (1612–1632) and the first Englishman to compile a Latin dictionary in which the English was printed before the Latin, the *Bibliotheca scholastica* (1598). It was revised and expanded by Francis Holyoke in 1606 and 1612, and became known as the *Rider-Holyoke Dictionary*. Herbert was likely consulting the revised edition.

"virga regalis, authoritatem habens imperantis,"[396] and, as Martial adds, *"qua ut pastor baculo / Oves regit."*[397] But enough upon this criticism.

The robe this great Prince wears is long and majestical; towards the skirt are folds, as is usually seen in large loose garments, but towards the shoulder 'tis somewhat strait like the rich copes used in cathedrals or those worn at the reception of ambassadors by the magnificos in Venice. Towards his head a mace is raised, which was an inseparable adjunct, it seems, when Princes sat in state, and on either side the King attend several great persons, on one side the nobles or Persian satraps, otherwise *homotimi* as Xenophon styles them, and on the other the Magi or priests. Two men also wait behind with great lamps, and some with rolls of parchments; opposite to them is a prisoner in chains, brought as it were to trial by the marshal, who formally leads the captive by one hand, the prisoner by the submiss[ive] bending of his body seeming to invite the court to mercy. Under these is placed a guard of six ranks of pikes, both men and arms in full proportion. Upon the left side of the throne stand several other flamens who hold rolls of parchment in their hands, and upon the right the nobles, who wear long hair, have antique garments upon their heads, bows in their hands, quivers full of long arrows fixed to their right sides and swords with plain guards unto their left. A select number of priests and nobles seem to withdraw apart and to expostulate or argue somewhat concerning the prisoner, who by this noble appearance and manner of proceeding may be conceived to be some person of eminency, but who he was the mysterious characters there engraven can best discover. And yet, seeing some imagine this structure was raised by the direction of Cyrus the Magnificent, who ruled *circa* A.M. 3400 and whose supreme officer the prophet Daniel for some time was, it may without offence be presumed Daniel, who when he was the president or chief of the hundred and twenty Princes mentioned in Daniel 6:2, by the envy of those ethnic Princes or governors he was accused of worshipping God contrary to that impious decree of Darius, for which he was arraigned, contemned and cast into the den of lions.[398] Otherwise it may

---

[396] M. Valerius Martialis (c. 38/41–102/04) was the pre-eminent Roman epigrammatist, whose writings had a great influence in the Renaissance. He wrote twelve books of epigrams, which were first edited by Niccolo Perrotti and Pomponio Leto (1471), and there were many subsequent editions; there was also an anonymous English translation of Book I, the *Spectaculum liber* (1674), and many English poets from the mid-sixteenth century onwards translated individual epigrams. The line reads: "The kingly wand, having the authority to command." The problem is that this is not a quotation from Martial.

[397] "As a shepherd rules over the sheep with a staff." This is another misattributed quotation, closer to Ovid, *Ex Ponto* 1. 8. 52 than to anything in Martial. Herbert's memory seems to be faulty here.

[398] The Book of Daniel, which Castel states was written "a little before 164 B.C." in the time of Antiochus IV, was compiled "to instill courage into the despairing faithful" (177) and is not considered historical, in spite of Herbert's wishful thinking.

represent Croesus,[399] that unfortunate Lydian king, who being deluded by the oracle's amphibology, engaging against the Persian became Cyrus his prisoner and had suffered, but by calling upon Solon in that his unfortunate condition, for seeing Belshazzar the last Assyrian monarch, to whose subversion Cyrus principally contributed was slain, it cannot properly represent that great conquest and revolution.

About a large stone's cast hence, over continued heaps of rubbish wherein doubtless are buried many rare pieces of art in which, as my thought prompted, that famous temple stood which was dedicated to Diana, there called *Anaya*, in its time reputed next to that at Ephesus the most curious piece throughout the world. At the east there rises a hill or rock, upon part of which, above fifty foot from the ground in like sculpture is the figure of a king, who with erected hands seems to adore the rising Sun, near which, so well as my sight would serve at such a distance, I fancied that I saw the Fire and a Serpent engraven, which being most obvious to wind and weather is most worn and least perspicable. The lifting-up of the hands in worship has of long time been a posture also amongst heathens. "*Omnes homines preces facturi, manus ad caelum tollant*," saith Aristotle, *Libro de mundo*; "*Duplices ad sidera palmae*," Ovid, and "*supinae ad caelum cum voce manus*," Virgil.[400] Moreover, that the Persians of old were polytheists may be proved by these three idols, for albeit the grand pagod by being the tutelary *numen*[401] of the place was in most repute, the Fire nevertheless was their principal deity, for with them it represented omnipotency as the sun the hieroglyphic of eternity and the Serpent time's revolution and sagacity. Besides these they had several other elementary gods, for as Herodotus in his first book relates, "*Soli, Lunae, Igni, Telluri, Aquae et Ventis Persae sacrificant* . . ."[402]

Scarce ten yards distant from these but upon the same declivity or front of the mountain in like sculpture is figured the image of their grand pagod, a demon of as uncouth and ugly a shape as well could be imagined, and, if reverenced by those wretches, sure it was not in love rather with a *ne noceat*,[403] base fear too

---

[399] Croesus was King of Lydia c. 560–546 B.C.E. He was renowned for his legendary wealth. In 547 B.C.E., when Astyages of Media had been deposed, he invaded Media to gain some territory, but Cyrus went after him and defeated the Lydians near Sardis. Cyrus claimed that Croesus had been captured, but in fact he had "followed oriental custom and immolated himself" (Olmstead, *History*, 40). Herbert also calls Belshazzar the King of Assyria; he was neither a king nor Assyrian, nor was he even the last Babylonian monarch (see above).

[400] All people making prayers lift their hands to Heaven (Aristotle). Palms held togther to the stars (Ovid, *Fasti* 1. 7. 5); Hands upturned to the sky, with voices (Virgil, *Aeneid* 3. 176–177).

[401] Divinity, spirit.

[402] "The Persians sacrifice to the sun, Moon, Fire, Earth, Waters and Winds" (Herodotus 1. 131).

[403] Literally, "lest he do harm," more freely, to avoid harm being done.

often drawing dastardly spirits into this vile subjection. It is of a gigantive size or magnitude, standing as upright as his deformed posture will permit, discovering a most dreadful visage 'twixt man and beast. Under his chin is a large maw or other thing like unto a satchel, but for what use 'tis a question whether the sculptor understood it. This monster has seven several arms on either side, as if descended from Briareus, and instead of hands he stretches forth his vulture's claws, his body being somewhat distorted. What the meaning of these seven arms should be is hard to guess, but according to my fancy they may signify on the one hand the terrene power and domination these kings had over so many kingdoms or provinces and on the other a mysterious type of the seven great planets which the Persians had in adoration; "*deus enim illos esse septem planetas, quos animatos credidit antiquitas,*"[404] saith Postellus. And albeit this pagod as to form be most terrible to behold, yet in old times it seems they gave it great reverence, and to qualify the dreadfulness of the figure, those more recent tell us that it represents the greatest Prince Persia ever had both in reference to extent of empire and to the power he had over infernal spirits whom by magic spells he used to bind and loose as he liked, so great a necromancer do they feign Jemshid to have been.[405] According to the course of their stories he lived about an hundred years after Kayumars, whom some imagine to be that Chedor-Laomer, *Kitter* in the Hebrew, so-called from the cydaris or royal cap he wore, who was vanquished by the patriarch Abraham. But having occasion in several places to remember this Jemshid, here I shall say no more.

Upon the King's left side are placed a stand of pikes, opposite to which in a little lower station is placed a man who by his posture and garb appears to be in a distressed condition, for albeit he be in the presence of the King he seems nevertheless to expostulate with some principal officers, and either from guilt or else upon view of that deformed monster to be in some kind of astonishment, so well as the sculptor's genius and hand could humour it. Below the guard are twenty flamens placed, some of which with their hands point upwards towards the King, others towards the sun and the rest downwards towards the Temple of Anaya. Two ranks of other flamens, sixteen in each rank, are placed on each side the altar, who by their mimic gestures and elevation and conjunction of hands express their *epinicia*[406] by this mode and manner of rejoicing, unless it were an antique mode of worship which probably they used often to their pagods. Some of these have their faces towards the King, who also had his share of adoration, but others turn their backs, glancing sideways upon the pagod, whom in this dance they

---

[404] "That those seven planets were gods, which antiquity believed to be alive" (Guillaume Postel, *De orbis terrae Concordia* [1544].

[405] "Greatness, royalty and the crown are mine," declares Jamshid; "who would dare say that any man but I was king?" (Ferdowsi, *Shahnameh*, 8). His pride, however, was punished by the gods.

[406] Victory-songs.

half environ. Lower are figured eighteen or twenty lions in a row, every couple looking towards one another. In the lowermost place, opposite under the altar, is a door or rather mouth of a cave, which gives entrance into the chapel that is supported by pillars. Mr. Skinner,[407] who travelled those parts more lately, assures me it is yet open and remaining in the same condition I have described.

Near these are the remains of a large sepulchre or coffin of stone, presumed to be the dormitory of some remarkable though unknown person, for both the villages thereabouts are silent in it, and 'tis the less enquirable, seeing that it was the custom of the monarchs of Persia to have their corpse let down into deep holes or pits purposely bored within the sides of mountains, where the bodies of the greatest number of those that preceded Alexander the Great were interred. About a bowshot hence to the southward upon the plain or lower ground is a high column in perfection, but of what use at such a distance I apprehend not.

To conclude, for *in magnis voluisse sat est*,[408] this is the sum of what I have to say relating to this uparallelled antiquity, and, when in perfection, incomparable structure, which has so far the precedency that Don Garcia de Silva Figueroa, ambassador *Anno Dom.* 1619 to Shah Abbas from Philip the Third of Spain,[409] upon his view not only prefers it before all he saw at Rome, but concludes that it is undoubtedly the only monument in the world at this day without imposture, yea, far exceeding, says he, all other miracles of the earth we can either see or hear of at this day. Give me leave therefore to add that here, where I may say *materiam superabat opus*, "the materials are rich but much more estimable the workmanship."[410] Nature and Art seem to conspire towards the creating amazement and pleasure both in sense and intellect, the present ruins retaining such a majesty as not only expresses the founder's magnificence but in the beholding strike a sensible impression if not of veneration yet of admiration in such especially as have a due esteem of silver-haired antiquity. Is it not therefore great pity that some illustrious Prince or other noble valuing rareties has not ere this sent some painter or other like artist to take a full and perfect draft of this so ancient monument, the rather seeing that the inhabitants of Shiraz, but principally

---

[407] Unidentified. He could be possibly Thomas Skinner (c. 1616–1695), a wealthy merchant who had interests in Indonesia and other parts of Asia, but Thomas had six brothers, all of whom were involved in Asian trade. Their names were Albertus, Daniel, Frederick (who was a factor in India), Lionel, Maurice and Robert. However, I have not found any indication that Thomas himself travelled. For details see Ruth Paley, "Skinner, Thomas (c. 1616–1695), merchant," *ODNB* 50: 869–70.

[408] "In great deeds, it's enough to have once wanted" (Propertius, *Elegies* 2. 10.5).

[409] Philip III of Spain reigned 1598–1621.

[410] Ovid, *Metamorphoses* 2. 5.

the villagers at Marvdasht[411] and other people thereabouts put no value on it, but contrarily (finding that albeit sometimes they gain, yet most times they lose by free-quarter of soldiers and others who out of mere curiosity repair thither) in barbarous manner spare not to deface and tear asunder what they can in spite and under pretense of serving their common occasions, albeit by the Dukes of Shiraz they have been at sundry times punished for it? Nevertheless I may here with thankfulness acknowledge how that upon my proposing it some years since unto that great Maecenas[412] of antiquity the late noble lord Thomas, Earl of Arundel,[413] he was so sensible thereof as to that end he dispatched a youth[414] thither whom Mr. Norgate[415] recommended to His Lordship for one he knew could both design and copy well, but I hear he died by the way at or near Surat before he could reach Persia, so as that worthy endeavour became frustrate.

To proceed. Little more then a mile hence is Marvdasht, which in a Spanish reporter[416] I find writ *Margatean* and in an Italian[417] *Mehrchoascan*, very much

---

[411] Marvdasht [*Mardash*] is now a 40-minute bus-ride from Shiraz, "a large industrial centre of no interest in itself" (Greenway and St. Vincent, *Iran* 300). Herbert thought otherwise in 1625 (see below).

[412] C. Cilnius Maecenas (c. 74–8 B. C. E.), the friend and adviser of Augustus and a great patron of literature who encouraged, amongst others, Horace and Virgil. His name became a byword for intelligent and generous patrons. He wrote a play, *Prometheus*, as well as some poetry, fragments of which may be found in J. Blänsdorf, ed., *Fragmenta poetarum Latinorum* (Stuttgart: Teubner, 1995).

[413] Thomas Howard, 2nd Earl of Arundel (1585–1646) was an art collector, bibliophile, and antiquarian. His particular interest was marbles, which is probably why attempting to preserve some of the monuments of Persepolis appealed to him. Arundel was not a politician, although he had worked as a special envoy to European Courts for both James I and Charles I. For details see Mary Hervey, *The Life, Correspondence and Collections of Thomas Howard, Earl of Arundel* (London: Oakley Books Reprints, 2008).

[414] The "youth" was Nicholas Wilford (c. 1608–1637), an artist who had been sent out by Charles I at Arundel's suggestion to study the silk industry and perhaps collect antiquities as well (see Introduction). Wilford unfortunately died at Bandar Abbas (not Surat) shortly after his arrival. For details, see R. W. Ferrier, "Charles I and the Antiquities of Persia: The Mission of Nicholas Wilford," *Iran* 8 (1970): 51–56. Ferrier reproduces a list of Wilford's possessions, amongst which was a copy of Herbert's book; he believes this to be the first mention of the book in Persia (56).

[415] Edward Norgate (1581–1650), son of Robert Norgate, Master of Corpus Christi College, Cambridge, was a heraldic painter, art expert and musician, employed by the Earl of Arundel to purchase art works and by Charles I to look after the royal musical instruments. He eventually held the office of Windsor Herald, and was the author of a work entitled *Miniatura, or the Art of Limning*. This book remained unpublished until it was recently edited by J. M. Muller and Jim Murrell (New Haven: Yale University Press, 1997).

[416] Don Garcia da Silva (Purchas 2: 1534).

[417] Pietro della Valle (*Travels* 3: 316).

differing from the right pronunciation. 'Tis a village consisting of near two hundred houses, such as they be, the people of which place were so transcendently superstitious that upon notice we were Christians not Mussulmans, according to their *Alcoran* what ground we trod or what places we entered, at our departure they sifted ashes and dust, apprehending we had polluted the earth by reason of our profession, which being done in our sight made us some pastime. This and the neighbouring villages, for that they are watered by aqueducts forced from the river Kur or al-Cyr, over which upon the Band-emir, a bridge so-called, we rode in the way from Shiraz to Persepolis, seem very delightful places, the gardens and fields by that refreshment appearing at most seasons extraordinarily pleasant and fruitful in variety of flowers and fruits and corn, Nevertheless, by those sluices, the mode of these parts, the main channel is so straitened that in several places 'tis very hardly discernible.

Rostam's Monument and Other Antiquities [illustration not shown]

Northwards about three English miles from Chehel-minar at the foot of that mountain which verges towards Persepolis, in like sculpture is carved the figure of a giant, which the Persians say is the representation of Rostam, which may the better be credited, seeing that in his memory the place is called Naqd, or as some pronounce, Naqsh-é Rostam, i.e. Rostam's monument. This Rostam was a hero celebrated in the old annals of Persia, which these modern times preserve but by tradition, so that uncertain it is what age he lived in, but as I gathered afterwards at Isfahan when I went to see his tomb, was in or about the reign of that great Artaxerxes or Ahasuerus who took to wife Esther the Jew, in whose wars 'tis likely he was some eminent commander, concerning whose strength and acts romance-like they report wonders. Nigh upon this same hill the images of several women and maidens are carved, one of which they say is the figure of Rostam's earthly goddess, of whose amours and adventures which like a knight-errant he performed for her sake the Persians tell many pleasant stories, as also how by the co-rivalship of Shughad his false friend, Rostam was destroyed by falling into a pit covered with boughs and earth, whence nevertheless with a dart he slew his adversary such time as he looked down into the pit to insult over Rostam by way of triumph.[418]

Not far thence, where the mountain in like manner is made smooth and even, are two other large figures of giants on horseback. The one has the royal tiara upon his head, with long crisped hair dangling under it, and upon his shoulders that royal veil which the sovereign Princes wear, as elsewhere described. In his left hand is a club with iron spikes at the end, not unlike that which painters

---

[418] Actually, Rostam persuaded Shughad to let him string his bow to keep wolves away, and then shot his enemy as he hid behind a tree when he realised the hero's real intention. See Ferdowsi, *Shahnameh*, 423–41.

usually give to Hercules. Opposite to this is the other chevalier, who wears a like vest upon his body with hair upon his head of equal length, but bare-headed. The horses in their posture face each other, as do the riders, who with their right hands stretched on high lay hold upon a round ring, seeming to contend about it and either to force it from each other or break it asunder. This probably is a symbol or emblem of that great Empire, and represents to all generations that great contest for the monarchy of the world which happened betwixt Darius and Alexander, or otherwise that 'twixt [Prince] Cyrus and Artaxerxes.

In another place, upon the precipice of the hill, is the effigy of another gigantic person, little different in habit and mounted upon a like Bucephalus. Within his right hand he holds a sword which is not so hooked as the *Damasco*[419] nor so close-guarded as ours, and with his left outstretched he grasps a footman that seems to oppose him, backed by another comrade bare-headed, who by this conquest over his fellow in submissive manner by the bowing of his body seems to beg the horseman's mercy.[420] There are several other images carved in the mountain which are lasting monuments and very well worth a traveller's notice, but these I lately named are the principal. Now whether these stupendous monuments may have been made by direction of some Persian potentate or of Alexander the Great, who had most pleasure in that kind of ostentation, and Lysippus the most expert statuary in the world at that time marching with his army, or whether they were formerly cut by the directions of that mighty monarch Nebuchadnezzar, the Hercules of the East, or precedent to him by the appointment of Semiramis, which last (as Diodorus Siculus *lib.* 2, Josephus *ex* Berossos *contra* Appian and other historiographers relate) in Chaldaea, Media and Persia to express her greatness but especially to eternise her fame planted gardens, dissected mountains, raised bridges and upon high places caused her own effigy and her husband's to be engraven, not only to the wonder of those times but admiration of all succeeding ages, which partly out of base flattery but principally out of fear the people first reputed idols and then worshipped, I am not able to determine, and therefore very willingly leave it to the further scrutiny of some future traveller who in these things may have a better genius, contenting myself only with the prospect and relation. At Kermanshah, a mountain near unto Pol-é Shah[421] in the way 'twixt Isfahan and Baghdad, the like curiosities are cut, and in all probability during the time these were erected. At Hamadan also the like and some few other parts of Persia, which being engraven upon solid stone at so great heighth and not upon the declivity, but hollowed within the precipice of those

---

[419] A curved sword or scimitar of Damascus steel.

[420] Herbert is referring here to the larger-than-life sculpture of King Shapur I triumphing over the kneeling figure of the Roman Emperor Valerian, whom he defeated and captured in 258.

[421] Literally, "the Shah's bridge."

mountains, as it endures the violence of wind and weather 'tis likely to continue as it is while the rock itself lasteth.[422] But to return.

Upon either side of this mountain near Chehel-minar, especially that which respects the south, the rock is cut smooth, and upwards above a hundred foot high in it are cut or pierced several holes, some being of larger size then other. The least is three foot square; also in the side of the hill some perspectives are engraven or at least designated. Now, seeing that Diodorus Siculus and other writers of those times acquaint us that when the Persian kings had the sovereign command of the world, their burial-places were not in cemeteries where most graves were usually made, but rather in deep holes purposely digged or fitted within the rock or marble mountains about Persepolis, whereinto the corpses, after they were embalmed, were let down by long cords or other engines fitted for that purpose, so as for the performing that last office there was no ascending without a ladder, which was only reared upon such solemn occasions. Albeit, it is not to be doubted how that this custom continued not many ages nor was practiced amongst all sorts of people, but during the time their Princes grasped the sceptre of the universe, and with those only that were of highest quality. For when the Greeks subverted this monarchy this mode was left, and that people conformed to the Greeks' customs, as appears by that stately funeral Hephaestion had and also that other of Alexander himself, where the corpses were neither interred in those deep holes nor burnt with fire but embalmed, coffined and kept after the manner of the Egyptians. Nor doth it appear what manner of funeral Statira,[423] the wife of Alexander and daughter of the last Darius had, whether according to the manner of the Macedonians or Persians, for albeit Justin, Diodorus Siculus, Quintus Curtius and Aelian make mention of her burial and of the burial of Darius, yet in what manner or in what place they were interred, albeit neither pomp nor cost was spared or the presence of the conqueror himself wanting for the greater honour of the obsequy, those historians are altogether silent.

Besides these, upon the same mountains some pieces of perspective are elaborately and regularly cut, resembling the noblest sort of ancient structure. The

---

[422] Herbert's references are not quite clear. Near Bisotun, a village not far from the town of Kermanshah [*Caramoon-Shahoon*] on the road to Hamadan, the visitor may see "famous bas-reliefs carved out of a dramatic mountain," which are actually Parthian rather than Persian, depicting Kings Mithridates and Gotarzes II (Greenway and St. Vincent, *Iran*, 323). Hamadan was once the summer capital of the Achaemenian Empire, but is now "a rather drab town" (327), although some of the ancient ruins may still be seen at Tappé-Yé Hekmatané (329).

[423] Statira [II] (d. 323 B.C.E.) was indeed the daughter of Darius III and she was captured after the battle of Issus by Alexander, who married her. Her sister Drypetis married Hephaestion (see Q. Curtius Curtius 3.11.24ff. and 4.10.18–19). However, she was murdered at the instigation of Roxana, Alexander's first wife (see Q. Curtius Curtius 8.4.23ff), who wished her own son (Alexander IV) to succeed to the throne.

lowest door or place of entrance is open, and as if it were to be ascended by steps; on either side the door are placed flat pilasters which sustain the architrave and other superstructure. Towards the summit are other doors shut, and the whole embellished with portraits of men which serve for ornament, something conform to that *Templum Solis* which long after by Aurelian[424] the emperor was erected upon Mount Quirinal in Rome, as expressed by Laurus. Upon the *culmen*[425] has been a pagod, which the inhabitants thereabouts say was Jemshid, he that succeeded Tahumers and he Husheng the son of Kayumars who ruled Persia *circa* A. M. 2000 and was contemporaneous with the patriarch Jacob, six hundred years before the destruction of Troy, then which, some presume to aver, no monument in the world precedes in time, "*nullam ante Troiana tempora monumentum apud ullos literis mandatum vel sculptum fuerat,*"[426] in which we ought not to be positive.

About three hundred paces southward from Chehel-minar there is a single column, entire from base to capital, but being so low and without company it is not easy to conjecture of what use it was, The pedestals of two other columns square in form are seen at no great distance thence, but uncertain what sort of column they bore, seeing that there is an empty hole in one of them, which some think served as an urn to keep the ashes of some dead bodies that were burned.

Some space from the mountain, towards the valley, are several coffins or troughs of stone, some whole but most broken, in which one may presume dead corpses have been laid. There are, moreover, the relics of some tanks or conservatories of water, towards which one may discern the aqueduct or water-passage was cut through from the top of the mountain so as by a pipe what rainwater fell at any time from the clouds was conveyed down into the cisterns. And with good reason: for albeit the city Persepolis had the benefit of the river lately-mentioned, yet the building expatiated most towards the north-east, which as towards the palace. Certain it is so great a distance needed these helps, wanting springs, the better to feed their places of pleasure as orchards, gardens, grots etc., which the city had plenty of, and those very large ones. The only ruin that remains of building in that part the city stood is a spacious square which had but one door for entrance. The walls are high and lasting, for they are of extraordinary large pieces of marble, and albeit the cement of these that joins the stones are visible, yet of what substance the single column is I lately mentioned I somewhat doubt, seeing 'tis so high and differing from the colour of that quarry, and by the curiosity of the cement seeming as if it were one piece of stone, so that the little time I stayed there would not suffer me to satisfy myself whether it was natural or artificial. Howbeit, since upon second thoughts I suppose it may be such plaisters in old times was made of flour with whites of eggs and the best sort of stone beaten into

---

[424] Aurelian [Lucius Domitius Aurelianus] was Emperor of Rome 270–75. Herbert is referring to his great Temple of Sol Invictus, whose worship the Emperor promoted.

[425] The top or summit, or perhaps here the ridge of the roof.

[426] The source of this quotation, which Herbert translates, has not been located.

powder, with which the outsides of some softer materials was natutally finished or pargetted. And of such a composition was that *piscina mirabilis* near Cuma,[427] which for colour and durableness even in those times gained admiration. To proceed now in our travel.

Meymand.

The eight and twentieth day of March we out foot to stirrup, and that night rode four and twenty miles to a town called Meymand.[428] In the mid-way 'twixt those two towns I observed a hill upon whose top, as the ruins showed, hath stood a castle so advantageously situated by nature as we judged was impregnable. A late rebellious Sultan manned it against Abbas his sovereign, who, to terrify others, came in person to reduce it, but such was the Sultan's resolution, such the heighth where the castle stood, so narrow the entrance and so desperately-defended that in six months he had but little hopes of taking it. What force could not do, magic (at least of gold) perpetrates, for an old wizard, covetous of gain, promises his best, and accordingly by spells so perplexed the deluded Sultan that upon the witch's assurance of fair quarter he descends, but the block rewarded him. Abbas acknowledges the enchanter merited his price, but while the wizard dotes upon his gold he sees not that danger was at hand, for the King, grudging the loss and knowing no better way to recover it but for being a witch, sends him to Satan without his head, making that the occasion of his justice, which but a little before he held useful though then disliked it. To return.

Meymand, a town of note upon the road betwixt Shiraz and Isfahan, is very delightfully-seated, enriched also with sweet water, excellent wine, plenty of wood store of grass and diapered with Nature's carpets. It belongs to their highly-honoured prophet Ismail,[429] whose tomb in a well-built *masjed* called Imam-Ismail is here seen, considerably-endowed through the liberality of many Princes, for towards its maintenance yearly twelve thousand maunds of rice and four thousand of barley is allowed.

Next night we lodged (slept I cannot say, we were so vexed with mosquitos) in Ujan,[430] a village consisting of thirty families, most of them prophets or

---

[427] Herbert is referring here to the ruins of the "wonderful" Roman thermal bath (*piscina*) at Cuma in Campania.

[428] Meymand or Main [*Moyown*] is seventy miles from Shiraz. The settlement there is 12,000 years old and there are many houses cut in the rocks. The town is now known for its almonds and rose-water production.

[429] Ismail bin Ja'afar (c. 721–753) was the eldest son of the sixth Shi'a Imam Ja'afar as-Sadiq and his designated successor. Unfortunately he died before his father, although some scholars say that he nevertheless succeeded to the Imamate in 748. He is much-venerated by Shi'a Muslims. Since he is thought to have died in Syria, the claims of this location as his tomb may be speculative.

[430] Also known as Aujun or Ujjan.

prophets' children. We still found least profit where such prophets dwelt, seeing they drunk no wine nor were grapes allowed to grow amongst them; not that wine there is held bad, but from some tradition, and probably that it is the blood of those giants who warred against the heathen deities. Nor was the water in their tanks so wholesome as might merit commendation, albeit the conservatory was as good as any we saw till then, being large and plaistered with a composition of lime and sand with some glutinous matter, as I apprehended, which made it both hard and smooth, so that it seemed to be no other then natural stone and better then that we call plaister of Paris. Such were the cisterns or tanks in old Rome, as Pliny tells us, and of like art were those slender marble columns our forefathers have seen cast or made for cathedral structures, reckoned *inter res perditas* by Pancirollus.[431]

Next day we rode over some craggy and steep hills, and at night made Tartang our *manzil*, a small town most remarkable in a *masjed* wherein we beheld a monument or tomb which was raised a pretty heighth from the ground and covered with violet-coloured velvet, under which lies buried a great-uncle of the King's. Next night we came to Asupas,[432] a place observable only in an old castle which was sometimes a garrison, in and about which inhabit, as we are told, not fewer then forty thousand Georgians and Circassians who by profession are Christians, albeit little better then captives, being forcibly transplanted hither.[433] They are a people having Saint George the Cappadocian bishop in veneration, being their converter and patron.[434] From Mohammedans they differ not in habit and mode but in their grey eyes and long white hair, which, after the mode of those antique gallants that be recorded by Pliny and Lucian, they wear tissued with fillets of silk and gold or silver. If any of these, which is too too oft, turn Mohammedan, they are *ipso facto* preferred beyond vulgar merit. Poor souls! Hearing that we were Christians they not only flocked about us but wept to see us, nor wanted we bowels of compassion to behold Christians in such a miserable thraldom and condition and under such temptations. Not far distance hence

---

[431] Guido Panciroli (1523–1599) was Professor of Law at the Universities of Turin and Padua. His principal work was *Rerum memorabilium sive deperditarum* (1599, repr. 1645), an encyclopaedic work about the lost monuments of the ancient world. A supplement about those in the modern world, such as the columns here mentioned, appeared after his death (1602). The Latin tag means "amongst lost things."

[432] The name means "strong guard" in Persian, but may have originally been named for Aspasia, the daughter of Artaxerxes II.

[433] Shah Abbas I had these unfortunate Georgians deported from Kartli between 1614 and 1617 after the defeat of King Teimuraz I of Kakhetia.

[434] St. George of Cappadocia (c. 257–303) is the familiar dragon-slaying St. George who became the patron saint of England, although Georgia is named for him. His fame as a Cappadocian knight was guaranteed by Jacobus de Voragine's story of his exploit in *The Golden Legend*. Whether he was an historical figure or not is debatable, but some scholars supply a conjectural date for him, which is given here.

is Thymar, memorable, if Bizzari[435] err not, in an ancient monument, by some Hebrew characters supposed to be the burial-place of Bathsheba, the mother of King Solomon, which probably may be mistaken for *Besh-shemeth*, which signifies a house dedicated to the sun. Howbeit, 'tis called *Meshed-é Soleiman*, i.e. Solomon's chapel, a place (if truly so) well worthy seeing.[436]

Next night we lay in Qumsheh,[437] next in Koshk-é Zard, next we came to Babarestan and next to Dehghanan, eight leagues from which place we rode over a mountain of black marble where doubtless are quarries of serpentine and porphyry, if the earth were examined. The descent was precipitous, so that save by ragged steps, and those not a little dangerous, was no riding down. Out of this part of the Perchoatrian mountains the Rhogomana River[438] springs, which, having watered Shiraz, runs into the Persian Gulf. Howbeit, down we got, and that night rode to *Gumbazellello*,[439] a village famous for a caravanserai and for the best wheat-bread in Persia. Next night we came to Yazd-é Khasht, a town which stands pleasantly in a narrow valley, the ground on each side declining gently, as no hill appears near it, the country round about for some miles being even and champagne, so as it is hardly to be seen or found till very near the place did not a castle point it out, which was built by Yazdegerd a Persian king, above the town long since, as this name partly intimates. Here is a very stately caravanserai, the best from thence to Bandar [Abbas] on the Gulf of Persia.

---

[435] Pietro Bizzari [*Byzar*] (c. 1525-after 1586) is briefly discussed in the Introduction. The work to which Herbert refers here is his *Persicarum rerum historia* (1583).

[436] The present-day Masjed-é Soleiman in Khozestan province is the site of Iran's earliest oilfield, which dates from 1908 (see Greenway and St. Vincent, 308), and the large city of Ahvaz is close by. Herbert seems to conflate the phrases "Masjed [or Meshed]-é Soleiman" (Solomon's Mosque) with "Mader-é Soleiman" (mother of Solomon), which refers to Bathsheba (see 1 Samuel 2:12–24 for the story), and the ruins which were believed to be Bathsheba's tomb (Malcolm, *History*, 125), but which in fact could be that of the Umayyad Caliph Suleiman ibn Abd al-Malik (715–17), the tenth in succession from Ali, and revered by Shi'ites for his benevolent rule. Whether Herbert's conjecture is correct or not I have not been able to discover, although some sources state the ruins are "Sassanian," which would make his guess about the sun a good one. There is also a Takht-é Soleiman (Throne of Solomon) near Tabriz and a Zendan-é Soleiman (Prison of Solomon). For details see Greenway and St. Vincent, *Iran*, 346–47.

[437] Now known as Shahreza, this town was famous for its hunting-grounds and contains monuments from the Seljuq period. It is named not for the ruler but for Imam Shahreza, who is buried here.

[438] The Khosht River.

[439] Foster guesses it as Gumbaz-é Ali, which means "tomb of Ali," but admits that "no place of that name has been found on the map in the position indicated" (*Herbert*, 314). However, the modern village of Gonbad, which is south-west of Shiraz and is situated in a wheat-growing area, seems to fit the bill.

Next day passing through Dih Maqsud Begi, we got to Aminabad,[440] by some called *Boyall*, a village of thirty families, most being apostate Georgians, enclosed to exclude their shame by a high, strong and round wall with battlements, which makes it to resemble a castle, albeit a village. It is commanded by Daud,[441] as they call Davit Khan, brother to the Duke of Shiraz, who for his apostasy was made an eparch and honoured with three temporal titles, but purchased, it may be, with loss of eternal happiness. Here is a neat caravanserai and banqueting-houses for his own delight; that I went into had five rooms upon a floor which were well-painted with imagery and embossed with gold. The gardens were formed into good order and, being the spring, which as Virgil, 2 *lib. Georg.* saith,[442] makes all things fair, amongst other flowers were tulips and roses of several colours, so as of house and gardens I may say "With various forms and curious figures there / The house and gardens of Daud Khan appear."

From Aminabad we rode next day to Cunaxa, a town boasting a thousand houses and especially in its great antiquity. The name it now bears varies not much from Cunaxa, which some make to be but three thousand and fifty furlongs from Babylon, where that memorable battle between Artaxerxes and his brother Cyrus was fought, whose death is attributed to the inhabitants of this city.[443] It may be, some think, either that same town which Pliny called *Parodoma* or *Orebatis* in Ptolemy.[444] Sir Robert Sherley was once commandant of this place under that wicked parricide and apostate Prince Kustandil Khan,[445] but it

---

[440] Aminabad [*Amno-baut*] is also known as Ujqaz.

[441] Davit Khan Undiladze [*Daud-cawn*] was the brother of Emamqoli Khan and the Governor of Qarabeg from 1627. He was instrumental in the good treatment of King Teimuraz I by the Safavid Court (Monshi, *History*, 3: 1285–86) and was responsible, together with Abbas I, for many great buildings in Isfahan. In 1632, however, he joined the revolt of Teimuraz against Shah Safi. In a speech delivered on 30 April 2007 President Saakashvili of Georgia made the preposterous claim that Davit Khan had actually founded the city of Shiraz!

[442] "It's spring that adorns the woods and groves with leaves" (Virgil, *Georgics* 2. 73).

[443] Cunaxa is on the left bank of the Euphrates, some 60 km north of Babylon. The battle between Artaxerxes and Prince Cyrus with his Greek mercenaries took place in 401 B.C.E. The retreat of the Greek mercenaries is the subject of Xenophon's *Persian Expedition*, also known as the *Anabasis*. Grant thinks it may be identified with modern Kunish, near Falluja in Iraq (*Guide* 198). See Xenophon, *The Persian Expedition* 46–51.

[444] Chardin also noted that Cornicha (i.e. Cunaxa) "is conjectured to be the Orebatis of Ptolemy" (William Mavor, *Voyages and Discoveries from the Time of Columbus to the Present* [London: E. Newbery, 1797], 11: 198).

[445] Konstantini I (1567–1605) [*Costandel-chawn*] briefly became King of Kakhetia (Georgia) in 1605, a position he attained by murdering his brother Giorgi, the heir-apparent, and his father Alexander (see below). He had been formerly taken hostage by the Persians (Monshi, *History*, 2: 400) and remained in exile, working for the Safavids becoming *amir al-omara* and Governor of Sirvan (1604). In 1605 he defeated an Ottoman

seems they bore small love to either of their memories, neither vouchsafing to bid him or us welcome, as most towns did we hitherto passed through, although I have omitted to speak the ceremonies, nor any accommodation there, though due to so noble a passenger. At this place Persia is bounded towards the north, for here Ayrac or Parthia takes beginning. Shapur, Ghanat-Sir, Nilgoonat, Kazerun, Firuzabad, Estahban, Naimabad[446] are towns in Farsistan which in this course I can but name, yet that you may the better go along, and for that the latest maps of Persia are erroneous both in rivers, situation of places and true names of towns (for to speak the truth, none that I have seen have five right names), I have therefore inserted this of the Persian Empire, in which, I presume, neither the position of places are much mistaken nor the names of towns in the least fictitious.

Map of the Persian Empire [illustration not shown]

Mehiar.

The next day we got to Mehiar, a considerable town, for it consisted of about a thousand houses, and albeit their houses were neat, yet were they in no wise comparable to their dovehouses for curious outsides. This reason they give: some of them, as tradition persuades at least, are descended not *a columba Noae*,[447] but from those who, being taught to feed at Mohammed's ear, not a little advanced his reputation, persuading thereby the simple people they communicated to him intelligence from some angel. Yet I rather think 'tis in memory of Semiramis, who, as Berossos relates, was at her death transformed into a dove, for which cause the Syrians and other oriental nations to this day have that bird in more then ordinary esteem amongst them.

---

army near the Aq-su river (Monshi, *History*, 3. 871). He himself was defeated and killed by King Giorgi X of Kartli a few months later when the Georgian nobles rose up against Safavid rule; his usurpation had not been approved by Shah Abbas, at least according to Monshi (*History*, 3: 882). I give the name as it appears in Monshi. Herbert is using the Persian form.

[446] Some of these towns are still of interest to tourists and archaeologists. Estehban was "once famous for its grapes;" Firuzabad has some Sassanian ruins, including those of a palace built by Shapur I. It had a Sassanian-era castle, now also in ruins. Kazerun has some bas-reliefs and Shapur a fire-temple ruin and a huge statue of Shapur I (Greenway and St. Vincent, *Iran* 302). The other have very little of note to recommend them.

[447] From Noah's dove.

Isfahanet.

Next night we were brought to Isfahanet by a servant of Mulai'im Beg, the King's fiscal,[448] who entreated the ambassadors to repose a day or two there till Isfahan could fit itself for their more solemn reception, where in this interim we may remember that most of these *manzils* we have passed from Chehel-minar to this place are 'twixt twenty and thirty miles asunder. The whole distance is somewhat above two hundred English miles, as I computed.

Sir Dodmore Cotton's entrance into Isfahan.

The tenth of April we left Isfahanet, which is a village six miles south from Isfahan. When we had gone a *farsang* further we were invited to a collation that was prepared in one of the King's gardens that was by the highway, whither the English agent and such other European merchants as were Residentiaries in Isfahan came to express their civilities unto the Ambassador. A mile nearer the city the Vizier,[449] the Sultan of Isfahan, Mula'im Beg and Khwaja Nazar[450] the Armenian Prince with about four thousand horse and innumerable foot came out to meet us. The highway for full two miles from the town was full of men, women and children; here also we found the banians in great numbers, who all together all the way in a volley of acclamations welcomed us with *khosh amadid*, the better sort with *khush geldün, safa geldün*,[451] in our language "welcome, welcome, heartily welcome," which with the kettledrums, fifes, tabours, timbrels, dancing-wenches, hocus-pocus and other antics past my remembrance, but according to

---

[448] Mula'im Beg [*Meloyembeg*], Abbas's Lord Treasurer, was described by Stodart as "one that doth much love the English" (*Journal*, 68).

[449] Shah Abbas's last Vizier was Kalifa Sultan, "a *sayyed* of high rank and a scholar of fine character." He was skilled in accountancy as well, "such that the records kept during his incumbency are free from error" (Monshi, *History*, 3: 1320–1321).

[450] Khwaja Nazar (d. 1636) was the *kalantar* or mayor of New Julfa (see below). The Armenian community appointed the *kalantar* themselves, and since they often referred to him as *ishkan* (Prince), Herbert assumed that he held that title. Nazar had succeeded his brother Khwaja Safar in 1618. His duties included tax collection, public order and judge in the community, as well as acting as the Shah's banker with the Armenians and controlling the silk trade. For further details see Sebouh Aslanian, "Social Capital, 'Trust' and the Role of Networks in Julfan Trade: Informal and Semi-formal Institutions at Work," *Journal of Global History* 1 (2006): 383–402. Curiously, Stodart refers to him as 'Sarphara Beg' (*Journal*, 72), which suggests that he thought Nazar was his deceased brother Safar; Denison Ross thought that "Herbert's Khwaja Nazar would seem to refer to the same man," but cites the *Court Minutes of the East India Company 1640–43* as stating that the "chief of the Armenians in Persia" was Safar (71 n. 1).

[451] As Foster correctly notes, this is Turkish, and means "welcome, heartily welcome." He also informs us that "Turkish was generally spoken at the Persian court and by the people of the better class" (*Herbert*, 314).

the customs of those countries, ennobled the entertainment. The bridge also over which we passed into the city was in like manner full of women on both sides, many of which, equally coveting to see and to be seen, in a fair deportment unmasked their faces. The first place we alighted at was Kun-é Padishah, a house of the King's at the west side of the *maidan*,[452] where some of the noblemen kneeled down and salaamed, three times kissing the King's threshold and as oft knocked their heads in a customary obeisance. Sir Robert Sherley, who was well-acquainted with the formalities of those parts and in all places habited like a Persian, *sizedaed*[453] also, which made him the more to be respected. A *qizilbash* concluded the ceremony in a panegyric that the Excellency of Shah Abbas had attracted a Prince and other gentlemen from the extremest angle of the world to see whether Fame had been partial in the report of his magnificence, but no wonder, since his beams spread themselves over the universe! That done, bottles of pure wine were lavished out, after which, with a continued clamour of the plebeians thereby expressing their joy, we were conducted to another house of the King's which was at the south-east end of the city, through which a broad sluice of water had its course into the Zayandé river, which made our lodging the more delightful.

The fourth day after our being in Isfahan, Mr. Burt the English agent and a very accomplished merchant, feasted our Ambassador, expressing a very noble entertainment and hearty welcome, where, according to the mode of Persia, there was store of odoriferous flowers and sweet water agreeable to the old custom mentioned by Plutarch in the *Life of Artaxerxes*, where the King, entertaining Antalcidas the Lacedaemonian, circled his brows with a garland of flowers wet with most sweet and precious oils which perfumed the place. At night a large tank of water was surrounded with lighted tapers, artificially uniting two contrary elements; squibs also and other fireworks, for the more honour of the feast, such as made the Persians admire. Next day Khwaja Nazar the Armenian Prince was visited by the Ambassador at his house in [New] Julfa;[454] a Christian he professes himself, but, I must be bold to say, his house was furnished with such

---

[452] Kun-é Padishah actually means "House of the King or Emperor." The *maidan* in question is Naghsh-é Jahan or Maidan-é Shah, built in 1591–1602, now renamed Emam Khomeini Square, "one of the largest in the world" (Greenway and St. Vincent, *Iran*, 195). It measures 512 × 159m.

[453] This is the *taqbir i-sijdah* or the *tasbih i-sijdah*. In the first the suppliant or worshipper drops on his knees, and in the second he "puts first his nose and then his forehead to the ground" (Hughes, *Dictionary*, 467).

[454] New Julfa or Jolfa was the Armenian quarter of Isfahan. Shah Abbas had compelled the Armenians to move there from [Old] Julfa (in the Tabriz area, for which see Greenway and St. Vincent, *Iran*, 158) in 1603, and it soon became not just a trade centre but the hub of Armenian culture in the Persian Empire. On the whole, relations were quite good between the Persians and the Armenians. See Anthony Ovanessian, *La Nouvelle Djoulfa* (Paris: Maison des Arts, 2007).

beastly pictures, such ugly postures as indeed are not fit to be remembered, for God calleth not to uncleanliness but to holiness. Yet forasmuch as he professed himself to be a Christian, that golden saying in Sedulius *lib.* 2 is fit to be writ upon his wall: "*Deus semper adest*,"[455] as also that which the prophet Jeremiah declares Chapter 44, verse 4, in the *odium* of that *infandum peccatum*, "It is unthinkable, for the Lord hateth it."[456] Amongst our other cates[457] I took most notice of a roasted pig, in regard it was the first we saw there, and is meat equally offensive to Jew and Mahometan. The flagons and bowls that we saw in his house were of gold, vials of sweet water for perfume and glasses of Shiraz wine were emptied for our better entertainment.

Georgian miseries.

These Georgians and Armenians are by some called Julphalins, from a suburb adjoining this city, but rather in memory of their metropolis which bears the name Ararat,[458] called *Ariamnes* by Tortelius.[459] The Georgians are the ancient inhabitants of that country and have little intermixture with other nations.[460] The soil is most part mountainous, much resembling Helvetia, where the Switzers live. From the tops of some hills they can discover, at least as they suppose, the Euxine[461] and Caspian Seas. They derive their name either from St. George their patron, or from the Gordian Hills[462] on which they inhabit, albeit the Greeks derive them from the word γεωγοί, for they are husbandmen. And indeed, the goodness of God is herein to be acknowledged, inasmuch as that respect by Turk,

---

[455] "God [in the present, the past, the future] is always there." The lines should read ". . . *Deus, praesentia, prisca, futura, / semper adest*" (Sedulius, *Paschale carmen* 2. 99–100).

[456] The verse reads "Howbeit I sent unto you all my servants the prophets, rising early and sending them, saying Oh, do not this abominable thing that I hate." Jeremiah was not delivering a message about pornographic pictures, but God's displeasure that Judah was worshipping the wrong gods.

[457] Dishes.

[458] Ararat is a region in southern Georgia as well as the famous mountain of that name.

[459] Giovanni Tortelio (1400–1466) was an Italian orthographer, humanist, theologian, and commentator on Juvenal from Arezzo. He wrote *De orthographia dictionum e Graecis tractatus* (1439), which appeared in print edited by Giorgio Valla, the son of the humanist Lorenzo Valla (Venice, 1495). Tortelius also served as a counsellor to Pope Nicholas V and was a friend of the elder Valla's.

[460] See S. Rapp, ed., *Languages and Cultures of Eastern Christianity: Georgian* (Aldershot: Ashgate, 2010), and *ODB* 2: 840–44.

[461] The Greek name for the Black Sea. It literally means "friendly to travellers," which Grant notes is "a euphemistic term" (*Guide*, 247).

[462] Named for Gordyene, a former kingdom in what is now the Turkish part of Kurdistan; these mountains are also known as the Gordysean Mountains.

Tartar and Persian who environ them, and tell them that all Anatolia and those
other countries that lie between the Euxine and Mediterranean, albeit they were
once altogether inhabited by Christians, are now overspread with those that embrace the Alcoran. They were interdicted communion with the Orthodox by Dioscorus, Patriarch of Constantinople,[463] nevertheless under Sapor [II] added to
the army triumphant 20,000 martyrs. At Albanopolis[464] St. Bartholomew was
buried, saith Sophronius.[465] Some call them *Ibri* and suppose that from them
descends the Spaniard. Constantine Porphyrogenitus,[466] if rightly-informed, de-
duces these Georgians are from David and Bathsheba, but that pedigree I suppose will be but badly proved. By profession they are now for the greatest parts
Nestorians[467] and Jacobites,[468] and more inclinable to arms then trading, as their
neighbours the Armenians be, but for comeliness of body, heighth of spirit and
faithfulness in trust are of that repute, especially with the Persians, that many of

[463] There was no such person as Dioscorus of Constantinople.

[464] A city in Illyria whose exact location is unknown; some modern scholars identify
it with a village near Kruja in modern Albania.

[465] Sophronius (560–638), a Syrian monk, theologian, and teacher of rhetoric, was
Patriarch of Jerusalem 634–38. He travelled to Constantinople and in Egypt (633) and
was executed by order of the Muslim authorities in Jerusalem, He wrote a collection of
poetry, the *Anacreontia*, and edited a now-lost selection of the writings of orthodox Greek
fathers, the *Florilegium*. St. Bartholomew was one of Jesus's disciples, and is traditionally
thought to have been one of the first apostles to Armenia (S. Der Nersessian, *The Armenians* [New York: Praeger, 1969], 74).

[466] Constantine VII Porphyrogenitus (905–959) was Emperor of Byzantium 908–
59. A retiring and learned man, he was an antiquarian, painter, and historian, and wrote
De administrando imperio, in which he included a history of the Empire to the year 817,
a work which contained a great deal of information on neighbouring countries and their
customs. It was first published in Latin by Johannes Meursius (1611), who supplied the
title, and there is a modern translation by Romilly Jenkins (Cambridge, MA: Harvard
University Press, 1967). Constantine VII also wrote the *Hippiatrica*, a treatise on horses
(printed 1530) and *De virtutibus et vitiis*, a kind of moral dictionary, which was printed
in Paris, 1634. See A. Toynbee, *Constantine Porphyrogenitus and his World* (Oxford: Oxford University Press, 1973). His surname means "born into the purple," i.e. emperor
from birth.

[467] The Nestorians were a sect founded by Nestorius (386–451), Patriarch of Constantinople. They believed that Jesus existed as two separate beings, one human and one
divine. Their view was formally condemned as heresy by the Council of Ephesus (431)
and Nestorius was deposed. This caused a schism in the Church; the "Assyrian Church,"
which was Eastern, followed Nestorius, and the Byzantine (Western Church) rejected
him.

[468] The Jacobites were the followers of Jacob the Syrian (c. 640–708), Bishop of
Edessa, a theologian, grammarian, and translator. His output included commentaries on
the Bible and liturgical writings in Syriac. Edward Brerewood dicusses them in Chapter
XXI of his *Inquiries* (185–90).

them are employed in places of command, especially against their turbulent adversary the Turk, and, as of old the Egyptian sultans had their mamelukes, so at this day the Persian king has the greatest number of his *qizilbashes* from thence, it being seldom heard that anyone of them is false, or having served the Persian ever turned to the Turk, notwithstanding which the Persian king in our times, upon some distaste given by Kustandil Khan, made war against that nation, as Sir Robert Sherley one time when we were travelling together gave us the ensuing relation.

Alexander,[469] a late Georgian Prince, had by a Circassian lady three sons, Alexander,[470] Terebeg and Kustandil. Terebeg enlisting himself under the Turk, Kustandil did the like under the Persian, but both for the preferment became apostates and turned *bozermen*.[471] Kustandil was the most active of spirit, albeit in body naturally deformed. Abbas, taking dislike against Alexander for his compliance with the Turk, the Prince so slightly excused the fact as exasperates Abbas the more. Ali Khan[472] thereupon was ordered to march against him with

---

[469] Alexander II of Kakheti (1527–1605) [*Scander*] reigned 1574–1601 and 1602–1605. Herbert's information about his murder and that of his son Giorgi III is not quite accurate; there were four sons, not three: Irakly [*Terebeg*], Davit (II), Giorgi (III), and Kustandil or Konstantini. Abbas deposed Alexander in 1601 and replaced him with his son Davit II (see below), but upon the latter's death in 1602 Alexander was restored, and in 1604 he associated his other son Giorgi III with him on the throne. As Governor of Sirvan, Kustandil had been sent (with his father) to reconquer the territory from the Turks. Giorgi (whom Monshi calls Gorgin Mirza) did not like having Kustandil "as a powerful neighbour" (*History*, 3: 869) and resented his conversion to Islam. The Persians did not quite trust Alexander, as he had hitherto been friendly with the Turks; they believed that he would sit on the fence until he saw the outcome of Abbas's war with them, which is why the Shah had sent them to Sirvan. Kustandil forced the issue by demanding they immediately attack in Sirvan; he argued with his brother and father, and they walked out of the room. As Giorgi left he abused his brother and they quarrelled; Kustandil "drew his sword, struck his brother and killed him" (*History*, 3: 870). It was Ali Khan Movafeq (see below), says Monshi at this point, who "drew his sword and killed Alexander Khan," after which "Kustandil took possession of his father's and brother's treasuries and commenced to rule in Georgia" (*History*, 3: 871). However, Monshi later contradicts himself by stating that Kustandil himself "had killed his father and brother" (*History*, 3: 880). They were killed on 2 March 1605.

[470] This is incorrect. Davit II succeeded Alexander briefly in 1601 but died the next year.

[471] Another name for Muslims. Foster suggests that it might derive from *busurman*, which apparently "is the popular name for a Muhammedan in modern Russian" (*Herbert*, 315).

[472] Ali Khan Movafeq (d. 1623) was "an Ottoman subject from Qarabeg" (Monshi *History*, 3: 862) who had known Kustandil since the latter had been a hostage at Abbas's Court. The Shah had made him a Khan and awarded him some land in Sirvan, which is why he accompanied Kustandil and Alexander.

ten thousand horse; in this expedition none was more forward then Kustandil (who with more credit might have mediated for his country) this administering occasion to put in practice his ambitious designs, yea, of such repute was he then at Court that he was joined in commission with Ali Khan. Having entered Georgia, Kustandil Khan under a pretence of duty gave his aged father a visit, who received him affectionately, but withal neglected not a friendly reproof for his apostasy, whereupon that night, after an invitantion to a banquet, he caused his father to be made away and then prevailed with the party he commanded, with whom some temporising Georgians complied, to salute him by the name of King. But so odious both to God and man was this parricide as he had little comfort in that forced greatness, for, not long after conflicting with Jegal-oglu's son,[473] who had entered Gheylan[474] with a party of Turkish horse, Kustandil received a prick in the arm and was constrained to retreat, but, which was worse, so suddenly and so unexpectedly was he assaulted in his tent by his own countrymen that albeit he himself made a shift to escape, they cut in pieces an accursed catamite[475] who was his bedfellow, and did him what further mischief they could.

Kustandil, being come unto the Persian Court, so provoked the King as he forthwith despatched him back for Georgia in the head of a gallant army, pretending to expel the Turk, but by his avant-couriers gave the Georgians notice of his cruel intent. The Queen, his late brother's wife, prevailing for an interview, Kustandil was shot by an ambuscade upon a signal given by this Amazon, who by that overreached his stratagem, having this or the like for excuse, "Nor can there be a punishment more fit/ Then he should die that first invented it."[476] But

---

[473] Jegal-oglu Pasha (d. 1606), the Ottoman commander-in-chief, was the Grand Vizier and the father of Mahmoud Pasha, the Ottoman *beglerbeg* of Sirvan. At the Battle of the Ak-su River, Kustandil was wounded just before he and Mahmoud fought (Monshi, *History*, 3: 871).

[474] Modern Ghal' é-yé Sang, now only "the limited remains of a walled town" (Greenway and St. Vincent, *Iran*, 261).

[475] Homosexual lover. There is, unsurprisingly, no mention of this in Monshi.

[476] Queen Ketevan (d. 1624), known as Didilal in Persian (Monshi, *History*, 3: 884–85) and now a saint in the Orthodox Church of Georgia, was the widow of Davit II and mother of Teimuraz I, serving as Regent 1605–1614. She did indeed organise a force against Kustandil, and the result was a battle at the river Mazu Keyvolan. Kustandil, charging ahead too fast to help one of his generals, found himself isolated in the battle and was killed by a group of Georgians on 22 October 1605 (Monshi, *History*, 3: 885). Abbas allowed Teimuraz to return to Georgia, but demanded hostages, and Queen Ketevan agreed to go to Persia, where the Shah attempted to force her to convert to Islam and even (according to some authorities) offered to make her his wife (he had married two Georgian wives already), but she refused. He had her tortured and burned. The eminent German dramatist Andreas Gryphius commemorated her in a tragedy entitled *Katherina von Georgien* (1657); Teimuraz himself had already commemorated her in a lengthy poem, *Tsigni da tsaneba Ketevan dedoplisa*, or *The Book and Passion of Queen Ketevan* (1625).

Abbas, glad of the occasion to discharge his promise, sends them word that as
they had treacherously slain his subject and servant, so he would have ample satisfaction. Nevertheless, by the friendly interposition of Ali Khan, who grieved
not one jot for the death of his competitor, Abbas alters his first thoughts and was
content that young Teimuraz by his appointment should be their King. Teimuraz, at the head of some thousand Persian horse, was received into Georgia with
joyful acclamations, but long his halcyon days continued not, for the Turks' ambassador then resident at Isfahan infuses jealousy into Abbas as if Teimuraz was
more the Grand Seigneur's[477] friend then his, and with like artifice Teimuraz
was abused, whereupon the young King, fearing to come to Court upon Abbas
his invitation, Lala Beg[478] presently marched into Georgia with thirty thousand
horse, foraging the country with fire and sword. The young King for his safety
first retired to the mountains, but there also being alarmed, he was forced to flee
unto the Turks, where he prevailed for such a force as not only reinstated him to
his own, but fell into Sirvan,[479] which so incensed the Persian King that drawing
together what force he could he resolved with himself to make quick work, and
not only to harass the Georgian country, but if possible to exterminate the people
from off the face of the earth, to which end in person Abbas enters his country, killing all that came in the way, firing churches and towns most lamentably
and cutting down all their mulberry trees, and having in that sort satisfied his
passion, returned and gave way to Teimuraz to take a review of his cruel execution.[480] Mourav,[481] a noble Georgian, not knowing any better way for retaliation,

---

There does not seem to be an English translation of this book, but see Donald Rayfield,
The Literature of Georgia: A History (London: Routledge, 2000), 105–6. In the 1634 edition Herbert devoted much more time to the tragedy of Queen Ketevan, whose story he
considerably truncates here, and seems to display little sympathy towards her, whilst the
earlier version is completely different (see Appendix).

[477] The Ottoman Sultan. In 1605 this was Ahmet I (1603–1617).

[478] According to Monshi, however, it was Shah Abbas himself who led the expedition to Georgia (see *History*, 3: 1081–83). He was assisted by Pir Budaq Khan, the Governor of Tabriz.

[479] Teimuraz defeated Abbas's general Ali Quli Khan at the Battle of Bohran in
1615. Herbert seems to be summing up events without giving the dates, which is confusing. For this battle, see Monshi, *History*, 3: 1107–1109.

[480] "The Arzad and Tayanat regions of Kakhetia were ravaged by the *qizilbashes* in
retaliation for the fact that the inhabitants had spirited Tahmuras out of the country,"
Monshi reported, adding that "Thirty thousand infidels were obliged to become Mussulmans" (*History*, 3: 1089). He does not mention church-burning, although the Shah did
fortify some churches, nor does he show any interest in mulberry-trees,

[481] Mourav Beg Gorji [*Morad*], born Giorgi Saakadze (1570–1629), was appointed
mourav (Governor) of Tbilisi in 1606. He defeated the Ottomans at the Battle of Ta-
shikari (1609) and became an adviser to King Luarsab II of Kartli (1606–1615), who
married his sister in 1611. Jealous nobles convinced the King that he was a traitor, and he

like another Zopyrus[482] disguises his face and flies to Qazvin to imprecate the King's revenge against Teimuraz for that wrong. Abbas, giving belief, orders a considerable force to fall into that late wasted country, but so soon as they were upon the Georgian confines, in the night, when the Persians dreamed of no enemy at hand, Mourav with five hundred confederates and as notable resolution as ever appeared in men, fell into the camp, cut in pieces seven hundred men and amongst others eleven khans and beglerbegs, the alarm striking such terror into the rest that they could not be persuaded when the day appeared to run any further hazard amongst those desperate men who had nothing left but their lives and for their fortresses inaccessible hills, since which Abbas, by the mediation of several of the *qizlbashes* who are Georgians, has given them an assurance of peace from thence, they on the other side promising to greater put a value on the friendship of the Persian.

A Georgian man and woman [illustration not shown]

The Armenians' tenets.

Now concerning Armenia, some derive it from Armenus a Thessalian, who was Jason's kinsman.[483] It is divided into Major and Minor; the lesser is in Anatolia, the greater is confined by Tartary to the north, Media and Assyria to the south, west and east with the Euxine and Caspian Sea, for it includes Colchis, Albania, Georgia, Iberia etc., countries which now be obscured in other recent names as Guria, Mingrelia, Turkmenia, Caraculia, Gurgen, Halaen and

---

fled to Persia, where he served Abbas I and converted to Islam. Abbas appointed him an advisor to King Simon II upon the latter's accession in 1619. Mourav Beg was then made chief of staff to the Persian general Qerciha Khan in Kartli, but turned against his new masters and defeated them decisively at the Battle of Martqopi (1625). He himself was beaten the next year and fled to Turkey, serving Sultan Murad IV in his Persian campaigns (see Monshi, *History*, 3: 1293–94). In 1629 he decided to return to Georgia and unite his countrymen to drive out the occupiers, but was captured on the way and executed by order of the Grand Vizier, Ekrem Hüsrev Pasha.

[482] Zopyrus, a Persian, was the son of Megabyzes, an advisor and friend of Darius I. The story (in Herodotus) is that he mutilated his own face and had himself whipped in order to ingratiate himself with the Babylonians and pose as a traitor and an exile. The Babylonians made him their general and he let the Persians into Babylon, whereupon Zopyrus was made satrap of Babylon by Darius. Historians doubt the truth of this story, as it looks curiously similar to the account of Odysseus spying in Troy just before the Trojan Horse was let into the city.

[483] "Armenus of Armenium, a Thessalonian city . . . accompanied Jason into Armenia, and Cyrsilus the Pharsalian and Medius the Larisaean say, who accompanied Alexander, say that Armenia was named after him" (Strabo 8. 11. 14. 9).

Sarlochia, in which place some say the Ten Tribes[484] were seated by Shalmaneser [V].

Two Patriarchs or Protomists[485] they have, one at Jerusalem, the other at Sina in Arabia, who nevertheless sometimes resides at Sir near Tarsus or Erevan in Sirvan, seeing that Antioch their old see they may not challenge. The three first General Councils they have in great honour; they study the Latin tongue very little, for it is rare in Asia. Twelve titular bishops they name, three hundred some say, very poor, which ought not to render them despicable. The Old and New Testaments they have in their mother-tongue, a Litany also, part of which is every Lord's Day read and expounded in the church. They allow but two sacraments, administer the Lord's Supper in both kinds, bread and wine, deny a Real Presence.[486] Baptism they celebrate after the Eutychian[487] sort, as Jacobus, father of the Jacobites and Johannes Philoponus,[488] *Anno Dom.* 550 mistaught them. Since Chosroes's time most of these Eastern Christians follow the contemned opinion of Nestorius, a heresy encouraged by Chosroes the Persian apostate in hatred to Heraclius the Emperor,[489] for by forcing it upon the Christians who were his subjects it spread like a leprosy or ill air wellnigh all over the Orient. The proselyte gentiles or Mohammedans they sign in the forehead with a burning cross, others they baptise with two fingers and sign the infant with the cross, as glorying in that hieroglyphic which Jews and Mussulmen esteem so ignominiously of. They are great lovers of tradition, pray not for the dead, imagining that till the general day of doom they are without either joy or torment. Five sabbaths every year they abstain from flesh, fish, cheese and butter in memory of those five ages wherein their gentile forefathers used to immolate their children to the old red dragon. Wednesdays and Fridays, except 'twixt Easter and Ascension, they

---

[484] The Ten Lost Tribes of Israel were those who were sent into exile by Shalmaneser V; only Benjamin and Judah were left, and it is from them that modern Jews claim descent. There is much speculation about who was "lost" and where they went, if anywhere.

[485] Herbert might mean *Protomisthos*, which means "first servant."

[486] The Real Presence is the belief that Christ is actually, not symbolically present in the Eucharist .

[487] Eutyches of Constantinople (c. 380–456) is said to have taught that the human nature of Jesus was overcome by his divine nature. The Council of Chalcedon (451) declared this belief heresy.

[488] Johannes Philoponus (c. 490–580) was an Alexandrian monophysite polymath, commentator on philosophy and exegete. See *ODB* 3: 1657.

[489] Herbert refers here to the long drawn-out wars between the Sassanian King Chosroes II (591–628) and the Byzantine Emperor Heraclius (610–42). It is true that the Nestorians were under the protection of the Persian rulers, but the Armenians had resisted, and had contemned Nestorianism at the Council of Dvin (506); amongst "heretics" they placed Eutyches, "showing that the Council took a definite position against the Monophysite doctrine" (Der Nersessian, *Armenians*, 77).

fast, and by what I have observed I suppose that no other Christians are stricter Lent-observers, for they not only refrain their wives during that time but abstain from flesh, fish, cheese and butter, through forty days feeding upon oil, bread, honey, dates, cucumbers, melons, herbs and the like, and drink only water, but at other times eat flesh of all kinds, yea, can dispense with hog's flesh and account it a dainty. Howbeit, before this great feast they fast twelve days. They marry ofttimes at nine or twelve years of age, the laity twice, ecclesiastics but once; trigamy to all is hateful!

The Presbytery are honoured. Imagery in the churches they approve not of, contemning the Greeks therein, but in their houses can endure the pictures of Venus and Priapus.[490] The Cross they regard, but worship not, nor do they believe there is a purgatory. Their temples are but mean. Obedience and respect to the better and elder sort they practice; theft and adultery they punish. In some things they are but refined idolators, for in burials they have a custom to lead about the church an unspotted lamb, which they divide and distribute to each a bit, a symbol obliging one another to love and charity. Peradventure this is a custom derived from that of the Hebrews, who used to divide a calf, as Moses records in Genesis 15:19 and as Jeremiah 34:18–19.[491] On Good Friday they represent the Passion and Burial of Our Saviour, during which they express sorrow in their faces. On Easter Day they joyfully celebrate the Resurrection by a representative body, using that morning, as do the Greeks, the old salvo "He is risen indeed;" an angelical note they call it. That day they celebrate as a great festival, the Mohammedans and Jews not daring, as not being permitted, to mingle among them; the King allows them that privilege. They fast upon the Nativity.

The Jesuits have been industrious to knit them unto Rome, but in vain. They insist much upon antiquity, and have a catalogue of two hundred bishops since their first conversion;[492] some were noble martyrs but of late years the report of an envious Doeg[493] that they had submitted to Rome and acknowledged the Pope their head made Abbas causelessly jealous of their loyalty, which would receive no qualification without the sacrifice of some of their lives made an offering

---

[490] A Greek fertility-god and protector of gardens whose principal feature was a large erect penis.

[491] "And he said unto him, Take me an heifer of three years old . . ." (Genesis 15:9); ". . . when they cut the calf in twain and passed between the parts thereof . . . and all the people of the land, which passed between the parts of the calf" (Jeremiah 34:18–19).

[492] Christians were already being persecuted in 110 C.E., but Armenia became one of the oldest Christian nations in about 301 when the King of Armenia was converted by St. Gregory and proclaimed Christianity the state religion, although historians have moved the event forward to about 314 (Der Nesessian, *Armenians*, 75).

[493] Doeg was an Edomite herdsman who betrayed the whereabouts of David to the wrathful Saul with dire consequences for the priests of Israel. For details, see 1 Samuel 21–22, and also Psalm 52, supposedly written by David at the time of the event.

to his cruelty, upon which the rest implore help from the Turk, which raised a bloody scene of ensuing troubles. Ludovic Grangier,[494] a Jesuit, 'tis reputed lately crossed the Black Sea into Mingrelia,[495] where Teimuraz Khan[496] treated him civilly, and that by his instruction they are much purged from superstition, which, if so, his name should be of more fame amongst them. In the year 1011 overrun they were by the savage Tartar. Mingrelia, part of Armenia, was of old called Colchis,[497] after that *Lazorum regio*, and Dioscurias[498] was the metropolis, once so famous and considerable that Timosthenes[499] spares not to report how that three hundred several languages were spoken there, so as the Romans' affairs in those parts were managed by no less then a hundred and thirty interpreters, whence it probably came to pass that Mithridates, King of Pontus[500] spake twenty-six several tongues, having had his education first and after that a free commerce and alliance with that his neighbouring country.

---

[494] Louis Grangier (1562–1616) was a Jesuit; born in Dijon, he became Professor of Rhetoric at Tournon, and in 1614 was sent to Mingrelia with Fr. Etienne Viau at the request of Prince Levon II, whose ambassadors in Constantinople recommended them as missionaries. Viau died in Mingrelia, but Grangier returned to Constantinople infected after assisting plague-victims, and died there (Borromeo, *Voyageurs*, 2: 61). There is a commemorative plaque in a church there; for which see J. Crétineau-Joly, *Histoire réligieuse, politique et littéraire de la Compagnie de Jésus* (Paris: Paul Mellier, 1845), 5: 4. Herbert apparently knew of Grangier's *Lettres envoyés du Levant par le Père Louys Grangier au Réverent Père Claude Acquaviva . . . Escrites à Moqui en Mingrélie, le deuxième jour de Mars de ceste année* (Paris, 1616).

[495] Mingrelia is in Western Georgia bordering on the Black Sea. The rulers of Mingrelia during Herbert's time were Prince Manuchar I (1590–1611) and Prince Levon II (1611–1667). Theatine missionaries came to Georgia with the Capuchins (1606); their order had been founded by, amongst others, Giovanni Carafa, afterwards Pope Paul IV (1555–1559), who had been Bishop of Chieti (Theate) in southern Italy. They made the first study of the Georgian language, and published the *Alphabetum Ibericum, sive Georgianum, cum oratione Dominicali* (1629), which Herbert probably used for his citation of Georgian words.

[496] Teimuraz I [*Threbis-Cawn*] (see above) was actually the ruler of Kakhetia, not Mingrelia.

[497] Colchis, in western Georgia, was an ancient kingdom in which Jason sought the Golden Fleece.

[498] The old name for the modern city of Sukhumi in Georgia.

[499] Timosthenes of Rhodes was an admiral under Ptolemy II Philadelphus (r.282–246 B.C.E.) who travelled around the ancient world and made a survey of the Mediterranean. He wrote several books, none of which are now extant; they include *On Harbours* and *On Islands*, as well as a *Chart of Distances*. Fragments from these books appear in the works of Eratosthenes and Strabo.

[500] Pontus, on the south coast of the Black Sea, was in north-west Anatolia, now in Turkey.

The Armenians at this day are the greatest travellers east and west of any Asiatics, desire of gain and affectation after novelties inducing them, albeit indeed the advantage they have in their situation, so near neighbouring the seas Caspian, Euxine, Mediterranean and the Palus Maeotis, give them more then ordinary encouragement. And whence it comes at this day the generality more inclining to merchandise then Mars, notwithstanding that the Turk, Tartar and Persian are oft causelessly quarrelling with them, and that the Turk and Persian by turns domineer over them. Learning is not now in that repute it was formerly, those frequent interruptions probably being the cause of it; howbeit, schools they have and universities. Their alphabet consists of 28 letters; they write from the left hand to the right but in their character nothing agreeing with the Greek, as do the Georgians, who have but 32. The Armenian letters and language is so very difficult that I had much ado to take these following words after their guttural pronunciation, excepting those they borrow from the Turks and Persians, which be easy, and the greatest mixture of their vulgar language.

Isfahan.

Fearing I have made too large a deviation, let me now lead you into Isfahan, metropolis of this great kingdom, yea, not inferior to the greatest and best-built city throughout the Orient:

Must Babel's lofty towers submit to this?
Tauris, Ninevah and Persepolis?
Shushan, Arsacia and Nabarca fall,
Before thy seat and power provincial?
Had that ambitious Nimrod thought on this,
Cambyses or the proud Semiramis,
With all those Princely rulers which did sway
The Eastern sceptres when thou didst obey,
It would have quelled their pride and let them know
All humans' actions have both ebb and flow.
The greatest monarchs cannot conquer fate;
Time doth by turns advance and subjugate.
Now royal Abbas rules, Spahawn[501] must rise;
Where kings affect, there most men cast their eyes,
There flock the people! 'Tis his power, not thine
Which hath eclipsed their light to make thee shine.
    Then use thy fortune so, that none from thence
    May wish thy fall or grudge thy eminence.

[501] *Spahawn* is the Middle Persian name for Isfahan; Herbert consistently uses it when referring to Isfahan, but in all other places it has been modernised.

Isfahan has Arctic elevation 32 degrees 39 minutes and longitude 86 degrees 30 minutes, differing a little from Don Garcia's accompt, whose heighth exceeded not 32 degrees 30 minutes, in whose description if I seem prolix, impute it to the desire I have to give what I found observable. And first, in regard some suppose her, like Agra, an upstart town, I will trace her in her antiquity and variations so far as my little reading will afford it us.

That it was Ecbatana, as Niger thinks, is ridiculous to imagine, Tabriz by suffrage of most writers being taken for that city.[502] Two thousand three hundred years ago it was called *Dura*, but whether that which Ptolemy calls *Dera* (not probable, seeing he places it in Susiana), or that *Dara* which was built by Arsaces[503] the first Parthian emperor after his victory over Seleucus, as Justin records in his 41 Book, I know not, but probably this old name has misled those that judge it to be *Dura* in that province where the mighty Assyrian erected his golden colossus. *Hecatompylos* is the next name I find it had, recorded by Apollodorus,[504] Polybius,[505] Ptolemy, and Pliny *lib.* 6, *c.* 8, and so dominated from her hundred gates, albeit the name be given also to Thebes, "*quae centum iacet obruta portis.*"[506] In Hyrcania also there was another of that name, and one in Libya that was built by Hercules, Diodorus Siculus mentions, whereby we may imagine her in those days a great city, and though in Alexander's conquests Curtius names her not, it seems she was then varied into that Greekish denomination. For of this name goes a tradition that Demetrius [II] Nicator, Soter's son, upon his treacherous killing Antiochus [VI], Alexander's son, he was affronted by Tryphon, lieutenant of Syria, and forced to fly to Arsaces [VII] the Persian king for succour, who, being acquainted with his unnatural desire not only denied him the

---

[502] Ecbatana was in northern Media, and is now known as Hamadan in west-central Iran. It is certainly not identifiable with Tabriz.

[503] Arsaces I, the founder of the Parthian Empire, reigned c. 250–248 B.C.E. Malcolm Colledge, however, gives only 247-? (*Parthians*, 178), as the regnal dates of Parthian kings are often uncertain and/or approximate.

[504] Apollodorus (b. c. 180 B.C.E.) was a Greek grammarian, historian and mythographer. His works include a chronicle of history to 144 B.C.E. and an essay on the gods, *De diis*, which was first printed in 1599 and again in 1661. The encyclopaedic mythographical work known as the *Bibliotheke* is now known not to be by him; it was edited by Benedetto Spoleto in 1555.

[505] Polybius (c. 200–after 118 B.C.E.), tutor to the Roman general Scipio Africanus, was a Greek historian from Megalopolis who had travelled quite widely in the Mediterranean region. His best-known work is the *Histories*, which is extant in an almost complete version. Herbert was likely using the edition by Isaac Casaubon (1609), which contains a great deal of exegesis and supplementary material. W. R. Paton has translated it in six volumes for the Loeb Classical Library (Cambridge, MA: Harvard University Press, 1922–1927).

[506] The actual quote should read "*atque vetus Theba centum iacet obruta portis,*" which translated "and ancient hundred-gated Thebes lies in ruins" (Juvenal, *Satires* 15. 6).

law of hospitality but sent him prisoner to Hecatompylos, where he was held in fetters till upon submission he was released and by Arsaces reseated in his own dominion.[507]

After that this city was called *Nymzamena*, which signifieth "half the world," a like hyperbole being given to Rome, which some call *Epitomen Universi*. By ben Jonas, who was here *Anno Heg.* 540, of Our Lord 1160 'tis called *Ashbahan* or *Acspachan*, who reports also that it had then twelve miles compass. By Cluverius 'tis called *Hagistan*, by the Arabian geographer "*Asbahawn, etenim sub Algebal,*" i.e. the mountainous part of Media, "*sunt urbes perillustres quarum maximum sunt Hamadan, Asbahawn, Deinar & Comm. Asbadana*"[508] after that and under the true latitude. By Mandeville our countryman, three hundred and forty years ago, *Saphaon*; at this day 'tis called *Spahawn*, or, as they sibboleth,[509] *Sphawhawn*, but by writers differently-spelled, as *Spaha, Spachen, Achaban, Aspachan, Izpaan, Spahan* and *Hispahan*, errors springing from length of time and diversity of idioms, but from whence the name *Spahawn* derives itself is not known unto the natives. I may, nevertheless, venture a conjecture of the etymon, that it is either that old town *Spada*,[510] where eunuchs were first gelded, or from a compound of *aspa*, which signifies "a horse," and *chahna*, "a house or stable," as the city Pasagardae, which signifies "a horse," and the rather in that the hippodrome, the body of the great *maidan*, was an old accustomed place for viewing of horses, and not unlikely to be that *Aspadana*[511] which Ptolemy in his fifth Table of Asia places amongst the cities of Persia and in the same degree of latitude, which gives it the greater probability, for *Aspa* in Ptolemy is thirty miles more towards the south then that which he calls *Hecatompylon Regia*. But I can no means close with those who are

---

[507] The chronology of these Antiochid rulers of Syria is a little complicated, and Herbert is not very clear, especially as he supplies no dates. Demetrius I Soter reigned 162–150 B.C.E., followed by Alexander Balas 150–145. His successor Demetrius II Nicator reigned jointly with Antiochus VI Dionysus, who was a child, from 145–142, and alone 142–141, after which he was deposed. Deposing first Antiochus VI, Tryphon succeeded in 142, reigning (after deposing Demetrius the next year) until 138, and he was likely responsible for the death of Antiochus VI; he himself was killed by supporters of Antiochus VII Sidetes, who reigned 138–129. It was at that point that Demetrius II made his comeback with help from Arsaces VII (also known as Phraates II) of Persia (r. 136–127); his second reign was 129–125.

[508] There are famous cities, of which the greatest are Hamadan . . .

[509] Pronounce it like non-native speakers.

[510] This mysterious town is probably a fiction. The earliest eunuchs were probably employed by the Assyrians and the ancient Chinese. The Romans referred to some eunuchs as *spadones*, derived from the Greek *spadon*, from which in turn comes the American slang word 'spade.'

[511] This is not a city but the name of the large audience-hall at Persepolis.

confident that this Isfahan was that old city which was called *Hecatompylos*,[512] for albeit I deny not that such a place there was, as called by our Greek historians, and that placed in this country, nevertheless, by comparing their several latitudes, it may be concluded that Kasbin or Qumis was that *Hecatompylos* which Ptolemy places in the latitude of 37 degrees 50 minutes, and both Ptolemy, Pliny and Strabo all agree that *Aspa*, as without peradventure Isfahan was then called, had no more northern elevation then 36 degrees, and withal placed in Parthia.

Give me leave to speak what I find acted whiles called Isfahan, and with that to couple our present observation. If I exceed, this may excuse it, *"praestas de Carthagine tacere, quam pauca dicere."*[513] A. D. 641, of the Hegira 25, by command of Omar [I][514] then Caliph of Mecca, Sa'ad bin Abi Waqqas[515] with some troops of Arabian horse invaded Persia to pluck violently away from Yazdegerd [III]'s head the tottering diadem, which at the third pull, having twice overthrown him, he effected, the splendour of that kingdom then eclipsing. Bin Abi Waqqas sacked his two best towns, *viz.* Almodin in Chaldaea (built *Anno Dom.* 520 by Chosroes, son to Kavadh [I],[516] howbeit the Alcoran says it sprung out of Hell), and Isfahan in Persia. *Anno Heg.* 400, Mahmud the Caliph of Baghdad,[517] after his conquest of Gujarat in India,in his return homewards plundered Isfahan. Toghrul Beg, commonly reputed Lord of the Seljukian family and ancestor of the Ottomans, in the year 1030, Edward the Confessor then ruling England, Gruffudd ab Llewellyn Wales,[518] was then entreated by Mohammed, Prince of Persia to aid him against *Pisastris* an encroaching Babylonian,[519] which Toghrul Beg

---

[512] Hecatompylos in western Khurasan was the capital of the Parthian Empire under the Arsacids. It is now Sahr-é Qumis in Iran.

[513] "Of Carthage I think it's better to be silent than to say but a little" (Sallust, *Bellum Jugurthinum* 19).

[514] Omar I ibn al-Khattab was caliph 634–44. He was eminent "for having chiefly contributed to the spread of Islam" (Hughes, *Dictionary*, 650).

[515] Sa'ad ibn Abi Waqqas [*Siet-ben Abivakez*] (c. 584–664) was one of the ablest of Omar I's generals; he completed the conquest of what was then the two Iraqs and facilitated the overthrow of the Sassanid Empire.

[516] Kavadh I reigned 488–531; Chosroes I Anushirvan succeeded him and reigned until 578.

[517] Herbert is referring here to Sultan Mahmud of Ghazna, who was not Caliph of Baghdad; he calls him "Mohammed."

[518] Edward the Confessor reigned 1042–1066; Prince Gruffudd ab Llewellyn of Gwynedd ruled 1055–1063. Neither was ruling in 1030. Canute was king of England in 1030 and Iago ab Idwal was prince of Gwynedd.

[519] By "Babylonian" Herbert means Iraqi or Kurd. "Two groups of these Orghuz turned to attack Ray and Hamadan" (Boyle, *History*, 38). They were threatening the rule of the Kakuyids (see below). There is no-one called *Pisastris* in the Arabian histories. Juan de Persia calls him *Pysasyri* (93); Le Strange identifies him with one al-Basasiri, "a Daylamite Captain of the Guards, an ardent Shi'ah who made a conspiracy to dethrone

did and prospered in, and after that defended him against the invading Indian,[520] in recompense of which good services the Turk only desires leave to pass through his country and over Araxia, which a bridge doth scorn (*"ponte indignatus Araxia," l. 6 Aeneid*), to visit his countrymen who lived betwixt the two seas Caspian and Euxine, a request how reasonable soever it seemed was nevertheless rashly denied by Mohammed, who indeed thought the Turk had a worse design. But this denial was so unkindly resented by the Turk that after some passionate expressions he kept his party for some time secretly in the Carmanian Desert and soon brought under command all that country which neighbours the Persian Gulf, and vexing to be so confined soon after he marches against the King and at Shiraz both armies meet, where albeit the Persians were seventy thousand horse and foot and more numerous then the Turk, yet was he vanquished. Mohammed, rallying another army of treble the number, nevertheless could not resist his destiny, for after a short but hot dispute near those plains, the Persian army was routed and so fiercely pursued by Toghrul that some thousands of the Persians were slain and many made prisoners, Mohammed saving himself in the field by the swiftness of his horse, which brought him to Isfahan, where, in amazement falling from his beast, he broke his neck. The Turkish forces pursuing and without resistance entering Isfahan, which when it had acknowledged Toghrul victor, with little opposition he made an entire conquest of Parthia. Rashid Billah also, son of Mustarshid, was slain by Masu'd,[521] *Anno Dom.* 1130, of the *Heg.* 510 and buried in Isfahan, which few for many shall speak her antiquity in the name she is now triumphant in.

I have told you how that in the story of Ibn Abi Waqqas a thousand years since it entitles Isfahan a city but gives us no further particulars concerning it. Ben Jonas, who saw it four hundred and seventy-six years ago, affords her twelve miles compass as she was at the time, saying further that she was rich

the Abbasid Caliph Qaim . . . Basasiri was captured and put to death by Toghrul Beg" (Juan de Persia, *Relaciones*, 318). This identification seems reasonable; Arslan al-Muzaffar al-Basasiri first appeared in around 1025. He may have been a Turkish slave in origin.

[520] Ala al-dawla Abu-Ja' afar Mohammed was the Kakuyid ruler of Isfahan 1007–1041. He was replaced by Toghrul Beg's appointee, his son Abu Mansur Faramurz (1041–1051), who "managed to exasperate Toghrul Beg," and was deposed when the latter captured Isfahan (1050), although he did compensate him with other territories (Boyle, *History*, 38–39). Herbert seems to have conflated the two Kakuyid rulers.

[521] Herbert's dates are a little inaccurate here. The Abbasid Caliph al-Mustarshid Billah reigned 1118–1135 and was assassinated; his son al-Rashid succeeded him and was deposed the next year (1136). He in turn was murdered in 1138. Mas'ud was the Seljuk Sultan of Hamadan (1134–1152). These Sultans exercised a great influence over the Caliphs of Baghdad; it was Mas'ud who defeated al-Mustarshid and deposed al-Rashid, but he did not murder him; this was done by "a group of his Khurasanian soldiers" (Boyle, *History*, 129); Hughes credits "the Assassins" with the murder of them both (*Dictionary*, 267).

and populous. Mandeville, *Ann. Dom.* 1300, which is above three hundred years since, reports that in his time it was a noble city. *Ann. Dom.* 1474 Iosafà Barbaro was here in Uzun Hassan's reign, and then by the name of Isfahan it was a city both great and famous, peopled with 150,000 souls, the town and suburbs being ten miles in compass. Rabbi Benjamin and Contarini the Venetian Ambassador eighty years ago relate that then she had twenty Italian miles in circuit, and Lemos the Portuguese,[522] sent by Albuquerque to Shah Ismail [I] *Ann. Dom.* 1513, reports her to be a very great city.

Suspending my judgment concerning their relations, I shall give you the truth of what I observed. Isfahan, metropolis of the Persian monarchy, is seated in the Parthian territory, now called Ayrac,[523] and as umbelic to that spacious body which at this day is awed by the Persian sceptre. From the Persian Gulf she is removed a hundred seventy-nine *farsangs*, of English miles five hundred thirty-seven, from the Caspian Sea three hundred and sixty miles English, from Shiraz two hundred twenty-two, from Babylon four hundred and fifty, from Kandahar eight hundred and seventy and from Qazvin two hundred and seventy. She is in compass at this day about nine English miles, including towards seventy thousand houses and of souls, as may be conjectured, contains about two hundred thousand, for besides natives there are merchants of sundry nations as English, Dutch, Portuguese, Pole, Muscovite, Indian, Arabian, Armenian, Georgian, Turk, Jew and others drawn thither by the magnetic power of gain. It has several good buildings, but the most observable are the *maidan, masjeds, hammams* and palaces, as be the gardens, monuments, and Julfa, a suburb adjoining.

Isfahan city is most pleasurable in its situation, elegant as to building, populous for inhabitants, rich in trade and noble by being the usual residence of the Court, eminent for all sorts of exercise, sufficiently-watered by the Zayandé, fruitful in its soil, and for air so pure and quick that I very well remember we found it much warmer in more northern cities which had greater latitude, and seeing Quintus Curtius saith of Persia "*regio non alia in tota Asia salubrior habetur*,"[524] I may in praise of this place add then the air of Isfahan no part of Persia is more healthy. Howbeit, 'tis of no great strength, and yet has a mud-wall about, and towards the

---

[522] Fernão Gomes de Lemos, Senhor de Trofa, was a Lisbon merchant and explorer. He was sent in 1515 to Persia with a gift which was worth twice the amount of the one which Ismail sent to Albuquerque as well as quantities of arms and ammunition. He later (1522–1524) served as Captain-Major of Ceylon, the last person to hold this office. Lemos was the third envoy from Albuquerque; the first was poisoned at Hormuz (1510), and a second was sent in 1514. For details, see K. G. Jayne, *Vasco da Gama and his Successors 1460–1580* (New York: Kessinger Reprints, n. d.), 108–10.

[523] Iraq.

[524] "In the whole of Asia there is no other region to be found more salubrious" (Curtius Rufus 5. 4).

outside of the city a large castle unflankered but moated about and several houses within, which guard the treasure, arms and ice there stored.

Let me lead you into the *maidan*, into which ere I can bring you we pass over a well-built several-arched bridge of hewn stone[525] which is towards the south-west end of the city, supported by five-and-thirty pillars through which the Zayandé from the mountains streams gently,[526] spreading in rainy seasons here wellnigh so broad as the Thames, but very shallow, for in summer her channel is contracted and so shallow that children usually wade or pass through it, for that the citizens for the better watering of their gardens by sluices drain it and divide it into many rivulets, insomuch that the course of the river is spoiled, and, which is strange, lost in some valleys not may leagues distant thence, where 'tis drunk up without ever emptying itself like other streams into any sea or ocean, especially by the pipes which feed the two great and famous gardens belonging to the King called Bagh-é Hezar Jarib and Chahar Bagh,[527] which for beauty contend with all others in Asia.

The *maidan* is without doubt as spacious, as pleasant and aromatic a market as any in the universe; it is a thousand paces from north to south, and from east to west above two hundred, resembling our Exchange[528] or the Place Royal[529] in Paris, but six times larger. The building is of sun-dried brick and an uninterrupted building, the inside full of shops, each shop filled with wares of sundry sorts, arched above in cupolas, terrace-wise framed at top and with plaister like that of Paris pargetted. That *maidan*, being the noblest part, is placed as it were in the heart of this city, the King's palace[530] or *chonna-Padishah* conjoining it upon the west side, possessing a

---

[525] This is the Allah Verdi Khan Bridge, now Si o Sé Bridge (Bridge of the Thirty Arches). It was built by Abbas I in 1602–1608 as a tribute to his great Georgian general and friend, and at that point divided the Chahar Bagh; on one side (the Chahar Bagh-é Abbasi) was the Jahan Nama Palace and on the other the Hezar Jarib Palace and Garden (Upper Chahar Bagh). The word *bagh* means "garden."

[526] "The Zayandé river starts in the Zagros mountains, flows from east to west through the heart of Isfahan, then peters out into the Kavir desert. It separates the northern part of the city from the Armenian quarter in Jolfa" (Greenway and St. Vincent, *Iran*, 193).

[527] The Chahar Bagh is now a square, originally a pleasure walkway and garden built by Abbas I in 1596.

[528] The Royal Exchange in London was founded by Sir Thomas Gresham in 1565 as a centre for trade and commerce.

[529] Now the Place des Vosges, it was built to celebrate the marriage of Louis XIII and Anne of Austria (1612). Herbert is, of course, alluding to his own trip to France by casually throwing out the name.

[530] This is the Ali Qapu Palace, built by Shah Abbas in 1597. The decorations to which Herbert refers are probably the paintings by the Shah's great Court painter Reza Abbasi (1565–1635). What visitors see now is the palace as it was repaired and restored under Abbas II (1642–1667) and Suleiman (1667–1694). Sir John Chardin, a few years

large space of ground backwards, but juts not to the street further then the other buildings, which are uniform to the street, so as to passengers it gives not any bravery, her greatest gallantry being in the trim, for it is pargetted and painted with blue and gold interlaced with posies of Arabic, which after the *grotesco*[531] manner makes it very pleasant. Within the rooms, according to the common form there, are arched, enlightened by trellises; the room is embossed above and painted with red, white, blue and gold, the sides with sports and landskips. The ground or floor was spread with curious carpets of silk and gold without other furniture, terraced above, garnished with a pharos overtopping many mosques, and the garden or wilderness behind the house was filled with airy citizens privileged from hurt or affright and for which they return their thankful notes in a more melodious consort and variety then if they were in the exactest *voilure*[532] in the universe. Within the hippodrome many of the cavalry use to ride; as Xenophon in the *Life of Cyrus* instances, so do the Persians at this day, daily repairing to the Court gate mounted with lances in their hands, *shamsheers*[533] or swords and quivers by their side, whereafter they have praced awhile they depart, unless the King prepare to go abroad, for then they give their due attendance.

The north side of the *maidan* hath eight or nine arched rooms usually hung with lamps and latten candlesticks, which being lighted (as 'tis usual, especially at the Festival of Lights, which they call *Ceraghan*)[534] give a curious splendour. Thither the Padishah and others frequently resort for pastime, as tumbling, sleight of hand, dancing-girls and painted catamites, that *nefandum peccatum*[535] being there tolerated. At the furthest end north is the Mint, where we saw one day silver coined, gold the second and next day brass. Not far thence are cooks' shops where men use to feed the helpful belly after the busy eye and painful feet have sufficiently laboured.

Afore the King's door are one and thirty demi-cannons of brass and twelve iron culverins unmounted, brought thither, as I suppose, after some overthrow they gave the Portugal or Turk, from Hormuz and Babylon. Opposite this palace

---

later (1672), called this palace "the finest in the world" (*Travels*, xxviii) and prefaced his book with an illustration of it. A new book on the palaces of Isfahan by Sussan Babaie, *Isfahan and its Palaces: Shi'ism and the Architecture of Conviviality in Early Modern Iran.* (Edinburgh: Edinburgh University Press, 2008) is now available.

[531] An architectural style which uses rough stonework to imitate caves, from Italian *grotesco*, a cave.

[532] A collective noun referring to all the sails of a ship.

[533] Scimitars or curved swords.

[534] This would be the Charharshanbe Suri, which is celebrated on the last Tuesday night of the old year as part of Nau Roz.

[535] A sin contrary to divine command, i.e. homosexuality. Literally. "the unspeakable vice."

is a fair temple or *jama masjed*[536] but that at the south end is the most noble.[537] The outside of this is stone, not formed according to the cross, the hieroglyphic of our salvation, as ours be, but round as were the Jews,' either from the Talmud, figuring our eternity, or from the *al-Kaaba* in Mecca, the shape whereof they say was revealed to Abraham out of Heaven, patterned, *quis hoc credat*,[538] from that which Adam reared in Paradise. Within, this here is distinguished into aisles; the walls are lined fifteen foot high from the sole with white well-polished marble. It is cupolaed, compassed with walls and open to the air, the aisles excepted, where the people resort to prayer and prostrations, which are covered, and without are some seats to rest in. In the centre is a large tank and at the portal another, octangular, filled with pure water, which first glides round the inside of the *maidan* through a stone course or channel six foot deep and as many broad, which after a pleasant murmur drills into this tank, whence it is sucked out by subterranean passages and distributed into private houses and gardens for use and for refreshment. Within the *maidan* the shops be uniform, trades usually having their shops together, of which some be mercers, lapidaries some and (not the fewest), such as sell gums, drugs and spices, showing also greater variety of simples and ingredients of medicine then ever I saw together in any one city of Europe, and such as may give encouragement to physicians both to view and judge both of their nature and quality as well as temperature of the climes they come from, which such as are ignorant cannot distinguish. And indeed, the drugs and spices here so perfumed the place that it made me since give the better credit to that monostich of an old poet, "We suck'd the aromatic air of Persia."

---

[536] This is the Masjed-é Lotfollah, named for Abbas I's father-in-law Sheikh Lotfollah (d. 1622), who was a holy man. This mosque was begun in 1602 and completed in 1618. It is also known as the Shah's Oratory (perhaps because it was used for private prayers) and the Women's Mosque. "This beautifully-proportioned mosque," write Greenway and St. Vincent, "with some of best mosaics from the era, took nearly twenty years to complete" (*Iran*, 196). Robert Byron, writing in 1933, liked "the flowered saucer-dome . . . skewed sideways over a blue recess. Symmetry; but not too much" (*Oxiana* 149). For further details see Boyle, *History*, 784–86. The Persian term, strictly, is *Jam-é Masjed*.

[537] Herbert refers here to the Masjed-é Shah (Royal Mosque), designed by Ustad Ali Akbar al-Isfahani for Abbas I, completed by Shah Safi and now known as the Masjed-é Emam (1612–1638). "This magnificent mosque is one of the most stunning buildings in Iran . . . The tiles of the mosque take on a different hue according to the light conditions" (Greenway and St. Vincent, 195–96). Robert Byron admired "the blue portal . . . with dome, divan and minarets clumped obliquely behind it in the direction of Mecca" (*Oxiana* 148). For further details see Boyle, *History*, 786–89. The pools or tanks Herbert mentions are probably the ones Boyle says are the ones in the madrassas close to the sanctuary (*History*, 87). They are also noted by Byron, who thought they spoiled the effect somewhat (*Oxiana*, 149).

[538] "Whoever believes this" (Seneca, *Epistolae morales ad Lucilium* 91).

The outside of this noble bourse or building has this form, so well as my memory would serve, for I must acknowledge I forgot to take the draft during my being upon the place, in which I am blameworthy:

*The **maidan** or great market in Isfahan [illustration not shown]*

Other mosques, here called *Dayr*[539] and *Sunna*, are orbicular for shape, part thereof having large cupolas for sight, but low and indifferently pleasant, a great part being open to the air and some of which have their *alkirans* that are high, slender round steeples or towers, most of which are terraced near the top like the Standard in Cheapside,[540] for the better conveniency of the boys at the accustomed hours to sing aloud in and for placing the lights at the *Keraghan* or Feast of Lights, which is annual. The materials of these mosques are sunburned bricks, varnished on the outside and beautiful with painted knots and fancies. Few are without their tanks or cisterns of water, wherein Mussulmen wash their hands, arms and eyes, having formerly bathed their face, ears, breast and feet as an operative work to purge sin and to confer holiness. The female sex during worship use to approach no nearer then the door of that mosque.

Hamams in this city be many and beautiful; some are foursquare, but most be globous. The stone of which they are built is for the most part white and well-polished, the windows large without, crossed and inwardly made narrow; the glass, where glass is, is thick, annealed and dark, the top or outside covering round and tiled with a counterfeit turquoise which is perfect blue, very beautiful and lasting. The insides of these hothouses are divided into many cells and con-camerations, some being for delight, others for sweating in, all for use, for the truth is, bathing with these is, at it was with the Greeks and Romans, no less familiar then eating and drinking, yet the excess doubtless weakens the body by making it soft and delicate, and subject to colds. Howbeit, they may better there use it then we in Europe, by reason that they drink water, eat much rice, polo[541] and the like food of easy digestion, which makes their bodies solid and hard, so as little fear is that the bathing will make them frothy; besides, their much sitting and little exercise makes them sweat less and need more bathing. These baths be of pure stone paved with black or chequered marble; men frequant them commonly in the morning, women towards night. The price for bathing is very small, but so much used as makes the gain more abundant; 'tis accounted a catholicon[542] against most diseases, especially colds, catarrhs, phegm, aches,

---

[539] *Dayr* is the Persian word for "monastery" (Foster, *Herbert* 315).

[540] A site where criminals were executed, the Standard is at the west end of Cheapside.

[541] Polo is a very popular Persian dish made with cooked rice, which is mixed with meat, vegetables, and spices. It is related to *pilaf* and *pullao*.

[542] Universal remedy.

agues, *lues Veneres*[543] and whatnot. The women's being there is known by a linen cloth usually displayed afore the door, which serves to forbid men any approach during that time.

The city is built upon a level ground and of oval form, having many streets and scarce any house but is accommodated with large gardens full of cypress trees. The city wall is of no force against cannon, but of use against horse and shock of any lance; some parapets and bulwarks it has of more ornament then use, the Persian magnanimity ever choosing to die rather then be besieged. It has a dozen portresses or gates, of which four are lately shut up, *Gouidest*, *Chaly*, *Mergh* and *Cherbaugh*, which are lately made the entrance into a royal garden. The other eight are *Hazena-baut*, which opens towards Shiraz and the Gulf; *Decridest*, to Babylon and Ardehal; *Tockzy* or *Tabriz-abaut*, to Kashan, Qum, Kasvin and Tabriz; *Kerroen*, to Yazd and Khorasan; *Lamboen*, to Hamadan; *Shabdiz*, *Madayan* to Kandahar and India, *Yowbara* and *Dalwatt*.[544]

Palaces here are few; the King's house in the *maidan*, that also where we lodged belonging to the King but made ready for our Ambassador. Khanan-é Mula'im Beg, Mir Abdullah, Tahmasp Quli Beg and Haram-é Beguma were those and indeed all I saw worth the remembering. The first is low-built, pargetted and painted without, but gilt within and spread with carpets, the usual furniture of this country, all of which have large gardens beautified with flowers, being plentifully-watered. The last, which is the Royal Seraglio, is famous for the treasure and beauties it contains, of which, being dangerous to inquire, we will be silent. The castle is large, strongly-walled and moated, made defensive with some pieces of brass, but more by a troop of lean-faced, beardless, memberless eunuchs, who, though Cyrus made such esquires of his body, now, like so many malignant sagittaries, have no other duty save to guard the ladies. The battlements it has are pleasant to look upon, but the horizontal plain which is easily discovered from thirty rising turrets there yields most pleasure.

Gardens here for grandeur and fragour are such as no city in Asia outvies, which at a little distance from the city you would judge a forest but withal so sweet and verdant that you may call it another Paradise. At the west end of Isfahan is that which is called Bagh-é Hezar Jarib,[545] a garden deservedly famous. From the *maidan*, if you go to this garden, you pass by Chahar Bagh, through an even street near two miles long and as broad as Holborn[546] in London, a great part of the way being garden-walls on either side the street, yet here and there

---

[543] A general term for venereal diseases.

[544] Foster supplies some information on the names of the gates, which I can find nowhere else. They are Ku-é dasht, Shahi, Marg, Char Bagh, Hasanabad, Dardasht, Tughchi, Karran, Lunban, Sayyid Ahmadiyan, Jubarah and Darwazah Daulat (*Herbert*, 315).

[545] Its name means "a thousand acres" (Foster, *Herbert* 316).

[546] A London street dating back to Anglo-Saxon times; it runs from St. Giles's High Street to the Holborn Viaduct, across both Westminster and the City of London.

bestrewed with *mahals* or summer-houses, all along being planted with broad-spreading *chenaer*-trees, which besides shade serves for use and ornament. Being come to the garden, or rather fruit forest of Hezar Jarib, you find it circled with a high wall which is about three miles in compass, entered by three gates which are wide and well-built. From north to south it was a thousand of my paces, from east to west seven hundred, and the prospect from one end to the other easily and fully discovered by reason there is a fair open aisle like that in Fontainebleau, which runs along and is distinguished into nine easy ascents, each surmounting or rising above the other about a foot, all being very smooth and even. In the centre or middle of the garden is a spacious tank formed into twelve equal sides, each side being five foot, set round with pipes of lead which spout the liquid element in variety of conceits, and that sort of pastime continues to the North Gate, where is raised a pile for prospect and other sort of pleasure, antickly-garished without, and within divided into six rooms. The lower part is adorned with tanks of white marble, which fume out a cool breeze by quaffing so much crystalline water as makes it bubble there by a constrained motion, the aqueduct being brought by extraordinary charge and toil thither from the Coronian mountain.

The higher rooms are beautified with variety of landskips, which represent their manner of sporting: hawking, fishing, riding, shooting, wrestling, courting and other fancies. The roof upon the parget was gilt and painted with blue and other colours. In this summer-house by some gentlemen who were *qizlbashes* of the Georgian nation I was invited to taste some Shiraz wine. They expressed very high civility and gave me leave to drink what I pleased; nevertheless I was sorry to see them in that exercise so over-liberal, which the custom of the place reproves not, but professing themselves Christians, have for their instruction that of the Psalmist, "*vinum laetificat cor,*" yet withal "*in iucunditatem creatum est non in ebrietatem,*" Ecclesiasticus 31:28.[547] But what seemed to me most pleasant was the view we enjoyed from our terrace, that afforded us a curious prospect into a great part of the city, which, save at Rostam's Tomb upon a hill two miles thence, elsewhere by reason of the level cannot well be obtained. This garden is replenished with trees of all sorts, for medicine, shade and fruit, which are all so green, so sweet and pleasant as may well be termed a compendium of sense-ravishing delights, or Abbas his Paradise.

Monuments of antiquity I could find but few, burial-places as in other Asiatic cities and agreeable to the Law of the Twelve Tables being commonly without the towns. Yet some here are, as Rostam's Tomb we were directed to, which we found two miles from Isfahan behind the garden we late spake of, a tomb scarce

---

[547] "Wine that maketh glad the heart of man" (Psalm 104:15). The full passage from Ecclesiasticus reads "Wine is as good as life to a man, if it be drunk moderately; what life is then to a man that is without wine? for it was made to make men glad" (Ecclesiasticus 31:27).

to be discerned by reason of its ruin, but by the Gabrs'[548] cabala preserved from oblivion. To see it, we foot it to the very top of a hill not easy to be ascended, where we found a hollow cave, whether cut by art or nature scarce discernible. His grave is here, as they say, but his image we found at a place near Chehel-minar (from his gigantic shape engraven upon the side of a black marble mountain) now called Nagsh-é Rostam, a brave chevalier (as report makes him) such time as Artaxerxes, Queen Esther's husband, wore the diadem. Some disgust happened between Rostam and his brother Shughad, who at a time when Rostam was in hot chase of some beast, it seems he fell into a pit which Shughad had digged and deceitfully-covered with boughs as if it had hatched no danger, but in prosecuting his hate and looking into the pit the more to glut his unbrotherly revenge, he was slain by a dart Rostam flung up to retaliate him.[549] Such was the end of Rostam and his brother, of whom the Gowers (the old Persians) fable no less then what we find others do of Bellianis[550] or Ogier the Dane.[551]

Nearer the city is Darius, or rather Xerxes his mount, a rising hillock which the people showed us whence Xerxes, upon view of the innumerable army he had in that large plain, wept upon a meditation that in five years none of them should be living, a notion true and sooner then he had predicted,for what by Themistocles on shore and Leonidas at sea, at Salamis and Thermopylae, his huge army melted away and quickly became less numerous. Howbeit, some say his second view of the army was at Abydos near Hellespont.

Not far from thence we rode to the hills now called Damavand,[552] of like name with those of Epirus known to Ptolemy, through which Abbas, who thought nothing impossible or unfeasible for the accommodation of the citizens, is forcing a

---

[548] A name for the Zoroastrians. See Gabr-abad below, the Zoroastrian quarter of Isfahan.

[549] Herbert has already repeated this story, with a slightly different twist. See above, 000.

[550] Herbert is referring to *The Honour of Chivalry: The Famous and Delectable History of Don Bellianis of Greece* (1545; English translation 1650), a romance written by Jerònimo Fernandez, a Castilian lawyer, and later continued by his nephew Andrés (1579). One of its characters is the Persian Prince Perianes. This work was very popular and was reprinted several times; its admirers included Cervantes, who cited it in *Don Quixote* (1605), and Dr. Samuel Johnson. There is a reprint of the English version (New York: Kessinger Reprints, 2003).

[551] Ogier the Dane is the eponymous hero of one of the poems in a medieval French romance, the *Geste de Doon de Mayence*. Ogier was one of Charlemagne's "paladins," although they had their differences, and he is mentioned in Pynson's printed edition of Mandeville's *Travels* (1493), which is where Herbert may have seen his name. He could also have found it (as 'Octher') in Hakluyt (*Voyages*, 40–41).

[552] Damavand [*Demawend*] is both a city and a mountain, actually a volcano, the highest in Iran. It is still famous for its aqueduct, and is mentioned in the *Shahnameh*. Herbert describes the town in more detail later.

passage, though he effect it not in less then twenty years' time by the incessant toil of 40,000, sometimes 100,000 men, to force a river to Isfahan that runs contentedly to itself fifty miles thence, and by this I suppose is effected, which aqueduct, when accomplished, will appear of more use then pomp and may compare with that intened by vainglorious Nero 'twixt Ostia and Avernus, now called Licola, or that other of Ficinus, which Claudius cut three thousand paces long by the incessant eleven years' labour of 30,000 men to bring the water to Rome, costing him 1,400,000 crowns, and with better success then Nero had in his vain attempt to cut the isthmus in Achaia or then Xerxes had by what he did at Mount Athos.

Within Isfahan I found that column or pillar of heads of men and beasts which was erected as a *salvo* and expiation of the King's oath. At the base 'tis twenty foot round and threescore high or thereabouts, for the truth is I forgot to measure it. The occasion of erecting this dreadful monument was this. *Anno* 1500, *Heg.* 880, such time as Shah Tahmasp ruled Persia[553] and Guneh Khan[554] added to the lustre of the diadem, this city, surfeiting with luxury, for "*ubi uber, ibi tuber,*"[555] refused not only to contribute a reasonable sum unto the King, albeit at that time infested with Turk and Tartar, but audaciously opposed his entrance, a rebellion so insufferable as made him vow a suitable revenge. With speed therefore and fury he assaults and in rage enters, firing a great part of the city and in hostile severity pillaging each house. To conclude, regarding neither the outcries of old men, weak women nor young children, in two days he put to the sword 30,000 Isfahanians, and "*in terrorem aliorum*"[556] erected a pillar of their heads, upon which might properly have been writ, "*heu, quo discordia cives perduxit miseros!*"[557]

Pillar of heads in Isfahan [illustration not shown]

---

[553] Herbert has the wrong Shah. In 1500 the Shah was Ismail I. Tahmasp did not succeed until 1524. Neither Boyle nor Eskandar Monshi mentions Ismail or Tahmasp doing anything like this. However, piling up the heads of enemies outside cities was a fairly normal practice. However, Timur was said to have massacred 70–90,000 people when he took Isfahan (1387) and piled up the heads into a pyramid.

[554] Della Valle mentions a "Khan of Erevan" named Emir Guneh Khan [*Guin-Shaw* in Herbert] and calls him "a general in these parts" (*Travels*, 2: 288). Foster seems to support this identification, but states that the rebellion mentioned here does not appear in the histories either of Malcolm or Sykes (*Herbert* 316). The editor cannot find it in modern historians, either. In 1604 one Guneh Khan Qajar had occupied Qarabagh by order of Shah Abbas; they appear to be the same person, and perhaps this is the "rebellion" alluded to here.

[555] "Where the soil is rich, you'll find roots" (Apuleius, *Apologia* 18.11). The pun does not work in English.

[556] For the terror of others.

[557] "Alas, where has discord brought the unhappy citizens?" (Virgil, *Eclogues* 1. 49–50).

In like manner Abbas, by the hasty death of father and elder brother, impatient
of co-rivalship, for 'tis true that "No faith in fellow-rulers, power or state/ Admits of comfort to participate," lops off such branches as he thought might eclipse
his greatness, and speeding to Isfahan to justify his title to the crown, expecting
to be welcomed, the citizens unadvisedly upbraid him with the death of Emir
Hamza[558] his brother and old Mohammed [Khodabanda], which so exasperates
Abbas that by his father's soul, the Seven Orbs, Bismillah[559] and Mohammed,
he vows revenge. For a month's space they held out and defended the city against
the King, but in the end victuals grew short, and upon his diverting the river, as
Cyrus when he took Babylon, so many as could did steal away, choosing any hazard rather then endure a famine. Abbas takes the advantage of it and by storm
enters, killing for two hours men, women and children without mercy, making good what a noble poet of ours in his monarchic tragedy well notes, "What
misery more great can be devised, / Then in a city when by force surprised?,"[560]
commanding forthwith a pillar to be advanced of the rebels' heads as a memorial of his justice and their disloyalty, wherein probably he took for example those
three towers of heads Tamerlane caused to be created of those he massacred at
Damascus. And doubtless the tragedy had been acted had not the Mufti, imitating Aurelian, who when he took Tyana,[561] having sworn the death of them

<hr />

[558] Prince Mirza Hamza (1564–1586) was proclaimed heir in 1578 by Mohammed Khodabanda, who had bowed to considerable pressure from his emirs (Monshi,
History, 1: 372). He became Governor of Isfahan on the accession of his father (1577)
and commanded armies against the Turkmen and Ottomans, winning victories against
both, Shortly before this, Shah Ismail II (1576–1577) had ordered Hamza, together with
Prince Abbas and their father to be murdered, but died before this could be carried out.
According to Monshi, the Prince was murdered by his barber whilst on campaign in
Azerbaidjan (Monshi, History, 1: 483–487). "It has been claimed, though never proven,"
Boyle writes, "that the murderer, a barber by the name of Khudvardi, had been hired by a
group of conspirators among [Hamza's] officers" (*History*, 261). Mohammed Khodabanda
abdicated, and may have been imprisoned, but he died of natural causes in 1596 (Monshi,
History, 2: 692).
[559] Literally, "In the name of God." It is an oath "frequently taken at the commencement of any undertaking" (Hughes, *Dictionary*, 43).
[560] Abbas did encounter some opposition in Isfahan, but not on the scale that Herbert describes. Yoli Beg, the Governor, welcomed the Shah, but did not allow access to
the fort at Tabarak. Later on, after feasting the Shah in his own house, "he retired into
the citadel with his officers," Monshi relates, "and defended the battlements with cannon
and muskets" (Monshi, *History*, 2: 603) He then arrested the men whom the Shah sent to
negotiate. After more fighting, Yoli Beg capitulated; no massacre appears to have taken
place, at least according to Monshi. For the full story, see Monshi, *History*, 2: 602–4. In
1597–1598 Abbas transferred his capital from Qazvin to Isfahan.
[561] Aurelian captured the Cappadocian city of Tyana in 272, after declaring that "he
would not leave a dog alive once he had captured the town" (Watson, *Aurelian*, 71). A

all, by a merry equivocation made all the dogs to be hanged up, in commiseration feigned a vision from his Prophet which declared that so a pillar were raised of heads, no matter though it were beasts' heads, and interceded for pardon, to which Abbas after so sufficient slaughter condescended, forthwith commanding a speedy destruction of all kinds of beasts (the innocent suffering for the nocent), of whose heads and those men already slain this monument of merciless mercy was reared, outbraving for heighth many mosques in Isfahan, though now grown ruinous. Such another in *Sumdeby* 'twixt *Erez* and Derbent[562] upon the like occasion, which some would have to be dedicated to the sun, like those four obelisks, each of which was forty-eight cubits high and raised by Sochis the Egyptian king as an expression of his zeal to that deity, as Pliny *lib.* 36, *c.* 65.[563]

The site of Julfa resembles Pera which is opposite to Constantinople or as Southwark is to London, the River Zayandé interposing. 'Tis called a suburb, as be those others of Gabr-abad, Abbas-abad, Shams-abad, Ghasem-abad and Shaikh Shaban,[564] though indeed they are peopled with men of one persuasion. Julfa is governed by a peculiar podestate, an Armenian Christian Prince (as they style him), Khwaja Nazar by name, though a merchant by profession, having superintendancy over them. He and his enjoy freedom of conscience, but for money matters and public taxes are at the sole disposition of the King. In Julfa, named so from another of that name in Armenia, the people inhabiting this suburb are numbered ten thousand, and in Azena-bad four thousand families. By some 'tis writ *Golfa* and *Chiulfa*, but I have better hit our dialect. The Julfans are habited like the Persians but differ in aspect, most of these and the Georgians having brighter hair and greyer eyes. They are for the most part merchants, many of them factors for the King, who exacts an account especially at their death, and, if of considerable estates, declares himself heir and disposes of what he thinks best, none daring to contradict him. They profess Christianity, taught them

---

legend states that he spared Tyana after having a vision of Apollonius of Tyre. See Alaric Watson, *Aurelian and the Third Century* (London: Routledge, 1999), 71–3.

[562] Derbent, now in modern Dagestan, is the southernmost city in Russia. Known as "the Gates of Alexander," it was settled in the eighth century B.C.E. Derbent is situated on a narrow strip between the Caspian Sea and the Caucasus Mountains. Herbert will describe it in detail later.

[563] Herbert is not accurate here. He cites Book 36, Chapter 8, but the reference is to [Chapter] 65. "Sochis" is actually spelled "Sesothis" by Pliny, who himself is not consistent, the name appearing as "Sesostris" elsewhere. The four columns, about 80 feet high, are at Heliopolis and were built by Seti I.

[564] Gabr-abad or Gabrian [*Gower-abaut*] is the Zoroastrian area; Abbas-abad [*Abbas-abaut*] contains historical gardens; Shams-abad [*Chanz-abaut*] is in northern Isfahan; Ghasem-abad [*Azen-abaut*] and Sheikh Shaban [*Cheigh-Saban*] are both in western Isfahan. I am indebted to Dr. Reza Abouei of the Department of Architecture, Sheffield University, for the last three identifications.

erroneously by Jacobus the Syrian Monophysite,[565] and have two protomists, one in Julfa and the other sometimes at Sis[566] near Tarsus, other times at *Ecmeasin* not far from Kivan, as with their tenents I have spoken of.

Gabr-abad, another suburb, takes its name from the Gabrs that inhabit it, nicknamed from their idolatry, being relics of the ancient Persians such as at this day the Persians be in India. The Persians have them in small account partly for that they are the ordinary people of that country, partly for that by their industry they shame the Persians in their idleness. These, if we may credit tradition, differ from all others in that they never built any temple to the sun as most idolators have done, but give a pretty good reason, for, say they, no place on earth could be sufficiently capacious, seeing that *"mundus universus est templum Solis."*[567] Zoroaster was their lawgiver and no other then Zoroaster whose ashes, if the Greeks may be believed, were consumed by lightning, invocating Orion. Nevertheless some think that he was Nimrod, but more certain it is that he was that Zoroaster who first taught the Persians magic and judicial astrology, howbeit some there be that imagine Zoroaster was that Perseus the Grecian hero who first gave Persia the name, and upon his Pegasus is said to fetch that fire from Heaven which they after idolised, albeit the Mohammedans apply the name *Gabr* to Christians, seeing it signifieth an unbeliever.[568] These Gabrs adored the sun, called Mithras, a representator of a more powerful deity; their flamens were a sort of Platonists, seeing that albeit they acknowledged many creatures to be excellent yet no way comparable to the Creator, who is, even as they accompt, the centre of all perfection; nevertheless they have declined that, and at this day deify an elemental Fire, which, like that of the Vestals, if we may believe, doth not extinguish.

An old inhabitant of Persia [illustration not shown]

Their marriages were such as I have related amongst the banished Parsis that live in India, but their burials differ, for in reverence to the fire, these not only forbear to burn the dead, fearing to offer it an unclean thing, but even hold it a crime to spit into the fire, which they yet repute sacred. Howbeit, in the oriental parts of India amongst the Brahmans the dead are exposed to the fire, albeit in the Occident it came first in request by Sulla the Dictator, who, having abused the dead corpse of Gaius Marius, fearing like sauce ordered that his dead body should be burned, which was done, and after practiced by the succeeding Roman

---

[565] A Monophysite believes that Christ incarnate had only a single nature, a combination of the human and the divine.

[566] Capital city of Cilician Armenia.

[567] "The whole world is the temple of the sun" (Latin proverb).

[568] In later centuries this name often appears as "Giaour," which admirers of Byron may remember is the title of one of his poems.

Princes.[569] But whereas the Egyptians powder the dead with salt and spices to preserve them from putrefaction, the Parsis in India expose the dead to the sun's rage till he has eaten them. And these Gabrs ofttimes put them in the hollow of a tree standing upright, supported by the bole till observation release them, for if the vulture pick out his right eye first, then they conclude he is in Paradise; if the left, then a cacodemon vexes him, and they feast or fast by that observation as joy or sorrow is occasioned. Contrary to the Persian satraps, who had their graves so deep in the sides of rocks and mountains that they were usually let down by cords or otherlike device many fathoms, the corpse first being embalmed. These people are for the most part mechanics or husbandmen; few of them either scholars, soldiers or *soldagars*, as they term their merchants. Their habit varies but little from the common mode, save that their headpiece is fashioned to the garb of Hyrcania. Their women show their faces, a thing in these parts very rare, and their apparel and hair is tinctured with yellow, resembling the burning embroidery of the sun, for a flame-coloured scarf hangs loose behind them, of use among the Roman women, as Lucan *lib.* 2, "Her face wanted a yellow veil to hide/ The amorous blushes of a shame-faced bride," and in his 3 *lib.*, "Whose hair and clothes with saffron colour dyed."[570] Howbeit, many of them, either out of zeal or poverty, go barefoot, for they use neither shoes nor sandals.

The Portuguese friars also have two houses here, and are of the rules of Carmel and Augustine;[571] their chapel is neatly-gilt and adorned with ornaments as organs, altars, crucifixes, images, candles etc., with which they endeavour to convert men to the Papacy, but for the Armenians, they are spectators rather then auditors and love no innovation, and the Persians 'tis their principle to contemn images. Nevertheless they are of some use, seeing they usually serve to send intelligence to Goa and other parts of Christendom.

We entered Isfahan the tenth of April and on May Day departed thence towards the Court, which was then at Astarabad in Mazanderan, about four hundred miles distant northwards from Isfahan.

---

[569] Lucius Cornelius Sulla (c. 138–78 B.C.E.), the Roman general and dictator who defeated King Mithridates VI of Pontus (84 B.C.E.) vied for political ascendancy over a number of years with Gaius Marius (157–86 B.C.E.). The latter, also a general, was five times consul and was outlawed by Sulla (88 B.C.E.). Their rivalry began a long period of civil strife and disorder in the Roman Republic.

[570] Lucan, *Civil War* 2.360–61; 3.20.

[571] The Augustinian Order was established in Persia by Fr. Antonio de Gouvea, whom Philip III sent as his first ambassador to the Persian court in 1602. The Carmelites, sent by Pope Clement VIII in 1604, settled two years later in Isfahan.

Tajabad.

Our first night's journey was to Bagh-é Rezvan, an hour's riding from Isfahan. Thenceforward, by reason of the intolerable heat, we were forced to travel in the night, all day refreshing ourselves in the caravanserai, good resting-places when goats forbade it not. From Bagh-é Rezvan we travelled to Sar Dahan,[572] sixteen English miles hence, called *Sarraca* by Ptolemy *lib.* 6, *cap.* 2, and next night we made *Whomg*[573] our manzil, being seven and twenty miles from Sar Dahan. Next we came to Tajabad, a house and garden of the King's, which for beauty and sweetness is comparable to any other in Parthia, and the more observable for that it is seated in a barren sandy soil; "The blushing rose grows here, the violet/ And Parthian myrtle in choice order fit!" Nevertheless, for five hundred paces every way it gives a pleasant prospect of most sort of trees familiar to that climate, as also of Persian fruits and flowers, *viz.* pomegranates, peaches, apricots, plums, apples, pears, cherries, chestnuts, damask red and white roses and other flowers in great variety watered with streams beautified with artificial grots, having also *hamams* of stone paved with white marble. The Mahal or Summer-Lodge brags also of a dozen chambers which were delightful to the view, rich in embossments of gold and paint of various colours and proud in the architect, and all safeguarded from sand and stealth by a defensive wall so high as hinders, save in one rising artificial hillock which is raised in midst of six descents, the affrighting sight of a circumvolving wilderness. A traveller is not to imagine pleasure his object, for pain and misery will entertain him oftenest, otherwise I would have lulled myself in this paradise, but on we must to try the difference.

Sandy desert.

From Tajabad next night we came to Bad Rud, which was six *farsangs* or eighteen English miles distant, nothing being memorable save an old castle in the way, which by reason of the darkness of the night we could hardly discover. From Bad Rud we got by break of day to Ab-é Garm;[574] both of these are the King's houses, who using this road lies at every twelve miles' end a lodge between Isfahan and the Caspian Sea, wherein our Ambassador had the honour to repose and found reasonable accommodation. And now the danger is part; let me tell you, part of the last night we crossed over an inhospitable sandy desert which was ten miles broad and in length (as they told us) little less then a hundred, where here and there we beheld the ground covered with a loose and flyting sand, which by the fury of the winter weather is accumulated into such heaps as upon any great wind the track is lost and passengers too oft overwhelmed and stifled by that

---

[572] Now part of Isfahan.

[573] Unidentified. Foster was also puzzled, stating that it "remains a mystery" (*Herbert*, 317).

[574] Ab-é Garm [*Obigarmy*] is a small town now noted for its hot springs.

impetuous tyrant. Yea, camels, horses, mules and other beasts, though strong, swift and steady in their going, yet sometimes are not able to shift for themselves but perish without recovery. Those rolling sands, when agitated by the wind, move more like sea then land, and render the way very dreadful to passengers. Howbeit, which was some amends, the dryness of these parts gives less advantage to the sun by exhalation to occasion winds then in hotter places and near the sea is observed, and indeed in this place I thought that curse was fulfilled which is mentioned in Deuteronomy 28:24, where the Lord by Moses threatens instead of rain to give them showers of dust,[575] for albeit the King, to do as much as may b e for the prevention of harm and preservation of passengers, has raised at every three miles' end a wall or castle, yet by the unstable foundation, in March and September, in despite of their best props it is piecemeal torn asunder, that little or no remains appear of their late standing. This our last night's travel was thirty miles.

Salt desert.[576]

Next night we rode one and twenty miles to Safid-ab,[577] an old weather-beaten caravanserai well-agreeing with the situation, being placed in an unsociable desert. Our next night's lodging was at Siyahkuh,[578] ten *farsangs* or thirty miles English, a place that made amends for the last, this being notable in her caravanserai, which is built from the ground of good free-stone, white and well-polished; yea, to the best of my remembrance, unless at Tang-é Dalen, this was the first building of that material I saw in eight hundred miles riding, most of the building as we passed being of brick well-hardened in the sun, as is common in these hotter parts of Asia. A word of our last night's journey: the most part of the night we rode upon a paved causeway broad enough for ten horses to go abreast, built by extraodinary labour and expense over a part of a great desert which is so even as that it affords a large horizon. Howbeit, being of boggy loose ground upon the surface it is covered with white salt, in some places a yard deep; a miserable passage! For if either the wind drive the loose salt abroad, which is like dust, or that by accident horse or camel forsake the causeway, the bog is not strong enough to uphold them but suffers them to sink past all recovery. This causeway has some resemblance with those ancient *viae militares* whose foundations were laid with huge piles or stakes pitched into a bog and fastened together with branches or

---

[575] "The Lord shall make the rain of thy land powder and dust; from Heaven shall it come down upon thee, until thou be destroyed."

[576] The Dasht-é Kavir, which extends across to the border with Afghanistan.

[577] Safid-ab [*Suffedaw*], which means "white water," from the waterfalls cascading down from the nearby mountains, is in modern-day Gilan province. Far from being insignificant, it is now the site of a major Upper Palaeolithic archaeological dig.

[578] Siyahkuh [*Syracow*]. Its name means "Black Mountain."

withes of wood upon which rubbish was spread and gravel or stones afterwards laid to make the ground more firm and solid. That of Trajan's was notable, but a dreadful passage this was, and the more to be feared because some forlorn hopes of highwaymen many times pillage passengers. God be blessed, we escaped this, but not another which was little less formidable, for we had no sooner passed this salt desert but of necessity we were constrained to climb over and about the hills called *Cartandae* of old, so high they were and glomerating, but for the easier ascent formed as if Olympus had been cut into labyrinths.

From Siyahkuh we rode next night two and twenty miles; most part of the way was over another salt desert wherein (we were told) thousands have unhappily perished, and would yet run like hazard did not a large and well-made causeway secure the passage. Here we pitched; old Terminus[579] in this place limiting Parthia from reaching farther north, from whose high tops look we back and memorise her that was once formidable to the Roman emperors and mistress of the greatest part of Asia. In the Scythic tongue she signifies "an exile or stranger," as Justin in his 41 book. The Parthian diadem was once garnished with two and twenty kingdoms comprehending the greatest part of Asia, from which magnificence she fell, yet after a long eclipse by virtue of the Sophian stem recovered a great part of her former brightness. 'Tis now called *Hyerac*, surnamed *Agemy* to distinguish it from that including Babylon. Her old provinces were *Rhagaea*, *Apamea* (not that near Seleucia in Assyria), *Tapiria*, *Choams*, *Araciana*, *Semina* and *Mizia*, her mountains Orontes, Abicoronii, Mardoranii and Parchoatri, not much above 800 miles in circuit.[580] And albeit most part was hilly and sterile, it bred nevertheless men in their time both wise and valiant, yea, in such repute with the Apostles that in the First Epistle of St. John the dedication was "*ad Parthos*," as some old copies have it.[581]

Next night, the moon making our way the easier, we rode to Gaz,[582] a pretty lodge belonging to the King distant from our last manzil eighteen miles. Near

---

[579] The Roman god of boundaries, whose story may be found in Ovid, *Fasti* 2. 61, 64. Also see Herbert of Chirbury, *Pagan Religion*, 271.

[580] *Hyerac* is Hyrcania (Old Persian *Varkana*) on the eastern shore of the Caspian Sea; *Rhagaea* is Rhagiane in Media; *Apamea* is Aparni or Parni, named for the Iranian nomads who became the Parthians (Malcolm Colledge, *The Parthians* [New York: Praeger, 1967], 16); *Tapira* is Tapuri on the Caspian Sea; *Choams* is Choarene, south-east of Tapuri; Mizia is probably Mesene, which borders on Syria. These locations are from Colledge's map of the Parthian Empire in 51 B.C.E. (18–19). *Orontes* is Mt. Aurvant, which is to the west of Ecbatana (Olmstead, *History*, 29)

[581] This "dedication" does not appear in the King James Bible (1611). The error arose from a misreading of the Greek "*pros parthenous*" (To the virgins), which somehow got translated into Latin as "*ad Parthos*" (To the Parthians).

[582] Now known as Bandar-é Gaz.

this place we overtook some of these Creats[583] or wandering herdsmen old authors commonly called nomads, either for that they descended from Numidians
or because they were named by the Greeks "*a pascando; quasi in pascuis inter armenta degentes.*" "From 'grazing,' as though living among livestock in pastures."
From the definition of 'nomad' om Stephanus's *Dictionarium* of 1654. Fixed stations these keep none, but for mixed profit and delight remove from place to
place as fancy and good pasturage invites, with all their family and sustance treasured up in long waggons that be covered with felt and so high as that they admit of a division into two stories. The lowest, the place of usual residence, is even
with the ground and they have six wheels to draw with. Little is the difference at
this day from what Strabo *l.* 21 of old reports concerning them in saying "*errant
semper sine lare vel dicta penate . . . sine fixis sedibus, sine legibus etc.*,"[584] a people
albeit now of no accompt amongst the Persians. Yet time was, when called Parni,
by their courage as well as numbers they obtained for Arsaces their countryman
the Parthian Empire.

But, having spoken elsewhere of this sort of people, I shall give you a brief
account of our last night's travel, which for the greater part of the way was
through the bottom of part of Taurus, level with the ground, though the top ordinarily moistens itself in the middle region. This is that strait (and not straits
in the plural, though the name be such) or narrow passage which is so much famoused in authors; by Pliny 'tis called *Caspiae Portae*,[585] who also terms it "*ingens naturae miraculum*," a great miracle of nature, Bertius[586] *Caspiarum Claustra*,
Strabo and Ptolemy *Pylae Caspiae*, and others *Meole, Zagriae, Zarzae, Zaraxae*;
Diodorus Siculus *Caspiae Portae*, Priscian[587] *Caspiadis tangunt portas*, some (and
not improperly) *Pyla Semiramidae*, albeit different from those we call *Caucatae*

---

[583] Foster notes that this word "means a nomadic herd of cattle driven from place to
place for pasture," but is here "applied to Eastern nomads" (*Herbert*, 317).

[584] They are always wandering, they have no household gods or settled homes, they
are without laws . . .

[585] The Caspian Gates, according to Pliny's translator John Healy, are "a narrow pass
on the west shore of [the] Caspian Sea, near Derbent [Russia]" (*Natural History*, 381).
Herbert seems to think otherwise, as he calls the narrows near Derbent the Caucasian
Gates. See note on Derbent below.

[586] Petrus Bertius or Bert (1565–1629) was a Flemish geographer and mathematician at the University of Leyden, where he was also Librarian. In 1618 he was appointed
Official Cosmographer to Louis XIII. He re-edited Ptolemy (1618–1619), but his main
work was the *Tabularum geographicarum contractum* (1600), an atlas which came out in a
convenient small-sized edition and contained detailed historical notes.

[587] Priscian (fl. 500 C.E.) was a Latin grammarian who may have come from Caesarea and possibly taught Latin in Constantinople. His primary work was the *Institutio
grammaticae*, a carefully-worked systematisation of Latin grammar which became the
standard textbook in that subject for centuries. Not much is known about him; even the
date is only established because he wrote a panegyric to the Emperor Anastasius I (490–

Portae or *Iberiae*, which are near Derbent, and wherein doubtless Maginus is mistaken in saying that the *Caspiae Portae* are in Turkmenistan, which he places in *Zagatbay*, or Altai as now called. This narrow strait is not more then forty yards broad and eight miles long, but the mountain on either side is precipitous and so high as it is much above what an arrow could reach at twice the shooting were it possible to begin the second where the first shot ended, and is one of those three noted passages through the great mountain Taurus, which from Persia and the south and western parts lead to Armenia, Hyrcania and the Caspian Sea, and which doubtless gave this the denomination. Through this it was the fair Amazonian came to Alexander, for that mentioned in Pliny which Nero threatened the Parthians to pierce through was in Armenia, and formerly spoken of.[588]

Now, albeit some have attributed this pass to the spirit of Semiramis, who to express her power and to eternise her memory to posterity effected wonders, certainly it is rather the work of Nature, God's handmaid, the height and hardness of the mountain rendering it an endeavour vainly to be attempted, if not impossible to be effected by man. Albeit, the Persians (merrily, I thought, till I perceived them displeased with my incredulity) assured me that it was done by Ali's arms with the help of his Zulfikar,[589] which, say the Persian chronicles, was eighteen cubits long, but by equal faith you are bound to believe Ali's arm was proportionate. Now to confirm this for a truth they tell us Ali, being in pursuit of the Gabrs (so then they called the Christians), unsheathing his Zulfikar, for the quicker execution it parted in two (at least was double-edged), with which he so hewed his enemies on the right hand and on the left that at some blows he beheaded hundreds, which made the rest fly to purpose. In the pursuit, the better to overtake his enemies, he clove rocks and mountains in twain and then, as I suppose, made his smooth passage, to which I have but this for answer, "*hanc fabulam longi temporis mendacia finxit,*"[590] for would they give that credit unto Pliny he deserves, they might know how that long before Ali's birth, speaking of this

---

518). From Vindelin de Spira's edition (1470) onwards there were many printed versions of Priscian available.

[588] In 54 Tiridates I, brother of Vologaeses I of Parthia, became king of Armenia with Parthian support, which provoked a Roman intervention by the general Cnaeus Domitius Corbulo, who was sent by Nero to enforce Roman claims to control of Armenia.

[589] Zulfikar was the legendary sword of Ali, who was given it by Mohammed. It was used by Husain ibn Ali, the last Shi'ite caliph, at the Battle of Karbala (680) against Caliph Yazid I, but Husain lost the battle and was killed. It is the sword which appears as a symbol on several flags and insignia of Islamic countries. Its name means "the Lord of the Vertebrae of the Back" (Hughes, *Dictionary*, 717).

[590] "A long-standing lie concocted this fable." The source of this quote seems to have been Leupold von Bebenberg, *Tractatus de juribus regni et imperii Romanorum*, in an edition by Hieronymo Balbi (1624). Leupold (1297–1363) was "the first synthesizer of German constitutional law" (Anthony Black, *Political Thought in Europe 1250–1450*

passage he says *"ruptura est montis longitudine octo mille passus angustissima etc.,"*[591] a description rightly agreeing with what we found it.

But of more certainty is what a Persian then in our company told, how that a dozen years since a valiant thief with five hundred horse and three hundred muskets defended this narrow road against all passengers, none passing or repassing without some acknowledgement, albeit the King of Larijan, whose dominion lay amongst the mountains, frowned at his sauciness and threatened him, but such storms rather made good music to the thief's ears. Howbeit Abbas also, upon affront, grows choleric to be so bearded, yet scorns to honour his overthrow by an army, well-knowing that he had many chevaliers about him by whose courage he little doubted to reduce him, but such was the fame that went out of this thief's fortitude that by their demur Abbas apprehended their fear, and for anger grows pale at it. Nevertheless, ere he could give his rage a vent an Armenian undertakes the work, whom the King embraces, and having breathed fresh courage into the hardy Christian, being excellently-mounted as a passenger he singles out the thief, who doubted not to master so fair a beast with small opposal. Such confidence had he in his valour that it was his custom to give fair play, usually commanding his company to look on at a distance, albeit more then one entered the strait, so that in short space this pair met and engaged each other with sword and buckler. The Armenian followed his blows with such dexterity that after some bloodshed, upon a close he gave death a free passage, a victory nobly-attained yet so irksome to his men, whose lives depended upon his safety, that like robbed bears they fell upon the victor, who doubtless had then and there expired had not some *qizlbashes* who were spectators relieved him, by whose sudden falling on the thieves were quickly sacrificed unto their master. The Christian, thus returning to Court crowned with laurel, Abbas adds to his lustre and gives him a command, so unsupportable to the weak soul of this champion that to cajole the King he denies his faith and turns infidel, though abundance of tears were shed by his countrymen as dissuasives from it. But see one end of his apostasy; the King, albeit he had cause to favour him by reason of his good success against the Tartars, yet jealousy, or rather Divine Vengeance, so stung old Abbas that without any known occasion or acquainting any man with his reason, he commanded Lala Beg to cut off his head such time as he was singing a lullabye to his good fortune.

[Cambridge: Cambridge University Press, 1992], 101). See G. W. Bowersock, *Lorenzo Valla on the Donation of Constantine* (Cambridge, MA: Harvard University Press, 2007).

[591] There is a very narrow space in the mountains eight thousand paces in length.

Hablarud. Firuzkuh.

Our next *manzil* was at Hablarud,[592] eighteen miles from Gaz, a village pretty well-built and delightfully-seated, and where the earth was mellowed by a sweet rivulet that purls from the tops of Taurus; also, the ground was most part of the year apparelled in green, requiting the painful husbandman with a due acknowledgment of olives, walnuts, rice, wheat, wood and other things. Bidding an unwilling farewell to that pleasant place, the next night we rode twenty miles to Firuzkuh,[593] i.e. a broken or divided mountain, and by the position thereof may probably be the issue of that which Ptolemy calls *Arsitis*. The town is sometimes honoured by the King's residence, not that the beauty of his house, which is ordinary, allures him, but for that there is choice hawking, pheasants and other game more abounding here then in most other parts of Parthia. The pole is here elevated six and thirty degrees. The town is refreshed with very sweet water; the situation is upon the brow of a high, well-wooded but (agreeable to its name) divided hill, having on each side a steep access whose top has been crowned with a large castle which now by age or war, the canker-worms of all temporaries, is moth-eaten-- her ribs only appear, expressing desolation. One Mohammed then commanded the town, and albeit trusted with the sword and scale, I fear he was Astraea's corrupted servant. No marvel, then, if in a discontented humour he left the earth, for we can witness that in Persia, especially in Firuzkuh, justice was corruptly-balanced. At our entrance into the town, to extort a bribe from our Ambassador, he hanged one Persian, at least we were so made to believe, cut off another's nose and mutilated a third to show that his laws, like Draco's,[594] were writ in blood. Their delinquency was for the felonious stealing a trifle of two shillings' value from a footman serving the English agent. Another was ready to be trussed up, but secret notice was given our Ambassador that if he pleased to beg his life, upon presenting the Governor with something, it should be granted him. This was the main design, and although well enough seen, our Ambassador very gladly ransomed him. Complaint was also then made against a farmer for thrashing a whore against her will; the Persian Rhadamanth,[595] 'twixt jest and earnest, bids geld him and hang his stones at his ears as two pendants, such as

---

[592] Hablarud [*Halvary*] is mentioned by Stodart, and Foster notes that it is located "in a valley of the same name" (*Herbert*, 317). There is also a Hablé-rud river basin in Tehran province. The village of that name appears to be in the river basin.

[593] Firuzkuh [*Periscow*] is in the Elburz Mountains, east of Teheran in modern-day Teheran province. In spite of its reputation as a place of natural interest, Greenway and St. Vincent do not say anything about it, but Robert Byron (in 1933) mentions it as being at "the second step of the Elburz" and the location of Reza Shah's new railway tunnel through the mountain (*Oxiana*, 225).

[594] Draco (seventh century B.C.E.), the Athenian lawgiver whose name has become synonymous with unreasonably strict penalties.

[595] Rhadamanthus is one of the three judges of the dead in the Greek underworld.

to him the Gulf of Persia offered none so precious. The poor wretch humbly besought him to spare his useful parts, the like did his astonished wife, so as after mediation of friends and thirty pound fine, upon promise to grind in his own mill ever after, the execution of the sentence was remitted, but each man cried out "A severe censor is this *daruga*," who never read, as I suppose, how that "*nemo iure natura cum detrimento alterius locupletior fieri debet*,"[596] or, which might be his own lesson, that "*avarus omnibus est malus, sed sibimet pessimus.*"[597] The barbarous Gauls indeed had such a custom, but here many times these satraps have such tricks to extort bribes that the subject has good cause to clamour out "Gold forfeits faith, perverts the poor man's right;/ Gold makes the law a slave, where shame wants sight," verifying what another merry poet sings: "*munera crede mihi placant hominesque deosque/ placatur donis Iuppiter ipso datis.*"[598]

After two days' repose in Firuzkuh we continued our travel, the Court then being little more than a hundred miles distant from us. Our first night's journey from Firuzkuh to *Gheer*[599] was four and twenty long miles and tedious in the passage, for some part was over rugged hills, other part through whistling days, in both which we were weather-beaten with a storm of wind and hail bred in Tartary and forced over the Caspian Sea, which from hence, if the season had permitted, we might have seen, as for some time not only took away our sight and hearing but threatened our brains, for in despite of our best skill to keep together we lost one another, insomuch as we had hardly recovered our company had not the unmelodious noise of braying mules and jingling of the camels' bells (being to windward) brought us together and helped us out of thoese Caspian or Zagrian Straits, through which when neither sun nor moon nor star befriends whoever after travel, let them be sure to borrow Theseus his thread or be content to wander in some kind of labyrinth. From Gheer we rode next night four and twenty miles to a small village whose name I have forgot, but remember very well that the frogs, the bulbuls or Philomels of this marish[600] place, assembled in such numbers and chirped such loathsome tunes that we wished Homer would have given them another king, for as one writes, "The prattling frog, thinking his language good, / Croaks fruitfully in his beloved mud." Nevertheless, frogs are of

---

[596] "No-one through natural law may make a profit to the detriment of someone else" (Justinian, *Digest of Roman Law*, Book 50, Title 17, 206). This is a phrase from equity law which Herbert would know well.

[597] "A miser is bad for everyone, but worst for himself" (Publilius Syrus, *Sententiae*).

[598] "Believe me, gifts please both gods and men; / Jupiter himself is pleased with presents" (variant text of Ovid, *Ars amatoria* 3. 653-654).

[599] Stodart gives *Jeere*, but neither Ross nor the present editor could find it on any map. Foster also says that it "remains unidentified" (*Herbert*, 317).

[600] Marshy.

great virtue if physically used, for there is no part of them but what is medicinable, if Aldrovandus[601] in his report be rightly-informed.

To Aliabad[602] one and twenty miles from the town of frogs, we rode next night, a very pleasant place for earth, water and wood, and where we found store of pheasants, a bird abounding in these Hyrcanian towns, but near the River Phasis[603] in Mingrelia, emptying itself into the Euxine near Trebizond, originally breeding. Jason and his Argonauts first made them known to Greece when thence he forced their sheep bearing fleeces of gold or gold-meriting fleeces. Next night we got to Nikar, five and twenty miles from Aliabad, observable only in the King's house and for that their common mansions and churches differ not from ours of the ordinary sort in England. Here, as in some other parts of Hyrcania, it being summertime, we were exceedingly pestered with flies and gnats, whose vexatious stings made some of us when we arose look as if we had the measles. And when we came near the sea, we were no less troubled with snakes, for if so be we left the road and rid through the green pastures, then they would wind about our horses' legs without other harm then affrighting and serving to persuade us into the common path again. This is not strange, seeing that Pompey, after he had subdued Tigranes the Armenian, marching into this country was constrained to retreat by reason of the infinite number of snakes and serpents that offended the army, as Plutarch, *Vita Pompeii* writeth.[604]

---

[601] Ulisse Aldrovandi (1522–1605) was an Italian nobleman. doctor, and scientist, Professor of Logic and Philosophy at the University of Bologna. In 1568 he became Director of the Bologna Botanical Gardens. His works include the *Ornithologiae* (1598), *De animalibus insectis* (1602), and the posthumously-published *Historia serpentum et draconum* (1640), which is likely Herbert's source for the information about frogs.

[602] Aliabad [*Aliavar*], a town near modern-day Gorgan (Asterabad). It has been mentioned recently in connection with the Iranian nuclear programme.

[603] The Phasis is now known as the Poti or Rioni River in Georgia.

[604] Cnaeus Pompeius Magnus (106–48 B.C.E.), eminent Roman general and statesman, rival of Julius Caesar and victim of political murder in Egypt. He was victorious in three wars against Mithridates VI of Pontus, deposed Antiochus XIII of Syria (64 B.C.E.) and captured Jerusalem (63 B.C.E.). He also fought against the Armenians. Tigranes II "the Great" of Armenia (c. 140–55 B.C.E.), reigned 95–55 B.C.E. He warred against the Parthians and Seleucids, and although he was defeated by Lucullus at Tigranocerta (69 B.C.E.) he fought the Romans to a standstill the next year and continued to wage war against Pompey, who replaced Lucullus as general.

Sir Dodmore Cotton's arrival at Court. Astarabad.

Next night we got to Astarabad,[605] a city upon the Mare Caspium. The Emperor of Persia was here at this time expecting the Ambassador, unwilling to remove until he came, and, as we thought, resting there so long both that we might see the extent of his Empire and likewise have a prospect of the better parts of Persia. The Sultan of the town, attended with fifty *qizlbashes*, met the Ambassador three miles from the Court, and having civilly brought us into Astarabad ushered us to our lodging; I may say "us," for the ceremony was very much below the quality of so eminent a person as an Ambassador.

Astarabad or *Abashabad*, and yet I dare not say so, named from Ahasuerus, is distant about two miles from the Caspian Sea. It is seated in a low ground, many salt marshes circumvolving her, and is but meanly-watered, no other but a small spring (*Maxera* in Ptolemy) streaming from the Taurisian mountains drills in two branches through it, the broader of which is not five yards over, yet was in former times a river of good breadth.[606] But it is no wonder we crossed over so few that we could call rivers, seeing the people cut them into many small sluices so that ofttimes the true channel is not to be discerned. This practice is no new thing, no less ancient then Cyrus the Great, who to retaliate the loss of his men which were drowned in passing the River Gyndes,[607] a branch of Euphrates in Assyria, divided it into above three hundred little streams so as the main channel became lost. This was in revenge for the loss of his white palfrey, a beast which was of the Nitaean breed, the best Media, nay the world, brought forth, as Seneca, *De ira, lib.* 3, *c.* 23. Howbeit, the ground is reasonable fat but uncultivated, the greater part of her inhabitants ploughing *in Campo Martio.*[608] I judge two thousand families live in this town, and no doubt increase daily, the King having but late affected this place. His palace is pretty large and but newly-finished, and

---

[605] "Two gardens and a palace," writes Robert Byron, "still mark this royal pleasaunce, where Shah Abbas received Sir Dodmore Cotton in 1627. Seen from a distance, the palace on its wooden hill looks like an English country-house. But it is really very small, its tilework is coarse, and it is planned with the incapacity to make convenient use of a given space usually found in Persian secular buildings . . . The two gardens are more romantic" (*Oxiana*, 225). Compare Herbert's description below of the palace as "large," although he, too, admired the gardens. In 1937 Astarabad was renamed Gorgan. Greenway and St. Vincent state that "it's still little more than a provincial market town," but "contains a couple of interesting buildings" (*Iran*, 381). For historical details, see also James J. Reid, "Rebellion and Social Change in Astarabad, 1537–1744," *International Journal of Middle Eastern Studies* 13 (1981): 35–53.

[606] Astarabad or Ashraf is on a tributary of the Qareh River, 37km from the Caspian Sea.

[607] The Gyndes River, now known as the Diyala, is on the road to Babylon.

[608] The Campus Martius in Rome was used as a place of exercise and for peoples' assemblies. However, Herbert may also be suggesting that the people here are more interested in war than in agriculture.

Farahabad,[609] the Hyrcanian metropolis, but five miles well-removed from here, where the seat royal in that country has been kept for some generations. Abbas-abad also is not above two miles hence and surpasses for a curious summer-house excelling all his other for prospect, painting, *hamam*, waterworks and a forest which is stored with game of several sorts, so as it attracts the King, who wher-ever he stays long makes cities of small villages.

The bazaar here is but ordinary and the *masjeds* are not to be admired.[610] The palace is large and looks into very pleasant gardens, albeit the building itself be not very regular, but rather confusedly divides itself into four mahals or banquet-ing-houses which we gorgeously-painted. Were these united, they might better delight the eye and cause the architect to be commended, but more of it at the Ambassador's audience. *Abbasabad* signifies 'Abbas his garden,'[611] and though I find a town mentioned in Ptolemy called *Abasena* in his time, I may not conclude it to be this, seeing he places that in Media.

The pole Arctic is here elevated eight and thirty degrees, seventeen minutes. It is due north from Isfahan; as we observed in our starlight travel (for in the summer season the days are raging hot and not to be travelled) Arcturus[612] was ever right before us. From the Gulf as we travelled from Hormuz to this place are a thousand English miles, from Isfahan three hundred and fifty or thereabouts, as we reckoned.

The Ambassador's entertainment at Court.

Before I give you a brief survey of Hyrcania, let me present a short narration of our Ambassador's audience and entertainment. After four days' repose the King assigned him his day of audience; it was the five and twentieth of May, our Sab-bath and the fag-end[613] of their Ramadan or Lent, advantageous to the Padishah though I will not say it spared him the charge of entertainment. Sir Dodmore Cotton our Ambassador had Sir Robert Sherley in his company, with myself, seven or eight other English gentlemen his followers. Good reason it was that some sultan or other should convoy and show him the way, the Court being a

---

[609] Farahabad (formerly Tahan), which means "place of joy" (Monshi, *History*, 2: 1059) was developed as his winter palace by Shah Abbas I from about 1600 onwards. Monshi writes that it was "the envy of all" and that the Shah was happiest when he was there (*History*, 2: 1060). Herbert describes the town in detail later.

[610] Greenway and St. Vincent mention only the Jam-é Masjed, "a single storey mosque with a traditional sloping tiled roof and an unusual minaret," which dates from the fifteenth century (*Iran*, 382).

[611] Herbert is referring to the Abbas Bagh, a beautiful garden planted by Abbas I. Foster mentions that after its destruction by the Afghans in 1723, it was restored by Nadir Shah, but "is now (1928) ruined and desolate" (*Herbert*, 318).

[612] The brightest star in the constellation Boötes.

[613] The refuse or inferior part of something; originally it was a clothier's term.

quarter of a mile distant from our house, but what ill office was done at Court I am not able to divine, yet so it happened that notice was given only by a courier from Mohammed Ali Beg[614] the favourite. Howbeit, to the court His Lordship got, very few of the town having notice of his audience, as appeared by those few that came out either to see him pass or to view the manner of his reception, which was without doubt the product of the favourite's envy, occasioned through the spite he causelessly bore unto our noble countryman Sir Robert Sherley, for otherwise it might have been wondered at, seeing Abbas of all sorts of honours counted to have strangers at his Court the highest.

At our alighting an officer bade us *khosh amadid* and ushered us into a little house which stood in the centre of a large court wherein was no other furniture save a few Persian carpets which were spread about a white marble tank filled with water. Here we reposed, and for two hours were entertained with polo and wine, nothing so good as the material they served in, flagons, cups, dishes, plates and covers being all of gold. Thence we were conducted by some sultans thorough a spacious garden which was curious to the eye and delicate to the smell, whence we were brought into another summer-house which was rich is gold embossments and painting but far more excellent in a free and noble prospect, for from the terrace thereof we had a delightful horizon into the Caspian Sea towards the north and southward at a great distance could discern the great mountain Taurus. The chambers were large and square, the roof arched and richly-gilded. Below, the ground was spread with carpets of silk and gold; in the midst were tanks full of sweet water, an element of no mean account in these torrid regions, and

---

[614] Mohammed Ali Beg (d. c. 1643) was originally a shepherd whom Abbas met by chance and conversed with; impressed with his intelligence, the Shah invited him to come to court, gave him his name and title, and made him *nazar*, the Intendant of the Household. He appears to have served Abbas diligently and honestly (he did not take bribes) until the Shah's death and then remained in office under Shah Safi. Jealous court factions tried to discredit him, but Safi supported him. However, some accounts say that he fell out of favour and was made ambassador to India as a punishment or to remove him from harm's way. Whether he could be called a "favourite" in the sense that this word is used in Western courts is a moot point, and whether he really was "the Shah's chief minister," as Jackson and Lockhart state (*History*, 396) is debatable. He does not seem to have been the equivalent of, say, the Duke of Buckingham at the Court of Charles I, with whose status Herbert would have been acquainted. 1634: Herbert wrote that "his birthplace was Parthia" and that "having a large bulk to maintain and no chameleon, his education being simple, he became costermonger, and by that became wealthy and capable to maintain himself. In a happy hour the King, then in the hippodrome and in Isfahan, took notice of him, viewed him, liked him and preferred him, so as in small time he became sole favourite" (126). See also Stodart, *Journal*, 29–34, 59–64. There is a portrait of him painted about 1632 by Hashim (c. 1598–1654) in the Fisher Fine Arts Library Image Collection, available online at www.imagesvr.library.upenn.edu.

round about the tanks were placed (*pomparum fercula*)[615] goblets, flagons, cisterns and other standards of massy gold, some of which were filled with perfumes, other with rose-water, with wine some and others with flowers.

After we had refreshed so long as we might at full feed our hungry eyes with that food of ostentation, we were conducted into another square large upper chamber where the roof was formed into an artificial element, many golden planets attracting the wandering eye to help their motion. Here the ground was covered with richer carpets then the former, the tank was larger, the materia more rich and the purling stream by pipes forced up into another region. This sea was so deep and so capacious that it seemed a litle ocean where the spoils of shipwracks were conjured out to please the most avaricious Mammon, for so much gold transformed into vessels for use and ornament were set for us to look upon that some merchants then present made an estimate of their incredible value. Another watery magazine there was, circled with a like wall of golden vessels; most of the flagons, cups and other plate were garnished with rubies, diamonds and like stones such as might compare with Cleopatra's furniture in that great feast made to Mark Antony. "*In quo convivio,*" saith Cedrenus *lib.* 4, "*omnia erant aurea, gemmis magnifice distincta, arteque elaborata.*"[616] But the chamber by the length of it was more resembling a gallery then a room of state; the ceiling was garnished with gold and pencilled with story in lively colours, all which seemed to strive whether art or nature to a judicious eye would be more acceptable. One John, a Dutchman who had long served the King, celebrated his skill here to the admiration of the Persians and his own advantage.[617] The floors also in this room were overlaid with such large and rich carpets as befitted the monarch of Persia. Round about the room were seated several tacit mirzas, khans, sultans and beglerbegs, who like so many inanimate statues were placed cross-legged, joining

---

[615] Dishes of ostentation.

[616] At that banquet, everything was of gold, set off with gems and carefully-worked with consummate skill.

[617] Jan Lukaszoon van Hasselt (d. 1653) arrived in Persia in 1617 and gained the favour of Shah Abbas, who made him a court artist; he painted the palace at Ashraf, described by Herbert, and he seems to have gained some influence at court (Willem Floor, "Dutch Painters in Iran during the First Half of the Seventeenth Century," *Persica* 8 [1979]: 147). He was also instrumental in persuading the Shah to send the first Persian embassy to Holland (1625) under Musa Beg, and he accompanied the ambassador to the Netherlands; he also seems to have worked in the silk trade, operating for the Shah in the Caspian provinces. In 1628 he returned to Persia, where he remained until 1630; after his return to Holland he was made a special agent for Abbas I in that country. Willem Floor states that he was "not always a nice and agreeable person" (159), as Herbert's account certainly confirms. For further details, see Hermann Goetz, "Persians and Persian Costumes in Dutch Painting of the Seventeenth Century," *The Art Bulletin*, 20 (1938): 280–90. My thanks to Dr. Willem Floor for his generous help with information on Dutch painters under the Safavids.

their bums to the ground, their backs to the wall and their eyes to a constant object; to speak to one another, sneeze, cough or spit in the Padishah's presence being ever since the time of Astyages held no good breeding, nor may they offend the King, who by the fulgor of his eye can dart them dead as soon as speak the word, as Caesar said unto Metellus. The Ganymede[618] boys, in vests of cloth of gold, rich bespangled turbans and embroidered sandals, curled hairs dangling about their shoulders, with rolling eyes and vermilion cheeks, carried in their hands flagons of best metal and went up and down proffering the delight of Bacchus to such as were disposed to take it. What Valerius reports to have been the custom here of old, *"circum pateris it Bacchus et omnis aula silet;" pueris tanquam surdis, quid facta opus esset indicabant, et ferens poculum, dedit poscentibus*[619] was here the mode and duly acted.

At the upper end, surmounting the rest so much only as two or three *mastabas*[620] or white silken shags[621] would elevate, sat the Padishah, beloved at home, famous abroad and formidable to his enemies. His grandeur was this: circled with such a world of wealth, he clothed himself that day in a plain red calico coat quilted with cotton, as if he should have said his dignity consisted rather in his parts and prudence then *furtivis coloribus*,[622] having no need to steal respect by borrowed colours or embroideries. Cross-legged the Padishah sat; his shash was white and large, his waist was girded with a thong of leather, the hilt of his sword was gold, the blade formed like a hemi-circle and doubtless well-tempered, the scabbard red and the courtiers, *regis ad exemplum*,[623] were but meanly-attired.

The Ambassador's audience.

The Ambassador, by Dick Williams his interpreter (*callimachee*[624] the Persians call him), acquainted the King that by his master's command he had undertaken a very great journey to congratulate his success against their common enemy the Turk, as also to promote trade and see Sir Robert Sherley vindicate himself from Naqd Ali Beg his imputations, and withal to desire a perpetual league of friendship might be continued 'twixt the two powerful monarchs of Great Britain and Persia. The Padishah, raising his body, returned this answer. To the

---

[618] Ganymede was a handsome Trojan prince abducted by Zeus and made cup-bearer to the gods.

[619] Bacchus goes around with the drinking vessels and the whole hall is silent (Valenius Flaccus, *Argonautica* 2. 348-349). Though the servants were deaf, they indicated what needed to be done, and, bearing the cup, he gave it to those who asked.

[620] An Arabic word meaning "raised platform."

[621] Shag carpets.

[622] "Plundered lustre" (Horace, *Epistles* 3. 20).

[623] "According to the example of the king" (Claudian, *De quarto consulatu Honorii Augusti panegyricus* 209).

[624] Foster explains that this is "really a Mongolian word, *kelemchi*" (*Herbert*, 319).

first, the Turks were a mean people compared with the generous Persians, as appeared by several battles he had given them ample proof of, and that then the Turks no people in the world were more inconsiderable; nevertheless, he wished unity amongst Christian Princes, the Ottoman grounding his conquest upon their discord. Concerning trade, the King of Great Britain should, if he pleased, receive ten thousand bales of silk at Gamrun every January, and for payment he would by way of exchange accept of so many thousand English clothes as should be adequate in value, for, as he well knew, the silk was a greater quantity then he could use in his own dominions, so were the clothes to him, but he would hazard the vending them by his merchants to serve his neighbours, so neither we nor he should need to traffic or hold correpondency with the Turks. It would infinitely be to his satisfaction to disappoint the Grand Seigneur of that yearly custom he was forced to when his caravans go by way of Aleppo or Trebizond to the Venetian, Genoan, French or other European merchants so as the Janissaries were maintained by those customs; what was this but to sharpen his enemy's sword to his destruction? Concerning Sir Robert Sherley, he had been long of his acquaintance, and expressed as many considerable favours towards him, though a stranger and a Christian, as to any of his born subjects. That if Naqd Beg had aspersed him unjustly he should have satisfaction; it argued, indeed, Naqd Beg was guilty, in that he rather chose to destroy himself by the way then adventure a purgation. "In some sort he presaged my rigour, for had he come and been found faulty, by my head (an oath of no small force) he should have been cut in as many pieces as there are days in the year and burnt in the open market with dog turds. Now, touching upon a friendship with the King your master, I cheerfully embrace it, and concerning yourself you are truly welcome, and seeing you have done me the honour none of my predecessors ever had before, for as you are the first ambassadors that ever came from Great Britain in that quality into my country you may deservedly challenge the more respect. Yea, as I account your master chief of the worshippers of Jesus, so do I of yourself in a superior degree to any other ambassador now present."

This said, the King sat down again, and whereas all Mohammedans knock their heads against the ground and kiss his garment, in a friendly manner he pulled our Ambassador near him and seated him by his side, smiling that he could not sit cross-legged, and, calling for a bowl of wine, there drunk his master's health, at which the Ambassador stood up and uncovered his head, which, having been noted by the Padishah, the more to oblige he lifted up his turban, and after an hour's entertainment dismissed him with much satisfaction.

But as it is a real truth that *"aures atque oculi regum sunt multi,"* [625] so we found, though not the occasion, that the King's goodwill became soon diverted, for from that day till we arrived at Qasvin, albeit no offence was given, neither

---

[625] "The eyes and ears of kings are many", a Latin proverb quoted by many authors, including Erasmus in his *Adagia*.

was the Ambassador cajoled at court nor saw he the King, neither did any sultan invite or visit him, all which was imputed to the envy of Mohammed Ali Beg, who by bribery was made our enemy, one that for his faculty in diving into other men's actions and informing the Padishah with his observations made a shift to engross the royal favour, insomuch as most business of state passed through this impure conveyance, so that it came to this at length: whom he loves the King honours, such as he hates the King crushes all to pieces. To have his good opinion each great man outvies others, insomuch that his annual comings in *viis et modis* was bruited to be sevenscore thousand pounds sterling, and well might be, since *Myter-beg*, the Overseer of the King's Harem, has a hundred thousand pounds yearly if it be true that some there assured me.

Sors nostra humilior![626] Tamar Beg's house at the north end of the town entertained us twelve long days and nights (so long the Court stayed after we got thither) where the sun darted his outrageous beams so oblique upon us as made us believe we felt not more heat then when we were within the burning zone than we did in Astarabad at that present. Nor did the sun, we thought, more torment us in the day then did those innumerable swarms of gnats, mosquitos and like vermin in the night season. Howbeit, our comfort was that if it were so for any continuance, our short stay there was some sort of prevention; and yet, though our suffering were great in one sense, the extremity of the Padishah's justice, or rigour I may better call it, was more in another as his miserable subjects felt it in a higher degree. I shall give but a few instances of it.

Shah Abbas his cruelty.

A poor distressed wretch, following a long and tedious pilgrimage from Kabul to this place upon some little business, ere he knew what the success would be, unhappily rested his weary limbs upon a field-carpet, choosing to refresh himself rather upon the cool grass then to be tormented within the town by the merciless vermin. Poor man; he fell *de malo in peius*,[627] for snorting in a climacteric hour at such time as the King set forth to hunt, his pampered jade startling, the King examines not the cause but sent an eternal arrow of sleep into the poor man's heart, jesting as Iphicrates[628] did when he saw his sleepy sentinel, "I did the man no wrong; I found him sleeping and asleep I left him." Poor wretch, happy only

---

[626] "Our more unhappy lot!" (Valerius Maximus, *Facta et dicta memorabilia* 6. 8).

[627] "From bad to worse" (Latin proverb).

[628] Iphicrates (d. c. 353 B.C.E.) was an Athenian general who was famous for making reforms in the army's weapons. The story of him killing a sentry is told by Sextus Julius Frontinus (c. 40–103), a Roman senator and general, in his *Stratagemata* (3.12.1), a famous work on military tactics. There is a modern translation of this work, which is undoubtedly Herbert's source, by C. E. Bennett (Cambridge, MA: Harvard University Press, 1925).

in this, *"Aeneae magni dextra occidit!"*[629] The courtiers also, as the negros in Mani-congo, who when their captain receives a hurt by war or accident sympathise by voluntarily maiming themselves, to applaud the fact practically made him their common mark, killing him a hundred times over if so many lives could have been forfeited. This is not unlike the practice of Artaxerxes his great ancestor, who, riding to hunt the lion, caused Megabyzus, a noble youth, to be beheaded for no other fault then darting a roused lion that made at him before the King began to throw, as Ctesias[630] relates, a punishment far exceeding the offence, undoubtedly. I prefer that noble pagan before him who had this excellent maxim of Juvenal, "delay cannot be long where life's concerned" [Satires 6. 221].

A soldier's wife, having fed too high, in a lustful bravado petitioned the King for natural help, her goodman proving impotent. A dangerous impudence! The King finds it to reflect upon himself, old at that time and master of four thousand concubines, so as he promises her speedy justice, calls his physicians, and when phlebotomy[631] was held too mean a remedy for her distemper they gave an asinago an opiate-potion, which so enrages the beast as by force he basely became her executioner.

There are *mollissima fandi tempora*[632] which are not always light upon, as appeared in a needy soldier, who, drawing up a catalogue of his good services, closing it in want and humbly entreating some stipend from his god of war for such and such good services. *Non hic peccatur*, for his sauciness he was drubbed with many bastinados[633] on the soles of his feet well-nigh to death, and imitating Piso the judge in Seneca *lib.* 1 *cap* 16, examines who it was that writ it? The clerk makes his apology, but the King, suffering passion to predominate over reason, that he should never write worse makes his hand to be cut off, giving the poor

---

[629] "He was killed by great Aeneas's right hand," Herbert's altered version of *"Aeneae magni dextra cadis"* (Virgil, *Aeneid* 10. 830), "You fell by the right hand of great Aeneas."

[630] Ctesias of Cnidus (fourth century B.C.E.) was a Greek physician and historian who accompanied Artaxerxes I on his campaign against Prince Cyrus the Younger. He wrote the *Persica*, a history of Persia and Assyria in twenty-three books, extant only in fragments, but an epitome was made by the Byzantine scholar and theologian Photius (815–897), which is likely Herbert's source. Ctesias also wrote a *History of India*. Photius's version was printed in Venice (1499).

[631] Bloodletting.

[632] "The most favourable occasions for speaking" (Virgil, *Aeneid* 4. 293–4).

[633] Bastinadoing, beating people upon the soles of the feet with a rod or paddle, was a common punishment in Turkey and Persia, but also used in Europe. It was also used by the Koreans to punish the Dutch castaways' escape attempts in 1653 (see Hendrik Hamel, *Journal and a Description of Korea* [1669], trans. Jean-Paul Buys [Seoul: Royal Asiatic Society, 1998], 14 and *passim*).

wretch just cause to ingeminate "*Oh! Quam vellem nescirem literas.*"[634] Thus we see
the worst tyranny is law upon the rack; "*summum ius, summa est iniuria.*"[635]

Two needy knaves were arraigned in the Divan and contemned for stealing;
many grievous taunts the Padishah levelled, saying they deserved death for daring only to come so near his Court so ragged. They confess they therefore stole
that they might wrap themselves in better clothing. Abbas, not satisfied with
their excuse, commands two new vests to be brought, but winding-sheets had
been more proper, for the executioner forthwith dragged them away and upon
two sticks staked them upon their fundaments.

Such and such other was his inhumane pastime during our stay at the Caspian Sea, but enough, or rather too much upon such a subject, especially relating to
so great and generous a Prince, as notwithstanding these mistakes is beloved as
well as feared at home and abroad no less highly honoured. Therefore, to record
the variety of tortures here too much used by men-eating hags of Hell, cannibal-
hounds, *capigi*[636] and their death-twanging bowstrings ripping up men's guts and
the like, what could be the effect but an odious and unnecessary remembrance?
For by these few sad instances we see that strait is the single path that leads to life
[Matthew 7:14], but to death many roadways appear, and life, albeit Calanis the
Brahman, arguing with Alexander, maintained that nothing is more despicable
and made it good upon himself, therein being *felo de se*,[637] yet St. Augustine has
a contrary opinion, for he put that value upon life as induced him to maintain
that a fly is to be preferred before the sun, which hath no life as the fly hath. And
albeit nothing be more commendable in Princes then justice, for it is that which
makes them gods, yet clemency is of greatest exaltation, by being most honourable. Tully, though a heathen, affirms as much in his oration to Caesar for the
life of Ligarius: "Thy clemency, O Caesar, is most excellent, yea, more honourable then thy other virtues; Fortune hath made thee great, but Nature hath advanced the higher in thy inclination unto mercy." Nor can they well be separated,
seeing that a Prince exalted above others in dignity is tied to an impartial way,
neither hating nor fearing any but rewarding and punishing as cause required,
without which contempt or confusion followeth. But to these irregularities of
Abbas I may not give the attribute of justice, since if the punishment exceed the
fault, justice then degenerates into cruelty, a vice odious to God who is the father
and fountain of mercy, and unto men, who are too apt to imitate bad examples,

---

[634] "Oh, I wish I had been illiterate," Herbert's altered (or slightly misremembered)
version of "*vellem litteras nescirem*" (Seneca, *De clementia*, 2. 2. 1).

[635] Lit. "The highest point of law is the highest point of injury/ injustice" (Cicero,
De officiis 1. 33). The pun does not work in English, unless it can be read satirically as "the
highest point of justice is injustice."

[636] Herbert probably means *qapucibasi*, in Ottoman Turkish *qapijibasi*, which means
"chief doorkeeper" (Savory, in Monshi, *History*, 2: 1390).

[637] Suicide.

conceiting any act, though never so unnatural (if moulded after such a pattern) commendable. Yet we see that heathen potentates, swerving from the divine rule of justice, pamper the corrupt habit of their minds out of a monstrous opinion that they may every way inebriate their lust without control, as appears by those inhumane games exercised in the Roman amphitheatres, by that barbarism Xerxes, as Xenophon notes, practiced on Masistes his brother and other satraps;[638] such in Deioces, father to Phraortes,[639] who laboured utterly to exterminate the Persian generosity, and may add the miserable tragedy of [Abbas's] son, memory whereof is recent through part of the greater Asia.

Abbas by divers wives[640] had several children, for whose education neither cost nor care was spared. Of most hope were Ismail, Safi Mirza, Khodabanda and Emamqoli, four brave young Princes, the two first being begot on Gordina, daughter of Simon Khan, the latter two of Marta, daughter of Alexander Mirza, both Georgians, both Christians, the first lady brought by Qarcaqay Khan,[641] the other by Shah Tahmasp Quli Beg being both Persians, both favourites, all of them so dear to Abbas that it seemed he then had got the elixir of earthly

---

[638] Masistes (d. 470 B.C.E.), Xerxes's brother and a military commander, had the bad luck to have a wife whose beauty and virtue attracted the King's attention, and he fell in love with her. Xerxes then ordered her daughter to marry his son Darius, "in hope that the mother would be more amenable." However, Xerxes then fell in love with the daughter, who "proved more compliant," but after the King presented her with a robe woven by Queen Amestris, the latter "demanded the wife of Masistes at the New Year's feast when the king must grant every requested gift," and she had the woman mutilated. Masistes, together with his family, fled to Bactria but "he was overtaken and put to death" (Olmstead, *History* 266–67)). The full story may be read in Herodotus (9.107–13), but is probably ahistorical. See H. Sancisi-Weerdenburg, "The Personality of Xerxes, King of Kings," in L. de Meyer and E. Haerinck, eds,, *Archaeologia Iranica et Orientalis Miscellaneia in honorem Louis van den Berghe Peeters.* (Ghent: Brill, 1989), 549-61.

[639] Deioces or Daiaukku was the founder-king of Media (709–656 B.C.E.); he was succeeded by Phraortes (656–633 B. C. E.), defeated and killed by Asshur-bani-pal.

[640] Ten in all. They were (1) Mahd-é Oliya, which is actually a title (m. 1587); (2) Oglan Pasha Khanum (m. 1587), the widow of Abbas's brother Prince Hamza; (3) Wali Ahad (m. 1591); (4) Fakhr-é Jahan (see below); (5) Yakshan Begum (b. 1586), whom Abbas married in 1602; (6) Tzarievna Marta (see below); (7) The daughter of Rostam Khan Daghistani (m. 1607); (8) Daughter of Masum Khan, Governor of Tabaristan (m. 1604, div. 1614); (9) Peri Lala Fatima, née Tinatin, daughter of Peykar Khan of Kakheti; Foster identifies her as Herbert's "Gordina," but states that she was the sister of King Luarsab II of Kartli (*Herbert* 320). There is some confusion here about origins; (10) Daughter of Shaikh Haider Moksi, Governor of Maraghah (m. 1610).

[641] Qarcaqay Khan [*Kurchiki-cawn*] (d. 1624), originally an Armenian Christian, rose to be the Commander-in-Chief of Iran [*Sepahsalar-é Iran*], *amir-al-omara* and Governor of Mashad and Tabriz. He was murdered by Mourav Beg after a revolt in Kartli (Monshi, *History*, 3: 1246). The Georgians then plundered his camp and killed his son as well.

happiness. [642] His wives were so incomparably beautiful, his favourites so exactly faithful and his sons so lively, the characters of his person, policy and courage reciprocally joying the aged King and overjoying the warlike Persians, but it is commonly observed that as the most excellent things alter soonest and that no day is so serene that is not shadowed with some clouds, for this candour and perfection in these youthful Princes quickly vanished. For Ismail, when by reason of his delight in arms and quick signs of magnanimity the Asian world gazed and admired him, in an infernal cloud of poison went down to an untimely grave at nineteen, in the meridian of his splendour. [643] Safi Mirza, dogged by a like adverse destiny, though elevated at first for revealing a conspiracy, was in the end at equal years thrown down and crushed to death after the dumb *qapucibashi* had got a hateful victory, mere jealousy in the King commanding it. [644] And Emamqoli, ere his popular applause could hatch his ruin, upon conference with a witch that understood the *almuten* [645] of his nativity, perceiving that short life attended him, grows fearful of his sire's inconstancy, and in a deep disconsolate melancholy evaporates his sad spirits, leaving the expectation of hatred and sovereignty to Khodabanda Sultan, surnamed Safi, [646] who, made wise by his brother's miseries,

---

[642] Herbert's account is somewhat inaccurate. Abbas's sons were Ismail Mirza (1601–1613); Mohammed Baqar Safi Mirza (1587–1614), of whom more later; Mohammed Razak Khodabanda (1591–1632); and Emamqoli Amanullah (1602–1632), both later executed by Shah Safi. Abbas did indeed marry two Georgian women; Fakhr-é Jahan, daughter of King Bagrat VII of Kartli (r. 1615–1619), whom he married in 1597, and Tzarievna Marta, daughter of King Davit I of Kahkheti (r. 1603–1604). Abbas married her in 1604 and they were divorced in 1614. There were also three other sons, Hassan Mirza (1589–1591), Husain Mirza (1591), and Tahmasp Mirza.

[643] Prince Ismail, "who was twelve years of age, fell ill at Isfahan and died on 29 Jomada II, 1022/ 16 August 1613" (Monshi, *History*, 3: 1083). No mention of poison, and Herbert has his age wrong.

[644] Prince Mohammed Baqar Safi first got into trouble, according to Monshi, through "a seditious relationship with [Farhad Beg Cerkes, the falconer]," who had encouraged the Prince "to commit various disloyal actions of the sort that lead to revolt" (Monshi, *History*, 3: 1096). Farhad was executed (1614), and for a while "the Shah still refused to suspect his son," in spite of the efforts of "court sycophants" to influence him to act against the Prince. Monshi says that the Prince was murdered by one Behbud Beg, a *golam* (non-Mussulman soldier) who said that "since the Prince had been heard to make treacherous remarks . . . he had murdered him as a mark of fidelity and to clear the Circassian *golams* of suspicion" (*History*, 3: 1099). The Prince had been made Governor of Hamadan at the age of four (1591), but he evolved into a competent and successful military commander against the Turks (see below).

[645] The *almuten* is the planet which bears the strongest influence in a nativity.

[646] Herbert is wrong about both these Princes. In 1626 Emamqoli, "through certain unwise actions . . . was blinded," but not put to death. "Emamqoli Mirza," Monshi writes rather evasively, "had committed various acts which were displeasing to his father" (*History*, 3: 1288). Khodabanda was also blinded (1621), because when Abbas was seriously ill

so prudently behaved himself in duty to the King and in a pleasing and safe distance to the people, that Abbas dotes, the people celebrate, and an uncontrollable good fortune seems to dandle him.

Affability, bounty, loyalty, courage and experience in arms at home and abroad, the Persian monarchy Turk, Arab, Mughal and Tartar admiring, fearing and commending him in several eulogies so as his own left nothing unsaid or uninvented that might honour him, and his enemies without, giving their thoughts the lie, could not but idolise him, who for all that, not like our common spirits efflated by every vulgar breath upon every act deify themselves and conceit all great additions of honour below their merits, stood immovable, sorry he grew so popular, chiding them for flattery and contemned himself of hypocrisy by suffering his victories to be so gilded, since what he had or did was but a reflex of his father's virtue, which he doubted might suffer an eclipse by his accumulation. Oh how execrable is this marrow-fretting scab of jealousy and envy! It converts that reason which only makes us men without any regard of justice into brutishness, yea, to exceed in cruelty the most unreasonable and most violent creatures! Is [Mohammed Baqir] Safi Sultan Mirza a Prince his son? On whom can he more justly confer his love? In whom should virtue rather dwell? Where can there be a better centre? Poor Prince! The path he treads to add lustre to his father's diadem and to oblige his country betrays his steps and entices him to an affrighting precipice, for the more he indulges his father it serves as fuel to an unjust jealousy; the more he dignifies his country by his good success against the Turks, the more applause the people crown him with . But Abbas fears more his popularity, yea, so far fears, so much degenerates from paternal piety that without pity or regard of justice (which make kings more beautiful then when circled with diadems), he contrives his speedy ruin.

During these his cabinet-machinations, the Prince brandishes his steel in proud Arabia, where after several conquests the victor himself became captivated, for an Arabian Princess of great beauty (and in such bodies usually are impaled the fairest souls) fettered him, but such was his bravery and worth as he quickly redeemed himself and made her his prisoner. Such magic and interchanges are in love, such magnetic power has Princely virtue. By this lady he has two children, Safi and Fatima, a name given her, as I suppose, in memory of Fatima, the wife of Ali, though not unlike both in name and perfection to that lovely Phaedymia who was the daughter of Otho a noble Persian, mentioned in the 3 *lib.* of Herodotus. [647] This young Princess Fatima was no less-loved by Safi Mirza the sire then doted on by the grandsire Abbas, a strange affection to distinguish

---

"the Prince spent his time in merrymaking, celebrating the fact he would soon be king, forgetting that kingship is at the disposition of God alone" (*History*, 3: 1187). It was left to Abbas's successor Shah Safi to have them executed.

[647] The "noble Persian" was called Otanes, and his daughter Phaedymia married Cambyses II, The full story may be read in Herodotus 3. 68–80.

so unnaturally,[648] to separate where Nature had so strongly united, to hate the graft and to endear the fruit! But that his hate might grow more currently and less suspected, he looks one way and aims another, seeks to enrage by abusing him whom he loved most dearly, Magar an Arab, the Prince's tutor, a faithful and prudent servant, and indeed "*vir bonus solus est prudens*,"[649] Aristotle tells us in his *Ethics*. Such was Magar, whom Abbas calls for, and in lieu of rewarding him for his son's generous affection darts him a stern frown, accusing him of pride and charging him that he had betwitched the Prince with a disloyal ambition. Magar, for all his prudence, sees not the venom prepared, and therefore in an humble but confident innocence excuses and endeavours to quiet him, but the more he vindicates himself and the clearer he makes Mirza's loyalty appear, the more he exasperates the King, so as the higher was his rage enflamed. At first the King amazes him with a volley of defamations, and in this maze gives the sign. A dreadful sign, for forthwith the bloodthirsty *qapucibasis* break in and strangle him! A barbarism, an act so unbecoming that famous King that with the vulgar sort to this very day it will not be credited! Nevertheless, Fame's shrill-mouthed trump sounds it abroad so that the Prince, then in action against the Tartar, has notice upon it, whereupon as a man void of sense he immediately leaves the camp, and, being come to Court, after many signals of sorrow beseeches the King that he may know the reason of Magar's death, who flashes him with this thundering retort: "For thy ambition!" The Prince calls Heaven to witness his loyalty, but Abbas provokes him further, to have more colour to satisfy the world in his designed destruction. The Prince, inflamed with passion, in that distraction imagines he saw Magar a-strangling, and in that ecstasy unsheaths his sword, vowing to rescue him. In the greatest, nay, I may say the wisest of men, reason hath not at all times the predominacy over passion, as we find exemplified in Shah Abbas, an

---

[648] On examination of Safavid genealogy, Iskandar Monshi and Boyle turned up no Princess Fatima, at least as the daughter of Prince Mohammed Baqir Safi Mirza. Herbert seems to have confused or conflated this Prince with his brother Mohammed Razak Mirza Khodabanda. The latter was not killed by his father, but Abbas did have him blinded in 1621 (see above). The former was killed, possibly by his father's orders, in 1614 (see above). Prince Mohammed Baqir was the father of two sons, Safi Mirza (1611–1642), who succeeded Abbas as Shah, and Suleiman, who was also blinded in 1621 on Abbas's orders and subsequently executed (1632) by his own brother! Prince Baqir (as we will call him to avoid confusion) married Princess Dil Aram (d. c. 1647), a Circassian or Georgian, not an "Arabian," as Herbert claims; Sykes, following Herbert's account, repeats the Fatima story but makes her Khodabanda's daughter (267). He too confuses the two Princes. Unfortunately, Christopher Buyers in *The Royal Ark*, an extensive and usually accurate genealogy of non-European royal families, has Prince Baqir marrying Fakh-é Jahan and Marta, both of whom were also cited as wives of his father Abbas I!

[649] "Only the good man is prudent." Herbert seems to be thinking of Horace's "*vir bonus et prudens versus reprehendit inertes*," which means "an honest and sensible man will condemn lifeless verse" (*Ars poetica* 445).

illustrious Prince and at some times reputed to be an indulgent father, but now so far from that that he sorrows not the least at his distraction, but upon this misearable advantage, by some fair terms first disarming him, invites him into another room, and, pretending he was not very well, withdrawing himself, commanded seven big-boned villains, deaf and dumb, through a trapdoor to issue into the room armed with bloody minds and deadly bowstrings, whose very looks as well as habit and weapons quickly bewray their office and intention, which needed no other interpretation. The Prince innocently admires the cause, and if oratory or other way of entreaty could have wrought remorse in these Hell-hounds only till he knew the ground of this cruel command he had afforded it, but well-knowing they were without reason and inexorable, with an incomparable rage and vivacity he flew upon those monsters, now one then another receiving testimonies of his courage, that ere they could fasten upon him their ghastly twanging bowstrings he sent three of them to the Devil, and for some time defended himself, offending those bloodhounds with admirable courage and dexterity, insomuch that had he mastered but any weapon he had doubtless saved himself and sent them packing, but wanting it his breath failed and longer his valour could not nourish him, so at last they fastened their nooses upon him who now for want of breath was a dead man, and the villains had triumphed in his further torture had not the King, who it seems was not far off, prevented it, commanding them only to pinion him, and before he could recover sense and strength, by drawing a flaming steel before his eyes made him stark blind, forbidding him the sight of what he most loved, wife, babes, friends and Magar's carcase, by which impiety Asia lost her fairest jewel, Persia her crown of honour and Mars his darling.

The loss of this brave Prince was quickly rumoured; all Persia mourns and in many threnodies sigh his farewell. The army also swells with passion, but seeing no remedy, by a forced silence murmur their imprecations. The Prince, when he perceived his own undoing (the eye of reason lent him such a sight), having cursed his birth, his fame, his loyalty, and, which is most sad, his parent, by many frantic threats vows his destruction, but finds his revenge impossible, yet at that conceit roars hideously and not to be comforted till Suleiman Beg, Qarcaqay Khan and other his kinsmen and *quondam*[650] favourites flocked about him and by their miserable examples dictate patience, none of which but in some measure had swollen big with the King's infusion in their times, and through his jealousy were made blind or crushed and damned to perpetual imprisonment.

In those discontented times Abbas kept his orb, moving like another Saturn, for now he imagines his crown fixed close to his head, nothing appearing that might disturb his quiet, and amongst his delights nothing so much pleased him as young Fatima. No Siren was melodious in song, no creature delicate in feature save pretty Fatima. If any stood in fear, who could compose his passion

---

[650] Former.

but Fatima? Court and kingdom admired his love to this pretty favourite and no less rejoiced at it, for by this innocent lady they oftimes found the way to expel his rage and how to pleasure him. The prisoners also by Fatima got livelihood, for want of which they were oftimes wellnigh famished, none but she daring to mediate, and thus by this good infant gained they what formerly they pined for, food and comfort. But what joy has the blinded Prince, since he cannot participate? Revenge delights him more; that word as music best pleases the infernal fancy of this melancholy Mirza, not caring how detestable so Abbas suffered. The Devil inspires new rage, and blows the coals of more then cruel assassination, for albeit he passionately loved Fatima, yet, hearing how his father doted on her, that afresh begins his hate yet hatches the innocent's confusion. Oh, in him behold the savage and transcendent cruelty of cursed man! Revenge had plunged him headlong into a whirlpool of unnatural barbarism, insomuch as when the pious child came in an unlucky hour to bring him comfort and by all symptoms of duty to express a lvely obedience, the wretch grasps and in a lymphatic fury whirls her neck about, unable to untwist herself from his wrathful hands, miserable Fatima expiring by her Hellish father, and in her the joy of parents, delight of Abbas, candour of Persia and comforter of the distressed vanishing. The astonished Princess his wife cries out his sight deceived him, that it was Fatima, little dreaming that he therefore martyred her because Fatima, and, as if that had not been enough, to prevent the King of a successor, hearing young Safi's voice dolorously crying out for Fatima, winged with rage he gropes for him, but by the Princess interposing the child escaped or else had lost what he now enjoys, the Persian diadem.[651]

Abbas, when he had notice of this tragedy, grows so outrageously passionate that many feared he would become his own executioner, but when he had drenched his sorrow in a sea of tears he moderates his spleen and revives upon hopes of additional punishment, vowing to retaliate his distracted act in the height of cruelty, which, being told the Prince, had so terrible a reply with a million of dismal curses added that the King was as one astonished. To conclude, after he had tired out a few more minutes with much impatience, the third day he put a period to his life by quaffing up a cup of poison. *"Non malum est mori, sed mori male,"*[652] saith St. Chrysostom; nevertheless, the King showed needless ceremony in his obsequies. The disconsolate Princess sequestered herself from the sight of man, but since her son's coming to the crown, whether he hath by his benign aspect banished her discontent and in some measure assuaged her sorrow I could not learn.[653] But for Abbas himself, he bade the world farewell a little after our departure.

---

[651] Herbert should have emended this: Shah Safi died in 1642.

[652] It is not bad to die, but to die badly.

[653] 1634: "Except now her son Safi Shah, succeeding his royal grandsire Abbas in the Persian dignity and crowned at our coming thence, hath since dissuaded her from

Now, after this digression, give me leave to give you a brief survey of the quality and condition we find Hyrcania at our being there.

Hyrcania

Hyrcania, now under the dominion of the Persian king, hath to the east Margiana, to the south Mount Taurus, to the west Armenia and parts of Media Atropatia, and north the Caspian Sea. Treble it is in length from east to west what it is in breadth from north to south, a country known in several ages by several names, for Mercator names it *Diurgament*, Angiolel[654] *Strava*, and 'tis also called *Coroa*, *Casson*, *Steana* and *Caspis* by other authors, but by the Hebrews it was called *Hadorum*, by the Tartars *Kabonchara* and by Pinetus *Kyrizath*, which last gives some occasion to imagine that it was into this place the Assyrian transplanted those inhabitants of Damascus that are mentioned in 2 Kings 16:9.[655] Josephus also gives the like name, for he terms it *Kyrene* but places it in Media, as in more due place will be remembered. Nevertheless, at this day not part, as some would, but whole Hyrcania is by the Persians named Mazanderan.[656]

By the several days' journey we rode within the kingdom I observed that it is in most places of a good soil through the benevolence of the clime, replenished with grass, fruit, corn, flowers and the like, and hath cattle in great plenty; moreover, for their manner of husbandry, buildings and civility more resembling ours of Europe then any other we had hitherto observed in Asia. And though the soil be good, the earth no doubt is much bettered by those many rivers and rivulets that, springing from Taurus, stream abundantly and de lightfully through the country and empty themselves into the Mare Caspium. Such are Cyrus and Cambyses, which gave two Great Kings their names and near which the *Obareni* and the *Oleni* inhabited, Araxes and *Obsel*, four rivers that deduce their springs near each other in Mount Ararat, Cambyses, which divides Media from Hyrcania, *Mozeran*, *Bundama*, Hardz (issuing, some suppose, out of the Desert of

---

that solitary and unfitting life, and to afford her some joy then, rather then for ever to live without it" (104). Herbert seems to have done some more research and decided that this was not the case.

[654] Giovanni Maria Angiolello (c. 1451–1525) was an Italian scholar who was enslaved by the Turks (1470), learned Turkish, and by 1480 had been appointed Treasurer to Sultan Mehmet II. After the Sultan's death he became a merchant in Persia, where he remained until 1515. He published the *Relazione* (1524), a history of Persia from 1467 down to the accession of Tahmasp I. Parts of this work appear in all editions of Ramusio.

[655] ". . . for the king of Assyria went up against Damascus and took it, and carried the people of it captive to Kir, and slew Rezin [the king of Syria]."

[656] 1638: "The Hyrcan language is understood by every Persian. Their habit resembles the Irish trews; upon their heads they wear pyramidal caps of cloth lined with delicate sheep's wool" (177).

Lop), Aragus (falsely said to drill from the Molossians) and others, which after
a long trickling race, having mellowed the earth, disembogue[657] themselves into
the Caspian.[658] Near the mountains they have sometimes a distempered channel, for after great rains or melting of snow they commonly overflow the lower
grounds, but the best is those land-floods meliorate the earth and are of but very
short continuance. I could neither see nor hear of that which Strabo in his 11 *lib.*
reports concerning some rivers here which fall so violently from the rocks that
men may pass under the water as under an arch without any wetting. Some water-
works indeed there be at Abbasabad, which is the King's prime garden, that by
art have that very resemblance, but in old times it so superabounded with wood
as that the whole was called *Sylva Hyrcana*, and whence in probability it was that
the Scythians termed it *Hercoon*, i.e. a solitary place in their language, which
nevertheless nourished offensive creatures of several kinds as snakes, which we
saw abundance of, but more especially lions, wolves, foxes, wildcats, boars and
tigers, which last a Roman poet mentions with an emphasis, saying "Them with
their dugs Hyrcanian tigers fed."[659] Albeit, since the woods have been destroyed,
towns built and the country inhabited, it is much altered, for tigers we saw none.
But (as a good exchange) plenty of cows, buffalo, horses, camels, sheep, mules,
deer red and fallow, antelopes, hogs, goats and other like beasts, and of birds
store of hens, pheasants, partridges, nightingales, pouts, quail, woodcock, thrush
and other birds; of fish, especially near the Caspian, sturgeon, mullet, mussels,
dogfish, eels, tunny and others; a grain also of small sorts and fruits and roots in
great variety. But that tree called *ochus,* which is said to distil honey, we found
not, but one that had sweet sap or juice, which 'tis likely gave the occasion of that
report, but of oak, elm, ash and most in mulberry-trees there is great plenty.

 In former times *Tambrace*, that was in vain besieged by Seleucus Callinicus,[660]
Telebrota, Saramanne, Adrapsa, Socanda or *Socoman, Asmuria, Tapen*, Carta and
Manzaca were towns of store, but now totally lost unless they be revived in Fara-
habad, Astarabad, Abbas-abad, Ferozkuh, Amol, Chaghapur, Kavand, Bildigh,

---

 [657] Empty into, or flow out into.
 [658] The Aragus or Aghkhay River [*Atrak*] is in north-west Iran bordering modern
Turkemenistan; the Hardz River [*Hydero*] flows past Mt. Damavand near Larijan; the
Molossians lived in Epirus, "a territory that now lies partly in northwestern Greece and
partly in southern Albania" (Grant, *Guide*, 241), hence Herbert's doubts. The Desert of
Lop extends from Korla eastwards to the Tarim River, and is now situated in the Xinjiang
Uighur Autonomous Region of China. It was once a saltwater lake.
 [659] Virgil, *Aeneid* 4. 367.
 [660] Seleucus II Callinicus reigned in Coele-Syria 246–225 B. C. E. He attacked
Parthia, whose leader Arsaces had annexed parts of Hyrcania, in about 228, but "was
hastily recalled to Antioch to settle further internal troubles" (Colledge, *Parthians*, 27).

Baz, *Darabgier,* Shamakhi, *Erea* and Baku,[661] nigh which last is a spring of that rare kind of oil or clammy substance which some call *neste,* but whether of that kind we find mentioned in 2 Maccabees 1:36,[662] which Nehemiah sprinkled the wood with that was laid upon the altar after it was enhausted from the pit wherein the priests had concealed the holy fire at such time as they were led captive into Persia, I cannot say, save that the same naphtha and *nepesi* there mentioned, as well as the quality, have some resemblance. This naphtha is an oily or fat liquid substance in colour not unlike soft white clay, of quality hot and dry, so as it is apt to inflame with the sun's beams or heat that issues from fire, as was mirthfully commented upon by one of Alexander's pages, who, being anointed, with much ado escaped burning.

Many such strange springs have been found; Aristotle mentions one in Carthage; at Ochus in Thessaly another such was, as Pliny reports; near Oxus, as Curtius, and the like near Babylon, for that at Cardavus in Saxony near Brunswick is rather a sort of bitumen, not unlike that is evaporated in the Mare Mortuum. This strange spring puts me in mind of another memorable water we so first at *Chacaporo,*[663] a town about twelve miles west for Farahabad, both of them upon the brink of the Mare Caspium. For eleven months it is sweet and potable, but one month every year so brackish as renders it unfit to drink or to dress meat with. Plutarch [in] *Vita Antonii* relates how that Mark Antony, having marched through Media into Hyrcania, besieged Praaspa,[664] the principal town of that

---

[661] *Tambrace,* called *Talabroce* by Strabo (8.146) and Polybius (Book 9), was, according to Ralegh, "the chief city of Hyrcania" (V, 102); *Saramanne,* which is Ptolemy's name (6. 9. 141), is *Samariane* in Strabo (7.147); *Adrapsa* is an error made by Ptolemy (6. 9.141) for Gadrapsa, a city in Bactriana (see H. L. Jones's note in Strabo, 7.147); *Soconda* is also known as Socana, but does not appear in Ptolemy unless it is *Sinica* (6. 9. 141) and may have been *Abaskun,* a port in the Gorgan (Astarabad) region now submerged in the Caspian Sea; *Asmuria* is *Amarusa* in Ptolemy (6. 9. 141) but otherwise unknown; *Tapen* is called *Royal Tape* by Strabo (7.147) and may be Tak, a city near Darghan in modern Iran (Hopkins, "Index" n.p.n.), formerly in Parthia, not Hyrcania; Carta, identified by Jones only as "a city in Hyrcania" (8.282), is in Strabo (5.251) but not Ptolemy; *Manzaca* is Ptolemy's *Maesoca.* None of these Hyrcanian cities has yet been located by modern scholars. Amol [*Omeal*], is a city on the banks of the Haraz River. It was the principal city of Mazanderan from Sassanian times to the Ilkhans; Herbert provides more details of Amol later. See also Greenway and St. Vincent, *Iran,* 374. Bildigh [*Bildith*] is across the peninsula from Baku towards Derbent; *Chacaporo* is unidentified; *Baezd* is Baz in north-west Iran; *Darabgier* is possibly Darucheh-é Namak; *Bachu* is Baku; *Erea* may be Arad in Fars; *Sumachy* is Shamakhi in the vicinity of Baku, the scene of a conflict between Shah Abbas and the Turks (1607).

[662] "And Neemias called this thing Naphthar, which is as much to say, a cleansing: but many men call it Nephi."

[663] Unidentified.

[664] Praaspa [*Phraata*] was the capital of Media Atropatene.

province, but his battering engines, being surprised by Phraates[665] the Parthian king and wanting victual, Antony was forced to retire, haste to enjoy his Cleopatra adding to his speed, so as after seven and twenty days he passed the Araxes, over which he had built a bridge which was broken by the enemy. In that march he lost 4000 horse and 20,000 foot, most of which died of fluxes and thirst. The reason I make mention of this is in regard the story says he passed a river that to the view appeared very clear, but the soldiers, thinking to assuage their thirst, found it increased by the brackish water, for it gnawed their guts and put them into other distempers.

Now, seeing some take Farahabad for the relics of Praaspa above-named, it is very likely that this salt-stream at Shamakhi was the same which Plutarch takes notice of in that expedition, and that there are springs and rivers of several tastes as well as colours is in no wise to be questioned, for thence it is that some conclude a *spiritus mundi*.[666] Now, concerning colours I have already instanced, and as to taste, the sea, experience teaches, is salt, not by nature but by agitation partly, and partly through the power and efficacy of the sun, which by his heat and beams attracts the small parts that be in the superficies of the saltwater. Philosophy also as well as experience acquaints us that in summer the sea is salter then it is in winter and that the east and south seas are most salt; yea, by common trial it is so observed. Moreover, the seawater is much thicker and stronger to bear, as we find by common experience, then fresh, whereby it comes to pass that ships leak and sink oftener in fresh waters then they do in the ocean. Besides, seeing salt has heat, we may perceive how that saltwater inflames rather then extinguishes fire, and for proof thereof have sundry examples in *lib.* 7 of Macrobius[667] and 10 *Symposium* of Plutarch, the reason being evident, seeing dryness is a quality that makes it a friend unto the fire, for as Aristotle, nature's principal secretary, observes, saltwater has a sort of fatness and oiliness incorporated,

---

[665] Phraates IV (r. c. 38–2 B.C.E.) defeated Antony's army outside Praaspa (36 B.C.E.). The Roman siege-engines did not get there in time, and Antony "was forced to construct great mounds of earth to replace the customary siege-engines" (Colledge, *Parthians*, 44). Phraates then attacked the Roman baggage-train as the other soldiers were occupied in doing this; he slaughtered ten thousand Romans (Herbert's figures are inflated), captured many others and completely destroyed their baggage-train, which contained the siege-engines. For details of Antony's defeat see Colledge, *Parthians*, 45–46.

[666] Literally "the spirit of the world," another name for the quintessence or fifth element.

[667] Aurelius Ambrosius Theodosius Macrobius (fl. 400) was a Roman grammarian and mythographer whose principal work was a commentary on the *Somnium Scipionis*, a lost work of Cicero. This work in turn was based on an incident in Plato's *Republic* where one Er, son of Arminius, returns from the dead and tells his tale about the Underworld. Macrobius was very popular in medieval times, being cited by, amongst others, Chaucer. His work was printed in Florence (1515). His *Saturnalia* has been translated by P. V. Davies (New York: Columbia University Press, 1969).

and albeit water in itself, like the purest oil, naturally is without smell or taste, nevertheless *per accidens* it may have both, according as it doth participate with the quality of the earth through whose veins it floweth, and from thence arises both colour, taste and smell, as we usually observe in such things as derive heat and tincture from sulphur, steel, vitriol, juniper and the like. Now that the fat or oiliness of the seawater inflames I could give many instances, but shall only when was proved in that memorable sea-fight 'twixt Mark Antony and Augustus Caesar at Actium in the Gulf of Lepanto, as recorded by Plutarch and other historians. To return.

The natives for the most part are exceeding courteous to strangers and hospitable, and no less industrious in husbandry. They speak Persian yet have a peculiar dialect of their own which they the less use since they became subject to the Persian, who oftimes would be very merry with them, but we could perceive it was in a degrading way, either occasioned from their imperfect speech (as the Parisian mocks the Norman and Gascon) or simplicity of heart or with the report they meet with of the women's courtesies, which though we saw little reason for, yet Strabo *lib*. 12 writes that "here the Tapiri inhabited of old, who after they have had three or four children commonly lend their wives to other men to breed upon, and to which the women as willingly condescended," a custom now abrogated yet probably not wholly forgotten. For the men, we found them, as I have said, of a very pleasant disposition and delighted with novelties. Of old their ancestors, as the Abbot of St. Albans did with the Norman conqueror, thought to have prevented Alexander's desired entrance, but with the same hand an instrument the Gordian Knot was cut, these Hyrcanians and their ways were mastered.

A Hyrcanian [illustration not shown]

Silkworms.

A great part of the country through which we passed was champagne, and near the town enclosed with quick-set. One time I left the road to ride through a pleasant green field, but many snakes twisted about my horse's legs without further harm then putting us both into an affright, and as it were advising me another time to keep the road. We also passed through great woods, but of all the trees I saw, none which for number as well as use exceeded the mulberry. For thirty miles' riding that tree had the pre-eminence, and larger of that kind I never saw, nor bearing more fruit, albeit 'tis the leaves they most value. The berry, if white, pleased our belly best, the colour our eye, the leaves our observation, for indeed in most villages and cottages we saw sheds filled with laborious people minding their enriching silkworms, an insect whereon Naure hath expressed so much art as it is scarce comprehensible. This worm, as in quality, in diversity of shape also varies from other worms, for her first generation rises from a small round sperm less then mustard-seed, which by laying in the sun or other moderate heat increases to an inch, the first shape it assumes being like palmer-worms,[668] from which resemblance in six months space it twice changes. The male after copulation dies, whom the female soon follows so soon as she had laid her eggs or seed, which you please to call it. Her food is usually the leaves and boughs of mulberry-trees, the white most delighting her, strewed every day fresh over her shed, which must be kept sweet and warm. The worm, being shut up, eats greedily, frequently raising her little head, and being as it were tired, sleeps two days together, during which she casts her skin and then eats with a fresh appetite. Soon after that she four several times casts her coat, and then, having discharged her belly, falls to work, in short space making her lawn both winding-sheet and sepulchre.

The silk happens to be of such colours as are commonly-laid before her, and is usually either white, yellow, green or sand-coloured, but being shut up, such is the transparency of the excrement that the fly is discernible. The exterior part is in colour like pale gold mixed with lemon, the silk rough and hairy; the interior part more hard and of an oval form, the better to inhume the fly, whose task being done, sometimes she dies, other times she breaks forth and then the worm is metamorphosed into a butterfly. Sometimes the silken balls are exposed to the scorching sun, through whose ardour the poor worm is broiled to death, not unlike a miser that voluntarily sacrifices himself to death so it be to contemplate his rich idolatry, but by this expansion the silk, they say, becomes finer then if suffered to break her habitacle. After this the cods are thrown into a cauldron, the water being moderately hot, then with a cane the people stir them about, at once drawing the slimy silk from as many as the instrument can conveniently lay hold upon, and with a wheel draw off the silk raw, which, being dry, is folded. During the winter season the slikworms sleep without eating, so as they seem dead, but in the spring being laid in the sun, revivie again, a perfect type of the resurrection. From the Seres of Regio Serica, part of Scythia towards Industan, this worm first came into Persia not long before Alexander's time, but until the Emperor Justinian's time, which was about the year of Our Lord 530,[669] it was not known in Europe, the first being presented by the Persians unto the Emperor at Byzantium as a rarity. That they afford honey, yield wax, build nests and are a sort of spider Aristotle and Pliny so think, but I think the Persian king finds it most from hence extracting 7600 *batmans* of raw silk yearly.

---

[668] A species of caterpillar which devours fruit-trees and leafy vegetables, so-called because it suddenly appears in great numbers, like pilgrims (palmers) flocking to a shrine.

[669] Justinianus [I] was Byzantine Emperor 527–65. For the silk story (in Procopius), see *ODB* 3: 1896–97.

Farahabad.

Upon Whitsun Monday we bade farewell to Astarabad, Shah Abbas the same
time removing his court to Qazvin. The reason why he went one way and we another was, as I suppose, that we might have the better prospect of his country, for
he went by Ferozkuh, we by Larijan. The first night after we left Astarabad we
lodged in Farahabad, which is five miles from Astarabad.

Farahabad is a town upon the southeast side of the Caspian Sea, probably
taking name from Farah-bagh or Farah-zad; *bagh* signifies "a garden" and *zad*
"a son," who succeeded Ferraz, son to Hormizd that was predecessor to Yazdegerd the Hyrcanian king slain by the Romans about the year of Our Lord 595,
five and twenty years before the era of the Mohammedans took beginning.[670]
Some, how truly I know not, take this for the remains of old Amarusa,[671] but I
rather imagine it the relics of that *Socanda* I find mentioned in Ptolemy. Nevertheless, othersome there be that by writing this city *Phraat-abad* suppose it to be
that Praaspa which Marcus Antonius besieged such time as he invaded Media
to be revenged for the death of Crassus, that rich and powerful Roman general
who with thirty thousand of his men was slain but lately before by Phraates the
Parthian,[672] returning *re infecta* with but half his men, the bridges being broken
by the Parthians that gave him particular passage over the rivers Araxes and
Cyrus. Ulugh Beg calls it *Strabat* and Teixeira *Estrabad*, names borrowed, as I
imagine, from the 6 *lib.* of Pliny, *c.* 16, where 'tis said "*Stauri, gentes sunt circa mare
Caspium.*"[673] The situation of this city is upon a flat, the soil rich and beautified
with gardens full of fruit, watered by a stream of sweet water[674] about forty paces
broad, which, springing from Taurus, the mother of a fruitful womb, after a long
and circling race at this town incorporates with the briny Caspian. The air nevertheless is not so pure here as we could find it was in most other places higher
up, but whether caused from some insalubrious marshes that are there or from
the vapours that usually rise from the sea a little mile thence, I am not able to
determine. Instead of walls it hath a deep moat or graff, willows and other trees

---

[670] Either Herbert's history or chronology needs a little adjustment here. Ferraz
[*Shezyr* or *Shaw-zyr*] could be Vistakhm, who ruled in Khorasan 592–96 and was the uncle of Chosroes II (591–628). Hormisdas or Hormuzd V [*Jazzay-Zeddah*] reigned briefly
in 592. Neither Yazdegerd II (440–57) nor III (634–52) fits here, and neither was killed
by the Romans. Furthermore, the Hegira took place in 622, not 620, as this computation
seems to suggest.

[671] Amarusa was a town in Hyrcania.

[672] Phraates is the wrong Parthian king. M. Licinius Crassus was defeated by the
forces of Orodes II (c. 57–38 B.C.E.) at the Battle of Carrhae (53 B.C.E.), largely due to
the inspired generalship of Suren. Crassus perished in a scuffle after the battle. For details
see Colledge, *Parthians*, 38–43.

[673] That the people around the Caspian Sea are the Stauri.

[674] The Tejna-rud river.

being planted upon the banks, which are broad enough to walk on, so as it gives both shade and ornament. The houses differ from the common form of Persia, for they are not flat above but like ours in England in the roof, and tiled and glazed according to the English custom.

This town has about three thousand families; the streets are broad enough, not regularly-built but rather in an irregular manner. The *mesjed* is not extraordinary, and two bazaars it has, yet neither of them singular. Few houses but have their gardens continuous, which together make a combined beauty though seeming separate. Of most note is the King's house at the north end of the town,[675] from whose balconies we had a large and delightful prospect to the sea as far as Talca or Tazata,[676] as the isle was then called, and some of the gardens extend to the brink of the Mare Caspium. This palace has two large square courts railed about, and the ground by the elaborate gardener was formed into grass-plots and knots of several sorts and replenished with variety of trees and flowers, which makes the place seem exceeding pleasant, and amongst others tulips and roses were there so plentiful that what is said of another is properly applicable to this, "*hic rosas nutrit, nitidosque flores veris amoeni,*"[677] and amongst other trees the spreading chenores, sycamores and chestnuts surround the place with so much beauty, and every part of the house affords so amiable a prospect as makes the eye and smell contend which shall surfeit soonest of variety. The mulberry of both colours at that time presented us with choice fruit no less wholesome then pleasant, so as by way of gratitude give me leave to tell you the Egyptians made that tree the hieroglyphic of wisdom, and upon this account: knowing that frost is its deadly enemy, it seldom or never buds until the cold weather be wholly gone, and then as by instinct it puts forth speedily and as quickly ripens to maturity.

This house of the King's, though it be spacious, yet it is low-built, but the rooms are high enough, arched and of sufficient length, rather resembling galleries then rooms of state. Three of those chambers were more richly-furnished then the rest, for the sides were adorned with looking-glasses, the ceiling of the roof arched and richly-painted and in some part embossed with gold, and the windows were of Muscovian glass, cemented with gold or what resembled it. Glass it was of large panes and very clear, which sort of glass, if that be its proper name,

---

[675] Herbert is describing the additions Shah Abbas had made to the palace. For details, see Monshi, *History*, 2: 1059–61. Foster informs us that this palace, "now a mass of ruins," was the one in which Shah Abbas died (*Herbert*, 320).

[676] Some scholars identify this with Idak Island on the Russian side of the Caspian Sea.

[677] "It grew roses and the luxuriant flowers of the pleasant spring" (Bernard Andreas, *Historia regis Henrici septimi* 35). Andreas (fl. 1500) was a friar from Bordeaux who worked for Henry VII as Prince Arthur's tutor and became a sort of poet laureate. His book was edited by James Gairdner (London: Longman, Brown 1858).

is taken out of a rock called slate in Karelia[678] near to the River Dvina in Russia, and by being soft is easily cut in pieces, sliced into thin flakes and preferred before other glass both for that it is clearer and not so brittle, nor apt to burn as glass or horn. The floors we could not enter with our shoes on; "*accurrant servi solers detriabunt*" in Terence[679] his *Heiauticon* was here observed, but with good reason, seeing they were spread some with velvet-stuff, with down or fine bombazine,[680] others with rich carpets and *calzoons* of bodkin[681] and cloth-of-gold. Howbeit, in winter-time the Padishah sleeps in sheets of costly sables or rich short curled shag of the sheep of Khorasan. In the gallery where the mirrors are not only on the sides but on the arch overhead in story or landscape is pencilled several immodest sports and symbols, such as if Aretine[682] had given the directions, lavoltas[683] which so much offended our eyes with shame that they are in no wise fit to be remembered, nor have I more concerning this save it is the opinion of some that Farahabad was the birthplace of that great physician and philosopher al-Farabi, who, as bin Kassem writes, so much admired Aristotle's book of physic that he read what is entitled *De auditu* no less then forty times over, leaving this world in the year of the Hegira 339 in his great climacteric.[684]

---

[678] Area in Russia and Finland.

[679] Publius Terentius Afer (c. 195/185–159 B. C. E.), Roman comic dramatist. Terence's plays were in print from 1477, and were extremely popular during the Renaissance. They were translated many times, from Nicholas Udall's selections in *Floures for Latine Spekynge* (1533), the well-known version by Richard Bernard (1598; reprinted to 1641) to Herbert's own day and Charles Hoole's translation (1661). The play Herbert refers to here is *Heauton timorumenos*, or *The Self-Tormentor*. The quote reads: "The servants, with great skill, took care lest it become worn."

[680] Bombazine was a fabric made of silk and wool.

[681] Bodkin, or cloth-of-bodkin, was a stiff fabric which required a bodkin (similar to a modern darning-needle) to sew it.

[682] Pietro Aretino (1492–1556) was the eminent Italian poet, playwright, and pornographer. Herbert is referring to his *Sonetti lussoriosi* (1524), which were written to accompany a series of erotic engravings illustrating sexual positions after paintings by Giulio Romano entitled *I modi*, or *The Sixteen Pleasures*. For a Puritan, Herbert seems to know quite a lot about this subject, as he has already mentioned similar paintings of "postures" on the walls of Khwaja Nazar's house in New Julfa. John Wolfe printed the Italian text of Aretino's *Ragionamenti* twice in London (1585, 1597), but there were no translations available to Herbert.

[683] The lavolta was a lively dance which involved the man picking up the woman by a special handle at the front of her dress and turning around. As a man with Puritan leanings, Herbert appears to have disapproved of dancing, although not all Puritans did so.

[684] Al-Farabi died in 951.

The Caspian Sea.

The Caspian Sea is deservedly ranked amongst the wonders of the world, for greatness, taste and colour justly challenging the name of sea, albeit without intercourse with the ocean, and, which is admirable, never overflowing its bounds, although many great and notable rivers, namely Volga, of old called *Rha* and *Edel*, into which Oka runs near Novgorod; Araxes, now Arash; Cyrus, now Kur; Cambyses, now Iori; *Coraxia*, now *Coddors*; Ural, Ridagnus,[685] *Socanda, Mazeras,* Ziarat,[686] Hardz, *Stao,* Atrak, *Ilmens, Syrto,* Jaxartes, Amur Darya, *Dynodore, Jebun, Habyn* and others continually ran into and thereby swell her concave womb so that a wonder it is it overflows not, albeit by its crooked shore it becomes of vast receipt not less then three thousand miles in compass.[687] The shape is usually rather oval then round, the diameter from north to south, that is to say from Astrakhan to Farahabad, accompted six hundred English miles, the other one-third more, so deep that in some places the ground is not felt in four hundred fathoms, where the greatest ships may sail boldly, but towards the shore is so full of straits and shoal water that vessels usually passing seldom draw above eight foot water when they are full-laden, and yet find the way very hazardous.

Map of Caspian Sea [illustration not shown]

By several names 'tis called; by the Arabians, like all other lakes *Bahr el Qazvin*; by the Russians *Chualenska Mor*;[688] *Mare de Baba, Sala, Gunnar* by the Georgians from those three port towns near Derbent; Gungestan, Tabarestan and Khorasan by the neighbouring inhabitants, but by the Romans *Mare Hyrcanum* and by the Persians Darya-yé Khazan and Mazanderan, by which name Hyrcania is now called, albeit Maginus in his adjunct to Ptolemy's maps erroneously places Mazanderan at the south-east side of this sea where indeed Margiana[689] ought to be. Upon the north it has Tartary, on the east Zagatbai[690] or Bactria and Margiana,

---

[685] The Ridagnus River [*Rhodago*], now known as the Nikha, joins with the Ziarat (see below and Curtius 6.4.6).

[686] The Ziarat River [*Ziobetis*], which originates at the foot of the Taurus Mountains, is described in detail by Curtius (6.4.4–7), who is probably the source for Herbert's description below.

[687] The Caspian Sea is 1210 km from north to south, 436 km from east to west. It is not a sea at all, but the largest lake in the world.

[688] The Russian name for the Caspian Sea is actually *Kospiyskoye More*. For a detailed explanation of names for the Caspian Sea, see Mohammed Ajam, "Names of the Caspian Sea," *Iran Chamber Society* (2007), www.iranchamber.com

[689] Margiana or Margush (modern Merv in Turkmenistan) was successively a sub-satrapy of Bactria and then a Seleucid eparchy (Olmstead, *History*, 48 and n. 74).

[690] Herbert refers here to Bactra-Zariaspa (modern Balkh), which was the capital of Bactria under the Achaemenids.

to the south Hyrcania and to the west parts of Media and Armenia the Great.[691]
Surrounded 'tis with lofty hills, save in some part of Mazanderan towards the
shore, a sea that has no commerce with any other, unless it be with the Euxine,
which then must be imperceptible and underground, and if so, 'tis wonderful, the
distance considered, being little less then three hundred of our miles and the way
very uneven and mountainous that interposes. Now, albeit there is not the least
sense or discovery of any in-draught in this sea towards the Armenian shore that
expresses such a subterranean *meatus*[692] in its course towards the Euxine nor in
the Euxine of its reception, yet undoubtedly some secret vent or other it needs
must have, otherwise this pond, according to reason, would overflow its banks by
that great surcharge or pouring-in of water which it continually entertains from
Volga, Oxus and Araxes, three mighty rivers, and those others I lately mentioned. Besides, that it has some secret and unknown intercourse with the ocean
may be presumed by its producing those kinds of fish which delight only to swim
in the sea and like salt-waters, namely porpoise, conger, gudgeon, thornback,
turbot, cuckrel, skates, soles, oysters, lobsters, crabs, sturgeons (of whose roe
they make caviar, which we had plenty of) and mullet, the roe of which makes
botargo,[693] with many others that delight not in floods or like fresh waters. And
that it rather mixes with the Euxine then the Gulf of Persia may be imagined,
for that besides Mount Taurus, Hyrcania, Parthia and Persia are interposing in a
distance quadruple to that it has from the Euxine, which intercourse nevertheless
was hinted at by that great geographer Strabo, speaking of this sea: "*sinum oceani
ad Boream esse tradunt*," and also by that great schoolman St. Basil in his *Homilies
4 Hexaemeronis*, "*mare unum est, ut illi dicunt qui orbem perlustraverant, etiamque
cum Hyrcanum et Caspium mare per se perforata sunt; haec tamen duo maria in pon-
tum Euxinum sese insinuant*,"[694] which is possible to him with whom nothing is

---

[691] Armenia the Great or Armenia Major referred in classical times to that part of
Armenia comprising "the major plateau east of the Euphrates" (Grant, *Guide*, 65), which
became an independent kingdom in 190 B.C.E. under Artashes. Sophene, east of the
Euphrates, was the other part and remained independent until the reign of Tigranes II (c.
94–56 B.C.E.). Lesser Armenia was beyond the Euphrates, and was annexed by Mithridates Eupator of Pontus (Der Nersessian, *Armenians*, 26).

[692] Path or course.

[693] Cured fish-roe (Italian or Spanish). Herbert spells it *potalgo*.

[694] St. Basil the Great (c. 329/33–379) was a lawyer, theologian and churchman
from Cappadocia, brother to St. Gregory of Nyssa and one of the Holy Hierarchs of the
Eastern Orthodox Church. The work to which Herbert refers is his collection of Lenten
sermons on the *Hexaemeron*, the theory that the world was created in six days, which Basil wrote in about 370. The whole passage translates: "The sea is one, as they say who have
travelled throughout the world, even if the Hyrcanian and Caspian seas have passages
leading out of them; these two seas pass into the Black Sea" (*Homilies* 4.5).There is a modern translation by Blomfield Jackson in *A Select Library of Nicene and Post-Nicene Fathers*

impossible. But in making *Hyrcanum et Caspium duo maria*[695] I understand not, being but one and the same sea under two several denominations, and therefore believe it is misprinted.

Now that I may *parva commovere magnis*,[696] sundry examples we have of subterranean channels for water, as Zioberus, one of those rivers that empty themselves into this sea, over which Alexander marched a flying body of horse when from Persepolis he pursued Bessus,[697] resting some time at Zadracarta, at that time the metropolis of this country. Zioberis springs fromTaurus but in its midcourse to the sea falls into a chasm and after thirty miles invisible running underground rises again near Ridagnus, another stream with which it mixes and then in an expiated channel they flow togther in one into the Caspian. The conqueror, at the request of his master Aristotle, made trial thereof by forcing in two oxen that confirmed the report. The like is reported of those two great rivers Niger and Nile, and the same of Tigris in Mesopotamia, Lycus in Asia,[698] Erasinus in Argolica near Peleponessus,[699] Anas that separates Boetica from Portugal and Tanais the Scythic river that divides Europe from Asia, for after long courses underground these re-appear in their open channels. But in this *meatus* of the Caspian we neither discover fall nor rise, so as amongst other hidden secrets of nature, though the knowledge thereof be incommunicated unto men, it is nevertheless well known to the God of Nature. Howbeit, so desirous have some Princes been of old to make an open intercourse between these two seas that notwithstanding the vast distance of place and surging grounds that interpose, they have attempted to cut such a sluice as should give passage to vessels from each other. Seleucus Nicator is one, who with incredible toil and charge undertook to make them communicable, but before he could finish this great design he was unhappily slain by Ptolemy Ceraunus[700] the Egyptian king, as Erasmus noteth. Some Persian monarchs also, whose immense power made them think nothing

---

of the Christian Church, 2nd Series, Volume 8. It may be found complete at the following website: www.newadvent.org/fathers.

[695] The Hyrcanian and the Caspian two seas.

[696] Compare small things with great.

[697] Bessus (d. 328 B.C.E.) was one of the generals of Darius III and satrap of Bactria. He commanded the Bactrian cavalry at Gaugamela, and after Darius's death (which he engineered) proclaimed himself Artaxerxes IV (331–328 B.C.E.) in opposition to Alexander. See Curtius, particularly Books 6–7.

[698] The Lycus river is a tributary of the Maeander, flowing near the city of Tripolis in Phrygia.

[699] The Erasinus river is located near Lake Stymphalos in Arcadia.

[700] Ptolemy Ceraunus (c. 318–279 B.C.E.) was not an Egyptian king but the son of Ptolemy I; he was passed over as heir to the Egyptian throne and went into exile, first to the court of King Lysimachus of Thrace and Macedon and then to that of Seleucus I, whom he murdered in 281. He reigned as King of Macedonia 281–279. When the Gauls invaded Macedonia he was captured and executed.

impossible, attempted the like, until by fruitless endeavours they were made to understand their vanity. And yet this has not that property other seas commonly have, that is to say *"fluxus et refluxus maris,"*[701] for so to satisfy my curiosity I well remember that I stood some hours one day upon the strand purposely to observe its motion; now albeit there was little or no wind at all stirring at that time, yet the water was somewhat turbulent and rolling, especially near the shore, as we see it is usual during calm weather in our narrow seas, and in its waves resembled an ebb and flood, but that it was really such I dare not be positive, so as what to conclude I know not, seeing Scaliger[702] that great scholar in his *Exerc. [ad]versus Cardanum* has this note: *"in ----- oceani--------nullus est-----,"* which probably may be the condition of this Mare Caspium.

Astrakhan.

In eight days they usually cross from Astrakhan to Derbent or Farrahabad, albeit by reason of adverse winds Sir Anthony Sherley, a noble traveller upon that account, was eighty. These vessels resemble our old curragh[703] recorded by Caesar and Lucan, for they are sewed with hemp and cord, and comparatively with ours have but little iron. We also saw many canoes or troughs of one large piece of oak, of which Hyrcania has store, so large as could receive six men and launch a pretty way without danger. At Farahabad and ports thereabouts were other small vessels and fisherboats, most of which were flat-bottomed, such excepted as trade to Derbent, Sala and Hachu along the shore, for compass they have none. The greatest exceed not thirty ton and in such they usually pass to Astrakhan, or, as some call it, *Citra-Khan*, which is forty-seven degrees north latitude, an isle which is twelve miles long and three broad. The town bearing the same name is seated upon a rising ground, the houses not many nor well-built, yet sufficiently-peopled, for albeit the soil be barren and the air bad, yet such is the trade it has in furs as sables, wolverine, luserus, ermine, miniver,[704] fox, beaver, otter, squirrel and the like from Russia and those northern parts, as also caviar, botargo[705] and that plenty of salt they extract from salt-water that is much resorted to by merchants of several countries, isomuch as it brings a considerable yearly custome to

---

[701] Ebb and flow of the sea.

[702] Julius Caesar Scaliger (1484–1558) was an eminent Italian humanist, doctor, and philosopher who spent much of his career in France. The work to which Herbert refers here is *Exotericarum exercitationum de subtilitate ad H. Cardanum* (1537), in which Scaliger attacked the work of Hieronymo Cardano in "the most savage book review in the bitter annals of literary invective," as Anthony Grafton noted. For details, see Grafton, *Cardano's Cosmos* (Cambridge, MA: Harvard University Press, 2000), 4ff.

[703] A small oval-shaped boat or coracle.

[704] Pure white fur from stoats; it was often used to line the robes of English peers.

[705] Tuna or mullet roe, sometimes known as "poor man's caviar."

the Great Duke of Muscovy,[706] who since he took it from the Negay Tartar,[707] which was *Anno Dom.* 1494 hath erected a castle of good defence, as appeared when Johannes Basilius the Emperor about six years after gave Selim the Great Turk two several defeats at such time as he brought his army thither in defence of the Tartar, and the like not long after by his son Basiliades, since when it has continued peaceably under Russian subjection.[708]

Six leagues from that town runs the river we call Volga, others *Wolga*, which springs out of a hill one hundred miles from Yaroslavl[709] in Russia, where the channel is wellnigh as broad as the Thames at London, but after near two thousand English miles' course enlarging near this place, in several ostiums it empties itself upon the north side into the Mare Caspium. This great river, were the depth answerable to breadth, would be much more frequented by those of Europe then it is, in regard it gives a nearer and easier passage into Persia and India then we have by way of Aleppo or Trebizond, and much sooner then by compassing Africa. For ships setting out from London in April with a fair wind they usually arrive in two months at St. Nicholas,[710] where the Pole is elevated sixty-six degrees thirty minutes, whence by water we go to Vologda[711] in seven days and from thence by horse or sled to Yaroslavl, which is a town upon Volga, and from Yaroslavl by boat to Astrakhan is under one month's sail, the whole from St. Nicholas to Astrakhan, most of the way by water, being commonly reckoned 2600 miles English, which is the utmost. From Astrakhan by boat to Derbent, which is upon the western shore, the passage is not above three days' sail, so the wind be fair, but the water by reason of shoals is dangerous in sundry places.

---

[706] Ivan III "the Great," who ruled 1462–1505.

[707] Anthony Jenkinson wrote of "a land of the Tartars called Turkemen is called the country of the Magnat or Nagay," and stated that they "were all destroyed in the yeere 1558 . . . through civill warres, famine, pestilence . . . " (Hakluyt, *Voyages*, 2: 204).

[708] Vasily III "the Blind" [*Basiliades*] r. 1505–1533. The "Johannes" suggests a conflation with his predecessor Ivan III, the "Great Duke of Mucovy" who defeated the Tartars. Since Selim I succeeded in 1512, Herbert must mean Vasily III. If *Basiliades* means "son of Basil," Herbert might mean Ivan IV "the Terrible" (r. 1533–1584), but the chronology would not fit.

[709] Yaroslavl is 250 km north-west of Moscow. It was founded in 1010, and by the seventeenth century was the second-largest city in Russia.

[710] St. Nicholas later developed into the city of Archangelsk on the White Sea; when Anthony Jenkinson landed there in 1557 he called it "the roade of St. Nicholas" (Foster, *England's Quest*, 17).

[711] Vologda is a Russian city whose name means "Pure One." It was founded in 1147. The Russia Company had a station there which had existed since the time of Jenkinson's journey.

Derbent.

Derbent[712] is a port town upon the Caspian shore of great antiquity, being supposed that the foundation thereof was laid by Alexander the Great, who also erected that great and strong castle adjoining it which is called Kastov, from whence he likewise drew a running trench as far as Tiflis,[713] the greatest part of which was countermured with a wall of stone through which was the only passage from Mingrelia and those parts into Media and Hyrcania, and usually called *Caucasiae vel Iberiae portae*,[714] which, though made by art, is nevertheless by Pliny termed "*ingens opus Naturae*," so as thence may be gathered, it was no less defensive in its natural situation. That historian also gives us the dimension, "*ibi transitus patet duntaxat 300 passus*,"[715] and was worthily reckoned among the wonders of Asia. Besides that, from the town unto the sea, which is more then a mile, two walls are raised which be eight foot thick and thirty foot high, the distance betwixt the walls being about eight hundred foot or eightscore paces. Moreover, the town itself for trade is not inferior to any other upon that sea, most of the noted places thereabouts, as also from Trebizond and other ports upon the Euxine frequently repairing thither for commerce, which enriches the town and makes it the more populous. Besides, as it is a garrison 'tis made more defensive by regular fortifications which have been occasionally added to the old wall, that of itself is both large and strong altogether, of that account as by a good reporter it is called "*urbs totius Orientis munitissima*."[716]

Derbent, which by transposition is *Ben-dar*, i.e. "the port town," is situate in that part of Armenia which is now called *Ziaria* and *Myral*, but Albania of old, and in some writers known by other names, as *Marcosa* and *Demir-capi*, i.e. "Iron Gates." From Shamakhi 'tis removed a hundred and twenty miles, and from Bildigh a hundred and eighty; the North Pole is there raised one and forty degrees and fifteen minutes, a place of that account as for many years it had been a bone of division betwixt the Turk and Persian, for it is indeed the key that gives entrance into Mazandaran, Gilan, Sirvan[717] and other considerable provinces insomuch as it has made that part the stage of war and by the various successes it

---

[712] The Persian name is Darband, Bab al-Abvab in Arabic.

[713] Tiflis or Tblisi [*Teflys*] is now the capital of Georgia. Situated on the Kur River, which is known in Georgian as the Mtkrani, it was founded in the fifth century by Vakhtang I of Kartli (r. 452–502), who incidentally led the movement to liberate his country from Persian rule.

[714] The Caucasian or Iberian Gates.

[715] A huge work of Nature . . . having passed across at that place stretching 300 paces, as far as one could guess.

[716] The most-fortified city in all the Orient.

[717] Gilan [*Gheylam*] is a "largely rural" province (Greenway and St. Vincent, *Iran*, 362) west of Mazandaram; Sirvan [*Shervan*] is no longer the name of a Persian province. It had been an indpendent kingdom until Shah Ismail I conquered it in 1509–1510; direct

endured has borne no small share in either's misfortune. More especially, in the year of Our Lord 1586, *Heg.* 948, at such time as Hamza Mirza with smoke and flame unkennelled Osman Pasha[718] with his varlets, the Persian Prince making the inhabitants then feel the temper of his sword and the houses the fire of his revenge, to this day showing the signs of his displeasure.

'Twixt this city and Derbent is that noted emporium[719] some call Arrash,[720] and not improperly, seeing it is watered by a stream flowing from the swift River Araxes, but according to others *Erec* and by othersome *Serce*, from which and from that abundance of raw silk which is here vended the country thereabouts is by some mistaken for the *Syrica regio*, albeit the truth is silk is extraordinarily plentiful here, and upon camels in large quantities carried to Kashan,[721] where the manufacture of carpeting and several sorts of silk-stuffs are in perfection, not a little to the town's advantage. At this place also is store of cotton-wool and galls, which merchants value, but of pistachios, pomegranates, grapes, melons, oranges and like fruits which travellers esteem of here in abundance. From hence to Baku, a noted town upon the Caspian shore, are about eighteen English miles, and thence to Bildigh fourteen more; the country is for the most part level and fruitful by being thoroughly-watered by both Araxes and Cyrus. Returning to Farahabad.

Zadracarta.

We travelled along the seaside and came the first night to Zadracarta, which is about twelve English miles west from Farahabad. The way we rode was close by the shore; this town lies open to the sea, which beats oft so outrageously against her banks that the inhabitants are oft put to charge in maintaining them. Here we crossed over a fresh water that was about a stone's cast over; one month in the year 'tis salt, as the inhabitants told us, but not the reason of it. This is that salt

---

rule was imposed in 1588 by Tahmasp I. In 1820 it was "finally incorporated into Russian territory" (Savory, in Monshi, *History*, 1: 131 n.121).

[718] Osman Pasha Ozdemiroglu (1526–1585) invaded north-west Persia and captured Tabriz (1585). Prince Hamza was sent "at the head of inferior forces" (Boyle, *History*, 261) against him, and failed to recapture the city, even though he managed to defeat the Turks in several skirmishes (see Monshi, *History*, 1: 444–46). His colleague Farhad Pasha continued the war against the Persians, defeating them at Baghdad (1587) and overrunning most of Lorestan and Khuzestan.

[719] Trade centre.

[720] Arrash, also known as Ashraf or Eres, was an important silk-trading city on the left bank of the Araxes. "No trace of the city of Eres now appears on the map," notes Le Strange (*Juan de Persia*, 325, n. 4). A royal residence was built there by Abbas I in 1613 (Stodart, *Journal*, 48 n.4).

[721] Kashan is in Isfahan Province, "renowned over the centuries for its ceramic tiles, pottery, textiles, carpets and silk" (Greenway and St. Vincent, *Iran*, 206). Shah Abbas loved it so much he wanted to be buried there. Herbert describes it in detail later.

stream I lately mentioned in the march Marcus Antonius made from Praaspa. Next night we rode to Barfrush,[722] a large town, pretty well-built and no less well-peopled, but the sea does not as much advantage them as the land, by reason of that plenty of silkworms they nourish, and indeed the place appeared to us the pleasanter by reason of that plenty of wood and water it had, which was as good as plentiful. Here they would drink no wine; the law prohibits it, but the ground of that law we could not learn, though we did suppose it was from that ridiculous tradition of the miscarriage of Harut and Marut, the two debauched angels.[723] From Zadracarta this place was twelve long miles; the inhabitants, we could perceive, delighted much in archery, an exercise these countries have even from the infancy of time been not a little famous for, and which gave the best of Latin poets the occasion to celebrate their neighbours of Ithyra[724] in the 2 of his *Georgics*: "The yew into Ithyrian bows is forc'd to bow . . ."[725]

Amol.

The next town of note we came to was Amol, which some take for *Zarama*, others for that Zadracarta[726] where Alexander refreshed his army in that pursuit he made after Bessus that infamous Bactrian, though others there bethink it the remains of that Nabatea where the Oracle of Dreams was famoused.[727] Howbeit, built it is under the north side of the imperious mountain Tauris, and of such grandeur that not less then three thousand families there inhabit. They were then a mixture of several nations: Armenians, Scythians, Persians, Jews, Kurds, Banians, Indians and Muscovians, who albeit they make a Babel of several languages yet live harmoniously, and, which is no less remarkable, being tolerated their own forms, for in the matter of conscience they question none where there

---

[722] Barfrush, also known as Babol, "once a busy and pleasant river-port with its habour at Babolsar (likely what Herbert means by *Barfrushdea*, the name he gives, Ed.). Nowadays it's a sprawling, drab commercial centre" (Greenway and St. Vincent, *Iran*, 375). It is 30 km east of Amol and 24 km from the Caspian Sea. Abbas I built a palace there.

[723] Harut and Marut were the two angels who were so compassionate about humans that they were sent to experience human life, which included temptation. They both succumbed, and when it came to their punishment God asked them whether they would prefer it now or in the hereafter; they chose to endure now, and "were suspended by the feet at Babel in a rocky pit, where they are great teachers of magic" (Hughes, *Dictionary*, 168). Herbert is probably deriving his story from equating "Babol" with "Babel." The full story is in the Quran, Sura 2:96.

[724] A city in Parthia.

[725] ". . . of yew trees it's the way Parthian [*Ituraeos*] bows can be made from their bent branches" (Virgil, *Georgics* 2. 448).

[726] The chief city in Hyrcania; however, its exact location is in dispute.

[727] Nabataea is an area now in southern Jordan where Petra is located.

is no breach of peace. They observe wellnigh several Sabbaths successively each after other, the Banians having Thursday for their sabbath, Friday the Persians, Saturday the Jews, Sunday the Armenians, Monday the Peguans,[728] Tuesday the Gabrs and Kurds or fire-adorers who are indeed the ancient Parthians, so that if any of the Scythians beyond Bokhara were there they would complete the week in that variety. But in this what is best worthy our observation, is that in the distribution of days the seventh day upon which God rested in contemplation of his six days' labour has worthily the pre-eminence over all the rest of the weekdays in which the structure of the universe was created, for the excellency of that day we may perceive by this is morally-acknowledged by most nations whether civil or barbarous.

To proceed. The town is built in a large level, but withal a very pleasant and fruitful soil, happy in her present prosperity and former greatness, her visible ruins making good the report that once it was this country's metropolis.[729] Nor are her buildings of the meaner sort or the castle unworthy notice, seeing it gives place to none I saw in all that province for beauty or strength, being fortified by a deep moat or trench it has that is full of water and compasses the castle, so as the only entrance is by a bridge which they draw and let down at pleasure, serving as a place of good defence to secure themselves against the rhodomontades of the neighbouring Taurisians and other mountaineers, and few houses but have their gardens. Yet of best note is the cathedral or *jama masjed*, in which, as we were told, are entombed four hundred forty-four Princes and prophets, whose sepulchres, though they be not so magnificent as that which with 1000 talents Alexander raised for his friend Hephaestion near this place, yet such they are as raise veneration amongst the people if not admiration with passengers, especially that of Mir *Agowmadeen*[730] to which they chiefly offer the mysteries of their religion.

---

[728] The Peguans were the inhabitants of the old Kingdom of Pegu, also known as the Mon kingdom of Hamsavati, of which Pegu was the capital, in the Irawaddy Delta, Burma, known today as Bago. Accounts by people such as Varthema, Conti, and Vasco da Gama speak of them as great traders; they were also mentioned in Ramusio, all authorities used by Herbert (see also *HJ* 693). Camoens (*Lusiads* 10. 122) mentions "the throne of Pegu / Once peopled by monsters" (221). For details of Peguan history the reader may be referred to Sir Arthur Phayre, *History of Burma* (London: Routledge, 1883), Chapter III. Herbert has more to say about Pegu in Part VI.

[729] Amol, on the Haraz River, was the capital of Tabarestan in succession to Sari from the ninth century until Mongol times. The mountain is actually Mt. Damavand. "Sadly," write Greenway and St. Vincent, "the town is no longer of any great beauty" (*Iran*, 375), and Foster described it earlier as "much decayed" (*Herbert*, 321). It is a very ancient town, having been inhabited before the arrival of the Aryans.

[730] Herbert is probably referring to the Mashhad-é Mir Bozorg, a tomb built during Abbas I's time to rehouse the remains of Mir Qavvam ed-din Bozorg, a holy martyr whom Foster states was "a saintly monarch of Mazanderan in the fourteenth century" (*Herbert*, 321). Greenway and St. Vincent mention that the "tomb box" dates from 1623;

When I entered I found about a score of ancient grave Arabians or Zophilars[731] sitting cross-legged in a circle near the Prince's dormitory with each an Arabic book laid before, out of which both modestly and musically they performed their exercises. This, as I supposed, was the *Parentalia vel sacra funesta in honorem mortuorum.*[732] After the Eastern mode they wagged their bodies, bowing their heads and battologising[733] the names "Allaho akbar" and "Mohammed"[734] very often, wherein they were so seriously composed that albeit I entered unexpectedly amongst them and in my own country habit (which gave most safety in travel and elsewhere was sufficiently admired), nevertheless they continued their service without disturbance or deviation, yet was no sooner ended but that they arose, very civilly bade me welcome, and showed me withal what antiquities the place afforded and as they thought might be acceptable to a stranger.

Thence passing to the riverside, over which upon a bridge of stone we rode the night before, to refresh myself under some poplars, for as says a poet of another like place, this had "Beds of grass and walks in shady woods, / And meadows ever green with crystal floods," seven or eight more beautiful then bashful damsels, like so many nymphs, sprang out of the water as, I suppose, to admire my habit, but I, no less admiring their confidence, quickly left them, having this in thought, *"quod non vetat lex, hoc vetat fieri pudor,"*[735] for the truth is I took them for *amorosas* and violators of the bounds of modesty until from better satisfaction I was made to believe it was simplicity and the opportunity they took to see a stranger, for when the sun mounts to his meridian the men commonly go to sleep and the women then have the benefit of the river, where they use to swim and probably cool their heat, in both kinds, 'tis feared, too much there abounding. The habit of these Dorids[736] was a fine *chudder*[737] or lawn embroidered at the neck, wrist and skirt with a border of several-coloured silks and threads of gold, but in public they go veiled according to the common mode with a long sheet which from top to toe covers them.

---

the building has "a huge dome and brick construction" (*Iran* 374). There are also tombs there dating from the fifteenth to the eighteenth centuries.

[731] Sufis. From *Sufi-lar* (Foster, *Herbert* 321).

[732] The *Parentalia* were [Roman] rites performed for parents or ancestors; the quote thus reads "ancestral rites or funeral rites for the dead." The rites were stretched out over twelve days in February.

[733] Repeating unnecessarily.

[734] *Allaho akbar* means "God is great."

[735] "When the law does not forbid it, let modesty do so" (Seneca, *Troades* 334). Herbert thought the women might be courtesans (*amorosas*).

[736] Literally sea-nymphs, the daughters of Doris, who was mother of fifty of them.

[737] "The ample sheet commonly worn as a mantle by women . . ." (*HJ* 217). The modern word *chador* is the Persian cognate. Herbert uses the version of the word from India.

The Taurus Mountains.

From Amol we travelled to Lahijan[738] or *jun* (as some pronounce it), being probably that *Jonaca* I find mentioned in Ptolemy. This place is from Amol thirty miles, and here the kingdom of Hyrcania is terminated by Mount Taurus,[739] a mountain reputed the greatest in the world both for length and heighth, for in one continued ledge of hills it makes way from the lesser Asia unto the furthest part of East India, not less then 3000 miles, and for proof of its greatness I vouch Aristotle, who affirms that *"Taurus mons omnium est maximus,"*[740] and Maginus, that *"Asiae totius longe maximus, mons Taurus est,"*[741] and Dionysius of Alexandria, that *"totius orbis terrarum maximus est Taurus. Sic dictus, quod instar Tauri, elato capito incedit . . .,"* for which reason, saith Eustathius,[742] *"veteres omnia grandia et robusta, Tauros vocavere,"*[743] so that upon the whole I may fitly apply what Lucan hath done to one much inferior, the Apennine, "Then which no earthly part more high doth rise, / Or whose approach comes nearer to the skies" [*Civil War* 2. 396-398] so high as the labour we endured was very great in the ascending. For albeit our travel in and over the mountain was sometimes through narrow inhospitable straits, otherwhiles it was over extraordinary hills, such hills as after two days winding and painful climbing (for I may so call it, seeing that oftimes we durst not ride), we got so high that we could clearly see the clouds hanging a great way below us and obscuring the earth, and by the sensible alterations of the air might well perceive we were mounted a good way up into the middle region, so different was it from the weather we found below and to our sad remembrance that rationally could not otherwise be expected, ascending from a hot and descending into a hotter country, for a gentleman of our company and of our country died soon after, and myself, not minding to alter my thin habit, by the like cold I took upon the mountain and in our descent into a very hot soil fell into so violent a dysentery as in eleven days gave me a thousand stools, most of blood. But

---

[738] Usually spelled Lahijun, it is now "a fairly unexciting town" (Greenway and St. Vincent, *Iran*, 370) with few tourist sights either now or in Herbert's time, as he does not describe any. If readers are curious, there is the Masjed-é Chahar Oleya, the "Mosque of the Four Guardians" which has some thirteenth-century tombs, as Greenway at St. Vincent mention (*Iran*, 369). It is actually about a hundred miles from Amol, not thirty.

[739] Actually, they were now crossing the Elburz Mountains, which Herbert describes later and calls *Albors*.

[740] Taurus is the largest of all the mountains.

[741] Throughout the length of Asia, mount Taurus is the largest.

[742] Eustathius of Thessalonica (c. 1110–1198) was a Professor of Rhetoric who held the posts of Bishop of Myra and then Archbishop of Thessalonica. He had an encyclopaedic knowledge of Greek literature, and besides writing the usual homilies and epistles wrote extensive commentaries on ancient poets, being especially respected for those on Homer.

[743] The ancients used to call all great and strong things Tauruses.

whether it had any influence upon those honoured persons Sir Dodmore Cotton
and Sir Robert Sherley I cannot judge, albeit they both were in good health when
we passed those hills and left this world for a better within a month after. Plutarch writes concerning Lucullus that pursuing Tigranes the Armenian king he
had like experience of the air here, differing so much from the air of the country
more remote as put the army into a distemper, but more especially this gives me
occasion to call to mind what Acosta the Spaniard[744] reports concerning those
high Peruvian mountains called *Peria-Cacae*,[745] which in passing over put him
into a distemper he could not better resemble then to a sea-sickness, vomiting so
much that he thought he should have died, caused through the subtlety of the air
and the sublimity of those hills, which he says surpass the Alps and the Pyrenees
mountains no less then lofty towers do ordinary cottages.

Now, the ascending this mountain Taurus was not more troublesome, I
thought, then the descending, for in some places we had the path so uneven and
so unskilfully-cut that we were in danger of tumbling down a deep and dreadful
precipice, at the bottom of which we could hear what we could not see, a hollow
murmuring water. But one part of the mountain was a more frightful passage
then the rest, agreeable to that in Ovid, *"per compendia montis precipita via,"*[746]
this for the space of three miles being cut or forced through the side of a perpendicular hill, the top and bottom of which was undiscernible, the widest part
not being above a yard, insomuch as if two horsemen should chance to meet, I
saw not how they could safely pass by one another unless they made like shift
the two goats mentioned in Pliny did, who accidentally meeting in such a place
had no way to preserve themselves but by the couching of the one whiles the
other passed over. That passage at Penmynmawr[747] 'twixt Aberconwy and Beau-
maris in little resembles this, but for danger is not comparable; a very wretched
pass, and good cause have I to remember it, for whiles I was sometimes through
a needless curiosity looking up, wondering at the great heighth above and anon
darting my sight down, no less marvelling at the depth below unawares, a rock
that jutted ill-favouredly out of order unexpectedly struck me such a blow that I
was somewhat astonied and happily delivered from a fall into that abyss, a rock,
I may say, that demands an uncivil tribute of heedless passengers!

---

[744] José de Acosta (1539-c. 1600) was a Jesuit and Professor of Philosophy at the
University of Ocaña, travelling to South America after being appointed Principal of Peru
(1571). On his return to Spain he became Superior of Valladolid, and wrote the *Historia
naturas y moras de las Incas* (1591), which was translated by Edward Grimston as *Of the
ancient superstitions of the Mexicans and Indians of America* (1604).

[745] The Andes Mountains.

[746] "The way ahead was a mountain shortcut" (Ovid, *Metamorphoses* 3. 234–235).

[747] Modern-day Penmaenmawr in Conwy County, Wales. Herbert is referring to
Bwlch Sychnant or the Sychnant Pass, which links Conwy to Penmaenmawr and is today
a popular tourist spot.

Howbeit, out of that formidable path of death we got at length to the top of that imperious mountain, which by its evenness for full fifty miles (such was its breadth from Amol to Damavend) and incomparable prospect is afforded made some amends for the danger we had lately passed, for from thence we raised our prospects so well as the interposing mists would suffer, not only over the breadth of Hyrcania but far into the Caspian Sea as we apprehended (for certain we could not be, seeing it was above a hundred miles distant) so as the sky and it were but one horizon, and save that it was a delight to have an uninterrupted object, little other use could we make of whatever we saw at that distance, our sight was so imperfect and the object so indistiguishable. But without doubt, from hence, for Taurus and Caucasus differ not, that ancient astronomer Prometheus, brother to Atlas, first observed and instructed the Assyrians in the motion of the firmament, the achronical rising and setting of the stars and bodies celestial, and found out the causes of meteors, eclipses and other occult causes and curiosities in nature, and whence it was that the fabulous Greeks report that by Mercury he was chained to a rock and his heart continually gnawed by a vulture at the command of Jupiter, the penalty being inflicted for his felonious stealing celestial fire from Apollo's chariot-wheels to enliven his inanimate statues, albeit Pallas was accessory, by whose persuasion Hercules shot the vulture at the marriage of Thetis.[748] Howbeit, Geraldus[749] finds out a contrary mythology, defining him only for a melancholy person; being overcharged with anxiety, griping care gnawed his heart as if it were a vulture.

Tartary.

Now from this highest terrace of the world look we towards the north-east and fix our eyes upon that part of Tartary which this mountain visits where it salutes Imaus.[750] Tartaria is so large a country as it contains not only a third part of the continent of the greater Asia but extends itself a great way into the most eastern part of Europe, comprehended in these three, *Sarmatia Asiatica*,[751] *Scythia* and *Cathaya*, which some divide into five, *viz.* 1. *Tartaria Antiqua*; 2. *Zacathai intra Imaum*; 3. *Cathai extra Imaum*; 4. *Deserta* or *Sarmatia Asiatica*; 5. *Minor Tartaria*, which includes the *Praecopense* with those that live 'twixt Tanais

---

[748] Thetis married the mortal Peleus and became the mother of Achilles.

[749] Lelio Gregorio Giraldi or Geraldi (1489–1552), a scholar from Ferrara, was a mythographer and writer on poetry. He was also the Apostolic Prothonotary to three popes, but never occupied an academic position. His most famous work of mythography is *De deis gentium* (1548), to which Herbert likely alludes here. There is a modern facsimile of this work (New York: Garland, 1976). I am indebted to the editor at MRTS for supplying this reference to "Geraldus," which I mistakenly attributed to Giraldus Cambrensis!

[750] Imaus or Emaus is a name for the Himalayas.

[751] Sarmatia is the southern part of Russia.

and Borysthenes.[752] The name, as some apprehend it, is from the Hebrew and signifieth "a remnant" or "scattered generations;" othersome derive it from the River Tartar which runs through those provinces they call Mongolia, we Gog and Magog, altogether populated by vagrants or such as are without certain habitations, their wealth solely consisting in their cattle, who go to and fro they know not whither, the Pole Star or the two Bears being their directors. Polygamy they allow; in marriages refrain only their mothers and sisters. A fierce, perfidious and crafty people they are, by continual practice made expert in riding, darting, and no less-exercised in footmanship, have little or no civility save in Zagathai,[753] where they associate in townships and are taught it by the commerce they have with their civilised neighbours. Bread they eat very seldom, for mare's milk, flesh half-boiled, sow's milk and herbs are their greatest dainties. About the Year of Our Lord 1200 they first embraced Mohammed; nevertheless many Jews are commorant among them, so as both sects now use circumcision. Amongst them are some hordes that profess Christ, albeit infected with the far-spread heresy of Nestorius, who being once the Constantinopolitan Patriarch, fell into that foul error that in Christ were two persons as well as two natures, a tenet because opposed by the Emperor Heraclius was so forcibly imposed by Chosroes the apostate upon the Christians within his dominions that it was submitted to by many and like a gangrene hath since spread itself through most parts of the Orient. By the power of the Muscovite image-worship is nevertheless introduced, at least for ornament in paint, but not in sculpture, which they think only violates the commandment. The rest are gentiles. The first that sovereignated over them that we read of was Genghis Khan, who by help of some associated hordes first subjected Unc Khan, by some styled Prester John (distinct from him in Ethiopia), after that Arghun, and at length died in Karakorum A. D. 1228. in this most memorable, that he was the immediate ancestor of Tamerlane, from whom the present Mughal is in a direct line descended.

Margiana.

But seeing Margiana is near us, for Zagathai, which is but a new name imposed by Za, or rather Chaghatai, father of Ogadai, father of Tamerlane, though I rather apprehend the derivation from *Saca*, it being part of that the Persians call Scythia, and adjoining Cathay takes the name of *Sacathay*, comprehends

---

[752] Borysthenes, also known as Olbia (its earliest name), now known as Izmit (Turkey), is "a city of Bithynia (northwestern Asia Minor) at the head of the Gulf of Astacus . . . near the Gulf of Izmit" (Grant, *Guide*, 431). It was refounded as Nicomedia by Nicomedes I of Bithynia in 265 B.C.E. and became the provincial capital of Bithynia-Pontus when the Romans conquered it under Vespasian (74).

[753] A territory comprising Turkestan and surrounding areas which was given to Zagathai, son of Genghis Khan, and was afterwards named for him.

Margiana, Bactria and Sogdiana, in which last was the Massagetes' country, to the north being terminated by the River Chesel, by the Mare Caspium to the west, by Imaus or rather Parapamisus to the south and to the east by the wilderness called Lop, which Margiana by Pinetus is termed *Tremigben*, by Castaldus *Jeselbash* by reason of the green turbans which they wear, as he was misinformed, for 'tis true that in the Turkish tongue *bash* signifieth "head," yet *jesel* is not "green," so it rather seems to take the denomination from the River Chesel, a noted river called Jaxartes of old, which waters that country and flows into the Caspian, a country so fruitful in corn and wine as gave Strabo the occasion to report how that one bunch of grapes presented Alexander filled a basket two cubits about, which encouraged him to found that city after which his own he named Alexandria. It was after called *Antiochia* and *Seleucia*, but since *Indion*.[754] Fifty miles hence is Marand, at which town Shah Ismail the Persian king gave a notable defeat to one of the Great Khans of Tartary.[755] But most remarkable is this region for that (as is believed) the patriarch Noah soon after he forsook the ark here planted, and either he or some other to his memory built the city of Nisa,[756] so-called by Ptolemy in his seventy table of Asia *cap.* 10, a derivative questionless from *Noassa* rather then *Niseus*, as those who write it who pretend that Bacchus be the founder of it, unless they be one. Hence also Nimrod and the rest, departing into the vale [of] Shinar[757] through the confusion of speech occasioned by the impious design they had in raising Babel, dispersed themselves, so as from them in few years after the greatest part of the earth became more or less inhabited.

Sogdiana.

Sogdiana adjoins this province, watered by the River Oxus, a fatal place to the Persian and Assyrian monarchs by being a boundary to their boundless ambition, but contrarily from thence have issued such swarms of people as at several times have wellnigh overspread the universe. This province was subjected to

---

[754] Grant informs us that Alexander actually built six towns in "the oasis of Merv," which is ancient Margiana (*Guide*, 26), but this one is the only one mentioned by historians and geographers such as Strabo and Curtius. Herbert's identification of it with Antiochia is correct; it was refounded by Antiochus I Soter. His identification of it with Seleucia, however, is wrong.

[755] Marand is "a city lying north of Lake Reza'iya (formerly Orumiya)" (Savory in Monshi, *History*, 1: 37 n. 8). The "Khan" was actually Sultan Baysonqur, who ruled the White Sheep Turkmen 1491–1492, not one of the Great Khans.

[756] Nisa or Nysa, also known as Scythopolis, is a town in Judaea on the nrothern border of Samaria (and now in Israel) which "claimed (like nearly a dozen towns listed by Stephanus of Byzantium) to be the legendary Nysa, where the infant god Dionysus had been nursed by the nymphs" (Grant, *Guide*, 570). The name Scythopolis was given the city under Ptolemy II Philadelphus (289–246 B.C.E.), who settled the Scythians there.

[757] Shinar is another name for Babylonia (cf. Genesis 11:2).

the Persians, for here Cyrus built another Cyropolis[758] to keep out the invading Tartar, and Alexander another Alexandria Oxiana in 44 degrees, as also Alexandria Ultima in 41,[759] and at this which was built by Cyrus it was where the victorious Greek received such a blow on the head from the besieged that for some time he was reputed dead, but being taken, for that churlish entertainment was levelled to the ground.

Bactria. Samarkand.

Bactria has Margiana to the west, to the east and north Sogdiana and the River Oxus, and to the south Aria and part of Parapomisa, now known by the name of Khurasan, which too is part of Zagathai and under the Persian, but I rather take the southern part to be so called. In former ages Samarkand,[760] which has 28 degrees (called *Maracanda* in Ptolemy, *Samracanda* in Chalcondylas[761] and *Paracanda* in Strabo), was the most noted emporium not only of Bactria but of any thereabouts, yea, for some ages the mart 'twixt India and the Roman subjects, famous also for that it was the place that gave both birth and burial,[762] though some say at *Anzar*, unto Tamerlane the great victor who in eight years subjected more countries then the Romans could in eight hundred, where also the traitor

---

[758] Modern-day Chojend. Cyropolis or Cyr was captured by Alexander (see Arrian 4.2–3; Curtius Rufus 7.6.16).

[759] Alexandria (or Seleucia) on the Oxus is a site "which cannot be securely identified with any attested Alexandria, though it may have borne that name for a time" (Grant, *Guide*, 576). Its modern name is Aï Khanum near the border between Afghanistan and Russia. Alexandria Ultima is Alexandria Eschate ("the furthest") or Alexandria on the Tanais, a town founded in 327 B.C.E. in Central Asia on the border with Sogdiana and now in Tadzhikistan. For details, see Grant, *Guide*, 25–26 and P. M. Fraser, *Cities of Alexander the Great* (Oxford: Oxford University Press, 1996), 151–61.

[760] Samarkand, as Marcanda, was actually the capital of Sogdiana (Grant, *Guide*, 596; Olmstead, *History*, 47) and is not in Bactria. Olmstead calls Marcanda "the predecessor of fabulous golden Samarcand, where, amidst gardens and orchards, the great mound under which slumbered the remains of the original settlement was remembered until Moslem times" (47).

[761] Laonicus Chalcondylas (c. 1423–1490) was a Byzantine historian who wrote the *Historiae libri decem*, an account of history covering the period 1298–1463 and dealing with the fall of the Byzantine Empire. Herbert had access to two versions of this work; it was translated into French by Blais de Vignère (1577), and a Latin edition by J. B. Braumbach was published in 1615. He is not to be confused with his brother (or cousin, depending on the authority) Demetrius Chalcondylas (1423–1511), the better-known Byzantine scholar renowned for his work on Homer.

[762] Herbert is wrong. Timor was born in Shahrisabz, now in Uzbekistan, and died in Otrar, an important trading centre on the Silk Road which is now little more than extensive ruins in modern Kazakhstan.

Bessus, surprised by Spitamenes,[763] was by him delivered to Alexander, who re-warded him answerable to his demerit, but his rash putting to death at this place Cleitus, that saved his life at the Battle of Granicus,[764] puts such a stain upon Alexander as all the tears he shed when sober could not wipe off the blemish. It is now become a poor place and gives precedence to Bokhara, which elevates the Pole Arctic forty degrees, called of old *Bactra* and before that *Zoroastes* and *Zoroaspa*,[765] probably from Zoroaster their first king, who was slain by Ninus.[766] This Zoroaster was the greatest astronomer in his time and practitioner in arts Magic, in which, and the fire-worship, he first instructed the Persians. Those books he writ concerning liberal arts and the cataclysm in fourteen pillars half-brass, half-brick, like those attributed to Enoch before the Flood, Ninus defaced. No less famous is this by being the birthplace of that great naturalist Avicenna, in the Eastern world called Husain Ali ibn Sina,[767] born *Anno Domini* 980, *Anno Hegirae* 370, those 90 books he writ concerning physics, chemistry and

---

[763] Spitamenes (d. 327 B.C.E.) was, as Herbert notes, the man who arrested Bessus. He did not come when Alexander summoned him, and he ambushed a force of Macedonians sent to enforce the King's orders in 329. He then fled to Bactria (he was a Bactrian aristocrat), but he was murdered by his own wife, "who delivered his head to Alexander" (see Curtius 8.3.1–16); however, Arrian states that Spitamenes was killed by the Massagetae (4.17.7). In any event, it was not Alexander who punished him. It was Spitamenes who arrested Bessus, the murderer of Darius III who had proclaimed himself Artaxerxes IV (see Curtius 7.5 *passim* for details).

[764] Cleitus or Clitus (d. 327 B.C.E.) was one of Alexander's cavalry generals. The account of his saving the King's life may be found in Curtius (8.1.39); soon after he had been designated the new satrap of Bactriana-Sogdiana, Alexander killed him in a drunken brawl at Maracanda (Curtius 8.1.20–52).

[765] According to Olmstead, [Bactria's] "chief city was . . . named Bactra, though the older Iranian name of Zariaspa long clung to the citadel" (*History*, 48). It is now known as Wazirabad or Balkh in northern Afghanistan (Grant, *Guide*, 97).

[766] Ninus was the legendary king who founded Nineveh, the capital of Assyria. He was sometimes identified with Nimrod (see Genesis 10) because he is also said to be the son of Bel, who becomes equated with Cush, which makes him Nimrod (according to the Torah), but scholars have more recently thought that he might have been Sargon of Agade (fl. 2300 B.C.E.), who may have had other names, if "Sargon" is a reign-name. The name Ninus is derived via the Greek *Ninos* from the Sumerian *Nina*, another name for the goddess Astarte. Lord Herbert of Chirbury discusses Ninus in *Pagan Religion* (153–54), and may well have been Herbert's source. Herodotus makes him a descendant of Herakles, and some accounts make him the husband of Semiramis, with whom he had a son, Ninyas (see below).

[767] Ibn Sina (980–1037) was an eminent Persian physician, philosopher, and commentator on Aristotle, the most important and best-known Islamic writer of his times and one of the few such known to intellectuals in mediaeval times, hence the corruption of his name to Avicenna. The *Avicennae opera* were translated and published in Venice over a lengthy period of time (1495–1546).

philosophy not a little advancing learning, which town also at this day submits to Khorasan, that gives name to the whole province (called *Coraxia* in Pliny, *Corziana* in Procopius,[768] *Corasophy* in Ptolemy and *Korasmia* in Athenaeus), subdivided into Heri, Farghan and Tocharistan.

Aria.

Heri, in former times called Aria,[769] which some mistake for Sablestan, that we now call Kandahar, but is included betwixt Hyrcania and Parapomisa, and in our times had for its governor Shah Abbas, during the life of his emulated elder brother. Eri,[770] the principal town in this province, is three miles about and not thirteen as some report, but so abounding in roses that the fame thereof is spread over a great part of the Orient and the *gul-ab*, as they call rose-water, so plentiful that it serves the neighbouring provinces, being so exceeding sweet as by much it excels what we have distilled in Europe. Rose-water is made use of in sherbet, banquets and other entertainments, where guests usually sit upon flowers and have flat-sided glasses filled with rose-water broke upon their heads, which, falling down upon the herbs and flowers, perfumes the place delightfully, for indeed the rose-water of Persia is so good that better is not in the world, so as much of it when ships pass from Gamrun to Surat, which is towards the spring, is vended in many parts of India.

---

[768] Procopius ofCaesarea (c. 500-565), historian of Justinian's wars and activities. This citation is from *Buildings* 3. 3. 9. See A. Cameron, *Procopius and the Sixth Century* (Berkeley: University of California Press, (1985); B. Baldwin, "Prokopius of Caesarea," *ODB* 3: 1732; A. Kaldellis, Procopius of Caesarea (Philadelphia: University of Pennsylvania Press, 2004). There was a 1607 edition of the *Buildings* published at Augsburg.

[769] Aria was "a territory in what is now western Afghanistan, watered by the rivers Arius (Heri, Hari) and Murghab, and bordered by Parthia to the west, Margiana and Bactria to the northeast, Drangiana to the south" (Grant, *Guide* 63). The old Persian name was Haraiva (Olmstead, *History*, 46).

[770] Now known as Herat; the old name for the city was Artocoana.

Tocharistan.

Tocharistan[771] takes its name from *Tochara*; "*Seres atque Tochares gentes prope Indiam*,"[772] Tzetzes mentions. The originary seat it is of the Torcs, the posterity of Togarmah son of Gomer,[773] a people confined or shut up by Alexander and not adventuring into the world till roused by Heraclius in his long and fierce war with Chosroes the Persian, and about two hundred years after, rushing through the Caspian Strait, some hordes seated themselves in that part of Armenia which was since called *Turcoman*, where they served Mohammed, Sultan of Persia, against his enemy the Caliph of Baghdad,[774] and, being abused by Mohammed, under Toghrul Beg their captain made themselves masters of Persia, as in a more proper place I have spoken of. Howbeit, as obscure as they were, some glimpse of them, it may seem, appeared to Rabbi ben Jonas, for that in his itinerary he oft mentions the name Turk, and amongst other things observes that the captived Jews transported by Shalmaneser [V] associated themselves with the Turks of Nishapur or *Nisa-pur*, i.e. "*Noë civitas*," by Haython the Georgian and Ulugh Beg the Bactrian also frequently commemorated, but until the year 1200 the name was not heard of in Europe, and the foundation of that vast Empire was not laid until the year 1300, such time as Osman,[775] chief of the Oguzian family, by conquest of Pontus and Bithynia[776] (now called *Bursa* from *Prusa*, the Ottomans' seat before the conquest of Constantinople) and other parts of Anatolia, left so great an army to Orhan[777] his son as gave him the first delightful prospect into Europe, since which under three other Princes and eleven emperors, a title assumed by Mohammed the Second[778] about the year 1450 upon his subduing

---

[771] An alternative name for Turkmenistan. Herbert is correct about the "hordes;" as Der Nesessian notes, "the different nomad tribes, in particular the Turkomans, penetrated in larger numbers into the country, dispossessing the Armenian peasants" (*Armenians* 42).

[772] The Seres and the Tocharians are people [who live] near India.

[773] Togarmah was the third son of Gomer and great-grandson of Noah through his son Japheth (Genesis 10:3). There was also a city called Togarama (Til-garimmu to the Assyrians) after him near Carchemish, possibly modern Gürün (*IBD*3: 1574).

[774] Herbert's history is a little tangled again. Sultan Mohammed Jalal ud-Dowlah was the ruler of Ghazna (1030–1031; 1041), but the main conflict was between Ma'sud I (1031–1041), Mohammed's successor, who was defeated by Toghrul Beg at the Battle of Merv (1038). Toghrul Beg did indeed become master of Persia in 1055, after he captured Shiraz. For the relationship of Toghrul Beg with Caliph al-Qa'im of Baghdad (1031–1075), see 000/ xref.

[775] Sultan Osman I, founder of the Ottoman Empire, reigned 1281–1326.

[776] Bithynia is in north-werstern Asia Minor adjoining the Black Sea. It was part of the ancient kingdom of Pontus and Bithynia, and then a Roman province of that name.

[777] Sultan Orhan reigned 1326–1359.

[778] Sultan Mehmet II "the Conqueror" reigned 1451–1481. In the West, he is known chiefly for his conquest of the Byzantine Empire and capture of Constantinople (1453).

Constantinople and Trebizond. Within the space of three hundred years they have enlarged their dominions over much of Africa, more of Europe and most of Asia, thereby reducing many late flourishing kingdoms under the worst of tyranny, prophesied of, as some imagine, by Jeremy in the 6 Chapter, 22 verse, and accomplishing that prophecy of Ezekiel Chap. 38, verse 2 under the name of Gog and Magog, to which the 20 Chapter of the Apocalypse has reference, as some imagine.[779]

Many considerable towns there were, but of best note are Tus, which is under 38 degrees and the more famous by being the birthplace of Nazar-ed-din[780] that great mathematician, translator and commentator upon Euclid whose works were lately printed at Rome in Arabic, Sarakhs,[781] *Gelack* and others, terminated by *Nycaphrac*, which springs out of the *Sariphaean* hill that is part of Imaus. There is a part of this country which some call Maurenabar,[782] which hath to the south the River *Jehun* (called also *Gihon* and *Gichon*, i.e. *magnus fluvius*, and by the likeness of the name some suppose it may be *Gozan*), to the south-east Ghazna, a large but desolate country now, albeit otherwise when Eusebius *lib.* 6 *Evang. praepar.* reported that it was so well governed as murder, adultery and theft was punished there and unchaste women discountenanced, yea, albeit environed with gentiles, they disallowed idol-worship, which discrimination from the rest was either from the light they received by the exiled Jews or else by the preaching of the apostles St. Thomas and St. Andrew,[783] whose labours were successful and manifested through the greatest part of Tartary and the Indies.

He then attacked the Empire of Trebizond, but did not capture the city until 1461, when the Emperor David II surrendered.

[779] "Thus saith the Lord, Behold, a people cometh from the north country, and a great nation shall be raised from the sides of the earth" (Jeremiah 6:22); "Set thy face against Gog, the land of Magog, the chief priest of Meschech and Tubal, and prophesy against him" (Ezekiel 38:2); "And shall go out to deceive the nations which are in the four quarters of the earth, Gog and Magog, to gather them together to battle: the number of whom is as the sand of the sea" (Revelation 20:8).

[780] Tus [*Tuzz*], which "was sacked [by Timur, Ed.] in 1389 and abandoned in the 15th century" (Greenway and St. Vincent, *Iran*, 236) was the regional seat of government before Mashhad, and is now known as Ferdowsi because it was that great poet's birthplace (940). Ruy Gonzales de Clavijo, the ambassador sent to Timur in 1403 by Henry III of Castile, reported that it was then "a most pleasant township" (Boyle, *History*, 415). "Nazar-ed-din" is Abu Nasir Mohammed al-Farabi (890–971), for whom see above.

[781] Sarakhs [*Sarchas*] is now on the border of modern Turkmenistan, and at one time was an important station on the Silk Road.

[782] Turan in Transoxiana.

[783] St. Andrew (fl. 1st century C.E.), usually known for being the patron saint of Scotland, was the first of Jesus's disciples to be called. "Later accounts of his life are unreliable," writes Donald Attwater; "They associate him with Scythia and Epirus and say he was martyred by crucifixion at Patras in Achaia" (*Dictionary*, 42).

Scytho-Sacaea.[784]

More north and north-east the Scythians beyond Imaus inhabit, by some said to be under the Great Cham's dominion, but Chams (or Khans, rather) there are many. Of old it was called *Regio Serica*, by reason of the abundance of silk and the excellent manufacture in tapestry and carpeting there found, which spread their fame into the most remote parts of the universe. This silk and delicate wool gave Sidonius Apollinaris[785] occasion for that monostich *"Assyrius gemmas, Ser vellera,"*[786] and to Tertullian[787] of *"Serae nerent, Babylonii intexerint,"*[788] and Tzetzes of *"Seres texturas pulcherrimas lana operiantur,"*[789] the true position of which is not rightly understood at this day, though most take it for Cathay, part of Zagathai, which also is derived from the Sacae, and what of old was *Scytho-Sacae*, by which name the Persians understand all Scythians, a name nevertheless mentioned by Strabo, whose Oriental limit is the ocean. And, notwithstanding geographers have filled their maps and globes with the names of *Tenduc, Tangart,*

---

[784] Herbert is unsure, as he tells us, of exactly what constitutes Scythia. Grant states that it was "the name loosely given by the Greeks to the entire area between the Carpathians and the river Tanais (Don), or even extending as far as the Caspian Sea" (*Guide,* 569). He also notes that the term included "the nomad Sacae and others who invaded Seleucid territories in Iran before and after 300 B.C.," and one group of these, the Parni, "evolved into the Parthians." In the 2nd century B.C.E. "the Sacae overran the Greek (Indo-Greek) communities of central Asia" (570). Colledge calls Scythians "a generic term in antiquity for the nomad tribes to the north of Iran" (*Parthians,* 46). They also made incursions into Colchis, now in Georgia (Lang, *Georgians,* 81–3).

[785] Sidonius Apollinaris (c. 423–480), Bishop of Clermont, was a Roman statesman and poet from the Lyons area. He married the daughter of the future emperor Avitus, and enjoyed a public career under several emperors. His poetry was modelled on that of Virgil and Horace. Sidonius's works were first printed by Vinetus (1552); further editions appeared in 1614 and 1652. There is an English translation by W. B. Anderson (Cambridge, MA: Harvard University Press, 1965).

[786] "The Assyrian gems, the Scythian wool" (Sidonius Apollinaris, *Carmina* 5. 22).

[787] Tertullian, *De cultu feminarum* 1. 1, *PL* 1. 1305 B. I am indebted to the editor at MRTS for tracking down this quote. Quintus Septimius Tertullianus (c. 160–235) was a lawyer, theologian, and early Christian polemicist, the first significant writer from the tradition of Latin Christianity, although he wrote much in Greek. His *Apologeticus pro Christianus* attacked other beliefs as superstitions and affirmed Christianity as the "true religion"; it was the first of his works to be printed, edited by Bernadinus Bernalius (Venice, 1493). It was translated into English as *Tertullian's Apology* by H. Brown (1655). There was a *Collected Edition* of Tertullian prepared by Beatus Rhenamus (Basle, 1521), and many editions of individual works, including translations into French, German, and Spanish.

[788] The Scythians spin, the Babylonians weave.

[789] The Scythians would produce the most beautiful weaving in wool.

Tamsur, Cando, Camul[790] and other hobgoblin words obtruded upon the world by those three errant monks Haython, Marco Polo the Venetian and Varthema, who, fearing no imputations, make strange discoveries as well as descriptions of places, and, *inter alia*, of Cambalu, the Khan's metropolis watered by *Polysanga*,[791] which also waters *Quinzay*[792] in China, as most credit. No Armenian or Jew, who are doubtless the greatest travellers in the world as merchants, was ever there or knows such a city, that ever yet I met with.

For my part I conceive we are in a deep ignorance as to the truth of those places, as I have already hinted, those nearer regions which interpose 'twixt Zagathai and Lop and the north part of China being to us, nay, to the civilised inhabitants about Kabul and Kandahar, little-known other then that the Tartars neighbour the Chinese to the north and north-east as the sea does to the south and to the west the *Barman* or Brahman. For that of Abu'l Fida the great Arabian cosmographer is no new discovery but what we easily believe, how that the ocean runs far beyond China from the east towards the north, but that it circles west above the north-east of Russia, as he says, and takes its course about Lapland, and that the sea fetches a compass about the east and north-east parts of Asia and Europe I know he has it only by speculation, which nevertheless may serve as a spur to encourage the further discovery of a north-east or north-west passage towards China and the East Indies. For the same Arabian, borrowing his light from our writers, calls the inhabitants of that part of the Asian continent Gog and Magog, which with better consideration is conjectured by Strabo *lib.* 1, that by reason of the vast deserts, the fierceness of people, noisome beasts and deep snows, especially near the mountains Imaus, which towards the north surge more and more to an incomprehensible height to penetrate other countries, with security is held impossible, the rather for that, as he says, the people and languages there are not to be numbered, and yet where known comprehends them under one denomination of Scythians, for *"omnes cognitas regiones versus septentrionem uno nomine vel Scythe vel Cesto-Scythe appellantur."*[793] But the character of what we now found true concerning them, makes them of the same piece with the other Tartarians, *"vicinia inter se nulli fines. Agrum non exercent, domus nec tectum habent, uxores liberose secum in plaustris trahunt. Armenta et pecora semper*

[790] Tenduc was described by Marco Polo as an eastern region ruled by descendants of Prester John with a capital city of the same name. Scholars now identify it as being around Hohhot, Inner Mongolia, near Shang-tu, where Kublai Khan had a palace.

[791] The Yangzte river.

[792] The city of Xuntien or Hangchow in the Yangzte Delta, about 200 km southwest of Shanghai.

[793] All the known northern regions are known by one name, Scythia or Cesto-Scythia.

pascentibus; argentum spurnunt, lacte et melle vescuntur,"[794] which how strange so-ever it seems now to us, in the infancy of time it was doubtless the course or manner of life which most nations practiced, but found inconsistent with civil states in after-ages when men assumed their several properties, and, incorporating themselves, formed a weal public, as we may observe among the Romans and Carthaginians. But fearing this subject has made me wander too far, I shall present the reader only with the habit of some of them as I took it, and conclude:

An Uzbeg man [illustration not shown]

Elburz. The pyres.
Now concerning Taurus, if we were to give that mountain the several names it bears in the different countries it runs through, varying indeed according to their sundry idioms, it would be endless; I shall therefore content myself in taking notice of that part thereof which came in our way, and by the natives called Elburz, a mountain of great fame if not infamous rather by reason of that pyre of idol-fire which, if tradition may be credited, had continued unextinguished for full fifty generations, of which place Strabo speaks in his *lib.* 15, Procopius also *lib.* 2 and Benjamin ben Jonas in his journal. The fane[795] was round, typing out eternity; in the midst an altar was raised five steps from the ground, under which a trench of fire was placed. The small round top of the pyre was open, the better to let in the air, which is the soul of fire, but this fire, if they may be believed, was not like our *focalis ignis*[796] fed with wood, coal, turf or like common combustibles, but, as they gave out, a flame so pure and rarefied as came nearest to those celestial bodies which the Stoics say be real fires, and, as the element of fire is supposed to resemble those *ignes aeterni* or Vestal Fires which Virgil mentions in his 2 *lib. Aeneid,*[797] so these have a cabbala[798] that Zoroaster was their first instructor in that idolatry. But 'tis probable that Zoroaster is the same, the name not varying much, for his opinion also it was that fire was most worthy divine effects, seeing that "*omnia ex uno igne sunt genitae.*"[799] The sun and moon

---

[794] "Amongst them there are no neighbourhood boundaries. They do not till the fields; they have no houses. Their wives freely go around with them in waggons; cattle and flocks are always grazing, [and] they spurn silver, feeding on milk and honey" (Justin 2. 2).
[795] A temple, or any sacred place.
[796] Kitchen-fire.
[797] Virgil describes Helen as "lurking beyond the door-sill of the Vesta" (*Aeneid* 2. 742).
[798] Esoteric knowledge.
[799] "Everything is generated from one fire" (Ficino, *Theologica Platonica* 1. 92).

are heavenly fires, whence their idol-fire was by them termed Mithra,[800] and this their god has singular properties, for fire is a comfortable creature distributing both heat and light, helping both against cold and darkness, the two greatest enemies unto sense, a learned man well observeth. "Fire," saith Agathias,[801] "so powerful and insatiable as all the world, were fire let alone, would not be able to suffice its appetite". That battle it received by Canopus the Egyptian idol,[802] which extinguished it by the water it held, was but a merry sleight, as *Roffensis lib. 2 Hist. Eccl.*[803] and *Suidas In Canopo* acquaint us. Moreover, by Procopius *lib. 2 De bello Persico*, the Pyreae at this place is also remembered; "*hic magnum Pyraeum est*" saith he, "*quod Persae deorum maxime venerantur, ubi igne, perpetuum Magi custodiant.*"[804] These Magi or flamens some call *Magusi* and *Magusei* (ironically from their incestuous marriages), who lived in great repute until Abdas,[805] a zealous Christian bishop of the primitive times, prevailed with the Persian king both to discountenance those Chemarins and to destroy their temples, after which they were massacred by *Waceck*, whom some call *Uvaceck the Saracen*,[806] as

---

[800] Yazata Mithra or Meher in the Zoroastrian religion is a creation of Ahura-Mazda who appears in the *Zend-Avesta* as the protector of justice and truth; he is also the source of cosmic light.

[801] Agathias of Myrina (c. 536–594) was a poet, historian, lawyer, and commentator on Pausanias, the Greek travel-writer. The work to which Herbert refers is the *Myrensis historiarum*, a continuation of Procopius, in which he dealt at length with the struggle between Justinian I's general Narses's wars against the Persians, Goths, and others and which contains a lengthy discussion of Persian religion in Book 2. Smith calls it an "honest and impartial work" (*Dictionary*, 1: 63). Baldassare Vulcanius (see below) edited the work (1594), and there is a modern edition by Averil Cameron (Oxford: Oxford University Press, 1970).

[802] Canopus was an ancient Egyptian city where Serapis was worshipped. The god's name seems to have got conflated with that of the city at some point in time.

[803] Herbert refers here to the *Textus Roffensis*, a collection of Old English manuscripts at Rochester, one of which is a copy of Bede's *Ecclesiastical History*, or *History of the English Church and People*. There is also a *Historia Roffensis* attributed to William de Dene (fl. c. 1350), a history of the Bishops of Rochester. Herbert's knowledge of this must have come from his assisting Sir William Dugdale in the *Monasticum Anglicanum* (1655–1683).

[804] This is the great pyre which the Persians worship as the greatest of their gods, where the Magi guard the eternal fire.

[805] Abdas or Audas (d. 420) was an early Bishop of Susa. He burned down the Zoroastrian temple, and was ordered by Yazdegerd I to pay for its restoration. He refused, and with twenty-eight other Christians was executed, thus becoming a martyr. Herbert appears to have got the story wrong; the Persian authorities were not responsible for Abdas's actions.

[806] "The story of the outright massacre and expulsion of the Zoroastrians from Persia by the Arab conquerors is without historical foundation," stated Marmaduke Pickthall, citing the Parsi historian G. K. Nariman, in a lecture entitled "Causes of the Rise

we learn from Tarikh in his story of Persia, from which we may conclude that as the Devil is restless in his labours to form his worship after the best pattern, so the original of this was probably either in allusion to the types of ceremonial law of the Jews are recorded in Leviticus 9:24[807] or else in imitation of that fire which for a divine end Moses, in Leviticus 6:13[808] commanded should neither be extinguished nor profaned, and for preservation whereof when the Jews were led captives into Persia, the priests took fire from the altar and hid it privily in a dry and hollow pit, which many years after was by Nehemiah's direction at his return from Persia to the Holy Land drawn out, and though at first sight it appeared like thick water, yet therewith sprinkling the wood that was upon the altar and the sun at that time reflecting his beams, it became a great fire quickly and consumed the sacrifice, 2 Maccabees 1:19,[809] so as by this word "fire," whereout Zoroaster would have all things produced, God was questionless intended, according to Deuteronomy 4:24 and Hebrews 12:29, where God is called a consuming fire,[810] so as of fire we may say what Plato the divine philosopher doth of light, "*est umbra dei; deus vero est lumen luminis,*"[811] to which I may add this truth, that "*totius rerum natura, causa et origo est Deus.*"[812]

In these pyres sometimes they not only immolated their children but men of more years then discretion.[813] The ceremony after the dedication usually was first to be anointed by the *Jesop*, crowned with garlands, and lastly to be attended by a multitude, then giving the survivors the same reason for that fact Mandanis

---

and Decline of Islam" (HTML version, n.p.n.). However, *Waceck* probably refers to Saad ibn Waqqas, Caliph Omar's general, who conquered Persia in 651.

[807] "And there came a fire out from before the Lord, and consumed upon the altar the burnt offering and the fat: which when all the people saw, they shouted, and fell on their faces."

[808] "The fire shall be ever burning upon the altar; it shall never go out."

[809] "For when our fathers were led into Persia, the priests that were then devout took the fire of the altar privily, and hid in in an hollow place of a pit without water, whence they kept it pure."

[810] In order, as follows. "For the Lord thy God is a consuming fire, even a jealous God;" "For our God is a consuming fire."

[811] "It is the semblance [shadow] of light; God is the light of lights" (Plato, *Politicus* 6).

[812] "God is the cause and origin of everything in nature." This (possibly another Platonic tag) and the above quote may also be found in Sir Walter Ralegh, *History of the World* 2. Thanks to the MRTS editor for identifying these.

[813] There is no tradition of human sacrifice by either Zoroastrians or Magi. Xenophon noted in his *Education of Cyrus* that "by Magian rule, bulls are to be sacrificed to Zeus and to the other deities, but horses are reserved for the sun" (cited in Olmstead, *History*, 477 n. 71).

the Brahman[814] did Alexander upon the like farewell, "*Mortem votis expetero, quae sine ------ senio carne liberatum, in puriorem melioremque vitam immutaret,*"[815] then, whiles the music makes a noise, throws himself into the fire, with which he thinks that he incorporates, from which gymnosophists[816] the Gabrs and Parsis differ but little at this day concerning that tenet. Furthermore, upon this high mountain it is, say the inhabitants, that Isfendiyar,[817] son to Gushtasp, who in Jacob's days ruled Persia, "endowed with power of not dying,"[818] with thirty other immortal Chirons[819] who by Zoroaster's doom are to continue there till Doomsday, so as if any could find the place they may, in another sense, if thieves meet them, likewise be immortal.

Here also upon Kharkesh's[820] high hill are some relics of the furious giantess Lamassus and of Arneost[821] her husband, a giant of monstrous shape and proportion; how many cubits he was high is incredible, but armed, as the Persians fabulously report, with two horns as big as the tusks of an elephant. His eyes also were proportionately big and his tail was like to a cow's, but in fight he was as

---

[814] Mandanis or Dandamis, a gymnosophist, accused Kalanos or Kalyana (see below), a fellow-gymnosophist, of arrogance. The story is reported by several biographers of Alexander the Great; the source was Megasthenes (Fragment XLIV in Strabo, 8; also Arrian 7. 2. 3–9). See J. W. McCrindle, *Ancient India as Described by Megasthenes and Arrian* (Calcutta: Thacker, Spink and Co., 1877).

[815] "In prayer I long for death without [fear], for it is liberation from old age and it changes life to a purer and better state."

[816] This term literally means "naked philosophers," and was used by ancient writers such as Strabo, Plutarch, and Diogenes Laertius (to cite some of Herbert's sources) to denote several different types of Indian mystics, wandering holy men, or *sadhus*, who were (and are) often naked. They believed that such things as food and clothing were a barrier to their purity.

[817] Gushtasp or Vishtaspa is the semi-legendary ruler traditionally associated with Zoroaster, and whose story is told in the *Shahnameh*, where he is the son of King Lohrasp (see Ferdowsi, *Shahnameh*, 369–70). His son, to whom he delegated his royal power, was Esfandyar (also known as Spendoclata or Spandodata), whom Herbert calls *Pischyton*; Ferdowsi tells us how he successfully established the religion of the fire-worshippers (*Shahnameh* 369). Gushtasp was succeeded by his grandson Bahman. Some scholars give him a date as flourishing c. 550–after 521 B.C.E., but this is conjecture.

[818] Not according to Ferdowsi; in the *Shahnameh* Esfandiyar falls to an arrow of Rostam (*Shahnameh*, 370).

[819] A centaur who was renowned for wisdom and benevolence. He was tutor to Achilles and perished after he allowed fire to be brought down from heaven as a benefit for the human race.

[820] Kharkesh [*Quequit*] is usually known as Kuh-é Kharkesh, a mountain in Gilan province.

[821] The *lamassu* in Sumerian mythology is the protective deity which Herbert described earlier on when he visited Persepolis; females were known as *apsasu*. Herbert's *Ameost* seems fairly close to the latter, but if so he has inverted the gender of the deities.

powerful as Hercules. This great thief and his wife were nevertheless both slain by *Ham-sha-Hortooin*, such another soldier as was Saint Roman[822] at Rouen.

But leaving these, let me draw your eyes to our ensuing journey. After many laborious steps we got to a village called Reine,[823] twelve miles short of Damavand, where we beheld a castle so built upon the best advantages of art and nature that to us it seemed impregnable, for above it wanted no ground either for peace or war. It had sweet gardens adorned with fruits and flowers, made happy in a rivulet of pure water which springs there and thence delightfully streams in many meanders into the bottom, but both by its situation and description may be that of which Procopius writes *"Caeli et aquarum salubritate praestat."*[824]

[The Story of Malek Bahman Larijani]

In this place (as a Persian of quality travelling in our company told us) not above five and twenty years ago lived Malek Bahman,[825] who commanded many hills and dales in Gilan and Taurus, a Prince albeit confined to the middle region, nevertheless forced with cost and care to uphold his dignity against both Tartar and Persian, his great and quarrelsome neighbours, wherein such was his good fortune and such the mutual love 'twixt him and his subjects that though often invaded he stood secure, yea, lived to observe the ruin of many his emulous neighbours, his aim only tending to preserve what his predecessors had made him heir unto and that his grey hairs might go in peace to an eternal dormitory. Thus thought Bahman, who also added his endeavours to complete his thoughts, but Abbas, returning from the conquest of Mazanderan, having forced Salim

---

[822] St. Romanus (d. 639) was Bishop of Rouen, about whom there is very little authentic information other than that he devoted himself to stamping out paganism.

[823] Reine [*Ryna*] is described by Greenway and St. Vincent as a "pretty village," and they found, like Herbert, that it "is not particularly easy to reach" (*Iran*, 185). It is the point where a visitor begins the exploration of the countryside around Mt. Damavand. Modern guidebooks do not mention the castle, so one must assume that it is now ruined or gone altogether.

[824] "It stands out by the health of the air and waters" (Procopius, *Wars of Justinian* 8. 13).

[825] Malek Bahman Larijani (d. 1597) ruled an extensive area of Tabarestan (Mazanderan) which included the city of Amol and Larijan. Monshi relates that he was "descended from Kayumars b. Bisotun b. Gostaham, who in the time of Timur was ruler of the whole of Rostamdar and commandant of the fortress of Nur" (*History*, 2: 696).The story of his resistance against Abbas and his generals is told in full by Monshi (*History*, 2: 693–98); Herbert's chronology of "not more than twenty-five years" is mistaken. Unlike Herbert, who obviously got the story from a source that admired Malek Bahman, Monshi is uniformly hostile to that ruler; "cunning and guile . . . were second nature to him," he declared (*History*, 2: 694), and went on to accuse him of "constantly stirring up trouble" (*History*, 2: 697).

Mirza son of Abdollah Khan[826] to become his pensioner, unhappily looking up towards this part of Taurus which seemed to threaten him, resolves to be no longer bearded by that mountainous king, but according to that motto of Tacitus pretends that from his lofty dwelling he usually pried into his two kingdoms of Media and Mazanderan, by that having advantage to ransack his towns, rob his caravans, allure his women, anticipate his progress to the Caspian Sea and divert many rivers into other sources, which, springing upon Taurus, streamed into Hyrcania and Shirvan and without whose course those provinces would become barren if not useless. Malek Bahman readily finds his drift, and comparing him with that fable of the wolf who, drinking at the spring-head, quarrelled with the lamb for troubling his draught when he was quenching his thirst at the spring below, premeditates what answer to return, whiles Abbas in an impatient delay resolves to try the chance of war, appointing Mahdi Quli Beg[827] to prosecute his design and not to return without victory.

This could not be so secretly intended but aged Bahman had intelligence. At first it troubled him, in that his grey hairs were more propense to ease then war, yet lest his subjects from his example might be encouraged, he throws away all dull thoughts and as a common father provides for safety, with arms and victuals furnishing his citadel[828] for many years' siege, yea, omitting nothing that might entitle him a careful and expert soldier. In each defensive place he plants a garrison, and other parts lays naked where the enemy might come, that in nothing the country might relieve the Persians. That done, he mews himself, his queen, his two sons and ten thousand select men in his castle, in that posture not fearing anything they could attempt.

---

[826] Mir Abdollah Khan was the maternal grandfather of Shah Abbas (his daughter was Queen Mahd-é Oliya) and hereditary Governor of Mazanderan under Shah Tahmasp I and subsequently murdered by his cousin Mir Soltan Morad, who "challenged his authority" (Monshi *History*, 1: 358); Monshi states that in 1596–1597 "there was no male descendant of that line fit to govern his ancestral domain, so the province [Mazanderan] came under control of the Shah both by inheritance and right of conquest" (*History*, 2: 693). Salim Mirza [*Shalley-mirza*], also known as Jahangir Mirza, was not the son of Mir Abdollah but of Malek Soltan Mohammed, ruler of Rostamdar and Kojur (r.1576–1595), who submitted to Shah Abbas (Monshi, *History*, 2: 678–80). Abbas annexed Mazanderan in 1596, Lahijan in 1595 and Gilan in 1592 (Boyle, *History*, 169).

[827] Mahdi Quli Khan Samlu was appointed Governor of Gilan in 1592 and of Sustar in 1595; however, the commander in charge of the campaign against Malek Bahman was Farhad Khan Qaramanlu (d. 1599). Monshi states unequivocally that Abbas "instructed Farhad Khan to subjugate the province and assume the governorship [of Mazanderan]" (*History*, 2: 693). Mahdi Quli Khan did campaign against the Afsars in 1597 and in the Heart area in 1602 (see Monshi, *History*, 2: 700–01; 810–13). Herbert or his source appear to have confused the two generals.

[828] Larijan.

The Persian general, in the meantime, with thirty thousand men marches against him, and at their first ascent find the way dangerous by those many showers of darts and stones he thundered on them, so as they first grumbled and then would have tumbled down, had not Mahdi Quli Beg by promises and threats encouraged his men, exposing his own head in the front of danger, so as after some skirmishes he laid close siege to the castle, where he was told the King and victory was included. Having well viewed this inaccessible fortress, he despaired of taking it, such was the height thereof and such thr perpendiculat ascent two excellent defences, art and nature, had enriched with it. Nevertheless some attempts he made, but invalidable; to shoot their arrows at it was one with aiming at the Moon. Small shot they had and lances good store, but of small force to batter rocks, so that after many tedious assaults and bravados wherein the Persians had stones in requital, the general, well knowing that what strength was not able to do ingenuity as the most forcible engine oft effects, he beat a parley, and with many protestations assured them of friendship, yea, that he might the better shadow pretended truth presents the aged King with turbans, scimitars, pearls and other gilded baits, means enough to angle for a kingdom, entreating him withal to descend and taste a banquet,[829] solemnly swearing by Ali, the head of Shah Abbas, Paradise, the Eight Orbs and other usual protestations that he should come and go with safety, no other reason inducing this invitation but a hearty goodwill he bore him and from the hopes he had of coming to some agreement. The peaceful King, unsued to deceit and war's rotten stratagems, swallows the tempting hook and believes all for truth, albeit his wife and sons dissuade, giving him instances of like dissimulation, but neither those nor the tears his men shed to beg his stay, vowing their constancy to the last, could avert his destiny, but down he goes without hostages, where he finds the crocodile ready to embrace him with tears of joy, but after a short banquet gives him an iron bed, regarding neither vow, honour nor engagement, so as Bahman now too late repents his dotage. The Persian general now thinks all his own and therefore sends his sons a message of entreaty, but upon a spear's point, the substance being that if they wished their father's safety they should come down and have his word engaged for their safe return, otherwise he would show the old man no mercy.

Nature enriches us with reason but Time with knowledge and experience, hence the two gallant youths, regardless of the rodomontades of that treacherous enemy, make this answer: they would believe he was a man of honour and honesty when according to his promise he gave the King their father his due liberty, otherwise he might account them idiots, his breach of faith to their father being so notorious, and that from equal reason he might demand the castle and crown, as them by whom those were preserved, adding withal that the King of Persia's ill-grounded ambition would never prosper, for though he had carefully avoided

---

[829] According to Monshi, it was Malek Bahman who "tried to persuade Farhad Khan to enter the fort and be his guest" (*History*, 2: 697).

the epithet of a tyrant, this would rub afresh his former injustice, yea, anatomise him so as all Asia would esteem him ignoble, yea, the world would tax him of dishonourable avarice, who, commanding over many large and fruitful provinces. could not rest contented without subjugating a nation never wrongdoing him and vassalling a King whose predecessors had in a larger series and for more ages governed Larijan than Ismail's posterity had done Persia, being withal a country so cold and barren that in the conquest more then title he could not boast of.

"*Sua retinere privatae domus, de alienis certare regia laus est,*"[830] says Tacitus; whiles private men think their own enough, great ones conceive all too little for their ambition, and accordingly Abbas will not be circumscribed, this being the usual return great spirits make, "*ius mihi obiectas, accincto gladio?*"[831] so as without further treaty he invites them from their consolidated cloud to view their father's head off. They, imagining innocence a sure guard, resolutely bid him do if he durst but withal call to mind that murder is inexpiable even in their Alcoran. Mahdi Quli Beg, having torn his fox's skin with over-scratching, sees this device prove air, and knows no way now to blow them up, himself being, as it were, undermined. Yet, giving rage a vent, he stormed it, but the besieged made so good defence that several *qizlbashes* there breathed their last and so many others were also maimed that without more ado they fell into a mutiny, resolving to return whiles they had a possibility, upbraiding the general that he knew not how to use a victory, seeing Bahman was theirs, Mount Taurus theirs, and doubted not the besieged would do homage if the Shah would accept of it and that with more credit and less hazard they could oppose the Turk or Indian. The general, in so great a strait, knew not well what to do, for on the one side, though he could ensure patience and make them stay, he knew not how to take the fort, and on the other, if he returned without conquest he as well knew his head would off, Farhad Khan, Allah Verdi Khan, Qarcaqay Khan and other captains for like miscarriage having that year been so rewarded.[832] Therefore in conclusion he resolves upon this wicked device: he releases Bahman, assuring him that his confinement was only to try his temper, that leave was therefore granted to him either to go or stay as pleased him, Abbas his master having sent for him and that he should depart with full satisfaction could he but see his sons, whom for their valour he had in a high esteem, and that if articles might be signed to it would fetter him in a thousand engagements.

Bahman, in no wise considering his craft, was overjoyed at this proposition, for never did music to his dull ears sound more melodiously, so as 'tis thought

---

[830] The full quote reads: "A private individual can satisfy his prestige by holding his own, but a monarch can only do it by claiming other people's property" (Tacitus, *Annals* 15. 1).

[831] Are you throwing rights in my face when I've already got my sword on?

[832] This is completely inaccurate; none of these men was executed that year. Farhad Khan was executed in 1599 (for details. See Monshi, *History*, 2: 761–63).

some spell infatuated him. He believes the Persian and dictates a pathetic letter, and is permitted to show his joy to his sons at a distance. A messenger delivers it and bewitches the Princes with such *pishkashes*[833] and presents of worth as were sent them, which, being accepted (fearing to irritate so potent a neighbour, the Queen also provoking them down) contrary to the soldiers, who by many submissive dissuasions presaged their ruin, they signed the articles, and, relying on the general's word, descend and were straight conducted to their endeared father, 'twixt whom was expressed as much love and obedience as possible. The general also seems to bear a part and invites them to a banquet, where death attended, for when these three were smiling in a mutual consent of love the general gives the sign, so as in one instant three *qizlbashes* with their slicing scimitars whipped off their heads, all three at one instant being made immortal,[834] and ere this villainy was divulged they made themselves masters of the castle, some receiving quarter, othersome destruction. Such was the miserable end of Malek Bahman and his two hopeful sons, who were forgetful of war's subtleties and how Ala al-Dowla[835] their neighbour, King of the Black Mountains, for playing fast and loose with Selim [the] First, Emperor of the Turks, by equal credulity gave a like issue to his life and kingdom. Opposite to this castle is erected the sepulchre of Bahman's beloved queen in the highway as we passed; 'tis of four equilaterals, raised above eight yards high, the material of stone, well-squared and very apparent and comely. The land here was well-wooded, for in old times hereabouts grew many lofty trees, which are rare now in these high places, such as induced the noble poet Lucan in his 3 *lib.* to remember them: "Then Taurus's lofty wood forsaken was."[836]

---

[833] This word is a Persian variant of *baksheesh*, itself a Middle Persian word, which is, of course, a bribe or "consideration." It can also mean simply "a present." However, by this time it had come to mean a gift given from an inferior to a superior person, which may have annoyed the English if they had known it. For details, see Ann Lambton, "'Pishkash:' Present or Tribute?," *Bulletin of the School of African and Oriental Studies* (1994): 145–58.

[834] Again, completely false. Malek Bahman was persuaded to come down from the fort by Farhad Khan, who sent him to court, where the Shah "took no immediate action against him." However, Abbas later handed him over to Malek Sultan Hoseyn Lavasani, whose brother Malek Bahman had slain, and this man "put him to death in revenge for the death of his brother." Monshi ends by stating that "the subsequent history of Malek Bahman's sons, and of the capture of their fortresses, will be given later, God willing!"(*History*, 2: 698).

[835] Ala al-Dowla was the ruler of Diar Bakr province; Selim I attacked him and annexed the province in 1516–1517 (see Monshi, *History*, 1: 71–2).

[836] Lucan, *Civil War* 3.225.

High peak of Damavand.

A long mile from this sepulchre and higher up into the air is the high peak of Damavand, by Strabo in his 11 *lib.* called *Jasonia*,[837] whose top, shaped like a pyramid, surmounts, as some think, all other parts of Taurus, up which defatigating hill nevertheless we scrambled but with difficulty, and from whence we had an unlimited horizon, for we could discover thence the Caspian Sea, albeit eightscore miles distant, and not so mistakenly as Alexander, who upon the prospect judged it to be some outbreaking of Palus Maeotis. Above it is compounded of sulphur, which causes it to sparkle each night like Etna, a pleasant object to the eye but so offensive to the smell that it requires a nosegay of garlic in the ascending.[838] Hence most part of Persia and Chaldaea has their brimstone. The reason why we rode up was out of curiosity to see the baths so generally resorted-to, which have springs, the one hot, the other cold, issuing out of this mountain. Three, which be private, are encircled with stone walls; the other two are open. The first are for those of quality, the other be more in common, and hither in August diseased people flock apace in very great multitudes, who receive notable cures from those waters, which by their great virtue and medicinal heat deservedly draw thither that concourse of people not from several parts of Persia only but more remote countries. These hot baths questionless receive their virtue from the mineral veins through which they pass, but what sort of minerals the water has either its heat or tincture from, whence from sulphur, vitriol, steel or the like, our short stay would not discover, and I could learn little of the people, for they were ignorant. The earth, says Aristotle *lib. De mundo*, has within it not only fountains of water but also of spirit and of fire, some of which flow like water, whence it comes that the water it ejects is sometimes scalding hot and at others lukewarm and temperate, but the causes and effects of this I leave to better disquisition.

> How are we tossed by Fortune! When we keep
> At sea, we see the wonders of the deep,
> And tremble at the danger where we dive
> Under the hideous waves. When we arrive
> On land, we think us happy, but ere long
> We must to work again and climb the strong

---

[837] Jasonia, although used by Strabo (5.231) and others in connection with Mt. Damavand, is a name which appears more than once in ancient geography. It denotes a place supposedly visited by Jason and his Argonauts, and this location is just one of them.

[838] Mt. Damavand is now "the most popular and accessible mountain" in the Elburz range, at least according to Greenway and St. Vincent, who, like Herbert, duly note its "sulphuric fumes at the top (which are strong enough to kill any stray sheep)," and that "it was first climbed by a westerner in 1837" (*Iran*, 121). They do not seem to have known about Sir Thomas Herbert!

And craggy mountains reaching up to Heaven.
Each down-cast look is death, each way uneven
Daunts our thick-panting hearts, lest if we miss
One step, we headlong fall the precipice.
The top, like fierce Vesuvius, sulphur spits,
The mid-way wholesome baths which cure all fits
Of agues, aches, palsy and the stone,
All epileptic fumes; as if alone
Nature had chose this place, to plant in this
The art of Galen and Hippocrates.

Noah's ark.[839]

Now, whether this mountain derive its name from the adjacent town called Damavand, or the town from it, others may better determine then myself, but from the etymon of the word in the original language or dialect of these parts, it signifies a "second plantation," whence it is that the Jews, who in great numbers inhabit hereabouts (having, as they report, been seated there ever since that memorable transplantation from Canaan by Shalmaneser [V], which is mentioned in 2 Kings 17:6[840]) spare not to aver, but from a Kabbala or received tradition from their ancestors, that upon this mountain of Damavand Noah's ark rested. About the place where the ark rested hath been no small contest amongst writers, so as to my apprehension that high place has been so clouded or depressed through variety of conjectures that it will be a labour of some difficulty to discover it. The most-received opinion I well know is that the ark, after that universal deluge, rested in Armenia the Greater, for [in] Genesis 8:4[841] we read that the ark stayed upon the mountains of Ararat, which word some interpret Armenia, and, running current with most, probably gave occasion to the poet Avitus in

---

[839] This has been a topic of great controversy from ancient until contemporary times. Mount Ararat is actually now in north-eastern Turkey, some 35 km south of the modern Armenian border; the Armenians still attach important symbolism to it. The name *Ararat* is now believed to be a Hebrew corruption for the ancient *Urartu*, which was not known to Herbert. In 1887 one Prince John Joseph Nouri of Baghdad, a Persian nobleman who was the Grand Archdeacon of Babylon, claimed to have found the ark on the summit of the mountain, and as late as 2006 the same claim was made by an American expedition.

[840] "In the ninth year of Hoshea the king of Assyria took Samaria, and carried Israel away into Assyria, and placed them in Halah and in Habor by the river of Gozan, and in the cities of the Medes."

[841] "And the ark rested in the seventh month, on the seventeenth day of the month, upon the mountains of Ararat."

his fourth book to say that "*Armeniae celsis instabat montibus arca.*"[842] Boccaccio[843] and Haython the Armenian are no less positive in reporting that "*in toto orbe terrarum non est mons altius quam Arash, cuius in cacumine arca Noae post diluvium stetit,*"[844] but where this Ararat was has not a little been controverted by divines and geographers of the greatest rank, for by Ararat, they say, is understood Caucasus and Taurus, which for length and height is reputed the greatest mountain in the world, stretching from the most northerly part of Armenia as far as India until it be affronted by Imaus, which in a contrary course divides Scythia, all of which tract or ledge of hills is usually comprehended under these three names: Ararat, Taurus and Caucasus, which for the greater half seem to environ the Mare Caspium.   Nevertheless, the names of these three imperious hills are lost in many places through length of time and the several idioms of speech which vary according to the different dialect of the sundry kingdoms and provinces they pierce through, as, for example, where Ararat rises in Armenia, there the most culminating peak or top is commonly called *Masis*, *Baris* and *Lubaris*, part of what we properly call the Gordiaean Hills, which some name *Kardu*.[845] In Media Atropatia[846] it multiplies into the *Coraxi*, out of which Araxes springs, *Moscichi*, *Pariadri* and *Baranta*;[847] where it crosses the most northerly part of Parthia nearest Media, *Caspii*, *Jasonii*, *Zagriae*, *Gadae*. Passing through Hyrcania it bears the names of *Sariphi*, *Coatri* (famous for trees of marvellous heighth, "*Aethera tangentes silvas liquere Choatra,*" Pliny *l. 6, c. 7*),[848] *Orontes*, *Coronii*, *Acrocerauni*, by which last the Greeks sometimes comprehend the whole province. Through Aria and Parapomisa 'tis called *Heniochi*, *Pharphariadae*, *Bomarei*, *Mandradani*,

---

[842] "The vessel stood on the high mountains of Armenia" (Avitus, *De spiritualis historiae gestis* 4. 539). Avitus, bishop of Vienne (c. 470–523), is known for his letters and the Latin poem cited here, which deals with various biblical themes. Books 1–3 have been edited by Daniel Nodes (Toronto: Ponitifcal Institute of Medieval Studies, 1985).

[843] Giovanni Boccaccio (1313–1375) is, of course, best-known for the *Decameron* (1349–1352), but he was also a mythographer and historian. Works which Herbert might have consulted here include *Genealogia deorum gentium* (1360–1374), and *De casibus virorum illustrium* (c. 1360) which was printed in Paris (1620). From this short quote it is impossible to track down the origin.

[844] In the whole world there is no mountain higher than Arash, upon whose summit Noah's ark rested after the Flood.

[845] Herbert is correct; the Gordiaean Mountains in Armenia are also known as the Carduchians. They were said by scholars to be north of Babel, and also part of the Ararat range.

[846] Media Atropatia or Atropatene is known now as Azerbaijan.

[847] The Coraxi were an ancient Colchian people; the Moschi were a tribe in southern Georgia or Cappadocia said to be descended from Meshech, the son of Japheth; the Pariadri, according to Strabo, are a range of mountains located in what is now Sper province in south-western Georgia. Baranta I have not been able to identify.

[848] Actually not Pliny, but Lucan, *Civil War* 3. 246.

Gassarii, *Oxiatri* (vicinating the River Oxus), and then Caucasus, where the Scytho-Sacae live in view of Imaus, all of which multiplications are comprised in the first three, whence it is that the quest is so obscure, Taurus, Caucasus and Ararat being indeed one and the same hill, for "*Caucasus est pars Tauri, et totum Taurus Caucasi nomine intellegi debet*," saith Philostratus in his 2 *lib*. With good consideration therefore, that glory of our nation for learning Sir Walter Ralegh in his map placed *fol*. 108 gives those names of Ararat, Taurus and Caucasus promiscuously to the whole hill in its full extent from Armenia to Margiana, so that albeit we read in Berossos *lib*. 2 that

> *in vertice Gordiaei montis, Noe quievit post diluvium. Noem tamen Scythae*
> *omnium deorum maiorum et minorum patrem appellaverunt et humanae*
> *gentis authorem et chaos et semen mundi agnoscant. Tyteam vero uxorem*
> *eius Aretiam vocant, in quam semen chaos posuit et ex qua tanquam*
> *ex terra cuncti homines prodierant.*[849]

Yet Annius,[850] Goropius and others fix the ark in that part of Margiana that joins to Hyrcania where it views Scythia, and not without reason, seeing some of the most learned in this sort of curiosity judge that the first seminary after Noah's descent from the ark was in Margiana, which is a luxurious soil fitted for grapes and what else might encourage his plantation, where, as we find in Ptolemy *Septimus tabula Asia* is the city *Nysca* in 41 degrees, either built by Noah or to his memory, and for the clime none fitter for grapes, which being showed Alexander the Great, he admired and thereupon there built Alexandria, and so the Scythians branching from the first seminary are properly called *gens semper antiquissima*[851] and may be preferred before the Phrygians and Egyptians in their claim concerning antiquity. Besides, from the concinnity[852] of name and tradition that

---

[849] Noah rested after the Flood on the summit of the Gordiaean mountains. The Scythians called Noah the father of all the greater and lesser gods and founder of the human race; they acknowledged him as the originator of the world from Chaos. His wife Tytea they called Aretia, in whom Chaos deposited his seed and from whom all the people were produced as though from the earth.

[850] Annius of Viterbo or Giovanni Nanni (1432–1502) was a Dominican monk and archaeologist in the service of Pope Sixtus IV. Unfortunately he was also likely a forger and a charlatan (he claimed he knew Etruscan); he wrote the *Antiquitatum variarum* in 17 volumes (Venice, 1499) in which he collected writings he claimed were pre-Christian Greek and Latin fragments or excerpts, through which he declared the course of ancient history would be altered. He said he had found old manuscripts of these in Mantua. See A. Grafton, *Forgers and Critics* (Princeton: Princeton University Press, 1990).

[851] Always the most ancient people.

[852] Similarity of the tone.

Bacchus there lived, whence it has the name Nysa,[853] which some nevertheless
suppose to be Agra, a city built upon a branch of Ganges and some say took its
denomination from Nisa, Bacchus his nurse, which with Jupiter's gave him the
name of Dionysus, to whose memory a city also was built in Media, of great esteem for breed of horses, and another in Margiana near the River Hydaspes, a
branch of Indus, remembered by Lucan in his 6 *lib.* "*ex qua Nytaeus Hydaspes.*"
From that analogy or resemblance of *Nytaea* of *Noachus* and *Bacchus* and the delight both took in vine-planting, it has induced Goropius and others to fancy that
they were one, and in India both of fame at this day, they rather, in regard Noah
made not his peregrination with Nimrod and his party, who settled in the Vale
of Shinar at the confusion of tongues, for Elam, Shem's son, returned the way he
came from Noah and seated himself in Persia, but Ophir and Havilah, sons of
Joktan, travelled further east, first to Lahore and after into Bengal, where, and
at and about Melaka, 'tis found they fixed their plantation, the places retaining
their names to many descending generations, by which and much more I might
observe 'tis apparent opinions differ concerning the place where the ark rested;
give me leave therefore to offer my own upon this report of the Jews inhabiting
at and about Damavand, that this was the place. .

First, Goropius and others are so far from agreeing with Haython that Ararat is in Armenia more then in any other place where the mountain uninterruptedly runs as far as Margiana, which is easterly to the Caspian Sea, as Strabo and
most geographers place it, albeit mistaken in making it a part of Tartary. And yet
Ptolemy in his fifth Table of Asia places it between Media and Armenia, which I
marvel at, and may properly bear that name; that he inclines rather to fix it in the
most southerly part of Scythia, which I think too far-stretched and rather agree
to that of St. Jerome, who says that Ararat is not only a hill so-called, but in a
larger signification a champagne country near which Araxes runs, over which,
albeit Virgil *lib.* 8 *Aeneid* says Araxes scorns a bridge,[854] Alexander and Caesar
built two not far distant from the foot of Taurus, which description brings it
very near our Damavand. Elmacin[855] also, in his first book, relates how that the
Emperor Heraclius, pursuing Chosroes the Parthian king into Hyrcania, was by
some then in the army showed a high hill which they called *Geudi*, upon which

[853] Nysa is the name associated with Scythopolis, now in Israel. However, there
were several towns of that name, which "claimed (like nearly a dozen other towns listed
by Stephanus of Byzantium) to be the legendary Nysa where the infant god Dionysus had
been nursed by the nymphs" (Grant, *Guide*, 570). Cf. above, 429 n. 754.

[854] "Here, vexed at being bridged, the rough Araxes" (Virgil, *Aeneid* 8. 986).

[855] George Elmacin or al-Makin (c. 1223–1274) was a Coptic Egyptian historian,
known to Arabs as Ibn Amid. He wrote the *Historia Saracenica*, a chronicle of events from
the time of Mohammed to 1118. Herbert could have availed himself either of the excellent Latin translation by the eminent Dutch Orientalist Thomas van Erpe (Erpenius) of
Leiden (1625) or a French one, *L'histoire Mohammedane* (1657).

they persuaded him the ark rested, which *Geudi*, says the author, was near unto a villa at that time called *Themain*, a name differing not much from Damavand,[856] the *D* and *Th* being sometimes alike pronounced. *Geographicus Nubiensis*[857] hath also some concordance with it, saying *"mons Jemanni, in qua requievit navis Nohae, legi debit Themanim,"* which name upon this occasion sundry Greek writers commemorate, saith Agathias. Furthermore, Vulcanius[858] in his 4 *lib.* gives us this further testimony, that upon the high mountain *Toman* Noah's ark rested, a name little different from what Damavand is now called, the various dialects of speech in many places occasioning a greater difference, and for proof may note the different pronunciation of London, Tredagh and Antwerp by our transmarine neighbours.[859]

Nor does that of Procopius upon *Genesis* weaken, but rather fortify this my conjecture, in saying that *"Ararat excurrit in medium inter Armeniam et Parthiam versus Adiabenam ad aquilonem, non ad orientem Babylon,"*[860] seeing that Damavand's situation is 'twixt Armenia and Parthia, being also the more strengthened from that of the commentator upon Berossos, who persuades his reader that the ark rested upon those Caspian hills that separate Armenia from Media, which description as with a finger to my apprehension directs unto this mountain of Damavand.

---

[856] It should be noted that Herbert always spells Damavand "Damoan," which makes the cognates he posits sound more alike.

[857] This epithet, which means "the Nubian geographer," refers to Abdullah al-Idrisi Ash-Sharif (1099–1166), a Spanish Muslim scholar from Cordoba who worked at the court of Roger II of Sicily. He wrote the *Kitab nuzhat al-mushtaq*, which became the first twelfth-century work of Arab geography printed (1592). A Latin translation was made in Rome (1619), which is likely where Herbert got this information. The quotation translates "it ought to be read that the mount of Jemmanus, on which Noah's ship rested, was called Themanim."

[858] Bonaventura Vulcanius (1538–1614), a scholar and poet born in Bruges, was Professor of Greek at the University of Leiden. He edited the *Syntagma Arateorum* (1577), a version of Germanicus Caesar's *Aratus* which became the standard version of the work of that much-edited and revised astronomer. Vulcanius was also known for having been the teacher of Hugo Grotius. It is likely that Herbert used his version of Aratus in the present work.

[859] Herbert probably means *Londres* for London, *Anvers* for Antwerp and *Drogheda* for Tredagh in Ireland.

[860] "Ararat rises mid-way between Armenia and Parthia towards Adiabene in the north, not to Babylon in the east" (Procopius of Gaza, *Commentary on the Octateuch*, CPG 7430).

Transplanted Jews. [861]

But, having peradventure presumed too far upon this supposition, I leave the disquisition to a more accurate observer, and only take leave to acquaint you with what the Jews hereabout inhabiting report how that part of the idolatrous tribes of Dan, Zebulon, Asher and Napthali were by Shalmaneser commanded to abide in these parts, Tiglath-pileser the Assyrian monarch having transplanted the half tribe of Manasses, Reuben and Gad to Jarri and other places within the Kingdom of Lar, as I have already observed. The inhabitants of Damascus also were removed by this great Prince to Kir in Media, 2 Kings 16:9[862] about the River Cyrus, which is so pronounced, but the Cushites were moved to Samaria in the place of those Jews, which Cushites,[863] as I gather from Josephus in his *lib.* 10, were inhabitants of this region, at that time called by the name of *Chusha*,[864] by which word some mistakenly have understood whole Persia, albeit more likely to be Khuzistan, as Susiana is oftimes called, a country extending from Lar westward as far as the Altars of Hercules,[865] the utmost cities of which were Apamea and Ctesiphon. And albeit *Gihon* be a ganeral name for great rivers, nothing indeed has puzzled scholars then to find where *Gozan* run, for albeit Ptolemy make it, if it be that *Gozana* which he mentions in his 6 *lib.* 16 *cap.*, a branch of Oxus, yet insomuch as *Hara*, which some erroneously take for *Chara* or *Charan* in Mesopotamia, where the patriarch Abraham sometimes dwelt, and Halah and Habor are cities in Media, as is recorded in the 2 Kings 18:11,[866] near

---

[861] Traditionally, the twelve tribes of Israel, each named for one of Jacob's sons, occupied areas what is now the modern state of Israel. In the East were Judah, Issachar, and Zebulon; in the South Reuben, Gad, and Simeon; in the West were Ephraim, Manasseh, and Benjamin, whilst Dan, Asher, and Napthali settled in the North. The tribe of Levi remained as "Levites" to look after the Temple in Jerusalem. Of course, from this migration spring all the legends of "lost tribes," whose "descendants" claim to be living in North America, Persia, Ethiopia, and other places to this day.

[862] ". . . for the king of Assyria went up against Damascus and took it, and carried the people of it captive to Kir . . ."

[863] The Cushites, also known as Elamites, were the original inhabitants of Persia; remnants of this group may be found in northern Iran and may also include the so-called "Marsh Arabs" of Iraq, whom ethnographers say are not Arabs at all. The term also applies to the Sabaeans.

[864] "Now as to Shalmaneser," Josephus writes in *Antiquities* X, "he removed the Israelites out of their country, and placed therein the nation of the Cutheans [*sic*], who had formerly belonged to the inner parts of Persia and Media, but were then called *Samaritans*" (*Works*, 222).

[865] Herbert seems to intend the *Pillars* of Hercules, promontaries in the Strait of Gibraltar.

[866] "And the king of Assyria did carry away Israel unto Assyria and put them in Halah and in Habor by the river of Gozan, and in the cities of the Medes" (2 Kings 18:11). There is a great deal of uncertainty about Gozan, including doubt as to whether

the River Gozan, it is not probable to be that Gozan which mixes with Oxus, since no part of Media is within three hundred miles of it. Gozan then either must be in Media, which may be, seeing that Araxes waters Armenia and runs into the west side of the Caspian Sea, or else this river here, which is of a great breadth, streaming from Taurus both into Media and Hyrcania and cut in many small rivulets by the people to draw her many ways. And the Jews inhabiting here confirm this conjecture, saying also that when they were brought hither captive they were dispersed into many several places and have here rested unremoved during many overtures and changes of the Persian monarchy.[867]

Moreover, albeit the Israelites had for the extent of their dominion what was from the Red Sea or Wilderness of Sin[868] to the River Euphrates and the Great Sea, as the Mediterranean is called Exodus 16:1 and Joshua 1:4, which was accomplished in David's reign, yet the territory they inhabited strictly called Judah and the portion of the twelve tribes was but small in comparison, scarce amounting to the third part of France, so as wonderful it is to consider what increase they had both by what we read upon numbering the people by Joab, and the force they brought him when Asa out of the two tribes of Judah and Benjamin drew into the field against Zerah the Ethiopian 580,000 men, as also by what Josephus writes were assembled in Jerusalem when besieged by Vespasian and his son.[869] Yet since they were banished their own country they have not since either had King, High Priest, country or town they could call theirs, but live scattered over the

---

it is a river at all, although more than one scholar claims that it is that part of the Volga near Khazan. Benjamin of Tudela, who thought that the Khazars were one of the "lost tribes," said it was in Ghazna. Biblical references do not help much; Isaiah 37:12, for example, refers to Gozan as a nation: "Have the gods of the nations delivered them which my fathers have destroyed, as Gozan and Haran and Rezeph . . .?" which contradicts 2 Kings 18:11.

[867] Briefly, the Persian Jews, many of whom claim to be of the tribe of Ephraim (see above), settled in what is now Khorasan after being relocated by Shalmaneser V in 722 B.C.E., and were further displaced by the Babylonian Captivity (586 B.C.E.). There are also Persian Jews in Afghanistan, Kyrgyzstan, Uzbekistan, Turkmenistan, and northwest India. Under the Safavids the Jews had rather mixed fortunes; Shah Abbas I allowed them to settle in Isfahan and his successor Safi left them alone, but in 1656 they were expelled and forced to convert to Shi' a Islam. In 1661 Abbas II (who had expelled them five years earlier) permitted them to return and practice their faith, but they were obliged to wear a distinguishing patch on their clothes.

[868] Whilst the Bible locates this area between Elim and Mount Sinai (Exodus 6: 1, for example), its location is unknown. Sir Leonard Woolley and T. E. Lawrence both tried to find it. See T. E. Lawrence, *The Wilderness of Zin* (London: Cape, 1919).

[869] Titus Flavius Vespasianus was Roman Emperor 69–79; in 70 he sent an army under his son Titus (later Emperor 79–81) to put down the revolt in Judaea. Titus captured Jerusalem and laid waste to the Temple there. For Josephus's account, see *Wars of the Jews* VIII.

face of the whole earth, so as they who once were the chosen people of God, and in consideration of whom all others were of no esteem for sanctity, whose dread was to be upon all the inhabitants under Heaven, whose name should make the universe to tremble whiles they obeyed the Lord, for their apostacy and idolatry are now rejected, and that dreadful prophecy of Jeremiah 24:9 pursuant to that curse of Moses pronounced Deuteronomy 28:37 and of Ezekiel 5:15,[870] where God threatens to deliver them to be removed into all the kingdoms of the earth for their hurt to be a reproach and a proverb into all the kingdoms of the earth to be a byword and a curse in all places whither he would drive them, to the full extent we see accomplished. For indeed not only what the Christians retort them for their hatred to Christ, the prophets and the apostles, the very heathen accused them as enemies of mankind towards whom they bore an irreconcilable hatred, as say Diodorus Siculus and Tacitus *lib.* 5[871] being of all nations the worst, as Ammianus[872] *De Marco Imperatore*, and as people that of old time moved sedition, so Ezra 4:15,[873] insomuch as they were termed "men avoiding the very sight of them if by chance they met them." And though I am persuaded by what I have seen they are at this day the most for number of any one people in the world were they drawn together into a body, yet being dispersed they appear as if they were few. Further, albeit when they were in the Promised Land, of all others they were the most prone to idolatry even when they had light and all the other world besides sat clouded in darkness, yet being now under captivity and severe subjections wherever they inhabit, they keep strictly to the traditions of their ancestors,

---

[870] "And I will deliver them to be removed into all the kingdoms of the earth for their hurt, to be a reproach and a proverb, a taunt and a curse, in all places whither I shall drive them" (Jeremiah 24:9); "And thou shalt become an astonishment, a proverb and a byword among all nations whither the Lord shall lead thee" (Deuteronomy 28:37); ". . . it shall be a reproach and a taunt, an instruction and an astonishment unto the nations that are round about thee . . . I the Lord have spoken" (Ezekiel 5:15).

[871] Tacitus, discussing Nero's alleged scapegoating of the Christians for the fire in Rome, nevertheless states that they "were hated for their enormities" and that Christianity was a "pernicious superstition" (*Histories* 5. 4).

[872] Ammianus Marcellinus (c. 330–400), Roman soldier and historian, known as the last major pagan historian of Rome. He admired the Emperor Julian, in whose campaigns, including that against the Persians, he served. His book, *Res gestae libri XXXI*, tracing the Roman Empire from Nerva to Valens (several books are lost), has been translated as *The Later Roman Empire* by Robert Wells (Harmondsworth: Penguin Books, 1989). It was edited by Castellus (1517) and Gelenius (1533); an English translation was made by Philemon Holland (1609). Marcus Aurelius is reported to have exclaimed during the Jewish revolt of 139, "O Marcomanni, O Quadi, O Sarmatians, at last I have found others more useless than you!" (Book 22. 5.5).

[873] ". . . know that this city is a rebellious city, and hurtful unto kings and provinces, and that they have moved sedition within the same of old time." In its context, this is Artaxerxes of Persia complaining about the inhabitants of Jerusalem.

reading the Pentateuch and abhorring idols, so that though by reason of the curse aforementioned and their unbounded avarice they be the most contemned people upon the earth, yet by us they are to be pitied, being the offspring of Abraham the friend of God, and forasmuch as that in Isaiah 14:3 'tis promised the Lord will in the end give them rest from their sorrow and from their fear and from their hard bondage.[874] For, as Deuteronomy 30:4,[875] albeit they should be cast out even to the ends of the earth, yet from thence will the Lord gather them and bring them to their own land, where he will cause them to dwell in safety, which some think will be accompanied by their conversion, according to that of Zechariah 12:10, "they shall look upon [me] whom they have pierced" and shall express their repentance by lamenting for him "as one mourneth for his only son," for in that day the Lord will oppose himself against all nations that shall come against Jerusalem. In the meantime (with grief be it spoken) we find them everywhere in a most obdurate condition. But to return.

Neyaveran.

East of Damavand's high peak is a town called Neyaveran,[876] in which were about a hundred families. A young man, son to Hajji Shahsavar or *Ashuerus*, the Persian merchant that died in London *Anno Domini* 1626 and brother to Mohammed whom we buried at sea, hearing of our passing by, came out accompanied with several of his friends and kindred to invite us to his house, which was about a mile away. He was apparelled in a robe of cloth-of-gold, had upon his head a tulipant[877] of silk and was gallantly-mounted. His mien was good and so was his civility; prevailing with the Ambassador to go a little out of his way to accept a collation such as the country and small warning could provide, it was with such cheerfulness as gave His Lordship and the rest in company good satisfaction. Thence we hastened towards Damavand, where, as we descended down a steep hill, we passed by a black tent pitched in a pleasant place near the road, filled with above thirty women and men, who at first I thought were solemnising their *Baalia* and *Paganalia*, but it proved a wedding. Staying there a while we saw the bride; she was about ten years old, but the groom thirty. Many bridesmaids came out to admire us, whom we no less wondered at, for their faces, hands and feet were upon that solemn occasion painted in various forms with birds, beasts, castles and flowers. Their arms and legs were chained with *manilios* or voluntary

---

[874] Herbert is paraphrasing Isaiah closely enough that no reptetion is needed.
[875] "If any of thine be driven out unto the outmost parts of Heaven, from thence will the Lord thy God gather thee, and from thence will he fetch thee . . ."
[876] Neyaveran [*Nova*] "has some lovely gardens" (Greenway at St. Vincent, *Iran*, 183).
[877] *Tulipant*, a word which "from the Turks passed . . . into European languages" (*HJ* 943), is a turban.

bracelets or rather fetters of brass and silver, which in their *moresco* made them appear not unlike the Arcadian shepherdesses as described in romances. Having presented them with a small offering we left them, that night making Damavand our *manzil*.

Damavand.

Damavand, whether it be the relic of Habor or Hala is uncertain, but by the Jews, in these parts called *Jehuda*, their long captivity and abode here, seems to be one of them, and that the Avae and Cuthaei[878] were transplanted by the order of the Assyrian monarch into Samaria from these parts is imagined. It is a town of good repute amongst the Persians; some write it *Damawand*, but I took it according to their pronunciation. The North Pole is there elevated six and thirty degrees twenty minutes, and longitude is twenty-eight. It is included by a skirt of Taurus in the Kaboncharion province (part of Gilan)[879] and is this way the limit of Media to the north. In old times here lived the Parasittacenae,[880] mountaineers mentioned by Strabo in his 11 and Herodotus in his 1 *lib*. A town pretty well-watered it is, for a branch of Gozan[881] refreshes her. Ben Jonas, whose travels Arias Montanus[882] had a good opinion of, draws this Gozan all over the Persian dominion wherever any Jews were planted, but erroneously, for it is restrictive. Damavand is peopled for the most part with Jews, who in this place are two hundred families. The bazaar is built aloft and scarce worth the climbing to, except it be to buy wine and fruit, which is had here in plenty and at easy prices. Two days we stayed in Damavand to recreate our weary bodies, but on the thirteenth of June we departed and that day rode to Varamin,[883] five and twenty miles from Damavand.

---

[878] The Cuthaei occupied Samaritan territory after the Babylonian captivity. Some authorities, including John Selden (*De iure naturale et gentium* 4. 7. 521; online edition at books.google.ca/books), believed them to have been Persians. The Avae are undentified.

[879] Kaboncharion is north of the border with Media.

[880] The region where these people lived is known as Sittacene, and it is partly in Assyria, partly in Babylonia. Pliny (6.205–6) places it between Chalonitis, Persis (mod. Fars) and Messene in Parthia. Strabo (5.309) calls it *Apolloniatis* (mod. Uluborlu in Turkey) and Curtius *Satrapene*.

[881] At this point "Gozan" becomes the Damavand River.

[882] Arias Montanus (1527–1598), a Spanish humanist who served Philip II as chaplain (after turning down a bishopric), edited the so-called *Polyglot Bible* (1572) and was the author of a nine-volume work on Jewish antiquities (1593), which was well respected and translated into several languages.

[883] Varamin [*Bomaheem*], which has Mongol-period ruins, "is still designated a village, though it will soon become part of southern Tehran" (Greenway and St. Vincent, *Iran*, 185)

Media derived.

And now we are in Media, a word of her. Media, saith Polybius, is situated in the centre of the greater Asia, accounted a rich and noble country. The fictitious Greeks persuade that it takes its name from Medus, son of Jason and Medea, Aeetes's unfortunate daughter; more certain it is that the name derives from Madai, Japhet's third son, son of Noah, for the Medes and Persians before Cyrus his time in scripture as well as profane stories are ever called *Madai* or *Medi* or *Elamitae*. By the Greeks sometimes you find them called *Harae* from a city and river there, by the Arabs *al-Gabal*, by reason it was hilly. And none more worthy it is what Mela *lib.* 4 *c.* 3 observes concerning the descent of the Medes from the Sarmatians (from whence the Saxons also): "*Madae*," saith he, "*a Sarmatis Sarmatae Medorum sunt soboles.*"[884] and from thence as Pompeius Trogus, *lib.* 41, "the Sarmati are called Sarmedai," which is a pretty conjecture. It was anciently divided into two, *viz.* major and minor; the minor was *Atropatia* (*Tropatena* in Ptolemy, *Atropataena* in Pliny) from Atropates,[885] one of Alexander's captains, and Media Major or *Azirka*, at this day *Sirvan*, i.e. "milky plain," where Ecbatana the metropolis once stood.

At this day 'tis divided into Gilan (*Gheylae* in Ptolemy, *Caddusia* in Pliny); Deylam, Vaspurakan[886] and Thezican, those are Atropatia, in which we might include part of Armenia, Julfa there being seated, and Nakhitchevan[887] (*Artaxata* of old). Sirvan has Aderbayon, Harran, Soltaniyé[888] and Tabrizstan, which are in Media Minor. To the north it has Mount Taurus, Parthia to the south, Bactria confines it east and on the west it has Greater Armenia and part of Assyria; Pausanias[889] errs in calling it Aria. A rich and puissant country it was in the world's

---

[884] The Medes are the offshoots of the Sarmatians of Median Sarmatia.

[885] Atropates was actually one of Darius III's satraps whom Alexander retained in office; he "ruled the northern wilds of Media and proved so memorable that his name . . . passed into the province's new title of Azerbaijan" (Robin Lane Fox, *Alexander the Great* [London: Allen Lane, 1973], 410).

[886] Vaspurakan [*Vaaz-pratan*] is now in eastern Armenia and was once an independent monarchy.

[887] Nakitchevan [*Nassivan*] is in the south of Armenia; it is not Artaxata or Artashat, which was established as the newArmenian capital by Artashes (Arsaces) soon after he took over the kingdom in 190 B.C.E. This city "was situated on the Arax river at its confluence with the river Metsamor" (Neressian, *Armenians*, 25).

[888] Soltaniyé [*Sultania*], "this once-great Mongol city . . . is now now no more than a large village," although it does contain the tomb of Sultan Oljaitu "with one of the largest domes in the world" (Greenway and St. Vincent, *Iran*, 335).

[889] Pausanias of (?)Lydia (2nd century C.E.) travelled widely in the ancient world; he visited, amongst other places, Jerusalem, Egypt, Rome, Greece, Macedonia, Mycenae and the site of Troy. His *Guide to Greece* was first edited by Alfonso Bonaccioli (1593–1594); there is a good modern translation in two volumes by Peter Levi (Harmondsworth: Penguin Books, 1984).

infancy, but whether by the confirming hand of war or God's justice in revenge of so many holy Christians that Chosroes massacred, I cannot say, but now it is a barren and miserable soil compared with the Phoenix of Isles, Great Britain, who, all things considered, equals the best-compacted pleasures of these Asiatic provinces. Nevertheless it has been fruitful, you may say; Pope Pius the Second took his information right out of Strabo as that an *hippotobos* or horse-pasture there should flourish fifty thousand breeders, of which the Nytaean race was most of pride, so-called from the city Nysa, one of Bacchus his towns which Hydaspes watered and concerning which Lucan *lib.* 8 has this remembrance: "*Qua rapidus Ganges et qua Nysaeus Hydaspes accedunt pelago.*" [890]

Here also Alexandropolis was founded by Alexander, of which at this day nothing remains, and albeit by their report of writers this country was then verdant and pasturable, yet little grass is to be found at this day, not only here but over most part of the Persian monarchy save in valleys and where rivers are, but instead thereof many camels abound, who make a shift to live even in sandy deserts and crop the boughs of trees or shrubs, which rarely they meet with. The dromedary and it are of one descent, but vary according to the country they breed in. In Bactria or Persia they have but one gib or bunch, the Arabian being ofttimes double. [891] The males in rutting-time burn with too much heat and grow foaming frantic towards copulation, yet, as some write, in that distraction will by no means commit incest nor will they go willingly without their comfort. They couple backwards, go great ten months, commonly have but one at a birth, which they suckle two years apart from company, not losing their milk by a second conception. They live threescore years, labour much, feed little, refrain drink three days but then quench their thirst immediately. Their milk is cordial, the flesh rank and lean, yet in Asia preferred before beef, veal or pork, which I suppose that Mohammed's Alcoran, or rather Osman's parody, commends it. From Varamin we came to Tehran.

Tehran.

Tehran, by her continued greatness, antiquity and situation, seems to be that *Rhazunda* [892] which Strabo mentions. Seated it is the midst of a large level or plain, and albeit at a distance it be environed with hills, yet one way it affords a large horizon. The air is temperate in the morning and towards sunset, but in

---

[890] "Where rapid Ganges and Nysaean Hydaspes reach the sea" (Lucan, *Civil War* 8. 227–228). The location of Nysa, which has associations with Bacchus, is unknown, but may be Scythopolis. For details, see Grant, *Guide*, 570.

[891] Herbert gets his camels mixed up; of course the "Arabian" camel has one hump, the Bactrian two.

[892] The old city of Rhages was quite near to Tehran, which may have resulted in this confusion.

the sun's meridian we found it very hot. The houses are of white bricks hardened by the sun; the city has about three thousand houses, of which the Duke's and the bazaar are the fairest, yet neither to be admired. The market is divided into two; some part is open, the other part arched. A rivulet in two branches streams through the town, serving withal both groves and gardens, who for such a favour return a thankful tribute to the gardener. Adjoining the city the King has a very large garden fenced with a high wall of mud no less in circuit then the city.[893] The house where we lodged overtopped all the rest, from whose high terrace early one morning I took a prospect both of city and country; I could perceive thence that most of the masters of families slept nightly with their seraglios upon the tops of their houses, which were spread with carpets. Some, I easily perceived, had three, some six women about them, wrapped in *cambolines* or fine linen,[894] but this curiosity (or rashness, rather) had like to have cost me dearly, the penalty being an arrow into his brains that dares do it, which, but for the privilege of the place and that I was in my own country habit, had been executed. The caravans' lodge here for elegancy far exceeds the *mesjed*; the inhabitants are pretty stately, the women lovely, and both curious in novelties, but the jealousy of the men confines the temper of the weaker sex. Yet, by that little they adventured at, we might see "*vetitis rebus gliscit voluntas.*"[895] Zeynal Khan[896] was Sultan of this city, a man of little worth in our apprehension, for albeit he had been Ambassador from Shah Abbas to Rudolph the Second,[897] which no doubt instructed him in some punctilios of good breeding and expressing of civilities to strangers, nevertheless, whether his late employment or his favour with Abbas, or his wealth, or rather his vexation for Naqd Beg his cousin, all or some of these made

---

[893] It was Tahmasp I who first saw advantages in Tehran, which, although not "one of the world's loveliest capitals" (Greenway and St. Vincent, *Iran*, 154) has, as Herbert notes, has numerous "green spaces," as we would call them today. He built the walls and laid out most of the gardens. Palaces in Tehran today are much more recent; it was only declared the capital in 1789 by Agha Mohammed Khan, who became Shah in 1795.

[894] "Not fine linen," says Foster, "but coarse woollens" (*Herbert*, 322).

[895] Desire grows for them when things are forbidden .

[896] Zeynal Beg Begdilu Samlu, a soldier and Sufi, was one of the Shah's closest friends and advisers. He was also an experienced diplomat; although Monshi does not mention the embassy to Vienna (embassies to Europe are typically of little importance to Monshi), he notes that Zeynal Beg was Ambassador to the Mughal Court (1622–1623) an appointment which elevated him from *tusmalbashi* (Superintendent of the Royal Kitchens). In 1624 he was sent to deal with Arab troubles in Iraq, an assignment he carried out successfully (Monshi, *History*, 3: 1240–1242), and the next year he was chosen by Abbas to negotiate with the Turks in Baghdad. He held the rank of *Esiq-aqasibasi*, the equivalent of a Field-Marshal, and was "one of the six principal officers of state" under Shah Abbas (Savory, in Monshi, *History*, 3: 1388). He was one of the nobles who ensured Shah Safi's peaceful accession in 1627 (see Monshi, *History*, 3: 1302).

[897] Rudolph II was Holy Roman Emperor 1576–1612.

him so very discourteous that albeit our Ambassador in civility sent to visit him, he returned a slight thanks without a revisit, which we thought barbarous. The Pole Arctic is elevated in Tehran thirty-five degrees forty minutes, fourscore in longitude.

Karaj.

From Tehran we travelled to a village called Karaj,[898] an inhospitable place, for it afforded us instead of sustenance torment such as the scalding sand and frying sun could operate. Nevertheless, in old times this has been of that repute as gave name to the country round about it such time as it was called *Kyr* or *Chir*, but not that mentioned in Amos 1:5.[899] Josephus places it in Media Superior and by him misspelled *Cyrene* or *Kyrene*, and by reason that thither the Assyrian Prince Tiglath-pileser transplanted the inhabitants of Damascus, 2 Kings 16:9, undergoing the like destiny their neighbours the Jews tasted under Shalmaneser. Sometimes by some it has been called *Syro-Media*, mentioned in Isaiah 22:6,[900] where 'tis said that Elam bare the quiver and Kir the shield. This is more likely to be that *Kyr* then *Karizath*, as Hyrcania is called by some, as I lately observed, but at this day save this small glimpse nothing remaineth. From hence to Tabriz is two days' riding. The caravanserai is thus shaped:

Caravanserai [illustration not shown]

Tabriz.

Tabriz,[901] the late Median metropolis, is situate in that part of Media which of old from one of Alexander's great officers was called Atropatia. The Turk and Persian call it *Taberyz* and *Teueris*, but in the world's adolescency 'twas known by other names, as of *Achmetha*, which we find in Ezra, after that *Ecbatana*[902] in the Apocrypha; Ctesias in his *Persica* calls it *Achbatana*, *Amatha* the 72

---

[898] Karaj [*Charah*], which Herbert calls "inhospitable," is described by Greenway and St. Vincent as "ugly urban sprawl," although the Karaj Dam is "picturesque" (*Iran*, 120).

[899] ". . . and the people of Syria shall go into captivity unto Kir, saith the Lord."

[900] "And Elam bare the quiver with chariots of men and horsemen, and Kir uncovered the shield."

[901] Herbert did not visit either Tabriz or Shamakhi. His account of these cities is cobbled together from writers such as Don Juan de Persia. It is impossible to trace the exact sources, but he cites a number of authorities for the historical and geographical information he provides.

[902] This, of course, is wrong. Ecbatana (Old Persian *Hangmatané*) is in northern Media on the site of what is now Hamadan.

Interpreters,[903] *Cordina* others and some *Tigranoama*, who by analogy have mis-placed her in Syria from a city there called *Egbatana*, converted into *Epiphania* by Antiochus [IV]; by othersome called *Arsacia*, of which there were divers, and *Europus*, which Ptolemy mentions, and places under thirty-seven degrees north. The premier founder of this noble city is not agreed upon; [in] Judith 1[904] it is said that Arphaxad[905] built it, he that was slain in the mountains of Ragan[906] by Nebuchadnezzar the great monarch of Assyria, who, after he had destroyed that city, returned to Nineveh. Othersome say Deioces the Mede *Anno Mundi* 3296, others that Seleucus [I] built it, but Diodorus Siculus attributes it to Semiramis, who with incredible roil brought the water thither through the mountains Oron-tes.[907] Howbeit, Josephus assures us that it, or rather a royal palace for the King, was built by the prophet Daniel: *"Aedificavit Daniel regiam Ecbatanam Mediae opus elegantissimum et arte mirabili constructum."*[908] *"Ubi,"* saith Diodorus Siculus, *"sepulchra regum et templum Anaiae maxime nobilitarunt,"*[909] a temple dedicated to Diana, whom they called Anaya, whose pillars were overlaid with gold as was the roof, and the pavement was mosaic marble of various colours, so excellent as gave Polybius *lib.* 10 occasion to say *"urbes omnes alias Ecbatana opibus et magnifi-centia longe superasset."*[910] In that temple the great Artaxerxes sequestered the fair Aspasia, whose beauty made him and his son competitors, as Plutarch in the *Life of Artaxerxes.*

To return. By the name of Ecbatana she was best-known and had then her most magnificence, for, saith Strabo, it was fifteen Italian miles, having walls strong and stately, seventy cubits high and fifty broad, beautified with many lofty

---

[903] The Seventy-Two Interpreters were traditionally thought to have translated the Torah into *Koine* Greek, in which it is known as the Pentateuch, at the request of Ptolemy II Philadelphus. Their number was conveniently rounded off to seventy, so the work be-came the Septuagint. Scholars have since dated the translations as being done between the 3rd and 1st centuries B.C.E.

[904] "In the twelfth year of the reign of Nabuchodonosor, who reigned in Nineve, the great city; in the days of Arphaxad, which reigned over the Medes in Ecbatana."

[905] Arphaxad was a son of Shem (Genesis 10:22, 24).

[906] Ragan or Raga is the location "from which a second Media took its name." It is "on the road north-east to Qazvin and then east . . . Tehran, the capital of present-day Iran, is the true successor of Raga, though the ancient site is somewhat to the south, where it was followed by the Rages of the Greeks and the Rai of medieval times" (Olm-stead, *History*, 30).

[907] See also Don Juan de Persia (182). Foster notes that Le Strange gives the location as Mount Valiyan (*Herbert*, 323).

[908] "He built a tower at Ecbatana, in Media; it was a most elegant building, and wonderfully made" (Josephus, *Works* 227).

[909] Where the tombs of the kings and the temple of Anaia were made all the more famous.

[910] Ecbatana had for surpassed all other cities in riches and magnificence.

turrets and battlements, and the like we have in Judith. Within were numbered many noble palaces, but that which Daniel built, the mausoleum afterwards of the Median kings, was most magnificent, which remained entire and undemolished in Josephus his time and some whiles after. That built by Darius was no less splendid, for most part was of cedar-wood, the roof being studded and plaited with burnished gold, of both which nothing now remains save memory, and I can hardly say memory, since some (but frivolously) make question whether Tabriz be old Ecbatana and whether it be in Media or no. But if to be under *Baronta*, if to be in 36 degrees 50 minutes, if to show the ruins of Tobias his grave,[911] if to be the burial-place of kings, if to be the metropolis time out of mind, if to be the city from Jerusalem N. E. four hundred *farsangs* can make it Ecbatana, or if the authority of Ananias,[912] Pietro della Valle, Leunclavius, Teixera[913] and of Ortelius will serve, it will then appear to be Ecbatana in Media, and the rather from this additional authority out of Polybius: *"Media sita in meditullio Asia, regio est opulentissima, eius caput est Ecbatana,"*[914] upon whose destruction by the Assyrians Raga, mentioned *lib.* Tobit[915] and called *Ara* formerly, became the head city of Media, but Ecbatana afterwards recovered its liberty, though not former glory. Pliny also hath this note: *"Ecbara* (meaning Ecbatana) *condita est a Seleuco Nicator rege; distans a Caspiis partis 20,000 passus,"*[916] so as Ptolemy's conceit of Tabriz (mistaken in the *tau*, a *gamma* being printed erroneously for it) to be in Assyria, of Cedrenus and Haython in Armenia, of Chalcondylas in Persia, of Niger in Pers-Armenia and of Paulus Venetus in Parthia—what were these conjectures but taking rise from the monarchic titles of Assyrian, Armenian or Parthian as they swayed them, but chiefly from the mistake how Armenia was divided, part of Armenia extending south from Araxis into Atropatene, Artaxata being the

---

[911] Tobias is often used interchangeably with Tobit.

[912] Ananias of Sirak (c. 600–650) was an Armenian theologian and geographer who studied in Trebizond. Apart from exegetic writings which included a work on the date of Christmas (translated by F. C. Conybeare in 1895), he also wrote an autobiography. His best-known work is the *Axarhac'oyc'* or *Geography*; this book has been translated by Robert Hewsen as *The Geography: The Long and Short Recensions* (Tübingen: L. Reichert Verlag, 1991). Hewsen has also written an informative article on this little-known geographer, "Science in 7th Century Armenia: Ananias of Sirak," *Isis* 59 (1968): 32–45.

[913] João Teixeira Albernaz (c. 1580–1662) was a Portuguese cartographer whose maps ranged from Brazil to Africa to a world atlas. He was appointed Chief Cartographer of Guinea and Africa (1605) by Philip III; Herbert is probably referring to his *Livro das plantas das cidades e fortalezas fa conquista da India Oriental* (1648).

[914] Media is situated in the middle region of Asia; it is a very prosperous area whose capital is Ecbatana.

[915] "In that day Tobit remembered the money which he had committed to Gabael in Rages of Media" (Tobit 4:1).

[916] "Ecbara was founded by king Seleucus Nicator; it is 20,000 *passus* distant from the Caspian region" (Pliny, *Natural History* 6. 43).

metropolis, and from whence the name Pers-Armenia was compounded, which is not above 36 degrees, though Ptolemy makes it 40? For by Abu'l Fida, Ulugh Beg and other geographers of those parts, the latitude of Tabriz best agrees with the situation of Ecbatana.

Tabriz, then, is a city both great and populous, famous for an inland trade and so well-governed that it is no terror to such as repair to buy and sell there, for all it is a garrison. The situation is near the mountain Orontes, or rather Beronta, which is part of Taurus. It is compassed with a mud-wall five miles about; the houses, after the common mode, are flat at top, their material sun-dried bricks, the bazaar large, the gardens lovely. That to the south-east was planted by King Tahmasp, and much spoken of, but the Turks' horse have lately grazed there. It has but a small supply of fresh water, yet what it lacks in that fire and flame supply, the sun, war's rage and civil broils having more then sufficiently parched her. To pass by the revolutions of the Empire, the Turks' first passage six hundred years since, Tamburlane's rage and the like, remember we only those irreconcilable factions the Envicaydarlai and Namidlai, that for three hundred years so persecuted one another with implacable wrath as they engaged in their quarrel nine other provinces, who at length grew so engaged amongst themselves that not only this city but Media and Armenia became wellnigh depopulated, the Ghibellines or Roses[917] parties or factions out-matching them so as in fine they made an easy entrance to any invader. Selim the Grand Seignior was the first espied it, and to become an eyesore to Tahmasp, son of Ismail their inveterate adversary, sends a pasha thither with an army, who ransacked it *Anno Domini* 1514, *Heg.* 894 without much resistance, and *Anno* 1530, Suleiman seconded it with so much fury that it flamed many days, the insatiate Turks pillaging without mercy, turning topsy-turvy all they met with, and into a chaos those elaborate walks and gardens which Shah Tahmasp so much delighted in. Reviving again, it was made prostrate to Ibrahim Pasha's[918] luxury, sent by Suleiman at the instigation

---

[917] Herbert refers here to the Guelph-Ghibelline feud in Florence during the thirteenth century, alluded to by Dante, and the Wars of the Roses in England, where the Houses of Lancaster (whose symbol was a red rose) and York (the white rose) fought a decades-long civil war which culminated in the death of Richard III and the advent of the Tudors under Henry VII in 1485. The Envicaydarlai and Namidlai are unidentified.

[918] Ibrahim Pasha Pargali (d. 1536), a Greek by birth, became Grand Vizier to Suleiman II in 1523. He attacked and captured Tabriz (1533) because Shah Tahmasp had ordered the death of the Ottoman Governor of Baghdad, and the Governor of Bitlis had defected to the Persians. Suleiman II actually invaded Persia on four different occasions between 1530 and 1536. Ibrahim was a great friend of Suleiman's, but even this did not, in the end, prevent the Sultan from eventually ordering his execution (after first getting religious clearance). Herbert's tortuous syntax needs unravelling: Ibrahim married Suleiman's sister Princess Asiye, and was the Sultan's brother-in-law.

of Olama,[919] a Persian traitor, albeit brother-in-law to the King, at which time the Turks plundered it, but *Anno* 1585, *Heg.* 965, it groaned under the greatest suffering when Osman the wrathful Pasha, slave to Murad the Third,[920] subduing it perpetrated all manner of horrible cruelty, till thirty years after[921] by that incomparable Prince Emir Hamza Mirza, elder brother to Shah Abbas, it was regained, rebuilt and fortified against the future insolence of those barbarians, for 'twixt this city and Ardabil[922] he gave the Turks a notable defeat, and after that Abbas himself *Anno* 1619 near the same place did the like, which for the future has quieted it under the Persian governrnent. Taurus is distant from Qazvin seven days' easy journey and from the Mare Caspium as many; from Arash, a city of good commerce in silks and through which Araxes streams, six; from Derbent eight; from Isfahan seventeen; from Shiraz thirty; from Hormuz sixty and from Jerusalem fifty; from Aleppo thirty and from Babylon thirty or thereabouts.

Shamakhi.[923]

Three days' journey from hence is Samakhi, which some pronounce *Shamaki*, a town consisting of four thousand houses or thereabouts, well-peopled and of good resort by merchants from Russia and Armenia, being thence the roadway to Qazvin. The North Pole is here elevated 39 degrees; situate it is in that part of Media called *Atropatia* by old writers, and pretends that it had its foundation laid

---

[919] Olama Sultan Takkalu [*Ulemus*] (d. 1537), brought up at the Safavid court (although he did not marry the Shah's sister), he had done good service as a military commander and had risen to the rank of emir, after which he was appointed Commander-in-Chief of the forces in Azerbaijan. He defected to the Turks and commanded a detachment of their soldiers during Suleiman's third invasion of Persia. According to Monshi he became "puffed up by ambition and aspired to become *vakil* and chief executive in matters of state" (*History*, 1: 110).

[920] Sultan Murad III [*Amurath*] reigned 1574–1595.

[921] Herbert's chronology is completely wrong. Prince Hamza Mirza was murdered in 1586. Tabriz was recaptured after forty-eight days of Turkish occupation (see Monshi, *History*, 1: 445–52).

[922] Ardabil [*Ardaveil*] "is really a long way from anywhere, and only useful for people travelling to or from Azerbaijan . . . The city is not a dull place, but there is nothing much to see" (Greenway and St. Vincent, *Iran*, 359). However, Monshi gives details on Abbas's building projects there, which included restoration of the tombs of Shaikh Jebra'il (an ancestor of the Shah), Shaikh Zahed-é Gilani and Shaikh Sehab al-Din Ahari. Around the latter he built "a beautiful garden" (*History*, 1: 536); this tomb is also mentioned by Greenway and St. Vincent (*Iran*, 359).

[923] Shamakhi or Shemakha was the capital of the province of Sirvan, now in Azerbaijan, from the ninth to the sixteenth century. In 1742 the Derbendids re-established the Khanate of Shemakha there, which lasted until 1828. An English factory was established there by Anthony Jenkinson, who voyaged to Persia in 1561 (see Hakluyt, *Voyages*, 91–102 or Foster, *England's Quest*, 31–33 for details).

by Shamakh ud-dowlah *Anno Dom.* 990, *Heg.* 370, from whom it probably took its name, having some coherence with it. The ground is good in which 'tis seated, and watered by a pretty river so as it bears corn and grapes in plenty, and though the place be level, it nevertheless has a large and delightful prospect towards the north-west. It was the royal seat of several kings, the last of which was Abdollah Khan,[924] who died and was here buried *Anno Dom.* 1566, leaving behind him a son called Sirvan Shah,[925] who, finding himself unable to sway a sceptre so near to Abbas the Persian king, prudentially submitted his royalty and enrolled himself a tributary Prince under his Empire. Now, albeit the city is commonly reputed of good defence, yet it was unable to keep out the Turkish army at such time as that old fretful wretch Mustapha[926] with fire and sword invaded those parts and turned most of the towns and villages into ashes, this place especially parching by the heat of his wrath and the inhabitants suffering under the edge of his merciless sword, the heads of so many of the besieged being upon the surrender whipped off as raised a monumental pillar which served as a trophy to express his savage fancy.

Next night we made our *manzil* at Sangarabad,[927] a town consisting of an hundred cottages. In this place we buried a civil gentleman Mr. Wellfleet, our comrade and countryman, under a broad-spreading chenoar-tree, and fixed a brazen scroll over him which spake his name and nation. This was the utmost we could do in that posture we were. Nevertheless, *ut te postremo donarem munere mortis,*[928] give me leave to add this distich to his memory: "We have deplored thy death; th' ensuing years / Thy kin will pay thee tribute with their tears."

---

[924] Abdollah Khan Ustalju [*Obdolo-chawn*] was "both the nephew and son-in-law of Shah Ismail" (Monshi, *History*, 1: 135–36), as Ismail's sister married his father and he himself married Ismail's daughter. He ruled in Shamakhi 1550–1566. He was defeated by the Turks when Suleiman II invaded in 1554.

[925] "Sirvan Shah" is not a name but a title. In 1538, for example, Shah Tahmasp I had elevated his brother Alqas Mirza to the post of *Sirvanshah*, which means "King of Sirvan" (see Savory in Monshi I, 115 n. 92). Abdollah was succeeded by Aras Khan Rumlu (1566–1576), who evacuated Sirvan and was killed after being defeated by Osman Pasha (see Monshi I, 354). Aras Khan was, of course, "a tributary Prince" of the Persian crown, and it is to him that Herbert is likely referring.

[926] Mustapha Pasha, also known as Lala Pasha, was the guardian of Suleiman II and the commander of a Turkish invading army numbering, says Monshi, 100,000 men. He defeated the Persians at Coldor (1579), but his army was beaten by Prince Hamza Mirza the next year and Sirvan was allocated to Mohammed Kalifa Zu'l Qadar (Monshi, *History*, 1: 356). In 1607 the Ottomans again besieged Shamakhi (see Monshi, *History*, 2: 921–23).

[927] Sangar or Sangarabad [*Sangurrabaut*] is now little but a "small Urartian citadel" (Greenway and St. Vincent, *Iran*, 348) about 30 km from the Turkish border.

[928] "That I might render you the last dues of the dead" (Catullus, *Carmina* 101. 3).

Shahin Dezh.

Next night we slept in the open fields under a bespangled canopy, the firmament, the next in Shahin Dezh, i.e. the King's Town, or his purgatory rather, if a conspiracy of loose and scalding sand, burning sun and mean cottages can make one, for the houses there differ little in shape or closeness from ovens, so as the people all day bake themselves in them instead of caves and grots, which serve well to abate the extreme ardour of the sun, a people so discourteous that our misery nothing afflicted them. Now, in regard that the heat derived from the sun arises from the reflection of his beams darted upon the surface of the earth, where the sun casts his beams perpendicular, which is only within the torrid zone, the heat where the reflex is most must by consequence be the greatest. But that the heat should so exceed here at such a distance from the tropic was doubtless from the quality of the earth and inflamed air that render it so intemperate to us, though better endured by the natives, who from their cradles are enured to it. Custom is a second nature. In probability this was the Land of Nod, i.e. banishment, into which Cain wandered after he departed from the presence of the Lord, for this country is east from Eden. And whereas he built Enoch[929] the city, albeit it has lost the name, the mountains *Enochi* nevertheless are not far distant, being part of Taurus and neighbouring the Bactrians, albeit that name is found also near Pontus and Albania, as some have placed them. From that hateful town we hasted, and next night got into Qazvin.

Qazvin.

Qazbin, or *Qazvin*[930] after the lisp of Persia, is that same city which was known to ancient topographers by the name of *Arsacia* or *Arsisaca* which Strabo mentions, so-named from Arsaces that valiant Persian who ruled here A.M. 3720, and from whom the ensuing kings *honoris gratia* were styled Arsacidae. This was two hundred and fifty years before the Incarnation of Our Saviour Christ, and is accounted the first that made Media an empire in despite of that Seleucus who was son to the great monarch of Syria Antiochus, surnamed Theos. By command of Nicanor[931] it was afterwards called *Europus*, but lost that name when it bended

---

[929] See Genesis 4:17. Herbert is correct about its derivation.

[930] There are still variants in the spelling. I have used "Qazvin" as it appears in Debenham's atlas as well as in Savory's edition of Monshi. It may be spelled "Kazvin," and Greenway at St. Vincent use "Ghazvin." Herbert uses "Casbyn" or "Cazbyn" as a rule.

[931] Nicanor, "probably a general of Seleucus I Nicator," gave this name to the city of Dura, also known as Qalat es-Salihiya in eastern Syria "overlooking the right bank of the River Euphrates," at the end of the fourth century B.C.E. (Grant, *Guide*, 223). From about 114 B.C.E. the city was in Parthian hands. Qazvin is definitely not Dura-Europus, because that city was completely destroyed by the Persian king Shapur I in 257 C.E.

under the next conquest. It is likely this was Rages,[932] a city in Media as appears in Tobit, whither the angel went from Ecbatana to receive the ten talents (of our money about three thousand pounds) Tobias was to receive from Gabael, son to Gabrias his kinsman. Their talent of silver contained 3000 shekels, i.e. 375 pounds, the Greek talent being but 175 pounds sterling, but a talent of gold was twelve times as much. I am not ignorant that some make Edessa in Mesopotamia[933] to be Rages, but that is unlikely, for what business had they from Nineveh to go to Ecbatana (in the way, no doubt, or not far deviate to Rages) a contrary way leading to Edessa, which was situated between Tigris and Euphrates? Besides, it is said in the Apocrypha that Rages was in Media, which Edessa is not, and whereas no part of Media is nearer then a thousand miles from the Holy City, Edessa is not above five hundred. In one author I find it called *Hispian*, meaning *Hispahan*, and if so he is much mistaken, that city being two hundred and seventy miles from Qazvin. Whence the word "Qazvin" is fetched I could not learn,[934] but I suppose from *cowz-van*, i.e. "a vale of barley," as *shir-van* is "a vale of milk," or else from King *Cazvan*, as they call *Acem-beg* the Armenian, or may it not be the relict of *Cashira*, an old city which Strabo placed here, for if I should deduce it from *Chezib*, as the Seventy Interpreters translate it in Genesis 38:5,[935] it would relish of too much affectation. The signification of *exile* is unknown by interpretation or occasion to the inhabitants, except the broacher of that conceit had recourse to the idiom of the old Parthians. Heylyn in his *Geography* makes this city and Isfahan to be one, in which conjecture he is exceedingly mistaken.

The North Pole is here elevated 36 degrees and 15 minutes, longitude 85 degrees 50 minutes. By King Tahmasp, son of Ismail, it was made metropolis of this monarchy, the better to affront the Ottomans. The kingdom it stands in is Media, the province Sirvan, that part which is called Deylam, removed from Tabriz a hundred and eighty miles English, from Hamadan (the sepulchre of Queen Esther and Mordecai) a hundred and ten. Now, concerning the derivation

---

[932] For Rhages, which is actually very near modern Tehran, see above. It is not identifiable with Qazvin, either. Herbert has already noted the connection with the story of Tobit.

[933] Edessa is now in southeastern Turkey, which used to be northwestern Mesopotamia (Grant, *Guide*, 229). Its rivers are actually two tributaries of the Euphrates, not the larger river itself.

[934] Herbert makes some interesting speculations, all of them wrong. The city takes its name from the Cas, an ancient tribe who lived south of the Caspian Sea, which also derives its name from the same people. It was actually founded by the Sassanid Emperor Shapur II in about 250 C.E. "King Cazvan" is unidentified.

[935] "And she [Shua] yet again conceived, and bare a son; and called his name Shelah: and he was at Chezib, when she bare him." Chezib is thought to have been the same as Achzib in southern Judah.

of Hamadan, it is obscure, so that whether built or named in memory of Hemdan the son of Dishan the son of Seir the Horite mentioned in Genesis 36[936] I know not, but famous it is at this day especially for being the burial-place of Avicenna (born at Samarkand), a man in his time of incomparable learning and industry as to nature, as may appear by near a hundred books he wrote concerning physic and philosophy, as also a dictionary of stones and herbs, poems concerning the soul etc. From Soltaniyé, the residence of six sultans, 'tis ninety (some say fifty), from Ardabil, the seigneury of the Abbasians, eighty, from Gilan seventy, from Farahabad two hundred, from Samarkand five hundred, from Hormuz eight hundred, from Babylon five hundred, from Jerusalem a thousand, from Isfahan two hundred and seventy, from Kandahar five hundred and fifty miles English or thereupon.

Qazvin at this day is for multitude of buildings and inhabitants the chief in Media, and equal for grandeur to any other city in the Persian Empire, Isfahan excepted. It is seated in a very large and fair even plain, no hill of note in thirty miles' compass overlooking her; a champagne it is, yielding grain and grapes, but little wood for growing there. Here Hephaestion, Alexander's favourite, was buried, but the monument upon which the Macedonian conqueror expended twelve thousand talents is not now to be seen, for Time has devoured it. It has a small stream flowing from *Abonda* (*Baronta* of old) which gives the thirsty drink and mellows the gardens, from whence by its refreshment and the people's industry they have abundance of fruits, rice, roots and flowers in variety. I think the reason why we saw no great rivers in any place is from their forcing it into sluices to bring it by subterranean passages to such towns as have none but by that kind of derivative, insomuch that if Indus, Euphrates and Ganges were amongst them, I mean where the country is most peopled, doubtless they would make them kiss the sea in five hundred ostiums or breaches. Such fruits as I remember we saw here were grapes, oranges, limes, lemons, pomcitrons, musk and water melons, plums, cherries, peaches, apricots, figs, gooseberries, pears, apples, pistachios, filberts, hazlenuts, walnuts, almonds and excellent pomegranates. Dates there were also, but such as came from Larestan. And several gardens we saw here very pleasant, for being furnished with trees of several sorts and watered with fresh springs, they become replenished with fruits and flowers of several kinds besides those lately mentioned, which together with the warbling birds that are numerous there, render the place extraodinarily delightful.

Qazvin is circled with a wall, but of little force against an adversary; the compass is about seven miles, families are towards twenty thousand and the people not fewer then two hundred thousand that live there. The bazaars are large

---

[936] See especially Genesis 36:20–30. These are the generations of Esau. However, the name comes from Old Persian *Hangmatana*, which the Greeks transliterated as Ecbatana, the more familiar name; it has nothing to do with Esau or anything biblical. Greek historians believed that the city had been founded by Deioces, the first Median king.

and pleasant but inferior to some about here. The *maidan* is uniform and beautiful; the King's palace and harem are nigh the great market. Low it is, built of raw bricks, varnished after the mode of paynim painting in blue, red and yellow tinctures mixed with Arabic knots and letters of azure and gold. The windows are large, trellissed and neatly-carved. Within it is of usual splendour; most of the rooms be arched, the roofs and sides neatly-painted in grotesque; the ground was also spread with carpets of silk and gold, then which no potentate in the world has more or better.[937] And here 'tis worth remembering what Saad ibn Waqqar, Omar's general, took from Yazdegerd the Persian King when he was vanquished: a carpet that was sixty cubits square, very curiously-wrought with figures and precious stones of several colours resembling flowers whose border had representations of the earth beautified with herbs and flowers as in the spring, and the materials with which it was woven were silk, silver, gold and stones of inestimable value, by which it appears this excellent art of carpet-making was anciently practiced in Persia.

Near the palace gate is a great tank or magazine of water made at the common charge and almost finished at our being here. The *hamams* or sweating-places are many, and resplendent in the azure pargetting and tiling wherewith they are circulated; the vulgar buildings also content the inhabitants, but to a discerning eye yield little admiration. The gardens are many and large, but with those in Isfahan and Shiraz are not to be compared. The *mesjids* are not two-thirds so many as John of Persia computed[938] long ago to be above 600, nor those so fastidious in pyramidical aspirings nor curious in architecture nor inside glory as in many lesser towns, so as I cannot enlarge her praise save that in spring and autumn I believe it may be a temperate and inciting climate, but in summer and winter are extreme in contraries, the sun frying them with his oblique flaming glances and Hiems a while no less benumbing them with his icicles.

Law regidly executed.

Here we met the Padishah again, who got into Qazvin two days afore us, and at his entrance into the seat-royal, instead of distributing the accustomed royal benevolence of giving a crown piece to all the women at his return after a long

---

[937] Unfortunately, as Greenway and St. Vincent note, Qazvin is now "only a shadow of its former splendour" (*Iran*, 337). Abbas moved the capital to Isfahan in 1598, and there have been several devastating earthquakes. There are two splendid mosques surviving, one quite ancient (although it has Safavid additions) and the other wholly Safavid. The palace described by Herbert no longer stands.

[938] John of Persia's "computations" are somewhat different from Herbert's. He states in the *Relation* (1604) that Qazvin had 450,000 inhabitants (to Herbert's 200,000) and that he had, "for curiosity, counted many times over its mosques, and of these there are more than 500," which Herbert elevates to 600 (*Juan de Persia*, 40).

process, which the ancient kings of Persia ever used, and Alexander doubled to those that were with child, and for omitting which Ochus[939] was taxed, Abbas exercised his severity. For it seems that forty camels entering loaden with tobacco out of India, the drivers being ignorant of a late prohibition, the King sometimes commanding and refraining as reason of state invited, Mohammed Ali the favourite, wanting his *pishkash*, commanded the penalty to be executed, which was to crop their ears and to snip their noses, offering withal to his angry justice a dismal sacrifice of forty load of tobacco, which was put into a deep hole that served as a pipe, and, being inflamed, in a black vapour gave the citizens *gratis* for two whole days and nights unpleasing incense.

Mohammed Ali Beg's undue practices.

After some stay, Sir Dodmore Cotton, to quicken his despatch, visited Mohammed Ali Beg, who, according to his education, entertained the Ambassador with a supercilious look, advising him to trust his success to his cabinet, wherein, as he would have him to understand, the mysteries of the whole state were locked, the King by reason of other great affairs expressing a willingness that it should be so. The Ambassador in any other place then Persia might have slighted his proposition, but perceiving no remedy and desiring to haste home, imparted so much as he saw necessary, in answer to which he soon perceived that touching Sir Robert Sherley he was to expect no further satisfaction, his adversary being dead, and at the Caspian Sea the King had sufficiently honoured him, but to speak truly, the Padishah had then no affection for him, who probably by reason of his old age he was disabled to do him further service, adding (but out of an enemy's mouth) that his embassies to the Princes of Christendom were but compliments of ordinary moment. But when our Ambassador objected he was in person there to justify his commission, that he had the King's letter of credence signed and stamped by the Shah himself and it had been a dangerous presumption for Sir Robert Sherley to look Shah Abbas in the face had he been an impostor, the favourite was convinced, we thought, for he had no further objection save that so our Ambassador pleased to lend him that *firman* Sir Robert Sherley brought for his justification, he would return it him next day with his master's sense concerning it.

It was no small vexation to our Ambassador to treat in this sort by proxy, but "*necessitas cogis ad turpia*"[940] is an old saying, and three days passed ere Mohammed Ali Beg would either vouchsafe to return the letter or give that satisfaction he promised. Howbeit, at length he came in person and told the Ambassador that the King had looked upon it, denied it to be his, and in passion burnt it, and that Sir Robert Sherley had liberty to depart. Now, albeit our Ambassador very well knew this undue practice, yet it was in vain to challenge the pragmatic

---

[939] Artaxerxes III (359–338 B.C.E.) was surnamed Ochus.

[940] "Necessity brings out the worst in one" (Latin proverb).

pagan, nor knew he any recourse by justice to ease himself, such was the constitution of that time and place, and by the inquiry then made it was very well understood how that he never showed it to the King nor had made any further scrutiny concerning it. The truth is he was bribed, but by whom it is not necessary to be mentioned, for Abbas by this got the worst, seeing in this transaction he was dishonoured, otherwise his justice and prudence would have appeared more to his vindication. Besides, the discontent he expressed against Naqd Ali Beg (as noted) and Ebrahim Khan his son, who durst not appear at court whiles Sir Robert Sherley was there nor many months after till Zeynal Khan[941] had mediated his peace, albeit not he but his father had offended, made as apparent as the sun that there was juggling. The truth is the wicked practice of these parts is such that when any are superannuated, according to the proverb "seeing they can do no more work they are to expect no more wages," and accordingly Sir Robert Sherley through old age being disabled to serve the Persians, that made them both slight his person and retrench his pension even then, when he most expected munificence and merited their best acknowledgements. But this bad requital of good service is no new thing in Persia, witness that in which Plutarch *De vita Artaxerxis* relates concerning Antalcidas, a noble Spartan, who whiles that state was paramount no man in the Persian court was more regarded, but suffering an eclipse at the battle of Leuctra (attributed to the good conduct of Epaminondas), the Spartans dispatched Antalcidas to the Persian king for supplies, whose reception was then as slight as formerly as it had been hospitable.[942]

The death of Sir Robert Sherley.

And hence came those discontents, nay, that arrow of Death that arrested him, for upon the 13 of July,[943] in less then a fortnight after our entering Qazvin, he gave this transitory world an *ultimum vale*[944] in his great climacteric, a family of so good antiquity that the naming serves to illustrate it without any hyperbole or other like addition. This gentleman also made good the old proverb that 'tis better to die honourably then to live with obloquy, and, wanting a fitter place for burial, we laid him under the threshold of his door without much noise or

---

[941] Actually Zeynal Beg.

[942] Antalcidas (d. 387 B.C.E.) had brokered a treaty between Artaxerxes II and the Greek city-states. In 387 B.C.E. the Persian king insisted that they sign to signify their obedience to the treaty, and he refused to allow the Thebans, who were part of the Boeotian League, to sign on behalf of the Boeotians themselves. He sent Cleombrotus II, the Spartan king, to attack Thebes unless they disbanded the League, which they refused. Epaminondas, the Boeotian commander, defeated the much larger Spartan army at Leuctra. Antalcidas committed suicide in shame.

[943] 1638 gives 13 June, which Foster calls "an obvious error" (*Herbert*, 205) and says that Sherley died of "fever and apoplexy."

[944] Final goodbye.

any other ceremony. He was brother to two gallant gentlemen, Sir Anthony and Sir Thomas Sherley,[945] deservedly-ranked amongst the greatest travellers in their times, and by their great experience qualified for most eminent services both civil and martial, so as in the due encomium of such, give me leave to apply what learned Casaubon has observed upon Strabo: *"Etenim, poetae prudentissimos heroum pronuntiavunt eos qui multis peregrinationibus usi sunt et varia loca pervagati, multorum vidisse hominum cum moribus urbes,"*[946] together with that of Ecclesiasticus 34:10–12, where (in the old translation) 'tis said "A man that hath travelled understandeth much, and he that hath good experience talketh of wisdom, but he that hath no experience knoweth little. When I travelled to and fro I saw many things and my understanding was greater then I was able to express; oftimes was I in danger of death, but by those things I had deliverance," in some measure verified in these brethren, who in passing through strange countries escaped many dangers, wherein nevertheless they reaped much honour and in which variety this gentleman had his share and no less tasted of sundry Princes' favours, for by Rudolph the Second he was created a Palatine of the Empire, by Pope Paul III[947] an Earl of the Sacred Palace of Lateran, from which he was empowered to legitimate the Indian bastards, and from the Persian monarch he received several honourable commands and for whom he performed some memorable services, but when he most expected found least, in his old age, even when he best deserved, yet in that not unlike Belisarius, which I speak not by report. And therefore, seeing he wants gilded trophies to adorn his sepulchre, albeit his virtues can out-brave those bubbles of vanity, till some will do it better, accept this *ultima amoris expressio*[948] from him who so long travelled in his company and so much honoured him:

> Lo here, the limits to whose restless brain
> No travels set, this urn doth now contain.

---

[945] For Sir Anthony Sherley (1565–1635), see Introduction. Sir Thomas Sherley (1564–c. 1630), the least-known of the three brothers, was an MP and a pirate. This last profession landed him in Turkish captivity (1603–1605); he was arrested again in England two years later and imprisoned in the Tower of London for shady dealings with the Levant Company.

[946] Isaac Casaubon (1559–1614), the great Swiss humanist and classical scholar from Geneva, was regarded in his time as one of the most learned men in Europe. His great edition of Strabo was published in Geneva (1587). Casaubon spent some years in France, and subsequently found great favour with James I, who invited him to England in 1610, where he spent the rest of his life. The quote reads: "For indeed, poets say that the most judicious heroes are those who undertake many journeys and travel to various places observing many peoples and cities together with their customs."

[947] Wrong pope. Herbert means Pope Paul V (Camillo Borghese), who reigned 1605–1621.

[948] Final expression of love.

A German count I was; the Papal state
Empower'd me th'Indians to legitimate.
Men, manners, countries to observe and see
Was my ambition and felicity.
The Persians last I viewed, with full desire
To purge my fame, blurred by a pagan's ire,
Which done, Death stops my passage. Thus the mind
Which reached the Poles is by this porch confined.
    Reader, I live happy still in home contents,
    Since outward hopes are but rich banishments.

After land-sweats and many a storm by sea,
This hillock aged Sherley's[949] rest must be;
He well had view'd arms, men and fashions strange,
In divers lands, desire so makes us range.
But, turning course, whilst the Persian tyrant he
With well-dispatched charge hoped glad would be,
See Fortune's scorn! Under this door he lies,
Who living had no place to rest his eyes.
    With what sad thoughts man's mind long hopes do twine,
    Learn by another's loss, but not by thine.

The Lady Sherley in distress.

Let it not seem impertinent if I add somewhat to the deserving memory of his wife, that thrice-worthy and heroic Lady Teresia.[950] The country she first drew breath in was Circassia, adjoining Georgia, that which Pomponius Mela calls

---

[949] Not that aged, even by the standards of the time; Sir Robert Sherley was born in 1581. The 1634 edition says that Sherley's age "exceeded not the great climacteric, which, being seven times nine, was looked upon as a specially critical period" (125), as Foster says. However, he takes issue with 1581 as the date of Sherley's birth as given in the *Dictionary of National Biography*, although he gives no reasons (*Herbert*, 324).

[950] Lady Teresa Sampsonia Sherley (1590–1669) was probably, as Herbert states, a Circassian who came to the court of Abbas I by way of a relative, probably a maternal aunt, who introduced her to "the Sultana," likely Tzarievna Marta, a Circassian herself. Several writers at the time claimed that she was a relative of the Shah's, but, as Herbert points out, this is unlikely. She was probably the daughter of a chieftain named Ismail Khan. There has been a fair amount of speculation about her religion, too; it is likely that she was an Orthodox Christian who converted to Catholicism, her husband's faith, and after his death she found shelter with the Carmelites. Sherley himself had converted in 1608, the year of their marriage. She arrived in England (1611) and was presented to James I. After Sherley's and Abbas's death she found herself denounced as a Christian, but defended herself vigorously before Shah Safi (1629) and left Persia in 1634. More information about her may be found in H. G. Chick, ed., *A Chronicle of the Carmelites in Persia and the Papal Mission of the XVII and XVIII Centuries* (London: Eyre and

Sargacia near Palus Maeotis, adjoining Georgia and 'twixt the northerly parts of the Black and Caspian Seas. She was of Christian parentage and honourable descent; her first relation to the court was being sent up to attend the Sultana, and by that means became sequestered to the harem, where there are many hundred virgins admitted whom the King seldom or never sees, and for ought I could hear, to the King she was no otherwise related. He nevertheless has power to dispose of such of them as he pleases to his officers, who esteeem it no small honour to receive a wife from his royal hands, according to which custom the Emperor of Persia presented her to Sir Robert Sherley as a testimony of his respect, which lady was a constant companion to him in all his fortunes until death.

Such time as her beloved lord lay dead and she half-dead through a long dysentery, one John, a Dutchman (rather a Jew), a painter, regarding neither her sex, profession nor disconsolate condition, complots with Mohammed Ali Beg to ruin her, pretending an engagement her husband was in to one Croll, a Fleming,[951] and, knowing he lay dead, referred himself to the testimony of the defunct to witness it, having no other evidence, it seems, to prove the debt. She might have paid them by like sophistry, that if the dead man would affirm it she would satisfy it, but the pretended creditors hasten to the *qadi* for a warrant to attach her goods. Howbeit, a faithful honest gentleman of our company, Mr. Robert Hedges by name, happily having notice, hastens to her house and advises her to make quick conveyance of her goods, which the poor lady readily hearkens to

---

Spottiswoode, 1939), in Chew, *Crescent*, 302–3; 336–38, and in William Neville, *The Three English Brothers* (1607), a compilation of the exploits of all the Sherley brothers and an account of Robert's marriage to "the Emperour of Persia his Neece." For the Catholics in Persia, see Carlos Alonso, "Clemente VIII y la fundación de la misiones catolicas en Persia," *Ciudad de Dios*, (1958): 196–240. An excellent article by Bernadette Andrea discloses a great deal more information about her and makes some interesting literary points as well. See B. Andrea, "Lady Sherley: The First Persian in England?" *Muslim World* 95(2005): 279–95. My thanks to Professor Andrea for sending me a copy of this fascinating article and information about sources.

[951] The exact identity of this Dutch artist is not known. Evelyn Sherley thought that he had painted a portrait of Sir Robert Sherley (99), which is also mentioned by Chew; he says that "a Flemish artist named Cole, under pretence of an old unpaid loan to Sherley, conspired with Mahomet Ali Beg and obtained a warrant to seize the widow's goods," which was prevented by Hedges (336 and n. 2). In the 1662 edition Herbert has "Croll," also in 1665 and 1677. Herbert's "John the boor" seems to refer to Jan van Hasselt rather than "Croll" himself. Willem Floor confirms that van Hasselt was "probably . . . John the Dutchman who tried to force his attentions upon Robert Sherley's widow" (159). The 1634 edition states that John "served the king of Persia twenty years" (125), but this is obviously incorrect, and also tells us that Sherley had "long since borrowed of him [Croll]" (125).

and forthwith tears the satin quilt she lay upon,[952] showing that virtue a stronger could not have bettered, and taking thence a cabinet which contained some jewels of value, being indeed all that was left her, entreats that worthy gentleman to safeguard them till the danger was over. He readily obeys, and was no sooner departed when John the boor enters with his catchpoles, who, without any apology for their rudeness or pity to her distress, broke ope her chests and plundered her of what was valuable, for some rich vests, costly turbans and a dagger of great price they took away, but finding no jewels such as they had seen him wear, and the rich ostrich-feather also (which they had worried in their ostrich-appetite), they were madded at that disappointment and made her horses, camels and asses (being all the personal estate they could then come by) bear them company, not caring if the lady starved. The gentleman, as soon as the storm was passed, returned, and besides words of comfort gladdened her heart in delivering her jewels again, of double value by that escape, without which I am persuaded her other fortune reached not to fifty pounds, a small provision for so noble a lady, especially seeing money is so useful in those uncharitable regions. But God provided better for her and beyond expectation, having, as I hear since, placed her in Rome, where of late years she lived with more freedom and outward happiness.

The death of Sir Dodmore Cotton.

"*Omnia quae de terra sunt, in terram convertentur,*" as we learn from Ecclesiasticus 40:11,[953] and in order thereto, like discontents, long conflict with adverse dispositions and fourteen days' consuming of a flux, occasioned, as I thought, by eating too much fruit or sucking in too much chill air upon Taurus, brought that religious gentleman Sir Dodmore Cotton our Ambassador to an immortal home. The 23rd of July, eleven days after Sir Robert Sherley's death, he bade this world adieu. Our duty commanding us to see him buried in the best sort we could, we obtained a dormitory for him amongst the Armenian graves, who also with their priests and people very civilly assisted the ceremony. His horse, which was led before, had a velvet saddle and cloth across his back; his coffin was covered with a crimson satin quilt (black they account not of) lined with purple taffeta. Upon his coffin were laid his bible, sword and hat; Mr. Hedges, Mr. Stodart, Mr. Emery, Mr. Molam, Dick the interpreter and such others of his followers as were

---

[952] 1634: "she tore a satin quilt with her feeble hands and trusted him with her treasure, a cabinet, some jewels, rich stones and the like, with which he was no sooner gone then the pagan sergeants, with John the Fleming, entered her chamber, carried away what was valuable or vendible: his horses, camels, vests, turbans, a rich Persian dagger and some other things" (125).

[953] "All things that are of the earth shall turn to the earth again."

healthy attended the corpse, and Dr. Gooch,[954] His Lordship's chaplain, buried him, where his body rests in hope till the Resurrection. Now, though his singular virtue and memory will not perish, seeing 'tis acknowledged that *"evenit ad Aethera virtus,"* I wish nevertheless with all my heart that he had a monument more befitting him as some more eminent memorial, for I may truly say he was *"vivum omnis virtutis exempla,"*[955] and therefore wish I could better express that *supremum officium amoris*[956] I owe then by decking his hearse with these unpolished epicedia:

> *Quod procul a patriis iacet hic qui conditur oris,*
> *Nullum crede nefas illum pepulisset, viator.*
> *Regis amor populique fuit, pietate colenda,*
> *Quorum iussa tulit per mille pericula Persis*
> *Legatus; sed Fata premunt, nec foedera curant.*
> *Si virtus, si prisca fides, si gratia morum*
> *Ossa beant, tumulus sacer est. Quid tenderis ultra?*
> *Mecca silet, Divum resonat Cazbena Britannum!*[957]

Lo, noble Cotton far from home hath found
A resting-place in the Assyrian ground.
His country's love and duty to his King
So far a willing heart from home did bring.

---

[954] Henry Gooch (c. 1584–1657), from Trinity College, Cambridge, was ordained in 1610 and became Vicar of Longstanton in Cambridgeshire, receiving his D. D. in 1623 soon before he left England, with the help of Cotton, who solicited Charles I's assistance. After Cotton's death he appears to have been the most senior man in the delegation (as well as one of the more unpleasant), and simply assumed authority, not without some opposition from Cotton's attendants. As soon as Cotton died, Stodart relates, "Doctor Googe called for all his keyes into his hands . . . I delivered them, for which I was very sory within a while after I considered what I had don" (*Journal*, 56–7). Gooch even gave away or sold some of Cotton's possessions (Stodart, *Journal*, 59), and he has a lot to say about the "degeneracy" of the entertainment given the English by the Shah, indicating that he attended all the festivities. For more details, and Gooch's account of his experiences in Persia, see Introduction. Gooch became Rector of Cheadle when he returned, but in 1645 lost his position because he was a royalist.

[955] A living example of every virtue.

[956] Last office of love.

[957] "Because far from home he lies buried on these shores, traveller, do not think that it was some wrongdoing that drove him away. It was love of king and people, since piety had to be observed, whose orders he bore through a thousand dangers as ambassador to the Persians: but the Fates pressed hard, nor did they regard treaties. If virtue, old-fashioned faithfulness, and grace of character bless his bones, his tomb is sacred. Why go any further? Mecca is silent: Qazvin resounds (in praise of) a godlike Briton." This much-improved translation comes from the MRTS editor.

Harden thy tenderness, no danger fear
The way to Heaven; alike is everywhere.

The burial of our three[958] Ambassadors, you cannot otherwise imagine, was no small discouragement to the progress of our travel, being as a body without a head, for although the Padishah seems to commiserate us as persons left desolate in a strange country, as an assurance of his respect having sent each of us two vests of cloth of gold,[959] yet we were convinced that he may well call himself a miserable man whose welfare depends upon the smiles of Persia. We prepared therefore to be gone, but could not till Mohammed Ali Beg gave his consent; long attendance we danced ere we could procure a *firman* for our safe travel, but at length importunity prevailed so as we got it, wrapped up in a piece of cloth of gold fastened with a silken string, with a stamp of Arabic letters curiously gilded upon paper very sleek and chamletted with red and blue agreeable to the mode of Persia. The King's *firman* was thus interpreted:

> The High and Mighty Star whose Head is covered with the sun, whose
> Motion is comparable to the Firmament, whose Imperial Majesty is
> come from Asharraf[960] and hath dispatched the Lord Ambassador
> of the English King etc. The Command of the Great King is that
> his followers be conducted from Our Palace of Qazvin to Saveh,
> by the Daruga of Saveh to the City of Qum, and by the Sultan
> of Qum to the City of Kashan through all My Territories. Fail not
> My command. I also command them a safe travel.
>   July. Bahman. *Heg.* 1008.

Mohammed Ali Beg described.

After thirty days' stay in Qazvin, about the midst of July we willingly bade farewell to the Persian court, but ere we go far, let me give Mohammed Ali Beg our small friend his reward that others may know him. His birthplace was Parthia, from *parah*, which signifies "to fructify." His *almuten* calculated, the aspect was found happy, and in him the Machiavellian motto was verified, that a dram of good fortune is better than a pound of virtue. In a happy minute Abbas, by accident casting his eye upon him, magic intuition it had, it seems, for from a very

---

[958] Chivalrously, Herbert is including Naqd Ali Beg.

[959] It was one of these vests which Dr. Gooch threw down at the bearer's feet (see Introduction), after which the English delegation left. Herbert's account suggests that they wanted to leave and that Mohammed Ali Beg tied them up in red tape; Stodart and Gooch stated that they were packed off rather quickly.

[960] This is *al-Asaru 'sh-sharif*, or "the sacred relic," which could be hair from the Prophet's head or moustache, or perhaps one of his footprints (for details see Hughes, *Dictionary* 28).

mean condition he was called to court, robed in gold and quickly made the magnet of Persia, so that we see there is no soul so base but is capable of some degree of exalted virtue, as appears in this example, for by being a favourite he quickly became of that reputation that he was acknowledged for the idol of his time, instructed by the King, and in short space acquainted not only with the intrigues of state but quickly learned to steer the helm of Persia. [961] His yearly income at our being there by many was estimated *viis et modis*[962] upwards of 100,000 pounds sterling, which may well be, seeing scarce any mirza, khan, sultan or beglerbeg that depended upon the Padishah's smiles but in aweful compliment had no other way to make him their friend but by some annual *pishkash* or other. His presence was comely, his countenance pleasant, made the more amenable by many complimental smiles. He was of a big full body; large eyes and nose he had and moustachios in excess; at this time aged about forty, a third of which he had been Fortune's minion. But no sooner was old Abbas by impartial Death struck from the helm of Persia and young Safi[963] made the royal steersman, when Mohammed's looks were humbled, yea, his splendour in the setting of his master quickly darkened, so as we see that true which says that ordinarily advancement and honour change men's minds from better to worse. "*Solus imperantium Vespasianus,*"

---

[961] 1634: "His birth-place was Parthia . . . and near Isfahan. His parentage was worshipful, that he knew no further then his father, a man both mean and poor. Mohammed, it seems, had no stomach for the wars, and having a large bulk to maintain, and no chameleon, his education being simple, he became a costermonger, and by that became wealthy and capable to maintain himself. In a happy hour the King, then in the hippodrome and in Isfahan, viewed him, liked him and preferred him, so as in small time he became sole favourite that was feared and honoured everywhere among the Persians" (126).

[962] By ways and means. This is a legal phrase.

[963] Shah Safi [*Suffee*] (1629–1642) had a habit of exterminating people whom he thought had climbed too far and might become a threat to his imperial power, such as Abbas's natural son Emamqoli Khan (not the "Duke of Shiraz," whose similar death Herbert describes below), whom Monshi accused of "claiming the throne" *History*, 3: 1303) and not a few of his own closer relatives. He was not actually in his "nonage" when he came to the throne, as Herbert suggests, but about nineteen. The 1634 edition in one place has "aged sixteen" (127). Monshi describes his accession and wishes him well as he "set foot on the throne of kingship" (*History*, 3: 1304). Monshi also hoped to chronicle the reign of Safi, but did not live to do so. In 1634 Herbert wrote: "But of what courage, ingenuity or inclination King Safi shows himself, I cannot give the reader satisfaction in, in that we parted thence just at his coronation, and his years cannot yet beget discretion in full measure (being not above fifteen), but it appears partly that he is truly of the Abbasian pedigree, for so soon as he got security of the diadem, he cut off Mohammed Ali Beg's head" (104). This is inaccurate: Safi did not execute Mohammed Ali Beg. And by 1677 the error seems to have been corrected.

says the historian, *"mutatus in melius;"*[964] for Mohammed Ali Beg, his imperious disposition and avarice heaped most men's contempt upon him, insomuch as any now dares brand him with becoming epithets, and his estates being so vast the very weight threatened to press him to ruin.

Of all others the Shirazian dynast most affrighted him when he darted him frowns of death, but,*"nec semper feriet, quodcunque minabitur,"*[965] a black mist of unexpected destruction fuming from young Safi's brow, of the right stock, sent Emamqoli first to an untimely grave and soon after the *beglerbeg* his son to bear him company, neither to be descended of loyal and Princely sires, to have Abbas his oath of safety, to be protector of Persia during the nonage of the infant King, to have famoused the Crown by many heroic services, nor to be Emamqoli Khan could repel the deadly shaft of jealousy, but in the meridian of his course and glory, in the extreme of his hopes and when so long a farewell was least thought on, he and his are hewed down, making good that of the satiric poet, *"Ad generum Cereris sine caede et vulnere pauci discedant tyrannis,"*[966] his pride among the natives, perfidy to the English and cruelty at Hormuz and in Arabia crying for revenge, in which examples we see fulfilled that as nothing is more proud, so nothing is more miserable then man, whereas Mohammed Ali Beg shakes off his rags of discontent and afresh ingratiates himself, at this day moving in a sphere of happiness.

Shah Abbas.

Abbas the Persian emperor was of stature low, of a quick aspect, his eyes small and flaming without any *palpebrae*[967] or hair over them. He had a low forehead but a high and hawked nose, sharp chin, and after the mode of Persia was upon the chin beardless; his moustachios were exceeding long and thick, and turned downwards. He was born in the year of Mohammed 938, King of Aria fifty years, Emperor of Persia forty-three, and died aged seventy in the year of our account 1628, of their era 1008 in Qazvin.[968] His heart, bowels and carcase were parted and buried in Ali Meshed, in Qazvin, in Ardabil (or at Qum, some say), so as few, it seems, know the certainty of this distribution.

Shah Abbas [illustration not shown]

---

[964] "Of the emperors, only Vespasian changed for the better" (Tacitus, *Histories* 1.9. 50). The Emperor Vespasian (69–79), a good man, was deified after his death.

[965] "[The bow] will not always hit the mark aimed at" (Horace, *Ars poetica* 350).

[966] Herbert seems to intend these lines: "Battle and slaughter / See most kings off; few tyrants die in their beds" (Juvenal, *Satires* 10.112-113).

[967] Eyebrows.

[968] Abbas died in Farrahabad, not Qazvin, on 8 January 1629 (N.S.).

The Eastern monarchs at this day continue the custom of their predecessors, who delighted more in epithets of virtue then in titles of kingdoms. They accounted it an effeminate vainglory to stuff their letters, or when they sent their ambassadors to foreign states to gild their greatness by accumulation of names of provinces, in which respect the German Emperor got little in the late letter he sent Abbas, the beginning of which was so filled with titles of his empire that after he had heard half a dozen he had no patience to stay the reading of the rest, which is also the reason that the Muscovite, unless necessity enforce, seldom or never thither sends his ambassadors. Nevertheless, the prolixity of titles and epithets is no less redundant in another kind, adorning his letters and dispatches with hyperboles of his resemblance to the sun, his affinity to the stars and agreement with the sweetest and rarest sort of fruits, flowers, gems etc., as also with the epithets of wise, famous, sweet, victorious, and agreement with the sweetest and rarest sort of fruits, flowers, gems etc., as also with the epithets of wise, famous, sweet, victorious, merciful, just, beautiful, courageous etc. Howbeit, the titles of the Persian monarch may be these:

Abbas, Emperor or Padishah of 1. Persia; 2. Parthia; 3. Media, 4. Bactria 5. Ortispana; 6. Khorasan, and 7, Aria; King of the Uzbeks 8; Tartars 9; Hyrcania 10; Draconia 11; Evergeta 12; Parmenia 13; Hydaspia 14; Sogdiana 15; Parapomisa 16; Drangiana 17; Arachosia 18; Margiana 19; Carmania 20; Gedrosia 21; as far as The Indus 22; Sultan of Hormuz 23; Khora 24; Arabia 25; Susiana 26; Chaldaea 27; Mesopotamia 28; Georgia 29; Armenia 30; Iberia 31; Mingrelia 32; Mirza or Prince of the Imperious Mountains of 33 Ararat; Taurus 34; Caucasus 35 and Periardo 36; Commander of all Creatures from the 37 Caspian Sea to the 38 Gulf of Persia. Lord of the Four Rivers of Paradise 39; Euphrates 40; Tigris 41; Araxes 42 and Indus 43; Of true descent from Ali, Governor of all Sultans, Emperor of Mussulmen, Bud of Honour, Mirror of Virtue, Rose of Delight etc.

Bubbles of ostentation.

And although to the modest reader a great deal of ostentation appear in these blustering titles, yet will they seem but small when we parallel them with kings of old and at this day in other places. For such was the amplitude of Nebuchadnezzar's kingdom that in Daniel 2:39 'tis recorded wherever the children of men dwelt, beasts in the field or fowls of the air, he gave under Nebuchaznezzar's hands. To Ahasuerus "*omnem terram et omnes maris insulas fecit tributarias,*" Esther 10:1.[969] To Cyrus the Lord God of Heaven gave all the kingdoms of the earth, Ezra 1:2,[970] and by monarchs of the then known world Xerxes,

---

[969] "[And the king Ahasuerus] laid a tribute upon all the land, and upon the isles of the sea."

[970] "Thus saith Cyrus king of Persia, The Lord God of heaven hath given me all the kingdoms of the earth . . ."

as Aeschines[971] writes in his letters, proclaims [himself to be] "Sovereign Lord of all men from the rising of the sun to the going down thereof." Domitian, like Pharaoh scoffing "Who is the Lord?" in his proclamations thus: Your Lord God Domitian, and Caligula entitled himself "*Deus optimus maximus et Jupiter Latialis.*"[972] Now, if he could have satisfied his atheism with the title of an earthly god or of Jove, Menander and Tzetzes had defended him, saying from Homer "*rex est viva Dei imago in terris, et reges omnes olim vocaverunt Ioves.*"[973] Shapur, son to Hormisdas the Persian, *Anno Domini* 315, also began his letter to Constantine the Emperor in this sort, as *lib.* 17 of [Ammianus] Marcellinus "I, Shapur, King of Kings, Equal to the Stars and Brother to the sun and Moon,"[974] which kindred to the sun was also claimed by Mark Antony that noble Roman, who called the two children he had by Cleopatra Sol and Luna,[975] both which nevertheless were led captive by Augustus and to this end it might be inferred that both sun and moon were his inferiors. Khusrau also, Hormisdas's son, in the year of grace 620 (the first of the Mohammedan accompt), scorning those of *Deus Terrebenus* or of *Homo a Deo secundus*, blows himself up in this blaspheming proem to Mauritius the Emperor[976] "Khusrau, Great King of Kings, Lord of Lords, Ruler

---

[971] Aeschines (389–314 B.C.E.) was the great Athenian orator and statesman best known for his opposition to Demosthenes in the form of three great speeches. He ended his career in exile as a sophist and teacher of rhetoric. Herbert's source for Aeschines's letters is probably Jacques Amyot's translation of Plutarch's *Opera moralia*, in French *Les oeuvres morales et meslées de Plutarch* (1572). Some modern scholars dispute whether the letters ascribed to Aeschines are in fact his. The tag actually translates "[proclaims] himself to be Lord of all men from the East to the West," but Herbert translates the spirit rather than the letter.

[972] Titus Flavius Domitianus reigned 81–96; Gaius Caligula reigned 37–41. Both gods were assassinated. Caligula's title translates "Jupiter Latialis, the Greatest and Best God."

[973] Menander (c. 342–290 B.C.E.), author of over 100 plays (mostly lost) and the greatest writer of the "New Comedy" in Athens. It is likely that the quotation from Homer may be found in the *Dyskolos*, which until recently was the only complete play by Menander available. The Latin translates "the king is the living image of God on earth, and all kings once were called Jupiters." Maurice Balme has made an excellent translation of all available plays and fragments (Oxford: Oxford University Press, 2001).

[974] Shapur I reigned 309–79, succeeding his father Hormisdas II (303–09). The Roman emperor Constantine I "the Great" reigned 306–37, although Herbert writes "Constantius," which suggests Constantius II (337–61), but he does give the date 315, which would suggest Constantine I.

[975] The children were Cleopatra Selene [Luna] or Cleopatra VIII (c. 40–6 B.C.E.), who married Juba II of Numidia; Alexander Helios [Sol] (b. c. 40 B.C.E.) and a third, not mentioned here, Ptolemy Philadelphus (b. 36 B.C.E.).

[976] Khusrau or Chosroes II was king of Persia 591–628 in succession to his father Hormisdas IV (578–91). Flavius Mauricius Tiberius or Maurice was Byzantine emperor 582–602, which means that Herbert got the wrong emperor. In fact, he means Heraclius

of Nations, Prince of Peace, Salvation of Men, amongst Gods a Man good and ever amongst men a God most glorious, the Great Conqueror arising with the sun, giving eyes or lustre to the night and a hero in descent," from which affected pride those idolatrous slaves were induced to worship and to clamour out "*Tu es nostra salus et in te credimus*,"[977] and whence the poet, to illustrate his bees, sings "Egypt nor Lydia do their kings obey, / Nor Medes nor Parthians half so much as they."[978] From which examples others in later times have arrogated to themselves no less supereminency, for Suleiman the wrathful Turk proclaimed himself King of Kings, Lord of Lords, Emperor of Constantinople and Trebizond, Ruler of Europe, Africa and Asia, Commander of the Ocean and Conqueror of Assyria, Arabia etc. Also Murad his grandson styled himself God of the Earth, Captain of the Universe, Sacred Angel, Mohammed's Beloved etc.[979]

At length the home-bred Chinese[980] but the other day sending his ambassadors to Abbas with an epistle directed "To his slave the Sophy of Persia the undaunted Emperor of the World (a well-read man) sends greeting," but neither the ambassador's brags that his master had six hundred great cities, two thousand walled towns, a thousand castles, sixty millions of slaves and a hundred and twenty thousand millions of crowns yearly revenue could make his King there to be admired or privilege his ambassadors from dirty welcome, the haughty Persian turning him back again to assure his master they neither believed him to be the Beauty of the Earth nor, as he writes himself, Heir-Apparent to the sun. His next neighbour and he being at odds for the title, the Tartar I mean, vulgarly the Great Khan, a Khan indeed in his mistaken genealogy, for, as some have writ, forgetting that his great-grandsire Genghis Khan was a blacksmith, he blasphemously proclaims himself son to the highest God and quintessence of the purest spirits, whence (as some travellers merrily report) is engendered that fantastic custom, some days after dinner to have his herald by sound of trumpet echo out to other potentates of the world that he has dined, so as then they have the liberty to go to dinner. What may we then think of the Peguan monarch, of him of Mattacala and Manicongo, who nourish so high a conceit of their radiancy that heathen ambassadors and others are required to creep like worms and to hide their faces lest their eyes should be bleared in gazing on such a lustre? Or of that fastidious Monomotapa,[981] who seldom goes abroad or shows himself, in

---

(610–42), who fought a long war against Khusrau II. The Latin states "Man is second after God."

[977] You are our safety and we believe in you.

[978] The poet is Virgil, and he sings about his bees in Book IV of the *Georgics*.

[979] The Turkish sultans here are Suleiman I "the Magnificent" (1520–1566) and Murad III (1574–1595).

[980] Herbert is likely referring to the Ming Emperor Wan-li, who reigned 1572–1620, but it could possibly be Tiang-qi, who reigned 1620–1627.

[981] The name of a great fourteenth-century ruler of what is now Zimbabwe.

compassion to his people lest they should be struck blind in eyeing him, a curtain weakening the beams that would otherwise issue from his face, but are permitted to use their ears to admire his champs when he eats and the gulps when he drinks, but pay soundly for it; at every gulp and cough (he coughs sometimes, you may suppose, of purpose) they shout for joy, and Stentor-like[982] make the place to ring again. And seeing the like pride appears in the Papal Prince Boniface VIII, we find in *Fasc. Temp.*[983] that not content with the title Universal Bishop he entitled himself Lord of the Whole World, but Sixtus IV,[984] his successor, soared a strain above him, in that panegyric upon the triumphal arch as he first entered Rome being writ "*In terris, crederis esse Deus.*" Therefore we may less wonder that Prester John (Negus they call him, having never read St. Cyprian[985] *Ad quirites*, "*In nullo gloriandum est, nam nostrum nihil est*") adorns his mitre with fifteen provincial titles, adding that he is Head of the Church, the Favourite of God, the Pillar of Faith, issued from Solomon, David, Judah and Abraham, Sion's Prop, Extract from the Virgin's Hand, Son of St. Peter and St. Paul by the Spirit and of Nahu by the Flesh, in these more vagrant then his other restless notions, in vain secluding himself from the view of man by a thin lawn, since in his swelling imposthumes his portrait is discovered, a cancer also spreading north as far the other way to that other kind of Christian, by name Ivan Vassilievich,[986] a tyrannic Muscovite whose coronation *Anno Domini* 1584 was celebrated with wonderful magnificence, besides his furs loading himself with two and thirty bubbles of

---

[982] In the *Iliad*, Stentor was a Greek warrior renowned for his extremely loud voice, hence "stentorian."

[983] Herbert refers here to Werner Rolevinck's *Fasciculus temporum omnes antiquorum chronicas complectens* (1474), a history of the world from the Creation to the reign of Pope Sixtus IV. Rolevinck (1425–1502) was a Carthusian monk from Westphalia whose popular work was reprinted many times from 1474 onwards. An online facsimile has been made available by the Biblioteca Valenciana.

[984] Pope Boniface VIII reigned 1294–1303; his papacy was marked by his conflict with Philip IV of France; Pope Sixtus IV reigned 1471–1484; he is known for building the Sistine Chapel and for having declared a crusade against the Ottoman Empire. The quotation means "On earth you are thought to be God."

[985] St. Cyprian (c. 200–258) was a Roman barrister who converted to Christianity and became Bishop of Carthage (248). When Emperor Decius persecuted the Christians (250–51) he hid, but re-emerged and pursued a successful career until a new persecution began under Valerian in 257, when he was executed for refusing to sacrifice to Roman gods. By *Ad Quirites* (*To the Citizens of Rome*) Herbert means the *Testimonia ad Quiritum*, which first appeared in print along with other works in 1471. The quotation translates "Nothing is worthy of boasting about, because nothing is ours" (*Testimonia* 3.4, PL 4. 734).

[986] Ivan IV "the Terrible" was Tsar of Russia 1533–1584. The date of his coronation is inaccurate, unless it is just a misprint for 1534.

ostentation, all which considered we well may say, well fare Aurelius,[987] Saladin[988] and Tamberlane, heroes as great as victorious and as terrible to the world as any of these we have lately named, who so detested flattery that they blushed at their deserved praises, and some at their burials causing their winding-sheet to be displayed as an epitome of all they merited, proclaimed aloud *pulvis et umbra sumus.*[989] But to return; let us now proceed on in our journey.

Saveh.

We left Qazvin about ten at night, thereby avoiding the sun's too much warmth, and at his first discovery from the Antipodes got into Farsian[990] a small town, but memorable in the sweet cool water we had there to quench our thirst with, an element more useful then fire in sunburnt Asia. Our next *manzil* was at *Asaph,*[991] at *Begun*[992] our next, observable in a royal caravanserai or hospital of charity erected at the cost and care of Tahmasp, late King of Persia, and did the water, which is blackish and unhealthy there, but correpond with other delights it has, it might merit better commendation. To Saveh[993] we got the next night, a town both great and fruitful, but that it is the ruin of old Tigranocerta, i.e. *Tigrani Civitas* as Bonacciolus[994] guesses, I cannot credit, seeing most place that city in Media Superior or Atropatia, neighbouring Armenia,[995] but that it was Messabatha or

---

[987] Herbert may mean Marcus Aurelius Antoninus, Roman Emperor 161–180 and noted Stoic philosopher, but it seems more likely that Aurelian [Lucius Domitius Aurelianus] (270–275) is intended, as the epithets "victorious" and "terrible" befit him more than they do his milder predecessor.

[988] Salah-ed-din Ayyub (1138–1193) was Sultan of Egypt and Syria 1174–1193, whose conflict with the Crusaders in general and with Richard I of England in particular is the stuff of legend.

[989] "We are dust and shadows" (Horace, *Odes* 4. 7. 16).

[990] Farsian [*Perissophoon*] is located in modern Golestan province. The identification is from Foster (*Herbert* 214).

[991] Tentatively identified as modern Ashraf. Foster has "Asaph" (*Herbert*, 214).

[992] Tentatively identified as modern Begim Aqa. However, della Valle mentions a place called "the Begum's caravanserai" (*Travels.* 2: 579), which Foster says was built by Zainab Begum, daughter of Shah Tahmasp and wife of Shah Abbas (*Herbert*, 326).

[993] Saveh, once an important regional trading centre, is in Markazi province between Tehran and Hamadan. Tradition has it that the Three Wise Men are buried here (as Marco Polo mentions in Book I), and now it is "of interest to travellers principally for its two extremely fine minarets" (Greenway and St. Vincent, *Iran*, 189).

[994] Alfonso Bonaccioli (1502–1581) was an Italian nobleman and humanist from Ferrara. He made Italian translations of geographical works by Strabo (1562–1565), Martianus Capella (1578), and Pausanias (1593–1594). Herbert's reference is to the Strabo translation.

[995] Der Nersessian states that Tigranocerta's site "has been identified by some scholars as that of the medieval town of Martyropolis (modern Farkin or Mayafarkin) at the

Artacana I more easily believe.[996] The Pole is here raised 35 degrees 7 minutes. A city I may call it, pleasantly upon a rising hill giving ground to twelve hundred houses, a sweet rivulet[997] from the mountain Baronta refreshing it, from which and the people's industry, the thankful earth retributes a tribute in variety of choice fruits and grain, as wheat, rice, barley, figs, pomegranates, olives and honey, the seven the Promised Land in Deuteronomy 8:8[998] is commended for. I am sure of this: no place I ever came in more delighted me for aerial music, and of all the choir, the nightingale twenty together (here called bulbuls) claiming the pre-eminence, whose excellency the second best of Roman poets thus celebrates:

> I must salute the curious Philomel,
> Which all the birds in singing doth excel.
> Come, pretty friend, my solace in the night,
> In all the grove I find no such delight.
> A thousand warbling notes thy throat displays,
> Which thy sweet music chants as many ways.
> The vulgar birds may strive to equal thee.
> Yet never can attain like harmony.
> Their mirth doth last no longer then the day,
> But thine doth chase the silent night away.

Charras.

Our next night's travel was over large plains, raised in many places by artificial mounts here and there cut into trenches, notable no doubt in many gallant encampings and memorable in Lucullus his captivating Mithridates, that learned King of Pontus, but what that grand epicure fortunately got, Marcus Crassus the covetous and richest Roman lost after his impious sacrilege at Jerusalem, ravishing thence the holy relics and so much treasure as outvalued six tons of gold. Puffed up with so much wealth and his victories amongst the Jews, he resolves with fifty thousand men to forage Persia, but Orodes [II], son of

---

foot of the Taurus mountains, on the north bank of the Tigris" (*Armenians*, 26). Most information about it comes from Appian of Alexandria. Saveh is "an important transit centre . . . on one of the two main roads between Tehran and Hamadan," and was important before the Mongols destroyed it in the thirteenth century (Greenway and St. Vincent, *Iran*, 189). It is definitely not the site of Tigranocerta.

[996] Saveh is not Artacana, although the location of the latter is disputed. Artacana may be Dara or Ardakan, a desert town in Yazd province (Greenway and St. Vincent, *Iran*, 217), or possibly Herat in Aria (modern Western Afghanistan).

[997] The Mazdaqan River (Foster, *Herbert* ,214).

[998] "A land of wheat, and barley, and vines, and fig trees, and pomegranates; a land of olive oil, and honey."

Mithridates the Third,[999] courageously opposed him hereabouts, and, following his army into Mesopotamia, near Haran the Romans were overthrown and the avaricious consul by Surena the general was made his prisoner, yea, to glut his thirst, divine vengeance so ordering as Tomyris[1000] did to Cyrus, the Parthian served Crassus so, forcing him to quaff a health to death in pouring down his throat molten gold.[1001]

Charras was formerly called Haran[1002] Acts 7:3, and is the place where Abraham once dwelt before his removal to Ur in Chaldaea, where Terah[1003] was a fire-idolator; called *Urche*, and by some authors *Orche* and *Orchoa*, near the Desert Arabia. In Genesis 10:11 'tis called *Calah*, in Ezekiel 27:23 *Canneh*, and after that *Calanneh*, as Appian supposes, albeit some think the great city Seleucia upon Tigris, not far thence, to be it.[1004] The country about it and part of Arabia was inhabited by the Semites.

But to return. By this overthrow given Crassus, the Roman power was exterminate in Parthia, fifty three years before the death of Christ. Yet long the Romans sorrowed not, for Mark Antony five years after by his general affronted them with better success; when the Parthians' flight nor fight helped them, their

---

[999] Mithridates III was actually the brother, not the son of Orodes II. As a reward for co-operating in the murder of their father Phraates III, Orodes made his brother co-ruler, with his headquarters in Media. He ruled 57–54 B.C.E. and was deposed for cruelty. He was defeated by Surena and captured in Babylon, where he was later killed.

[1000] Tomyris (fl. 550–531 B.C.E.), hardly "an obscure Saka queen" (Olmstead, *History*, 66) was the ruler of the Massagetae. Her forces defeated Cyrus II, who was mortally-wounded and died soon afterwards (539 B.C.E.). The story of his death which Herbert alludes to is fictitious, but is found in ancient sources who include Herodotus, Strabo (5.263; he mentions Cyrus's defeat but not Tomyris by name), Polyaenus (all used by Herbert) and the sixth-century Byzantine historian Jordanes in *De origine actibusque Getarum* (551). We will hear more of her later.

[1001] This is pure fiction. After a meeting to discuss terms with Surena after the battle of Carrhae, a scuffle ensued between the Parthians and Octavius, one of Crassus's officers, during which Crassus was killed (Colledge, *Parthians*, 41–42).

[1002] This surmise of Herbert's is incorrect; Haran is a city not in Iran but south-east of Edessa in Turkey, "on the main route from Nineveh to Aleppo" (*IBD* 2: 608). It was indeed the city where Terah (see below) lived with Abram, later Abraham (Genesis 11:31; Acts 7:2, 4).

[1003] Terah was Abram's father (Genesis 11:26–32). He moved his family from Ur to Haran and from where Abram migrated to Canaan (Genesis 12–21).

[1004] Calah, known to the Arabs as Nimrud and the Biblical Haran, is about 30 km south-east of the modern Iraqi city of Mosul. It was the capital of Assyria until 710 B.C.E., and was destroyed by the Babylonians in 612 B.C.E. It is certainly not the same place as Seleucia, which was situated on the western side of the Tigris river in Mesopotamia, and whose ruins were likely not visible in Herbert's time. Herbert is correct in identifying it with Carrhae, the site of Crassus's defeat.

Prince Pacorus[1005] by his death disanimating them, affrighted in great measure when Phraates[1006] (Mezentius, some name the parricide) deposed the valiant Orodes from crown and life, treason, the Devil's virtue, perpetrating that the Romans could not do by generous conflict. Yet Antony attempts revenge, but adverse Fortune suffered him not to thrive; such was the resistance he found by the Satrapeni inhabiting Media and the Armenian forces led by Tigranes, a captain that formerly worsted Lucullus. Howbeit, Augustus, in whose reign our blessed Saviour became flesh and Janus's temple was opened, by treaty easily effected what his predecessors could not do by force, prevailing with Phraates to veil bonnet to the Roman diadem. But two hundred years after, one Ardashir, a native Persian and royally-descended, shakes off that servitude, not only outbraving the Romans but by a three days' fight and victory over Artabanus[1007] revived the Persian name, which for full five hundred years had been subject to Parthia. But Alexander Severus, from Julius Caesar the four and twentieth emperor, succeeding Heliogabalus the lustful,[1008] receives a pragmatic letter frrom the new king to restore what anciently adorned the crown of Persia. This repugned the Roman majesty, and thereupon marches to give him an account, but in careless passing-over of Euphrates, the army was so suddenly charged by Ardashir that the Roman Emperor was routed totally, his bad luck not ending there, for Maximinus the Thracian soon after bereaved him of his Empire, and the German assassinates him of his life, his virtuous mother Mamaea, Origen's[1009] proselyte,

---

[1005] Pacorus I (d. 38 B. C. E.) was likely associated with his father Orodes II on the throne from about 52, although this is not certain. He was killed in Syria fighting the Romans (see Colledge, *Parthians*, 43–44).

[1006] The first act of Phraates IV was to "murder first his father and then all his brothers" after Orodes II handed over the throne to him (Colledge, *Parthians*, 44). The name Mezentius is probably an allusion to the mythical cruel and ruthless king from Virgil's *Aeneid*, who wreaks havoc amongst the Trojans until slain by Aeneas.

[1007] Artabanus V (c. 213–24/26) was the last Arsacid king of Parthia. There were actually three battles between Artabanus and Ardashir, but in the last the former was killed and "Parthia fell into the hands of Ardashir, who was cronwed king in Ctesiphon" (Colledge, *Parthians*, 173).

[1008] M. Aurelius Alexander Severus reigned 222–235; he succeeded M. Aurelius Antoninus, surnamed Heliogabalus or Elagabalus because of his Sun-worship. He reigned 218–222, and was known for his cruelty and dissolution.

[1009] Origen of Alexandria (c. 185–254) was one of the earliest and most prolific Christian theologians and biblical exegetes. He wrote commentaries in both Greek and Latin on practically every book in the Bible, and his most famous doctrinal work is the *De principiis*. Origen's *Homilies* were the first works to appear in print (1475), and from 1512–1679 there were many editions of all his extant writings. Erasmus edited Origen shortly before he died (1536). The Greek writings were edited by Bishop Pierre Huet (1668).

associating the Emperor in his death as she had formerly in his glory.[1010] Licinius Valerianus,[1011] surnamed Colobus, undertook then to rule the Empire and took upon him to overrule the rising Persian, but neither his eloquence, which was notable, nor his army, which was great, could do what a Supreme Judge had decreed otherwise, for Shapur with an undaunted party denied him entrance, and in the end the Romans were defeated, but, which was worse, Valerian himself being taken prisoner, was to his dying day and to the astonishment of all tyrants made a footstool for Shapur to tread upon whever he mounted, the justice of God herein being singularly manifested by compensating the Emperor in this singular abasement and odious servitude for his cruelty and extreme rigour extended to the orthodox Christians, many thousands of which he had martyred, and amongst the rest St. Lawrence[1012] that noble witness, who upon a gridiron was in a most horrid and inhuman manner broiled to death. But have I not wandered too far in reviving the memory of Parthia, for by this we are entered Qumis, where, having refreshed our scorched and wearied bodies three days, of so noble a place I could not choose but make this following observation.

Shahr e-Qumis.

Shahr-e Qumis,[1013] in the latitude of 34 degrees 40 minutes, is a city at this day of special note in Parthia, and placed in the mid-way betwixt those two royal cities Qazvin and Isfahan, a city which, if some say true, for antiquity and quondam greatness gives place to no other in Persia, whether considered in the name *Gauna*, a name it once bore and by assimilation thought by some to be that *Guriana* which in old times was a town of singular note, but erroneously as I conceive, seeing that was under five degrees further latitude and by Ptolemy placed in Margiana, or from the name *Arbacta*, so-called from Arbaces the Mede, who in the year from the Creation 3146 laid the foundation, or rather new-imposed

---

[1010] Maximinus I Thrax, "the Thracian," reigned 235–238. Julia Mamaea (d. 235), whose association with Origen is doubtful, was Alexander's mother and the sister of the Empress Julia Soaemias Bassiana, who was also murdered, together with Alexander Severus, probably on the orders of Maximinus.

[1011] Valerian did not succeed to the imperial throne until 253.

[1012] St. Lawrence (d. 258), one of the Seven Deacons of Rome, was martyred because when asked to turn over the treasure of the church to the Romans, "he assembled the poor and the sick and presented them to the [Roman] prefect." The story about the gridiron is probably fiction; "it is more likely that in fact he was beheaded" (Attwater, *Dictionary* 208–9).

[1013] Shahr-e Qumis, which Herbert confusedly calls *Qum* and which the Greeks called Hecatompylos ("many-gated"), was the capital of the Parthian (Arsacid) Empire from about 217 B.C.E. A ruler possibly known as Tiridates (I), brother of Arsaces I, moved the capital to this former Seleucid city, "a site," Malcolm Colledge says, "as yet undiscovered, but which lay on the main trade route across Iran" (*Parthians*, 27).

the name soon after the destruction of Nineveh, to whose overthrow he most contributed, or in *Coama*, which is a name I find recorded in Ptolemy and Diodorus, and being then of that eminency as gave the adjacent part of that province the name *Coama* and *Regio Cominsena*,[1014] as I find in Strabo *lib*. 11 and also in Ptolemy. Notwithstanding, some there be, and that of approved authority, who take this city rather than Isfahan to be that which by reason of its hundred gates the Grecians termed *Hecatompylos*, and may be granted, seeing the latitude is the same which Ptolemy gives it.

Nor was this place less considerable for magnitude then antiquity, for by Arabian geographers it is one of the four best cities that empire had, and the inhabitants have a tradition that for bulk it was once comparable unto Babylon. Friar Odoric de Friuli[1015] also reports it to have been full fifty miles in circumference, and that for greatness it gave not place to any other city in Asia.[1016] Howbeit, the circuit it then had cannot by any marks now extant be discovered, but that it was a large town is discernible both by the rubbish appearing in several places and the foundation of temples and other public structures. Now, seeing some travellers have vouchsafed this city so immense a body, it gives me the invitation to take a restrospect of other great and famous cities, which, if it be a vanity, I have no better excuse then by remembering that St. Augustine made it one of his three wishes to have seen Rome in its glory.

The greatest cities compared.

The greatest of cities that ever were without all peradventure were Babylon and Rome, with which I might rank Nineveh. They were imperial during such a time as those monarchs swayed their sceptres over the universe. That hyperbole mentioned at Shiraz, which derisively terms Cairo and Damascus villages, I willingly

---

[1014] Comisene was an area on the south-east coast of the Caspian Sea.

[1015] Friar Odoric (c. 1265–1331), who was beatified by Benedict XIV (1755) was born at Pordenone in the Friuli district, hence Herbert's reference. His travels began between 1314 and 1318 in Venice, and from there he went to Constantinpole and across to Persia. He visited Tabriz, Soltaniyé, and Kashan in Persia on his way to Yazd, subsequently turning west towards Mesopotamia and thence to India and China. An English version of his *Relatio* appeared in Hakluyt (1599); in Italian it was published by Ramusio (1574) and a Latin edition made in Antwerp (1643) would also have been available to Herbert.

[1016] What Odoric says is that "I came to a certain city by the name of Comerum, which formerly was a great city . . . The compass of its walls is a good fifty miles, and there be therein palaces yet standing entire, but without inhabitants" (*Travels*, 72). The translator, Sir Henry Yule, states that "this locality has not been placed with accuracy," and he suggests that Odoric may be describing not Qum but Persepolis (72 n. 16). Greenway and St. Vincent mention nothing like this; there are no buildings in Qum older than the ninth century burial-place of Imam Reza's sister (*Iran*, 190).

pretermit,[1017] for since their fall new Babylon and new Rome, that is to say Cairo
and Constantinople, are by most ranked amongst the greatest cities of the world.
Concerning Babylon, being now so near the place, I shall here only note her circuit, which Solinus, who gives the largest measure, reports to be four hundred
and eighty furlongs, which according to our measurement is about threescore
English miles, and Rome, in Nero's time at full growth, had fifty, of which last
the extent may best be imagined by the number of those denizens enrolled into
census that were able to bear arms, which, as Lipsius[1018] and others relate, were
463,000, and could not exceed one-third of the whole, women, children and servants comprehended. Now, whereas I named Cairo and Constantinople as the
greatest cities of recent times, it was partly for their being adopted into the names
of those two former, and some travellers as yet continue that repute concerning
them, although I am of another opinion, for Cairo is well-known to be a long
and narrow scattering piece, or rather pieces of towns patched together, and that
it falls much short of that grandeur some report it. Besides, no small part of the
number of her inhabitants are merchants and non-residentiaries. And, concerning Constantinople, it is a great and populous city, yet has not above twelve English miles compass, but were their circumvallations[1019] treble what they are they
would fall short of what old Rome and Babylon are reported. Those also, when
I consider the many and great gardens and orchards they then probably had,
(for without doubt that high-raised garden which Nebuchadnezzar erected upon
arched pillars was for admiration and prospect over the city which was founded
upon a level ground rather then that there wanted garden-room in Babylon) as
at this day, Constantinople and Cairo have, and according to the recent mode of
Isfahan, Agra and other the greatest and noblest cities of the Orient (for as to the
greatness of those in China I give little credit), I am persuaded that those vacant
and pleasurable places took up well-nigh half the ground within those cities, so
as by what I have considered and observed I am not afraid to say that it is probable that some of our European cities are not less numerous in houses and fixed
inhabitants as those I named. For albeit in Spain, Italy, Germany and the Netherlands there are very many large and beautiful cities, yet there find I none that

---

[1017] Pass by without mentioning.

[1018] Joost Lips [Justus Lipsius] (1547–1606), Professor of History and Latin at the
Collegium Trilingue in Leuven from 1592, was a Dutch philosopher whose primary interest was the revival of ancient philosophical traditions, and he was particularly respected for his work on Stoicism, the *Manductio ad Stoicam philosophiam* (1592). Herbert may
have found this reference in Lips's *Poliorceticon* (1596), which is a discourse on fortified
towns. His *Omnia opera* appeared in 1637; *Six Books on Politics and Civil Doctrine* (1594)
was translated by William Jones, and his most popular work, *De constantia* (1584), had
four English translations between 1594 and 1670. See also *Justus Lipsius Concerning Constancy*, ed. and trans. R. V. Young, MRTS 389 (Tempe: ACMRS, 2011).

[1019] A line of fortifications usually built around cities by besiegers.

for greatness and populousness are comparable to Paris and London, which two, like the reflex of the two great luminaries, appear the greatest, and of those, to which the precedency should be given is work for a more accurate observer.

Nevertheless, though by the vogue of most travellers I well know that Paris has the first place attributed, I grant it is so increased since I was there, being upwards of twenty years, that I am not qualified to give a judgment. But on the other side, London is also increased since then even to admiration, so that were the length of London drawn into a circle, the shape that Paris bears, taking in all that building which is contiguous, it is believed the diameter would equal if not exceed Paris. And as to the number of inhabitants, the addition it has from the sea by people from exotic places gives it a capacity above Paris and as by the weekly Bills of Mortality[1020] is presumed. Moreover, the number of gardens, cemeteries and like places adjoining religious houses and churches, colleges in the University, besides those belonging to the King, Princes and other of the nobility there, with the great number of tennis-courts in Paris, take up much more spare space then London doth, which especially within the walls is most compact and thronged with houses, with few gardens or like vacant places interjecting. But supposing that the narrow lanes where coaches, and alleys where men can hardly pass, which also are good buildings, were expatiated and extended to an equal breadth with the broadest street, doubtless either of those cities would then swell beyond the compass either of Babylon or Rome or any other, which nevertheless is submitted. This digression I have the rather adventured, observing how that foreign writers either out of ignorance or envy speak sparingly of our metropolis and in rank place it amongst cities that be but of a second or third magnitude. Therefore, to return.

Qumis.

The name this city bears has been variously pronounced according to the different dialect of nations; some call it *Coim*, others *Kom* and *Kome*. Odoric calls it *Comerum* but the Arabian geographers *Comm*. The situation nevertheless is unanimously agreed to be in a large and delightful plain, the country for some miles about very fruitful in its soil and the air exceeding sweet, seldom clouded with fogs or parched with heat save when the sun passes from the Vernal Equinox to the Northern Tropic. The breezes seldom fail them, which allays the heat, likewise abated by those fruitful gardens they have, whose trees are the best umbrellas for refreshment as well as shade, bearing store of delicious fruits, namely grapes, pomegranates, melons of all sorts, pomcitrons, apricots, plums, pears, pistachios, almonds, quinces, cherries, figs, walnuts, small-nuts, berries and the best wheat in Persia. The peach or *mela Persica* is here abounding, a fruit and leaf

---

[1020] The Bills of Mortality were printed public announcements about how many people died, who they were, and what they died of.

so much resembling man's heart and tongue that the Egyptian priests dedicated it to their goddess Isis as the hieroglyphic[1021] of affection, probably that which Virgil in his *Georgics* refers to: "Media yields pleasant apples of harsh juice,/ 'Gainst step-dames' poison nothing more in use."[1022]

The city has about two thousand houses, most of them more then common structure, well-built, well-formed, well-furnished. The streets are spacious, the bazaar beautiful, but the city is now unwalled, according to the usual mode of cities in Asia. The mosque is famous and venerable, having been richly and beautifully adorned by enshrining the body of once-amiable Fatima,[1023] Ali's wife, daughter and heir to their Prophet Mohammed. The *mesjid* is of Epirotic[1024] form, the tomb raised three yards high, covered with velvet, and the ascent by three or four steps of refined silver, and more then this there is *nullum memorabile nomen*[1025] that I could light upon, for Shah Safi, who succeeded Abbas, was here since buried.

Such time as Tamburlane the victorious Tartar (so I may well style him, since in eight years he conquered more then the Romans could do in eight hundred, as his acts writ by Albacen the Arab and translated by Jean de Bec, abbot of Mortimer[1026] do testify) returned loaden with spoils of war, having hammered the brazen

---

[1021] Francis Quarles wrote in the Preface to his *Hieroglyphics of the Life of Man* (1634) that "before the knowledge of letters, God was known by hieroglyphics. And indeed, what are the Heavens, the earth, nay, every creature, the Hieroglyphics and Emblems of his glory?"

[1022] Virgil, *Georgics* 2. 126–128.

[1023] Fatima (c. 616–634), also known as a-Zahra (the beautiful), was the daughter of Mohammed and Khadija, the wife of Ali, and ancestress of the Fatimid caliphs. From her sons Hasan and Husain descend the *sayeds*, the issue of Mohammed. Her father called her one of the "four perfect women." Unfortunately, Herbert has the wrong Fatima; the one buried in this mosque, known as the Hazrat-é Masumeh, is actually the sister of Imam Reza (d. 817), the eighth grandson of Mohammed, who is himself buried in Mashhad (Greenway and St. Vincent, *Iran*, 223). The surrounding building complex was started by Abbas I, who wanted to establish the place as a centre of Shi'ite worship. Like Rayy, Qum was from early times regarded as a centre of Shi'ism.

[1024] Epirotic architecture is renowned for its stonework. The name refers to Epirus in north-western Greece.

[1025] "Nothing worthy the name" (Servius, Preface to *Aeneid* 1).

[1026] Abu Ali al-Hassan al-Haytham or al-Hazen (965–1039) was an Arab polymath from Basra who wrote scientific treatises and works on mathematics, as well as philosophy and optics. However, Herbert is citing the so-called *Memoirs of Timur*, ascribed to al-Hazen, printed in an English version by William Ponsonby in 1599. "Alhacen" is mentioned in connection with this work by Purchas, who is one of Herbert's main sources, and this is likely the source here; obviously the dates do not fit, and the actual author of the biography of Timur was Ibn Arabshah (d. 1450), whose book was translated into Latin by Gelius (1636) and French by Vatier (1658). For further information on ibn Arabshah, see Howard Miller, "Tamburlaine: The Migration and Translation of Marlowe's

face of the Turkish insolence *Anno Dom.* 1397, *Heg.* 777. This poor Qumis, among others, parched in the heat of his fury, not from any eye of rage or envy he darted, but from an impudent provocation and affront which *Hoharo-mirza*, called *Badr Khan*,[1027] causelessly jealous, put upon the triumphant Tartar, so ill-resented that no less then the loss both of his life and crown would expiate, making also many men and towns sharers in his misery. This place especially, which but for the Ardabilian *sayed* his requesting mercy, had been levelled with the earth, ploughed up and salted, but in the sable weed she is now apparelled we see towns can die as well as men, and may sigh with melancholy Statius, "Death is the common friend,/ For whate'er had beginning, shall have end" [*Theboid* 9. 280].

From Qumis we rode to Sin-sin,[1028] of old *Zoara*, and thence to Kashan, *Cassaim* Cluverius misspells it, a city from Qumis removed six and thirty miles, the way being easy and plain, albeit sandy.

Kashan.

Kashan,[1029] where the Arctic elevation is 34 degrees 7 minutes, longitude 86 degrees, may worthily be reputed the second town in Parthia for grandeur, wealth and beauty, distant north from Isfahan sixty long English miles and from Qazvin south two hundred and ten or thereabouts. Whence the name derives itself the illiterate Kashanians could not tell, but my conjecture is that 'tis borrowed from *cushan*, which in the Syriac signifieth "heat" or "blackness," or from Hassan, son to Husain, son of Ali, or from Shah Hassan, son to *Axan*, begot by Toghrul Beg *Anno Heg.* 582, of our account 1202, subjected by the Great Khan, or, which best pleases me, if ancient enough. From Uzun Hassan the Armenian (or Hassan Beg some call him) who in the Year of Our Lord 1470, of Mohammed's flight from

---

Arabic Sources," in Carmine di Biase, ed., *Travel and Translation in the Early Modern Period* (Amsterdam: Rodopi, 2006), 255–66. Timur himself did not go to Qum. See F. J. Goldsmid, "Perplexities of Oriental History," *Transactions of the Royal Geographical Society* n. s. 2 (1885): 365–89. Goldsmid says that Ibn Arabshah did not write the *Memoirs*, but modern scholars think otherwise.

[1027] Unidentified.

[1028] Sin-sin [*Zenzen*] is known now only for its attractive mosque and a caravanserai.

[1029] Kashan has been inhabited since Achaemenid times, and survived successive invasions by Arabs (637) and Mongols six hundred years later. The Safavids actually spent a good deal of time there, and the city was famous for textiles and ceramics. "Some say that the name comes from the type of glazed tiles produced there in the area, called *kashi*, others argue that the city was named after the Kashou tribe which originally inhabited the area. Poets claim that Kashan is based on the ancient word for 'temple,' and one Iranian lexicographer said that 'kashan' is a type of home made from bamboo. If that isn't enough to confuse everyone, a famous local historian has written that the name of the city comes from *key ashan*, which means 'place of rulers'" (Greenway and St. Vincent, *Iran*, 207). Herbert's conjectures may now be added to the list.

Mecca 850, vanquished Abdullah Khan, who was the last of Tamburlane's progeny that ruled Persia.

At this day it is a city both great and lovely, and ancient too, for Odoric eni-
titles it a noble and renowned city as in his time, and as now, it is well-seated,
comely-built and abundantly-peopled, overtopped by no hill, unseasoned by no
marshes nor watered by any great stream, which chiefly augments the heat when
Sol approaches Cancer, but which rages there in no less violence in Scorpio, not
that in the Zodiac, but real scorpions, which in number engender here, a little
serpent of a finger long (which makes me wonder at Cedrenus, who says there are
scorpions two cubits long in the Brahmins' country, i.e. India) but of great terror
in the sting, and so inflaming as with their envenomed arrow some die, few avoid
madness at least for a whole day, the sting proving most dangerous when the season is hottest, which is when the Dog-star appeareth. And, as it was said of another, "*Una eademque manus fert vulnus opemque*,"[1030] so in this malady is no such
remedy as by the oil of scorpions. The poet so advises: "The serpent's head joined
to the wounded part / Fitly is said to heal th'infected smart / Like Telaphus cur'd
by Achilles's dart,"[1031] whence is that Persian adage or rather execration, "May a
scorpion of Kashan sting thee," but, which is more remarkable, agreeable to what
Pliny in his *Natural History*[1032] reports of the scorpions in Mesopotamia. They say
it, and we found it true, some of them creeping into our rugs as we slept, they seldom or never hurt a stranger. Hollar[1033] affirms how one who exceedingly loved
the smell of basil being dead had a scorpion found in his brains; howbeit, the
Ethiops say that to eat basil is an antidote. The Africans report that 'tis a present cure to anoint with garlic, and Pontanus[1034] writes how that one stung with

---

[1030] "Let the same hand bring both wound and remedy." This Latin adage is an adaptation of Ovid, *Remediae amoris* 44: "*una manus vobis vulnus opemque feret.*"

[1031] Telaphus or Telephos, king of Mysia, was a son of Heracles; he was wounded in
a battle by the Achaeans, and later his wound was healed by Achilles, the man who had
thrown the spear.

[1032] Pliny, *Natural History* 28. 5. 248.

[1033] Vaclav (Wenceslaus) Hollar (1607–1677) was, of course, the great engraver from
Prague who settled in England under the patronage of the Earl of Arundel and produced
many wonderful collections of engravings, particularly excelling in architectural scenes.
Amongst his works which might have interested Herbert we might number his illustra-
tions of forts and towns in Tangier (1668) and sketches made for John Ogilby's *Africa*.
See also Introduction.

[1034] Giovanni Gioviano Pontano (1426–1503) was a humanist, poet, and diplomat
from Spoleto who moved to Naples and served the ruler there, founding an academy and
writing on such diverse subjects as botany and architecture. Herbert was likely familiar
with his *Eridanus* (1491), a collection of Latin elegiac poems in which Pontano ranges
over a vast array of subjects, many taken from everday life (such as scorpion bites) and
including personal topics. They were vivid, lively, and immensely popular with educated
readers.

a scorpion was helped by drinking frankincense with the sculpture of a scorpion resolved into powder. Howbeit, the Persians' usual remedy is to bleed and bathe the affected part with scorpion's oil, or otherwise to hold it over the head of the scorpion, first being soundly bruised.

This noble city is in compass not less then York or Norwich, about four thousand families being accounted in her. The houses are fairly-built, many of which are pargetted without and painted. The mosques and hamams are in their cupolas curiously ceruleated with a feigned turquoise, the bazaar is spacious and uniform, furnished with silks, damasks and carpets of silk, silk and gold, and of course thrummed wool, no part of the world having better or better-coloured. Here are also store of spices and other merchandise; besides, the people here, the fruit of industry, be more civil, no less active and as trim and rich in their attire as I could observe in any other part, and by reason they allow few to be idle. Here are full manufactures of silks, satins and cloth-of-gold curiously-wrought and coloured, no better in the world, and in such plenty that one Cartwright,[1035] an English merchant who was there about the year 1600, spares not to aver that there was then more silk brought in one year into Kashan then broadcloths are into London.

Here also they have a singular art in dyeing or colouring of silks and staining of linen-cloth like the Indian *pantados*. They also make very curious flowers and knots, and in beautiful colours upon leather, which are very lasting and for several uses; in a word, a more industrious and civil people or a town better-governed Persia elsewhere has not. Here is no want of pleasure neither, abounding in gardens, fruits and corn, by the elaborate *tymars*[1036] made to fructify, which, being cultivated, retribute a gainful acknowledgement. The caravanserai in this city is a very noble, I may say unparalleled fabric of that kind, by many degrees preceding all other caravanserais we saw in Persia, this being both large enough and fit enough to lodge the court of the greatest potentate in Asia. A royal foundation it is, being built by Abbas for travellers to repose in gratis and to express

---

[1035] John Cartwright (fl. 1600–1625) was the first Englishman to visit Babylon, Nineveh, Persepolis, and Susa. Leaving England in 1600, he did his travelling in the company of John Mildenhall (d. 1614; see Introduction), an employee of the East India Company, and published an account enigmatically called *The Preacher's Travels* (1611), in which he never mentions preaching at all, nor is there any evidence that Cartwright was anything other than as Herbert says, a merchant, although Foster calls him "the Reverend" (*England's Quest*, 175). His account concentrates on the Sherley brothers, Anthony and Robert. For details and an extract, see K. Parker, ed. *Early Modern Tales of the Orient* (London: Routledge, 1999), Chapter 6.

[1036] 1638: *tymariots* (214). Foster notes that the *OED* gives both versions; the word means 'attendance,' and is derived from the Turkish *tamar*, "hence a fief held by military service; from this they have been extended to signify one holding such a fief. Here Herbert uses the word as equivalent to a farmer or agriculturalist" (*Herbert*, 326).

his magnificence as well as charity. The whole building is grounded with marble, rising from the ground six foot; the residue is brick refined in the sun, pargetted and adorned with knots and fancies of Arabic characters in azure, red and white colours laid in oil after the mode of Persia. It is a perfect quadrant, for each angle from one another are two hundred paces, the whole eight hundred. In the umbelic of this court is a square tank filled by an aqueduct with crystalline water. This royal house has also adjoining it such gardens as rather exceed then want to display the founder's munificence.[1037]

Persian Magi.

Here is not any other memorable antiquity that I could hear of, save that Tekuder Oglan, the usurper who died frantic, was buried here *Anno Heg.* 655, and he scarce worth the memory, more then which I have not to say concerning this city other then that several conjectures by learned men have passed whence the Wise Men came that presented Our Blessed Saviour with their offerings, who were without doubt the first fruits and called of the gentiles, waiting the accomplishment of Balaam's prophecy mentioned in Numbers 24:17: "There shall come a star out of Jacob and a sceptre shall rise out of Israel and shall smite the corners of Moab and destroy the children of Sheth," which was gathered more from this of their prophet then any other astrologic computation. Now that they were gentiles is evident, but from what city or province no less disputable then the place of their burial. The word *Magus* is proper to Persia, Persia is east from Bethlehem, so as some are of opinion they came from hence, others from Susa, where then flourished an academy. Nevertheless, the people here have a tradition that those three Wise Men or Kings went hence, which some say were entombed in Gilan; howbeit, Melchior[1038] persuades us they came from Sheba in Sabaea. *"Ex orientali Arabiae regione reges ad colendum Christum venerunt,"* saith Postellus, "the kings came from the east part of Arabia to worship Christ." Others labour no less to

---

[1037] Herbert is describing the Bagh-é Tarikhi-yé Fin, "this famous and beautiful garden with its pools and orchards . . . this classical Persian vision of paradise has always been prized for its natural springs and still contains the remains of [Abbas's] two storey palace" (Greenway and St. Vincent, *Iran* 207). These gardens owe their beauty to the skills of the great architect Shaikh Baha' al-Din Amili (1576–1621); according to Boyle, they "served as a model for the more famous Shalimar Gardens of Lahore" (*History*, 668). It was constructed in its present form by Shah Safi; in 1852 it was the scene of the assassination of former Prime Minister Amir-é Kabir.

[1038] Melchior Hoffmann (c. 1495–1542) was a German anabaptist and follower of Luther. He wrote a commentary on Daniel (1526) and *Prophecy from Holy and Divine Scripture* (1530), from which Herbert takes this citation. His view was that all may be saved, particularly those who become regenerated, but that anyone who sins after regeneration is damned; his followers were known as Melchiorites.

bring them from the Omerites[1039] in Ethiopia, south. From Babylon othersome think they came, from Hormuz some would have them, a conjecture as likely as it was Paradise. Ceylon and Taprobane[1040] have been thought their country, but if you please to trust Friar Odoric of Friuli, Kashan was it.[1041]

But seeing this is a work of such difficulty, let me rather busy my brains in quest of what a Magus was, since Simon Magus[1042] through his black art has in common acceptation rendered the name odious and under which title witches, sorcerers, enchanters, fortune-tellers or pretending calculators of nativities, hydromantics, pyromantics[1043] and other diabolics have cloaked their trumperies, altogether unworthy the name of the Persian Magi, which was an honourable epithet and peculiar to Persia, which nevertheless has been attributed, though under other names, to such as amongst other nations were studious in philosophy and the liberal sciences, such as after the dialect of their countries were called Gymnosophists, Brahmins, Tallapoi,[1044] Chaldaei, Druids, Bards etc., who in

---

[1039] The Omerites or Homerites (Graeco-Roman nomenclature) were the inhabitants of the Himyarite Kingdom in what is now Yemen. They were the pre-eminent power in Arabia until 525 C.E., conquered lands as far as Sabaea (Sheba) and had their capital at Sana'a, still the capital of Yemen.

[1040] Taprobane [*Taprophan*] is an old name for Ceylon (Sri Lanka). The name is used by Pliny, who notes that it "is in the Eastern Sea and stretches along the side of India from east to west" and goes on to describe it and its people in some detail (6. 82–91).

[1041] "I halted at the city of the three Magi, called Cassan, a royal city and of great repute" (Odoric of Pordenone, *The Travels of Friar Odoric: Cathay and the Way Thither*, trans. Henry Yule (1886) [Grand Rapids: W. B. Eerdmans, 2002], 70). Yule notes that Odoric is the only authority locating the Magi in Kashan (*Travels*, 70, n. 14).

[1042] Simon Magus (fl. 30–60) was a Gnostic whose attempt to buy the Apostles' ability to perform miracles is recorded in Acts 8:9–24 and in the non-biblical *Acts of Peter*, and who is mentioned unfavourably in the writings of Irenaeus, who attacked gnosticism in *Adversus haereses* (c. 180) and in Justin Martyr. He met the Emperor Claudius in Rome, and some believed that he was God in human form, which of course did not endear him to Christians; fragments of his *Apophasis megale* or *Great Pronouncement* are extant.

[1043] Water-diviners and fire-diviners.

[1044] *Tallapoi* is a name used for Buddhist priests. Speculations about its origins are contradictory; Foster, for example, states that it derived from the words *tala poe* in the Talaing (Mon) language of Pegu, which mean "my lord" (*Early Travels* 36). Fernao Guerreiro thinks it comes from the Sanskrit *tala-pattra*, which means "fan-palm leaf," which the priests used to shade themselves (*Early Travels*, 270 n. 7). *HJ* has an entry for *talipot* with a similar explanation (892). European contact with Buddhism probably began in 1254, when Willem van Ruysbroeck, a friar, visited Karakorum and entered into a dialogue with Buddhist monks. In the 1634 edition Herbert stated that "these Tallapois' houses are in trees, to secure them from the tigers," and he tells an anecdote about how when one of them prayed for him he offered wine, "which he, contrary to his law, tasted of, and liking it, bid me fill his horn. I did so, and he, bedlam-like, made but one draught of it, then, gravely elevating his eyes, hands and one leg, he cried out to Mortis Ali his

their times were contemplative and studious in the secrets of nature, which in the worst sense and vulgarly as commonly-accepted is called magic, but judicial and natural astronomy in a more favourable and by the most learned. And in which our most ancient philosophers the Druids, long before the Saxons' entrance, were excellent, as I might prove by many instances, but that one out of Pliny's *Natural History* may serve, that the Britons were so addicted unto magic as in that art they were the first that instructed the Persians, an authority that serves well to reprove Tully,[1045] who rashly entitles the Britons barbarous, albeit I suppose he did it on the general account, as they usually styled all those nations who derived neither their laws nor language from the Romans, and in that the Greeks were even with them when they comprehended the Romans under that attribute.

Now, the differences 'twixt Magi and pseudo-Magi are these. Common custom, saith St. Jerome, apprehends that magicians are no better then enchanters, such as impostors nowadays are rightly-termed, who usually delude their customers with fallacious words and species or otherwise practice an unlawful correspondence with Satan in his black arts, like those Jannes and Jambres who resisted Moses,[1046] and either by a *deceptio visus*[1047] or diabolical enchantments imitated Moses until by a supreme vindictive hand upon themselves by that plague of lice they were constrained to acknowledge the omnipotency of God and that *digitu Dei* those wonders were performed by his servant Moses, which they were not able to counterfeit, Exodus 8:19,[1048] in which rank were Elymas, i.e. the Persian sorcerer mentioned [in] Acts 13:8[1049] and Simon surnamed Magus, his co-disciple, both of which used infernal arts and were accordingly discovered and punished by the apostles, whereas contrarily it may be presumed by the character given the right Magi, such as those who came with their offerings unto Christ, that theirs was lawful, for, saith Peter Martyr, "by the word Magi we understand wise and honest men," and is the more credible seeing that the definition of *magia* is no other then 'an elevated wisdom and science of the harmony and contents of universals in nature,' in which the Magi took an unexpressible delight.

Now, it will not be denied that the pleasures of the intellect do far exceed those of the affections, for in pleasure there is satiety which is not attained to in knowledge, satisfaction and appetite, saith the Lord Verulam, being perpetually

---

prophet in the Arabian tongue" (196). At this point, Herbert seems to have thought the Tallapoi were Shi'ite Muslims!

[1045] Cicero; from Tullius, his second name.

[1046] Jannes and Jambres were two Egyptian magicians who tried to imitate the "magic" of Moses and Aaron in order to discredit them. For details, see Exodus 7:11 and 8:7.

[1047] Optical illusion.

[1048] "Then the Magicians said unto Pharaoh, This is the finger of God."

[1049] "But Elymas the sorcerer (for so is his name by interpretation) withstood them, seeking to turn away the deputy from the faith."

interchangeable, and Apuleius[1050] withal, in his *Apology* tells us that *"Persarum lingua Magus est, qui nostra sacerdos,"*[1051] which is probable, seeing that the Jews themselves had it in such estimation as it was a rule how that in *"Geneara-lege non adscisci in Sanhedrim Magiae non ignaros et 70 linguarum peritos,"* with which agrees that out of another, *"is Magus est qui divinorum erat cultor et interpres,"* and Pencerus[1052] *De divinationibus, "praeerant Magi religioni Persicae ut in populo Dei Levitae, studiisque verae philosophiae erant dediti, nec usquam rex Persarum poterat esse, qui non autea Magorum disciplinam scientiamque percepisset,"*[1053] which we may the better credit, seeing Cyrus, in that memorable conspiracy he made against his brother Artaxerxes persuading the Greeks to confederate with him, amongst other praises vainly arrogated to himself one was that he was more capable of ruling then his brother for that he was the greater magician, intending thereby his proficiency in the liberal arts, languages and astrology. Plutarch also in his *Life of Themistocles* acquaints us that of so high esteem were the Magi with the Persian kings as they frequently delightfully heard their lectures touching philosophy and arts magic. Mantuan[1054] also very rightly thus defines them: "A Persian Magus call'd he is / Who knows herbs, stars and deities. / All three learn'd in Persepolis," so as upon the whole it appears that the Magi were so-called from their laborious scrutiny into hidden causes, by their practice and experience in

---

[1050] Lucius Apuleius (114–after 170) of Madaura in Africa is, of course, known as the author of *The Golden Ass.* However, he had a serious side, and was also a mythographer. He wrote *De daemone Socratis,* a work dealing with spirits in which he posits them as an intermediary life-form between the gods and mortals. The work to which Herbert refers is the *Apologia,* also known as *Pro se de magica,* the text of a very long and extremely funny speech he gave in defence of himself against a charge of magic. It was edited by Stephanus. For details, see T. N. Winter, "The Publication of Apuleius' *Apology,*" *Transactions and Proceedings of the American Philological Association* 100 (1969): 607–12.

[1051] In the language of the Persians 'magus' is what we call in our language 'priest.'

[1052] Kaspar Pencer (1525–1602) was a German astronomer, mathematician, and physician who was successively Professor of Mathematics (1554) and Medicine (1560) at the University of Wittenberg. The son-in-law of Philipp Melanchthon, he was imprisoned for a number of years for his Calvinist beliefs, but eventually became Rector of the University of Wittenberg. Herbert is citing his *Commentarius de praecipuis divinationum generibus* (1551). Pencer was often quoted by writers on witchcraft.

[1053] The Magi were in charge of the Persian religion the way the Levites were [of that of] the people of God; they were dedicated to true philosophy, neither was there any Persian king who did not learn from the discipline and wisdom of the Magi.

[1054] Baptista Mantovano, known as Mantuan (1447–1516), was an Italian poet whose *Eclogues* were very popular with Protestants because he was highly critical of corruption in the Catholic church. They were translated into English by George Turberville (1567) and Thomas Harvey (1656); there is a modern translation by L. Piepho (New York: Peter Lang, 2001). See also 25 L. Piepho, "Mantuan's Eclogues in the English Reformation," *Sixteenth Century Journal* 25 (1994): 623–32.

astronomy proving the theory as well as the practic part. For, by their careful observing the celestial motions they comprehended their probable influences and from thence divined many strange and notable events in nature as earthquakes, inundations, eclipses, distemperature in weather, revolutions of state and the like, but, which was more considerable, by their contemplating the wonderful order, harmony and providence by which the creature is made they duly magnified and admired the Creator, and from their customary diving into occult causes of nature were thence called magical, albeit no other then a connection of agents and patients in nature respecting each other, and by learned men discovered to produce such effects as to such as are ignorant of their causes appear strange and wonderful. But after this digression I proceed upon our travel.

To Babylon.

The 23 of August we came to a village called Abu Zaydabad, which was about eighteen miles from Kashan; there we rested but one day. The next night we got to Natanz, which some call *Tane*, and in all probability takes name from *Nanta*, for Diana was there so-called and worshipped. There goes a tradition likewise that the last unfortunate Darius there breathed his last through the treachery of that perfidious Bactrian Bessus, which, if so, then I may make this observation: the village and lodge, ashamed of such barbarism, seems to hide itself betwixt two lofty hills, so as until near the place 'tis hardly to be discerned. Nevertheless, from the top of either of those hills we had a delightful prospect, for from thence we could see several country villages watered by small rivulets. That night's travel was full thirty miles. The next night we got to Reig, but more then that it was one and twenty miles from Natanz, not worth remembering, and that from Isfahan it is distant three *farsangs*, but from Qazvin two hundred and fifty or thereabouts. Whence to Baghdad, the first day is to *Corranda*, and then successively to *Deacow*, *Miscarroon*, Karind, *Laccary*, *Corbet*, *Nazareil*, Shuburgan, near which is Pol-é Shah and *Caramoon-Shahoon*, formerly called Cunaxa,[1055] where was decided that contest for the Persian crown 'twixt Artaxerxes and Cyrus recorded by Xenophon, and in memory thereof in the concave of the adjacent mountain is engraven portraits resembling those I mentioned of Rostam near the ruins of Persepolis, only here are added the figures of elephants and other beasts such as are well-worth the observing. *Baldat*[1056] is next to Shuburgan, whence it is but one day's journey to Baghdad upon Tigris, the total being a hundred and

---

[1055] For details of Cunaxa see below, 000. Some of the other places are: Khorandi [*Corranda*], Dih-é girdu [*Deacow*], Mesarqan [*Miscarroon*], Khorin [*Corryn*], Lachari [*Laccary*] and Khorbeh [*Corbet*], Shuburgan [*Subber-cawn*], all in modern Iran. None of these places is mentioned by Greenway and St. Vincent. I have not been able to identify *Nazareil*.

[1056] Baldah in Iraq.

thirty *farsangs*. Howbeit, from Isfahan there is another road, first travelling to *Golpichan*,[1057] which is forty *farsangs*, thence to *Tossareban*, forty more, to *Mando* fifty, to *Hemoometzar* seven, and then by *Baroc*[1058] to Baghdad seven more, in all a hundred forty-four *farsangs,* the passage more easy though of greater distance, and therefore more travelled, especially by caravan, of which city old and new suffer me to give a brief description. And first of Babylon.

Babylon.

Babylon was of old a city in that country which in Genesis 11:2[1059] is named Shinar, a vale watered by the River Euphrates, one of those that stream through Paradise. The country afterwards was called Chaldaea, *Keldan* and *Arcalder* by Berossos, but the Land of Nimrod, Micah 5:6,[1060] and after that Babylonia. To the east it had Susiana, to the west Mesopotamia, and to the south part of the Persian Gulf. The name was imposed upon that memorable confusion of speech happening there about a hundred and twenty years after the Flood, which de-feated that design the race of Ham (for Heber's family would not join with Nim-rod in that attempt) had hatched to secure themselves from a second deluge, the promoting which impious work is attributed principally to that Nimrod who is Genesis 10:9 is styled "the mighty hunter," such as his tyranny became a proverb, by Berossos called *Nimbroth*, who with his confederates intended such a pile the top whereof should reach into Heaven, *"Aedificamus nobis urbem et turrim cuius caput sit in coelis,"* Genesis 11:4.[1061] Berossos adds *"ad altitudinem et magnitudinem montium,"*[1062] and accordingly *multorum manibus*, there being, as good authors report, no less then five hundred thousand men by full thirty years' incessant la-bour that stupendous work, whose basis was nine miles about, had its superstruc-ture advanced to a proportionable height, five thousand paces, say some, which make 25,730 foot, a height hardly to be believed when we consider how that wonder of the world the greatest of the Egyptian pyramids exceeds not a thou-sand foot, says Heylyn, five hundred foot save one, says Greaves,[1063] whose report is most to be credited since he measured it, which pyramid, if but five hundred

---

[1057] Goliyan in modern Iran.

[1058] Probably Baroshki in Iraq.

[1059] ". . . they found a plain in the land of Shinar; and they dwelt there."

[1060] "And they shall waste the land of Assyria with the sword, and the land of Nim-rod in the entrances thereof . . ."

[1061] ". . . let us build us a city and a tower, whose top may reach into Heaven."

[1062] To the height and size of the mountains.

[1063] John Greaves (1602–1652), mathematician and antiquary, was the Savilian Pro-fessor of Astronomy at Oxford from 1643 and the author of the first accurate survey of the pyramids at Gizeh, *Pyramidographia* (1646), based on data collected during his trip to Egypt in 1638. He collected Greek, Arabic, and Persian manuscripts, and published an-other work which would have interested Herbert, *Elementa linguae Persicae* (1646).

foot, equals the height of Paul's when the pyramidal spire stood upon the steeple.
Yet Herodotus reports this tower was in height four thousand paces; St. Jerome
exceeds him, making it sixteen thousand, but seeing the stair or passage to ascend by was circular, and of that breadth also, if we may credit Verstegan,[1064]
as afforded scope sufficient for horse and carts to turn, 'tis probable the paces
mentioned by St. Jerome and Herodotus rather relate to the compass then to the
perpendicular, which consideration can best qualify that Jewish hyperbole we
meet with in the *Yalkut*,[1065] averring that it was seven and twenty miles high, an
edifice, let the height be what it will, so wonderful as gave occasion to a heathen
poet to feign his gigantomachia *"montes montibus superponere, ut Iovem de sua sede
detruderent,"*[1066] and, as the poet, "The Heavens look' d pale with wonder to behold / With what attempt and rage the giants bold / Sought to affront the gods
by raising high / Mount upon mount, to inhabit in the sky."[1067] But he who from
his supreme seat beheld their arrogance, to check the progress of that impious
design confounds their language from one which was the Hebrew (*"ex quo fonte
orientales et meridionales linguae dimanant,"*[1068] saith Postellus) unto seventy-two
(saith Goropius, by that cause of separation *"naturale idioma et primum a parente
rerum naturae Deo munus concessum, illic erat mutatum"*)[1069] dispersing them into
several parts, the better to plant the world.

Now, albeit the tower was never finished, for it was, as one says well, *"opus
ultione divina incompletum,"*[1070] although Alexander by wonderful expense and
labour of men many hundred years after in vain attempted it, and before him

---

[1064] Richard Verstegan, also known as Rowlands (1548–c. 1636), was an Anglo-
Dutch antiquarian, poet, and publisher. Herbert is referring to his *Restitution of Decayed
Intelligence of Antiquities* (1605), in which Verstegan attempted to revive an interest in
places and artifacts he considered needed to be examined further and had been neglected
by scholars. He also wrote a similar work about archaeology in his own country of origin,
Nederlandsche Antiquiteyten (1613), which ran into many editions, and which, amongst
other interesting snippets of information, contains the earliest account of the Pied Piper
of Hamelin.

[1065] The *Yalkut Shimoni* was a compilation of Old Testament exegesis and rabbinical
wisdom. Its authorship has been disputed; amongst others, Lord Herbert of Chirbury
believed that it was written by Rabbi Simeon ha-Darshan, a thirteenth-century scholar
from Amsterdam (*Pagan Religion*, 88 and n. 19), but modern scholars have also ascribed it
to Rabbi Simeon Kara, an eleventh century French exegete. A Latin version was printed
in Venice by M. Prinz (1566).

[1066] "Mountains piled upon mountains so that they could thrust Jove down from his
throne" (Ovid, *Metamorphoses* 1. 152–153).

[1067] Virgil, *Aeneid* 6. 582–584.

[1068] From which source originated all the languages of the east and south.

[1069] The natural language that was first granted as a gift by God, nature's father, was
changed from thence.

[1070] A work left incomplete by divine vengeance.

Semiramis, say the fabulous Greeks, or rather Nebuchadnezzar, the city nevertheless swelled into a vast extent, for Nimrod, living there six and fifty years, increased its buildings, was the first that sovereignated over men and that taught them idolatry, so as dying they deified him by the name of *Sudormin*, which the Romans after converted into Saturn. Arphaxad, Shem's son, planting Chaldaea and Elam his brother Persia, Belus[1071] surnamed Jupiter Babylonicus succeeded at Babylon, A.M. 1800. By some he is called *Baal* and *Bel*, whose son Ninus, called *Amraphel*, having conquered Libya, Arabia, Media and Bactria is accounted the first monarch of the earth, and the more to express his magnificence, built, or rather enlarged (for in Genesis 10:11 Asshur or Nimrod is said to build) Nineveh the Great upon Tigris, formerly called *Nisith* and *Reubaboth*, and since Mosul,[1072] which rather is the ruins of Seleucia, by Nebuchadnezzar afterwards made the capital city of Assyria, which yet gave pre-eminence to Babylon. After two and fifty years overruled by that virago Semiramis he was buried in the temple he himself had built and dedicated to Belus his father, Juno his mother and Rhea his grandmother, whose golden statues he erected in the middle of the city to be worshipped, agreeable to what we find mentioned in the Wisdom of Solomon 14:15–18:

> When a father mourned grievously for his son that was suddenly taken away, he then made an image for him that was a dead man, whom forthwith he worshipped as a god, and amongst his servants ordained ceremonies and sacrifices, so as in process of time that wicked custom prevailed and was observed as a law, and idols by the commandment of tyrants became to be adored. And for such as were so remote that they could not worship them presently, they counterfeited the visage and made the gorgeous image of a king whom they honoured, flattering him that was absent as if he had been present.[1073]

[1071] Belus, known to the Canaanites and Phoenicians as Baal, and to the Babylonians as Bel-Marduk, the god of war, was also the ancient legendary king who founded Babylon, and of course the two are confuted. Eusebius notes that Belus, a giant, escaped destruction fromthe gods and went to Babylon, where he built the Tower of Babel, drained a sea and founded a city, Babylon, around which he constructed a wall and then vanished (*Praep. ev.* 9.18). Diodorus Siculus mentions a "Tomb of Belus" which was restored by Alexander the Great after being destroyed by the Persians (17.112–13), and this same tomb is described by Strabo (7.199); scholars have suggested that they may mean the ziggurat at Babylon. Herbert's citing of Greek and Roman names for Belus is correct; however, they were terms used in the Hellenistic period and later.

[1072] Mosul is on the west bank of the Tigris; the ruins of Nineveh are on the east bank.

[1073] This is Herbert's own translation of the Latin (Vulgate) version, which has been omitted. It is one of the books of the Apocrypha.

By the Chaldaeans, Ninus is called *Hercules*, by the Assyrians *Jupiter*, and *Amraphel* by others; vanquished by the patriarch Abraham after his departure from Ur[1074] (so-called because there the fire was worshipped) to Haran to avoid idolatry, which place was between Babylon and Nineveh, where before the Flood was the terrestrial Paradise.

This brave active Princess reigned forty years, during which she enlarged the Empire from Ethiopia to India. Of that courage she was, that news being brought as she was dressing her head how that Babylon had revolted, she presently vowed never to perfect her dress till the city was reduced. Semiramis, as she enlarged the Empire, so did she her fame by sundry great and memorable acts, for besides the elegant gardens she made in Media, at Babylon upon many high pillars of stone she made a garden, which for the manner and curiosity thereof was accounted one of the Wonders of the World, after that cutting the Caspian Strait, contracting Euphrates and building over it the noblest bridge any story ever mentioned, raising two obelisks in Babylon, the least of which was a hundred and thirty foot high and five and twenty in thickness, hewn and brought thither down Tigris from Ararat.[1075] She also erected two incomparable palaces on either side Euphrates, one towards the east, the other towards the west end of Babylon, the first extending thirty, the other sixty furlongs, and each compassed with a stately wall. But transcending those, in the centre or middle of the city she raised the noblest building in the world: it was a square tower of black polished marble, every side being a thousand paces, entered by four gates of burnished brass, the height of the first being a quarter of a mile. Eight towers rose one upon another, gradually diminishing, in little imitated by that *Mausoleum Augusti*[1076] which was built many ages after in Rome 'twixt the Tiber and Via Flaminia, thought to resemble that which Artemisia dedicated to the Carian king. At the culmen or top was a chapel or cupola in which were placed three golden images representing Jupiter, Ops[1077] and Juno, i.e. her father-in-law Belus, her husband

---

[1074] Now Tel el-Muqqaya in Iraq.

[1075] Peter Clayton, in a chapter entitled "Some Forgotten Wonders," notes that Diodorus Siculus thought that this obelisk "should be numbered amongst the seven most notable works of his day" (P. Clayton and M. Price, eds., *The Seven Wonders of the Ancient World* [London: Routledge, 1989], 158). The "Hanging Gardens of Babylon," however, are described by Diodorus Siculus, Berossos via Josephus, who ascribes them to Nebuchadnezzar II, Curtius Rufus, and Philo of Byzantium (fl. 250 B.C.E.). All of these writers, except Philo, are cited by Herbert. There will be more on these gardens below. See Irving Finkel, "The Hanging Gardens of Babylon," in Clayton and Price, *Wonders*, 38–58.

[1076] Augustus erected his mausoleum in 28 B.C.E. on the Campus Martius. It is now a bare but nevertheless impressive ruin, apparently too dangerous for tourists to be admitted.

[1077] Ops was the Roman goddess of plenty; Lord Herbert of Chirbury writes in *Pagan Religion* that "Ops, Cybele, Vesta, Rhea, Ceres and others were goddesses in the same sense; they represented the Earth or the things it produced" (216).

Ninus and herself, statues twelve cubits high and of pure massy gold, continuing amongst those idolators for many succeeding generations the most reverenced idols in the world, the rather for that (as Herodotus) in that temple was yearly consumed in frankincense to the value of 100,000 talents. Undefaced until about the year from the beginning of the world 3490, in a frantic fit it was demolished by Xerxes after his beating by Leonidas and Themistocles, the Grecian land and sea generals. This grand idol had for many ages been had in divine veneration, so as the reformation had been commendable had it proceeded from a better principle. From the top of the highest tower and by reason of the continual serenity of the sky the Chaldaean astrologers (whose skill in that art, they say, was practiced 3600 years before Alexander's conquests, which, if true, reaches to Enoch's time) precisely observed the planetary motions, and though they could not hear their rolling harmony, yet thence they had the exact light and magnitude of the stars, their heliacal, acronical, matutine and vespertine motions, rise and fall, the progress of the sun, the constellations, aspects and influence of planets etc., for in that art during those times they had the greatest knowledge of any astrologers.

Now, though the heart of Semiramis was put into an orb of gold above, yet her body was interred below, and, as Xerxes, ransacking for treasure above, in lieu thereof, having opened the place where Belus, a great astrologer was well as king, was buried, there only he found a large vessel of glass which contained his body swimming in oil, and for full 1600 years had, it seems, continued in that condition. So Darius, afterwards in like hope of wealth violating her tomb below, discovered her coffin, upon the opening of which such a pestilential smell vapoured thereout as not only killed some that were spectators, but infected the greatest part of Asia. The like memorable example happened *Anno Dom.* 170, upon a man's forcing open a shrine of gold in the temple of Apollo, where instead of the treasure that avaricious wretch expected, there issued forth such an infectious breath as first killed the man then infected the whole city, and soon afterward overspread such a vast space of the earth as it is thought half of mankind died of that pestilence, which ceased not till it had unpeopled the greatest part of the universe. Concerning which great empress accept that short character Berossos gives, "*Haec virago militia, triumphis, divitiis, victoriis et imperio omnes mortales antecessit; nemo etenim huic feminae comaparandus est.*"[1078]

And as to the city, albeit Nimrod[1079] begun, it was exceedingly beautified and enlarged by Semiramis, concerning whom *dicitur altam*—"*coctilibus mures*

[1078] This virago came before all mortals in warfare, triumphs, riches, victory and empire; no one can be compared to this woman.

[1079] Nimrod, legendary founder of Babylon, is described in Genesis 10:10 as being king in "Babel, and Accad, and Calneh, in the land of Shinar." Muslims say that he was the son of Cush and that he reigned for five hundred years; he is mentioned in the Quran (Sura 2:160; 21:68–9). Shinar "can be identified on a map of modern Iraq" and included well-known ancient cities such as Ur of the Chaldees, Lagash and Uruk (Leonard

cinxisse Semiramis urbem," and another poet, "*Persarum statuit Babylona Semiramis urbem,*"[1080] not only encompassing it with a wall but with such a wall as worthily was accounted principal of the world's Seven Wonders, for as Solinus reports, it was four hundred and fourscore furlongs about, which makes threescore our miles; Diodorus Siculus three hundred sixty-five, Quintus Curtius three hundred and fifty-eight, the height and thickness holding proportion. The height, say the same authors, was two hundred cubits (the common cubit is the length of the arm from the elbow to the longest finger's end, which is half a yard; the holy cubit was a yard, the geometrical cubit three). Fifty cubits of the largest measure, saith another, and the thickness was forty foot; fifty cubits, say others, and so broad that six chariots could well drive together at the top, and so battlemented that they could not fall. A broad graft or trench it also had, filled with water that went round the wall, which was entered by a hundred gates of brass, and what made this wall no less beautiful then strong was for that it was so arched so as under a piazza men might walk as in a shade. Semiramis begun, but finished it was for the recreation of Amytis,[1081] wife of Nebuchadnezzar the Great, or, as some allude, by Nitocris[1082] his daughter, who as Josephus *ex* Berossos *lib.* 1 *Contra Appiano* and Herodotus *lib.* 1 says, emulated Semiramis. Seconded by such a palace as gaining even his own admiration extorted from him that impious boast, "Is not this great Babel that I have built?," the city so strong that Cyrus, albeit by that success obtained at Borsippa[1083] he had the opportunity to wreath his brow with the Median diadem, yet was he unable to master it until he turned Euphrates another way, as Semiramis had done when she built the bridge, by which he

---

Cottrell, *The Land of Shinar* [London: Souvenir Press, 1965], 15). Nimrod's historicity has been much debated.

[1080] Semiramis surrounded the city with walls of burnt brick (Ovid, *Metamorphoses* 4.58). Semiramis established Babylon, the city of the Persians (Propertius, *Elegies* 3.11.21).

[1081] Amytis (b. c. 623 B.C.E.) was the Median wife of Nebuchadrezzar II. According to Ussher she was the daughter of Astyages, but others make her father Cyaxares II. Ussher is also the seventeenth-century authority for claiming that the Hanging Gardens were built for her because she was homesick, and that the king planted trees there from her homeland (*Annals*, 881). Berossos was probably Ussher's source; in the *Babyloniaca* (cited also by Josephus) he tells the same story, as does Diodorus Siculus (2.10). Finkel thinks the Amytis story is plausible (Clayton and Price, *Wonders*, 41–43).

[1082] Nitocris (fl. 600–575 B.C.E.) is an enigmatic figure. Ussher states that she was the wife of King Amel-Marduk of Babylon (562–560 B.C.E.), the biblical Evil-Merodach, whom she married in 583 B.C.E. Others believe she was the wife of Nabonidus and the mother of Nebuchadrezzar III, who ruled briefly 521–520 B.C.E., and still others (othersome, as Herbert would say) that she was a wife of Nebuchadrezzar II and the mother of Belshazzar. Herodotus is the source for some information (*Histories* 1.185–87).

[1083] Modern Birs Nimrud in Iraq; there is a ruined ziggurat on the site.

made his happy approach whilst Belshazzar, carousing amongst the Princes of his Empire, fell asleep, a perpetual sleep as called in Jeremiah 51:57,[1084] being after that dreadful apparition upon the wall that night slain by Darius, as recorded in Daniel 5:30,[1085] a city so great that, as Aristotle reports, one part in three days (hours, says one) after it was taken knew not that the enemy was entered, but that one post should run to meet another to show the king of Babylon that his city was taken at one end we read in the prophet Jeremiah 51:31,[1086] and that at the noise of the winning of Babel the earth was moved and the cry heard amongst the nations, Jeremiah 50:46,[1087] a city so imperial that for many generations it was the usual place of residence for the monarchs of the whole world. Honoured with the court of nine and forty emperors from Nimrod to Belshazzar for about 1600 years, the Empire terminating in that Prince was transferred to Darius and after to Cyrus by the victory he obtained over Astyages his grandfather, A.M. 3400. A city so beautiful and so stately as that Pausanias [called it] "the greatest and the most glorious of cities that ever the sun beheld," so that besides the superlative praises profane writers give, Holy Writ styles her the Princess and Glory of Kingdoms, as in Isaiah 47,[1088] and in Jeremiah the praise of the whole earth, Jeremiah 51:41.[1089]

Now, where could the wit of man find out a better to to inhabit then that local place which Adam in his innocency enjoyed, in which Babylon was situated, so rich that Alexander, when he became master of this place, found treasured there two hundred thousand talents of gold, every talent being in ours £4500, and what fitter place could that great monarch choose to bid farewell to the world then in what was "*epitomen universi,*" as one calls it, and at a time when ambassadors from all parts of the universe attended to acknowledge him sovereign, and where a parliament of the whole world was assembling to consult how to preserve what his victorious arm had purchased? But, to show the incertainty of this world's glory, this great victor in the meridian of his splendour and strength quaffing, some say, too great a draught of ox blood, as the richest wines there were called, to Hercules his eminent progenitor departs, with this epithet

---

[1084] "And I will make drunk her Princes, and her wise men, her captains, her rulers, and her mighty men: and they shall sleep a perpetual sleep . . . "

[1085] "In that night was Belshazzar the king of the Chaldaeans slain."

[1086] "One post shall run to meet another, and one messenger to meet another, to shew the king of Babylon that his city is taken at one end."

[1087] "At the noise of the taking of Babylon the earth is moved and the cry is heard among the nations."

[1088] Herbert appears to be referring to Isaiah 47:5, which reads "Sit thou silent, and get thee into darkness, O daughter of the Chaldaeans, for thou shalt no more be called, the lady of the kingdoms."

[1089] "How is Shaddach taken! and how is the praise of the whole earth surprised! how is Babylon become an astonishment among the nations!"

given by an envious critic, *"Terrarum fatale malum et sidus iniquum gentibus,"*[1090] having disturbed the world about twelve years, whose spirit, how heroic soever it was, is nevertheless censured by a Roman historian in these words: *"nihil aliud quam bene ausus est, vana contemnere."*[1091]

Now, according to natural motion, as all things when at the highest descend, so this triumphant city, by the revolution of succeeding times unable to resist the uncontrollable decree of Heaven signified by the greater prophets, had this judgment pronounced, "the proud walls of Babylon shall be utterly broken, and her high gates be burnt with fire; she shall become an heap, a dwelling-place for dragons," and that it should be said "how is Babylon become an astonishment, a hissing and a desolation amongst all nations?," Jeremiah 50:51. And as in the old, so in the new; in Revelation 17 the like judgment is denounced against mystical Babylon, for the old was then destroyed: "Babylon the Great is fallen, is fallen, and become the habitation of devils," of that astonishment both to the kings and merchants of the earth, that standing afar off they weep and wail, saying "Alas! alas for that great city, but the righteous do rejoice, seeing that in her was found the blood of the prophets and of the saints and of all that were slain upon the earth," which how far applicable unto this I intermeddle not, nor concerning her have more to say then that the utter desolation of this great city may well serve as a mirror for all others of that kind to view their destiny, for even the greatest cities die and have their periods. Give me leave therefore only in her present state to erect a monumental pillar unto her memory, whereon in capital letters I may affix this inscription:

BABYLON
Nil nisi NOMEN habet.

Nevertheless, as was her rise, her destruction was not at one time, but languished by degrees. The greatest blow was given by Seleucus Nicator, A.M. 3645, who about 306 years before the Incarnation of Our Saviour, in that very place where Cush once stood built a city at the place where Tigris and Euphrates meet, for some space making one channel and after his own name called it Seleucia,[1092]

[1090] Herbert truncates this passage, which should read: *"terrarum fatale malum fulmenque quod omnes / Percuteret pariter populos et sidus iniquum / gentibus."* Translation: "a fatal evil for the world, and a lightning-bolt that struck all people equally, a star fateful for the nations" (Lucan, *Civil War* 10.34-36).

[1091] "He dared, nothing but well, to despise vain things." (Livy, *Histories* 9.17).

[1092] In 321 B.C.E. Seleucus was appointed Governor of Babylon, but, as Grant notes, the city "lost its position as a major entrepot of commerce between east and west to the newly-founded Seleucia on the Tigris" (*Guide*, 96). The Seleucids did, however, restore the temple of Marduk at Babylon. Seleucia on the Tigris was built on the site of Opis, a Babylonian village "at the narrowest point between the Euphrates and the Tigris," and it was on this site that "Seleucus I Nicator founded the colony of Seleucia (307/300) which

but before that Calneh and Calah, one of those four cities over which Nimrod ruled, mentioned in Genesis 10:10–11,[1093] being fifty miles to the north of Babylon, by the diminution of one the other increasing, for partly by persuasions but principally by menace, that great Prince forced six hundred thousand souls out of Babylon to people Seleucia, agreeable to the prophecy of Jeremiah 51:45,[1094] which says that the people should go out of her. Strabo also *lib.* 16 in brief remembers as much: "*Babylonia partim Persae dicuerunt, partim consumpsit tempus, partim negligentia Macedonum, praesertim postquam Seleucus Nicator condidit Seleuciam ad Tigrim, stadiis tantum 300 a Babylone distans,*"[1095] by reason of which voisinage Seleucia is but erroneously by some taken for Babylon rather then Baghdad, for that Babylon which is in Egypt was built by Cambyses the Persian king, son to Cyrus, but since named *El-Cairo* by Gebir, lieutenant to the Babylonian caliph, *caire* in Syriac and British signifying 'a city.' Memphis and Latopolis[1096] stood there, or very near the place, as Leo [Africanus] in his *History of Africa* acquaints us.

Baghdad.

Baghdad, raised out of old Babel's ruins, is in 36 degrees 20 minutes north, in 82 of longitude, built in that part of Mesopotamia the Persians call *Iraq*, the Turks *Diarbec*, the Arabs *Jazeera*, the Armenians *Meredin*, albeit some place it in Susiana. The name Baghdad,[1097] I suppose, is either from *bag-deb*, 'a lordly city,' or from *bagh-dat*, 'a Princely garden;' howbeit, some say from *Bugiaser* the Babylonian caliph, who distributed two million of gold to re-edify it after that devastation which was made there by Amalric, King of Jewry.[1098] But long she enjoyed

---

replaced Babylon as the principal city of the country and became capital of his empire" (Grant, *Guide*, 576).

[1093] "And the beginning of his kingdom was Babel, and Erech and Accad, and Calneh, in the land of Shinar. Out of that land went forth Asshur, and builded Nineveh, and the city Rehoboth, and Calah."

[1094] "My people, go ye out in the midst of her, and deliver every man his soul from the fierce anger of the Lord."

[1095] The Persians say that, partly the ravages of time, partly the neglect of the Macedonians destroyed Babylon, especially after Seleucus Nicator founded Seleucia on the Tigris, 300 *stadia* (1 *stadium*= 607 feet) distant from Babylon.

[1096] Modern Esna, on the lower west bank of the Nile.

[1097] The name probably derives from the Middle Persian *bhaga*, 'God,' and *dad*, 'gift.'

[1098] Amalric I was King of Jerusalem 1162–1174. He twice invaded Egypt and the adjacent areas (1163, 1169) to exact tribute from the Fatimid rulers, and defeated the Grand Vizier Dirghan at the Battle of Pelusium (Tel Farama). The Caliph of Baghdad at the time was al-Mustanjid (1160–1170), who here appears as *Bugiaser*, unless Dirghan is meant.

not that splendour, for Ket-Buqa,[1099] a Tartarian Prince, by order from Hulagu his brother not only sacked it with a barbarous rage but withal cruely tortured the then Lord Caliph al-Mustasim.[1100] Howbeit, in the year of Our Lord 762, *Heg.* 142, al-Mansur,[1101] the three and twentieth caliph, by art magic observing a precise time when by a good influence of the Heavens it might in future times be fortunate, begun to rear her up again, and as a peculiar act testifying his devotion built the mosque in that place where one *Bagdet*, an eremite, had made his hermitage, and from whose memory it took the denomination.[1102] Al-Mansur nevertheless, as Tarikh [al-Tabari] the Persian historian says, gave it another name, *viz. Medina al-Islam*, i.e. 'the City of Peace,' or, according to *Ben Casen, Deer-Assala*, i.e. 'The church of Peace.'[1103] This, as I suppose, is that great al-Mansur who every month, to alter his grey hairs to black, was at the charge of two thousand drams of musk.

An evil spirit, it seems, predominated this place, for she no sooner began to take breath and to deck herself in summer livery when another cold northern blast benumbed her; Toghrul Beg or Sadek, Lord of the Seljukian family and father of the Ottomans, in despite of the Arab and Persian, *Anno Domini* 1031, *Heg.* 411 for some time forcing her to bow under the yoke of Turkish bondage.[1104] However, once more an Arabian caliph, Najm al-din by name, son to Emir al-Mumin, set her at liberty, after whom *Addae-daul* and Sayed Saif ud-dowlah enlarged her, and to them, according to Ahmed abu Bakr, followed al-Mustazhir

---

[1099] Ket-Buqa [*Chyta*], "a Nestorian Christian, famous afterwards as the Mongol commander at 'Ain Jalut" (Boyle, *History*, 342) was not Hulagu's brother. He was one of three generals involved in the taking of Baghdad.

[1100] The capture of Baghdad by Hulagu Khan's forces occurred in 1258. Al-Mustasim was "rolled up in a carpet and trampled or kicked to death, to avoid the shedding of his blood, such being the Mongols' method of executing their own Princes" (Boyle, *History*, 349).

[1101] Herbert's wording is ambiguous, although his chronology here is correct. Baghdad was in fact *founded* by Caliph al-Mansur (754–75), who was the twenty-first (not twenty-fourth) caliph after Mohammed. In 762 he built Baghdad, which he called, ironically, "the City of Peace," as Herbert notes, to replace Haran as his capital (Albert Hourani, *A History of the Arab People* [Cambridge, MA: Harvard University Press, 1991], 33).

[1102] This is one story about the origins of the name that has no foundation in history.

[1103] Al-Tabari writes that when al-Mansur arrived, "at the site of the palace there was then a priest's church. He spent the night there, and awoke next morning having passed the sweetest and gentlest night on earth. He stayed, and everything he saw pleased him. Then he said, "This is the site on which I shall build" (al-Tabari 145, cited in Hourani, *History*, 33).

[1104] According to Hourani, the Seljuks "established themselves in Baghdad in 1055 as effective rulers beneath the suzerainity of the Abbasids" (*History*, 84). Their rule ended in 1194, during the caliphate of al-Nasir (1180–1225).

Billah, son to al-Muktadi,[1105] who ruled there *Anno Dom.* 1100, *Heg.* 480, which several caliphs, as they were excessively rich, so they spared neither cost nor pain to redintegrate her memory, after which Shah Ismail conquered it from Bajazet, but Suleiman his successor regained it from Shah Tahmasp. From Suleiman the Persian king Mohammed [Khodabanda], son of Tahmasp, recovered it *Anno Dom.* 1566, *Heg.* 946; entering unsuspected in the disguise of merchants, fifteen hundred of his men in like habit driving into Baghdad a caravan of three thousand camels, and giving the watchword, immediately threw off their disguise and brandished their glittering blades in the eyes of the astonished garrison. The Persians by that stratagem kept it till the year of Our Lord 1605, *Heg.* 985, when it again reverted to Turkish thraldom, howbeit Shah Abbas the Persian *Anno Dom.* 1625, *Heg.* 1005 by force beat the Turks thence, as also their confederates the Tartars from Van in Armenia, since which the Turks by a like stratagem have regained and at this present hold it. Let us now into the town.

In the city is little more worthy observation then the bridge, the mosque, the *coho*-house,[1106] the bazaar and the gardens. The bridge resembles that at Rohan in Normandy, having passage over thirty long boats which are boarded and chained one to another and made to separate at pleasure. The mosque, built in the west side of the city, is large, round and pleasantly-raised of white freestone brought down Tigris from Mosul. The Sultan's house, that adjoins the bazaar or great market, is large but low, and near it are some brass pieces which the Turks brought hither or from Hormuz when it was taken by the Persians. A little chapel also, *Panch Ali* by name, is memorable by reason of that impression of five fingers which Ali made in the solid stone there. Coho-houses are houses of good fellowship, where towards evening most commonly many Mussulmen ordinarily assemble to sip coffee, a Stygian liquor, black, thick and bitter, brewed out of *bunchie* or *bunnin*[1107] berries, more reputed of, if they hold to the old custom that is recorded by Herodotus, how that not a woman here but once in her lifetime sat in Venus's temple, but most esteemed from a tradition they have that Mohammed sipped no other broth then this, which was invented by Gabriel. In the coho-house they also inebriate themselves with *arak* and tobacco. The bazaar is pretty large and square, the houses comely and the gardens sweet, yet all put-together are no way comaparable to many late upstart towns about her.

[1105] Al-Mustazhir Billah was Caliph of Baghdad 1094–1118 in succession to al-Muktadi (1075–1094). Herbert fails to mention that Baghdad was captured by Timur (1401) who "ordered a ruthless massacre of her citizens" (Jackson and Lockhart, *History*, 67), but was rebuilt by Sultan Ahmed Jalayir, its former ruler, who returned after a short exile in Egypt. He was expelled again, returned once more and was killed in 1411.

[1106] A corruption of the Arabic *kahwa*, 'coffee.'

[1107] "The word *bunn* is the word given to the [coffee] plant, and *bun* is the existing name in Shoa [Ethiopia, Ed.]. The name is also that applied in Yemen" (*HJ* 232).

Twelve miles lower, towards Euphrates, a confused mount is seen, which some imagine to be the rubbish of Nimrod's tower, and the rather because that slimy bricks and mortar may be digged out of it. I rather imagine this to be the ruin of that great and memorable temple which was erected by Semiramis in honour of Bel or Jupiter Belus. At a distance it is better perceived then when nearer hand, the insensible rising all the way, it may be, occasions it. What more or more properly can I apply then that of Ausonius[1108] in one of his epigrams: "Why wonder we that people die, since monuments decay,/ Yea, flimsy stones with men's great names, Death's tyrannies obey" [*Epigrams* 37.9-10].

Baghdad is distant from Aleppo forty days by caravan, of which above two-thirds of the way be through the deserts, but by water it may be done in fewer, for in one day we pass from thence to Fallujah, in sixteen days more to Birber, from whence in two days to Aleppo in Syria, from Aleppo by caravan to Tripoli under Mount Libanus in seven days. Aleppo is twenty leagues from Antioch, but to see old Susa is neither unworthy our labour nor out of our way, for it gave name to Susiana, which has Assyria to the north, the Gulf south, Persia east and to the west Babylon.

Susa.

Susa,[1109] everywhere famoused, was one of the three royal palaces the Median monarchs so much gloried and delighted in, *viz.* Babylon, Susa and Ecbatana. Xenophon thus distributes the court-motion, *viz.* three spring months in Susa, two summer months in Ecbatana and seven winter months the King spent in Babylon, meaning when the sun was remotest, for their winter is equal to our summer in heat when the sun rises to his meridian. This was built by Darius son of Hystaspes, *Anno Mundi* 3444, as Pliny in his 6 *lib. c.* 28, who rather beautified it with many palaces. Some say Laomedon[1110] built it such time as

---

[1108] Decimus Magnus Ausonius (c. 310–395), poet, lawyer, rhetorician, and soldier, the tutor of the Emperor Gratian. His most famous works were the *Mosella* and the *Septem sententiae*. Unlike most poets, he enjoyed a successful political careeer culminating in the consulship (379). His *Epigrams* were edited by J. C. Scaliger (1574) and there is a recent edition by N. M. Kay (London: Duckworth, 2001). See also H. Sivan, *Ausonius of Bordeaux* (London: Routledge, 1993).

[1109] Herbert uses the form *Shushan*, which, with *Shush*, is an earlier form of the name than the more familiar Susa, which I have used here (Grant, *Guide*, 610). He is correct in ascribing the foundation of the "new" town to Darius I, although we now know that as a settlement it is much more ancient, going back to 4000 B.C.E. or further. See also below.

[1110] Laomedon was the son of Ilus and King of Troy; he built the city walls of Troy.

Tola[1111] judged Israel. Others make Cyrus, the first founder of Pasagardae (so-called from Pison,[1112] a branch of Hiddekel) to be the architect, in memory of his good success obtained in that very place against Astyages the Median. It is spoken of in the first chapter of Esther that there Ahasuerus, *Anno Mundi* 3500, feasted his lieutenants over an hundred and twenty-seven provinces a hundred and eighty days. Both Nehemiah and Daniel, whose burial-place it is, call it *"Susis castrum in Elam regione,"*[1113] thereby making Susiana part of Persia. And, notwithstanding the many mutations and miseries it suffered, yet it was to smile on Alexander when he extracted thence to pay his soldiers and fill his bags fifty thousand talents in bullion and nine millions of coined gold, and well may be, since Cassiodorus[1114] in his 7 *lib.* 15 *Epistle* reports for truth that Memnon, son to Tithonus, reckoned by Herodotus *lib.* 2[1115] the first founder, and to have called it *Memnonia*, so gloried in his work that he cemented the stones with gold, which made Aristagoras[1116] proclaim unto his men of war that if they could but master it, every soldier there might then compare with Jove for wealth.

[1111] Tola, whose name means "scarlet worm," judged Israel c. 1210–1190 B.C.E., according to R. P. ben Dedek's *Kings' Calendar* dating (which is disputed by some scholars). For details, see Judges 10:1–2.

[1112] One of the so-called Four Rivers of Eden (Genesis 2: 10–14). Scholars have tentatively identified it with the Wadi Bahin river system, now dry, which runs into the Euphrates and drains central Arabia. For details, see David J. Gibson, *The Land of Eden Located* (1964), www.Nabataea.net/eden.html.com

[1113] "Susis, a fortified place in the Elam region." Susa was the capital of the ancient Elamite Empire (the *Keturim* in Esther, Daniel, and Nehemiah) until 2300 B.C.E., when it was taken by Sargon I of Akkad. It passed back into Elamite hands briefly in about 2240 B.C.E. and again in 2004, after which it reverted to the Akkadians. Asshur-banipal flattened Susa in 647 B.C.E., but it revived until Cyrus took it in 538. Chardin says that Susa is modern Hamadan (*Travels*, 143), but in fact Hamadan is Ecbatana.

[1114] Flavius Magnus Cassiodorus Senator (c. 490–585), Roman statesman, theologian, and historian, possibly of Syrian origins (although he lived in S. Italy) who pusued his career under King Theodoric of the Ostrogoths. He retired from public life and founded a monastery. Amongst his works are the *Chronica*, a survey of history to 519, a discussion of the function of the liberal arts and the *Gothic History*, which survives only because of an abridgment by Jordanes. Cassiodorus was first edited by Guillaume Fournier (1588), and a new edition by Jean Garet appeared in Herbert's lifetime (1679), too late to be used here. L. W. Jones has edited the *Institutiones* (New York: Columbia University Press, 1946). See also J. O'Donnell, *Cassiodorus* (Berkeley: University of California Press, 1979).

[1115] Herodotus is not discussing the founding of Susa, but describing a colossal statue on the road "between Sardis and Smyrna." He states that "some people . . . guess the figure is Memnon" (2.106). This is the only mention of the legendary Memnon in Herodotus.

[1116] Aristagoras was made satrap of Miletus by Darius I. He ruled the city 502–497 B.C.E.

The name Susa is much controverted. Athenaeus defines it from 'plenty of bellies,' but where fetched I cannot apprehend, the Arabic nor Persian having no such etymon[1117] or signification. As well I might say from *suzan* or *shuzan*, which in the Persic tongue signifies 'a needle or a glass bottle,' but rather believe it was derived from Cush, Noah's grandson, Susiana from him being called Chusiana and at this day not much discrepant in the name Khuzistan, and not *Elaran* as some have fancied, more probable in that Cush, Ham's son, planted a colony here ere he removed into Ethiopia, a mistake which made the Septuagints imagine Nile as one of those four streaming from Paradise, his sons also hereabouts inhabiting, *viz.* Nimrod in Chaldaea, Seba in Arabia, one Havilah in Susiana (for the other Havilah, the son of Joktan, removed into India), Raamah into Arabia first and after that into Carmania.

At this day 'tis called *Valdac* or *Baldach* as Paulus Venetus, and not far from the Gulf and watered by Choaspes, which, arising from the Jaroonian mountains streams very pleasantly to this place, and not far from Basra participates with the Gulf of Persia, where also Euphrates, called *Phras*[1118] *and Al-makheer*, from Libanus[1119] some say, from Mount Abo in Armenia say others, and Tigris, now called *Diglat*, *Tegil* and, of old, *Hiddekel*, from Taurus, or *Nyphates*, which is part of Taurus, embowel themselves, a river of such account with the Persian emperors that no water but this of Choaspes, no bread but from Assus in Phrygia, no wine but Chalybonian in Syria, no salt but what they had from Memphis in Egypt could please their dainty palates. Daniel calls it *Ulai*, Pliny *Eulaeus*, now *Tirtis*, an anti-stream of which glides to Shiraz.

Susa is under thirty degrees, but Ptolemy makes it four more; it was in compass an hundred and twenty stades or furlongs, so Strabo. Polyclitus[1120] numbers two hundred, which is above twenty miles English. The wall about it was quadrangular. In building, walls, houses and temples, in little it resembled great Babylon. The royal palace here, some say, was built by Mordecai, and of that magnificence that it was not inferior to that other which Daniel formerly built at Ecbatana. The outside and the pavement of this were mosaic or small pieces of chequered marble, arched also and supported by pillars which were richly-gilded and set with stones of lustre. The roof was painted after the resemblance of the starry firmament, and in all parts so beautiful in the art and so rich in the material as sufficiently expressed the founder's greatness as well as the architect's

---

[1117] The literal sense of a word.

[1118] Modern Firat, Iraq.

[1119] Herbert is probably referring to Mount Libanus, which is "a region extending for about thirty miles from north to south behind Berytus (Beirut) in Phoenicia (Lebanon)" (Grant, *Guide*, 344).

[1120] Polyclitus of Larissa was a historian who accompanied Alexander the Great on his expeditions and wrote an account of Alexander. He is cited by Aelian, one of Herbert's references, and by other later historians.

ingenuity. By Cyrus it was made choice of for the delight of his most beautiful Panthea,[1121] a lady celebrated by writers in those times and on whom Cyrus the Great passionately doted. Xenophon also ennobles this city from the plenty it had of springs of pure water streaming into Choaspes, which for the delight of the Persian monarch took to drink of occasioned the poet Tibullus to observe that ". . . where Choaspes springs / Which once was the delight of kings."[1122] famoused also for that bitumen which some call naphtha, being an oily liquid substance like clay, but set on fire would inflame the very air. It was showed Alexander near Ecbatana as one of the rareties of Asia. The like is at Hait,[1123] a hundred sixty-nine miles from Baghdad upon Euphrates in the way to Aleppo. From Babylon, Ecbatana and Susa had equidistancy.

Paradise.

Paradise, or the place of the terrestrial Garden of Eden (*Hegea-del-Holan* the Indians name it, *Gan-Eden* the Hebrews, *Geserta* now, wherein God placed Adam) is much controverted, and where it was no less doubted of, some making it an allegory, others a local place. Strange it is to consider the variety; some say it was in the middle region of the air, whence they draw those four great streams that water Paradise, some place it in the Mountains of the Moon in Ethiopia, whence Nilus springs, othersome in the circles of the Moon and others under the circle, supposing that thence the four rivers flow under large deep seas into Paradise. Nevertheless, there be some that think the four rivers signify four cardinal virtues, the word 'Paradise' being a metaphor of delight, man's fall the banishment and the Torrid Zone the fiery sword, fanatic fancies such as made the brainsick Hermians[1124] and Seleucians aver there never was a Paradise, but some, and those well-read, imagine it was ten miles about, the province Mesopotamia, the place Eden, to this day retaining both name and memory. St. Augustine judges it was in the Happy Arabia, amongst the Tartars, dreams Goropius (in

---

[1121] Panthea was the wife of Abradatas, King of Susa. In 538 B.C.E. Cyrus defeated and captured Abradatas, and his magnanimous treatment of Panthea led to the reconciliation of the two enemies. When Abradatas was killed in battle with the Egyptians, Panthea took her own life. The full story is told in Xenophon's *Cyropaedia*, also known as *The Education of Cyrus*. William Barker translated it into English (1552), and there is a new translation by W. Ambler (Ithaca: Cornell University Press, 2001).

[1122] "The kingly streams / Of royal Choaspes" (Tibullus, *Elegies* 3. 7. 142–143). This poem is the "Panegyric of Messalla," which is not by Tibullus but part of the *Tibullan Collection*.

[1123] Modern Hit, Iraq.

[1124] The inhabitants of what became Seleucia on the Calycadnus, "the most important city in Rough Cilicia (Cilicia Tracheia, Aspera; southeastern Asia Minor) on the right (west) bank of the river Calycadnus (Gök Su) . . . on the site of an earlier habitation centre variously named as Hermia and Hyria" (Grant, *Guide*, 575).

Holland, he might as well have said), under the North Pole, thinks Postellus, in Syria Beroaldus,[1125] upon the banks of the Tigris Xenophon, everywhere before Adam sinned, thinks Ortelius. Some say it comprehended Mesopotamia, that part called *Padan* or *Phadan-Aram* and *Aram-Naharaim*, i.e. Syria *fluvii*, Armenia, Mount Taurus, encircling Shinar. Others carry it further as that it included Nilus and Ganges, a too great limit for a garden! For Nilus, arising from Zaire in Africa, empties itself into the midland sea, and Ganges from Siba near Imaus in Scythia into the Bengalan Ocean. The inhabitants in Ceylon say it was in Egypt, Syria and Judaea, that the Tree of Knowledge grew on Mount Calvary, the second Adam suffering where the first Adam offended. Some also dream that it is in a mountain above the sky, where Enoch and Elias are.

The most probable is this, that Nile and Ganges had no being there, the Septuagints mistake arising from their supposition that *Pison* was Ganges and *Gihon* Nile. Mesopotamia no doubt was east from Arabia, where Moses, the first that ever wrote history, about the year from the Creation 2430 completed his Pentateuch, and as questionless, the Garden of Eden was watered with Euphrates and Tigris, who in their several fluxes, one from Periardo in Armenia, the other from Libanus,[1126] divide themselves into four branches, Pison one (streaming through Pasagardae in Persia), Gihon the other, which after became a proper name for all great rivers in Persia, commixing with Choapes, both run into the Gulf at Basra. For, whereas it is said Pison compasses the land of Havilah,[1127] we must not imagine it to be that Havilah which is in India, but that rather which was in Susiana, where Havilah son of Cush planted before he removed into south Africa. Or if that will not content, make Mount Taurus a wall unto it east and north, and Euphrates, Tigris, Araxes (or Gozan, if you please) and Indus the four rivers to water it; [it] will be a sufficient extendure, and in the adolescency of the world, as the name interprets, most delicious, and, till Noah's flood, most think, undefaced.

The author's sickness and recovery.

Can I choose a better place to seat your patience then here? After the death of some gentlemen my course came next, though not to die, yet to put my feet into the grave. Whether through cold I got on Mount Taurus, where I wantonly sucked in too much cool air, or that I played the epicure too largely upon

---

[1125] Filippo Beroaldo (1433–1505) was Professor of Rhetoric and Poetry at the University of Bologna. His edition of Pliny appeared in 1498, and he also published editions of Julius Caesar and Florus. He wrote commentaries on Ovid's *Metamorphoses* and produced a historical chronicle.

[1126] The Libanus mountains run from north to south in Syria.

[1127] Havilah has been identified with Ha'ill in N. Arabia, which has several dried-up river beds connecting to the Euphrates.

fruit, or that diversity of meridians or so long quaffing variety of waters might be the cause, I cannot say, but some or all of these by God's appointment upon our descent into Media put me into a violent dysentery, so as by continuance in that disease I was like a skeleton and reduced to so much weakness that I may be bold to say scarce could any man be more enfeebled. I wanted not the advice and help of the archiater,[1128] the King's doctor, who albeit he was doubtless a very skilled physician, yet did me little good, so malignant was my distemper, albeit I took what he prescribed, part of which, I well remember, were pomegranate pills, barberries,[1129] sloes in broth and sundry other things, and returned what he expected,[1130] so that it was hard to judge whether my spirits or gold decayed further. In this sad condition and misery I was forced to travel three hundred miles hanging upon the side of a camel in a cage resembling a cradle.

Murad, the Aesculapius of Persia, seeing I would rather die then part with more fees (for when it was gone I knew not where to borrow; merchants were strangers to me and I had above thirteen thousand miles home by the southwest of Africa) limited my life to five days' existence. But he that sits on high, in comparison of whose wisdom all human knowledge is mere folly, in four and twenty hours after, as it were by a miracle, proved this oraculiser mistaken in his crisis, for I had then attending me an Armenian called Magar and a Tartarian woman who, sore against my will, would for my recovery be often invocating her heathenish deities, but finding they had no power, whether to accelerate Murad's sentence or to possess my linen or apparel, of which I had good store, I know not, but no doubt well-knowing that wine was by the doctor forbidden me, she nevertheless in an agony of thirst presents me with a vial full of intoxicating wine which both looked and relished curiously and I poured down no less insensibly without wit or measure. But, as if opium had been steeped in it, it quickly banished my senses and put me for four and twenty hours into a trance, so as in that time, had not a friend or servant resisted, I had been buried alive, they thinking I was dead, "*nam nec color, nec sanguis, nec sensus, nec vox superasset,*"[1131] as was said of another in like condition. But through God's mercy this desperate potion recovered me, for after I had disgorged abundantly I fell into a deep sleep, Nature's nurse, and, as one aptly terms it, the parenthesis of all our cares, not having done so for a month before, the people admiring the operation, so that by the benefit of that little rest and binding quality of the wine, but chiefly through God's mercy towards me, that body which was reduced to such weakness and like a crazy rotten vessel leaky on all sides, was through mercy, as it were, careened, launched

---

[1128] Anglicised version of the Greek word for 'chief physician.'

[1129] Culpeper writes that the barberry "is so well known by every boy or girl that has but attained to the age of seven years that it needs no description" (*Herbal*, 33), but this is no longer the case. It is used to make a purgative.

[1130] Paid him what he asked for.

[1131] For no colour, blood, senses, or voice were left.

out into the world again and in a few months became strong and perfectly recovered. Howbeit, my desperate doctress, whiles my other servants slept, when she thought me dead opened my trunks and robbed me of my linen and moneys, for all which I would not pursue her, the law is so strict there against felony, especially in behalf of strangers. I will therefore say with David, Psalm 7: "O, what troubles and adversities hast thou showed me, and yet didst thou turn and refresh me, yea, and broughtest me from the deeps of the earth again," for which I render praises unto thee, and seeing thou hast delivered my soul from death, wilt thou not also deliver my feet from falling? "Oh that I might walk before thee in the light of the living," Psalm 56:13.

Noah's Flood.

Now, concerning the kings and other Princes ruling over this Empire in the first and second monarchies of the world, it would require a volume to proceed in the method of an historian, but, seeing the chorography of those parts is what I chiefly aim at, I will only present the reader with a summary of their successions, interwoven with such public matters as I coceive may specially relate unto the places observed in our travel, and in that I shall trace it to the first original.

God, perceiving that the wickedness of man was great in the earth and that all the imaginations of the thoughts of his heart were continually evil, repented that he had made man, Genesis 6:5, so as by the flood of waters he destroyed everything in whose nostrils the spirit of life did breathe, whatsoever were in the dry land, Noah only finding grace in the eyes of the Lord, escaped in the ark together with his wife, their three sons and their wives, being in all eight persons. The face of the earth was covered with water one hundred and fifty days, fifteen cubits above the highest mountains. In the seventh month the ark rested upon the mountains of Ararat; in the tenth month the tops of the mountains were discovered. Forty days after Noah opened the windows of the ark after which, at the end of the second month, Noah and all that were there preserved as seed to replenish the earth issued out and in thankfulness to the Lord and as evidence of his faith he built and altar and of every clean beast and fowl offered a burnt offering thereon unto the Lord. God having blessed Noah and his sons, he had them bring forth fruit, multiply and replenish the earth; the sons of Noah were Shem, Ham and Japhet, of whom the whole earth was overspread. Noah began to be an husbandman, planted a vineyard and lived after the Flood 350 years; the whole course of his life was 950 years, and then died A.M. 2006. Concerning Ararat and the place of Noah's plantation after he forsook the ark I have elsewhere spoken.

In the space of a hundred and thirty years after the Flood Noah, having peopled the Orient to the end the middle and more western parts might be likewise planted and the world distributed amongst his children, he gave several of them their mission, who accordingly travelling from the east came into the Vale of Shinar (as far as the great River Euphrates) where they rested, for they found that place fit for plantation, after which, as well to get themselves a name for their better association, or, as some imagine, for the better securing themselves from a second cataclysm, Nimrod by thirty years of incessant labour of that company built a city and tower whose top they intended should reach Heaven, Genesis 11:4. But the Highest, perceiving their impious design, descended, and by confounding their language (for till then they were *populus unius labii*[1132]) made them desist, and from thence scattered them abroad upon the face of the whole earth, by which multiplication of that original idiom of speech the place was called *Babel*, in Hebrew and most other tongues signifying 'confusion.'

Now albeit this was miraculous, it might be well worth our labour to consider whether speech proceed from art or Nature. The most learned agree that "*arte humana et non Natura loquela et nomina rerum sunt imposita*,"[1133] but do not think it fit in this place. Soon after the Creation Adam and his children planted the world from Eden, reputed the navel or centre of the earth, albeit Strabo by his story of the two eagles which begun their flight from east to west and met at Pytho in Phocis[1134] would have that the meditullium, so Noah's children near the same place commenced theirs, thence dispersing themselves into the most remote places. Shem's posterity chose Asia the Great, Ham's Africa and Japhet's Europe, albeit the *Liber de generatione* published scarce two hundred years hence by Abraham Zacuto,[1135] a Jewish Kabbalist, tells us, but not his authority, that the five sons of Noah first planted all that part of the greater Asia which is betwixt Euphrates and the Indian sea as far as Ganges, but of more certainty 'tis in Peleg's[1136] time, about three hundred years after the Flood, the world was set out into partition, and as their numbers increased, so were colonies dispersed for better and more universal plantation.

[1132] A people of a single tongue.

[1133] By human art, not nature, were speech and the names of things imposed.

[1134] Phocis is "a territory of central Greece including the valley of the river Cephisus to the north and the plain of Crisa on the Corinthian Gulf to the south" (Grant, *Guide*, 502).

[1135] Abraham ben Samuel Zacuto (c. 1450–1510) was a Spanish-Jewish astronomer, historian, and mathematician from Salamanca, Professor at Zaragoza and Salamanca Universities. He moved to Lisbon and became Court Astronomer to Manoel I. His works include an *Almanach perpetuum*, a history of the Jews to 1500 called the *Sefer Hayushasin* (1504, reprinted in Cracow, 1581) and the work Herbert cites, a commentary on Aristotle's *De generatione et corruptione* (1498).

[1136] Peleg was the great-grandson of Shem; "in his days was the earth divided" (Genesis 10:25).

Nimrod, the first monarch.

Nimrod, whether by reason of his more then ordinary stature and strength (for Berossos reports him to be ten common cubits high, which make 15 foot) or from the eminency of his birth or else by consent of his brethren, usurped a sovereignty over is diversely-conjectured, but an eminent writer observes "*is primus erat qui cepit regnare super homines; ignem quoque adorare*,"[1137] the first-noted idolator and that presumed to lord it over his brethren. Cyril,[1138] nevertheless, *Contra Julian l. 4*, alludes it to Belus or Arbelus his son, "*Arbelus vir arrogans, primus dicitur a subditis accipisse nomen deitatis*,"[1139] howbeit in sacred and profane story he is also acknowledged the first monarch of the earth, for as the first foundation of Babel is attributed to him, so is the first kingdom, as appears by Genesis 10:10, where 'tis said "The beginning of kingdoms was Babylon, Erech, Accad and Calneh in the land of Shinar," and "out of that land Ashur (or as some translations, Nimrod) went forth and builded Nineveh and Calah which is a great city." This is he whose name, derived from the Hebrew *marad*, renders him "*rebelis contra Deum et Naturam*,"[1140] he who by reason of his tyranny became a proverb, "*quasi Nimrod robustus venator coram Domino*,"[1141] by Berossos called *Nimbroth*, by others *Saturnus Babylonicus*, whose father was Cush or *Jupiter Belus* and his father Ham, called *Jupiter Chamon*, agreeable to that of Tzetzes, "*reges omnes olim vocaverunt Ioves*,"[1142] and after five hundred years as king died about the Year of the World 1844, his body being buried at Babylon, say most, albeit one author I met with finds some part of him at Persepolis.

To Nimrod succeeded Belus his son, styled *Jupiter Babylonicus*, *Baal*, and *Bel*, which in Chaldee signify 'the sun' or 'sovereign Lord.' This Prince at the age of threescore years gave place to Ninus, who, imitating his great ancestors, added to his empire Arabia, Armenia and those countries that verge upon Bactria, and to deify his father Belus erected his statue in gold, which he commanded to be worshipped. This is the first idolatry any story mentions. After fifty years Semiramis,

---

[1137] "He was the first to set himself to reign over men and to worship fire" (Peter Comestor, *Historia Scholastica* 1. 37, PL 198. 1088).

[1138] St. Cyril (c. 373–444) was Patriarch of Alexandria from 412. He is best known for his controversy with the Nestorians over the divinity of Christ, but he alienated many others by "exercising his authority with a hastiness and violence that led to much trouble" (Attwater, *Dictionary*, 98). Julian is, of course, the Emperor Julian the Apostate (r. 361–63), whose sun-worship and philosophical writings did not appeal to Cyril.

[1139] Arbelus was an arrogant man, the first, it is said, to accept the name of a god from his subjects.

[1140] As a rebel against God and Nature.

[1141] Like Nimrod, who was a mighty hunter before the Lord.

[1142] All kings were once called Joves.

the daughter of Derceta[1143] an Askalonite, her father not known in history, being made his wife so captivated his reason then in dotage, as prevailing that she might command the Empire five days, made such use of her power as within that time the King was sent to his long home, so as she swayed the sceptre without control, and being of a masculine spirit so greatly enlarged the Assyrian Empire that she not only added to it Egypt and Bactria but also the East Indies, "*quo praeter illam et Alexandrum nemo intravit*," saith an old historian,[1144] but of that last had little reason to boast, seeing that she was, though unwillingly, forced to a retreat over Indus by Staurobates, in passing which all but twenty of that great body of thirty hundred thousand foot and ten hundred thousand horse with nearly a hundred thousand chariots miserably perished. Nevertheless, to recount the wonderful things together with the memorable conquests she effected both at Babylon and other places would be to report what is spoken concerning this virago in the late description of Babylon and other parts. Her death after forty-two years' rule is variously reported, some affirming she was slain by her son Ninus[1145] in his father's vindication, others that she died a natural death or was metamorphosed into a dove, which in her memory the Babylonian princes bore afterwards in their royal banner or ensign.

Ninus her successor, by some writers called *Ninias*, and by othersome *Zaneis*,[1146] *Mars* and *Amraphel*, is supposed to be that Prince whom Abraham overthrew with Chedor-laomer the Persian king near Damscus in the rescue of his nephew Lot, as recorded in Genesis 14:1.[1147] Chedor-laomer king of Persia, whether that was his proper name or given him from the regal tire or garment he wore upon his head, which was named *chedar* or *cydaris*, or that he was called *Kedar* from his dusky complexion is doubtful, but more certain he is that same which the *Tarikh* calls Kaiumers, father to Saiamuk,[1148] to whom in order

---

[1143] "Others report [Semiramis] to be the daughter of Derceta, a courtezan of Ascalon . . . others say, that this Derceta or Dercetis, the mother of Semiramis, was sometimes a recluse, and had professed a holy and religious life" (Ralegh, *History of the World* I, Ch. XII, Sec. III, 407).

[1144] "Where except for her and Alexander no-one had entered" (Pompeius Trogus [Justin], 1. 11).

[1145] Usually designated by the variant form 'Ninyas.'

[1146] See, for example, Jordanes, who says "Zaneis, who is Ninyas, the son of Ninus and Semiramis, 38 years, the overthrow of whom in thirty years was promised to Abraham, who was 75 years old" (*De summa temporum vel origine actibusque gentis Romanorum*, ed. T. Mommsen [Berlin: Weidmann, 1922], 15).

[1147] "And it came to pass in the days of Amraphel king of Shinar, Arioch king of Ellasar, Chedor-laomer king of Elam, and Tidal king of nations; that these made war . . ." (Genesis 14:1–2ff).

[1148] Saiamuk was not a king, but the valiant son of Kayumars who fell defending his father's kingdom from "a hideous Demon / Who . . . aspired / To work his ruin" (Ferdowsi, *Shahnameh*, 16–17).

succeeded Husheng, Jemshid, Zohak, Feridun, Minuchihr, Nauder, Afrasiyab (whom some suppose Achaemenes[1149]), Barzu, Kai-Kobad, Solomon, Kai-Kaus, Lohurasp etc.[1150]

Miserable end of Sardanapalus.

But, being as yet in quest of the Assyrian line, return we to Ninias, who began his reign A.M. 2000 and finished it after thirty-eight years' rule being succeeded by Ariaeus,[1151] by some called *Thuras*, after whom followed seven and thirty emperors, the last of whom was Sardanapalus,[1152] who begun his reign over that great monarchy A.M. 3124, but by all historians said to be a Prince so degenerating from the warlike spirit of his great ancestors that he is styled *"vir muliere corruptior,"*[1153] and not without reason, seeing he was so effeminate that he not only wholly sequestered himself from men but gave himself up to the society of his wives and concubines both in habit and exercise imitating them, a Prince that wanted Plato for his tutor, who was so far from Sardanapalus his opinion that thanked God he was a man and not a woman, so as it was not without difficulty Arbaces his Median lieutenant obtained admission into his palace at Nineveh, where he found the Emperor delicately attired not with an *ornamentum virile,*[1154] but in ladies' dress he spangled with rich jewels and spinning of silk among the

---

[1149] The legendary ancestor of the Achaemenids. If he existed, scholars date him about 700 B.C.E. and believe him to have been a tribal leader, not a king. There are no historical records of his existence; however, he may have been an ancestor whom Darius I appropriated after took the kingdom. Plato identified him with Perses, whom the Greeks believed to have been the ancestor of the Persians, and some scholars identify him with a ruler of Elam called Hakhamanish. The editor is not qualified to make any judgments on this.

[1150] All these legendary Persian kings (except Solomon, who should not be in the list) are chronicled by Ferdowsi in the *Shahnameh* as follows (numbers refer to the Davis translation except when noted): Hushang (3–4); Jamshid (6–8); Zahhak (9–28); Feridun (28–36); Minuchihr (47–63); Nauder or Nozar (111–12); Afrasiab (115 *passim*; not a king but the enemy of Rostam and Kay Kavus); Barzu (Levin, trans., *Shahnameh*, 250–58; a rival of Rostam and King of the Tartars); Kay Qobad (95–99); Kay Kavus (142 *passim*); Lohrasp (361).

[1151] "Ariaeus, 30 years. In his tenth year Abraham at 100 years old begat his son Isaac" (Jordanes 16). Ralegh states that Ninyas "associated to himself Arius, king of Arabia" (*History*, 329), but whether this is the same person or not I do not know.

[1152] As noted above, this is Shamash-shum-ukin, King of Babylon 668–648 B.C.E. He did perish in the fire, but at Babylon, not Nineveh. The son of Esarhaddon of Assyria, he was assigned Babylon by his father whilst Assyria went to his brother Asshur-banipal (669–631 B.C.E.) and rebelled against him. Ctesias is the original source of the self-immolation story.

[1153] "A man more corrupt than a woman" (Justin 1.3).

[1154] Manly clothing.

females. Astonished, the general withdrew, but so dissatisfied with the state of a monarchy where so many sons of Mars should be subjected under so pusillanimous a Prince as he immediately sounded the trumpet of rebellion and drew Belochus the Babel prisoner into his conspiracy. Whiles Sardanapalus was handling his distaff the generals brandished their swords and marched up with all their forces against Nineveh the Great, so-called in Jonah 4:11,[1155] threescore miles about, saith Herodotus, and so gallantly-seated upon Tigris that by the prophet Zephaniah 2:13[1156] she is styled "a glorious city."

The rebels quickened their march, thinking to surprise the city, which, notwithstanding the King's neglect, was so well-foreseen, victualled and manned, but, which was most, commanded by so faithful a Governor that it not only bade defiance to the besiegers, but issuing out at convenient times forced them sundry times to retreat to a further distance.[1157] The city by this means held out upwards of two years, insomuch as the conspirators despaired of taking it, had not a superior Power who set periods to all dominions so disposed that by the overflowing of Tigris (as foretold by the prophet Nahum 1:8 and 2:6) near twenty furlongs of the wall fell, a wall that was a hundred foot high and withal so broad that upon the rampire three chariots might pass on breast, that great unexpected breach giving the enemy desired entrance. The miserable Emperor, then in despair, retired to his palace, and, inviting his women into the place where his jewels and treasure lay, sets fire to the place, whereby all was quickly consumed with himself for company. Such was the woeful exit of that great Prince, who, as Justin observes, "*hoc solo imitatus est virum.*"[1158] The coin then melted in that flame is by consent of writers computed one hundred millions of talents in gold and one thousand millions of talents in silver, which in ours amounts to twenty thousand and five hundred millions of pounds, a some incredible did not the greatness of that Empire and the long time his frugal predecessors had been amassing it, convince towards it.[1159]

[1155] "And should not I spare Nineveh, that great city, wherein are more than sixscore thousand persons that cannot discern between their right hand and their left hand, and also much cattle?"

[1156] "And he will stretch out his hand against the north, and destroy Assyria; and will make Nineveh a desolation, and dry like a wilderness."

[1157] According to Diodorus, Sardanapalus, far from sitting around in his palace enjoying himself, "led forth the forces of the rest of the provinces against [the rebels]; whereupon a battle being fought, the rebels were totally routed, and with a great slaughter were forced to the mountain 70 furlongs from Nineveh" (131–32).

[1158] "In this alone did he imitate a man" (Justin 1. 3).

[1159] The whole Sardanapalus story is fiction, or at best confused history. Asshur-banipal actually starved *Babylon* (not Nineveh) into submission, after which King Shamash-shum-ukin (Sardanapalus) immolated himself in his palace (see above). Nineveh fell to the Medes and Babylonians in 612 B.C.E.; King Sin-shar-ishkun, whose fate is unknown, disappeared from history. His successor (and possibly brother) Asshur-uballit II

Thus this great monarchy, which had continued gloriously commanding the world about 1350 years, had its first though not ultimate period in a succession from Nimrod, and, being divided between the two great captains, Arbaces arrogated to himself Media and Persia with the adjacent provinces, albeit some give Persia to Achaemenes, son of Persis, who contributed a considerable assistance to the two other conspirators in this great enterprise, and from whose loins Cyrus the Great descended, who afterwards subjected the Assyrian and Median Empires under that of Persia. But Belochus[1160] took for his share Babylon and the east of Assyria, Nineveh included.

Scythians expelled.

Arbaces by this fall of Sardanapalus raised to himself the sovereignty of Media, and dying was succeeded by Mandanes, but some, omitting him, say Sosarmus, who after thirty years gave place to Madius,[1161] and he after five and twenty, says Heylyn, forty says Ralegh, did the like to Cardicas, who after thirteen years' rule bequeathed the royal sceptre to Deioces, as Sir Walter Ralegh calls him. The difference concerning the time of his reign is no less, the one giving him seventeen, the other fifty-three years in government. This Deioces first founded Ecbatana, says Heylyn, by Doctor Ussher the reverend Primate reputed Arphaxad, whom Nebuchadnezzar slew in the mountains of Ragan, Judith 1:15.[1162] Nevertheless, I find that the distance of time between Deioces and Nebuchadnezzar to be upwards of eighty years, so that how to make Deioces and Arphaxad one is more difficult then to agree the foundation of the town, seeing Arphaxad is not said to build the town but the walls and towers thereof, [Judith] 1:4.[1163]

Now, albeit the city was sadly plundered and defaced or demolished by the Assyrian Emperor, nevertheless it was repaired in his time if it be true what good authors report, that Daniel the prophet re-edified a royal palace for the King

---

(612–609 B.C.E.) set up a court in Haran and held out for two or so years; after Haran was in turn captured he met his death trying to regain it with the help of Necho II of Egypt.

[1160] Belochus is dated by Smith to 1587 B.C.E., but at the same time he notes that "no records of this and of several succeeding reigns have been preserved" (*Sacred Annals* III, 148). Jordanes states "Belochus, 30 years. When he was king young Joseph had the dream about his brothers . . ." (20).

[1161] Madius was actually a Scythian. He ruled the Medes 652–625 B.C.E.

[1162] "He took Arphaxad in the mountains of Ragau, and smote him through with his darts, and destroyed him utterly that day." Herbert (or Heylyn) refer, of course, to Bishop James Ussher (1581–1656), whose dating of the Creation in his *Annales pars posterior* (1654), the sequel to the *Annales veteris testamenti* (1650), has already been discussed.

[1163] "And he made the gates thereof, even gates that were raised to the height of seventy cubits, and the breadth of them was forty cubits, for the going forth of his mighty armies, and for the setting in array of his footmen."

which for elegancy of structure and value of materials was comparable to any other then extant. Deioces dying A.M. 3191 was succeeded by Phraortes,[1164] a Prince of great courage and success, who died before the walls of Nineveh leaving the Median crown unto Cyaxares his son, who during his forty years' rule prosecuted the Assyrian war and laid close siege to Nineveh, but was forced to withdraw, having notice that a great body of Scythian horse had invaded his country and there rested. This was an unexpected chance of war, and as Herodotus *lib.* 1 reports, had no other way to recover his right then by inviting the most considerable field-officers of the Scythians to a banquet, and picking a quarrel with some in their cups, upon a signal given by Cyaxares all their throats were cut, which was of that dread to the other Scythians that they willingly found their way back again into their own country with this character from Justin *lib.* 1, "*Scythos magis ebrietate quam bello vincuntur.*" Astyages his son upon his father's death was proclaimed and with all due ceremony crowned King. Astyages is mentioned in that Apocryphal story of Bel and the Dragon,[1165] and by some supposed to be that great Prince Ahasuerus who married Esther the Jew, but the ground of that conjecture I neither find nor credit, seeing that by the best authors either Darius Hystaspes or Artaxerxes, by the Greeks called *Machrochyr*, one of them was undoubtedly that Prince.[1166] Besides, the distance of time betwixt those two kings is not less then a hundred and twenty-nine years. Of this Astyages little is recorded save that for the richness of his apparel none ever excelled him; his daughter Mandane,[1167] whom he had by Ariana[1168] his wife, he gave in marriage to Cambyses the Persian,[1169] father of Cyrus the Great. Astyages first dreamed that his daughter made so much water as drowned all Asia, and another time that the sun, being under his feet, thrice he proffered to embrace it but it still avoided him, which upon the astrologers acquainting him that it related to his grandson Cyrus, which signified the sun, he endeavoured (but in vain) the child's

---

[1164] Phraortes reigned 675–653 B.C.E. With Persian help he attacked the Assyrians, but was killed. For details see Olmstead, *History*, 29–31.

[1165] "And king Astyages was gathered to his fathers, and Cyrus of Persia received his kingdom" (Bel and the Dragon 1:1).

[1166] Ahasuerus is another confusing name. In the Book of Esther he is Artaxerxes II, who marries the fictional Esther. In Tobit 14:15 he may be identified as Cyaxares I of Media, who with Nabopolassar of Babylon (whose troops were likely led by his son Nebuchadnezzar, as he is the Babylonian king mentioned) attacked Nineveh (see above).

[1167] Mandane (c. 584–559 B.C.E.) was the daughter of Astyages, as Herbert says. Herodotus's story may simply be propaganda to link Cyrus and the Medes; she would have to have been born after 585, which was when Aryenis (see below) married Astyages.

[1168] Aryenis or Ariana was the daughter of Alyattes, king of Lydia (r. 619–560 B.C.E.).

[1169] Cambyses I ruled 589–550 B.C.E. in Anshan, which was the old capital of Elam, now in Fars province, north-western Iran. He was a vassal of Astyages.

destruction. To him succeeded Cyaxares, whom some call Darius the Mede,[1170] whom Cyrus succeeded A.M. 3406.

The Assyrian Empire terminates.

To Belochus, now settled in the Assyrian Empire about the Year of the World 3146, succeeded Pal Asshur, called Tiglath-pileser,[1171] who in 2 Kings 15:29 is recorded to have ruined Galilee, one of the three principal provinces of Canaan, of which province Samaria was the principal city, and carried all the inhabitants of Naphtali and Damascus captives into Assyria. After three and twenty years' rule he gave place to Salmanassar,[1172] by some called Nabonassar, who, prosecuting his father's design, plundered Samaria, and in the reign of Hoshea King of Israel, who neglected the payment of his tribute, after three years' siege took Samaria, and the Almighty, being provoked by his people through their idolatry and conforming themselves to the heathen that were round about then, so ordered that the Ten Tribes were also removed out of his sight, none being left "but the Tribe of Judah only," 2 Kings 17:18.[1173] Those of the captives were placed in Halah and Habor by the River Gozan and in the cities of the Medes.

This Assyrian Prince after ten years' rule was succeeded by Sennacherib,[1174] who, going to fight against Taharqa[1175] the Ethiopian king, by the way sent a blasphemous summons to King Hezekiah[1176] by his servant Rab-shakeh, for which, upon the prayer of good Hezekiah and pursuant to the prophecy of Isaiah, one hundred fourscore and five thousand of the Assyrians were in one night slain by an angel of the Lord, which made Sennacherib hasten back to Nineveh, where, as he was worshipping in Nisroch's temple he was slain by his sons Adrammelech

---

[1170] "Darius the Mede" is actually Cyaxares "II" (c. 617–537 B.C.E.), son of Astyages and brother of Mandane (see below), although he was not technically a king at all, but the Regent of Babylon whom Cyrus appointed in 539 B.C.E. He was in fact Cyrus's elderly uncle; neither Herodotus nor Ctesias make mention of him, although Xenophon does in the *Cyropaedia*. Herbert acknowledges this a few pages later (see below).

[1171] Tiglath-pileser III was king of Assyria 745–727 B.C.E. "In the days of Pekah king of Israel came Tiglath-pileser king of Assyria and took Ijon, and Abel-beth-maachah . . . and Galilee, all the land of Naphtali, and carried them captive to Assyria" (2 Kings 15:29). Pekah was king of Israel 735–732 B.C.E.

[1172] For Shalmaneser V (727–722 B.C.E.); see above. Hoshea was king of Israel 732–724 B.C.E.

[1173] "Therefore the Lord was very angry with Israel, and removed them out of his sight: there was none left but the tribe of Judah only."

[1174] Herbert is wrong here. Shalmaneser V, who ruled for five years, not ten, was succeeded by Sargon II (722–705 B.C.E.) and then by Sennacherib (705–681 B.C.E.).

[1175] Taharqa [*Tirhakah*] was king of Ethiopia (Nubia) and Egypt 690–664 B.C.E.

[1176] Hezekiah was king of Judah 716–687 B.C.E.

and Sharezer, who escaped into Armenia, and Esarhaddon[1177] his son reigned in his stead, 2 Kings 19:37. Esarhaddon, having taken revenge upon the parricides, by that confusion then happening between the two brethren gave occasion to Merodach the Governor of Babylon to rebel, and succeeding therein deposed the King, and thereupon transferred the seat royal from Nineveh to Babylon. Merodach-baladan, as called 2 Kings 20:12, swayed the ceptre, of whom little mention is made albeit he reigned 40 years and left the imperial crown to Ben-Merodach his son, who after twenty years gave place to Nabopolassar the triumpher over Pharaoh Necho the Egyptian king, and at the end of 25 years was succeeded by Nebuchadnezzar, who by reason of his many victories and triumphant reign was called the Hercules of the East.[1178] This great Prince was the golden Head of that terrible image mentioned in Daniel 2:32,[1179] to whom the Highest gave a kingdom, power, strength and glory, commanding not only wheresoever the children of men dwelt but also the beasts of the field and the fowls of the Heaven were given into his hand as ruler over them all, so as it will be too great a labour in this small circle to enumerate his conquests, his victorious arm subduing wherever it was extended. Egypt he made a province of his Empire, Jerusalem he destroyed and fired the Temple, carrying Zedekiah and his people prisoners to Babylon, the last of the four Kings of Judah, *viz.* Manasseh, Jehoiakim, Jehoiachin and Zedekiah,[1180] who by the Assyrian kings were led captive to Babylon. Syria and Arabia were likeiwse subjected under the stroke of his sceptre, and part of Ethiopia. The pride of Nineveh he abased, agreeable to the prophecy of Nahum 3:7,[1181] and, Tobit 14, slew Arphaxad and spoiled Ecbatana. In a word, the extent of his

---

[1177] Esarhaddon was king of Assyria 681–669 B.C.E. Herbert paraphrases 2 Kings 19:37.

[1178] Herbert's chronology is thoroughly inaccurate here. Esarhaddon was succeeded by Asshur-bani-pal (669–631). "Merodach-baladan" is actually Marduk-apal-iddina II, who reigned in Babylon 721–710 and 703 B.C.E., when Sargon II was King of Assyria. Sargon and Sennacherib actually took direct control of Babylon 710–703. Marduk-apal-iddina was succeeded by Marduk-zakir-sumi II (703), Bel-ibni (703–700), Asshur-nadin-sumi (700–694), Nergal-ushezib (694–693) and Mushezib-marduk (693–689), at which point Sennacherib took over again, then Esarhaddon. At the latter's death in 669 Shamash-sum-ukin (Sardanapalus) became King of Babylon. His successor Kandalanu (648–627) was the only one of these kings (after himself) who lasted twenty years. There is no "Ben-marduk."

[1179] "This image's head was of fine gold, his breast and arms of silver, his belly and his thighs of brass."

[1180] Their reigns are as follows: Manasseh (687–642); Jehoiakim (609–598); Jehoiachin [*Jeconias*] (598–597), who was deported to Babylon, and Zedekiah (597–587), the last king of Judah, also made captive and deported.

[1181] "And it shall come to pass, that all they that look upon thee shall flee from thee, and say, Nineveh is laid waste: who will bemoan her? Whence shall I seek comforters for thee?" Tobit 14 is cited several times above.

dominion was not strained within less bounds then the confines of the then-in-habited world. But to particularise his many sumptuous and magnificent structures, especially that at Babylon, would be no less tedious, for he not only beautified old Babylon but added to it a new city upon the opposite side of the river, which he enclosed with a triple wall of brick, and for the delight of his Queen, whom some name Amytis, supposed to be the daughter of Astyages the Median king, and for the recreation of his daughter Nitocris (who in spirit and noble buildings she afterwards made seemed another Semiramis) by extraordinary cost and incredible number of hands raised such stately arches of stone as for height and breadth seemed a mountain, which gave a curious prospect not only over that mighty city and river but into the country round about, which was level and the horizon uninterrupted by any hill, so that besides the delightful walks it had he planted it with all manner of fruit and flowers insomuch as it seemed a paradise, which, with the rich and stately palace he erected for his royal seat, reputed one of the wonders of Asia and continuing perfect to Alexander's time, begot such admiration in the King himself as occasioned that expression "Is not this great Babylon which I have built?," which boast drew upon him the most memorable judgment any story mentions, for seven years spending his time amongst savage beasts, yet through divine mercy restored to sense and dignity, all the remainder of his life acknowledging God's power most sovereign and everlasting.

This mighty monarch after four and forty years' rule paid Nature her last debt and was buried in Babylon, having first bequeathed his crown and sceptre to Evil-Merodach, a friend unto the captived Jews and in particular to King Jehoiachin, as we find in Jeremiah 52:31,[1182] nevertheless, a son very unlike the father. Much of what the one by prudence and valour got, the other lost by want of judgment and too much pusillanimity, for Egypt under Amasis[1183] revolted from him, Media by the good conduct of Astyages and Persia by the lively spirit of Cyrus withdrew from under his subjection, and marching with resolute armies against him in the end deprived Evil-Merodach both of life and reign, whom nevertheless Balthazar, called Belshazzar[1184] in Daniel, succeeded, a Prince of that

---

[1182] Amel-Marduk or Evil-Merodach was king of Babylon 562–560 B.C.E. In Jeremiah 52:31 we find "And it came to pass in the seven and thirtieth year of the captivity of Jehoiachin king of Judah, in the twelfth month, in the five and twentieth day of the month, that Evil-Merodach king of Babylon in the first year of his reign lifted up the head of Jehoiachin king of Judah, and brought him forth out of prison."

[1183] Amasis or Ahmose II of Egypt reigned 570–526 B.C.E.

[1184] More inaccuracies. Amel-Marduk, who was not deposed or killed by Cyrus, was succeeded by his brother-in-law and assassin Nergal-shur-usur or Neriglissar (560–556), Labashi-Marduk (556) and, finally, Nabonidus (556–522), for whom, as we have seen, Belshazzar acted as regent (not ring) for the last eight years of his reign and on and off at other times. Under Belshazzar's tenure "misrule and graft were rampant, the peasants were oppressed, and their fields went out of cultivation" (Olmstead, *History*, 45).

tyrannical and disobliging nature as rendered him no less contemptible abroad then hateful at home, so as the period of that great Assyrian Empire, which from Nimrod to this Prince had flourished upward of 1600 years under a series of fifty monarchs, had its ultimate period. For Belshazzar too securely and impiously feasting a thousand of his lords, those gold and silver vessels consecrated to the Lord and by his grandfather Nebuchadnezzar brought from the Temple at Jerusalem to Babylon being profanely used by the King, the Princes, their wives and concubines, *digitu Dei*,[1185] judgment by Daniel's interpretation was pronounced against that miserable Prince and execution immediately followed, for the Medes and Persians who then besieged the city entered forthwith and mastered Babylon, yea, that night was Belshazzar the King of the Chaldaeans slain and Darius the Mede, then sixty-two years old, saluted king, Daniel 5:31,[1186] where we are to note that this Darius the Mede, as the Persians call him, by the Greeks is called Cyaxares, as we find by Xenophon. He was uncle to Cyrus the Persian, and obtaining the diadem when he was old held it but two years, and dying issueless gave Cyrus an uniterrupted admission unto the whole, for as we read in Ezra 1:2, the Lord God of Heaven gave unto him all the kingdoms of the earth, and Esther 1:1 had his Empire extended from India to Ethiopia, which comprehended 127 provinces.

Croesus and Babylon subdued.

The siege of Babylon, the metropolis of the world, may not be pretermitted without a little notice. Cyrus was the son of Cambyses and Mandane, daughter of Astyages the Median king; Cambyses was the son of Cyrus, son of Darius, son of Achaemenes, son of Perses, who, saith Isidore, gave Persia its name, a Prince of that virtue and repute as gave that race for many years the usual surname of Achaemenids. Cyrus, whose name being derived from *chyr* signifies 'the sun,' some years before calling to mind the mischief intended to him at his birth by his jealous grandfather, ambition predominating over parental respect, he marched against him with an army of Persians under the command of Harpagus, whom Astyages had ordered to destroy Cyrus, but abhorring that cruelty preserved the infant, who lived to recompense the fact and were ministerial together in the subduing Astyages, whom they sent prisoner into Hyrcania in Evil-Merodach's time, where in an anguish of mind he soon departed, and after the death of Cyaxares his son, old when he entered upon the government, Cyrus both by birth and conquest claimed that crown.

[1185] "by the finger of God." Herbert alludes to "It is by the finger of God that I cast out demons . . ." (Luke 11:20).

[1186] "And Darius the Median took the kingdom, being about threescore and two years old."

The Chaldaean Emperor, not liking his success, proclaimed war against Cyrus, and drew Croesus, the rich and puissant King of Lydia, into his league. Howbeit Cyrus, who well knew the Babylonians' tempers and the intended place of rendezvous, with a great body of horse quickly got into Cappadocia and interposed 'twixt the Babylonians and them, and soon engaging the Lydians, though the fight was smart, by night compelled them to retreat. Cyrus, early preparing to renew the fight, found no enemy, but intelligence that Croesus had withdrawn himself into Sardis, his best city and strongest hold, dismissing most of the army into quarters. But Cyrus drew before the garrison, and after some assaults not only took the city but in it an incredible mass of treasure, and, which was most considerable, the King himself, whom the conqueror, notwithstanding his alliance, set upon a high pile of wood, which when ready to be inflamed he lamentably cried out "Solon! Solon!," which Cyrus, demanding the reason of, was by the relation so convinced both as to his own mortality and the chance of war as in Princely prudence he not only repealed the sentence but restored him, though not to the kingdom yet to his good opinion. The people nevertheless, soon after endeavouring their liberty, were not only utterly disarmed but in policy so trained up in ease and licentiousness that they who before were a redoubted and warlike nation became effeminate and amongst men of honour of no esteem.

The Chaldaeans, by this blow given their friends began to apprehend their approaching troubles and that Cyrus would make their country the seat of war, so that in the first place they victualled Babylon with provisions of all sorts sufficient for a twenty-years' siege, but Cyrus, pre-ordained for the conquest of that city and Empire, not so much from that prophetic acclamation of Nebuchadnezzar which some allude to, "that a mule should subdue Lydia and subvert the Assyrian monarchy," the mule signifying his mixture of blood, as from that election of the Almighty, Isaiah 44:28, above 100 years before his birth: "That as his anointed he should subdue nations, loose the loins of kings . . . and [*which was his greatest trust*, Herbert's note] fulfil the pleasure of the Almighty, saying to Jerusalem, Thou shalt be built, and to the temple thy foundation shall be laid," which accordingly he piously endeavoured in the first year of his reign, making a decree[1187] to build God's house, restoring the sanctified vessels (which Nebuchadnezzar took thence) to Shesh-bazzar,[1188] one of the Princes of Judah, Ezra 1:8

[1187] Olmstead cites a decree issued in 538 B.C.E., Cyrus's first regnal year, which reads "As for the house of God which is at Jerusalem, let the house be built, the place where they offer fire sacrifice continually . . . Also, let the gold and silver utensils of the house of God, which Nebuchadnezzar took from the house of God and brought to Babylon, be restored and brought again to the temple" (*History*, 57–58).
[1188] Shesh-bazzar is described in Ezra 1:8 as "one of the Princes of Judah," and he was certainly appointed Governor by Cyrus. "On the orders of Cyrus," Castel tells us, "he began the construction of the temple but was quickly forced to stop the work because the country was too poor and too lacking in unity" (*History*, 152). Olmstead notes that the

and 5:14, which was a commission very warrantable for this great enterprise. The city was compassed with a wall so high and thick as deservedly made it one of the Wonders of the World; it was, saith Diodorus Siculus, 365 furlongs about, in height 365 foot and so broad that six chariots could well pass in front. The great River Euphrates ran through the middle of the city, wellnigh double the breadth of the Thames at London, which Semiramis nevertheless made communicable by a bridge, the like whereof was not in all the world. The garrison also was wll-manned, so abundantly-victualled and provided with necessaries of all sorts and barricaded with brazen gates so strong that the besieged held it impregnable. But God, having decreed the end, directs the means, for as prophesied in Jeremiah 51:11, ". . . the Lord hath raised up the spirit of the kings of the Medes, for his device is against Babylon, to destroy it."

Accordingly Darius the Mede and his nephew Cyrus, perceiving how impossible it was to take the city by battery or storm, and how well they within were furnished with victual, contrive another way, probably taking their design from the Princess Nitocris, who when the bridge was built diverted the stream by sluice, for a large, deep sluice she cut a mile above the city, which turned the channel and gave it another course till they had laid their foundation and raised the superstructure so high as needed. Accordingly, whiles Belshazzar was lulling himself in his vain confidence, Cyrus by several sluices and trenches which the pioneers and many hands easily cut and effected in that soft and easy ground so drained the usual channel that it became dry, as foretold by Jeremiah 51:31,[1189] and whiles the besieged Prince was carousing with his satraps, their wives and concubines, as formerly remembered and recorded by the prophet Daniel 5:2 and by Jeremiah 51:57,[1190] the besiegers made the easier entrance so as the city was surprised and the besieged then found it their best play to save themselves by flight, in which many fell by the sword, others in the city, amongst whom Belshazzar himself, whom wine and sleep had miserably prepared for it, by which subversion this great city, that formerly knew no subjection but sat as Empress of the World, now begun to relish the mutability of fortune and was forced to bow under the Persian yoke, for the victor, not content with disrobing her of her imperial dress, gave her as a prey to the insulting soldier. A sad judgment, but no doubt by divine dispensation, both to bring her to a strict account for her

name Shesh-bazzar is "clearly Babylonian, perhaps Shamash-apal-usur, but . . . he *might* have been, as was later claimed, a Jewish Prince" (*History*, 58).

[1189] Herbert repeats the passage in Jeremiah about "One post shall run to meet another . . ." There is nothing here relating to Cyrus's engineering feats.

[1190] "Belshazzar, whiles he tasted the wine, commanded to bring the golden and silver vessels which his father Nebuchadnezzar had taken out of the temple which was in Jerusalem; that the king, and his Princes, his wives, and his concubines, might drink therein" (Daniel 5:2); "And I will make drunk their Princes, and her wise men, her captains, and her rulers, and her mighty men . . ." (Jeremiah 51:57).

notorious idolatry and to compensate the cruelty and taunts upon sundry occasions expressed towards the captivated Jews, as we find particularly denounced by the prophet Jeremiah 51:24, "And I will render unto Babylon and to all the inhabitants of Chaldaea all their evil that they have done in Zion in your sight," and also that the world by the ruin of this matchless place might know there is a set time for the undoubted dissolution of the whole.

Death of Cyrus the Great.

The fame of this great enterprise was such as with little trouble served to reduce the rest of Asia the Less, but unable to forbear giving the reins to his boundless desire his great spirit would not be satisfied whiles his Empire had any bounds, so that with a numerous force he marched against the Scythians. Tomyris, Queen of the Massagetae (a people some deduce from Magog, but I rather think from *massag*, i.e. 'mixture' in Hebrew) the Princess he formerly courted in vain for his wife affronted him with an army equal for number and not inferior for resolution, so that both sides appearing desirous to engage, after a hot dispute the Queen became victorious, and having Cyrus in her power, the death of her son Spargapizes (to whom Cyrus refused quarter not long before) coming fresh in memory, she commanded his head should be off and then threw it into a vessel filled with blood, with this expression: "Cyrus, now drink thy fill," so writes Herodotus and Justin. Nevertheless, Valerius Maximus[1191] and Strabo report otherwise, that at the age of seventy years and the nine and twentieth of his reign he died in peace and was with all due ceremony buried at Pasagardae, a city in Susiana which he had founded, with which agrees Xenophon, *lib.* 8, so that how uncertain soever the place and manner of his death be, 'tis more certain that his body was entombed at Pasagardae, seeing that Alexander the Great, returning thither out of India inconsiderately put to death Orsin, a Prince of the blood-royal of Persia upon the suggestion of that malicious eunuch Bagoas[1192] that he had violated Cyrus his tomb, upon which was only this plain epitaph: "O man, I Cyrus am, Cambyses's son, / Who first the Persian monarchy begun. / The Asiatic Empire I controlled; / Envy not then that this small place I hold."

[1191] Valerius Maximus (fl. 20 C.E.), Roman rhetorician and statesman, consul (14) and Proconsul of Asia from 27. He wrote *Facta et dicta memorabilia* in 9 books, a work which was a compendium of information used for many years by rhetoricians who were looking for stories and quotes to illustrate points. It was printed by Aldus Manutius (1502), and Herbert could have known the later edition of Pighius (1657). There is a modern translation in the Loeb Classical Library by D. Shackleton Bailey (Cambridge, MA: Harvard University Press, 2000).

[1192] Bagoas (d. 330/29 B.C.E.), one of the intimates of Darius III, achieved eminence when he helped in the murder of King Arses, which secured the throne for Darius in 336 B. C. E. Bagoas also engineered the death of Arses's father Artaxerxes III; "by his murder," writes Olmstead, "Bagoas destroyed the Persian Empire" (*History*, 489).

Cambyses's frantic pranks.

To Cyrus the Magnificent (for so he is called) succeeded Cambyses his son, a Prince in nothing resembling the magnanimity of his father, being infamous for his cruelty and prodigious lust, but his reign was short, not exceeding nine years, yet turbulent, for having subdued Egypt and Ethiopia as far as Elephantine, whose neighbour the Troglodytes,[1193] never having been tributary to any, refused so much as to send him of their earth and water, which last they could ill spare, in token of their subjection, so well-fenced they were with rolling sands and heat intolerable. In a jealous humour by the hands of that villain Prexaspes he made away his only brother Smerdis,[1194] and having no issue of his own the anguish thereof disposed him so to frenzy that it increased upon the tidings brought that fifty thousand of his men whom he had sent to burn the temple of Jupiter Ammon which stood in Barca,[1195] that confining part of Cyrene formerly called Marmarica,[1196] were buried in those hideous waves of sand which Satan, who oftimes commands the air, had raised for the preservation of his worship, a storm against which there was no shelter nor evasion, as Herodotus *lib.* 2, albeit precautioned by the Psyllians,[1197] who suffered the like fate for that simple challenge they gave the south winds for the injury they did them in drying up their few rivulets, with which not being admonished but rather hardened, in revenge he forthwith demolished the temple of Anubis at Memphis, broke the neck of

---

[1193] "Troglodytes" are actually 'cave-dwellers,' and this word is misused here. There were actual troglodytes in Libya, Morocco, and Tunisia, but Herbert mistakenly uses the word instead of *Trogodyae* or *Trogodutai* (in its Greek form), who were an Ethiopic people living in what is now northern Sudan and southern Egypt. Seneca refers to them as "the Trogodytae, whose houses are underground" (*Quaestiones naturales* 4. 2.18), which might be the source of the error. See also Pomponius Mela, *De chorographia* 1. 38.

[1194] Smerdis (d. 522 B.C.E.), or Bardiya in Persian, a full (younger) brother of Cambyses, proclaimed himself king whilst Cambyses was still in Egypt (11 March 522 B.C.E.), and when Cambyses died on his way home (possibly by suicide) he was recognised as king by most of the Empire. He was eventually killed by Darius on 29 September, having ruled for eight months (Olmstead, *History*, 92–93). Herodotus says that Cambyses had sent Prexaspes, "the Persian he trusted most," to kill Smerdis, because he had had a dream "that a messenger came to him from Persia to tell him that Smerdis was sitting on the royal throne with his head touching the sky" (*Histories*, 3.30).

[1195] "A coastal city of Cyrenaica (Libya) located in front of a narrow plain beneath the lower spurs of the Jebel-el-Akhdar," and re-named Ptolemais by Ptolemy III (246–221 B. C. E.) after he attached it to his new city of that name. The modern name is Tolmeta (Grant, *Guide*, 525).

[1196] Marmarica is on the coast of northern Africa between Libya and Egypt.

[1197] The Psyllians or Psylli lived in the Sahara. They are mentioned by Pliny as being very knowledgeable about snakes (*Natural History* 28. 30).

that beastly deity,[1198] of great veneration with the Egyptians, and at Damascus going about like pranks, which had been good had the zeal been rightly-grounded, he was casually wounded by his own sword so mortally that he could not be recovered but in that extremity died frantic[1199] and unpitied.

The deputy he had left to superintend Persia had a son that resembled Smerdis, whom he vested with the imperial robe and crown which Cyrus left, and that device passed current until the imposture was discovered by a lady of his own seraglio who was daughter to Otanes,[1200] a satrap of no mean account, who one time telling her father what she observed, he acquainted the seven subordinate Princes how that the pretended Smerdis "wanted his ears." Quickly they found the means to give him his desert, after he had worn the diadem eight years.[1201]

The seven princes who had the superintendancy of the realm, not knowing of any right heir to the crown, found out no better expedient for an election then by agreeing that he should reign whose horse neighed first next morning after the rising of the sun, which being published, that night Darius his ingenious groom made his master's horse cover a mare in the place appointed, so that he no sooner entered the field next morning but the horse, mindful it seems of his late entertainment, fell to neighing courageously, which the rest of the competitors,

<hr/>

[1198] Herbert has the wrong "beastly god." Cambyses, at least according to Herodotus, killed Apis, the bull-god; he stabbed the animal and it starved to death (Herodotus 2.27–29). Olmstead states that this never happened, and that the Apis-bull died when Cambyses was in Ethiopia; "the next Apis-bull," he states, "born in the fifth year of Cambyses, survived to the fourth year of Darius." As evidence, he describes a stele which shows Cambyses, in Egyptian dress, *worshipping* the Apis-bull (*History*, 90).

[1199] The Egyptians thought Cambyses's mania was Apis's revenge (Herodotus 2.30). However, Olmstead categorically writes that "tales of the mad doings of Cambyses in Egypt must be discounted" (*History*, 90). For details and evidence, see Olmstead, *History* 89–91.

[1200] Otanes (d. c. 513 B.C.E.) was a member of the royal family, the brother of Cambyses's mother and the father of his wife Phaedymia. He was probably also the father of Amestris, the first wife of Xerxes I. After assisting Darius to the throne, Otanes was appointed satrap of Samos, which Darius had sent him to conquer in 517.

[1201] Herbert's account of Gaumata or Pseudo-Smerdis is completely wrong. He seems to have misread Herodotus, who says that the pretender was the brother, not the son of "the man Cambyses had appointed steward of the household in his absence," one Patizeithes, that he was also called Smerdis and that he was a Magus (3.61). On 1 July 522 B.C.E., Gaumata, as we shall call him to distinguish him from the real Smerdis, "took for himself the kingdom" (Olmstead, *History*, 108), and soon afterwards Cambyses died, as Olmstead believes, by his own hand. His reign lasted less than four months, not eight years; "Darius," Olmstead writes, paraphrasing Herodotus, "slew that Gaumata and his allies . . . on September 29" (108). The full account may be read in Herodotus (3.61–78). Herbert also consulted Justin, who says that the pretender was actually the brother of Prexaspes, and called Oropates; he also retells the story of Otanes's daughter (1. 9).

ignorant of that craft, accepted as an undoubted presage of his merit, and with all due ceremony saluted him with the regal name. At Pasagardae the arch-flamen put upon his shoulders the vest and upon his head the crown or royal tiara which the great Cyrus had on at his coronation. Howbeit, by being lineally descended from Arsames,[1202] who was grandson to Cyrus the Great, as saith Herodotus, he had a title to the crown, albeit others are of a different opinion, believing that descent was invented after his accession to the crown. Howbeit, seeing he acquired his greatness by the favour of his horse, inasmuch as 'a horse' in the Persian tongue was then and yet is called *asp* and *aspis*, it hath induced me to think that his agnomen of *Hystaspes* was thence derived.[1203]

Darius his great army routed.

During the interregnum Babylon, not yet well-acquainted with the yoke, revolted, but by the faithfulness of Zopyrus was reduced.[1204] This is that Prince [Darius, Ed.] whom the captived Jews minded of Cyrus his great ancestor's good intention to the Holy City and Temple which Nebuchadnezzar had destroyed and stirred up his heart to rebuild both. In the interim he expressed much kindness to the Jews, whence it is that some of their rabbis will needs have him to be that Ahaseurus who upon the repudiating of Vashti[1205] married Esther, Mordecai's niece, after which he prosecuted the Grecian war and extended his bounds beyond the Hellespont. The war was upon this occasion: he despatched ambassadors to Amyntas[1206] the Macedonian king, *"ut aquam et terram traderunt*

[1202] Arsames, in Persian Arshama (c. 615–521 B.C.E.), was the grandfather of Darius and the ruler of Parthia and Hyrcania, but described by Olmstead as "at best, a petty kinglet" (107). He was still alive when Darius ascended the throne in 522 B.C.E., at least according to a stele of Xerxes I (Olmstead, *History*, 214).

[1203] It's not; the name comes from his father, Vishtaspa.

[1204] It was a little more complex than this. After the fall of Babylon, Nabonidus's elderly son proclaimed himself Nebuchadrezzar III (522 B.C.E.). After two battles he was defeated at killed at Zazana on the Euphrates river. This was not quite the end: a man called Arakha, who claimed to be another son of Nabonidus, declared himself king as Nebuchadrezzar IV (September–November 521 B.C.E.). He occupied Babylon, but was captured by Vindafarna, one of the "seven Princes" Herbert mentions above; he was impaled by order of Darius (Olmstead, *History*, 115). Zopyrus was not involved in either of these campaigns.

[1205] In Esther, Vashti is the wife repudiated by Ahasuerus in favour of Esther. The *Midrash* (Jewish commentaries, as Herbert notes with the "rabbis") makes her a greatgranddaughter of Nebuchadnezzar. She has sometimes been identified as Amestris (d. c. 440 B.C.E.), daughter of Otanes and wife of Xerxes I, but most scholars do not believe this. Given the largely fictitious nature of the Book of Esther (see above), Vashti is probably a fiction too.

[1206] Amyntas I was king of Macedon 547–498 B.C.E.

Dario."[1207] Whiles his council was deliberating what answer to make, the King in civility invited the ambassadors to a banquet where several ladies were, to whom the ambassadors, either from their intemperate drinking or the haughtiness of their master's Empire, expressed such rude behaviour that soon after at a like collation the ambassadors were slain by some of the Macedonian youth who had disguised themselves in women's habit. A rash attempt, for being known to Darius, albeit he expressed his dislike of the ambassadors' misbehaviour, which he would have punished, yet he looked upon it as a violation of the Law of Nations and consequently an affront towards his own person, which he was so sensible of, that having first acquainted them with his apprehensions, with all possible speed, making this the colour of that war, he marched towards them with a royal army and without much resistance harried them as far as Marathon, a town near Athens, where the Athenians with a small force encountered that great army of the Persians, who by apparitions were put into that panic fear that they were shamefully put to flight, not rallying till they had passed the Hellespont, a victory albeit attributed to the singular courage and good conduct of Miltiades,[1208] yet by the ingrateful state of Athens, to their everlasting infamy, was most unworthily requited. This great defeat, aggravated by the revolt of Egypt and the dissension amongst his sons about their title to the crown, and some add the grief he took for being disappointed of his hopes to enjoy Anthina's lovely daughter, were of that force that they broke his great heart. After he had reigned six and thirty years, having ordered that his body should be buried at Persepolis and directing, notwithstanding that Artobazarnes[1209] was his first-born son, that Xerxes his second son, born after Darius had obtained the crown, should succeed in the throne.

[1207] "So that they might hand over earth and water to Darius." Earth and water were traditional symbols of surrender.

[1208] Miltiades (c. 550–489 B.C.E.), the Athenian general, defeated the Persians at Marathon (490), but his subsequent military failure on the island of Paros led to him being charged (unjustly) with treason, which resulted in his flight to the protection of the enemy.

[1209] Artobazarnes, the elder brother of Xerxes, was, it is said, passed over as heir by Darius because Queen Atossa, the daughter of Cyrus, wanted her son to be king. However, as Olmstead tells us, "he [Xerxes] is already recognised as successor by 507" (*History*, 214). He also believes that in fact Artobazarnes was the son of a commoner (the daughter of Gobryas, whose name has not been preserved) and that he was born before Darius was anywhere near a throne. Herodotus mentions a harem struggle (*Histories* 7.2–3), which of course also may have occurred; he describes Atossa as "all-powerful" (7.3).

[The reign of Xerxes I]

Xerxes the first year of his reign reduced Egypt, and the next made what preparation he could to prosecute the war against Greece, the disgrace his father received at Marathon was so fresh in his memory. The army he raised was so prodigiously great that men thought it was not only great enough to overrun Greece but the whole universe, no less, as most historians say, then eighteen hundred thousand foot. Herodotus heightens them to five millions, two hundred eighty-three thousand two hundred and twenty men and also fourscore thousand horse. His navy also were a thousand ships, which Justin *lib.* 2 centiples, *"naves quoque decies centum millia numero habuisse dicitur."*[1210] With that monstrous body this great monarch marched undisturbed as far as the Hellespont without seeing the face of an enemy. There he took the second muster of his army; it is reported that from a sudden consideration of the mortality of his men he could not refrain from weeping. Ominous tears, for they presaged what happened sooner then peradventure he apprehended! To join the two worlds he forthwith caused above six hundred great boats to be coupled and planked, and thereby made a bridge over the Hellespont 'twixt the two castles Abydos, which is on the Asian shore, and Sestos in Europe, where the sea, albeit a mile broad, is narrowest. Having thus passed his army, to express equal care for his fleet and withal to leave some signal of his magnificence he converted the peninsula where Mount Athos stood into an island, the place he cut being about two miles. This great body of horse and foot, which as they drank the River Cyssus dry, devoured also such a world of provisions that the providers found it impossible to subsist long in those ruinous quarters, so as it forced the Persian monarch to engage the Grecian army sooner then otherwise was intended, which albeit they wisely delayed, nevertheless waiting for an advantage, the Persians were no sooner advanced to Thermopylae, so-called from the hot baths there, a strait or narrow passage not exceeding half an acre of ground, but that Leonidas[1211] the Spartan king with three hundred Lacedaemonians, the remainder of five thousand that first appeared, defended the pass with such incomparable resolution that for two days they withstood that world of men, an opposition so memorable as albeit Leonidas with his men were slain, yet so noble a sacrifice lives and will live in Fame's honourable roll to all posterity, so as not without cause the Greeks in that place raised him a statue with this inscription, *"aliquando hic contra myriados cum trescentis hominibus pugnavit Leonidas."*[1212] Howbeit, Xerxes after this smart entertainment marched as far as Athens, which being abandoned by the inhabitants he easily fired, by the way having plundered the temple at Delphos, which was marvellous rich by the offerings of many Princes and people of preceding generations, sacrilege, for so

---

[1210] "He was said to have had a hundred thousand ships" (Justin 2. 10).

[1211] Leonidas I was king of Sparta 489–480 B.C.E.

[1212] Once Leonidas with three hundred men fought here against tens of thousands.

'tis called, seeing he acknowledged Apollo for one of his gods, so notorious, says Herodotus and other historians of those times, as occasioned many fatal calamities to pursue him. For first, his great armado was soon after beaten and sunk by Themistocles the Athenian admiral with his four hundred sail near the Isle of Salamis in the Gulf of Negroponte, and such havoc made by the incensed Greeks that "*non victi sed vincendo fatigati inter ingentes catervas stratorum hostium occiderunt,*"[1213] saith an author, a fight or execution so dreadful to the Persian king that his spirits sunk so as he could not think himself safe amidst his royal guard so long as he continued on the wrong side the Hellespont, and accordingly, leaving Mardonius,[1214] his general and uncle by marriage, three hundred and fifty thousand select men, he hastened to Sestos, where finding the bridge disordered by a late storm, he was necessitated to ferry over in a small cock-boat, thence giving one historian occasion to say he was "*primus in fuga, postremus in praelio,*"[1215] and to another, and that very truly, "*eius introitus in Graeciam non tam terribilis quam discessus fuit turpis . . .*"[1216]

Temple of Belus destroyed.

Nevertheless, to dissemble his grief for that instability of fortune he began to play such mad pranks as rendered him more and more ridiculous, for in the first place, to be revenged for the breaking his bridge and loss sustained at sea, he commands a sea-captain to give the water three hundred lashes and having the images of Neptune, Boreas and Proteus brought as delinquents before him to express his own greatness (being brother to the sun and Moon, as he generally styled himself) and what low esteem he had of those marine or inferior deities, he committed them prisoners to his Provost-Marshal, who was ordered to manacle their hands and load their legs with fetters during pleasure, for which irreverence and impiety, as they imputed, the Greeks proclaimed him "*deorum immortalium hostis,*"[1217] but he in requital thereof and to show that he loved to

---

[1213] "Tired out not as the conquered but as victors they killed a huge number of the enemy's troops" (Justin 2.10).

[1214] Mardonius (d. 479 B.C.E.) was the son of Gobryas, whose daughter Artozostra was a wife of Darius I. He fought with distinction at Thermopylae and Salamis, but when his fleet was destroyed he was actually in Thrace. He had pushed Xerxes to avenge Darius's defeat at Marathon, and he continued urging the King to attack Greece again after each defeat. He was made Governor of the occupied areas of Greece, defeated Alexander I of Macedon, and recaptured Athens. He offered to rebuild the city in return for a truce, but the Athenians refused. Mardonius was killed at the Battle of Plataea (see Herodotus, Book 9 for details of his career).

[1215] "First in flight, last in fight" (Justin 2. 10).

[1216] "His invasion of Greece was nowhere near as terrible as his retreat was disgraceful" (Justin 2. 10).

[1217] The enemy of the immortal gods.

imitate Cambyses his ancestor, chained the Palladium[1218] and fired the temple of Minerva, the rather for that she was the Athenians' tutelary goddess, and with like frenzy burned the temples of all other gods interposing his return, that of Ephesus excepted, whence so soon as he understood how that the rest of his great army was wholly broken by the overthrow given Mardonius at Plataea by land and Artayntes[1219] at Mycale by sea in one same day, he continued his flying march as far as Babylon, where to show that he put not his confidence in those strong walls he causelessly pulled down part thereof and then also without the least provocation first defaced and then after that demolished the noblest structure and piece of antiquity that was at that time extant throughout the world, the temple of Belus which Semiramis with charge incredible and art incomparable had erected and dedicated to the memory of her husband's grandsire Belus. It was a square pyramid, saith Strabo *lib.* 13, *c.* 3, made of brick; in the midst rose eight towers, the first of which was one furlong high, and the rest proportionable, so high and so curious that it superadded to the other Seven Wonders of the World. He also ravished thence the statue of Belus, which was twelve cubits high and of massy gold, and as Herodotus *lib.* 1, slew divers of the flamens that would have rescued it.[1220] Howbeit, this act of his, albeit historians reproach him for it, nevertheless seems alluded to by that memorable prediction of Jeremiah 51:18, where inveighing against the gross idolatry of the Chaldaeans the prophet concludes: "They are vanity, the work of errors: in the time of their visitation they shall perish," and in verse 44, "And I will punish Bel in Babylon . . . yea, the wall of Babylon shall fall."[1221] Thus having satiated his humour against those imaginary gods, with like barbarous outrage his exercised his tyranny against men, most inhumanly putting first the wife of Masistes the Bactrian lieutenant and after that himself and children to death, with several others of whom he conceived some causeless jealousy, so as becoming more feared then loved. Artabazus,[1222]

[1218] The Palladium was an image of Athene (Minerva) which was supposed to protect the city of Troy and which, according to legend, came to Athens and then to Rome.

[1219] Artayntes was one of Xerxes's senior admirals. The battles of Mycale and Plataea took place the same day. Mycale was not actually a naval battle, and Artayntes escaped after the defeat, only to be castigated by Masistes, Darius's son, and accused of cowardice. Artayntes reacted angrily; Herodotus tells us that "in a rage he drew his *akinakes* [a short straight Scythian sword, Ed.] against Masistes," but he was wrestled to the ground by another man (9.107).

[1220] Herbert took the description of the statue from Herodotus, but increased the priestly casualties. "Xerxes did take [the statue]," Herodotus writes, "as well as killing the priest who was telling him not to touch it" (1.183).

[1221] Herbert cites the Vulgate in both [Latin] passages. I have substituted the King James version.

[1222] Herbert confuses (in spelling only, it seems) Artabazus, a satrap and military commander, with Artabanus (d. 465 B. C. E.), the powerful and influential Captain of the Royal Guard, although he identifies Artabanus's position correctly. "Near the end of

his uncle and Captain of the Guard, conspired with Mithridates[1223] a eunuch, his Chamberlain, and having found a wicked opportunity to execute their treason, they cut him off, a fact fully recompensed by Artaxerxes his son, who succeeded in the throne.

Now, notwithstanding these prodigious extravagances of Xerxes, that he had some virtue and bravery intermixed appears by Alexander the Great, who at his entering Persepolis perceiving a statue of Xerxes thrown under foot by the soldiers, viewing it for a while said to some officers standing by he was considering with himself whether in respect of his virtue he should set it up again or let it lie upon consideration of that mischief he had done in Greece. Xerxes was buried at Persepolis.

Themistocles dies in Persia.

Artaxerxes began his reign *Anno Mundi* 3500 and ruled the Empire most honourably full four and forty years. This Prince is usually called Longimanus, *"qui dextra fuit longior quam sinistra,"*[1224] so long, standing upright he could touch his knee with his right hand, by the Arabians *Tamas-Sharshi* and by the Persians *Ardashir-Bahman*. Affected with the loss his predecessors had sustained by the Grecian war, he despatched his ambassadors in the first year of his reign to conclude a peace with the Athenians, inclined to it by Timagoras,[1225] who had received a bribe of ten thousand darics[1226] or saggitaries, which cost him his life. He had the better means to reduce Egypt, which he effected in the end. During that, Themistocles the great Athenian captain incurred the jealousy of his own and the Spartan democratical states and had the sentence of ostracism inflicted, so as forced by his ingrateful countrymen to shift for himself, he adventured to the court of Persia where he received as generous entertainment as could be devised, of such high esteem was a noble enemy with the Persian, but soon after being by the Persian king desired to serve under him in Egypt, he chose rather

---

465," Olmstead relates, "Xerxes was assassinated in his bedchamber. At the head of the conspirators was Artabanus" (*History*, 289). Artabanus was killed as he tried to assassinate Artaxerxes, having decided to usurp the throne himself.

[1223] This is the wrong name. The Chamberlain was Aspamitres and the other conspirator Megabyzus, the son of Zopyrus (Olmstead, *History*, 289). Herodotus does not give an account of Xerxes's death; his account of that king ends with the Masistes incident (see above). Aspamitres was later killed, and Megabyzus later fell in battle.

[1224] Whose right [arm] was longer than his left.

[1225] Timagoras (d. 367 B.C.E.) was the Athenian who, together with Antalcidas, failed to conclude negotiations with the Persians over the attempt of Artaxerxes II (*not* Artaxerxes I, as Herbert has it here) and was "accused of making adoration to the king and having accepted from him a bribe of forty talents." He was condemned to death (Olmstead, *History*, 410; Diodorus Siculus 15. 81.3).

[1226] A heavy Persian gold coin (about 8.4 grams).

to bid farewell to the world in a cup of poison then to engage against his country, notwithstanding their cruelty.

The rest of this great monarch's reign was peacable and full of honour. He was a Prince of great civility and a constant well-wisher to the Jews, in Ezra 7: [11–26] and Nehemiah 2: [1–10] much spoken of, and therefore by most is taken to be that Ahasuerus who for the most part kept his court in Susa, and the rather for that Artaxerxes by the Persians is pronounced *Artaxasha*, which some make Ahaseurus, but that Nehemiah, Ezra and Zerubbabel[1227] were by this *Rex Regum*, as he styles himself, permitted to return to build and inhabit Jerusalem is by none I meet with so much as questioned. He was contemporary with the High Priest Jehoiakim, which gives Krenzheimius[1228] and others to affirm that Esther was the wife of this Prince. He died at a ripe age and was buried at Persepolis.

[The reign of Darius II].

Darius the bastard, by the death of Xerxes [II] and Sogdianus (Queen Esther's children, 'tis thought) for some time established the Empire to himself.[1229] Egypt in his time rebelled,[1230] and contracting a defensive league with the Athenians, utterly expelled the Persians thence and preserved their liberty during his and his successor Artaxerxes Mnemon's reigns. In the interim, to his illegitimation he added incest, for by Parysatis his sister he had Artaxerxes whom we lately named and Cyrus his brother, that for some years governed Asia the Less, a Prince of

---

[1227] Zerubbabel was a descendent of the royal family of Judah. Cyrus (not Artaxerxes) allowed him to bring the Jews out of exile in 538 B.C.E., and he was still alive when the Temple was rebuilt in 515.

[1228] Leonhard Krenzheim (1532–1598) was a Polish Calvinist minister and theologian from Legnica in Silesia who worked with the famous humanist Philipp Melanchthon. He was the author of a historical chronology and of *Coniecturae piae et eruditae de impedentibus in ecclesia et imperiis. . . .* (1580).

[1229] Some clarification is needed here. First, neither Xerxes nor Sogdianus were sons of Esther. Secondly, Xerxes II, son of Queen Damaspia (d. 424), was recognised as king in Persia and ruled for 45 days in 424 B.C.E. Thirdly, Sogdianus or Secydianus, the son of Artaxerxes by Alogyne of Babylon, ruled in Elam 424–423 B.C.E., ordered the murder of Xerxes II, and was himself assassinated a few months later. Lastly, Ochus, the son of Artaxerxes I by Cosmartidene of Babylon and husband to Parysatis (see above; his half-sister, which Herbert brands below as "incest"), ruled in Media, Babylon, and Egypt. After the death of Sogdianus he became the sole ruler of Persia as Darius II. For details, see S. Zawadzki, "The Circumstances of Darius II's Accession," *Jaarbericht Ex Oriente Lux* (1995–1996): 45–49.

[1230] Amyrtaeus the Saïte was King of Egypt 405–399 B.C.E., the only king of Dynasty XXVIII and the man who led the revolt against Persian rule in 405 B.C.E. He was succeeded by Naiferaaiurtu (Psammetichus of Mendes or Nepherites as he was variously called) who founded the XXIX Dynasty and maintained an independent Egypt.

equal magnanimity to any in his time but withal so ambitious that his father still kept him at a distance, being indeed jealous of him, and the more, observing that the Queen passionately affected him.

Fight betwixt Artaxerxes and Cyrus.

After nineteen years' reign Darius died and his son Artaxerxes was placed in his throne. The greatest of this Prince's troubles took rise from the restless ambition and pursuit of his brother Cyrus after the crown, heightened thereto by the partial favour of the Queen Mother and the secret insinuations of Tissaphernes[1231] his pretended friend, who first made him believe he had most right to sway, being born after his father was king, but finding that project not likely to succeed, faced about, informing the King of the Prince's intent, which occasioned a summons to be sent him, and appearing being secured but in fetters of gold, at the importunity of his mother Parysatis he was soon set at liberty and restored to his lieutenancy of Lydia and the adjacent provinces, at that distance ruminating how to compass his ambitious ends under colour of revenge for that late disgrace he suffered, and having a considerable interest in Greece they were willing to widen the difference thereby to make Persia the less capable of offending them, so as they readily furnished him with ten thousand auxiliaries expert in war, but the preparations that Cyrus made made it appear he was in earnest and that he resolved to win the crown or find a grave. Accordingly, with a considerable army of horse and foot he passed through Syria into Assyria and without opposition possessed himself of the two principal seats of the Empire, Babylon and Susa, which made him believe the rest his own and was no less the opinion of both. Howbeit, at length intelligence being brought that Artaxerxes was advancing with nine hundred thousand men, it somewhat altered his former apprehension. Cyrus nevertheless prepared for fight; what he wanted of number was supplied by skill. Both armies, being on their march, at or near Cunaxa, about 4000 furlongs from Babylon, came first in view of each other. The generals, having disposed their men into such order as they thought best, quickly engaged; for many hours victory seemed doubtful. Cyrus for his part expressed as much resolution as man could do, for first with his own hand he killed Artagerzes, a Caddusian[1232] Prince, soon

---

[1231] Tissaphernes (d. 395 B.C.E.) is described by Olmstead as "the ablest and most unscrupulous diplomat that Persia ever produced," beginning his career under Darius II by successfully defeating a revolt by the satrap of Sardis in 413 (*History*, 358–59). His influence grew by degrees, and he could be described as the chief adviser to Artaxerxes II and the enemy of Prince Cyrus, consolidating his power after the death of Prince Cyrus at Cunaxa. Queen Parysatis became his nemesis, and her intrigues and influence led to his eventual execution. "Tissaphernes was decapitated," Olmstead tells us, "and his head was then forwarded to the king. Parysatis had her revenge" (*History*, 384).

[1232] Caddusia was in north-west Persia or Media Atropatene, now Gilan and Ardebil provinces.

after made way into the thickest of his enemies, and personally charging Arta-xerxes, gave him such a testimony of his valour that the enemy, who with a shout applauded the fact, it was thought he had been slain, but the King, being rather inflamed thereby, requited him so with his sword that Cyrus had no further de-sire to engage the King. In fine, perceiving the Imperial ensign, which was an eagle of gold, advance, Cyrus resolved to put it to an issue, so as too eagerly ex-posing his own person it happened that his tiara or regal cap, which he wore as pretending right to the crown, fell from his head, which being observed by Mi-tradates a Persian youth, with a bold thrust he wounded the Prince in the face, so that he was forced for some time to withdraw out of the fight, and towards night was accidentally and miserably slain by by some pioneers, inhabitants of Cunaxa who by mistake fell into his naked quarter.

In this expedition Xenophon the historian had commanded, but so soon as the whole army fell into a rout, in despite of the Persians he made a safe and memorable retreat through the Caddusians' country into Georgia and crossed the River Phasis to Trebizond, where he embarked for Byzantium and thence with honour brought his countrymen into Greece. In this great fight many thousands were on both sides slain; nevertheless Artaxerxes becoming master of the field, taking a view of those that were slain, amongst others Cyrus was discovered by the long hair he wore. His head was quickly severed from his body and presented the King, and Mitridates, to whom his death was imputed, albeit the King would have had the honour himself, was highly rewarded, but soon after by the craft and cruelty of Parysatis the Queen Mother in a most horrid manner was put to death, as we find by Xenophon and Plutarch in the *Life of Artaxerxes*, who not satisfied therewith also made Statira the queen away by poison only for express-ing her detestation of the fact.

Amidst the spoils it happened that Darius the young Prince light upon Aspasia,[1233] a lady of extraordinary beauty that Cyrus upon the first sight became amorous, and after some discourse so passionately affected that without her he could not live. The aged King, upon the report of her beauty, would needs see whether Fame spake truth, and upon view became equally captivated, so as this unhappy competition occasioned a difference not to be reconciled 'twixt father and son. The King, nevertheless perceiving how extremely the Prince's soul was en-deared to her, and considering that *indecora sunt intuta*,[1234] gave way to his son, en-deavouring all he could to abate his own desire, which though smothered a while, broke out at last into such a flame that he violently seized her from his company, and pretending that it was in zeal, sequestered her within the Vestal temple of Anaya, as they call Diana at Ecbatana, which enraged the Prince, and being fur-ther heightened in his jealousy by Tiribazus, a eunuch in near relation to the King, without the least consideration, finding no other way how to recover Aspasia, he

---

[1233] Little is known of Aspasia other than that she was a Greek from Phocaea.
[1234] "Shameful things are dangerous" (Tacitus, *Histories*, 1. 33).

practices how he might assassinate the King his father in his closet, a treason of an ugly dye, and according to its demerit no sooner known but that the conspirators were slain in the attempt, and the Prince himself, though heir-apparent, secured, tried by a Council of War, most of which were Princes, contemned, and the sentence put in execution.[1235] Now albeit the King for his own preservation approved thereof at first, yet afterwards the loss of so hopeful a Prince so overcharged his thoughts thatin a languishing condition it at length broke his heart. Such was the end of this great monarch after six and thirty years' reign, being likewise buried at Persepolis in or about the Year of the World 3600.

Darius [III] elected King.

Ochus his third son was crowned King, who during his six and twenty years' rule acted as many tragic parts as the worst of his predecessors ever did, so as of him 'tis said *"nulla non sanguinis, non sexus, non aetatis misericordia permotus est."*[1236] And for example, not content with the cruel persecution he made abroad against Egypt, which he reduced, and the blood he spilt in the conquest of India, Syria and Cyprus, where he gave little quarter, at home he made away his two brethren, and as he was contriving more bloodshed was himself cut short by Bagoas the eunuch, who finding it impossible to ascend the throne mounted the right heir Arses[1237] thereon, whom nevertheless he soon after slew, fearing he would revenge his father's death. In this unhappy Prince the royal race of Cyrus the

---

[1235] Tiribazus [*Terebates*] was a powerful satrap who did in fact persuade Prince Darius to rebel against his father, who had associated him in the kingship. The Aspasia story has no historical foundation. "The conspiracy was betrayed by a eunuch," Olmstead writes, "and Darius was caught in the royal bedchamber; tried by royal judges who gave written decision in the king's absence, he was condemned to death" (*History*, 424). This episode was followed by the suspicious suicide of Prince Ariaspes, who with Darius and Ochus (the future Artaxerxes III) was a son of Statira, and the poisoning of Prince Arsames, a natural son of Artaxerxes II "celebrated for his wisdom," after which "the aged Atraxerxes died of grief" (Olmstead, *History*, 424). For further details, see Diodorus Siculus 15. 93; Justin 10. 1–2. There are also accounts in Aelian and Plutarch's *Life of Artaxerxes*.

[1236] "Neither blood [ties], sex, nor age could induce him to pity" (Pompeius Trogus 10. 3, in Justin). Olmstead noted that Artaxerxes III "was reputed the most bloodthirsty of all the Achaemenid monarchs . . . No sooner was he seated on the throne than he killed off all his relatives without distinction of age or sex" (*History*, 424).

[1237] Arses was King of Persia 338–336 B.C.E. He was the youngest son of Artaxerxes III and Atossa, and was placed on the throne by Bagoas as a puppet ruler. However, "Arses objected to the tyrannical control exercised by [Bagoas] and attempted to poison him, but he himself fell a victim to the draught . . . all his children were slain, and Bagoas presented the empty throne to the forty-five year old Darius" (Olmstead, *History* 491).

Great took end, having ruled the Persian Empire about two hundred and thirty years.

Bagoas, albeit of great power, was nonetheless so hateful to the subject by reason of his treasonable practices that he saw it was in vain in his own behalf to attempt the crown, so that not knowing how to secure himself better then by obliging his friend he pitched upon Codomanus, who at that time was Lieutenant of Armenia by commission from the late King. Codomanus nevertheless was of the blood of kings,[1238] and of such noted valour and courtesy that it was no sooner proposed then generally approved of. Having the royal sceptre in his hand, according to custom he assumed the name of Darius, the better to ingratiate himself with the people, who had that name in veneration. This is he whom the Greeks call *ultimus Darius*, the Persians *Parvus* or *Cowcheck* from his misfortune rather then from want of prowess, in which and other Princely virtues he was equal to any of the greatest monarchs that preceded him. But the Supreme, who from his highest throne disposes of monarchies and states as to his divine wisdom seems best, set a period unto this, as foretold by the prophet Daniel 11:4.[1239] And in order thereto, albeit Philip[1240] the father of Alexander, so soon as he could prevail with the Grecian states to be their captain-general, had invaded part of the Lesser Asia by Parmenio his lieutenant-general and Attalus his field-marshal, and laid a foundation for Alexander's prosecution of the Persian war.[1241] Nevertheless, he was so opposed by Memnon, a Rhodian officer under Darius, that Philip made but little progress in that work, for the design was laid aside upon that unhappy death of Philip, who was slain by Pausanias, a Macedonian youth whom Attalus against nature had abused, and being complained on to Philip, receiving but a slight return provoked the young man in a treasonable way to vent his passion upon the King, so that it appeared the overthrow of the Persian monarchy was clearly designed for Alexander, who no sooner had composed his domestic broils at home, which gained the son the same reputation with the Grecian Princes and states the father had, to retaliate the Persian

---

[1238] Darius III was the son of Arsames, son of Ostanes, a brother of Artaxerxes II. This fact, Olmstead comments, "shows how completely the main line of the royal house had been wiped out" (*History*, 490).

[1239] "And when he [a mighty king] shall stand up, his kingdom shall be broken, and shall be divided toward the four winds of Heaven; and not to his posterity, nor according to his dominion which he ruled: for his kingdom shall be plucked up, even for others besides those."

[1240] Philip II of Macedon reigned 359–336 B.C.E.

[1241] Parmenio (d. 330 B.C.E.) was the senior general of Alexander the Great and served him until he was assassinated by fellow-officers. "He had gained many successes without Alexander," Q. Curtius wrote, "while Alexander had achieved nothing of significance without him" (7.33). Attalus (d. 331 B.C.E.), who was the uncle of Queen Cleopatra, Philip II's last wife, was murdered by Parmenio on Alexander's orders, Alexander fearing he was plotting his assassination (see Q. Curtius 7.1–3).

for the many invasions and vexations they had given Greece, but principally to quench his ambitious thirst and to give the reins to his boundless spirit, he first disposed his own kingdom to Antipater's[1242] trust, and then distributed most of that he had amongst his friends, giving this reason to Parmenio: "*spes sola et Asia mihi sufficent.*"[1243]

Inconsiderable was the number he raised for so great a task, not exceeding thirty thousand foot, five thousand horse and one hundred and eighty ships, which nevertheless expressed the greatness of his mind, yet notwithstanding is not to be too much censured, seeing what his army fell short for number and bravery was supplied by courage and skill, most of them being veteran soldiers who had received many honourable scars in the wars under Philip his victorious father, "*ut milites et militiae magistri fuerunt,*"[1244] whereas on the contrary Darius infinitely exceeded Alexander in numbers and wealth, and that through long peace and plenty most of them were richly-clad and delicately-fed, yet withal were given over to luxury and grown effeminate.

Alexander, whom the Persians called *Skander* and *Alkandar*, then crossing the Hellespont, gave defiance to the Persians by throwing a dart. He landed without much opposition and had leisure to offer a solemn sacrifice upon Achilles his ancestor's tomb. The first encounter he received was near the River Granicus, which divides the Trojan territories from the Propontis in the Adrastian Field; the more noted place this is, not only from this first battle with the Persians, but for that Pompey the Great at Stella near this place defeated Mithridates the great King of Pontus and Tamerlane the like to Bajazet with his five hundred thousand men, of which two hundred thousand lost their lives that day in the field. In this first fight Spithridates[1245] the Persian general performed the part of a gallant commander; nevertheless, being slain, the rest fled, "*quos terrore nominis magis armis vicit,*"[1246] saith Plutarch concerning Alexander. The victory was Alexander's, who in that fight expressed so much skill as well as valour that the glory of the day was wholly his. Of the Persians fell above twenty thousand, says Quintus Curtius; Plutarch reduces them to two thousand, but of the Greeks not above thirty horse and foot, to whose memory Alexander forthwith caused statues of brass to be erected by Lysippus, the best statuary at that time in the world.

[1242] Antipater (d. 319 B.C.E.) was Regent of Macedon from 334 until his death. He was also a military commander who defeated the Spartans and organised the raising of further troops when Alexander needed them. There were rumours that he had Alexander poisoned (see Q. Curtius 10.10, 14–18).

[1243] Hope alone and Asia are enough for me.

[1244] They were soldiers and masters of soldiers.

[1245] Spithridates was the satrap of Ionia (see Diodorus Siculus 17.19.3–5; Book 2 of Q. Curtius is lost).

[1246] Whom he defeated by fear of his name rather than by arms.

Curiosity of Darius his march.

This success gave him the command of most parts of Asia the Less, and not only furnished him with recruits but what they most wanted, provision. Passing through Phrygia towards the Euxine, at Gordis with his sword he dissolved that knot upon which the conquest of Asia by oracle was said to depend. Darius by this time found the maxim true that the meanest enemy is not to be contemned, much more so great a soldier as the Macedonian, so at length he resolved in person to engage Alexander, and like himself advanced with an army of three hundred thousand foot and an hundred thousand horse, according to Justin; Plutarch doubles their number. Concerning the method of this march Curtius and others give us this strange relation; in the van of the army the arch-flamen carried the Holy Fire, attended by the priests and three hundred sixty-five youths all clothed in red. Next followed the chariot of Jupiter drawn by white horses, the riders being apparelled in scarlet and holding rods of gold in their hands. After them came the chariot dedicated to the sun, which was attended by ten other sumptuous chariots richly-wrought with silver and gold; the vanguard of horse was forty thousand, consisting of several nations and habits. The King's own regiment of foot, which the Persians termed 'Immortals,' were adorned with chains of pearl, their coats embroidered with gold and sleeves powdered with oriental pearl, after which marched fifteen thousand more splendid then the former, apparelled like women. They were called the kindred of the Great King, next whom rode his life-guard, excellently-mounted and clad like servants of so great a monarch, and after them Darius himself, sitting in a triumphant chariot which was of burnished gold embellished with glittering stones and supported by several gods of his great Empire. Upon his head was the royal tiara, and the head of the chariot resembled a *sombrero de sol*, two eagles spreading their wings over him. On either side were two little pagodas or pillars, all being gold set with precious gems; two hundred satraps or rather Princes of the blood with rich partizans went nearest his person. In the last place came Sisygambis[1247] the Queen Mother and the wife of Darius, whose attire was so rich it was not to be valued; they also were drawn in chariots of gold, with fifteen *cajuas*[1248] in which sat the King's children and nieces and a large train of Persian ladies with an infinite number of concubines, and their guard of eunuchs as richly-apparelled as the rest attended them. Near these marched the Treasurer at War with his charge, which was so great that it burthened two thousand camels and mules, after which followed two hundred thousand foot and fifty thousand horse, an army so nice in diet, so rich in habit, so different in language and generally so effeminate as without doubt it was their

---

[1247] Sisygambis (d. 323 B.C.E.), daughter of Artaxerxes II, was the wife of Arsames, son of Otanes, and Darius III's mother. She later married her grand daughter Statira to Alexander the Great after he had defeated Darius at Issus. After Alexander's death she committed suicide by starvation.

[1248] The Portuguese version of *cadjowas* (see above).

very numbers they thought would amaze that little force Alexander was in the head of, who though few were so little frighted with their great body that upon the description was made of their wealth had their courages so inflamed that they thought it not long ere they engaged.

The fight was soon begun, but continued not long, for the Persians, more minded to preserve what they had then to run the uncertain hazard of war upon such unequal terms or to adventure their golden robes and jewels against those coarse despicable fellows that with iron and steel advanced against them. In this short fight the Persians lost 100,000 foot and like number of horse, saith Q. Curtius; others say 60,000 foot and 10,000 horse, most of which fell in the chase. Darius himself was so pursued that fearing to be known in that posture he threw the crown from his head. The treasure also was all taken, but, which was of more note, his mother, wife, children and kin were Alexander's prisoners, who used them like a noble Prince, for albeit they were of incomparable beauty yet commanded his affection so as they had not the least violation or disrespect given by any, the victor also ordering that what jewels they lost should be forthwith restored. Yet the spoils were many and rich, even to admiration, amongst which I only mention a cabinet of gold thick set with diamonds and other precious stones, which for materials and art was reputed the best jewel in the world. Alexander, taking that in his hand and showing it to Perdiccas[1249] pleasantly demanded what was fittest to put therein? Some saying gold, others pearl and stones of price; "No," says he, "nothing but Homer's *Iliad*." Pliny, *lib. 7, c. 29*.

Alexander enters Jerusalem.

Soon after this conflict Parmenio routed Prince Memnon's[1250] brigade near Damascus, in which flight the Prince was slain and the daughter of Ochus the former King, together with the wives and daughters of most of the nobility of Persia taken prisoners, as also a further mass of Darius his treasure, amounting to 6200 talents of money coined and in bullion 500 talents, over and besides other wealth which was inestimable. Phoenicia also and most of Syria prostrated themselves to Alexander upon this victory, who likewise after seven months' siege mastered the city of Tyre and for their obstinacy made the inhabitants feel his wrathful temper. Gaza also made him some resistance, but being taken, Alexander advanced without further interruption to Jerusalem, out of which, to entertain the

---

[1249] Perdiccas (d. 321 B.C.E.) was Alexander's infantry commander at Issus and a trusted friend of the King's. Heckel states that "he was the most powerful individual in Babylon at the time of Alexander's death" (Q. Curtius 318), and may have been considered a successor by Alexander. He was murdered by some of his own officers in Babylon.

[1250] Prince Memnon, son-in-law of Artabazus (see above), was a Rhodian who led a mercenary army in the Persian service. After his death at Damascus, his wife and son were captured by Parmenio (Q. Curtius 3.13.14).

conqueror, issued Jaddua[1251] the High Priest attired in his pontifical robe with a mitre upon his head and attended by the priests and Levites in their sacerdotal habits, which, saith Josephus, was so full of gravity and state that Alexander first admired and then prostrated himself before the High Priest for his benediction, who for his better satisfaction likewise entertained him, amongst other things, with the prophecy of Daniel which in express terms presaged his victories.

Thence he marched into Egypt, which submitted, and having an ardent desire to visit Jupiter Ammon's temple, albeit the way was exceeding difficult, nevertheless after five days treading the loose and scalding sands, in all that desert seeing neither grass nor tree, beast nor bird, being at length arrived at the place he was saluted with the affected title of Jupiter's Son, as the parasites interpreted the equivocal Greek word wherewith the oracle entertained him. Returning to Memphis he quickened his march towards the north part of Assyria called Adiabene, where he had notice that the chaste and beautiful wife of Darius, notwithstanding her Princely usage, was so overwhelmed with grief upon the thoughts of the declining condition of her husband that death only could give ease to her affliction.

Soon after this the Persian King proffered Alexander his fair daughter with thirty thousand talents, together with Egypt and all Asia the Less for portion. But Alexander, who had these already in possession and the sovereignty of the world in his idea, replied that the firmament could not endure two suns, so that they prepared on either sides for another fight. Darius recruited an army to five hundred thousand horse and foot; some authors make it much more, and Alexander his to fifty thousand foot and eight thousand horse. These great bodies soon met and engaged each other; this battle was much better-fought then the former, most of them having gained experience. Darius expressed sufficient personal bravery that day, and the soldiers, the one side for liberty, the other for conquest, stood so well and so equally to their charge that Victory stood hovering a good while with doubtful wings ere it appeared to which part she would incline, but Alexander, who well knew that upon this the whole depended and would decide the quarrel, expressed such extraordinary valour as well as experience in the fight as at length, albeit he lost three hundred of his best men and that Parmenio, Perdiccas and Hephaestion were hurt in the fight, he renewed the battle with such fresh courage that the Persian army were constrained to give ground and then fled, Darius himself in the last place, who in the battle having given great proof of his courage, in this condition would have slain himself. In the pursuit more were slain then in the fight; 30,000 says Arrian, 40,000 says Quintus Curtius, but Diodorus Siculus makes them double the number.

[1251] Jaddua or Yaddua was High Priest of Israel c. 371–320 B.C.E. He is the last of the High Priests to be mentioned in the Bible (see Nehemiah 2:10–11), and is sometimes referred to as Simeon the Just.

How uncertain soever the number be, this day's victory over that part got him conquest over the whole. "*Quo praelio*," says Justin, "*Asiae imperium rapuit Alexander; cuius tanta fuit felicitas, ut post hoc, nemo rebellare ausus est. Persae enim, post imperium tot annorum, iugum servitutis patienter acceperint,*"[1252] which words of the historian were true, for the reputation of this battle quite broke the heart of the Persian nobility and set the Imperial crown upon Alexander's head, who pursued the victory, forcing the remains of the Persian army to disperse themselves into divided quarters and such places where they could find best shelter. Invitations also came from provinces and cities in most places thereabouts to Alexander to take what he had victoriously acquired by right of war. Arbela was the first that rendered, nigh where the battle was. Arbela is a city under 37 degrees, called by Ptolemy *Arbelitis*, by Marcellinus *Gangabela*, and is about fifteen leagues north from Nineveh in that part of Assyria which was then called *Arrapachita*, severed from Armenia by the Nyphates Hills.[1253] Babylon was next in this kind of complement, which place for a long time had been the object of Alexander's desires, so that thither in the best equipage he could he cheerfully marched with the greatest part of his army, having first sent some horse after Darius, who with a flying party was passed the mountain that divides those parts from Media, to preserve himself where he could find most safety.

Alexander enters Babylon and Susa.

Alexander therefore, marching through the country called Adiabene, which is 'twixt the Arrapachites[1254] (corruptly from *Arphashite*, that part of Assyria being the first plantation of Arphaxad son of Shem) and the Garamantes (before the Flood the same where Eden or the Garden of Paradise stood), at length the victor came in sight of the high walls of Babylon, which put him into an ecstasy of joy, for indeed that was the place he coveted, having as it were from the beginning of time struck terror not into Greece alone but all other kingdoms and

---

[1252] By which battle Alexander seized the empire of Asia; after this everything became so happy that none dared rebel. After an empire lasting so many years, the Persians patiently accepted the yoke of servitude.

[1253] The exact location of Arbela is not known, and the battle is now usually more accurately referred to as Gaugamela. Recent studies have suggested that the site may be east of Mosul in Iraq.

[1254] A province of northern Assyria. Herbert likely got this information about Arphaxad, which does not appear in earlier editions, from Bochart's *Geographica sacra seu Phaleg et Canaan* (1646). Samuel Bochart (1599–1667), a distinguished French Huguenot scholar with whom Herbert could have been acquainted, had studied at Oxford and knew Arabic, Hebrew, and Syriac. For details on this see Samuel Sharpe, "Remarks on the Topography of Nineveh," *Original Papers read before the Syro-Egyptian Society of London*, Vol. I, Pt. II (London: James Madden, 1850), 26.

provinces through the world. To welcome the conqueror Mazaeus,[1255] a Persian satrap who was at that time Governor of the place, had faithfully promised his master Darius that he would keep it for him not only against Alexander but all the world, falsely issued with the Captain of the Castle and the Treasurer, who presented Alexander with a particular of his charge, being no less then fifty thousand talents of silver in bullion, or, as some report, two hundred thousand talents in gold, followed by the Magi or Chaldaean astrologers, as forward as the rest to adore this rising sun, accompanied with an infinite number of horse and townsmen all in their full livery, having ordered that the way all along should be strewed with flowers and altars erected smoking with incense, with what other symbols of joy and submission they could possibly express to make his entrance more acceptable and magnificent, without the least outward appearance of fear or terror for their inevitable subjection and loss which they were sure would follow this new chance of war. Alexander, rapt with admiration, beheld the stateliness of the place, the height and strength of the walls, the beauty of the towers, the many noble structures and places of pleasure all along the River Euphrates, that especially which was supported by arches, the greatness and curiosity of the royal palace then which the world had not its superior, that excepted of Persepolis, and no less magnifying the Temple of Belus which Xerxes had defaced. Alexander gave immediate order for repair thereof, but having a little before spoken more particularly of this place I may not repeat. Nevertheless, such contentment Alexander found here that he spent more then a month's time in banqueting and other excess, which had wellnigh vitiated the spirits of his countrymen who had been educated after another manner of diet in a strict but wholesome discipline of war.

At length, leaving the superintendancy of the place with Mazaeus the former Governor, the conqueror marched directly towards Susa. His way into Susiana was through Sittacene or Satrapene, close by the Altars of Hercules, which he viewed for the honour he bore that hero, whom he ever emulated. Into Susa he was received by Abulites, according to his principle still adoring the rising sun, who expressed little less ceremony in his entertainment then Mazaeus had formerly at Babylon. Here the Treasurer presented the conqueror with an invoice of his charge which was nine millions of gold and fifty thousand talents of silver not put into the mint, as say most writers, albeit Plutarch mentions only four thousand talents and in purple silk to an equal value.

The pleasure of this noted place detained him longer then he intended at his first coming, for indeed the curiosity of the gardens and the magnificence of the palace were not to be parallelled. Alexander, at a Princely banquet which he

---

[1255] Mazaeus (d. 328 B.C.E.) fought against Alexander with some distinction, especially at Gaugamela, but in 331 he surrendered Babylon to the Macedonians. However, Alexander retained his services as Governor of Babylon, in which post he remained until his death (see Q. Curtius 5.1.17).

made Hephaestion and other prime officers of the army with several of the Persian lords, sitting in Darius his state there, which was of pure gold most richly-set with precious stoned, could not forbear exulting and to confess what he had long desired was now accomplished, *viz.* to be master of Xerxes his magnificent palace, and having here as at Babylon placed a considerable guard, he hasted towards Persepolis, invited thither by Tiridates, the fearful Governor. By the way, as I noted in our passage near Jarri, he was to march through the strait called *Pylae Persidis*, where Ariobazarnes, a noble Persian, gallantly defended the pass with a small party of well-resolved Persians, so that Alexander, after the loss of more captains then in the two first battles against Darius and many companies of foot, was forced to find another way, at which the noble Persian hasting to Persepolis in defence of his master's right was basely refused entrance by Tiridates, so that wheeling about he immediately fought the Macedonian victor, in which attempt he found an honourable grave.

Greatness of the Persian exchequer.

Persepolis, albeit the gates were opened to give Alexander leave to enter in a friendly and submissive sort, nevertheless such was the spite they bore this gallant place for the mischief Xerxes had done in Greece that the soldiers had leave to kill and spoil as they listed. This was the metropolis, the principal seat and burial-place of the Persian monarchs. No place in the world being put into the balance with this city would have weighed it down, for after the soldiers had loaded themselves with three days' plunder of money, plate, jewels, images of gold and bullion in abundance, the conqueror had as his share a hundred and twenty thousand talents in coin, but not content therewith he set the city and palace on fire at the instigation of an infamous strumpet, concerning which I have more particularly spoken in the description of Persepolis.

And not finding any fitter place to take a survey of the Persian exchequer, which clearly appears by the several vast sums Alexander seized in this itinerant war to be prodigious, suffer me a little view that it may evidence how properly the Persian kings arrogated to themselves the title of King of Kings and Lord of All Men etc., their annual revenue being answerable to the amplitude of their Empire, which extended one way from the north side of the Hellespont to the River Ganges and the other way to the *Ara Philenorum*[1256] and country of the Garamantes, so as if only from India they extracted yearly three hundred and threescore talents of gold, out of the rest of the 127 provinces how great must be the receipt? For no less was yearly brought into the exchequer, say good authors, then 40,500 talents of gold, every talent, according to the Hebrew, amounting unto 4500 pounds, so as the several vast sums which Alexander disposed out of these several treasuries may well be credited. Let it not then be lost labour to

---

[1256] The "Altar of the Phileni" is now known as Adjabiya, in Libya.

enumerate those sums as I found them registered and probably agreed with the accompt then given Alexander.

At the Battle of Issus Alexander took from the Treasurer at War 6200 talents of coins designed for the pay of Darius his army and 500 talents more in bullion unminted. What the silver talent was is doubtful, for if it were the Babylonian talent that was 218 pounds, if the Alexandrian, 375 pounds, if the Egyptian, 275 pounds, for I observe that the Attic and Euboeic[1257] with the talents in different kingdoms were not the same, no more then was the weight, which had its equal variation, and such as hath occasioned sundry mistakes amongst historians. At Memphis he found 800 talents, at Damascus 2600, at Babylon 50,000, at Ecbatana 26,000, at Susa 50,000 unminted and nine millions of gold, at Pasagardae 60,000 and in Persepolis 120,000 talents, or, as Strabo reports, if he mean not rather the total, thirty-two millions seven hundred and fifty thousand pounds, so that the 30,000 talents or eighteen millions of crowns which Darius proffered Alexander with his daughter Statira in portion and the 10,000 talents for ransoming of prisoners would have easily been paid, seeing that prodigious mass of treasure Alexander sent thence into his native kingdom was so great as loaded five thousand camels and ten thousand mules.

Moreover, seeing I am upon this subject, suffer me to balance these with other stupendous sums I meet with in authentic stories. And first, concerning that which Sardanapalus sacrificed with himself in flames when Nineveh was taken by Belochus, it is reported to be no less then one hundred millions of talents in gold with a thousand millions of talents in silver, which in our money amounts unto twenty thousand and five hundred millions of pounds, scarce credible if the vast extent of that Empire and arbitrary authority of those kings were not considered, and compared with what King David amassed together out of a far less dominion, for David, as appears 1 Chronicles 22:14, bequeathed Solomon towards the building of the Temple one hundred thousand talents of gold and ten hundred thousand talents of silver, which in our money amounts to eight hundred sixty-seven millions three hundred eighty-two thousand and five hundred pounds sterling or thereabouts. Marvellous it is likewise to consider where and in what manner Cyrus scraped so vast a sum together out of his lieutenancy in the Lesser Asia such time as he marched against his brother Artaxerxes, being as Xenophon reports one hundred and five and twenty millions of pounds.

Now as in the first I gave but one instance out of the tax that was yearly raised from India, so in the last I shall only mention Egypt, which in Cleopatra's time brought every year into the public treasury twelve thousand and five hundred talents of gold, which according to our computation makes 7,500,000 crowns, sums so very great as puts to silence that mass of plate which was offered Pizarro, a Spanish commander in America, by Atahualpa the Peruvian King for his

---

[1257] Euboea is "the largest island, after Crete, of the Aegean archipelago" (Grant, *Guide*, 246).

ransom.[1258] Oh, how has our Mother Earth groaned through the violence that
has been offered by extracting this Mammon of darkness! How many millions
of lives have been spent in mines for the producing that which misused has
helped to put the universe into a combustion? And seeing the very entrails of the
Earth has been thus incessantly torn for this precious ore, as the world esteems
it, strange is it to consider what is become of this accumulated heap, appearing
that the exchequers of most potentates at this day, as in most former times, are
rather empty then full, and that all nations complain for a supply, and yet those
many public treasuries would hardly amount to what embodied in one exchequer
in the world's adolescency, insomuch as it may presumed that the greater part is
lost and buried in the sea where it is irrecoverable, but not to be lamented, seeing "covetousness is but idolatry," and 'tis not wealth but content that makes men
happy. Nevertheless, that great wealth the Persian kings were masters of made
them so reputable with the Romans that by them they were styled *"reges beatis-
simi,"* as, amongst others, Horace has an allusion in his *"Persarum rege beatior,"*[1259]
concluding this parenthesis with that invective against avarice, *"ullum est officium
vel locum aut solemne quod avaritia violare non audet?"*[1260] And drawing our eyes
from the prospect of these enchanting metals, I have the more liberty to follow
Alexander into India with this caution, *"Non alienis castris tanquam explorator, sed
viator."*[1261]

Lamentable death of Darius.

Alexander then having intelligence brought him how perfidiously Bessus had
dealt with his declining Prince and the death's wounds given him by those traitorous hands,[1262] delayed not to give order for a speedy march in quest of Bessus,
the rather for it was told him that Darius at his death retained so grateful a

[1258] Francisco Pizarro (1471–1541) was the conqueror of the Inca Empire and the
founder of the city of Lima. Atahualpa (c. 1502–1433) was the last Inca of Peru. He
reigned 1532–1533 and was murdered by the Spaniards.

[1259] "More blessed than Persia's king" (Horace, *Odes* 3. 9. 4).

[1260] Is there any dutiful action or place or rite which avarice does not dare violate?
(adapted from Cicero, *Pro Quinctio* 6).

[1261] "I am not in foreign camps as a scout, but as a traveller." This may be adapted
from *"solo enim et in aliena castra transire, non tanquam transfuga, sed tanquam explorator"*
(Seneca, *Ad Lucilium 1.2.5*).

[1262] Arrian's account says that at Gaugamela, "Bessus and his friends did not at once
abandon the attempt to get Darius away . . . but when Alexander was close upon them,
Nabarzanes and Bartaentes struck him down and left him" (3.21–2). Q. Curtius noted
that Bartaentes "fled into India" to escape punishment (6.6.36). However, for Curtius the
real villain seems to have been Nabarzanes, a cavalry commander, who "prepared the way
for their nefarious plan" with Bessus (5.9.2). For details of the assassination, which differs
from Arrian's version, see Curtius 5.13.1–25).

memory for the civility expressed to his nearest relations that he heartily invocated all his gods Alexander might have his desires as to an universal conquest of the world accomplished; *"precatur superum inferumque numina et regales deos ut Alexandro imperium orbis terrarum contingat,"*[1263] with which words he expired and with him Persian freedom. *"Vitam pariter cum Persarum regno sic finivit,"* Justin *lib.* 10.[1264] Revenge quickened Alexander's march towards Bactria, serving withal to quicken his desired entrance that way into the Indies, so that selecting twenty thousand foot and three thousand horse, with those few he designed the prosecution of his universal conquest.

Marching therefore first through Parthia, in fifteen days he passed through Hyrcania, which by the natural defence it had in woods and fastnesses might easily have obstructed his passage had Bessus but endeavoured it, but self-guilt sufficiently tortured him for he was now become the reproach of men and found it accordingly, for upon Alexander's coming into Margiana he was apprehended by his own party and brought bound to Alexander, who abhorring his sight, ordered that he should be delivered to Oxathres[1265] the brother of Darius, to be disposed of as he should think fit. *"In ultimum perfidiae fratri Darii excruciandum tradidit,"*[1266] saith Justin *lib.* 12, which done, the conqueror gave order for the interment of the embalmed royal corpse, which was done in military form and with as much ceremony and exoression of sorrow that was possible, but Alexander being the principal mourner, by the sadness of his countenance sufficiently discovered the anguish of his spirit, a generous compassion and so well-resented, yea, having so forcible an impression upon the souls of the Persian Princes then attending the obsequies as albeit the country was formally subdued. Not till by those tears he shed could he make an entire conquest over their affections.

Nysa and Mount Meru.

This great funeral thus performed, Alexander then passed his army over the River Oxus and afterwards the like over Jaxartes, which Plutarch calls *Oraxartes*. The Greeks, it seems, not very expert in geography, took it for Tanais,[1267] *"urbem*

[1263] He prayed to the deities above and below and the royal gods that Alexander might achieve rule over the world.

[1264] He ended his life together with the kingdom of Persia.

[1265] Oxathres, who was indeed Darius III's brother, commanded the Persian reserves, and after fighting bravely at the Battle of Issus he was captured. Alexander later enrolled him amongst his "friends," a closely-knit band of warriors whom he favoured. Herbert's source for the handing-over of Bessus (Artaxerxes IV, as he called himself) to Oxathres is Q. Curtius (7.5.40–1). Arrian, who does not mention Oxathres at all, simply states that after his humiliation, Bessus was "sent away to Bactra to be executed" (3.30).

[1266] In his last treachery he was handed over to Darius's brother for torture.

[1267] Tanais is "a site now under water near Taganrog (in the province of Rostov, southern Russia) on the gulf of that name in the northern part of Lake Maeotis (the Sea

Alexandriam super omnem Tanaim condidit,"[1268] and in seventeen days compassed it with a wall six miles about, a great mistake, this emptying itself into the Caspian Sea and that into Moeotis or *Mare de Tanna*, which in 48 degrees flows into the Euxine, the distance 'twixt those two rivers being little less then two thousand miles. Alexander, still thinking the conquest of India, directs his course through the most southerly part of the Massagetes' country, leaving the Paropamissan Hills and Arachosia on the right hand, during which he laid the foundation of twelve cities, but falling into some riot, in that distemper slew Cleitus, his old and trusty servant, after which he intended to repose at the city Nysa, built by Bacchus upon the banks of the Hydaspes, of great repute in those days for the sacred Mount and incomparable vines there abounding, which from thence and the neighbourhood to Ararat in Margiana and the name it bore gives some good cause to fancy that it was built by the Patriarch[1269] and was his first plantation. Here he constituted his *Argyraspides*,[1270] who had their armour damasked and filetted with silver.

Porus, a valiant and powerful Indian Prince, having notice that Alexander advanced towards his country, which comprehended a great part of what the Mughal now holds in Industan, waited for him upon the banks of Hydaspes with a great body of horse and foot and many elephants of war, where they fought and gave the Greeks such testimony of their valour that albeit Alexander got the better of the day it gave the Greeks nevertheless fresh cause to rest satisfied with such victories as they had got, without further hazard into the Orient, to put which out of thought Alexander let loose the reins to all manner of debauchery, for at the mountain Meru he celebrated the Bacchanalia and for fifteen days glutted the army with those mystic fopperies, after which he forced his way through Daedala and Acedira,[1271] after which he took by assault a fort situated upon an inaccessible hill which could not be subjected by Hercules. After that Mazaga[1272] and Nora, over Acesines, another branch of Indus, and then set foot in India, for so saith the historian, which I note only to show that Indus and this river are one in that story, all which he apprehended his own by that little possession, the

---

of Azov) . . . the site of an archaic market town or fishing settlement that was known as Tanais" (Grant, *Guide*, 621).

[1268] He founded the city of Alexandria over all Tanais.

[1269] Noah, whose ark is said to have come to rest on Mount Ararat.

[1270] A crack Macedonian division commanded by Nicanor. Herbert's description is accurate.

[1271] "From here [Nysa] they came into the area called Daedala, the inhabitants of which had abandoned their homes and sought refuge in some remote, tree-clad mountains. Accordingly Alexander pressed on to Acedira, also burned and deserted by its fleeing inhabitants" (Curtius Rufus 8.10.19).

[1272] Mazaga, which Arrian calls "Massaga, the largest town in this neighbourhood" (4.26), proved difficult to take.

consideration whereof made him to acquaint his great officers with his design to penetrate as far as Ganges, which they seemed to approve of. But, being known unto the army, the length of the way, the increase of heat, wasted quarters, infinite numbers of Indians assembled in their own defence, the difficulty of passing over Ganges, which was reported to be thirty furlongs broad and a hundred fathoms deep, these and the like had so vive an impression in their fancies that as one and all they expressed their discontent, so as finding that neither by threats nor promises he could allay the mutinous humour of the camp, at present he dissembled his thoughts and seemed to rest satisfied, albeit soon after he made several of them feel the weight of his displeasure, so that the horse he marched through Patalena upon the eastern banks of the River Indus, and most of the foot in boats passed merrily down the stream until they came to what we call Diu,[1273] formerly Patala, near the Tropic and in view of the ocean, where drawing his horse and foot into a body he straightway invaded the country of the Oxidracans, stormed the principal place of defence the Mallians had, and temerariously both mounting the parapet and violently leaping into the town to the amazement of the barbarians, followed but by two officers, for a while sustained the darts and other weapons the enemy sent, and by that inconsiderate act, if the historian say true, had perished, had not the army as men desperate in his rescue enforced their speedy entrance.

Afterwards he subdued the Brahmans' country, and preparing for his march against the more remote Indians assembled near the banks of Ganges, the camp broke out into a fresh murmur, so that albeit he used all possible means to persuade their further march, vehemently declaring that unless they opposed their fortune against the numerous but naked preparations about Ganges which gave them a bold defiance, they would retreat with shame, and, saith Plutarch *Vita Alexandri*, all they had thitherto done was not thanksworthy, notwithstanding which the army, having the old idea before their imagination, glutted with victory, overcharged with rich spoils and tired with travel, first they showed him their white hairs and the many maims received in battles, and then with tears besought him to put a period to his conquests and ambition, by which they gave him cause sufficient to understand their unwillingness to scorch their bodies, which already looked like mummy, any longer in those fiery reasons, so that in fine he was forced to condescend.

[1273] Diu in Gujarat. Earlier, Herbert had stated that it was known as both Patalena and Patala. The name refers to both the island and the town situated at the eastern end. For Alexander's siege, see Arrian 6.17.5 or Q. Curtius 9.8.28; he calls the city "Patalia."

Alexander admires the ocean.

Nor was it ill-resolved; duly considering the great way they should have marched ere they arrived at Ganges, the intolerable heat they must endure, the uncertainty of provisions and loss probably they might have undergone in an enemy's country, who having no dependence upon the Persians were not at all shook by the fall of the Persian Empire, but rather as one man embodied upon the banks of Ganges, part of which, namely the Gangaridae and the Prasii,[1274] were reputed two hundred thousand foot and fourscore thousand horse, besides eight thousand warlike elephants, all bent in his opposal, withal finding upon a muster that albeit in the fight against Porus and the Mallians[1275] his army consisted of an hundred and twenty thousand foot and fifteen thousand horse, full three parts of that number were since dead, part being slain in fight but most dying of flux and fevers occasioned through excess of grapes at Nysa and their other intemperance at the celebration of the frantic orgies. Alexander therefore seemingly submitted at length to a return into a more moderate clime, and the rather that he might recruited with those fifteen thousand men he had notice were advanced as far as Jasques. He thereupon published his resolution to retreat, which was received with general acclamations of joy, and after a month's rest upon the *aestuarium* of the River Indus prepared for a march towards Hormuz, whiles the conqueror himself, heedfully observing the flux of the river, the situation of the maritime coast and that large horizon the place afforded, was infinitely delighted with the novelty but especially with the prospect of the ocean.

The earth and ocean compared.

Now give me leave to pause a while and consider why Alexander had the ocean in such admiration. The ocean was deservedly the subject of his wonder, for Pella, the place of his birth, being situate near the Thessalonic Gulf which neighbours the archipelago, without doubt gave him not only the prospect of that but in the course of his conquest had the view of other seas, as the Mare de la Tana, now *Ziabache*, the Euxine, the Mediterranean and the Mare Caspium, all which may well be properly called the ocean. The Mediterranean we find called *Mare Magnum*, the Great Sea, in Exodus and in Joshua 1:4. Pontus Euxinus also has the name of *Mare Maggiore* and well deserves that attribute, seeing it is wellnigh three thousand miles in compass, so great as warranted Ovid and other Roman poets to denominate all other

---

[1274] The Gangaridae and the Prasii, whom Curtius tells us lived "on the far bank of the Ganges," were ruled by King Aggramenes, "who was now blockading the roads with a force of 20,000 cavalry and 400,000 infantry" (9.2.3). Diodorus says the King had 20,000 cavalry and 200,000 infantry, not to mention "2000 chariots and 4000 elephants" (17.93.2).

[1275] The Mallians or Malli had their capital at what is now the modern city of Multan.

seas by that, as "*Omnia pontus nil nisi pontus.*"[1276] And as for the Caspian, though by reason it is everywhere encompassed with land [and] it indeed rather resembles a great lough or pond then sea, nevertheless from its greatness and other properties is worthily-ranked *inter dei magnalia*,[1277] and by cosmographers in the catalogue of other seas, for Pliny terms it "*ingens*" and Maginus "*vastum mare*," a large and vast sea, albeit the circuit be usually taken for little above a thousand miles. And for the *Mare Tanais* or *Palus Moeotis*, 'tis also great, seeing that from the middle part land can hardly be discerned, so that upon the whole I may conclude the sea is great, for it is "a collection of many waters joined unto the ocean," but comparatively the disproportion is great betwixt the ocean and the sea, for if I may so resemble, such as loughs are to the sea so may the sea be compared with the ocean, which is so great that in Genesis 1:2 'tis styled "*facies abyssi*,"[1278] for then it was an overspreading element in extent and depth exceeding all other seas, but as in verse 10, when the waters were gathered together unto one place, that collection was then called *maria*. Also, the circumfluent ocean "*universam circumambiens terram*," on every side surrounds the earth, giving life both to all springs and receiving into its womb all rivers, from which it is aptly-termed "*fluviorum fontiumque pater*,"[1279] by Virgil "*patrem rerum*"[1280] and by Homer and Orpheus "*patrem deorum hominum et aliorum*," the Father of gods and men and all other things, for that in the constitution of all sublunary bodies moisture is necessarily required. Mela also calls it "*immensum, vastissimum ac infinitum pelagus*,"[1281] and Seneca that "nothing is endless or bottomless save the ocean."

Moreover, as it exceeds the sea for magnitude, so doth it in depth, for the sea in most places may be fathomed, yea, it is well-known that the deepness of the sea usually answers to the height of mountains, which seldom exceed three miles perpendicular, but in our narrow seas is scarce found half so much, so that albeit the earth as most ponderous be ordinarily assigned the lowest station, nevertheless Solinus authoritatively maintains that the ocean is deeper then the earth, so profound that in a vulgar acceptation, albeit erroneously, it is styled bottomless. For though in sounding the narrow seas they seldom fail of ground, 'tis otherwise in the ocean, and I very well remember that in the great ocean in the mid-way betwixt the two great continents of Africa and America, when we were several days becalmed, the captain of our ship to satisfy his curiosity one time let fall

---

[1276] "All is sea, nothing but sea." Herbert seems to be conflating two quotes here: 1. *Nil nisi pontus erat*, "nothing but the sea" (Ovid, *Heroides* 13.22); 2. *Omnia pontus erant, derant quoque litora ponto*, "all was sea, sea without a shore" (Ovid, *Metamorphoses* 1. 292).

[1277] "amongst God's great works."

[1278] The face of the waters.

[1279] The father of rivers and fountains.

[1280] Father of things.

[1281] The huge, vast and infinite sea.

his lead, which had all the logline he could possibly make or borrow, probably upward of three thousand fathom, and having veered it out to the very end could find no ground, so as he would have persuaded us it was abyss, albeit that trial gave no such consequence.

I may observe this further difference. Albeit in our narrow seas there is commonly a *fluxus et refluxus maris*, an ebb and flood, the Euxine and the Mediterranean have but their flux in most places discernible, for the one streams through the Thracian Bosphorus and Propontis into the archipelago, but both through the Strait of Gibraltar into the great Atlantic Ocean, "*sic dictus ob velocitatem et per interiora maris discurrens*,"[1282] from its bellowing near the shore by poets usually styled *tauriceps*, and by painters represented in that similitude. Nevetheless, the ocean where far from land and when undisturbed by wind is *placidus in loco*, in its own place still and pacific, and yet it may not be denied that for the preservation of its purity and the life of its inhabitants it has both motion and internal Aestivation, so having spoken this little concerning the greatness of the sea, forasmuch as sea and land make but one sphere, give me leave to contemplate the earth with like admiration Alexander did the ocean.

That the Almighty created the first chaos out of nothing is evident [from] Genesis 1:1 and Wisdom of Solomon 11:14, which sufficiently convinces Aristotle's supposed *materia prima*, for out of that mass both the Heavenly and elementary bodies were constituted and formed.[1283] By the *fiat* of the Almighty the subtercelestial waters were separated from the supercelestial, so that the third day the earth was visible and appeared firm and distinguished from the waters, yea, in such a beautiful and harmonious manner that both earth and water had their bounds, so as the water, which first overpowered the earth, was gathered into one place, limited, and not suffered to invade the earth's proportion. "*Occlusit mare valvis*," he shut up the sea with doors; "*dicens, huiusque venies et non amplius*," [saying] hitherto shalt thou go and no further; "*fluctuorum tuorum superbie litus hic opponit*," here shall thy proud waves stay, Job 38:8. And both not as Ovid fancies, "*ponderibus librata suis*,"[1284] poised or balanced by their own weight, but by the direction of the great Architect hung in the air, or, as Job 26:7, "*Terram suspendit super nihilum*," the earth hung upon nothing, with which that of the Psalmist differs not, "*Terram fundavit super maria*," he founded the earth upon the waters, the waters compassing the earth and mixing with it in the most intrinsic places,

[1282] So-called for its swiftness, running through the midst of the sea.

[1283] See, for example, Martin Ruhland, *Lexicon alchemicae, sive dictionarium alchemisticum* (1612), where *materia prima* is defined as "A crude mixture of matter, or another name for *materia prima* is Chaos, as it is in the beginning" (323). Aristotle believed primal chaos to be the foundation of reality.

[1284] Ovid, *Metamorphoses* 1.10.

whence probably it it [that] Thales of Miletus[1285] was of opinion that the earth floated and was aptly resemblable to a ship swimming in the water.

Now whereas Solinus maintains that the ocean is larger and deeper then the earth, as lately-mentioned in an experiment we are to understand that the terrestrial sphere is a globe or round body comprehended within the superficies of the earth and water, which though by some supposed to be equally disposed, nay, by the ancients who comprised the earth within an hundred and eighty degrees of longitude, had attributed scarce one half of the sphere, that dimension is increased very much since land has been discovered within the polar circles and by the addition of that vast *terra firma* in America. Howbeit, Scaliger in his 38 *Exercitatio* is of opinion that were it possible to level the earth by spreading the lofty mountains and making them even with the plain ground, the water would be overspread and have no place, which *Rec. Cos. lib.* 4[1286] exceeds, in averring that the earth is ten thousand times greater then the sea, an hypothesis very much differing from most cosmographers, but what authority he has I cannot apprehend, unless he take that for his guide we find in Esdras 4:47, where it is said "that the waters were gathered," at the Creation, I suppose, "into a seventh part, so that six parts of the earth were kept dry," which for that it is apocryphal how far it may be credited for truth I leave to better judgments then my own and in reverence to the author forbear further to question.

But how disputable soever the disproportion be betwixt the earth and water as to magnitude, the profundity or depth is more satisfactorily demonstrated, for notwithstanding the ocean be usually styled bottomless, and in the deepest parts, which may be presumed where it is broadest, albeit there are rising grounds and mountains in the ocean where the plummet or lead may touch, yet in other places I believe it is not or at least never hitherto has been fathomed. Howbeit, the judgment of most is the deepest exceeds not thirty miles, an uncertain conjecture but commonly taken from that simile of answering to the height of Tenerife or other the highest mountains, yea, granting that the depth were an hundred, nay, a thousand miles, yet will it not adequate the crassitude or thickness of the earth, whose diameter is acknowledged to be seven thousand and two hundred miles, allowing the circumference to be one and twenty thousand and six hundred, nay, it will fall short of the semi-diameter, seeing that from the centre to the superficies of the earth are reckoned three thousand and six hundred miles, which as to depth clearly gives the earth the superiority, and in comparison of which depth in the narrow seas is very inconsiderable, being evident that the logline in most ships, when veered out, usually finds ground, as I have sometimes observed, and find likewise reported by Priscian concerning Julius Caesar, who for his private

---

[1285] Thales of Miletus (fl. 600 B.C.E.) was a Pre-Socratic Greek philosopher and mathematician who held that all things had their origin in water. Our knowledge of his thought comes only through secondary sources.

[1286] Unidentified.

satisfaction fathoming the seas found it not to exceed thirty *stadia*, which make about three miles and a half English, although Solinus allows fifty-four *stadia*, which doubles the former.

Now in this parallel, although I have noted a seeming difference in those two, they nevertheless agree in one centre, which is an imaginary insensible small point fixed in the mid-part of the earth, from whence height is to be measured rather then from the superficies of the towering earth or sphericity of the swelling water, though both are practiced. But the more to admire this wonderful fabric and thereby to glorify the Creator, such as the centre is to the sphere of the earth the great terrestrial globe is no other then when it is made the centre of that vast immeasurable circle of the celestial motions, comprehensive only by him who is infinite and incomprehensible. Howbeit man, the microcosm, duly considered in his admirable structure of body together with the faculties and abilities of the soul, is a miracle far surmounting not only the earth and ocean but Heaven itself with all the rest of the creation, such as induced the prophet to acknowledge with this acclamation: "He was fearfully and wonderfully made; yea, the Lord hath given him dominion over the works of his hands and subjected all things under him," Psalm 8:5 and [Psalm] 139:14, which abundantly obliges man to praise the Lord.

Alexander's *ne plus ultra*.

These and the like rightly-weighted, Alexander, albeit a scholar to Aristotle, was not amiss in that his admiration, who for his further recreation would needs adventure upon that element he admired, and accordingly went aboard his admiral then riding near Diu, and having a gentle gale quickly weighed anchor, hoist sail and launched so far that "Lands no longer do appear, / Heaven and sea being everywhere," probably twenty leagues south-west into the ocean. A great adventure for such a person and upon such an occasion, being merely to satisfy his curiosity, but the contrareity of the element having its usual effect, it soon became unpleasant to him, but more when the sky threatened a storm and the wind in a loud and churlish tone seemed to proclaim that although he had triumphed over the land and, as the poet said afterwards, that over the seas kings may assert a jurisdiction, yea, seeing *"nec tellus eadem non parit omnia,"*[1287] that by their ships they associate the remotest nations and communicate to one another whatever Nature or industry hath provided. The winds, nevertheless, are not under their subjection, but reserved to his sole dispose who as he is supreme governs all, which having acknowledged, he willingly returned ashore, finding that merry ironic proverb to be true, *"Prope aquas dulcissima est ambulatio, navigatio iuxta terrae."*[1288]

[1287] "Not every crop is grown on every soil" (Ovid, *Ars amatoria* 1. 757).
[1288] A walk near water is very pleasant—a voyage close to land.

The boundure of Alexander's march into India being in the tract obscure, I take leave also to offer my own apprehension in short concerning it. Historians, some fix his *ne plus* at the River Indus, others at the River Ganges, nor is there any that leads it further that I meet with. Now, for his penetrating India as far as Ganges, if he went so far, as no doubt he did in his desire, ofttimes saying that Caucasus and the Aemodian Mountains should be the limits of his dominion, having likewise sundry times expressed his emulation of Bacchus and Hercules, whose pillars being raised near Gibraltar and Babylon he had heard were erected further upon the eastern banks of Ganges, and for Bacchus that he pierced both *intra* and *extra* as far as China, which granted, I know not by what authority a great historian writes "*Praeter Semiramim et Alexandrum nemo Indiam intravit.*"[1289] If Ganges were the boundure, then probably his march was soon after his battle with Porus, and his nearest way as men now travel was 'twixt Lahore and Agra, where the River Jamuna at Praije streams into Ganges. But if he passed down Indus, as Arrian puts us out of doubt, then his way was to Cambay by Ahmedabad, which made it near a thousand miles ere he could attain the Aestuarium, which is not improbable, that thereby he might have a view of his navy, which, as most imagine, sailed little beyond Suwali Road or Choul, albeit the direction Alexander gave his admiral seems to infer that some of the fleet adventured as far as the Gulf of Bengal, for he commanded him to set a compass about and to leave India upon the right hand, which he could not do without doubling the promontary called Cape Camrin, as we read in Plutarch, *Vita Alexandri*, and by the relation which Onesicritus[1290] gave may be thought that he discovered Taprobane, but this inquest being to discover the extent of Alexander's march, I shall only follow that.

Pliny writes that "*Hypasis Indiae fluvius Alexandri fuit terminus;*"[1291] now, to find that river is no less difficult. I suppose it is the same which Philostratus *Vita Apollonii Tyanae* mentions in that memorable expedition Bacchus and Hercules made into those oriental countries when they were opposed by the

---

[1289] Except for Alexander and Semiramis, no-one had been to India. cf. above, 521 n. 1139.

[1290] Onesicritus of Astypalaea (see Curtius 9.10.3), who studied under the famous Diogenes the Cynic, was the chief helmsman to Alexander. He accompanied Nearchus (see above, Part I) on his voyage to the Euphrates, and wrote a book called *How Alexander was Educated*. He is cited by Diogenes Laertius and Arrian, amongst others. Heckel recommends a study of Onesicritus by T. S. Brown, *Onesicritus: A Study in Hellenistic Historiography* (Berkeley: University of California Press, 1949). See also Heckel's note in Curtius (317).

[1291] "The Hypasis (Bibassis), a river of India, was Alexander's stopping point." (Pliny, *Natural History* 6. 62). It is the Beias or Vipasa river.

Oxidracans,[1292] people inhabiting between the River Hydrastes[1293] and Ganges, being by artificial thunder and lightning forced to retreat. This most understand to be ordinance, which the Eastern world pretend to have had the knowledge of many hundred years before Swart the German Franciscan friar in his chemical experiments invented about the year 1330.[1294] Hydrastes is in my opinion no other then Hydaspes, now called Hyrotis and the same which Strabo calls *Hypanis*, "*ultra quam Alexander progredi non ausus est*," beyond which Alexander marched not, but Ptolemy in his 10 *Tab. Asiae* calls it *Bibassis* and from Imaus makes it flow into Indus under 35 degrees.[1295] And the ignorance we are in concerning the Oxidracans' country makes the quest still more dark, for that they were of India is evident, albeit some there be that place them amongst the Oxiani[1296] in Margiana, the Oxyatri in Scythia[1297] and the Oxidrancae,[1298] whom Ptolemy finds inhabiting near the Sogdian mountains in the latitude of 46 degrees. Therefore, seeing in the *Life of Alexander* that fighting against the Oxidracans from the parapet Alexander gave a "thundering leap" (as Plutarch calls it) into the town, and amongst the thickest of the enemy exposed his single person for a little time, and notwithstanding the admiration the barbarians were in of his attempt had perished, had not his men, fearless in that exigence of the greatest danger to rescue their general, taken it by storm. Though the name differ, the story does not from that already mentioned against the Mallians. Now that the Mallians, or Malli, are those we now call *Malna*, not much varying the name, 'twixt Indus and Gujarat, is apparent, which granted, then it will follow that Alexander was not so far east as Ganges, albeit Craterus, his favourite and of great command in the army, in a letter which he writ unto his mother Aristopatra then in Greece, concerning their march, reports that Alexander was advanced into India as far as Ganges,[1299] with which Lucan seems to agree, for having spoken of Ganges in *lib.* 3 [.233-234] he subjoins: "Here Alexander stopp'd, being taught to find / The world was

---

[1292] The Oxidracans were an Indian people who lived on the banks of the Ravi near Multan. See also Philostratus, *Life of Apollonius* 3. 14.

[1293] Hydrastes is an ancient name for the Ravi river; Hydaspes is the Jhelum.

[1294] Berthold Schwartz (fl. 1330), also known as Constantine Anelzin, was a Franciscan friar and alchemist born in Freiburg. He was the reputed inventor of guns and gunpowder, although some scholars doubt this attribution and suggest that he was in fact himself no more than a legendary figure.

[1295] Ptolemy links the Bibassis river with the Zaradrus as rivers "flowing from the Imaus mountains" (150–1).

[1296] A people of Sogdiana on the Oxus River.

[1297] The Oxyatri were a Bactrian tribe.

[1298] Herbert (or Ptolemy) may have confused these with the Oxiani (see above). They are not mentioned by Arrian, Curtius, Grant, or Olmstead.

[1299] Craterus (c. 370–321 B.C.E.) became Alexander's second-in-command after the death of Parmenio. He married Princess Amestris, daughter of Darius III's brother Oxyathres, and was killed in battle against Eumenes of Cardia.

larger then his boundless mind," and in the 10 *lib.* [.32-33] by like poetical authority speaking of Alexander, "'Mongst those strange floods that bloody did appear, / The Persian Phrat and Indian Ganges were," notwithstanding which, observing the course of history it appears how that after his fight with Porus he passed down Indus, where he stayed two months to refresh his men and withal to observe the ocean, but it is writ that in the other five he subdued the Brahmans' country.[1300] Now, Burma is *extra Gangem*; I answer 'tis true, at this day that place is so-named, but of old so was all that about Calicut and Narsingha, where the customs of the old Indians are as yet retained; yea, in Alexander's time the country about Cambay, Diu, Burhanpur and all the Indian coast from Indus to Cape Comorin were Brahmins or gentiles, so that Alexander, in subjecting the country about Choul and Broach may properly be said to subjugate the Brahmins' country. Besides, upon the discontent the army expressed when given out that Alexander intended for Ganges, we find that returning he was quickly in Gedrosia, which Indus washes, so that upon the whole, to me it is most likely his furthest progress was not much beyond the River Indus. The *melius inquirendum* I leave to others, and return to Alexander.

Alexander, having given his admiral instructions to surround not only Arabia but all Africa, it seems that rodomontade was more to express the greatness of his mind then to expect the possibility of so great an adventure, and by the course Nearchus steered, which was up the Persian Gulf to Basra, it appears no less, for Alexander in the meantime continuing his march came before a city which Ambiger[1301] had manned against him, and after an assault took without quarter to the defendants, for, to the greater terror of the Greeks, they had their weapons envenomed so as such as were wounded hardly escaped, and amongst others Ptolemy, who after Alexander's death was King of Egypt, was miraculously cured by virtue of an herb which Alexander dreamed he saw in the mouth of a serpent. There he laid the foundation of Barce, the last of seventy he built in that his nine years of government; there also he paid his vows and supplicated his gods that no mortal might exceed the bounds of his conquest. Also, as an everlasting monument of his fame and to amuse succeeding generations, or rather to show he was a Greek of whom 'tis said "*ex musca scire faciunt elephantem*,"[1302] he caused armours, bits and mangers to be made of an extraordinary size and height,

---

[1300] The terms are confusing here. Francesco Pinto, writing about 1545, speaks of "the King of Brama," and Mandelslo (1639) refers to "Brahmans" (*HJ* 131), the term that Herbert uses here. Both writers are referring to Burma and its people. Herbert is correct; Alexander did not get anywhere near Burma. They are not to be confused with Brahm*i*ns, who are also mentioned here.

[1301] The name Ambiger is probably derived from Justin, who calls him 'Ambus' (12.12.2) or perhaps from Orosius, where the name appears as 'Ambira' (see Heckel in Curtius 296 n. 53). The city was Harmatella (see Curtius 9.8.22).

[1302] "Out of a fly they could make an elephant" (Erasmus, *Adagia* 1.9.69).

by this artifice of representing things greater then indeed they were, albeit of admiration to simple spectators in after ages, to the ingenious nevertheless they gave just cause to have the truth and reality of his great achievements suspected, a fit requital for such a delusion. He also erected twelve great altars which he dedicated unto Hercules, such as not only attracted those in after ages to admire but to adore, and amongst others the Persian kings, who for some generations there presented their accustomed oblations, which had they been upon the banks of Ganges would have been too far for their progress, Indus being the terminus of their following empire, so that after he had (saith the historian) with a few men overcome innumerable armies and travelled to the utmost parts of the earth, to behold which was beyond the hopes of man, and extended his dominions from India to Ethiopia and Libya, from Danube to the Indian Ocean and from the Ionic Sea to Tanais, which soon after was subdivided into thirty great kingdoms, again with a sigh bidding farewell to India and the ocean he advanced into the country of the Orytes, where the penury he encountered was compensated with that plenty he after found in Gedrosia, whence also marching along the coast near the city of Arbis under the Tropic of Cancer he met his recruits, not a little to the rejoicing of his wellnigh-spent army.

But again, forgetting the sad event of his former luxuriance, he fell afresh to the frantic solemnisation of the feast of Bacchus, soon after at Thapsacus viewed his new fleet and took some recreation again at sea. But that tradition of coasting about the south of Arabia and landing at Socotra is of little credit, after which he removed his camp to a convenient place for pitching his rich and glorious tent, wherein he intended to give audience to an hundred ambassadors who with noble presents were come from the remotest parts of India on this and on the other side Ganges to congratulate his victories and to crave his alliance, by the earth and water some of them brought implying, at least as Alexander fancied, a total subjection. These strangers he entertained, and after audience, seated most magnificently upon an hundred beds of burnished gold, at which time he also presented each of them with plate suitable to his greatness, but their astonishment. Which done, he marched through Carmania to Lar and thence to Pasagardae, where Orsines, a Prince of the blood royal of Persia, was lamentably destroyed at Alexander's crediting Bagoas,[1303] a eunuch that mortally hated him. The accusation was that he had violated Cyrus his tomb, in which was no wealth as informed but a sword and bow; howbeit, upon further examination the farud being discovered, the eunuch had the like reward and his house and furniture were

---

[1303] Bagoas (d. 323 B.C.E.) is not the same man who poisoned Artaxerxes III and Arses and helped Darius III get the throne. This eunuch was a friend of Nabarzanes, one of the plotters against Darius, and saved his life by intervening with Alexander, over whom he came to have considerable influence.

given Perdiccas, estimated at six hundred thousand crowns.[1304] There Kalyana the Brahmin, in contempt of death and to show that life is but *somnium umbrae brevissimum*[1305] built his funeral pile, predicted Alexander's death in Babylon, and taking a solemn farewell of his acquaintance in the camp, according to the Indian mode burned himself to ashes.

Alexander after that returned to Susa and married Statira the Persian Princess, whose sister he then gave to his dear Hephaestion and so other Persian ladies to as many great officers of his army, for the greater magnificence of which marriages he prepared a most ample and royal feast for nine thousand guests, to each of which he gave a cup of gold to use in their sacrifices, and as a more abundant testimony of his love to the army as well as to express his own greatness he also discharged out of his own treasurty the debt which his Macedonian soldiers had contracted, which amounted to nine thousand and seventy talents, being in ours five hundred millions and seven hundred thousand crowns, and easy for Alexander to spare; at his death, which soon after happened, being found coffered up at Babylon an hundred thousand talents, as Justin reports, in ready coin, which some others double, and his revenue at that time being three hundred thousand talents *per annum*. Nevertheless, having some apprehensions of fear in going to Babylon, for sundry prophecies were rumoured that he should die there, he turned with his army towards the north and came to Ecbatana, where his favourite Hephaestion, notwithstanding his physician's utmost care, died of a fever, whose death Alexander so passionately bewailed as Justin taxes him that "*contra decus regum diu luxit.*"[1306] But for the greater solemnity, for seven days a general howling, in which the *praeficae*[1307] expressed their art sufficiently, was made; all the horses in the army were shorn, the battlements and walls of houses thrown down, instruments of music put under silence as not the least noise appeared, yea, to compliment the conqueror the sacred fires in each *pyreae* were by the Surena extinguished. A monument lastly was erected upon which was expended twelve thousand talents, which is seven millions of crowns, and having offered up his afflicted doctor as a sacrifice, for which Alexander is worthily reproved, the altars were made to smoke with incense and the dead corpse worshipped as a deity, the highest honour he could ascend to.

[1304] Prince Orsines (d. 323 B.C.E.) was a direct descendant of Cyrus who served as Darius III's commander at Gaugamela. Arrian states that he made himself satrap of Persia without first clearing it with Alexander (6.29.2). The account of Bagoas poisoning him is in Curtius; Bagoas was furious because Orsines had presented many splendid gifts to Alexander but not to him, which is why he poisoned Orsines after falsely accusing him of stealing gold from the tomb. For details, see Curtius 10.1.24–38.

[1305] A very brief dream of illusion.

[1306] He mourned a long time, which was not in keeping with the dignity of kings (Justin 12.12).

[1307] Female mourners.

Alexander dies at Babylon.

Now whiles the obsequies were in hand, Alexander had notice that the ambassadors attended him at Babylon, not only from Carthage and other African parts but also from several kings and states in Europe, namely Spain, Sicily, France, Sardinia and most parts of Italy, Rome excepted, which though but growing to what is aspired of, yet being four hundred years old from the foundation laid by Romulus[1308] was then so great that Plutarch reports it could send out an hundred and thirty thousand warlike citizens. These came to congratulate his success in the East, to divert his journey west and to crave his alliance, yea, being become so terrible to the world as all nations courted and seemed to acknowledge him their sovereign. Then was accomplished that prodigy of those two eagles observed to light upon the highest pinnacle of the court of Pallas that whole day on which Alexander was born, and as others, "*universarum terrarum imperium infanti portendebant,*" the infant conquest of the universe.

The access of those extraordinary ambassadors from the furthest occidental parts (I may so say, seeing the Morini[1309] in Picardy are by Lucan called *extremi hominum*),[1310] these, or rather his inevitable fate, accelerated Alexander's remove to Babylon, which being near, the Chaldaean magicians interposed and prevailed with him to turn aside for some time to Birsa beyond Euphrates, whence by Anaxarchus the philosopher, who derided their arts, he was induced to return to Babylon, though not without some bad omens at his entrance, which nevertheless was as splendid as art and cost could invent. After audience given, summons issued for the holding of a parliament of no less then the whole world and entertainments as sumptuous as luxury in the highest degree could set forth then took place, during which this great conqueror died, "*qui,*" as Justin relates, "*cum nullo hostium unquam congressus est quem non vicerit; nullam urbem quam non expugnaverit, nullam gentem adiit quam non calcaverit, denique florea aetatis suae ac victoriarum non virtute hostili sed fraude et suorum insidiis ereptus est.*"[1311] His death was not without suspicion of poison given him by Cassander[1312] his cup-bearer

---

[1308] The traditional date for the foundation of Rome by Romulus is given as 753 B.C.E.

[1309] The Morini were an ancient Belgic tribe living in the area of modern Boulogne and Calais.

[1310] Herbert is mistaken; the quote is found in Virgil, *Aeneid* 8. 727.

[1311] "Who, while he met with no enemy that he did not defeat, no city that he did not capture, no people he encountered that he did not subdue, was undermined in the flower of his age and victories not by the courage of enemies, but stealthily by trickery and the plotting of his own people" (Justin 1. 16).

[1312] Cassander was the son of Antipater, the Regent. There is no real evidence that he poisoned Alexander. He was passed over as Regent in favour of Polyperchon, but he later ruled as King of Macedon 305–297, after a brief interregnum at the death of Alexander IV.

and not without the treasonable directions of [Cassander's] father Antipater, who with the son afterwards prosecuted their cruelty even to the utter extirpation of all Alexander's royal progeny. Such was the exit of this great Prince, in the three and thirtieth year of his age and twelfth of his reign, whom living one world would not suffice, but dead a grave contained, as Lucan *lib*. 10:

> That check alone,
> Nature gave this king's wild ambition
> Who to his grave the world's sole empire bore
> With that same envy it was got before,
> And wanting heirs, left all he did obtain
> To be divided by the sword again.

For so soon as his body was conveyed by Ptolemy Soter to Alexandria in Egypt, where with all due solemnity it was interred, the corpse being so well-embalmed that the two first Caesars, at their being there two hundred and fifty years after his death opening his tomb found him perfect and incorrupt.[1313] The disposition of his Empire to the worthiest seemed to revive the bones of Pyrrha afresh, for ambition and self-opinion so inflamed those great and emulous captains, by that word each supposing himself pointed at and principally concerned that "*virtus mihi numen et ensis / quem teneo*"[1314] was, as may be thought, each man's motto, for as albeit the crown was by suffrage of the army given to Arrhidaeus,[1315] natural brother to Alexander, and Perdiccas[1316] assigned his governor, both were soon after slain, the first by Olympias,[1317] the last by Ptolemy. The Empire nevertheless was piecemeal rent asunder, and albeit sufficient to satiate their ambition, by the sword was nevertheless in a short time reduced under four, of which Seleucus was one that grasped the Syrian sceptre and made Persia a subordinate province of his own Empire.

[1313] For details of Alexander's death and what modern scholarship has to say about it, see Chugg, *Lost Tomb*, 1–33.

[1314] "Valour, and the sword / Here in my hand" (Statius, *Thebaid* 3. 615).

[1315] Philip III Arrhidaeus reigned 323–317. He was the son of Philip II by Philinna of Larissa, a concubine, and thus half-brother to Alexander.

[1316] Perdiccas (d. 321 B.C.E.), one of Alexander's generals, was regent of Macedon after the death of Alexander. He was killed during an attack against Ptolemy I of Engypt.

[1317] Olympias of Epirus (c. 376–316 B.C.E.) was the fourth wife of Philip II. She murdered Philip III so that her grandson Alexander IV (r. 317–309) could become king; her other victims included Caranus, another son of Philip II, Cleopatra Eurydice, the last wife of Philip II, and Caranus's sister. She tried to ensure that Cassander never came to the throne, but he defeated her forces and had her executed by his agents.

Beginning of the Parthian Empire.

Thirty years was Persia held under that subjection, notwithstanding the discontent of the Persian nobility, until Theodatus,[1318] Governor of Bactria, which was then entitled "a kingdom having a thousand cities," by the advantage he had through distance from Syria and the engagement that crown was in against the Lesser Asia, he revolted and took upon him the supreme title, by whose example the rest of the Orient threw off the Macedonian yoke and elected to themselves kings being natives of their own country, amongst whom Arsaces, one of an obscure birth as his name partly implies, *Ar-Saces* or *Sacan*, i.e. Scythian, but sufficiently famous for his active life though ill-employed, for with a crew of profligate associates he commanded the hills and extorted tribute from caravans and passengers, observing what Theodatus had done and being well-instructed with the discontents Persia was in, but principally moved with ambition, suddenly enters those countries in hostile manner, defeats Andragoras the Lieutenant of that province, overruns Hyrcania, and upon Theodatus his death enters into confederacy with the young King, so as by that supply he lent he dared to affront Seleucus surnamed Callimachus in the field, and having after a sore fight obtained a clear victory, utterly abolished the Syrian government in those parts and thereupon arrogated to himself the name of conqueror, yea, in memory of that victory commanded that day to be annually observed with solemnity. By this acquisition, which was *Anno Mundi* 3718, he invited the Scythians to share in his good fortune, and by that elevation the country was new-named Parthia, which signifies 'exiles' in the Scythic tongue, Justin *lib.* 41, people who during the monarchy of the Assyrians and Medes were the least-known throughout the Orient, but by this change the Persians were nevertheless kept under subjection.[1319]

Arsaces enlarged the bounds of his dominion wellnight from Euphrates to Indua, living so highly-honoured by his subjects that Cyrus was not in greater esteem with the Persians, Ptolemy with the Egyptians nor Romulus with the Romans then this Arsaces with the Parthians. Arsaces was he that built Dara,

---

[1318] Diodotus I, whom Justin calls Theodatus (41.4.5), rebelled against Antiochus II of Syria in about 255 B.C.E. He ruled as the founder-king of Bactria c. 255–238.

[1319] Malcolm Colledge states that "the two early accounts of Strabo and Trogus (in Justin's epitome) are . . . credible" (*Parthians*, 25). It appears that Andragoras, the Seleucid satrap of Parthia, himself revolted in 245 B.C.E., and Diodotus II of Bactria (238–228), son of Diodotus I, followed. Seleucus II was defeated by "Celtic invaders" (Colledge, *Parthians*, 25) at the battle of Ancyra in 238, at which point Arsaces allied himself with Diodotus II (Herbert's "young king") attacked Andragoras and overran Parthia. Arsaces [*Arshak* in Parthian] himself was the ruler of the Parni from about 250, and within three years had made himself into Arsaces I, King of Parthia. He reigned until 211 B.C.E.

since called Aspadara,[1320] after that Isfahan. The ninth from him called Orodes had the honour to give the Roman general Crassus a memorable defeat at Carrhae in Africa, and Phraates his successor forced Marcus Antonius with loss sufficient to retreat over Araxes into Syria, albeit Ventidius his lieutenant two years after redeemed his credit, Pacorus the Prince being slain and the country reduced, had not Antony, envying his glory, recalled him thence. Nevertheless, of such terror was the Roman name by that defeat that then and not till then they acknowledged subordination to Caesar Augustus, who having deposed the parricide elected another Phraates[1321] in his room. At this time was echoed *"pacem te poscimus omnes,"*[1322] the Prince of Peace our Saviour Christ then taking flesh of the Virgin Mary and for some time dwelling amongst the sons of sinful men.

To Phraates succeeded Orodes, whom some call Doridaeus; him, Vonones, to whom Tiridates the last of the Arsacidae, slain by Artabanus whom the Persians call *Arda-Bahman*, twelve of whose blood successively swayed the Parthian sceptre after each other until the last, bearing the same name as the first, was treacherously slain by Caracalla the Roman Emperor, Septimius Severus his son, who to the ignominy of the Roman majesty, after he had perfidiously slain most of the Alexandrian youth, also, under pretence of marriage with a daughter of the Parthian king, *contra fidem datam*[1323] massacred the King and such of the Parthian nobility as attended him for the consummation of the wedding union, which breach of faith so highly incensed the Parthians that they maintained a gallant and desperate fight against the Romans, nor could be reconciled till they understood how that Macrinus[1324] the general had revenged their quarrel upon Caracalla's person. Nevertheless, they were so out of heart by those several losses that Artaxerxes,[1325] an active and valiant Persian, observing the opportunity to recover their freedom (to all dominions the Almighty having set a period), in

---

[1320] Dara is now thought to be near the modern town of Abivard, "but the site was found to be unsuitable and for the next capital the town of Hecatompylus was chosen" (Colledge, *Parthians*, 67).

[1321] Phraates V, also known as Phraataces, reigned 2 B.C.E.–4 C.E. Herbert is wrong about him; he was placed on the throne by his mother Queen Musa, who poisoned Phraates IV and then married her own son. Augustus sent Gaius Caesar to restore order, and "Phraataces and Gaius were able to settle the matter amicably in the Roman favour" (Colledge, *Parthians*, 47).

[1322] The full quote runs: *"Nulla salus bello; pacem te poscimus omnes"* (Virgil, *Aeneid* 11. 360), "There is no salvation in war; we all seek peace from you."

[1323] "Against [his] pledged word" (Paulus Diaconus, *Historia Romanorum* 5. 8).

[1324] M. Opelius Severus Macrinus, Roman Emperor 217–18, "purchased peace for a huge sum" because the Parthians were winning battles in Mesopotamia (Colledge, *Parthians*, 171–72). He did not revenge the death of any Parthians.

[1325] Artaxerxes, usually known as Ardashir, revolted against Artabanus V in 220, and the rebellion grew to include other subject peoples. Artabanus was defeated in 224 (or 226) and killed, and Ardashir I was crowned king of the new Sassanian dynasty of

order thereto this Persian suddenly headed a considerable party by whose courage abundantly expressed by three days' fight he broke their yoke asunder and once more restored freedom to the Persian, *Anno Dom.* 230, after near six hundred years subjection under the Greeks and Parthians.[1326]

Valerian the Emperor embased.

Macrinus, enjoying the purple robe but one year, was succeeded by that monster Heliogabalus, who after three years more gave place to Alexander Severus that was buried at York.[1327] Artaxerxes, whom the Persians call Ardashir, i.e. 'father and lord in war,' was no sooner invested in the Persian throne but taking a retrospect of the ancient greatness of that Empire, upon much of which the Romans had encroached, by his ambassador he demanded restitution, to answer which Severus with a considerable army advances towards Persia, and having divided his body into three, the part he led himself was so weakened by that distribution that the Persians, by continual alarms having broken that which marched into Media, the second part was put into a panic fear, so as the Emperor, *re infecta*,[1328] retreated, and though little blood was spilt, yet helped it to heighten then the Persian spirit and reputation so as Valerianus about twenty-five years after, during which seven emperors intervened, marched thitherward in hopes (hearing that Artaxerxes was dead) he should succeed better then his predecessor Severus had done, but fell out much worse, for Sapor the Persian King beat the Roman army and took Valerian surnamed Colobus[1329] prisoner, whom to his dying day he made his footstool, a greater contempt having never formerly been expressed

---

Persia, whilst Vologaeses VI and Artavasdes, the son of Artabanus V, kept fighting for another two years.

[1326] Orodes III (4–7 C.E.) was murdered, and to avoid anarchy the Parthians requested Augustus to send them one of the sons of Phraates IV. This was Vonones I (7–12), who was defeated by Artabanus, king of Media Atropene, who succeeded as Artabanus III and reigned until 38. Caracalla (M. Antoninus) was Roman Emperor 211–217; at this time there were two joint Parthian kings, Vologaeses VI (c. 207–27) and Artabanus V (213–24/26), who actually *refused* to give his daughter to Caracalla, which led to a Roman invasion and a Parthian counter-attack after the death of Caracalla. The story Herbert tells about the massacre is untrue. For a complete list and genealogy of Parthian rulers, see Colledge, *Parthians*, 179.

[1327] Untrue. Alexander Severus was murdered at Sicula, the modern town of Sicklingen near Mainz, Germany; his mausoleum in Rome was on the Via Latina. The only Roman Emperor reputed to be buried at York is Constantius I Chlorus (d. 306), father of Constantine the Great.

[1328] The business being unfinished.

[1329] The term *colobus* is derived from Greek, and means 'short' or 'mutilated.'

to the Roman chief.[1330] But this judgment some impute to his severity against the Christians, whom he cruelly persecuted, and for his inhuman broiling that blessed martyr St. Lawrence[1331] to death, which Eusebius in his ecclesiastical story at length mentions.

Gallienus[1332] succeeded Valerian, but so bad was the other's entertainment that albeit Sapores survived four other of the Roman emperors he had no further molestation from any of them, which gave him the more leisure to exercise his tyranny at home, but *Anno Domini* 272, Death giving him a *supersedeas*, he bade the world an unwilling farewell after twenty years' rule during which he had exceedingly disturbed the world, having with his army walled in Syria, Cilicia, Mesopotamia, Cappadocia, and returning, amongst his trophies had intermixed many curses for his cruelties, which too had been requited had not the Roman general been treacherously made away by Philip,[1333] an Arabian renegado, during his siege afore Ctesiphon, once the seat-royal of the Arsacidae. Howbeit, Trebellius in *Gallicanus* affirms that Sapores was slain by Odenathus[1334] the Palmyrian king, Divine Justice so directing, in the same place where Gordianus[1335] was murdered.

Hormisdas[1336] reigned after Sapores; the Persians call him Kirmanshah, who ruled thirteen months, and after him Varanes three years.[1337] Narses[1338]

[1330] Ardashir I reigned 226–41. Valerian invaded Persian territory in 258, when Sapor (Shapur I) had been reigning for seventeen years. Shapur reigned until 272.

[1331] St. Lawrence (d. 258), a Christian deacon, was put to death in Rome, the story goes, "by being roasted on a grid" (Attwater, *Dictionary*, 209), and Valerian's defeat was seen by Christians as retribution for this gruesome martyrdom, although Eusebius and others actually blame Macrianus, the Prefect of the Guard, for turning Valerian against them. Eusebius, in his account of Valerian's persecutions, does not mention St. Lawrence (for the full account, see Eusebius 7.10–11).

[1332] P. Licinius Egnatius Gallienus, the eldest son of Valerian, was sole emperor 260–68. He had been associated with his father from 253. He was too busy dealing with usurpers to have any time for the Persians.

[1333] Philip the Arabian (M. Aurelius Philippus) reigned 244–49. He probably did not murder his predecessor, although there were rumours and accusations, due to the fact that Philip did not prove a popular emperor.

[1334] Publius Septimius Odenathus was king of Palmyra c. 258–67/68. He fought the Persians as an ally of Rome, and twice besieged Ctesiphon. He was Emperor of the East in all but name, and shared triumphs with Gallienus.

[1335] Gordian III (M. Antonius Gordianus) reigned 238–44. His army was victorious over the Persians at Retaena (243) but may have suffered defeat at Misiche, now the modern city of Fallujah in Iraq, although Roman accounts do not mention this. Trebellius's account in the *Historia Augustae* states that Philip claimed that Gordian had died of a fever (31.2), but historians are doubtful about the exact cause of his death.

[1336] Hormizd [*Hormisdas*] I reigned 272–73.

[1337] Bahram (Varahran) I reigned 273–76.

[1338] Narses (Persian *Narseh*), uncle of Bahram III, reigned 293–302. Herbert is confused about dates here and mixes up Bahram II (276–93) with Bahram III, who reigned

(Yazdegerd, say the Persians) followed him, who after sixteen years left the crown to his son Varanes II, surnamed Saganshah; the Persians call him Bahram. He, after a few months, gave Narses, albeit an alien, leave to succeed. This Narses with all possible rage prosecuted the war against the Armenians and Mesopotamians, in whose aid Galerius[1339] the Roman general fought with bad success at first, yet trying the second bout was victor, which so disanimated Narses that in the height of despair and impatience he burned himself after eight years of government. Mizdates[1340] reigned seven years after him, after whom came Shapores[1341] or King Porus, by Teixeira called *Shahur*, by Schickard *Xabul Xabulketaph* (in Spanish authors the *x* is sounded as our *sh*), to the Romans a restless adversary, to the Persians tyrannical and to the Christians most malicious. This is he that was acknowledged sovereign before he was born, the crown being at adventure set upon his mother's belly before she was delivered. Julian the Apostate raged not more against the Christians in the Lesser Asia then Sapores did at the same time against them in the Great, the Jews aggravating the King by persuading him that the Christians were unalterable in their loyalty to the Romans, so as in ten years from the year 337 to 347 he massacred above thirty thousand Christians, as Metaphrastus[1342] reports, it being the practice of those primitive Christians in all the time of their persecution to oppose the word of those under whose

---

for a few months in 293 and who technically was only King of the Sakas in Eastern Iran, hence his name "Saganshah." Yarshater states that "the fate of . . . Bahram III is not known" (1.129). Narseh invaded Armenia and Mespotamia (*Cambridge History of Iran*, vol. 3.1–2 [Cambridge: Cambridge University Press, 1986], 1.294) and defeated Galerius at Callinicum. The Romans came back in 297 and Galerius was victorious, as Herbert states. Narseh sued for peace, which he obtained, but on terms favourable to the Romans. He did not burn himself, but abdicated in 302. For his reign see Yarshater, *History* 3. 1, 129–31.

[1339] Galerius was Roman emperor 293–311. An able and experienced general, he was made Caesar in 293 by Emperor Diocletian (285–305) and persecuted Christians. When Diocletian abdicated he became Emperor.

[1340] Hormizd II reigned 302–09, "a hard and strong man who none the less was well-liked" (Yarshater, *History* 1, 131).

[1341] Shapur II reigned 309–79, one of the longest reigns of any ancient monarch. Herbert's account of his wars with Rome and his cruelty towards the Christians is largely accurate. The story about the crown on his mother's belly appears to be quite true. For his reign see Yarshater, *History*, 1.132–40. The identification with Porus (see above 000) is erroneous; this name was never used for Shapur. The usual Western version of the name is "Sapor."

[1342] Simeon 'Metaphrastes' (fl. c. 960) was a Byzantine chronicler and hagiographer, also known as Simeon Logothetes. The name used by Herbert means 'the worker-over,' which refers to his habit of adjusting his accounts of saints' lives to suit his times. He is chiefly-known for the *Menologion*, a work on saints compiled, it was said, on the order of Emperor Constantine VII. See *ODB* 3: 1983–84.

jurisdiction they lived with evangelical fortitude and vanquishing patience, the Church's arms being no other then prayers and tears, and of sufficient advantage against the enemy, reaching no less way then into Heaven, yea, graciously submitting their cause to the good pleasure of God, albeit in his dispensation and as a symptom of his displeasure his strokes are as to human apprehension towards all sorts of men undistinguishable, as with an equal hand afflicting the innocent with the nocent, but with several operations. In those days the Oriental parts for the greater part embraced Christ, and in Sozomen[1343] you have the particulars.

Julian the Apostate's sad end.

Julian not only out of cruelty to Christ's flock but in ambition invading his territories, under the walls of Ctesiphon was mortally wounded by an invisible hand, a judgment of that astonishment and conviction that with horror of mind throwing his blood into the air, he expired with this despairing exclamation, "*Tandem vicisti, Galilee!*" and Jovian, who then commanded the field, with the joyful acclamation "*Omnes sumus Christiani!*" was saluted Emperor in his place, for "in those times it was an ingenious thing to be a Christian," saith a good author, whose attempts proving of little force against the Persian, in his return towards Constantinople to the inexpressible sorrow of the army he was arrested by grim death after he had been but eight months Emperor.[1344]

[More Sassanid rulers].

About this time Shapur, also being at *Mopsierive*, a town under Mount Taurus, sighed out his affrighted ghost at the age and reign of seventy-one, *Anno Domini* 379, leaving Artaxerxes[1345] his brother to rule after him, who in the eleventh year

---

[1343] Salminius Hermias Sozomenus (c. 400–455) was an ecclesiastical historian from Gaza. His surviving work, the *Historia ecclesiastica* (c. 440), traces church history from Constantine I to the accession of Valentinian III (425). It was first edited by Estienne (1544), and John Christopherson, bishop of Chichester, edited it in 1612.

[1344] Julian (361–63) led his army into Persia and attacked Ctesiphon. Accounts vary as to who had the advantage, but since the Emperor was mortally wounded it hardly mattered. His exclamation "You have won at last, O Galilean" is probably wishful thinking on the part of Christian historians, as is the joyful shout "Now we're all Christians!" at Jovian's accession. Flavius Claudius Jovianus (363–64), a Christian, succeeded him, and proceeded to make peace with Shapur in order to get the Romans out of Persia while they could still go. Jovian is revered for having issued the Universal Declaration of Toleration (364), which effectively returned the Roman Empire to the Christian fold. He is said to have died of suffocation from an overheated brazier in his tent.

[1345] The dates of these Sassanid rulers, which Herbert gets wrong, are as follows. Ardashir II (379–83) who was not Shapur's brother, unless he was "very elderly" (Yarshater, *History*, 1:140); Shapur III (383–88) was a son of Shapur II, "mild and well-disposed

of his reign gave this world a farewell. Shapur after five years followed him in
that inevitable path, Varanes after him ten, Yazdegerd, a constant friend unto the
Romans, succeeding him, who, as Socrates Scholasticus reports, was converted
by Marutha,[1346] Bishop of Mesopotamia, sent into Persia to that end by Pope Innocent and Theodosius the Emperor,[1347] by whose persuasion he destroyed the
pyree or idol-temple and extinguished that fire which for many preceding generations had by those gentiles been heathenishly worshipped. The Persian stories
give out that he apostasised, but who can tell the truth? However, this is certain,
that in the twentieth year of his reign, *Anno Domini* 420, he died, and Varanes
V,[1348] or Bahram as the Persians term him, inherited his royalties. By some this
Prince is taxed for his perfidy and cruelty, especially against the Christians, in
whose defence Theodosius sent Anatolius with a gallant army. Varanes, diffid-
ing in his own, requests aid from Alamandurus[1349] an Arabian Saracen, whose
armies, when they met, were so numerous that they covered the earth for many
miles. At Babylon was their rendezvous, but ere the battle began such a panic
fear struck the pagans that they fled amazedly; by land some perished, but more
by water, for Euphrates without pity engulfed an hundred thousand of those
miscreants, and by that loss the Persian king was heartbroken, seeing a hand of

towards the nobility" (*History*, 1:141); Bahram IV (388–99), probably the son of Shapur
III, was "vulgar and neglectful" according to the historian al-Isfahani (Yarshater, *History*,
1:142–43) and Yazdegerd I (399–420), whose alleged persecution of Zoroastrians, here
praised by Herbert, as well as his friendliness towards Christians, is, Yarshater states, be-
lied by "many of the acts of Christian martyrs" in his reign (1:143), although he stopped
persecutions through the good offices of Bishop Marutha (see below). As for his "apostasy," Ferdowsi dubbed him "Yazdegerd the Unjust" (*Shahnameh*, 601–21).

[1346] Marutha (d. c. 420) was Bishop of Maiferqat, or, as some scholars state, Tagrit
(modern Tikrit). As Herbert states, he was sent to Persia by Emperor Theodosius II and
won the esteem of Yazdegerd I. In addition to commentaries on the Gospels, Marutha
wrote the *Acts of the Persian Martyrs* as well as compiling a Syrian liturgy and compos-
ing hymns.

[1347] Theodosius II was Eastern (Byzantine) emperor 408–50. Pope Innocent I
reigned 401–17.

[1348] Bahram V (420–40) was surnamed *Gur*, 'the wild ass,' from his hunting skills.
Herbert has Bahram IV, which is wrong, and after this his dates are wildly inaccurate.
He did persecute Christians, but after Theodosius II refused to extradite some who had
fled Persia he became more reasonable (Yarshater, *History*, 1:145). Ferdowsi wrote that
"Once Bahram was established in his reign / Grief fled, and pleasure flourished once
again" (*Shahnameh*, 622).

[1349] Al-Mundhir I (431–72) was the Lakhmid king of Al-Kufah in Southern Iraq.
He is mentioned by John Donne as being a convert famous for resisting the Eutychian
heresy, which, Donne explained, meant believing "that the divine nature in Christ, the
Godhead, suffered as well as the human" (Sermon XXII). He invaded Arabia and sup-
ported Bahram V, as Herbert states. See I. Shahîd, *Byzantium and the Arabs in the Fifth
Century* (Washington, DC: Dumbarton Oaks, 1989).

divine vengeance outstretched against him, so that he made his exit after twenty years, and another Varanes succeeded in his stead.[1350] This Prince made truce with Marcianus[1351] the Emperor and died in the fourteenth year of his reign.

Peroz succeeded him, called Firoz by the Persians, a Prince more rash then valiant; in the twentieth year of his reign the wars of Scythia made an end of him. Valens, or *Belax* and *Jalas* as some say, was then chosen king, after him Cabades, called also *Kobad*, who was deposed by Zamasp in the eleventh year of his greatness, which Zamasp was also deposed by the nobles of Persia in the fourth year of his reign for that he had published a brutish edict that women should be used in common, and Cabades was re-established in the throne again, but at last, through his too much lenity and indulgence to his brother he was unexpectedly made blind and the tyrant restored again.[1352]

At this time great wars were commenced 'twixt the Romans and Persians, Kavadh the Persian storming extremely that by their means his potent neighbour and ally Tsathes, son to Gubaz king of the Lazars,[1353] a part of Colchis, had received baptism at Constantinople, the Emperor Justinian as godfather witnessing for Tsathes at the font and most of the nobility of Asia honouring the

---

[1350] Herbert is mistaken here. Bahram V was succeeded by Yazdegerd II (440–57), who renewed the war against the Byzantine Empire, but once again Anatolius negotiated a peace with the Persians (Yarshater, *History*, 1:146).

[1351] Flavius Marcianus was emperor of the East 450–57. He is famed for his benevolent rule and defiance of Attila the Hun and for convening the Council of Chalcedon. By the time Anatolius got to Persia, he had succeeded Theodosius II.

[1352] This account also is not very accurate. Yazdegerd II was succeeded by his son Hormizd III (457–58), but he was deposed by his brother Peroz I (458–84), who was defeated and imprisoned by the Hephthalites, a Bactrian people (469). After his captivity he had to contend with the Armenians, but in 482 the Hephthalites again defeated Peroz and killed him two years later. His next brother, Balash (484–88), made peace with both the Hephthalites and the Armenians, but was deposed and replaced by Kavadh I [*Cabades*] (488–96, first reign), son of Peroz, himself deposed and confined by a conspiracy of nobles because he had become a Mazdakite, which was a Zoroastrian heretic sect. His final brother Zahmasp [*Lambases*] (496–99) replaced him, but Kavadh escaped from prison to the Hephthalites, who helped him get his throne back. Yarshater and other historians do not mention Zahmasp's repressive edict against women. This time, Kavadh remained on his throne until 531. For details see Yarshater, *History*, 1:147–52.

[1353] The Lazars, as Herbert calls them, were the people of Lazica or Egrisi, a West Georgian kingdom in the South Caucasus, a Byzantine vassal state sometimes occupied by the Persians. Gubaz II [*Gurgenus*] reigned c. 539–54; he requested Persian help against the Byzantines (541) and then turned against the Persians (548), whom he expelled some years later with Byzantine assistance (551). His new allies betrayed and killed him (554), although it should be noted that Justinian had the killers executed. Tsathes [*Zotus*] was not Gubaz's son, but his brother. For details, see D. Braund, *Georgia in Antiquity: A History of Colchis and Transcaucasian Iberia 550 B.C.–A.D. 562.* (Oxford: Oxford University Press, 1994).

solemnity, so that after this Persian tyrant had gorged himself with the slaughter of many thousands of the Lazars and Armenians, Death summoned him to an unwilling accompt after thirty years' reign, and Khusrau his son (they call him *Chezir-buzurgh* or 'great,' *Anushirvan* Teixeira and *Nasir-avan* the Arabs) was with accustomed solenity crowned King. About this time the Roman monarchy in the West took end.[1354]

The Cruelty of Khusrau.

Of all the tyrants that ever were in Persia this Khusrau was the most wicked, for first, albeit he had concluded a peace for an hundred and ten years with Justinian the Roman Emperor, he quickly broke it and to the utmost exasperated him. 'Twould be endless to speak his restless motion, his barbarism, his hypocrisy; take a few for many. In mere malice he first put to death his brother Balash and then Aspebides his aged uncle, which the people murmured at, but to provoke them the more he commands them to follow him into Syria, where he desperately engaged them in a desperate war against the Palmyreans, by whom under Zenobia's conduct they were soundly beaten, in revenge whereof he plundered Barbosa, Antioch, Seleucia, Apamea and other parts thereabouts.[1355] In Phoenicia also he enacts more mischief; there he violently forced Euphemia, a Christian lady, and of her begot Hormizd, who succeeded him.[1356] He also compelled the chaste nymphs of Daphne to offer incense to him as a deity, which they excused by fearing he would have ravished them. He then consumed the stately temple dedicated to St. Michael the Archangel, accounting it no sacrilege to rob other

---

[1354] Khusrau I Anushirvan reigned 531–79. His name actually means 'of immortal soul' (Yarshater, *History*, 1.153). Far from the tyrant described here, he was an enlightened ruler, "the most illustrious of the Sassanian rulers," Yarshater states, "comparable to Shah Abbas in Safavid times" (*History*, 1.152). Furthermore, in regard to Khusrau's religious policy, he notes that "we hear of no systematic persecutions during his reign, although some of his underlings at times showed a too-zealous attitude in regard to minority faiths" (1:161). Ferdowsi says that he "ruled with justice and glory, and . . . became renowned for his righteousness and generosity" (*Shahnameh* 684). Why Herbert places the end of the "Western Roman monarchy" in his time I do not know; Romulus Augustulus, the last Roman Emperor, had abdicated in 476.

[1355] Khusrau did indeed invade Syria and invest Antioch, which he took and plundered (540). In 541 the Persians captured Petra (not Palmyra) and other Byzantine cities. Again, Herbert's historical senses seem to have left him, as Zenobia, Queen of Palmyra, was defeated by the Emperor Aurelian in 273. Khusrau was held up at Edessa and forced eventually to pull back (Yarshater, *History*, 1:155–56). Herbert places this event, too, in the wrong chronological order (see below).

[1356] Not true. Hormizd IV (see below) "was the son of a Turkish Princess who had been given in marriage to cement good relations between the two states" (Yarshater, *History*, 1:162). There is no evidence for Herbert's claim about Euphemia.

churches. After this he besieged Sergiropolis, but being forced thence with dis-honour he attempts the spoil of Jerusalem, yet hearing that Belisarius[1357] (in his time the most rich and after the poorest of men) was approaching, to avoid that storm he renews his league with the Romans, never purposing to keep it, for next year with a great force of horse he ravages Armenia and then Phoenicia, where he killed Narses *Anno Domini* 556,[1358] in requital whereof Justin[1359] the Roman Emperor enters Mingrelia and by the death of Nachorages the Persian general obtains a victory. Nevertheless, restless Khusrau next year assaults Edessa, but fruitlessly, for at Sagaribon the Christians vanquished him. *Anno Domini* 547 he commands Adharmahan[1360] with a very great army to invade the Lesser Asia, which accordingly they did, and unpeopling Antioch, into Iberia also and Ar-menia they entered with no less voracity, but by the Armenians were forced to a shameful retreat.[1361]

First conversion of the Armenians.

At this time the Armenians received the Christian faith and the Romans about the same time received complaints from the Christians of Khusrau's cruelty. Jus-tin the Emperor sends Tiberius[1362] (elected Caesar) to relieve them; his army was great and consisted of many several nations, as French, Italians, Poenians, Illyrians, Mysians, Isaurians etc. Towards Armenia he marched to meet with

---

[1357] Flavius Belisarius (c. 505–565), a famous general under Justinian, was fighting Persia in the south, but had been recalled and sent to Italy by 542. Khusrau's forces de-feated the Byzantines the next year, but were stopped at Edessa (see above). Belisarius is best-known for his victories against the Vandals (534), his capture of Rome and defeat of the Ostrogoths (536), and his campaign against the Bulgarians (559).

[1358] Narses (478–573), an Armenian eunuch who became a distinguished general under Justinian, was nowhere near Persia in 556. He commanded the Byzantines against the Ostrogoths (552), defeated the Alemanni and Franks (554), and then served as Gov-ernor of Italy until 565. He continued to work well into his nineties. He is not to be con-fused with the Narses who led the armies of the emperor Maurice or the Persian king of that name.

[1359] Justin II reigned 565–78. He invaded Persian territory after an Armenian revolt and besieged Nisibis (572), which he failed to take and had to retreat, later being forced to make peace after the Persians captured Dara and attacked Syria.

[1360] Adharmahan [*Artabanus*], a Persian general, attacked Syria and captured Apa-mea (573). He later began a successful campaign in Mesopotamia (581–82), although he was defeated at Constantia by Maurice.

[1361] Khusrau invaded Armenia in 575 and won at first, then lost a battle against the Byzantines (see below), who in turn moved into Persia. However, the next year, whilst they were negotiating, the Persians "won a great victory" (Yarshater, *History*, 1:159). Fighting was still going on when Khusrau died in 579.

[1362] Tiberius II Constantinus reigned 578–84. He had become co-emperor in 574, when Justin II went insane. See *ODB* 3: 2083–84.

Khusrau, who upon notice took the field with a numerous army besides Persians, having a supply out of Bactria, India, Arabia etc. Caesarea, the Cappadocian metropolis, was soon mastered by Tiberius, who after a long march came in view of the enemy. The two armies with equal courage hastened to face each other, and being met the signal was given and the armies quickly engaged. Khusrau wanted neither skill not personal resolution; nevertheless, perceiving that the number of the Roman army was great and orderly-embattled, and having a sting in his conscience that set before him his many cruelties, especially against the innocent Christians, he could not but vent many sighs and apprehend his danger, so soon as he perceived Curs,[1363] a Scythian commander, who at time led the right wing of the Roman horse, with good order first to charge and then soon after to rout the enemies' left and after that the main body, which after some resistance they broke, leaving many Persians dead upon the place. The chase was pursued for many miles, in which more fell then in the field. This proved a victory of extraordinary advantage to the Romans and delivery to the Christians, who in this battle did good service. Khusrau himself escaped narrowly, passing the Euphrates upon an elephant; with a sad heart he resents this loss, which he feared would draw along with it other prejudices, but what most aggravated his trouble of spirit was the loss of his fire-god, which fell into the enemies' hand, who made sport with it, for recovery whereof he made some attempts, but in vain, so that finding himself scorned by his adversaries, disaffected by his subjects and forsaken, as he thought, of his god, his heart broke and his body was buried at Ctesiphon, a city in Susiana not far from the Altars of Hercules, after he had reigned forty-eight years, leaving this report behind him, that to the Christians he was cruel, to the Greeks perfidious and to the Persians tyrannical.

In his place his son Hormisdas, named from *hor*, i.e. *ignis* or fire, Hormizd by the Persians, was crowned King, *Anno Domini* 579.[1364] His eight years' rule was troublesome, for in his third year Mauritius, son-in-law and lieutenant to Tiberius and also Emperor afterwards, entered Persia with an army, foraged where he pleased, and perpetrated all manner of hostility, albeit to prevent it

[1363] Curs was a Scythian commander in the Byzantine army who had been a colleague of the Byzantine general John Mystacon under Tiberius II. In the Armenian campaign he and John attacked independently; Curs may have been annoyed because he had been passed over as *Magister militum* in favour of John, but in any event they quarrelled. He was instrumental in the Byzantine victory at Melitene (576), along with Justinian, the *Magister militum* of the East.
[1364] Hormizd IV reigned 579–90, eleven, not eight years. "Some Islamic sources," writes Yarshater, "praise Hormizd as being more just than his father . . . others condemn him as tyrannical and cruel. The Christians of the Sassanian empire considered him friendly and praised his reign" (*History*, 1.162). Ferdowsi wrote that "As Hormozd established his power . . . his evil nature became apparent and he strayed from the paths of righteousness" (*Shahnameh* 717).

Tamkhusrau[1365] the Persian, Adharmahan the Mede, al-Mundhir the Scenite[1366] and Theodoric the Scythian did what they could to oppose the torrent. *Anno Domini* 589 Philippicus[1367] with some Roman legions, having passed Amida entered Persia especially to comfort the poor Christians in those parts who were threatened by the Magi to be slain that year, if not by massacre yet by miracle. Kardarigan[1368] the Persian general fancies to himself that they were brought hither by some uncontrollable destiny to be destroyed, but the event proved contrary to the Magi's predictions instead of the Christians above thirty thousand Persians being slain by the valour and diligence of the three great captains Philippicus, Heraclius (father to the succeeding Emperor)[1369] and Vitalian.

Bahram,[1370] a noble Bactrian, by hap escaped from the Romans, but no a second disadventure, for Hormizd grew so distracted by reason of this late

[1365] Tamkhusrau (d. 582) was a Persian general who had defeated the *Magister militum* Justinian in Northern Iran (577), but was killed at the Battle of Constantia when the Persians were defeated by Maurice.

[1366] Al-Mundhir V was the Lakhmid ruler of Al-Kufa 576–82. A scenite is a person who lives in a tent.

[1367] Philippicus (c. 550–614) was the brother-in-law of Emperor Maurice. When the latter became Emperor in 582 he gave up his position as *Magister militum*, but "his successor in the field was wholly incompetent" (Yarshater, *History*, 1.163), and Maurice had replaced him with Philippicus. He invaded Persia in 584 and defeated the Persians at Solachon (586), but after failure to capture the fort at Chlomoron he gave up his command to Heraclius Senior. After the Persians recaptured Martyropolis he was recalled (589). He was later sent to Armenia by Heraclius (613), but was defeated by the Persians and had to retreat.

[1368] Kardarigan [*Cardarigas*] had been the victor over the Romans at the Battle of the River Nymphios (582). The battle Herbert describes here is the Battle of the River Araxes (589).

[1369] Heraclius the Elder (d. 614) was the *exarch* of Carthage, and he had enjoyed a long and distinguished military career. He was later responsible (610) for moving against the tyranny of Phocas (see below), sending a fleet commanded by his son Heraclius and an army under his nephew Nicetas to invest Constantinople. Under his administration Carthage was "the single part of the empire which at that time enjoyed peace, prosperity and good government" (Jenkins, *Byzantium*, 20).

[1370] Bahram Chobin, who came from Rayy and was an Arsacid (Yarshater, *History*, 1.163), became King of Persia as Bahram VI (590–91) and a legendary hero celebrated in the *Shahnameh*. He had been a largely-successful general under Hormizd IV, winning victories in Balkh (588) and in the Caucasus. At first he was successful against the Byzantines, and he recaptured Martyropolis from them, but his defeat at the Araxes allowed Hormizd IV, who was jealous of his success, to dismiss and humiliate him, which led to Bahram's rebellion and his eventual accession to the throne. Details of all this may be found in Theophylact of Simocatta's chronicles, which are discussed in M. Whitby, *The Emperor Maurice and his Historians: Theophylact Simocatta on Persian and Balkan Warfare* (Oxford: Oxford University Press, 1988). Ferdowsi gives an account of Bahram's

overthrow that in scorn he forces Bahram to put on women's apparel and with a distaff in his hand to disport the insulting multitude, which jeer cost him dear, for Bahram's returning into such parts as affected him and prevailing with Farrokhan[1371] and Banduy,[1372] a Persian nobleman of account whom the King had also disobliged, by this confederacy they speedily raise so great a force and pass to Shiraz so privately that ere many knew of their approach they enter the city and seize upon the King, yea, that same day they deposed him they crowned his son Khusrau in his place, into whom the soul of his cruel grandsire seemed to be translated. The barbarous traitors, not content therewith, execute their wrath upon the Queen and her innocent children, whom most cruelly they sawed asunder, at which Hormizd expresses the symptoms of a distracted man, his son not being able to comfort him because his beloved wife was irrecoverable. Khusrau, fearing his passion might make him accomptable for his usurpation, commands some villains to assassinate the wretched King, whom the people had in that high esteem as they deified him; "*Oromasdes fuit deus Persarum*,"[1373] saith Plutarch. It appeared an act so infernal that all Persia abominated him as an unnatural parricide; this makes him an absolute tyrant, but Bahram that had mounted him with the same hand thought to pull him down. The King, having notice of his latest intent, gives order to raise some force for his security, but into such hate was this Khusrau grown that none would appear upon the service, whereby to save his life he flies with Shirin[1374] his wife to Byzantium, his parent's dreadful

---

humiliation by Hormizd; the King "ordered that a black box should be brought containing spindles, cotton and various other undignified articles such as . . . female pantaloons and a yellow veil" (*Shahnameh*, 23.6-7 Levy translation).

[1371] Farrokhan is the given name of Shahbaraz, Khusrau's general (see above), who reigned briefly as king April–June 629.

[1372] In the *Shahnameh* Banduy [*Byndois*] and Gostaham or Bistam turn against Hormizd IV and denounce him to the army, accusing him of trying to kill his son, after which the King is seized, deposed and blinded (*Shahnameh* 72.9 Levy translation). They were Hormizd's brothers-in-law (Yarshater, *History*, 1:164). Banduy helped Khusrau escape from Bahram when he was pursued to a monastery by Bahram's soldiers (*Shahnameh* 39, Levy translation).

[1373] Hormizd became a Persian god.

[1374] Shirin or Shireen [*Cesarca*] (d. 628) was first Khusrau's mistress and then his wife. She was probably a Nestorian Christian who later converted to the West Syrian Church. When Khusrau captured Jerusalem (614), she is said to have obtained the true cross and taken it back to Persia. Some historians accuse her of plotting against Khusrau and even of poisoning him, but the evidence is not by any means conclusive. Ferdowsi writes that she committed suicide on her husband's grave after proposals of marriage from his successor and probable murderer, Siroes (*Shahnameh* XXXIX, Levy translation). Her romance with Khusrau found its way into the *Arabian Nights* in "The Story of Khusrau and Shirin." W. Baum has written a recent study of her, *Shirin: Christian-Queen-Myth of Love* (Piscataway: Gorgias Press, 2004).

ghost everywhere haunting him, but by the Christian Emperor Mauritius and his Empress[1375] is with his Queen and little ones courteously received.[1376] After he had reposed awhile in Thrace and pretended a desire to become a Christian, he prevailed with the Emperor to assist him with an army commanded by Narses[1377] and Comentiolus[1378] to re-invest him in his Empire. The Emperor's kinsman Domitian, Bishop of Melitene[1379] and Gregory the Patriarch of Antioch[1380] bearing Khusrau company, the better to instruct and confirm him to the Christian faith.

The cruelty of Khusrau.

Into Hieropolis they entered without resistance; at Daraz the rebel Bahram affronted them with an army of Scythic Persians, but such was the courage of the Christians that Bahram was vanquished. Khusrau returns the Emperor his thanks with tears of joy, and knowing it would better please them then his conformity to religion he first presented them with a rich cross of great value in gems and gold, and then returns that other which Theodora the wife to Justinian had devoted, brought from Antioch by Khusrau the elder, and dedicates another, made at his own charge, circumscribed with:

> *Hanc crucem ego Chosroes Rex Regum etc. quoniam ope Sancti Sergii*
> *Martyris honorabilis contra Baranum iniquissimum adepti sumus, votum*
> *fecimus etc. Nos auream crucem lapillis distinctam ad eius templum*
> *missuros etc., una cum cruce quam Justinianus Imperator ad templum*

[1375] Maurice was married to empress Constantina (c. 550–605).

[1376] The fate of Hormizd IV is a matter of dispute, although most sources agree he was blinded. Theophylact, for example, states that he was killed by Khusrau a few days after his blinding (4.7), but Sebeos in the *History of Heraclius* states plainly that he was murdered by his courtiers and that Khusrau had nothing to do with it (10.75; translation by Robert Bedrosian [1985], http://rbedrosian.com).

[1377] Narses (d. 603) was a Byzantine general who held a command in Mesopotamia under Maurice. When that Emperor was deposed and murdered by the usurper Phocas (602–10) he courageously refused allegiance to the new Emperor, and was rescued from Edessa by the Persians. He later went to Constantinople as an envoy, where he was seized and burned alive by order of Phocas. See *ODB* 2: 1438.

[1378] John Comentiolus (d. 610), the brother of emperor Phocas and *Magister militum* in Spain, was a general and diplomat under Justin II, by whom he was sent to negotiate peace with Persia in 567. He was defeated by the Avars (598) and in 601 was replaced as *Magister militum* by Philippicus. He supported his brother's usurpation but there is no evidence that he was involved in Maurice's murder.

[1379] St. Domitian, bishop of Melitene (d. 602), was Emperor Maurice's cousin. Herbert mistakenly calls him "bishop of Malta," presumably because *Melita* is the Latin name for Malta and he mixed it up with *Melitenus*.

[1380] Gregory I was Chalcedonian patriarch of Antioch 571–94.

eius misit, et quam Chosroes Rex Regum etc. filius Cabadi nostri proavi
etc. hunc advehit etc., ad aedem Sancti Sergii mittendum curavimus.[1381]

as at large is memorised by Baronius.[1382] A chalice of gold also he devoted, with this inscription, *"Ego Chosroes Rex Regum filius incliti Hormizdi, haec in disco inscribenda curavimus, non ut spectuntur ad hominibus;"*[1383] nay, he went further yet in his hypocrisy, for he gave out that he would delay no longer to become a Christian.

Khusrau baptised.

But how subtle soever he was, his Queen Shirin knew him to be a dissembler. She, good lady, therefore, to espouse Christ, fled to Constantinople and there received baptism, Khusrau following her with 60,000 men, but when he saw she was not to be recovered by force or without he would become a Christian he also was baptised and such as followed him, to the admiration of the Persians and amazement of the Asiatic world, as Paulus Diaconus in his 4 *lib.* 16 *ch.*, in Victor also, and in John, Abbot of Biclar[1384] is extant in these words: *"In his ergo temporibus quibus Deus omnipotens prostrato veteris haeresis veneno, pacem suae restituit ecclesiae, Imperator Persarum Christi fidem suscipiens et pacem cum Imperatore Mauricio firmans . . ."* Nevertheless, if I should here relate his apostacy, his cruelty against the Christians and those other barbarisms which he soon after perpetrated, it would require a volume. In brief, so soon as he heard of the massacre of Mauritius with

---

[1381] I, Chosroes, King of Kings etc., since I obtained it by means of the help of St. Sergius the honorable martyr against the mos wickd Bahram, have dedicatd this cross as a vow. As we are about to send the golden cross adorned with precious stones to his shrine, along with the cross which Emperor Justinian sent to his shrine, and the one which Chosroes King of Kings son of Kavadh, our ancestor ets., brought here, etc., we have taken care to send it to the shrine of St. Sergius. See E. K. Fowden, *The Barbarian Plain: Saint Sergius Between Rome and Iran* (Berkeley: University of California Press, 1999).

[1382] Cesare Baronio (1538–1607), cardinal and historian, wrote the *Annales ecclesiastici* (1588–1607), the history of the Church to 1198. This work corrected numerous historical errors; however, according to Cross and Livingstone, "on many matters . . . his information was scanty and in error, and throughout his critical powers failed to support his good intentions" (F. L. Cross and E. A. Livingstone, *The Oxford Dictionary of the Christian Church* 2nd ed. [Oxford: Oxford University Press, 1997], 135).

[1383] I, Khusrau, King of Kings, son of the renowned Hormizd, have caused this to be inscribed on the vessel, that it may not be questioned by men.

[1384] John of Biclar (c. 540–after 590), a Goth who became an abbot in Spain and subsequently Bishop of Gerona, wrote a Latin chronicle covering the years 567–590. See Joan Ferry, *John of Biclar and his Chronicle* (Houston: Rice University Press, 1990), which includes a translation of the work. Bishop Prudencio Sandoval of Pamplona edited the text in 1615. Translation: "Therefore in these times in which, once the poison of ancient heresy had been laid low, Almighty God restored peace to his church, the emperor of Persia taking the Christian faith and making peace with the emperor Maurice."

his wife and children by Phocas,[1385] a captain of his army, and the arrogance of Boniface the Romish Bishop,[1386] who about that time assumed the title of Universal Bishop, he makes this the pretended ground of his new war.

Accordingly, first he rejects Lilius the Roman ambassador, and then denies Christ, but vowing to sacrifice himself in Mauritius his quarrel, and thenceforward reassumed his pagan titles of Khusrau, King of Kings, Lord of Lords, Ruler of Princes, Salvation of Man etc., by such his blasphemy giving the Persian idolaters what assurance he could that he was returned to his former heathenism, and, which was worse, enforcing such as would continue Christians to suck in the heresy of Nestorius, who held that in Christ were two persons as well as two natures, an error that has wellnigh infected all the Orient. This done, *Anno* 603 with an army of an hundred thousand men he entered Syria, there in Palestine and Phoenicia doing all the mischief imaginable. The Lesser Asia parched also with his fury; the poor Christians he chased as far as Chalcedon, after that took Capessa and Edessa,[1387] and to his satisfaction *Anno Domini* 610 hears of the untimely deaths of Narses and Phocas his enemies, who were beheaded by Heraclius the Emperor.[1388] That year also he sacks Apamea, Caesarea, Cappadocia etc., at Antioch also was overjoyed with a victory he obtained against the Christians, which encouraged him to overrun Palestine and in hostile manner to enter Jerusalem, where he derided Zacharias the venerable Patriarch,[1389] the more to vex the poor Christians inhabiting that once holy city, then he ravished

---

[1385] Flavius Phocas was Byzantine Emperor 602–10. "His administration is remarkable," Romilly Jenkins writes, "for nothing but disaster abroad and bloodshed at home: and people said commonly that it was doubtful whether the more destructive enemy were the Persians without or the Emperor within" (*Byzantium: The Imperial Centuries A. D. 610–1071* [Toronto: University of Toronto Press, 1987], 19).

[1386] Pope Boniface III (19 February–12 November 607) maintained good relations with Emperor Phocas, from whom he obtained "a formal declaration that Rome . . . was Head of all the churches" (J. N. D. Kelly, *The Oxford Dictionary of Popes* [Oxford: Oxford University Press, 1988], 69). See also D. Olster, *The Politics of Usurpation in the Seventh Century* (Amsterdam: Hakkeit, 1993).

[1387] When Khusrau entered Edessa, which had in fact "opened its gates" to him because the people refused to recognise Phocas, he proclaimed one Theodosius as "son of Maurice, the true emperor" (Yarshater, *History*, 1:167). He was able to do this because there was a rumour that the real Theodosius had escaped Phocas's massacre of Maurice's family.

[1388] Heraclius did indeed have Phocas executed, but it was the latter who had ordered Narses burned (see above). For Heraclius and his Persian wars see W. E. Kaegi, *Heraclius, Emperor of Byzantium* (Cambridge: Cambridge University Press, 2003).

[1389] Zacharias was patriarch of Jerusalem 609–632. When Khusrau took the city and "ravished" the Cross (May 614), he also enslaved the Patriarch, but after Heraclius had defeated the Persians Zacharias was restored to his position. The Cross was not restored until 629, when King Shahbaraz made peace with Heraclius.

the Cross from thence and brought it into Shiraz, where for some four years it was forcibly detained. After that he subjected Egypt and part of Libya, yea, made the black-faced Ethiopians admire his frenzy.

The Roman Empire, not without cause, was troubled when they felt his wrath in Anatolia, chiefly in Ancyra the Galatian metropolis. 'Tis reported how that in this frantic outbreaking he massacred not less then three hundred thousand Christians, partly-occasioned by the Jews who followed the camp and paid ready money for many whom, as story says, without mercy they slaughtered. Heraclius, having his hands full elsewhere, sent seventy Roman gentlemen to treat of peace. Taes, the Persian general, puffed up with success, accounting them no better then spies, in savage sort made them return again, which Heraclius resented as so high an indignity that with a choice number of men he fought with Taes and had the victory; Taes for his ill success was by Khusrau's command flayed alive and Shahbaraz[1390] made general in his place. Heraclius in the interim wintered in the Pontic region, whiles Shahbaraz with a great army of horse passes through Cilicia and one moonshine night assailed the Romans, whom he thought to have found unprepared, by that haste lost 50,000 of his men, which gave, as it were, new life to the drooping Christians.

Khusrau, not content with this, next year sent Shahbaraz against the Roman army, but the Romans, having other work near home, Heraclius desired a cessation. Khusrau, not considering that war is the effect of God, offended Providence, but rather suffering his reason to be enslaved by a revengeful passion, vows never to give himself rest until he had exercised the utmost of his power to exterminate the Christians, notwithstanding he had many that lived inoffensively under his Empire. To that end he sends Shahin[1391] into Trebizond, but at Azotus Heraclius fought with him and gained a seasonable victory. At Gazacot[1392] Khusrau dares the Roman Emperor again with an army of 50,000 Persians, most of which were horse; never was battle better-fought nor more doubtfully, but at length the Persians fly and Khusrau himself upon a swift Arabian courser disdained not to post to Theobatman, hoping there if anywhere to find safety, but such was the general hate he had plunged himself into that he durst not trust that sanctuary.

[1390] Shahrbaraz (d. 630), whose given name was Farrokhan, was one of Khusrau II's most effective generals in the war with Heraclius. The king apparently became suspicious of him and contemplated having him executed, but the threat did not materialise and Shahrbaraz went on to become king of Persia for a brief time (629–30), for which see below. The name, which is actually a title, means "Boar of the Empire." See *ODB* 3: 1887.

[1391] Shahin [*Sathyn*] (d. 628) was the Persian general in charge of the northern army. He was leading the troops who invaded Anatolia and besieged Chalcedon (615). In 623 he commanded an army in Azerbaijan; he was killed in battle against the Byzantines and his body desecrated by Khusrau II (see below).

[1392] Caesarea Mazaca, the principal city of Cappadocia. Heraclius drove the Persians out in 611. Herbert's chronology seems to be all over the place at this point.

Several pyres demolished.

Heraclius therefore, resolving to ferret him, pursues the tyrant, but Khusrau, hearing of his approach, thinks it more safe to fly into Media then look for help from that helpless deity. Heraclius, when he had throroughly searched that idolatrous place and could not find him, was sorry he missed his aim, but rejoices again that his idols were there to execute his wrath upon, and in some sort to expiate for the cruelty he had showed the Christians who were then under the Roman subjection, so that of the people some he slew, the rest he banished. The flamens he sacrificed to their idol, the pyre he extinguished and made other common fire to be commixed with that imposture, and together made it active to consume the whole city into ashes. At Gazacot he did the like, where was another pyre much resorted-to and worshipped by those gentiles, as Cedrenus tells us, an abomination taught them by Zoroaster in Vishtaspa's time, and seems either that which Moses forbade the Israelites, that they should not let their seed (or children) pass through the fire to Moloch, a brazen, hollow, heated statue, or of the Sepharvites, of whom 'tis said that they burned their children in the fire to Adramalech and Annamalech,[1393] gods of Sepharvaim, as in Leviticus 18:21 and in 2 Kings 17:17 and 31,[1394] concerning which, who desires further satisfaction let him read Lucian, Strabo *lib.* 15, Procopius *lib.* 2 *De bello Persico*, Agathias *lib.* 2 and others. Amongst other things which Heraclius found in that temple dedicated to the sun was a remarkable image of Khusrau which the people fondly worshipped. The frame was round, remembling heaven; Khusrau's head was wreathed with the sun, the rays whereof spread themselves to the umbelic of the image. Upon the one side was the sun, on the other the Moon and Stars, his brothers and sisters painted, and under his feet the angels with crowns and sceptres, as it were adoring him. Now albeit the work was curious and the materials rich, being most part of refined gold glittering with stones of price, yet did the good Emperor throw all into the fire to incorporate with that deity.

Khusroes, not quite out of breath, by this had gathered a fresh army out of Hyrcania and gave order for Shah Raplakan[1395] to forage Albania, but having

---

[1393] The Sepharvites or Sepharvaim were the people of Sepharvais, an ancient town which may have been located near Damascus. Adramalech was a god brought by the Sepharvaim to Samaria, and children were sacrificed to him; Annamalech was a companion-god whose name is linked with 'An, "the male counterpart of 'Anat" (*Illustrated Bible Dictionary* 1:48), a Phoenician goddess. See also Lord Herbert of Chirbury, *Pagan Religion*, 87–88.

[1394] "And thou shalt not let any of thy seed pass through the fire to Molech . . ." (Leviticus 18:21); "And they caused their sons and daughters to pass through fire . . ." (2 Kings 17:17).

[1395] Shah Raplakan [*Sha-Rablecca*] (d. 627) was probably the Governor of Persian Armenia of that name mentioned in Byzantine chronicles. Theophanes calls him "an energetic man puffed up with great vanity" (*Chronicle*, trans. Harry Turtledove [Philadelphia:

intelligence that they were in a good posture of defence, Raplakan returned, until Shahbaraz with new forces forced him back again, and much hurt in all probability would have they done had not Heraclius speedily interposed and happily defeated both those armies in one day, neither knowing of the other's loss. Mohammed the pseudo-prophet was a common soldier in Heraclius his army all this while,[1396] soon after which commences his *Hegira* or flight from Mecca, whose inhabitants at first threatened to kill him for his innovation, *Anno Domini* 632 and of the Emperor's reign 13. Shahbaraz the Persian general, by command of Khusrau his restless master, takes the field again with a numerous army and without much resistance marches over Euphrates, of purpose to try the fortune of war once more against Heraclius, who so soon as he was acquainted with his advance gave him reason to repent his confidence, the good Emperor himself discharging his duty so excellently that day and with such admirable personal valour and resolution that it is reported how that Shahbaraz, upon view thereof cried out to Cosma his companion, "O Cosma! Seest thou with what courage the Emperor fights? Certainly he alone is able to vanquish all our multitudes." And accordingly, after a short but hot dispute, the Romans had the victory. Many lost their lives that day, but the Persian general with some horse made a safe retreat.[1397]

First appearance of the Turks.

That winter the Emperor marched to Sebasteia,[1398] and crossing the River Halys[1399] made Paphlagonia[1400] his rendezvous. Khusrau yet swells with passion, and by diabolical witchcraft invents how he might vex the Christians, against whom he raged with all sorts of cruelty, and ere he made his last exit once more

---

University of Pennsylvania Press, 1982], 308.29); he was appointed by Khusrau to take command in Albania (624) and in 627 was sent to relieve Tiflis.

[1396] There is no evidence of the truth of this statement anywhere. Neither Salahi nor Hourani mentions anything about Mohammed's military service. The only contact, which was indirect in any case (if it happened at all), between the Prophet and Heraclius came much later, when Mohammed, in writing, was supposed to have enjoined both Heraclius and Khusrau II to embrace Islam. See M. A. Salahi, *Muhammad, Man and Prophet* (Shaftesbury: Element Books, 1995), 519–22, and J. Howard-Johnston, *Witnesses to a World Crisis: Historians and Histories of the Middle East in the Seventh Century* (Oxford: Oxford University Press, 2010), 402–7.

[1397] Herbert is describing the Battle of the River Sarbaros (625), which was actually a draw.

[1398] "A city of Pontus (northern Asia Minor)," which used to be called Megalopolis, was in later Roman times the capital of Armenia Prima (Grant, *Guide*, 571).

[1399] The Halys river in Anatolia is now known as the Kizilirmak.

[1400] Originally "a territory in northern Asia Minor on the (Euxine) Black Sea," which later became a Roman province "with its capital at Gangra . . . though a certain amount of Paphlagonian territory was detached" (Grant, *Guide*, 472).

adventures a battle with the incensed Romans; 150,000 men he musters, marches and divides in three. To Shahin he distributes one part, to Shahbaraz another
and to himself a third, imagining by some or all of these to attain his end. Shahin with his 50,000 hastens against the Emperor, Shahbaraz with his 50,000
marches against Constantinople, and Khusrau stays upon the frontiers with the
rest. Heraclius, having intelligence of his force and drift, divides his also into
three, the one to hasten into Thrace, the other to bestow a camisado upon Shahin's quarter, and the last he led himself into Lazic territories, to which place the
Khazars, a sort of Turk, came to serve with the Roman army.[1401] Theodore, Lieutenant-General to Heraclius, hastened to meet the enemy, and notwithstanding
the Persian bravery and courage of a regiment of the Chrysolocae which Shahin
had most confidence in; the Persian army was routed, and no wonder, seeing the
Christians, most of the Roman army being then sad, had Heaven to friend, so
terrible a shower of hail so dreadfully thundering against the Persian horse that
it was visible how God appeared in their defence. In fine, the Persians fled and
Shahin lost his life in the field; the Persians nevertheless redeemed Shahin's body
with a considerable sum, which being brought into their quarters, instead of a
decent burial the Persian tyrant commanded that his carcase should first be arrayed in rags, perfumed him then with dog-turds and lastly slashed his senseless
trunk into many pieces.

That year the Khazars, to gratify Heraclius, under the conduct of Ziebel[1402]
broke through the Caspian Straits and did the Persians much mischief, but to
the Roman army expressed no small service by that action. This was the first
appearance or time that the Turks were taken notice of, who from so obscure a
begnning in few years after made a conquest of most of Asia with a great part of
Europe and Africa. *Anno Domini* 626 Shahbaraz with a very great force entered
Thrace, pillaged Chalcedon, a town built by Jason and Argias, much traded to,
being in view of Byzantium and the Bosphorus. After that they laid siege to Constantinople[1403] and for ten days more or less stormed it, but such was the noble
resolution of the Christians and such her natural defence that the Persians could
not enter, so as upon notice that Heraclius was approaching they raised their
siege and made a dishonourable retreat into their own quarters. *Anno* 627, the

---

[1401] The Khazars, who lived in the Caucasus region, made the alliance with Heraclius in 627. Herbert's calling them "a sort of Turk" is somewhat misleading, as this
phrase refers to the West Göktürks, who were also with Heraclius in the Caucasus (627–
28) and whose army sacked Derbent and helped the Byzantines besiege Tiflis. They were
a Central Asian people who had territory in China, N. Asia and E. Europe, and were the
first Turkic tribe to actually call themselves "Turks."

[1402] Yabgu Khak'an or Ziebel [*Ziebit*] was king of the West Göktürks 618–30. It was
actually his nephew Buri-sad who commanded the army which raided Persian territory.

[1403] By now the Persians had the Avars as their allies when they attacked Constantinople, which was gallantly defended by the forces under Patriarch Sergius I (610–38).

Emperor having decided to requite the Persians for their former violence against the Romans and their friends, with a considerable army entered Armenia, and in a long-fought battle obtained a great victory over the Persian,[1404] after which he pursued Khusrau and made a forcible entry into Ctesiphon, which after he had soundly plundered, he totally domolished and fired. Ctesiphon was a city in Susiana not far from Apamea and Babylon but upon Tigris; not a little famoused in writers, it was built by Belochus, who by the death of Sardanapalus began the Assyrian Empire, albeit Ammianus *lib.* 23 writes *"Vardanes instituit Ctesiphon et rex Pacorus amplificavit."*[1405] The Persian kings used to keep their court during the winter season there; Basil, Cyril, Nazianzen[1406] and other grave authors are of opinion that at this city the Tower of Babel was erected. Howbeit, most are of another opinion, for other writers place it in the Vale of Shinaar where Babylon upon Euphrates was built, being about two days' journey from Ctesiphon, nor are there any remains of Nimrod's tower at Ctesiphon. To return. Khusrau, when he heard that Shahbaraz had sped but ill in Thrace and had redelivered Chalcedon to the Christians, inflamed with passion he sends an assassin to murder him, but by strange hap the Emperor's son, having notice thereof, in honour acquaints the general therewith, who by this ingratitude of Khusrau raised a very dangerous rebellion. Khusrau, when he saw things succeed this unfortunately, fell into a fever first and then a flux enfeebled him so that upon his death-bed he nominated his son Merdaza,[1407] begot of Shirin his beloved wife, but ere he could set the crown on his head Merdaza was slain by Siroes his brother before his father's face, an act so horrid that Khusrau bitterly curses the fratricide, but Siroes, as bloody a viper as ever lived, heaps great sins upon his head by commanding some villains to shoot Khusrau. At that instant his loathed soul, calling to mind his like cruelty to Hormizd his father, could not but acknowledge that God was just in that retaliation, insomuch as that in anguish of soul he breathed out his wretched spirit, having reigned or rather troubled the world full fifty years.[1408]

[1404] Herbert is probably referring to a great battle which took place near the ruins of ancient Nineveh (627) in which the Persian general Rhazates, himself actually an Armenian, was killed, after which Heraclius moved towards Dastagird, where Khusrau had gone. The King then fled to Ctesiphon (Yarshater, *History*, 1:170).

[1405] "Vardanes founded Ctesiphon and king Pacorus enlarged it." This is incorrect; Vardanes I of Parthia reigned c. 40–47 C.E., and Pacorus II reigned 78–105. Ctesiphon was founded in the 1st century B.C.E.

[1406] St. Gregory of Nazianzus (329–389), Bishop of Sasima (372) and one of the four Greek doctors of the church, was briefly Bishop of Constantinople (380), but spent most of his life near his birthplace of Arianzus. He was closely-connected with St. Basil in the defeat of the Arian heresy (Attwater, *Dictionary*, 157).

[1407] The account of Merdaza and his untimely death is accurate.

[1408] Khusrau was arrested when the rebellion broke out, and at the end of February 628 he was murdered. Siroes, also known as Kavadh II, reigned February–September 628. According to Yarshater he was not murdered, but "died, probably of the plague"

Persia subjected to the Arabians.

So soon as Heraclius heard of Khusrau his death he hoped that the old quarrel was at an end; that year hereafter he travelled to the Holy City and presented Zacharias the Patriarch[1409] with the Cross of Christ found by Helena, a British lady, *Anno Domini* 323,[1410] ravished thence by Khusrau and rescued by Heraclius, as lately-remembered. His triumphant entering there was the 17 September 628, the same year that Boniface published to the world his Catholic supremacy[1411] and in or near which time Mohammed divulged his Alkoran.

Siroes, by Teixeira called *Chobad-Xirvihe*, in the *Tarikh* or annal of time *Scyrviah*, in the sixth year of his reign had the reward of a parricide, for he was cruelly murdered by Shahbaraz.[1412] Shahbaraz is by the Persians called *Shahriyar*, by Schickard *Sharibar*, who in the third month of his reign also slew Ardashir, right heir to the throne, but eight months after that himself was slain by Shin Shah,[1413] lord of that part of Taurus now called Larijan. The successors to this Prince are incertain; the Roman authors from him to the conquest of

---

(*History*, 1:170). Ferdowsi certainly thought Siroes had murdered Khusrau, and has Shirin say "May this man who has shed his father's blood never more keep his stature. . . . I will never look on this malefactor even from a distance" (*Shahnameh*, 39, 401, Levy translation).

[1409] St. Zacharias was Patriarch of Jerusalem 609-632. He spent fourteen years in Persian captivity as a slave to king Khusrau, and was liberated through the good offices of Heraclius. The cross, known as the "Precious Cross," was apparently with Zacharias in Persia all the time.

[1410] Empress Helena (c. 255–330) was the Christian wife of Emperor Constantius I Chlorus (305–06) and the mother of Constantine the Great. "There is no historical justification" for her British birth, states Attwater; "she was almost certainly born at Drepanum in Asia Minor." Similarly, again as Attwater notes, whilst her name is associated with the Cross, "the earliest writers do not mention St. Helen as having anything to do with it; she may, indeed, have been dead before it happened" (*Dictionary*, 163). For details, see J. W. Drijvers, *Helena Augusta* (Leiden: Brill, 1992).

[1411] Herbert is mistaken. Boniface III died in 607 (see above). The Pope in 628 was Honorius I (625–38).

[1412] Siroes was succeeded by his son Ardashir III (born 621), who "reigned" 628-30. As Herbert states, he was murdered and supplanted by Shahbaraz, who himself reigned only April–June 630. For Ardashir III, see Ferdowsi 40; here, he is murdered by Piruz the son of Khusrau, who, "seizing the king's mouth, kept his hand over it until the monarch was dead" (Levy, *Shahnameh* 407).

[1413] Ferdowsi, between Ardashir III and Purandokht, inserts one "Goraz, known as Farayin," who may be identified with Herbert's *Shin Shah*, whom Ferdowsi says had "an evil character" (41; Levy, 408–9). Ferdowsi does not list Shahbaraz as a king at all (although Don Juan de Persia does), unless Goraz is another name for him, or Herbert and Don Juan are confusing him with Shahin, who died in 626 and was never king. Herbert seems to have been following Don Juan de Persia (85–6), who himself used Agathias as a source, "the proper names throughout being very incorrectly given," as Le Strange

Mohammed reckon three Kings of Persia, the Arabs six, the Persians five, the *Tarikh* four, Teixeira seven, the Armenians eleven, which it will be difficult to reconcile. Shin Shah at the end of three months was banished by Purandokht,[1414] natural daughter to Khusrau. She had as bad a fate, for at the end of sixteen months she was made away by poison but died much-lamented. To her followed Gushnasp Bandeh,[1415] by the *Tarikh* called *Ian-ku-kar-connah*, who ruled nine months and then died. To him succeeded Azarmidokht,[1416] Khusrau's youngest daughter, who after sixteen months' government died and left Khurrazad[1417] to succeed her. He also at the end of six weeks was slain by Farrokhzad[1418] (*Shahriyar* some call him), who after a like way died of poison, and Yazdegerd followed, who was forthwith made away by Bornarym, and he by Hormizd, captivated and the kingdom conquered by Mohammed and his Arabians, being the last of those twelve vanishing turrets which Khusrau in a perplexed vision saw one night after he had been reading and admiring Aristotle, as he himself related.[1419]

---

comments (*Juan de Persia*, 316). Don Juan also cites Joseph Scaliger as a reference (85). Herbert could also have referred to al-Tabari's rather confused account.

[1414] Queen Purandokht [*Turan Doct*], also known as Boran, reigned 629–30. She was the daughter of Khusrau II, and Ferdowsi says that "she ruled the land with gentleness so great that even the wind of Heaven did not leap upon the dust" (42; Levy translation 411); she made peace with the Byzantines and disposed of "the tyrannous man" Piruz (411). Purandokht was the first female ruler of Persia. There is no evidence that she was poisoned. Sebeos mentions that she married one Khusrau-Hormizd, who was killed by the palace-guards as he was returning home one night (*Chronicle* 28.89–90).

[1415] Gushnasp Bandeh, a cousin of Khusrau II, reigned November–December 630. Herbert misses out the shadowy Khusrau III, a son of Hormizd IV, who reigned October–November 630. I cannot identify *Iazan-Zeddah*.

[1416] Queen Azarmidokht [*Azurmy Doct*], sister of Purandokht, reigned 630–31. Farrokh-Hormizd, father of Rostam Farrokhzad (see below), attempted to force her to marry him, but she refused and he was killed. Rostam deposed and blinded her. Ferdowsi does not mention her at all.

[1417] Khurrazad [*Shezir* or *Kezir*], a grandson of Khusrau II, reigned March–April 631.

[1418] Farrokhzad [*Phorog-Zeddah*], brother of Khurrazad, reigned April–May 631. For him, see Ferdowsi, *Shahnameh*i 43, 412. Shahriyar was the name of Yazdegerd III's father; he was a son of Khusrau II (Yarshater, *History*, 1:171).

[1419] The final Sassanid succession is as follows. Hormizd V, a grandson of Khusrau II, reigned (in Nisibis only) 631–32; Khusrau IV, a grandson of Khusrau I, reigned January–March 632; Peroz II, his brother, reigned March–April 632; Khusrau V (b. 629), possibly a posthumous son of Khusrau II, was placed on the throne April–June 632. The last Sassanid ruler was Yazdegerd III (632–51), under whom, as Ferdowsi put it "the standards of the kings of the world came to an end. Gold vanished and farthings took its place . . ." (*Shahnameh* 44, 413). After the defeat of the Persian army under Rostam, who was killed at the Battle of Qadisiyya (636), Yazdegerd fought on, but after another defeat at

Now as in all massy bodies there appear certain trepidations and waverings before they are able to fix or settle, so by these various revolutions of state in this perplexed Persia the Almighty seemed to decree the period of those that claimed a right by succession and to bring it under the stroke of a foreign authority, such time as [Yazdegerd]¹⁴²⁰ after five years' rule (ten, some say, others six) was slain by Omar, the second Caliph after Mohammed. This great change happened in the Year of Our Lord 640, of the world 4510, and from the Year of the Hegira 20, by whose fall Persia, after long glory, sets in an ecliptic cloud and becomes fettered and forced for a time under the iron yoke of Saracenic bondage, for after an interrupted succession of 28 kings from Ardashir who ruled Persia *Anno Domini* 232, *Anno Mundi* 4184, after Alexander the Great 540 years and after 400 years' obedience to those Persian kings, Mohammed, then under the Roman army, first putting his Arabian brigade into a mutiny for want of pay, revolted, and being made their general quickly reduced Arabia, Egypt and Syria, which great Mohammed I have formerly a little spoken of.

To Mohammed succeeded Abu Bakr,¹⁴²¹ Abdullah Abu Bakr some name him, by Elmacin in his *Saracenic History* called *Abubeer-justus*, and is said to have warred against the *Abassines, Dybanes* and *Bernagassoes*. In the great climactic year he died, having sat as Caliph and King of Persia two years. Omar succeeded him; he is called *Hoshmar* and *Homer*, son to Abdul Qattab, a wealthy merchant. Ali, son-in-law to Mohammed, for pretending to the caliphship was by this restless Caliph everywhere pursued, and having advanced a great army he sacked Basra, an Arabian city, and as an overflowing torrent rushed as far as Gabata, tyrannising over Syria and Egypt.¹⁴²² After that he forages Palestine and Iberia, and as an unlucky comet blazes with fire and sword into Assyria. At Baghdad, which he made his headquarters, he resolves to repose, and dedicates the small remainder of his time to the exercises of devotion; nevertheless, studying how to disturb the world and to enlarge his empire, by an irrefragable vow he obliged himself *per fas per nefas* to endeavour to the utmost the extirpation of Christianity, which he judged the surest way to propagate the *Alcoran*, so as giving a commission to Mavi, he sends him with a numerous army of Arabs first against the Syrians, and with small opposition took Damascus,¹⁴²³ a city at that time wealthy

---

Nihavand (642) and some years of wandering, was betrayed and assassinated by order of the *marzpan* of Marv, one Mahoe, in 651 (see Yarshater, *History*, 1.172).

¹⁴²⁰ Herbert (incorrectly) has "Hormisdas."

¹⁴²¹ Abu Bakr, the first caliph, reigned 632–34. His daughter Ayesha was Mohammed's wife, whom the Prophet married when she was nine. Elmacin's epithet of *Justus* (the Just) is a Latin translation of *as-Siddiq*, which means "the Veracious" (Hughes, *Dictionary*, 7).

¹⁴²² Syria was invaded in 634, beginning with the Battle of Yarmuk, and Egypt in 641. Basra was refounded in 637.

¹⁴²³ Omar's army took Damascus in 635.

and so full of delights as Mohammed acknowledges he durst not trust himself there for fear of temptation, for of all the cities in the world Damascus may worthily be placed in the first rank both for antiquity, commerce and beauty. The Hebrews call it *Damasseq*, Julian in his *Epistles* calls it *"veram Iovis urbem."*[1424] All agree that it is *totius Orientis oculum*;[1425] the Turks *Shani*, and not a little famous from what tradition commonly reports, that Adam and Eve are buried there, there Cain slew Abel, the tomb of Zechariah,[1426] father of John the Baptist is there showed with other antique rarities of that kind. In like sort he sends sundry other officers with considerable forces to reduce other countries by their sword, the best way he could devise for spreading the Alcoran. Accordingly Rostam Beg[1427] with fifteen thousand horse enters Khuzestan[1428] but at the siege of *Escair-Mecron* was slain and in the army Moses surnamed Ashar[1429] commanded after him. This Arab forcibly entered the city and made *Abawaz, Sabur, Arckan, Khorasan, Jarri* and *Lar* acknowledge Mohammed and enrol themselves Omar's tributaries. Abu Obeid ibn Mas'ud[1430] also with thirteen thousand horse subjected Iraq, walled Rastack, [and] of a poor town made it a city and new-named it Kufa or *Kalufa-ophrat*,[1431] since which time it has been the place of coronation for several kings of Persia. Forty miles from Babylon is Kufa, and conjoins Mesjed-Ali, the burial-place of Ali, saint, king and prophet of the Persians.

[1424] Truly the city of Jupiter (Julian, *Epistola* XXIV).

[1425] The eye of all the Orient.

[1426] Nothing is known of Zechariah except that he was a priest (Luke 1:5).

[1427] Rostam Farrokhzad (d. 636), Prince of Azerbaijan and governor of Khurasan, was actually Yazdegerd III's "chief minister and commander of the central army" (Yarshater, *History*, 1:172). After an initial success over the Arabs via his general Bahram, he was defeated and killed at the Battle of Qadisiyya (636). Some authorities believe that he was the historical figure behind the legendary Rostam, but given his character, this seems unlikely (see above, n. 964); the source is Ferdowsi, who calls Rostam "a man of alert mind, sagacious, warlike and one who had been a conqueror. He was a calculator of the stars, of great perception" (*Shahnameh* 44, Levy translation 413).

[1428] The Khuzestan campaign took place 638–40.

[1429] Abu Musa al-Ashari (d. 662/72), one of Mohammed's "companions," was a successful general under Omar and the Governor of Basra and Kufa.

[1430] Abu Obeid ibn Mas'ud (d. 634) was defeated and killed by an army commanded by the Persian general Bahram at the Battle of the Bridge.

[1431] Kufa was re-founded in 637.

Abu Ubaydah[1432] next year subdued Ta'if upon Dijlah,[1433] a town afterwards aggrandised by Abdul Malik[1434] *Anno* 705, *Heg.* 85. Emesa he also attempted to take, but in the trial lost five thousand men, and in the storm Ubaydah was slain himself and the Saracen army forced to retreat. Omar reanimates his men and persuades them that the Elsheerians overcame them by magic, which he also knew how to practice. They dare not disobey their Prophet, but return again to Elsheer, where that siege was renewed under Sa'ad ibn Abi Waqqas, who had such luck through Omar's skill that Emesa was taken and forced to feel his tortures. At Elqadisiya, a frontier town, in that angry mood he slew five and twenty thousand Persians and at Galula, Isfahan and Yazd at several times made Yazdegerd[1435] the Persian general fly, who had no heat left in him when he beheld how fortunately Omar himself subjected Khusistan, Parc, Kerman and Iraq, and in Mesarqan, Jarri, Dehaq, Lar, Shiraz and Meymand had made all men there submit and swear themselves Mussulmen.

Yazdegerd dies, and Hormizd[1436] heads his party and labours to repel the Saracens, but in vain, an uncontrollable decree hastening Persia's bondage, for fifteen thousand men with himself he sacrificed as farewell to the liberty of his country. Omar nine months after this battle was slain treacherously by a varlet,[1437] and in the al-Kaaba in Mecca near to Abu Bakr his predecessor was buried. Osman, in despite of Ali, succeeded him; Omar sat twelve years, this man ten and four months in the Pontificacy.[1438] By *Hucba* his field-marshal, to whose conduct he committed a great body of horse, he subjected divers parts of North Africa,

---

[1432] Abu Ubaydah ibn Jarrah (581–639), one of Mohammed's most able generals, who was with him in all the wars of his career. He became one of the ten Patriarchs of Islam, and went on to serve Caliph Omar with distinction. Herbert is probably referring to the sieges of Ta' if [*Wafit*] (630) and of Emesa [*Elsheer*] (639). It was during the latter that Abu Ubaydah died of plague; he was not killed in the battle.

[1433] Ta'if is a medium-sized city in modern Saudi Arabia, about 100 km south-east of Mecca. It is now used as the summer-capital of the country. The river Dijlah is also known as the Digla (Herbert has *Diglas*).

[1434] Abdul Malik was the Umayyad caliph of Damascus. He reigned 685–705.

[1435] Yazdegerd III. Herbert seems not to have realised that he was actually the last Sassanian King of Persia, unless one counts "Peroz III" (see below).

[1436] In 651 Yazdegerd III's son Peroz (III) started using the title "King of Kings," and twice even sent an envoy to China asking for help against the Arabs. In 677 he himself went to China where he spent the rest of his days (Yarshater, *History*, 1, 176). The Hormizd to whom Herbert refers is probably a general known as Hormuzan, who surrendered to the Arabs at Tostar (642) and later settled in their territory with a pension from Caliph Omar.

[1437] The dates are wrong. Omar I was assassinated by a Persian called Peroz in 644. Yazdegerd III was murdered in 651.

[1438] The dates are wrong again. Omar I reigned ten years as caliph, Osman (644–56), twelve years.

viz. Numidia, Mauretania, as far as Tunis or Carthage. Mu'awiyya,[1439] Sultan of Damascus, in the Caliph's behalf overran Syria [and] Egypt, and in 1000 galley-foists transferred such a swarm of Saracens into Cyprus that upon their entry they seemed enough to cover it. There they sacked Constantia or Ceraunia,[1440] a city built by Cyrus; thence they fell upon Rhodes, where they prepetrated much savage cruelty, and amongst other spoils they demolished the Colossus which was built by Chares of Lindos, scholar to Lysippus, in twelve years, and in regard 'tis said that the sun shines daily in that island, was to the sun dedicated. This huge image was of gilded brass and eighty cubits high, the thumb as big as a large man. The legs stood on either side the river so wide that thereunder might pass a large vessel in full sail. In the one hand it held a javelin which it pointed to the east; on its breast was a mirror wherein those that dwelt in the isle might descry ships sailing at a distance. This wonder of the world, which cost three hundred talents, Mu'awiyya sold to Emissa a Jew for two hundred pounds sterling, who demolished it and with the brass thereof loaded away nine hundred and thirty camels.[1441] In that isle he also defaced an hundred other colossuses, and most barbarously of costly monuments seventy thousand.

Heraclius the Roman Emperor died *Anno Domini* 641 after thirty years' reign and in his place Heraclius Constantinus succeeded, who in the seventh month of his empire was poisoned by Martina[1442] his stepmother, the better to advance

---

[1439] Mu'awiyya ibn Abu Sufyan [*Mavia*] (d. 680) was viceroy of Syria under the first two Caliphs, and himself ruled as Caliph Mu'awiyya I 661–80. He attacked Cyprus, as Herbert states (649), and captured Rhodes (654). He is considered the founder of the Omayyad Dynasty of Caliphs. Only his struggle for power with Caliph Ali after Omar's death in 656 stopped him from invading the Byzantine Empire and attacking Constantinople.

[1440] Probably Ceryneia in southern Greece, the site of Hercules's labour involving the Hind of Ceryneia. There is no known connection with Cyrus.

[1441] Chares of Lindos began work on the Colossus of Rhodes in 294 B.C.E. It took twelve years to finish, and was about 110 feet high. It was actually destroyed by an earthquake in about 226 B.C.E., according to Strabo (3.107). The Arabs captured Rhodes in 654, and shipped the pieces "across the strait to Asia Minor and sold them to a Jew *from* Emesa [not a Jew *called* Emissa, as Herbert states here, Ed.]. Tradition has it that he removed them to Syria on the backs of 900 camels" (Higgins, in Clayton and Price, *Wonders*, 127, 137). Herbert is again using Don Juan de Persia as his source (88).

[1442] Empress Martina (c. 585–648) was actually Heraclius's niece by his sister Maria and married her uncle in about 613; she was co-ruler with her stepson Constantine III (641). For details, see Lynda Garland, *Byzantine Empresses: Women and Power in Byzantium AD 527–1204* (London: Routledge, 1998), 61–73; Howard-Johnston, *Witnesses*, 252–53.

Heracleonas her son, but unexpectedly both of them were exiled by the people, their noses and tongues cut out and Constans saluted Emperor in his place.[1443]

The Saracens subject Tartary.
Osman, having finished his paraphrase upon the *Alcoran*, digested it into seven small tracts which he subdivided into an hundred and fourteen chapters.[1444] It so happened that by accident he lost a ring of gold which Mohammed as a legacy had bequeathed him, but was to descend unto the succeeding caliphs. The virtue of it was supposed great and probably not unlike that magic ring mentioned by Philostratus's *Vita Apollonii*, said to be effected by a constellation of planets, so as no means was unattempted to recover it, which taking no good effect, he conceals the loss and counterfeits another like it of silver, embowelling a motto to this purpose, "O upright ones, O penitents!" from which pattern most Mohammedans to this day wear rings of silver.

Now forasmuch as Mohammed's persuasion is with a naked sword to embrace the Alcoran, in the second and third sura promising the greatest share in Paradise to such as shall destroy most unbelievers, Osman, having done his church-work, devises with himself from that doctrine how to enlarge his Empire, but yet under a pretext of charity to teach other nations their way how to attain Paradise. India in those days was rich and well-peopled; to any who would undertake the conquest he promises, besides other advantages, his blessing, which is as a thousand benedictions. Abdullah ibn Amir,[1445] a man both valiant and superstitious, accepts the task and with thirty thousand horse hastes thitherward, but by new instructions from Osman, who had considered how long a business 'twould be to subdue so remote a continent, he directs his course towards Tartary. Aria he enters and easily subjugated, after that Khorasan, Maurenabar, Ghazneven, and then with little opposition took the cities of Naishapur, *Thalecan* and Tocharistan, yea, all Dilmon[1446] to *Rulk*, as far as *Jebun* and *Ardoc* would give leave, rivers beyond Oxus. A wonderful progress in war and enlargement of empire these new Mohammedan popes made, no less to the terror and amazement

---

[1443] Constantine III (sometimes called Heraclius II) was the son of Heraclius and his first wife Eudocia. He ruled for a short time in 641. He was co-Emperor with Heracleonas, Heraclius's son by Martina. Constantine III died of natural causes, not poison, and Heracleonas then briefly ruled with Constans II (641–68), who was Constantine III's son. In December 641 Heracleonas and Martina were overthrown; Martina had her tongue slit, Heracleonas his nose. For details see Theophanes, *Chronicles*, 347.

[1444] Herbert is correct; Caliph Osman undertook "the second and final revision of the sacred book" (Hughes, *Dictionary*, 655), although his role is disputed.

[1445] Herbert is probably referring to Amr ibn al-As, who campaigned in Egypt (639–42) and eventually conquered it, moving from there to Tripoli. He defeated the Byzantine general Theodore at the Battle of Heliopolis (640).

[1446] Dilmon is an old name for Bahrein.

of the world then to the spreading of the *Alcoran*, Satan at about that time, as 'tis thought, being let loose. Osman the Caliph, by these acquisitions of conquest made himself the most puissant and redoubted Prince then living. Nevertheless, how victorious soever he was abroad, he died miserably at home by poison, which he sucked voluntarily rather than be slain, as story says, by the enraged multitude, in the eighty-eighth year of his age in the fifth year and eighth month of his caliphate. In his place Ali the right heir, attended with ten thousand Persians and twenty thousand Arabians, at Mecca is saluted Caliph. His reign was full of misery, for Mu'awiyya the Syrian, storming at Osman's fall and thinking himself worthy to succeed, with an hundred thousand men enters Arabia with a resolution to depose Ali, but in the encounter was well-beaten and lost ten thousand of his men. Howbeit, at the second trial Ali lost not only the day but his life and mitre. Of the Egyptians in this bloody fight were slain fifteen thousand, and of Saracens twenty thousand, by which victory Mu'awiyya was saluted King. Ali died aged sixty-three and was buried near to Kufa[1447] upon Euphrates at Masjed-Ali; Karb-Ali some have miscalled it. He left a ring with which the Persian kings wed their kingdom; its motto is to this purpose: "With a sincere heart I venerate God." By the Persians he is sometimes called *Amir al-Mu'minin*, i.e. 'Prince of the Faithful.'[1448] By Fatima, Mohammed's sole child, he had Husain,[1449] who after a few months pretended rule died poisoned, *Anno Domini* 666, *Heg.* 46, and was buried at Mesjed-Ali; his symbol was "God alone is powerful." Mu'awiyya, Ali's tormentor, soon after Husain's death slew eleven of his children; the twelfth escaped, Musa Qasim or Mohammed Mahdi[1450] by name, from whom the Kings of Persia at this day say they are descended. This Mohammed Mahdi is thought still alive and to return again, which causes the King to have a horse ever ready

---

[1447] Kufa or al-Kufah is a city 170 km south of Baghdad. Caliph Ali moved the capital there from Medina (656), and after his murder it became the centre for the partisans of Imam Husain under al-Mukhtar (see below). The Abbasids captured it in 749, and for a short time (until 762) it regained its status.

[1448] Ali (656–61) "was struck with a poisoned sword by Ibn Muljam at al-Kufah, and died after three days" (Hughes, *Dictionary*, 13). He was briefly succeeded by al-Hassan, the fifth Sunni Caliph (661), who was later poisoned by his wife at the instigation of Yazid, son of Mu' awiya I (Hughes, *Dictionary*, 168).

[1449] Husain [*Hocem*] (624–680), second son of Ali and Fatima, brother to Caliph al-Hassan, is revered by the Shi'as as their Third Khalifa or Imam. He was killed during a conflict with Caliph Yazid I (680–83), and his death, considered a martyrdom, is commemorated by Shi'a Mussulmans "every year during the first ten days of the Muharram" (Hughes, *Dictionary*, 185). Herbert's claim that he was poisoned is not accurate, and he gets the date wrong.

[1450] Herbert is probably referring to Mohammed Abu'l Qasim, the Twelfth Shi'a Imam, "who is believed to be concealed in some secret place until the day of his manifestation at the end of the world" (Hughes, *Dictionary*, 304). The term 'al-Mahdi' means 'the Expected One.'

for him, though I believe the horse is rather continued from the old custom of that horse which was dedicated to the sun, as I have elsewhere related.

Treachery and cruelty.

Mu'awiyya, Lord of the Ommayan family, having stated himself in the government, sent *Suzindus* his kinsman with a great force against the Grecians. Accordingly *Suzindus*[1451] besieges Syracuse and after that Byzantium, but by Constantine the Emperor,[1452] successor to Heraclius, was slain with thirty thousand other Saracens of his army. That same year the plague raged so terribly in the Mohammedan Empire that the like was never formerly known; amongst the rest Mu'awiyya expired aged seventy-seven and in his reign over Egypt etc. twenty-four, his symbol this, as was reported: "Beg for forgiveness," which Mu'awiyya was so implacably bent against Ali and his race that not content to have him destroyed and eleven of his grandchildren, he caused an anathema to be daily used in their common prayer against him, continued by the Ommayan family for eight descents until by Omar[1453] the fifteenth Caliph abolished. It was requited by Abu'l Abbas,[1454] the ancestor of Abbas now reigning, who was the two-and-twentieth Caliph, and no sooner seated but that he extirpated root and branch the Ommian race, *Anno Hegira* 132, and that with such barbarity as never to be paralleled, for inviting all the family to receive their fealty, eighty of them being assembled and suspectless of harm, upon a signal which Abu'l gave they were all knocked down, and contrary to Nature, which abhors cruelty, he caused them to be laid together in a carpet spread over them, upon whose wretched carcases he feasted, insulting in the sad groans which many of them, who were not quite dead, made, and causing this dirge to be sung: "For the day of Husain and his eleven sons," and nothing else, so that his "Beg for forgiveness" was a motto very necessary to be remembered.

[1451] This must be Abdullah ibn Sa'ad ibn Abi as-Sarh, the foster-brother of caliph Uthman I, Governor of Upper Egypt and the founder of the first Egyptian naval force. He captured Tripoli (647) and defeated the Byzantines at the battle of The Masts (655).

[1452] Constantine IV (668–85), "a man of energy and ability" (Jenkins, *Byzantium*, 42) succeeded Constans II. In 674 Mu'awiyya's forces attacked Constantinople and were soundly defeated, largely due to the invention of "Greek Fire," which destroyed the Arab ships. In 675 they attacked again, but were driven off and their fleet decimated. Constantine IV's generals, Florus and Petronas, defeated them once more in another land engagement "and put thirty thousand of them to the sword," as Theophanes gleefully related (*Chronicles* 353–54). The battles were at Syllacum (677) and Cyzicus (680).

[1453] Omar II (715–17) was the eighth Omayyad caliph. He was poisoned.

[1454] Abu'l Abbas as-Saffah was the founder of the Abbasid Caliphate after the defeat and death of Marwan II. He reigned 749–54. His surname actually means "the Blood-Shedder" (Hughes, *Dictionary*, 1). He was the nineteenth Caliph.

To Mu'awiyya followed as caliph Yazid or Yezid, memorable for his vein of poetry.[1455] He it was that put the Alcoran into rhyme. His riot and venery so exasperated Mu'awiyya ibn Abdullah as at the age of forty he made him away, having ruled but three years. Mu'awiyya was quickly dethroned by Abdul ibn Yazid; some are of opinion that Husain and his eleven sons were slain by this Caliph, not by Mu'awiyya. Marwan, after he had sat nine months, dispossesses him, as he was by Abdul again, but both by Abdul Malik were of life and kingdom bereaved. *Didacus* dethroned and forced Malik to flight, *Oleydore Didacus*,[1456] and Suleiman by the help of Justinian the Emperor[1457] slew *Oleydore*. Malik returns from banishment, expels Suleiman and to the utmost took revenge of Mu'awiyya's murderers.[1458] The Christians were the worse for this establishment, for Malik forthwith ravaged Syria, Armenia and Thrace, and in the fifteenth year of his Empire died, ordaining al-Walid successor in his stead. This Caliph died of grief, for the armies he had sent into Spain revolted against him.[1459] Suleiman succeeded him; him, Omar, deposed by Yazid, son to Malik the late Caliph. Ibrahim marched off after him, a Prince foolhardy and unfortunate.[1460] After his death the Empire was divided 'twixt Yazid and al-Walid, who having sped so well in Asia and Africa, with all the forces they could make they invade Europe;

[1455] Caliph Yazid I (679–83) was known to have been a poet, but little of his poetry survives; there is no evidence that he versified the Quran. He is hated by the Shi'as for having killed Hussein.

[1456] There is no-one called *Didacus* or *Oleydore* in the succession of caliphs.

[1457] Justinian II "Rhinotmetus" (Slit-nose) reigned 685–95; 705–11. After his deposition and mutilation he was succeeded by Leontius (695–98) and Tiberius III Absimarus (698–705).

[1458] The succession to Yazid I is as follows: Mu'awiyya II [*Mutar-Mavia-ben Abdulla*] (683), who was deposed; Marwan I [*Marvan*] (683–84), who was poisoned; Abdul Malik [*Melec*] (684–705); al-Walid I [*Uvalid*] (705–15), under whom Arabia was conquered (for him, see Don Juan de Persia, *Relaciones*, 89–90); Suleiman [*Zulziman*] (715–17), who, "defeated before Constantinople, dies of grief" (Hughes, *Dictionary*, 266). Al-Malik was not deposed by Suleiman. Herbert gets the dates of al-Walid I wrong; he was Abdul Malik's successor. Don Juan de Persia gets it right (88–89).

[1459] Al-Walid I's army attacked Spain in 710–12. He was, says Don Juan de Persia. "this same Caliph who was generally called 'The Sword of God'" (*Relaciones*, 90). The Arabs were victorious in Spain; it would appear that Herbert is confusing al-Walid with his successor Suleiman. No accounts mention a mutiny (see above, n. 1000).

[1460] Yazid II reigned 720–24, following Omar II (see above); Herbert seems to have omitted Yazid's successor Hisham (724–43). Al-Walid II (743) was murdered and succeeded by Yazid III (743–44), who "died of the plague" (Hughes, *Dictionary*, 266) and Ibrahim (744). It was al-Walid I, not II, who invaded Spain (see above). Don Juan de Persia has Hisham succeed in 748, succeeding Yazid II, but at the wrong time. Marwan II (744–49), the last caliph of this line, is made to succeed Hisham (90). "The names in the text," states Le Strange, "are in great confusion" (*Juan de Persia*, 317).

into Spain marched al-Walid's army, led by Abdurrahman, first having in vessels crossed the strait, and Yazid's forces led by Abd al-Rahman[1461] entered France. The first had better fortune then the second, for those under al-Walid conquered Granada and rooted themselves for seven hundred years in Spain till Ferdinand of late expulsed[1462] and his successor forced them back to Barbary. Those that entered France, albeit they were invited thither by Eudes, Duke of Aquitaine,[1463] who hated Charles Martel[1464] mortally, were resisted by Martel and thirty thousand French gallants, Eudes the West Goth upon better consideration siding with the Christians, so as after a long and smart fight near Turin in Piedmont the Saracens were beaten, and of their numberless company three hundred thousand slain, July 22, 726, as Bede and others at that time living do testify. The two Caliphs died mad when they heard of these misfortunes.

The Tartars overrun Persia.

Marwan[1465] was placed in their stead, in whose time *Hyblin* his general purposed to invade Tartary with an hundred thousand men, but in the way was assailed by *Sophy Salyn*,[1466] Saint *Azmully's* son, of descent from Ali and *Lamonis* the

---

[1461] Abdurrahman ibn Abdullah al-Rafiqi [*Sha-Rablan*] (d. 733) was Governor of Andalusia (721 and 731–32). He defeated Eudes of Aquitaine at the Battle of Bordeaux (731) but was himself defeated at Tours the next year. He is not to be confused with his namesake the Caliph of Cordoba (see below).

[1462] Abdurrahman I became the first Caliph of Cordoba in 755, after the overthrow of the Omayyads. This caliphate lasted until 1236, when Cordoba was taken by Ferdinand I of León and Castile. The Caliphate then re-established itself in Granada; Abdu'illah as-Zaggal, also known as Boabdil, the last of the line, was overthrown by Ferdinand V of Aragon in 1492.

[1463] Eudes, Duke of Aquitaine, reigned 681–736. He fought at Toulouse against the Arabs (721) and twice defeated forces under the Amir Ambiza (725–26).

[1464] Charles Martel (686–741), Duke of the Franks and Mayor of the Palace under successive Merovingian kings, was the virtual ruler of most of France. His triumph over the Arabs at Poitiers or Tours was a landmark victory for the Christian cause, but even after that "the Mussulmans continued to hold Narbonne and to ravage Burgundy and the Dauphiné" (Stanley Lane-Poole, *The Mohammedan Dynasties: Chronological and Genealogical Tables with Historical Introductions* (1893) [New York: Frederick Ungar, 1965], 5). The Caliph at the time was Hisham (724–43), not al-Walid or Yazid.

[1465] Marwan II was defeated and killed at the battle of the Zab by Abu'l Abbas as-Saffah, who became the first Abbasid caliph (749).

[1466] Probably Zelma, the fictitious son of Abu Mussulman. Herbert took the name *Salyn* from Juan de Persia, who says that he caused the death of Marwan II (91), and who also gives the size of Marwan's army as 300,000 men (90). Unfortunately, "Zelma . . . is unknown to Moslem history" (Le Strange, *Juan de Persia*, 317). *Hyblin* remains a mystery.

Arabess,[1467] in which conflict *Hyblin* was slain. Marwan in revenge with three hundred thousand Saracens enters Persia, where *Salyn* encounters him and near to Isfahan vanquished the Arabian, an hundred thousand of his men being slain and scattered. Marwan, affrighted at this loss, flies from Babylon to Mecca and thence into Egypt, but thither also Salyn pursues him, and by his banishment or death put an end to the race of his inveterate enemies the ibn Humians, begun by Mu'awiyya, by Marwan ended.

The family of Ali or ibn Abbas in this man begun again to recover the sceptre of Persia, *Anno Domini* 750, *Heg.* 130, for albeit *Abuballa*[1468] awhile opposed Saint Abu Mussulman,[1469] *Asmullah*[1470] was crowned king at Kufa and sat as Caliph also. Authors here a little vary, for some say it was *Asmullah* who brought so great a force out of Khorasan that he made Marwan fly from Persia to Egypt and thence into Barbary, where he seated in Fez in Morocco and peopled divers parts of North Africa, the Alids[1471] being from them descended, distinguished from the Berbers or mountaineers, which are the old inhabitants of those countries. And about this time it was that the Turks living then in the most northerly parts of *Zogethai* made an eruption through the Caspian Straits and for some time located themselves in Turkomania, a province in Armenia the Greater. This *Asmullah* is he that revived Mukhtar's[1472] tenets to the honour of Ali and disgrace of the three successors of Mohammed, published by *Sayed Gunet* of Ardabil.

Saint Abu Mussulman being dead, his son *Salyn* was saluted King, who after three years dying, al-Mansur[1473] succeeded him, *Anno Domini* 758, *Hegira* 138. This is he who repaired Baghdad. Al-Mahdi Abdullah followed, by some called Najmuddin Fidal Ali, to whom Al-Hadi Mirza, father of that *Amir al-Muminin*

[1467] Possibly Layla, Ali's fifth wife.

[1468] Possibly Ubaydullah ibn Ziyad (d. 687), the Governor of Basra.

[1469] Suleiman Abu Mussulman ibn Aqil raised support for the followers of Husain in Kufa (682), but never became caliph, although Don Juan de Persia says he did (*Relaciones*, 91).

[1470] Probably Abdullah ibn Zubayr (624–92), who proclaimed himself caliph in Syria, Iraq, and southern Arabia in 680, splitting the caliphate between himself and Marwan I (684–86). He was defeated and killed by Abd al-Malik.

[1471] This is incorrect; the Alid Dynasty in Morocco (788–992) was founded by Idris ibn Abdullah, a direct descendent of Caliph Ali, following a revolt in Medina by Ali's supporters (786), which was crushed, forcing Idris to flee first to Egypt and then to Morocco, where he reigned as Idris I (788–93). For details, see Lane-Poole, *Dynasties*, 35–6.

[1472] Al-Mukhtar ibn Ali Ubayd al-Thakafi (d. 687), the avenger of Husain's death, raised a revolt against the governor of Basra (see above) and took power in Kufa (686). He defeated and killed ibn Ziyad, but was himself killed soon afterwards. He did not drive Marwan I out of Persia.

[1473] Al-Mansur, whom Don Juan de Persia calls "a man of great astuteness" (*Relaciones*, 90), reigned 754–75. His predecessor was Abu'l Abbas (see above).

of whom the French speak so much. In his time, viz. 798, Charlemagne flour-ished, and this our isle under Edgar altered its name from Britain to England.[1474] 'Twixt this *Amir al-Muminin* or Harun, King of Persia and the Christian Em-peror Charles was great amity, ambassadors and presents being reciprocally sent from each other, as we find recorded by Eginhard[1475] his secretary and Aemilius, *lib.* 3.[1476] This Harun, some say, died a Christian. In his time many fanatic schol-ars in the sight of thousands undertook to fly, but in the trial from one rock to another, notwithstanding the height of the wind, perished.

Harun after three and twenty years' rule died and al-Amin his son reigned five years after, al-Mamun after him, who, when he had for some time raged against the Christians and troubled divers of the islands in the Mediterranean Sea, died and was succeeded by al-Mutasim, who equally vexed the Christians, disturbed Italy and alarmed Rome, but he also in short space vanished and was succeeded by these Caliphs successively: al-Wasiq, al-Mutawakkil, al-Muntasir, al-Musta'in, al-Mu'tazz, in whose time happened the greatest earthquake that ever was felt in Asia, al-Muhtadi, al-Mutamid Billah, al-Mutazid, al-Muqtafi, al-Muqtadir, al-Qahir, ar-Razi, al-Muttaqi, al-Mustaqfi, al-Muti, al-Tai', al-Qadir, i.e. 'God's servant,' who ended the Caliphs of the Arabic or Persian stem,[1477] for then *Anno* 1030, *Hegira* 410, came the Turkomen led by Toghrul Beg who had his first call into Persia by Mohammed the then Sultan to assist him against

---

[1474] Al-Mahdi reigned 775–85, followed by Al-Hadi 785–86. *Amir al-Muminin* is a title meaning "Prince of the Faithful," referring here to the great Harun al-Rashid [*Aar-on*] (786–809), who figures prominently in *The Thousand and One Nights*, but who certain-ly did not become a Christian. Charlemagne was Holy Roman Emperor 800–14; Edgar "the Peaceful" was King of England 959–75. Herbert may have intended Egbert, King of the West Saxons (802–39), who became King of England in 829.

[1475] Eginhard or Einhard (c. 770–840) was a Frankish statesman, historian, math-ematician, and diplomat. One of Charlemagne's chief advisers, he wrote the definitive history of his master's reign, the *De vita Caroli Magni*. Modern translations include that of Lewis Thorpe (Harmondsworth: Penguin Books, 1969) and T.F. X. Noble (Philadel-phia: Penn State University Press, 2009).

[1476] Paulo Emilio di Verona (c. 1455–1529) compiled by order of Charles VIII a Lat-in history of the French monarchy, *De rebus gestis Francorum* (1517; French translation, 1581). He also wrote a work on ancient monuments in France, *In Franciae antiquitatem libri tres.*

[1477] The chronology of the caliphs is as follows: al-Amin (809–13), claimed as the founder of Baghdad by Don Juan de Persia (*Relaciones*, 92); al-Mamun (813–33), al-Muta-sim I (833–41), al-Wasiq (841–47), al-Mutawakkil (847–61), who persecuted Christians; al-Muntasir (861–62), al-Musta'in (862–66), al-Mu'tazz (866–69), al-Mahdi (169–70), al-Mutamid (870–92), who re-established Baghdad as capital; al-Mutazid (892–902), the conqueror of Persia; al-Muqtafi I (902–08), al-Muqtadir (908–32), al-Qahir (932–34), al-Razi (934–40), al-Mutaqqi (940–45), al-Muti (945–74), al-Ta'i (974–91), and al-Qadir (991–1031).

the Babylonians, but the Turk, after he had freed Mohammed from the danger which Pisastris threatened, desiring leave to go into Armenia to visit his kindred who were lately seated there, resents the denial with such impatience that Mohammed, ere he could appease the wrathful Turk, was bereaved both of life and kingdom. In his death the family of Saint Abdullah was eclipsed till Shah Ismail dispelled the interposing cloud and revived the splendour of his ancestry. The Buwayhid Kings who begun *Anno Heg.* 319 ended *Anno Heg.* 480. In the *Juchasin*[1478] they are chronicled, and at Shiraz I have spoken concerning them.

The successor of Toghrul Beg was Osman son of Ertughrul, who in the year 1300, *Heg.* 680 laid the foundation of the Turkish Empire in Europe and Asia, and the Seljukian, of the same extraction, governed Persia, begun by Toghrul Beg, son of Seljuk, son of Yakak,[1479] a Turkman or Tartarian. Toghrul Beg, some say, was slain by treason; his successor was Farrokhzad, Ma'sud's son, slain by Alp Arslan, Prince of Ghazna. To him followed Ibrahim ibn Ma'sud, whose son Mas'ud married the daughter of Malik Shah, King of Turkestan.[1480] Mas'ud from Khorasan entered Persia with a great army and near to Tabriz slew al-Mustarshid Billah, [the] Caliph, and in another fight ar-Rashid his son at Isfahan. To Mas'ud in Ghazna succeeded Shah Arslan, slain by Bahram Shah his brother, to whom ruled Khusrau his son, who after he had foraged India died *Anno Heg.* 555, and in him took end the Subutarque family.[1481]

In those times as Caliphs of Baghdad and part of Persia were Jalal al-dowlah,[1482] whose seventh successor Mustansir was slain by Genghis Khan, *Anno Heg.* 580, and al-Mustasim Billah governed in his place. Of those Tartars I have spoken; descend we then to the year of Our Lord 1415, *Heg.* 795, such time as

[1478] The *Juchasin* or *Book of Genealogies* was compiled by Abraham ben Samuel Zacuto (see above), and contains lists of Popes, Kings, Emperors, Caliphs and Sultans. It was printed in Cracow (1581).

[1479] Yakak [*Didacus*] was "a Turkman chieftain in the service of one of the Khans of Turkestan" (Lane-Poole, *Dynasties*, 150). Seljuk [*Salgbucius*] (fl. c. 1000–1038) "migrated ... to Jand in the province of Bukhara, where he and his people enthusiastically embraced Islam" (Lane-Poole, *Dynasties*, 150). They eventually overran Khorasan in about 1037, having defeated the Ghaznavids.

[1480] Malik Shah ruled as Great Seljuk 1072–1092. Mas'ud was the Seljuk sultan of Hamadan (1133–1152), not to be confused with sultan Mas'ud I of Ghazna (1030–1040).

[1481] Herbert's chronology is a little confused. The dates of the rulers of Ghazna are as follows: Toghrul Beg seized the throne for a short time in 1052, and was followed by Farrokhzad [*Pharag-zed*] (1052–1059), Ibrahim [*Ebraim*] (1059–1099), Mas'ud III (1099–1114), Shirzad (1114–1115), Arslan Shah [*Sha-Aesolan*] (1115–1118), Bahram Shah [*Babahun-sha*] (1118–1152), and Khusrau I [*Gosrhao*] (1152–1160).

[1482] Jalal al-Dowlah was the Buwayhid ruler of Iraq 1025–1043; caliph al-Mustansir (1226–1240), an Abbasid, was killed fighting against Genghis Khan. His successor was al-Mutasim (1240–1258), who was slain by Hulagu Khan.

Qara Mohammed the Turk re-entered Persia. He ruled three years and left Qara Yusuf to succeed him, who also after three years died at Qazvin, and left six sons, viz. *Pir-buda-cawn*, Iskander Mirza, Jahan Shah, Abu Said and *Mirza Abdal*, all which died untimely. Of those seven Jahan Shah was the last, who also was slain with Hasan Ali his son by Uzun Hasan, so at that time the family of [the] Qara Koyunlu or Black Sheep ended and the Ak Koyunlu or White Sheep took beginning. The first of these were Turks, the last Armenians.[1483]

During this the Ottoman race so enlarged their conquests in the Lesser Asia that the Grecian Princes, to stop the impetuous torrent, by their ambassadors represented their sad condition unto Tamerlane, who at that time was highly-famed for the victories he had a little before obtained over Tokhtamish,[1484] a Scythic Prince and some inroads he had made into China if Paulus Giovius in that be not mistaken, so as that noble Prince in commiseration to those distressed Christians, but principally detesting the insolencies of the Turk from whom he had but lately received some affronts near the River Borysthenes and contempt done to his ambassadors, with a willing heart and all the force he could make marched against Bayezid, who with equal numbers and more spite marched against the Tartars. Near Mount Stella, the plain where Pompey worsted Mithridates,[1485] was maintained a long and bloody fight, but the Almighty being pleased that a hook should pierce the jaws of that Turkish leviathan, the spirits of the Christians were so animated that the victory rested with Tamerlane, who in the flight slew many thousand Turks, and the better to choke the insolence of Bayezid, put him in an iron cage as accustomed to wild beasts and carried him in that ridiculous posture through all his marches, after which without any consideration he subjected the rest of the Turkish provinces and received acknowledgement of his subjection from all that part of Asia and Africa, for besides the Lesser Asia and Armenia, all Assyria, Syria, Egypt and other parts of Africa, Asia, Persia and the

---

[1483] This chronology is completely inaccurate. The rulers of the Black Sheep Turkmen were as follows: Qara Mohammed [*Ghara-Mahumed*] (c. 1378–1388), Qara Yusuf [*Kara-Issuph*] (1388–1420), Qara Iskander [*Scander-Mirza*] (1420/21–36), Jahan Shah [*Joon-sha*] (1436–1467), killed by Uzun Hassan of the White Sheep, and Hassan Ali [*Acen-Ally*] (1467–1468/69), in whose time the dynasty ended. Jahan Shah was not the last ruler. Qara Yusuf's sons were Ispend (d. 1438), who led the Sadlu tribe and occupied Tabriz until 1429; Abu Said [*Abuzedda*] (d. 1431) was made ruler of Tabriz by the Timurid Shahrukh (1429) and then executed by his brother Iskander, himself murdered by his son Kubad. *Pir-buda-cawn* and *Mirza Abdal* are unidentified, but they are not sons of Qara Yusuf, who had four, not six sons.

[1484] Tokhtamish [*Calisho*] (d. 1406) was Khan of the White Horde (1378–1380) and of the Golden Horde (1380–1395). He took Tabriz (1385) and invaded Transoxiana two years later, but was defeated by Timur at the River Terek (1391) and the River Vorskla. He was deposed and wandered around for some years before his death. It is true that Timur had plans to invade China (for details, see Jackson and Lockhart, *History*, 80–83).

[1485] This was in the Tauric Chersonese; Mithridates VI died near it in Panticapaeum.

dominions under that crown he added to his Empire all those Eastern countries
that stretch as far as Ganges, so that for extent of dominion and speedy conquest
he is without parallel.[1486]

Sheikh Safi visited by Tamerlane.

The Persian annals further acquaint us that Tamerlane, returning through Media towards Samarkand, gave a friendly visit to Syed or Sheikh Safi,[1487] a reputed saint at that time living in Ardabil, a town under 37 degrees 30 minutes
about seventy English miles to the north-east of Qazvin and half that distance
from Soltaniyé, who, perceiving that by *Hoharo-Mirza's* advice the conqueror
had destined many thousand prisoners, of which the most number were Persians,
to perpetual slavery or death, the Sheikh begged their liberties, which Tamerlane granting, the mercy was deservedly attributed to Safi and highly increased
the opinion of his holiness,[1488] soon after which, *Anno Dom.* 1407, *Heg.* 787 the
Tartarian Emperor died, and almost three years after the Persian saint followed
in that inevitable path, being no less ceremoniously entombed at Ardabil, albeit some say at Shamakhi, concerning whom give me leave to apply that which
Horace did not more aptly to another, "*Crescit occulto . . . velut arbor aevo / Fama
sophii . . .*"[1489]

Safi left behind him a son called Syed Junaid,[1490] for of such esteem was his
father's sanctity that as *ex traduce* they held it requisite to give the like attribute of

---

[1486] The battle with Sultan Bayezid I (1389–1402) was fought on the site of present-day Ankara; "the most likely date," say Jackson and Lockhart, "is . . . 28 July 1402"
(*History*, 78).

[1487] Sheikh Safi or Safi-ed-din al-Ishaq (1252–1334), a descendant of Mohammed,
was known as a Sufi saint and philosopher. He founded a Sufi monastery in Ardabil, in
which he advocated the teachings of one Murshid Gilani, a Sufi. Safi was the ancestor of
the Safavids and his sect was known as the Safaviyya; it was a group "based on religious
principles with an unmistakable orientation towards political influence and claims to
secular power" (Jackson and Lockhart, *History*, 38). Some few poems by Safi still survive.
Herbert gives his date of death as 1409, which is incorrect. Curiously enough, his chronology then gets better, skipping forward over one hundred years to Uzun Hassan.

[1488] It was not to Safi but to his grandson Khwaja Ali (d. 1429) that Timur made this
concession in 1404. The prisoners were "Sufiyan-i Rumlu, who were the descendants of
liberated prisoners of war from Anatolia" (Jackson and Lockhart, *History*, 56, n.2).

[1489] The full quote translates: "The glory [of Marcellus] grows like a tree through /
secluded generations" (Horace, *Odes* 1. 12. 45–6).

[1490] Syed Junaid (d. 1460) was actually Safi's great-grandson. He was the leader of
the Safaviyyas from about 1447 (Jackson and Lockhart, *History*, 200), and even used the
title "Sultan." He was driven out of Ardabil by Jahan Shah of the Black Sheep Turkmen,
and took refuge with Uzun Hassan (1456), whose sister Khadija he married. "There is no
doubt," Jackson and Lockhart state, "that [Junaid] gave military training to the adherents

'Syed,' i.e. 'Saint' unto him, who also at least by a pretended zeal seemed merito-riously to acquire that epithet, which nevertheless he made rigght use of towards the pulling down the Black Sheep's race, of which Jahan Shah the son of Qara Yusuf at that time only remained, to which end he hatches this design. First he invited Uzun, otherwise called Uzun Hassan, the Armenian King, to the con-quest of Persia, which by the death of Jahan Shah, *Anno Dom.* 1467, *Heg.* 848 he quickly effected, and thereby reduced under subjection the provinces of Hyer-ac, Iraq, Aderbayan, Cabonchara, Mazanderan, Sirvan, Kerman and Khuzistan, during which there was that amity 'twixt the victor and the Saint of Ardabil that he was so far from opposing the new model of church affairs Junaid had compiled for the better-fancied, perceiving the Syed's drift to make a perpetual schism or rent from the Turk in their persuasion as he gave it all the countenance he could and imposed the New Quran, as they termed it, on the Persian, who from the belief they had of the Syed's learning and holiness without dispute or further examinations freely accepted of it, in no wise considering that the introducing a novel doctrine is no other then an affectation of tyranny over the understanding and belief of men. For albeit till then Abu Bakr, Omar and Osman, the three succeeding caliphs after Mohammed, were venerably esteemed of by the Per-sians and reputed prophets, yet now being told by Syed Junaid that those were no prophets but impostors and intruders into the caliphship which Ali the Per-sian, matching with Fatima, Mohammed's sole child, had most right unto, which notwithstanding Ali was not only by their power and subtle practices kept out of possession during their lives but by their procuration slain by al-Muljam the Syr-ian general, and not therewith satisfied his race so prosecuted that Husain, Ali's son, was likewise cut off and his other sons, eleven in number, destroyed; the twelfth, called Musa al-Qasim,[1491] by miracle only escaping, of whom the crafty Syed Junaid himelf descended.

Haidar marries Uzun Hassan's daughter.

Those and other like conditions so wrought that it was thought those three pre-tended prophets should be reputed rather devils then saints, expunged their cal-endar and instead of invoking, the Persians were instructed to execrate them as heretics, and as it is related, the Turkish mufti not many years since upon some occasion declared it an article of his faith that he held it a more meritorious work to destroy one Persian then a hundred Christians. Howbeit, this great breach, purposely designed by Junaid the better to advance his own tribe and to make

---

of the order who lived in his retinue and used them in military operations" (203). He was killed in battle with Khalil-Allah, the Sirvan-Shah.

[1491] Musa al-Qasim (d. 799) was not the son of Husain, but of Ja'afar, the grandson of Husain. "The great body of the Shi' ahs," states Hughes, "acknowledge Musa al-Kazim and his descendents as the true Imams" (*History*, 574).

his access the easier to the crown, was not so secretly-contrived but that Jahan Shah had some whispering of it, which so soon as the Syed understood he wisely withdrew himself into the Arabian territories, where he took the opportunity to quicken Uzun Hassan towards the invading Persia, as lately mentioned. But the Armenians' giving law unto the Persian was so badly resented that Junaid perceived it contributed not a little towards the attaining his ambitious ends, which Uzun Hassan was altogether ignorant of, otherwise he would not so easily have condescended to match his daughter Marta, whom the Persians call *Kadayun Hatun*, begot of Despina the daughter of Calo-Joannes the good Emperor of Trebizond,[1492] with Haidar Mirza[1493] his son, whom Paulus Giovius calls *Harduelles*, by which high affinity he made his nearer approach to the throne. Nor was the match much to the young lady's disliking, for she had liberty granted her to continue the possession of that religion which her Christian mother had instructed her in, nor was it held an undervaluing, seeing that Haidar's descent was in a direct line drawn from Ali and Fatima, the daughter and heir of Mohammed, in an uninterrupted stem of thirty-five Princes and saints, some of which are as follows: Abbas had Abu Talib the father of Ali, who by Fatima had Husain father of Mirza al-Qasim, whom some name *Moheddin*, from whom Mutar, Saint Abu Mussulman and Salyn descended, and from whom Sheykh Safi ed-din al-Ishaq, who for his learning and sanctity was declared *Qutb al-ullah*,[1494] to whom succeeded Sheykh or Syed Musa, who was the father of Mirza Sadr al-din, the father of Sheykh Ali, father of Sheykh Ibrahim,[1495] father of Sheykh Safi, father of Syed Junaid, father of Sheykh Haidar, who by his wife Marta had Ismail surnamed Safi.

[1492] John IV Palaeologus was Emperor of Trebizond 1429–1459. Herbert has his sobriquet confused with that of John II Comnenus, Emperor of Byzantium, known as Calo-Joannes (1118–1143), which means 'the Good,' as Herbert states. Despina Hatum, formerly known as Theodora Comnena, was John IV's natural daughter. Halima, the daughter of Uzun Hassan and Despina, was the mother of the future Shah Ismail I.

[1493] Sheykh Haidar Mirza (1460–1488) led the Safaviyya until he was slain in battle by Yakub Khan of the White Sheep Turkmen. He did marry Princess Marta, Uzun Hassan's daughter, as Herbert states. "The name Qizilbash for the followers of the Ardabil sheikhs undoubtedly goes back, together with the introduction of the red turban, to the time of Haidar" (Jackson and Lockhart, *History*, 207). Juan de Persia gives a lengthy account of his career (*Relaciones*, 107–11) and compares his account with that of Botero (2:171).

[1494] Literally, "Axis of God." *Qutb* is often used as an honorific for Shi'a saints.

[1495] Sadr al-Din (d. 1392) was the son of sheykh Safi (see Jackson and Lockhart, *History*, 199, n.4); Khwaja Ali (d. 1429), for whom see above, n. 1032; Sheykh Ibrahim (d. 1448) was governor of Ardabil under Jahan Shah and remembered by Christian chroniclers for his cruelty.

Uzun Hassan's happy reign.

Uzun Hassan son of *Tecritt-cawn*,[1496] expelled his country by Bayezid [I] and reinvested by Tamerlane, happily kept what he had conquered and spent the remainder of his reign with peace, maintaining a good correspondence with Mehmet the Great Turk, to whom by his ambassadors amongst other things, if worth the memory, he presented a pair of playing-tables which were of crystal, the dice and men of gold set with precious stones, being part of the spoils which Tamerlane left after he had foraged Persia. To this great Prince many Christian Princes dispatched their messengers, and amongst others Zeno[1497] came ambassador from the Venetians to engage him against the Turk for some loss they had received but upon pretence to repossess his wife's brother of Trebizond, in order whereto he invaded the Turks' dominions and engaged at several times the two great pashas Mustapha and Murad, and had the better awhile, but at last was overpowered and worsted by Mehmet, insomuch as his son Zeynal Khan, who commanded the army, was forced to retreat to Tabriz, whither at that time the Turks feared to follow. At length, either for grief at that bad success or age, in the year 1477 Uzun Hassan died at Qazvin, where he was royally interred.

He left seven sons behind: Ogurlu Mirza, Sultan Khalil, Yakub, Yusuf, Maksud Beg, Masih Beg and Zeynal Khan,[1498] most of which came to untimely ends, for Ogurlu was destroyed by poison, Khalil was slain by Mas' ud Beg, Masih and Zeynal Khan died in fight against the Turk, Yakub was murdered by a whore at Tabriz and Yusuf died of an imposthume.[1499] Their children also had little better destiny, for Baysonqur and Alwand Beg, sons of Yakub the third son of Uzun

---

[1496] Incorrect. Uzun Hassan's father was Ali ibn Qara Yülük, Khan of the White Sheep Turkmen 1436–1438.

[1497] Caterino Zeno [*Zenus*], the Venetian ambassador, was in Persia 1471–1474. His grandfather Antonio was also a traveller. Jackson and Lockhart note that "he was particularly well-equipped for his mission," as his wife, a cousin of David Comnenus, the last emperor of Trebizond (1459–1461), was a niece to Despina Hatum, Uzun Hassan's wife (*History*, 176). Venice had been, in fact, already at war with the Turks since 1463, and this alliance with the Turkmen did not make Sultan Mehmed II happy. The "loss" Herbert mentions was Venetian territory in the Greek islands. Zeno wrote an account of his experiences, *Commentarii del viaggio in Persia* (Venice, 1558), also published by Ramusio. His dates of birth and death are not known.

[1498] Herbert's information about Uzun Hassan's sons is not very accurate. Ogurlu Mohammed (d. 1474) rebelled against his father; Khalil Mirza [*Sultan Chalil*] (1443–1480), who was the eldest son (not Ogurlu, as Herbert says), served as governor of Shiraz and was khan of the White Sheep Turkmen 1479–1480; Maqsud Beg [*Maczud*] (d. 1474), who connived at Ogurlu's rebellion, was put to death by his father; Yakub Beg [*Jacob*] (d. 1491) was khan of the White Sheep Turkmen 1480–1491. His forces destroyed Sheykh Haidar; of Masih Beg [*Josias*] and Yusuf [*Issus*], not much of note can be said; Zeynal Khan was commander of the forces against the Turks in 1476.

[1499] An abscess.

Hassan, for some time strove who should first grasp the royal sceptre, and albeit
Baysonqur prevailed, long he enjoyed it not, being by Rostam son of Maksud
Beg, Uzun's second son, forced to fly for safety of his life, but returning out of
Armenia the next year with a considerable party died by the way, which made
Rostam think he would not meet with any further disturbance, yet it happened
otherwise, for Mohammed Mirza, who was son to Ogurlu the eldest son, having
most rights at length found friends who settled him in the throne, notwithstanding which after a few months he was dethroned by Qasim[1500] and *Hayb-Sultan*,
two powerful rebels who were quickly dispatched out of the world by Alwand,
Baysonqur's brother, and in Isfahan lie buried.[1501] Alwand by that means stepped
into the royal seat and ruled peaceably full five years, but upon the suggestion of
Yaqub, who had a jealousy of Haidar his brother-in-law, grown popular by his
sanctity but more by reason of his match with their sister, and most of all for his
high descent, could not think himself safe as long as Haidar lived, so that very
treacherously he caused the Syed to be murdered, and not therewith satisfied,
gave order for the like to Ismail his son, but he had such timely advertisement by
a secret friend that withdrawing to Pir Ali,[1502] the Governor of Mazanderan, he
found security.[1503]

[1500] Qasim ibn Djihangir [*Kacem*] was emir of Mardin 1469–1503.

[1501] The chronology of the White Sheep Turkmen is as follows. Baysonqur [*Baisan-gor*] son of Yaqub reigned 1490–1493 in Transoxiana; Rostam son of Maqsud reigned 1493–1497; at this point Herbert is in error, because Rostam's successor was Ahmad Govde (1497), whose name means 'the Dwarf' (Jackson and Lockhart, *History*, 188) and who was actually Ogurlu's son, himself followed by Murad, son of Yaqub (first reign 1497–1499), of whom more below, then Alwand [*Elvan*] (1499–1502), son of Yusuf, of whom more below also; Mohammed Mirza [*Hamet*], son of Yusuf, not of Ogurlu, reigned in Fars (1499–1501), and finally Murad again (1502–1507), until he fled from Baghdad to Turkey.

[1502] Kara Kia Mirza Ali was the Governor of Lahijan, "distinguished from and su-perior to the other governors of Gilan by virtue of his rank and station, his noble lineage, the excellence of his character and shrewdness of insight" (Monshi, *History*, 1:40). He helped save Ismail from Rostam's men and looked after Ismail for five years (1494–1499) until hostilities broke out between Alwand and his brother Murad.

[1503] There is some confusion here. Sultan Ali, the son of Haidar, had helped Ros-tam get the throne in 1493, but Rostam's soldiers killed him in 1494 when Rostam be-came worried about Haidar's power. It was in fact Sultan Rostam who tried to kill Ismail as well, not Alwand. Furthermore, Sheykh Haidar was killed in battle by the Sirvan-Shah Farrokh Yasar (r. 1465–1500), not Alwand, after attacking Samakhi (1488). Ali was killed by Yaqub.

The signification of *Sophy*.

Ismail in the meantime, as his years increased so did his reputation, especially with his countrymen the Persians, who perceiving in him and extraordinary in-egnuity as well as courage, wished for an opportunity to advance him higher. The name *Sophy*, some say, was given by the Greeks, his mother's countrymen who were his instructors and followers, albeit I find that some of his ancestors had that attribute or surname given, so as 'tis dubious. Murad or Amurath, Alwand's brother, aiming at the crown was disappointed of his hopes by the rout of his party; nevertheless, that competition gave Ismail opportunity to raise what force his friend Pir Ali could upon the just pretence of securing himself and revenging his father's untimely death, so that with speed he possessed himself of Samakhi, which he fortified. Alwand, to suppress this rebellion, immediately advanced against him with what horse and foot he could, but the Taurisians, mindful of some late rigour he executed there,[1504] failed his expectation, which put him into that disorder as wellnigh distracted him, increased by the intelligence he also had that his brother Murad had so far insinuated into Bayezid the Great Turk's favour as he not only gave him his daughter to wife but commanded the Governor of Babylon to assist him against Alwand, notwithstanding all which so happy was Alwand in that first expedition that Murad was worsted and forced to fly for safety into the Stony Arabia. Howbeit, otherwise was his success with Ismail, who by the additional recruits he had from Tauris, Ardabil and other parts of Sirvan, but principally out of Arzenion, where the great tribes or hordes collected, the Afshars, Rumlus, Saffaviya, Ostaljus, Qajars, Samlu, Zul-Qadars etc.[1505] gave him assistance, so as he first slew Farrokh-Yasar his father's murderer and then thought it advisable to engage his uncle Alwand so soon as possible, and accordingly at or near Sharur, the midway between Isfahan and Shiraz, the two armies met, and after an hour's fight Ismail had the better of the day. Alwand's army fled towards Shiraz, himself being slain by a private soldier in the chase,[1506] and no nother claimant appearing, Ismail surnamed Safi both by right of blood and conquest gat the sceptre and then entered the city of Shiraz, where he was

---

[1504] "While Esma'il was advancing on Arzenjan by way of Terjan," Monshi writes, "Alvand entered Tabriz and began to extort money forcibly from the populace" (History, 1:45).

[1505] Herbert is listing some of the major Turkmen tribes who helped Ismail in the foundation of what would become the Safavid Empire; however, "the survival of tribal loyalties," as Jackson and Lockhart note, "had serious repercussions for the Safavid state" (215). Indeed, the Afshars and the Qajars would provide Persia with ruling dynasties after the collapse of the Safavids. We have already met members of the others acting as generals, advisers and statesmen under Abbas I.

[1506] Inaccurate. Monshi, for example, states that Alwand "died in Diar Bakr in 910/1504" (*History*, 1:45). For details see Jackson and Lockhart, *History*, 211–12 and Monshi, *History*, 1:42–45. Herbert's sources are Don Juan de Persia and Botero.

welcomed with such demonstrations of joy as is usually afforded conquerors, but what made this change the more acceptable was the long-wished restoration of the diadem to a Prince of the blood of Persia.[1507]

In Persia I endeavoured to inform myself concerning the genuine signification of the word *Sophy*, a name usually attributed to the kings of Persia, but the natives could give me little satisfaction. I find it was not more ancient than Ismail at his coronation, either, as I suppose, in memory of his ancestor who bore that name and indeed laid the first foundation of Ismail's greatness and whence, *honoris gratia*, it might be attributed according to that ancient custom of the oriental and other nations, for in Egypt the Pharaohs and Ptolemies, in Syria the Antiochi, in Persia the Achaemenes and Arsacidae and the Caesars amongst the Romans were in use as now the Sophy. Nevertheless, it seems to me that either the agnomen might be given by the Greeks upon Haidar his father's marriage with Marta the daughter of Despina daughter to Calo-Joannes Emperor of Trebizond as lately mentioned, and by reason of his prudence probably might merit that name as John did *kalos*, i.e. 'good,' and according to the ancient usual custom of the kings of England, France and other places, but if the Greek derivation will not serve, if I may criticise without offence I do observe that in the Armenian idiom *sophy* signifies 'wool,' of which the shashes were made the Persian kings then used to wear, or otherwise may relate to the word *shoff*, as I find the shash in ancient times was termed, which differed from the turban now worn, for it was a high, narrow-peaked cap lined with the rich wool of Khorasan resembling the *cydaris*, which some say Cyrus first invented, but in the Slavonian it signifieth 'studiousness,' and by reason hereof Bayezid was surnamed *Sophy*, he that was son to Suleiman by Roxolana,[1508] as appears in the Turkish history *Vita Solimanis*. But though to me the word *shoff* seems to me derived from *shah*, i.e. 'king,' yet seeing that in the Scythic tongue *soffey* is 'famous,' and that much of the Persian language as well as their extract flows thence, the greater is the probability that hence the name may be deduced, and the rather for that the word *Mughal* is imposed by the Tartars upon the race of Tamerlane ruling Industan, which word in

---

[1507] Some clarification of events is needed here. Ismail's army defeated and killed Farrokh Yasar at a place called Jabani near Shamakhi (December 1500). Alwand, who was not Ismail's uncle but, like him, was a grandson of Uzun Hassan, began collecting his army in the spring of 1501, "moving like a victim to the slaughter" as Monshi put it (I, 45). His victory was not over Murad, but over Qasem Beg Pornak, whom Alwand defeated at Mardin (Monshi I, 45). Alwand was defeated by Ismail at Sharur (July or August 1501). Murad was still a threat, and he too was defeated by Ismail, not by Alwand, at a battle near Hamadan (June 1503). He took refuge with Ala al-dowla, the Zul-Qadar ruler of Maras and Albestan, and in 1507 again raised an army; whether there was a battle or not was disputed (Monshi I, 50–51).

[1508] Roxolana [Alexandra Lisowska], also known as Hürrem (c. 1510–1558), of possible Ukrainian or Ruthenian lineage, was the wife of Suleiman the Magnificent.

their speech imports 'great' or 'illustrious,' though in the first original 'laborious,' but again, when I consider that several of the intervening kings since Ismail have intermitted that word, namely Mohammed surnamed Khodabanda, Tahmasp and Abbas, it may be granted that the word *Sophy* is a proper name and that the former is *datum et non acceptum*, given by the Europeans but not taken by the Persians, for the Prince that succeeded Abbas having his name Safi, as they pronounce, the present king succeeding him is called Abbas, so as it appears to be a proper and alternate name without any further relation.[1509]

'Tekelli' burnt.

To return. The crown was no sooner set upon Ismail's head but by proclamation he ratified the reformation that his grandfather had contrived, declaring thereupon the Turks to be heretics.[1510] This glorious rise continued to the meridian, for to give the Turk some better assurance of his fitness to rule and animosity to the Ottomans, he forthwith entered Diar Bakr with a considerable army, most horse, with which he reduced that, as soon after Armenia, Albania, Iberia and Circassia, which he challenged as his right by descending from Uzun Hassan and quieted the possession with his sword to the inexpressible joy of the Persians but amazement of the Turks, and dread too, perceiving they should now have work enough with the Persians. About this time, *viz.* 1506, that Tekelli,[1511] Haidar's

---

[1509] The problems with it likely arose from European confusion of the name 'Safi' with 'Sufi,' and the fact that both names sound like the Greek *sophia*, which means 'wisdom.' Don Juan de Persia, however, states categorically that "the word *Sophi* does not mean 'wise,' as some erroneously-instructed have said," and he confirms the derivation from the word *soff* (*Relaciones*, 111).

[1510] Savory calls this action "a turning-point in the history of Iran" (Monshi, *History*, 1:45 n. 10). What it did was to effectively impose Shi' a Islam on the country.

[1511] Tekelli [*Techelles*] is Shah Quli from the province of Teke-Ili in Turkey (Anatolia), "who hailed from that area but whose origins are unknown" (Jackson and Lockhart, *History*, 220). Herbert and his sources (see Juan de Persia, *Relaciones*, 113–15, for example) seem to have derived their version of his name from his province; Juan de Persia says that the Turks called him "Tekelli Qizil Bash," which means 'the qizilbash from Teke-Ili' (113). He raised an army and started attacking people in the area, destroying villages and desecrating mosques. Herbert is only partially correct about these events; Lockhart and Jackson state that "although Shah Quli had begun as a supporter of the Safavids, in the later stages of his revolt he had been worshipped as God, Prophet and Mahdi, and had thus relinquished his support for Ismail" (*History*, 221). In fact, he had proclaimed himself caliph in succession to Ismail. As for the burning, it was not Shah Quli who was burnt; in 1504 Ismail had put down a revolt led by one Emir Husain Kia Colavi in Firuzkuh and Damavand, whose corpse he had ordered burned (Monshi, *History*, 1:49). Herbert or his sources seem to have conflated the two incidents. Monshi does not mention his brother Hassan, and neither do Jackson and Lockhart; Juan de Persia, however, says that 'Tekelli' was the *son* of 'Hasan Khalifah' (*Relaciones*, 113); he likely means "successor."

disciple, out of zeal to propagate these new-broached opinions and to force the erroneous Turks to a conformity, with a considerable party of horse which Ismail gave liberty to raise and to be equally-divided betwixt him and Hassan his co-disciple, by some ironically called *Khalifa*, which enterprise for some time gave a notable disturbance to the Turk and not a little advantage to the European Christians, had they made right use of it. Strange it is to consider with what confidence these reputed saints with a small party[1512] advanced against a numerous and the most formidable enemy at that time in the universe, which nevertheless zeal in their apphensions rendered easy to be effected, having therefore in the first place having adjudged the Turks heretics and proclaimed them enemies to the Mussulmanish faith and worthy to be prosecuted with fire and sword, in hostile manner they first entered Anatolia with 20,000 horse and foot, and at Iconium near Lycaeonia[1513] gave Qurqud, who commanded those parts in chief under his uncle Bayezid,[1514] a notable defeat. Soon after he did the like to Qara Qush, the Pasha of Anatolia, so as without let he entered and sacked the rich city of Kutahiyah,[1515] after which, hearing that Ali Pasha was advanced against him with a great body of horse and foot, soldier-like he drew out and met the Turks in the plains of Ancyra,[1516] whom he worsted, the general Ali Pasha in that conflict being found dead in the field,[1517] a success that got Tekelli so high a reputation that even Bayezid himself was startled as if Tamerlane's ghost were revived,

---

[1512] Don Juan de Persia states that it was "an immense multitude of various tribesmen" (*Relaciones*, 113).

[1513] "A section of the southern central tableland of Asia Minor . . . generally thought of as bounded by Galatia, Cappadocia, Isauria, Pisidia and Phrygia." Iconium, now Konya, became the capital of the region in c. 371 (Grant, *Guide*, 363–64).

[1514] Prince Sultan Qorqud [*Orcan*] (d. 1512), governor of Anatolia, a noted Islamic scholar but no general, was Bayezid's son, not nephew (Stanford J. Shaw, *History of the Ottoman Empire and Modern Turkey* [Cambridge: Cambridge University Press, 1976], 1. 77). The battle took place on the plains of Alashehir near Konya (June 1511); Don Juan says that Tekelli "might easily have taken him prisoner or even killed him, but . . . contented himself with putting Qorqud to an ignominious flight" (*Relaciones*, 113). Qorqud was put to death by Selim I in Anatolia.

[1515] Qara Qush [*Garagozes*] (d. 1511) was the beglerbeg of Anatolia. This battle was in Bithynia, and after his defeat Qara Qush fled to Kutahiyah [*Cutbes*] in Galatia, but Tekelli captured the city and put him to death; Juan de Persia says that he was impaled (*Relaciones*, 113–14).

[1516] Now Ankara. It was the capital of Galatia.

[1517] Grand Vizier Khadim Ali Pasha (d. 1511), along with Prince Ahmet, Bayezid II's son, actually defeated Shah Quli at the Battle of Sivas (1511), which, however, "ended in a catastrophe for both sides; the Grand Vizier was mortally-wounded and Shah Quli was killed either during or soon after the engagement" (Jackson and Lockhart, *History*, 221), although Juan de Persia says he escaped and joined Ismail in Little Armenia (*Relaciones*, 115), but Ismail, far from welcoming them, had their leaders executed (Jackson

insomuch as if Ismail had but furnished his captain with recruits and given him that due countenance he deserved, 'tis thought he would have succeeded better in that military progress, which failing, he was forced to maintain his men upon free quarters, so as the pillage the soldiers got made many steal away to secure their booty, which also alienated the affections of the province wherever he came, who formerly gave him an uninterruped entrance amongst them, as the Persians well perceived when they drove their cattle and withdrew themselves to the mountains without giving him any help by men, victual or intelligence, an advantage the crafty Turk quickly espied, so that he marched towards him with a great army, which the Persians by reason of their inequal numbers feared, so as they made what haste they could to secure themselves in the high mountains of Anti-Taurus, whither the Turks pursuing, the Persians made a hasty retreat into Media. And by the way some of them unadvisedly plundering a caravan of raw silk belonging to the merchants of Tabriz and consigned for Trebizond, Tekelli, as soon as he came into Tauris was secured and by Ismail's appointment, seemingly to gratify the Turks, burned or otherwise miserably put to death with several of his officers.

Bayezid, observing Ismail's prudence and good conduct, apprehended he would not only disappoint his aims, the extending of his Empire as far as Indus but by his courage and restless motion prevent his western progress and designs against the Christians, so that he thought it wisdom to firm a truce for some time with the Persian, that he might with more liberty prosecute his other design, for to undertake both at once would be too great an enterprise, and it was not without cause that he dreaded Ismail, whose virtue and martial success was such that he not only stood his ground against the Turk but made the Tartar and Mughal sensible of his discipline, which so elevated his fame that ambassadors from sundry kings and Princes had been with him to congratulate, and amongst other admirers the Jews were so taken with him that they mistook him for their Messiah, but by the just hand of God had so unexpected a return as quickly made them feel their error, finding him rather a second Vespasian. During this short peace, as Bayezid was one way active so was Ismail another, for well knowing the ancient boundary of his territories he forthwith reduced all Sirvan and after that Gilan towards the north, as also what other Princes were not feudatory in Herat, Khuzistan, Kerman and Makran,[1518] but made Qum his usual headquarter and

---

and Lockhart, *History*, 221). There is no basis in historical records for Herbert's claim that Shah Quli was burned alive. The title 'Khadim' means 'eunuch.'

[1518] Ismail conquered Khuzistan to dislodge the independent kingdom of Haviza "ultra-Shi' i sectarians who had lived there since 840/1436" (Jackson and Lockhart, *History*, 216); he attacked Herat because it had been taken over by the Uzbeks in 1506. Herbert describes the campaign against the Uzbeks below, which was extended to move against them in Khorasan as well; Ismail defeated them at Marv (1510) but a Persian army was beaten in Khorasan at the Battle of Ghudjuvan (November 1512). The subjugation of

by Elyas Beg[1519] he infested the Uzbek Tartar, having by that way forced most of Mazanderan to submit. Howbeit, near Varamin[1520] his success was otherwise, by an ambuscade laid by Husain Beg Colavi, Lord of Hablarud and Firuzkuh, who albeit he had news that Ismail was personally advancing thitherward and found himself unable to keep the field, nevertheless fortified some places of defence, in one of which he immured himself, having a great opinion of his men and that the castle was tenable, so that at some distance being summoned he refused to yield, but a royal army drawing before it 'twas expected he would then resign, yet such was his great heart that he kept the place till flux and famine constrained him, whereupon submitting, his former confidence in defying his army so inflamed Ismail that Husain and fifty others suffered under his displeasure, but the rest were pardoned.[1521]

Ismail invades Tartary.

During this, hearing of some resolution the Prince of Mazanderan[1522] had to prevent his recruits, he [Ismail, Ed.] fell speedily into into their country and did them no small mischief, and having taken hostages for their future good behaviour returned to prosecute his intended war against the Chagatai. With twenty thousand horse he entered that country in hostile manner, and albeit he understood by good intelligence that the Tartars had got together near three hundred thousand horse and foot led by *Vlacuc-cawn*[1523] he declined not the fight, which

---

Sirvan had already begun with the defeat of Alwand (1501), "which opened up for Ismail the way to Tabriz, the Turkmen capital" (Jackson and Lockhart, *History*, 212).

[1519] Elyas Beg Eygus-Oglü [*Elias*] (d. 1504), a Turk, was sent by Ismail to attack Husain Kia Colavi [*Ocen-beg Gheloley*] (see above, n. 1052), but was surprised by the rebel before he could muster his troops. Holed up in Varamin, he was persuaded to treat with Husain Kia, whose troops murdered Elyas Beg and his officers as they talked peace (see Monshi, *History*, 1:47–48).

[1520] Herbert has "Boghar," which is incorrect (see Monshi, *History*, 1:47).

[1521] Herbert's account is confused. According to Monshi, Ismail first attacked Gol-é Kandan, a fortress, and then went on to capture Firuzkuh, which was defended by Ali Kia, Husain's brother, whom the Shah spared. Husain and his army "shut himself up in the fortress of Osta, which was the strongest castle in those parts," but in the end they surrendered because of famine and thirst, as Herbert states, after which Ismail ordered a general massacre. Husain was placed in an iron cage but managed to kill himself, after which his body was burned (Monshi, *History*, 1:48).

[1522] This was Aqa Rostam Ruz-Afzun (d. 1510), "who had subjugated and seized control of the province of Mazandaran," and who had "consistently acted in a hostile manner toward officers of the Safavid court" (Monshi, *History*, 1:62).

[1523] Unidentified. However, Herbert may refer to Jan Vafa Mirza (d. 1511), from whose army Sahi Beg split off, leaving him in Herat, from which he eventually fled (Monshi I, 60). He was killed fighting at Mahmudabad [*Maran* in Herbert] with Sahi Beg Khan (see below).

the Tartar, notwithstanding their odds, did for some time, so that Ismail took up his winter quarters in and about *Taran*, but with the first opportunity of weather entered Tuz and enlarged his quarters as far as Samarkand, which was formerly spoiled. That summer he engaged Sahi Beg Khan,[1524] who commanded thirty thousand horse and foot selected from those under *Vlacuc-cawn*, for Sahi Beg Khan on the death of Husain Beg had, it seems, usurped the crown of Khorasan, and Husain's son not being in a condition to defend their right, took the advantage of Ismail's presence, so that having declared the wrong they suffered and voluntarily proffered subjection to his Imperial Crown, he undertook their defence and accordingly entered Rum,[1525] where after a sharp but short dispute at Marv Sahi Beg Khan was slain, and Husain Ali, son to Husain Kia Colavi, upon doing his homage was placed in his father's stead.[1526]

Ismail, having thus enlarged his dominions, with all the force he could make directs his march towards Oxus, and having passed the river, in a pitched field slew Jani Beg Sultan, the Maurenabar king,[1527] yea, without much opposition he harassed far and wide those Scythic provinces. By storm he also took the strong castle *Aelcam*, and after that Dargozin,[1528] Farghana,[1529] *Azfaker* and several other considerable forts in Sogdiana, Ghazna, Maurenabar, Rum and Turkestan, and far beyond Balkh, the Uzbek metropolis, most of which garrisons he slighted, so that Ismail, crowned with victory and his army loaden with spoils of war, upon

---

[1524] Sahi Beg Khan (d. 1510), a descendant of Genghis Khan, usually known as Mohammed Khan Shaibani or Sibani, annexed Transoxiana in 1507 and made himself the ruler there after he had destroyed the Timurids. He ruled "all the land from the farthest reaches of Turkestan to the borders of Persian Iraq" (Monshi, *History*, 1:59). He attacked Kerman in 1510 and was defeated and slain by Ismail's army at Marv (December 2). For details of the battle, see Monshi, *History*, 1:61–62. The Emperor Babur, also, has quite a lot to say about Sahi Beg (*Baburnama* 247ff).

[1525] Rum was populated by Turkmen who were Ottoman subjects. Its inhabitants rebelled against the Turks a few years later (Jackson and Lockhart, *History*, 222).

[1526] There is some confusion here. Ismail appointed Husain Beg Lala as Governor of Herat (Monshi, *History*, 1:65); who Hassan Ali [*Acem-Ally*] might be, I do not know and cannot find a reference in Monshi to any son of Husain Colavi with that name.

[1527] There were two separate actions in Maurenabar (Transoxiana). In the spring of 1511 Ismail, narrowly avoiding a battle, made a truce with Jani Beg Sultan [*Cham-Silha*] and other leaders, but, as Monshi relates, "the Uzbeg sultans . . . did not remain loyal to the treaty," and when Ismail had left "they began to rais the periphery of the Safavid empire" (*History*, 1:64). That led to Ismail giving Babur Mirza (later Emperor Babur of the Mughals) permission to attack them, which he did, defeating them and killing their leaders. It was Babur's victory, not the Shah's; Babur occupied Transoxiana until March 1512, when he was driven out. Unfortunately, the *Baburnama* has a gap from 1509–1519, so we have no account from Babur's own pen about this campaign.

[1528] A city north of Hamadan.

[1529] A city in Uzbekistan, about 150 km south-east of Tashkent.

notice sent him that Bayezid, at the importunity of the Tartars, was drawing near the confines of Persia with a great body of horse and foot,[1530] he retreated and by the way sacked revolting Tuz,[1531] Sakalkand,[1532] and some other offensive towns that interposed. Thus, having sufficiently retaliated the Tartar for the inroads and disturbances they had several times given the Persians to oblige the Turk and for the depredations he had suffered from those vagrant tribes which take their name from the Qara Qoyonlu or Black Sheep, he marched through Mazanderam to Persia in triumph, the country all the way he passed sending in provision and expressing their rejoicings by all the merriments and modes they could, very much to Ismail's satisfaction, and in magnificent manner making his *intrada* into Qum, his reception was with all possible demonstrations of love and joyful acclamations.

In a few days intelligence was brought him how that the Turks were drawing towards Erevan, so that by way of diversion Ismail with fifty thousand horse fell into Diar Bakr, which he harrassed to purpose upon this occasion. The Mesopotamians under the Turk, so soon as they had certain notice that the Persians were invading Tartary, through treachery got into Baghdad, which they plundered, and used the Persians who were soldiers of that garrison very barbarously, for not content to call them *raffadins*, which signifies 'heretics,' they cut off the noses and thumbs of several of them and in that savage manner expulsed them the town, to revenge which Ismail made that spoil in the Turks' quarters, and engaging the enemy near Karamit[1533] had the better of them, insomuch as he had the chase to the very banks of the Tigris, which effected, he returned to Qum, where for the greater provocation of the Turk he caused a swine to be nourished in the court and named it Bayezid. But what immediately followed more perplexed the Turk, for *Anno Dom.* 1511, *Heg.* 891, Ismail recovered Baghdad, into which he was permitted to enter at a postern which Bariq Beg had for a sum of money opened, so unexpectedly to Mohammed Pasha the Governor thereof that without the least resistance he made what haste he could to leave the fort and save himself,

---

[1530] This is not true. Bayezid II, after a revolt led against him by Prince Selim in 1511, was effectively deposed and died in 1512. Monshi notes that far from being overtly hostile and marching against Ismail, the Sultan "had always observed the protocols necessary for a policy of close friendship and alliance" (*History*, 1:67); Bayezid had protested Ismail's harshness against Sunnis after the Shah captured Baghdad in 1508, but he had not sent an army (Shaw, *History*, 76). There seems to be some confusion here with the army that Bayezid sent against Shah Quli. Selim I succeeded and went about eliminating his brothers and other rivals; in 1514 he invaded Azerbaijan, which led to the Safavid disaster at the Battle of Calderan (see below).

[1531] Ismail did not sack Tuz; after the Safavid defeat at Godjovan (November 1512), he merely "sent a number of emirs and a detachment of men in the direction of Tuz," which caused the Uzbeks to retreat across the Oxus (Monshi, *History*, 1:66–67).

[1532] Sakalkand is a town in Tocharistan (northern Afghanistan).

[1533] Karamit in modern Turkey is also known as Amida-Nigra.

believing that the soldiers were all likewise corrupted.[1534] This year Lemos[1535] a Portugal agent was civilly-treated by Ismail at Kashan and by *Mirza Abucaca*[1536] the field-marshal showed the army encamped, who at his return to Goa told Albuquerque, at that time Viceroy, that he verily thought Ismail had not fewer then fifty thousand tents in which were lodged a hundred and thirty thousand men.

Memorable fight in the Chaldiran Plains.

Bayezid was that year, as 'tis reported, poisoned by a Jew,[1537] and his son Selim succeeded, about which time it was that Murad[1538] or Amurath, son to Sultan Ahmet, Bayezid's eldest son, whom Selim had put to death for self-preservation, fled to Ismail, his brother Ala-ed-din doing the like to Qansuh al-Ghuri the Egyptian Sultan, where both were welcomed, though soon after it cost them dear, for it was the occasion of the utter ruin of one and of a quick and sharp war with the other.[1539] Ismail nevertheless seemed glad of any occasion to engage his adversary and to obviate the invasion threatened by Selim. Hearing that Ibrahim Pasha was hastening towards Armenia, he put Murad at the head of ten thousand horse, promising that[1540] with twenty thousand more should second him, in confidence whereof Murad advanced as far as Erzerum, but there having intelligence that Selim was hasting that way, he thought it most advisable, with leave

---

[1534] Barik Beg, a Turkman, had control of Iraq, and Ismail sent him "a gold-embroidered hat, a sword-belt and a special robe of honour" to induce him to submit. Barik, however, wavered in his new-found loyalty, but Baghdad eventually surrendered to Ismail's general Husain Beg Lala. Barik Beg "slipped across the Tigris at night and joined Sultan Morad Aq Qoyunlu in headlong flight toward Aleppo" (Monshi, *History*, 1:54–55). Mohammed Pasha is not mentioned by Monshi.

[1535] Fernão Gomes de Lemos's mission was in 1515, not 1511 as Herbert states here.

[1536] Unidentified.

[1537] Not true. Bayezid II abdicated on 24 April 1512, and died a few months later of natural causes.

[1538] Prince Murad (d. 1514) fled from Selim's approaching army to Isfahan, where he "entered [Ismail's] service" and "was received with favour" (Monshi, *History*, 1:68). However, he died soon afterwards,

[1539] Prince Ahmet (d. 1513), contesting his brother Selim's accession to the throne, sent his son Ala-ud-din to capture the city of Bursa and make it his capital. He set up an administration there, collected taxes and ran a 'government' from Bursa. In the summer of the same year Selim forced Ahmet out and the Prince fled to Cilicia, after which he sought help from Sultan Qansuh al-Ghuri and his Mamluks, because he was anti-Shi'a and would not seek aid from Persia. Selim finally defeated Ahmet at the Battle of Yenisehir (15 April 1513) and had him executed soon afterwards.

[1540] Ustacaoglu Mohammed Khan [*Ustreff-Oglan*] (d. 1514), one of Ismail's chief emirs, would command the left wing of the Persian army at Chaldiran and was killed there.

of Ala-ud-dowla the Prince of Anti-Taurus,[1541] to retreat, well-knowing that his
uncle would hunt after him.

Ismail, upon the first intelligence of Selim's approach, in good order marched
against him with thirty thousand horse and threescore thousand foot, say the
Turk, albeit the Persians allow not above half that number. The Turkish army,
upward of three hundred thousand horse and foot, without opposition passed as
far as the River Araxes, and with help of their great guns being over, both armies
resolved to engage. The Emperors were both there in person and drew up in a
large even place called the Chaldiran Plain, not far from Khoy and near unto Na-
sivan, where for a full sixteen hours a most memorable field was fought with such
fierceness and equal resolution that the Turkish annals call the battle "the day of
doom," in which such was the singular personal valour Ismail expressed that the
Turks themselves spare not to give their enemy high commendations, also gallantly and in such good order his cavalry appeared that had not the noise of the
Turks' artillery affrighted their horse more then their numbers did their riders,
'tis thought the Persians had obtained a clearer victory, for every single Persian
ten Turks being found dead in the place. Now insomuch as there was no chase,
but rather that part of either army kept in a body all the night, until next day they
drew off on either side leaving the country people to bury the dead. The mastery
of the field is not decided by indifferent writers, who yet agree in this, that fifteen thousand men lay dead upon the ground. The Turkish history nevertheless
speaks partially in their own behalf, but this is equally acknowledged, that Selim, immediately after the fight, probably disliking his entertainment and satisfied with the sight of Persia, retreated with his whole body by the skirts of Armenia into Carmania, by the way causing Ala-ud-dowla the Anti-Tauran King to be
strangled for his conrrespondency with Ismail and his nephew Murad,[1542] soon

---

[1541] Ala-ud-dowla Zul Qadar [*Aladules*] (d. 1512/15) ruled in Khamak, "lying west
of Arzinjan on the left bank of the Western Euphrates. His little kingdom appears to
have extended down into Lesser Armenia" (Le Strange, in Don Juan de Persia, *Relaciones*, 321, n. 3). In 1506 Sultan Murad of the Aq Qoyunlu had taken refuge with him,
and he fought against Ismail at Mount Dorna (1508). Monshi, however, states that some
scholars thought that "no battle took place," and whilst he disagrees, he ends by saying
"God knoweth best which is true" (*History*, 1:51). Monshi states that Ala-ud-dowla was
killed fighting the Turks in 1512 (*History*, 1:53), but has Selim I marching against him
right after the Battle of Chaldiran two years later (*History*, 1:71). Juan de Persia has him
strangled by order of Selim I in 1515 after being captured (*Relaciones*, 120), with which
Herbert concurs. Anti-Taurus is a name used by Strabo to designate a range of mountains
parallel to Taurus across the Seyhan River in south-east Turkey, running to the Cappadocian plateau (5.319).

[1542] There is little doubt that Chaldiran was a Turkish victory, largely due to the
Turks' overwhelming superiority in troop-numbers and artillery. The Persians scorned
the use of the latter on a large scale, although they were certainly cognizant of its use and
effectiveness quite early in the history of firearms. Monshi reports a Persian commander,

after with all the force he could make invading Egypt. By the treachery of Khair Bey the Sultan of Aleppo[1543] he vanquished Qansuh al-Ghuri and reduced their kingdom into a province, which from Sultan Saladin *Anno Heg.* 680 had continued in that race to the year *Heg.* 896, and albeit the recovery was in vain endeavoured by Tuman Bey,[1544] the Turk holds possession unto this day.

While Ismail, retiring to Qazvin, took care of his wounded soldiers, and having recruited his army prosecuted the subjection of Mazanderam, and withal for the better preservation of his person and honour and in imitation of the Mamelukes who then guarded the person of the Egyptian king, instituted a lifeguard called *qizlbashes*, which at first consisted of an hundred horse, most of them Georgians, but since the number increased to a thousand, into which order none are admitted until they are experienced in arms and are of more then ordinary repute, in the execution of which trust they accordingly have extraordinary pay, which they well deserve, for I have been in the company of many of them and at all times found them exceeding civil as well as sociable, and especially to strangers. Paulus Jovius and some others report that in memory of the twelve sons of Hassan son of Ali, from whose youngest son Mirza Mahdi Ismail drew his descent, this order had its beginning and that their *mandils* or turbans were folded in twelve plaits and the tag or point like the end of a sugar-loaf piercing the turban was red, and from that colour takes the name of *qizlbash*, i.e. 'red head.' Howbeit, for several months I was conversant with these *qizlbashes* in Persia, and to the best of my remembrance never observed that the fashion of their *mandil* or turban was such, or to differ from that form you see represented in this narrative *fol.* 165 and 226, and if any difference be it is in the elevation. But for

---

Durmis Khan, stating "with arrogant pride" when another officer spoke of Selim's firepower and suggested attacking the Turks when they were on the move, "I am not a caravan-thief. Whatever is decreed by God will occur" (*History*, 1:68). It did; Jackson and Lockhart call Chaldiran "a shattering defeat" (*History*, 224), although Monshi cites Hasan Beg Rumlu, a Persian historian, as saying that "five thousand men were killed, of whom three thousand were Ottomans" (1:71). Historians concur that after the battle Selim did enter Tabriz, but did not stay long due to his men's near-mutinous state, and withdrew soon afterwards to his own territories (see Monshi, *History*, 1:71; Jackson and Lockhart, *History*, 225).

[1543] Khair Bey [*Caer-beg*] (d. 1552), a Circassian, was appointed Governor of Egypt by Selim I in 1517 as his reward for delivering the country into Turkish hands. Selim created him the first Pasha of his reign, and Egypt became a vassal state. By the Egyptians his name was changed to *Khain*, which means 'traitor,' from *Khair*, which means 'good' (Afaf Lutfi al-Sayyid Marsot, *A History of Egypt from the Arab Conquest to the Present* [Cambridge: Cambridge University Press, 2007], 45).

[1544] Al-Ashraf Tuman Bey II [*Toman-beg*] (1516–1517) continued the struggle against the Turks after the death of Qansuh al-Ghuri. He was defeated at the Battle of Raydaniyya (22 January 1517) and at Giza (3 April), after which he fled to the village of Damanhur, where he was captured and hanged two weeks later by order of Selim I.

the tag or point I am sure I never saw any nor any of that shape worn unless it be
in the *coola* or cap that is usually by the inferior sort worn in Mazanderam and
other parts of Persia, being cloth on the outside and shag or fine and short curling sheep's fleece on the inside, sharp like the top of a sugar-loaf at the point and
rising a span from the head, as you may see resembled. But concerning the name
I have the less scruple, albeit the truth is when I demanded the signification of
the name from some of them they pleaded ignorance as we understand it, as also
the ground of their institution.[1545]

In that interval, Tabriz by a party from Diar Bakr suffered by Ibrahim
Khan,[1546] afterward a favourite to Suleiman the Magnificent, upon the invitation
of Olama Beg a discontented Persian, who notwithstanding he had the honour
to marry Ismail's sister, yet upon some special favour expressed to Zeynal [Beg]
held a treasonable correspondence with the Turk, and not content therewith, so
corrupted Mohammed Ali Beg,[1547] then Governor of Baghdad, that the place
was treasonably delivered up to Suleiman to the extreme vexation of the Persian
king and little comfort of Ali Beg, who soon after received the reward due unto
such treachery. This year Shah Tahmasp was born at Ardabil, and in the five succeeding years after, but by several wives, Ismail had Alqas Khan, Sam Mirza,
and Bahram Khan otherwise named Elyas Beg.[1548] *Anno Dom.* 1520 Selim the

---

[1545] Juan de Persia says that "it was Ali who instituted this form of headgear, which
was a bonnet or high-hat made of cotton-stuff or wool, of a red colour. This is what the
words *Qizil Bash* signify, namely "red head," and it is for this, as we shall find later, that
the Turks call the Persians the Qizil Bash" (*Relaciones*, 110).

[1546] The account of his Ibrahim's execution (1536) given below by Herbert is inaccurate.

[1547] Mohammed Khan Saraf al-Din Oglu (d. 1547), whom Monshi calls, contrary
to Herbert, "a genuine Sufi and a single-minded supporter of the Safavid house," actually abandoned Baghdad on orders from the Shah "cut the bridge, and with about three
hundred followers who were loyal to the Shah went via Basra to Defzul and from there
to Shiraz." The garrison then welcomed the Turks into the city (*History*, 113). Mohammed Khan served as *amir al-omara* of Khorasan and received Emperor Humayun when
he visited Herat (1545).

[1548] Alqas Mirza [*Hel-cawn*] (1515–1550), whom Monshi calls "that ignoramus,
that ingrate" (*History*, 1:115) and a "foolish Prince" (1:116) was Sirvan Shah (1538–1547).
He rebelled and defected to the Ottomans, under whom he was given military command
(see Jackson and Lockhart, *History*, 242–43), supported Olama Takkalu, and was captured, pardoned by Tahmasp and imprisoned at Alamut (1549), dying soon afterwards
in captivity (Monshi, *History*, 1:124). Sam Mirza [*Sormiza*] (1518–1567) was Governor-
General of Khorasan (1521–1529; 1532–1534) and Governor of Ardabil (1549–1561). He
also rebelled and was imprisoned after being pardoned. Bahram Mirza [*Barbon-cawn*]
(1518–1550) served as Governor-General of Khorasan (1529–1532), Governor of Gilan
(1536–1537) and of Hamadan (1546–1549). He remained loyal to his brother Tahmasp
and served him in both administrative and military capacities.

Great Turk died, succeeded by Suleiman,[1549] five years after which Shah Ismail died in the twentieth year of his reign and fortieth of his age, and was buried near his ancestors at Ardabil, in his place Tamas or Shah Tahmasp, as some call him, being crowned king.

The Turk beaten by the Portugal.

Babylon thus taken, it gave the Turk the easier reduction of Diar Bakr and part of Khuzestan, with all those adjacent countries that confine the north of Arabia, inasmuch as with very little resistance they became masters also of the Rivers Tigris and Euphrates, which gave them a desirable prospect into the Gulf of Persia with some further hopes of all those regions that extend as far as Indus, and that they might have the opportunity of requiting Tamerlane's issue for that memorable loss they suffered at Mount Stella under Bayezid. In order thereunto, the Grand Seigneur forthwith appointed a great quantity of timber to be cut in Cilicia, now called Kerman, and shipped it thence for Pelusium and Cairo, whence by camels it was drawn to Suez, where a navy consisting of an hundred vessels great and small was in short space built and fitted for sea, which was no sooner made ready but he appoints Suleiman Pasha[1550] to put ten thousand soldiers aboard at the port of Mocha, and coasting the south of Arabia to endeavour the surprise of Diu; those were his instructions, which great design how secretly soever it was managed was seasonably communicated to the Portugal, in whose hands the castle was, albeit they pretend they had no notice until the fleet was discovered near the place, so that albeit they could not so well provide against their landing as they would, yet the Turks being ashore and marching immediately towards the fort, which without a summons they rudely stormed, were so gallantly repulsed by the Portugal that many Turks there breathed their last, and finding that the castle was neither so weakly-manned nor flanked as they were made believe and that the Portugals were in a gallant posture of defence, but which most amazed them, the Mohammedans thereabouts gave them little encouragement to stay, the frigates from several parts also embodying threatened to intercept them in their return, those and other considerations not only hastened them aboard but made them hoist sail, for all which they were so well-beaten by the Portugal that a great part of the fleet was sunk and dispersed, so as few of them came safe back to Aden, those that got ashore near Muscat and other parts of Arabia being also so coarsely-enterteined by the natives that not above one-third of the number got back to Aden, a success so gtaeful to the Persian that he congratulated the Christians and the Mughal expressed the like sense, altogether dislining such a neighbourhood.

[1549] Sultan Suleiman I 'the Magnificent' was Ottoman emperor 1520–1566.

[1550] Serjeant prints the full account of the attack on Diu by the Turks written by an Arab chronicler (*Portuguese*, 86–94).

Suleiman, heartily vexed, nevertheless thought fit to colour this loss the best
he could, and therefore draws all the horse he could out of Diar Bakr and Carmania, with which he fell so unexpectedly into Media that he entered Tabriz[1551]
before Shah Tahmasp could be in a posture to resist. Most miserably was that
poor city used by the enraged Turk, albeit no opposition was made, for not content with plunder they cut down their fruit-trees and trees for shade, yea, levelled
with the ground the King's palace and such other houses of the nobility as might
best express their malice, and then laden with spoil marched back to Carandab
in Diar Bakr, where for some time they rested.

Deli Mohammed beats the Turk.

Tahmasp and the Persian nobility, sufficiently incensed, were not idle in the
meantime to find means to retaliate, for having ordered Deli Mohammed,[1552]
one that had many times engaged the Turks, with six thousand horse to follow
close in the rear, he so galled them with continual alarms that Ibrahim Pasha,
not well enduring because not formerly acquainted with such a bravado, made
a stand and next to Bitlis, then a Persian garrison, drew up with a resolution to
fight, and well might, being upwards of two hundred thousand horse and foot,
notwithstanding which inequality the Persian horse, taking the opportunity of
the darkness of night, fell into their enemy's quarters with such courage and good
order as if they had been treble the number, seconding that with such courage
and good order as the Turks by this unexpected alarm after a little resistance fell
into great confusion, inasmuch as at length they fled whither they apprehended
they could best secure themselves. In the pursuit five sanjaks, eight hundred janissaries and twenty thousand private soldiers were slain, forty pieces of cannon
taken, Olama Beg the Persian rebel and the two pashas narrowly escaping, but
what madded old Suleiman, they took his seraglio which was then upon camels,
and all were beauties he not a little doted upon, a victory not more joyous to the
Persian, for 'tis annually celebrated upon the third and tenth of October, then
vexatious to the Turk, and of that present influence that Ibrahim the great Pasha
from thenceforward declined in his master's favour, for unwilling that the Pasha

---

[1551] Actually Ibrahim Pargali occupied Tabriz first (July 1534) and Suleiman himself arrived two months later (Jackson and Lockhart, *History*, 241). The Turks held the
city only until the next year.

[1552] Deli Mohammed [*Delimenthes*] is probably fictional. Juan de Persia, the source
here, recounts how on October 13, 1536 "Deli Mohammed . . . took them [the Turks] by
surprise in the darkness, when an immense number of the enemy were put to the sword"
(*Relaciones*, 125). Monshi does not mention this event, neither do Jackson and Lockhart;
we may therefore conclude, as Le Strange does, that Juan de Persia's account "appears to
be a patriotic invention" (323, n. 12). Tahmasp sent Princes Bahram and Alqas to Tabriz
and followed a little later, and by the time they got there "Sultan Suleiman had left Tabriz
and was advancing on Iraq" (*History*, 1:111).

should *in bello bis peccare*[1553] he first remanded him to court and so ordered that without seeing his face he was immediately strangled by a mute, who surprised him sleeping. By that delinquency the vast wealth he had heaped together whiles he was a favourite and in great command was then also seized by Suleiman, who presented a great part of it to his chief delight the fair Roxolana, who, the truth is, for his siding with Mustafa[1554] against her son had principally contrived and after this manner effected this late great Pasha's destruction.

Roxolana's sons' sad end.

About this time Bayezid,[1555] Suleiman's son by Roxolana, was worsted by his brother Selim,[1556] so that he fled for safety to Tahmasp, whom he found at Qazvin, where he was really welcomed, but Suleiman, imagining that he would provoke the Persian to an unwished invasion, having then bent his whole design against the Christians, peremptorily sent to demand his son, which being denied he seconds it with a cominatory letter yet withal assuring Tahmasp that he came designedly to assassinate him, so that contrary to his faith and honour

---

[1553] [One should not] blunder twice in war. The full phrase is a Latin proverb, *non licet in bello bis peccare.*

[1554] Prince Mustafa of Manisa and Amasya (1515–1553) was Suleiman's heir-apparent, the son of his first wife Gulbadar Sultan. In fact, he conspired with Roxolana and Grand Vizier Damat Rustem Pasha against his father, and was first arrested, then executed, as Herbert relates below, although he seems to have confused the chronology; Prince Mustafa died several years before Prince Bayezid.

[1555] Prince Bayezid (1521–1562) had done good service by quelling a revolt in Thrace (1554) and as Governor of Kutahiya, but in 1554 Suleiman dismissed him and replaced him with his brother Selim (see below). Bayezid refused to be dismissed and attacked Selim, who defeated him in Konya (1559). He attempted to make peace with his father, who responded by sending another army to capture him, at which point he fled to Tahmasp. "Bayezid maintained his haughty and arrogant demeanour," Monshi reports; he was "an arrogant, reticent, and cold-natured man" (*History*, 1:168). Monshi supports Sultan Suleiman's claim that Bayezid wished Tahmasp no good; he "revealed his secret self . . . and conspired to inflict injury on the Shah's person" (1:170). He was handed over, not to Hassan Aga but to Khusrau Pasha; "it never entered the Shah's head," Monshi writes, "that the Ottoman envoys would do harm to Bayezid while he was on Persian territory, but as soon as he was handed over, he and his four sons were immediately put to death on instructions from Sultan Suleiman" (1:172).

[1556] Selim II "the Drunkard" was Ottoman Sultan 1566–1574. There was a fourth brother, the hunchback Prince Cihangir (1531–1553), who seems to have died of natural causes. Suleiman also had three children by various concubines; of these only Prince Mehmet (1521–1543) survived to adulthood, and died of smallpox.

he unadvisedly delivered up the poor Prince to Hassan Aqa,[1557] the Turk's
ambassador, who thereby had the opportunity not only to murder the Prince
but also four of his children, namely Omar, Murad, Selim and Mehmet, to the
everlasting shame and reproach of them that so counselled the King and to the
immoderate anguish of Roxolana's spirit, though to the seeming satisfaction of
an enraged father whom Tahmasp thought would have been pacified with such
a victim and that by his compliance had put a lasting obligation upon the Turk,
which he quickly found otherwise, whiles Suleiman, upon a pretence of righting
Alqas Mirza, one of Ismail's sons and at that time Governor of Sirvan but retired
to Derbent, with a considerable party, most horse, enters Armenia, surprised
the city Van, and persuading the Mirza to go to Baghdad the Turks drew back,
whereupon the Governor of Baghdad having received a large bribe delivered the
poor prince up to Shah Tahmasp, who after a month's imprisonment caused him
likewise to be strangled.[1558]

Notwithstanding which, Suleiman next year in the head of an hundred and
fifty thousand men enters Persia, to oppose whom Shah Tahmasp, having by sad
experience found the advantage the Turks had by their great ordinance, prevailed
with the Viceroy of Goa to furnish him with five thousand Portugals from Hormuz, Diu and other garrisons, who were the more willing for the late invasion
the Turk made against Diu near Indus. The Portugals were all foot and brought
along with them a train of twenty pieces of cannon, which in the fight was so
unexpected that it both amazed and mischiefed the Turks, inasmuch as the Persians had the better of that day's contest, the success whereof they attributed and
accordingly gave the Christians a due acknowledgement of that good service, and
from that day forward the Persians were acquainted with the use of guns, and of
small shot they have attained the mastery.

Suleiman by this mischance was constrained to draw back into Anatolia,
during which Mustafa, another of Roxolana's sons, incurred his father's high
displeasure, and forgetful of his brother's tragic end simply commits himself to
the favour of the Persian King, who having first exclaimed upon the villainous
Pasha Hassan, then gave the Prince assurance of his life during his abode, notwithstanding which Suleiman, who was pretty well-practiced in the roadway
to Persia, marches thitherward with eighty thousand men, Turk-like doing all
the mischief he could, albeit to prevent further spoil Tahmasp advanced with
all the force he had as far as Erec, where coming to an engagement the Persian
horse, not yet enduring the noise of guns would not be ordered, so that many
of the Persians were killed by shot and the rest forsook the field, leaving poor

---

[1557] Hassan Aqa was actually Suleiman's chief taster; he was sent with Ali Pasha, the
Governor of Maras, "to fetch Bayezid" (Monshi, *History*, 1:171–72). In 1559 he was one
of the ambassadors to the court of Shah Tahmasp (1:192).

[1558] Herbert's facts are largely correct but his chronology is wrong; Alqas died a captive in 1550.

Mustafa to shift for himself, who by some sinister advice flying to his father's tent and prostrate at his feet in a lamentable manner beseeching pardon even for his mother Roxolana's sake, the cruel and inexorable Turk (unworthy the name of father), forthwith commands him to be strangled, albeit he was the only son by that venter then living. But long he lived not after this savage cruelty, for that year 1566 he sighed out his affrighted ghost at the siege of Szigeth in Hungary.[1559] Ambassadors from most parts, according to custom congratulating his successor's access to the crown, Shah Tahmasp despatched Shah Quli Khan to Istanbul; this man was both well-known and feared amongst the Turks and Indians. In his passage to court being gallantly attended, one time he gave a visit according to form to the Vizier Pasha and was shot at by a desperate *jemoglan*[1560] upon no other provocation then for that he was a heretic. He narrowly escaped, but the *jemoglan* being apprehended, his blind zeal could not prevent his immediate torture.

[The Death of Shah Tahmasp].

The Turk in the interim took Nicosia and Cyprus from the Venetians, which occasioned a perpetual league with Spain and all the Princes of Italy; yea, Vincentio d' Alessandri,[1561] a Secretary to that Republic, was despatched unto Persia to awaken that King. This gentleman had the Slavonian tongue, insomuch as he passed through Poland down the Danube into the Euxine and so incognito and in disguise to Trebizond, whence by Erzerum, a Cappadocian town on the outskirts of Armenia, he came safe to Qazvin. There, having produced his credentials, he was very civilly entertained, and albeit no rhetoric wanted not argument to enforce the Persian to fall speedily into the Turkish quarters, seeing he had drawn all his force against the European Princes, yet such was his propensity to ease or else the dread he had of the Turkish puissance that no persuasions would at that time serve to make a satisfactory return unto the Venetians, still imagining that the Turk would gratify. Now, the thanks he gave was this:

[1559] Suleiman I invaded Persia on four occasions: 1533, 1534–1535, 1548–1549, and 1553–1554. Details of all these invasions may be read in Monshi, who devotes an entire section to them (*History*, 1:109–22; 124–31). Szigeth is the modern city of Szeged, near the Serbian border.

[1560] A kind of Turkish infantryman, especially a musketeer.

[1561] Vincentio d' Alessandri visited Persia in 1571. Pope Pius V had hoped for an anti-Turk alliance, but d' Alessandri had written that "little or nothing could be expected from Tahmasp. The Shah had, he said, been immured in his palace for eleven years and cared only for women and money; the country was in a bad state, there was much injustice and the roads were unsafe" (Jackson and Lockhart, *History*, 384). His reports may be found in Charles Grey, ed. *A Narrative of Italian Travels in Persia in the Fifteenth and Sixteenth Centuries* under the title *The Narrative of the Most Noble Vincentio d' Alessandri*, trans. W. Thomas and S. Roy (London: Hakluyt Society, 1873).

Amurath¹⁵⁶² no sooner put an end to the Cyprian war (*Anno* 1575) and recruited himself after that great and memorable defeat given him at Lepanto¹⁵⁶³ but he fell afresh to quarrel with the Persian upon no other pretence then the death of Ercas Mirza his late friend. Accordingly he prepares to renew the war, whiles the Persian king, ignorant of those preparations, with what force he could invades the Uzbeks' country and happily took Kabul, but hearing that the Turk intended to prosecute the Persian war, he forthwith retreated to Qazvin, where amidst his martial consultations and provisions Death gave him his *supersedes*¹⁵⁶⁴ and summoned him to another world after fifty years' rule¹⁵⁶⁵ and fourteen days' sickness, at the age of sixty-eight giving up the ghost, so that at Ardebil with all due ceremony he was interred near to his royal ancestors.

The tragic end of several Persian Princes.

Shah Tahmasp left behind him twelve sons and three daughters. The sons were Mohammed, Ismail, Haidar, Suleiman, Emamqoli, Murad, Mustafa, Ali, Mohammed, Hamza, Hasan and Ahmed Khan.¹⁵⁶⁶ Mohammed by right of primogeniture claimed but could not have the crown, so strong a faction was raised

---

¹⁵⁶² Murad III was Ottoman sultan 1574–1595. He broke the Treaty of Amasya (1555) and invaded Azerbaijan in 1576–1577. Ercas-Mirza is unidentified; Monshi makes no reference to him in his account of Murad's activities. He may be the beglerbeg of Rumelia, Murad's favourite. Herbert always uses the form "Amurath," which I have emended to Murad from this point. Murad III was known as a patron of the arts and a composer of mystical verse.

¹⁵⁶³ The Battle of Lepanto took place in 1571, when a fleet sent by Sultan Selim II was defeated by a combined force of Venetians, Spaniards, Genoese, and others under the command of Don John of Austria. The Turks took Cyprus in 1570.

¹⁵⁶⁴ A legal term meaning "order, judgment or proclamation."

¹⁵⁶⁵ Actually, fifty-three years. The trouble with the Turks did not begin in his reign, but shortly after the murder of his successor Ismail II (see below). Tahmasp died on 14 May 1576.

¹⁵⁶⁶ Tahmasp actually had twenty-three sons and thirteen daughters alive at the time of his death (Monshi, *History*, 1:206). Those mentioned by Herbert are noted here. Mohammed became Shah Mohammed Khodabanda; Ismail II succeeded Tahmasp; Haidar (1555–1576) was "a man of integrity, chaste, compassionate, kindly" (Monshi, *History*, 1:215) who had aspirations to be shah; Suleiman (1554–1576) served as Comptroller of the Imam Reza Shrine and Governor of Mashad; Emamqoli (1562–1577) was governor of Lahijan; Mustafa (1557–1576), described by Monshi as "extremely capable and talented" (1:216), was Governor of Gilan; Hassan (1558–1576) was made governor of half of Mazanderam. They were almost all killed by order of their brother Ismail II. However, Prince Ali (1562–after 1616) was still alive when Monshi wrote his chronicle 1:218). Herbert mistakenly adds Prince Hamza (1564–1586) to the list; he was actually Tahmasp's grandson (for him see above, n. 345). Monshi gives details of them all (1:206–21) and of their murder, which he calls "martyrdom" (1:309–15).

by his virago sister Pari Khan Khanum[1567] in the behalf of Ismail the second brother, Samkal Khan[1568] joining in the conspiracy, pretending that by reason of Mohammed's imperfection Tahmasp had nominated Ismail to succeed, so that Mohammed for the safety of his life was forced to fly into Georgia, the conspirators in the interim putting Haidar and eight others of the sons of Tahmasp to untimely deaths. Ismail soon after was served with the same sauce,[1569] for one night expecting the admittance of some of his harem, Pari Khan Khanum with four young Sultans disguised in women's apparel entered his chamber and took off his head, a cruelty quickly requited by Mohammed, for enforcing his way with 12,000 horse the Georgians and Kurds supplied him with, he was no sooner seated on the throne of his royal ancestors but command was given Salman Mirza,[1570] General of the Horse, to retaliate his Amazonian sister, and accordingly her head with her long curled hair dangling down was on a spear's point presented Mohammed, who in the beholding it was affrighted as if he had viewed Medusa's head.[1571]

[1567] Pari Khan Khanum [*Peria-Conconna*] (1548–1578) "did everything she could to promote the cause of Ismail" (Monshi, *History*, 1:218). She became too powerful for her brother Ismail II, whom she considered owed his accession to her, and she appears to have alienated many powerful emirs at court, including her brother, who took exception to a woman having so much influence; this did not stop her from becoming Regent when Ismail was killed. She was strangled at the accession of Shah Mohammed Khodabanda, the murderers "acting on orders," as Monshi put it without saying whose orders they were (*History*, 1:337).

[1568] Samkal Sultan Cerkes (d. 1578) was the maternal uncle of Pari Khan Khanum and the man who strangled Prince Suleiman (see above). His daughter married Ismail II (1576). Samkal was also involved in the murder of Prince Haidar (Monshi, *History*, 1:306). On the accession of Mohammed Khodabanda he was himself murdered by Aslan Khan, an emir (Monshi, *History*, 1:337).

[1569] Monshi's account of Ismail II's death (25 November 1577) differs from Herbert's. One night he took a large dose of opium and died the next morning, but "the physicians discovered traces of poison in the Shah's body," and some people speculated that Pari Khan "had conspired with maidservants of the harem to arrange that poison be inserted in [Ismail's] electuary mixture" (Monshi, *History*, 1:27). However, no Persian source mentions "sultans" disguised as women. Jackson and Lockhart state that the Shah died "in an unexpected and mysterious fashion" (*History*, 253). The story of men in women's clothing is reported by Juan de Persia, Herbert's likely source (*Relaciones*, 132).

[1570] Salman Mirza Jabiri (d. 1582) was Superintendent of the Royal Workshops. Ismail II appointed him Vizier in 1577 and he managed to retain his position after the Shah's death, by helping Mohammed Khodabanda succeed. His daughter married Prince Hamza, the heir-apparent, and he became very powerful, but he was soon murdered by some emirs for "behaving in a dictatorial way" (Monshi, *History*, 1:420). He did not have anything to do with the murder of Pari Khan Khanum.

[1571] Herbert's account of Pari Khan's death does not agree with Monshi's. According to the latter "some of Kalil Khan's men, acting on orders, strangled Pari Khan" (History,

Emir Hamza Mirza's success against the Turk.

These intestine broils so weakened the common interest that the Turk, who wants no foresight espying his advantage, prepared with all the force he could draw out of Asia the Less, Diar Bakr and parts about Baghdad to make an entire conquest or at least to overrun the Persian, which country alone had spent him more men, treasure and time than all Anatolia and Morea had done by reasons of the divisions that happened in most of those provinces, and having the like hopes of Persia by these divisions, Mustafa the cruel and perfidious Pasha was ordered to undertake that task, which being agreeable to his nature was readily accepted, so that albeit the haste the Turk made was great, yet the preparations being such also, Mohammed in the interval got himself quietly possessed of the crown, insomuch as at the first notice of the Turk's approach Sultan Toqmaq,[1572] who was at that time Governor of Revan[1573] and famous for an expert soldier so as he was both known and feared by the Turk, with a very gallant body of horse encountered the enemy upon the frontiers of Armenia, and in a speedy engagement expressed so much resolution that day as albeit Mustafa had treble the number, the van led by Bairam Beg[1574] was routed, and prosecuting that charge broke through the whole party, most of which was cut off, without giving the least quarter, which so enraged the wrathful Pasha that immediately ordering his whole body to advance, by their numbers they overpowered the Persian, so that albeit they fought most desperately and in that charge slew above 10,000 Turks they were nevertheless in fine forced to retreat and to leave 4000 of their company dead in the place, with whose heads and those of his own whom the Persians had slain the savage Turk faced a great bulwark, inasmuch as nothing could be seen but ghastly faces and heads, which made it a terrible object, and this he erected as a trophy of his victory, or rather barbarism, but represented to his master in the best sense as if the slaughter had been much more then it really was, for all which Mustafa, disliking his late entertainment and hearing that

---

1:337) and there is no mention of the head being shown to Shah Mohammed. However, Juan de Persia writes that "her head, all bloody and dishevelled," was "stuck on a lance-point, thus exposed to public view" (*Relaciones*, 135).

[1572] Mohammadi Khan Toqmaq Ustalju (d. 1580), Beglerbeg of Cokur-é Sad, was a soldier and diplomat. He represented Persia at the coronations of Selim II and Murad III, and was Governor of Revan and of Tabriz. The battle described here is the Battle of Khildir or Coldor (August 1578). It is reported in some detail by Monshi (History, 1:350–51).

[1573] Yerevan in Armenia. This city was finally captured by Murad IV (1635) during the Ottoman-Persian war.

[1574] Bairam Beg was one of the commanders described by Juan de Persia, who calls him Bahram Pasha, as "valiant warriors and excellent commanders" (Relaciones, 137). He also took part in the defeat of Toqmaq (138), although Monshi does not mention him at all.

Salman Mirza was advancing with a fresh party of horse, withal finding upon a muster he took that 40,000 of his men were lost by fluxes, his enemies' sword and the bad weather they endured passing the montains in the way to Tiflis. Those considerations swayed with him to retreat, but by the way being encouraged with a large recruit of men conducted by Manuchar a Georgian Prince, Alexander his brother and son to Levanti Beg[1575] taking like care of his victual, he now resolved to re-enter Sirvan. For more expedition and and better safety part of his army marched through unfrequented paths showed them by the apostate Georgian, and other part through Armenia, which the Persians had made desolate to prevent the Turk of relief, and having notice that towards Derbent a great part of the cattle of the country were driven away, in the first place he ordered a party of horse that way for forage, which Toqmaq the Persian general no sooner had notice of but that with the like spriteful party he beat up the Turks' quarters as they lay dispersed in a valley which was wellnigh compassed with the River Kanak,[1576] a river that of itself is sufficiently rapid but by some late rains so increased that the Turk in flying from the enemy lost by the sword and torrent 10,000 of his men, the Persians by their pursuit losing also a considerable number in the stream, which was so fierce that the Turkish general himself, upon the alarm making all the haste he could to succour his men, is said to lose 8000 more in the river and in Araxes, into which Kanak and Kur run.

Notwithstanding these abatements Mustafa continued his march as far as the city Erec, where he expected some opposition, but the people were all fled and had removed much of their goods into the mountainous parts so that the town was left desolate and once ordered to be burnt, but upon second thought spared and garrisoned with 5000 men, most of which were Georgians forced thither by the sons of Levanti Beg. This done, they took Samakhi without resistance, which they might well do, the Governor being withdrawn. Mustafa, overjoyed with this success, first constituted Osman Beg[1577] commander-in-chief in those parts, and then with the greater part of his army fell back towards Erzerum his usual headquarter, while Osman in the meantime was pinched in Sirvan with want and not a little disheartened by the running away of many of his men, whereby and by the janissaries' advice he fell back to Tiflis, yet not so secretly but that in passing through Georgia he was so hotly alarmed by the country people who had

---

[1575] Manuchar (Minuchir) I Dadiani was later Prince of Mingrelia 1590–1611. Alexander (Iskander) II was King of Kakheti 1574–1605, the son of Levanti or Levan II, who reigned 1520–1574. Manuchar married Nestan-Darejan (d. 1597), the daughter of Alexander II, and was therefore not his brother but his son-in-law. Juan de Persia makes the same mistake (*Relaciones*, 40).

[1576] Le Strange notes that the River Kanak [*Conac*], "a left bank affluent of the River Araxes," no longer appears on maps (Juan de Persia 325, n. 4).

[1577] Osman Pasha Ozdemiroglu is the same general who sacked Tabriz (see above, n. 467). Lala Mustafa Pasha made him beglerbeg of Sirvan (Monshi, *History*, 1:353).

abundantly smarted by the insolence of the Turk as with sufficient loss he continued his march till he attained Erzerum. There he took up his winter quarters, but dispersed his army into several villages thereabouts, Mustafa being removed during this the Precopence under the command of Adel Geray[1578] marched through the Circassian territories with 30,000 horse and foot, in all their passage along the Caspian shore as far as Derbent not meeting with the least interruption, which gave them the greater confidence to enter Sirvan. At and about Genje[1579] were quartered all the Persian horse under Emamqoli Khan;[1580] Aras Khan,[1581] having notice, drew all his horse together, resolved with the first advantage he could spy to welcome the uninvited Tartar, but Adel, by the good intelligence he had, prevented that design and contrarily began with the Persian, and with that courage as most of the Persian horse was routed and many officers and soldiers slain, and Aras Khan himself, doing what he could to rally, was taken prisoner and sent to Osman, who without any consulting with a council of war, caused him to be hanged up in that garrison. Such was Aras his sad exit, but in this alarm Emamqoli Khan, albeit he narrowly escaped a surprise, yet could not he prevent the taking of his harem, which extremely troubled him, there being some beauties which were presented the Turkish general.

Mohammed, surnamed Khodabanda by the Turk for that he was purblind,[1582] though as I apprehend it may be rather from *Cognabanda*, as the place was called where he had both birth and education, by his first wife had several sons,[1583] namely Ismail,[1584] Mustafa, Mir Khan, Junaid and Safi Mirza. Ismail, by the malice and

---

[1578] Adel Geray Khan [*Abdul-Chery*] (d. 1580), "a gallant youth" (Juan de Persia, *Relaciones*, 149), was the younger son of Dowlat Geray I (r. 1551–1577), the khan of the Crimean Tartars (Monshi, *History*, 1:354). His story is told in more detail below.

[1579] Modern-day Ganca in Azerbaijan. It is renowned for its carpets.

[1580] Emamqoli Khan Qajar (d. 1588) served as governor of Ganja and of Qarabag. He is not to be confused with Emamqoli Khan the son of Allah Verdi Khan, whom Herbert met in Shiraz.

[1581] Aras Khan Rumlu [*Erez-chan*] (d. 1580) was the *amir-al-umara* of Sirvan. After his evacuation of Sirvan he was captured and executed by the Turks, as Herbert relates.

[1582] Nearly blind.

[1583] Herbert's list is wrong. Mohammed's sons were as follows. Hassan Mirza (1558–1578), Governor of half of Mazanderan (1569–1577), put to death by Ismail II. His mother was "the daughter of Mir Abd al-Azim Seyfi Hoseyni, a respected Gilani emir" (Monshi, 1:208); Hamza Mirza (1565–1586), who is discussed at length by Herbert (also see above, n. 365); Shah Abbas I (1571–1629); Abu Talib (1574–1619), proclaimed heir-apparent (1586), blinded and imprisoned by Abbas I; Tahmasp (1576–c. 1592), also blinded and imprisoned. The mother of these four was Mahd-é Oliya Qeyr al-Nisa Begum.

[1584] Ismail Mirza (b. 1584) was actually the son of Prince Hamza, and therefore Mohammed Khodabanda's grandson. The other three persons mentioned are not Shah

power of Masum Beg,[1585] the King's favourite at that time, was first confined and then famished to death in the castle of Caykahe near Tabriz, and the rest came to untimely ends. By Mahd-é Oliya[1586] Princess of Heri he had likewise four sons, *viz.* Emir Hamza, Haidar,[1587] Abbas and Tahmasp, of which Hamza[1588] was reputed most valiant and popular, but Abbas most politic and ambitious.

Emir Hamza Mirza's success against the Turk.

Emir Hamza, Mohammed Khodabanda's eldest son, during these broils was practising the rules of Mars, and having some experience in the Indian war, so ill endured these continual bravados of the Turks that he never gave over soliciting the King until he commissioned him to raise what horse he could to oppose the Turk. In the head of twenty thousand horse this valiant Prince prosecuted the enemy with such resolution and speed and attended with so good success that through all Asia his fame quickly spread, inasmuch as the Turks gave out that Castriot[1589] was revived, for first with twelve thousand horse this hopeful Prince, the Begum his mother in company, set out of Qazvin, followed by Mirza

---

Mohammed's sons, and I can find no reference to them in either Monshi or modern historians.

[1585] Sultan Masum Khan of Sava was one of the leaders of a Takkalu-Turkman rebellion put down by Prince Hamza, who ordered his lands and possessions confiscated as a punishment (Monshi, *History*, 1:478).

[1586] Istibah Bilqis uz-Zamani, usually known as Mahd-é Oliya Qeyr al-Nisa Begum (c. 1532–1579) was the daughter of Mir Abdullah Khan, the ruler of Mazanderam. She was very powerful, and virtually ruled Persia from the accession of her husband to her murder by the *qizlbashes*. "Nothing was done without her order," Monshi states (History, 1:338); she promoted her son Hamza Mirza and attempted to curb the power of the emirs, supporting her husband in every way she could. For details, see Monshi, History, 1:367–71. She was also the mother of Shah Abbas I, Prince Abu Talib and Prince Tahmasp.

[1587] Haidar Mirza (1585–1597) was not Mohammed's son but the younger son of Prince Hamza. He had been sent as a hostage to Istanbul and died there of the plague. "It was not fitting that a Safavid Prince . . . and a Shi' ite of pure faith should sire children while he was in Ottoman hands," Monshi comments;"it was a merciful providence that decreed he should die a natural death . . . before he had had any children" (History, 2:707).

[1588] Herbert has "Ismail," which is obviously incorrect.

[1589] Prince Gjergj Kastrioti Skanderbeg (1405–1468), the great "warrior-king" of Albania and the country's national hero. He led resistance against the Ottoman Empire, and defeated the Turks in three battles, beginning with Torrioll (1444), then negotiating with them whilst keepin Albania independent. He became something of a hero in Europe, another Christian warrior struggling valiantly against the infidels. The Turks here paid a great compliment to Prince Hamza by comparing him to Skanderbeg.

Salman with eight thousand more. In the first place he defeated Kaytas Pasha[1590]
and his party that were foraging those parts; he then took Arrash by storm and
caused all the cannon which Mustafa had planted for defence of that garrison to
be drawn out and sent to Qazvin as a royal present to the King his father, the
first fruits of his contest with his inveterate adversary the Turk. This done, without the least unnecessary delay, having intelligence where and in what manner
the Tartars were quartered, he gave them such a thundering alarm that the Pre-
compence, being amazed and in disorder, gave the Prince the opportunity with
ease to destroy most of his men, the rest flying every way they could, confounded
with shame and fear, the Persians following the pursuit as far as the Caspian Sea,
where not being able to fly further they begged quarter, which was given them,
but Adel Geray the general could not escape, the Prince taking him prisoner and
using him with good respect. This prosperous success gave him fresh courage
to prosecute the Turk; accordingly, approaching with his victorious army before
Samakhi he summoned the garrison to yield, but Osman, demanding time to return an answer, being in the interim certainly informed of the Tartars' defeat and
finding no fence against fear, that night he fled secretly out of the town, spurring
all the way till he got to Derbent. The garrison next morning understanding their
condition offered to yield the place upon condition of mercy, but being exasperated by their late easy submission to the Turk, the Prince bade them stand to
their arms, which they refusing to do the army entered without opposition, and
the Prince selected some to make examples of his rigour. The rest he pardoned
upon fine, but the Turks were made prisoners of war, and thus the Turk's army of
seventy thousand men by the valour of this gallant Prince was broken in pieces
so as for some years after the country hath rest.

The Prince of Tartary miserably abused.

The Turks in this sort being happily expulsed, Emir Hamza, loaden with spoils
as well as victory, in a triumphant manner returned into Qazvin, where he was
embraced by the King, his mother and the Tartarian youthful Prince being in
company. The Tartar, giving his parole to be a true prisoner, had what liberty he
pleased and more then did him good, for being of a comely aspect and for courage of good report, his character took so deep an impression in the Queen that
albeit she had purposed a marriage 'twixt him and Emir Hamza Mirza's sister,
the better to make an alliance with the Crimean [Khan][1591] to whom Adel was
son, she nevertheless became amorous herself and could not be satisfied till she

---

[1590] Kaytas Pasha was the Turkish commander at Arrash. He had been left there
with a garrison of 5,000 and 100 small cannon known as "Esmeriles" by Mustafa Pasha
(see Juan de Persia, *Relaciones*, 147; 150–51).
[1591] They were also known as Khans of the Krim, which is the name Herbert uses.
Their dynasty was founded in about 1420 by Hajji Geray and lasted until 1783.

enjoyed him. To effect it she found opportunity to her wish, but in the dalliance spent so much time and took so little care for secrecy that albeit Mohammed either could or would not see, the sultans nevertheless took notice, and envying the repute a stranger had got they contrived his death. One evening, after observing his passage to the Queen's usual place of retirement in the gardens, they so secured their way that before the Queen or Adel had any warning the sultans rushed in, and finding them too familiar first removed the Queen then castrated the Prince, and in a very barbarous manner displayed them to the people without, who enraged therewith, quickly took away his life, which in some respect was a mercy. Howbeit, that act so disobliged the King and Prince that the conspirators received other rewards then probably they expected; for this dishonour and for the murder of the Prince the Crimean [Khan] also was so provoked that he soon after joined with the Turk to be the more revenged.[1592]

Mustafa Pasha dies in disgrace.

Murad [III] also, upon the sad account he received from Osman then in Derbent, and how formidable the Persian Prince was like to appear the ensuing spring, gave Mustafa fresh orders to levy a greater army then he had before and to prosecute the war with fire and sword, but the Persians by their emissaries having timely intelligence of these preparations accordingly provide for their defence.

[1592] This anecdote is related by Juan de Persia (*Relaciones*, 152), but he (unlike Herbert) dismisses it as being motivated by "a feeling of petty jealousy against the Tartar Prince, a sentiment that had been aroused in their minds at the sight of the intimacy he had gained in the affections of Shah Muhammad Khuda-Bandah" (153). Juan's source for the story (and possibly Herbert's) is Giovanni Tommaso Minadoi (1540–1615), an Italian historian and traveller who wrote *Guerra fra Turchi et Persiani* (Venice, 1588), translated into English by Abraham Hartwell as *The history of the warres betweene the Turkes and Persians* (1595). Persian sources do not mention it; Monshi does note that "after Adel Geray had been in residence in the state apartments for some time, differences of opinion arose among the emirs and principal officers of state concerning him," but only because they thought he should be treated more like a real prisoner. Shah Mohammed Khodabanda told them that "Since we started off by treating the Tartar Prince with respect . . . we would acquire a bad name if we were now to incarcerate him in a fortress," and he refused to take action. The emirs disagreed, and took matters into their own hands; Monshi tells us that Adel, "since he was familiar with the ways of the *qezlbas*, thought they had come to kill him, and he and the group of Tartars who were with him stupidly seized their weapons and started to fight." The result was a melée in which Adel was slain (*History*, 1:356–58). His brother, khan Mohammed Geray III (r. 1577–1584) joined Osman Pasha at Derbent (Monshi, *History*, 1:374). As for Mahd-é Oliya, there is no truth in the accusation that she had an affair with Adel, and her murder took place sometime later under completely different circumstances (see Monshi, *History*, 1:368–72).

Aliqoli Khan,[1593] late Governor of Genge, was constituted general for the Persian, whiles Mustafa, glad of the occasion to vindicate himself, drew together all the cavalry the Turk had either in Syria, Assyria or Armenia the Great and Less, and of foot a numerous body, and Hassan Aga,[1594] one of the Vizier's sons, in the van marched to Tiflis, where he encamped, whither Osman also repaired with all the horse and foot he could make.

In the Persian army commanded by Aliqoli Khan, amongst other noble personages was Simon or Zeynal Khan,[1595] an exiled Prince of Georgia but feudatory to the Persian. Of known courage in fight he was and of approved affection to the Persian and constant to his Christian profession, but the contrary was his brother Daud or Davit,[1596] who did what in him lay to oblige the Turk and offend the Persian. Hassan, again rising with his party with an intent to fall into Sirvan, the Persian general had so good notice of his design that taking the advantage of a pass he fell upon the Turk and so seasonably divided their party that after a notable execution the rest fled towards the hills, Hassan by the speed of his horse very narrowly escaping. This success persuaded them to hunt the enemy in the woods, where whilst they were too carelessly riding, suspecting little danger,

---

[1593] Aliqoli Khan Samlu (d. 1589) was Governor-General of Herat and husband to Zaynab Begum, daughter of Shah Tahmasp, whose funeral he organised at the command of Ismail II. He became very close to Prince Hamza and also tutor to Prince Abbas and consequently an enemy to Prince Hamza (see below); Shah Mohammed appointed him Govenor of Khorasan. He fought the Uzbegs in a heroic defence of Herat (Monshi, *History*, 1:557–59), but became embroiled in court disputes and even rebellion, which led first to Shah Mohammed defeating him in Khorasan (although he allowed him to retain his Governorship) and to his murder later on. Herbert confuses him here with Emamqoli Khan the governor of Genge, who was in command against Osman Pasha, not Mustafa (see above, n. 1115). Don Juan de Persia does not (*Relaciones*, 1:56–58), which suggests that Herbert had other sources.

[1594] Hassan Pasha Sokollu was the son of the Grand Vizier Mehmet Sokollu Pasha, who held office 1565–1579. He was Beglerbeg of Damascus, and was described by Juan de Persia as "a good general" (*Relaciones*, 156).

[1595] Simon [*Synon*], king of Kartli, reigned 1556–1569 and 1578–1599. He had fought against the Persians in 1556 when his father Luarsab I had been mortally wounded at the battle of Garisi, and he himself had continued the fight until his deposition by his brother Davit or Daud (see below) after several battles, at which point he went to Persia, but ended up in prison for refusing to convert to Islam. However, because of his anti-Ottoman stance Tahmasp I released him and reinstated him.

[1596] Davit XI was king of Kartli 1569–1578. He, unlike his brother, had submitted to Islam (1562) and was rewarded by being made sub-king of Lower Kartli and Tblisi by the Persian shah. In 1569 he began a war against his brother, but was defeated in two battles (1567, 1569) before finally gaining the upper hand at the Battle of P'artshkhisi (1569) and taking the throne. In 1578 he himself was deposed and fled to the protection of Murad III in Constantinople, where he settled and wrote medical treatises. Davit died there in about 1580/81.

the subtle Turk, having ambushed a thousand horse in those uncouth passages charged the Persians with so great haste and outcries that the unexpectedness striking more terror then needed into their adversaries' hearts, they fled after little opposition but much loss, albeit the Georgian Prince with his party made a better retreat, but, which was of most import, the Persian general himself was taken prisoner and under a guard sent to Erzerum, and the Turks refusing both ransom and exchange, so continued for three years, at length making his escape such time as Ferhad Pasha[1597] invaded Persia.

Hassan Aga, being now master of the field, advanced to Tiflis for the seasonable relief of many half-starved men, whence constinuing is march towards Derbent the Georgian Prince with a small party of horse gave the enemy so unexpected a charge in their rear and with such admirable courage that the Turk was first disordered and then put to flight. Hassan and Osman, again making use of their spurs, left their men to the mercy of the Persian swords but their train and treasure as a due unto their valour and a testimony of that memorable defeat. At Tiflis old Mustafa had taken up his quarter, intending to follow Hassan with the rest of his force, but when Hassan himself brought the Pasha the first tidings of this loss, so great was the old man's passion that he had forthwith caused him to be strangled had not his taking the Persian general prisoner and, no less, his relation to the Grand Vizier, been good argument in his behalf.

This disaster and the approaching winter put Mustafa upon new resolutions, so that instead of prosecuting his instructions, which were to fall upon Sirvan with fire and sword, he disposed his whole army into winter quarters, so divided that it would require some time to rendezvous, the Persians by that gaining a breathing-time and space to prepare against the spring. But Murad the Great Turk had no sooner notice of the little effectual progress his old favourite had made, his enemies at court also representing everything in the worst dress, that albeit Hassan Aga by his father's interest had a favour expressed from Murad, who as an acknowledgement of the signal service he had done in taking prisoner the Persian general had a silver battleaxe double-gilded and set with precious stones sent unto him with a shield of pure gold embellished with pearl and a vest of cloth-of-gold, Mustafa contrarily not only being discharged from his command but summoned to Istanbul to answer his miscarriage, so as notwithstanding his late favour with Murad, with whom he was educated from a child, and the many considerable field-services he had done against the poor Christians, so industrious were his enemies at court and so powerful his old back-friend Sinan

---

[1597] Ferhad or Farhat Pasha (d. 1584), an Albanian whose original name was Sokolovic, was Grand Vizier under Selim II, Second Vizier under Murad III and beglerbeg of Bosnia. He is known for having built a famous mosque in Banja Luka and for having defeated the Hapsburg general Auersperg at the Battle of the River Radonja (1575).

Pasha[1598] that both his life and estate had gone had not the Sultana by mediation of some ladies about her interceded in the old man's behalf. Notwithstanding, he had a *supersedeas* and, which vexed him most, his antagonist Sinan Pasha, for prosecuting the Persian war was appointed general in Mustafa's place.

During this, the jealousies and fears so increased in the Persian court throughout the different interests of the two brothers Emir Hamza and Abbas, the latter of which was the Governor of Heri or Aria, and entrusted with the management of the war against the Mughal, that the necessary preparations to oppose the more then threatened invasion of the Turks was wholly laid aside, the Persian King forgetting the late success he had, by the advice of Salman Mirza, whose daughter Prince Emir Hamza had married, choosing rather to send [Shahqoli Tabat-oglu][1599] ambassador to Murad with a rich present to usher in his propositions for peace. The Persian ambassador took his way through the skirts of Armenia to Trebizond, where finding a fit vessel he embarked and by the benefit of a fair gale made a short and easy passage to Istanbul, into which port he was with due ceremony received, and after four days' repose had audience and acceptance of his present, which indeed as such as well-deserved the Grand Seigneur's thanks. At this time Mustafa Pasha died; of age and grief, say some, but othersome rather think that he was poisoned, and the Emperor by his

---

[1598] Sinan Pasha (d. 1596), an Albanian by birth, was governor of Egypt (1569–1571) and was appointed Grand Vizier by Murad III in 1580 after a distinguished military career. He "arrived in Tiflis temporarily to take command," Juan de Persia writes, "superb and in his glory" (*Relaciones*, 159). Murad replaced him after Mehmet Pasha's defeat near Tblisi with Ferhad Pasha (Monshi, History, 1:424), but he came back twice after being disgraced, serving as Grand Vizier again in 1589 (although appointed Governor of Damascus), deposed and banished by Mehmet III in February 1595, and being re-appointed the same year in August.

[1599] Herbert has *Maxut-chan*, which may be Mahsud Khan. However, Juan de Persia writes that in 1580 Mohammed Khodabanda sent Haidar Aga to Sinan Pasha to propose peace, which was accepted preliminarily by Murad, and then followed up by sending Ibrahim Khan as ambassador plenipotentiary to Istanbul in 1582 (*Relaciones*, 161). Monshi also states that Shahqoli Sultan Tabat-oglu Zul Qadar "accompanied Omar Aqa [a Turk] when the latter returned to report to the Ottoman sultan" (*History*, 1:389). This may be the same embassy which Juan de Persia, without naming the ambassador, says "returned without having been able to effect anything of moment" (159). Monshi also states that the "plenipotentiary" mentioned by Juan de Persia was not Haidar, but his son Ibrahim Khan Tarkan Torkman, Governor of Qum (*History*, 1:390). Furthermore, no peace was made, for "Ibrahim Khan remained at Istanbul for seven years, until finally, after the accession of Shah Abbas, he obtained permission to return to Iran" (*History*, 1:391). Herbert mentions Ibrahim Khan's detainment in the next section (see below). Again, there seems to be some confusion here; who *Maxut* stands for is a mystery. I have placed Shahqoli Tabat-oglu's name in square brackets, taking Monshi as more authoritative, as this mission is described by Herbert as unsuccessful.

death made himself heir to his great personal estate. [Ibrahim Khan], pressing the Vizier for a dispatch, brought it to this issue, that peace would be granted for what time he would propose; conditionally, the Persians would deliver Tabriz, Qazvin and all Sirvan to the Turk, to be forever enrolled in the list of provinces under that crown. But the ambassador, wisely desiring further instructions from his master ere he could give answer, by his courier acquainted his master with the unreasonableness of the Turk's demands, grounded upon the division of the two Persian Princes and the expectation he had of Sinan Pasha's success in prosecuting the war, which being taken into consideration by Shah Mohammed, who to that end had convened most of the considerable officers he had unto Qazvin, the result was that not one inch of earth should be given their insolent adversary more then he could master with his sword, to prevent which a great force should forthwith be drawn unto the frontiers of Armenia, which the victorious Prince Emir Hamza should command, and that Abbas Mirza with another army should prosecute the war against the Mughal towards Kabul. This being agreed in Council was put in speedy execution, and being thought fit to recall [Shahqoli Tabat-oglu], he made his return through the enemy's quarters, purposely to discover their order and force, and being come to Qazvin so well satisfied the King with his discreet carriage in that trust as induced him to make him his Treasurer,[1600] an office not only honourable but of great profit, which nevertheless acquired him great envy at court, and amongst others Emir Khan,[1601] who never loved him, so as making use of his favour with the King he so insinuated and suggested false apprehensions into his weak brain that the Treasurer, perceiving the King's kindness lessened and his countenance changed, and that the craft of his adversary was likely to take place, rather then suffer further under their power he chose to withdraw himself and his family with some portable goods into the enemy's quarters, where being friendly received by Sinan Pasha he had the liberty to live peaceably at Van.

[1600] Ibrahim Khan Turkman was made *daruga* of Isfahan by Shah Mohammed (Monshi, *History*, 1:501).

[1601] Emir Khan Turkman (d. 1585) was the beglerbeg of Azerbaijan and Governor of Tabriz. He loyally served Shah Esmail II, who had been twenty years in prison under Tahmasp, and he had been betrothed to Fatima, Tahmasp's daughter (Monshi, *History*, 1:374). According to Monshi he was himself the victim of slander; "Emir Khan," he writes, "was a man concerned with the general good," but he had, it seems, also "been guilty of various improper practices" (*History*, 1:429). He was also an intimate of Prince Hamza, but enemies contrived to destroy this relationship, too, as Emir Khan was given to high-handedness. When the Turkman-Takkalu revolt broke out he was implicated and executed. His full story may be read in Monshi, *History*, 1:322–28; 429–30.

Erzerum. Persian ambassador abused at Constantinople.

Emir Hamza Mirza during this drew towards the Turk, and having entrusted
Simon Khan the Georgian and Toqmaq the Persian, with six thousand horse
they disposed part of that body into an ambuscade and with the rest fell on Sinan's quarters, whence being repulsed and counterfeiting some fear drew the enemy to a loose pursuit, till being past the place where their men were hid, breaking out upon their rear Toqmaq faced about, so that the enemy was charged both
ways, who finding themselves to be entrapped, rather sought how to escape then
adventure the fight. Howbeit, above six thousand of the Turks were lost, the rest
escaping to Erzerum, which the old Pasha had made his head-quarter at that
time.

Erzerum is a town of great strength both by its situation and art, and by
reason of its voisinage to the Persian dominions usually the place of rendezvous
when the Turks have any design against that Empire, a place of great import to
them in that besides the advantage it gives of recruits it affords portage of necessaries both from the Midland, Euxine and Caspian Seas. The country it stands in
is Cappadocia, *Leuco-Syria* of old, divided by the River Euphrates from Armenia
and on the other hand Carmania, which comprehends those provinces in former
times were called Lycia, Cilicia, Pamphylia and Caria,[1602] places now totally under the Mohammedans, who have extinguished the Christian light and interest
as if it had never been. But to return.

Murad, resolving to fall into Hungary and those parts, thought fit to call
home Sinan Pasha to advise concerning that war, to which end he constituted Mehmet Pasha,[1603] nephew to Mustafa, general against the Persians. At Erzerum he took the muster of all his army, which was so numerous and the season
so good that he forthwith took the field and marched unresisted as far as the
River Araxes, now called Arrash, burning and doing all the spoil he could. Emir
Hamza, by his scouts having notice of their numbers and approach, ordered Toqmaq with Simon the Georgian, the Persians' approved friend, to hinder the
further entrance of the Turks so well they could, the general following with the

---

[1602] Lycia is on the southern coast of modern Turkey; Cilicia was an Armenian kingdom extending from the south-eastern coast of modern Turkey to Cyprus and comprising
a large part of modern Anatolia; Pamphylia was a region of southern Asia Minor located
between Lycia and Cilicia; it extended from the Mediterranean to Mount Taurus; Caria
was a kingdom of western Anatolia which extended south to Lycia.

[1603] Mehmet Pasha, beglerbeg of Erzerum, assumed his command in 1583, replacing Rizvan Pasha. The "apostate Georgian Prince" is Manuchar; Mehmet regarded him
with suspicion, and at Qars their differences came to a head when Mehmet tried to have
the Georgian killed. In the ensuing melée Mehmet was wounded and Manuchar escaped. Sultan Murad III put the blame on Sinan Pasha, "who, he said, had kept him ill-
informed throughout" and whom he dismissed as Grand Vizier. For full details see Juan
de Persia, *Relaciones*, 162–65.

rest of his horse and dragoons. The Turks, animated by the success they had and by the running away of the people still where they came, supposing no force near, continued their march towards Tauris, till upon a sudden the Persian horse discovered themselves and engaged with so great haste and valour that notwithstanding the inequality of numbers the Persian horse made good the ground until they were overpowered by some reserve of horse Mehmet ordered to renew the charge, but by some prisoners he took understanding that the Persian Prince, whose name was terrible to the Turk, was at hand, he thought it the best way to retreat, and accordingly marched back with double the haste he came on, which the Persian Prince no sooner knew but that with unusual speed he followed the enemy in the rear and with such advantage that in their over-hasty passing the rivers many of the Turks were drowned and no less number killed in the field, a loss so discouraging the youthful Pasha that after he had reproached the apostate Georgian Prince as if he had occasioned that mishcance he ceased not marching till he arrived at Tiflis, not daring to look his enemy in the face until he had recruited his force. At about this time Ibrahim Khan, ambassador from the Persian King, received an unusual affront at Constantinople at the circumcision of Mehmet, eldest son to Murad, without any provocation from the ambassador, being *contra ius gentium*[1604] made close prisoner for some time and his attendants likewise confined in houses infected with the plague. The design was principally to let the other ambassadors see how little the Grand Seigneur valued the Persian King.[1605]

Shah Mohammed, albeit the misusage of his servant was ground sufficient to defy the Turk, yet seemed to take little notice of that affront, so unhappy was he in the difference 'twixt his two sons, which grew to that height as made it seem past reconciliation, and at length threatened a civil war. For Abbas, albeit the younger brother, having courage enough and much more craft then Emir Hamza, was not afraid to proceed in his disloyal practices to supplant his brother and vex his father, whose age inclined him rather to pursue peace then war, notwthstanding which, perceiving Abbas restless in his designs, he was by the advice of his great officers persuaded to proclaim him rebel and with a considerable power to march towards Aria to reduce him if he could. Abbas, so soon as he understood of his father's intent, first prepared for fight, but through the advice of some friends he had about the King was at length prevailed with to submit, and by the King upon promise of future obedience embraced and pardoned, to the great dislike of Emir Hamza and also of his father-in-law Salman Mirza, the last of which through the subtle and false suggestions of Abbas to the King was soon after made shorter by the head,[1606] and was but introductory to Emir Hamza's

---

[1604] Against the law of nations.

[1605] Prince Mehmet's circumcision ceremonies took place June–July 1582.

[1606] This is not accurate. Shah Mohammed did not quite order Salman's execution, but allowed his enemies the emirs "to do whatever they liked with him," after which he

approaching ruin, for Abbas, perceiving that his brother was not to be overcome by force, by fraud attempted it. In the meantime Farhad Pasha was made commander-in-chief over the Turks against Persia, and having prepared all things a mutiny unexpectedly happened in the camp, which grew to that height as lost him that summer's opportunity and made him continue about Erzerum, but gave the greater advantage to the Persian.

Emir Khan, at that time Governor of Tabriz, falling (how justly is not known)[1607] into the King's displeasure, had his eyes thrust out, and being under close restraint in a few months died, thereby having some ease, but his command was given to Ali Quli Khan [Samlu], who being taken prisoner by the Turks in their march through Georgia made his escape from Farhad Khan. He, having done as little as those before him, was called home, and Osman Pasha succeeded in his place.[1608] This Pasha was quick of resolution and by nature fierce; from all those parts of Asia as far as Babylon he had power to draw together what force he pleased, and resolving with himself to harrass the Persian territories with fire and sword, he embodied at the usual place of rendezvous two hundred thousand horse and foot, and with a suitable quantity of great guns he drew from Trebizond through the Georgian country, passed uninterruptedly into Media almost in view of Tabriz, destroying the enemy's quarters all the way. Emir Hamza the Persian general, formerly acquainted with the Turks' manner of march, advanced against them with ten thousand good horse, the King following the Prince his son with eighty thousand horse and foot more, so that a more gallant army was not seen nor better-commanded in Persia in the memory of man.

The Turkish army again worsted.

Five leagues to the southwards of Tabriz the Persian Prince encamped, expecting the coming of Osman, who continued his march, and having the advantage both in numbers and a large train of artillery, which he heard the Persian horse would not endure, resolved to try the fortune, as they call it, of the field. The Persian

---

was arrested, dismissed from office and murdered by being stabbed. "Glory be to God!" exults Monshi; "The more man is concerned with his own good, the more evil the outcome" (*History*, 1:419–20). The murder took place late in 1582.

[1607] Prince Hamza had dismissed Emir Khan from office because of various offences and slights, including his refusal to attend a festival and absenting himself from the Asura, which is a day on which the martyrdom of Hussein is celebrated. Various emirs, taking advantage of Prince Hamza's anger, parlayed Emir Khan's actions into an intention of rebellion, and when the Turkman-Takkalu revolt broke out it "signed the death-warrant of Emir Khan, who was executed at Qahqaha" (Monshi, *History*, 1:434). Monshi says nothing about blinding.

[1608] Osman Pasha, now (Spring 1585) made Grand Vizier and commander-in-chief, had been ordered by Murad III "to conquer the whole of Azerbaijan, if not Iraq" (Monshi, *History*, 1:438). Tabriz fell to the Ottomans in September 1585.

Prince, desiring his father to quicken his march, resolved the like, so as the city Tabriz interposing and garrisoned by the Persian, Ali Quli Khan being Governor, Osman thought it not safe to have so considerable an enemy in his rear, and therefore drawing before the place, ere he could summon it the Governor made so brave a sally that above a thousand Turks were slain and the Persians made a retreat with little loss. This exasperated the Turk, so that making his approach and planting his battery he played so furiously upon the city wall that a breach was made, and being resolved to storm, the besieged, perceiving their danger, beat a parley and upon conditions to march out soldier-like they surrendered the town, which had fair quarter afforded till such a time as report was brought the general how that some Janissaries going into a stove[1609] were by some of the inhabitants secretly made away, which so incensed the Turk that he gave them free liberty to do what they list, whereupon the town was plundered, unarmed men killed by the sword, women abused and all sorts of violence exercised, some few prisoners escaping to the Persian camp, which served to exasperate their minds and so inflamed the Prince Emir Hamza that he immediately drew out a small party of horse, with which he faced the city walls, which Osman could so ill endure that albeit he himself was at that time under a sore distemper of the flux he nevertheless ordered Mehmet Pasha[1610] to beat him thence. The Pasha accordingly drew out forty thousand horse and foot with a small train of artillery, but the Persian seeing the number so inequal held it prudential to retire, yet with so moderate a pace as expressed their valour, and only till he reached some part of his army, so that when he had twenty thousand more horse added, he drew up with a resolution to fight the enemy, who had the same desire, so that they soon met and skirmished, and after that engaged the whole armies, but the Persians having the better, the Turks by the help of their train made a pretty good retreat, leaving towards six thousand men to the mercy of the enemy's sword.

Upon this the Prince sent a defiance to the Turkish general, who accepting the challenge, within five days drew out what force he had, being upwards of an hundred thousand horse and foot, the Persians scarce amounting to half that number, but seeing it falls out that in great armies the far lesser part only engage, the Persians had so much the superiority in resolution that day as that after the Pasha of Qaraman[1611] was observed to fall by Emir Hamza's sword the

---

[1609] A public bath-house. "On one occasion," Monshi relates, "the bath attendants at some public baths in the backstreets murdered an Ottoman soldier and threw his body down a well. This incident finally broke Osman Pasha's patience" (*History*, 1:443).

[1610] Mehmet Pasha (d. 1585) was the Ottoman beglerbeg of Diar Bakr. He is not to be confused with Mehmet Pasha, beglerbeg of Erzerum (see above, n. 1135). Mortally-wounded and taken prisoner in this battle, he was decapitated (Monshi, *History*, 1:445).

[1611] Murad Pasha, beglerbeg of Qaraman, was not killed in this battle but taken prisoner (Monshi, *History*, 1:446). Later, after his release by Shah Abbas I, he became Grand Vizier to Sultan Ahmet I (1607) and negotiated peace with the Persians.

Turks gave ground, and in the confused haste they made lost more men then had formerly been slain in the field, and amongst others fell the Pasha of Trebizond, six *sanjaks*[1612] and twenty thousand common men, so that had not their great guns disordered now and then the Persian horse, they had doubtless obtained a full victory. The Persians lost two thousand, but Osman was so daunted with Emir Hamza's high courage that having constituted Ja'afar Khan,[1613] who had been Governor of Tripoli, the Governor of Tabriz, and leaving there a great part of his army, with the rest he marched back to Erzerum, the better to recover of the flux.

Now albeit Osman with a good guard of horse passed thither undisturbed, yet his foot and train, that could not march above their usual rate, were interrupted by the Persian horse, who by a nearer way got before and skirmished with them to so good purpose as near Shenb-Ghazan[1614] they seized upon their caravan, which had above six thousand camels and mules and valuable burthens, besides asinagos in abundance, loaden with provisions of all sorts necessary, and the rest of the Persian horse being come up they engaged the whole army, which was so well-commanded, though Osman was not there, as for some hours a fiercer fight was not known then that in the memory of any then present, but, as at other times, the Persian Prince expressed so great personal courage and dexterity that by his example there was a general resolution in the Persians to die or conquer, so that in conclusion they had the victory though with considerable loss, yet requiting the enemy by the loss of twenty thousand of his men who then gasped their last, and had pursued the Turks had not night and the continual firing their cannon prevented the Persian, and yet some stories report that in the discharging their great guns at random the Turks had the greatest loss. That part of the army which escaped made so unpleasant a relation unto Osman that it increased his distemper, insomuch as within few days after he gave up the ghost, leaving the conduct of his army to Jegal-Oglu, a good soldier and a wary, and who in a retreat he made towards Van gave the Persian a notable blow, yet when he came to Erzerum and took the musters of his remaining force found that in this unhappy

---

[1612] A *sanjak* or *sanjak-bey* is an Ottoman provincial governor.

[1613] Ja' afar Pasha Khadim [*Giafar*] was the Ottoman Governor of Tabriz. A skilful military commander, he repulsed a Persian attack and held the city after the death of Osman Pasha (Monshi, *History*, 1:447–48). Juan de Persia confirms that he was the former Pasha of Tripoli, and adds that Osman gave him "the right to collect the tribute of the Tabriz district during three coming years, also leaving with him a garrison of 12,000 men" (*Relaciones*, 184).

[1614] Shenb-Ghazan [*Sancazan*] is the site of the tomb belonging to Ghazan Khan (r. 1295–1304), the Mongol ruler of Persia whom Boyle calls "the greatest of the Il-Khans" (*History*, 396). Herbert's spelling indicates that his source is either Minadoi or Juan de Persia, who adopts the former's "queer spelling," as Le Strange remarks (*Juan de Persia*, 328, n. 15). Juan de Persia himself was present in Prince Hamza's army at this battle.

expedition Osman one way or other had lost a hundred thousand of his men. The Persian Prince, not thinking it advisable to follow the enemy too far, returned back to Qazvin where he was embraced by his aged father, honoured by all the officers and little less then adored by the vulgar sort, but after a little refreshment also remembering that Tabriz continued under the power of the Turks, most of which had huts in a large fort or barbican Osman with great labour and expense had raised and fortified notably with great ordinance, so that Ja'afar with his 15,000 foot having victualled the forts, supposed then that he was able to defend the place against all the force Persia could bring.

Abbas Mirza's envy to Hamza Mirza. [The murder of Prince Hamza].

In this interim Mohammed Khan[1615] had the command of the Armenian auxiliaries, who were upwards of 10,000 men, with whom he marched towards Tabriz, which he summoned in vain, and being without order from the Persian general knew it would be ill-resented. Therefore, as one in despair and to increase his account he proclaimed Mirza Tahmasp, Mohammed's youngest son, King, and with joyful acclamations directed their way towards Qazvin. The old King marvelled at this insolence and forthwith sent Emir Hamza against this conspirator, who for some time stood his ground againt the Prince, but being worsted took to his heels, and being close-pursued was apprehended near Kashan, and his head being cut off presented to the King then at Qazvin, but the poor abused Prince upon the acknowledgement of his fault, which he neither designed not well could help, was forgiven, albeit for some time confined to his house.

These alternate outbreakings of the King's sons not only disturbed the old King's rest but retarded the necessary perparations to oppose the Turk's fresh forces that were ready to march the reducing the city of Tabriz, withal perplexed the spirit of Emir Hamza, whose whole design was the public welfare of his country and an honourable defence against the Turk. But his brother Abbas had other designs in his head, which were by what means he might make his quickest access to the crown, and his unnatural wish, as wicked as it was, wanted not instruments to effect his desires, amongst which was Aliqoli Khan [Samlu], who in mere envy bore a constant ill-will unto Prince Emir Hamza and as occasion

---

[1615] Mohammed Khan Mowsellu Turkman was the Governor of Kashan. He abducted Prince Tahmasp (1586) and proclaimed him heir-apparent (not Shah). Allied with the Takkalu clan in an extensive rebellion, Mohammed hoped to undermine the power of Prince Hamza and get revenge for the death of Emir Khan, but the rebels were defeated at the Battle of Abhar and Mohammed was captured. Contrary to Herbert's account, his life was spared by Prince Hamza. He subsequently became Emir of Ardabil and is mentioned as paying homage to Shah Abbas on his succession (Monshi, *History*, 2:549). Juan de Persia, an eye-witness again, mentions that the rebel Saqali Khan, the brother of Emir Khan, was captured and beheaded (*Relaciones*, 200).

served was still ready to eclipse his splendour and to lessen him in his father's repute, which was the easier to be done, the Emir's victories and popular applause
drawing most men's eyes and expectations upon that rising son, which made him
jealous of his own estate and of the others setting before his time.

Farhad Pasha in the interim with a great army, most of which were drawn out
of the garrisons in provinces round about, quickens his march for the seasonable
relief of Tabriz, which though not besieged was distressed for victual and by fluxes and other distempers had lost many of its men. The Persian King, roused by
this advance of the enemy, by the persuasions of his son Abbas commissioned Aliqoli Khan his friend to go commander-in-chief of an army distinct from that his
brother Emir Hamza commanded, for which end he drew what horse he could
from his government in Herat and Mazanderam, having order also to join with
Emamqoli Khan, who from his government about Lar and Shiraz[1616] brought
about 15,000 horse, the Prince intending to follow with the main body of horse
and foot, which was about 40,000. Emamqoli Khan by the Prince's direction
hastened to discover the enemy, and in beating up the quarters of Zeynal Khan
near Salmas[1617] made some execution and with like good hap the Pasha of Re-
vian, which accelerated Farhad's march, but so soon as Aliqoli Khan saw the
Turkish army, without the least resistance he drew back, encouraging the enemy
to prosecute their way, harassing the country wherever they came, suffering him
to relieve Tabriz and to waste the greatest part of Sirvan.

This treacherous act of Aliqoli Khan was well worth the punishment, but the
enemy overspreading the country with his horse hindered the Prince to give that
opposition he intended had his brother Abbas his men been at his command, so
that instead of looking towards the enemy he marched after Aliqoli Khan, who
fearing to encounter the Prince kept on his way towards Kabul and marched after
such a rate that the Prince thought it not best to prosecute that wretch at that time,
but rather to return and join with Emamqoli Khan, which being done and many
volunteers coming in beyond imagination to serve the Prince against the common
adversary, he was so overjoyed therewith that he was fully resolved speedily to
encounter Farhad in the open field. But alas, when he was in the meridian of fair
hopes and in a place thought most free from any treasonable attempt, he was by a
corrupted eunuch murdered whilst he took some rest upon a pallet in his tent, supposed by the procuration of Aliqoli Khan and not without the suspicion of Abbas
his knowledge, who by his brother's death was undoubted heir unto the crown, an
act so villainous and at such as time as gave the Turks cause to rejoice, but Persia
became overwhelmed with amazement and grief. The army likewise had such sad
apprehensions, as if in the Prince's death they had all gone with him to the grave,

---

[1616] Emamqoli Khan Qajar was not governor of either Lar of Shiraz. Herbert seems
to be confusing him with Emamqoli Khan, son of Allah Verdi Khan, who was governor
of Lar.

[1617] A town some 850 km south-east of Tehran.

seeming careless and heartless to give any further resistance to the Turk, so large a share had this generous Prince in the hearts of the people, yea, the whole nation by the setting of this bright star seemed clouded and veiled with everlasting night, their light being thus miserably extinguished by the baseness of a treacherous valet employed by base and cowardly men, but the eunuch after strict examination was exquisitely tortured whiles the body of this great Prince was with all possible demonstrations of love in September 1586 conveyed to Ardebil, where he was interred near the dormitories of his royal ancestors.[1618]

Farhad Pasha the Turkish general, though as a noble enemy he could not refrain some show of sorrow for this hero's death, yet let not slip his advantage, but in short time made tributary the whole territory about Genje and forced contribution from Shamakhi and all the country 'twixt that and the Caspian Sea, notwithstanding which good service being called home, and succeeding worse in the Transylvanian war the next year he was summoned by the Vizier of Istanbul and by a secret order put to death.

Turkish ambassador affronted at the Persian court.

Jegal-oglu Pasha, the Governor of Baghdad, by order from the Royal Porte succeeded Farhad in his charge for the Persian war. He wasted the Median territories which lie upon the frontiers of Mesopotamia called Diar Bakr, which were quarters that had not been spoiled of long time, but whiles Mohammed was ordering Emamqoli Khan to attend Jegal-oglu's motion, Murad, the better to prosecute his intended war in Europe, by his ambassador desired a cessation of arms with the Persian, the better to enlarge his dominion towards Kandahar and Kabul, willingly condescended unto so as articles were agreed and signed, and hostages on each side given according to form, and peace proclaimed at Constantinople and Qazvin. Howbeit, in less then three years, the Persian hostage dying at Constantinople, inasmuch as he was the King's nephew his body was embalmed and by sea conveyed to Trebizond and thence into his own country where he was honourably buried amongst his friends.

Shah Mohammed, to put a period to his disconsolate life, died in the Year of Our Lord 1595,[1619] and with all due ceremony was entombed by his

---

[1618] This is inaccurate, at least according to Monshi's account. Prince Hamza was murdered by his barber (see above). Monshi further adds that "he left Aliqoli Khan's tent, drunk as a lord" (*History*, 1:483). This is Aliqoli Beg Fath-oglu Ostalju. Monshi does not implicate either of the two Aliqoli Khans in the murder, Shah Mohammed himself slew the assassin (Monshi, History, 1:485). Prince Hamza was murdered on 4 December 1586, not September as Herbert has it.

[1619] Shah Mohammed Khodabanda abdicated in 1587, after which he lived in retirement until his death. Herbert actually gives 1597 as the date of his death, which I have emended.

princely ancestors. In his place Abbas his son was proclaimed and soon after crowned King.[1620] Ambassadors from most parts of the world were addressed to congratulate his access to the crown, amongst whom one from the Great Turk who was rather a *fecialis*[1621] or herald then an ambassador, for no sooner was that ceremony over but in an insulting manner he menaced war unless Abbas would send his son or some other eminent officer hostage in his place that was lately dead, which being done in the face of other ambassadors the manner of it was so highly resented by Abbas that to let him and the rest know how little he valued the Turk his master's amity, he commanded him forthwith to be gone, which the ambassador smiling at gave the King so great offence that in high passion he commanded him to be slain, but the great officers of the court, disliking such a precedent and well-knowing it was in passion the order was seemingly given, to satisfy the King and to be quit for some uncivil treatment a former ambassador from Persia had at Istanbul, with a cane they only chabuched him upon the soles of his feet and then posted him out of the country miserably disgraced, an act very much below the report that went of Abbas for his prudence, and indeed to the violation of the Law of Nations, which holds the persons of ambassadors as inviolable, nor was it otherwise resented by Murad, who upon the return of his ambassador first blasphemed and then breathed defiance,[1622] vowing the utter extirpation of the Sophian race, which nevertheless was a while deferred by reason of his war in Hungary and some intestine troubles occasioned through the revolt of a great part of his forces in Anatolia, so that albeit he received additional and unwelcome tidings of the loss of Tabriz, he was not then in a condition to make good the threats he thundered out against Persia or to endeavour the recovery of the town, soon after being arrested by impartial death in the Year of Our Lord 1603, Sultan Ahmet succeeding as Grand Seigneur in his place.[1623]

[1620] It was not that straightforward. Shortly after the death of Prince Hamza certain emirs of the Samlu and Ustalju factions proclaimed Prince Abu Talib as Shah. Thanks to Ali Quli Khan Samlu, however, who "had succeeded in spiriting Prince Abbas off to Mashhad" (Jackson and Lockhart, *History*, 261), supporters of Abbas managed to get him to Qazvin and make him Shah, at which point Mohammed Khodabanda agreed to abdicate. Abbas succeeded on 16 October 1587.

[1621] In ancient Rome a *fecialis* or *fetialis* was "one of a college of priests responsible for formally making war or peace" (Simpson, *Dictionary*, 246).

[1622] Herbert's story about the ambassador is inaccurate. However, according to Juan de Persia, Mehmet III (see below), not Murad III, sent an embassy under Mehmet Aga to Persia with a demand that Abbas send his son Safi to Constantinople as a hostage. After the Shah refused and the ambassador became angry, Abbas "gave command that they should shave off the beard of [Mehmet's] ambassador and send the same as a gift to the Sultan" (*Relaciones*, 232).

[1623] Herbert is mistaken. Murad III died in 1595 and was succeeded by Mehmet III (1595–1603), to whom Ahmet I succeeded and reigned until 1617. Juan de Persia notes that "at the moment of our writing these pages" Mehmet III "is still the reigning Sultan

Baghdad taken by stratagem.

Ahmet, notwithstanding his being thus bearded by the Persian and that his predecessor bequeathed unto him the taking revenge for that affront done his ambassador, was so intent upon the prosecution of the entire conquest of Hungary to come the nearer unto Vienna, the seat-royal of the German Emperor, that Abbas had the more advantage to recruit and encompass his designs. In the first place, therefore, understanding how that by order from the Imperial Porte Jegal-oglu Pasha with all the force of horse and foot he could make against Zel Ali,[1624] a famous rebel formidable in his time, and by the auxiliaries sent him out of Persia hearing of Jegal-oglu's advance was so far from affright that he marched towards his adversary and in the Palmyrean territories engaged and routed Jegal-oglu, who was forced to leave the field and some thousands of his best men dead in the place. Abbas, taking the opportunity of the Governor's absence caused several of his officers and *qizlbashes* to be disguised like merchants, and under colour of a caravan entered Baghdad unsuspected and by that stratagem quickly became masters of the place.[1625] Jegal-oglu, having a good interest at court, had this ill success interpreted in the best sense, and having received fresh orders to levy a powerful army to invade Persia and being master of the field to lay close siege to Baghdad, accordingly the next spring he rendezvoused at Erzerum and fell upon Abdullah Khan the Viceroy's quarters in Sirvan, committing what spoil he could, but young Emir Hamza Mirza, Abbas his eldest son, inheriting his uncle's virtue as well as name, with a strong body of horse and dragoons confronting the Pasha near to Soltaniyeh gave him such a brush that the Turk retreated as far back as Van, where in a second encounter the Persian had much the better of the fight, many being slain upon this place on both sides, but by the flight of

of the Ottoman Empire" (*Relaciones*, 223). He also wrote that Mehmet III "showed every sign of wishing that the capitulations of the peace treaty should hold good" (224). Herbert omits any mention of Mehmet III.

[1624] Zel Ali, who had served in the Hungarian campaign, was promised the title of pasha of Bosnia by Mehmet III. When he was not appointed he rebelled (1603), defeated the governor Ja'afar Pasha, and entered the city of Baghnaluk, proclaiming himself ruler of Bosnia. He refused a summons to Istanbul, and was eventually left in charge by the Sultan.

[1625] Herbert has already told us how the Persians *lost* Baghdad in 1587 and 1605 (see above); he story he repeats here about the disguised merchants actually happened some years earlier during the reign of Shah Mohammed. There is nothing in Monshi or modern historians to substantiate what Herbert says here, and it's in any case doubtful that the same ruse would have worked twice! Baghdad remained in Ottoman hands until 1622. Herbert states later that the Persians lost Baghdad "by treachery," which we must assume means in 1605. From this point onwards there are many repetitions and inaccuracies in Herbert's account of some of the years following. Jackson and Lockhart note that Minadoi's account, likely one of Herbert's sources, contains errors, only some of which were corrected by Don Juan of Persia (*History*, 387).

Jegal-oglu and the Pasha of Trebizond the Persians kept the field and had the spoil of those that were dead, and by that day's success in little more time cleared all the Persian provinces of the Turks. [1626]

Shah Abbas, now moving prince-like in his own orb, for the better spreading of his fame and engaging against his inveterate adversary the Turk dispatched ambassadors to several parts of the world. Zeynal Khan was sent to Rudolph the Emperor, [1627] Mahdiqoli Khan [Samlu] to the King of Poland [1628] and *Yuzbashi* Hassan [1629] to Henry IV of France, Philip IV of Spain [1630] and the

---

[1626] Monshi records that in the winter of 1604 Jegal-oglu "decided to retire to Van" because he was running out of provisions and because Shah Abbas was waiting for him with a large force on the other side of the River Araxes (*History*, 2:860). Abbas did not have a son called Hamza; Herbert has mistakenly repeated the story of Abbas's elder brother Prince Hamza (see above). For details of Abbas's sons, see above, n. 419. Jegal-oglu was decisively defeated at the battle of Sufian (7 November 1605) by Shah Abbas himself (see Monshi, *History*, 2:886–93), and again retreated to Van. It is difficult to work out which one of these engagements Herbert refers to here, or whether he mixed them up due to inaccurate sources.

[1627] In 1599 Shah Abbas sent Hussein Ali Beg Bayat as ambassador to Prague, accompanied by Sir Anthony Sherley, Hussein's nephew Ali Quli Beg, and Uruch Beg (later Don Juan de Persia); Emperor Rudolph II "treated them with great consideration" (Jackson and Lockhart, *History*, 387). They then went on to see Pope Clement VIII in Rome; Abbas also wrote letters to Popes Paul V and Urban VIII. In return Rudolph sent Stefan Kakasch de Zalonkemeny to Persia (1603), but he died in Lebanon and his successor Georg Tektander took over the embassy. Mahdiqoli Beg went to Prague in 1605, where his portrait was engraved by Aegidius Sadeler; another delegation followed in 1610.

[1628] The contact between Persia and Poland is interesting. In 1601 Sigismund III Wasa (r. 1587–1632) sent one Sefer Muratowicz, a merchant of Albanian descent, to order some carpets in Persia. He was received by Shah Abbas, who was amazed to find that Muratowicz spoke Persian; although he explained that he was not an ambassador, the Shah duly gave him some carpets for the King, which Sigismund later presented to his daughter as a wedding-gift. Muratowicz's account is printed in Adam Walaszek, ed., *Trzy Relacje z Polskich Podrozy na Wschod Muzumanski w Pierwszej Powie XVII Wieku* (Krakow: Biblioteka Jagiellonski, 1980). It is not available in English, but is discussed in that language by Jolanta Sierakowska-Dyndo, "Poland and Persia during the Safavid Period," available at www.polandiran.blogspot. com

[1629] Not a name but a military title. Savory translates it as "centurion" (Monshi, *History*, 2:1392), because he is in charge of a hundred soldiers. Herbert's "Hassan" may be a mistake for "Hussein" (see below).

[1630] Hussein Ali Beg Bayat's delegation also went to Spain, where Ali Quli Beg and Uruch Beg converted to Christianity with Philip III and Queen Margarita as godparents! The later ambassador to Spain was not Hassan, but Dengiz Beg Rumlu (d. 1613), who went to Spain in 1608 with Antonio de Gouvéa (see details of his embassy and subsequent execution in Monshi, *History*, 2:1074–1075; also Jackson and Lockhart, *History*, 391). In

Venetian Republic,[1631] with instructions to treat with them about commerce with Persia and a joint league against their common enemy the Turk, and Mohammed *Rosarbeg* to Shah Selim the Great Mughal.[1632] Ahmet, having intelligence how active the Persian was to disturb his progress abroad against the Christians, to find him work at home commands Nasuh Pasha[1633] to draw all the forces of horse and foot he could to the usual place of rendezvous in order to the prosecuting the Persian, but those levies came to little effect by reason of the peace that upon the Persian ambassador's repair to Constantinople was soon after agreed between those two great Mohammedans, contrary to the Persian's late proposition and unhappily to the disappointing the Christian princes' design.

In the year 1613 Shah Abbas, for the better establishing that truce and more vigorously to proceed in his war begun with the Mughal, sent Qazi Khan his ambassador with an extraordinary present to the Imperial Porte. The ambassador was treated with extraordinary respect and so cajoled by the Vizier that it is reported he was tempted to exceed his instructions, for he condescended that his master should as a feudatory pay to the Turk's exchequer an annual sum or acknowledgment for the terrritories in and about Sirvan and Gilan, which was denied by Abbas and the ambassador at his return, none daring to intercede in his behalf, was for that mistake put to death.[1634]

1614 Philip III sent Don Garcia de Silva y Figueroa as ambassador; he finally arrived in 1617 after being detained at Goa by the Portuguese (Jackson and Lockhart, *History*, 392). Philip, who was also King of Portugal, wanted Abbas to expel English merchants, a request with which the Shah did not comply. Philip IV did not succeed until 1621.

[1631] Abbas's ambassador to Venice was Hajji Mahmud Shahsavar, for whom see Part I. An earlier embassy to Doge Marino Grimani had been sent in 1603.

[1632] No-one of this name was sent to India. The first ambassador sent by Abbas was Yadegar Sultan Rumlu (1590–1597), followed by Zeynal Beg (1620) and finally Takta Beg Ustalju (1627), all of whom are mentioned by Monshi. The last two were sent to Emperor Jahangir (Shah Selim).

[1633] Nasuh Pasha (d. 1614) was beglerbeg of Diar Bakr and later Grand Vizier under Ahmet I (1611). He negotiated a treaty with the Persians, and according to Monshi he wanted to be "the person responsible for bringing to an end the warfare between two such great monarchs" (*History*, 2:1058). His enemies at court brought about his downfall and execution. He was succeeded as Grand Vizier by Mehmet Pasha, known as Oküz, which means "the Ox." He commanded the Ottoman army which was sent to Persia in 1617 by Sultan Mustafa I (1617–1618).

[1634] This is inaccurate. Qazi Khan (whom Herbert mistakenly calls Ali Khan) accompanied Nasuh Pasha to Istanbul, and when he returned to Persia the Shah "received Qazi Khan and the Ottoman ambassador with favour" (Monshi II, 1076). He was certainly not "put to death." Monshi also gives full details of the territorial negotiations (History, 2:1076–77).

Insolency of the Janissaries.

The Turks soon after this, *viz. Anno Dom.* 1618, by way of Erzerum entered Media, the army being commanded by Kalil Pasha,[1635] who taking opportunity of the King's absence in Kandahar, passed unopposed as far as Ardabil, which he plundered, and harassed the country about, Qarcaqay Khan[1636] the Governor of Tabriz and at that time President of those parts not doing anything considerable for prevention. Upon the advance of Emir Hamza Mirza the Turks retreated to Van and a truce was presently concluded, but the Turk ere long insisting upon the restitution of the city Tabriz, the war was freshly prosecuted. The command of the Persian army was given to Emir Hamza the Prince, who in the expression of his courage, quickness of execution and happy success appeared to the Turk no other then as if his uncle had been revived, and withal so prudent in managing the war that though he well knew it was attended with jealousy and accidents of several kinds, which rendered the event uncertain, nevertheless such was the excellency of his spirit and so just and honourable the work he was upon that to engage against that insolent enemy was his choicest recreation, insomuch as the Turks, albeit they could not but commend his courage, yet failed they not by secret artifices at court to destroy this gallant person by an invisible hand, amongst other engines secretly insinuating into the heart of Abbas the danger he was in through the popular esteem of his active son, so as what the enemy could not effect by dint of sword was compassed by base deceit, the Prince first being made blind and soon after away by the treachery of his barber, as was commnly reported. However, his death was sudden and without question by foul practice of some who whiles the King was engaged in the wars of Khorasan thought to have seized the crown, but more certain it is that albeit the King was at first worsted in Mazanderan, nevertheless by the seasonable recruit brought him by Farhad Khan[1637] he quickly recovered that loss, quieted those parts about Larejan and returning beat the rebels near Qazvin, where having made a terrible slaughter, amidst his passion Emir Hamza by the King's command was made blind by a

---

[1635] Kalil Pasha was appointed Grand Vizier in 1617 in succession to Mehmet Pasha. Herbert mistakenly calls him "Ali Pasha."

[1636] For Qarcaqay Khan, see above. "In order to protect lives," Monshi writes, "he removed all civilians from regions through which the Ottomans were likely to march and he also evacuated all civilians from the city [Tabriz] itself. He then awaited orders from the Shah" (*History*, 1:1152).

[1637] Herbert's chronology is completely skewed at this point. Farhad Khan Qaramanlu (d. 1599) was a distinguished military commander. He campaigned in Gilan and Khuzestan, suppressed revolts in Gilan, Kerman and Khorasan, and was Governor of Fars, Azerbaijan, and Gilan. He was commander-in-chief of Persian forces in Khorasan and Mazanderam. "His overweening pride caused his downfall," Monshi states (*History*, 2:761) and he was executed after losing a battle in which the Shah's life had been in danger.

hot polished steel drawn afore his eyes, which having formerly related needs no repetition.[1638]

Abbas, not staying for the Turks as the custom of his ancestors had been, thought fit to begin with them, and taking the opportunity of their being engaged in Hungary, with the entire conquest whereof the Turk is restless in design, in the head of a royal army he quickly cleared Sirvan, then expelled the enemy out of Van and Tiflis and soon after mastered Basra and Baghdad, the last of which through treachery was soon after retaken by the Turk. The Persian King had in this interval good intelligence from Istanbul concerning the distractions of that place, which was welcome news to the court of Persia. For indeed, so insolent appeared the Janissaries there at that time as upon some slight disgust given by Delavar the Grand Vizier they broke in upon the Pasha and by violent hands put him to death, an outrage so intolerable that Osman the Grand Seigneur could not choose but reprove them for so rash a fact, but to such a heighth of presumption were they soared as they first secured the Emperor under a guard and soon after murdered him, not without the secret insinuations, as some imagine, of his uncle Mustafa, whom thereupon the mutinous Janissaries first mounted into the throne and as quickly dethroned, having a better opinion of [Ahmet] the brother of Osman, whom in that confusion they proclaimed King.[1639]

This uproar at the Imperial Porte gave the Christian princes some hopes that great body would burst through its own weight and intestine distemper, the

---

[1638] Herbert is mistaken again. First, it was Qarcaqay Khan who defeated Kalil Pasha "at a place called Pol-é Sekasta" (Monshi, History, 2:1153), after which Kalil decided to re-open peace talks. Secondly, he has repeated the story about Abbas's *brother* Hamza (Abbas did not have a son of that name), who was killed by his barber Khudaverdi. Thirdly, Princes Emamqoli and Khodabanda, who *were* Abbas's sons, were blinded by Abbas's orders, not Prince Hamza.

[1639] Herbert has most of this right. When Ahmet I died (1617), Mustafa I ascended the throne. However, he was mentally incompetent and was deposed the next year, being replaced by his nephew Osman II (1618–1622), a boy of twelve, but evidently one of some spirit, for he immediately set about trying to curb the power of the Janissaries with the help of his new Grand Vizier, Delavar Pasha, who was appointed in 1619. The Janissaries murdered the Vizier in 1622 and soon after they killed Osman II as well, replacing him with his deposed and mentally-unstable uncle Mustafa, whose second "reign" lasted until 1623. At this point Herbert is inaccurate again; Mustafa was succeeded by not by Ahmet but by Osman II's brother Murad IV (1623–1640), a skilled poet and composer as well as one of the great warrior-sultans. It is possible that Herbert may have written "Achmet" instead of "Amurath," the alternate to "Murad." Herbert may have known Sir Thomas Roe's *A true and faithful relation presented to his Majesty and the prince, of what hath lately happened in Constantinople, concerning the death of Sultan Osman, and the setting up of Mustafa his uncle. Together with other ememorable occurrents worthy of observation* (London, 1622).

rather for the Pasha of Anatolia, Abaza Pasha, or *Apaphy* as they pronounce,[1640] taking advantage of that disorder thought fit to try what he could do to set up for himself. Abbas, equally valuing that opportunity, with a considerable body of horse and dragoons invaded Diar Bakr, and having with a round sum corrupted one of the principal officers in Baghdad, he not only appeared but got entrance to the city before Ahmet the Governor had any timely notice for prevention, so that having mastered the town, the Governor durst not trust unto the citadel and barbican within, so as he secretly withdrew with a small party of horse into Carmania, which sight so discouraged those he left behind as upon first summons the forts were delivered up, yea, such was the reputation of mastering that important place that not only Misdin and Mardin, two other notable forts, yielded to Abbas, but the whole province dispatched persons to acknowledge their submission, insomuch as all those people who inhabited the countries through which Tigris and Euphrates run even from Armenia to Basra upon the Persian Gulf, terrified with this sudden and successful inroad, as one man submitted to the Persian crown. The reduction of those warm countries encouraging several Persian subjects to repair thither to plant, whiles the Turks, such as would not list themselves under the Persian, utterly defected those parts and in several bodies retired, some into Syria, others into Egypt, where by the Persians had the sole dominion over those provinces both to the heightening the Persian reputation abroad and the consternation of the Turks that by this time were composed at home, and Ali Pasha, who had the command of those revolting countries, for his negligence was made shorter by the head.

Anatolia also was in a trembling motion at that time, for Abaza Pasha stood upon his guard. It so happened that the Persian, judging he was really revolted, doubted not but that he would contribute what he could to espouse the Persian in his defence, and for trial they tempted him to deliver Erzerum into their hands. The crafty Pasha, counterfeiting a willingness, so disposed of his own men that a thousand, most of them Georgians, of the five thousand that were sent to take possession, were cut off, an act so welcome to the Turk as ingratiated him at court, insomuch as rich presents were sent him from Istanbul with solemn protestations of oblivion for his revolt and an increase of force and continuance of command, all

---

[1640] Mehmet Abaza Pasha [*Abbasi-Bassa*] was the Ottoman beglerbeg of Erzerum. In 1623 he moved against the Janissaries, executing some and seizing property. Monshi states that "he gathered a band of ruffians and brought under his control the provinces adjacent to . . . Erzerum" (*History*, 3:1235), after which he marched on Istanbul with the intention of deposing Sultan Mustafa I and replacing him with Prince Murad, but failed and returned to Erzerum. Mustafa was deposed anyway by other factions and the Prince became Sultan Murad IV. Abaza then "thought it prudent to make overtures to the Safavid court" (Monshi, *History*, 3:1238), and although he did not trust him, Abbas accepted them, but his suspicions proved correct, as Abaza changed sides twice and eventually returned to Istanbul.

which so well satisfied the young Pasha that after a return of thanks he immediately fell into Diar Bakr with all the force he could make, and near Mosul happily gave a notable defeat to a considerable party of horse and foot which the Persian had ordered for the better security of the garrison and country thereabouts.

This loss startled Abbas somewhat, but more when he received news how about that time the Georgians, who were in alliance with the Turk, had killed many of his men near Van, and as further evidence of their hatred sent their heads to the Imperial Porte as a testimony of their service, which compliment was received with thanks from thence, but otherwise soon after by Abbas, who paid them in their own coin for their future instruction. Abaza Pasha in this interim improved his time, for being master of the field he both ranged and harassed that miserable country without any mercy. Abbas by those that fled had notice of the Turk's strength and of his drawing before Baghdad, which resolutely refused his summons, and for the better preservation thereof in the head of thirty thousand horse marched towards the enemy, notwithstanding they were double his number. The Turks nevertheless resolved to continue the siege; Abbas by a herald challenged the Turks, but by the advice of a Council of War it was held adviseable rather to entrench themselves and to straighten the siege rather then to draw off and fight. Howbeit, the Persian horse gave them continued alarms and so cut off provisions from abroad that in less then thirty days they were reduced to more want then they within the town, which so perplexed the Turk that to the amazement of even their own camp, taking advantage of the night Abaza drew off, and having got the Tigris 'twixt him and his adversary made the best retreat he could with bag and baggage, but having a train of artillery withal to draw, could not make such haste but that the Persians got over the Tigris at length and had a nimble pursuit of the Turks for ten days and with such effect as very few of them escaped, a victory so remarkable and obtained with so little loss as in twenty years' time a greater was not recorded, so as the memory of it at this day lives fresh all over Persia, as appeared by several sonnets amongst them at my being in that country about five years after.[1641]

Abbas, having sufficiently scoured those western parts, was no less active and successful elsewhere, for the next year, *viz.* 1627, by the good conduct of Qarcaqay Khan he totally expulsed the Turk out of Sirvan and Gilan and reduced the natives to their allegiance, and by Tahmasp Quli Beg likewise annexed Mazandaran to his Empire, having done the like by Lala Beg and Emamqoli Khan in the conquest of Lar, Kerman, Hormuz, Khusistan, Makran and part of Ajman and Juzirey, so as he extended his territories one way from Indus to Euphrates and the other from the Caspian Sea to Babylon and the Gulf of Persia, which to this day they keep, to the honour of that crown and consternation of the neighbouring potentates.

[1641] Baghdad was recaptured in 1623 (see above and Monshi, *History*, 3:1225–1226).

Deaths of Shah Abbas and [Shah] Safi.

In this sort Abbas, after he had attained to a higher elevation of glory then any of his race, the whole course of his command being full of splendour, died in the year 1629, *Heg.* 1037, after he had lived full fourscore years and ruled the Empire forty-three. His body was from Qazvin translated to Ardabil and buried near the corpses of his great ancestors, and in his place Safi his grandson was proclaimed King, who after he had swayed the sceptre about fifteen years being likewise summoned by impartial death was buried at Qum and succeeded by his son Abbas, a Prince of great courage and prudence at this day and likely to preserve what his royal progenitors committed to his inspection and government.[1642]

Thus, having run over the series of their kings, in the next place I shall offer my mixed observations concerning that kingdom, together with a little supplement relating to their religion, after which I shall proceed in our travels. But first, suffer me to take a farewell of Persia in this epidicticon.[1643]

> Why do the windings of inconstant state
> Molest us weaklings, since the selfsame Fate
> Turns kings and kingdoms with an equal doom,
> Whiles slaves too oft possess their master's room?
> So pricking thistles choke our fairest corn,
> And hopeful oaks the bugging ivies scorn.
> Men are but men, and be they strong or wise,
> All their designs subject to hazard lies.
> Millions of helps cannot support that crown
> Which sin erects; Fate justly pulls it down.
> Witness fair Persia, large and rich of ground,
> The fitter nurse of war; in it was found
> Even in those golden times which poets vaunt
> Victorious Cyrus, who yet did supplant
> His father. Oh, that men would learn to see
> What life were best, not what doth please the eye!
> But out, alas! When they have drank of blood,
> That bitter potion's sweet, yea, even a flood
> Of lives' food cannot their hot thirst allay,

[1642] Shah Abbas I died on January 19, 1629. Monshi called him, amongst other epithets, "a radiant sun, in the shadow of whose justice men had lived in tranquillity . . . a bright star which had shed security and well-being upon all men" (History, 3:1301). Monshi then quotes a letter from Pope Urban VIII addressing Abbas as "the refulgence of the infinite divine grace and the refuge of all mankind . . . a king who is the model and source of guidance for people throughout the world" (*History*, 3:1305). His age was sixty, not eighty, and he had ruled for forty-two years. Shah Safi (1629–1642), who has already been mentioned above in several places, was succeeded by Abbas II (1642–1667). By the time Herbert died the shah was Suleiman I (1667–1694).

[1643] A rhetorical display.

Till Tomyris that blood with blood repay.
So happed to Cyrus, whom th' insulting Queen
Upbraids with bloodshed. Vengeance is too keen,
For in a bowl of gore dead drowned lies
His crowned temples and insatiate eyes,
That King aspired, and for his itching vein
Two hundred thousand subjects there lay slain.
Thus fares it still with thee, fair Persia,
Whose various native beauties freely may
A stranger's love entice. Thy breath is sweet,
Thy face well-made, a nursery of delight;
Thy breasts not dry of milk, thy arms are strong,
Thy belly fruitful, legs both clean and long;
Thy veins are large, blood pure, quick spirits hast,
But for thy back, oh stay! There lies the waste.
To this fair symmetry of outward parts,
The Giver great, to egnage by great deserts,
Infused hath into thy children wit,
Wisdom and courage best to manage it.
Nor wast thou barb'rous or indisciplined,
For had thy ear unto its good inclined,
Thy country prophetess foretold thee how
Hell and its wrath by Christ to disfavour.
Since which thy sages, kings or more then kings,
If I mistake thee not, their offerings
Unto my infant God humbly present.
O faith exceeding almost faith's extent,
See how this Light of Lights on earth did shine,
See how thy virtues retrograde decline!
Holy Thaddeus,[1644] whom Saint Thomas sent
To cure thy kings thy flamens did present
With Hellish torments, and with like foul hands
Simon the Canaanites good news withstands.
In after-times thy Khusrau, Persia, made
A pond of Christian blood; nor here thou stayed,
But in despite of Christ the Arabian thief
Thou chose to be thy unlearned judge and chief.
Hence, hence proceed those gross impieties
Which swallow'd, greedily delight thine eye!
Bloodshed and lust, the foulest out of kind,
Which my chaste Muse is fear'd to name; the mind

[1644] Thaddeus was one of the twelve Apostles; he is identified by scholars with 'Judas [the son of] of James' mentioned in Acts 1:13 and by Jerome, who says that he was "sent on a mission to Abgar, king of Edessa" (*Illustrated Bible Dictionary*, 3:1553). This appears to be what Herbert alludes to here.

Thou only keepst of zealous awe, the heart
Is foul defil'd, for so thou learnd'st the art
Of lust and pride from thy cursed Mahomet,
Whose thoughts unbounded all on thrones was set.
Nor did his successors as prophets live,
But one another murder'd; all did grieve
At neighbours' diadems. The God of Peace
For those thy sins, thy power will sure decrease,
And thou, that oft hast felt a foreign power,
Once more mayst feel as Scythic race so sour
That all the world shall know how greatest kings
Are thrall to change as well as weaker things.

[Part VII]

The various names of Persia.

Having given a brief memorial concerning their kings and revolutions of state, I shall think it worth my labour to add some miscellaneous observations I made relating to the men and manners of the country. And first, concerning the country itself, then which no other, as I suppose, has had greater variations, for in Nimrod's days it was exiled *Chusa* or *Cuth*, a name assumed from the son of Ham, who removed thence into Arabia and after that into south Africa, but in Chedor-Laomer's and till Daniel's time it was named *Elam*, from Elam son of Shem, brother (if profane authors say true) to Madai or Atlas Maurus son of Japhet, and thence called *Elamita* and *Elamis*. The next it changed was to Persia; "*Persae sunt vocati a Perseo rege, qui nomen eius subactae genti imposuit*," saith Isidore.[1] A Grecian hero he was and son to Jupiter by Danae the daughter of Acrisius, albeit others rather think it is derived from *parasp*, i.e. 'a horse' in Persian, or *peresh*, which in the Hebrew signifies 'a horseman;' howbeit, in that language it signifies 'a ram,' as typified in Daniel, and in the Chaldaean 'a horse's hoof,' 'a hooked nose,' or 'a division.' The Greek entitled it *Panchaia* and *Cephoene*, in memory of Cepheus who was after King of part of Ethiopia, a brother to Cadmus, Agenor's children. This Cepheus was father to Andromeda, wife to Perseus and parents of Perses the renowned archer, who flourished in the world before the building of Rome twelve hundred and seventy years. *Gog* and *Magog* some have named her, and *Magusea* othersome, but ironically. Such time as Achaemenes son to Aegeus, King of Athens ruled it had an Achaemenian denomination, as Megasthenes the Persian historian, Lucan, Herodotus, Suidas, Cedrenus and others observe, after which it was named *Arsaca* from Arsaces the heroic Parthian, *Artea* after that by themselves, importing a noble country from whence many illustrious persons assumed their forenames, as Arta-xerxes, Arta-banus, Arta-aspes etc. But the Tartars, in their overrunning this and a greater part of Asia, named it *Chorsoria*, or rather *Corsace*, for the Persians called them *Sacae*, as Strabo *Lib.* 11[2] and Solinus note. The Arabians *Anno Dom.* 598, such time as Mohammed subjected

---

[1] "The Persians were named by king Perseus, who imposed his name on the conquered people by force" (Isidore, *Etymologiae* 9.2)

[2] Strabo 5.261.

it, *Saracenia*, *Azemia* by the Turks for that it was part of the Assyrian Empire. By the same reason the Scythians called them *Aramei* by neighbouring the Syrians, but in envy to Syed Junaid the late reformer of the Alcoran *Etnizaria* and *Agamia*, since when they have added those of *Sophiani*, *Jezel-bashi*, *Izmaelitae*, *Sheykh-Hayderii*, *Khorasaniae* and other names unworthy the notice, save that Time herein seems to disport and please itself with this kind of variety.

The Empire is terminated on east, west, north and south with India, Arabia, Mesopotamia, the Caspian and Persian Seas. From Kandahar to Babylon, east and west, it stretches four hundred and forty *farsangs*, of English a thousand three hundred and twenty miles, in seventy days usually travelled and from Julfa near Van[3] in Georgia to Cape Gwadar[4] is twenty five degrees, the furthest part of Gedrosia or Makram upon Indus, north and south, four hundred ninety and six *farsangs*, which are a thousand four hundred eighty and eight English miles, in eighty days commonly journeyed, from whence we may compute the circuit according to our miles is not less then four thousand. The north and east part of the country is fruitful in grass, corn and fruit, for there they have plenty of beneficial showers and a temperate season. The south and west, except where rivulets are, appear to be sandy, mountainous and sterile, for the vehement heat scorches the earth and makes it barren and from whence the soil yields no exhalations, the mother of clouds, and consequently wants rain to moisten the earth, but instead whereof God vouchsafes them frequent breezes. But, all considered, no part of Asia yields a more healthy air; only as the Empire is large, so the temperament of places differ in heat and cold according to the variety of latitudes.

Shah Abbas his exchequer.

Concerning the public revenue of this kingdom, as there is not anything amongst civil affairs more subject to error then a true and intrinsic valuation concerning the wealth, power, policy and force of an estate, so in this conjecture I must go upon incertainty, but howsoever it seem to others, the Persian nevertheless makes many sorts of harvests, filling every year his coffers with above three hundred

---

[3] Van is now in eastern Turkey. It was once the capital (as Tushpa) of the ancient kingdom of Urartu, and passed through the hands of various occupiers. Alexander the Great captured it in 331 B.C.E., after which it was controlled by the Seleucids, Armenians, Persians, Arabs, and Seljuks. From 1502 to 1520 it was contested by the Ottomans and the Safavids, finally falling to the Turks in 1548. John Cartwright visited Van in 1602 (Foster, *England's Quest*, 175), probably the first Englishman to go there.

[4] Gwadar is the name for the region of the south-western coast of what is now Pakistan. It is close to the Strait of Hormuz and the Persian Gulf, and is located in the area formerly known as Gedrosia. The "cape" is really a headland on the Pakistan-Iran border.

and fifty-seven thousand *tomans* (a *toman* is five marks sterling),[5] in our money about 1,190,000 pounds sterling, a revenue more to be admired since he extracts it principally from raw silk, customs and cotton, albeit he thinks not any way dishonourable that brings in money. So thought Abbas, and thence derived that custom of sending into the market his daily presents of fruits and flowers, a kind of thrift ordinarily practiced by the greatest potentates in Asia and of which he not only boasted, not as Agesilaus [II] did of his polt-foot,[6] but seemed to complain of the nicety of other Princes in that particular. Nor is he without example, for we read in 1 Chronicles 17[7] King David, notwithstanding his enlarged empire and conquests, thought parsimony a revenue and thence neglected not the increase of his exchequer, at home appointing officers to oversee his labourers that tilled the ground, his vineyards, olives, fields, sheep, camels, asses and the like, which was a good example to his subjects and not held dishonourable, "for the profit of the earth is for all and the King himself is served by the field", saith Solomon, Ecclesiastes 5:9. They also had their merchants, and no doubt, if all the potentates of the earth were enquired after, none would exceed Abbas in frugality, for albeit as he had a *merum imperium*[8] could command what he pleased, nevertheless was delighted more in his artifices, by letter confessing his admiration upon sight of some massy piece of plate, which if he but commended they knew the signification. And in gold having received a present, if rich and heavy then it was commendable work though never so lumpish, for he values more by weight then workmanship. Ninety walled towns are under his command and villages above forty thousand, few of which one way or another escape this kind of courtship, for though they practice nothing less then goldsmiths' work and imagery, yet upon an imaginary report, desiring to see whether Fame had not been niggardly in their commendation, they dare not but return him as an acknowledgement of their thanks the best sort of metal, considering which that great treasure which is commonly taken out for ostantation at the reception of ambassadors or travellers of note is the less to be admired. But his genius travels with other fancies, for he hath many factors abroad whom he dispatches through the universe, some of which return in three, in five some; few pass seven years without giving an account to his Commissioners. If they return empty they are rarely sent abroad again, for his is a strict auditor, but when they return full straight and to his liking he rewards them considerably, further gratifying them with a woman out of his harem, a horse, a sword, a mantle or the like. Under such hopes and promises they live.

---

[5] The *mark* was a measure of weight for gold; the *mark sterling* was two-thirds of a pound sterling.

[6] Deformed or distorted foot; perhaps here implying a club-foot.

[7] This reference seems incorrect.

[8] This legal term may be rendered as "pure command" or "absolute command."

Again, from Industan, Tartary and Arabia every year move towards Persia many caravans that import merchandise of several sorts, as China ware, satins, silks, stones, drugs, tulipants etc., of whose approach he has early notice and sometimes for reasons of state prohibits his subjects to trade with them, whereupon none dare traffic, but by that artifice bringing them to his own price, or else his factors meet them upon entering his dominions with a report that the passage is not only long but dangerous, or that the late dearth makes the country incapable to buy, by such devices so startling them that rather then run their risk or incur his displeasure they oftimes condescend to a reasonable mart, sometimes receiving money for their goods or by exchange for what the Persian Emperor can best spare, to his own subjects and others his merchants then dispersing those new merchandises at good rates and having coin or bullion, to prevent its pilgrimage into other regions moulds it into plate of large assize too heavy to go far, work poor in show but not in value. Besides, by a customary law he makes himself heir to whom he pleases, so that few rich men die but that he claims a propriety, none daring to call his claim in question. He also, according to the old mode, expects annual presents. One man's offering a year or two before our being in Persia is remarkable; it was the Duke of Shiraz who presented the King in Lar the value of four hundred sixty and five thousand florins, forty-nine goblets of gold, seventy-two of silver and such other rareties as in all burdened three hundred camels, a royal present from a subject.

His policy.
Yet this might be tolerated if Astraea[9] were abroad, but contrarily corruption oft renders this brave Prince too much distempered, so as "Where money overrules what good do laws? For there the poor are crushed without a cause." Nor do the Persian kings resemble their great ancestors who were governed by the statute laws, for in Daniel 6:7 it is recorded that "the Presidents of the Kingdom, the Governors, Princes, Councillors and Captains consulted together" to ordain a royal statute established by Darius his signing, which expressed the royal assent, but rather what the same prophet told Belshazzar that Nebuchadnezzar assumed, Daniel 5:19, "Whom he would he slew, and whom he would he kept alive." He set up and pulled down as he listed, and according to that pattern the eastern provinces, whether Mohammedan or Gentiles, demean themselves, usurping an absolute dominion, against which the civilians in defence of the Law of Nature complain "*quod Principi placuit, legis illum habet vigorem*,"[10] made adequate to the will of the ruler. A memorable precedent we have in that fearful

---

[9] Astraea is the goddess of Justice.
[10] "Whatever pleases the Prince has the force of law" (Justinian, *Digest*, 1.4.1). There is a modern translation of this important work by Peter Birks and G. McLeod (Ithaca: Cornell University Press, 1997).

shift or exposition the Magi gave one of the Persian kings when he desired to marry his daughter, telling him there was no law to warrant such a fact, but a law they found that the King might do as he list, but "*ad libitum mutare leges, quia regnum datur propter regem*"[11] was no good comment, for it was a maxim that "*omnia regni potestas referri debet ad bonum regni,*"[12] whereas a Panbasilay[13] levels princes with peasants.

And indeed in this glass I wish we that live under Christian kings and states could see our own freedom and happiness, especially above those that live in unnatural bondage under such as acknowledge Mohammed, for not without due acknowledgement be it remembered that in Europe the subjects under most Christian kings and states are governed by wholesome laws, have lives and properties preserved, yea, besides, municipals have the *jura naturalia* which are held immutable, preserved agreeable to that great aphorism of Nature "*quod fieri non vis alteri ne feceris,*"[14] upon which basis all our wholesome laws are founded. Cicero also *l. 4 De legibus*, "law is the foundation of liberty." And again, "laws," saith he, "are enacted for the preservation of cities and men, to the end they may enjoy a happy life," yea, for that it is the Apostle enjoins us to "pray for kings and all that are in authority, that under them we may live a quiet and peaceable life" [1 Tim. 2:2], the true reach of the law being only to maintain property, to secure the persons and estates of men and to order all things so as may conduce to public good. Such is the happiness we enjoy, but in viewing the reverse shall find that in Persia, Turkey and other Mohammedan countries it is otherwise, for there the princes exercise a *merum imperium*,[15] not enduring to be limited or bounded by any law, so that the fence being broken down what defence is there for the poor subject against rapine, lust or what may otherwise destroy and render the outward man as to this life most miserable? Nay, the inward, too, albeit there be a seeming toleration, for how many affronts and massacres acted upon trivial pretences are they that profess Christ subject to? How oft are their children ravished

---

[11] "To change the law at will, since the kingdom is given for the sake of the king." Sir John Fortescue says the opposite, but with similar wording: "*non potest Rex Angliae ad libitum suum leges mutare regni sui,*" or "the King of England may not change his laws whenever he feels like it." He also cites the previous quote from Justinian on the same page (Sir John Fortescue, *De laudibus legum Angliae* [London: Lawbook Exchange Ltd., 1999], 232).

[12] Fortescue, *De laudibus* 234.

[13] Herbert's anglicisation of the Greek word for 'ruler of all,' or 'despot' (παμβασιλεύς).

[14] The Golden Rule: "don't do to others what you don't want done to you." Amongst authors who were Herbert's contemporaries, this can be found cited in Hobbes.

[15] "Pure command," which the Roman lawyer Ulpian defines as "*gladii potestatem,*" or "power of the sword." It has no connection with jurisdiction (Justinian, *Digest of Roman Law*, Title 2, 1s3).

from them and forcibly circumcised, with other cruelties too many to be here
remembered?

High esteem of the Persian kings.

That therefore which the Persian kings of old so much gloried in, "*se esse dominos
omnium hominum*,"[16] is now their doctrine, for they have the power of life and
death, condemn without hearing, dispose of men's persons and estates when and
as they please without any respect of right, especially at men's deaths where there
is any considerable estate, the heir not presuming further then to inventory, seeing the King hath the sole power of disposure, and so as in the dividend 'tis well
if a tenth come to the right inheritors, as we understand right. Such, alas, is the
custom and constitution of those eastern countries, where the best reason they
have is that in all ages they have been nuzzled under that sort of government and
through long custom used to adore their King, so that as of old they are not content to reverence him as the image of God who, as Plutarch in the *Life of Themistocles*, albeit a gentile, doth confess, by his infinite wisdom governs and preserves
all things, with Orpheus account him "*animata Dei imago in terris*,"[17] and with
Homer the best-beloved son of Jove, but have a more transcendent esteem and
opinion concerning him, for they retain the same repute as in former times their
ancestors did of their elemental deities, from that reverence not daring to spit or
cough in their presence or in public assemblies to appear other then inanimate
statues, and as of old pull their hands within their sleeves in sign of servitude,
forbearing for those times in his presence to speak to one another or probably
to think amiss, for the simpler sort suppose he knows their very thoughts, so as
at the receipt of any letter from him they first give it a *mubarak*[18] or solemn respect by the bowing of their bodies and kissing the paper before they read, and
swear usually by his head, as *shahin bashi* and *sar-é shah*,[19] then which they have
not a more solemn attestation. But herein they imitate others of old, for in Genesis 42:16 we find Joseph swearing by the life of Pharaoh. The Greeks also, as
Juvenal observes, were used to swear by one another's head, which the Romans
themselves likewise imitated, as appears by Ovid in his *Epistles*, "*perque tuum
nostrumque caput quod iunximus una iuro*,"[20] and by Silius *lib*. 10, "*adiuro teque
tuumque caput*."[21] But the Persians besides the head swore by the King's right

---

[16] To be the masters of all men.

[17] The living image of God on earth.

[18] An Arabic word meaning 'blessing.'

[19] These phrases mean, in Turkish and Persian respectively, 'the King's head' (Foster, *Herbert*, 327).

[20] "By your head and mine which we laid side by side" (Ovid, *Heroides* 3. 107).

[21] "I swear by you and your head" (Catullus, *Carmina* 66. 40). It is not by Silius
Italicus.

hand, for that was the oath Darius gave Tertus the eunuch when chosen to attend the Princess Statira, afterwards married to Alexander; yea, they apprehend the King sees in all places, as may be presumed by pointing their finger to the eye and saying *chashm*, i.e. 'the King sees,'[22] and his words esteemed apothegms are many times registered as well as deeds in cedar tablets gummed with cinnabar, his name usually writ with gold upon paper of a curious gloss and fineness, varied into several fancies effected by taking oiled colours and dropping them severally upon water, whereby the paper becomes sleek and camletted[23] or veined in such sort as it resembles agate or porphyry. In a word, they spare not to parallel their King with Mohammed or Ali, and, as accustomed of old, "By loss of ours the Gods preserve thy life." Yea, the better to illustrate his perfection, amongst other his provincial titles they give him the epithets of amber, nutmegs, roses and such sweet odours and flowers as most delight the sense, which also is the form of most countries in the Orient, so that upon the whole under most miserable servitude these wretched Mohammedans do live, which they better endure, not knowing what a free subject means, and for that they are indulged to the height of corrupted appetite. And yet, although the King himself be incircumscriptable and have his *sic volo, sic iubeo*[24] allowed him, nevertheless, well knowing that maxim true "'tis justice that supports the crown" and that "without law, what do kingdoms differ from places of robbery?" for the avoiding confusion and preservation of the peace, laws or rather customs they have, which are strictly executed. For the soldiery, they are subjected under ordinances of war, the rest under a kind of Imperial Law which serves to distinguish *meum* and *tuum* betwixt the subject, for which end in most cities and great towns *qazis*[25] and other magistrates are appointed, who have power from the King to call persons, examine witnesses and to hear and determine business 'twixt party and party, yea, to award judgment in causes civil and criminal with little charge and short attendance, and in criminals no place affords more severe proceedings, which is the reason the country is so secure and travellers can scarce find a more quiet place then Persia. But, seeing the *qazis* have a latitude allowed them in adjudications and accept of gifts, I fear they may be corrupted and biassed, which too oft blinds the eyes and makes innocence the delinquent.

---

[22] Foster comments that whilst *chashm* means 'eye,' Herbert has mistranslated. "The expression as used by the Persians," he tells us, "(an abbreviation of *ba-chashm*), means 'willingly' or 'with pleasure' (*Herbert*, 327).

[23] From 'camlet,' which refers to a woven fabric originally made from camel or goat hair. In this context it means 'woven.' Herbert uses the term again below, repeating what he says about Persian paper.

[24] "Thus I want, thus I order." Adapted from Juvenal, "*hoc volo, sic iubeo*" (*Satires* 6. 223).

[25] A general term meaning 'magistrates.'

Oriental mode concerning hair.

Now concerning the natives, they are generally well-limbed and straight; the zone they live in makes them tawny, the wine cheerful, opium salacious. The women paint, the men love arms, all affect poetry; what the grape inflames the law allays and example bridles. The Persians allow no part of their body hair except the upper lip, which they wear long and thick and turning downwards, as also a lock upon the crown of the head by which they are made to believe their Prophet will at the resurrection lift them to Paradise, a figment whether proceding from Mohammed's own brain or the apostate monk his associate uncertain, but probable it is he had read the scripture, and there in Ezekiel 8:3[26] and in the apocryphal story of Bel and the Dragon[27] finds Habakkuk so transported from Judaea to Babylon, for elsewhere their head was shaven or made incapable by the oil, being but thrice anointed. This has been the mode of the oriental people since the promulgation of the Alcoran, introduced and first imposed by the Arabians, but that the wearing hair and covering the head was otherwise of old appears in history very plainly.

Hair was worn according to humour of several nations and agreeable to the temperature of the place, for in countries more incling to the poles then the Equinoctial usually men fenced their heads from cold with long hair, but in more temperate climes hair was curt and commonly exposed to the air for refreshment, but within the torrid zone their head was kept warm to ward off the penetrating beams of the sun, whose ardour would not be endured. But the Romans, living in the mid-way 'twixt the tropic and the polar circle, shaved not their heads yet rather wore their hair short according to the modern fashion of the Spaniard, as may appear by medals and other antiquities in which the Caesars for the first two centuries are represented, albeit the first was so-called for having a bush of hair upon his head at the birth. Amongst the Jews also of old it was the custom to wear it short, as may be gathered from 1 Corinthians 11:14, where by way of interrogation the Apostle saith "Doth not nature itself teach you that if a man hath long hair, it is a shame unto him?" Nevertheless, in some cases long hair was allowed, as to the Nazarites, who separating from the world dedicated themselves to the Lord and by that vow suffered no razor to come upon their heads, but permitted their locks to grow full-length, Numbers 6:5,[28] as exemplified in Samson, Samuel, the Baptist and others, for albeit Our Saviour in Matthew 2:23

---

[26] "And he put forth the form of an hand, and he took me by a lock of mine hair, and the spirit lifted me up . . ."

[27] "Then the angel of the Lord took him by the crown, and bare him by the hair of his head, and through the vehemency of his spirit set him in Babylon over the den" (Bel and the Dragon 36).

[28] "All the days of the vow of his separation there shall no razor come upon his head . . ."

is called a Nazarite,[29] that was rather from the city Nazareth, seeing he refrained not wine, as may be supposed by the marriage in Cana in Galilee and the institution of the Eucharist. But that princes and persons of quality in those times wore long hair is evident by certain precedents; I shall only instance Absalom, who wore his hair so long and so large that cutting it once every year it is said to weigh two hundred shekels by the King's weight, which made six pound and four ounces, allowing the shekel half an ounce, not mentioned by way of reproach, albeit what he made his pride became his judgment, for it is said "that none in Israel was so praised for beauty as Absalom," but rather as an ornament. Nor can it be denied but short hair at some time and in some places was a symbol of servitude. Besides, it appears by the effigies at Chehel-minar, where I touched a little upon this subject, that most of the monarchs of old wore their hair very long and crisped, and as particularly instanced by Plutarch in his description of Astyages. The Gauls also of old were denominated from their hair *Comati*, and the Britons our ancestors of old, as now, imitated their transmarine neighbours, as appears by antique coins and otherwise, so that albeit the monks from a tradition shave the upper part of their head by way of distinction from the laity, yet therein they differ from the Levitical priesthood, who except in lamentations, as in Isaiah 15:2,[30] were not suffered to make bald parts upon their head, shave their beards nor make incisions in their flesh, Leviticus 21:5,[31] which last is now practiced amongst Mohammedans.

The Persian mode concerning their heads.

But not to run into extremes; as amongst the primitive Christians it was a reproach to wear long hair, so was it to be bald, therefore to avoid that contempt such as had short hair wore raised caps and such as shaved wreathed their heads with rolls of linen not only for ornament's sake but to expel the sun's piercing rays and for defence against an enemy, for undoubtedly those large turbans the Turks wear over a flat-crowned quilted cap is a very serviceable headpiece. Those in Persia are excessive large and valuable, albeit commonly they are of calico, for the superior sort of people have them woven with silk and gold with a rich fringe or tassel of gold and silver at the end, but at feasts, entertainments and gaudy-days I have seen them wreath their shashes with ropes of orient pearl and chains of gold set with precious stones of great value. That which the King himself has on differs not in shape from others, unless it exceed for magnitude; all the difference I could observe was that he wore it in the contrary way and more erect then others, which put me in mind of that which Plutarch observes concerning Artaxerxes,

---

[29] "And he came and dwelt in a city called Nazareth . . ."

[30] ". . . on all their heads shall be baldness, and every beard cut off."

[31] "They shall not make baldness upon their head, neither shall they shave off the corner of their beard, nor make any cuttings in their flesh."

who in his old age causing his son Cyrus to be proclaimed king gave him the royal preogative of wearing the peak or top of his *cydaris* upright, not permitted any subject. Some glimpse of that head tire or tiara we have in Plutarch *Vita Antonii*, which noble Roman gave order for a high and rich tribunal to be erected in the most public place of Alexandria where he and Cleopatra seated themselves in chairs of burnished gold. Two of a smaller size were set for their two sons; the eldest was called Alexander, to whom his share of the world he allotted Parthia, Media and Armenia, who that day wore a rich tiara which resembled a high-crowned hat and upon his shoulder a long vest according to the royal robe of Persia. But Ptolemy, the younger, to whom he bequeathed Macedon and other parts of Greece, upon his head had a broad-brimmed hat about which was a fillet or band richly set with stones, upon his shoulder a long cloak after the Macedonian sort, and upon his feet were embroidered sandals.

With these shashes the Persians go covered all day long, not excepting the presence of the King nor their set times of devotion, for to bare or uncover the head is held irreverent. Now as the Europeans in their salutes usually take off their hats in presence of the betters to bare their heads, the Mohammedans signify the same only by a moderate deflection of the head and directing their hand towards their heart, by which they usually express their complement, but this custom came in with the Alcoran, before which the oriental people, Persians and others, wore a sort of hat and bonnet as yet continued in China, where unless by the late invasion of the Tartars Mohammed is not acknowledged; yea, both at salutations and in presence of superiors they were uncovered. So say Eustathius and Dionysius, two credible witnesses, and Plutarch attests the like, for, saith he, "in fight we cover our heads against our enemies, but in saluting our friends are uncovered," a practice not only recommended by St. Paul, 1 Corinthians 11:4, where it is said that at the exercise of religious duties to be covered the head thereby is dishonoured, for that a man ought not to cover his head at those times appears by the seventh verse, but as to the other sex it is otherwise.[32] Now, how rigid soever the Turk may seem in abhorring the moving his turban, especially towards a Christian in salutations, the Persians nevertheless have more generosity, for with them it is a maxim and might be so with others, that singularity is discommendable as being an humour either slighting order and degrees of men (allowed angels), or otherwise the civil customs and good manners of countries in things indifferent and merely ceremonial, serving only to cement affection. And albeit to one another they are strict enough to that mode or custom of being covered, nevertheless at Astarabad after Sir Dodmore Cotton had his audience, at which Shah Abbas was present with the Ambassador, the King his master's

---

[32] 1 Corinthians 13–15 deals with whether men or women should pray covered or uncovered. "Is it comely," Paul asks in verse 13, "that a woman pray unto God uncovered?" Men should not have long hair, but for women, "her hair is given her for a covering." Herbert has already cited the verse about men's long hair being unnatural.

health being by Sir Robert Sherley remembered, the Ambassador standing up uncovered. The Persian king, frolic at that time, or rather in civility, took off his tulipant. Another time, as I heedlessly crossed the court where the King was sitting in an open tent hearing petitions, I made my due respects by uncovering my head and bowing towards the King, who was so well pleased therewith that he raised his turban a little from his brows, both to honour me the more and express his satisfaction especially for that I appeared in my own country habit, otherwise it had been a presumption punishable, but, as it proved, a grace that procured me the more respect especially with the better sort, wherever I passed. The King indeed took great delight and esteemed it an addition of lustre to his court to behold exotics in their own country habit, so that the greater the variety appeared, he would say the more was his court and country honoured at home and in estimation abroad, insomuch as upon any affront done a stranger, if in his own habit, he should be sure of due reparation, but in case he went in the habit of the country where he travelled, undistinguishable when the injury was offered, it wuld be otherwise upon address for vindication, the emphasis, it seems, wanting that inclined it. Such was then the rule of the court and populous places, albeit in travel foreigners have their liberty to please themselves as to their garb and without cause of exception to any.

Habit.

The Asiatics wear no bands; their *jobba*[33] or outside vest is usually of calico stitched with silk or quilted with cotton, but the better sort have garments of parti-coloured silk, some being satin, some gold and silver chamlets, and some of bodkin and rich cloth-of-gold figured, for variety best pleases them. No colour displeases but black, which is not worn because they hold it dismal and unlucky. Their sleeves are strait[34] and long, varying from the Turks, who have them wide and short; their close-coat usually reaches to their calves and bears round. Their waists are girt with fine towels of silk and gold about eight yards long; those and the sashes distinguish the quality of those that wear them. Dukes and other of the noble sort have them woven with gold; merchants and *qizlbashes* with silver, of silk and wool those of inferior rank.

---

[33] The *jobba*, or *aljoba* as Herbert calls it, was a loose-fitting gown made of silk brocade. It could be long- or short-sleeved and was usually worn open or unbelted. Herbert did not mention that it could also be fur-lined. For a good summary of Persian clothing of this time (in spite of the title), see Melinda Haren, "Persian Clothing in the 16th Century," www.roxanefarabi.com/clothingPgs/Clothingarticle.htm. The author cites Herbert, Chardin, and other travellers from the sixteenth and seventeenth centuries, and there are illustrations.

[34] narrow

Next their skin they wear smocks or demi-shirts of cotton, in colour resembling Scotch plaid; their breeches, like the Irish trews,[35] have hose and stockings sewed together. The stocking falls not always into their shoes, but from the ankle down gives to the eye two inches of leg naked. Their shoes are of leather, well-sewed but without latchets and of what colour you can fancy, sharp at the toe and turning upwards, the heels high and small, shod with iron or nails engrailed. This also I noted, they do not wed themselves to these iron hemicycles for thrift or ease; they seldom journey far or go swiftly, exercise and spare diet never agreeing, but to tread in a venerable path of antiquity, a custom also derived from their forefathers, either symbolising with Mohammed, whose arms was a crescent Diana, his motto *"Cresco,"* else borrowed from the *cygales* of the Athenians or from the Romans, who wore crescents or half-moons upon their shoes as an ensign of honour, by Martial and Pancirollus termed *"lunati calcei, lunata nusquam pellis,"*[36] and by Statius in his *Boscages, "primaque patricia clausit vestigia Luna."*[37] Over all the Persians, especially such as travel, throw short calzoons or coats of cloth without sleeves, furred with sables, foxes, *mushwhormaws,*[38] squirrels or sheepskins, which is a fur highly-prized. In hottest seasons they endure to wear short wide stockings of English cloth heeled with leather and serve sometimes for boots, howbeit they want not such.

Gloves are of no esteem amongst them nor rings of gold, for silver rings are most worn; not that gold is less valuable, for in other utensils they have it, but because Mohammed, according to tradition, had one of silver which was left Osman for a legacy and charmed with singular properties. None have their rings of iron except those of a baser sort, a metal some account a symbol of slavery. They paint their nails and hands with henna into a red or tawny colour, which besides the ornament it gives cools the liver and in war makes them, they say, valiant. Their nails are discoloured with white and vermilion, but why so I cannot tell, unless it be in imitation of Cyrus, who as an augmentation of honour commanded his great officers to tincture their nails and faces with vermilion, serving both to distinguish them from the vulgar and, as did our warlike Britons, in fight to appear the more terrible.

In their rings they wear agates or turquoises, which stones most delight them; some have their names or some word out of the Alcoran engraven in it,

---

[35] Trews are not quite trousers nor breeches, but form-fitting garments which cover the legs and lower abdomen and are gathered above the knee. Scholars have noted that they are depicted in the Irish *Book of Kells,* an early origin indeed.

[36] "Shoes bent into crescent-shapes, nowhere a crescent-shape on the skin" (Martial, 1.1. 50).

[37] Statius, *Silvae* 5. 28(adorns your first steps with the crescent moon of nobility). Herbert rather quaintly translates *Silvae* as *Boscages* (Woods).

[38] This is Herbert's version of the Persian term *mush-i-kharma,* which in Persian means a 'marten.'

with which they sometimes stamp their letters, for not one swordman amongst a thousand knows the use of letters, the mullahs and clergy engrossing that science, who when they write frequently do it kneeling, either because that posture is easier or that what they dictate in that form is reputed holy. Goose-quills they write not with, but reeds or canes, in which they imitate the ancients. Their paper is very glossy, and by dropping oiled colours camletted[39] and veined like marble; the materials are not rags or skins but bombazine[40] or cotton-wool, coarse and requiring much toil to perfect.

In washing they are not less ceremonious then the Jews, whom they seem to imitate by joining the tops of the fingers of both hands together with the thumb, which is parabolical; this they do not only afore and after meals but when they ease nature, and to that end have boys who carry an ewer filled with water, which in the open streets they are not afraid to make use of.

Their cavalry. Their arms.

Their swords, *shamsheers* they call them, are like crescents, of pure metal, broad and sharp as any razor, nor do they value them unless the arm be good and at one blow they can cut in two an asinego. The hilts are without ward, being of gold, silver, horn, ivory, ebony, steel or wood, sometimes of the *rizbuba* or morses'[41] teeth usually taken at Pochora in Russia. The Persian scimitars were of that esteem in old times that as Herodotus *lib.* 4 writes, it became the Scythians' god, being accounted no less then *simulacrum Martis.*[42] "*Scythae Acinaci sacrificant,*" saith Lucan in *Jove tragoedia,*[43] and Arnobius *lib.* 6, "*ridetis priscis temporibus, Persis fluvias, Arabas informen lapidem, Scythas Acinacem coluisse.*"[44] Their scabbards are of camel's hide, on solemn days covered with velvet embroidered with gold and stones of price. They seldom ride without bow and arrows, the quiver

---

[39] Camlet is a woven fabric of silk and goat's hair.

[40] Bombazine is a fabric made from silk, wool, or both. It was introduced into England during the reign of Elizabeth I.

[41] A morse is a walrus.

[42] The image of Mars. For Herodotus on the Scythians, see *Histories* 4.1–142.

[43] Unidentified. Lucan is not known to have written anything with this title. The quote translates "The Scythians sacrificed to [the river] Acinaces."

[44] Arnobius of Sicca (d. c. 330) was a Numidian theologian whose chief work was the *Adversus gentes*, which was an early attack on paganism and from which Herbert is quoting here (6. 11, PL 5. 1185). A fairly learned writer, Arnobius draws on such sources as Varro and Lucretius; he is assumed to have been a Christian writer, but very little is for certain known about him. The first edition of Arnobius was that of Faustus Sebaeus (1543); there were many other editions available to Herbert including those of Gerhard Elmenhorst (1603) and Salmasius (1651). The quote translates: "You'll laugh that in ancient times the Persians worshipped streams, the Arabs a formless stone, and the Scythians an acacia tree."

and case oft wrought and cut very artificially, the bow short but strong, the arrows long and well-headed, and albeit some think incomaparble in execution to
a gun, yet time has been they have with that, as we in France, in many parts of
Asia obtained memorable victories, the most remarkable wherein Crassus lost
his, Valerian and others, occasioning those dirges of the Roman poets, *"terga con-
versi metuenda Parthi,"*[45] and Lucan, *lib.* 1, "More swift that Parthian back-shot
shaft,"[46] and Virgil in his 4 *lib. Georgica,* "Thick as a summer shower / Or as a
cloud of arrows in their flight / When the bold Parthians are engag'd in fight,"[47]
and Ovid in their commendations *"Gens fuit et campis et equis et tuta sagittis . . .,"*[48]
by Lucan at the battle with Crassus said to be envenomed, "Nor were their trusty
shafts steel'd at the head / Alone, but also deadly poisoned," at this day of little
credit in archery unless they can in a full career cleave an orange which is hung
puprosely athwart the hippodrome, and, when past the mark, with another hit
the rest, turning in his short stirrups and Morocco saddle backwards.

In this weapon and their sword they more delight then in great ordinance,
which nevertheless they have mounted, as we could perceive, at Jask, Hormuz and
Gamrun, most of which were taken from the vanquished Portugal. Some cannon we see mounted at Lar, some unmounted at Shiraz, Isfahan and other places,
but seldom use them in a train upon field-services, which in some late battles has
given the Turk no small advantage over them, especially by disordering the Persian
horse, who with that terrible noise are not a little frighted. The use of muskets they
have had only since the Portugals assisted King Tahmasp with some Christian
auxiliaries against the Turk, so as now they are become very good shots. Howbeit,
Cedrenus in his *History* relates that Khusrau the Persian king ,who lived about the
sixth century, invented an engine which *"guttas demitterat tanquam pluviam et toni-
trui sonitus resonaret,"*[49] but of what use gives no relation, and *"apparatae,"* saith another, referring to this place, *"sunt fulgorum imitationes et fragores tonitruis similes"*[50]
which I apprehend were in imitation of those *"claudiana tonitruana"*[51] mentioned
by Jerome, *Magium lib.* 1, *Miscell. c.* 1 and probably take their model from that
"machina Salmonei" noted by Virgil, Homer, Valerius and others.[52]

---

[45] "The Parthian retreat is to be feared." This is a quotation from Seneca, but its location is unknown.
[46] Lucan, *Civil War* 1.230.
[47] Virgil, *Georgics* 4. 312-314.
[48] A nation whose plains, horses and arrows made them safe (Ovid, *Fasti* 5. 581).
Herbert mistakenly writes *terris,* 'lands,' for *campis,* 'plains.'
[49] Sent down showers of rain and resounded with thunderclaps.
[50] There were brought in imitations of lightning and thunderclaps.
[51] "Claudian thunderclaps" (Erasmus, *Adages* 3. 2. 19).
[52] Salmoneus was the son of Aeolus, the keeper of the winds; he got people to worship him as Zeus by devising a machine that imitated thunder, for which presumption the
real "Thunderer" struck him with a thunderbolt.

Persian women. Their habit and behaviour.

The women here, as of old in other parts of Asia, veil their faces in public. This veiling the face is very ancient both amongst the Jews and Romans. Rebecca, when she approached Isaac covered her face, Genesis 24:65,[53] yea, amongst men it was a note of reverence, as we find by Elijah and by the Apostle intimated 1 Corinthians 11:10,[54] yea, by the Romans used, for the bride was commonly presented to her husband with a yellow scarf thrown over her face. Sulpicius Gallus, the first that found out the eclipse,[55] repudiated his wife for showing her face when she went abroad. But to describe them; I observed that generally they are low of stature yet straight and comely, more corpulent then lean. Wine and music fattens them; the spleen is curable where passion rules not, and as to complexion, it is usually pale but made sanguine by adulterate fucuses. Their hair is black and curled, their foreheads high, skin soft, eyes black, have high noses, pretty large mouths, thick lips and round cheeks. Honest women, when they take the liberty to go abroad, seldom speak to any in the way or unveil their faces. When they travel or follow the camp the vulgar sort ride astride upon horses, but those of better rank are mounted two and two upon camels in cages of wood, covered with cloth to forbid any man the sight of them.

A Persian woman [illustration not shown]

Nor is this a new custom, for Plutarch in the *Life of Artaxerxes* mentions the like, saying that the Persians were so jealous that to speak to or touch any of the King's women was no less the death, nay, to approach near their coaches when they travelled, and instances some particulars, as in the story of Darius when he begged the fair Aspasia for his concubine, whose perfections had captured the King also. And in that story of Themistocles the exiled Athenian he relates how that the Persians, jealous of their woves and concubines, keep them strictly mewed up at home, but abroad carry them in close coaches or *cajuas*, which were so covered about that no passenger could so much as see them, nor were they drawn with horses but travelled hanging upon camels. In one of these Themistocles, disguised in a woman's habit, was secretly conveyed out of Greece to the court of Artaxerxes, where he found more safety and better welcome then amongst his ungrateful countrymen. In one of these the last Darius was conveyed into Margiana by Bessus, that had shackled him with golden fetters, Justin *lib*. 11. Agreeable to this, we oftimes had a prospect of the travelling seraglios and could well

---

[53] ". . . therefore she took a vail, and covered herself."

[54] "For this cause ought the woman to have power on her head because of the angels."

[55] Sulpicius Gallus, a Roman general and scholar, predicted an eclipse before the battle of Pydna (168 B.C.E.) in which King Perseus of Macedon was defeated by the Romans.

perceive that their guards were pale lean-faced eunuchs, who are so jealous of their charge that as we travelled 'twas the hazard of our lives if we neglected to hasten out of the way so soon as we saw them, or else throwing ourselves upon the ground to cover us with some veil or other that the eunuchs might be satisfied we durst not view them.In one of these, for ease and warmth I myself was forced to travel upon a camel above three hundred miles, being so enfeebled by a flux as I was not able to ride on horseback, and to keep company with the caravan was necessitated to this kind of accommodation. Howbeit, that the custom was otherwise appears by that sumptuous entertainment which Belshazzar made to a thousand of his lords then cooped up in Babylon, where the King and his princes, his wives and concubines drank wine in those golden vessels Nebuchadnezzar brought thither from the House of God which was at Jerusalem, Daniel 5:3,[56] and likewise at that magnific feast which Ahaseurus made for an hundred and eighty days to the nobles and princes of his Empire, as in Esther 1:11,[57] where it is said that the King, sitting in his throne at Susa the palace commanded the eunuchs to bring Queen Vashti with the crown royal to show the people and the princes her beauty, which was excellent. Plutarch also in the *Life of Artaxerxes* notes how Statira the Queen Mother usually sat with the King at meat in public and was placed near the King in an open chariot when he took the air abroad, the beholding of which, says the author, gave great content to the people. But the *amorosas* or those of the order of Laïs,[58] like those *ambubaiae* of old amongst the Syrians,[59] the most sociable have most freedom, and in this region are not worst esteemed of. No question, but to free themselves from jealous husbands many there would be of that order; those therefore that are such are not admitted without suit and giving money, after which toleration none dare abuse them, being company for the best or greatest, in which respect they go no less richly-habilimented then what is recorded by Heliodorus in his *Ethiopian History*. Upon

---

[56] "Then they brought the golden vessels that were taken out of the temple . . ."

[57] "To bring Vashti the queen before the king with the crown royal, to shew the people and the princes her beauty . . ."

[58] Laïs of Corinth was a famous courtesan who lived at the time of the Peloponnessian War (431–404 B.C.E.) and was celebrated both for her beauty and her greed. Ancient writers, however, often confounded her with a slightly younger contemporary, Laïs of Hyccara, and it is very hard to determine which one is being discussed in the numerous stories told about them. She is mentioned by Athenaeus (13. 26), who is one of Herbert's sources.

[59] More properly *ambubae*. The word is the Latin version of *embuba*, which is a form of a Syrian reed instrument known as the *mizmar*. It was played often by women entertainers, and was known to the Romans; in fact the name often refers to the musical group as well as to the instrument itself.

Theagenes his ushering Arsaca the Persian lady, "*inducebatur,*" saith he, "*vestem Persicam, ornabaturque aureis torquibus et monilibus, distinctis gemmis.*"[60]

Their hair, curling, dishevels about their shoulders, sometimes plaited in a caul of gold; round about their face and chin usually they hang a rope of pearl. Their cheeks are of a delicate vermilion dye; art oftener then nature causes it. Their eyelids are coloured coal-black with a fine pencil dipped in that mineral kohl, which Xenophon saith the Medes used to paint their faces with, which was the old way of painting, and from the Vulgate translation of the Bible, where 'tis said "*Jezebel depinxit oculos suos stibio,*" 2 Kings 9:30,[61] may be presumed that she was so painted, with which antimony the Grecian dames in old time coloured their eyebrows, now also used in Turkey. They have also artificial incisions of various shapes and forms, as have the *enamoradas* likewise. Their noses are set with jewels of gold embellished with rich stones and their ears also have rings of equal lustre. In a word, to show they are servants to Dame Flora, they beautify their arms, hands, legs and feet with painted flowers and birds, and in a naked garb force every limb about them to dance after each other, elaborately making their bells and timbrels answer their turnings. Their habit, not unlike themselves, is loose and gaudy, reaching to their mid-legs, under which they wear drawers of cloth-of-gold, satin, tissued stuffs or costly embroidery. This kind of creature is of no religion save that of the last Assyrian monarch, whose doctrine was *ede, bibe, lude,*[62] for these look temptingly, drink notably and covet men's souls and money greedily. They scorn, nay, upbraid the soberer sort with epithets of "slave," "rejected," "unsociable" and unworthy their notice, so as true it is at this day what Pompeius Trogus observed long ago, "*Parthi uxoribus et feminis non convivia tantum virorum, sed etiam conspectus interdicebant,*"[63] and yet Xenophon in the *Institution of Cyrus lib.* 1 says that the Persian custom was to kiss each other at meeting and parting, and in Chapter 15:11 of the Apocryphal part of Esther 'tis said "*Tulit auream virgam et posuit super collum eius et osculatus est eam.*"[64] Howbeit, that manner of salute is now very offensive to the Persian.

---

[60] She was brought in [wearing] Persian clothes, decorated with golden necklaces, bracelets, and precious gems.

[61] ". . . and she [Jezebel] painted her face, and tired her head . . ." The quote from the Vulgate translates "Jezebel painted her eyes with antimony."

[62] "Eat, drink, have a good time."

[63] The Parthians forbade their wives not just parties, but even their being seen.

[64] "And so he held up his golden sceptre, and laid it upon her neck" [and kissed her—omitted in the KJV *Apocrypha*].

Royal ensign.

Concerning the arms of Persia, Zonaras[65] in his first book and nineteenth chapter out of an ancient monument observeth that in old times they bore Luna, an eagle crowned of the sun, displayed Saturn, which continued for many descents their royal ensign, till Cyrus (as in the Empire, in escutcheon also) made an alteration. Xenophon gives us the view thereof: *"Erat Cyro figuram aurea aquila in longa hasta suspensa, et nunc etiam id insigne Persarum regibus manet,"*[66] borne till Crassus perished by them, at which time a sagittary was blazoned in their royal standard, a fit emblem of that people, who for skill in horsemanship and frequent riding might properly be resembled to a sagittary, from whence also that coin of Darius came, a round piece of gold, fifteen shillings in our money, Darius being stamped on the one side and a sagittary, his coat-armour, on the other, memorised by Plutarch in the *Life of Agesilaus*, who complained that his design of conquering Asia was prevented by thirty thousand sagittaries, meaning a bribe of so many pieces of gold bearing that stamp given to betray his enterprise.[67] But Mohammed, when he had yoked their necks under a twofold bondage, the other was rejected, and a symbol of greater mystery in their banner displayed, *viz.* Mercury, a crescent Luna with this *impresa, "Totum dum impleat orbem,"* alluding to an universal command, which was since borrowed by the French, how properly I know not, but may appear to such as go to Fontainbleau, where that device I saw iterated. But Mohammed's prediction failed when that *santoon* of Ardabil invented a new ensign, *viz.* Venus, a lion couchant Sol and as a tie of amity accepted by the Great Mughal and other neighbouring princes in India. But the khans, beglerbegs, sultans (the same the Greeks called *homotimi*, i.e. Persian nobles, *satrapae* the Romans), agas and qizlbashes bear no coat-armour, not that they are entitled slaves but from their ignorance in heraldry, for no honour there is hereditary. Nevertheless, this I can say in praise of the Persian: they are very humane and noble in their natures, differing in their ingenuity and civility to one

---

[65] Joannes Zonaras (twelfth century) was a Byzantine soldier, chronicler, and theologian. His *Epitome of History* is his best-known work; it traces human history from the Creation to the death of the Emperor Alexius I Comnenus (1118), and is drawn largely from the histories of Josephus and Dio Cassius. A Latin edition (1557) was printed at Basel, followed by a French translation ten years later and many other editions. See *ODB* 3: 2229.

[66] Cyrus had the golden image of eagle suspended on a long spear; it still remains as an insignia of Persian rulers.

[67] Agesilaus II was King of Sparta 401–360 B.C.E. In 361, at the age of nearly eighty. he was asked by Djedhor or Tachos, King of Egypt, for military help against his brother Nectanebo II, who wished to depose Tachos and become sole ruler of Egypt. However, when Nectanebo offered Agesilaus a large sum of money, the Spartan king supported him instead and Tachos was duly overthrown, escaping to Persia and spending the rest of his life there.

another but much more to strangers very much from the Turks, who are rugged and barbarous, for the Persians allow degrees amongst themselves, and of other people have a due esteem according to their birth and quality, yea, give respect agreeable to merit.

[Religion and marriage amongst the ancient Persians].

In old times (commonly or corruptedly so-called, seeing as one says well our times are the ancient times in that the world is now ancient and not those we count so by a retrograde computation) they were idolators such as the Gowers be now, the Kurds in Syria, the Parsis in India, the Peguans etc., but by converse with Greeks and Romans abolished their celestial worship and, as Strabo relates, received demonomy, continued until Mohammed. The firmament they called Jupiter, the *primum mobile* of other gods; him they feared, but Apollo the sun, or Mithras as they termed him, they most affected and to whom they dedicated many temples, attiring him with epithets of honour, health and gentleness, as yet memorising his image in the stamp and coat-armour of their emperors. The Moon also had adoration amongst them, supposing her espoused to Apollo, as yet continued, for upon the first view they give it a *mubarak*. They also had reward and punishment ranked in the catalogue of their deities. Venus had equal reverence, the Earth also; Water, Air, and Fire wanted not the names of deities, Fire and Water especially. Zoroaster charged them to keep a continual fire, not fed with common fuel nor to be kindled with profane air, only such as should come from the beams of that glorious eye of Heaven the sun, lightning, flints or the like. The water also was by no means to be corrupted with dead carcases, dirt, urine, rags or what expressed sordidity or nastiness. Images they esteemed but indifferently, usually actuating their rites in groves, mounts and other places.

Their marriages were commonly celebrated in the spring, such time as the sun makes the *aequinoctium*, the bridegroom the first day junketing on nothing save apples and camel's marrow, a diet they thought proper for that day's festival. Polygamy they liked of, the King giving the example, honouring them with most applause who proved fathers of most children. They seldom saw their infants till past four years of age, from which to twenty they learned to ride and shoot, also to fare meanly, lodge hard, watch, till the earth and be content with small things. In the *Institution of Cyrus lib*. 3 mention is made of a soldier, that sneezing at a court of war the whole company bowed and blessed the gods, that sign serving as a good omen to the business they were about, a custom continued amongst the Persians.

[Clothing and various customs].

The old men went plain, but the young men's habit was rich, their arms and legs fettered with voluntary chains of burnished gold or brass, whose fulgor they delighted in from its conformity to the sun. In war their attire was either steel or mailed work curiously-linked, and their brass plates scaled. Their targets were of ox-hides large and round, their cap was linen multiplicated, darts, bows, swords and axes their arms, all which in excellent good order and through long practice they managed dexterously. Parallel to these is what Xenophon says, [that] in Cyrus his time their common arms were bow and arrows in quivers, short crroked scimitars, battleaxes, light shields and two lances apiece, their arrows greater then they are now, for the bow they drew was not less then three cubits. Children from the fifth year of their age to the twentieth used little other exercise, saith Herodotus (1. 136), then these, *viz.* to ride the horse, shoot and speak truth. Cyrus was their first instructor, before whose time it was rare to see one ride, but after as rare to see a Persian of any rank afoot. Howbeit, Dionysius reports otherwise of Parthia. That it was "*regio plana, ob quam rem, accommodata . . .,*"[68] which we found otherwise, and this custom was imitated by Arsaces when he introduced the Parthian: "*Equis omni tempore vectantur; illis bella, convivia; illis publica et privata officia obeunt; super equos ire, consistere, mercari, colloqui. Hoc denique discrimen inter servos et liberos. Quod servi pedibus, liberi non nisi equis ineunt;* Justin, *lib.* 41.[69]

A Persian qizlbash [illustration not shown]

The great men's tables were splendid in rich furniture and dishes of gold, but in meats very ordinary and sparing. Bacchus their countryman taught them the art of drunkenness, insomuch as no matter of moment passed current save what relished of Bacchism; their ordinary negotiations and bargains were seldom ratified unless consolidated in froth and drunkenness. Nevertheless, their compliments were hearty, to equals affording embraces, to superiors the head and knee, which mode is to this hour continued without alteration.

Superstitious they are, as may be noted from our adverse fortune as we travelled, for in some places when we stood at their mercy to provide us mules, camels or horses, how hasty soever we appeared they cared not to set us forward except by throwing the dice such a chance happened as they thought fortunate, a ceremony deduced from the Romans, who had their *albi* or *atri* or *fasti* and *nefasti*

---

[68] A flat region, and, on account of that, agreeable.

[69] They ride horses all the time, at war or when entertaining, publicly and privately. They entertain courtesy on horseback, they go, rest, trade, and gather together. Finally, this is the distinction between slaves and free men; those who serve are on foot, whilst the free never go out without horses.

dies.[70] In msichances also or in sickness some use sorecery, prescribing charms, cross characters, letters, antics or the like, taken commonly out of the Alcoran. Necromantic studies they applaud because profound and transcending vulgar capacities, for as many in those parts make a living of it; few *syeds* there but can exorcise. Friday is their sabbath, licentiously kept and may therefore be supposed such a sabbath as Plutarch speaks of from Σάβαζιαι or Bacchanals, for Sabazius[71] is Bacchus.

Militia.

Amongst them four degrees are most remarkable: *khans*, *qizlbashes*, *agas* and *chelebi*; the *tiniars* or *turkmars* are more despicable. Upon muster the Persian king can march, as appears by roll and pension, three hundred thousand horse and seventy thousand foot or musketoons; such force he can readily advance, but seldom exceeds fifty thousand, enough to find forage or provender in such barren countries. For example, Fateh Mirza has in his brigade fifty sub-pashas of note, each of them commanding three hundred. Horse-officers are Emamqoli Khan Duke of Shiraz, who commands thirty thousand horse; Daud Khan his brother; Qazi Khan Lord of Samakhi, Asur Khan Lord of Marv-é Shahijan; Sadr Lord of the Kadi*s*; Magar Sultan of Tabriz each command twelve thousand horse; Safiqoli Khan Sultan of Baghdad, Ahmed Khan Lord of Mesarqan, Safiqoli Khan, Gushtasp Khan Sultan of Qum, Zaynal Khan Lord of *Tyroan* each hath a charge of fifteen thousand horse; Isa Khan twenty-four thousand, Itimad al-Dowla the Vizier seventeen thousand; Peykar Khan Lord of Gorgestan,[72] Husain Khan Lord of Herat, Mansur Khan and Zeynal Khan Lord of Sigestan ten thousand each; Mohammed Governor of Ganja eight thousand; Hamza Khan of Dora seven thousand; Ali Quli of Firuzkuh four thousand; Murad of Arasbar six thousand; Badr Khan the *daruga* six thousand and Dargahqoli, son to Khan Ali Khan Sultan of Kandahar four thousand;[73] three hundred and twenty thousand

---

[70] *Albi* or *atri dies* are "white or black days;" they were also known as *fasti* and *nefasti*, days on which business could or could not be conducted without impiety.

[71] Dionysus Sabazius was the god of barley.

[72] Gorgestan was another name for Georgia.

[73] Emamqoli Khan and his brother have already been noted; Qazi Khan [*Kaza-can*] "was a Sufi *seyyed* from Qazvin and a descendent of the vizier Qazi Jahan;" he held the rank of *sadr* or Head of a Religious Institution (Monshi, History, 3:1317, and see above, n. 1536). Herbert cites his title *sadr* as "Zedder" and calls him "Lord of the Caddies," i.e. *kadis*, but thinks this is a separate person; Asur Khan Cegani [*Assur-chawn*] became governor of Marv in 1623; Safiqoli Khan, governor of Baghdad, commanded against the Ottomans (1622–1623) and again two years later, when he heroically defended Baghdad against them (Monshi, History, 3:1269–71; 1316); Safiqoli Sultan was "one of the great emirs" (Monshi, *History*, 3:1316). Herbert has mixed up the two Safiqolis; Zeynal Khan is probably Zeynal Beg Begdilu Samlu, for whom see above; Isa Khan [*Isaac-beg*] is

horse or thereabouts, wonderful when I consider the little pasturage and other
provender the country affords, for their horses have but chopped straw and a little
barley to serve the turn, yet this diet renders them less apt to diseases and keeps
them in as good heart as ours having better provision.

In peace they are not always idle, solacing their active bodies in sundry sorts
of warlike exercise. They dance not, except as Pyrrhus[74] taught the Epirotes, but
love to hunt and chase the stag, the antelope, gazelle, tiger, boar, goat, hare,
fox, jackal, wolf and the like, in which pastimes they express singular courage
and dexterity. They also know well how to use the bow, dart, scimitar, guns and
javelin. Their arquebus is longer then ours but thinner; they use that very well
but detest the trouble of cannon and such pieces as require carriage. They have
greyhounds, large and not unlike the Irish, of courage to encounter a lion, have
spaniels also, but not so good as their hawks may challenge. Eyries they have of
eagles, lanners, goshawks and hobbies,[75] but their best falcons are out of Russia
and the Scythic provinces; they fly at hares, jackals, partridge, pheasant, ern,[76]
pelican, poot,[77] ostrich etc. Their lures and hoods are sometimes embroidered
or richly-set with stones of price. The vulgar sort delight in morris-dancing,
wrestling, assaulting, bandying, swinging upon ropes, ram and cock fighting, in
which exercises they spend much time, nor do they value their money, to see boys
dance or lavoltas upon the rope, in which sleights they are excellent.

---

probably the governor of Kakhetia whom Abbas appointed in 1614, but there are several
people of this name; *Etemad al-dowla* is actually a title held by the Vizier, not a name,
which means "trusted support of the state" (Savory, in Monshi, *History*, 3:1388); Peykar
Khan Igirmi-dort [*Perker-cawn*], emir of Qarabag and governor of Barda, fought unsuccessfully against Teimuraz I of Kakhetia (1616); Husain Khan Solvizi was governor
of Lorestan; Mansur Khan was governor of Arabestan from 1622–1623, but was dismissed; Mohammed Khan Ziad-oglu Qajar was beglerbeg of Qarabag and governor of
Ganja (1611), from which post he was dismissed in 1627 for "negligence and slackness"
(Monshi, *History*, 3:1289); Murad Khan Sultan Baybordlu was an emir and governor of
Arasbar (Monshi, *History*, 3:1321); Badr Sultan Bayat was "governor of various places in
Cokur-é Sad" (Monshi, *History*, 3:1312); Dargahqoli Sultan Qoroglu Zul-qadar was an
emir and "governor of various districts in Fars" (Monshi, *History*, 3:1310).

[74] Pyrrhus II was King of Epirus 306–301 and 297–272 B. C. E. Plutarch noted
that he liked "the joyless dance" of Phoenician women, because it had no accompanying flute-music (9.8.3). Pyrrhus himself was said to have mentioned this in his (now lost)
Memoirs. However, there is also a "Pyrrhic dance" connected with Neoptolemus or Pyrrhus, the son of Achilles, which was a war-dance with flute accopmpaniment. The Pyrrhic dance came to symbolise Pyrrhus's "victories," which were won at great cost, hence
"Pyrrhic victory."

[75] The lanner is a kind of falcon, which is found in Africa, south-eastern Europe and
parts of Asia. Hobbies are small falcons.

[76] An ern or erne is a sea-eagle.

[77] Probably an abbreviated form of 'puttock,' a kite.

Merchants here are in estimation; they adventure into Turkey, Russia, India and other parts of Asia, and more seldom into Europe. Such mechanics as be amongst them are industrious and ingenious, whether you consider those that labour in silk and bombazine or that dye and weave carpets, or other arts with which their bazaars abound. Besides, they have a rare art to print flowers of all sorts in leather and in colours, of which they make buskins, sandals, saddles and furniture for houses; also they stain linen cloth, which we call *pantados*.

Physicians. Calculations.

Their physicians are great admirers of nature, doting so much thereon as they make that oftimes the first causer which indeed is but instrumental or secondary; moral men they be, humane in language and in garb, both which beget esteem from all that converse with them, and did not avarice (a vice predominating there and by occasion of sickness in me full dearly exemplified) and magic studies too far sway them, I could value them above the rest. They have degrees transcending one another in title as their skill and seniority merits; so well as I could apprehend these are learned in the sciences and few but are philosophers. Nevertheless, their libraries are small, their books usually Arabic, but choice and useful, wherein they agree with that rule in Seneca, "*Non refert quam multas sed quam bonas habent*,"[78] commonly such as advance their practice and profession, and in their proper art perceived that they prefer plants and other vegetables before minerals. Some schools I visited and observed (as I formerly mentioned near Lar) that according to the old adage "*necessarium est silentium ad studia*"[79] they affect silence, and sitting cross-legged wag their bodies, imagining that such motion advantages study and serves for exercise. Indeed, Seneca seems to be of that judgment "*mihi tamen necessarium est concutere corpus, ut si aliqua causa spiritus densior erat, extenuaret illum iactatio quam profuisse mihi sensi.*"[80] The doctors are named *hakims*; it may be radically from the Hebrew word *hachabaim*, that is 'a learned man' or *chachan*, which in Old Persian signifies 'great' or 'a philosopher,' or the same that *Magus* was and a preserver of life, *Mulay* in the Arabic,[81] but a mountebank or impostor is nicknamed *Shaitan-Tabib*, or the Devil's chirurgeon. They are masters of much knowledge and are not ignorant of the mathematics.

---

[78] "It doesn't matter whether they have a great deal, but whether what they have is good" (Seneca, *Epistolae morales ad Lucilium* 45).

[79] Silence is necessary for studies.

[80] "For me, though, it was essential to have a physical shaking, whether if for some reason breath is thicker, that shaking would thin it beneficially" (Seneca, *Epistolae morales ad Lucilium* 55).

[81] Literally 'a schoolmaster,' but may stand for any learned man and sometimes for an imam or priest.

Many Arabic writers, learned both in natural philosophy and the mathematics, have flourished in those parts, most of whose books they read, namely Hippocrates, to whom the great Artaxerxes wrote an invitatory letter, Galen, Averroes, Alfarabi, Avicenna, ibn Isa, Abu Ali,[82] *Mohammed Abdullah, Ben Eladib,* Abubir, Rhazes,[83] Al-Ghazzali and Albumazar.[84] In geography Abu'l Fada the great Arab cosmographer whose works they have, one of whose maps I saw at Gamrun and I thought differed from ours both in lands and seas; it was to be sold, but what money I had would not be accepted, as also Alphraganus,[85] from whom they better their discourse, and by such helps become admirable. Nor want they knowledge of herbs, drugs and gums, witness the *maidan* in Isfahan, then which no place in the world, I think, shows greater plenty of herbs and drugs, having also no less choice of fruits, gums and odours. I observed that to such of us had fluxes they gave sloes, rice, cinnamon, pomegranate, barberries; to purge melancholy aloes, senna, rhubarb; for phlegm turbith; for colds and sweatings oils of beaver, leopards, jackals, *Herba maris,*[86] Our Lady's Rose etc., besides which the country affords plenty of galbanum, scamony, armoniac, manna, pistachios, dates, oppoponax, sarcocolla and asafoetida, which last is in greatest measure found about Lahore and other parts near the River Indus.[87] Howbeit, sweating

---

[82] Possibly Abu Ali of Balkh (fl. 970–1000), a historian and poet who wrote a prose *Shahnameh* (Frye, *History,* 625).

[83] Mohammed ibn Zakariyya al-Razi (864–925), born in Rayy, was the first writer to describe smallpox and also "converted alchemy into a science of material substances or chemistry" (Frye, *History,* 412). He wrote more than fifty works on medicine alone, including his book on smallpox and measles, which was translated as *Opera parva alubetri.* He was also a philosopher of note, who admired Socrates and composed in all over two hundred books "dealing with nearly every branch of learning" (Frye, *History,* 424). His work was well-known in Europe since at least medieval times, as he is mentioned by Chaucer.

[84] Hunain ibn Ishaq, who translated Greek medical writers into Arabic.

[85] Mohammed ibn Kathir al-Farghani (d. c. 865) was an astronomer from Transoxiana. His best-known book, which was very popular in Europe from the twelfth to the seventeenth century in many Latin translations, was the *Elements,* which summarised the Ptolemaic system of astronomy. He was also a distinguished poet and Sufi.

[86] Seaweed.

[87] I list only the more unfamiliar names. For barberries, see above. Turbith is a climbing plant used as a purgative. Galbanum is an aromatic gum used for making perfume; Herbert, uncharacteristically, missed the biblical reference, "And the Lord said unto Moses, take unto thee sweet spices, stachte, and onycha and galbanum . . ." (Exodus 31:34). Oppoponax is a resinous gum from Africa and the Middle East; it is used to produce myrrh. Scamony, which Culpeper dismisses as a weed, is a purgative found in Smyrna and Aleppo. Armoniac is usually known as "Armenian bole." It is a red clay found in Synope, Armenia, which contains magnesium and has medicinal qualities. Sarcocolla is a resinous shrub used by Arab doctors to treat wounds. Culpeper calls it "Saracen's

is the epidemic physic there, of least charge and most useful, insomuch as some citizens have above threescore *hamams* or baths, some say three hundred.

In antique paths of ignorance they choose rather to tread then by any new invention to call in question the reverend judgment of their ancestors. Hence it is that they continue their maimed calculations, out of a blind conceit that antiquity commanded them, for they have used to compute their years rather by the moon then by that motion of the sun, affirming that the firmament or eighth Heaven finishes its revolution in two and thirty years, which is false, his diurnal motion from east to west completing itself in four and twenty hours, his other from west to east but one degree in an hundred years, such is the violence of the First Mover. Notwithstanding, it is probable they mean the Heaven of Saturn which adjoins it, whose revolution comes near their time, finishing its journey from west to east in thirty years. Hence their lunary account is become subject to error, reckoning from the autumnal equinox twelve moons, the number of days in a whole year three hundred fifty-three, so that our solar computations exceeds theirs twelve days at least every year, whereby it comes to pass that thirty of our years make one and thirty of theirs, whence the difference arises 'twixt us and them in their *Hegira*, which by protract will doubtless occasion more confusion.

Their era. Poetry.

These differences in accompt were observed of old, for the Chaldaean astronomers who kept the Registers of Time persuaded Callisthenes,[88] Aristotle's nephew and attendant upon Alexander at Babylon, that their records ascended forty-three thousand years, which Diodorus Siculus, *lib*. 8.1, by reducing to months, found to reach precisely unto the Creation and no further. The Egyptians used the like accompt, for they, as Solon reported, pretended annals of nine thousand years, which Plutarch by like computation found to intend months of moons rather then years, but the Iberians, who boasted of the antiquity of their knowledge in letters and of having precedents of six thousand years, their year was found to consist of four months, which being likewise calculated was found to fall short of the time that Moses lived. But wherefore the Jews ever computed their times by jubilees, the Christians by indictions, the Romans by *lustrae* and the Greeks by Olympiads, these that follow Mohammed have a different epoch

---

Wound-wort" (Nicholas Culpeper, *The Complete Herbal* (1653) [Ware: Omega Books, 1985], 261).

[88] Callisthenes (d. 327 B.C.E.) was Alexander's "official" historian. He opposed the deification of Alexander, and was wrongly implicated by the King, possibly in retaliation for his outspokenness, in a conspiracy against Alexander's life, for which he was executed, in spite of being the nephew of Aristotle, who had been Alexander's tutor.

to accompt by, as the *Aera Gelalina* from Jalal ed-din,[89] *Aera Yezdegerdina* from Yazdegerd, besides the *Hegira* they have from Mohammed, which is their epoch or accompt of time.

Such as practice manufactures have an inferior repute to the soldiers; nevertheless they live plentifully and more secure from the jealous eyes of the King then do the great ones, who oft deceive their thoughts that they are happier. The peasants here, as elsewhere in Asia, are slaves; they dare call nothing their own, such is the rapine of the Begs of that country, nay, every *qizlbash* dares domineer, as we could perceive in our travels, yet upon complaint the Kadi ordinarily yields them reasonable justice.

The Persians had this character of old, "*cunctarum hominum sunt mitissimi*, of all men the most civil," which disposition they reserve unto this day, being generally of a very gentle and obliging nature, facetious,[90] harmless in discourse and little inquisitive after exotic news, seldom exceeding this demand, "if such a country have good wine, fair women, serviceable horses and well-tempered swords?" Few of them can read, yet honour such as can, that science being monopolised by churchmen, clerks, *santos*[91] and merchants. Some little skill they have in music, that they have resembling the Doric and Phrygic, a soft and lofty sort of comfort. Above all poetry lulls them, their common ballads resounding out the merry disports of Mars and his mistress, to which saints they dedicate their amorous devotion. Abu'l Hassan,[92] who lived *A. Heg*, 385, Al-Ghazzali, Ibn al-Farid[93] and Al-Farghani are their principal poets in those fancies, nor have I read that amongst the Romans or in any other parts poetry has been better rewarded, witness poet Marwan, who for those 70 distichs which he presented Mohammed the great al-Mansur's son received as a reward 70,000 staters.[94]

---

[89] Jalal ed-din Rumi (1207–1273) was born in Balkh, now in Afghanistan, and was therefore technically a Persian. After 1215, when his family fled from the Mongols, he lived in Konya, Turkey. His great collection of poems, the *Mathnawi*, is one of the pivotal Sufi texts and he is probably the best-known Sufi poet in the West today. His followers are the *mevlevi* dervishes of Turkey. There is a good modern translation of his works by Coleman Barks, *The Essential Rumi* (Edison: Castle Books, 1997).

[90] Not used in a pejorative sense; here it means 'witty' or 'amusing.'

[91] Holy men.

[92] Abu'l Hassan Kharraqani (fl. 950) was a Sufi poet and mystic, "considered the *qutb* (pole) of his day and whose special spiritual relation with Bayezid is related so beautifully in the *Tadkhirat al-auliya* of [Farid ud-din] Attar" (Frye, *History*, 461).

[93] Omar ibn al-Farid (1181–1235), a distinguished and well-loved poet, was not actually a Persian at all; he was born and died in Cairo. His best-known works are *The Sufi Way* and *The Wine Ode*. There is a modern translation of his poems by Emil Homerin (New York: Paulist Press, 2001). He was also a Hadith specialist. 1638: Herbert called his poetry "amorous and exact" (269).

[94] Herbert's source may be mistaken or exaggerating. A more modern historian notes that Marwan ibn Hafsa [*Mervan*] wrote a sonnet in praise of the caliph Harun

Tahir,[95] who was general to Caliph al-Mamun, for three verses which a poet gave him requited him with 300,000 pieces of gold, and Abdullah[96] his son, he who for fear of a consumption fed only upon lion's flesh boiled in vinegar, of which confection he took two drams daily, was no less liberal to that art, and as I might instance, many other princes of the Sophian pedigree of later times, not a little to their reputation. And how lame soe'er the verses are, their graceful chanting and quavering (after the French air) gives it to the ear harmonious, so that in my opinion it was rigidly said by a Father when he called poesy *"vinum daemonum,"*[97] for, says the Lord Verulam, poesy not only refreshes the soul by chanting things rare and various, but also exalts the spirits with high raptures, and being joined with music sweetly insinuates itself, so as it has been esteemed of even in the rudest times and amongst those nations which were accounted barbarous.[98] And albeit the men affect not to dance themselves, though anciently dancing was in request with men, as stories tell us, nevertheless dancing is much esteemed there, for the Ganymedes and Laïsians (wanton boys and girls) foot it even to admiration; Myrmillonian dances I may properly call them, seeing the bells, brass armlets, silver fetters, timbrels, cymbals and the like so revive Bacchus, in this kind of dance being so elaborate that each limb seems to emulate, yea, to contend

---

al-Rashid (786–809) and received "a purse of 5000 golden pieces, a robe of honour, ten Greek slave-girls, and one of his own steeds to ride on" (William Muir, *The Caliphate: Its Rise, Decline and Fall* (1898) [Beirut: Khayats Reprints, 1963], 488 n. 2). Harun was not the son of al-Mansur, but his grandson. His father was Caliph al-Mahdi (775–785).

[95] Tahir ibn al-Husain (d. 822) "the great-grandson of a Persian slave belonging to an Arab chief" (Muir, *Caliphate*, 491) reduced the whole of Arabia to the Caliphate and captured Baghdad (813), defeating al-Mamun's brother Caliph al-Amin and helping al-Mamun get the throne. He became Governor of Baghdad (820) and was "a generous patron of learning and poetry." He was also renowned for a letter he wrote to his son "on all the duties of life, social and political . . . justly regarded as a model, not only of perfect writing, but of culture and precept" (Muir, *Caliphate*, 505).

[96] Abdullah ibn Tahir (d. 844), son of the above, conquered Egypt (816) and was appointed Governor of Ricca (819). By the 830's he had become the almost-independent ruler of Khorasan and defeated an uprising in Azerbaijan in 837. Remaining loyal to the Caliphate, he defeated another rebellion in Tabaristan and continued to rule with the Caliph's approval until his death. Frye quotes the Arab historian Yaqubi as saying that Abdullah "ruled Khurasan as no-one had ever done before, so that all the lands were subject to him" (*History* 100–1).

[97] The wine of demons. Herbert got the phrase from Bacon's essay "Of Truth," where he says "One of the Fathers, in great severity, called poesy *vinum daemonum* because it filleth the imagination" (Bacon, *Major Works*, 341).

[98] ". . . poesy serveth and conferreth to magnanimity, morality, and to delectation . . .[and we see that] joined also with the agreement and consort it hath with music, it hath access and estimation in rude times and barbarous regions, where other learning stood excluded" (Bacon, *Advancement of Learning*, 2. 186–87).

which can express the most motion, their hands, eyes and bums gesticulating severally and after each other, swimming round and now and then conforming themselves to a Doric stillness, the Ganymedes with incantating voices and distorted bodies sympathising, and poesy, mirth and wine raising the sport commonly to admiration. But were this all, 'twere excusable, for though persons of quality here have their several seraglios, these dancers seldom go without their wages and in a higher degree of baseness the pederasts affect those painted antic-robed youths or catamites in a sodomitic way, completing the Roman proverb "*Persicos odi puer apparatus,*"[99] a vice so detestable, so damnable, so unnatural as forces Hell to show its ugliness before its season. Hear St. [John] Chrysostom: "*Cogitato, quem grave illud sit peccatum, ut quod ipsam Gehennam etiam ut ne tempus apparere coegerat,*" and for the detestation whereof Alexander is honoured to all posterity.[100]

The art of painting the face has been a mode more ancient then commendable, and sufficiently blemished by Jezebel. Xenophon by an example he gives makes it appear that men likewise used it, for in the description of Astyages the Median king he tells us that his face was sanguined with vermilion, his eyes struck with a semi-circle of azure and his neck adorned with a carcanet or rope of pearl and sometimes with a chain of gold, in use then amongst such as were favourites or princes of the blood, an ornament more ancient then Astyages amonsgt other nations, for Pharaoh, when he promoted Joseph to be second in the Kingdom of Egypt, amongst other the regal attire was put about his neck a chain of gold, Genesis 41:42. Daniel at Babylon had the like by order of Belshazzar, Daniel 5:29, Zerubbabel by Darius, Esdras 3:6 and by like order of the Syrian king Alexander there was sent unto Jonathan the High Priest a chain of gold, as the custom was to such as were of the King's blood, 1 Maccabees 10:20.[101]

Eunuchs.

Persia continues the ancient custom of emasculating youths, practiced to preserve the excellency of their voice but principally for guarding the seraglios of great persons, which although it sufficiently effeminate them, yet some eunuchs have neither wanted courage nor reputation, seeing that both Barbary and other Mohammedan countries out of them have elected generals for the field, but

---

[99] "Boy, I hate the fancily-adorned Persians" (Horace, *Odes* 1. 38.1).

[100] Herbert has already translated this phrase.

[101] The references are cited in order. "And Pharaoh . . . put a gold chain about his neck;" ". . . they clothed Daniel with scarlet and put a chain of gold about his neck;" "he shall have . . . a chain about his neck;" Zerubbabel was one of the builders of the Second Temple. "He sent him a purple robe and a gold crown;" The Syrian king was Alexander Balas, who appointed Jonathan Maccabaeus High Priest in 153 B.CE. and then governor of Judaea in 150.

in the execution of their ordinary trust about women find them mischievous enough, for being armed with sword and target, bow and arrows they express their jealousy too oft, to the prejudice of ignorant and careless travellers. They are of most ancient standing, for we read of them in Scripture in oldest times, especially in this Empire, so that Donatus in Terence and Petronius Arbiter[102] spare not to aver that Persia made the first eunuchs, by which word is sometimes understood 'chamberlains' or those great officers whose nearest attendance was upon the King, but those other that wait upon the harems have their testicles cut off, which so enervates nature or at least the exercise that they are utterly disabled as to procreation, and yet it is of the opinion of some that when the testicles are forced away there is such a remainder of seed stowed up in the glandules of generation which be spermatic that it is possible for eunuchs to generate, notwithstanding which, until a jealous Turk observed a gelding to cover a mare, the extreme now used was not practiced. Honest women rarely show their faces, to strangers eclipsing by a white sheet, the note of innocence, those beauties which are exsquisite, no man daring to praise any of that sex, especially another's wife; such is their jealousy.

Their circumcision.
Now concerning circumcision, it is here used and accounted so necessary that without it no-one calls himself a Mussulman. Men and sometimes women conform to it, the men for Paradise, the women for honour's sake, or ibn Sidi Ali[103] lies who so paraphrases. From nine to fifteen the females may, and in Cairo and the adjacent parts at this day it is frequently practiced, nor is this a recent custom, for Strabo *lib.* 16 in that case makes this physical observation, "*Quemadmodum viri praeputium habens, mulieres habent etiam quondam glandulosam carnem quam nympham vocant, non ineptam accipiendo characteri circumcisionis.*"[104] The males at Ishmael's age (whom they imagine was Abraham's best-beloved) are enjoined it,

---

[102] Gaius Petronius (c. 27–66), a Roman courtier under Nero noted for having written the *Satyricon*, a farcical story about low-life characters written in a mixture of prose and verse, at once satirical, bawdy, and extremely funny. The name "Arbiter" was bestowed on Petronius because of his position as a kind of model of elegance and wit at Nero's court. There was no English translation of the *Satyricon* until that of William Burnaby (1694), but Herbert could have used the editions of P. Pithoeus (1564), Joseph Scaliger (1571), or Daniel Heinsius (1629). There is a brilliant modern translation by Sarah Ruden (Indianapolis: Hackett, 2000).

[103] Possibly Abu Ali ibn Muskuya (d. 1040), Arab philosopher, theologian, and physician, one of the pre-eminent Shi'a writers of his time (Frye, *History*, 478).

[104] Jones has a problem with this; his translation reads "they rear every child that is born, and circumcise the males, and excise the females" (8.153) and adds in a note that "[they] remove portions of the *nymphae* and sometimes of the *clitoris*" (8.153 n.2). Earlier on Strabo says only that "they mutilate their bodies" (7.339). The correct translation

ere twelve hoping he may be able to speak his profession. Howbeit, the Arabs practiced it before Mohammed's time, yea, some think he himself was not circumcised, nor that he imposed, but suffered it only to please the Arabians. A fee is to be paid amid the ceremony, for want of which the poorest sort are seldom cut. The ceremony is more or less according to the difference of their degree, acted either at home or in the mesjeds; if son to a mirza, khan, sultan or *chelebi*[105] it has more pomp, for his kindred and friends in their best equipage assemble at the parents' house, as a symbol of their joy presenting him with gifts of sundry prices, and after small stay mount the boy upon a trapped courser richly-vested, holding in his right hand a sword, in his left a bridle. A slave goes to either side, one holding a lance, the other a flambeau, neither of which are without their allegories. Music is not wanting, for it goes first, the father next, and according as they are in blood the rest follow promiscuously; the *hajji* attending at the entrance into the mosque helps him to alight and hallows him. To work they straightway go; one holds his knee, a second disrobes, a third holds his hands and others by some trivial conceit strive to win his thoughts to extenuate his ensuing torment. The priest, having muttered his orisons, dilating the prepuce in a trice with his silver scissors circumcises him and then applies a healing powder of salt, date-stones and cotton wool, the standers-by, to joy his initiation into Mahometry throwing down their *munera natalitia*,[106] salute him by the name of Mussulman. But if the ceremony be at home, they then provide a banquet, before which the boy enters well-attended; he is unclothed before them all and circumcised, and in commemoration of such a benefit (imitating therein Abraham when Isaac was weaned) continue a feast three days together, at the end whereof the child is led about in state, bathed and purged, a turban of white silk put upon his head and all the way as he returns saluted with joyful acclamations.

But such as turn apostates, to swill in luxury the more or to robe themselves with some title or advancement (forgetting that for a base and momentary applause or pleasure they disrobe their soul of everlasting happiness, such as run parallel with the lines of eternity) are brought before the Kadi, who upon this signification leads him into the mosque and without much ceremony, only cutting the foreskin, are thereby made Mohammedans, which done, those devils incarnate, to witness their new persuasion or rather to aggravate and indeed accelerate their damnation spurn with their feet the Cross, the hieroglyphic of our salvation, which in the primitive and purest age was of that honour amongst Christians as not only they used it in baptism but upon their foreheads to despite the Jews and heathens and to glory in that same thing the more which the enemies of Christ upbraided the Christians with as calumny. Superstition I detest,

---

should be: "Like having the foreskin of a man, the woman even has a sort of gland-like part of flesh they call *nymphae*. Not unsuitable for receiving the mark of circumcision."

[105] *Chelebi* in Turkish denotes "prince" or even "gentleman."

[106] Birthday presents.

but that it should become a derision is miserable and to be pitied. To return: the renegade in token of defiance spits thrice at it, having this misbelief that Christ never suffered but Judas, and then exults in the usual battology "*La il-laha ilallah wa Mohammed rasul Allah*, God is first, praise him, and next him, Mohammed,"[107] after which imprecation the wretch holds up one finger, thereby renouncing a Trinity. Three Mussulmans then dart three staves three times towards Heaven, and ere any touch ground his new name is imposed, which done, he is led slowly on an ass about the city that everyone may note him for a denizen and proselyte to Mohammed, but (praised be God) I have not heard of any European Christian who in this country of late times hath denied his faith, which is cause of rejoicing.[108]

Weddings and Burial.

Their weddings have not much variety.[109] First, observe that polygamy is tolerable for Mohammed to excuse his own infirmity, but borrowing it from the Romans honours such most as have several wives and beget most children, wherein they argue with Scaliger that the pleasure of generation is a sixth sense, but their common excuse is to furnish the Emperor with soldiers for defence, Paradise with saints and to resound the meritorious praises of their Mohammed, the dervish, an order of begging friar, excepted, who from a transcendent conceit of their own purity forbear matrimony but suppose Nature's blackest villainy no sin, producing Mohammed for their prototype, who both by precept and example defended it. I have peradventure tied your chaste ears too long to so impure a subject. Such therefore as dare wed provide a sum of money and buy her goodwill, her parents being no further charged then to bathe and purify her. They choose their wives more from report of others then particular acquaintance, the friends of either party commonly recommending and concluding. The day being come, the bride is veiled in lawn and bravely mounted, a troupe of friends accompany her to church, in the mid-way being met with an equal number of friends; all

---

[107] Actually it means "There is no god but God, and Mohammed is the prophet of God."

[108] Herbert has his basic facts correct. Muslims are certainly not believers in the Trinity; the Quran states "They are surely infidels who say 'God is the third of three'" (Sura 5:75); they do refer to Christ as "the Messiah," but qualify it by saying he was "only a prophet" (Sura 5:77). They deny that he was crucified, for the Quran says "they slew him not, and they crucified him not, but they had only his likeness" (Sura 14:156). "Muslim tradition," Rogerson explains, "would later add the story that Yehuda (Judas) took his master's place and died on the cross full of remorse for his treachery" (Barnaby Rogerson, *The Prophet Muhammad: A Biography* [London: Abacus Books, 2003], 142).

[109] Herbert might be saying this because for Muslims marriage is a legal contract, not a religious ceremony. His description of the festivities and other activities is quite accurate (for further details see Hughes, *Dictionary*, 318–23).

aggrandize the ceremony. Entering the mosque, the Mulay takes the protest of their good liking; she demands three things (such as the Jewish women did of old): bed-right, food and clothing. Their fathers having declared themselves content, the priest circles them with a cord, conjoins their hands, takes a reciprocal oath and calls Mohammed to witness, after which the Kadi enrols their names, the hour, day, month and year of nuptial, and with an *euge* dismisses them. The first day vapours away in tobacco, feasts and other joviality, the men and women being severed; at night the bride enters a stove where she is washed and perfumed that her degree may the better appear and her person be the better accepted of. Next night they bathe together and seven days after, during which the feasting holds in some measure according to the old custom of *septem ad convivium*,[110] at which time if he discover her to be no virgin she is returned to her parents with dishonour and likewise kept till Death makes the divorce. The Alcoran allows incestuous marriages, pretending that thereby love is better contracted and conserved.[111] In case also the man be weary or that she be barren, he acquaints the Mulay therewith, who Jew-like gives a Bill of Divorce upon his allowing her a dowry,[112] after which if he require her again and they agree, they are secondarily married, yea, five, six, seven times rejecting and revoking as hate or love can stimulate, by that disorder love vanishing, jealousy building, rage advancing, clamours roaring and by which many times the fathers neither know their own children nor they their parents. They marry none of another religion, but use such as slaves or concubines, refrain them in their diseases; four wives the law tolerates, in concubines [they] are unlimited, never wed common prostitutes, give suck two years and permit not widows to marry again till an hundred and twenty days be expired.

Their burials revive some ceremonies that of old were used amongst the Jews and gentiles. At his farewell to the world the next of kin close the eyes, as did Joseph in the 46 of Genesis and Telemachus in Ovid.[113] The nobler sort of people had their sepulchres in the sides of mountains or hills about Persepolis. Howbeit, some used to embalm, the brains being exhausted by a silver engine; the belly, so soon as dissected and the bowels extracted, cleansed with wine, farced with cassia, myrrh and other spices, was then closed and buried in extraordinary deep pits or vaults, or in places bored in the sides of mountains. But the poorest sort used only bitumen or else the juice of cedar, which resists putrefaction. Howbeit, the most usual way of burial is this: first they wash the corpse with clean water,

---

[110] Seven [days] at the feast. From *"septem diebus iussit convivium"* (Esther 1; Vulgate Bible).

[111] This is not true. Amongst "legal disabilities in marriage" under Islam Hughes lists *"Consanguinity*, which includes mother, grandmother, sister, niece, aunt, etc." (*Dictionary*, 316). Incestuous marriages were, however, common in pre-Islamic Arabia.

[112] For details of Mohammed's teachings on divorce, see Sura 2:26.

[113] Ovid, *Heroides* 3.

as we find practiced to Tabitha in Acts 9, and then they carry it orderly and with silence to the grave. They then lodge the carcase not in the mesjed or churches but churchyards, and where none lay formerly, supposing it a vile part to disturb the dead, whom in the grave they think sensible of torment. They place his head towards Medina, and according to the old *septem ad luctum* for seven days the next of kin watch, to keep if possible the evil angel from his grave, incessantly warbling out elegiac threnodies as the last expression of love he can show, but *"Vidi enim lachrymas, et est pars fraudis in illis."*[114]

Others thus: in the first place go those of his blood, next them his varlets naked to the waist, the rest in trews, who to express their zeal burn or scratch their arms and breasts and cut and print circles in their flesh (a mode borrowed from the Jews, prohibited by Moses [in] Leviticus 19:28 and in Deuteronomy 14:1)[115] so that the blood oft trickles in many places. Next them are ranked some youths whose shoulders bear some texts out of the Alcoran, mixing with them eulogies of the defunct, which they ingeminate. Next these follow many persons of best rank, each putting his hand to the cord that draws the hearse, and on every side throng the multitude, some bearing in their hands laurel or cypress, others garlands of flowers, fruits and what best befits the season; some semi-naked horsemen play along, and oftimes to demonstrate their love spare not to wound their carcases. In the last place go the *presicae* or women hired to weep and howl, who tear their false hair, probably smell to onions (*hinc ille lachrymae*) and use such impostures as did the antic Romans noted in Livy, who make it an art to mourn and by their counterfeit tears and shrieks to provoke others to passion and like lamentation. These we find mentioned in Jeremiah 9:17,[116] which custom the people of God borrowed from the heathen. They are also noted by Ovid in his 3 *Artes amandi*: ". . . discunt lacrimare decenter,/ Quoque volunt tempore, quoque modo,"[117] and Juvenal in his 6 *Satura*, "Fruitful in tears, tears that still ready stand / To sally forth, and but expect command."[118] In this decorum they march slowly and with commendable silence, but at his dormitory ululate *"La ilahah"* etc., "Let us praise God." There, first unclothing and then cleansing the carcase, his sins thereby, as they say, vanish; then they anoint him with unguents, and so wrapped in fine linen bury him, placing his head towards Mecca, his face towards Heaven (the rather noted, in that the other sex are buried with their faces downwards) and his arms spread as prepared to embrace his prophet Mohammed. Upon the grave they fix two stones at head and feet,

---

[114] "I have seen their tears, and there is something of falsehood in them" (Ovid, *Heroides* 12. 93; variant text).

[115] "Ye shall not make any cuttings in your flesh for the dead, nor print any marks upon you;" "Ye are the children of the Lord your God; ye shall not cut yourselves, nor make any baldness between your eyes for the dead."

[116] "Consider ye, and call for the mourning women, that they may come . . ."

[117] Ovid, *Ars amatoria* 3. 291–292.

[118] Juvenal, *Satires* 6. 274–276.

which in Arabic characters engraved and coloured notes his name, quality and time of burial. There they leave him, but give not over twice a day to sing his requiem, beseeching Mohammed to succour him against his bad angels, of whom as part of their creed they nourish this opinion.[119]

So soon as any Mussulman is buried, forthwith Munkar and Nakir,[120] two ugly devils, assail him; the one is armed with an iron club, the other with a hook of flaming brass, in which frightful posture they view the carcase and in an imperious or rather insolent manner command him to lift up his head, to fall prostrate upon his knees and beg his soul, which it is supposed was till then departed. The dead body re-entertains his soul and together give an account of their past life; now, upon concession if it appear his life was good, the devils as spirits fly away and give way to two good angels,[121] apparelled in white to comfort him, to the day of doom not budging from him nor seeming unwilling to protect him, but in case his life upon examination or confession appear bad, then the black-eyed cacodemon[122] with the iron club hits him so pat upon the head as thumps him ten yards deep into the ground, where he sleeps not long, for the other Hell-hound with the flaming hook pulls him up again, in that horrid sort tormenting him till Mohammed calls a parliament and gives deliverance.[123] In one place of his Alcoran he promises to save them all, but in another, forgetting his promise, appoints them to pass over the Bridge of Judgment, each man carrying his sins in a bag behind him, but in passing over, with such as have heavy loads the bridge breaks and they fall into Hell, such as have less weight into purgatory etc.[124]

[119] This is a fairly accurate account of the burial-customs. For further details, see Hughes, *Dictionary*, 44–47. However, he does not say anything about women being buried face downwards.

[120] Munkar and Nakir [*Muengar* and *Quarequar*] are not "ugly devils," but "the two angels who are said by Muhammad to visit the dead in their graves and to interrogate them as to their belief in the Prophet and his religion." Their names mean "The Unknown" and "The Repudiating." They are black with blue eyes (Hughes, *Dictionary*, 420).

[121] Herbert may be referring here to the *Kiramun Katibun*, "the two recording angels who are said to be with every man, one on the right hand to record his good deeds, and one on his left to record the evil deeds" (Hughes, *Dictionary*, 279).

[122] An evil spirit which often has the form of a monster.

[123] According to the *Mishkat* of the Imam Husain al-Baghawi (d. c. 1242), a celebrated Quranic authority, "the wicked will be struck with a rod and they will roar out" (Hughes, *Dictionary*, 353). Another authority, Abu Hurairah (c. 713–791) said that "then the ground will be ordered to close around him, and it will break his sides and turn his right side to his left, and he will suffer perpetual punishment till God raise him therefrom" (cited in Hughes, *Dictionary*, 27). Herbert seems to have heard both versions.

[124] After judgment "those who are to be admitted into Paradise will take the right-hand way, and those who are destined to Hell-fire will take the left, but both of them must first pass the bridge, called in Arabic *as-Sirat*" (Hughes, *Dictionary*, 544), after which "the righteous will pass over it with the swiftness of lightning but the wicked

In former times they used to burn the bodies, as did the Romans and most ethnics. The carcase was folded in linen called *linum vivum*, made of the stone asbestos,[125] which was both spun and woven, and being put into the fire would not consume but preserved the ashes from mixture with other things, and so was committed to the sepulchre. This precious sort of linen at the first was sold at a high rate, but afterwards became more common, for such time as Sulla besieged Athens it was observed that what was anointed with that oil became free from burning. Pliny also reports that he saw napkins frequently used, which when dirty or foul were cleansed by fire and not by water, a rare kind of washing!

Food.

Now concerning the furniture of their houses, call him to mind who by the foot of Alcides[126] found out his other dimension; a pan, a platter and a carpet is the epitome. Their diet is soon dressed, readily eaten and is quickly-digested as described. Their table is usually the ground, covered with some slight sort of carpet over which they spread a pintado cloth. Afore each man they lay five or six thin cakes of wheat or pancakes, for other bread they make none, and this some tear asunder when they eat it, with their ten fingers representing, forsooth, as some imagine, the Ten Commandments, and carelessly scattering many wooden spoons, their handles being above half a yard long and the spoon itself so large as my mouth could seldom master. They have a meat resembling the old *maza*, which was meal mixed with water and oil with gobbets of flesh. They have withal little pasties of hashed meats not unlike the Turkish *sanbousaks*.[127] They seldom go beyond *polo*, but in that dish express, they think, a witty invention, setting before you sometimes forty dishes called by forty names, as *polo, chelo, kishmy-polo*,

---

will soon miss their footing and will fall into the fire of Hell" (Mullah Ali Qari, cited in Hughes, *Dictionary*, 595). "Purgatory" is the closest Herbert can get to the state of *barzakh*; the Quran says "behind them is *barzakh*, until the day when they shall be raised" (Sura 23:99). It is defined by Hughes as "an intervening state between death and the Day of Judgment" (*Dictionary*, 39).

[125] *Linum vivum* (see Pliny, *Natural History* 19. 19) is actually asbestine, a fire-resistant magnesium silicate compound which was used to make towels and napkins, as Herbert states here. This quality meant that anything made from it could be cleaned by being thrown into the fire.

[126] Hercules.

[127] *Sanbusak* is a dish made from dough, butter, eggs, sesame seeds and filling, which Claudia Roden says is "popular in Syria, the Lebanon and Egypt," but also quotes a poetic recipe from the time of Caliph al-Mustakfi (944–45), who gave a memorable banquet featuring this dish (*A New Book of Middle Eastern Food* [Harmondsworth: Penguin Books, 1985], 132–33). The Turkish version is actually called *börek*.

cherry-polo etc.,[128] albeit indeed it differ but in the cookery: all are of rice, mutton and hens boiled together, some having butter, some none, some having turmeric and saffron, othersome none, some having onions and garlic, some none, some having almonds and raisins, some none and so on *ad infinitum*, making us also believe they make gallant cheer and great variety though the ingredients be one, differing only in colour, some coming to the table black as coal, some as white as curds, others (that you may know their cooks are witty) be yellow, green, blue, red or in such a colour as they fancy. Wot you, forsooth, why rice is so generally eaten and so valuable? Not that it exceeds wheat or other grain in goodness, fineness, roundness or the like, though I cannot deny but it is a solid grain and in boiling swells so much that a pint unboiled will increase to near four pints in boiling, but from a tradition delivered by their grand annalist Yaqub ibn Said Ali, who affirms that on a time Mohammed being in prayer was conveyed into Paradise, whence earnestly beholding its varieties, at length he cast his eyes upon a glorious throne, and fearing that he should be punished for his presumption blushed for shame and sweat for fear, but loath to have it discovered wipes from off his brow the sweat with his first finger and threw it out of Paradise. It was not lost, it seems by the story, for therewith divides itself into six drops; the first was metamophosed into a fragrant rose, and thence it is rose-water is much used and in honour of the rose an annual feast yet solemnised. The second was coverted into a grain of rice, a holy grain; the other four became four doctors: Abu Hanifa, Abu Abdul Mailk ibn Anas, Mohammed al-Safi and Ahmed ibn Hanbal,[129] who

---

[128]   *Chelo* or *chilau* is boiled, steamed rice, used often as a base for meat or chicken. Greenway and St. Vincent, unlike Herbert, are more appreciative of the rice-dishes. "Saffron is frequently used to flavour and colour the rice," they tell us, and "If the rice is served with a slab of butter on top, lovingly blend the butter into the rice for a few minutes as the Iranians do; it really livens up the rice if it's a bit bland or dry" (*Iran*, 109). Cherry *polo* is made with rice and sour cherries; by *kishmy* Herbert may mean *khoreshta*, sauces, "aromatic and textural symphonies, the result of centuries of traditional harmonizing, creating and enjoying" (Roden, *Middle Eastern Food*, 403). Herbert, it seems, was no gourmet!

[129]   These are the Four Imams, from whom the four Sunni Islam sects are descended. Their dates are as follows: Abu Hanifa [*Abu-hamet*] (700–780), "the great oracle of Sunni jurisprudence" (Hughes, *Dictionary*, 8); Abu Abdul Illah Malik ibn Anas [*Melek-zeddah*] (716–795), "considered to be the most learned man of his time" (Hughes, *Dictionary*, 312), whose teachings are still followed in North Africa; Mohammed Idris Al-Shafi [*Shec-Vassaim*] (780–824) founded the Shafi sect in Egypt and Arabia; Ahmed ibn Hanbal [*Achmet Sembelim*] (780–855), who founded the fourth orthodox Sunni sect in Baghdad and whose teachings "the modern Wahhabis are supposed to follow" (Hughes, *Dictionary*, 188). As they were not Mohammed's contemporaries they certainly did not help him with the Quran. The story of the sweat has its origins in the *Hadith*; in one version, Mohammed began to sweat from modesty and his rose-flavoured sweat turned into the souls of prophets. Another states that scholars, martyrs, and believers came from the sweat that ran down his chest. See also M. H. Fadel, "Schools of Jurisprudence," in

assisted Mohammed to publish if not compose his Alcoran.[130] They have salads, achars and hard eggs which usually are variously-coloured and hard that their stomachs might not be deluded in too quick a digestion. Mutton there is sweet, but far principally in the tail, the weight commonly ponderising twenty pounds; in Turcomania they weight sixty pounds and may balance the rest of the carcase. Camel, goat and pheasant the country yields and the law allows the eating, but not of beef, veal, swine's flesh, hare and buffalos, which are prohibited. Camel's flesh they sell us in the bazaars roasted upon skewers or cut in mammocks and carbonadoed;[131] three or four spits are sold for twopence. Bad pastrymen they are, for I have seen them put a lamb whole into an oven and take it out as black as a coal. They say it tastes the better, but I thought otherwise.

The poor are not so voluptuous; they content themselves with dry rice, herbs, roots, fruit, lentils and a meat resembling thlummery.[132] Dates also, preserved in syrup mixed with buttermilk, is precious food, but to memorise their cheese and butter will either make your mouths water or turn; in good earnest the worst any ever tasted of, both that it wants art and material, for 'tis dry, blue and hard, ill to the eye, bad to the taste and worst for digestion. The worst is towards the Gulf, the best in Mazenderam, but neither of them praiseworthy. Their butter usually comes from the *guspans'*[133] tails, which saves them churning; howbeit, some boil the cream in a raw skin so it is commonly very sluttish, full of hairs and unsalted. This sort will keep fresh (sweet, I do not say) six months, but when we drew our

---

Medieval Islamic Civilization: An Encylcopedia, ed. Josef W. Meri (New York: Routledge, 2006), 2: 702–4.

[130] Mohammed himself never "published" the Quran; like other holy books, it was believed that it came as a revelation. Caliph Abu Bakr, who was worried that since so many of the people who had committed parts of it to memory were dead, the wisdom might be lost, commissioned Zaid ibn Sabit to collect and write down what he could, who is recorded by al-Bukhari as having done so, until finally "[Caliph] Usman compiled them into one book" after retreiving the final portions from Caliph Omar's daughter Hafsah. The Caliph asked Zaid ibn Sabit, Abdullah ibn az-Zubeir, Said ibn Alas and Abdur Rahman ibn al-Haris ibn Hisham to undertake the "definitive" edition (Hughes, *Dictionary*, 486). At any rate, the early history of Mohammed and the Quran is shrouded in mystery and uncertainty. See G. Schaefer, *The Genesis of Literature in Islam* (Edinburgh: University of Edinburgh Press, 2009), 11; G. S. Reynolds, ed., *The Quran in its Historical Context* (London: Routledge, 2008).

[131] "Mammocks" are "chunks" of no particlar shape; "carbonadoed" means "grilled."

[132] This word is usually rendered as "flummery," and denotes a sweet dish made from eggs, milk and flour. Its name derives from the Welsh *llymru*, and the "thlu" sound is the best the English can do to approximate it. Herbert likes to sprinkle his narrative with Welsh terms whenever he can.

[133] A *guspan* is a fat-rumped sheep.

knives through it a thousand slut's hairs came along with it; they nevertheless commend it.

Their liquor is sometimes fair water, sugar, rosewater and juice of lemons mixed, and sugar coated with citrons, violets or other sweet flowers, sometimes a mixture of amber; this we call sherbet. Wine they also drink, having, as they pretend, a peculiar privilege from Ali and from the indulgence Syed Junaid in his *Commentary* offered them, which the Turks are not worthy of, heartily laughing at the reason the Turks give for their abstinence. The Turks indeed forbear wine upon a tradition that two angels, Harut and Marut by name, being sent down to instruct the Turks in morality and amongst other things to forbear drinking of wine, it seems fell under that temptation, for they themselves having drunk above measure became enamoured of a beautiful virgin and solicited her to wantonness. But the damsel, understanding whence they came, dissembled her consent upon condition they would teach her the *Al-fath*[134] that would carry her up to Heaven, which they no sooner did but she immediately ascended and informed against the angels, who were thereupon excluded Heaven, but the virgin was metamorphosed into the Morning Star. From that accident wine is abhorred and refrained.

Coffee. Opium. Diet.

Arak or *aqua vitae* they also drink and tobacco sucked through water (that it inebriate not) by long canes issuing from a round vessel, and above the rest affect coffee, a drink black as soot, thick and strong-scented, distrained from bunchee, bunnin or bayberries beat into a powder and boiled in water, wholesome but not toothsome they say, but if sipped hot comforts the brain, expels melancholy and sleep, purges choler, alleviates the spirits and begets an excellent concoction; yea, however ingrate or insapory it seems at first, it becomes great and delicious enough by custom, but not regarded for those good properties so much as from a romance that it was invented and brewed by the angel Gabriel to restore Mohammed's decayed moisture, who never drunk it but made it a matter of nothing to unhorse forty men and in Venus's camp with more then a Herculean fortitude amongst women to effect wonders. But sure 'tis more ancient then Mohammed, for story says that the Lacedaemonians were stronger then their neighbour Greeks by shunning excess and keeping to their 'black broth,' which when Dionysius would have drunk, the cook told him he must also use exercise.

Opium, the juice of the poppy, is of great use there also; good, if taken moderately, bad, nay mortal if beyond measure, but by practice they make that familiar which would kill us, so that their medicine is our poison. They chew it much,

---

[134] This word means 'the victory,' and is the title of Sura 45 in the Quran, which speaks of the "victory" that God gives people over their sins, "that God may pardon thee thy former and later sin." For Harut and Marut, see Sura 2:96 and Part IV.

for it helps catarrhs, cowardice and the epilepsy, strengthens (as they say) Venus and, which is admirable, some extraordinary foot-posts they have who by continual chewing this with some other confection are enabled to run day and night without intermission, seeming to be in a constant dream or giddiness, seeing but not knowing whom they meet though well-acquainted, and miss not their intended places, by a strange efficacy expulsing the tedious thoughts of travel and rarely for some days deceiving the body of its seasonable rest and lodging. Opium, coffee and the root of betel, tears of poppy and tobacco condense the spirits and makes them strong and allegre, which both make the Persians believe they expel fear and enable them to run continually. And how strange soever this report of the foot-posts may seem, yet this out of Mizaldus[135] *Cent.* 2:55 something resembles it: *"Avicenna refert quendam peregre profecturum, libram unam olei violacei cum adipe mixti bibisse, et inediam absque ulla fame decem dierum sustenuisse."*[136] Olympiodorus of Alexandria also writes that in his time a certain man lived without sleep, having nothing else to sustain nature save the air and light of the sun. Besides soporiferous pellets which the foot-man chewed, *pedibus [timor] addidit alas*,[137] but however mysterious it be, I persuade not every man to imitate Velleius the Epicure,[138] who feared nothing so much as to doubt of everything.

They commonly eat in earth or porcelain, not valuing silver, the King by such attracting it to his own table. They have another reason, but ridiculous, that Mohammed at his descent into Hell, seeing the devils at dinner, observed that they were served in silver. In feeding they use not knives or employ one finger or two, three or four being enjoined them from tradition, nor do they cut their bread but break or rend it, equally fictitious, for Osman in his parody assures them the Devil (*Shaitan*, they call him) doth cut what he eats, which makes it no fable, seeing he eats not. And for the mode of breaking bread, Osman borrowed it from the Jews who had that custom, practised likewise by the gentiles as we find in Xenophon in his description of the Persians. Nevertheless, ignorance makes them attribute all to miracles. At meals they are the merriest men alive; no people in

---

[135] Antoine or Antonio Mizauld (1510–1578) was astrologer and physician to Queen Marguerite de Valois. He first came to prominence with a treatise on weather prediction (1546), but his most famous works were on the subject of astrological medicine, *Harmonia coelestium corporum et humanorum* (1555) and *Secrets de la lune* (1571). He also wrote on botany in *Historia hortensium* (1575). Herbert cites here Mizauld's book on natural curiosities, *Centuriae XII: Memorabilium utilium ac iucundum in aphorismos arcanorum omnis generum locupletes* (1566).

[136] Avicenna relates that when someone was setting out on a journey, he drank one pound of violet oil mixed with fat, and was then then able to refrain from food without feeling any hunger for ten days.

[137] "Fear gave wings to his feet" (Virgil, *Aeneid* 8. 224).

[138] Gaius Velleius (fl. c. 50 B.C.E.) was a Roman senator and Epicurean philosopher. He features prominently in Cicero's *On the Nature of the Gods*, where he is used in Book I as a spokesman for the followers of Epicurus.

the world have better stomachs, drink more freely or more affect voracity, yet are harmlessly merry, a mixture of meat and mirth excellently becoming them, for here "*Qui canit arte canat; qui bibit arte, bibat*,"[139] jovial in a high degree, especially when courtesans are in company. The men account that for good manners which we thought barbarous: when in complement or rather squalid wantonness they would overcharge their mouths with polo and by an affected laughter exonerate their chaps, throwing the overplus into the dish again, and as a symbol of good-will offer others to eat what they had chewed formerly.

To end, having soaked their *hulsinees* or water-bags, wine-bottles are then usually emptied; at that exercise they sit long and drink soundly, condemning that precept in the Alcoran as an idle toy invented by Osman that it is giants' blood, the blood of those the Greeks call *Theomachoi*[140] or the Devil's gall as some have resembled it, albeit the Turks forbear to drink it partly from that persuasion. Nevertheless, the Persians in this are commendable, that they never quarrel in their cups nor compel they any to sit longer or drink more then he pleases, nor drink they healths or one unto another, a civil custom but too much abused amongst Christians. Minos, a heathen, strictly forbade it the Cretans, as Plato rehearses in his dialogues, but compared with these of old are without resemblance, these being homely, those full of excess. Dio[141] and Ctesias give some instances, as that in old times the Persian monarchs made many feasts and many times invited no less then fifteen thousand men, in every entertainment expending four hundred talents, which amounts in our money to two hundred and forty thousand crowns, and at private feasts where forty or fifty were entertained, as Ephippus Olynthius[142] reports, a supper stood in a hundred *minae* of gold, each *mina* or *dyna* in our money valuing six and twenty shillings and eight pence, a large amount in that juvenility if true, for we say "*plures opes nunc sunt*," yet credible when the vast revenue of the Persian Empire extracted from many nations is considered, for what accrued out of those hundred and twenty-seven provinces

---

[139] "Whoever sings well, let him sing; whoever drinks well, let him drink" (Ovid, *Ars amatoria* 2. 220).

[140] Literally "fighters against the gods." Herbert refers here to the giants who tried to storm Olympus and displace the gods from their high seat. It also appears in Acts 5: 39 and in the writings of Athanasius as a term for heretics.

[141] Dio Chrysostomos of Prusa (c. 40–120) was a philosopher, historian of the Roman Empire, and rhetorician. His major extant work is the *Discourses* or *Orations*, which deal with political and moral subjects, and are renowned for their balance and toleration; eighty of them are preserved complete and there are also some fragments. It has been translated by J. W. Cohoon and H. L. Crosby (Cambridge, MA: Harvard University Press, 1932–1951).

[142] Ephippius Olynthius (fl. 330–after 320 B.C.E.) was a Greek historian who wrote about Alexander the Great and is cited by Athenaeus, who says that he "outlived Alexander" (1. 12, 18). He may also be the "Ephippus of Chalcis" mentioned by Arrian as being appointed "superintendent" over the "Secretary of foreign troops" (5.4).

was not less then forty thousand and five hundred Attic or Euboeic talents, in our account forty hundred thousand crowns or thereabouts.

Present revenue.

Nor is the crown revenue at this day much less, albeit his treasury be not half so great, for Tahmasp *An. Dom.* 1560 received eight millions of crowns gathered from fifty sultans who farmed his income, besides annual presents from great officers, some of which may be considered by the wealth of a late neighbour of theirs, the Governor of Lahore, who at his death bequeathed unto his master three millions of coined gold, a great quantity of bullion, jewels of great price and many elephants, camels and horses of great value. It is well-known that Levanti Beg seldom failed to send him yearly the value of twenty thousand crowns as a New Year's gift; twelve thousand horse the Kurds 'twixt the two seas also yearly presented, and Abbas at this day from silk and other duties receives yearly above nine millions, fourteen millions and two hundred and eighty thousand florins, some say, three hundred and fifty thousand tomans in Persian money, which in ours is about eleven hundred and ninety thousand pounds sterling.

Now though the ground be for the mist part barren, yet especially towards the north the soil is rich, and elsewhere, where rivers or springs make the improvement. And it hinders not that her womb is uberous, for besides that plenty of marble we could from her bosom oftimes discover many minerals and stone of lustre, as jacynths, chrysolite, onyx, turquoise, serpentine and granites; bezoars and pearls also (then which no part of the world has better) are no less valuable. The mines of gold in old times have here been found, as Plautus in *Sticho* is proof in that particular: "The Persian hills he may deserve to hold,/ Which (if the proverb lie not) are of gold," and Varro[143] by like allusion, "The Persian mountains nor the Lydian state / Our minds from care or zeal can separate," but at this day of small esteeem the natives either wanting skill or will to discover them.

Coins at this day used are the *abbasi*, in our money sixteen pence; *larin*, ten pence; *mohammadi*, eight pence; *shahi*, four pence; *sadi*, two pence; *bisti*, two pence; double *qazbak*, a penny; single *qazbak*, a half-penny; *fals* (like the Turk *aspars*) ten to a *qazbak*. But the gold coins are *sultanis*, equal to a Venice sequin; *dinars*, alike in value and name to the old *darics*, thirteen shillings and four pence, but few seen; all but the *qazbakis* and *fals* are of pure silver, the rest are brass but

---

[143] Marcus Terentius Varro (116–27 B.C.E.) was a Roman soldier, politician and philologist. He wrote the *Antiquitates rerum hominum et divinarum*, which contains much information about religious customs in the Empire, and the celebrated treastise *De lingua Latina*, which is not extant in complete state, Book IV being mostly missing and other books in fragmentary form. It was first edited by Denis Godefroy (1585). There seems to have been no English translation until 1710; there is a modern translation by R. Kent (Cambridge, MA: Harvard University Press, 1951).

current all over the monarchy.[144] Now, 'tis to be observed that no Mohammedan prince stamps his coin with images, but letters purporting their names or some text out of the Alcoran; howbeit, before the eightieth year of the Hegira, certain it is they commonly used images and not letters.

I have elsewhere described their buildings; their beds are cots of two foot height or four low posts strengthened with girth-web, a shag or *yopangee*[145] spread on top, of double use for it serves as an umbrella abroad and at home for a coverlet. In summer their slaves attend about them, some to waft and beget cool air, others to scare away the gnats and suchlike buzzing vermin, which during hot weather pesters them extremely. The men account it a shame to urine standing; their reason is because dogs use that posture. They have slaves attending with ewers of silver filled with water to cleanse pollution.

The better sort are so oft on horseback as they hate to see men walk; such they think distempered in mind. A madder thing to see them ride, though not half a stone's cast! Their horses, especially for service, are of the Arabian breed, bodied like jennets, swifter and of more courage; they curb their mettle with sharp bits, a ring of iron helping them. Their bridles are long and sometimes studded with gold; of gold ofttimes are their pommels and stirrups. Saddles of the better sort are usually of velvet, high and close like our great saddle; the trees are curiously-painted. That form they borrow from the Tartar is hard, small and close; sure, but not easy. Generally in good liking are their horses, albeit their fare be mean; a little bag filled with barley and chopped straw hung about their heads is both livery and manger. They strictly tie them to a certain proportion. Mules are no less valuable then their horses, of better service where the passage is sandy or mountainous. Men use horses, women mules and camels; every camel is loaden with two *cajuas*, which hold two women. The cage is of wood covered with cloth, so low as suffers them not to stand upright, but less grievous in that for the most part all sorts fit and endure not long standing. When any harem travels they are guarded with eunuchs armed with bows and swords, both for defence and offence.

---

[144] Jackson and Lockhart supply the following information about Persian currency. The silver *dinar* [dura] was introduced by Ghazan Khan (1295–1304) and the "unit of reckoning" was the *toman* at 10,000 dinars. The *abbasi* was a 200 dinar piece; the *mohammadi* (named for Shah Mohammed Khodabanda) was 100 dinars; the *bisti* 20 dinars; the *shahi* 50 dinars. The *qazbakis* were 5 and 10 dinars respectively. The *sadi* is another name for a double shahi, worth 100 dinars. The *larin* we have already met; it is "a double twist of silver purl, stamped on both sides" and worth 10 dinars. The *fals* (which Herbert calls *fluce*), is actually a copper (not brass) coin worth 10 dinars. Further details may be found in Jackson and Lockhart, *History*, 556–67.

[145] From Turkish *yapinjaq*, which means 'a shaggy cloak' (Foster, *Herbert*, 331).

The Persian's characters.

Their alphabet is writ in their proper character:

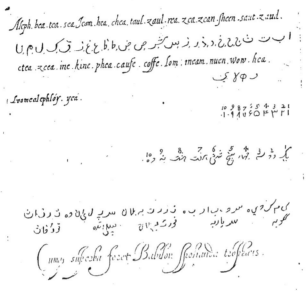

Examples of writing [illustration shown above]

To which, if I add somewhat of their language it may both show the affinity it has with the Saxon, who after their descent from Ararat first planted in Saca, a part of Bactria, and after in Sarmatia, before their progress into the Cymbric Chersonese, from whom we borrow our Teutonic, and peradventure be of some use to the future traveller.

List of words [illustration shown on pp.704–8]

English.	Perſian.	*English.*	Perſian.
GOD	*Whoddaw*	Gentleman	*Awgaw*
Heaven	*Afman*	Merchant	*Soldager*
the Sun	*Afta*, & *Samon*	Souldier, or Golden-	
the Moon	*Maw*	head.	*Cowzel-baſh*
a Star	*Starra*, & *Navſh*	Lord Ambaſſadour	*Elchee-beg*
the Skye	*Kabowdas*	Preſident	*Viſier*
Wind	*Baud*	Judge	*Cauſee*, or *Caddi*
a white Cloud	*Sephyte*	Juſtice	*Darraguod*
the Earth	*Zameen*	Phyſician	*Hackeam*
Emperour	*Pot-ſhaw*	Chancellour	*Mordati*
King	*Shaw*	Conſtable	*Calentar*
Queen, or Empreſs	*Beggoon*	Purveyor	*Mammandar*
Prince	*Mirza*	a Chriſtian	*Franghee*
Duke	*Cawn*	a Mooriſh believer	*Muſſulman*
Marqueſs	*Beglerbeg*	a Jew	*Jehewd*
Earl	*Sultan*	an Armenian	*Armenee*
Lord	*Beg*	Perſian	*Pharſee*
Lady	*Conna*	Indian	*Mogul*, or *Indee*
Lords Son	*Beg-zedday*	Georgian	*Gorgee*

English.	Persian.	English.	Persian.
Sarcaſtrian	Carcáſh	Belly	Shykam
Turk	Torc	Yard	Kery
a Church	Dear	Stones	Sekym
a High Prieſt	Muſtaed-dini	Matrix	Cus
an Archbiſhop	Kalyph	Thighs	Roam
a Prieſt	Mulai	Knees	Zoanow
a Holy Man	Hodgee	Foot	Poe
a begging Friar	Abdal	Wine	Sherap
a Saint	Meer & Emyr	Water	Obb
a Prophet	Emoom	Fire	Attaſh
a Prophets Son	Syet & Emoon-zedda	Wind	Bawd
a Church	Machit or Meſquit	the Sea	Deriob
a Great Church or	Jewma-machit	a Ship	Kiſhtee
Cathedral		a Boat	Kiſhtee-cowcheck
a Holy Father	Padre	Fiſh	Mohee
a Father	Bobbaw	a Sheep	Guſpan
a Mother	Mamma and Madre	a Goat	Booz
a Brother	Broder	Roaſt-meat	Cobbob
a Siſter	Qhvaar	Rice	Brindg
a Son	Zedda	boyled Rice	Pelo
a Daughter	Daughter	Wood	Tzom
a Boy	Oglan & Piſſar	Apples	Sib
a Girl	Daughter	Pomgranads	Narr
a Maiden	Whotoon	Musk-melons	Corpoos
a Couſin	Choul	Water-melons	Hendeon
a Friend	Memam	Myrobalans	Allilha
a Slave	Colloom	Dates	Wehormaw
a Servant	Marda	Almonds	Bodoom
a Foot-man	Shooter	Raiſins	Kiſhmiſh
a Groom	Mitar-baſhe	Walnuts	Gardow
a Cook	Aſh-paſh	Sugar	Sucker
a Butler	Suffrage	Small-nuts	Piſtachoes
a Barber	Syrtraſh	Sirrop of Dates	Dooſhab
a Doctreſs	Dayah	pleaſant Liquor	Sherbet
a Mountebank	Shytan-Tabyb	Bezar	Pezar
a Scribe	Vikeel	a Roſe	Gull
an Interpreter	Callamache	Grapes	Angwor
a Speech or Lan-	Zavoan	Figs	Anger
guage		Orange	Norenge
a Mechanick	Oaſtad	Lemmon	Lemoon
a Man	Adam	Carroway-feed	Giznees
an old Man	Pyrh-adam	Annife-feed	Zera
a Woman	Zan	Nutmeg	Gooſe
The Head	Serry	Cloves	Mekut
Hair	Mow	Mace	Bashas
Eyes	Chaſin	Cinamon	Dolcheen
Eye-brows	Browz	Spice	Filfill
Noſe	Bymry	Ginger	Gingerfill
Ears	Gouſh	Pepper	Pepperfill
Cheeks	Row	Ophium	Triack or Theriack
Face	Tahom	Rhubarb	Rhubar
Muſtachoes	Sibyl	Onions	Peoſe
Lips	Lab	Spikenard	Sembul-tib
Teeth	Dandoon	Manna	Sheer-queſt
Chin	Chynoſer	Sena	Machyi
Arm	Bozow	Poppie	Puſtie
Breaſt	Sinow	one Year	Teck Sol
Hand	Daſt	one Month	Teck-Maw
Finger	Anguſht	a Day	Rowſe

English.	Persian.	English.	Persian.
to day	*Amrowſe*	a Door	*Darr*
Yeſterday	*Dig-rowſe*	a Table	*Taghtah*
to morrow	*Subbaw*	a Chair	*Curſee*
two dayes hence	*Paſt-ſubbaw*	a Cup	*Paola*
Night	*Shaue* or *ſhab*	a Candle	*Sham* & *Mum*
Soon	*Zood*	a Candleſtick	*Shamdom*
Much	*Piſhaar*	a Bed	*Maſruſh*
More.	*Diggar*	a Pillow	*Nazholiſh*
Good	*Cowbaß*	a Quill	*Callam*
Bad	*Baddaß*	a Garden	*Baugh* or *Bawt*
Naught	*Cowb-nees*	a Town	*De*
Great	*Buzzurk*	the Devil	*Shytan*
Little	*Cowcheck*	Hell	*Jehendam*
Small	*Kam*	Rogue	*Haramzedday*
Leſs	*Andac*	Slave	*Colloom*
Write	*Binwees*	Whore	*Cobba*
Sing	*Bowhoon*	Cuckold	*Ghyddee*
Bread	*Noon*	Fool	*Dooamra*
Butter	*Rogan*	Baſtard	*Haram-zedda*
Cheeſe	*Paneer*	old Whore	*Moder-Cobba*
Milk	*Sheer*	the Kings Evil	*Boagma*
ſowr Milk	*Moſſe*	Dog	*Segg*
Vinegar	*Sirca*	Cat	*Chat*
Roſe-water	*Gule-ob*	Mule	*Aſtor*
Honey	*Dow-ſhabb*	a Goat	*Buz*
Salt	*Namak*	Cow	*Gow*
Water	*Obb*	an Aſs	*Owlock*
Rain-water	*Ob-baroon*	an Elephant	*Behad*
Salt-water	*Ob-namak*	a Nightingale	*Bulbul*
Hot	*Garmas*	a Camel	*Shoutor*
Cold	*Sermawas*	Mule-man	*Aſtor-dor*
a Book	*Catobb*	Camel-man	*Sheuter-dor*
a Cheſt	*Sandough*	Horſe-keeper	*Myter*
a Carpet	*Collee*	a Horſe	*Aſp*
a League	*Farſang*	a Saddle	*Zeen*
half a League	*Nym-farſangas*	a Saddle-cloth	*Zeen-puſh*
a reſting placo	*Manzeil*	a Shooe	*Coſh*
a common Inn	*Carravans-raw*	a Nail	*Cheat*
a Nurſery	*Haram*	Shepherd	*Uloch*
a Houſe	*Conney*	Bird	*Quoy*
a place	*Joy*	Beef	*Gouſt de gow*
Straw	*Jo*	Hen	*Morgh*
Barley	*Cow*	Hens-eggs	*Tongh-morgh*
Wheat	*Gandowm*	Boiled	*Poaĉtas*
Money	*Zarr*	Half boiled	*Nym-poaĉt*
Iron	*Pholot*	Paper	*Coggeſh* & *Cartas*
a Knife	*Cord*	Thred	*Reſpun*
a Sword	*Shamſheer*	All boiled	*Hamma-poaĉt*
a Gun	*Tophangh*	Kitchen	*Mawdbaugh*
a Glaſs	*Shuſha*	Old	*Chonnay*
Ink	*Moora-kabbas*	New	*Novas*
Silk	*Abruſhumas*	I, Thou, He	*Man, San, O*
Lace	*Chytoon*	Nothing	*Hech*
Buttons	*Dougma*	a High way	*Raw*
a Furr	*Fuſt*	a Tree	*Drake*
a Dagger	*Hangier*	a Turquoiſe	*Pheruzay*
Spur	*Mahamis*	a Paſport	*Rhyrman*
Boots	*Chagma*	a Cap *or* Turbant	*Mandeel*
a Window	*Pangera*	a Coat	*Cabay*

English.	Persian.	English.	Persian.
a Key	*Cleet*	Stop	*Baſt*
a Ring	*Hanguſter*	Waſh	*Buſhur*
a Tower	*Mynar*	the Market	*Buzzar*
a Needle	*Suſan*	the great Market	*Mydan*
a Looking-glaſs	*Dina*	You lie.	*Drugmaguee*
a Whip	*Chabuck*	You ſay true.	*Roſmaguee*
a Towel	*Dezmal*	Very right.	*Dreuſtas.*
a Gift	*Piſcaſh*	Near, far off.	*Nazeecas, duras.*
a Platter	*Langaree*	Bring it hither.	*Bear ingee.*
a Plate	*Nalbachee*	What ſay you?	*Che-cheſas ?*
Colour	*Raugh*	Go, call him.	*Bro, awaſcun.*
White	*Sevittas*	He is aſleep.	*Cobbedat.*
Red	*Sourck*	He is abroad.	*Swarſhudat.*
a Miſ-believer	*Caffar*	He is not within.	*Conney neeſe.*
a Privy	*Adam-conney*	He is beheaded.	*Shaw cuſht.*
a Cloſe-ſtool	*Ob-conney*	He eats and drinks.	*Moughwherat.*
a Cradle	*Cajna*	Come quickly.	*Zood beaw.*
a Glaſs-bottle	*Shuzan*	Go quickly.	*Zood burroo.*
a riding-Coat	*Bolla-puſh*	Know you? yes.	*Medamny ? baly.*
a Hill	*Achow* or *Kowby*	Where is he?	*Quo jaas ?*
a Hot-houſe	*Hummum*	Who? my Father?	*Che ? pader man ?*
a Sweet-heart	*Jonanam*	I know not.	*Che medannam.*
a Cap	*Koola*	Can I tell you?	*Che cunnam ?*
a Turbant	*Mandil* & *Duſtar*	Not far off.	*Dure-neeſe.*
a Bridge	*Pully*	What ſay you ?	*Chemi-gwee ?*
a River	*Root-connah*	I drink to you.	*Eſco-ſumaw.*
Strength	*Zoor*	I thank you.	*Bizmilla.*
Full	*Pooras*	With all my heart.	*Allhumderalla.*
Strait	*Tanghea*	Much good do it you.	*Awpheat.*
Weak	*Sanghe-nees*	Give me.	*Biddy.*
In health	*Choggea*	Do you love me?	*Dooz me daree ?*
Sick	*Na-choggea*	Take away.	*Verdure.*
Dead	*Mordaſs*	You trifle.	*Bazi-mecunnee.*
Gone	*Raſtas*	Fill full.	*Pour kum.*
Here	*Ingee*	Boil the meat.	*Gouſt-buppoſe.*
Above	*Bolla* & *bollanda*	Stay a while.	*Andac wieſt.*
Below	*Poin*	Even ſo.	*Humſhee.*
Angry	*Janghea*	Beat him.	*Beſome.*
Hungry	*O jam*	It is day.	*Rowſ-haſt.*
Sope	*Saboon*	It is night.	*Shah-haſt.*
Broken	*Shekeſtas*	It is dark.	*Tareekas.*
Laden	*Barkonnas*	Say thou.	*Guſta.*
Loſt	*Gumſhottas*	I have forgot.	*Man varamaſheardam.*
Found	*Paydcun*	Bravely done, or ſaid.	*Barra colla.*
Tabaco	*Tombacco* & *Tutoon*	Brave game, or good	*Tamas-ſhaw.*
a Tabaco-pipe	*Calliown* & *Lula*	ſport.	

English.	Persian.
Peace be unto you.	*Sallam-alleekam.*
The like peace I wiſh you.	*Alleekam-ſallam.*
Whither do you go?	*Quo ja merue ?*
Not far.	*Dure neeſe.*
How do you to day?	*Chaldery,* or *Che-haldory amrooz ?*
Well, I praiſe God.	*Choggee, Shoocoro-Whoddaw.*
Good, I am very glad thereof.	*Koobas, Whoddaw baſhat.*
Where have you been?	*Quo ja boodee ?*
Not far.	*Nazeechas.*
I am your Servant.	*Man merda ſumaw.*

God

English.	Persian.
God thank you.	Whoddaw-negatur.
Welcome, Sir, heartily welcome.	Hoshomodee, Agaw, Suffowardee.
Tell me, how you do? healthy?	Gufta, chehaldery? chogee?
Where is your house? at Babylon?	Quo jaas chonna sumaw? Bagdat?
Have you a Wife?	Zan daree?
Yea truly, fifteen, Sir.	Bally, pounzdata, beg.
How old are you? Twenty four.	Chan sol daree? Char-beest.
How are you called?	Che nom daree sumaw?
My Name is called Teredoro.	Noma mannas Teredore.
Is this the way to Tauris?	Een raw hast Tabyris?
Yea, but how many leagues thither?	Bally, o chan Farsangas untraf?
I suppose 'tis twenty.	Man medonam, beest.
Is the way good or bad?	Raw koob o baddas?
Is there good Wine?	Unjee koob sherabbas?
Yea, in the high-way.	Bally, raw hast.
Whose Garden is that?	Een baugh mally chee?
'Tis the great King's.	Mally-Pot-shawbas.
Know you Cazbeen?	Cazbeen medanny?
I do, Sir: Have you seen it?	Man bali beg : sumaw dedee?
Why not? I know all Persia.	Cheree-na, hamma Farsee dedaw:
Come hither, good Boy.	Ingee bear, koob Pissar.
Give me some Wine, soon.	Sherap be dee, zood.
Fill me but one Cup.	Pourcun yeck paola:
Then saddle my horse.	Asp zeen pushee.
I thank you, Sir.	Whoddaw-negaturat.
It grows dark, I'le sleep.	Tarreekas, man mechobed,
Give me some Water, Slave.	Ob bedee, colloom.
Here, Sir; take it.	Ingee, Agaw, hast bedec.
Much good do it you, Brother.	Awpheat bashat, Broder.
What business have you here?	Che Corr daree sumaw ingeas?
Little: But stay a while.	Coocheck; Andac wyst.
I have some occasion.	Man corr daram.
Tell me; where is the King?	Gufta; Pot-shaw quo jaas?
I believe in Hyrcania.	Man medonam Mozendram:
God bless you.	Whoddaw bashat.

English.	Persian.	Turkish.	Arabick.
One	Yeck	Beer	Wahad
Two	Do, or Dew	Ekee	Tenyne
Three	Se	Ewch	Telaty
Four	Char	Dewrt	Arba
Five	Panch	Beash	Xamse
Six	Shesh	Altee	Sitte
Seven	Haft	Yedtee	Sabaa
Eight	Hasht	Seckez	Temania
Nine	No	Dockez	Tissaa
Ten	Dah	One	Ashra
Eleven	Yauzda	One-beer	Hedash
Twelve	Dozda	One-ekhe	Tenash
Thirteen	Sezda	One-ewch	Telatash
Fourteen	Charda or Chaharda	One-dewrt	Arbatasli
Fifteen	Pounzda	One-beash	Xamtash
Sixteen	Shoonzda	One-altee	Sittash
Seventeen	Hawda	One-yedtee	Sabatash
Eighteen	Hashda	One-seckez	Temantasli
Nineteen	Nouzda	One-dockoz	Tissatash
Twenty	Beest	Ygarmy	Ashreini
Twenty one	Yec-beest	Ygarmy beer	

The Alcoran.[146]

Now concerning their religion, if such I may term it, being as one says rather a confused hodge-podge or mass of superstition, at this day it varies not from the Turks in any particle of the Alcoran, yet account they one the other heretics, being no less divided in their possession then we and the Papalins.[147] A schism began *Anno Domini* 1420 by a syed of Ardabil, the better to advance the Sophian title, derived from Ali, who was both kinsman and son-in-law to their prophet Mohammed, which Ali, albeit by those relations he had right to sit as Caliph at Mecca after Mohammed, yet three others stepped up before him who during their lives excluded him. They were Abu Bakr, Omar and Osman, by the Turks venerably accounted of, but by the Persians, as appears by the commination invented by Syed Junaid, reputed heretics, from whence arises such hatred betwixt these two mighty monarchs that to Europe's good they divide and prosecute each other as it were with hatred irreconcilable.

Mohammed's coadjutors in the Alcoran.

Mohammed, son of Abdullah a pagan and Amina a Jew, was born at Jathrib, or *Itarip*, Postellus calls it, in Arabia, the year from Creation 4544 and of Christ Our Blessed Lord and Saviour 574, Justinian [II] at that time governing the Roman Empire and Khusrau father to Hormizd the Persian.[148] His parents were poor, therefore as an apprentice with much patience he served Zayed ibn Hartab,[149] a

---

[146] It is difficult to work out which edition or translation of the Quran was used by Herbert. A. Hinkelmann printed an Arabic text, *Al-Coranus, seu lex Islamitica* in Hamburg (1649), but not a Latin translation. The first was commissioned by Peter the Venerable in the twelfth century. That medieval Latin translation, *Lex Mahomet[ae] pseudoprophetae*, by Robert of Ketton (who was an Englishman) and Hermann of Dalmatia (1143), appeared in print (1543) published by Theodore Bibliander; this was also translated into Dutch, Italian (1547), and German (Hughes, 523). Herbert may have known André du Ryer's French version (1647), and there was also another German translation by Schweiger (Nurnberg, 1616). The first English translation, which Herbert may have used, was hardly a translation at all; Alexander Ross (1592–1654), Charles I's chaplain, issued *Mahomet's Alcoran, Translated out of Arabique into French, by the Sieur du Ryer . . . and newly Englished, for the satisfaction of all that desire to look into the Turkish vanities* (London, 1649). See further T. E. Burman, *Reading the Qur'an in Latin Christendom 1140–1560* (Philadelphia: University of Pennsylvania Press, 2007).

[147] Roman Catholics.

[148] Mohammed's father was Abdullah ibn Abd al-Muttallib [*Abdar*] (545–570) and his mother was Amina bint Wahabi [*Emma*] (d. 577), not a Jew but a member of the Banu Zohrah clan of the Quraish tribe. He was actually born in 570 in Mecca. "Justinian" should be "Justin."

[149] Possibly identifiable as As-Sa'ib ibn Abu As-Sa'ib, who was Mohammed's early business partner before he started working for his future wife Khadijah (Salahi, *Muhammed*, 39–40). After Mohammed's mother died he went to live with his paternal

rich merchant, who dying left his servant a considerable legacy, but by reason of those broils 'twixt Khusrau and the Romans traffic decayed and most men were compelled to dance after Bellona's music, so as Mohammed amongst others enlisted himself and served under Heraclius and after that the Persian, not caring who was vanquished so he gained. Nor did he err in his imagination, for by the great estate left him by ibn Hartab and acquired in the wars, he had the credit to command so many Tartars and Arabians that at length he adventured to set up for himself and had the hap first to beat the Christian forces and soon after the Persian, which got him more reputation, insomuch as having acquainted his army with the discord at that time happening in the Roman state, for so it was that Phocas, having slain his master Mauritius the Emperor and allowed Boniface the title of Universal Bishop, so much to the dissatisfaction of the Christians that agreeable to the character Gregory the Great[150] gave John the Constantinopolitan Patriarch[151] they called them Antichrist, and not without some show of reason, seeing that sixty good Bishops of Rome from Linus,[152] seven years after the Passion, to that Pope more minded to feed Christ's flock then to arrogate to themselves lordship over men and much less an universal supremacy, convinced himself that he was ordained from the beginning of the Creation not only to eclipse the pride of that Pope but withal to instruct the world in a better way then either Moses did the Jews or Christ the Christians, most blasphemously withal giving out that he was the Comforter promised, and yet says he came to give his Law by the sword and not by miracle and to advance the Arabian name and dignity above all other in the universe. The Jews also, seeing his glorious rise, cried him up for the Messiah[153] till they perceived him to eat camel's flesh and then they abhorred him, but the illiterate savages admire, and though some thought meanly of him, most part hoped he could effect his promises and accordingly credit his pretended revelations.

---

grandfather Abd al-Muttallib; when he in turn died (578) he was taken in by his uncle Abu Talib, where "tradition . . . has it that he immediately started work as a herdsman for his uncle" (Rogerson, *Muhammad*, 48), gradually gaining experience and becoming a merchant himself. "Half his life," Rogerson writes, "from the years 582 to 610, would be spent on the caravan trade" (*Muhammad*, 52). As we have noted before, there is no evidence that he fought for either Heraclius or Khusrau. For further discussion, see Howard-Johnston, *Witnesses*, 295–418, 445–60.

[150] Patriarch John II of Constantinople reigned 429–41. He was a Nestorian and was criticised by Lactantius.

[151] Pope St. Gregory I "the Great" reigned 590–604.

[152] St. Linus, whose existence has been debated, was Bishop of Rome c. 66–78.

[153] Herbert may be referring to the acceptance of Mohammed as the Messiah by certain Jewish groups as the Muslims became more and more powerful. For details of his dealings with them, see Salahi, *Muhammad*, 208–11, 277–86, 492–501; Rogerson, *Muhammad*, 140–42, 150–52.

But ere he could finish this new model, by him called an Alcoran,[154] or Laws, more resembling ordinances of war then instructions to conquer lust, as one has noted, the Persian suddenly broke in among them and in memory of their late hostility and plunder retaliates them so to purpose that Mohammed, to save his life, made use of his dromedary, leaving the rest of his company to the fury of the Persian. With a sad heart Mohammed hastens back to Mecca, *Mocura* and *Munachiates* of old and then the Stony Arabia metropolis, but when he calls to mind his miserable estate, by this last defeat being defeated both of his money and men, yet such men whose impulse was prepared to propagate his Alcoran, consumes in the meditation, and by his fretfulness and incessant vexing had at that time like to have made Death his executioner. Some safer way he therefore ruminates, and in the first place, to solace his unquiet spirit and enrrich himself, lays close siege to Khadijah,[155] a woman of great wealth and by some thought Queen of Khorasan, whom after an amorous assault he won and of her begot three sons and three daughters, namely Ibrahim, Tayeb and Taher, which three died young, Fatima and Zaynab, both married to Murtaza Ali, Umm Kalthoum and Ruqqaya, wives to old Abu Bakr.[156] But his stomach growing weak, one sort of meat began to loathe him, for Khadijah was stale and others better fancied him; in his Alcoran he therefore thought fit to allow carnal liberty, the better to excuse himself, who was so insatiably libidinous that he was not ashamed to become a precedent and countenance his incontinency by a law. Accordingly and with solemnity, as ibn Qasim, a writer of his belief reports, he espoused Aisha, the beloved child of his son-in-law Abu Bakr, a child (though Mohammed's wife) I may well call her, for at that time she exceeded not six years, yet soon after so acceptable to her husband that he calls her his best-beloved, dictates a whole

---

[154] The term *Quran*, according to Hughes, "is derived from the Arabic *Qara*, which occurs at the commencement of Surah XCV"; it means "to read" or "to recite" (483). It does not mean "the Law."

[155] Khadijah bint Khuwaylid ibn Asad (555–623) was the daughter of a wealthy businessman. She first employed and then married Mohammed, but in fact she was the one to initiate the union, which she did through an intermediary. The marriage, a love-match, was very happy and Mohammed took no other wives until after Khadijah's death (for details see Salahi, *Muhammad*, 40–43; Rogerson, *Muhammad*, 72–74). Herbert's translation of a title she was given, *Amirat-Quraish*, is wrong; it means "Princess of the Quraysh [tribe]."

[156] Mohammed and Khadijah had two sons, both of whom died as infants: Qasim (d. 605) and Taher, also known as Abdullah (d. 615). Ibrahim (d. 630) was the daughter of Mohammed and Maria al-Qibtiyya (see below), and also died an infant. Ruqqaya [*Rachya*] (d. 634) and Umm Kalthoum [*Om Kaltom*] (d. c. 630) both married Utbah ibn Abu Lahab and were both divorced from him. Neither married Abu Bakr; however, Ruqayya married again, this time to Osman ibn Affan, who later reigned as Caliph Osman I (640–56). Zaynab (d. c. 629) married Abu'l Abbas ibn al-Rabiah, one of Mohammed's companions, not Ali; for Fatima Zohra (c. 616–634), see Part IV.

chapter in her commendations, and for her love to him and civility to others, for her witty conceits and skill in story and languages she is made superlative and entitled 'Mother of the Faithful,' and contrary to a tenet in his Alcoran asked to be buried in her grave, as by old Abu Bakr his survivor afterwards was performed.[157] His third wife was Miriam or *Mameya*, which is Mary, of whom he begat Ibrahim Qasim, who at the age of six months by the arrow of death was directed the inevitable way. Zaynab, the repudiate of al-Hartab, was his fourth and last wife, for of concubines he had above an hundred, but in no author are their names recorded. This was a lady credulous of visions, and "*magnes mendacii credulitas*, credulity is the magnet of lies,"[158] for she verily believed that his epilepsy was occasioned by an angel's conferring with him, so that amongst Mohammedans she also is surnamed a Mother of the Mussulmans or True Believers.[159]

But that his doctrine might not want a confirmation by miracles, some of those his bosom friends and other his familiars taught doves to feed out of his ear and camels to expect their food of him, which blazoned his holiness, albeit ever since Semiramis her time, who was fed and educated amongst doves, in the oriental parts doves have a more then common estimation. However, by this practice he not only deluded his familiars but also put all Arabia into an

---

[157] Aisha bint Abu Bakr (c. 610–678) was "betrothed by her father but did not physically become Mohammed's wife until she was considered sexually mature" (Rogerson, *Muhammad*, 137), an event judged to have taken place when she was nine, not six. Herbert does not mention that Mohammed married, at the same time, Sawdah bint Zama (c. 593–674), a widow, with whom he remained after his marriage to Aisha (for details see Rogerson, *Muhammad*, 135–36). After Ali became caliph (656), Aisha raised an army against him but was defeated; Ali simply sent her to live out her days in Medina. She was revered by Muslims because she had possession of many Hadiths of Mohammed.

[158] Cited by Francis Bacon in "Of Church Controversies" (Bacon, *Major Works* 7).

[159] Mohammed's fourth wife was Hafsah bint Omar (606–666); the fifth was Zaynab bint Khuzayma (d. 624), who died eight months after she married Mohammed; she was followed by Hind bint Abi Omayya or Umm Salama (c. 596–680); Rayhanah, a convert from Judaism, whose relationship with Mohammed is disputed, but who may have married him in about 628, although Rogerson says she "begged to be kept a concubine" (*Muhammad*, 167); Zaynab bint Jahsh (c. 596–632), the divorced wife of Mohammed's adopted son Zeid, "a marriage which was ordered by Allah" (Salahi, *Muhammad*, 455); Juwayriyah bint Al-Harith ibn Dirar (b. 608), the daughter of a defeated enemy with whom Mohammed reconciled (Salahi, *Muhhamed*, 448); Ramlah bint Abi Sufiyan (c. 595–662), known as Umm Habiba, the daughter of another enemy of the Muslims (Salahi, *Muhammad*, 448–51); Safiyya bint Huqaiq (c. 610–670) and Maymouna (c. 593–674), a widow and relative of Mohammed (Hughes, *Dictionary* 308) . Herbert's mention of 'Mariam' refers to Maria al-Qibtiyya ('the Copt'), whose son Ibrahim we have already mentioned above. She died in 637; Rogerson states that she, too, was a concubine, but Mohammed liked her so much "that his other wives began to complain that he visited her day and night" (*Muhammad* 180). The Shi'as say that Mohammed had twenty-two wives; "eight of these," states Hughes, "never consummated the marriage" (*Dictionary* 400).

expectation of some extraordinary consequence, so as having by the help of Sergius an Italian,[160] a nest of uncleanness, a monk, a Sabellian,[161] a discontented wretch for missing the bishopric of Byzantium, and of John of Antioch, an unsound and heretical Nestorian, two subtle spirits, who, as Lactantius saith, by mixing truth with falsehood and sowing the seeds of error disturbed the tranquillity of all things, by such help or rather by the help of such, he finished his Alcoran in the Year of Our Blessed Lord 620, at that time being aged forty-six. It so transported him that from Mechat to Mecca he goes to have it credited, but therein his predictions failed him, for so soon as the Arabs perceived his design (being formerly acquainted with his birth and breeding) they banish him, and but for his wives' relations there had crushed him and his cockatrice egg which was but then hatching, so that involved with more perplexity now then ever he was at his wits' end, and once resolved to burn his book and return to trading, but Sergius, whose interest was involved, pacified him, telling him so great a work could not but be attended with opposition. The disanimated prophet revives upon this and apprehends this affliction propitious to his memory, so that to Yathrib he goes, where for two years he secludes himself from company, therein imitating other lawgivers as Pythagoras, who concealed himself ten years, Zoroaster twenty and Socrates for some certain time, so that Mohammed, having finished his plot and commanding the accompt or era since observed by his sectaries to commence from his late persecution,[162] he again adventures and by gifts and other

---

[160] According to Newton, "Mahomet patched together his Alcoran (a book containing his pestilent doctrine and gross opinions) through the instinction and procurement of two heretical monks, John of Antioch and Sergius of Italy" (*History*, 120). Della Valle also refers to "Sergius, a Christian by profession but an Heretical Nestorian Monk" and "Abdala, a Jew," who helped Mohammed create "his most palpable Imposture" (*Travels*, 419). This was already a well-known legend; there is a painting called "Mohammed and the Monk Sergius" by Lucas van Leyden, which was done in 1508 (see R. A. K., "Master J. A. of Zwolle and Others: A Handsome Gift of Rare Prints," *Record of the Art Museum, Princeton University*, 20, [1961]: 30–42).

[161] Sabellius (fl. c. 215) was a priest and theologian from Rome, but may have been of African origins. He denied the Trinity and expounded a theology called 'modalism,' for which he was excommunicated by Pope Calixtus I (217–22). He believed that "Father, Son and Holy Spirit do not represent real distinctions in the Godhead but successive modes of its self-revelation" (Kelly, *Dictionary*, 13).

[162] Having previously, due to the hostility of the Quraish in Mecca, sent many of his followers and family to Axum in Ethiopia, where they received protection from the Emperor. Mohammed himself remained in Mecca facing opposition until 15 June 622, when he and others left the city for Yathrib, later known as Medina. This is Year 1 of the *Hegira*, or Flight from Mecca. "From this secure base," Rogerson tells us, "he began to wage war against the non-believers. There should be no mistake about one point in particular: the Prophet was the aggressor in the conflict . . . He wished to convert the Meccans to Islam; they essentially wanted to be left in peace with their wealth and their pagan deities"

persuasions attracted so many followers that within seven years his Alcoran was received in Mecca, from this root branching out so many sects as in short time infected all the Orient.

Mohammed, whose name Arabically signifies 'deceit,'[163] and many times *"conveniunt rebus nomina saepe sua,"* affording also the number 666, the mark of Antichrist, having accomplished his design was summoned to appear before the Lord of all flesh, the God omnipotent and Judge of all men's actions, at whose tribunal, no doubt, he hath received a just judgment for his impiety. He died in the year of his climacteric sixty-three,[164] of the *Hegira* 17 and of Our Saviour, say some, 637, others 666, ordaining Ali to succeed him and his carcase to be interred in Aisha's grave in Yathrib, which *per Antonomasiam* he new-named *Medinat al-Nabi*,[165] it or Mecca being that *Munichiates* mentioned in Ptolemy, albeit I rather think it Mecca, because I read that Medina or Yathrib was built *Anno Domini* 364 by *Aadbuddadaule* then King of Babylon;[166] by Osman allegorically called *Al-Baramain* and by others *Deasalem*, i.e. 'a holy place' or 'town of mercy,' none daring in the garb of a soldier tread east, west, north or south nigher then six one way, twelve, eighteen and twenty-four miles the other, upon pain of death.

His Alcoran or *Sunna*, i.e. *The Book of Truth*[167] *or* a legend for the Faithful, is stuffed with philosophy moral and natural, and mixed with so many fantasies and inventions as renders the whole full of absurdities and contradictions and forced with such trash as may powerfully provoke any sober student to a height of laughter. The preface is that the book was sent from God by Gabriel to Murtaza Ali (so say the Persians) but he, mistaking the right man, gave it to Mohammed, whom when God saw replenished with equal virtue the angel was not blamed but the gift confirmed. They report withal that so soon as he was born an angel brought him three keys made of three great Orient pearls, which he

---

(*Muhammad*, 119). Salahi, however, sees Mohammed's actions against the Quraish in Mecca as pre-emptive; "It was expected," he writes, "that the Quraish might before long try to launch an all-out campaign to eliminate such a challenge before it had a chance to gather strength" (*Muhammad*, 224), but he stresses that the Muslims got "permission" from a revelation of God to Mohammed "to fight the non-believers" when the occasion presented itself (225).

[163] It means nothing of the kind. The name signifies 'often praised' or 'worthy of praise.' Salahi notes that "it was a totally unfamiliar name in Arabia" (*Muhammad*, 23).

[164] Mohammed died in 632, Year 11 of the Hegira. For details on the prejudices against Islam in seventeenth-century England see Nabil Matar, *Islam in Britain 1558–1685* (Cambridge: Cambridge University Press, 1998).

[165] City of the Prophet.

[166] Medina was founded in the sixth century B.C.E. The first tribes who lived there were the Banu Matrawil and Banu Hawf, who claimed descent from Noah's son Shem.

[167] "A path or way; a manner of life" (Hughes, *Muhammad*, 622).

snatched from the angel and thereby got a triplicate dominion over law, victory and prophecy.

To begin, then. The Alcoran or Bible, by them called *Quran* from *kara*, which signifies 'scripture,' as Scaliger and Drusius[168] note, and *Al-salaam*, i.e. 'the Law of Peace,' or *Al-kakan*, i.e. 'judgment,' as it was digested by Osman fifteen years after the death of Mohammed, is a volume twice so big as the Psalms of David, divided into a hundred and fourteen *suras* or chapters, put by Osman into a kind of rhythm and writ originally in Arabic, a language so magnified by Mohammedans as they believe the angels in Heaven speak it, albeit 'tis well-known that till Mohammed's time the Arabian tongue was little different from the Chaldee. I might object that the Hebrew has the preference, it being the opinion of a great doctor that "*in caelo Hebrea lingua usuri sumus; nam Natura ibi redibit, quae primitus hanc linguam tenuit.*"[169] This Alcoran, then, is not so much a continued tract of devotion or direction to good life as a chaos or mass of his own acts, having intermixed the arts of war and peace, systems of rhetoric, mathematics and ethics borrowed out of *Applis*, as they call Aristotle, and other philosophers, but grossly and confusedly handled. His mother instructed him in the Jewish rites and Sergius in the Gospel, whence it is that in the seventy-one sura of *Nuh* and in the tenth of *Yunus*,[170] and in other chapters speaks of Enoch, Abraham, Moses, Elijah and David, whose songs called *Zabur Dawood*[171] or the Psalms of David and the *Taurat Musa*[172] or Pentateuch of Moses he extols highly. The *Injil* or Gospel of Saint Luke he quotes at large in the fourth sura of *an-Nisa* and in the fifth of

---

[168] Jan van der Driessche (1550–1616) was a Belgian linguist and writer on comparative religion who fled with his father to England in 1567 in order to escape persecution as a Protestant. He subsequently (1571) became Professor of Oriental Languages at Oxford; a few years later he returned home to the University of Leyden (1577) and occupied a similar post. He wrote a Chaldaean grammar (1602) and commentaries on the Pentateuch, the Book of Ruth and on Origen. His *Tetragrammaton vel De nomine dei proprio* (1604) was a work about the names of pagan gods, and he also wrote *De sectis Judaeicis* (1619).

[169] We will use the Hebrew language in heaven, for Nature, which originally held that language, will return.

[170] Noah, called *Nabiyu'llah*, 'Prophet of God' (Hughes, *Dictionary*, 435) is mentioned in several suras; Herbert is referring to Sura 71:27–29; Sura 10:98 is known as the *Suratu Yunus*; Jonah is also considered a prophet by the Quran.

[171] The prophet Enoch may be the *Idris* of Suras 19:57 and 21:85; the identification is made by early commentators such as Al-Baizawi (Hughes, *Dictionary*, 192). Abraham and Moses are both considered very important prophets by Muslims. The Quran considers that David was a prophet and that God revealed the *Zabur* (Psalms) to him. "He has no special title . . . as all Muslims are agreed that he was not a law-giver or the founder of a dispensation" (Hughes, *Dictionary*, 71).

[172] Literally 'the law of Moses.'

al-Maidah[173] names Christ *Ruhun min Allah* and *Hazrah*, i.e. 'Messias the Spirit or word and light of God, holy Jesus,'[174] not omitting his bodily ascension into Heaven in the light of his twelve Apostles, seventy Disciples and five hundred others, nevertheless does not confess him to be the son of God but that the Virgin conceived by smelling to a rose presented her by Gabriel, and that he was born out of her breasts.[175] Also, it was not he that was crucified but Judas or some other wicked thief, Christ being withdrawn from them by a cloud from Heaven that covered him; thence it is that the Cross is so ridiculous amongst them. They say also that he was the most holy, chaste and powerful saint that ever conversed upon Earth, and in the second sura of *Al-Baqarah* in the Alcoran it is declared that Moses and Christ shall save the Jews and Christians at the Day of Doom, yet in the next chapter of *Al-Imran*, forgetting, it seems, what he had said, avers that no soul shall be saved but by his Alcoran, he being sent into the world to moderate the strictness of the Gospel as Christ the severity of the law ceremonial, varying also from what it the twelfth sura he commands, that they should be held in equal repute with the Alcoran, running thus: "The holy and merciful god first sent the ceremonial Law and then the Gospel to direct all men in the right path, and lastly the Alcoran, a faithful book for instruction." No man therefore amongst them dares undervalue the old Law and the Gospel, but practice it no less then what is commanded in the Alcoran, from whence it is they venerate the Holy Sepulchre, visit saints' tombs, honour the memory of Our Saviour and abhor the Jews. Saint John Baptist he also speaks modestly of and of the Blessed Virgin with singular reverence, saying in the nineteenth sura to this purpose:

> Hail Mary, thou art blessed, yea in purity and holiness exceeding all other
> women; the meditation of God's laws was ever in thy heart, therefore
> He hath selected thee, refined thee and made thee his happiest
> dwelling. Thou art full of knowledge and mercy, free from pollution,
> hatred or ambition, yea thou, the Virgin Mother of the great Prophet

---

[173] *Injil* refers to "the revelations made by God to Jesus." However, it does not appear in Sura 4, but twice in Sura 3 and four times in Sura 5, amongst other references, of which there are twelve altogether (Hughes, *Dictionary*, 211). Sura 4 is entitled *Siratu 'n-Nisa*, 'the Chapter of Women,' and only mentions Moses as being asked to show God to the Jews; it has nothing to do with St. Luke. Sura 5's title means 'the Table.'

[174] *Ruhun min Allah* means "a spirit from God . . . The title *Ruhu'llah* is the special Kalimah for Jesus Christ" (Hughes, *Dictionary*, 229). *Hazrah* means literally 'presence.' However, as Hughes explains, "When applied to the names of prophets, apostles and saints it expresses the sacredness of his office and character, i.e. Our Saviour is called *Hazratu Isa*" (*Dictionary*, 170).

[175] I am not sure where Herbert got this from. Sura 3 'Alu Imran' and Sura 19 'Mary' deal with the birth of Christ, and in both the angel Gabriel, when Mary asks how she may conceive without a man, simply tells her that "God will create what he will" (19).

Jesus art only of womankind most lovely and perfect in the sight of the Almighty.

which I name not that his book is any way more valuable, the end considered, which was his plot for apostacy, but that the Devil and Sergius, his coadjutors, could not derogate from their majesty, and to whom we may say in the words of Our Saviour to the demoniac, "Hold thy peace," for as another says, *"ex ore tuo sordet."* [176]

Now albeit the Alcoran for its greater repute feigns that three angels, flying with Mohammed into a high mountain, one ripped up his breast and washed his guts with snow, the second opened his heart, thereout plucking a black kernel that was Satan's part, which the angel closed up and made perfect, then weighing him in a scale, many men not being heavy enough to counterpoise him the angel set him upon the lower Earth, saying no number shall be able to weight against him. [177] Now what these angels were appears by the book itself, which consists of heresiarchies against our Blessed Saviour, for with Arius [178] it denies the Divinity, with Sabellius the Trinity, with Macedonius [179] the Holy Ghost proceeding, with Manichaeus [180] the death of Christ and such like errors as those wretches broached. In the 32 Sura he politically commands that no man be so

---

[176] What comes out of your mouth is filthy.

[177] This story is reported by Ibn Ishaq (d. 767) in his biography of the Prophet, the *Sirat Rasul Allah* (*The Way of God's Prophet*), which he compiled from a collection he made of oral traditions about Mohammed. Further details of this and about Mohammed's visit to Heaven are discussed in J. R. Porter, "Muhammad's Journey to Heaven," *Numen* (1974): 64–80; F.S. Colby, *Narrating Muhammed's Night Journey* (Albany: SUNY Press, 2008). Herbert describes the event in much more detail below.

[178] Arius (fourth century C. E.), an Egyptian, "taught that the Son was both posterior and inferior to the Father" (Jenkins, *Byzantium* 357). The Arian heresy was condemned by Pope Sylvester I (314–35) in 325.

[179] Macedonius I (d. c. 366) was Bishop of Constantinople 342–46 and 351–60. An extremely controversial churchman, he established the ascetic Macedonian sect which was condemned by Pope Damasus I (366–84) in 374. Herbert is correct in asserting that the Macedonians denied the divinity of the Holy Ghost, and can thus dubiously link another "heretic" sect to Mohammed, who had probably never heard of them.

[180] Mani (c. 210–276) was a Persian who declared himself to be a disciple of Jesus and claimed succession to the prophets of the Old Testament. He called himself the "Paraclete" (Consoler), a name used often to refer to the Holy Spirit, and he proclaimed himself to be the Last Prophet, like Mohammed would after him. According to Rogerson, "he created a new spirituality from elements of Christianity, Mithraism and Zoroastrianism" (*Muhammad*, 86). He was known to Christians, and condemned by St. Augustine (a former admirer) as a heretic. Mani was put to death by order of Bahram I of Persia, although Shapur I, the previous king, had respected him. Linking Mohammed and Mani was a common Christian slur; however, it is possible that as Khusrau I three hundred years later persecuted the followers of one Mazdak, a Persian priest who followed Mani's teachings, so that they fled to Arabia, "the *hanif* of Mecca must have listened to those

impious as to question any particle of his Law nor to dispute about it, yet in another Chapter confesses 'tis stuffed with untruths.

Their commandments.

Their commandments are eight.[181]

1 Commandment. *There is one and but one great God and Mohammed is his Prophet.*
This every fourth hour the *muezzins*[182] and *talismani*[183] sing aloud from the steeple-tops of every mosque or Alcorans, as some allusively call them, *"Quia a cacumine turrium fragmenta Alcoranni pueri plerumque vociferant."*[184] The usual words are *"La ilahah ilallah wa Mohammed rasul allah,"* but the Persians, by Syed Junaid's direction to the honour of their Prophet, *"La ilahah ilallah Murtaza Ali vel bilullah,"* which they iterate as a word of praise borrowed from the Hebrew *hallelu-ja* or as by the old Persians used in the paean or warlike songs which commonly began with *"alala,"* as Xenophon *c.* 2 observes, or *"hillula"* and *"eluleus,"* a song to Bacchus. The acknowledgement one only God they borrow either from the Decalogue or fourth of Ezekiel, upon which also our ancient bards and druids beat, in those dark times making it an article of their faith.

2 Commandment. *'Tis neither good nor just that any Mussulmans live unmarried, lest the professors of the Alcoran be diminished,*
whence it ariseth that polygamy is tolerated, yea that such are thought most honourable who superabound in wives and concubines, Mohammed in the sura of Baqara boasting of his singularity therein and that he had strength at most times to satiate forty women. In that chapter of *Attabrim* he confesses that he had violated his faith and troth but that he had received pardon from God and had to witness Gabriel and Rachel, two angels. But who sees not in this precept he had respect to the natural disposition of the Arabians, better-pleased with freedom

---

creeds just as attentively as had St. Augustine, who first began his spiritual path as a Manichean 'hearer'" (Rogerson, *Muhammad*, 87).

[181] According to Hughes there are some problems with the exact number of commandments. In Sura 7 we are told that God gave Moses "nine clear signs," but scholars have said these are the miracles Moses performed in Egypt. Hughes cites the commentator Husain as saying that the commandments given in Sura 6 "are those Ten Commandments which in every dispensation are incumbent upon mankind" (*Dictionary*, 58). Della Valle also provides a similar listing (*Travels*, 420–21). 1634: Herbert calls these "The Persian's Commandments" (153).

[182] "The callers of the *azan*, or summons to prayer" (Hughes, *Dictionary*, 367).

[183] Herbert's meaning is unclear. The *tilsam*, plural *talasim*, which means "mystical characters" or "seals upon which such characters are engraved or inscribed" was corrupted through its plural form into the English 'talisman' or charm (Hughes, *Dictionary*, 627).

[184] Because from the top of the tower passages of the Quran are called out by boys.

and voluptuousness then virtue, not caring how, so by any magic he could yoke them under obedience?

3 Commandment. *It behoves Mussulmen to be charitable and to hate contentions.*

From this issues good to travellers, for whereas inns are not to be had in heathen countries there are buildings of purpose for the accommodation of travellers always open for entertainment and clean-kept, and near them is a large and convenient stable. In one of these inns fifteent thousand pounds ster;ing hath been disbursed upon a charitable account, yea, so remarkable is their charity that they not only erect hospitals for lame men and diseased but sometimes for aged, starved or hurt birds, beasts and such creatures.

Their invocations.

4 Commandment. *It behoves Mussulmans to invoke their Prophet every day five times at least and to attend his coming patiently,*

which they accomplish with such regard that when the muezzin is heard to cry aloud from the steeple of the mosque they fall to prayer though busied in profane talk, drinking, drabbing or the like. But before they enter the mosque they wash their feet, lay aside their shoes, and being assembled turn their faces all one way, and in the prayers shut their eyes, sometimes their ears, drop their beads and with a submissive voice or murmur ingeminate their devotions, bending, prostrating and kissing the ground or some relic of consecrated earth brought from the *Haram*[185] or the *al-Qaaba,* two chapels erected in Mecca, says the Alcoran, by Abraham from the idea or pattern of that which Adam built in Paradise, yet holding nevertheless that he stayed there not above one day and that it was translated by angels into Heaven at the general deluge. In every *al-Fatiha*[186] or prayer they *sizeda* or kiss the earth at every epithet or name of God and Mohammed, and after they have battologised *"La illahah"* or praises, they iterate another to this effect:

> In the name of the good and holy God. Praised be the Sovereign of all worlds, the only merciful God of doom. Thee we serve, thee we call upon; show us the best way, that which thou hast revealed to Mohammed, not that whereby thou punishest the ungodly.

---

[185] The *Haramu Makkah,* "the sacred boundary of Makkah (Mecca)" (Hughes, *Dictionary* 163).

[186] The first chapter of the Quran, which "is held in great veneration by Muhammedans and is used by them very much as the *Paternoster* is recited by Roman Catholics" (Hughes, *Dictionary,* 125).

This also they use, I have noted amongst them, being a tautology of the names of God and Mohammed:

> *Bismillah! Raugh mawn, a raugh-heam Albundill-Ally; Etto hyatto, almo bara-*
> *katto, asulmatto, attayo batto; leyla, beesallem, aleyka, I, jaana, uebeen rough*
> *meet Wallough heeweeber-catto. Essa-lamalena, wallah Ebadulla, hesolaheem*
> *Eshaddo. Awla el-abba, el-Allaho, Eshaddai, Mohammed resull-Allogh, l'alla,*
> *Essamalena Ebadulla Solaheem, Essamaleekam Essamaleeka. Allyhomma, Sul-*
> *Billula. Allaw Mohummed don Wallaw Wasaleem-chamma salleata, Albumder-*
> *Ally, whoddaw,*[187]

which form the Mohammedans in Arabia, Persia, India, Java and other parts have, or most parts of it.

Now though this be most usual, yet are they not without other set forms of prayer compiled by Osman in his parody and more largely by that famous Al-Mutannabi,[188] who in his high-flown conceits endeavoured to exalt his name and reputation above that of Mohammed. Their *al-fatihas* are either for the safety of their kings, a happy issue, welfare of their country, thanks that they are Mussul-men, *Bozarmen*[189] true believers or the like, five times in four and twenty hours exercising prayer. The hours commonly observed canonically are about daybreak, noon, three in the afternoon, sunset and midnight, called by them *Fajr, Zuhr, 'Asr, Maghrib, Isha.*[190] The first hour is acted by four *tashahhuds* and two prayers;

---

[187] Herbert's transliteration is very difficult to decipher. *Bismillah... heam* means "In the Name of God, the Merciful and the Compassionate," the opening to Sura 1 of the *Quran*, "al-Fatiha" (see above). Most of the rest is unreadable; *Eshaddai... Allah* means "I testify that Mohammed is the Messenger of God," the *shihada* formula which confirms that one is a Muslim.

[188] Abu Tayeb al-Mutanabbi ibn al-Husain (915–965), born in al-Kufa, is consid-ered one of the greatest Arab poets. His name means "he who claims to be a prophet," which he acquired whilst leading the Qarmatians in a revolt as a young man (932). After a rather chequered career (he appears to have been difficult and quarrelsome) he settled at the court of Saif ud-daula (r. 945–67), the ruler of Aleppo, and began to compile his great work, the *Diwan*. He also worked as a court poet in Shiraz. Al-Mutanabbi ended his life a victim to bandits near Baghdad. Frye remarks of his poetry that he "combined the smooth civility of the city-dweller... with a touch of the ancient savagery: hence his popularity" (*History*, 592). There is a modern translation of his poetry by Arthur Worm-houdt (Chicago: Kazi Books, 2003).

[189] By this term Herbert means the Bahshariyah sect of Shi'a Islam. They were the followers of Abu Hashim (d. 716), one of Ali's grandsons. They are also known as the Hashimis.

[190] These are the transliterations from Hughes. Respectively, the times are daybreak, midday (at the point when the sun declines), "midway between *zuhr* and *maghrib*," which is approximately three p.m., evening, and "when night has closed in" (Hughes, *Diction-ary*, 177). The exact times vary somewhat from month to month.

the second by ten times kissing the earth with five *al-fatihahs*; the third hour requires eight grovellings and four ejaculations; the fourth has five *sijdahs* and three orations; and the last hour has fifteen *tashahhuds* and eight repetitions; after that hour to daybreak 'tis held unnecessary to invocate. However, the Persians, since their reformation, think it enough to pray thrice in four and twenty hours, at *sob*, *zuhr* and *magrhib*, the Arabic words which signify 'morning,' 'noon' and 'night.' On the *Jumah* or Sabbath, by the Persians called *Jomé*, by Turks *Zuma-g'iuny*, *Jumaad* by the vulgar Arabs,[191] they assemble in the mosques (which are without seats and bells), first washing their face, hands and arms to the elbow, then kneeling with faces towards Medina, speak not to one another, spit nor cough if they can avoid it.

5 Commandment. *See thou observe yearly a month Lent or Bairam.*

The Lent or Ramadan, called also *Ramdan*, *Ramazan* and *Ramulam*, begins commonly at the sun's entrance into Aries, Libra other times, no time certain, and is in imitation of our Lent, or rather the forty days Moses was in Horeb, by some said in memory of Mohammed's forty days' obscuring himself in the desert when he fled from the rage of Mecca's inhabitants, and for that in this month he divulged his Alcoran, but most likely (as in the 47 Sura of himself, and 25, in which he treats of the excellency of the Alcoran[192]) from his being so long in the sixth Heaven called *Al-abal*,[193] where this anthropomorphite[194] blasphemously reports he had the honour to shake hands with the Almighty, which he says were seventy times colder then ice, and that being upon the Earth, to make the people credit him the more he commanded the Moon to descend, half of which he put into his own sleeve and the other half served as a zone or girdle for his son-in-law Murtaza Ali. Howbeit, to others' amazement he afterwards pieced it together and placed it in the same orb whence first he invited it.

During this Ramazan,[195] all day long they abstain from all sorts of viands or refection, he being counted the veriest heretic in the world that dare eat anything in the day, yet the sun is no sooner set but that they let loose the reins of their

---

[191] *Jumah* simply means 'Friday,' but there is a problem with Herbert's inclusion of the word *Jumaad*, which actually means 'the fifth (or sixth) month' (*Jumada'l-ula* and *Jumada l'ukhra*).

[192] These chapters are called, successively, 'Mohammed' and 'Furqan,' which translates as 'Quran' (Hughes, *Dictionary*, 490).

[193] Muslim tradition recognises seven Heavens; the sixth one's name translates as 'ruby' or 'garnet' (Hughes, *Dictionary*, 170).

[194] Someone who gives human form and characteristics to the non-human, in this case to God.

[195] Here Herbert uses the Persian variant, with which he was probably more familiar.

appetite, epicurising in all kinds of delights and pleasures possible. Prosper's[196] saying that "to fast from sin is the best fast" is here no good doctrine. So soon as the nine and twentieth day is passed (for though the Alcoran commands forty, yet by those of the late reformation it is limited to one moon), they begin the *Bairam*,[197] as we do Easter, and continue their merriment till the third day be ended; the two days after the *Bairam* are commonly called *Khusti-bairam*. The last hour of the last festival they usually resolve upon a pilgrimage to visit their Prophet's sepulchre, not magnetically-attracted, not entombed in an iron coffin as some report, but laid under a fair marble, polished and engraven with Arabic sentences out of the *Elesalem*,[198] and in the way, as we have observed, they wallow in all kind of turpitude, yet nowhere persecuted, being palliated with a pilgrim's coat and hypocritic sanctity.

Festivals.

The *Baqrah-id*[199] they solemnise in November or *Chodad-maw* (by the Turks called *Silcade*,[200] by the Arabs *Rabi'u 'l-Awwal),*[201] a feast observed in commemoration of the ram which was sacrificed by Abraham at such time as Ishmael, they say, should have been offered.[202] Other festivals they celebrate: the *Id al-Hassan*; the *Nau Roz*; *Imamy*; *Id al-kader*; *Jedt-Ousans*; *Auwtpatsian, Safyan*; the Roses; Daffodils; the *Aspand*; the *Mehregan*, the Feast of Brotherhood etc.[203]

---

[196] St. Prosper of Aquitaine (c. 390–after 455), a theologian and poet, was a member of the Papal Chancellery under Pope Leo I. He was the author of a chronicle of world history to 455. *De vocatione omnium gentium*, from which this quote is likely taken, is probably not by him (PL 51. 698 B). A modern translation as *The Call of All Nations* is available (Mahwah: Paulist Press, 1951). This quote may be found in [Pope] Leo I, *Sermones* 94. 1, (PL 54. 458); my thanks to Dr. MacCoull for this information.

[197] *Bairam* is simply the Turkish word for 'festival.' Herbert is referring to the "lesser *bairam*," which is celebrated three days after the end of Ramadan.

[198] A variation of al-Islam.

[199] The Baqarah-id [*Buccaree*], is, according to Foster, "celebrated on the tenth of Zul-Hijjah, the last month of the Hijra year" (*Herbert*, 332). This is the month "appointed for pilgrimage to [Mecca]" (Hughes, *Dictionary*, 717).

[200] Herbert could be referring here to Zulqa'adah, "the eleventh month" (Foster, *Herbert*, 332). Its name means "master of truce," and it is "so-called because it was the month in which the ancient Arabs abstained from warfare" (Hughes, *Dictionary*, 717).

[201] The third month of the Muslim year, "the first spring month" (Hughes, *Dictionary*, 531).

[202] Shi'a tradition says that Ishmael, not Isaac, was the intended sacrifice to God who was saved by the appearance of a sacrificial animal, "a black and white sheep . . . which had been pasturing forty years in Paradise" (Hughes, *Dictionary*, 219). However, Sura 37:90 seems to suggest that it was Isaac, not Ishmael.

[203] Herbert does not describe these last two. The *Aspand* [*Ispend*] is actually a Zoroastrian rite (not really a festival at all) involving the burning on charcoal of a herb called

The *Id al-Hassan* is from Hassan son of Ali, who was slain with seven of his sons by Muawiya the Caliph of Damascus, nephew to Osman, a festival begun (they say revived) by Syed Junaid, followed by Haidar and commanded by Shah Ismail as a triumph against the *Ben-Humians*, who left no means unattempted to have extirped Ali's family root and branch, which nevertheless was providentially preserved in one of that stem named Mirza Sherif (they call him Sheykh Azimullah), who at his birth was secretly conveyed into some good hands that preserved him from the Ben-Humian inquisition, from which Azimullah, who lived near an hundred years after Mohammed's flight from Mecca, Syed Junaid of Ardabil, son of that venerable saint or syed Sheykh Safi, of so great esteem for sanctity in Tamerlane's time as gave him the invitation to visit him in his march through Persia against the Turkish tyrant, is lineally-descended, which syed not only inveighed against the Turkish tenet concerning Mohammed's three successors Abu Bakr and the rest, but anathematised such as honour them, yea, he spared not those four other great *hajjis* or doctors who were contemporary with Mohammed, those four, if I be not deceived, whom Mohammed in fear for his presumption in Paradise wiped from the sweat of his brow and by miracle were metamorphosed into four learned men, by name Ahmed ibn Hanbal, Abu Hanifa, Malik ibn Anas and Al-Shafi, which new-broached opinion is so offensive to the Turks that of late the Mufti,[204] condemning an innocent Persian, swore a great oath he thought it a better act and a more meritorious to kill one Persian then seventy Christians.

Hassan, most agree, was slain treacherously by *Chuse*, a slave to Mu'awiya.[205] Mu'awiya was .accessory; the Persians therefore punish him yearly, though rotten a thousand years since, for first they frame a deformed image whose face is black, his nose pierced through with a dart and clad in straw, which done, they hurry it through the streets in a hurly-burly of thousands of people, who when they have dragged it sufficiently through the city, draw it to some rising hill where to all men's view they elevate this caitiff. The Qadi bawls out a pathetic oration to this purpose, that after strict search Ali had directed them where to apprehend the traitor, unworthy the least show of mercy, this being the same villain who slew

---

aspand in order to ward off the Evil Eye from children. The *Mehregan* [*Ceraghan*] is also Zoroastrian; Herbert is correct in saying it is a feast of brotherhood (friends and families). It takes place on the 196th day of the year.

[204] "The officer who expounds the law" (Hughes, *Dictionary*, 867). His job is to assist magistrates and to provide legal decisions when needed. Muftis may also be more exalted personages, such as the Grand Mufti of Cairo.

[205] According to Hughes, Hassan was "poisoned by his wife Ja'dah, who was suborned to commit the deed by Yazid, the son of Mu'awiya, by a promise of marrying her, which promise he did not keep," forcing her to marry someone else (*Dictionary*, 168). This version of Hasan's death seems actually to have been the most prevalent.

Hassan, Ali's son, and his eleven sons, Zein[206] only escaping, so that every good man is bound to curse him, yea, to help to torment him in the vilest manner possible. In token of joy they unanimously sing *epinicia* and cry aloud "*Ya Ali*," yea, strive to rend the clouds with their clamours. At a set time they cease, when fire is given to a train of gunpowder which sets divers squibs afire, blow up the detested Syrian, by a hideous noise making the air echo at his funeral. Hassan's ghost, they think, now sleeps quietly; each Persian commends one another's zeal and spends that night in merriment.

The Id al-Hassan was observed when we were in Isfahan. They have a tradition that Hassan, Ali's son, was lost in a wilderness, where thirst or rather Mu'awiya the Caliph killed him. Nine days they wander up and down, all that while having neither hair nor beard nor seeming joyful, but incessantly beating their breasts; some tear their garments, and crying out "Hassan! Hassan!" in a melancholy note so long, so fiercely that many can neither howl longer nor for a month's space recover their voices. The tenth day they find an imaginary Hassan, the Mohammedan tetragrammaton[207] that "*nunquamque satis quaesitus Adonis*,"[208] whom they echo forth in stentorian clamours till they bring him to his grave, where they let him sleep quietly until the next year's zeal fetch him out (*semper enim perdunt semper et inveniunt*)[209] and force him again to accompany their devotion, parallel to which is that in Ovid's *Metamorphoses*: "Our sorrow's monument shall ever last; / Adonis, thy death's image every year / Shall in our solemnised complaints appear,"[210] and may be in imitation of that annual custom which was observed by the Egyptians howling in like manner for their lost Osiris as the idolatrous Jews did for Tammuz, mentioned by the prophet Ezekiel 8 and 14[211] and first celebrated by the Phoenicians.

---

[206] Zein al-Abidin [*Sheresin*], son of Hussein (not of Hassan), was the fourth Sh'ite Imam. 1634: Herbert names him "Musa, or rather Mirza Cherisim or Prince Cherisim, by some called Mohammed Mahadin" (159).

[207] The Tetragrammaton, according to Lord Herbert of Chirbury, was "a word of four letters, which [the Jews] might have pronounced *Jave* or *Jehave*" and he believed that it originated from *Jah*, "one of the names of God." We derive "*hallelu-jah*" from it, he states, and "while they were dancing, the pagans used to shout the name . . . very loudly" (*Pagan Religion*, 73). Sir Thomas Herbert is suggesting that shouting Hassan's name is equivalent. The authority for both Herberts is van der Driessche's treatise on the Tetragrammaton (above, 707 n. 167).

[208] Herbert misquotes Ovid here; the god should be Osiris, not Adonis, "for whom her search is never-ending" (*Metamorphoses* 9. 693).

[209] "For they always lose and they always find" (Lactantius, *Divinae institutiones* 1. 21). Lactantius is referring to the cult of Osiris.

[210] Ovid, *Metamorphoses* 10.724–725.

[211] ". . . and, behold, there sat women weeping for Tammuz" (Ezekiel 8:14); Herbert may have conflated chapter and verse. However, in 14:3 we find the words "these men have set up their idols in their hearts," which may refer to the same worship of Tammuz.

The Nau Roz is in imitation of our New Year's Day, but they begin, after the old manner, in March, such time as the sun in his equal shine to either pole makes the equinoctium. A festival of joviality this is, for one prayer preying upon variety of pleasures; the talismans pipe now to Bacchus, Ceres and Venus. I have observed that in many parts for eleven months in the year we could see very few women of any extraordinary quality, and those we saw were veiled, being offensive in the streets or gardens to converse with any, yet these twelve days of the Nau Roz they have liberty, so as all places were full of them, yea, their naked faces discovered, frisking in amorous postures and drawing the eye by a forced magic. Gifts also and reciprocal presents are retorted up and down from one to another with garments of silk and gold, horses, fruits and *piskashes* of other sorts, nothing but riding the horse, drinking, cock-fighting, fortune-telling, singing, swinging in the air, courting and the like being observed to the last minute of that festival.[212]

The *Imamy* has some dependence on the Baqarah-id. This takes its rise from a camel, that from a ram; that for Ishmael, this for Mohammed. In November the Meccan Protomist sends a camel by an adopted son (sometimes natural), who is welcomed to Isfahan by many thousand Mussulmen, who show extreme joy for so holy a present. After they have tried and tired their voices, the *hajji* from an exalted place acquaints them with the cause of his long journey, persuades them to a thankful remembrance and blesses them. The multitude, without any respect of men or danger, throng about the beast, who is no sooner in the field where Death arrests him but that they fall upon him and pluck off his short hairs with an admirable dexterity, keeping them as sanctimonious relics prevalent against sudden death, though many die in the assult and thousands return maimed, hunger, thirst, poverty and whatnot, after which the tormented camel is by the *hajji* again signed for sacrifice. The *daruga* first transfixes his javelin; the Vizier beheads him and gives it the King. The carcase is then torn piecemeal by the foolhardy multitude, so greedy to obtain this charm of long life and plenty that immortality and the place where meat and drink is needless, oft in the essay entertains them.

The Tammuz cult originated in Sumeria but spread to Phoenicia and Syria; he was the husband of the goddess Ishtar. His story, as Herbert suggests, is parallel to that of Adonis and Aphrodite.

[212] Herbert is correct with the date; Nau Roz or No Ruz starts around 21 March, the spring equinox. "Even before the Achaemenian period," Greenway and St. Vincent note, "the coming of spring was celebrated on a large scale throughout Persia" (*Iran*, 102). Under the Parthians and early Sassanians it became an autumn festival (Boyce, *Zoroastrians*, 106), but was moved back again to spring (128). The New Year period is ten days before and after that date. It is one of the few traditional festivals left in the Islamic Republic of Iran. The "Greater No Ruz" is Zoroaster's birthday (Boyce, *Zoroastrians*, 180).

The *Id al-Ghadir Khum* is a feast in memory of Ali's victory over the three old caitiffs of Mecca, by Death, not Ali, conquered. After some threnodies many prayers are muttered, songs chanted and alms bestowed; the King is at most charge in this solemnity, the greater honour reflecting him, in regard of his ancestry.[213]

The *Auwptpatsion* or *Owdt-bapision* is in memory of Mohammed's baptism by Sergius.[214] Many of the ordinary sort of Mohammedans assemble, and after the *daruga* has put a period to his oration, promiscuously besprinkle with water one another's faces then soil their flesh with dirt and filth, and the great ones many times to please the King act the like among them. Lastly, they cleanse themselves with water, supposing all deformity washed off and their bodies cleanlier thereafter.

The *Safian* is a solemnity of fasting, feasting and praying for the prosperity of their King and continuation of the Safian pedigree.

The Feast of Roses and Daffodils is begun by a procession of santoons at the first budding of flowers and for thirty days celebrated with all manner of sports and recreations to be imagined. This annual feast seems to be continued from the custom of those memorable ones which in old times were celebrated in Persia such time as the kings thereof had the supreme monarchy of the world, as we read in the Book of Esther and elsewhere, for at the keeping of this feast we beheld an infinte number of tents pitched, with such a flux of men, women, boys and girls with arms, music, songs and dances as would make one think that either the Games of Olympus were revived or Bacchus his orgies.[215]

---

[213] This description is not quite accurate. The Id al-Ghadir Khum [*Id al-kader*] is actually in honour of Mohammed's designation of Ali as his successor. It takes place on 18 December. Foster, paraphrasing Hughes (*Dictionary*, 138) adds that "images of the three usurping Khalifs, made of dough filled with honey, are stuck with knives and the honey sipped, as typifying their blood" (*Herbert*, 333). *Ghadir* means 'pool' (Hughes, *Dictionary*, 138).

[214] Foster identifies this festival with the one described by della Valle as the "Abrizan" (*Travels* 3: 38), on which "the Persians exchange visits and sprinkled one another with water, perfumed or pure." He considers that "Herbert's explanation of the origin of the ceremony appears therefore to be incorrect" (*Herbert*, 333).

[215] 1634: "Other feasts are performed by the *abdals*, who take their name from Abdullah, father of Mohammed. These have no abode, vow poverty, lodge in churches (which made our lodgings lousy after them), and have provision brought them by the charitable. They are covered with a sheepskin, and, though yet poor, yet travel with dangerous weapons, with which 'tis often thought they do villainy and get by. A horn is tied around their neck which they use to blow in markets when they would have the people to hear orations" (167). The name means 'substitutes,' and, according to Hughes, there are seventy of them, "of whom forty reside in Syria and thirty elsewhere. When one dies, another takes his place, being so appointed by God" (*Dictionary*, 1–2).

6 Commandment. *Reverence thy parents,*
   which how they perform, many tragic stories daily inform.

7 Commandment. *Cursed be the slayer,*
   so well practiced in Persia that what by rigour of the laws and what from this one may travel in any place at any time without danger, and although they be generally martialists and affect much wine, yet I scarce ever saw any quarreller or homicide amongst them.

8 Commandment. *Do unto others as thou wouldst others should do to thee,*
   from whence they are humane and courteous, but bribery lately crept amongst them, [as] is easily discerned.
   The Alcoran then, being a miscellany, treats further in the 33 [Sura] how that *Dajjal*[216] *or Shaitan,* i.e. the Devil, shall at length be saved by Mohammed's means, and in the 72 Sura that al-Gehenni or the infernal ghosts shall after I know not how many years be freed. How far Sergius in this made use of Origen I know not. The 85 Sura treats of the Zodiac; the 91, 92, 93 of the Moon, night morn, the 113 of the firmament, but is philosophy of such coarseness that I may well say *"Discum potius quam philosophum,"*[217] for how can it well be otherwise, since in his seventeenth Sura he confesses he could neither read nor write but that all his learning was supernatural? In one chapter he is bold to say that Solomon was a great magician and that he learned it from Marut and Harut, two bad angels; with more reason we may say that Mohammed was skilled in that infernal wisdom if half of those miracles be true he records of himself. One is this: being one time compassed with a great assembly of Arabians he pointed at the Moon with his thumb and long finger. It seems it knew his mind, for the Moon in obeisance immediately clove asunder and in two pieces fell upon the hill of Mecca upon which Mohammed at that time stood. With a piece of his linsey-woolsey coat he patched and made it whole again, which after it had also, say the Persians, embraced Murtaza Ali in way of compliment, it reascended and from that time became the badge or coat-armour of bozarmen. In another he assures his proselytes that Mecca, Medina and Jerusalem be holy cities built by Adam in Paradise but framed in Heaven, and thence it is that Jerusalem is honoured by Turks as well as Christians. Four cities sprung out of Hell at the birth of Mohammed, at which time all idols fell and Lucifer was thrown into Hell, so deep into that abyss as he was some years ere he could get up again. The names of the towns are, as pleases Mohammed to say, Medina in Chaldaea, Antioch in Syria, Bubastis

---

[216] *Dajjal* [*Dagial*] means "false" or "lying," and refers to "certain religious impostors who shall appear in the world," the last of whom will be Antichrist (Hughes, *Dictionary* 64).
[217] Cicero, *De Oratore* 2.5.21

in Egypt and Erebuni in Armenia,[218] places that have this black vizard put upon them, probably for that they resisted the progress of his Alcoran.

Heaven described.

In the 47 Sura he records his pilgrimage or ascent into Heaven,[219] where he had a rare object, and thence brought a description of the several spheres, Heavens, Hells and Paradise, as also of angels and saints, judgment, the Resurrection, joy and pain etc., of which I shall afford you a compendium out of their own authors. One eve, as Mohammed was sporting privately at Mecca with Aisha his young wife, Gabriel (Seraphiel the Persians call him, the same, say they, that fostered Mohammed and Ali three years, such a Genius peradventure as haunted Brutus), in a flash of fire entering their chamber thus saluted Mohammed: "Hail, thou beloved man! I come to fetch thee; the God whom thou so zealously worshippest desires to see thee at his own habitation." Mohammed going to mount upon the angel's wings, of which he had seventy pair, demands what way he should take to ascend; thereupon, the angel shows him an ass, Buraq by name, and bids him mount. Mohammed, essaying to get up, could not, till he prayed for him. From Mecca he posted as swift as thought, for Buraq at four steps brought him to Jerusalem;[220] there dismounting, the angel took him into his protection. In few minutes Mohammed passed the Seven Seas and ascended Heaven, into which he

---

[218] Bubastis [*Vastet*] in the Nile Delta was the centre of the cult of the cat-goddess Bastet; Erebuni [*Eb-baran*], now a district of Yerevan in Armenia, was an Urartan centre founded in 782 B.C.E. It had a temple of Khaldi and later a fire-temple was built there under the Achaemenids.

[219] This is the *Miraj*, "the Ascent," and it is mentioned only once in the Quran, and that is in Sura 17:1 (see below). The full story is told in the *Mishkatu'l-Masabih*, described by Hughes as "a well-known book of Sunni tradition . . . compiled by the Imam Husain al-Baghawi" (d. c. 1130) and revised by Waliya ud-din some two hundred years later. Hughes notes that it was translated into Persian in the time of Emperor Akbar I (*Dictionary*, 353). The story does not mention Aisha at all; in fact, according to the tradition the event took place in 620 and he was widowed at the time (Rogerson, *Muhammad*, 112), but the name Buraq [*Albarack*] is recorded correctly (Hughes, *Dictionary*, 351), although Buraq was not quite an ass, but "a white animal between the size of a mule and an ass, having two wings" (Hughes, *Dictionary*, 44). I have seen a Persian painting in which "he" is depicted with a woman's face. The "night flight," as it is usually called, was a very important experience; "without the challenge of the mystical night flight," Rogerson states; "Islam would have become a very different religion in later centuries. The night flight would inspire generations of mystics to seek a similar experience of the divinity" (*Muhammad*, 114).

[220] Sura 17:1 states "Praise be to Him who has carried His servant by night from the Masjidu 'l-Haram to the Masjidu 'l-Aqsa." The two *masjids* are in Mecca and Jerusalem (Hughes, *Dictionary*, 351). This is the only mention of the "night journey" in the Quran. Everything else comes from the *Hadith*.

was let by Gabriel the porter, who keeps seventy thousand keys that open several divisions of Paradise. From one Heaven to another, according to his computation, is five hundred years' travel; howbeit Mohammed passed through all the seven in a moment. In those orbs he saw many strange things, but first take notice what metal the orbs are of.

The first, says he, is of refined silver, wherein all the glittering stars are fixed with chains of burnished brass. In this Heaven he saw a cock so great that standing upon the Moon, his comb reached into the imperial Heaven; every time this cock crowed all other chanticleers upon the Earth re-echoed him. The second Heaven is of gold, such as has been seven times tried in the fire; the third of pearl. In this Heaven he saw innumerable troops of saints and angels, each of which saluting him by his name, he prayed for them. Amongst the rest he took notice of Adam, Enoch, Abraham, Samuel, David, Solomon etc., all whom he knew by revelation and of which some he taxed, others he commended as occasion served. The fourth was of smaragd,[221] where he saw infinite companies of other angels, who made a mighty noise and incessantly praised God; every angel there was a thousand times bigger then the globe of the Earth. Each had ten thousand heads, every head threescore and ten thousand tongues, and every tongue praised God in seven hundred thousand languages. Amongst them he noted one especially, *Phatyr* or the Angel of Mercy, a creature of that vast frame that every step he trod was twelve times more than the distance is 'twixt both the poles. Mohammed enquired of him why he wept so; the angel replied it was in compassion to see the deplorable estate of man. This is that angel has the Holy Pen[222] in keeping, a pen of orient pearl so long that an Arabian courser in five hundred years' galloping can hardly reach to the further end of it. With this pen God registers all things past, present and to come; the ink he writes with is pure light, the character so mysterious that none but he and Seraphiel can read it. All the hundred and four Holy Books are written by this quill, *viz.* those ten which Adam received, Seth[223] had fifty, Idris or Enoch thirty and Abraham had the rest. It also writ Moses his law, David's psalms, Christ's gospel and Mohammed's Alcoran. The fifth Heaven was of diamonds, where he saw a mighty angel of all others the wisest; he had as many heads and tongues and voices as any two in the

---

[221] From Latin *smaragdus*, which means any green precious stone, but particularly an emerald.

[222] This is the *Qalam*, "the pen with which God is said to have pre-recorded the actions of men" (Hughes, *Dictionary*, 478). Sura 68 is called *Al-Qalam*. The Angel of Mercy is Israfil.

[223] The third son of Adam and Eve (see Genesis 4:25). His importance to Mohammed, Hughes states, is probably because "in the fourth century there existed in Egypt a set of gnostics calling themselves Sethians, who regarded Seth as a divine emanation, which will account for Muhammad classing him as an inspired prophet with a revelation" (*Dictionary*, 569).

inferior orb and had the keeping of that book wherein all men in the world have their names written. He did nothing but turn over leaves and blot out one name or another, for by that, as by the arrow of Death, they die suddenly.[224] The sixth was of turquoise, the seventh of *al-ahal*; some interpret it 'fire,' others 'pure light' or 'breath congealed.' All these circumvolve one another like pearls or onions; they be translucent and yet of metals! Above all is the Heaven of Heavens, full of light and silence, immense and within which all other bodies are comprised, but it is incomprehended. There Mohammed saw (or rather dreamed he saw) the highest Throne, rich beyond expression, very great also for it was supported by seven angels,[225] each of them so great that a falcon if he were to fly a thousand years could not go so far as is the distance of one eye from another. About the Throne hung fourteen candles everlastingly-burning; the length of one of those candles, as Mohammed conjectured, was from one end to another as much space as a horse can ride in five hundred years. There this blasphemer fails not to say he saw the Almighty, who (if it be lawful to mention) in sign of welcome laid his hand upon Mohammed's face. His hands, says this anthropomorphite,[226] were a thousand times colder then ice, for all which Mohammed, in acknowledgement of his own baseness, blushed for shame and sweat for fear, and with his long finger sweeping the sweat from his brow threw it into Paradise. Rare sweat, for each drop (he notes them to be six) turned into some rare thing; one drop became a rose, another turned into a grain of rice, the other four into four learned men: Ahmed ibn Hanbal, Abu Hanifa, Malik ibn Asan and Al-Shafi. After he had full instructions he descended with his Alcoran. What course he took to promote it, and being entertained how notoriously it has overspread the greatest part of Asia and Africa is too visible; here only let us note his *quatuor novissima*[227] concerning angels, judgment, Paradise and Hell.[228]

----

[224] Azrail is the Angel of Death (see Sura 32:11).

[225] These are the *Hamalatu al-arsh*, which means "bearers of the throne." They are mentioned in Sura 40:7. Hughes cites the commentator al-Baghawi as saying that there are eight of them "so tall that their feet stand on the lowest strata of the earth and their heads reach the highest Heaven." However, Herbert must have been reading a different version, as al-Baghawi says "it is a journey of seven hundred years from their ears to their shoulders" (Hughes, *Dictionary*, 160).

[226] A person who endows a deity with human form.

[227] The four last things.

[228] For the complete account from the *Mishkatu 'l-Masabih*, see Hughes, *Dictionary* 351–52. There are substantial differences between it and the version Herbert gives here, particularly in the way Mohammed meets the various prophets. Each is stationed in a Heaven, together with other prominent figures. Here Mohammed meets (in order) Adam, Jesus and John, Joseph, Enoch, Aaron, Moses, and finally Abraham in the seventh Heaven. He does not meet Samuel, David, or Solomon, at least not in this version, although there are stories in the *Hadith* which say he did. In fact, much of Herbert's information seems to come from the *Hadith*, a collection of "divine sayings" (*hadis*), which

Angels.

Angels are either good or bad. Both are subject to death, the good because they consist of flame, an element; to sin, because Lucifer, an angel, for his ambition was expulsed Paradise. Bad angels are imprisoned in dogs, swine, toads, wolves, bears, tigers etc. After the Day of Doom they shall be tormented in Hell, but in the end are to be delivered.

Judgment.

The great and general Judgment is as certain as the day of death and will happen suddenly, such time as all the world is wrapped in a careless security. The angels know not the time until Mohammed point it out by a great and fearful duel 'twixt Azrail and Death, whom in the end he vanquishes, thereby becoming so enraged that in this manner he destroys all living creatures in the world. New-arming himself with flaming brass, in each quarter of the world he sounds his dreadful trumpet, whose affrighting clangour makes not only men, beasts, fishes, birds and other creatures die, but the angels also give over living. Lastly, Azrail himself, whom God commanded to follow the rest in the inevitable path, who accordingly by wrapping his iron wings about strangles himself with such a dreadful noise as is unexpressible.

After this ensues an universal earthquake attended by a shower of purling brimstone which devours all grass, trees and vegetable creatures, yea, the palaces of the proudest tyrants, and turning topsy-turvy the earth, water and other elements reduces them into their original, a confused lump. Forty days it rests in this new Chaos, during which God grasps it in his fist and beholding it, speaks to this effect: "Where are now the haughty princes, the cruel tyrants, lascivious wantons and greedy earthworms?" Which said, for forty days and nights space he incessantly rains down a shower of mercy and by a gracious and gentle breath reduces the world into a fresh and glorious estate, which done he calls up Seraphiel and bids him take his trumpet in his hand. The trumpet is of gold and, speaking to common understanding, about five hundred years travel from one end to another. At the first sound ensues a revivification of angels and men; at the second angels reassume their glorious robes and men their naked flesh again. Michael the archangel, perceiving the tribune raised upon a high mount in Jehoshaphat's

---

consists not only of the Prophet's sayings but "a heterogenous collection of folk wisdom, Bedouin traditions, epigrams and *wasiyya*—the treasured deathbed sayings of the Arabs" (Rogerson, *Muhammad*, 228). Scholars attempted to sort these out and authenticate them, and eventually eight "editions" became accepted as "real" traditions, although, as Rogerson states, "no canonical edition has ever been accepted" (228). See also Syed Iqbal Zaheer, *Fake Pearls: A Collection of Fabricated Prophetic Sayings* (Bangalore: Iqra Publications, 2002). Zaheer maintains that despite the efforts of editors through the ages, many of the stories in the *Hadith* are simply false.

vale, approaches with his balance and poises every man's deeds in either scale. Such whose good out-balance their evil are put upon the right hand, the other on the left. After that, such as are loaden with their sins packed up in a satchel and tied about their necks pass upon a narrow and weak bridge towards Hell; such as have few sins get over safely but those that be heavy laden break the bridge and fall into an abyss. Upon the other side stands Mohammed transformed into a ram, and in his deep fleece lodges his sectaries, whom after long travel he brings to some gap which he finds in Paradise, where skipping in he disburdens himself and shakes them out, at that instant assuming new forms more lovely, more strong and every way more excellent, with eyes as big as the Earth, with eyebrows bigger and more beautiful then the rainbow.[229]

Hell. Paradise.

The Alcoran further tells you what and where Hell is, and what is Paradise. Hell is in the umbelic of the world, circled with a thick wall of adamant, entered by seven gates of flaming brass, divided into many cells, some of which are more loathsome and fuller of torment then others.[230] In it are divers holes or caves, some so deep that in a thousand years a millstone cannot find the bottom. In the descent are sharp swords and pikes placed purposely to torture souls in their falling. Some places be abyss[es] full of oil and brimstone ever-burning, and so terrible that the devils forbear not to howl and screech and rage there beyond measure. Other prisons there be that are full of toads, serpents and all other sorts of noisome creatures imaginable; the damned eat nothing there save the forbidden fruit,[231] which being in their guts inflames like sulphur and makes them roar continually. Some rivers be full of crocodiles, others so cold as makes them gnash and chatter. Howbeit, these pains of Hell must not abide for ever, say their doctors, for after each soul has suffered so many thousand years as the sins amount to they have committed Mohammed will deliver them and the devils also, first changing their affrighted shapes into shapes more tolerable and then bringing them to *Alcanzar*, a stream flowing out of Paradise, where they are to cool their

---

[229] A complete account of the Judgment Day (*Qiyamah*) may be found under "Resurrection" in Hughes (*Dictionary*, 536–44). He cites relevant Quranic passages and summarises different versions from the *Hadith* and other sources. Herbert's account shows that he is familiar with several versions of the event, and what he gives is largely accurate. A glance at Hughes's summary, however, will show that Herbert has omitted, or did not know, many other details.

[230] This is correct. The Muslim commentators give seven divisions of Hell. For details, see Hughes, *Dictionary*, 171.

[231] "No food shall they have but the fruit of the bitter thorn" (Sura 88:6). The *Mishkat* says in addition that "the infidels shall be drenched with yellow water, draught after draught . . . when they drink it it will tear their entrails to pieces" (Hughes, *Dictionary*, 177).

heat and wash away their black-scorched mummy,[232] and then they vary into a moist flesh whiter then the driven snow and thenceforth sing *Lala-billulaes*, which is "Praise be to God and Mohammed."

Paradise is a place of as much delight as Mohammed's carnal apprehension was able to imagine or his fancy contrive. He is uncertain of the local place, but supposes it will be upon the Earth after the Day of Doom, when all deformity shall be removed, for till then the souls and bodies of men sleep in their graves but be sensible of joy and torment. Paradise, says the Alcoran, is so many miles about as there be motes or atoms in the sun; it is enclosed with a wall of gold ninety times refined, ten thousand miles high and in thickness about three thousand, has seven gates to enter at (seven is a mystery).[233] Of carbuncle or purest ruby is the first gate; the other six be of pearl, emerald, turquoise, hyacinth, smaragd and amethyst, reflecting upon the spheres, divided into seven spacious gardens, subdivided into seventy times seven places of delight, each filled with inhabitants, music, wine and all sensual pleasures imaginable. All have cool refreshing rivulets of crystal drilling over pebbles of amber. Summer-houses it also has, shaded with trees ever-fruitful and verdant; in the centre of that Elysium is a tree higher then the mountains of the world were they heaped one upon another, so broad that Paradise becomes delightfully-shaded by it. The trunk of this tree is diamond, the leaves of gold and the boughs of jet; each leaf is wrought into an antic shape, in this most admirable, for that on one side in letters of light are the names of God, on the opposite the name of Mohammed. From several quarters four streams gush out of purest milk, water, coho and honey; these empty themselves into *Alcanzar*, whence this mixture of nepenthe[234] flows into other parts of Paradise. Aromatic flowers are there in abundance such as ravish both eye and smell; airy choristers, the meanest of which as far excel our nightingales as they do ravens. The air is a compound of sense-ravishing odours. Mohammedans there (for Christians, Jews nor gentiles have not such glory) are ever young and spritefull, a hundred times bigger and more frolic than ever was Mohammed. The women are severed from the men; not that they are kept from them, for Gabriel is never averse to let them in, but that by such a screen they may become more ardently amorous and affected to their damozels, who have such visages as fair Aisha had, Mohammed's best-beloved, their hairs being threads of gold, their eyes diamonds as big as the Moon. Their lips resemble cherries, their teeth pearl, their tongues rubies, their cheeks coral, their noses jasper, their foreheads

---

[232] Sura 74:29 "generally held to be the second Surah composed by Muhammad" speaks of one of the consequences of Hell as "blackening the skin" (Hughes, *Dictionary*, 171).

[233] The Quran was revealed to Mohammed in seven revelations or in the seven major dialects of Arabia, according to interpretation. There are seven verses in it containing the word *salaam*, which means 'peace' (Hughes, *Dictionary*, 569–70).

[234] A drug that causes forgetfulness; some scholars believe it to have been laudanum.

sapphire; round-faced, courteous and merciful. In this Paradise is, say they, a table of diamond seven hundred thousand days' journey long about which are chairs of gold and pearl for use and ornament.

The males are to be of Mohammed's favour and complexion such as their Prophet had when Gabriel mounted him towards Heaven; none but will be much brighter then the sun, with such eyes, eyebrows and ears as are scarce credible. To conclude, Gabriel the Porter of Paradise has seventy thousand keys which pertain to his office, every key being seven thousand miles long, by which you may imagine the doors are no pygmy ones! In a word, 'tis no less ingenious then the rest that Mohammed confessed he writ, three parts of four untruths in this his legend. To confute them would be a labour needless, though Melancthon has done it, so that I may well say as Seneca did to Lucilius, *"Non vaco plusquam ad tantas ineptias,"* for indeed, *"perfidias eorum recitasse superesse est."*[235]

Religious orders.

Such are the fanatic dogmas of the Alcoran, credited by most Asiatics wose disciples are above seventy sorts of orders or degrees, some of which with heed I have observed, and here, as the cover of their legend, shut up, ranking them in an alphabetic way lest I should in any way injure their seniority: *Abdalli, Alambeli, Alfaqui, Alfurcani, Anesii, Asaphii, Bedvini, Benesiani, Bosarmani, Buani, Caddi, Cadaleschi, Calyphi, Calfi, Choggi, Cobtini, Cumerati, Dephterdarii, Deruissi, Dervislari, Duanni, Emeri, Emawm-zeddi, Fyllali, Gularchi, Hodgei, Hugiemali, Imami, Kalenderi, Leshari, Malahedi, Melichi, Mendee, Morabiti, Morrabouci, Mudreessi, Mufti, Mulai, Mulevei, Muezini, Mustadini, Mutevelli, Muzulmanni, Naappi, Ozmanni, Papassi, Ramdani, Santoni, Seriphi, Shahi, Sophini, Sunni, Syetti, Talismanni, Tecknai, Torlaceni, Torlaqui, Zaidi, Zophilari* etc., whose tenets, how ridiculous soever they may be, yet are so esteemed of here that in their defence they will at any time become martyrs,[236] but Saint Augustine's definition

---

[235] "I don't have the time for so much nonsense; to have told of their treachery is to have survived it." This quotation is not from Seneca.

[236] This is a hodge-podge of sects, titles and other things, and Herbert's definitions, which follow, are often wildly inaccurate. Insofar as can be determined by matching spellings and approximations, which I have here reproduced, they are as follows. Those I have been unable to identify I have left in italics. Abdal: "substitutes . . . certain persons by whom, it is said, God continues the world in existence. Their number is seventy, of whom forty reside in Syria, and thirty elsewhere" (Hughes, *Dictionary*, 1); *Alambeli*; Al-faqir: a religious mendicant; *Alfurcani*; *Akhnasiyah*; Ashariyah: a sect founded by Abu'l Hasan al-Ashari (873–935; see below), who taught that "the attributes of God are distinct from His essence" (Hughes, *Dictionary*, 25); Bidiyah: they held that it is always a citizen's duty to obey rulers (Hughes, *Dictionary*, 569); *Benesiani*: Beni Isguene: a settlement founded by Ibadiya Muslims in the mid-eleventh century (Rauf); Bahsamiyah: the followers of Abu Hashim (d. 716), grandson of Ali; *Buani*; Cadi or Qadi; *Cadaleschi*; Caliphs; Khalfiya:

is true, that *"causa non poena facit martyrem,"*[237] and 'tis well-observed that these false teachers are so ravished and transported when they have found they have a dominion and sovereignty over the faith and consciences of men as no persecution or torture can ever make them to relinquish it. Now since this blasphemous anthropomorphite persuades his sectaries that at his ascent into Heaven the Almighty touched him with his hand, it seemed he was ignorant that God is infinite as well as eternal, and without any composition, so as that tenet of his is an error against the very essence of God, *"Maledictus est,"* says Augustine, *"qui deitatem ad hominis lineamenta refert. Deus enim non est humanae formae particeps,*

---

founded by Khalfu'l Khariji, who taught that "contrary to the general belief, the children of idolaters will be eternally damned" (Hughes, *Dictionary*, 268); *Choggi*; *Cobtini*; *Cumerati*; A *defterdar* is a Minister of Finance; Druses: a sect now mostly in Lebanon, Israel and Syria. Their founder was the Fatimid Caliph al-Hakim (996–1021). A detailed summary of their beliefs may be found in Hughes (*Dictionary*, 100–1); Dervishes, of which there are many kinds; Deobandis; amirs: noblemen or commanders; Imam Zadeh: the shrine of a saint; *Fyllali*; *Gularchi*; Hajji: a title of respect given to those who have gone to Mecca; Hujjatiya: a Sufi sect. The word *hujja* means 'argument' or 'proof;' Imamiya: they state that "the world is never left without an Imam of the Bani Hashim to lead the prayers" (Hughes, *Dictionary*, 568); Qalandars: a Persian order of dervishes; Lafziyah: they hold that although the Quran itself is not an "inspired writing," the instructions in it are from God (Hughes, 269); Makhlukiya; Malikites: a Sunni sect founded by Imam Malik ibn Anas (see above); *Mendee*; Morabites: followers of Mohieddin, grandson of Ali, but may also refer to scientists and theologians in African Muslim countries; *Mubarikiya*; Madrassa: a school; Mufti (see above); Mulay or *muallim*: a teacher in a religious school or mosque; Muezzin (see above); Murtaziya: a sect that says "it is lawful for a Muslim to fight against his Imam" (Hughes, 268); Musulman: a Muslim; Nabi: a prophet. However, Herbert might mean the Nahiya sect, "who say faith is knowledge" or the Najiya, "the Saved Ones" (Hughes, *Dictionary*, 569); Osmaniya: a Sunni sect; Papassi: fortune-tellers (Rauf, n.p.n.); *Ramdani*; Shaitaniya: those who "deny the personality of Satan" (Hughes, 568); *Seriphi*; Sha'iya: they believe once one has repeated the creed salvation is obtained (Hughes, 569); Sifatiya: also known as "Attributists," because they believe God's attributes "are eternally inherent in his essence without separation or change" (Hughes, 582); Sunnis; Syeds; Talismans (see above); *Torlaceni*; *Torlaqi*; Zaidiya: a Shi'ite sect who follow Zaid ibn al-Husain (Hughes, 698); Zafiraniya: they maintain that the Quran is "a created thing" (Hughes, 698). Further details may be found in Ijaz A. Rauf, "73 Divisions in Islam and One True Jama'at," www.real-islam.org.com, from which some of these definitions are taken, but which has no page-numbers.

   [237] "The cause, not the punishment, makes a martyr" (Augustine, *Epistles* 89. 2, PL 33. 310).

neque corpus humanum divinae.[238] Yea, Trismegistus[239] could say *"Anima est imago mentis, mens imago dei; deus enim mentis praeest, mens animae, corpori anima*; 'the soul is the image of the understanding, understanding is the image of God, God rules over the understanding, the understanding over the soul as the soul doth over the body.'"

Their rules are various. The Mufti is chief in hearing and deciding in case of errors, which, if he fail in, the Meccan Protomist determines it. The Qadi, *Cadaleschi* and *Mustadini* are next in ecclesiastical dignity. The Hajji, Emeri and Mulay: the first are expositors, the other mendicants eating the bread in idleness. The *Fyllali* converse most. The Druses are wandering wolves in sheep's clothing; "*deruisses oratores Persici*" are mentioned by Herodotus *lib*. 9. The Talismans regard the hours of prayer by turning the four-houred glass; the muezzins cry from the tops of mosques, battologising *La illahah ilallah*. The Qalandars, Abdals and Dervishes be pederasts and dangerous to meet in solitary places. The *Terlaqui* and *Cobtini* are of the Family of Love,[240] the *Lethari* and Papassi star-gazers and fortune-tellers. The sunni, *Naappi* and *Tecknai* vow silence and assassinate. The syeds and Imamiya sometimes pull out their eyes, having once seen Medinet al-Nabi; others of these have pulled out their tongues. The Hujjatiya sing amorous songs; some for penance go naked, othersome are covered in ashes. The Deobandis are fools or madmen, yet thought inspired. The *Mendae* afflect their bodies by thirst, lashing and wounding themselves and in charity carry burthens or do any servile labour gratis; some abjure flesh, fish, wine and rose-water; some live

---

[238] "Accursed is the man who reduces God to human features, for God is not a participant in human form, nor the human body in the divine" (Augustine, *Sermones* 234.7, PL 39. 2180).

[239] Hermes Trismegistus was the name given by Neoplatonists to the god Thoth, who was once credited with the authorship of various sacred writings; he became associated from the third century C.E. onwards with a work called the *Poimandres*, in which Divine Intelligence appears to a sleeper in a vision and expounds what is essentially a Neoplatonic philosophy. According to Jacopo da Bergamo's *Supplementum chronicorum* (1483), he also invented astronomy. The Hermetic myth was exploded by Meric Casaubon in the 1660s; not only was the claim that he predated Moses disproved, but doubts were cast on his very existence. He is cited several times by Lord Herbert of Chirbury (*Pagan Religion*, 135–36) and his works were available in a number of editions. There is a translation by B. P. Copenhaver, *Hermetica: The Greek Corpus Hermeticum and the Latin Asclepius* (Cambridge: Cambridge University Press, 1995).

[240] Herbert alludes here to a Protestant sect founded by Henrik Niklaes, a Dutchman, in about 1540. Their beliefs included advocacy of communal property rather than private, and that God's spirit in the true believer made anything possible. They believed that they could reach a state of perfect love with God. In England the movement was started in the 1550s by Christopher Vittels, and in spite of proclamations against it by Mary I and Elizabeth I, was still flourishing in 1610. Its members tended to conceal their beliefs with outward conformity.

eremites and some build houses to safeguard birds and beasts, feed them and have music to prevent their melancholy; othersome build hospitals, inns, baths, mosques and the like. Some are poetasters or mimographers,[241] othersome have seeds and charms to make women fruitful. Some scorch their skins in the sun, others of more pity and piety oil their naked bodies, and to allure the poor flies to pasture roll themselves in the burning sun. These and many other paths they tread, directed by the Alcoran the way to Acheron,[242] so as I shall conclude with that of Saint Jerome, "*Si non placet non legas etc*,"[243] and take leave with another to say "*Quid ultra dicam in re tam exulcerata ubi a capite ad pedem non est sanitas.*"[244]

Schisms in the Alcoran.

This more crafty then learned lawgiver [Mohammed], perceiving his divinity and philosophy insufficient to abide the trial, has this salvo, by commanding that none upon pain of damnation presume to question a syllable of it, and with good reason, for "*Suspecta est lex*," says Tertullian, "*quae se probare non audet*,"[245] from whence few, except they be ecclesiastics, trouble themselves to read or study it, hoping by a reverend ignorance and the collier's faith to be saved. But by your favour I will answer you out of Martial: "Others with words and pleasing looks / Thou may'st deceive; but me / Thou shalt not, for I know thee / A rank hypocrite to be."[246] Howbeit, the Persians, since Junaid's reformation, have contracted the Alcoran into a lesser volume; Osman's labours they slight, the four great doctors who had their original from the sweat of Mohammed's brow also execrate. These are the most material difference 'twixt Turk and Persian. And let none think that Syet's was the first schism, for Osman was no sooner dead but according to the adage "*Posthumi heresii filii*" Ibnul,[247] to enfeeble Osman's labours, commented upon the Alcoran and differed from his opinion. After him Ibn Abdul Hasan of

---

[241] People who represent the language of signs in writing.

[242] A river in the Greek underworld, but often used as a synonymn for Hell itself.

[243] "If you don't like it don't read it." This is not found in Jerome.

[244] What can I say further about something so disease-ridden that there's no health in it from head to foot?

[245] That law is suspect which does not allow itself to be tested. This is not found in Tertullian.

[246] Herbert is probably using Sir Richard Fanshawe's translation of Martial (*Epigrams* 4. 88. 9–10).

[247] Herbert may be referring to Mohammed ibn Ismail (fl. 740–after 785), one of the Imams of the so-called Ismaili sect of Muslims, now directed by the Aga Khans. He was the son of Ismail ibn Ja'afar (721–765), after whom the sect is named, and was believed to have been the last Imam of the Ismailis by those known as "Seveners." The Ismailis split into sub-sects; the Syrian branch, for example, became the Musta'ali sect. The Abbasid caliphs in Baghdad sporadically persecuted the Ismailis. Herbert's knowledge of these matters is somewhat confused, and calling a person *Ibnul* translates only as "son

Basra[248] by his austere life and eloquence not only opposed the Melchian,[249] but in comparison of whom Ibnul himself was counted erroneous. At his death they sainted him, but trusting to tradition, for they could never prevail with Hasan to commit anything to writing, his disciples differed so far amongst themselves that it came to blows, which has but coarse logic, not agreeing in any point, till *Elharu Ibnu-esed* of Babylon did his best in an elaborate paraphrase not only to reconcile them but withal to make canonical al-Hasan's expositions. It seemed calm weather for a while, but ere long a thunderclap was heard from Mecca's territories anathematising *Elharu-esed*, persecuting him and all his fautors, pursuant to which by Malik Shah's[250] command they not only burn his papers but excommunicate him from the converse and society of Mussulmen.

Nevertheless King *Cazel*[251] afterwards was induced to have a good opinion of *Elharu* and his tenets, and at that time being a favourite to his uncle the great Malik Shah (a Turk and late victor over Babylon) makes use of his power, desiring some favour for the late excommunicated men. Malik could not easily be persuaded, but Nizam al-Mulk,[252] another courtier of note and favourer of *Elharu's* doctrine, seconds *Cazel* and pervails to have the Asharite sectaries called

---

of," so it's anyone's guess who he might be; however, it appears that Herbert is alluding to the Ismailis.

[248] Abu al-Hasan ibn Ismail al-Ashari of Basra (874–936) was a theologian who founded the Ashariyya or Asharite school of Quranic interpretation in opposition to the Mu'tazilite school of his teacher al-Jubbai. He was known for attempting to reconcile science and faith (although he stressed the importance of not blindly accepting religious authority without proof), and in his *Maqalat al-Islamin* he collected together a great number of theological opinions. He held, amongst other things, that the Quran was eternal, uncreated, and he rejected anthropomorhism. He is said to have written more than three hundred books. Al-Ashari is revered by Sunnis as an Imam.

[249] Unidentified, but may mean "Meccan."

[250] Malik Shah I [*Melec-sha*], Great Seljuk Sultan 1072–1092, was a strong Sunni Muslim and opposed to any other forms of Islam. See also above. He was a cultured and enlightened ruler. Under Toghrul Beg the Asharites had been persecuted, but Herbert is correct in crediting Nizam al-Mulk (see below) with persuading his successor to be tolerant, and in fact because of this the Asharites gained considerable political power. Both he and Nizam al-Mulk were murdered by the Assassins (Hashashin).

[251] Probably Kilij Arslan I, later Seljuk Sultan of Rum 1092–1106.

[252] Abu Ali al-Hasan al-Tusi (1018–1092), a Persian statesman from Tuzz known as "Nizam al-Mulk [*Nydam Emul*]," which translates as "Order of the Empire," was no mere courtier but Vizier to Sultans Alp Arslan and Malik Shah I from 1063 to his assassination. A great reformer and educator, he not only founded schools which came to be known as Nizamiyyas and which developed into some of the great universities, but reformed the Seljuk army and finances as well. He wrote the *Siyasat-nama* (1091), a handbook for kingship and statecraft, and he gave support to al-Ghazzali against Islamic schismatics, making him Head of the Nizamiyya College in Baghdad. For details, see Julie Scott Meirami, *Persian Historiography to the End of the Twelfth Century* (Edinburgh:

home again. Al-Ghazzali, a nimble-witted man, undertakes it and by little less then miracle closes the late-made breach, so as now Mohammed shines without interposition, but an altercation quickly followed, for Saint Azimullah from the Caspian shore defies all such as thought well of Mohammed's three intruding successors. This seemed a terrible apostacy at first, but while all Asia were in admiration what the event would be, a crack of no less amazement comes from the west, where al-Mutannabi[253] exalts his own piety and learning above Mohammed's. This seemed intolerable, so that being apprehended, as a reward of his apostacy and to prevent any further schism that upstart doctor was put to a miserable death.

After this, both the clergy and laity grew exceeding voluptuous; a foolish thing it was then to affect learning or to appear honest. Lascivious poems was the only delight, and Mohammed's Paradise seemed then in being. This corruption in good manners was nevertheless enveighed against by *Essebraver Differaverd*, a Bactrian, whose severe satires so stung those epicures that many began to examine their lives and conversation, of which being convinced made them ashamed, and being perceived by Ibn al-Farid,[254] one well-learned in his time, he, as one well-acquainted with the humour of the Persian, sweetened all by his amorous poesy, which was seconded by al-Farghani, whose lines were applauded by some but by othersome exploded as a busy Cabbalist. A chaos seemed then to cover that face of Persia, till *Elifarni* a sober historian took upon himself to set right what was amiss. Seventy-two sects he reduced to two, the Leshariya and Imamiya, the first of which eulogically extols Mohammed and is received through all Morea, Anatolia, Egypt, Palestine and the Lesser Asia; the other Ali, which is received all over the Persian monarchy and beyond Indus. In the last place Syed Junaid displays his ensign to such effect as keeps its credit to this day in opposition to the Turk. It would here be tedious to rehearse their brawls, wherein I have gone too far already; I will therefore shut up with that of the Pastoral, *"Non nostrum inter nos tantas componere lites."*[255]

Edinburgh University Press, 1999), 145–88. She includes a detailed summary of the *Siyasat-Nama* in the latter part of this section.

[253] For al-Mutanabbi, see above, 712 n. 187. Herbert's assertions about his demise are false.

[254] For al-Farid, see above. Al-Farghani commented on al-Farid's *Ta'iyya*.

[255] "Not ours to arbitrate these great disputes between you" (Virgil, *Eclogue* 3. 108).

[PART VIII :
OTHER PARTS OF INDIA AND ASIA]

After this repose, let's abroad again and see what observation we can make in other parts of India, then which the world, for pleasure and wealth, has none more considerable. To encompass it we must to sea again, for without such helps it cannot be accomplished.

To which end, April 12 we took ship at Suwali, and being three or four leagues off at sea, the wind came fair and made the liquid billows swell so advantageously as next day we had sight of some noted towns, *viz.* Gandevi,[1] Daman,[2] St. John de Vacas,[3] Choul,[4] Dabhol[5] etc., most of which were subjected

---

[1] Gandevi [*Gundava*] is a small town in Gujarat.

[2] Daman, 100 miles north of modern Mumbai, had been in Portuguese hands since Martim Afonso de Sousa captured it in 1534; in 1559 Sultan Ahmed Shah II of Gujarat turned over the surrounding region to them. It remained under Portuguese control (along with Goa and Diu) until 1961, and still has a "lingering Portuguese flavour" (Singh, *India*, 656).

[3] Probably the fort on Ilha das Vacas (Isle of Cows) or Arnalla.

[4] Choul or Chaul was the scene of two battles fought by the Portuguese against the combined Egyptian-Gujarati navies which resulted in the consolidation of Portuguese control of the Indian Ocean. The second was celebrated by Camoens: "In Chaul the very seas will churn /," the poet wrote; "With blood, fire and iron resistance / As the combined fleets of Egypt and Cambay / Confront him [Almeida] with his destiny that day" (*Lusiads* 10. 29). Lourenço, Almeida's son, died in the first battle (1508). There was a third successful battle against the Gujarati fleet alone fought by Eitor de Silveiro (1529). Presumably Herbert is referring to the first one. *Hobson-Jobson* is "almost certain that this was the *Simulla* of Ptolemy's Tables" (210). It was visited by Afanasy Nikitin (*Voyage* 9) and Varthema in 1510 (*Travels*, 113).

[5] Dabhol [*Dabul*] was once the chief port of the Kingdom of Bijapur. Sir Henry Middleton arrived there (1612), as recorded by John Jourdain, but no trade was established until 1635, when a Convention was signed which allowed "active trade between the English at Surat and the Portuguese at Goa" (Foster, *England's Quest*, 318). Herbert's remark about its decline seems prophetic in light of the fact that Dabhol does not even merit a mention in Singh. Almeida, Camoens boasted, "before descending / In wrath on the coast of Cambay, / Plunges his sword in opulent Dabhol, / All its pretensions made contemptible" (*Lusiads* 10. 34). Afanasy Nikitin was there in 1470 (20) and Captain Walter Peyton in 1615 (Purchas, 1: 528). For details of Dabhol, see *Maharashtra*

by Albuquerque to the Crown of Portugal about the year 1512, Dabhol, *Dunga* of old, excepted, which yielded to the mercy of Andrade,[6] Governor of Choul, from whom 'twas soon rapt by the Deccanis, but by that made a basis of greater misery, for Francesco de Almeida a few years after recovered it by stratagem and burnt it to the very ground. Howbeit, by command of the Goan Viceroy 'twas again repaired, till Captain Hall[7] (if I mistake not his name) about the year 1620 took the town and made the daring Portugal know their bravados to the English were not terrible.

[Dabhol].

The south point of Dabhol, as I observed, has Arctic elevation 17 degrees 35 minutes, variation west 15 degrees 34 minutes. Heretofore it obeyed the King of Deccan, but at this day the Lusitanian, seated at the foot of a high, pleasant and fruitful mountain, whence streams a rivulet of fresh water[8] which is beyond measure useful in that hot climate. The road gives reasonable good anchorage, and the town itself, especially towards the sea, appears beautiful to such as view it, albeit the houses be but low and terraced at the top, a mode that best serves to qualify the extremes of heat and cold. An old castle and a few temples at this day are all she boasts of, for the bazaar is but ordinary and the streets narrow, nor is her mart now so considerable as at first, seeing that Surat and Cambay to the north, Goa and Calicut[9] to the south have eclipsed her so as now she condoles with other her disconsolate neighbours and is to acknowledge there is a destiny and decay in towns as well as other things.

State Gazetteers, ed. Arunchandra Pathak (Bombay: Directorate of Government Printing, 1962).

[6] Simão d'Andrade, younger brother of Ruy Freire. This unpleasant gentleman is remembered for his two incursions into China (1517 and 1519), after the second of which he began to kidnap Chinese women and children whom he later sold as slaves.

[7] Herbert was correct; Captain John Hall (not James, the captain of the *Mary*) had raided Dabhol in 1623. The English had already attacked Dabhol in 1621–1622, but they did not in fact take the city. The Dutch also attacked it in 1621. For details see Ashin Das Gupta, "Indian Merchants and the Western Indian Ocean: The Early Seventeenth Century," *Modern Asian Studies* 19 (1985): 481–99.

[8] The Anjawel (Vashishti) river.

[9] Modern Kozhikode in northern Kerala (see Singh, *India*, 949–51). Vasco da Gama landed here in 1498, when it was the chief city of Malabar and the centre of the Samorin's government. Camoens wrote of this: ". . . bright dawn broke in those heights / Where the River Ganges has its source, / As the sailors, aloft at the masthead / Saw mountains glimmering before the prow / . . . Then cheerfully said their Manlindinian pilot, / That land ahead is surely Calicut" (*Lusiads* 6. 92). It will be discussed in more detail a little later.

[Choul].

Choul, in Ptolemy's days called *Comane* if Castaldus guess right, is removed from the Equinoctial 18 degrees 30 minutes north, ravished from the diadem of Deccan by Almeida in the Year of Our Redemption 1508, and in which, to perpetuate his conquest, he erected a fort which he fortified with cannon. Howbeit, *Anno Dom.* 1571 it was for some months besieged by Misamoluc[10] the Deccan prince with a numerous army of horse and foot besides elephants, but by the gallant defence made by the Portugal were forced to rise with loss and shame. The inhabitants are a mixture of Portugals and Banians; it affords little else worth noting. Here the *Expedition* bearing up to speak with us, both fell foul one another's hawsers, through which mischance her bowsprit gave our mizzen-shrouds a churlish salute, but by a happy gale were parted without further damage.

Mangalore.

After five days' sail we were again nadir to the sun, his declination being fifteen degrees north. We were then close by the isle in which Goa is situated; ere long we were becalmed, whereby the air suddenly became inflamed, so as we were forced to sweat and live like salamanders. This extremity continued not above a week, for then we had a fresh gale, by help whereof the three and twentieth day we came to an anchor at Mangalore,[11] a city that obeys the Malabar. In the road we found towards forty Malabar men-of-war riding, who notwithstanding their numbers and appetite to do us mischief hoisted sail towards Goa, one only miscarrying, that suffered the *Jonas*'s barge to come up with her, but after variable strife by rowing and making more sail got away, yet not without some shot in her side which she unwillingly received. That night we came to an anchor in Mount Elly[12] or Delli's Bay, a port under the vassalage of the Malabar; we rode in nine fathom, not above three being near the shore, and gladly would have landed but durst not be too prodigal of our belief, for albeit the natives seemed willing to have us come ashore, we knew them to be treacherous, but seeing we would not trust them they came aboard our ships as daring to trust us, and in their canoes

---

[10] This is Herbert's version of the Portuguese *Nizamaluco*. It refers here to Murtaza Nizam Shah I, Sultan of Ahmednagar (see Part II). The siege actually took place in 1570.

[11] Mangalore was at that time a major port in Gujarat, and is now the chief port town in Karnataka State. Once it was the capital of the Alupa Dynasty, which ended in the fourteenth century. It is on the west coast of the Arabian Sea. The Portuguese took it over in 1520.

[12] Mount Deli or Eli [*Elly*] is an isolated mountain and an island near Cannanore, as Herbert's illustration shows. It was mentioned by Marco Polo as "Mount Ely" and has a famous temple to the god Hanuman, which is now the Mount Deli Lighthouse. It was "a conspicuous and well-known landmark to mariners" (William Logan, *Malabar Manual* [Madras: Government Press, 1887], 1: 82).

brought us cocos, mangos, jacks, green pepper, buffalos, hens, eggs and other
things, which we were glad to buy, though not at very easy prices. But for every tun of water a ryal[13] would not content them, albeit they had plenty, by this
barbarism infringing the very Law of Nature and Nations. Accordingly the poet
brings in his goddess, blaming the rustics for their inhumanity: "Why are these
waters stopped, whose use is free? / The sun and air dispersed to all we see, / Why
not those brooks? I crave community."

Nevertheless, what was wanting in water was supplied in fruit and other
rareties, for here we had the wood called *calambuco*,[14] a tree very much valued and
used at funerals. The richer sort have gums and odours of Arabia put in flames,
which is pure white, sweet and fine, or in taffetas of transparent fineness. Of all
sorts of wood they most affect that called *aquila*,[15] and nenjxt to that *calamba* or
calambuca, which some think *lignum aloes*, trees very rare, growing but in few
regions. It is sweet and delightful to the smell, high and even, and found commonly in the lofty mountain of *Chamoys*[16] in Cochin China,[17] and being rare and
hardly-got these people sell at excessive rates, both in regard the Banians delight
to have this wood in their obsequies and that the Japonians so much value it for
ornament in their houses. They imagine no pillow wholesomer, nothing more
conducing to health then that to sleep upon, extremely hating what is soft, for
they find that such both heats the blood and perturbs the fancy. Of old they used
to wrap those dead bodies that were to be burned and purified in the fire in that
kind of linen called *linum vivum* or asbestos, of which I have formerly spoken,
but I shall add the description out of Hierocles[18] treating of the clothing of the

---

[13] The ryal was a gold coin introduced by Henry VII (1485–1509) to replace the noble. It had a value of 6s. 8d. Mary I (1553–1558) and Elizabeth I (1558–1603) issued ryals
worth 15s (the spur ryal) and 22s (the rose ryal). Herbert is probably referring to James I's
rose ryal, which was worth 30s because the price of gold had increased. Some numisma-
tists call this a "double ryal." James's spur ryal was increased to 16s 6d in 1612.

[14] The Portuguese word for *calambac*, "the finest kind of aloes-wood" (*HJ* 144).

[15] This is also known as 'eaglewood,' defined in *Hobson-Jobson* as "the name of an aromatic wood from Camboja [*sic*] and some other Indian regions, chiefly trans-gangetic."
However, *Hobson-Jobson* notes further that eaglewood "is another name for aloes-wood"
(335).

[16] Probably the Shevaroys or Selvarayan Range in what is now known as Tamil
Nadu. The name means "beautiful ones" in Tamil.

[17] Cochin-China, which today would be in the southern part of Vietnam, was so-
called to distinguish it from Cochin in India, which is in Malabar. The name was derived
from the Malay name of Vietnam, *Kuchi*.

[18] Hierocles of Alexandria (fl. 430) wrote a commentary on the *Chrysa epe* (*Golden
Verses*) of Pythagoras and a treatise *On Providence*. He was frequently confused with a
Stoic philosopher of the same name, whose fragmentary *Elements of Ethics* was cited by
Stobaeus and others. There were many editions and translations which Herbert could
have used; his works were first edited by J. Curtenius (1583), and there was an edition

Brahmans: *"Indorum utuntur veste linea ex lapidibus, quod quidem texunt; mollia sunt lapidum stamina et membranae ex quibus panni fiunt, cui neque igne neque aqua expurgantur, sed cum sordes et maculas contexterunt, in flammis iniecti, albescunt et lucidi fiunt."* [19]

Rare Indian fruit.

Here we had the fairest lemons I ever saw. It is an old saying that life is upheld by the taste of some sweetmeats. Give me leave, therefore, to name some fruit that may be worth the notice: pawpaws, cocos, bananas and plantains, all very sweet and delicious; oranges we had also store of, which may be remembered, they were so succulent and dainty and of so curious a relish as affects the eater beyond measure. The rind also was no less pleasant than the juice, and seem to have dulcity and acrimony mixed together. The bananas were no less delightful; the tree is but low, yet spreads gracefully, the fruit is not unlike a sausage for shape, but in taste is most pleasant. They ripen though you crop them immaturely, and from a dark green turn into a bright yellow; the rind peels off easily and the fruit, being put into the mouth, yields an incomparable relish. The jack grows upon a tree which is very low yet not easy to be ascended, for in shape it resembles a pompion;[20] without, 'tis of a yellow colour mixed with veins, but within it is full of golden-coloured cloves, each of them being full of kernels, not unlike the largest sort of French bean but somewhat more globous. That is the fruit which hath in it a stone, which being boiled, the buffalos eat of. The fruit is somewhat unpleasant at the first gust, which as I suppose the heat and rareness causes, and 'tis glutinous in the mouth but of double benefit to the stomach, being restorative and good for the back and of singular use against that French disease [21] which was brought from the wars at Naples. In taste it has some resemblance with that the Africans call *kola*.[22]

---

by Meric Casaubon of *De providentia* (1655). Hermann Schibli has recently provided a translation of extant works and a discussion of Hierocles's philosophy in *Hierocles of Alexandria* (Oxford: Oxford University Press, 2002).

[19] Some of the Indians use linen clothing made from stones, which certain of them weave; the filaments of the stones are soft, and the membranes from which the garments are made can be cleaned neither by fire nor water, but, covered over with dirt and stains, they are thrown into the flames and become white and clear.

[20] Pumpkin. It can also be spelled *pompeon*.

[21] Venereal disease. The French, of course, called it *la maladie anglaise*.

[22] In west African countries the kola nut used to be passed round when friends visited each other; it also had public ceremonial and ritual uses. It is a red nut with a bitter taste which contains caffeine and stains the teeth. It was once used in many soft drinks, hence 'cola.'

The ananas[23] is not inferior to the jack in bulk, albeit the plant it springs from be no way equal, for it arises not from seed but a root like that of an artichoke. At maturity they rise not above two foot, whereby with less labour they enrich the gatherer; without 'tis armed with a moistless rind which is hard, but pleasant within, and though a little seem to satiate, yet experience teaches that the stomach covets it and admits an easy digestion. The durian resembles the jack; the shape is round and the outside beautiful, and yet that beauty exceeds not the inward virtue, for albeit at first opening it give a smell not unlike a rotten onion, which to many seems offensive, the meat nevertheless is of a whitish colour and divided with a dozen cells which are filled with stones as big as chestnuts, white and cordial. In Malacca and Java they abound most, and are worth the enquiring after, for it is a fruit both nutritive and dainty, yea, without an hyperbole the epitome of the best and rarest fruits throughout the Orient. Areca and betel are also here much in use. The areca tree grows very high and resembles the palmetto; the wood is fuzzy and soft and hangs like shaded grapes in clusters; the fruit is shaped like a walnut and of like bigness, white within and not easily penetrated, but like good oil hath neither taste nor smell, for they eat it not alone but wrap it in a leaf of betel or *betere*, which hath neither flower nor moisture, and chew it in morsels. Some, as I have noted, mix with it a kind of lime like that of oyster-shells, which together, if they say true, cures the colic, removes melancholy, kills worms, purges the maw, preserves the teeth, prevents hunger and stupefies the sense, which last virtue occasions the Indian women to chew it when they go to burning with their dead husbands.[24]

Mount Deli.
Mount Deli is 12 degrees latitude in 55 degrees 30 minutes longitude, variation 13 degrees, a place as eminent in hills as any other part we saw upon the coast of India, and limits the two rich and populous kingdoms of Deccan and Malabar. It gave this resemblance as we rode by it:

Mount Elly [illustration not shown]

---

[23] Pineapple. There is a long and interesting entry about how it came into Asia, where it existed long before coming to Europe from America, in *HJ* 25–28.

[24] This description is largely correct. There are many different species of areca palms, and betel is of the same family. There are varying accounts as to whether this was the narcotic used in *suttee* or *sati*, the practice of self-immolation by Hindu widows. Betel-nut is chewed today in civilisations from Malaysia to the Solomon Islands; however, it is now known to be a factor in oral cancers and its use is not as widespread as it was in Herbert's day.

An unhappy accident happened us here before we weighed anchor, for on the five and twentieth day descrying at the point of the bay a junk of seventy tons fraught with merchandise and bound for *Acheen* we could likewise perceive a Malabar pirate skulk near this junk, which he doubted not to board, being off at sea and past our help, as accordingly fell out, for being under sail the man-of-war gave her chase, so as the junk, perceiving the danger, chose rather to put herself under our protection than hazard the rapine of that frigate. But her condition (with grief I speak it) was little better, for the *Jonas* boarding her with a barge towed her to our admiral, where after short consultation she was adjudged prize. For my part I could not reach the offence, but this I could, that she had a cargo of cotton, opium, onions and probably somewhat under the cotton was most value, which was her crime, it seems. But how the prize was distributed concerns not me to inquire; I was a passenger, but no merchant nor informer. The seamen, it appeared, were to make what advantage they could unto themselves, for they first gave the Indians that were aboard a churlish welcome, by which they perceived they intended to make them slaves and sell them to the Javans, who usually give fifty ryals[25] for every slave, which rather then suffer threescore of those poor wretches threw themselves desperately into the sea, choosing rather to expose their carcases to the waves then the mercy of our men, if I may so call it, which seemed sport to some there but not so to me, who had compassion, nor could I be informed what provocation had been given our men to make such a proceeding. The canoes from shore showed them more mercy for they saved some of them, but those our boats took up resented our dealing so passionately as they seemed more willing to be drowned.

That night we had terrible weather, much rain mixed with thunder and lightning; this stormy weather is usual here when the sun is nearest and makes their summer, for then upon this Indian coast they have the greatest sign of winter, from the summer solstice to the autumnal equinox continuing wind and rain, which makes it exceedingly boisterous and unsafe to travel. These extraodinary rains are without doubt the causes of the yearly overflowing of Nilus, seeing that like weather at the same season is in the Ethiopian mountains. Howbeit, those months of June, July and August, albeit they may be stormy in India, are the fairest months of the year and calmest weather in the Mediterranean and those countries that are about that climate, but I looked upon it then as a sign of God's displeasure.

Coast of Malabar.

Thence we sailed due south and that evening passed by Cannanore, Montingue, Honwar and Batkul, which some repute part of Canara or Deccan, and then by Mangalore, *Mandagara* of old, in which, as the Jesuits report, were seventy

---

[25] An English coin originally worth about 10s., but by 1616 it was worth 16s. 6d. Cf. above, 000.

thousand Christians, Calicut, called *Camanes*; Cochin, *Colchin* in Ptolemy and the bay *Sinus Colchicus*, Cranganore, Coullam, and *Bryn John*[26] as far as Cape Comorin,[27] the utmost promontary, in seven degrees and a half north, variation 14 degrees, a cape well-known of old, for it is by Ptolemy called *Cory*, by Strabo *Conontancina*, by Pliny *Calasea* and *Comar* by Arabians, but by other cosmographers *Colaicum*, *Calligicum* and *Calingois*, where the *Mavo-Calingi* are by Pliny seated. Howbeit, at this day by the inhabitants 'tis called *Tuttan-Cory*,[28] where, ere we pass further, a little concerning the custom, habit and superstition of the Malabars, with such as mix among them, this serving for caution: "To observe the mode is safe; by moving much / Religious faith oft gets a doubtful touch."

Malabar is at this day a great and famous part of India, stretching along from Batkul, a port under 14 degrees, to Cape Comorin, which is about 7 degrees north from the Equinoctial, about four hundred miles in length but in breadth nowhere above a hundred, so populous that the Samorin of Calicut[29] is able upon occasion to take the field with 200,000 men to oppose the Narsingan, the

---

[26] Canara is a name "that has long been given to that part of of the West coast which lies below the Ghats from Mt. Dely [*sic*] northward to the Goa territory" (*HJ* 153). Cannanor, modern Kannur, is a city bordered by the Western Ghats. The Portuguese built a fort there in 1505. For details of the town, see Singh, *India*, 959–62. Montingue is a small port town near Cannanore; Herbert seems to be using the French form from Pyrard de Laval (see below), who visited it in 1601. Honwar [*Onor*] was the site of Fort Santa Caterina, erected by the Portuguese in 1568. Batkul or Bhaktal [*Batticala*], which means "round town," was established by the Portuguese in 1514. By 1542 it had declined in importance because of the rise of Goa; however, the English established a factory there in the seventeenth century. *Hobson-Jobson* gives its location as "just S. of Pigeon Island and Hog Island" (71) and Della Valle mentions it (*Travels* 2: 390). Cranganore is one of the oldest royal cities in Malabar. The Portuguese established themselves there in 1523 and built a fort. Ramusio and Barbosa mention it. Coullam or Coulao, also known as Quilon or Desinganadra and now called Kollam [*Cowlam*], was the location of the Portuguese fort of Sao Tomé, established in 1518. Herbert describes it in more detail below. Singh calls it "the southern gateway to the backwaters of Kerala" (*India*, 923). However, it had been a trading-port of significance since Phoenician times and was visited by Marco Polo in 1275. Bryn John is another example of Herbert trying to make everything Welsh; it is Brinjaon or Vilinjam, near Trivandrum (Foster, *Herbert*, 334).

[27] Pliny calls it *Coliacus* (*Natural History* 6. 380), not *Calasea*.

[28] Foster states that this is "a confusion with the town of Tuticorin" (*Herbert*, 334).

[29] The Samorin, also spelled Zamorin, or more accurately Sarmoothin, was the Hindu ruler of Calicut and its immediate area, effectively the whole of northern Malabar. The title means "Lord of the Sea." In 1498 Manivikraman Raja, then the Samorin, received Vasco da Gama; Camoens, rather more complimentary than Herbert, described him as "the mighty emperor," whose "expression was that / Of a venerable and prosperous lord; / His robe was a cloth of gold, his diadem / Studded with every kind of precious gem" (*Lusiads* 5. 57).

Deccan or Golcondan³⁰ kings his powerful neighbours.³¹ His country is most of the year verdant, and abounding with cattle, corn, fruit, cotton, silkworms, pepper, ginger, tamarind, cassia, cardamom, rice, myrobalanes, ananas, pawpaws, melons, dates, cocos and other fruits, and boasts also in several defensive towns and harbours as Coullam, Cochin,³² Calicut, Mangalore etc. And to say truth, the ocean itself forty leagues into the sea is all along the Indian shore so anchorable and so secure that the roads it affords are comparable to harbours in some other places, but for the better understanding of such part of the East Indies as is on this side Ganges this small map will serve to direct the eye to the most remarkable places, especially such as I shall have occasion to speak of.

Map of India [illustration shown on p. 750]

The Samorin.

And first of Malabar. It is a well-known region upon the western part of that great continent and sub-divided into sundry petty toparchies which are subordinate to the great Samorin, a naked negro but not a little puffed-up by being the principal brahman and no less tyrannical then proud, and not so much by provocation as wicked practice, which the people are so used to that they are the less sensible of that bondage and suffering.

---

³⁰ Golconda, which is located west of Hyderabad, was the capital city of the Qutb Shahs (c. 1364–1512) and later one of the five Muslim states making up the Deccan Sultanate. It finally fell to Aurangzeb and became part of the Mughal Empire (1687). The town is now ruined. Golconda was known for its diamonds. Portuguese, Dutch, and English all at one time established themselves there. Herbert probably knew William Methold's *Relation of the Kingdom of Golconda*, printed by Purchas.

³¹ Narsinga was a name for Vijayanagar, which Empire of that name controlled most of south India from about 1366–1565, at which time its armies were defeated by a Muslim alliance. The Empire was at its most powerful at the end of the fifteenth century. Camoens, writing in 1572 when the Empire was rapidly disappearing, called it "the powerful kingdom of Narsinga / Richer in gems and gold than in soldiers" (*Lusiads* 7. 21).

³² Cochin, modern Kochi, was first invested by the Portuguese under Alvarez Cabral, and contains the oldest Christian church in India, built by the Franciscans who came with him in 1503. A synagogue first built in 1568 but destroyed by the Portuguese was rebuilt by the Dutch after they captured Kochi in 1663 (Singh, *India* 939). Ralph Fitch was there in 1589, attempting to get a ship back to England (Foster, *England's Quest*, 104). Camoens writes "In Cochin you will see Pacheco Pereira, / That matchless hero, prove himself; / No poet ever praised a victory / So deserving of eternal glory" (*Lusiads* 2. 52). Duarte Pacheco Pereira was the conqueror of the Malabar coast.

Image published with permission of ProQuest. Further reproduction is prohibited without permission.

Datura. Nairs' pride.

The Nairs[33] are his magnates; they exercise no less authority over their inferiors then the Samorin doth over them, being freely tolerated an arbitrary liberty, life excepted, and withal are so extremely libidinous as no part of the world affords a more obscene generation, their beastly appetite not so much provoked by the heat as by the art and diet they invent towards provocation. Amongst others they

---

[33] The Nairs [*Nayroes*] were the caste of rulers in Malabar. For details of their customs, see Logan, *Malabar* 1: 131.

have the *datura*[34] in special request, both for that it contributes towards the accomplishing of their corrupt ends and with that security and mode as heightens their recreation. It is an herb or drug, which being infused or otherwise prepared and taken has a marvellous force, for it is not so much of a soporiferous quality to procure sleep as to stupefy and infatuate the intellect, since the patient or rather abused party sometimes appears merry as if a tarantula had infected him, and hath his eyes open, but sees no otherwise then if a *gutta serena*[35] or heated steel had deprived the optic, so as during the operation the Nair many times makes that his opportunity to visit and act his amours, whiles the goodman by that delusive spell is rendered a ridiculous spectator and seeming an assentor to their *méchanteries*.[36] I confess I never saw it practiced, but is related by Linschoten and other such as may be credited.

Maffei, in his belief that these Nairs are of the caste of *kshatriyas*, one of the descendants of Purusha and Parvati, in the foregoing more fully-mentioned, is not amiss, or in the report that they are generally proud and lazy, usually go armed and will not abate one jot of the common ornement of those oriental parts, which is to beautify or rather load their arms and necks with silver bracelets, ropes of pearl and other effeminate pieces of bravery, and so stately that they expect more then ordinary respect, as appears in passing through a crowd, only by striking his sword upon his target makes that voice serve both to express his dignity and to obtain a speedy and clear passage. Thévet, Varthema and Paulus Venetus go further, in saying that an inferior person dare not look them in the face or appear within fifty paces. But this is more certain, that as the sword awes the indefensive villager, so custom has enslaved them, and in such sort that in peace the common people seem dastardly but in war are found spirited, nor would one think otherwise when he takes the prospect of their visage and limbs, which express both ingenuity and strength sufficient.

Of colour they are rather black then olivaster; their hair crisps but grows longer then the Africans, and albeit they wear their hair, yet conform they to the mode of shashes, for about their temples they wreath a curious sort of linen sometimes wrought with silk and gold. Their waist is circled with a piece of calico, but from the thigh downward and from their middle upward are naked. The vulgar wear about their waist a parti-coloured plaid and pink their skin; the women veil themselves like other Indians. Their greatest pride is expressed in adorning their ears and noses, supposing them most courtly who delacerate their

---

[34] Datura [*deutra*] or *dhattura* (Sanskrit) is "*datura stramonium*, or thorn-apple" (*HJ* 208). Its connection with sexual peccadilloes seems to have been well-known; Samuel Butler speaks in *Hudibras* (1676) of "lechers and their punks with dewtry" who "Commit fantastical advowtry" (3. 1; cited in *HJ* 209), a novel use of half-rhyme.

[35] Loss of sight which could not be explained; it is now known as amaurosis. "So thick a 'drop serene,'" wrote Milton, "hath quenched these orbs" (*Paradise Lost* 3. 25).

[36] Wicked tricks.

ears widest, which they effect by many ponderous baubles which they hang there, and ring their snouts with jewels of silver, brass or ivory; their arms and legs also are richly-chained.

Concerning their marriages: formerly it was the custom that the brahmin had the first night's company with the bride, supposing the ground of better value by that holy seed, as they call it, a practice now wholly abrogated, and, which was no less rare, the Samorin to make sure work used to confer his command upon his sister's issue, assured, it seems, that she was of his blood and they of his by consequence.

The men are more addicted to arms then arts. The Portugals, at their first entrenching on their shore, thought them a very simple sort of people because unlearned and easy to overcome because most were naked, but both deceived them, for Nature instructed them in their own defence, and long contest with the Portugals taught them experience, so as in short time they learned how to use their bow and arrow, darts and targets well, and of late years have attained the art of making hand-grenados and other fireworks, wherein they are pregnant and of which they have such store that they proffered us as much and of what sorts we would for money. Their country abounds with minerals and stones of price, and no part is without plenty of fruit and other provision, howbeit the land, especially near the seashore, we could perceive was woody and mountainous.

Most of the people in their diet abstain from flesh, wine and strong water, contenting themselves with milk, rice, sugar, herbs and fruits of several sorts and spices, for they are of the banian persuasion, who have a detestation against any that for preservation of their own will take away the life of another. Ovid, 15 *Metamorphoses* has this in their apology:

> To shed the blood of man
> How wickedly is he prepared? Who can
> Asunder cut the throat of calves and hears
> The bellowing breeder with relentless ears,
> Or silly kids, which like poor infants cry,
> Stick with his knife, or his voracity
> Feed with the fowl he feed? Oh, to what ill
> Are they not prone, who are so prone to kill?[37]

Calicut.

Passing from thence, we came afore Calicut, ten leagues from that place where our men took the prize aforementioned, thought by some to be that town which Ptolemy calls *Canthapis*, a city in 23 degrees, an error broached by Niger and Bertius. Above a thousand years ago it was called *Callicaris*, then of some note but not so well-known as now, and had increased her fame by more trade had

---

[37] Ovid, *Metamorphoses* 15.463–468.

she prospered better against the continued differences it had with the Portugal, who when they could not conquer by force, as Seleucus did Babylon ruined her by policy, for they transferred their mart and staple to other towns, by which removal in small time this city became poor and desolate. It declines from the Equator towards the North Pole eleven degrees, and from its standing in the burning zone must needs be at some time of the year sulphurous. The earth is but meanly fruitful in grass; nevertheless, her gardens by industry and help of some brooks are most part of the year verdant and redundant in variety of fruits and flowers. The city of itself is large, but of small elegancy in building, for the houses are low, thick and dark, and the streets narrow. The harbour is a pretty way distant from the town and but indifferent to anchor in, yet shows the remains of two strong forts which were raised about the year 1515 by the Portuguese, in a sort demolished since by the Malabar. The Samorin in this place has his usual abiding, a Prince of great power and awe and not more black in colour then treacherous in disposition.

Many deformed pagodas are here worshipped, hacving this ordinary evasion, that they adore not idols but the demons they represent, most of which at one time or another have been defaced and destroyed by the Portugal. The chapel where the grand cacodemon[38] used to sit was uncovered and about three yards high; the wooden entrance was engraven with hideous shapes. Within, their beloved Priapus was enthroned upon a mount, *oculis mirabile monstrum*,[39] for upon his head he wore a diadem whence issued four great ram's horns such as Jupiter Ammon[40] in memory of the ram that conducted Bacchus and his female army through those deserts was represented, and being distressed for want of water it had given, upon his prayer to Jupiter, by a stroke of the ram's foot upon a rock, and if not that, typing out some other mystery hitherto concealed. His eyes were small and squint, his mouth large and opening like a portcullis, from whence branched four great tusks, but his nose was flat, his beard spread like the rays of the sun. His hands resembled the claws of a vulture, his thighs and legs were strong and hairy, feet and tail most like that of a monkey, which put together rendered the devil not unlike himself, wickedly deformed, and the men beyond measure gross idolators.

Other temples they had, stuffed with other pagods, ugly all yet differing as to invention, for some of them were painted black, others red, some devouring

---

[38] King James I had written in his *Daemonologie* (1597) that "we reade that in *Calicute*, [the Devil] appearing in forme of a *Goate*-bucke, hath publiclie that un-honest homage done unto him, by everie one of the people" (*Daemonologie* [New York: General Books, 2008], 29).

[39] "A monster wonderful to the eyes" (Virgil, *Aeneid* 8. 81).

[40] Jupiter Ammon, a Roman version of Zeus Ammon, himself a Greek version of an Egyptian god, was created by the Romans after they conquered Egypt. There is, of course, no connection with Hinduism or Buddhism.

fowls and usually such as were in Hell were white ones. These are of the old
stamp, for they seem to threaten or otherwise to express satisfaction in men's
offerings, but what they could not do their *chemarims*[41] effected, for each morn
the priest, a yogi,[42] perfumes and washes them; it seems the Devil ever leaves
a filthy smell behind, being his manner of benediction. Every new moon their
custom was to sacrifice a live cock, the symbol of lust and courage, which they
found themselves predominating. At this ceremony the priest was pontifically-
attired in lawn, armed with a sharp silver knife, his arms and legs garnished after
the morisco mode with bells or round silver plates which made a jingling, and
after he had sacrificed the yielding cock and filled his hands with rice, goes retrograde, not daring to look upon any other object save his idol, till being come
near an Acherontic[43] lake, suddenly he turns about and embowels his offering,
after which he advances his hands sometimes above his head and so returns,
supposing that his holocaust was accepted. The Samorin used not to eat it till it
were first offered and so acknowledged as food sent him from his demon; what
he leaves is not given to the poor, for it is the crows' pittance, and good reason
too — they think them his servitors. The people to this day, as they suppose, retain some incommendable customs, for they exchange their wives, nor seem the
women displeased at it, polygamy is so sufferable, but in this they differ from
other libidinous lawgivers; as the men have many wives, so one woman here is
allowed many husbands and the issue bequeathed as the nominates. The old custom of the world is here retained in the sedge and palmetto leaves they use for
paper, the pen being then a file of iron, but now a hardened piece of wood cut
sharp. Thence we passed by.

Kollam

Kollam,[44] a town and province called *Sopatpa* in Arrian and *Colay* in Ptolemy,
who places it in 13 degrees, but we found it in 9 degrees north, included in the
Travancorean[45] kingdom. Once it obeyed the Narsingan monarch and once the
Malabar, but at this day neither. About two hundred years ago the town was rich

---

[41] A Hebrew word which means "people dressed in black." It was a term used to denote priests of idolatrous religions.

[42] Here, *yogi* [*jogue*] means a Hindu priest who is an ascetic, and probably also practices yoga.

[43] Hellish; the word is derived from Acheron, a river in Hades.

[44] Kollam [*Coullam*], also known as Quilon and Culão, was the location of the Portuguese fort of São Tomé, established in 1518. Singh calls it "the southern gateway to the
backwaters of Kerala" (*India*, 923); however, it had been a trading-port of significance
since Phoenician times and was visited by Marco Polo in 1275 (*Travels*, 287–88).

[45] Travancore (Thiruvithamkoor) was a state whose territory covered most of the
southern part of Kerala and included part of modern Tamil Nadu. Its capital was Trivandrum. From 1180 to 1730 it was ruled by the Venad Dynasty of rajahs.

and great and populous, traded to by many Indians, enlarged by the Samorin and able to number a hundred thousand inhabitants, of such repute it then was for situation, trade and fidelity of the Coullamites. But now, the period of her excellency is outrun, for Calicut first and then Goa have not only monopolised but attracted the trade of this as well as other places.

Indian Christians.

Now albeit I have mentioned the banians in sundry places as I meet with them, here also along this coast they swarm in multitudes, sucking in the sweetness of gain by an immeasurable thirst and industry, but it is ravished from them by drones, the Moors and gentiles lording it over them. Alas, the banian is no swaggerer, no roisterer; he abhors domineering and fighting, yea, suffers himself to be fleeced by any man rather then resist or shed blood by breach of peace or making the least opposition. They love no tumult, no innovation, are content to submit rather then govern, and wish all were of their mind, that is to say morally honest, courteous in behaviour, temperate in passion, decent in apparel, abstemious in diet, industrious in their life, charitable to the needy and so innocent as not to take away the life of the filthiest vermin, and no marvel, seeing that if they should destroy any living thing, thereby they might dislodge their friends of a peaceful mansion or devour the souls of such as were dearest to them, for, as I have elsewhere noted, they verily credit the transanimation or passage of souls into beasts, a persuasion how strange soever it be to us, was not so of old to our countrymen the Druids, who not only believed the immortality of the souls of men but after separation from the body that they passed from one man into another. Ovid seems to allude unto it: "Let's home, and in brute beasts our bodies hide, / Where happily our parents may abide, / Our brothers or some by alliance tied, / One man or other sure!"[46]

But the country is not wholly overspread with these gentiles, for amongst them here and there are scattered Christians, and the Jesuits report that *Anno Dom.* 1554 'twixt Kollam and this cape were then about twenty villas of Saint Thomas Christians. More certain it is there ancestors were converted by Saint Thomas the Apostle, for both here and most other parts of the habitable world the apostles without doubt divulged the glad tidings of salvation as aforetold by the prophet David, Psalm 19: "Their sound is gone into all lands, and their words unto the ends of the world." Mantuan, also, gives this attestation:

As when the flood o'erspread, old careful Noë
His sons dispersed throughout the world to show
The law of God and sacred rites to pay;
So when Our Saviour would no longer stay

---

[46] Ovid, *Metamorphoses* 15. 458–461.

On earth, a mission of his scholars he
To th' utmost bounds of th' earth with charter free
Doth make, t' instruct the world both how to pray
And to appease God's wrath with sacred lay.

And accordingly, history abundantly acquaints us that in both the Asias the Gospel was throughly-preached, but for their ingratitude removed, and through the subtlety of Satan that carnal law of Mohammed hath since infected these parts, so as it hath spread itself almost through all the oriental islands and continent, notwithstanding which Christ has his flock, which though scattered, in due time will be gathered, for in Persia are many thousand and in India a no less multitude; nevertheless, compared with other idolators, but a handful, which must not discourage, seeing 'tis better go to Heaven alone then to Hell with a multitude. Arnobius of old could say *"Nationibus cunctis nos sumus Christiani,"*[47] and we find in many chiefly maritime towns of India that name of late years has been honoured, and that in Meliapore, Narsinga, Kollam, Carcara, Coorg, Beypore, Tannore, Bhatkal, Honawar, Cranganore, Goa and other places Christianity is owned, yea, in many of the Indian isles some are found.[48] And one reason is for that among the Mohammedans liberty of conscience is allowed, agreeable to a sura in the Alcoran which declares that none are to be dissuaded from the religion they sucked from their cradle, which gains them peaceful habitations and inclines them to live without disturbing the public.

Now, these Indian Christians have sundry ceremonies and forms of long time practiced amongst themselves and differing from those the Papacy use or the Reformed Churches of Europe. Their churches are low and poorly-furnished, yet neat they are and sweetly-kept, matted, without painted images which the Greek churches abound with. They assemble cheerfully, and at their entering shut their eyes the better to contemplate the exercise they come about with their own unworthiness; kneeling, they look towards the altar near which the priest is seated. Him they salute with humble reverence, who returns his blessing by the uplifting of his hands and eyes and at a set hour begins prayers, seldom exceeding two hours in the whole exercise. First, a brief confession is made, not unlike that in our liturgy, and assent to in an unanim amen. After that follows an ex-

---

[47] "We Christians exist in all nations" (Arnobius, *Adversus Gentes* 1. 16, PL 5. 738; *Christiani* does not appear in the original).

[48] Meliapore, or Sao Tomé de Meliapur, where it was claimed St. Thomas was buried (see below), was originally a Portuguese settlement; a church was built in 1523 and a colony started. By 1544 the Jesuits had arrived, and in 1614 a fort was built. By 1635 the town had its own Bishop. Today it is a suburb of Madras. Coorg [*Curigan*] is at the southern end of the Western Ghats; it remained an independent kingdom until 1834. Tannore or Tannur is a coastal town 20 miles south of Calicut whose ruler was subject to the Samorin. Beypore [*Bipur*]was colonised by Portugal in 1531. Honawar is a town in Goa. For further details, see P. J. Podipara, *The Thomas Christians* (London: Longman, 1970).

position of some part of scripture during which their attention, looks and silence is commendable. They sing a hymn and at parting out of the church resalute the minister, who ceases not to elevate his hands till all the people be departed. At home they usually read a chapter in either testament, both which they suppose they have incorrupt after the originals, translated for them by Saint Thomas the Patron of the Orient. The Chaldee also is not unknown, but few save the clergy understand what is writ in any other then their mother-tongue, for their schools are few and only teaches them to read, being without the academies or instructors in philosophy or like learning. Every first Sunday in the month the priest reads a homily, writ, as they say, by the Apostle or some of his disciples. They baptise commonly at the fortieth day if the parents desire it not sooner; they sign the forehead with the cross and then wash all over with water. The Lord's Supper they administer in both kinds and communicants receive it kneeling. They observe two days' preparation, during which they eat no flesh, revel not nor accompany with women, and in the church, if need be, make their confession. The clergy marry but once, the laity twice, and widows, if they marry before the year be expired, are ill-reported of. None, save in case of adultery, have licence to divorce. In sickness the priest is usually sent for, both to pray and give the Eucharist if desired, which done, they take a long farewell of wife, children and others and so rid themselves of worldly distractions which too oft hinder that last great work, so as by a contemplation of the joys of Heaven they strive to mitigate the grim aspect of approaching death. Being dead, the survivors rather joy then mourn, and having first washed the corpse they afterwards wrap it in clean linen, friends accompany him to the grave and place the body with the head west, either in respect of Jerusalem or the old local place of Paradise. Five days after they visit the family. Feast and fast as we accustom; their Lent begins in the spring and is observed forty days. Their year is the soligenian.[49] Our three chief festivals they celebrate; the first of July they also commemorate the martyrdom of Saint Thomas. They have many protomists, the chief of which used to reside at a house built upon a mountain nine miles from Cranganore, but since the Portugals have planted India shave their heads. Laics pay their *decima*,[50] affect justice, profess truth, practice humility and believe no Purgatory.[51]

---

[49] Also known as the Tropical or Astronomical Year; it is the time which the earth takes to go round the sun from one vernal equinox to the next, which is 365 days.

[50] The ten percent tithe.

[51] Briefly, the St. Thomas Christians belonged to the Syro-Malabar Catholic Church and were Chaldean Christians, "the convenient, if not very appropriate, title applied to the descendants of the ancient Nestorian Churches now in communion with the see of Rome" (*Oxford Dictionary of the Christian Church* 2nd ed., 263). The Portuguese arrived in 1498 and were originally friendly with these people, but later started to make an attempt to Latinise them, and in 1599 they renounced their Nestorianism, accepted a Portuguese-appointed bishop, and recognised Papal authority. By the time Herbert was there,

Ceylon.

May 7 we had eight degrees; ere sunset we were close by the high mountains called Bryn John, i.e. the Mount of John, a Cambrian word, but when or by whom imposed is past my finding. Next day we had 7 degrees 30 minutes, variation 14 degrees, then which place, that famous promontary of East India called Cape Comorin (*Tamus* by Mela) extands no further south towards the Equator. The next we sailed by the Maldive Isles memorised by Pyrard de Laval,[52] who reports that the King styles himself Emperor of thirteen provinces and twelve thousand islands.[53] Jerome de Santo Stefano[54] makes them eight thousand, the most and least of any king in the world, the Spaniard excepted, is owner of. Near these are the isles of Candu, Nicobar[55] and Sombrero, in view of Ceylon and Sumatra; all of them abound with date-trees or palms, of old celebrated that both spiritual and temporal victors have it in their triumphs. The poet also

---

however, there were problems between the Latinists and the Chaldeans, and by 1653 there was a schism. The story that St. Thomas was actually in India may be apocryphal; in fact, there is an alternative explanation concerning one Mar Thomas Cana, a Syrian merchant who was said to have landed in Cranganore during the reign of King Cheruman Perumal of Malabar (see below), with dates variously being given as c. 345 and 800 C. E.! The story of St. Thomas converting the ruler of Meliapore was related to Antonio Gouvéa, but its veracity has been questioned. See Ved Prakash, "The Myth of St. Thomas and the Mylapore Shiva Temple," *Ishwari Sharan Archives*, www.hamsa.org

[52] François Pyrard de Laval (1570–1621) was shipwrecked on the Maldive Islands, taken prisoner and held captive there for five years (1602–1607). In spite of bad treatment he not only learned the Divehi language of Malé Island, where he was confined, but made a study of Maldivian culture and history, which he published as *Discours du voyage des françois aux Indes Orientales* (1611). This was expanded (1619) with the help of Pierre Bergeron, whose method consisted of getting Pyrard drunk on several occasions, which induced him to talk about his travels; Bergeron then compared the accounts and if they coincided enough took them as truth (Alam and Subrahmanyam, *Travels*, 337). Albert Gray and H. F. Bell made a translation as *Voyage of François Pyrard of Laval to the East Indies, the Maldives, the Moluccas and Brazil* (London: Hakluyt Society, 1887).

[53] The number varies. According to Christopher Buyers, Sultan Ibrahim III (1585–1607), the ruler of the Maldives when Pyrard de Laval was there, styled himself "Lord of the Thousand Islands." However, many Maldivian sultans used "Lord of Twelve Thousand Islands" as their title.

[54] Girolamo di Santo Stefano, an Italian merchant, travelled to India and described his experiences in a letter written in 1499, which was published by Ramusio. In addition to a short visit to the Maldives, he spent a total of one day in Ceylon! The dates of his birth and death are not known.

[55] The Nicobar Islands are in the Bay of Bengal 1000 km. from the east coast of India. Singh notes that they, together with the Andaman Islands, "comprise 572 tropical islands (of which 36 are inhabited) with unique fauna, lush forests, white sandy beaches and exquisite coral" (*India*, 1037). Sir James Lancaster was there in 1592 (Foster, *England's Quest*, 141–42).

notes it in saying "The noble palm which high doth rise / Equals great men with destinies."

Thence our course was by Ceylon, one of those five isles which Ptolemy calls *Barussae*, albeit Cluverius thinks the Philippines to be them, not unown unto the ancients if that which Ptolemy called *Panigarensis* and since then by Arabian authors *Sisuara*, *Tenarisis*, *Nanigeris* and *Sarandib*, but at this day 'tis called *Chingal* by the inhabitants, who are a very comely people having good features and nothing like the Africans save in colour; besides, they are ingenious and excel in the mechanic arts. The better sort wear silks, but the vulgar are naked from the waist upwards. Now, this place must needs be hot, seeing 'tis so near the Equinoctial, severed from the Asiatic continent by a sea which is not forty leagues over, limited from eight to eleven degrees north latitude. The length is about seventy leagues, breadth forty and circuit two hundred and fifty or thereabout, famoused through some old erroneous conjectures that this was Paradise and that Solomon had hence his gold of Ophir. But in regard all or most fix the ruins of the one in Mesopotamia and the other in Malacca or thereabouts, that tradition is of little credit, but that Malik Perumal, king of this island, was one of those Magi, wise men or kings premonished by that prophecy of Balaam the Edomite[56] that as to a king, priest and prophet offered gold, frankincense and myrrh unto Our Blessed Saviour, foretold also by the Persian Sibyl and by a new star as by the finger of God miraculously-direrted, is the tradition of this place, and also that at his return he made known the mystery of God's Incarnation for man's redemption and by his laborious teaching many proselytes, which some to this very day maintain for truth.[57] But more certain it is that the seeds of Christian knowledge have there been sown whence sprung professors, though the greatest part

---

[56] For Balaam the Edomite, see Numbers 22–24.

[57] The source for this story may have been the Portuguese historian João de Barros (1496–1570), who travelled to Africa (1522–1523) and whose *Decadas de Asia* (1552; 1553; 1563; 1615), using Arab and Asian sources, was the most comprehensive account of the Portuguese enterprise in the Indies. The Magi story appears in the third *Decad* (1563), where the name of the king of "Ceilan" is given as "Primal" or Perumal. K. T. Rajasingham quotes Barros as saying that "a king of the island of Ceilan, called Primal, went in a ship . . . to join other kings who were going to adore the Lord at Bethlehem" (n.p.n.). We may identify this king with Cheruman Perumal, who was a semi-legendary king of Malabar or Rajah of Cranganore; the problem is that there were several kings with this name, and there is no firm proof that this one even existed. The Chera Dynasty ruled the area from the 8th century B. C. E. to the 9th century C. E. However, Rajasingham further notes in his article that the reference may be due to confusion on Barros's part; he writes that when Giovanni di Marignolli (c. 1290-after 1357), the Papal legate to the Great Khan (1341) landed at "Columban" (Kollam) in 1344 he went to see a personage he described as the "Queen of Saba," which he called "Yalapanam," the name for ancient Jaffna in Ceylon. Marignolli also visited Java and Sumatra. If this was Barros's source, it accounts for the confusion. This is compounded by Herbert's reference later to "Candace"

are since turned apostates; howbeit, this is obvious in history, that Candace's[58] eunuch baptised by Philip preached Christ in many parts of Arabia and sundry isles thereabouts, and India also, as Socotra, this and Taprobane or Sumatra, if Dorotheus Bishop of Tyre,[59] who lived in the days of the great Constantine, had good authority for the reporting it.

In Claudius Caesar's time some of the natives of this island, having made some shift to cross over into Malabar, travelled through Persia unto Rome, where albeit they pretended some knowledge in astronomy and the sphere bewrayed their ignorance by admiring to observe the sun contrary to what it was seen to be at Ceylon; "*solem a laeva oriri mirantur*"[60] are the words of the historian, which by the Romans might equally be wondered at, seeing that those Indians, by being within the burning zone, have their shadows on both sides according as the sun makes his progress to either tropic. Nevertheless, probable it is what understanding these Ceylonians had was borrowed from the gymnosophists, who had their light from Zoroaster the most ancient and in his time the most excellent philosopher. He lived full five hundred years before the Trojan War, saith Suidas, and was the first that gave name to the Magi of Persia: "*Zoroaster, Perso-Medus sapiens apud eos qui in astronomia excelluerat, etiam qui primus dedit nomen eis Magis, qui civilia tractarunt. 4 libros scripsit de naturae, 5 de astroscopeia et unum de pretiosis lapidibus...*"[61] And Picus Mirandolus,[62] from Ficino, *De dogmatis Chaldaicae theologiae*: "*Tum Persarum, Graecorum et Chaldaeorum in illam divina et locupletissima*

(see below). For details, see K. T. Rajasingham, "Was one of the Magi a King from Lanka?" *The Bahamas Writer*, No. 3 (January 2002): n.p.n., www.bahamaswriter.com.

  [58] Candace is a corruption of the title *Kandaka* or *Kendaces* held by ruling queens of Meroë or Kush. For the story of Philip the Evangelist (not the apostle of that name) and the Ethiopian eunuch, see Acts 8:27–39. The *Kandaka* in the story may have been Queen Amanikhatashan, who reigned 62–85.

  [59] St. Dorotheus, Bishop of Tyre (c. 255–362), is known as the teacher of Eusebius and as the possible compiler of the *Acts of the Seventy Apostles*, which is venerated by the Eastern Orthodox church. Exiled by the Emperor Julian, the ancient bishop met his death by martyrdom shortly afterwards.

  [60] "They wondered at the sun rising on the left" (Pliny, *Natural History* 6. 24).

  [61] Zoroaster was a Perso-Median sage who excelled amongst them in astronomy, and who first gave them the name of Magi, as they treated public matters. He wrote four books about nature, five on astroscopy [observation of the stars, Ed.] and one on precious stones.

  [62] "He related divine and most eloquent things of the Persians, Greeks and Chaldaeans." Count Giovanni Pico della Mirandola (1463–1494), the youngest son of the Prince of Mirandola, was a leading exponent of Platonism. His best-known work is the *Oration on the Dignity of Mankind*, which appeared posthumously (1496) and for which he is now mostly remembered. He also wrote the *Disputationes adversum astrologium divinatricem*, in which he attacked astrology as a pseudo-science. His *Opera omnia* were published in 1498.

enarravit..." And albeit at Kashan I had occasion to speak more largely concerning these oriental philosophers, I shall here but add that testimony which Porphyry[63] gives concerning their definition and the nature of their learning: *"Apud Persas,"* quoth he, *"qui circa divina sunt sapientes eorumque cultores, Magi appellantur. Hoc enim propria dialecto eius regionis, Magus significat."* Howbeit, the honour of the first European discovery we owe to Lourenço, son of Almeida, who about the year 1500 first arrived here but did not alter the name from what the natives called it.

Their horrid idolatry.

At present it is overrun with stinking weeds of heathenism, for, as said of another place, "Here grow those heaps of errors, which we see,/ Of all uncleanness and idolatry." It is so great that scarce any village or mount without its inanimate pagod, their supposed deities or *mali genii* such as Lactantius and Prudentius[64] describe: *"Cum portis, domibus, thermis, stabulis soleatis assignare suos genios perque omnia membra urbis perque locos geniorum millia multa fingere,"* and we are to observe that *"genii locorum sunt daemones."*[65] Amongst others, which I mention only for the imposture, was that infamous Hanuman or ape's-tooth god[66] which was highly-esteemed and resoted to by millions of Indians till Constantine[67] a late

---

[63] "Amongst the Persians, those who are wise and reverent in divine things are called Magi, for this is what *Magus* means in the particular dialect of that country." Porphyry (c. 232–305) was a Neoplatonist philosopher, a disciple of Plotinus and the editor of his works. He also wrote a treatise on theurgic practices which survives in fragments, and his own works were edited by Marsilio Ficino. His most famous works are his attack on Christianity, the *Adversus Christianos*, which has been translated recently by R. M. Berchman (Leiden: Brill, 2005) and his commentary on Aristotle's *Categories*, also known by its Latin title the *Isagoge*, translated by J. Barnes (Oxford: Oxford University Press, 2003).

[64] Aurelius Clemens Prudentius (349–after 400) was the pre-eminent Christian Latin poet. His chief works are the *Hamartigenia*, which deals with the origins of sin and from which this quotation comes, and the polemical *Contra Symmachum*, in which he narrates the conflict between St. Ambrose and the distinguished Roman statesman Symmachus. His poems were edited by Daniel Heinsius (1667). See M. A. Malamud, *A Poetics of Transformation* (Ithaca: Cornell University Press, 1989; M. Mastrangelo, *The Roman Self in Late Antiquity* (Baltimore: Johns Hopkins University Press, 2007).

[65] "You are accustomed to assign spirits everywhere, to doors, houses, baths, stables and all the parts of the city, to pretend that there are many thousands of places of spirits" (Lactantius, *Institutiones.* 2.15, PL 6. 333; Prudentius, *Contra Symmachum* 2. 446–449).

[66] Hanuman [*Hanimant*], a monkey-god, is the chief adviser to the Monkey-King Sugriva in the *Ramayana*, and he helps Rama in his fight against evil.

[67] Dom Constantino de Bragança (1528–1575), a scion of the Portuguese royal family, was Viceroy of the Indies 1558–1561. He conquered Jaffna (1560) and built a fort on Mannar Island. Historians such as C. R. Boxer have numbered him amongst the most re-

Goan viceroy, landing five hundred men at Colombo first forcibly took away that apish idol and upon their proffering a ransom of three hundred thousand ducats burned it to ashes, notwithstanding which a crafty banian so well-forged another counterfeit as was believed by the yogis to be the same (willingly to be deluded, it seems) thereby exceedingly enriching himself and joying not a little in these simple Ceylonians.

Another was that not far from Mattacala,[68] conspicuous in its standing, concerning which the Sinhalese and yogis report that many years ago *Johna*[69] their king nourished a conceit that this *diabolo* was no better then a senseless idol, but lo, a yogi by the Devil's craft so wrought that upon a time when Johna entered he beheld, as he thought, the pagod breathe out fire, his eyes seeming to be coloured with rage and the scimitar in his hand wrathfully bent against him, at which the amazed king cries out for help, accuses his infidelity and, having satisfied for his error, ever after became a zealous idolater.[70] The place where this grand pagoda stood was enveloped with a cloud of arms for its defence, and not without good reason, seeing it was their belief that upon the fall of that idol the final ruin of the universe should immediately follow by fire or otherwise. Now, without any countenancing that imposture, that the world shall be consumed is credited, but not till he that made it shall please to order the dissolution. Lucretius hath that observation: "*Inque brevi spatio mutantur secla animantum*,"[71] and the like of another Roman poet: "The time shall come when sea, when land, when all / The heaven's vast moving regions burning shall / Consume, and to their ancient Chaos fall."[72] And albeit of the ancient heathens we may say they had some seeming devotion

---

ligiously fanatical of the Portuguese viceroys, a characteristic illustrated by this story. The tooth in question is actually that reputed to be the Buddha's, and Dom Costantino's seizure of it constituted "Christendom's first direct assault on Asia's oldest-established religion" (Allen, *Search*, 31). For more details see Charles Allen, *The Search for the Buddha: The Man who Discovered India's Lost Religion* (New York: Carroll and Graf, 2002), 31–33.

[68] Also known as Batecala or Batticaloa. It is in eastern Sri Lanka, 69 miles southeast of Trincomalee on an island. The Dutch came there in 1602 and built a fort. For further details, see Richard Plunkett and Brigitte Ellemor, *Sri Lanka* (Melbourne: Lonely Planet Publications, 2003), 263–64.

[69] 'Johna' may refer to King Dharmapala of Kotte, who reigned 1551–1597. In 1557 he converted to Christianity and took the name Dom João Dharmapala. He was the last ruler of his dynasty. If he is 'Johna,' however, Herbert has the story a little garbled.

[70] Herbert may be alluding to the *Soma dagoba* (pagod) at Sairuwawilla in the Kottisar district of Sri Lanka. For further details, see Charles Pridham, *An Historical, Political and Statistical Account of Ceylon and its Dependencies* (London: T. and W. Boone, 1889), 1: 327–28.

[71] Lucretius is here referring to "violent earthquakes" which will "in a brief space, dash the whole world to fragments" (*On the Nature of the Universe* 5. 174).

[72] Lucan, *Civil War* 1. 74–76.

drawn from the very dictates of Nature, like those mentioned in Romans 2:14[73] who had a law written in their hearts, so as it was a maxim there was not any who had some spark of civility to men and zeal to some one or other deity. That principle nevertheless now seems extinguished amongst the gentiles we meet with in these regions.

Colombo. Tradition of Adam and Eve.

Upon Colombo's high peak, a place dearly-bought by the Portugal, was showed and credited the footsteps of old Adam, born and buried here if we will believe them.[74] Here also they show a lake of salt-water upon a high hill, said to be no other but the tears afflicted Eve shed a hundred years together for the loss of her righteous son Abel, a cabbala[75] how strange soever it be Friar Odoric of Friuli not only believes but vehemently persuades others to give credit to it.

The soil is good, and abounds with sundry sorts of spices as pepper, ginger and the like, but in most plenty with cinnamon, which gave the occasion to Ptolemy and Strabo to call it *Cinnamonifera regio*. Cinnamon is a precious bark; the tree is straight and the branches are in no way ruinous but grow in comely order. It resembles the olive-tree in height but the leaves are more like the bay or orange. The blossoms are exactly white, the fruit globous, hard and dark-coloured. It is apparelled with a thick rind, which in summer, when it may best discover its virgin nakedness, 'tis disrobed of and by the churlish peasant cut in many pieces, and being hardened in the sun so gathered. I might here present you many other rareties this noble isle affords, as oranges, dates, cocos, ananas, plantains and mastic[76] (which Coryate erroneously believed grew nowhere but in Siam), elephants, buffalos, cows, sheep, hogs etc., smaragd, rubies, diamonds, ambergris[77] and the like, which gave the Danes a fair invitation for commerce unto this place, their ships usually riding near the port of Kandy,[78] and put together

---

[73] "For when the Gentiles, which have not the law, do by nature the things contained in the law, these, having not the law, are a law unto themselves."

[74] Herbert must be referring here to Adam's Peak or Sri Pada, "a beautiful and fascinating place . . . where Adam first set foot on earth after being cast out of heaven." Apparently the "footprint" is believed by some to be that of St. Thomas and by others as the sacred footprint of Buddha as he left for Paradise (Plunkett and Ellemor, *Sri Lanka*, 187). It is actually near the town of Mahiyangana, east of Kandy.

[75] Used here to denote esoteric discipline or knowledge.

[76] Mastic is a plant related to the pistachio which produces an aromatic gum.

[77] Ambergris is a secretion with a distinctive smell produced by sperm-whales.

[78] The Danish East India Company was given its charter in 1616 by Christian IV. In 1618 Roelant Crappé went ahead with one ship to reconnoitre, and landed in Ceylon that November; he was to stay there until 1636. The rest of the Danish fleet under Öve Gjedde (1594–1660) arrived in 1620 and set about making a treaty with Rajah Senarat of Kandy. By 1621 the Danes were established at Tranquebar (Tharangambadi) near Naga-

seemed so attractive to the victorious Lusitanian Almeida that in despite of her united heptarchy he landed *Ann. Dom.* 1506 and for Manuel his king exacted an annual tax of two hundred and fifty thousand pound weight of their best cinnamon, which Sousa began to load away the third year after. But the King, more rich then crafty, to show how little he regarded the loss of so much useless barks of trees and to set a better edge upon the appetite of the Portugal, one day he invited them to see him walk upon a terrace in an embroidered coat thick powdered with gold, smaragds, pearl and diamond, altogether darting out rays of wonderful lustre, to which albeit the sun wanted not to increase the splendour, yet as if that were not enough, five hundred flambeaux or torches were, as story says, put in flames to make this Prince seem a greater object of astonishment, but it rather was as a *corpo santo*, for forthwith Silveira,[79] judging the cost and labour well worth his pains, built a citadel there under pretence to aid them against the Malabar junks, but rather to be his jewel-keeper, for in short time he so pursued the King that he became a ravisher of what he had, and by a forced nakedness learned him a future better way of politic bravery.[80]

Garcia de Orta, physician to the Goan Viceroy, reports that the King used to be served in dishes of lodestones not only for the rarity but the medicinable virtue thereof, as having a power to discover poison and to continue youth. Store of pearl-oysters have been taken 'twixt Cape Comorin and Ceylon of good value, and here is no want of gold, but the King thinks not that so valuable as to be served in dishes of other material.

---

pattinam and by the time Herbert saw their ships they had built a factory at Masulipatam as well. For further details, see Asta Bredsdorff, *The Trials and Travels of William Leyel: An Account of the Danish East India Company in Tranquebar, 1639–48* (Copenhagen: Museum Tusculanum Press, 2009) or *Danish Rule in India: Serampore, Balasore District, Nicobar Islands, Tharangambadi, Danish East India Company, Danish India, Gondalpara* (New York: General Books, 2010).

[79] There are two brothers of this name. Eitor de Silveira (d. 1531) defeated the Gujerati forces at Choul (1529), went on to blockade Aden (Serjeant, *Portuguese*, 172), then conquer Tannah and Bassein. He was killed at the siege of Diu, after which the Portuguese forces had to retire for the time being. Antonio de Silveira, whom we have already met, sacked Surat (1530) and Daman (1531).

[80] Herbert refers here to Lourenço de Almeida's treaty with the King of Kotte, Parakramabahu VIII (1484–1508). The King offered the Portuguese cinnamon and elephants, and some time later allowed them to build a residence in Colombo. After a while frictions arose between the Portuguese and the Sinhalese. For details, see C. P. de Silva, "The Portuguese Impact on the Production and Trade in Sri Lanka Cinnamon in Asia in the Sixteenth and Seventeenth Centuries," *Indica, 26* (1989): 25–38.

Coromandel.

From Ceylon we hoist sail for some eminent ports and maritime parts of India, lorded by black but daring pagans. The Mughal has encircled within his diadem many of those noble kingdoms or provinces. The rest— the Deccan, the Samorin, Narsingan, Peguan, Siamite and others, but the chiefest isles neighbouring this we last landed at are Sumatra, the Java, Borneo, the Manellie, the Celebes, Moluccas, Bande, Amboyna, Philippine etc., which I shall briefly speak of, and in order thereunto, first of the coast of Coromandel (Ptolemy calls it *Catagardamna*), which stretches above three hundred leagues from Cape Comorin under eight degrees north towards the aestuarium of Ganges or the Argaric Gulf, which now we call the Gulf of Bengal, *Magnum Gangis ostium* in Ptolemy, as far as Chatgaon under 22 degrees north. Upon that coast are sundry towns of note, *viz.* Nagapattinam, Meliapore (the burial-place of Saint Thomas the Apostle of India and of Saint Bartholomew, say some, but mistaken in that tradition, seeing ecclesiastical story leaves him buried at Albanopolis in Armenia), Pulicat, Armagon, Narsinga, Masulipatam, Petapoli and sundry more, in some of which the English, in others the Dutch have factories.[81] Here Strabo places the Assacani, from which some from the congruity of name derive the Assassins, whose wicked tenets have rendered them in more then name not to be mentioned.[82]

Ganges.

Now concerning Ganges, amongst rivers it is second to none, for after a flux of three thousand miles, having increased her channel by fifty other rivers that run into her, which for above an hundred miles double the breadth that Euphrates bears at old Babylon and thrice its depth, it divides India in two, branches itself into several streams and has many noted towns built upon her banks, affording them earth and water as good as any, and by the banians held sacred, as Lucan, albeit mistaken in its course, takes notice: "Sacred Ganges only cross doth run / Of any river to the rising sun."[83] At length, under the same tropic with the River

---

[81] Nagapattinam [*Nagapatan*], which was colonised in the 1520s, had been a trading hub for centuries and from the eighth to fifteenth centuries a centre of Buddhism. The Franciscans and Jesuits came there in the 1540's. A fort was erected (1643) and the Dutch took the town over in 1654. Pulicat [*Polycat*] was the location of a Dutch factory from 1610, "which before long became the headquarters of the Dutch on the Coromandel Coast" (Foster, *England's Quest*, 209). Armagon [*Armagun*] in Golconda was the site of an English factory until 1640; Petapoli [*Bipilipitam*], one of the main port cities of Golconda, had a Dutch factory from 1606. Its modern name is Nizampatam.

[82] The Assacani lived in the Swat and Buner valleys; Arrian refers to them as Indians. They are certainly *not* the notorious Assassins (Hashashin), a breakaway Ismaili Muslim group, who from about 1020 settled in Iran, Iraq, Syria, and Lebanon, and whom Hulagu Khan practically eliminated in 1292.

[83] Lucan, *Civil War* 3. 230–232.

Indus, in five great mouths or *ostia*, of old called *Cambysum, Magnum, Camberi-cum, Pseudostomum* and *Antibolum*, it empties itself into the Bengalan Gulf, as I have a little before mentioned. The banians have the water of Ganges in that divine esteem that in deadly fits they covet to have their mouths wet with it, and imagine that the rock whence it first flows bears the figure or shape of a horned cow, a creature with them of a singular respect, albeit a fancy others are also taken with, as appears by the River Po, according as Virgil *l. 4 Georgics* mentions,[84] and as might be instanced of other places, agreeable to what the ancient poets feigned of the ocean, which from the noise it makes they resembled to a bull's head and called it *Tauriceps.*

Nagapattinam.

Nagapattinam, i.e. 'a town upon the River Naga,' has 12 degrees latitude north, odd minutes, is in a climate hot and unwholesome both in regard the wind and rains there are for some part of the year high and unseasonable. The town nevertheless has good water, fruits well-relished and no less nutritive, notwithstanding which the people are much-vexed with fevers, fluxes and other distempers. Blockish they be and unapt for study or exercise; heat indeed here predominates and probably debilitates their appetite and invites them too much to ease, the mother of luxury. A small, thin, but fine *shuddery* or veil of lawn they draw afore their secret parts; their head has a small wreath about it, the rest being exposed to view and all sorts of weather. They want no gold, stones of value or such things as the merchant covets, for but a few years since they prized them little better then we do trifles. Here any religion is tolerable, and Virgil's *"Omnigenumque deum monstra"*[85] seems translated hither, but the manner of their marriages is extraordinary, for many times the priest with a cow and the man and the woman go together to the waterside, where the brahmin first mutters a short prayer and then links their hands about the cow's tail, pours upon them all his hallowed oil and lastly forces the beast into the river, whereinto she goes willingly so far as till they be to the middle in water, neither returns she nor do they disunite till the waves advise them, when being on shore they untie and hold that mysterious tie forcible and sacred ever after. Mr. Fitch[86] the merchant in his travels through these parts makes the like observation.

---

[84] ". . . the Po, the bellowing bull / Whose charging forehead has two golden horns—/ No river has more violent force than this" (Virgil, *Georgics* 4. 371–373).

[85] "Monster forms of gods / of every race" (Virgil, *Aeneid* 8. 698–699).

[86] Ralph Fitch (c. 1550–1611) was an English merchant who travelled extensively in Asia from 1583–1591. He sailed to Tripoli and Aleppo en route to Baghdad and Hormuz, where he and his colleagues were arrested by the Portuguese as spies and sent on to Goa, where they were eventually set free and proceeded to Agra, where they met Akbar (1585). Fitch then carried on alone through India and then to Pegu, Burma, northern Thailand,

Women burn with their dead husbands.

The heathen are averse to law and also to morality, as if in a malignant sort they resisted the very liberty of Nature for their preservation, as Plutarch in *[The Life of] Alexander*: "*Et quod Natura remittit invida iure negant,*"[87] as also may be observed by Dandanis the Indian[88] expostulating with Alexander against Pythagoras, suitable to which the people upon this allow the banians' wives the liberty to burn with their dead husbands,[89] so that Death, having cut in two their union, the relict conceits herself[90] a loathed carcase, and resolving to make herself an

---

and Malacca (1588). He then journeyed back the way he had come, finnaly arriving home in 1591. Shortly afterwards he wrote his *Account of the Voyage of Ralph Fitch, Merchant of London, to the Indies*, which was included by both Purchas and Hakluyt in their collections. Michael Edwardes has written a good account of Fitch in his *Ralph Fitch — Elizabethan in the Indies* (Oxford: Oxford University Press, 1973).

[87] "What nature gives up they deny with envious law" (Plutarch, *Life of Alexander* 65).

[88] It is curious that Herbert uses the form *Dandanis* here, when both Plutarch and Strabo (7.111; 7.121), who recount the story (which Herbert has mentioned twice already) use *Mandanis*. However, Francis Bacon, whom Herbert has cited before, uses *Dandanis* in *The Advancement of Learning*. The older source for this version of the name is actually Palladius Helenopolitanus (c. 363–425) in a Greek work entitled (in Latin) *De Indicis gentibus et de Bragmanibus*, which was available to Herbert in its Latin form edited by Joachim Kammermeister (1569). A century later Edward Bysshe offered a Latin translation in England (1669).

[89] This is, of course, a description of *sati* (Anglicised to *suttee*), which was practiceed in Rajasthan, the Vijayanagar Empire, and the Gangetic Plain area. When the god Shiva was humiliated by Dakhsi, his daughter Sati (Dakshayani) immolated herself as a protest. *Sati* was voluntary from ancient times (except at some royal funerals), but apparently was enforced in later times. The Mughals found the practice horrifying, as Herbert notes later on; Akbar wanted it banned, but failed to act decisively enough and made exceptions. However, Aurangzeb actually enacted a law against it which officials tried to enforce (1663). The Portuguese had banned it in Goa as early as 1515, but the Danes allowed it to be performed at Serampore until the 19th century. From 1798 the British tried to abolish it, but it took more than a decade, and the editor recently read of a instance in a rural community in 2007. It is interesting to note that Herbert slightly changed his original description of *sati* in the 1638 edition, and kept the later version in subsequent revisions. Kate Teltscher thinks that in the 1634 edition Herbert overtly states "what is only implicit in most accounts: that sati is no more than womankind's just deserts . . . a particularly potent counter to the heroic image of the sati" (*India*, 53). He wrote in 1634 that sati was "a just revenge for their [wives'] former too-much abused liberty, grown so audaciously impudent that upon the least distaste nothing but the lives of their harmless husbands would satiate their lustful boldness" (191). In the later version the banians "allow" the women to choose to die, and a generalised personified "Death" (not the lust of the women) is the cause.

[90] Persuades herself [that she is]. . .

holocaust, robes her body with a transparent lawn, her arms, legs and thighs also fettered with chains expressing love, but her ears, nose and fingers are adorned with pearl and precious stones. With one hand she holds a nosegay of flowers, in the other a ball, both of which are emblems of Paradise. She is attended with a great number, some accompanying her for love, others for civility, but most for her encouragement and honour of the ceremony. The priest, all the way she goes, describes the joys she is to possess and the assurance she has to enjoy her husband speedily in Elysium. She returns a modest smile, trips on, chewing something in her mouth that intoxicates her brain, and upon sight of the flame seems transported with satisfaction. So soon as she sees the carcase of her husband laid upon a pile and the fire burn, like a mad lover she whirls about the pit, and having bid farewell to parents, children and friends willingly incorporates with the fire, which quickly makes them one in ashes. Music of sundry sorts and acclamations of spectators yell aloud at the same instant both for the greater honour of the obsequy and that the screeches of the poor wretch may not be heard, whereby others may be discouraged. It seems that the Roman poets, though at a great distance, had some prospect of it, by this funeral song they have warbled out in their memorial: "They strive to die and who best speed shall make, / They blush, grim Death so slowly t'overtake; / The conquerors burn, their breasts yield to the fire, / And to their husbands their burnt lips aspire."[91]

Now, albeit some women of this persuasion living under a Mohammedan prince being denied this liberty to burn their bodies with their husbands' corpse have been known of late years to make themselves away, yet others more wise and less valuing a place in the catalogue of those fiery zealots, do refuse to burn, but in such cases by way of ignominy they are commanded to shave their heads and to sequester themselves from company, which is a punishment. Howbeit, this custom of burning is much more ancient with men amongst the brahmins of those parts then with the other sex, for with the latter it came not in practice until several of their husbands were made away with by poison which their lascivious wives would frequently administer upon giving them distaste or other slight provocation, for prevention whereof this Draco's law was devised and enjoined the relict, which though in its institution seemed severe, was to deter from that wicked practice, but long custom hath made familiar and reputable. We find it so recorded in St. Jerome *lib.* 1 *Ad Jovinian* and Aelian in his *Variae historiae lib.* 7, *c.* 8. but amongst men much more old, as I might instance from several authorities and examples, one of which may be that of Mandanis the gymnosophist, who as Strabo *lib.* 15 reports was courted by Alexander the Great to accept of a rich present he made the philosopher, but contemning it and his glory it (at least seemingly) so incensed the King that the brahmin for his arrogance was condemned to death, and being told he might be pardoned so he would but desire it, with no

---

[91] Propertius, *Elegies* 3. 13. 19–22.

less morosity answered he would indeed petition Alexander, not for life but for liberty to burn himself, that death was in no wise terrible where 'tis only an inlet into immortality in exchange of his old perishing flesh, expecting a more durable and excellent condition.

Besides this heathenish custom here are many other lewd practices, such and so many that *"Peccata sunt in delictis,"*[92] for Satan here seems to erect his throne and imperiously to display his banner of idolatry and under various dresses to proclaim a toleration for all manner of wickedness. Such is the miserable vassalage with which this wretched generation are enslaved and so far from any sense of their misery that they have devised sundry tragic scenes to heighten the reputation of their pagod, though with their own destruction, and amongst other *actus triumphales* a massy idol of orichalcum is placed upon a chariot with eight wheels, richly-gilded; the ascent is by several easy steps upon which especially on gaudy days[93] the yogis and many prostituting girls were placed. *O ignis infernalis luxuria!* Hellish zeal, seeing parents destinate their pretty children to unchastity merely to enrich the idol, not unlike those Babylonian votaries of Mylitta, as Venus was there called, who received their prizes with this excuse, *"Tanti tibi deam Mylitte imploro,"* and by the courtesans after offered to adorn her temple![94] Thus mounted, they go on in procession, a procession not unlike the *thensa*[95] used by the superstitious Romans or that idolatry of the Danes recorded by Ditmarus,[96] for happy is that man, be he rich or poor, great or base, that can lend a hand to draw the chariot, yea, they account them happiest who out of a frantic zeal temerariously throw their naked bodies in the way, to the end that by the ponderousness of the chariot they may be crushed that thereby they may become the Devil's martyrs, thus remembered by a poet, *"Vigor inde animis et mortis honorae / Dulce sacrum: gaudent natorum fata parentes / Hortanturque mori, deflent iamque omnis ephebum . . ."*[97] But concerning those a poet gives this caution, "What helps it thus to haste your destiny/ In all post-haste, since all this wretched fry/ Shall with full sail to Hell through Cocyt fly?"

---

[92] There are sins in pleasures.

[93] Festivals or celebrations.

[94] For details on Mylitta, see Lord Herbert of Chirbury, *Pagan Religion*, 104. The source is Herodotus 1. 131.

[95] The *thensa* was a vehicle used by the Romans to convey the images of deities to the circus games.

[96] Dietmar or Thietmar of Merseburg (975–1018) wrote the *Chronicon* (1012–1018), a history of the Saxon rulers of Germany and the earlier Holy Roman Emperors. Printed editions began to appear in the sixteenth century. There is a modern translation by David Warner (Manchester: Manchester University Press, 2001).

[97] The full passage reads: ". . . hence their high resolve / And swear the sacrament of glorious death, / Parents are gladdened by their children's fate / And urge them to their doom; the young men all are shedding tears, the mothers well content / To lay the wreaths" (Statius, *Thebaid* 4. 230–234).

Meliapore.

Which bad objects removed, we come to Meliapore, a well-known town upon the coast of Coromandel and in the Kingdom of Bisnagar.[98] The Arctic pole there has 13 degrees 20 minutes. It was first called *Salamina* then *Melange*, but Meliapore after that and now St. Thomas, for that in this place he suffered martyrdom. Distant is is from Cape Comorin two hundred leagues or thereabouts. At this day it is but small and poor and under a Moorish command; it yields little for trade save cotton-ware and such common commodities, howbeit is exalted in her memory in regard that according to tradition this was the place where that holy apostle finished his labours after he had published the glad tidings of salvation through Persia, Hyrcania, Bactria, Sogdiana and many parts of India, and by Divine Grace obtained many proselytes, and those converts not of the meanest sort, for Sygamus the Emperor[99] himself was baptised and by his good example several other of the nobles, who in testimony of their change converted the heathen temples, by some said to be three hundred, into houses of prayer and preaching of the Gospel. Howbeit, the Devil so wrought that some apostates enraged the multitude so as in a blind zeal the Apostle and the King both suffered, the one being shot to death, the other brained, but both crowned with glorious martyrdom. This happened about thirty years after Our Saviour's passion, and in memory thereof a commemorative feast is yearly celebrated the first of July by the native Christians through India.[100] And however Abdias Babylonicus, who writ that after death they appeared and preached against their former doctrine may seem questionable, this is more certainly reported and credited, that in memory of their ingratitude divine justice hath marked their posterity, as some Jews, how truly I know not, say the Tribe of Benjamin are to this day, who of all others were most fierce against Our Saviour who was of the Tribe of Judah, these having one leg bigger in the calf then the other, which 'tis probable gave Pliny *lib. 7, cap.* 23

---

[98] This name is a corruption of Vijayanagara. There is some confusion because 'Narsinga' refers to the Vijayanagara Empire and sometimes also to the town. Herbert seems aware of the confusion. Both names were given by the Portuguese. The modern name is Hampi; it is now a ghost town, "set in a strange and sublime boulder-strewn landscape that resonates with a magical air" (Singh, *India*, 873). After its sacking in 1565 (see below), the town declined, although *Hobson-Jobson* cites Wytfliet's *Histoire des Indes* (1611) as saying that the King of Bisnagar "est puissant" (97), presumably meaning the Adil Shah of that time, Ibrahim II (1579–1626). When Herbert was there the ruler was Mohammed (1626–1660). For details, see Fernão Nunes and Domingos Paes, *Chronica dos reis de Bisnaga* (c. 1535), translated by R. Sewell in 1900 as *A Forgotten Empire (Vijayanagar): A Contribution to the History of India* (New Delhi: Ministry of Information and Broadcasting, 1962)..

[99] This is fiction. *Sygamus* may refer not to a person, but to the Sangama dynasty, which ruled Vijayanagara 1336–1485; if it does, the dates are wildly inaccurate. Its first emperor was Harihara Raya I (1336–56).

[100] A story was told that St. Thomas had converted "the King of Meliapore."

the occasion to feign them to be the *Monocoli*, "*Qui umbra pedis se protegant*,"[101] and as a false light misguided our countryman Sir John Mandeville in his relation concerning them.[102] Notwithstanding the people's rage, the two martyrs had each his sepulchre there, honoured and resorted to by the Christians inhabiting India, till about fifty years since their skulls and bones were brought away and, as holy relics, at this day preserved in the Virgin Mary's Church in Goa, according to the command of John III, King of Portugal, who sent Manoel Frias (directed by Afonso Sousa)[103] to Meliapore for that purpose. By an old manuscript which Campanine the Jesuit translated out of Chaldean into Latin it appears also that the Apostle preached the Gospel amongst the Indians and after that unto the Chinese, where it is said that "*Per D. Thomam regnum caelorum volavit et ascendit ad Sinas . . .*," whose plantations were afterward watered by Frumentius[104] in the days of Constantine the Great by the encouragement of holy Athanasius the Patriarch of Alexandria, who in recompense of his labours constituted him the first Bishop of that great diocese. Many peristent stories might be added out of Spanish reporters, but the most warrantable is this: in the Year of Our Lord 883 as Malmesbury,[105] Flor[entius] Wigorn[ensis][106] and others assure, Sigehelm, Bish-

---

[101] "They protect themselves by the shade of their feet" (Pliny, *Natural History* 7, 23).

[102] Pliny does not say anything about Jewish tribes, but he cites Ctesias as his source and states that they "have only one leg and hop with amazing speed" (*Natural History* 7. 23). Mandeville takes this up and in some editions there are woodcuts showing people with a huge foot shading their heads from the sun.

[103] Dom Martim Afonso de Sousa (c. 1489–1564/71), the Portugese admiral and explorer whom Camoens called the "scourge / of French pirates" (*Lusiads* 10. 63), led an expedition to mainland Brazil (1532) and became its first Governor. He served also in the Indies from 1534, and captured Diu (1535), defeating the Samorin's fleet off Cape Comorin. He was appointed governor of the Portuguese Indies (1542–2545).

[104] St. Frumentius (d. c. 380) does not seem to have gone anywhere near China. In fact, "he is venerated as the first evangelizer of Ethiopia" (Attwater, *Dictionary* 141). Constantine the Great seems to have had nothing to do with it either; according to Attwater, Frumentius, after doing missionary work in Ethiopia, went to Athanasius and suggested that he send a bishop to Axum. Attwater states that "there is strong confirmation of the presence in Ethiopia of a bishop named Frumentius, consecrated by Athanasius about the middle of the fourth century" (141).

[105] William of Malmesbury (c. 1080/90–1143), a monk who spent most of his life at Malmesbury Abbey, was one of the most important of the early English chroniclers. His *Gesta regum Anglorum* traced the history of England from 449–1127, and this was followed by the *Historia novella*, which took events up to 1142. His *Gesta pontificorum* is a significant contribution to ecclesiastical history.

[106] Florence of Worcester (c. 1060–1118) was a chronicler to whom used to be attributed the *Chronicum ex chronicis*, a universal history based on the work of Marianus Scotus (d. 1052), an Irish historian, with additional material taken from Bede and the *Anglo-Saxon Chronicle*. In Herbert's time it was thought that Florence himself wrote the years 1030–1117 and that others, notably John of Worcester (d. 1140) continued it; schol-

op of Sherbourne in Dorsetshire, encouraged by Alfred,[107] a pious English king, travelled to this place as a pilgrim with alms and offerings. After nine years he returned home with many rareties and gave so good an account of his travel as from that time this place was famoused with most in Europe.[108]

In the Year of Our Lord 1277 Narasimha,[109] an atheist, conquered Narsinga and all the regions about Meliapore. This Prince is branded for extreme covetousness and for being a severe enemy to the Christians. Having one year abundance of rice and other grains and room enough to hoard it in, to depite the Christians the more no place would serve his turn to lay it in but the chapel where prayers were daily offered by those poor Christians. With all submission they entreat him to refrain, but that stimulates him to greater profaneness, for supposing himself fit to be worshipped he enjoins the people to that adoration. But see God's vindictive hand: that night an affrighting vision of the Apostle approaches, both threatening and with an iron whip proffering to lash the King, who suddenly awaking, relents and beseeches the Christians to pray for him and acknowledges his own infirmity, himself putting his hand to purge the chapel and satisfy for his sacrilege, a miracle not a little joying the mournful Christians, as the tradition of the place reports for verity. Near this are other towns, *viz.* Pulicat in 14 degrees, Armagon, Tenasserim[110] and Petapoli, all in our way to Narsinga and Masulipatam, some being in the Kingdom of Bijapur, othersome in Golconda and of late years made English factories. The natives differ in customs, colour and other things little from the Narsingans.

---

ars now believe that John probably wrote the whole thing based on Marianus, and that others continued it to 1295. The work was edited in 1592 by William Howard.

[107] Alfred "the Great" reigned 871–899.

[108] There are problems with this story, too. William of Malmesbury conflated Sigehelm I, Bishop of Sherbourne (909–32) with one ealdorman Sigehelm who was said to have been martyred in India, but "India" was then a very vague term. See David Pratt, "The Illnesses of King Alfred the Great," *Anglo-Saxon England* 30 (2001): 39–90, here 69–70.

[109] Rajah Narasimha III [*Myrangee*] was the ruler of the Haysala Empire in Karnataka 1254–1291 with the capital at Dorasamudra. He fought a civil war with his brother Ramanatha, who set up his rival capital at Cannanore (1253–1295). Christianity had been in this area from the eighth century, although there are also reports that one Theophilus came from the Maldives to India in 354 and preached the Gospel.

[110] Tenasserim [*Tanessery*] is a Burmese town which, according to Varthema, "lieth next to Pegu, a small kingdom and tributary to Siam." His translator notes that it is "some distance inland on the south side of the lower branch of the Kistna [River] which debouches at Masulipatam" (Varthema, *Travels*, 197).

Narsinga.

Narsinga is a noble part of India where some would have Coromandel to terminate. Famous it is all over Asia, confined by Malabar, Golconda, Bengal (*Baracura* and *Gandarida* of old) and the ocean, the King so rich that he despises his neighbours and so powerful as he values neither Mughal, Deccan, Samorin nor Peguan, the country so full of all things requisite for use and pleasure, as fair towns, strong forts, pleasant fields and choice minerals, also having rivers which so enrich the earth as abundantly produces corn, cattle, fruits etc. that with good cause he is reputed as considerable a monarch as any in India. This may appear by his annual revenue, which some compute to be no less then two millions of pounds, and by the victory he obtained against Adil Shah the Deccan,[111] leading into the field three hundred elephants, thirty thousand horse and double that number of foot, after which Tanassery was by him subjected. The banians swarm like locusts here and the brahmins are nowhere more reputed of, having several temples, albeit in the structure they boast of no great bravery, being most proud within by having many deformed idols.

Bisnagar.

Near this is Bisnagar, *Modura* of old, *Arcati* says Castaldus, *Pentagramma* one conjectures, but more likely to be that *"Binagra urbs Indiae intra Gangem"* mentioned in Ptolemy and once the metropolis, but being about one hundred years ago subjected by the King of Deccan, abated of its splendour by the remove of the court to *Pengard*, five days travel thence, and is now the second city for grandeur and trade in that Kingdom, circled with a wall of near four miles compass, regularly-fortified, well-built and no less wealthy. The haven also is good, and the city frequented by European ships and junks from Malacca, Borneo, Java, Sumatra, Ceylon and many other parts of India, Arabia, Persia etc. The custom heretofore was that a traveller, when he came to the court, usually had civil entertainment, many times invited by the King, the better to show his bravery. His coat was thick-set with stones and gems of lustre, which when robed with, for the resemblance they had was with the sun, which they worship, he was little less then adored, his court was so full of majesty and his guard consisted of a thousand men. Polygamy he affects, and therefore wrote himself husband of a thousand women, many of which have him all his life in such esteem that upon his death they voluntarily make his flaming grave their sepulchre.

---

[111] King Krishna Devi of Vijayanagar (1509–29) defeated Ismail Adil Shah of Bijapur at the Battle of Raichur (1520). However, the tables were turned by Ali Adil Shah I at the Battle of Talikoti in 1565, which effectively ended the Vijayanagar Empire and thus Hindu rule in the south came to an end.

Masulipatam.

More northward upon this coast is Masulipatam, by contraction commonly-pro-
nounced *Meslipatam*, a town removed from the Equinoctial 16 degrees and a half
north, now under the Golcondan king and in the skirt of the Bengalan Gulf.[112]
The province admits a mixture of idolators; the gentiles are most in number but
least in power since the Mughal subjected them. Mohammed was first blazoned
amongst them by a colony of Persians who were conducted there in the 28 Year of
the *Hegira*, of our account 648, by Abdul ibn Amir, a man of no small command
under Osman, then Caliph of Babylon, since which invasion their offspring have
here continued. The town itself now neither for bulk nor beauty is considerable;
one reason may be for that fifty years ago by a raging mortality and famine it was
almost unpeopled and made desolate. The streets are but few, and those narrow,
the houses low and the fields parched by the extremity of heat, which here rages
from March to July, from whence to November wind and rain as incessantly disturb them, so as of twelve months they have but four, that is to say from November to March salubrious and moderate. Howbeit the town, by reason the English
reside there and of late traffic for calico, rice and the like, begins to revive and
will increase unless the deceitful disposition of the people occasion their remove
thence into Armagon and Pulicat, towns upon the same coast neighbouring
Masulipatam, where they may sit down with more ease, less charge and have as
choice variety of merchandise. Bengal borders upon Golconda, Arracan[113] upon
that part of Bengal which is watered by *Chaberis*, Pegu upon Arakan, Siam and
Tenasserim upon Pegu and upon Siam Cochin China and China, which some
make the boundary of Bacchus his eastern conquests.[114]

---

[112] *Hobson-Jobson* notes that Masulipatam or Machilipatnam means "Fish-Town"
and that it is "sometimes vulgarly called *Machhlipatan* or *Macchli-bandar* or simply *Bandar*" (561). The Danes established a factory there in 1625. For details of its history, see
S. Arasaratnam and A. Roy, *Masulipatam and Cambay 1500–1600* (Delhi: Munshiram
Manoharlal, 2005).

[113] Arracan or Arakan is a puzzle, as the name does not appear to designate any particular geographical area, although it appears to refer to south-east Bengal. Some writers
use the form 'Rakan' or 'Rakhang' (*HJ* 35). Others identify it with Champa, an old kingdom in south-east Indo-China.

[114] Herbert alludes here to a story that the god Dionysus was in India. An Orphic
tradition claims that Dionysus was made crazy by Hera because he was the son of her
husband Zeus by Persephone, and that he subsequently wandered around until he finally
embarked for India from Thrace. When in India he conquered the sub-continent by over-
coming armies with his spells. There are also stories about Alexander the Great knowing the myth and wishing to emulate the god, who had preceded him in the conquest of
India.

Casta. Bacchus his orgies.

Hence remove your chaste eyes to an unchaste town, though Casta[115] by name, a town no less infamous for idolatry. The mosques show art in sculpture but are hateful in the stink of their devotion, for here the shapes the pagods bear have some resemblance with Priapus and Pan as they are described by Servius in the 2 *Eclogue*[116] of Virgil: great eyes, flat nose, wide mouth, four great horns, a long beard shaped like the radiance of the sun, having claws for hands and crooked-legged so as it is all over deformed.

Among other their solemn festivals the mystic fopperies dedicated to Bacchus in these parts are not utterly extinguished, as may appear by the dress, mimic frisks and nightly pastimes the women practice. They cover themselves with skins, adorn their heads and tresses with ivy, in one hand holding a leaved javelin and cymbals of brass or timbrels in the other, attended by many boys and girls who ramble like distracted people up and down, striving to rend the air with their continued clamours, little differing from that description as we find in Avienus[117] the poet:

> ....*hic chorus ingens*
> *Feminei coetus pulchri colit orgia Bacchi*
> *Producit noctem ludus sacer. Aëra pulsant*
> *Vocibus et crebris late sola calcibus urgent.*
> ....*non qua celeri ruit agmine Ganges*
> *Indorum populi stata curant festa Lyaeo.*[118]

---

[115] In the 1634 edition Herbert identifies Casta as "a city in Coromandel adjoining Narsinga, where the people differ not in colour nor condition" (103). It is probably modern-day Hospet, now a Shi'ite Muslim centre and 13 km from Hampi; Singh notes that during the Muharram Festival, which is held in memory of Imam Hussein, "the daytime preliminaries appear to be a bewildering hybrid of Muslim and Hindu ritual" (*India*, 870). The "pagods" Herbert writes about are probably the image of Lord Shiva and the *Shivalingam*, which Herbert equates with the phallus of Priapus. This is a short cylindrical pillar with a round top which denotes the primal energy of the Creator.

[116] Priapus is not mentioned in this Eclogue; for Pan, see 2. 32–34.

[117] Rufus Festus Avienus (fl. 360–390) was a Roman statesman who was also poet of history and geography, amongst whose works may be found the *Descriptio orbis terrarum* and *Ora maritima*, paraphrases of Dionysius of Alexandria and Aratus. Smith, having noted that Festus is not very original, does commend him for "considerable energy and liveliness of style" (*Dictionary*, 1: 432). The work was first printed by Antonio di Strata (Venice, 1488).

[118] "Here a huge chorus, a gathering of female beauty, cultivates the orgy of Bacchus, and the sacred enactment prolongs the night. They make the air echo with their cries and strike the wide ground with frequent footsteps . . . nor where the Ganges flows in its swift course do the peoples of India leave the feasts of Bacchus unattended" (Avienus, *Descriptio orbis terrarum* 751–757).

so that it may well be admired this licentious festival should survive all others
celebrated in memory of those ethnic deities, which as Varro enumerates were
not less then thirty thousand, and albeit Bacchus was the first-known conqueror
of the East, the first that circled his brows with a diadem and in an ivory chariot
drawn sometimes with elephants, at other times with lynxes, rode in triumph,
seconded some ages after by Tarquinius Priscus[119] at Rome, as Plutarch records
in his *Life of Romulus*, the great distance of place and time, for he was, some
think, contemporary with Moses, might have put this with others in oblivion.
But the vast extent these Bacchanalia spread is no less observable, either proceeding from the pleasure of the grape or toleration they gave to all manner of
debauchery, insomuch as under various names and attributes alluding to its several operations through most noted kingdoms of the world this wine-god has
been acknowledged, as in part may be collected from Elias Vinetus,[120] who thus
enumerates:

> *Orgia me Bacchum vocant.*
> *Osirim Aegypti putant.*
> *Mysi Phanacem nominant.*
> *Dionysum Indi existimant.*
> *Romana sacra, Liberum.*
> *Arabici, Adonem.*
> *Leucaniaci, Pentheum.*
> *Graeci, Nictileum.*
> *Tremolenti, Lyaeum.*
> *Fremibundi Bromium* etc.[121]

---

[119] Lucius Tarquinius Priscus was one of the semi-legendary kings of Rome. His
dates of reign are traditionally given as 616–579 B.C.E.

[120] Elie or Elias Vinet (1509–1587) was a French humanist scholar best known for
his edition of Ausonius's *Lectiones* (1574). He was a professor at the University of Bordeaux and at the Collège de Guyenne, where he later became Principal and where his
most illustrious student was Montaigne. Vinet also edited the *Epitome* of Florus (1554) as
well as Pomponius Mela and Solinus.

[121] This passage is also quoted by Lord Herbert of Chirbury in *Pagan Religion*,
where it is identified as Ausonius's "Epigram 29" (248). It may serve as some evidence
that Thomas Herbert was reading his noble cousin's book, although there are differences
in the transcription of the verse. Here it translates: "[The Ogygians — *orgia* is wrong] call
me Bacchus, / The Egyptians think I am Osiris, / The Mysi name me Phanaces, / The Indians consider me Dionysus, / To holy Rome I am Liber, / [To] the Arabs Adonis, / [To]
the Leucantaci Pentheus / [To] the Greeks Nictileus, / [To] those that tremble, Lyaeus, /
[To] those who roar I am Bromius." Phanaces means "the bringer of light;" Lyaeus is "the
releaser from care;" Bromios is "the noisy;" Pentheus was a Theban king who was torn to
bits by his wife and daughters at a Bacchic orgy. However, in Lord Herbert's version the
word appears as *Pantheus*, which means "the all-embracing god," and the people who are
called here the *Leucantaci* are rendered as *Lucanii* by Lord Herbert, i.e. the Lucanians.

A few of many, were not these too many, might be remembered.

Some of these nevertheless bid the world farewell when the corpse of their deceased husbands are incendiated, albeit some viragos rather choose to outbrave Death's terrors by going quick with him into the grave, a dreadful exit, but such, as they say, expresses most affection! Such and so many sad delusions Satan practices amongst his devoted votaries, and for his greater variety finds that Virgil's monstrous brood of deities are here exceeded, for not only the cow is equally adored with the old Egyptian Apis or pied bull, but the sun, Moon and Stars as souls celestial, and very much resembling those miserable idolators registered in *Libro sapientiae, cap.* 13:[122] "Who acknowledged the Fire, the Wind, the swift Air, the course of the Stars, the great Waters or the sun and the Moon to be the gods and governors of the world," not content with which, others there be who have rivers and trees in like veneration, parallel with the Celts our neighbours described by Tacitus, "*Qui nulla simulacra, nullum peregrinae superstitionis vestigium videre liceat.*"[123] Scarce credible are some solemn festivals they keep; in one of them they had a lewd custom to fasten sick or needy men, stupid by too much zeal, to an engine, which being hoisted elevates him equal with the pagod; the blood trickling from his wounded shoulders (it may be said "*excessit medicina modum*"),[124] at his descent as a meritorious sacrifice is dashed against a tree, and after he has invoked the demon to accept his offering, returns with hope to thrive the better ever after. This bloody or rather butcherly sacrifice is mentioned in 2 *lib.* Virgil *Aeneid*, "*sanguine placastis,*"[125] and of old was used by the Rhodians, Cretans and Carthaginians, who when their city was besieged caused two hun-

---

The identification of Bacchus with Osiris may also be found in Herodotus (2.48). Lord Herbert also has *Ogygia* in the first line rather than *orgia*, referring to the Ogygians rather than to Bacchic mysteries or orgies. There is a further problem with this text, however; Ausonius's "Epigram 29" has nothing to do with Bacchus. "Epigram 31," which consists of four lines of Greek, is entitled "Libero Patri" (To Liber Pater, i.e. Bacchus), but only mentions the identification of Bacchus with Osiris and the Mysae (Mistae in Herbert). The last three lines are a problem, too. The two poems are now Ausonius's *Epigrams* 32 and 33, which describe a statue in the poet's villa, which was designated "Lucaniacus." For details, see R. P. H. Green, *The Works of Ausonius* (Oxford: Oxford University Press, 1991), 75, 392–93. My thanks to Dr. Leslie MacCoull for this information.

[122] The *Liber sapientiae*, also known as *The Book of Wisdom* or *The Wisdom of Solomon*, is an apocryphal text which appeared in St. Jerome's Vulgate Bible, although he is at pains to leave out the name of Solomon because he considered the attribution spurious, hence the other name.

[123] "There are no images, and nothing to suggest that the cult is of foreign origin" (Tacitus, *Germania* 43).

[124] "[the] remedy exceeded the limit" (Lucan, *Civil War* 2. 242).

[125] "Blood, and a virgin slain/ You gave to appease the winds . . ." (Virgil, *Aeneid* 2. 160–161).

dred of their principal youths to be slain as a double hecatomb.[126] In Africa and America the like hellish custom is to this very day observed, as we read in Acosta. They oft offer in the night, but first make the streets bright with lights and then stuff their hands with rice and glomerate in dances, in every corner where a puppet sits throwing rice or fruits, but once being out of the ring haste away, not daring to look back lest the Devil tear them by way of gratitude, to which poor wretches give me leave to apply that in Ecclesiasticus 30:19, "*Quid proderis libatio idolo/ nec enim manducabit nec odorabit?*"[127] This [Benjamin of Tudela][128] and others witness, but many of those abominable practices are prohibited and discontinued since the Mohammedans have borne rule, who as bad as they are have nevertheless expressed their abhorrency against that custom.

They have a different kind of burial to what we find in most other places, for here the carcase is placed either in a deep cave which is long and narrow, or else betwixt two walls that be built of purpose, wherein the simple relict voluntarily immures herself, by that self-sequestration never after speaking to any, but expecting death by that arrow of Famine, which of all sorts of deaths as it is the most languishing is the most formidable. Their habit is for the most part nakedness, the zone by reason of its distemperate heat well excusing clothing. They delight in fishing and to sport upon the water in boats or *curry-curries* resembling the Venetian gondola, and thus shaped:

A Curry-curry or boat [illustration shown on p. 779]

Ophir.

But seeing we are now at Malacca and in or near the *Aurea Chersonesus*, places celebrated by reason of that plenty of gold has been brought thence, as induced several cosmographers and historians to fix Ophir there.[129] Nevertheless, finding

---

[126] Sacrifice; usually it consisted of a hundred oxen.

[127] "What good doeth the offering unto an idol? for neither can it eat nor smell . . ."

[128] Herbert has 'Tudalensis.'

[129] Herbert is correct about the genealogy of Joktan and about the gold. Modern scholars are as divided as ever about the site of Ophir (and Herbert himself has already presented some opinions in Part I). It may have been in the southern part of Arabia or southern Palestine, modern-day Oman, the East Africa coast (Somaliland or perhaps the Egyptian 'Land of Punt'), Supara, a city 75 km north of Bombay (which was Josephus's idea), and a number of other places, even including Great Zimbabwe (for details, see D. J. Wiseman's article in *Illustrated Bible Dictionary* 1119–20, from which this list is taken). Tomé Lopes, who sailed with Vasco da Gama, located Ophir in Sofala (Mozambique), a place Herbert mentions here; Milton in *Paradise Lost* (1668) writes of "Sofala, thought Ophir" (11:400), and there is a Portuguese tradition that it was Ofir, a town in the Espende district in Portugal. The endless fascination with this mysterious place is due to its

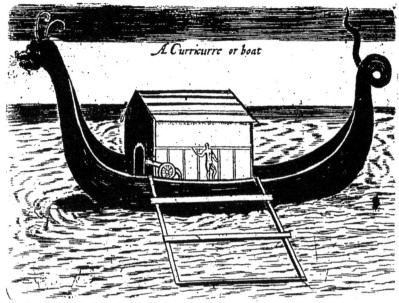

A Curricurre or boat

the local place no less controverted, and according to various apprehensions drawn into several contrary quarters of the world, albeit in that brief discourse I made concerning the Red Sea and Carmania where I made mention of the burial-place of Erythraeus there are some glances at it, I shall here nevertheless, as in the most proper place, speak a little further upon that subject.

And first, concerning the name. It is agreed by most that it is derived from Ophir son of Joktan mentioned in Genesis 10:30 upon the fixing his plantation, which albeit the Scripture cldars, nevertheless from analogy of the name and from abundance of gold and ivory found in several opposite parts of the earth, the place is tossed to and fro, whereby the discovery of the true place is obscured and becomes more difficult, yea, not any historical part of Scripture more controverted that I can meet with then is Ophir. Amongst many others I shall instance Rabanus Maurus, and from his light Christopher Columbus, whose authority Stephanus inclines to, and whose joint opinion it is a great isle that verges towards the Gulf of Mexico was Ophir, to which conjecture they are led by no other reason I can find then that the Spaniard has thence extracted a mass of silver, gold and precious stones, but no ivory, albeit what they have drawn thence is little compared with what other parts of the *terra firma* in America, especially

---

connections with Solomon and his gold-bearing ships, and it is still with us, as in John Masefield's "Quinquereme of Nineveh from distant Ophir / Rowing home to haven in sunny Palestine / With a cargo of ivory . . ."

about *Potosi*, have afforded, which mines nevertheless are far more uberous in silver then gold, the last being the emphasis of Ophir, a metal we see by daily experience much more plentiful in Africa and Asia then the new-found world that hath hitherto been discovered.

Howbeit, 'tis probable that removal of Ophir into the Occident, but especially the similitude of the name in like manner persuaded Goropius to infer, and not without some vehemency, that it was rather in Peru! Now the reason he gives is because Ophir and *Peruaym* are harmonious in sound, and indeed it is not denied that Ophir and *Peruaym* are terms convertible, as may appear by comparing I Kings 9:26 with II Chronicles 3:6,[130] where, for the better fortifying that conjecture, they with like reason persuade their readers that Sephar[131] is that mighty mountain or rather chain of hills now called the Andes, which surge to a marvellous height and penetrate the heart of Peru, not ceasing their course until they come in sight of the Straits called Magellan. Notwithstanding which, Ortelius, rejecting that of the Teutonic, persuades that he has made a more real discovery of the place in *Aegisymba* or South Africa, for in his *Thesaurus* he mentions a town and province called *Phura*, a part of Soffala, which was attainable by Solomon's ships from Ezion-geber without the help of any compass and where there is such store of gold, precious stones, ivory ane ebony (which some take for the algummin[132] wood) as no other part of the world affords more plenty; yea, to strengthen that imagination others suppose that by the word *Sophyra*, which is Ophir anagrammatised, mentioned in the 72 Interpreters, is intended or meant Sofala or *Sophura*, as to attain their ends they wrest it, albeit Saint Jerome by that name intends Sephar. But which is more strange, Pimente,[133] a learned man, for the greater honour of his country from the like analogy of name fancies that the Isle of Cadiz was Ophir, which Montanus dislikes and therefore removes it into Africa as far as Carthage, and some others, disproving his, into Guinea and the River Gambia, which for plenty of gold gives not place to any part of the

---

[130] "And he garnished the house with precious stones for beauty: and the gold was gold of Parvaim" (2 Chronicles 3:6).

[131] Sephar is mentioned as one of the "stations" where the Israelites stopped during the Exodus: "And they removed from Shapher and encamped in Haradah" (Numbers 33:23). Various locations have been suggested, such as Mt. Cassius (it had a temple to Jupiter Cassius) in the Mt. Seir range, now known as as-Sera. It is near the city of Petra on the Red Sea coast.

[132] Actually it is sandalwood, not ebony.

[133] Fr. Nicolao Pimente travelled in Goa, India, Pegu and Malacca, Nagapatam and the Vijayanagar Empire (1597–1599) as Jesuit Visitor to those areas. He published an account of his experiences, *Cartas que o Padre Nicolao Pimenta da Companhia de Jesus Visitador nas Parte do Oriente da mesma Companhia, escriveo ao Geral della A 26 Nouebro do Ano de 1599* (1602). Herbert inexplicably refers to him as "Pineda," perhaps confusing him with the explorer of that name, who only travelled (and met a particularly nasty death) in America.

universe. But Danaeus, no less taken with his conceit, pretends that he has found it at Hormuz, upon no other account I can find then the golden trade it had in his time, so that we see, merely to please the imagination several otherwise learned men have laboured to discover Ophir in several quarters of the world opposite to the opinions of Saint Jerome, Saint Augustine and other reverend and judicious authors who have more accurately suffered their reason to be directed by the unerring Rule, which plainly instructs that Ophir and Havilah with the rest of Joktan's sons had their dwelling "from Mesha as thou goest into Sephar, a mountain of the east," Genesis 10:30. East must be understood from Babel, where the first division was of the sons of Noah, and east also from Arabia, where 'tis presumed was writ the Pentateuch, and that, being infallible, convinces and puts to silence those opinions I lately mentioned, none of the places they assign being east from thence but *in diametro* opposite and repugnant to that of Moses his manduction.

But for the better manifestation of the true place, we are therefore to consider that Ophir *"est verbum profluens,"* *Obrizum* and *Opherizum* being the same, *"Quia ex insula Ophyr aurum est praestantissimum;* [from the island of Ophir] gold well-refined," as Pliny observes. It is also called Ophir in 1 Kings 22:48, but *Uphuz* and *Ophaz* in Jeremiah 10:9, Daniel 10:5 and in the *Targum*[134] or *Babylonian paraphrase Ophy*; yea, in some other ancient authors *Mophaz*, and *Urphee* by Eupolemus. Moreover, sometimes Ophir is glaced at under the name of *Tarsis*, but that Ophir's colony planted in East India, where Mesha[135] and Sephar in their vestigia may yet be found, I shall briefly demonstrate not only from the current of authentic writers but also from the names and memory of the originary planters, albeit rationally it cannot be imagined but that through length of time, revolutions of state and diversity of idioms they as well as other things have been subject to variations.

In 1 Kings 9:26, also in 2 Chronicles 8:18 it is recorded that "King Solomon made a navy of ships in Ezion-geber which is besides Eloth and the brink of the Red Sea in the land of Edom. And Hiram sent with the navy his servants who had knowledge of the sea with Solomon's servants, and they came to Ophir, and from thence brought four hundred and fifty talents of gold," in our money about three million and six hundred thousand crowns. In 2 Chronicles 9:10 Hiram and Solomon's servants who brought gold also brought algummim wood, and

---

[134] The *Targums* were Aramaic translations, interpretations or paraphrases of the Old Testament (except the Books of Nehemiah and Daniel) made after the Babylonian captivity. For details, see *Illustrated Bible Dictionary*, 3: 1516–17.

[135] Mesha, which is the limit for the land inhabited by Joktan's family, has been identified with Massa in northern Arabia, "but the probable location of Sephar in S. Arabia suggests a similar locality for Mesha, though no place of that name has been suggested in that region" (*Illustrated Bible Dictionary*, 2: 985). Herbert discusses Mesha in more detail below.

in 1 Kings 10:22 "Solomon had upon the sea the navy of Tharsis with Hiram's navy, and once in three years came the navy of Tharsis, which brought gold, silver, ivory, apes and peacocks," by which it appears the port from whence that fleet set sail was Ezion-geber. Therefore, to evince Ortelius, if the navy sailed from Ezion-geber to Sofala, the course they were then to steer would have been west from Guardafui, a cape-land that gives the first inlet into the Red Sea from the ocean, which is the contrary way or point of the compass to that part of the world Scripture tells us Ophir made his plantation. Besides, the port that fleet set sail twoards was certainly a much greater distance then Sofala, which from Ezion-geber with a fair wind might well be attained in a month's time, whereas the voyage to Ophir was triennial or in less then three years not to be accomplished. Not that they spent that time in providing the cargo, which probably by merchants and others was still in preparation, but rather through distance of place and the long way they made ere they could attain their port, for in regard they had no compass to direct their way 'tis likely they feared to put to sea without ken of land, but crept along the Arabian and Indian shores as at this day the Mughal's great *shahi* or junk uses to do when it sets sail from Suwali Road to Mocha in the Red Sea once in two or three years most richly-loaden. For albeit it cannot be denied that King Solomon was the richest prince in his time, seeing that in Ecclesiasticus 47 'tis said "he gathered gold as tin and silver as lead," so he was the wisest, for he was filled with understanding as with a flood; he furnished the earth with grave and wise sentences by reason of his songs, proverbs, similitudes and interpretations, for he discoursed of trees from the cedar in Lebanon to the hyssop upon the wall, and people from all the kings of the Earth came to hear and to admire his wisdom, 1 Kings 4:32, whence it may be concluded that his knowledge was admirable in Nature's secrets. Nevertheless, that he expressed his knowledge concerning the wonderful nature and use of the magnet is not mentioned in any of his that are extant, for the use of the magnet was found by Fla[vio] of Malfi,[136] a Calabrese, of such virtue and use, saith Bodin[137] *Cap.* 7 that *"Tota rerum Natura nihil admirabilis; usus enim eius est plane divinus,"*[138] so

---

[136] Flavio Gioia (fl. 1302) was an Italian pilot and captain who may have been from either Amalfi or Naples. He did not invent the magnetic compass, which had been known to the Chinese for centuries (of which Herbert was evidently unaware), but introduced it to Europeans and modified its design and appearance. He suspended the needle over a fleur-de-lys design pointing north, and put it in a case with a glass cover.

[137] Jean Bodin (1530–1596) was an eminent French jurist and political philosopher; he was Professor of Law at the University of Toulouse. His best-known work is *Les six livres de la république* (1576), translated into English by William Knolles as *Six Bookes of a Commonwealthe* (1606). Bodin also wrote against witchcraft and history; a posthumously-published work, the *Colloquium heptaplomeres de rerum sublimium arcanis ablati*, gives his views on the question of universal religion.

[138] There is nothing admirable about Nature, but making use of it is distinctly divine.

as had the use of the magnet been then known and practised, the voyage in all probability might have been overcome in six months' space, as ships at this day give frequent proof of. But we do not read that the virtue of the magnet was known or made use of in that age or long after by the Phoenicians, who nevertheless were the first that perfected navigation, for that the polary direction was altogether unknown unto the ancients is agreed by most, notwithstanding that noted speech Plautus writ two thousand years since, "the wind being fair, steer your course," seems applicable, for the most judicious rather think the tackling or sail by which the vessel was to be turned is meant by that direction. Nevertheless, that those parts abound with lodestones is well-known, seeing the King of Ceylon used them as others did porcelain, being in such plenty that some have from their attractive property marvelled how ships could pass with large anchors and iron skates, and no less that there is no greater increase of variation, as Pliny and Serapion[139] have imagined, for confutation of which we need no other example then that of Elba, an isle in the Tuscan Sea, where a store of magnets and but little variation are found and observed. But to return.

Forasmuch as Sacred Writ instructs us that Ophir and the rest of Joktan's sons, upon that memorable division of the Earth which happened in the days of Peleg, brother of Joktan, sons of Eber, had their partition or lot assigned them in the Orient, *viz.* from Mesha unto Sephar, without further argument that serves to confute those speculations of Columbus, Maurus and Stephanus as to the pretended discoveries of place in contrary quarters of the world, and in answer to Goropius concerning Peru by reason of the affinity it has with the word *Peruaym*, that criticism will not avail, seeing there are towns in Siam and the neighbourhood of Malacca now called Peru and Perua which better preserve the memory of old *Peruaym*, albeit, if I may be allowed the like liberty, the isle Taprobane seems most to shadow it, being according to the translation of Junius[140] and Tremellius[141] from the original writ *Tapronaym* and *Taperuaym*, words that have very little discordance with *Peruaym*, by which is understood Ophir. But that

[139] This may be St. Serapion, Bishop of Antioch (190–211), a Syrian theologian mentioned by Eusebius (5. 19).

[140] François du Jun (1545–1602) was a French Protestant lawyer, Hebraist, and theologian who assisted Tremellius (see below) at the University of Heidelberg. He was Professor of Divinity there from 1581 and became Professor of Theology at Leiden (1592). He produced a Latin Old Testament (1579), edited Tertullian (1597), and wrote an autobiography (1595) which shows that he had a very interesting life. His *Works* were published in 1613.

[141] John (Giovanni) Immanuel (Emanuele) Tremelli (1510–1580) was an Italian Hebraist from Ferrara of Jewish background, who became successively (and quickly) a Catholic (1540) and a Protestant (1541). He taught Hebrew at the University of Strasbourg until 1547, when he left for England and was appointed Regius Professor of Hebrew at Cambridge (1549). In 1568 he produced a Chaldaic and Syriac grammar. He translated the Bible into Latin from Hebrew and Syriac (1575–80) with Junius.

Taprobane is an island under or near the Equinoctial is agreed by all, although some difference there be whether Sumatra or Ceylon be it, Mercator's judgment being for Sumatra and Ortelius for Ceylon. Howbeit, most incline to Sumatra, both for that it is nearest the continent and consequently the more esaily discovered by Onesicritus, Alexander's admiral, who wanting the use of a compass doubtless crept as near the shore as well he might, and for that store of gold has both of old and yet is obtained at Sumatra more then in Ceylon, whence it was called *Aurea Insula* by the ancients. Howbeit, that great and learned expositor Saint Jerome in his paraphrase upon 1 Kings 22:48, where it is writ that "Jehoshaphat made ships of Tharshish to [go] to Ophir for gold," but broken in pieces at Ezion-geber, the Lord disapproving his design, from the word 'Tharshish' infers that "*Ophir est locus Indiae, in quo aureum optimum nascitur*; Ophir is a place in India where is the purest gold,"[142] and in another place "*Ophyri regio necessario posita est in Orientali India;* Ophir is without all doubt in the East Indies." Of the same judgment in Tzetzes, for, saith he:

> The golden Indian Isle by poets sung,
> A peninusula some call it, and no isle;
> The Hebrews name it Ophir in their tongue,
> All sorts of stones and mines of gold erewhile
> Are found there with the choicest Prasine stone.

A stone of price, abounding in the Prasians' country, saith Pliny *lib.* 6, *cap.* 18, from the name resembled to a leek, though probably the emerald, for it was of a greenish colour. But the country itself is most famoused for that resistance the citizens of Palibotra[143] made against Bacchus, and albeit by some it be more

---

[142] J. A. Thompson, the writer of the article on this name in the *Illustrated Bible Dictionary*, cites W. F. Albright as noting "that the very word Tarshish [*sic*; the usual spelling—Ed] suggests the idea of mining or smelting (the Akkadian word *rasasu* means 'to be smelted'), and in that sense any mineral-bearing land may be called Tarshish." However, he states that Pliny and Strabo, who thought it was in Spain "in the Guadalquivir Valley" might be correct, because "the mineral wealth of Spain attracted the Phoenicians" (3: 1519).

[143] The site of this city has been disputed. Megasthenes, who was there in about 302 B.C.E., is responsible for the name, which is Greek. He wrote that it was "where the streams of the Erannoboas and the Ganges unite" (Allen, *Search*, 69). Eighteenth and nineteenth century scholars suggested Kanauj and Allahabad (Prayag). For example, writing in 1833, Edward Archer noted that some thought it was near Patna, but he was nonetheless of the opinion that it should be identified with Allahabad (*Tours*, 2: 106). Finally, Sir William Jones established that it was in fact Patna, identifying Megasthenes's 'Erannoboas,' with the river Sone, which was also known as *Hiranyabahu* (Allen, *Search* 70–71). The modern name Patna was given to the city in the reign of Sher Shah Suri (1540–1545).

strictly confined to Bengal and that part, yet Strabo gives it a greater extent: calling all that coast Prasia "which lies betwixt Indus and Ganges," so that albeit the *Insula Aurea* be by Ptolemy and others placed here.

Yet the *Aurea Terra* and the *Aurea Chersonesus*[144] is not so well agreed-upon, for Josephus by *Aurea Terra* intends Ophir, and by that general consequently comprehends all those regions that verge easterly from the River Indus, seeing all that oriental part of the world even from Indus to *Polisanga* (if such a river be not feigned) and most islands from the Maldive Islands to Japan more or less have gold, which if so, I do not know by what authority Varrerius confines that metal to Pegu and Sumatra, maintaining that no other place in the East Indies produces gold on either side the River Ganges. His words are these: "*Citra et ultra Gangem nulla pars Indiae sit quae aurum gignat preter Peguam et Sumatram*,"[145] an hypothesis found mistaken by such as drive a trade for gold in those maritime parts that verge towards Cochin-China, upon which consideration it is, as I suppose, that Mercator stretches *Aurea Chersonesus* from Sumatra to Japan, both in reference to the isles and coast maritimate, too great a space, doubtless, and disagreeing with a peninsula. Therefore, upon better grounds it may be reduced to a less, as of some late have confined it to Malabar, albeit Ptolemy and Niger place it about Malacca, Java and parts thereabouts. But Solinus, converting the species, calls it *Argyra*, which Pomponius Mela *lib.* 3 *cap.* 8 seems to reconcile: "*Ad Tamum enim Indiae promontorium est insula Chrysae ad Gangem Argyrae*," by that promontory meaning either Cape Comorin or that other which shoots into the sea and becomes an equal boundary to the two straits of Sunda[146] and Malacca. And by Pliny *l.* 6 *c.* 21: "*Extra ostium Indi Chrysae et Argirae fertilis metallis; sed quod aliqui tradunt aurum et argentum cum eis solum esse, haud facile crediderim*," by which that author places it nearer Indus then Ganges. But that Ophir was at and about Malacca, at least in some contiguous maritime part of East India, and that Joktan with all or most of his sons planted in the East Indies, and that their colonies, though dispersed for better accommodation, were in the voisinage of one another, will appear by the continuation of the names of the principal planters, as may be imagined, yea proved, by what is this day extant, notwithstanding the alteration of names and change of language that unavoidably hath happened.

And first, concerning Mesha and Mount Sephar. That their station was thereabouts has been the constant opinion of most, until of late a modern writer, finding Mesha the son of Aram the son of Shem in Mesopotamia, thence

---

[144] Marco Polo identified Japan as *Aurea Terra* (Land of Gold); the *Aurea Chersonesus* (Golden Peninsula), mentioned by Ptolemy and others (including Milton in Book XI of *Paradise Lost*), is in south-west Asia.

[145] There is no part of India this or that side of the Ganges which produces gold except Pegu and Sumatra.

[146] Sunda is the strait between Java and Sumatra which connects the Java Sea and the Indian Ocean.

imagines those places are to be understood to be in that country, but that country being neither east from Shinar nor the Arabian Desert, that conjecture is not forcible. Another finds it in Arabia Felix, upon that old mistake in not distinguishing the plantation of Havilah the descendent of Ham from that other of Havilah who descended from Shem, which error also misled the Septuagint, by the River Gihon (a branch of Euphrates) understanding Ganges. But Ptolemy with better consideration finds it in East India, calls it *Mons Mazius* and places it under 36 degrees, notwithstanding all that large tract the same geographer extends from the promontory *Manancomum* to *Sabanna* being above 100 leagues is by Strabo termed *Terra Musicani* or *Meshicani*, as some write it. Nor is Sephar that mountain in the east at this day utterly forgotten, seeing some there be who find *Sepha* there as also *Syba* and *Sypha*, which differ but little from the ancient name it bore or from the latitude allowed *Mons Mazeus*, out of which it is supposed Ganges springs, albeit in the easterly part of Aria another *Sypha* is known of late to the east of *Mazeus*, whose distance may be salved by that of Caucasus, which keeps its name a vast distance and through several regions, but Postellus helps that supposition, for he takes the great mountain Bellaguate, which in that dialect signifies 'a high mountain,' to be Sephar, albeit Bellaguate branches from Imaus, and in a continued ledge of spiring hills pierces through the heart of Industan, Deccan and the Narsingan countries, in the middle betwixt the Gulf of Bengal and the Indian Ocean uninterruptedly as far as Cape Comorin, not unlike the Apennine, which in a chain of hills cuts quite through Italy. And concerning it, Saint Jerome [PL 23. 91A] vouches that *Sophyra*, as he calls Sephar, "*mons est orientis in India, iuxta quem filii Joctan habitaverunt*; Sephar is a mountain in the East Indies near which the sons of Joktan inhabited," so that 'tis very strange any would have Sephar to be the Andes in America, as I lately mentioned.

Concerning their several plantations it may warrantably be supposed that Joktan, the father of those thirteen sons mentioned in Genesis 10:26, seated himself somewhere near the River Ganges, the rather for that it is granted by some and those not the least-learned, that Noah, before Nimrod and his associates moved westward towards Euphrates, fixed his quarters somewhere in Margiana or upon the banks of Indus, that being the richest soil, and the first choice was doubtless allowed him both in the relation he stood as upon the account of seniority. Thence it is in some authors we find that river called 'Joktan' and alternately Joktan called by the name of 'Ganges.' Now the father, having made his selection, the sons in all probability dispersed themselves about contiguous places, yet so as to continue a neighbourhood, both for their better association and preservation. And accordingly by an easy inquisition we find the several plantations of Ophir, Havilah, Adoram, Abimael, Obal, Jerah and Sheba, seven of the sons of Joktan originally seated on either side Ganges, for those nations the ancients called the *Orites per apherisin*, the *Ophirites* and the *Tapiri*,[147] which

---

[147] The Orites were a tribe in Gedrosia encountered by Alexander the Great.

some who take a liberty to please their fancy without much torture of the word write *Tophiri*, were inhabitants *inter Gangem* and in good measure preserve the memory of Ophir their originary planter, who either removed or extended his dwelling towards Malacca and that maritime coast which is *extra Gangem* may be acknowledged, seeing it is the belief of some, both in regard Malacca is a chersonese and that it has its situation upon the sea, but principally for that in all ages there and in the neighbouring isles plenty of gold, ivory and ebony, which was most likely to be the almuggin-wood,[148] seeing it was used for the garnishing and trimming the stairs and pillars of the Temple, and there was none such seen before in the Land of Judah, which excludes cypress and cedar-wood, of which there was plenty, but of ebony nowhere but in India, if we credit Virgil, and in regard that apes, peacocks and precious stones have at all times been there, it is the mosr credible that Ophir was in that part of the world placed. For the name 'Malacca' is but new, and varied from *Tacola*, as I find it mentioned in some authors, and more particularly by Plutarch *Vita Alexandris*, where the people of that place are called *Taxili* or *Tashili*,[149] they who with the *Sabaei* were active for the defence of their liberties upon the Greeks' threatened invasion, after which it was named *Malaza*, where geographers of old placed the *Aurea Chersonesis*, and after that *Maleicola*, which with little alteration was contracted to *Malacca*, in which name it now resteth. And it is the better demonstrated for that the river which serves that town was called *Gaza*, a proper name where gold is hoarded, and holds the name in part as yet, and upon those banks it was that noted city *Barygaza* was built, whose foundation was laid by the *Aratrii*,[150] by some thought the Oriti lately mentioned, who first inhabited the Gedrosian territory near Cambay upon the eastern banks of the River Indus, so that upon the whole matter Malacca may warrantably be concluded the place which in old times was called Ophir, albeit the gold had at that particular place from the neighbouring islands come likewise under that general denomination.

Moreover, to trace the footsteps of the other sons of Joktan: in Pegu we find the memory of Havilah, seeing part of that country was now called Burma and *Brama* but of old *Brachmanorum regio*, is at this day called *Chava* and *Chavilah*, and a contiguous principality late a feudatory to the crown of Pegu and since to Tangu is called Ava,[151] which apparently continues the memory of Havilah brother of Ophir. Of Adoram the *Aramel* or *Aramite* in the Gujarat province are

---

[148] A precious wood, reddish in colour, which was given by the Queen of Sheba to Solomon for the temple (see 1 Kings 19: 11–12, where it is called 'almug').

[149] Herbert refers here to Taxila or Takshashila, now in Pakistan. It was a great Buddhist centre from the 6th century B.C.E., and the ruined city is now a World Heritage Site. It lies approximately 35 km west of the Pakistani capital, Islamabad.

[150] The Aratrii (Sanskrit *Arashtra*) lived on the Periplus, inland from Barygaza, which is another name for Broach.

[151] The old Kingdom of Ava in Burma.

descended. Of Abimael, i.e. *Pater Mallorum*, those planted the coast of Malabar; those also inhabiting Malva, a province in Industan, and the *Malli*[152] noted by Plutarch to live thereabouts, for so were those called of old, and at this day his name is continued by some considerable towns upon that coast, as *Malibe* and *Maleta*, all or some of which in all likelihood from Abimael deduce their original. Of Obal are the *Obalites* descended and the *Abelites* mentioned by historians and placed around Ganges. But concerning Jerah, albeit they of Jarri near Lar pretend some interest in that name, as I mentioned in that place; upon better view I may discover his *vestigia* near Malacca amongst his other brethren, seeing the town and province of *Jor* or *Jehor* and *Joor* (as some pronounce)[153] preserves his name in that part of Siam which confines Malacca and affronts the isle Sumatra to the east, for I likewise find that country called *Jeria* of old, part of which was watered by the River Cophen,[154] yea, by the names of *Seria* and *Siria* (doubtless mistaken by the amanuensis or in the transcript) glanced at by Josephus. And as to the last of the sons of Joktan, named Sheba, here are sufficient remains both from the *Sibae* and the *Sabaei*, who in confederacy with the *Tacolae* lately mentioned gave some stop to the Macedonian torrent, also from that river which streams not far from Johore through the Malaccan territories into the ocean and from that promontory likewise which thrusts its head into the saltwater near Sincapura,[155] Ptolemy and others called *Magnum*. The Kingdom of Siam withal was heretofore named *Sabannae regio*, as attested by Strabo in his definition of the *Terra Musicani*,[156] and not many leagues from Malacca there is at this day a town so-named. Dionysius also in his *Periegesis* makes *Sabolassa* one of the *ostia* of the River Ganges.

Gold of Ophir.

Now, albeit this may serve to point out Ophir, yet seeing Tarshish is an adjunct with Ophir and a word admitting a various signification, it will not be lost labour to discuss that a little, being a term that by curious pens has been no less argued then Ophir. But by a parenthesis first accept the description of what has been the subject of this disquisition, gold, discovered very rarely, for the *auraria* run not in mines and veins so apparently and so plentifully as silver doth, but for the most part is hid and undiscovered until found in shallow brooks and rivulets near to mountains, usually after storms and rains, sometimes in dust and powder, but at other times in grains which for bigness and shape resemble melon-seeds,

---

[152] For the Malli and Mallians, who nearly killed Alexander, see Arrian 6, *passim*.
[153] The Sultanate of Johore, now part of Malaysia.
[154] Now the Kabul River near Peshawar in the Hindu Kush.
[155] Singapore.
[156] The Musicani inhabited a very rich Indian kingdom mentioned by Arrian (6.17–18). Alexander built a fortress in their territory.

and that sort is most pure and needs least refining, the quality or nature of it such as exceeds silver twelve times in value, as it is not subject to rust and so solid as endures age and fire above all other metals, yea, most improvable in its product, for Pliny *lib.* 33 *cap.* 3 observes that one ounce may well be beaten with the hammer into seven hundred leaves, every leaf being four fingers broad and length proportionable. In Africa and Asia is store of this precious earth, so much being imported by David and Solomon as provision for the Temple that as mentioned in 2 Chronicles 9:22 Solomon excelled all the kings of the earth in riches and wisdom, for silver there was as plenteous as stones and cedars as the fig-trees that grow abundantly in the plains. And from those two parts of the world much more gold is brought into Europe, where the least quantity is concocted, then from America, albeit of silver ore America yields more then Africa, Asia and Europe put together. And yet I have not heard of any lump of gold so great as Oviedo[157] reports he saw in America, one of which was an entire grain or piece of gold of seven pound weight valuing seven hundred pesos (a peso is thirteen ryals); the other was five pound weight. Peter Martyr also saw an ingot there that weighed 3310 pesos entire of itself without any artificial addition, a rarity fit to be presented to the Portugal king, to whom it was accordingly carried in the *Boadilla*, but miscarried by tempest.

Tarshish.

Now concerning the word 'Tarshish', so much criticised, it is *verbum ambiguum* and admits a various sense, for sometimes it signifies a city, othersome a region, as also a precious stone of the colour of the sea, but at some time the sea itself, as may be gathered. That there was a city so-called in Cilicia appears by that of the Prophet Jonah, who being sent by the Almighty to admonish Nineveh took a contrary way and and Joppa[158] shipped himself for Tarshish, of which city St. Paul the Apostle was a native, Acts 22:3. The name is probably deduced from Tarshish the son of Javan, Genesis 10:4, who in the days of Peleg planted in that part of the Lesser Asia which the Turks at this day call *Hamza*. But whereas Tarshish is mentioned in 1 Kings 10:22 and in 2 Chronicles 9:21 that Solomon's

---

[157] Gonzalo Fernandez de Oviedo y Valdez (1478–1557), a notary, rose from an obscure birth to become Keeper of the Wardrobe to the Infante Don Juan of Spain and Inspector of Gold Foundries in America (1514–1515). After a stay in Italy, where he met people like Michelangelo and Leonardo, he went travelling in the Indies, but not before he had written and published a romance, *Claribalte* (1520). He travelled to India (1521) and Cuba (1523); his *Historia general y natural de las Indias* (1526) appeared in Ramusio and was translated by Richard Eden as *The Decades of the New World or West India* (1555). He is also responsible for the famous story of Ponce de Léon and the fountain of youth.

[158] Joppa is "situated in the central sector of the coastal plain of Judaea (now adjoining Tel Aviv to its south); the ancient city was built on a rock hill . . . which juts out onto the Mediterranean" (Grant, *Guide* 318).

ships went to Tarshish with Hiram's servants, every year once came the ships of Tarshish bringing gold and silver and ivory etc., seeing gold in the 10 verse of that chapter is called 'gold of Ophir,' with submission the word 'Tarshish' there may signify 'the sea,' for it appears by the 1 Kings 9:26 that King Solomon built his navy at Ezion-geber which sailed to Ophir, so as albeit 'tis styled 'the navy of Tarshish' and 'Hiram's navy' 'tis probable those two neighbour Princes were concerned in the return of that voyage, the Phoenicians at that time being more expert seamen then the Jews, notwithstanding which that those ships were either riding in the Mediterranean or upon the Nile, unless brought over by sledge from Coptos or Pelusium as Cleopatra's was, which is very improbable. For otherwise it will be said those navies went to Cadiz, which place at that time being called *Tarteshus*,[159] Pimente fancies were vessels belonging thereunto. Otherwise, passing that strait, they sailed through the Atlantic, and doubling Cape Bona Speranza made their way into the Red Sea, as some have conceited, but a vain conception it is, seeing the Scripture in express terms acquaints us that the navies were built at Ezion-geber near Eilat upon the shore of the Red Sea, so as had Ophir been in any part in or near the Midland Sea or come from Tarshish in Cilicia, then the voyage might have been accomplished in far less time then three years, seeing that Tarshish was not above a week's sail from Joppa, a port twenty miles west from Jerusalem and not above three days' sail from Skandrun, *Alexandretta* of old, the most noted Syro-Phoenician port at the bottom of the Straits, but those that think by Tarshish is meant Ophir or else that there was some country in India of that name are more to be credited.

Further, from 2 Chronicles 20:36, where it is written that Jehoshaphat "built ships in Ezion-geber, which being broken were not able to go to Tharshish," some judge that 'Tharshish' there signifies the sea, and the rather for that the word carries it in several other places, as noted by several learned expositors. Saint Jerome is one, who in his paraphrase lately mentioned speaking of Ophir. "*Locus est Indiae*," says he, "*in quo aurum optimum nascitur*," adds "*Tharshish vel est regio Indiae ut vult Josephus; vel certe omne pelagus Tharshish appellatur. Etenim Hebrei Tharshish mare dici generaliter autumant.*"[160] And in Isaiah also 23:1, "*Ululate naves Tharshish*" is interpreted "Howl, ye ships of the sea," and in the 6 verse, "Go over to Tarshish," in the Vulgar Latin it is "*Transita maris.*" In like sort "the daughter of Tarshish" is in the 10 verse translated "*filia maris*," and in Ezekiel 27:12, 25 "the ships of Tarshish" is rendered "*naves maris*" in that edition. But, by being thus variously construed, thence it is that by 'Tarshish' sometimes is understood

---

[159] The lost ciy of Tartessus is often identified as Tarshish and located in the Guadalquivir river in south-western Spain. For details and its connection with Ophir, see the article by J. A. Thompson in *Illustrated Bible Dictionary*, 3: 1517–1519.

[160] "There is a place in India where the best gold originated, for Josephus would either have Tarshish a part of India or he would call all the sea Tarshish, for in Hebrew *Tharshish* means 'the sea,' as they generally assert" (*In Isaiam* 6. 12, PL 24. 212C).

a chrysolite, for the colour of that stone hath a resemblance with the sea. Howbeit, to find it an Indian region, as that great author I lately named conjectures, is past my undertaking.

Malacca.

Return we therefore to Malacca itself, where the Pole Arctic is elevated five degrees, a city within this Kingdom of Siam, to whose sceptre it was subject until about the Year of Our Lord 1508, when by the Portugal it was forced from Abdul,[161] at that time king, whose life they also very inconsiderately took away, as appeared by a dangerous mutiny sson after happening in the town, which Albuquerque quitted, and by Sequiera's[162] advice was converted into a garrison. It had a sufficient number of ordinance planted to fortify the place, seeing it was reported there was no less then three thousand; also seizing the King's exchequer into his hands, by inventory then taken, so much minted coin came to the King of Portugal's particular share, albeit but a fifth, as amounted unto two hundred and fifty thousand ryals of eight. But the unexpected and undeserved death of the King was so ill resented by the Siam king[163] and the neighbouring potentates that by a general combination taking the advantage of Albuquerque's absence they suddenly appeared in a very great body before the town, and by a desperate storm mastered both city and citadel, the Siam king very generously giving the Portugals leave to ship themselves away, but withal commanding the works they

---

[161] Herbert is mistaken. When the Portuguese conquered Malacca for the first time (1508) Sultan Mahmud (1488–1528) lost his throne to his son Ahmed (1508–1511), but regained it and killed Ahmed; Albuquerque then attacked Malacca in retaliation (see below), captured it and plundered it, as Herbert relates. Mahmud, wounded in the hand, fled, but later returned with help from neighbouring monarchs. The Portuguese attacked Malacca again (1526) under Pedro Mascarenhas, and Mahmud fled to Sumatra. For a contemporary Portuguese account of Malacca, see Tomé Pires, *Suma oriental* (1516; modern edition by A. Cortesão, 1944).

[162] Diogo Lopes de Sequiera (c. 1465–1530) went to Malacca in 1509 (not the previous year, as Herbert suggests) to establish trade, armed with a letter from King Manoel I. Local factions intrigued against him and there was a plot to kill him, as it was felt that the Portuguese would threaten local traders' business with Asia and Arabia. There was violence, and some Portuguese were killed. Sequiera then "commanded that a man and a woman, who had come on board the ships the day of the affray, should have an arrow passed through their skulls, and thus they were landed in one of his boats as a present to the King" (João Barros, *Decad II*; quoted in J. A. Crawfurd, *A Descriptive Dictionary of the Indian Islands and Adjacent Countries* [London: Bradbury and Evans, 1856], 246).

[163] Rama Thibodi II was King of Ayutthaya 1491–1529. He ruled from the city of that name, which is about forty miles north of Bangkok (see below). He was famous for having established a code of law based on that of Manu in India (C. G. F. Simkin, *The Traditional Trade of Asia* [New York: Oxford University Press, 1968], 157).

had made to be forthwith slighted. Howbeit, some few years after it was reduced under the crown of Portugal and so continued, until lately it hath been wrested from them by the Hollander,[164] whose plantations are scattered through those parts, and naval power so increased by the encouragement of that rich Indian commerce as hath rendered that industrious nation very formidable and which indeed hath given them wellnigh the dominion of those seas and the opporunity of engrossing to themselves not only the Molucca Isles but in a sort the sole traffic of the Orient, to their exceeding great advantage but prejudice of many others, yea, more especially to the damage and diminution of the English trade and reputation in those parts, for which we are justly to be reprehended, and imputable to our want of industry or neglect of appropriating to ourselves some convenient place for plantation and increase of men and merchandise according to that example the Portugal and Dutch have both given, who by that means have made themselves lords of all or most of the maritime parts of the west and south coasts of Africa and Asia the Great, and in a manner now give law to the greatest part of those indefensive people, who though they want no will, want power to obviate those intrusions.

Whereas the English, by a joint stock and select company, content themselves in managing their factories under the superintendance and inspection of Presidents and Agents, who it cannot be denied live both in India and Persia with splendour and reputation and make frequent and considerable returns, nevertheless by living wholly amongst Mohammedans and gentiles in places where they exercise authority and heathenish superstition and idolatry, their men are under a constant offence to see God dishonoured and have not that protection and indulgence they expect and merit, seeing that many times they are subjected to the causeless bravados of the military as also the craft of the civil sort of Indians, and upon slight cause and false information have too often been exposed to the rapine and arbitrary disposition of those infidels, who of late times, if report say true, have been known to cast our merchants into prison, where they have been fettered with chains and not set at liberty without considerable sums extorted from them, and all this without any just cause or provocation, which affronts would have been avoided had our East India Company fixed plantations in some secure places either upon isles or sea-coast there where men might exercise their religion with more freedom and purity and with more security to their persons and estates then can possibly be expected in the moving factories they only for some time are resident. The Portugal found it so when they had Hormuz, Goa and Calicut, and the Dutch no less by their commanding in Cochin, Malacca and Jakarta, which they now call Batavia, a most considerable port and kept all along in despite of the numerous and resolute Javans. Upon which considerations, I have sometimes thought that if but one-half of those English which

---

[164] The Dutch captured Malacca in 1641; they held it until 1795.

have removed into the Carib isles and planted colonies in Virginia, New England and other parts of Norumbega[165] in the West Indies had, if the royal authority held fit, been employed upon plantations in East India, Madagascar, Mauritius or other fit places, that design in all probability would in far less time have made another kind of product, both as to command by land and power by sea enlargement of trade and propagation of the Gospel. The Orient countries being superlative to the Occident in reference to all sorts of mechanic arts and also to a more valuable commerce in jewels, gold, silks, spices and drugs then America, and the East being overspread with gross gentilism gives no less invitation for the preaching of the Gospel and rescuing those poor wretches out of Satan's tyranny then any part of the new-found world, which is and ought to be the chief end of all such generous and public undertakings. And this in all likelihood might have been compassed by such a number, for, as I apprehend, there are in our western plantations double the number of Portugal and Dutch now extant in the East Indies, and by persons of such ingenuity and so good a purse as might advance the hnour of our nation, growth of trade and several other public advantages.

But to return. This town of Malacca is a port of good account whether we consider her strength or trade, albeit by reason the land is low where 'tis situate, is not reputed healthy. The town in shape is rather long then round, extending almost two English miles in length but not half so much in breadth. The buildings are low and ordinary and the streets narrow, the bazaar being the only place that has anything either beautiful or pleasurable. It is watered by the Gaza,[166] upon whose banks Barigaza stood of old, formerly called *Mazotas*, sufficiently deep and broad, yet admitting a bridge, which makes the inhabitants on either side able without boats to communicate with each other, and for its better defence has a castle well-stored with cannon[167] and a wall about reasonable-flankered and bettered by a late grass and counterscarp. But the gardens and fields abound

---

[165] Norumbega [*Norumberga*] was a semi-mythical place in North America, thought by some to have been in what is now New England. It appears on a 1529 map of the world drawn by Girolamo da Verrazzano, the brother of the explorer Giovanni. He called it "Oranberga," and it was described some years later (1542) by the French pirate and navigator Jean Fonteneau, also known as Alfonse de Saintonge (1484–1544). Scholars now consider that it was simply invented to fill a gap in North American geography, although there is a possibility that its name derived from a native American language. Fonteneau's exploits are described in *Les voyages aventureux du Capitaine Jean Alfonse* (1559), which appeared in English as *The Rutter of Jean Alfonse* (1600).

[166] Now known as the Melaka River.

[167] This would have been the "the great Portuguese fortress of A Famosa," which Moore calls "Melaka's most enduring symbol," and which contained "within its massive laterite walls . . . a castle, two palaces, government buildings, five churches and two hospitals." All that remains now is the Porta de Santiago, which bears the date 1670, when the Dutch made repairs to the buildings (Wendy Moore, *West Malaysia and Singapore* [Lincolnwood: Passport Books, 1993], 171).

with fruits, amongst which the durian is the principal and the pineapple, albeit they want not corn or grain of several sorts, for the land being low and the soil fat gives the labourer sufficient encouragement. Nevertheless, being so near the Equinox the air is usually warm and at some time above measure, so that the *solis ostia*[168] are here placed. Here is frequent thunder, but qualified by the long nights and frequent showers and breezes. The Indians are numerous hereabouts; the better sort have rich apparel, the commoners go the most part naked. They are generally witty and hospitable, love music and novelties, civil in peace and fierce in war, yet deceitful if too much credited. Their language is of great extent, no less there then in the world elsewhere the Latin and Arabic. Singapore is the other *fretum* that divides this continent from Sumatra, so narrow as a msuket will reach over, and by reason of rocks very dangerous for passengers. Ptolemy called it *Similta*, but *Sinticora* Castaldus.

Pattani.

Hence to Pattani is not above twelve hours travel. Ptolemy calls that place *Pat-inga*, Castaldus *Balanga* and others *Perimula*, but all agree it is in the Gulf of Bengal, which of old was *Sinus Argaricus extra Gangem*. There the Arctic pole is elevated seven degrees. A town it is situated betwixt Malacca and Siam, of good trade by reason of the commodities it affords, which attracts merchants, under regal government, and the Princes derive themselves from one *Gingee*, son and pro-rex to the King of Delhi, here substituted when Pattani was subjected.[169] The Mughal his great neighbour has often threatened to dethrone him, yet he keeps his own, being safeguarded by interposing Ganges and some small but useful islets, where he advantageously fortifies. The town is by situation strong and by twelve pieces of great brass ordinance better strengthened, one of which our men call a basilisk, being twenty-six foot long and well-proportioned both in bore and squaring. Some temples of idolatry here as in Johore its neighbour are seen,

---

[168] Doors of the sun.

[169] Pattani [*Patania*], known as Langkasuka until the advent of Islam and now in southern Thailand, was a port-kingdom on the east side of the Malay peninsula. *Gingee* is unidentified. Stories of Pattani's foundation vary; one version says that in the fourteenth century a fisherman called Paktani was sent by a nearby ruler to look out for a suitable place for a new settlement and he chose this location. Another, perhaps more historical, has one Phaya Tu Nakpa as founder-king, who converted to Islam and ruled under the new name of Sultan Ismail Shah. He died in 1530; in his reign the Portuguese arrived under the command of Godinho de Eredia (1516). In 1563 Sultan Muzaffar Shah of Pattani invaded Ayutthaya (Siam), and for some decades after 1584 it enjoyed great power and prosperity under four successive queens-regnant. By Herbert's time the Dutch controlled the trade thereabouts, as the English had discovered in 1613 (Foster, *England's Quest*, 211–12), and although they managed to set up a factory there in 1618 it lasted only until 1623, when it was "dissolved as uprofitable" (Foster, *England's Quest*, 217).

but of better note are those ancient monuments of some of their kings who are there buried.

The people are black and by reason of the heat show most part of their body naked; great delight they take in chawing betel and opium. *Arak* or strong liquor they also drink exceedingly; the better sort usually eat in thin plates of gold, others in porcelain. The people usually speak three languages, the Malay, the Siam and that of China, but their writing differs, for the Malay write from the right hand to the left as the Hebrews use, the Siam from the left unto the right, as we, but the China down-right or perpendicular, all three usual and no less useful to those that traffic there. They are a mixture of Mohammedans and gentiles; the one so worship God as the others do their pagod, both erroneously. Hospitable they are to such as from desire of novelty or gain reside amongst them, and enquire not much of their country, business or religion, but so addict to vice as strangers that come as travellers or merchants have extraordinary need to pray for grace to resist temptation, for ths custom in some places allures them to lubricity and debauched courses. Such as if grace does not restrain have reason have reason to take heed of punishment, seeing adultery they nevertheless punish. Howbeit, the young women are carelessly frolic and fearlessly merry and the married melancholy, because strictly observed. Idleness and heat provokes them so as they wallow in all manner of turpitude; the grape moves them, they say, to wickedness, for they delight their gust and palate with choicest wines, waters, *arak*, rice and fruits, but by this their intemperance abbreviate their days, so as sixty years is accounted an old age, which if you contemplate their excess, death's harbinger, and the zone they seat in, may well be granted.

Siam.

Adjoining this is Siam, *Sabanna* and *Cortatha* of old, a city and kingdom so named, declining north from the Equinoctial 14 degrees, [which] is a great and famous part of India, having Pattani to the south, to the west Pegu and part of the Bengalan Gulf. Johore, Malacca, a great part of Pegu, Burma and Cambodia were tributary to him, Patani also, *Jamohay*, *Odjea* and other territories watered by Ganges also acknowledge him, so as his power is large and well-known that within the memory of man he was able to bring into the field five hundred elephants and two hundred thousand fighting men armed with good swords, bows and arrows, shield and lance. The King pretends to a large race of kingly progenitors. The zone is hot, which makes the men black, and in such places little clothing is requisite, so that they content themselves with a cambolin of lawn of a sad colour, which is trebled about their shoulders. Howbeit, some tie a leather skin about their neck and as a badge of devotion gird their middles with a thong and hold a sombrero in their hands to abate the heat, but wear no sandals, both that the scorching sands may mortify their flesh and that the Tallapoi may be thought meritorious.[170] Now, albeit liberty be allowed Christians and indeed Moors and other superstitions, nevertheless the natives are transcendent idolators, carving their deities after the shapes of Pan and Priapus with other goatish fancies, yea, in postures not fit to be remembered. They have groves and altars also, whereon they offer flesh, fruits, flowers, and many times when the Tallapoi tell them their demon is melancholy they warble out haromious music and do what they can to make him merry. Others by break of day run to their pagods with a basket of rice, hoping that day will be happier. The kings of Arakan,[171] Tenasserim, Siam, Pegu, Ava and Tangu[172] are all gentiles and have their temples stuffed with pagods.

The Tallapoi preach usually every Monday (their Sabbath) in the market, and assemble their auditory by the sound of a copper basin. These seem mendicants by profession, yet what by awe, for as some say the very infernal spirits obey their incantantions, and what by policy, for they contemplate humility externally very much, the people have them in high estimation by their prediction of future events and marvellous knowledge in things past and present, by magic and moral observation, resolving, dissuading, applauding, directing and delighting such as credit them, and credit most of these ethnics do, supposing them "Of gods th' interpreters and Phoebus's lays, / The three-legg'd charming stool, the clarion bays, / Planets, birds, language and all old assays." Such be their priests. And for the people, as report goes they have been detestable sodomites, a sin so hateful to Nature as is not to be named, for as an unnatural uncleanness it abhors it. Now, to deter these catamites a late Queen Rectrix[173] prudently commanded that all the male children should have a bell of gold in which was an adder's tongue dried put through the prepuce, which by custom took away the contempt and became rather an ornament, so as at this day some will exceed and have three or four of

---

[170] St. Francis Xavier, who was in Japan (1550–1551), described Buddhism as "a fraudulent law and an invention of the Devil," and Buddha himself as a "gymnosophist," which he most certainly was not (Audrius Beinorius, "Buddhism," 12). Matteo Ricci also ridiculed Buddhism, because of the belief in reincarnation and in the sanctity of animal life (Jonathan Spence, *The Memory-Palace of Matteo Ricci* [Harmondsworth: Penguin Books, 1985], 249).

[171] Arakan [*Arrachan*] was a city-state now located in Rakhine State, Burma. It is bordered by the Bay of Bengal in the west and Bangladesh to the east, and at one time its territory included Chittagong, the second-largest city in Bangladesh. It was not conquered by the Burmese until 1784.

[172] Tangu or Tuang-ngu was a kingdom and city of the Shan State in Burma. King Namdabayin (1581–1599) was the last ruler of the First Tuang-ngu Dynasty.

[173] Herbert may be referring here to Queen Shinsawbu (1453–1472), who reigned in Pegu (1453–1460) and then in Dagon (1460–1472). She was a rare istance of a queen regnant in the area. Herbert's description of this and other Peguan customs relies heavily (in fact, almost plagiarises it in places) on that of Ralph Fitch (see Hakluyt, *Voyages* 252–69).

those bells pendant, but when they have a mind to marry the midwife presents a soporiferous potion, during whose operation the bell is loosed from the flesh and fastened to the foreskin, and the unguent being applied, the cure is quickly perfected.[174] This practice and other the uncomely habit and lascivious practices of the women there Caesar Frederick[175] observes in his travels, as also Mr. Fitch a London merchant, Antonio Galvano and others, and how incredible soever it seems to some, I suppose there are both in London and other parts of Europe merchants and seamen who have been in those parts and seen what I have related. Here sedge and palmetto-leaves are used for paper.

The usual place of residence for the King is at Indy,[176] a town situate within an isle compassed wellnigh with the Menam;[177] his palace is large and pretty well-built and held tenable. Howbeit, most other houses are low and mean and the streets narrow, but available to keep out the extreme heat which at some time rages. Those of the coast of Coromandel one way and the Chinese the other traffic hither with satins, porcelains and other rich commodities, which makes the place the more noted. The boys ofttimes paint themselves with a celestial colour from top to toe and as an augmentation of beauty cut, gash and pink their skins,

---

[174] This deadpan passage (or the similar one in Fitch) came in for much hilarity as "Meriton Latroon," improved on Herbert's horrified description by noting that "the better sort [of women, Ed.] are covered with a fine transparent taffeta or dainty lawn, which by a cunning device is made to open, that as they pass along, the least air discovers all to all men's immodest views" (Richard Head, *The English Rogue Described in the Life of Meriton Latroon* [London, 1665], 443).

[175] Cesare Frederici, an Italian merchant, travelled during the 1560s–1580s in India and neighbouring areas, visiting Vijayanagara two years after its sacking (1567). His voyages were recorded by Ramusio and Hakluyt, and Thomas Hickock translated his account as *The Voyage and Travaile of M. Caesar Frederick Merchant of Venice into the East India, the Indies and beyond . . .* (1588). The dates of his birth and death are not known. Due to his limited literary skills, Ralph Fitch, Foster tells us, "eagerly availed himself of the help offered by Thomas Hickock's English version . . . of the *Viaggio* of Cesare Frederici" (*England's Quest*, 106), so it is not surprising to see Herbert mention him.

[176] The capital of Siam (since 1350) was Ayutthaya, which fits Herbert's description; I cannot trace where the name *Indy* came from. The palace Herbert mentions here is probably the one built by Rama Thibodi II in 1499. It is situated on an island at the junction of three rivers, one of which is the Chao Phraya, which also runs through Bangkok. The King when Herbert was writing his account was Jettha (1628–1630). For details of the old capital, see J. Cummings, *Thailand* (Melbourne: Lonely Planet Publications, 1990), 128–33 or Sibylle Bouquet, ed., *The Green Guide: Thailand* (London: Michelin, 2002), 84–91.

[177] *Menam* means "mother of waters." Crawfurd states that "it seems the only [word] in the Siamese language for a river. It is in fact a generic and not a proper name" (*Indian Islands*, 202). Here it probably means the lower Chao Phraya basin.

which they apprehend to be a noble and ingenious ornament, but to us rather bred horror then affectation; the men affect perfumes and practice compliment.

The *cabriz*-stone.

The soil notwithstanding, the River Menam is but indifferent for grass but uberous in rich stones as diamonds, chrysolites, onyx, magnets and bezoars. It hath plenty of *lignum aloes*, benjamin and cotton; it hath also mines of copper, silver being plentifully brought thither from Japan, but victuals and like commodities they have abundantly from other parts, which is the reason that they are bought here cheaper then in many other places. Amongst stones most memorable is the *cabriz* or bloodstone here generated, the marvellous virtue whereof is such as Osorius tells us that when the Portuguese had war with the Sumatrans, one time they descried a junk at sea, which after some resistance was boarded by Nakhoda Beg[178] the captain, but after long and smart fight the armed Portuguese, entering among the naked Indians, easily put to the sword all that begged not quarter, amongst others Nakhoda Beg himself, who bled not, albeit they had slashed and wounded him in sundry places. They were amazed at the sight and thought it magical, till having taken from his arm a bracelet of gold wherein was the *cabriz*-stone, the reason then appeared, for that was no sooner removed but blood issued abundantly from every wound he had. Doubtless this is the best bloodstone in the world, and could it prevent wounding as well as staunch blood, might worthily be ranked amongst stones most precious. The beast out of which this *cabriz*-stone stone is taken is called *cabral*; the Chinese residing at Bantam are best-acquainted with him, albeit some say that in Siam and the Java he is seen the oftenest.

Pegu.

Adjoining this is Pegu,[179] *Lestarum Regio* in Ptolemy, confined by Siam, Ganges and the ocean, a monarchy of greater extent fifty years ago and till the Siamite plucked forcibly from that crown several great and wealthy seigneuries;[180] howbeit, she is yet commandress of many large territories and islands, as *Monym*, Barongo, *Nogomallo, Duradura, Cocos*[181] and others. By Castaldus it is supposed to be that old *Triglipton* which is mentioned in Ptolemy and by him placed under

---

[178] This is not a name at all; *nakhoda* means "captain" in Malay.

[179] Modern-day Bago, Burma.

[180] In 1539 King Tabinshweti had annexed Pegu from its last king, Takayupti (see below for details).

[181] Barongo is an island in the mouth of the Sittang river in Burma; the other places are unidentified. The French writer and traveller Urbain Chevreau (1613–1701), in his *Histoire du monde* (Paris, 1686), also mentions *Triglipton* as being either Martaban or Pegu, and has a similar description of the temple, as well as the list of produce given

18 degrees; it has Arctic elevation 16 degrees 40 minutes. The city is walled with stone, beautified with turrets and to issue out and in shows four gates and thrice that number of posterns, but made most defensive by a deep graff that circumvolves her, so large and deep and has intercourse with the sea that crocodiles[182] are many times seen to swim there. The streets are not many, but those that be are large and broad, which is rare in hot countries, and seldom crooking. Afore most doors grow trees whose fruit and shade make them useful and acceptable. It is divided into the new and old; the old is greatest and best-inhabited. The country is now very bare in wood, albeit in old times it abounded with timber of great height, of which in his 2 *lib. Georgicon* seems to have some knowledge: "Of those great woods in th'utmost India bred, / Near the world's furthest border, whose high head / No shaft can well the tops thereof surmount, / Though shot by those we archers good account."[183] That these [people] are diabolical is evident by their *varellas*[184] which are observable, for most of their *varellas* are stuffed with ugly idols. That at Dagon[185] was the most remarkable for structure without and ornament within, out-braving any other in the Orient; the wilderness or garden about it and superstition there used are so strange as might very well challenge a large description.

This kingdom abounds with the most sorts of Nature's blessings, for here is store of gold, silver, lead, and iron, also smaragds, topazes, rubies, sapphires, garnets, emeralds, spinels[186] and cat's eyes, as also plenty of rice, *caravances*, long pepper, sugar, *benoyn*, musk, gum-lac, bamboo, cotton and callicoes, but all these if they were centipled are not able to make them happy, wanting the true Pearl, that which the godly merchant bought, though to obtain it he sold all his frail possession, for albeit the holy Apostle Saint Thomas brought them the tidings of salvation yet they love darkness more then light, delighting at this day in

---

below (II, viii, 518). It seems that Chevreau had read the French translation of Herbert's book.

[182] The crocodiles may be a detail borrowed from Ralph Fitch, who wrote about "a great ditch . . . full of water, with many crocodiles in it" (Hakluyt, *Voyages*, 261).

[183] Virgil, *Georgics* 2. 122-125.

[184] Herbert used the same term found in Fitch's account; a *varella* is a temple, usually with a gilded roof and "round like a sugar loaf," as Fitch noted (Hakluyt, *Voyages*, 263).

[185] Dagon [*Dogonne*] is the Shwe Dagon or Golden Pagoda, located on Singattana Hill. It was built between the sixth and tenth centuries. Ralph Fitch saw it in 1586 and described it as "of a wonderful bigness and all gilded from the foot to the top. It is the fairest place, as I suppose, that is in the world" (Hakluyt, *Voyages*, 264). In 1608 it was plundered by Filipe Brito, who made off with the bell. For further details, see Win Pe, *Shwedagon* (Rangoon: Printing and Publishing Corporation, 1972) and Cayetano J. Socorras, "The Portuguese in Lower Burma: Filipe Brito de Nicote," *Luso-Brazilian Review* 3 (1966): 3–24.

[186] A spinel is a red stone rather similar to a ruby.

obscure and loathed sins, and the *kyacks* are filled with filthy idols, insomuch as Bonferre,[187] an old Franciscan, after four tedious years' labour to reduce them to some conformity with the Church of Rome, came home professing that he had rather with St. Anthony preach among pigs then such a swinish generation. The truth is they believe they know not what, and *"Quaenam est ista simplicitas? Nescire quod credas?"*[188] says Jerome to the Luciferians. Yet somewhat, if all be true he tells, is worthy your notice, as that they believe the world, consisting of Heaven, Sea and Earth, had four creations (which tradition is from the banians), and that for impiety it was four times destroyed, *viz.* by fire, wind, water and earthquakes. Each age was governed by a tutelary *numen*, miserable in this, that he was transitory and not immortal. They reckon that the last destruction of the world and the death of their last God was thirty thousand years ago (in Plato's great year, perhaps) and that all shall once more suffer a chaos. They also imagine that a great Lord who is omniscient and omnipotent lives and rules in Heaven, but they do not worship him, in that Satan, who ever loves to cover truth in dark mists of ignorance, assures them he desires it not and doth them no hurt; howbeit, they worship that liar lest he do them mischief. They believe a revivification of the body after death, co-union with the soul and, as Bomferrus believes, confess a threefold receptacle of souls departed, *Nashac*, *Nishac* and *Shua*, i.e. Heaven, Hell and Purgatory, by which the Friar labours to convince us of more ignorance then these pagans.

Their habit is a thin, fine lawn; some call it a cambolin, which differs little from what they wear in Industan and Siam, but in this they vary: they wear no beards and had a fancy to dye their teeth black because dogs' teeth are white, whom they hate to imitate. They also cut and pink their flesh to become no less modish then their neighbours. The crows and parrots here are grey, as usually in Africa. The land is low in many parts and subject to inundation, but, which troubles them most, be ravenous beasts as tigers, wolves and the like offensive creatures, to avoid which they raise their houses upon arches or posts of bamboos that be large reeds, and they ascend usually by ladders.

About an hundred years ago the Peguan monarch was far more formidable then he is at present; his diadem then sparkled with the lustre of twelve wealthy provinces which acknowledged Pegu their sovereign. Some of those were Siam,

---

[187] Fr. Bonferre [*Bomferrus*] was actually a French Dominican, not a Franciscan. He was in Pegu (1554–1557) with Fr. Gaspar de Cruz as one of the chaplains for the Portuguese community. He was said to have studied the Mon language and he wrote an account of his experiences in Pegu, where his largely futile attempts to convert the local Buddhists were not appreciated very much (G. D. E. Hall, *Burma* [London: Hutchinson, 1960], 50). Samuel Purchas included a translation of Bonferre's report (*Pilgrims* 5: 507), from which Herbert quotes here.

[188] "What sort of nonsense is that? Don't you know what you believe?" (PL 23. 166C).

Ava, *Chavilan*, Burma, *Jangomer*, Tuang-ngu, Caplan[189] (where are found store
of rubies, sapphires, spinels and other precious stones which are digged out of the
rocks), Lavo, *Meliotalk* etc.,[190] out of which he yearly extracted two millions of
crowns and a million men to serve him upon all occasions. This hardly could content him (for what will satiate the ambitious?), seeing that by a too lofty conceit
of his greatness he had his neighbour Princes in contempt. Tyranny succeeded
his pride, and that begot destruction, for the Viceroy of Ava, whom he found no
privilege by being his uncle, nor that he unwillingly submitted under his government, broke asunder his silver yoke of servitude. However, ere he could ripen his
design the Peguan, having notice, suddenly arrests him, so that in amazement
he acknowledges his fault and begs the other's mercy. But the Peguan king, not
liking a reconciled enemy, quickly made his uncle shorter by the head, and to terrify others by that example made wife, children and forty others whom he most
respected bear a part in that tragedy. It was justice upon the rack, no doubt, and
served rather to exasperate others then to secure their loyalty, as appeared by the
Viceroy of Siam, who perceiving his own uncertain standing, the least cause being jealousy and the least jealousy ushering death, he suddenly rebels, and with
all the force he could raise, ere the Peguan returned from Ava, enters Pegu in a
hostile way. But the King, having proclaimed him a rebel and threatened terrible
revenge, marches against the Siamite with an army, as some report, of nine hundred thousand fighting men. That world of men could not contrary the decree
of the Almighty, for such was the confused haste he made, precipitated by fury,
such the hate his cruelty had gained him and such the affright his uncle's *malus
genius* everywhere presented, that after three hours fight his monstrous multitude
turn tail and yield themselves a prey to the enraged axe of war, which was glutted
with blood, so as by that day's victory the Siamite advances in triumph. Howbeit, not willing to make more haste then good speed, he returns and fortifies the
most considerable places in his own kingdom, whiles the Peguan king, winged
with rage, in the head of another nummerous army enters Siam with a resolution
to pursue him to his very door, but the Siamite, arming himself with the fox's
skin, refused to fight, not so much out of fear as resolved upon an easier way of
conquest, for whiles the Peguan darts many fiery defiances and calls him rebel,
coward and whatnot, the Siamite opened the sluices and gave way to the swift

---

[189] Caplan, Ralph Fitch noted (and from whom Herbert appears to be pilfering information), "is the place where they find the rubies and sapphires and spinels; it stands
six days journey from Ava in the Kingdom of Pegu" (Hakluyt, *Voyages*, 265). However,
there is no town of that name, and Jack Beeching, the editor of Hakluyt, suggests that
"this could hardly be a mangled hearsay version of Mogok, the ruby-mining centre in the
mountains north of Mandalay—but what else might it be?" (Hakluyt, *Voyages*, 441, n.
103).
[190] Lavo [*Lawran*] was a Mon kingdom of central Siam in the Chao Phraya basin.
Meliotalk is unidentified.

rivers Salwin[191] and Menam to break their banks, which flushed so violently into the Peguan army that for want of boast above seven hundred thousand of the Peguan army perished, and the rest with fear or famine totally destroyed. Nor was this strange, seeing that the Salwin and the Menam, like Nile and Niger, overflow and supply theirw want of rain, mellowing the earth so as it compares with Egypt for plenty and with any other part of India for rareties.

Nevertheless, it seems the King made shift to save himself from that inundation, for notwithstanding that incredible number their records say were destroyed by that accident, the ensuing year he used the means to raise another army which entered Siam, but with so little success as besides the rout of five hundred thousand men the death of his son was added to, so that he made a sorrowful retreat to Martaban with less then one-third of his army, but, which was worse then that, through these continued brawls of war his treasure impaired, his citizens were impoverished by want of trade and his kingdom in a sort depopulated through loss of so many men, which proved not motives of pity with the other subjected provinces but provocatives rather to unfetter themselves as Siam had done. Accordingly the Viceroys of Burma, of Taungu and of Arakan confederate, and whiles the King of Pegu was contriving new designs at Martaban enter Pegu with a desperate army, foraging and destroying such as the late famine had spared, where though they found few people and less food, yet got they riches incredible, for out of the city of Pegu they took no less treasure then loaded two thousand camels, and as a period not only made the wretched King crownless but crowned their conquest with his life, his wife and three sons sorrowfully accompanying him. Now this success was attended with misfortune of another kind, for the sovereign of Arakan and the other two, disagreeing about the dividing that great spoil, were beaten home by the Burman king, who also enjoyed it but a while, the Siamite entering so furiously that the Burman was content with a safe retreat, leaving the Siamite victorious, who since, upon a marriage 'twixt one of the royal family of Pegu and his daughter, has quit his claim and gives the right heir leave to repossess both city and kingdom, which a short peace has recovered to little less trade and beauty then it had formerly.[192] But, to facilitate our travel,

---

[191] The River Salwin or Salween [*Suḥan*] flows from Tibet to the Andaman Sea and passes through China, Burma, and Thailand.

[192] Herbert's history or his source's is confused. In a short a space as possible, this is what happened. In 1530 king Mahathiri Zerathura of Taungu died and was succeeded by Tabinshweti (1530–1551), an ambitious man who desired to reunite Burma as a kingdom with himself as its ruler. King Binya Ran II of Pegu had died in 1526 and had been succeeded by Takayutpi (1526–1539), but Tabinshweti asserted his own claim to Pegu and attacked it for the first time in 1534. Beaten back several times, Tabinshweti kept trying, and in 1539 he finally succeeded; Takayutpi fled to the neighbouring state of Prome, where his brother-in-law was king. Tabinshweti advanced on Prome, but held back because it was too strong; Takayutpi decided to break out and attack the enemy

accept an adjoining map to that, this describing India on the other side of Ganges. From Pegu to Bengal are ninety leagues; the second town of note is Martaban under 15 degrees, which some imagine to be *Triglipton* noted by Pliny, rather
then Pegu, as thinks Castaldus. The next good road is Negrais,[193] nigh which is
Kyonkadun, whence we pass to Pegu in *paros*[194] or boats by water. *Medon* is upon
that river, from whence we go to Dedaye, to Syriam, to Kaye and then come to
Pegu.[195] At Caplan we found stones of price, as merchants told us.

Map of Pegu and Borneo [illustration not shown]

---

himself, having failed to secure help from others for his restoration, and was killed, at
which point Tabinshweti was recognised as King of Pegu. Now Tabinshweti decided to
expand his territory and attacked the town of Martaban, which he destroyed (1540), followed by Prome, which surrendered after a tough fight to his forces in 1542. It was at
Martaban that the Burmese, having practically starved the town into submission, pretended to make a deal with the Viceroy, who came out with his family and was massacred; Herbert mentions this episode. In the next two years Tabinshweti's general Bayinnaung (later king) defeated the Shans of Ava and invaded Arakan in 1546. At this
point the Siamese intervened and attacked Tavoy in Arakan, which forced Tabinshweti
into retreat once more, but two years later he decided to invade Siam, and his huge army
(described by Herbert), under the command of Bayinnaung and including some Portuguese soldiers, got as far into Siam as Ayutthaya, but the defences were strong and soon
the Burmese army was starving, ridden with disease, and under constant attack from the
Siamese forces. Had they not managed to capture the son-in-law of the Siamese king,
Maha Chakrapat (1548–1569), they would have been defeated, but this allowed them to
negotiate a retreat from Siam. Soon after this Tabinshweti took to drink and Bayinnaung
assumed the regency, but he remained loyal to the King, who was eventually assassinated
in 1549 by a nobleman who was supposed to be looking after him when Bayinnaung was
away quelling a rebellion. Bayinnaung himself succeeded to the throne soon afterwards.
In 1550 Smim Sawhtut managed to regain the Peguan throne for a short time, followed
by Smim Htaw (1551–1553), but the Siamese soon recovered their conquest. There was
constant strife between Siam and the Burmese kingdoms; for further details and a good
account of the history, see Prince Damrong Rajanupab, *Our Wars with the Burmese: Thai-
Burmese Conflict 1539–1767* (Bangkok: White Lotus Press [1917], 2001).

[193] Cape Negrais is one of the mouths of the Irawaddy River in Burma.

[194] A fast-moving sailing or rowing boat, usually with a sharp end. The standard
(Malaysian) spelling is *prau*.

[195] Kyonkadun [*Cosmyn*], Dedaye [*Dela*], Syriam [*Cirion*], and Kaye [*Macao*] are all
towns on the way north to Pegu after crossing the Gulf of Martaban. *Medon* is unidentified.

The elephant adored.

To tell you what is reported of this monarch when he shows himself in his royal paradrome or when he is disposed to load himself with gems, his head, ears, arms, hands, legs and feet resembling a spangled firmament such as may amaze the sense and dazzle the eye, or of his deifying his elephants because milk-white and of greater bulk then usual would be but repetition. I will therefore content myself in giving you the prospect of that his deity, not that he is unknown in England but for other things then his shape rendering him worth the observation.

The elephant, for growth and understanding reputed the chiefest of unreasonable animals, has been the subject of sundry learned pens, as of Aristotle, Plutarch, Pliny, Strabo, Arrian and others. They go two, sometimes three years with young and have extreme torment in their labour. The teat is 'twixt their forelegs, which the young easily find and suck with eagerness; at three years of age they wean themselves and fall to other provent as herbs, boughs of trees, shrubs and like vegetables, but when in service have more dainty fare as corn, fruits, roots, sugar-canes, milk, whey and such as may increase both strength and courage. They grow till they be fifteen years old and are usually eighteen foot high, but some of the highest mount to four and twenty. Notwithstanding such marvellous greatness they are not dull and unwieldy, but quick and spirited; they can and easily do lie down and rise as other beasts, contrary to the report of some old writers. So active are they, notwithstanding their cylindrical form of leg, as at Rome in Nero and Galba's[196] time they were taught to dance upon a cable or great rope, as we find reported by Suetonius, and so full of courage as no story gives any more commendation to any beast then to the elephant that King Porus fought upon against Alexander. And albeit his tusks and his proboscis are his best weapons, yet can he frame his mighty body as occasion serves into offensive and defensive postures. In rutting time, which is commonly when the season is hottest, the males are mad and hardly to be ruled without the females' company. Some confidently report that their testicles are in or near their forehead, which being a tender part, is the reason the conductor sits there and with his iron rod or hook there corrects him; howbeit, Aristotle places his stones near his reins. His trunk is long and composed of small nerves which be full of strength and very agile; his skin is rough and ash-coloured, his teeth proportionable to his body. Some are thirteen foot long and weigh upwards of a hundred and thirty pounds. Muddy rivers and cool shadowed places best please, but swine, serpents and mice displease them; cock-crowing doth also offend them. The Persians call him the symbol of fidelity, Egyptians the hieroglyphic of justice, Indians of piety, Siamites of memory, Arabs the ensign of magnanimity, Sumatrans the emblem of providence. Pliny in 8 *lib. Natural History* gathers them together: "*Intellectus illi sermonis patrii imperiorumque obedientia officiorumque di dicere memoria, amoris*

---

[196] Servius Sulpicius Galba was Roman Emperor 68–69.

et gloriae voluptas, imo vera religio quoque siderum solique ac lunae veneratio.[197] I
shall sum up all in that excellent description Job 40, as by Mr. Sandys[198] is paraphrased:

> With thee God made the mighty elephant,
> Who ox-like feeds on every herb and plant.
> His mighty strength lies in his able loins,
> And where the flexure of his navel joins
> His stretched-out tail presents a mountain-pine.
> The sinews of his stones like cords combine,
> His bones the hammer'd steel in strength surpass,
> His sides are fortified with ribs of brass,
> Of God's great works the chief. Lo, He who made
> This behemoth hath armed him with a blade;
> He feeds on lofty hills, lives not by prey.
> About this gentle prince the subjects play;
> His limbs he couches in the cooler shades.
> Oft when Heaven's burning eye the fields invades
> To marishes he resorts, obscur'd with reeds
> And hoary willows, which the moisture feeds.
> The chiding currents at his entry rise,
> Who quivering Jordan swallows with his eyes.
> Can the bold hunter take him in a toil,
> Or by the trunk produce him as his spoil?

Musk-cats here are also store of. She exceeds the castor[199] for bigness; her head
is little, her eyes are clear and has a long muzzle, but her teeth be sharp and offensive, her hair parti-coloured, hard and bristly, yellow above and white downwards. Her pocket is near the genitory, except sometimes with a spoon or stick,
but when out of servitude of her own accord she parts with it, which by its fragor
is discovered by the careless passenger.[200]

---

[197] ". . . it understands the language of its native land, is obedient to orders, remembers the duties that it has been taught, and has a desire for affection and honour [as well
as] true religion and worship of the stars, sun and moon" (8. 1).

[198] George Sandys (1578–1644) was an English traveller, poet, and colonist who
lived in Virginia for ten years (1621–1631). There, amongst other activities, he found
time to translate Ovid's *Metamorphoses* (1626). His best-known work, however, is the one
quoted here, the *Paraphrase upon the Psalms and Hymns dispersed throughout the Old and
New Testaments* (1636). The reference here is Job 40:15–24. Richard Hooper has edited
the *Poetical Works of George Sandys* (London: J. R. Smith, 1872).

[199] The beaver.

[200] Musk-cats are a kind of civet-cat, also known as bondars and native to Bengal.
Ben Jonson mentions their "fragor" in *Every Man Out of His Humour*: "He sleeps with a

Sumatra.

Come we now to the Indian islands, the chiefest of which is Sumatra, that famous isle which Aristotle *Lib. de Mundo* and others of old call *Taprobane*,[201] and
from the plenty of gold found there supposed to be Ophir or Parvaim, and the
isle there thence called *Taparvane*, with which agree Junius and Tremellius, as
formerly noted. Odoric calls it *Simolta*, Josephus *Samotra*, others *Alramis* and *Za-
mara*, *Simunda* in Ptolemy, by the inhabitors *Salyca* or *Salutra*, and if Japan be not
an isle may truly be reputed the third great isle throughout the universe. Six hundred, some say nine hundred of our miles long it is, and in breadth somewhere
two hundred and forty, traded to, as some suppose, by Solomon, was unknown
to Alexander, unless, as Megasthenes thinks, by Onesicritus his vice-admiral
discovered. Iambulus an errant Greek was here two hundred years afore Christ's
nativity, if Diodorus Siculus had true information, and if so, may be reputed the
first discoverer, but of a Christian Alvaro Tellez[202] is thought the first, who *Anno*
1506 to find gold sailed whither wind and weather guided, since when most
merchants of the world have knowledge of it. 'Tis nadir to the Equinoctial, so
that the Pole-star is not in the southerly part of the island visible at all, but depressed under the horizon. Many petty kings there advance their sceptres, but
the richest crown encircles the ecliptic brow of that tyrant of Achin.[203] Howbeit,
all of them are well-stored with gold and stones, but miserable in their Mawmetry[204] and superstition. Most of them were not many years since so engulfed in
the abyss of paganism that they used to adore cat, rat, dog or devil, but since the
Alcoran has crowded in, the worship of these elementary creatures is abolished.
Both sexes go most part naked; the soil is good where rivers are near, but barren
where gold is obtained.

Several towns of note here be. The mediterranean are Manacabo, formerly
called *Sindacanda*, where is gold, but of best note are Achin, by them called
Aceh, not far from that cape called *Jovis promotorium* in Ptolemy, Padang, Painan, *Daya*, Tiku, Pariaman, Jambi, *Tykoa* (east of Jambi), *Baruzee*, Bukittingi,

---

musk-cat every night and walks all day hanged in pomander-chains for penance" (*Works*,
2.1: 108–9).

[201] They are wrong; 'Taprobane' denotes Ceylon (see above, several times).

[202] Alvaro Tellez, a Portuguese, was one of the captains in Tristao da Cunha's fleet.
He landed in Aceh (1506), as Herbert says. For details of the Portuguese in Sumatra, see
Mark Dion, "Sumatra through Portuguese Eyes: Excerpts from João de Barros' *Decadas
da Asia*," *Indonesia 9* (1970): 128–62.

[203] The Sultanate of Achin [*Acheen*], in northern Sumatra, is now known as Aceh,
with its capital at Banda Aceh. During Herbert's time it was ruled by Sultan Iskander
Muda (1604–1637), Herbert's "tyrant of Achin," who greatly expanded his territory in
eastern Sumatra and gained some in the Malay Peninsula as well. The Dutch, in spite of
considerable efforts, were unable to subjugate this powerful country until 1878.

[204] Mohammedanism.

Menantabo, Cambar, Aru, Darau and, though last, not least in gold, Pasé.[205] And in the strait 'twixt the island and the continent against Johore are the Barellae[206] and other small but very pleasant islands. The rivers flow with fish and might prove more delightful for the net and angle did not those hateful crocodiles, here more then in Nilus, frustrate both. *"Natura se potissimum prodit in minimis"*[207] has reference to Democritus his atoms, otherwise this might have challenged it, seeing these amphibii are observed to be one of the greatest wonders we meet with, in that from so small a beginning as an egg not much bigger then that of a turkey it increases to eight or ten yards in length. Their bodies are not longer then their tale, which is a weapon of like use with them the proboscis is to the elephant. Their mouth is very wide, at one gulp being able to swallow horse or man; their teeth are ingrailed,[208] have no tongue. They cannot move the upper jaw, and albeit the belly be penetrable, yet the back is hardly to be pierced. The brumal[209] quarter they fast from food, but the rest of the year devour all sorts of prey, and that with voracity. No less-notable is the number 60 in the female, for sixty days pass ere she lay her eggs, which are usually sixty in number; sixty days she conceals them and when she sits spends sixty days in the hatching. She

---

[205] Sumatra is now, of course, part of Indonesia. Minangkebau [*Manacabo*] was an island kingdom in west Sumatra famed for its gold mines. The first European there was Jean Parmentier (1529) and the Dutch East India Company was trading there in 1651; Padang is a town on the west coast of Sumatra, a major Dutch trading-post in the seventeenth century still with "some semblance of old-world charm" (Dorai, *Indonesia*, 182), as is Painan; Tiku was a pepper-trading port which Thomas Best visited in 1613 and 1615, followed by William Keeling in 1616; (Foster, *England's Quest*, 240, 245); Pariaman [*Priaman*], on the west coast of Sumatra, was a source of pepper and spices; Sir James Lancaster sent a ship there (1602) and Best traded pepper there in 1613; Jambi is on the eastern side of Sumatra; in 1615 the English began trading with its ruler, and, in spite of Dutch objections, established a factory there which stayed until 1681 (Foster, *England's Quest*, 246); *Tykoa* is unidentified; it does not appear on any map and may be a misreading of Tiku; Bukittingi [*Cattatinga*] is another west-coast town; its name means "Tall Hill," and it was a Dutch outpost (Dorai, *Indonesia*, 182–84); Minangkabau [*Menantabo*] must be another reference to the people rather than a place, as Bukettingi is the centre for that culture; Aru and Darau are the same place. Tomé Pires, a Portuguese official who was there in 1513, mentions that it was a source of rattan and slaves, amongst other things (Simkin, *Trade*, 165); Pasé [*Passaman*] was a port in Aceh which traded with the Peguans before the Europeans came; in 1529 a Portuguese attack was repulsed (Simkin, *Trade*, 183).

[206] Probably Karimun Island and others, although there are islands known as 'Varella' on the other side of the Malay Peninsula which are marked on the seventeenth century map.

[207] "Nature shows itself most powerfully in the smallest things" (Bacon, *De dignitate et augmentis scientiarum* 1: 541).

[208] Indented.

[209] Winter, which was sometimes known as 'brume.'

has sixty teeth and sixty joints, and sixty years is usually the age of this detested amphibium, whether it be beast, fish or serpent. By seamen it is called 'alligator', corruptedly from *allegardos*, a word compounded of Spanish and Almain;[210] the name we give it is a *croceo calore*, or *per antiprasin quod crocum timeat*. The most noxious of all sea-monsters it is, and rightly becomes the dissemblers' epithet: "*In quibus est astutia hyenae et pietas crocodili*,"[211] the Egyptians say of impudence, and yet as daring as it is we find them fearful of such as are bold and bold towards the fearful, awed by none more then the ichneumon,[212] who oftimes steals into his belly and gnaws his guts, whiles he opens his chaps to let the trochil[213] in to pick his teeth, which gives it the usual feeding.

Hence we sail by some small isles called *Marrah* and *Lampon*[214] in the Straits of Sunda,[215] so-named by Ptolemy, and from a point and town in the next great island. Of polygyny we might better speak then land, such bad luck by the malevolent Venus or ill diet had our late intended plantation there, where was such mortality of men that the name was ironically changed into 'Kill-abundance.' Sumatra is divided from Java by the Straits of Sunda, so-called from the isles 'Sundae' as Maginus imagines, but where Sunda is, is better known then the isles so-called.

Java the Greater. Bantam.
Java Major is an isle declining 7 degrees 40 minutes towards the Antarctic from the Equinoctial and placed in the 120th degree of longitude, a very great and noble isle, for from east to west it stretches one hundred and fifty leagues or of miles four hundred and fifty, and from north to south ninety leagues or two hundred and seventy miles English. The midland is for the most part mountainous and meanly-peopled, but the maritime low and very populous; the first is very subject to wind, but healthy, the latter marish and insalubrious. J. Scaliger calls it "a compendium of the world," for it abounds with all things that be either useful or excellent. The coast, by reason of trade for pepper, has towns best built and most

---

[210] German, from French *allemagne*.

[211] "In whom there is the hyena's intelligence and the crocodile's piety" (Mantuan, *Eclogue* 4. 196).

[212] The ichneumon wasp. It was thought to kill dragons and crocodiles by burrowing in mud and sticking its tail up their nostrils, then attacking. This story is related by Pliny in his *Natural History* (8.35–36).

[213] The trochilus is the crocodile-bird, which may often be observed sitting on the reptile's back.

[214] Tentatively, these may be identified as Lagundi Island and Merak, now an industrial city in Java which has an island in its harbour.

[215] The Straits of Sunda [*Sundy*] separate Sumatra and Java.

wealthy; upon the north side and to the north-east are Bantam, Palembang,[216] Jakarta (new-named Batavia by the Dutch but formerly *Sunda-Calapa* by the inhabitants, and not unlikely to be that city *Sunda* where the people used with a dead body to bury so many living fish as in his lifetime he had slain enemies), Japara, Tuban, *Jortan*, Gresik, Cirebon, Surabaya etc.[217]

Bantam is under Arctic declination or latitude 6 degrees 20 minutes and of westerly variation 3 degrees. It is the biggest city in the island, owned by the natives and stretched wellnigh two miles in length, the most remarkable places being the Pangiran's[218] palace, the bazaar, a few irregular streets and at the furthest end the Chinese, who there associate as do the Jews at Amsterdam, but nothing so splendid. The town of its own growth affords little save rice, pepper and cotton-wool, and pepper for the greatest part is brought thither by the infintely industrious Chinese, who each January come to anchor in multitudes in this port and unload their junks or *praus*[219] from Jambi in Sumatra, Borneo, Malacca and other places, making Bantam their magazine, out of which for ryals or by exchange they supply the English, Dutch and other nations. The Chinese are no quarrellers, albeit voluptuous, venerious, costly in their sports, great gamesters and in trading too subtle for young merchants, oftimes so wedded to dicing that

---

[216] Palembang is in southern Sumatra. It has been identified as the site of the capital of the ancient Buddhist Kingdom of Srivijaya. Its name derives from *limbang*, 'to pan for gold.' Now it has "little to entice visitors," although it is Sumatra's second-largest city (Stephen Backshall, *Indonesia* [London: Rough Guides, 1999], 420).

[217] Bantam or Banten was a major pepper town in west Java where the first Dutch ships, under "the incompetent and arrogant Cornelis de Houtman" (Dorai, *Indonesia*, 31) arrived in 1596. The sailors got drunk and disorderly and were expelled but the Dutch colonial era in Indonesia had now started. Best traded there in 1615. Japara was the capital of the Sultan of Mataram. After a recommendation for a factory by John Jourdain (1615) had failed, it was visited by Richard Bishop in 1618, and the next year a factor was appointed, but the Dutch attacked and burnt it. By 1620 the English were back, staying until 1648 (Foster, *England's Quest*, 247–48); Tuban is a coastal town on the northern side of the island; Gresik [*Greecy*] is a coastal town in east Java famous for its *ikat* textiles (Dorai, *Indonesia*, 90). Jourdain wanted an English factory established there (Foster, *England's Quest*, 246); Cirebon [*Chyringin*] is a port town on the northern coast containing the Sang Cipta Rasa mosque, "one of the oldest Islamic structures in Java, completed in 1480" (Backshall, *Indonesia*, 146); Surabaya, now the East Java provincial capital, was a major city by 1620 and now is Indonesia's second-largest city. Shortly before Herbert was there (in 1625) the city had been captured by Sultan Agung Hanyokrokusumo of Mataram (1613–1646), who three years later attacked Batavia twice, but was finally driven off by the Dutch. He ruled all of Java except Batavia and Bantam. For details of the city, see Dorai, *Indonesia*, 31–33; 159–61.

[218] The term *Pangiran* is often used to denote not the ruler himself, but a deputy or sub-ruler. The "Sovereign Prince" mentioned by Herbert a little later refers to Sultan Agung (see above). His title was *Panembahan*, which is similar.

[219] A *prau* is a long, narrow Malay sailing-boat with two sails.

after they have lost their whole estate wife and children are staked, yet in little time, Jew-like, by gleaning here and there are able to redeem their loss; if not, they are sold in the market for most advantage.

The isle has but one Sovereign Prince.[220] They entitle him the Mataram; he has four tetrarchs or deputies, his subordinates, is of that power (as reported) he can draw two hundred thousand men into the field upon occasion, ignorant in martial discipline at least according to our form, but of approved courage and dexterity and sufficiently ingenious as to the invention of their arms and execution. They commonly use lances, darts, arrows and shields, but their greatest bravery is in their *krisses*, a weapon that is commonly two foot long and four inches broad, waved, sharp both in the edge and point but contrary to the law of Nature and nations envenomed. The handle is usually of wood or horn, howbeit some have them of gold or silver or ivory, cut into the shape of a misshapen pagod, yet were they a thousand times more ugly these savages would dare to idolise, especially in that they ask the idol on their crest pardon after they have perpetrated an homicide, not unlike what was practiced by Lewis the Eleventh to the crucifix in his hat.[221] But withal, these Javans are drunk in demonomy and the more earnestly embrace it by how much their corrupt natures abhor honesty, whence it happens that they trade in murder, adultery, theft, rapine, deceit and all other wickedness. Magic also and astrology delights them, a study their priests are excellent in and in which Satan, 'tis thought, instructs them, the better to oblige their gratitude and to worship him as the Apollo of knowledge, which we may inculcate with that of the prophet Isaiah, Chapter 44: "Is there a God beside me? Yea, there is no God: I know not any . . . [He] maketh diviners mad, [he] turneth wise men backward and maketh their knowledge foolish," and in Jeremiah 10: "Learn not the way of the heathen . . . they are altogether brutish and foolish . . . his molten image is falsehood, and there is no breath in them . . . they are vanity . . . and in the day of account they shall perish. But in the Lord shall all true believers be justified and shall glory."

The natives till of late were not acquainted with navigation, but in the art of swimming, as most negros, very excellent, and seeing that they are not, for want of ships and marine knowledge, capable of affairs abroad, those that live some distance from the sea make hunting their chief recreation, and such sports as it tries their courage as well as agility, the isle having store of tigers, ounces and such beasts as give chase and resistance. The Alcoran is known of late years in most parts of the isle, and as an infectious air is spread into the most remote islands. Friendly they are towards the English, especially since the Dutch forced Jakarta from them, betwixt whom is such such variance that fifteen ryals has

---

[220] Sultan Agung Hanyokrokusumo.

[221] Louis XI was King of France 1461–1483. He was a ruthlessly efficient but superstitious ruler known for his cunning and secretive nature. The story of his crucifix is related by Philippe de Commynes in his *Memoires*, which were printed in 1524.

been given by either as a reward for a prisoner dead or alive, nor is there ever hope of true amity with barbarians. The *Orang-kayas*[222] are the prime sort of people, who are lazy and sociable but deceitful. They repute themselves descended from China and have a tradition that they landed there out of a junk which was seven hundred years ago forced upon that isle by tempest. They are a very proud race, wear their hair pretty long and about their heads sometimes wreath a valuable shash which none but themselves dare touch, but go elsewhere naked to the waist where the gird themselves with a particoloured mantle which falls no deeper then the knees. Their ordinary food (and not at easy rates) is rice, wheat, *pinange*,[223] betel, opium, goats, hens, eggs, cocos, plantains and jacks, for drink have excellent water and for wine *arak*, which, like the Irish whiskey drunk immoderately accelerates death, but temperately exhilerates the heart, cures fluxes, kills worms and helps digestion. These parts are for the greater part of the year subject to such loud thunders and flashes of lightning as are very dreadful to strangers.

Whence this noble isle is called Java[224] I confess my ignorance; from Javan, Japhet's son, 'twould be ridiculous to suppose, in that most agree his plantation was in the Lesser Asia, but in regard his brother Tharsis peopled these parts might he not from his brother's name and to his memory borrow the denomination? Niger apprehends that it is the same was called *Insula Iabadiae*, which sounds like *Java*; some call it *Jamboli*. There is another in Morea of that name; some also take it for Taprobane.

Nothing save pepper and cotton present themselves in this isle worthy our noting. Pepper is a seed first sown and in the growth like hops or vines supported by poles, till by maturity it gets the strength of a bushy, round and pleasant tree. The pepper hangs four inches in length and one about in many clusters, each yielding fifty or sixty corns which be full and round and fragrant. The smooth is best accounted of. Cotton is no less observable. The tree is slender but straight, a yard high and like a briar. Virgil in his 2 *Georgics* has this allusion to it: "Trees grow in Ethiopia white with wool,/ Where from the leaves the natives fleeces pull." At the top it divides itself into several branches, each of which is charged with many balls which contains the bombast, the shape whereof is round and equal to a walnut. At maturity the cod opens and discloses her treasure, but being cropped is in an entire heap with flails or suchlike useful though churlish instrument forced out and by the enriched owner cheerfully gathered.

---

[222] "Most seventeenth century European writers," Lach and Van Kley state, "talk about the *orang kayas*, by which they understand rich or powerful men or great aristocrats with political power" (*Asia*, 3: 1378).

[223] *Pinange* is betel-quid; it is composed of areca-nut, betel-leaves and lime. For details see Zhang Yangwen, *The Social Life of Opium in China* (Cambridge: Cambridge University Press, 2005), 42–3.

[224] Some etymological guessses include a derivation from *jawa-wut* or the Chinese millet, and *yava*, the Sanskrit word for 'barley,' which grows on the island.

Malayan language.

The Malayan, like those of the Industan's, have twenty-six letters in their alphabet and write like the Arabic. The language in these parts is no less epidemic in India then are the Latin, Arabic and Slavonian elsewhere. These few common words may be useful to a future traveller:

List of words [illustration shown on pp. 812–814]

English.	Malay.	English.	Malay.
A King	*Rutgeo*	a barrel of a Gun	*Sombo-bedyl*
a Noble-man	*Oran-kay*	a Looking-glass	*Sarmi*
a Lord	*Kay*	a Glass	*Lora*
a Priest	*Cadda*	a Lamp	*Pulita*
a Merchant	*Phetor*	a warm thing	*Penas*
an Interpreter	*Jorbiffa*	a Cap or Turbant	*Cayo*
a Man	*Oran*	a Marriage-maker	*Coemodo*
a Woman	*Paran-poan* and *Tadon*	a Command	*T'fuyka*
a Child	*Buda*	a Year	*Tanwa*
a Boy	*Catfion*	a Day	*Aris*
a Youth	*Monda*	a Book	*Nimoda. Kytab*
a Father	*Babba*	a Bed	*Bantell*
a Mother	*Mamma*	a good Day	*Tabea*
a Brother	*Addal-Ally*	a Royal of 8	*Serpi*
a Sister	*Adda-paparas*	a Christian	*Vrangby*
an Uncle	*Niana*	All	*Samoanga*
a Friend	*Marty-lowty*	the Head	*Capell. Coar*
a Strange man	*Oran-Leya*	Hair	*Ramboyet*
a Chirurgion	*Goething*	Ears	*Talinga*
an Iron Smith	*Goada*	Eyes	*Martic*
an Elephant	*Catgha*	Eye-brows	*Alys*
an Ox	*Cambi. Al omba*	Nose	*Irotdon*
a Goat	*Carbow*	Neck	*Goulon*
a Sheep	*Domba*	Lips	*Lambider*
a Dog	*Hanghe*	Tongue	*Ilat*
a Bird	*Borron*	Teeth	*Anton*
a Hen	*Ayam*	Beard	*Tianga*
a Duck	*Bebee*	Back	*Balacca*
a Musk-Cat	*Catto-Dalgalia*	Shoulder	*Baon*
a Sow	*Sabi. Sieleng*	Arm	*Backeyen*
a Fish	*Ican*	Hand	*Tangan*
a Water-Pot	*Laude*	Finger	*Jary-laree*
a Herb	*Oberbedil. Lancuas*	Belly	*Penot*
a Musk-Nut	*Palla*	Blood	*Darno*
a Ship	*Capel. Junck*	Privy part	*Perot*
a Boat	*Praw. Paca-fura*	Thigh	*Backy*
a Coat	*Naffee*	Leg	*Gula*
a Needle	*Nareon*	Foot	*Bhackhye*
a Custom	*Negry*	Toe	*Ghoumo*
a Rope	*Tali*	Fire	*Api*
a Stone	*Batu*	Air	*Baya*
a Ring	*Chinfin*	Water	*Eyer*
a Wimble	*Alforees*	Earth	*Zam*
a Shooe	*Apon*	the Sea	*Chay*
a Sword	*Ita. Padang*	Gold	*Maz. Cabo*
a Dagger	*Cryze*	Silver	*Peca. Salorca*
a Knife	*Piefon*	Brass	*Temba*
a Javelin	*Tomba*	Copper	*Tambagle*
a Shield	*Salviack*	Lead	*Tyma*
a Gun	*Bedyl. Pitfil.*	Iron	*Negle*

English.	Malay.	English.	Malay.
Money	Sarfi	the other day	Bulmari-dula
Scarlet	Facca-lata-miera	Early	Pagi
Death	Mattu	Night	Malam
Merchandife	Bayick. Dimana	to Morrow	Tfouck
Melancholy	Chinta	What fay you?	Abba-catta
Silk	Sabuck	Is he not here?	Beef?
Paper	Cartas	What's done?	Bigimana?
Qnills	Cazamp	Well done	Soofa
Ink	Mangfi	Where is it?	Manauten?
a Book	Khytab. Nymoda	Bring it back	Combali?
Wine	Aracca	Now	Bacabaren
Vinegar	T'fuka	How much?	Barappe itu?
Strong-water	Pinangha	Give place	Lalan
Bread	Sagu	Require it	Minta
Boil'd Rice	Braas	Regard	Nanthy
Fruit	Tacat	Let pafs	Ganga
Drink	Larnick	Near hand	Gila
Sugar	Gula	We will go	Maree
Salt	Garram. Matary	Leave it	Jangemaft
Oyl	Nuagia	I have	Ada
Flefh	Lalyer	It is found	Botonvum
Fifh	Ivack	It is	Dalan
Crabs	Horra	I will bring it	Addadizano
Plates	Pienig	I fee	Green
Pepper	Lada. Sihang	I thank you	Terimacache
Ginger	Alia	I underftand not	Tan, or Tyeda-taw
Mace	Bengo	I care	Tage
Cloves	Chocho. Sianck	I have hot	Tyeda-da
Cinamon	Cajumayns	I defire not	Tyeda-maw
Aloes	Garro	I am fick	Bite-fecata
Tamarind	Affa	to eat	Macan
Rice	Braas. Parce	to remember	Engat
Nuts	Calappen. Palla	to ftretch out	Dufta
Sweet Gums	Daringo	to beat one another	Baccalayo
Sweet Spices	Dingyn	to afhame	Malon
Plantaines	Gardang	to choofe	Damare
Cocos	Calapa	to pay	Chyni
Muftard	Sajani	to give	Bering
Eggs	Teloor	to buy	Bilby
Woe	Saya	to live	Jagava
Better	Parma	to poyfon	Ampo
Great	Bazaer	to obferve	Dodouer
Sweet	Manys	to be filent	Dyem
Heavy	Brat	to gain	Menang
Strong	Cras	to deftroy	Ilan
Needles	Calvenetten	to cover the head	Kocodang
Bags	Corni	to arife	Paffai
Hard Wax	Caju-lacca	to burn	Bacear
Friendfhip	Pondarra	to kill	Benue
I	Manyr	to fpin	Tnedda
Thou	Pakanera	to fell	Jouwall
He	Itowen	to do	Bretoon
We	Dep	to fwear	Sempa
Ye	Pachaneras	to help	Touloug
They	Itowe	to us	Quia-bota
She	Dya	to let blood	Bewang-darner
Sunday	Jon-maheet	to queftion	Betangia
to day	Mari	to know	Kyunal
Yefterday	Bulmari	to die	Bantaren

English.	Malay.	English.	Malay.
Take it	Ambell	Eleven	Sabalas
Not good	Tieda-Bayck	Twelve	Dua-balas
Sloth	Checho	Thirteen	Tiga-balas
Give thanks	Tarima. Caffe	Fourteen	Enpat-balas
Farewel	Tingat	Fifteen	Lyma-balas
One	Satu	Sixteen	Nam-balas
Two	Dua	Seventeen	Toufiou-balas
Three	Tiga	Eighteen	De lappan-balas
Four	Enpat	Nineteen	Sambalam-balas
Five	Lyma	Twenty	Dua-pola
Six	Nam	Twenty one	Dua-pola-fatu
Seven	Toufion	Twenty two	Dua-pola-dua
Eight	De lappan	Twenty three	Dua-pola-tiga
Nine	Sambalan	Twenty four	Dua-pola-enpat
Ten	Sapola	Twenty five	Dua-pola-lyma.

Bali.

Bali is an isle east of Java inhabited by gentiles. The women there as yet continue the custom of burning at their husbands' funerals more then in other places in India, especially where the Mohammedans have dominion.

Celebes.

Our course from Java to the Celebes is north-east, distant from Bantam two hundred leagues or thereabouts. Celebes, *Cassiteria* of old or that which Ptolemy calls *Solis insula* or *"quae nympharum rubent cubile dicitur,"* is now best-known by the name of Makassar,[225] from her best city so-called, an isle for quantity and quality very considerable, for it stretches from the Equator six degrees south. Oval in form it is and two hundred miles long at least, well-peopled, but with bad people, no place engendering greater demonomists, or till of late worse savages, agreeing with the old name Ptolemy gave the men, which was *anthropophagi* or men-eaters. Howbeit, Mohammed is now known among them, but by him *a malo in peius*,[226] for though he teacheth them there is one and but one God, yet seeing Jesus Christ is there unknown, at least unbelieved-in, how little does that knowledge advantage them, but the greater part of the inhabitants are gentiles,

---

[225] Makassar, now known as Ujung Pendang, "an animated, determinedly unpretentious port city" (Backshall, *Indonesia*, 786), is the capital of South Sulawesi (Sulawesi is the local name for the Celebes) and the centre of the Bugi people, who originated in Mongolia (Dorai, *Indonesia*, 301). By the early seventeenth century this area had converted to Islam. In 1545 the Portuguese, trading from Goa, erected a fort there, which was taken by the Dutch in 1667. The term 'Makassar' really applies to a loose confederation of western Bugi states.

[226] "From bad to worse." This is a commonplace Latin proverb.

"Nil praeter nubes et coeli lumen adorant,"[227] and yet Antonio Paiva,[228] a Lusitanian priest, reports that he converted many here to Christ, but at this day those footsteps are very rarely to be discovered. From Makassar to Cambyna west northwest are four and twenty leagues and to Nussasira eighty are reckoned.[229]

The isle is fruitful, though under the most frying part of the Burning Zone. The sun yields them day and heat enough, but night their complexion. The habit they wear differs not from their grandfather Adam's, a few fig or plantain leaves tied about their middles, and are elsewhere naked. The better sort, to vary from the vulgar, are tulipanted, and the better to set off their coal-black beauties shirt their skin with a pure white *shuddero* which does not lenify[230] the scorching heat so much as serves for ornament. The women have adulterated their first stamp not only by deforming their face and body with paint but by that vile lubricity their souls are spotted with. Impudence goes here unmasked, for contrary to the practice of most places, in the night these drink *arak*, which is their wine, and then seem amorous, but it were well travellers would remember that ancient verse, *"Nox et amor vinumque nihil moderabile suadent,"*[231] for such is their damned art that these sirens can sing safety to themselves when by the same pipe and weed they smoke others to death, a trick they will be perfect in though they die for it. Pythagoras made the wantons of Crotona modest and the men moderate; to these let me add with the poet *"Iam qui corrigat, alter erit."*[232] This artifice of these lewd ones may run parallel with that maid who by customary eating of *napellus*, the most dangerous poison, some say, of all vegetables, hurt not herself but poisoned such as had carnal knowledge of her, so as verily, that which Menander applied to the lewd Cypriots or Propetidae very properly alludes to these courtesans, "Who have no fear nor shame for their offence,/ But hardened are with brazen

---

[227] [The Jews] "worship nothing but clouds and the *numen* of heaven" (Juvenal, *Satires* 14. 97).

[228] There was a Fr. Antonio Paiva who possibly led a Portuguese mission to Ayutthaya (1544) and was rumoured to have converted king Phra Jairaja, but scholars are doubtful whether this story is true. Herbert could mean the same person, as the dates do fit.

[229] Cambyna is a large island near the southern entrance of the Bouton Strait near the Celebes; Nussasira [*Nossaseres*] is the island nearest the Celebes.

[230] Mitigate, alleviate.

[231] "The night and love and wine urge no forbearance" (Ovid, *Amores* 1. 6. 59–60).

[232] Herbert has truncated this citation. The poem reads: *"Scaliger annosi correxit tempora mundi / Quis iam, qui mores corrigat, alter erit?"* (John Owen, *Epigrammata libri III*, I, 16). Owen (1564–1622) was a Welsh schoolmaster who wrote several popular books of epigrams. They were translated (1677) by Thomas Harvey, whose English version of this one is: "Learned Scaliger the world's deformed times/ Reformed; who shall now reform men's crimes?" Dana F. Sutton has edited a hypertext critical version of Owen's book at www.philologiacl.bham.ac.uk.

impudence," resembling those mentioned by Pliny *lib.* 7, *cap.* 2 named Bythiae.[233] No less lewd and cunning in this hellish art Parysatis, the Queen Mother who poisoned Statira wife to Artaxerxes by carving her half a bird with a knife that was envenomed but upon one side, as you read in Plutarch, and, which is no less mischievous, the men use long canes or trunks called *sempitans*,[234] out of which they blow a little pricking quill, which if it draw the least drop of blood, it destroys immediately. Some venoms operate in an hour, others in a moment, the veins and body by the virulency of that poison corrupting and rotting presently, even to terror and amazement.

You cannot choose but think this a hell upon earth, though at our first approach upon sight of so goodly an island we thought it an Elysium, but remembering that *"impia sub dulci melle latens,"*[235] we hastened away for better places, the Moluccas I mean, which Ptolemy calls *Sinde*, then which no part of the universe gives more delight or greater variety of refreshment. By the way we cast our eyes upon many small isles, and, as we sail due east, upon Bali in 8 degrees 30 minutes and Timor in 10 degrees south, 20 minutes easterly from the last, both more rich in stones and spices then some greater isles about them. Leave we *Conio* and Seram[236] unspoken of, not that they are unworthy but because we haste to the Moluccas, in view now and where we mean to rest awhile.

The Molucca Islands.

The Molucca Isles, called *Solis Insulae* in former ages, confine India and are five[237] in number: Molucca, Galela, Ternate, Tidore and Maquian, in which last Magellan after his long voyage *Anno* 1520 ended his life through the treachery of those barbarians. The English were the first that ever traded to these isles of any Christians,[238] so as most of them have ever since acknowledged our King their

---

[233] A Scythian tribe thought by some, including Pliny, to be a race of wicked magicians and sorcerers.

[234] *Sempitans*, which are blowpipes still used in Borneo, are about two metres in length.

[235] "Wicked things lying hidden beneath sweet honey" (Ovid, *Amores* 1. 8. 104).

[236] Backshall describes Seram as "a moody eyebrow glowering north over a more urbane Ambon." It is the second-largest of the Molucca Islands (*Indonesia*, 870).

[237] These five are what were known as the 'Spice Islands.' There are actually a "thousand or more" islands making up the Moluccas, now known as Maluku (Backshall, *Indonesia*, 855).

[238] Sir Francis Drake was the first Englishman to *reach* the Moluccas in his voyage around the world (1579). Herbert is wrong, however, about the English and trade; the Portuguese were there in 1511, "locating Banda, Ternate and Ambon" (Backshall, *Indonesia*, 857) and in the 1520s the Spaniards. By 1605 the Dutch had displaced the Portuguese in Ambon (Amboyna) in Ternate and even executed some English would-be traders there in 1623, which might have been the source of Herbert's complaint (see details

sovereign, but by the Dutch it seems our men are now thrust out as if all India were theirs by title from the Creation!

Of these, Galela is greatest and Ternate the highest; all of them afford cloves, mace, nutmegs, ginger, pepper, oil, aloes and honey. Most of them have the Equinoctial for their zenith and by those diurnal showers and breezes, which fail them not, with the sun's voisinage the fruits ripen sooner, the earth smells more aromatical and the air seems more nutritive there then observed in most other places.

The clove-tree differs in proportion according to the place whence it receives its vigour; some are comparable to the bay, which it resembles, the leaves only somewhat narrower, others to box or suchlike trees of humble stature. 'Tis most part of the year green, having leaves long and small, distending into many branches. It blossoms early but becomes exceeding inconstant in complexion, from a virgin white varying into other colours, for in the morn in shows a pale green, in the meridian a distempered red and sets in blackness. The cloves manifest themselves at the utmost end of the branches and in their growing evaporate such sense-ravishing odours as if a compendium of Nature's sweetest gums were there extracted and united. They are produced thrice every year and gratefully retort a treble vintage; yea, though but perfected in three years yet counted an advantage, seeing physicians say they are hot and dry in the third degree, corroborate the stomach, benefit concoction and such up moisture so exceedingly that no other plant will prosper in its neighbourhood.

The nutmeg, like trees most excellent, is not very lofty in heighth, scarce rising so high as the cherry. By some it is resembled to the peach but varies in form of leaf and grain and affects more compass. The nut is clothed with a defensive husk like those of baser quality and resembles the thick rind of a walnut, but at full ripeness discovers her naked purity the mace, and chastly entwines with a vermilion blush her endeared fruit and sister, which hath a third coat, and both of them breathe out most pleasing smells. The mace in a few days like choice

---

below). Sir Henry Middleton tried to trade there (1605) but had been caught in the middle of hostilities between the Dutch and Portuguese (Foster, *England's Quest*, 166–67). Spain had sent an expedition under Magellan, one ship of which reached Tidore as early as 1522 (Simkin, *Trade*, 184), but did not actually capture it until 1606, holding it until the Dutch displaced them nearly sixty years later. Middleton was also at Tidore, where he helped rescue the Sultan of Ternate from a Tidore fleet but was welcomed by the Portuguese at Tidore after escorting the Sultan home and was able to trade in cloves (Foster, *England's Quest*, 166). In Ternate a Dutch fort was built in 1606, from which they helped the locals fight the Spanish. Ternate and Tidore had a trade-rivalry between the Portuguese, who had a treaty with the latter, and Spain, but the Spanish left Tidore in 1529, although they came back briefly in 1542–1545 and made further claims after they had founded Manila in 1570 (Simkin, *Trade*, 183–84). Galela is now "simply a knot of houses surrounding a small port" (Backshall, *Indonesia*, 885).

beauties by the sun's flames becomes twany, yet in that complexion best pleases the rustic gatherer. In these isles only are found those rare and beautiful birds of the sun which are commonly-called *Manucaudiatae* or Birds of Paradise.

Several other isles of note there are, some of which, namely Amboyna, was in the quiet possession of the English until disseised by the treachery and cruelty of some Dutch, who under a show of friendship invited our factors to a feast, where most perfidiously and to the perpetual reproach of their Christian profession amongst infidels, not content with the possession of the place they entertained those innocent persons with most cruel and exquisite tortures.[239] These isles are commonly called the Molucca Isles or Isles of Banda,[240] those two being accounted the principal.

Banda.

Banda is in 4 degrees 30 minutes, and from Amboyna twenty leagues; Amboyna is almost in the mid-way betwixt Banda and Molucca. Puloway is from Banda three leagues, from Puloway west north west are Lonthoire, the greatest of the

---

[239] The details of this incident are as follows. Sir James Lancaster had founded an English trading-post in Banten (1602), and seven years later the Dutch drove the Portuguese out of the area and had established themselves in Aceh. An English factory was built at Camballo near Amboyna (1615), which irritated the Dutch, who wanted a monopoly on the spice-trade and were prepared to use force to get it. However, in 1619 a treaty was signed between Holland and England, which gave the English the right to one-third of the spices, the Dutch to two thirds. However, the Dutch East India Company, under the new Governor Jan Pieterszoon Coen, claimed that as a private enterprise it did not have to honour a treaty made by governments, and refused to follow the terms. In retaliation the English then attacked Batavia and drove the Dutch out with Javan help, but the Dutch regained it almost immediately. In 1623 a rumour went round that the English and Portuguese, with help from some Japanese *samurai* mercenaries, planned to take Amboyna and kill the Dutch. That is when the Dutch arrested ten Englishmen, nine Japanese, and one Portuguese, tortured them and executed them in March of that year. Simkin, however, says only eight Englishmen were executed (*Trade*, 197).The English complained to Governor Coen in Batavia, and James I personally intervened with a diplomatic protest; the Dutch duly set up a commission of enquiry, which ended in acquitting those who had ordered the execution (1631). That this affair was not forgotten in England is demonstrated by the fact that John Dryden wrote a play about it entitled *Amboyna, or The Cruelties of the Dutch to the English Merchants* (1673), fifty years later! Some historians have argued that the Amboyna incident played a part in the two Dutch wars under the Protectorate and in the reign of Charles II.

[240] Banda is actually a group of volcanic islands on which grow the nutmeg trees which were the only world source for mace and nutmeg at the time. Antonio de Abreu (see below) led a Portuguese expedition there (1512), and another foray followed in 1529, but the people there remained independent, and no forts or settlements were built there. By the early seventeenth century the Dutch had established themselves on the islands.

isles of Banda, Batu Kapal, *Labataka*, Neira, *Ticonbassa*, Gunung Api, Selamon and others, all which, especially Puloway and Pulau Run, appear as if they were continued wildernesses of nutmegs and clove-trees, pepper, vines and olives.[241] Until some late violence was offered by our emulous neighbours, the two last commerced first with our English merchants and contracted a perpetual amity with our King, but in affront to them and us they have forcibly expelled our merchants thence and now entitle themselves lords of Banda, caring neither for our interest nor what right the Ternatensian nor Banda kings have over them, albeit 'tis well-known the Dutch traded thither after the English and that till the year 1595 they had no considerable trade in any part of the Indies, which how they have improved is understood to the terror and admiration of the natives.

Borneo.

Near these is Borneo, by some supposed to be that *Insula Bonae Fortunae* and *Porne* we find mentioned in Ptolemy, an isle nadir to the Equator, which in shape resembles an oval shield. The major part inclines towards the north, for her Antarctic elevation is not above 3 degrees, whereas the Arctic extends to 7 degrees odd minutes. The first discovery of any Christian European is attributed to de Abreu,[242] who in the Year of Our Lord 1523 accidnetally came to anchor at this island. At this day it groans for the most part under Spanish servitude, who where treasure is to be had become ingenious and indefatigable, but what artifices they use is well-known and that under pretence of sacred an insatiate thirst after gold is too oft discovered, albeit they cannot well be ignorant that "*Coelum nulla est reparabile gaza.*"[243]

It has many villages and consequently much people, but the one as to outward things are poor and the other wretched in their idolatry, so as did not that plenty of gold, diamonds and other merchandise as bezoar, *lignum aloes*, musk, civet, benjamin, amber, *sanguis draconum*, wax, rice and rattans or canes make her magnetical, the place would not be so attractive as it is to merchants and

---

[241] Puloway or Pulau Ay is a small island off the south-west coast of Sumatra; it is about 45 km in circumference. Lonthoir [*Lantore*] and Selamon [*Salamo*] are settlements on the island of Banda Besar, the largest of the Banda Islands. Neira [*Nero*], now known as Bandaneira, is at the present day the capital, "still dressed in the solid European architecture raised when this tiny island was the focus of the world trade in nutmeg" (Backshall, *Indonesia*, 873). Pulau Run [*Puloreen*] is a very small island only 3 km long and 1 km wide. The Portuguese were there as early as 1512, and the Dutch arrived in 1599, built forts and tried to secure a monopoly on the spice trade. In 1619 Coen invaded the islands and annexed them.

[242] Antonio de Abreu, who was at the conquest of Malacca (1511) and led the first Portuguese expedition to Timor the same year and to the Moluccas and Borneo in 1523.

[243] "Heaven returns no treasure" (Valerius Flaccus, *Argonautica* 6. 562).

travellers. Her best maritime towns and ports are Sandakan,[244] which is in 1 degree 35 minutes south and from Bantam north-east a hundred and sixty leagues or thereabouts, and Banjarmasin;[245] the rest be scarce worth the regarding.

Bezoar, or as the Persians call it, *pezar* and *pazahar*, is of two sorts, found both in Asia and America. Of Asia the best is had in Persia, Pegu and this Borneo, and is of more value then what is had in the new-found world. It is oft found in the stomach or maw of a goat in Pegu and upon the Indian mountains; some, nevertheless, how truly I know not, affirm it is no other then the congealed tears of a stag and that such as are taken from beasts feeding upon theriacal herbs are most sovereign and of greatest virtue to expel poison and other noxious distempers. The shape is also various, for some resemble a plum, some a date-stone, others dove-eggs and some are like chestnuts and goats' kidneys, but all blunt-ended. No less different are they in colour, for some are red, pale green some, othersome dark yellow and some sky-coloured. The last are best, consisting of many scales which like onions circumvolve one another and in which Nature has expressed far more curiosity then art's best imitation, for each inferior scale, not unlike the orbs, yields more splendour then the other, and as it diminishes its quantity increases its virtue according as it is in tenuity or thickness. Many are counterfeit, but to discover the fraud they use to pierce them with hot bodkins, or after they have weighed them steeping them in cold water four hours; if they crack not they are held good, and to know them for such they first wipe and balance them, observing that if they weigh never so little above the first weight 'tis a sure sign they are base and of small value. It is also observed that the bezoars of Borneo are not above half the value of those which are had in Persia.

Lignum aloes, according to the country where it grows, has diversity of nature. The Javans and Malayans name it *garreo*, the Indians and Portuguese *d'aquilha*, but the Chinese and Cochin Chinese *calambo*. It is framed of large round sticks of a clouded grain mixed with veins of an ash colour, pleasant to the eye and ponderous in the hand, but of a bitter relish and fitter for the fire then taste, for hot coals no sooner touch it but to the honour of its own funeral it expires and vapours out an odour so aromatic and confortable as no other is used by the Indians, Malayans, Siamites, Peguans, Cambodians or Borneans when they burn the corpse of their deceased parents, which with them is the noblest manner of burial.

Musk is bred in the navel of the cat and is either yellow, brown or black; the first is held the best, the last the basest. The choicest shows a deep amber colour not unlike spikenard and is clothed with a moist skin which sweats out

---

[244] Sandakan [*Socodania*] is on the coast of Sabah in the north of the island.
[245] Banjarmasin [*Bemermassen*] is on the south-western corner of Borneo. The Portuguese sent missionaries there in the sixteenth century and there had been some trade with England, but both "found Banjarmasin and its rulers squalid and dangerous" (Backshall, *Indonesia*, 745).

some bristly hairs, without stones, lead or like adulterous mixture, but withal of so strong a smell that to many it seems offensive, and tasted penetrates into the mouth if it suddenly dissolve, or in the hand if it be long a-melting. Those are the usual ways to discover the quality.

Civet, a sort of musk bred in a little bladder within the testicles of a certain creature not unlike a cat, is of different colours; deep yellow, as I have been told, is usually the best and the worst is white, for that is greasy and sophisticate. Nevertheless, when it is new it is observed to be pale, and gradually turns yellowish.

Benjamin, by the Malayans called *menyan* and by others *Indian's benyan*, is either white or yellow, but both are streaked. The gum issues from a tree which is high and small and furnished with fruitless branches; the leaves are not unlike the olive. Arabia has good, but Pegu and Siam better, whereas that from Sumatra, Pariaman and *Barrousse*[246] is coarse and bad, and more approved of at Java than in England.

Amber is of many forms: grey, brown, white and black. Grey is reputed best, the black is worst, the other two be indifferent. The best sort of grey is pure and interlaced with ashy veins and not subject to sink, for the most part got in Sofala, Magadoxa, Mombasa, Mozambique, Madagascar, Malindi and other parts of South Africa, found there at incertain hazards. Now concerning gems, I will but name their proper places, for in these I borrow reports from merchants. Coral, amber, emerald, chalcedony, onyx, sardonyx, bezoar, haematite and turquoise for the most part are had in Arabia, Industan and Persia; pearls, beryls, sapphires and adamants at Ceylon; jasper, carnelian, agate, heliotrope, jacinth[247] and chrysolite in Malabar, Narsinga and Cochin-China, which Cochin-China extends from 11 to 17 degrees north latitude and is confined by Champa, *Tonkin*,[248] Laos and the ocean, a country rich and pleasant, the people idolators yet civil to strangers. Diamonds come from Borneo and Golconda, Vijayanagar, Delhi and the isles near the greater Java; gold, silver, rubies and porcelain from Pegu, Siam, Bengal, Sumatra, Japan and China, enough to make poor men rich and rich men miserable. Now, albeit the best and most orient pearl in the world have for some years been got near Bahrein in the Gulf of Persia, where in some oysters have been found not fewer then 100 pearls great and small, formed, some say, of the dew of heaven, which in streams falls into gaping shellfish and there breeds no otherwise then as kernels do in hogs and stones in bladders or the kidneys. Nevertheless, store of small pearl is had in oysters, mussels and other shellfish all along the coast of India, as I could partly observe in our passage, for the natives in several places would adventure to the sides of our ships, though

---

[246] Possibly Pesesir in West Sumatra.

[247] A red-coloured zircon.

[248] Champa was an ancient kingdom in parts of south and central Vietnam, into which it was eventually absorbed in 1720. Tunkin [*Tunebin*] or Tonkin was the northern part, governed by the Mac Dynasty and nominally under the suzerainity of China.

under sail, with their small canoes to chaffer with us, and I well remember that amongst other things store of seed-pearl was proffered. Howbeit, sometimes great pearls are found, as may appear by the report of a sea-captain, who not far from Borneo saw a pearl was round and orient and of the bigness of a dove's egg, of great price and probably superior to that which Cleopatra dissolved, valued at 25,000 crowns and drunk to aggrandise Mark Antony's welcome. P. Martyr *Decad* 8 reports that he saw a pearl weighed 100 ounces which was offered to be sold the Duke of Medina Sidonia, a Spanish grandee, but the Mughal has pearls of incredible bigness or rarity.

Mindanao.

By a NNE course in a few hours we view Mindanao, an isle as big as Sicily branching from 6 to above 9 degrees north, north of which and neighbouring are the Philippines, named in honour of Philip II by Lopez de Legaspi,[249] who first discovered those isles and planted there *Anno Domini* 1565. Near them are the Manilas,[250] by Ptolemy called *Satyrorum Insulae*, isles for the greatest part nameless because numberless; the best and greatest is Luzon, under 14 degrees north latitude, whence in a direct azimuth west is Cambodia, a rich part of the Asiatic continent, but north from Luzon are Kyushu and Shikoku, best-known to the inhabitants if China and Japan, as is Korea, a long narrow peninsula famous in the site but infamous in her inhabitants, who are a people that live by spoil and doing mischief to their neighbours, more subtle than the Chinese or Japanese.

Japan.

Japan, unless Mercator's fancy be true that it was *Aurea Chersonesis*, was unknown to old geographers, albeit the name *Chryse* be given it by Niger and *Zipangri* by M. Paulus Venetus,[251] who rather than so great an isle should be without a name makes bold with his invention. But certain it is we owe its discovery to Motta, Peixoto and Zeimoto,[252] banished Portuguese who in the year 1542 wandering

---

[249] Miguel Lopez de Legaspi (c. 1510–1572) was in Mexico (1545) and later sent to conquer what became the Philippine Islands (1563). He occupied the Ladrone Islands near the Marianas (1564), then took possession of Cebu (1565) and Luzon (1570) with very little resistance. He was appointed the first Governor of the Philippines in 1566, and founded Manila in 1571.

[250] Modern Philippines.

[251] Marco Polo the Venetian. The name Cipangu or Zipangu for Japan was common amongst early travellers. Polo says only "We shall begin with an island that is called Japan" (*Travels*, 243). The name may have been derived from the Shanghai dialect word for Japan.

[252] Antonio de Motta, Francisco Zeimoto, and Antonio Peixoto sailed off-course in a Chinese ship from Siam and landed on Tanegashima Island in southern Japan. Whilst

abroad to seek their fortunes, were by storm shipwracked upon this isle, from which time it was well-known to them, but the English begun to trade here not till 1613[253] and the Dutch more lately, but whether it be an isle or no is disputable, albeit some pretend to know its dimensions and accordingly limit it 'twixt the degrees 35 and 48, and by like supposition the length to be 230 leagues and breadth 109 or thereabouts, most of which is barren and coarse, but fruitful in minerals. Towns of best note and traffic are Miyako, Osaka, Tajima, Funai, Fukato, Sakai, *Cratez*, *Tenkeday*, Uraga, *Amamgueyo*, Usuki, *Machma* etc.,[254] of

there they introduced the Japanese to muskets, which were soon being manufactured by local craftsmen, with the result that, as a historian notes, that "Life was made more dangerous for everyone from first-rank courtier to untouchable gravedigger when Western firearms were introduced by the Portuguese" (Jerrold M. Packard, *Sons of Heaven: A Portrait of the Japanese Monarchy* [New York: Collier Books, 1989], 145), which was demonstrated when Oda Nobunaga used firearms at the Battle of Nagashino (1575), Japan's introduction to modern warfare. A few years after the three shipwrecked mariners (1549), St. Francis Xavier arrived in Japan. For details, see Olof Lidin, *Tanegashima: The Arrival of Europe in Japan* (Copenhagen: Nordic Institute of Asian Studies, 2002). In 1544 Fernão Mendes Pinto landed in Funai on the Oita River and later claimed to have been the first Portuguese in Japan; Giles Milton, however, calls him "a garrulous adventurer" who "altered dates, borrowed stories and exaggerated his own bravado" (*Samurai William*, 9, 11). The English translation by 'H. C., Gent.' of his *Peregrinaçam* appeared in 1653 as *The Voyages and Adventures* (for full title, see Bibliography). Portuguese trading did not "officially" begin in Japan until 1571 (they had been trading in Funai since 1559), when a ship arrived at Nagasaki.

[253] The English first reached Japan by accident, too. On 12 November 1600, the pilot William Adams on the *Liefde*, a Dutch ship with sick crewmen, anchored near Funai. Herbert is alluding most likely to Captain John Saris, who anchored in Hirado Bay in 1613 (see above, Part I). The Dutch had actually arrived in 1606 and in 1609 under Jacques Specx of the Dutch East India Company, "who had been given the unenviable task of establishing a 'factory' or trading-base in Japan" (Milton, *Samurai William*, 140). The factory was established at Hirado.

[254] Herbert did not go to Japan; his description is lifted almost *verbatim* from John Saris's account and his phonetic spelling of Japanese names is atrocious at best. Miyako [*Meacco*] was a name for Kyoto, then the capital of Japan; the name means "seat of the Imperial Palace." By the time Francis Xavier, who had heard great things about Miyako, got there the city was almost in ruins—Herbert's description of it being not as beautiful as Florence is an understatement (and it was a lot bigger). Osaka [*Ozacca*], according to William Adams's account, was a very large city, "as big if not bigger than London" and location of a castle which was so impressive Adams was awestruck (Milton, *Samurai William*, 104–5) and Herbert mentions it later. Hirado, also known as Firando [*Fyrando*] in north-eastern Kyushu, became the site of an English factory (1613–1625) and is where John Saris landed in 1613. The Dutch East India Company had been there since 1609; Fukato [*Fuccato*] is a town in Tamagawa Prefecture, and Sakai [*Sacay*] is in Osaka Prefecture; it was a centre of trade and had foreign factories by Herbert's time. Uraga [*Oringaw*]

which Miyako, a mediterranean city, is reputed the metropolis, Suruga[255] the
next best, and next that Osaka, honoured with the court till about 1615, [when]
a great part of the city was fired and not only this, but many other towns in that
province. Miyako is as big as Florence but not so beautiful, watered by a river of
sweet water. The buildings are but ordinary; of best note are the fotics[256] which
are filled with *mannadas*, to which the Japanese are exceedingly addicted. The
Jesuits' industries, though great, produces little advantage; the people are so miserably drawn away by the example of their idolatrous neighbours the Chinese,
whom in nothing else they seem to agree with, and albeit there was at first a
seeming conversion to Christianity both in Xavier's time and since, yet they have
oft apostasised, and the greater number of inhabitants being gentiles have made
many massacres and destroyed such as were real professors, insomuch as at this
day there is little of Christ there owned, the wretches rather inclining to the
Alcoran which has of late years crept very near them and best agrees with their
sensual appetite, for it gives a large toleration to carnal men and has nothing of
austerity mixed with it, which best pleases.[257]

---

is at the entrance of Tokyo (Edo) Bay, which John Saris called "a very good harbour for
shipping" (quoted in Milton, *Samurai William*, 197). Uuski [*Vosuquis*] is in Oita Prefecture, and was the seat of the *daimyo* (feudal lord) Otomo Sorin (see below), who built
the castle there in 1562 and who received Pinto. The remaining names are very hard to
decipher. *Amamgueyo* may be Yamaguchi in the south of Honshu, where Francis Xavier
went in 1550; *Cratez* is probably Karatsu in Kyushu, a famous pottery and stoneware centre in the sixteenth century (Malcolm Davis, *Japan* [Boston: APA Publications, 1995],
356); *Tenkeday* may be Togendai on Lake Ashi near Hakone, but more likely may refer
to Kamakura; and *Machma* could be Matsuyama on Shikoku, near which a large castle
was erected in 1603.

[255] Suruga is a town near Hirado, quite close to the city of Nagasaki.

[256] The term *fotic* is a corruption of the Japanese *hotoke*, which can mean either the
Buddha himself or his statue, and can also refer to any objects of worship in Buddhist
temples. Sir Ernest Satow thought that *mannada* was a misprint for "Amida," the name of
Buddha, which does sound logical (Saris, 140, n. 4). Herbert uses both as generic terms
for 'idol' or 'image.' The 1638 edition suggests that Herbert might have had some idea
about the name, as he states that the Japanese "call them *mannadoes*" (335).

[257] The Japanese began acting against converts in 1611, and by 1614, after a monk
called Suden had presented Shogun Hidetada with a recommendation for expelling missionaries, a law was passed to that effect. However, there had been massacres of Japanese
converts in 1612 and 1619, but Sansom says no foreigners were killed until 1622, "which
was the year styled in the reports of the missions the year of the Great Martyrdom," in
which over fifty were burned or executed (George Sansom, *A History of Japan 1615–1867*
[Stanford: Stanford University Press, 1963], 40–41). This is inaccurate; Hideyoshi had
26 Japanese and foreign Christians crucified at Nagasaki in 1597. Herbert's assertion
that the Japanese were turning Muslim is nonsensical. Altogether the Shogunate executed "between five and six thousand Christians" in the period 1614–1640 (Mikiso Hane,

The government is monarchical, for above threescore petty princes do homage and prostrate their coronets afore the supreme diadem.[258] The country is most part mountainous, but full of rivulets which makes it abound with corn, grass and minerals; the north and east parts are less-peopled then the south and west. The old Roman execration *"Abin hinc in malam crucem"*[259] and manner of execution is here in use, a punishment not more full of torture then ignominy. The people are valiant and reasonable civil, affectors of novelties and beyond measure jealous if occasioned, revengeful if injured and devilish if exasperated. They pretend much to learning and especially to skill in geography, howbeit are ignorant of the European and African in the greatest part and totally concerning the American, nevertheless have no small opinion of their art in the division of the world, wherein they think themselves superlative and all others mistaken, for they divide the world into three parts, that is to say into China, Japan and Siam, which sufficiently expresses their abilities in that science, but in entertainments they are better skilled, for they sit long and fare well, and in eating use sticks or forks, and shift the table as new courses come. In riding they mount upon the right side, their alphabet exceeds not 20 letters, whereas the Malayan has 26; they, as the Chinese, have also many characters, of which every one stands for an entire word, as we use in short-writing. At funerals they wear white. They would, but cannot deny themselves to be descended from China, for certain it is they were banished about six hundred years ago upon some insurrection, in consideration whereof they continue and implacable animosity to each other. The islanders rob and prey upon the Chinese abroad on all advantages, yea, at home in their prayers abominate and in all compliments and ceremonies are opposite to one another as much as may be, no less then the French and Spaniard. Upon any trivial accusation the children are so sensible of their reputation that without any pause to evince the truth they will whip off a joint from their finger, with

Japan: A Historical Survey [New York: Scribners, 1972], 148); the most ruthless persecutor was Iemitsu (see below), who was Shogun when Herbert made his journey.

[258] Like most other Westerners, Herbert did not understand how the Japanese government worked. In his time the Emperor was Go-Mizunoo (1611–1629), but the real power was then in the hands of the Tokugawa Shogun, who was often termed 'Emperor' by Westerners. At this time it was Ieyasu (1603–1616; resigned title to Hidetada in 1605), followed by his son Hidetada (1616–1623) and then Iemitsu (1623–1651). The custom was for the Emperor to abdicate (often when the Shogun suggested he do so) and become a Retired Emperor, although Go-Mizunoo ('Go' means 'II') was "surprisingly assertive" and "regarded his position as the chief guardian of Japan's native virtues a primary part of the monarchy's much-depleted powers" (Packard, *Sons of Heaven*, 177). He abdicated on his own terms and named his daughter Meisho his successor. No foreigner ever actually saw the Emperor until the reign of Meiji (1867–1912), and few the Shogun (Will Adams and Francis Xavier did), but it was the latter, not the former, who received foreigners.

[259] "Go and get yourself crucified" (Plautus, *Persa* 2. 4. 17); it is usually rendered as "go and hang yourself."

this imprecation: "If true, I wish my hand may never heal again." Murder, theft, treason and adultery are punished severely, either by crucifying or beheading with a *katana*.[260]

Osaka is 80 leagues from Bungo;[261] it is a port of good note and in nothing more observable than the castle, which heretofore as reported was varnished, tiled and burnished in some places with plates of gold, a regular fortification and of excellent stone, the walls whereof were everywhere twenty foot thick and the whole work circulated with a large, deep trench full of water. The castle was entred by a dozen iron gates and some drawbridges.[262] Of late years it was made the prison of *Coja-zamma* Prince of *Tanzey*, eldest son of *Tiqua-zamma* the late Emperor, whose father *Faxiba-zamma*[263] subjected all the other princes of Japan and made them by oath and pledge acknowledge him their sovereign. *Coja-zamma* upon his father's sudden death was unexpectedly seized by *Ogosho-zamma*, who compelled him to marry his daughter, after which he was requited by confinement to that hateful prison.[264] On the other side the river Sakai, a town traded

---

[260] The Japanese long sword; Herbert probably got this word from Saris, who renders it as *cattana*.

[261] Bungo is the name usually applied by Europeans to Oita in Kyushu, which was one of the few Christian enclaves in Japan. St. Francis Xavier met the *daimyo*, Otomo Sorin (1530–1587), in 1551 and converted him; in 1559 Otomo opened Funai to Portuguese traders. He was usually referred to as 'the King of Bungo.'

[262] Osaka Castle is probably one of the most visited tourist sites in Japan today, although much of it is actually restoration. It was built (1583) by Toyotomi Hideyoshi, the great rival to Ieyasu. Ieyasu himself had been imprisoned by Oda Nobunaga in Sakai, but had escaped (1582). Milton describes Osaka Castle as a "rambling, elegant castle, whose scale and elegance far surpassed the Tower of London. It was one of the marvels of Japan, a building of such immensity that all who saw it were impressed." Will Adams noted the audience-chamber, which he called "a wonderful costly house . . . gilded with gold in abundance" (Milton, *Samurai William*, 105–6).

[263] This name must refer to Hideyoshi, who in fact "subjected all the other princes of Japan" in 1590. There is some confusion, however, as Hideyoshi was known in Adams's and Saris's accounts as 'Tyco-zamma,' a corruption of his Japanese title *taiko-sama*, 'lord high retired regent,' the name by which Hideyoshi was known after he had ceded power to his son. Hideyoshi's father was a man named Yaemon, a peasant who later became a soldier, and was certainly no samurai. *Tiqua-zamma* is closer to Hideyoshi's title.

[264] This is highly fanciful and inaccurate; Herbert never saw the castle anyhow. Osaka Castle was besieged by Ieyasu first in 1614 and again in 1615; after the second siege Hideyoshi's son and heir Hideyori committed suicide. Part of the confusion has to do with Herbert and his sources being unable to tell emperors from shoguns; the Emperors in the period immediately before Herbert's time were Ogimachi (1557–1586) and Go-Yozei (1586–1611), neither of whom could be described as aggressive rulers, but they nevertheless tried to assert themselves against the power of the shoguns. Who Herbert means by the names he gives is not clear, and events do not fit, either.

to by Christians, is situate. Edo,[265] not far thence, is a town strongly-walled and well-peopled; 15 leagues there is Yokohama, a town that affords good anchorage. Hirado is not less than 300 leagues thence if you coast thither; it is a chersonese and elevates the Arctic Pole 33 degrees 30 minutes, variation east 1 degree 50 minutes, where and at Fukato the English had for some time a noted factory.

Hakata is a pretty town watered with a sweet river and made defensive by a castle, a forest of lofty pines and spreading sycamores for three miles' space well-nigh compass the town, of force against the scorching sun, delightful to the eye, yea, more grateful then any other object did not idolatry render it ingrate, for under those green trees where are many small but richly-tiled fotics they adore pagodas in shape not unlike Pan and Priapus, yet Satan himself in his ugliest resemblance, for where the country is most in habited and garnished with greatest variety of trees and corn etc., as 'twixt Edo and Suruga, there are erected most fotics, and there the people are the greatest idolaters. In June and July they seldom fail of prodigious storms called typhoons[266] or hurricanes, that for 24 hours thunder in the air and tornado-like in that time veer round about all points of the compass.

In Miyako are 60 temples and colleges in which some have numbered 3333 *Chamaetinae* or little gilded demons of sundry shapes,[267] which according to the custom of the gentiles of old, parts of whose litany was *"Dii deaeque superi, inferi et medioxani, adiuvate."*[268] These poor heathens in like sort invocate; they call

---

[265] Edo is the old name for Tokyo. Ieyasu made it the capital in the early 1600s, but the Emperor remained cloistered in Kyoto.

[266] The word 'typhoon' probably originated from Mandarn *tai fēng* or Hakka dialect *tai foong*. I had originally transcribed the word as *tsunami* because the "ff" looked like the long "s" in my copy-text. In Japan, a letter from Lord Matsudaira Masamone to Shogun Ieyasu in 1611 recorded the word *tsumani* as being used by fishermen to denote a "harbour wave," and the same year a Spanish captain, Sebastian Vizcaino, also wrote about the same storm. In an article by Julyan Cartwright and Hisami Nakamura we find that the word *tsunami* first appears in English in a letter from the American traveller Eliza Ruhamah Scidmore in a letter to her brother, a consular official in Yokohama (1896). See Julyan H. Cartwright and Hisami Nakamura, "Tsunami: A History of the Term and of Scientific Understanding of the Phenomenon in Japanese and Western Culture," *Notes and Records of the Royal Society* 62 (2008): 151–66. My thanks to Professors Cartwright and Nakamura for clearing up this error.

[267] Herbert may be alluding here to the great Sanjusangendo Temple in Kyoto, which contains 1001 gilded images of Kannon (Chinese Kuan-Yin), the goddess of mercy. How many images there are in the rest of Kyoto's temples I do not know. Sanjusangendo was built in 1164, almost destroyed by fire in 1249, and rebuilt in 1266. The statues are all different, and are arranged around a large central "thousand-handed" Kannon with crystal eyes. Herbert's *Chamaetinae* probably means Kannon[s].

[268] "Help, O you high, low and middle-ranked gods!" (Plautus, *Cistellaria* 512).

them *manadees*, of which Sakyamuni and Amida,[269] say the bonzes,[270] have the highest rank in their calendar. Nevertheless, by *Tyco-zamma* a monstrous image was erected there of orichalcum,[271] so large as albeit his posture was sitting the chair was not less then 70 foot high and 80 broad; his head was capable to hold fifteen men and the thumb in compass was 40 inches, by which the rest may be conjectured. Near this grand pagod is a fotic, in the cloister whereof a memorial is registered how that the ears and noses of 3000 of the captived Koreans were there interred.[272] At *Dabys* such another colossus of concave copper was raised; it was an idol 24 foot high, notwithstanding which his posture was such as his buttocks rested upon his legs after the usual mode of the Orient.[273] But in such remembrances how can I proceed without an exclamation? Sedulius furnishes me with one very proper for the occasion:

---

[269] Sakyamuni [*Shaca*] means "Sage of the Sakyas." Gautama Buddha was a Sakya; they were an independent Himalayan kingdom. "*Namu Amida Butsu*" is a common address to Buddha which means "in homage to Amida Buddha." The title 'Amida' may be translated as "Infinite Light." Whoever invokes the name of Amida Buddha in genuine faith will be reborn in the Pure Land. This is one of the very few references to Buddhism in Herbert's book.

[270] This term is commonly used by early writers to refer to *bhiksus* or Buddhist monks and, more often, Chinese or Japanese monks. The Portuguese coined the word *bonzo* from the Japanese *bozu* or *bonsu*.

[271] A kind of brass or bronze, but less expensive than either. Herbert obviously did not know that this Buddha, which was about 48 feet high, had been destroyed by a fire in 1602 and replaced by a small wooden image. He is correct, however, in saying that it was built by Hideyoshi. The 1638 edition reads: "But more noticeable than the rest is that in Miyako, not unlike the Rhodian Colossus, huge and wonderful . . . its posture is sitting in a chair 70 feet high and so broad his head is capable to support fifteen men, who may stand together without pressing" (335).

[272] This probably refers to the 'Keicho campaign' against Korea. Hideyoshi, smarting from defeats inflicted on his troops by the Koreans and Chinese, invaded Korea again in 1597 and at the Battle of Sochon his victorious generals collected the ears "from 38,000 Korean and Chinese heads" and sent them to the Shogun (Cotterell, *East Asia* 126). In the 1638 edition Herbert calls the Koreans "a base, thievish people vicinating and infecting the Japonians" (335). See also description in Saris (*Voyage*, 141).

[273] More historical confusion here. One of these "images" is evidently the Great Daibutsu at Kamakura (Herbert thinks *Dabys* is a place, but it surely means 'Daibutsu'), which was erected in 1252. John Saris wrote that it was "in the likeness of a man kneeling upon the ground, with his buttocks resting on his heels, his arms of wonderful largeness and the whole body proportionable;" some of his men climbed inside it, where they "whooped and hollowed, which made an exceeding great noise" (Milton, *Samurai William*, 196). The Emperor at the time it was built was Go-Fukakusa (1246–1260). There is also a great Buddha statue at the Sanjusangendo temple in Kyoto, and others throughout Japan; without more specific information these cannot be identified with any certainty.

Poor wretched souls which dote on vanity
    And hallowing dumb idols in your heart,
Fear not your great Creator to defy
    By adoring works of your own hand and art!
What fury or what frenzy thus beguiles
    Your minds, foul ugly shapes so to adore,
With birds and nasty bulls and dragons vile,
    Half dog, half man, prostrate their help to implore?[274]

A notable imposture.

But of most remark was the fotic at Tenshodaijin,[275] where, if some speak truth, Satan ofttimes made an apparition. This temple was of more then ordinary structure and the bonzes numerous. Amongst other sacrifices or forms of worship one was that a damsel every New Moon was by the bonzes brought into the temple and placed right against the idol. The room was forthwith illuminated by a preparation of *lignum vitae*[276] with other costly perfumes put into lamps of gold; after a small space the lights, as it were by miracle, extinguish, and then in gross darkness the phantasma, having assumed a bodily shape or other false representation, accompanies her, at least as she imagines, because certain scales like those of fishes are left behind as an argument to persuade it was no phantasma, but unless the bonzes second that work upon this imaginary familiarity, the most is but a tympany or false conception. Nevertheless, for her applause at her issuing she is entertained with music and songs, and is of more repute with them ever after. Now to this notable piece of imposture of Satan, who in this doubtless makes a *deceptio visus et tactus*, I shall make no other disquisition then by applying to the credulous what the gloss upon the *Jus Pontificium*[277] expresseth in the like case or scruple: *"Credunt, sed male credunt, quia sunt phantasmata;* some believe, but they believe amiss, seeing they are but phantasms," and *"Eludit enim Diabolus aciem tum spectantium tum etiam cogitantium;* the Devil eludes the sense as well of the

---

[274] Sedulius, *Carmen paschale* 1. 242–247.

[275] Tenshodaijin [*Tencheday*] is not a place but a name of the sun-goddess Amaterasu no Omikami. Will Adams told John Saris about the "fotoqui or temple dedicated to Tencheday, to which image they make [a] devout pilgrimage," and that Tencheday "is thought to be the Devil" (Kerr, 9: 29). The rather garbled story about the "damsel" may be related to the fact that until the reign of Go-Daigo (1318–1339) an Imperial princess was chosen as the priestess of this temple, which is at the Ise Shrine. Herbert does not know the difference between shrines (Shinto) and temples (Buddhist).

[276] A very hard wood, known sometimes as *guayacan*.

[277] Herbert is probably referring to Petrus Gregorius (Pierre Grégoire)'s *Syntagma iuris universi* (1580), a pioneering work in comparative jurisprudence; Grégoire (1540–1617) was Professor of Civil Law at the University of Cahors (1570–1580).

beholders as those that so imagine," for "*imagine falsa visibus humanis magicas tribuere figura*," saith Sedulius *lib. 4 Carmina.*[278]

China.

Due west from Japan is China, the most easterly part of the continent of Greater Asia, a kingdom no less great then wealthy and as famous as great, but not well-discovered; their jealousy and discourtesy to strangers, for they suffer many to enter but few return, chiefly causes it. This is subject to several names, scarce any two strange people according in one denomination, and no wonder, since amongst themselves they affect variety, yea, it is a custom for kings to new-name both themselves and the kingdom at their coronation according to fancy.

It Ptolemy it is called *Sinorum Regio*, *Seres* by other geographers; the Moors in Industan call it *Cathaya*, the Arabians *Tsinin*, the Sia-mites *Cyn*, the Malayans *Tabenzo*, the Japonites *Than* and *Tsin*, the Tar-tars *Han* (from the metropolis Qinzhou[279] which they call *Hanshin*), Al-Hasan *Tajis*, Paulus Venetus *Mangi*; the inhabitants, say Pereira,[280] Riccius[281]

---

[278] "By means of a false image they present magical shapes to the human gaze" (Sedulius, *Carmen paschale* 4. 170–171).

[279] Qinzhou (also known as Yamchow or Yen Chow) is on the Gulf of Tonkin in Guangxi Province. It was founded in the Southern Dynasty period (420–589), and the name was changed from Anzhou (which may be what Herbert means by *Hanshin*) to Qinzhou during the Sui Dynasty (581–618). There are impressive Ming ruins near the city. It is about 120 km from the Vietnam border.

[280] Galeote Pereira was a Portuguese nobleman who began his travels by going to India in 1534. Between 1539 and 1548 he visited Malacca, China, and Siam. In 1549 he was seized and imprisoned by the Chinese authorities and some of his men were execut-ed. When the Chinese released the others and sent them to various towns in Fukien and Guangxi provinces, Pereira escaped (1553). He wrote a short account of his experiences in China (1565) which was translated by Richard Willes and included in his *History of Travayle in the Easte and Weste Indies* (1577). See C. R. Boxer, ed., *South China in the Six-teenth Century. Being the narratives of Galeote Pereira, Fr. Gaspar de la Cruz, O. P. and Fr. Martín de Rada* (London: Hakluyt Society, 1958).

[281] Matteo Ricci (1552–1610) was a remarkable Jesuit who started his Asian sojourn in 1578, leaving Lisbon for Goa and Cochin and then back to Goa. He left again in 1582 for Malacca, Macau, and then China, where he lived first in Zhaoqing and then other places, settling in Nanjing in 1599. He published a world map in 1584, which he revised in 1602, but was most famous for his *Treatise on Mnemonic Arts*, which he wrote in 1596. Ricci learned Chinese and translated Euclid into that language, as well as writing *The True Meaning of the Lord of Heaven* (1603) and the *Ten Discourses by a Paradoxical Man* (1608). Ricci also wrote the *Historia*, an account of his experiences in China (1608–1610). In China Ricci is best-known for his treatise *On Friendship*, in which he translated max-ims by classical and Christian authors into Chinese. For a very interesting work on this fascinating figure, see Jonathan Spence, *The Memory Palace of Matteo Ricci* (Harmonds-

and *Trigantius,*[282] *Tamen* and themselves *Tamegines.* But how various so'er that be, this is not so uncertain, that it is a spacious monarchy and extends from 17 degrees to 47 of north latitude, which to the south Canton and to the north Peking, two royal cities, seem to terminate. On the east and south it has the ocean, on the west the deserts of Industan, on the north the Tartars and on the southwest Cochin China and Pegu, and from every opposite side not less then 1500 English miles, as some have imagined, which granted, the whole compass will be 4000 and upwards. The country is full of sweet and navigable rivers, some of which are no less-inhabited then cities, which are reported to be 600; besides, the Jesuits report it has 2000 walled towns, 4000 unwalled, 1000 castles and villages scarce to be numbered, and many they had need to be, since they lodge, as some friars that inhabited there have undertaken to estimate, above threescore millions of men, women being uncounted, which if so, it has four times more then all France is supposed to have and well-considered excuses that conjecture Brerewood[283] makes in his inquiries, saying that if the whole world were divided into 30 equal parts, the Christians will appedar to be but 5 of the 30, the Mohammedans 6 and the gentiles 19 out of that distribution. The whole Empire is divided into fifteen provinces governed by so many *Quon-su* and *Lausiae* who have their *Tutons* and *Chyams,* as their deputies are intitled. Each of those provinces has a metropolis, but every way more excellent then the rest are Peking, by some called *Pasquin,* Nanjing, Canton and *Quinsay,* by them called *Ham-can,* of which four Peking hath now the precedency albeit *Quinsay* had formerly.

---

worth: Penguin Books, 1984). Po-chia Hsia, *A Jesuit in the Forbidden City Matteo Ricci 1552-1610.* Oxford University Press, 2010. I am indebted to Dr. William Poole, Galsworthy Fellow and Tutor, New College, Oxford, for drawing my attention to this book and for helping clarify and augment the notes on China.

[282] Nicolas Trigault (1577–1628) was a French Jesuit from Douai who first went to China for a short time in 1611, where he lived in Hangzhou. After a few years back in Europe raising money for missions, he returned to China in 1618 and spent the rest of his life there. Trigault translated Matteo Ricci's *De Christiana expeditione apud Sinos* (1615) from Italian into Latin, "he effectively censored [Ricci] in places, and changed the interpretation in others, in order to present a more acceptable interpretation of China to his western superiors" (Letter from Dr. William Poole to the editor), and he made transcriptions of Chinese letters and translated Aesop into Chinese (1625). He committed suicide after a long period of depression. A portrait of him in Chinese dress was painted by Rubens. See also Liam M. Brockney, *Journey to the East: The Jesuit Mission to China, 1579–1724* (Cambridge, MA: Harvard University Press, 2007).

[283] Edward Brerewood (c. 1565–1613), scientist, theologian, logician, and linguist, was Professor of Astronomy at Gresham College, London. The work to which Herbert refers here is his *Enquiries touching the Diversity of Languages and Religions through the Chief Parts of the World* (1614, 1622, 1635, and twice in 1674), a pioneering work in comparative religion and linguistics. There is a facsimile of the 1674 edition currently available (New York: Kessinger Reprints, 2007).

Peking elevates the North Pole 41 degrees 15 minutes and by late geographers is accounted the same city some call Cambalu, watered by Polisanga, differing in the latitude of Cambalu, which is placed in 45 degrees and country in which 'tis placed, but if Pantoja[284] and di Conti[285] say right, the China monarch[286] is that same Great Khan with M. Venetus and Mandeville, who doubtless were no further east then Industan and Bactria, and from the reports there met of the more easterly parts then made famous. The city Peking, as described by some which are without good authority, is not only the greatest and best-peopled city in all Asia but in all the world, if, as some report, it hath 30 Dutch leagues circumference, in which are many stately buildings and 24,000 Mandarin sepulchres, the meanest of which are not without some beauty, and a no less number of little gilded chapels, besides 3800 temples that be devoted to idolatry. It also has as many gates and posterns as days in a year, sixscore bazaars and above a thousand bridges. This city is distant about a hundred miles from that marvellous wall which some say *Crisnagol*, others *Zaintzan* the 117th king built 1000 years since to keep out the Tartar, a wall 1200 miles long, twelve yards thick and six fathoms in height, such as was seven and twenty years erecting by a continued labour of 750,000 men, which nevertheless could not hinder the Tartar of late, who not only forced his passage but with little opposition hath overrun and subjected this great Empire.[287]

---

[284] Diego Pantoja (1581–1617) arrived in Nanjing as a young priest in 1600 and accompanied Matteo Ricci to Peking, where he learned Chinese and seems to have made himself useful as a musician and composer, setting eight songs by Ricci which were performed in the Chinese court (Spence, *Memory Palace*, 198–99). He also revised the calendar for the Emperor and drew maps of Europe for the Chinese (1611). He published a work in Chinese, *Qi Ke* (1614), which explained the main tenets of Catholicism. Pantoja died in Macao after being expelled from the Manchu court.

[285] Niccolò di Conti (1395–1469) was a Venetian merchant and traveller who had a fascinating career travelling in South East Asia, India, and the Middle East, and who may also have gone to China, although some scholars dispute this claim. He began his travels in 1419 and returned to Venice in 1444, having married an Indian woman and converted to Islam so that he could travel as a Muslim merchant. Pope Eugenius IV commanded him to write an account of his travels as a penance for his conversion! Di Conti's book was finally published in 1492, after which it was included by Ramusio in his collection and translated into English (1579) by John Frampton, another merchant-traveller.

[286] During the time of Herbert's travels the "China monarch" was Emperor Chongzhen (1627–1644), the last ruler of the Ming Dynasty. However, by the time this edition was printed, the Mings had been overthrown by the Manchus (as Herbert notes below) and the Emperor was the great Kangxi (1662–1723).

[287] This description of the Great Wall is inaccurate. Herbert is probably referring to the wall built by the Ming Dynasty starting in 1386, "which is about 26 ft tall and 23 ft wide at its base" (Davis, *China*, 58). However, the first 'Great Wall' was built much further south by the Emperor Qin Shihuang (246–209 B. C. E.) in about 221 B. C. E., and

Nanjing, the second city for grandeur, was once the metropolis.[288] It elevates the Arctic Pole 35 degrees and is distant from the sea 8 leagues or thereabouts. The city is 12 leagues about, circled with three strong walls and ditches. The King's palace is vast; the other buildings many, for 200,000 are reckoned, but meanly-beautiful. The temples, such as they be, are above a thousand, the streets fair and the people industrious; from Peking it is removed east six hundred miles English, most part of the way navigable.

Canton is at the most southerly end, in 17 (some observe 25) degrees latitude, a town rich and spacious. The ships ride commonly in view of it,[289] from which to Peking is little less then two months' travel. Here merchants are permitted to come ashore, but when they enter the city-gate usually enrol their names in a book to the end that upon a penalty they return aboard at night, but of late have a little more liberty. In this place merchants trade for gold, musk, silks of all sorts, cabinets, porcelain and sundry other rich commodities.[290]

Qinzhou or *Ham-ceu* borders Cochin-China. Of old this city was the greatest, at this day the most remarkable for variety of antique rareties of any city in the Orient.

These are the most noted, and what is most notable in them are their *meani* or idol-temples.[291] The country is champagne and exceeding fruitful, the rivers abound with fish which the Chinese not only banquet upon but also upon frogs, snakes, rats, hogs, dogs and such food as many other nations abominate, and for their better dispatch they fish with cormorants. The people are olive-coloured, more black or white as they live in distance from the Equinoctial; they wear their hair long and filleted but their beards very thin, even to deformity. Their eyes are

---

it was for the building of that one that the Emperor "mustered nearly a million people" (Davis, *China*, 58). The 'Tartars,' in this case the Manchus, defeated the Mings in 1644.

[288] The Imperial Court was moved to Nanjing [*Nanquin*] under the first Ming Emperor, Hong Wu (1368–1398). The walls mentioned by Herbert include one built in the fourteenth century, which is still standing.

[289] 1638: "Our ships came almost in view of it" (337).

[290] Canton [*Cantam*], now known as Guangzhou, was a city first traded in by the Portuguese, who had reached China in 1514, although they were expelled from the city in 1522, resurfacing again by 1557 when they were allowed to rent what became Macao (Simkin, *Trade*, 185). "The Cantonese talent for business," states Davis, "was as keen then as it now," and although "at that time the Ming court in Beijing banned all foreign trade," the Cantonese defied the government, because, "as the saying went, the Emperor was far away" (Davis, *China*, 289).

[291] 1638: "None be without their *meani* or temples filled with *deastri* or idols" (337). *Deaster* was a neo-Latin word coined by Sebastien Castellio (1515–1563), a Calvinist theologian who wrote the *Four Books of Sacred Dialogues* (1542). According to a later theologian, this was "a word of no authority sacred or profane" (G. Campbell, *The Four Gospels, Translated out of Greek with Preliminary Discourses and Notes Critical and Explanatory* [Andover: Gould and Newman, 1837], 1: 369).

commonly black, noses little, eyes small, nails wellnigh as long as their finger but serving to distinguish their quality. The better sort are habited in silk and a slight sort of satin, the meaner in black cloth made of cotton; both wear their coats long and quilted, made to tie under the left arm after the usual garb of Asia. Their sleeves are long and at the wrist very strait; their shoes are of such stuff as their coats, but some have them richly-embroidered, the sole is cloth or calico. The greatest variety is in their head-attire, for some knit their hair in cawls of silk, of horsehair some but some with fillets of gold or silver; others wear high round caps made of fine twigs stitched with silk of divers colours, but others fancy an antique sort of hat which is high-crowned and round, but one-half without any brim, and no colour so much pleases them as that we call tawny. The women are modest and amongst themselves differ not in apparel, in that a cambolin or veil of white linen covers them, showing nothing but their polt-feet, which from their infancy are straitened so as to make them *à la mode*; many of them become voluntarily lame and crippled.[292]

They tolerate polygamy and that odious sin of sodomy,[293] yea, what else their idle depraved natures can imagine to please their effeminacies, and are not ashamed to expose them to public view in prints and painting.[294] They are a proud, lazy, jealous and voluptuous sort of people. Music, poetry, painting and stage-plays delight them exceedingly and [they] care not what they spend in luxury and fireworks. They eat in porcelain, which as Gonzalo de Mendoza[295] (a

---

[292] In earlier editions, Herbert is not so neutral on foot-binding; in the 1638 edition, for example, he says that "so as to make them *a la mode*, many of them are maimed" (338).

[293] Matteo Ricci had noted a few years earlier that "no less than the natural lusts they practice unnatural ones that reverse the order of things, and this is neither forbidden by law, nor thought to be illicit, nor even a cause for shame. It is spoken of in public and practiced everywhere . . . there are public streets full of boys got up like prostitutes" (*Fonto Ricciani* 1/98, cited in Spence, *Memory Palace*, 220–21). Galeote Perreira, too, wrote that "the greatest fault we find in them is sodomy, a vice very common in the meaner sort and nothing strange among the best" (cited in Spence, *Memory Palace*, 221). Both men were simply reacting as Catholics against any kind of sexuality that did not result in progeny. Herbert, of course, is reacting as a Protestant and a man with Puritan sympathies, although of course any form of sex other than that used for procreation would have been considered 'unnatural' by him anyway.

[294] Herbert may have seen some Chinese erotic art, which, like any other art of its kind, ranges from the tender to the vulgar. The high period of Chinese erotic art was the late Ming period; the Ming dynasty ended in 1644. Some of this art was claimed to be instructional, so that inexperienced young people would know what to do. It is uncertain why Herbert seems to single out Chinese art for censure yet does not mention Japanese *shunga*, but it may be from reading Ricci.

[295] Juan Gonzalez de Mendoza (c. 1540–1617), a Spanish priest, was sent by Philip II to China in 1580. He spent three years there, and then went on to Mexico, where he

gentleman sent thither by Philip II with a present) reports, is not earth of 100 years' preparation as commonly-spoken, but a chalky substance which digged or soaked in water yields a kind of cream above, but below the earth and sediment is coarse; out of that fine upper earth-like cream the purest sort of chinaware is made and the ordinary sort out of the other earth, which is less fat or oily. So soon as they be formed or baked in the sun they paint and gild them very curiously, and so put them into the furnace; howbeit, Pancirollus saith that porcelain is a compound of eggshells, lobster-shells and gypsum which is treasured 80 years in the bowels of the earth ere it be prepared. They have their diet in many small dishes, love their meat minced, which they take up with two sticks of bone or ivory. But some have their nails so long as serves for that exercise, for to touch either their mouths or their meat with their fingers is absurd. Their drink is commonly hot and by its taste and colour appears to be coffee;[296] they drink oft and little. The *liaos*[297] will be served on the knee; they sit on stools and eat on tables as the Europeans, and albeit no nation in the world be more idle and voraginous then they, yet are few or no beggars found, for if he be a young beggar he has the whip, if old or lame or blind he is provided for in the hospital.

Murder they punish with death, as also theft; the least punishment is the strappado, yet what laws they have most resemble the Imperial, which they vigorously execute. Their laws, it seems, are consistent with the condition of the country and disposition of the people, but the extreme rigour and execution thereof may be resembled to the grape, which being gently pretty yields wholesome wine, but too much squeezing renders it bad and unpleasant. 'Tis a difficult matter for man to establish any one law that will quadrate[298] with the humour of all places; their justice is severe, their prisons strong and their executions quick. The mandarins are honoured, the khans reverenced, the King little less then adored; no subject has recourse except by petition. His wives, children and eunuchs only have access to him; ambassadors enter not without presents of value.

---

stayed for two years. He was Bishop of the Lipari Islands and of Chiapas in Mexico. He wrote the *Historia de las cosas mas notables, ritos y costumbres del gran reyno de la China* (1586), which was translated into English by Robert Parke as *The History of the Great and Mighty Kingdom of China and the Situation thereof* (1588). It was a pioneering work in that Gonzalez was the first writer to publish and explain Chinese characters, of which he printed only two, and both were unrecognisable. "His explanation," Dr. Poole notes in a letter to the editor, "is also pretty dodgy." It has been edited by Sir George Staunton (London: Hakluyt Society, 1854).

[296] Herbert is probably referring to tea in this passage; the Chinese did not drink coffee. Tea came to England via Portugal (1662), when Catherine of Bragança, a keen tea-drinker, married Charles II. Portugal imported its tea from China.

[297] Bureaucrats (literally), or those who later became better-known to the West as mandarins. Herbert spells the word *louthayas*.

[298] square.

They are curious in novelties and love to see strange arts, which they delight-fully practice; few but has skill either in tillage, making china dishes or can paint, sing, play or do something that is useful and modest. The mathematics they af-fect, use not letters but characters, of which they have above 40,000;[299] they write neither to the right nor to the left, but downright, not with pens but pencils of horsehair such are as in use with painters. Their language is the most part mono-syllables; few but have a vein in poetry and music and are studious in all the liberal sciences. Scholars and merchants are more honoured then men of war; no people in the world more honour their King then they, for they suppose him too glori-ous to look upon. They obey his will in everything, fill his exchequer yearly with above a hundred millions of crowns, call him the undaunted Emperor, Lord of the Whole World, Son of the Sun and Beauty of the Whole Earth.[300] Nor do any people in the world express more filial respect to parents then they, for they obey them at all times and places, marry not without their consent, leave their children's names to them, honour them be they never so mean, relieve them be they never so poor, at their death express all symptoms possible of duty and in white linen, as did the Jews, seldom mourn less then two or three years. The longer they mourn, they think the better they express their observance and affection.

But they arrogate to themselves the invention of all arts and knowledge in the liberal sciences, and in cannot be denied but that some of them they have, as logic, rhetoric, music, arithmetic and astronomy; they are, say they, the most ancient and unmixed people in the universe, have all from their Minerva and borrow nothing from others. They boast how that they first invented charac-ters, guns, painting, tillage and navigation. Now, give me leave to say a word in our defence against the rhodomontades of these Chinese, who, as I suppose, in none of these parallel Europe. For their antiquity, I deny not but they have con-tinued without much mixture (yet admirable if so, since both the Tartars and Siamites have overrun their country) since the first seminary begun by Shem in those parts,[301] but if granted others in that may compare with them, namely the

---

[299] Herbert's source for this information may have been the writings of Gonzalez de Mendoza, Ricci, or other missionaries. Mei Yingzuo compiled a Chinese dictionary, the *Zihui* (1615), which contained about 33,179 characters, to which Zhang Zilie added a supplement (1627), but it's unlikely Herbert knew of these. Ricci and Michele Rug-gieri produced a Portuguese-Chinese dictionary (1583–1588) which was unpublished and then lost until 2001, and a second dictionary, by Ricci and Lazaro Cattaneo (1598) has also been lost and remains unrecovered.

[300] The usual title of the Chinese emperor was "Son of Heaven."

[301] On the basis of "Behold, these shall come from far: and lo, these from the north and the west: and these from the land of Sinim" (Isaiah 49:12) there was a belief that Shem and his descendents settled in China. The Sinim were equated with the Chin, which was in turn supposed to denote Shem. Later writers have even believed that the Shang Dynasty (dated by some modern scholars as 1600–1046 B.C.E.) in north-eastern China corresponded chronologically with Abraham's time.

Britons, Biscayans and others, for I regard not their legend of kings or such conquests as they obtained long before the birth of time a hundred thousand years ago, unless we qualify it by the ephemeris of the Arcadians, whose year had but ninety days, the Spaniards but four months, the Massagetes sixteen, or of the Egyptians who had twelve years in one of ours, following the course of the moon and not the revolution of the sun nor regarding the *dies intercalares*,³⁰² an error most of the oriental ethnics are plunged in. Very likely they imitate the Chaldee, who as Diodorus Siculus *lib.* 3, affirm the origin of their characters or astrology was three and forty thousand years before the overthrow of the last Darius, which did not Annius of Viterbo help in his paraphrase upon Berossos, would be laughed at, but Xenophon and others say that the years they accounted by were lunary, upon which reduction it will appear that 43,000 of their lunar years make but 3634 of our solar, but their hieroglyphics, though more ancient then letters, come short of the Egyptians.

Their guns, the use of which Bacchus taught them, are not above a span long, so that they rather resemble pistols than guns, their bore and squaring being less then ours, and for their painting it cannot be denied but that it is of good colours but their designs short of our invention. They draw the postures filthy and shadow meanly, which doubtless in painting makes the perfection. Horology knowledge they want, as may be supposed by the story of that King who upon first view of a watch presented by an European was so surprised that he verily believed it a living creature, till by winding it up he perceived the *primum mobile*.³⁰³ Their husbandry is without much art, for albeit the grain be good, the soil be rich and the zone moderate, yet their corn is neither so various nor so good nor so certain as in our harvests. Their navigation is lame; they build many ships yet without beauty or defence, nor have they much skill in sailing, having no good logarithms nor mathematic instruments to take the height of the sun by. Their compass is also defective, for it hath but eight or twelve points to distinguish by, nor is the magnet till of late known amongst them, notwithstanding they say they see with two eyes and those of Europe with but one and all other people are blind or at least purblind in ignorance.

They delight excessively in all sorts of games, and when they have lost care not, though they stake wives and children, whom they willingly part with till they can redeem them. They are hospitable to one another and believe a resurrection,

---

³⁰² Isidore of Seville, to whom Herbert is probably referring here, states "the days are called intercalary, since they are inserted to make a harmonious reckoning before the sun and moon" (*Etymologiae* 6. 17. 28).

³⁰³ The story of the Chinese emperor and his Italian clock (not watch) may be found in Matteo Ricci, who had presented a chiming clock to emperor Wan Li. In fact, the Chinese probably invented water-clocks, and there is a tradition of Yi Xing and Liang Yingzhan constructing one in the 6th century B. C. E. One Su Song appears to have invented a kind of mechanical clock (although water was still involved) in 1088.

for sometimes they will lend money to be repayed them in the other world.[304]
Interludes, masques, fireworks and such devices wonderfully take them, nor value they what money they expend in such disport so their expectation be not
frustrate. Their houses are meanly-built and as badly furnished, howbeit their
meani have no such grandeur nor external beauty as in a country so peaceful, so
rich and amongst a people so studious and superstitious might be expected, yet
though their outsides be but ordinary, they many times are lined with excellent
good porphyry, serpentine and like marble. Their colleges and temples express by
some invention or other their infernal art and familiarity with the old Magician,
to whom they devote enthusiastic boys who with their long-spread hair prostrate themselves afore the *mannada*,[305] and suddenly, as if some hag had terrified
them, start up and vibrate a spear or other weapon, whiles the spectators with
dejected looks warble out a soft Doric sort of music, departing not till the vatici-
nating[306] youths pronounce somewhat that points at his worship and obedience.

They celebrate their *Natalitia*[307] very solemnly a fortnight's time, spending the
days in pastime and the night with feasts; amongst the rest they have choice fruits
and wines, in which they take full liberty. The New Year they begin in March[308]
and is no less-observed there; at that time every man strives to exceed others in the
fancy of their pageants and adorning their doors respectively with paper arches and
images, and all the night long make them visible by lights and lanterns.

Funerals of the Chinese.

Their weddings have more or less ceremony according to the quality of the persons. Their funerals are after this sort: when any dies they first wash, then perfume and lastly apparel the corpse, and put his best clothes on, then cover his
head, and having set him in a chair, his wife entering the room first gives him
respect and then kisses him. After that she takes her farewell with as much sorrow as can be imagined, if it be not counterfeit; she is no sooner gone but his
children enter. They first kneel and then kiss the dead man's hand, yea, strive to
out-vie each other in their ejaculations, expressing their love by sorrowful countenances and gestures as beating their breasts and pouring out tears in abun-

---

[304] There is a mixture of Taoist and Buddhist ideas in the Chinese concept of the
afterlife. When people die, they come before Chenhuang, the god of walls, who conducts
a kind of preliminary hearing, after which the good are sent to a Buddhist paradise, the
abode of the Taoist immortals, or the tenth court of hell to be reborn. Bad people, after
forty-nine days, are sent to hell, after which their punishment or reincarnation is determined.

[305] Image.

[306] Prophesying.

[307] Birthdays.

[308] Chinese New Year is based on the lunisolar calendar and varies according to
which animal presides over the year. It can be in January to March.

dance. They being withdrawn, next his kindred act their parts, and lastly his friends and other more remote acquaintances. The third day they lay him in a coffin of precious wood which they cover with a silk cloth, and over it place his picture. For fifteen days in that sort the corpse rests, and each day a table is spread with meat which nightly the priests have liberty to eat, for 'tis they that burn the incense and offer sacrifice. When they carry it to the grave, women are hired to howl, the better to move others to compassion; sometimes upon his coffin they place the image of a dead man whom they expect should show him the surest and readiest way to Elysium. That done, the widow and children for some days exclude themselves, and when abroad go about dolorously-habited, for they put coarse sackcloth next their skin, have their clothes made long and plain and for three years' space are not seen to laugh or joy in anything, but to the utmost of their powers express their love by a continued lamentation, abstinence from feasts and pastimes, and in all their letters subscribe themselves such a one's disobedient and unworthy widow, or what may best set forth observance.[309]

Mauritius Island.

But, having launched too far, 'tis high time to look homewards, yet not till we have bid farewell to lovely Asia, into which when some have adventured this motto may be remembered: "Man's heart commands as many ways as stars find resting-places; / Who travels must disguise himself each way with Janus faces." How delightful and how magical the excellencies of the Orient are to most, yet Ovid's "*Nescio qua natale solum*"[310] was still the close of my observation, so that upon the seventh of June after long sail, some storms and much patience, we again descried land. It bore NNW from us, but at the sun's first blush the ensuing morning, we knew it was Diogo Rodrigues, an isle above fifty miles about and in 20 degrees south latitude; there we anchored not, knowing that Mauritius was but 90 leagues distant thence upon a WNW course, a place where we doubted not of some refreshment. This *Digarroys* was first discovered by the Portuguese, but except some Welshman gave it the name I know not whence called *Digarroys*, seeing that *digarrad* in the British dialect fitly complies with it, the condition

---

[309] It is uncertain whether Herbert is describing Taoist or Buddhist rituals here. "Funeral rituals," Ludwig states, "are the most serious and protracted of all traditional Chinese rituals" (221). The washing, funeral garments, and mourning could apply to either religion, and the clothes used in the mourning-procession are indeed made of "coarse sackcloth" as Herbert states. "The intensity of mourning and the length," Ludwig writes, "are determined by how closely one is related to the deceased" (222). Herbert does not mention the "soul-tablet" which has the name of the dead person on it and which is set up on a chair (the corpse is not—it is in a coffin dressed in a grave-jacket).

[310] The full quotation reads: "*Nescio qua natale solum dulcedine cunctos / ducit et immemores non sinit esse sui*" (Ovid, *Epistolae ex Ponto* 1 .3. 35–36). Translation: "Our native soil draws all of us, by I know not / what sweetness, and never allows us to forget."

being a desolate island, desolate in human inhabitants, for in other things 'tis replenished, as with wood, tortoises, dodos and like fowl.[311] To our view it gave itself not very high at a league distance, but this also I remember, that at then south-west end are shoals which are long and dangerous. By benefit of a constant wind, we soon arrived at Mauritius.

The bay of Mauritius [illustration not shown]

Mauritius.

Mauritius is an isle situate within the Burning Zone under twenty degrees five minutes Antarctic latitude, longitude from the meridian of Cape Comorin twenty degrees and as many minutes and variation four and twenty degrees and nineteen minutes. To what part of the world it belongs is questionable, seeing that it participates both with America in respect of the vast Southern Ocean and inclineth towards the Asiatic Sea, washing India, Java and other isles, and with Africa also, to which most properly she appertains if you think fit to make her subordinate to that Empress of Isles Madagascar, which seems to shadow her and from whose eastern banks she is removed a hundred leagues or thereabouts. But however doubtful to which three it appertains, of this there is no doubt, that for variety of temporal blessings she may compare with most places in the universe.

It was first discovered by the Portugal, whose industrious arm and ingenious fancy ere America was discovered by Columbus gave us the first full knowledge of the East and names to many places formerly innominate, and amongst others the name *Do-Cerne* unto this, but how properly I know not, if we should allude to that in Pliny *1. 6 c.* 31, that *Cerne*[312] being placed near the Gulf of Persia and of the same name that we meet with some elsewhere in old authors amongst the Azores and other places. After that it varied into the names *Roderigo* and *Cygnaea*, lastly to *Mauritius*, which whether in memory of Graf Maurice[313] or of a ship so-named that by age or accident laid her ribs there I know not, but by equal authority I may deduce the name from some Cambrian, the relics or glimmering of whose speech we find gasping in many of these remote quarters of the world, in the word *mawr-ynisus* or 'bigger island,' fitly so-named if compared

---

[311] Diogo Rodrigues Island [*Digarroys*] was named for Diogo Rodrigues (d. 1577), the Portuguese explorer who found the three islands and called them the Mascarenas, after Pedro Mascarenhas (see below). This island was named after Rodrigues in 1528; the Dutch began coming there in 1601, but it was never used as a name for Mauritius. Herbert's version of the name is a corruption and the Welsh derivations here and below are nonsense.

[312] Cerne or Cirne is another name for St. Apollonia, not for Mauritius (see below).

[313] Prince Maurice of Orange-Nassau was Stadholder of the Netherlands 1584–1625. The Portuguese visited Mauritius in 1507, but some Dutch ships, blown off course, landed there in 1598, naming the island after their ruler, as Herbert guesses correctly.

with those other lesser neighbouring isles Digarroys, England's Forest, Dozimo, St. Apollonia etc., and by a more euphonaisical concision *Maur–isius*.[314] But grant it be so-called by the Hollander, yet it follows that they have more right to it than the English, they themselves knowing and acknowledging that the English landed there a dozen years before them, who no question had new-named it but that they knew the Portugal had done it before. This also be remembered, that in the year 1505, when Francisco Almeida, of all the Portugals the most renowned for Eastern conquest and discovery, subjecting many maritime parts of Aegisymba in Quiloa, Mombasa, Malindi, Mozambique etc. reports that there and in some isles (I suppose this one) where he erected forts and castles of defence he found crosses and other symbols of Christianity which made him confident that Christ had formerly been served there, and therefore in humility would not esteem himself the first Christian discoverer.[315] But how incertain that may be, it is without doubt that it is an isle abounding with and capable of all things requisite for the necessary use of man and requirable for the zone 'tis placed in.

Ebony. Palmetto-wine.

The land, especially where it respects the sea, is high, but elsewhere champagne and plain, the shape rather oval then round and the circuit of English miles not much above a hundred, the greatest extent being from the north-east to the south-west, the air exceeding good and the soil, though incultivated, so full of vigour that it procreates without seed, withal luxuriant in grass and herbs and such flowers as Nature usually diapers the earth with when dressed in summer livery. Nor can it be denied that by reason of the temperature of the air, and those daily breezes and showers which fall, the earth is meliorated and fitted for grain of most sorts, as also for plants, fruits, flowers and what else may be thought fit by the ingenious planter either for use or ornament. And seeing Heaven and Earth conspire and contribute to the action and advantage of the life of man, how much more abundant cause hath man to magnify his Maker, who is the liberal dispenser of those rare trees and fruits which naturally offer themselves to what man's appetite can rationally covet or lay claim unto, for we find it replenished with trees of several sorts, some of which are good for timber, others for food and

---

[314] Herbert is a little confused with the names. *Dozimo* is probably a corruption of Dina Moraze, another name for Diogo Rodrigues Island. St. Apollonia, named by the Portuguese in 1513, is now Réunion; the French arrived in 1638 and in 1642 renamed it Isle de Bourbon, which was changed to Réunion in 1792 during the French Revolution. *England's Forest* is another name for the Mascarenhas Islands (see below).

[315] In 1598 two ships from a group commanded by Benjamin Wood were wrecked near Martaban, and seven survivors found a canoe in which they managed to get to Mauritius, "then uninhabited" (Foster, *England's Quest*, 141). They were probably the first Englishmen to reach the island.

all for use. Among the rest I observed store of ebony; Virgil in his *Georgics* reports that ". . . no place save India / Black ebon wood doth bear, men say,"[316] which granted, then consequently Mauritius must be reputed a member of the Indies. But that ebony is found growing in other parts and particularly in the Egyptian territories, Lucan *l.* 10 gives us his authority: "The island Meroë/ Rich in black ebony,"[317] which reduces this isle again to Africa. Wood it is of different colour and for use of no less variety, for we found what was black and red as also white and yellow; black is most valuable. The tree is commonly high and very strait, the outside covered with a smooth bark, here found in great plenty till of late years destruction hath been made, especially by the Dutch and French, who have imported such store thereof into Europe and other their Indian plantations that it is much abated.

Here also is that phoenix in nature, the palmetto, for it is but one in the origin. We call it dactyl or date, seeing that *palma* translated is 'date' in English, a tree which both for quality, duration and fruit is usually attributed to both heroes and conquerors. The trunk is slender but very high and round, not branching save near the top as the coco doth, and those rather resemble round sedge then boughs which are evergreen. Under the sedge appears a soft pulp not unlike the cauliflower, which being cut and sod tastes very like it, but for that the vegetative virtue consists in that the tree prospers not after that is severed, as Xenophon also observeth. Whiles that substance remain it yields a liquor like the toddy, in colour and relish not unlike must or sweet wine, which effades not out of the pierced bark, so as in a hour's space the quantity of a pottle[318] may be gathered. In some old authors we read that there was tree-honey as well as bee-honey, or, as they call it, tears or blood dropping from trees. By that description it should be the palmetto-wine, of which wine and amber-coloured nuts, which being polished were by the Persians usually set upon tables or cabinets amongst other curiosities. Xenophon takes notice in his travels; seamen usually have a cane or quill which they suck with, so as two or three trees being pierced, in an hour's space they repletiate the greediest appetite, though he booze his bellyfull! To drink with moderation it comforts the spirit, albeit cold in the digestion. It also purges and helps obstructions and kills worms, but immoderately taken intoxicates the brain and disposes to fluxes; howbeit, exposed two days in the sun turns acid, in which quality it is binding.

Here also are coco-trees male and female, both which bear blossoms, but the female only is fruitful and not so neither unless a flowering branch be inoculate, for by that mixture of seed she fructifies. the shape of which two trees, according to my small skill, take thus resembled.

---

[316] Virgil, *Georgics* 2. 116–117.

[317] "Far and wide by your divided / stream is Meroë surrounded, fruitful for her black farmers,/ rejoicing in her foliage of ebony" (*Civil War* 10. 302–304).

[318] A two-quart drinking vessel.

Trees and a bird [illustration shown above]

Their several virtues are thus summed up by Sylvester:[319]

> The Indian isles most admirable be
> In those rare fruits call'd cocos commonly,
> The which alone far richer wonder yields
> Than all our groves, meadows, orchards, gardens, fields!
> What, would'st thou drink? The wounded leaves drop wine;
> Lack'st thou fine linen? Dress the tender vine,
> Dress it like flax, spin it, then weave it well;
> It shall thy cambric and thy lawn excel.
> Long'st thou for butter? Bite the pulpy part,
> For never better came to any mart.
> Dost need good oil? Then bolt it to and fro,
> And passing oil it soon becometh so.
> Or vinegar to whet thine appetite?
> Why, sun it well and it will sharply bite.
> Or, want'st thou sugar? Steep the same a stound,
> And sweeter sugar is not to be found.
> 'Tis what you will, or will be what you would;

---

[319] This is from Sylvester's translation of Du Bartas's *Works and Days* (1605).

Should Midas touch it, sure it would be gold,
And God, all good, to crown our life with bays,
Had done enough if He had made no more
But this one plant, so full of choicest store,
Save that the world, where one thing breeds satiety,
Could not be fair without so great variety.

Praises it very well deserveth, and concerning the palmetto the relish is so perfectly good that none of us who tasted of it thought it nauseous, but rather pleasant and dainty. We also took notice that we were no sooner gone but the lizards would make haste to suck this distilling nectar and were intoxicated with it, a creature so exceedingly delighted with beholding man's visage and what in them lies, expressing so much affection that we would not injure them in that senseless condition. Parrots and other birds also would be tasters, which made it of more repute with passengers.

Trees. Dodos.

Several other sorts of trees there are, which differ no less in quality then in form. One I took special notice of was above five yards about and of a reasonable height, but umbriferous [320] it was not, for albeit it had many branches yet it was without leaf or flower, the bole so soft as with a knife I could almost as easily write my name in it as with a stick one may in sand. In curiosity I put some of the wood into my mouth and chewed it; what the virtue may be I know not, but this I did, that for half an hour my mouth was inflamed as if I had taken so much vitriol! Near that was another which was but low of growth yet large-spread in its branches; upon it hung fruit or seed like ash-keys, [321] only these were larger and thicker, resembling the ginny-beans or caravances, but safeguarded with sharp prickles and by such a defence one might have thought what was within should have been considerable. The shell or cod was very hard, but being broke found in it six or eight nuts, each of which was less then a dove's egg but in colour and shape not unlike the beezer. The kernel tasted like an acorn; what the quality was I could not tell, save that by some experiment the surgeon made it was found little less then poison. The Africans at Sierra Leone have such a tree as this they call *ogu*, with which they envenom their darts; this, peradventure, may be of that kind. Many other we saw here, some of which were like pines, others like limes and sycamores, and do not remember that we saw any oak, cedar, fir or cypress, nor was the fruit or seed they bore such as we knew, though we could resemble them to pineapples, artichokes, plums, nuts, cherries and the like, but as to their names and properties utterly ignorant. Yet observe we could; nothing was lost,

---

[320] Shady.
[321] The winged seed of the ash-tree.

for what was food for birds the tortoises would eat, and what the tortoises refused the hogs did devour, so as by one or other all was tasted.

Again, this noble isle, as it is as prodigal in her water and wood, so she corresponds in what else a fruitful parent labours in, not only boasting in that variety but in feathered creatures also, yea, in the rareness of that variety. I will name but some, and first the dodo, a bird the Dutch call *walchvogel* or *doed-aars*.[322] Her body is round and fat, which occasions her slow pace or her corpulence, and so great as few of them weigh less then fifty pound. Meat it is with some, but better to the eye then stomach, such as only a strong appetite can vanquish, but otherwise through its oiliness it cannot choose but quickly cloy and nauseate the stomach, being indeed more pleasurable to look upon then feed upon. It is of a melancholy visage, as sensible of Nature's injury in framing so massy a body to be directed by complemental wings such as indeed are unable to hoist her from the ground, serving only to rank her amongst birds. Her head is variously dressed, for one half is hooded with down that is of a dark colour, the other half is naked and of a white hue as if lawn were drawn over it. Her bill hooks and bends downwards, the thrill or breathing-place in the midst, from which part to the end the colour is of a light green mixed with a pale yellow. Her eyes are round and bright, and instead of feathers has a most fine down; her train, like to a China beard, is no more then three or four short feathers. Her legs are thick and black, her talons great, her stomach fiery, so as she can easily digest stones, in that and shape not a little resembling the ostrich. The dodo, cockatoo or parrot and one of the hens, take so well as in my table-book I could draw them.

---

[322] There is a great deal of literature on the dodo. Readers might like to know that Herbert was correct about the names (which he does not translate, however); *walchvogel* means 'disgusting bird' or 'nauseating bird;' the English word 'dodo' is a corruption of the Dutch *doedaars*, which means 'fat arse,' so-named because there was a lot of fat on the bird's rump. The Dutch bestowed this rude name on the bird in 1598; they were also the first to draw one, an illustration made by a sailor on the Dutch East India Company ship the *Gelderland*, which was in the Indies 1601–1603. The Dutch artist Roelant Savery (1576–1639) painted the dodo in 1626; a copy of this delightful and highly-detailed work made by his nephew Jan Savery (1589–1654) may be seen online at www.en:Image:ExtinctDodoBird.jpeg.com. The last confirmed sighting of a dodo was in 1662, and scholars believe now that it was extinct by 1690. Herbert was most certainly the first *Englishman* to draw a dodo. For details, see Errol Fuller, *Dodo: A Brief History from Extinction to Icon* (New York: Universe Publishers, 2003). Foster, too, has something to say about the dodo, telling us that the word *walchvogel* means "another extinct bird called the Giant," and that "the name *dodaarsen* was given to that bird by the Dutch sailors because it somewhat resembled a dabchick," thus diplomatically avoiding having to give the ruder definition above (*Herbert*, 335).

Image published with permission of ProQuest. Further reproduction is prohibited without permission.

Cockatoo, hen and dodo [illustration shown above]

Here are also aeries of hawks and sundry other birds, as goshawks, lanners, hobbies, flamingos, geese, pouts,[323] swallows, kites, blackbirds, sparrows, robins, herons that are white and beautiful, in their flesh good but in their feathers more valuable, cockatoos, a sort of parrot whose nature may well take name from κακὸν ὡὸν, it is so fierce and so indomitable; bitterns, hens and many other which I forbear to enumerate, but the parrots in their feathers were curious and more esteemed for their much prattle. Such their curious liveries and such their language as they are not unaptly-called Ανθρογλοτὸς, a right epitheton. "The parrot human's language knows so well / That to his lord says 'save you' and 'farewell,'" out of which was by a good poet celebrated with this epitaph:

> Parrots, birds light, her lord's well-tongued delight
> And painful figurer of human voice
> Dies; of air's citizens the fairest light,
> The green commander of the Eastern choice,
> Whom Juno's bird with curious painted tail
> Nor pheasant of cold Phasis could prevail
> To out-beauty. Kings he could salute and name
> Caesar, to whom discourse he'd friendly frame.[324]

---

[323] A pout is a large turkey-like bird.

[324] This might be Herbert's paraphrase of Ovid, *Amores* 2. 6.

Here are also innumerable bats or reremice,[325] and those of extraordinary bigness, for some of them were not less then goshawks; seamen strip them of their skins and then eat them.

The manatee and torpedo.

In the rivers here we found no less variety of fish. Such as we took and tasted of I noted; the manatee was the rarest, for both in taste and shape it equally opposes feeder and beholder. This fish doth use both elements; those very fins which steer them in the sea serve as stilts ashore to creep upon, in which exercise their paps also befriend them, and though fish, differs little from veal in taste but more in show, for the ribs and entrails, as also their face. Some say it is like an elephant when the proboscis is wanting, but from the cow have their denomination, for it is verily thought the land has not that creature which the watery citizens resemble not. They affect shoaled waters and to be near the shore to graze upon; their eyes are very small, bulk about three yards long and in breadth but half as much, famoused for a gentle fish delighting to behold the visage of man, most valuable in a stone that is consolidated in the head, which being pounded and put in wine and drunk fasting is, as are the brains of sharks and tuberons, sovereign against the stone and colic, yea, of more prize then other his great teeth, which yet to him are far more useful. Andrew Evans, captain of our ship, struck one of them with a fizzgig, and for quicker dispatch leapt into the sea, and swimming towards it with a stiletto wounded the fish in several places; as the victor he would needs get up upon her back, but the triumph cost him dearly, for the manatee labouring under pangs, circling its body so crushed the captain by that forcible embrace as the brute made him spit blood to his dying day, which happened soon after.

Give me leave to name what fish we took. They were dolphins, eonates, albacores, *cavallos*, porpoise, grampus, mullet, bream, tench, trout, sole, flounders, tortoise, eel, pike, shark, crab, lobster, oysters, crayfish, cuttlefish (which though its blood be black as ink caused by a high concoction is nevertheless meat very delicious), rockfish, limpets and a speckled toadfish or 'poison-fish' as the seamen from experience named it, which albeit last-named came first to net and eaten too greedily by the heedless sailors was an error that cost some no less then their lives, others for some time their senses. In shape it was not unlike a tench but more black and deformedly-spotted: "The poisonous sea-fish drink learn to beware/ Whom the deep channels of the seas prepare; / Her scales have bane, her oils like purging are." Other strange fish we had which met with as strange stomachs, who either out of appetite or curiosity would not be afraid to taste; some had the shape of hedgehogs, others of cats. Some were globous, others triangular,

---

[325] A now-obsolete synonym for 'bat,' usually spelled 'rearmouse.'

such as Gorraeus calls *lupus marinus*.[326] The torpedo or crampfish also came to hand, a fish, if Pliny write true, that by hiding itself with mud and dirt catches lesser fish very strangely, for by his frigidity he benumbs such fish as swim over or lodge near him, and so preys upon them. Amazed (not knowing that fish but by its quality) we were when a sudden trembling seized us; a device it has to beget liberty as well as to catch his prey, for by evaporating a cold breath it stupefies such as touch, nay, which is more, as hold a thing that touches it.

Torpedo-fish [illustration not shown]

Hear Oppian:[327]

> Along her stretched guts two branches rise,
> With fraud, not strength, endued; these patronise
> The fish, which who so wounds, his joints decay,
> His blood congeals, his limbs move not, they say;
> His powers dissolve, he shakes, and falls away.

---

[326] "Sea wolf." Jean de Gorris (1505–1577) was Professor, then Dean of Medicine in the University of Paris from 1549. His *Definitionum medicarum libri XXIII* (1564) was one of the best-known encyclopaedias of medical terms compiled in the Renaissance. For further details see Michael Stolberg, "Die *Definitionum medicarum libri XXIII* der Humanisten und Hippokratikers Jean de Gorris," www.haraldfischerverlag.de/hfv.com.

[327] *Halieutica* 2. 63–67. Oppian of Corycne (c. 142–172) lived in Malta, an island to which his father had been exiled for inadvertently slighting the Emperor Lucius Verus when the latter had visited Corycne. However, when Verus died (169) Oppian's father was pardoned by Marcus Aurelius and the family returned to Rome, where Oppian died of the plague. He wrote the *Halieutica*, a 3500-line poem in Greek on the subject of fishing which was well received by the Emperor. A Latin translation by Laurentius Lippius appeared in 1478, printed along with a treatise on hunting by another Oppian (of Apamea), with whom this one was often confused. The fishing part alone was printed several times; Herbert could have used editions from 1515 and 1549. There was no English translation until that of William Diaper in the early eighteenth century, so Herbert probably did his own here.

The remora. Tortoises and bats.

The remora or echeneis[328] is by Fracastorius[329] said to be of the same nature: *"Remora ex natura torpedinis est: effunditur e corpore suo humorem quandam viscosissimum et frigidissimum, qui eam aquam quae et circa gubernaculum navis vehit, congerat ad morsum reddatur inhabilis,"*[330] which last qualities I leave to better enquiry.

Remora [illustration not shown]

Albeit 'tis frequently so reported, and a memorable story thereof painted in the Viceroy's palace at Goa, which how far it may serve for proof I shall not here determine, but being dead it has not this quality.

Moreover, this isle affords goats, hogs, beeves and land-tortoises, tortoises so great as suffer two men with ease to sit and so strong as carry them, yea, as some report, fifteen men have at once stood upon it. Sailors affect to eat them, but are better meat for hogs in my opinion; they make pretty sport but are coarse food, so are their rats, bats and monkeys, most of which useful and unuseful creatures were first brought hither by the Portugal for refreshment in their return from India, but at this day the English and Dutch reap their harvest. Birds had here at no charge and little labour are hens, bats, herons etc.; the hens flock together twenty and forty in a company. If you catch one you may catch all; the surest way is by showing them a red cloth, for it seems that colour exasperates their spleen, as appears by the assaults they will make, for when one is struck down the residue budge not. They eat like parched pigs if you roast them. The bats, through a long-continued security ignorant of the deceits of men and unused to the smell of powder, are as easily taken, for if one be shot the other take not wing, neither knowing nor valuing danger, such is their care to condole their late associates, but if my stomach deceive me not, worse meat cannot easily be tasted. A fierce, ill-favoured carrion it is; it is ever squeaking, and in offensive noise calling to one another make bad melody. This is the only four-footed beast that's volant,[331]

---

[328] The remora is a sucker-fish; the echineis is a legendary creature which was said to live in the Indian Ocean and stick on ships, slowing their progress. This must have been quite a feat, as it was only six inches in length!

[329] Girolamo Fracastorio (1478–1553), a Professor at the University of Padua from the age of nineteen, was a poet, physician, astronomer, and geologist, one of whose many contributions to science was the proposal of a 'germ theory' of disease in his treatise *De contagione* (1546). He was also a pioneer in the study of veneral disease and wrote a lengthy poem about it entitled *Syphilis, sive de morbo gallico* (1539). It was probably not well received in France.

[330] The remora is sluggish by nature; it emits from its body a very oily and cold humour, which collects in the water around the rudder of a ship and renders it unmanageable.

[331] Capable of flight.

and therefore whether more properly to be ranked amongst birds or beasts as yet undecided, and in this is further observable, that no bird but the bat doth urine, a rare creature but so offensive to the orgies that, as poets say, nothing more destroys it then the smoke of ivy, which is dedicated to Bacchus. Bats, flying fish and seals be participles of Nature and species of a doubtful kind, participating both bird and beast, but these *vespertilios*[332] hang in swarms upon the boughs of trees by claws fixed at the extreme part of their wings, their monkey-faces in that posture ever turning downwards, as I have delineated upon the coco-tree a little before mentioned. We took another fish, an eagle-fish I imagined it; the eyes were five-quarters asunder. From one fin-end to the other were above four yards, its mouth so wide and teeth so long as it resembled a small portcullis; the tail also was very long and small, a fish, take it altogether, rather to admire than junket on.

An eagle-fish [illustration not shown]

In this isle are several good places to anchor in, howbeit two are most frequented; that at the north-west side bears the form of a hemicircle and elevates the Pole Arctic 19 degrees and 30 minutes, the other at the south-east directly opposite to the other, where we found 20 degrees 15 minutes and longitude from Cape Comorin 20 degrees 20 minutes, but from The Lizard 99, both which bays seem landlocked and have oozy ground, so as ships may ride safe there in five, ten, fifteen or twenty fathoms, being nowhere dangerous. The soil of itself is stony towards the shore but at more distance has rich mould covered with grass and herbs and bearing wood in abundance; it hath also some springs of good water and nothing wants that may either delight the eye or satiate the taste. And, after so long a voyage, give me leave to recreate a little:

> Here radiant flowers, the meadow's vive delight,
> Vary their nature, rising to the sight
> In shining beds, where spreads the tender grass,
> Not breaking careless sleep of the dainty lass.
> The attendant troops make thy large house resound,
> But here birds chirp, streams murmur on the ground.

The sleep-charming streams gently drill from the rocks and delightfully trickle along the valleys, and not only by their meanders mellow the ground but by their harmonious murmur afford an irresistible magic to ease and meditation, yea, to charm the sense by moving a gentle attention to the spirits as without labour stills the soul's natural and discussive faculty. And, which is not to be forgotten, ambergris is often found floating about this island, but how generated, whether

[332] Bats (Latin).

in the whale, the forth of the sea or otherwise is not determined. Coral, white and pleasant to look upon, grows here in abundance; this is the only vegetable that has branches and no leaves , but how tobacco came hither, whether by art or Nature I know not, but it roots and thrives equally with the Irish potato. To conclude, notwithstanding all these excellencies this *insula beata*, this pleasantest of Asiatic isles, *terra suis contenta bonis,*[333] was then uninhabited save by beasts and birds inasmuch as it gives the better invitation to more suitable inhabitants without dread of lion, tiger, wolf, fox, dog or suchlike offensive creatures, but upon condition to pay a grateful tribute to such as scarcity or foul weather direct thither for refreshment.

The sun's excellencies and properties.

I have dwelt somewhat long in the description of this isle, but may be excused by the delight I took there after long being at sea and some sickness at land, so that I could have been content we might have rested there. Nevertheless, as soon as the wind came fair aboard we went and in three hours' sail lost sight of the Mauritius. Now, forasmuch as this delightful place is within the Torrid Zone, I cannot but take notice of that opinion Aquinas and several others both fathers and philosophers held, how all that vast space of earth comprehended within the Burning Zone was not only uninhabited but even the ocean itself, especially under the Equator, not navigable, a tenet which took rise from a vulgar error and observation that forasmuch as heat within the Temperate Zone was more or less according as the place is in distance from the Tropic, the like reason overruled that betwixt the Tropics it consequently increased by how much it had its nearer approach toward the Equinoctial, where the heat, as they imagined, was intolerable. For answer: it is very true the sun, being limited his course within the Burning Zone, by reason of that constant residence emits his beams and shines with utmost ardour upon those parts and people, whether his glances be oblique or perpendicular, and from thence it is that the continent is more especially parched through the extremity of heat and the air inflamed. Nevertheless, such is the wonderful wisdom and goodness of God that in some parts upon the *terra firma*, but principally in islands and places wellnigh compassed with water, the earth is commonly fruitful and the sun delightful and advantageous. Give me leave eulogically to enumerate a few of those many attributes have deservedly been given that glorious planet: in Genesis 1:4 it is called the great luminary which the Almighty placed in the Firmament of Heaven to illuminate the Earth and rule the day as the moon the night, and in the 19 Psalm the prophet David declares:

---

[333] "A land satisfied with its own blessings" (Lucan, *Civil War* 8. 445) This phrase also appears on Ortelius's map of Egypt (1601).

There is the sun's pavilion set,
Who from his rosy cabinet
Like a fresh bridegroom shows his face,
And as a giant runs his race.
He riseth in the dawning East,
And glides obliquely to the West.
The world with his bright rays replete
All creatures cherisheth with heat.

And Ecclesiastes 11:7, "Truly the light is sweet, and a pleasant thing it is for the eyes to behold the sun." *Sol est fons lucis*, the fountain of light, "ever in motion, never resting, and with his light discovering all things." Nor is its light less extensive then its heat, for light is the chariot by which heat is conveyed about the inferior orbs and though in its own body limited to heaven, by its influence goes to and fro and visits all the corners of the earth. At once it irradiates every province, views all cities and other parts within the hemisphere, embraces both sea and land, with equal respect salutes the cottages of peasants and courts of princes, merrily frisks up and down without differencing prisons from palaces, gilds the mountains and causes the valleys to glister, cheerfully dances upon rivers, makes the meadows fragrant and the fields fruitful, solaces youth as well as age, revives, yea, provokes decayed Nature, and though inanimate of itself gives life to vegetables, insects etc. It renders all things fair, saith Virgil,[334] and Orpheus in his lyrics sings "all things are made truthful and flourishing by the sun."[335] Now albeit from these and other properties the gentiles have this excellent creature in adoration, which Job reproves, saying "If I beheld the sun when it shined . . . and my heart hath been secretly enticed so as my mouth kissed my hand, should I not thereby deny God which is above?"[336] imitated by the Jews, reproved in Ezekiel 8:17,[337] where the 25 idolatrous elders set their backs towards the temple, and turning their faces to the east worshipped the sun, this was by an erroneous attributing to the second what was due unto the first, for it is the power of God that gives virtue to the sun to exhale vapours, which vapours are formed into clouds containing rain, and it is rain both qualifies the air and makes the earth in due season to bring forth her increase, yet so as those and all other subordinate causes together with the sun itself would be altogether ineffectual were it not for that operative faculty wherewith the Almighty hath endowed those creatures, for it is by his direction the sun not only helps the generation of all sensible bodies,

---

[334] Virgil, *Aeneid* 4. 607.

[335] Herbert must be making his own version here, as the *Orphic Hymns* were first translated into English by Thomas Taylor in 1792.

[336] Job 31: 26–28.

[337] "Then he said unto me, Hast thou seen this, O son of man? Is it a light thing to the house of Judah that they commit the abominations which they commit here? For they have filled the land with violence, and have returned to provoke me to anger . . ."

but as St. Augustine observes, that nourishes and brings its work into perfection, therefore we must acknowledge with St. Ambrose, "the sun certainly is good where it actuates as a servant, not a sovereign."[338] Moreover, albeit by its benign influence ordained for the comfort of man, this isle and many other places within this Zone are observed constantly verdant and admirably fruitful; nevertheless, it has its shadow, for it cannot be denied but in the mediterranean parts of Africa the country is generally a-dust and the earth for want of moisture converted into sand, as Alexander observed in his travel from Egypt to Libya upon a visit of the temple dedicated to Jupiter Ammon, for five days neither bird nor beast, tree nor grass appearing, saith the historian, a fit place for Ham's posterity and agreeable to that of the Psalmist where 'tis said that "a fruitful land is made barren for the wickedness of those that dwell therein,"[339] in those troglodyte regions the earth for the most part being sapless and without springs, which makes both earth and air scorching and insufferable. This consideration gave subject to one poet of that romance concerning the Psylli[340] their challenging the south wind, and to another how "That barren land / During all seasons doth unaltered stand / Through Nature's disrespect, for that burnt earth / Unto a few small herbs only gives breath/ Which to the Aethiop is great cause of mirth."

Withal, let us observe that the heat is more intense and violent under the Tropic by reason of the solstice in June then under the Equinoctial in March or September, at which times the sun only cuts their zenith, for under the Equinoctial I have been four several times, and the like under both the Tropics, and so it was, whether *per accidens* or otherwise I know not, but I could perceive the heat was more extreme under and near the Tropics where the sun for some short space of time seems to have its station, so that both by what I then felt and since heard from others of experience the heat is greater at Hormuz in the Gulf of Persia, Mocha in the Red Sea and at Berenice and Syene[341] near Egypt during the summer solstice then we find in most Asiatic regions under or near the Equinox, as those that are conversant in Ceylon, Sumatra, Borneo, the Celebes and Molucca Isles, which are nadir to the Equinoctial, have related and can best witness. Now the reasons may be these: first, that through the like goodness of God the heat near the Tropic is very much allayed by those tempestuous storms of wind and

---

[338] Ambrose, *Hexaemeron* 4. 1. 4 (PL 14. 189 B).

[339] Psalm 107: 34.

[340] See above, where they are called 'Psyllians.' The poet is unidentified; these mysterious people are mentioned in Strabo (6.31; 8.117), Pliny and Herodotus.

[341] Syene is now called Aswan, and is situated on the eastern bank of the Nile just below the First Cataract. In connection with the sun, Grant notes that in about 250 B.C.E. the geographer Erastosthenes was there and "by comparing the size of the sun's shadow with Alexandria, he was able to estimate the circumference of the earth" (*Guide*, 613). It has many ancient sites, including the gate to a temple of Alexander IV, the ill-fated son of Alexander the Great. Now, of course, it also is the site of an important dam.

rain which during that season usually rage in that climate not only for six weeks obscuring and consequently assuaging the beams of the sun, but occasioning the overflowing of Nile and Niger and several other rivers in Africa, and of Ganges and Mehan or Suhan[342] and others in India, insomuch as they seem to have most winter during the summer season, I mean when and where the sun is nighest, for otherwise the heat under the Tropics, by reason of the comorrance of the sun for some time and that the days there are longer then under the Equator must needs be greatest, whence we may likewise note that the sun, when it returns to the vernal Equinox, and for those following six months comes into our hemisphere after he has made the Arctic Pole his horizon. Those regions within the Polar Circle, which have the same distance the Tropics have from the Equator, albeit more resembling night then day when the sun is depressed and disappearing, yea, by reason of a continued darkness and extremity of cold are places by us not to be endured. Nevertheless, by this reappearing of the sun and its constant residence for half the year above the horizon, the Earth receives plenary amends and becomes habitable, yea, produces fruits proper for warm countries and such as will not maturate with us in England. Secondly, several other accidents I may note which contribute to the temperature of those parts, for besides the monsoons or anniversary winds, which for three months blow constantly one way and six the other, these hot countries have frequent breezes which like the *Etesiae*[343] breathe gently every morning and evening from the east and south, which qualifies the earth and air exceedingly, so as during that breeze the extremity is very little perceived. Moreover, by the interposition of the Earth, the nights, expecially near the sun, are equal or longer then the day, during which the moon, that has power to govern the night as the sun the day, abundantly compensates, and being commonly attracted by mists, dews, fogs and vapours lenifies the air and moderates the ardour of the sun, as that distich of the poet speaks very properly: "What the outrageous sun inflames by day,/ The night's cool dews do equally allay," for together with the frequent showers of rain that fall through the rich mercy of the Creator and under him attritbuted the influence either of the *Praesepe* and Aselli[344] or some other unknown constellation, as also the springs and rivers that abound there more and more consequently dispose to a better temperature, yea, the like is from the delight as well as the shade the trees afford, who by reason their sap retires seldom or never to the root, are all the year long so attired in their gayest livery and the fruits in great variety are so juicy and cooling as refresh exceedingly, all which considered it will appear that those parts are not only habitable, but seeing Nature is nowhere more prodigal, no place is more luxuriant for pleasure in any part of the universe. Nevertheless, not to the natives but to such

---

[342] The Suhan is a river in the Upper Punjab region.

[343] The Etesian winds "blow for forty days every year about the dog-days" (Simpson, *Trade*, 220).

[344] These constellations are The Manger (or Beehive) and The Donkeys.

as repair thither out of colder climates let me give this advice, that they study their preservation both in the careful ordering their habit and diet, especially till they be seasoned, for the air is very subtle and pure and enters the pores insensibly, so as without due care and moderation the strongest and healthiest bodies by flux or fever will probably become quickly indisposed and endangered.

England's Forest.

Being under sail, the first day we descried land which bore south-west. By its height and position we imagined it was what we call England's Forest, which next day we ascertained. This name was imposed *Anno* 1613 by Captain Castleton,[345] commander of the *Pearl*, but who made the first discovery is doubtful, seeing some of late have given it Senhor Mascarenhas[346] his name, purporting he was the first, yet some there be that call it *Pulo-puar*, an Indian name, but by whom or when so darkly-writ as is not very legible. This pleasant isle has above fifty English miles circuit; the South Pole is there elevated 20 degrees and 55 minutes from the Equator. Its longitude from Mauritius is not more then 1 degree and a half, and distant thence about seven and thirty leagues, but the variation of the compass is 23 degrees, the ground very high and raiseth itself a good way into the middle region, the earth everywhere green, especially in trees which mount more then ordinarily to a sublimity. It had no creature in it save birds till our captain sent his longboat with some hogs and goats of both kinds ashore, that by a happy multiplication the future passenger might be revived. Here is also plenty of fish, of which the eels are notable, some of them weighing thirty pounds, whereby we may judge them to be congers, and not odious in their corpulency, for to the taste they render themselves sweet and moist. Birds here are many and rare, but most of them being such as are spoken if in Mauritius, need no repetition.

---

[345] Captain Samuel Castleton (d. 1616) led an expedition to Sumatra in the *Pearl* (1611–1613), and in 1615 he was dispatched by the East India Company to the Banda Islands, which he reached in 1616. Off the Bandas he ran into a Dutch fleet, but after negotiations was permitted to proceed. For further details see Foster, *England's Quest*, 263–65, or John Tatton, *A Journal of a voyage made by the Pearl to the East India wherein went as Captain Master Samuel Castleton of London* (1625), which is Purchas's source (3: 43).

[346] Pedro de Mascarenhas (1470–1555) was appointed Portuguese viceroy of Goa (1526) but lost the post through intrigues and ended up in prison. The name was given by Diogo Rodrigues (see above). The Mascarenhas Islands are off Madagascar, and eventually became a French colony (Simkin, *Trade*, 248).

The whale.

In a few days by the benefit of propitious winds we launched far into the *Mare del Sur*, where Magellan's cloud, *Stella nebulosa*,[347] scarce visible without a glass and more resembling part of the galactea then stars, they are of so small a magnitude, with several other Antarctic constellations more and more discovered themselves unto us and approached our zenith. But long since those happy *Favonii*[348] continued not, for the wind veering into a contrary quarter, the sky overspread with clouds so as the sea laboured with a dreadful tumour. For seven whole days and nights this termpest lasted, and forced us all that while to lie by the lee without more sail then the mizzen. Howbeit, *post multos una serena*,[349] still launching through the ocean the sky cleared up and fair weather ensued. For many hundred miles we were recreated with many shoals of fish which played about our ship, although it was of great burden. In bigness the whale exceeds any other creature, for usually it is toward 40 cubits long and a fourth part in thickness, yea, Nearchus told Alexander he saw one that was 50 cubits, but Pliny in his *Natural History* that there are some be 960 foot long,[350] which is wellnigh four acres.

A whale [illustration not shown]

I have formerly said somewhat concerning this sea-monster and therefore shall only farther note that by the greatness and force of this leviathan the Almighty setteth forth his omnipotency by the marvellous works of the creation, as we have most elegantly described in Job 41 and by Mr. Sandys thus paraphrased:

> This wonder of the deep his mighty force
> And goodly form shall furnish our discourse,
> Who can divest him of his waves, bestride
> His monstrous back, and with a bridle ride,
> His head's huge door unlock, whose jaws with great
> And dreadful teeth in treble rank are set,
> Arm'd with refulgent shields together join'd
> And seal'd up to resist the ruffling wind?
> The nether by the upper fortified,
> No force their combination can divide;
> His sneezing sets on fire the foaming brine,
> His round eyes like the morning eyelids shine.
> Infernal lightning sallies from his throat,

---

[347] There are actually two of these irregular dwarf galaxies, the North and South Magellan Clouds. They are visible in the southern hemisphere and were thought to orbit the Milky Way, a theory disproved in modern times.

[348] West winds.

[349] "After many (stormy days), one calm" (Tibullus, *Elegies* 3. 6. 32).

[350] Pliny, *Natural History* 32. 10.

Ejected sparks upon the billows float.
A cloud of smoke from his wide nostrils flies
As vapours from a boiling furnace rise.
He burning coals exhales and vomits flames,
His strength the Empire of the Ocean claims.
Loud tempests, roaring floods and what affright
The trembling sailor, turn to his delight.
The flakes of his tough flesh so firmly bound
As not to be divorced by a wound;
His heart's a solid rock, to fear unknown,
And harder then the grinder's nether stone.
The sword his armed sides in vain assails,
No dart nor lancce can penetrate his scales;
He brass as rotten wood and steel no more
Regards then reeds that bristle on the shore.
Dreads he the twanging of the archer's string,
Or singing stones from the Phoenician fling?
Darts he esteems as straw asunder torn,
And shaking of the javelin laughs to scorn.
He ragged stones beneath his belly spreads
For his repose as soft as downy beds;
The seas before him as a cauldron boil,
And in the fervour of a motion foil.
A light stroke from the floods detects his way,
Who covers their aspiring heads with grey.
Of all whom ample Earth's round shoulders bear,
None equals this. Created without fear,
Whatever is exalted he disdains,
And as a king amongst the might reigns.

Saint Helena.

Aristotle 2 *lib. Meteores* is of opinion that no great blasts of wind blow from the
south; doubtless had he travelled in our company he would have retracted that
opinion, for from that meridional quarter many gusts and storms assailed us.
Ovid in his 4 *lib. Ex ponto* agrees with that learned Greek and may be granted in
our hemisphere: "Rough Boreas our domestic ruleth here, / And takes his vigour
from a place more near; / But the mild South, from adverse quarter sent, / Comes
far, blows gently and more impotent."[351]

But as it was, after threescore and ten days' further sail we attained sight of
Saint Helena,[352] where the ocean bellows on every side so fretfully as the place

---

[351] Ovid, *Ex Ponto* 4.10. 41–44.

[352] They arrived at St. Helena on 8 October. As Foster notes, "Herbert omits the fact
that the fleet called at Table Bay, remaining there from 7 to 21 September" (*Herbert*, 335).

might fear an inundation had not the extraordinary height, but chiefly that Supreme Providence which hath set the sea its bounds safeguarded it. It has no neighbouring isles great nor small, but seems equidistant from those two noted ports called Rio Grande and Cape Negro, in Brazil the one, the other in Congo, both in one elevation and parallel with Saint Helena, from that in America distant 400 leagues, from the other in Africa not much less, if any, from that number. It had its name given by John de Nova[353] in or about the year after the Incarnation of Our Saviour 1502, so-called for that in his return from India to Lisbon it was discovered the 3 of May, a day consecrated to the memory of Helena the Empress, who first found the cross [and] was the most religious of ladies in her time, mother to the first Christian Emperor Constantine, both of them glorious in their age, Britons both, bright gems of this our nation. This isle is removed south from the Equator sixteen degrees, from the utmost promontary of South Africa it hath two and twenty degrees of longitude, and where the needle varies five degrees and thirteen minutes, but from the land's end of England distant 4500 English miles, from the Cape of Good Hope 1740, Madagascar 3000, Surat 6600 and from Bantam 6900 or thereabouts. In that bay which takes name from the chapel the isle has this resemblance.

St. Helena [illustration not shown]

But to what part of the inhabited world it appertains may be queried, seeing the vast Ethiopic Ocean so largely circles it; to Africa I imagine rather then America. It is but small, not exceeding thirty English miles circumference, yet excssive high, for it veils its head often in the clouds, where opening a wide mouth it gulps down sufficient moisture to cool its ardour, which, by reason of the clime 'tis in, cannot be but sometimes intemperate, and but for the affinity it has with the Middle Region, which envelops it as with a chill-cold tulipant, and long nights, it has that extreme heat which the sun darts constantly twice every year perpendicular upon this isle, would doubtless make the entrails inflame (had it sulphur) like another Vesuvius. Nevertheless, the land is not more eminent in its height then the ambient sea is profound in the depth, so deep that as there are mountains in the sea as in the Earth is not to be doubted, seeing that upon the casting of the lead, log or plummet will scarce find ground, which is the cause

---

[353] João de Nova (c. 1460–1509) was actually born in Spain but was sent to Portugal, where he settled and became Mayor of Lisbon in 1496. He was appointed commander of the third Portuguese expedition to India (1501), and on the way there was the first European to see Ascension Island (1501) and St. Helena (1502). After returning home he set out again with Francisco de Almeida (1505), but was back the next year and again went to sea, this time with Tristao da Cunha, but was arrested by order of Albuquerque because he wanted to sail to India, not Arabia, where the Duke wanted him to collect supplies to attack Hormuz. De Nova died in Cochin a few years later.

the mariners do sometimes carry their anchors ashore that they may moor or ride the more securely. By reason of the depth I could hardly discern either flux or reflux near the shore, seeming as if we were in the mid-ocean where neither ebb nor flood is to be discerned. Howbeit, the saltwater plashes and froths to see itself so suddenly resisted, but the moist breath usually vapouring in or upon the seas makes it sometimes turbulent.

The isle is hard to be ascended; not that the passage is craggy, but that it is so precipitous. The sailors have an ironic proverb, 'the way is such as a man may choose whether he will break his heart going up or his neck coming down,' but being up, no place can yield a more large or a more delightful sea-prospect. The land is very even and plain above and swells nowhere to a deformed rising. Some springs above be sweet, but below are brackish; the reason may be for that in their drilling descent they may relish of the salt hills through which it cuts an usual passage, so as they become salt both by their own composition and the salt breath which the sea evaporates. Nevertheless, there are but two noted rivulets; one bubbles down towards the Chapel, the other into the Lemon Valley, so-called from a lemon tree and chapel built at the bottom of the isle by the Spaniard *Anno* 1571, and by the Dutch of late pulled down, a place once intended for God's worship but now disposed-of to common uses.[354] There are some ruins of a little town, lately demolished by the Spaniard so that it became a magazine of private trade in turning and returning out of both the Indies. No other monuments or antiquities are there found; you see all if you look upon the ribs of a weather-beaten carrack and some broken pieces of great ordinance which albeit left there against the owner's liking, serve some instead of anchors. Human inhabitants there are none, nor ever were, save that in the year 1591 Captain Kendall,[355] weighing anchor sooner then was expected, one Legar a mariner was accidentally left ashore. Eighteen months after, Captain Parker[356] coming to an anchor found poor Legar alive and well, but so amazed or rather overjoyed at his arrival that

---

[354] Lemon Valley is renowned for its interesting rock formations, and is now a World Conservation Monitoring Centre. The chapel built by the Portuguese was described by Cavendish on his first voyage around the world in 1588 (Hakluyt, *Voyages*, 295–96). Cavendish (see n. 356 below) also believed the chapel had been built in 1571; the Portuguese attempted to keep their discovery of St. Helena secret.

[355] Captain Abraham Kendall of the *Royal Merchant* put in at St. Helena on his way to India in 1591 because of a sick crew, one of whom, John Legar (Herbert has *Segar*, as do some other writers), was left behind. Kendall's ship was part of the first fleet of East Indiamen, and he was also one of Ralegh's Roanoke colonists. He fought against the Spanish Armada in Drake's squadron (1588).

[356] Captain William Parker (c. 1545–1618) was the captain of the *Prudence*, in which he sailed to the Cape Verde Islands (1601) and then landed on St. Vincent the following year, capturing and burning the town. He then went on to sack Margarita Island and capture the Spanish governor, after which he did the same on Puerto Bello (1602). Parker also served with Sir Anthony Sherley, the brother of Sir Robert. However, Foster says

he died suddenly. Howbeit, of hogs and goats here are plenty, who agree well-favouredly and multiply even to admiration, happy in their ease and safety until ships arrive there for refreshment; the goats leap wildly from rock to rock and to avoid the reach of our small guns keep their sentinels.

Here with little labour we got also good store of pheasants, pouts, quails, hens, patridge, and, which was no less acceptable, divers sorts of grass and roots as wood-sorrel,[357] three leav'd grass, scurvy-grass[358] and the like acid herbs sovereign against the scurvy. We also had basil, spinach, fennel, anise, radish, mustardseed, tobacco and some others, which by a willing hand directed by an ingenious eye may soon be gathered, brought hither and here sown by Fernando Lopes[359] a Portugal in the Year of Our Lord 1515 for the good of his countrymen, who nevertheless at this day dare hardly to land to oversee their seminary or own their labours, the English and the Dutch in the churlish language of a cannon sometime disputing the propriety. *Anno* 1588 Cavendish[360] our countryman

---

that it was not Parker, but Lieutenant Edmund Barker who actually rescued Legar in 1593 (*Herbert*, 336). Barker wrote *The Narrative of the First Voyage of Sir James Lancaster.*

[357] Wood-sorrel, according to Culpeper, is used for "hindering putrefaction of the blood and ulcers in the mouth and body." It "groweth upon the ground," he says, and is "made of three leaves like a trefoil, but broad at the ends" (*Herbal*, 273).

[358] Culpeper states that scurvy-grass "hath many thick flat leaves, longer than broad, and sometimes longer and narrower; smooth on the edges and sometimes a little waved." It has "many whitish flowers, with yellow threads in the middle" (*Herbal*, 267). He says that English scurvy-grass "is more used for its salt taste," but that Dutch scurvy-grass "is of better effect, and chiefly used by those that have the scurvy" (268).

[359] Fernão Lopes [*Fernandus Lupius*] (d. 1545) had a very interesting story. Left behind at Goa by Albuquerque in 1503 to command a garrison, he and some others converted to Islam and supported Indian resistance to their own countrymen. Lopes was captured, tortured, and mutilated, but stayed in India until 1515, when he decided to go back home. When his ship stopped in at St. Helena, Lopes and four African slaves asked to stay on the island, and Lopes remained there until 1533, returning to Portugal and telling his story to King Joao III, who sent him on to Rome where he obtained an audience with Pope Clement VII. The Pope offered to help him in any way he could, and Lopes asked to be sent back to St. Helena. This time he did not return to Portugal, and died on the island. For details, see H. Clifford, "The Earliest Exile of St. Helena," *Blackwood's Magazine* (1903): 625–33, and a recent book by Beau W. Rowlands, *Fernao Lopes: A South Atlantic Robinson Crusoe* (London: George Mann, 2007).

[360] Thomas Cavendish (1560–1591) began his career by going to Virginia with Sir Richard Grenville (1585), and the next year decided he would sail around the world in his ship the *Desire*. It was on 8 June 1588 that Cavendish spotted St. Helena, "at which no English ship had hitherto touched" (Foster, *England's Quest*, 121). In 1591 Cavendish again set sail, but after many adventures, including fights with the Portuguese, he was lost somewhere near Ascension Island. His account, *The Voyage of Thomas Cavendish around the Whole Earth* (1588) and *Last Voyage* (1591), may be found in Beeching's edition of Hakluyt (270–98).

landed here in his circumnavigating the globe; then he found store of lemons, oranges, pomegranates, pomcitrons, figs and dates, but how the alteration comes who knows, for none of those grow there now that I could either see or hear of, one lemon-tree excepted.

To conclude: in the old chapel here were buried our Captain Andrew Evans, whose death's wound, as formerly told, was unhappily given him by a manatee at the Mauritius. He was an expert seaman and no less vigilant then expert, and so doubtless the company had a great loss of him. "*Cretensis nescit pelagus?*"[361] was an old adage setting forth the excellencies of those islanders in maritime affairs, for it is without controversy that in those times they instructed other nations in the art of navigation, but upon subversion of the Persian monarchy by the Greeks and of theirs by the Romans it was transferred to our quarters. Questionless the Portugals, by their ingenious and industrious discovery of the sea-passage into the East Indies somewhat less then 200 years since gave that art its greatest perfection, but who is now the most excellent let Keckermann[362] decide the question, which learned observator in his treatise of the Spanish and Portugal discoveries makes this result: "*Hoc tamen certum est, omnibus hodie gentibus navigandi industria et peritia, Anglos esse superiores.* Of all nations the English for sea-affairs are reputed the most excellent; "*Post Anglos Belgas, et inter hos Flandros, Hollandos, Zelandos*; and next the English the Dutch, amongst which the chiefest in that art are the Flemings, Hollanders, Zeelanders," so as by the judgment of that indifferent[363] and learned writer it appears the English have the first place in sea-knowledge and and navigation attributed them. And amongst the best sea-commanders this late captain of ours very well deserved with the first to be ranked.

The Gorgades [Cape Verde Islands].

But to return. That this is a very delightful isle cannot be denied, and its admirable prospect and other pleasures were sufficient to induce our longer stay, but stay we might not, so as after a week's refreshment we discharged our reckoning in a hearty farewell, and by the invitation of a prosperous gale upon a N.W. course swiftly cut our passage through the yielding ocean, insomuch as on the sixteenth

---

[361] "Is there a Cretan who doesn't understand the sea?" (Erasmus, *Adages* 1. 2. 31).

[362] Bartholomew Keckermann (1571–1609) was Professor of Hebrew at the University of Heidelberg (1600) and of Philosophy at the University of Danzig (1602), a rhetorician, astronomer, mathematician, geographer, and writer on education. He was also one of the earliest systematic theologians. His major work was the pothumously-published *Systema compendiosum totius mathematices* (1617), and his *Opera omnia quae extant* were issued in Geneva (1614). See Joseph S. Freedman, "The Career and Writings of Bartholomew Keckermann (d. 1609)," *Proceedings of the American Philosophical Society* 141 (1997): 305–64.

[363] That is, unbiased; as Keckermann is not English he does not have to make this claim.

of October we were once more nadir to the sun, which at that time was in its Antarctic progress. The third day after we had sight of Ascension Isle, so-named by John de Nova in the year 1501, because upon that feast-day it was he first discovered it. The isle is south from the Equinoctial about 7 degrees, little more then thirty miles in circuit, well-wooded and watered but little else observable. We were miserably pestered with that variable weather, till then being frequently entertained with loud blasts of wind, nasty showers of rain with terrible thunder and lightning, but God put an end to it. The eleventh of November we were parallel to Cape Verde and those isles poets call the *Gorgades*, who feign that those three islands were the habitations of the three Gorgons, Medusa, Sthenno and Euryale, whom they make furies rather than beauties, ill-requiting Perseus his reports that they were the much-famoused daughters of Phorcys the son of Neptune. Their yellow hairs curling like snakes and dishevelling about their naked shoulders so much set forth their beauty and gained such admiration in the beholders as if they were transformed into statues.

America.

But leaving these upon a more westerly course we coasted parts of the American continent, *viz.* Guiana, Florida, Virginia, New England and other parts of Norumbega, which with the several adjacent isles as we passed by, [I] shall in this place have no other observation then that the sea in many places as we sailed was so covered with green weeds even where the water was not to be fathomed, that it rather seemed a field of grass then the ocean. But what was most to be noted, those weeds or branches like nets were entangled and drawn along by the barnacles, which in those long voyages usually breed upon the sides of ships and exceedingly pester and retard their way in sailing.

Desiring rather in this place to vindicate the truth, which of long time hath been either defamed or so eclipsed as the reality of the first discovery is not well-known, being nevertheless attributed to Columbus, I shall therefore in the first place see what either by prophetic pens or reason otherwise is upon record that may point towards that great, nay greatest part of the world, which for upwards of 5000 years and during those mighty contests for an universal supremacy by the monarchs of the Earth was concealed, so as until the only-wise God thought fit to give more perfection to navigation, it seemed totally unknown and undiscovered.

Plato, who was contemporary with Alexander the Great and flourished about the 3580 Year of the World, is one of the first. He, in his dialogue 'twixt Timaeus and Critias discourses, but obscurely, of a large occidental island, which being without a name, from the view he seems to make into the Atlantic Sea gives it the name of *Atlantis*, land in greatness comparable to Asia and Africa united.[364] Aristotle his co-disciple approves of his conjecture, albeit he takes it only as a supposition. Theophrastus also, in his *Book of Rareties* published two thousand years ago, amongst other things relates how that some merchants, sailing through the Straits of Gibraltar, were by storm driven further west then they desired, by which accident they descried land but found it unpeopled. It is the opinion of most that land was the Azores, for the isles Columbus first found out when he made his first discovery were fully-planted. Hanno the Carthaginian is the next; his sea-voyage is very incertainly-related, for some suppose that he doubled Cape Buona Speranza, and amongst other places pretend the discovery of several western isles, but the course he steered is queried. Some say south and others west; Pomponius Mela and Lampridius[365] say the land he discovered was south, and if south then not the West Indies, for it may be presumed that seeing the use of the compass was then unknown, his way was not without ken of land but rather crept near the shore, for had he been in the mid-ocean he had been lost, and in his human reason irrecoverable. Virgil in the 6 *lib. Aeneid*, foretelling the greatness of Caesar's dominion, has this allusion:

Stretching his great command
Past Garamants and India, lies a land
Beyond both year and sun. Atlas the sky
That bears the star-fraught Pole, doth wheel hereby.[366]

about the right sense whereof is no small variance, for Servius thinks the poet only means the Ethiops, which Laudivius dislikes, not allowing any part of Ethiopia to exceed the Tropics, to make which good he supposes that the word *extra* signifies *per extra*, and by like evasion Donatus[367] understands *solem pro die* and *annum pro nocte*, which is no grammatical procedure. But Ludovicus de la Cerda[368] with better consideration interprets Virgil's meaning to be that Augustus Caesar

---

[364] Plato tells part of the story of Atlantis in the *Timaeus* (25a ff.) and continues in the *Critias*, which is subtitled *The Island of Atlantis* (1217–1238). However, the discussion breaks off rather suddenly.

[365] Aelius Lampridius (fl. c. 330) was one of the supposed authors of the *Augustan Histories*. He wrote lives of, amongst others, Alexander Severus and Commodus.

[366] Virgil, *Aeneid* 6. 794-797.

[367] Aelius Donatus (4th century C.E.) is best-known for his *Ars grammatica*, work which became the most popular grammar book used in schools from the Middle Ages onwards, and which was reprinted innumerable times. Hardly anything is known about the author other than that he was the teacher of St. Jerome. A *Life of Virgil* is also attributed to Donatus.

[368] Juan Luis de la Cerda (1560–1643), a Jesuit scholar, was well known for his editions of Virgil and as a commentator on that poet's works. He produced an annotated version of the *Eclogues* or *Bucolics* (1608) as well as the first six books of the *Aeneid*, but also edited Tertullian and the *Psalms of Solomon* (1626), the first edition of those works.

should extend his sceptre beyond Atlas into the more meridional parts of Libya or South Africa into lands without the zodiac, and so the words *extra sidera* are to have zodiacs adjoined, but granting that it makes nothing for the discovery of America. After that Seneca the philosopher in his *Medea* gives us this prediction:

> The time shall one day be
> Guided by Providence, when men shall see
> The liquid ocean to enlarge her bounds,
> And pay the Earth a tribute of more grounds
> In ample measure. For the sea gods then
> Will show new worlds and rereties to men;
> Yea, by his leave who all things doth command,
> See Thule less north by far then other lands.[369]

These are but dim lights to show the way into the Western world, so that upon the whole it may be granted the discovery of that vast continent was reserved for a succeeding generation. The first we meet with is Madog[370] son of Prince Owain Gwynedd, who for thirty years ruled Wales after his father Gruffydd ap Cynan had at St. David's done homage to William the Conqueror for lands he held on the other side Severn. He was in direct line descended from Rhodri the Great, a Prince famoused for his success against the invading German, especially at Berthen, Bangelu, Monegid and Angelsey about the year 846, such time as Burghred ruled over the Mercians and Aethelwulf the West Saxons.[371] The annals of that time acquaint us that Owain was no sooner dead but that the custom of *gavelkind*,[372] which some think has ruined most families in Wales,

---

See Andrew Laird, "Juan Luis de la Cerda and the Predicament of Commentary," in *The Classical Commentary*, ed. R. K. Gibson et al. (Leiden: Brill, 2002), 171-203.

[369] Seneca, *Medea* 375–381.

[370] Prince Madog (c. 1150–1180) was perhaps a natural son of Prince Owain. Disgusted with internecine bickering after his father's death, he was supposed to have set out from Wales in 1170 on an expedition from which he never returned. A legend says that Madog landed in Florida or Mobile Bay and that he travelled upriver, coming into contact with native tribes as he went. Herbert may have found confirmation for his ideas from reading George Peckham's *A True Report of the late Discoveries of the Newfound Lands* (1583) or David Powell's *History of Cambria* (1589). Hakluyt also included an account of Madog's adventures, for which there is no historical evidence.

[371] Owain Gwynedd ab Gruffudd was king of Gwynedd 1137–1180; his father Gruffudd ab Cynan was king of Gwynedd 1081–1137 and thus contemporary with William I 'the Conqueror,' who reigned 1066–1087. Rhodri Mawr 'the Great' was king of Gwynedd 844–878. contemporary with Burghred of Mercia (852–74) and Æthelwulf of the West Saxons (839–58).

[372] Gavelkind, which varied from place to place, was in Wales a custom of tribal succession by which when a landowner died, his land was not divided amongst his sons,

occasioned great division amongst his sons, of which Iorwerth or Edward surnamed 'Drwyndwn' by reason of his broken nose, was eldest, but withstood by
Hywel and Daffydd the younger sons by reason of that and other his imperfections. Hywel also was objected against for that his mother was of Ireland, 'twixt
which countries war was proclaimed, so Daffydd was best-approved of though
youngest, both in respect of his comely personage and ingenuity but principally
for that he had gained the affections of the Lady Emma Plantagenet, sister to
King Henry II. Howbeit, this indirect practice was soon after questioned by Llywellyn ab Iorwerth, who with the assistance of Hywel ab Mareddud and Cynan
ab Owain his popular kinsmen, gave battle to Daffydd, and having the better of
the day possessed himself of that principality *Anno* 1195 and preserved it.[373]

These intestine broils were no way pleasing to Madog, who by that discord
foresaw their ruin (for what destroys a nation sooner then division?) and the Norman's speedy conquest. Therefore, to avoid that storm and provide for himself
he resolves upon a sea-adventure, hoping to find out some place abroad where
he might plant securely and not be liable to invasion. So tradition, and it is not
unlike that so generous a Prince was not unacquainted with those authors lately
cited, but to deviate a little, more certain it is that the song penned by Taliesin[374]
a prophetic bard was then accomplished, written *Anno Dom.* 490, such time as

---

but put into a common stock and then redivided amongst members of the sept (clan division).

[373] Prince Iorwerth ab Owain 'Drwyndwn' (1145–1174) was killed at the battle of
Pennant Melangell; Prince Hywel ap Owain (d. 1170) was a distinguished Welsh-lan-
guage poet who composed the first attested love-poetry in that language. He was driven
out of Gwynedd by his half-brother Daffydd ab Owain and then killed at the battle
of Pentraeth. Daffydd ab Owain reigned as Prince of Gwynedd 1170–1195 and fought
against his brothers. He did marry Emma of Anjou (d. c. 1214), the sister of King John,
and he was deposed and then imprisoned (1197) by his cousin Llywellyn ap Iorwerth,
who became Llywellyn I of Wales (1195–1240), also known as Llywellyn 'the Great.'
Daffydd escaped from prison and spent the rest of his days in England. For details, see
Kari Maund, *The Welsh Kings: Warriors, Warlords and Princes* (Stroud: Tempus Books,
2006), 186–87.

[374] Taliesin (c. 534–599) is believed to be one of the earliest Welsh poets known to
us by name. His poems appear in the fourteenth-century *Book of Taliesin*, and some of
them are considered genuine by scholars. Herbert probably knew the legendary accounts
of Taliesin written by Ellis Gruffydd in the sixteenth century and John Jones in 1607. W.
F. Stene translated the poems into English (1858) and there are now modern translations
of the legendary poems attributed to him by Marged Haycock, *Legendary Poems from the
Book of Taliesin* (Aberystwyth: CMCS Press, 2007) and the putatively historical poems
in praise of Urien Rheged and other 6th century rulers were edited by Ifor Williams, *The
Poems of Taliesin* (Dublin: DIAS, 1968). My thanks to Professor Marged Haycock of the
Department of Welsh, Aberystwyth University, for this information.

Ambrosius Aurelianus,[375] brother to Uther Pendragon,[376] repaired hither from Armorica[377] to command in chief against the Saxon, in which the bard foretells that at such time as the fell to discord amongst themselves and to idolatry, the British splendour should be eclipsed: "*Eu Nar a folant/ Eu Hjaith a gadwant/ Eu tir a gothlant / Ond gwyllt Wallia*; Whiles Cambria's issue serve the Lord their maker,/ Whiles with no other language are partaker, / Whiles so with glory they their own shall keep, / Whiles other nations in oblivion sleep." Taliesin also in the same song reproves the pride and avarice of the clergy, who to despite the Welsh gave out that Augustine the monk was their first converter, who had embraced Christ long before by the preaching of Joseph of Arimathea and Simon Zelotes,[378] as Baronius and other annals witness, whence came that religious boast that Britons had pre-eminence by having the first Christian king, emperor

---

[375] Ambrosius Aurelianus was a semi-legendary British hero who organised resistance against Saxon invaders. He is mentioned by Geoffrey of Monmouth and by Gildas in *De excidio et conquestu Britanniae*, which was edited by Polydore Virgil in 1525 and translated by John Josseline in 1568. Bede also writes about him, dating him as flourishing during the reign of the Eastern Roman Emperor Zeno (474–491). Gerald of Wales calls him "Merlin Ambrosius," who foretold the destruction of Britain (248).

[376] Uther Pendragon is well known as the father of King Arthur, an identification which originated in Welsh poetry. Geoffrey of Monmouth makes him the son of Emperor Constantine III (407–411), who reigned in Britain, and calls him Ambrosius Aurelianus's brother. When Ambrosius's throne was seized by Vortigern Uther defeated the usurper and became king.

[377] The ancient region of Armorica included modern Brittany and the area between the Seine and Loire rivers in France.

[378] Simon Zelotes (the Zealot) was an obscure disciple of Jesus, whose name does not denote his membership in a radical Jewish movement but merely his zeal for the Law. His deeds were collected by Isidore of Seville, whom Herbert cites earlier, or he could have found them in Jacobus de Voragine's *Golden Legend* (c. 1260), which had existed in an English translation since 1438 and was printed by Caxton (1483) and many times afterwards. There is a tradition that Simon was in Britain, but it is also claimed that he was martyred in Colchis (now in Georgia) or in Persia where some scholars (including Lipsius, another one of Herbert's sources) say he was sawn in half. He also proselytised in Egypt and Armenia. See Jacobus de Voragine, *The Golden Legend: Selections*, trans. Christopher Stace (Harmondsworth: Penguin Books, 1998), 285–90.

and monastery in the world, made good in Lucius, [379] Constantine and Bangor. [380] The canzon was this:

> *Gwae'r offeiriad byd*
> *Nis angreisseia gwyd*
> > *ac ny phregetha*
> *Gwae ny cheidw ygail*
> *Ac eff yu vigail*
> > *ac ny's areilia*
> *Gwae ny theidw cyc ddevaid*
> *Rhaew bleidhie, Rhufeniaid*
> > *a' i'ffon g'nwppa.*

> Woe be to that priest y-born
> That will not cleanly weed his corn,
> > and preach his charge among.
> Woe be to that shepherd I say
> That will not watch his fold always,
> > as to him doth belong.
> Woe be to him that doth not keep
> From Romish wolves his silly sheep
> > with staff and weapon strong. [381]

---

[379] Lucius was a legendary second-century king of Britain mentioned by Geoffrey of Monmouth, Bede, and the *Liber Pontificalis*, all of which are cited by Herbert. In about 178 he was supposed to have written a letter to Pope Eleutherius (174–89) asking for missionaries, to which the pope responded by sending Duvianus and Fuganus, who converted King Lucius (who was later canonised) and many of his people followed suit. Lucius was also traditionally said to have founded St. Peter's Church in Cornhill, London. See Alan Smith, "Lucius of Britain: Alleged King and Church Founder," *Folklore*, (1979): 29–36.

[380] Bangor on Dee Abbey in Flintshire, Wales, may have been founded by one Dunawd, father of St. Deiniol, in about 510. Another tradition makes St. Iltyd the founder, but there is little evidence. It was visited by St. Augustine of Canterbury in about 598, and at one time housed about two thousand monks.

[381] This poem, entitled "Difregwawd Taliesin," may be found in its earliest form included in *The Red Book of Hergest* (c. 1400). Herbert's version is a little garbled and sometimes untranslatable from the way he gives the Welsh. The text from *The Red Book of Hergest* reads: "*Gwae offeiriat byt ny agreitho gwyt* (MS *ywyt*) *ny phregetha, / Ny wercheidw y geil* (MS *gell*) *ac efyn uugeil nys arheila / Ny differ y deueit rac bleideu ribynnyeit a chyffas da*," which translates "Woe to the priest of the world [i.e. people] who doesn't condemn sin, who doesn't preach. / Who does not defend his sheepfold, and he a shepherd, who does not look after it, / Who does not defend his sheep from ravening wolves through urging [to confession]." For details, see Marged Haycock, ed. *Blodugerdd Barddas o Ganu Crefyddol Cynnar* (Swansea: Cyhoeddiadau Barddas, 1994), 349–65. I am indebted for this information and translation to Professor Marged Haycock.

But to digress no further. Madog, having ships, men and provisions ready, with his Prince's license put to sea from Abergwylli in the year 1170. Wind and see favouring so good a design, after some weeks' sailing west he descried land, probably Newfoundland, but whetever it was overjoyed him. Madog then, ranging the coiast, so soon as he had found a convenient place sat down to plant; after he had fortified he left a hundred and twenty men, and by Providence, the best compass, and benefit of the Pole Star returned safely to his own country, where having recounted his voyage, the fruitfulness of the soil, the simplicity of the savages, the wealth abounding there and facility of enlargement, after some months' refreshment in ten barques loaden with necessary provisions they put to sea again and happily recovered their plantation. They found few of those they left there yet living, caused either by too much eating, the novelty of that climate, which though never so good yet causes alteration in new inhabitants, or treachery of the natives, so as Madog, having the assistance of Encon and Edwall his brethren, quickly put it into good order, where they stayed some time in expectation of a fresh supply of men, but their expectations proved vain, for in the overturn of that state by the indiscretion of that unhappy Prince Llywellyn ap Gruffudd married to Eleanor, daughter of Simon de Montfort, Earl of Leicester and Eleanor daughter of King John,[382] Gruffudd being slain *Anno* 1282 at Buellht. Madog and his company returned no more, nor is there any record that the Welsh attempted to prosecute their former adventure.

Nevertheless, albeit Madog and his Cambrian crew be dead and their memory moth-eaten, yet their footsteps are plainly traced, which the language they left, the religion they taught and the relics there found do clearly evidence, otherwise how come those British words, not much altered from the dialect used at this day, amongst the Mexicans, whence they had the use of beads, crucifixes etc., all which the Spaniards, as we read in Lopez de Gomara[383] and others, found amongst those of Cuzco and Culhuacan at their first landing in America? Yea, whence comes that tradition amongst the Mexicans that a strange people came thither in curraghs who taught them the knowledge of God and by whose instruction they became civilised, as it is related by Columbus, Postellus, Lopez, Cortez and other Castilians? That of Fernando Cortez, who *Anno Domini* 1519

---

[382] Llywellyn II ap Gryffudd was the last prince of Wales; he reigned from 1255 to 1282. He married Eleanor de Montfort (1252–1282), daughter of Simon de Montfort, sixth earl of Leicester (1208–1265), the prominent leader of the opposition to Henry III and the man associated with the founding of Parliament. De Montfort's wife was Princess Eleanor Plantagenet (1215–1275), daughter of King John.

[383] Francisco Lopez de Gomara (1511–1565) was a Jesuit historian from Seville who had accompanied Hernan Cortes as chaplain when the latter went to Algeria. Lopez wrote the *Cronica de la conquista de Nueva España* (1552), which was translated into English as *The pleasant History of the Conquest of West India, now called New Spain* (1596) and the *Historia de las Indias* (1552).

was ambassador and general for Ferdinand and Isabella, is most remarkable, for in some discourse 'twixt him and Moctezuma II, son of Ahuitzotl and father of Cuauhtemoc the last King of Mexico,[384] the ambassador, observing the Indians to have many ceremonies which the Spaniards used, demanded who first instructed them. The answer was that many years before a strange nation landed there who were such a people as induced his ancestors to afford them civil reception, but how they were called or whence they came could not satisfy. Another time, in a panegyric Moctezuma returned them he had this expression: "One chief cause of my affection to your nation is I have many times heard my father say how that he heard his grandsire affirm that some generations before his progenitors came thither as atrangers in company of a noble man who abode there awhile and then departed, but left many of his people behind, that upon his return most of those he left there died and that from him or some of them they supposed themselves to be descended," by which narrative it may be presumed the people he meant were Welsh rather then Spaniards, and the records of that voyage writ by many bards and genealogists confirm as much, as may appear by the learned poems of Cynwrig ap Goronwy, Gutun Owain who lived in Edward IV's time and Sir Mareddud ap Rhys, which last lived in the year 1447, and of Madog has this eulogy: *Madog wif' mwydic wedd; Iawn genau Owen Gwynedd/ Ni funnum dyr, fyenaid oedd/ Nada mawr ond y'm orodedd*; Madog ap Owen was I call'd;/ Strong, tall and comely, not enthralled/ With home-bred pleasures, but to fame;/ Through land and sea I sought the same."[385]

By their language also, Welsh names being given birds, rivers, rocks, beasts etc., as *gw'rando*, which signifies 'to hearken,' *pen-gwyn*, 'a bird that has a white head' and rocks of that resemblance. Isles there are called *Chorboesso*; there is also Cape Britain; *gwyndwr*, 'white water;' *bara*, 'bread;' *mam*, 'mother;' *tate*, 'father;' *dawr*, 'water;' *pryd*, 'time;' *buch*, 'a cow;' *clugar*, 'a heathcock;' *llynog*, 'a fox;' *wy*, 'an egg;' *calaf*, 'a quill;' *trwyn*, 'a nose;' *nef*, 'heaven' and others. Nor is it a fantasy of yesterday, since learned men both of late and former times have taken notice

---

[384] Ahuitzotl reigned 1486–1502, and was in fact the father of Moctezuma II (1502–1520). At the expense of being pedantic, Cuauhtemoc (1520–1521) was the nephew, not the son of Moctezuma; after Moctezuma had been murdered by the Spaniards he was succeeded by his son Cuitlahuac (1521), who died soon after his accession from smallpox, an imported disease.

[385] Cynwrig ap Goronwy is a mystery. There was a fifteenth-century poet named Cynwrig ap Dafydd Goch, but Dr. Bleddyn Owen Huws wonders "whether [Cynwrig ap Goronwy] might have been one of Iolo Morganwg's creations" (letter to editor from Professor Marged Haycock); Gutun Owain (fl. 1460–1480) was a poet from Shropshire and a student of the great Daffydd ap Gwilym; Sir Maredudd ap Rhys (d. 1447) was a poet from Powys whose subjects were mainly love and nature. Edward IV was King of England 1461–1483.

of: such are Cynwrig ap Goronwy, Maredudd ap Rhys, Gutun Owain, Lloyd,[386] Powell,[387] Price,[388] Hakluyt, Broughton,[389] Purchas, Davies[390] and others whose learning and integrity have credit and abundantly convince the ingenious so as no doubt had it been known as merited then had not Christopher Columbus, Amerigo Vespucci,[391] Magellan nor others carried away the labour of so great a discovery, nor had Madog been defrauded of his memory nor our kings their just title to the West Indies, at least to that part of it which a secret Fate, as it were, renewed their claim to by Columbus his proferring the discovery to King Henry VII, nor then had His Holiness or His Catholic Majesty had that plea which

[386] Humphrey Lloyd (1527–1568) was a Welsh doctor and antiquarian who served as private secretary to Lord Arundel when the latter was Chancellor of Oxford. His principal work was the *Commentarioli descriptionis Britanniae fragmentum* (1572), which was translated by Thomas Twyne as *The Breviary of Britain* (1573). Lloyd was also a cartographer; he prepared a map of England and Wales which was included by Ortelius in the supplement to his atlas (1573).

[387] David Powell (c. 1552–1598) was a cleric, the first graduate of Jesus College, Oxford (1573) and the first editor of the works of Gerald of Wales (Giraldus Cambrensis), although Lewis Thorpe, the modern editor, tells us that "he took great liberties with the text" (52). He published Gerald's *Topographia Hiberniae sive de mirabilibus Hiberniae. Expugnatio Hiberniae. Itinerarium Cambriae . . .* in 1585. Powell's main original work was his *History of Cambria, now called Wales* (1584).

[388] Sir John Price (c. 1502–1555), notary, Prior of St. Guthlac's monastery, MP and Secretary to the Council of Wales under Henry VIII, was a great antiquary and collector of Welsh manuscripts. He transcribed Welsh poetry, produced a Welsh bardic grammar, and wrote a description of Wales translated by Humphrey Lloyd and included in David Powell's *History of Cambria*.

[389] Hugh Broughton (1549–1612) was an eminent Hebraist and translator who worked on the King James Bible. He was a Fellow of Christ's College, Cambridge and Reader of Divinity at Durham (1574). His principal work is the *Consent of Scriptures* (1588), a chronology of world history from Adam to Jesus Christ.

[390] John Davies (c. 1567–1644), Rector of Mallwyd, was a distinguished Welsh scholar who played a large part in the translation of the Bible into Welsh (1620). His own output included two important reference works, the *Antiquae linguae Britannicae rudimenta* (1621), which was a Welsh grammar, and the *Dictionarium duplex* (1632), the first comprehensive Welsh dictionary.

[391] Amerigo Vespucci (1454–1512) was an Italian (not Spanish, as Herbert thought) merchant and explorer whose career was largely in Spain, where he had gone as an agent for the Medici banking cartel. He made his great voyage to South America (1499–1502) and rose to become Pilot-Major of Spain (1508). Herbert is referring to two letters supposedly sent by him, one to Francesco de' Medici (1503) and printed as *Mundus novus*, which described the South American voyage and was widely read in Europe, and the other to the Florentine statesman Piero Soderini. In this letter (1504) Vespucci said that he made four voyages to the Americas between 1497 and 1504. Their authenticity has been disputed.

they now ground upon the Genoan's discovery, as the Jesuits and others have so vehemetly disputed for.

Columbus. Americus. Magellan.

Far be it from me in the least to detract from Columbus, albeit 'tis supposed that his confidence arose from another's direction, who by stress of weather was driven upon those parts and to him communicated, or else from Columbus his apprehension of the improbability that so much of the 360 degrees should be sea, as ordinary charts do make, and that he might as well discover westward as the Portugals had done east to the other Indies. Be it therefore remembered that his voyage was after the other of our countryman three hundred and two and twenty years, so as possession is the Spaniard's best plea, for he cannot arrogate to himself a right upon pretence of the first discovery.

Columbus was born at Nervi not far from Genoa,[392] a man of a modest nature, studious and well-read in the mathematics and chiefly in navigation. His first encouragement was, say the Spaniards, from pursuing an ephemeris written by a Spanish mariner who had been forced into the West Indies by tempest and died at Columbus his house after his arrival. This, some think, was invented to the end an Italian should not master so much glory; whether Columbus had any light from poets or heard of Madog's voyage who knows, for what nation formerly knew not the acts of Englishmen better then themselves, otherwise Polydore Virgil[393] had not undertook to our shame and wrong the English chronology nor Verstegan alias Rowley the confidence to render wellnight all the considerable gentry of this land from the etymology of their names Teutonic. Columbus, well-assured of this discovery, sent his brother to King Henry VII to propose the business so he would accept the undertaking, but the improbability of the design togther with the obscure quality of the stranger made the King give little credit to the proposition, for in his passage he had been imprisoned by pirates, who stripped him before they set him at liberty. Upon the King's refusal he applied himself to the French king, who in like manner, hearing that King Henry had refused, gave him the like dismiss, so as he had rested under a final discouragement had not Ferdinand the Spanish king accepted the motion and given him

---

[392] The birthplace of Columbus is still disputed. Scholars seem to favour Savona, near Genoa, over Nervi, but many other towns in the vicinity of Genoa have claimed the honour.

[393] Polydore Virgil (c. 1470–1555) was born in Urbino and came to England in 1499 in the service of Henry VII, rising to become Bishop of Bath and Wells (1504) and enjoying the favour of Cardinal Wolsey during the early years of Henry VIII. In 1515 he ended up in prison, having lost Wolsey's favour, but soon regained most of his status and wrote the *Historia Anglica* (1534; written 1512–1513), in which he questions Geoffrey of Monmouth's veracity, and *Liber de prodigiis* (1526).

the command of two hundred men in two small ships at the request of Juan Perez
de Marchena,[394] at that time Rector of the Monastery of Rabida, a great Maecenas to industry, with which, after threscore days' sail (in that time having no
small ado to quiet the mutinous Spaniards) Columbus descried land, that part
called *Guanahami*, by Columbus new-named *San Salvador*,[395] a part of Mexico,
and southward to the place where Madog formerly landed, a discovery no less
joying them than if thereby they had got the Empire of the World, a prize so
worthy that from the year 1492 to this they have brought home no less gold and
silver then all Europe enjoyed formerly. Columbus died *Anno* 1506 in his fourth
return out of the Indies.

Anno Dom. 1497 Amerigo Vespucci, a Spaniard, before his voyage into the
Orient also adventures south, where with small roil he found more land, but part
of what was formerly discovered. Nevertheless, as if Columbus had done but
little, he arrogates to himself the honour of the discovery by calling the whole
continent, which stretches almost to either Pole, America, but injuriously, seeing
others preceded him in the discovery. Magellan after that sails more southerly
then Vespucci in the year 1519, through that *fretum* which with better reason is
called Magellan's, and since that many others have given their names unto ports,
hills, rivers, rocks etc. Only Madog sleeps in oblivion; howbeit, such as value
Madog's memory will not easily pretermit those living monuments without some
due acknowledgement, but after this long parenthesis I return.

The Azores.

The beginning of December[396] we had sight of the Azores[397] or Flemish Islands,
which the name seems to infer were first found out by the Dutch, for according to
tradition a merchant of Bourges, bound for Lisbon in the year 1449, was by stress

---

[394] Juan Perez (d. c. 1513) was confessor to Queen Isabel I and Father Guardian of
the Convent of La Rabida near Palos. He met Columbus in 1484/85 and became a firm
supporter, persuaded him to seek help from Queen Isabel, even accompanying Columbus
on his second voyage (1493) and becoming the first priest to say mass in the New World.
He became Guardian of the convent which Columbus established in San Domingo, after which nothing further was heard from him. The name Marchena is that of a separate
person, another priest supportive of Columbus's ideas. The historian Gomara conflated
them by stating that the Father Guardian of La Rabida was "Juan Perez de Marchena,"
when in fact they were two people, and he is Herbert's source here.

[395] Now San Salvador de Atenco.

[396] Foster states that the *Expedition*'s log gives the date as 30 November (*Herbert*,
336).

[397] The Azores are comprised of nine islands: Corvo and Flores (the Western Group);
Graciosa, Terceira, Faial, Pico, and São Jorge (the Central Group); and Sao Miguel and
Santa Maria (the Eastern Group). The first one to be discovered was Santa Maria by
Diogo Silves in 1427, not by the Dutch, although some scholars, like Robert L. Santos,

of weather driven so far west as unexpectedly 'twixt the latitude of 38 and 40 degrees he descried several small islands in view of one another, but at time without show of human inhabitants. These he called Flemish Islands; howbeit, coming soon after ashore in Andalucia and reporting his adventure, the Portugals by his compass easily found their way and quickly planted them with men and what else was necessary, at which time they gave them the names of Sao Jorge, Sao Miguel, Santa Maria, Faial, Pico and the Terceiras, comprehended it at first under the name of the Terceiras but afterwards of the Azores, so-called from the many aeries of hawks they found there, albeit Ortelius rather supposes the name to be derived from the Spanish word *essorer*, which signifies 'to dry' or 'to wither,' for the old name given it by geographers, if rightly apprehended and granted to be the name which Theophrastus mentions in his *Book of Rareties*, was *Uxiana*, but the new denominations imposed by the Lusitanian are not improper, for Terceira is so-called for that it resembles three isles, Faial has its name from the beech-trees with which it then abounded, Pico from the pyramidal shape it bears, Flores for that it was overspread with flowers and the rest from saints to whose patronage the captain thought most fit to recommend them. Of these Terceira is greatest if not the fruitfullest, for it abounds with wine and oil, corn and fruit etc. Angra[398] is her best town and Brazil the strongest fort, which also commands the haven, the best that island has, though not very good to anchor in.

The Azores [illustration not shown]

Terceira is not famoused for anything more then for the defence it gave Prior Dom Antonio the titulary King of Portugal[399] against the Spaniard, as may

---

believe it was Goncalvo Velho Cabral who discovered it in 1432. The Church of Our Lady of the Assumption was built there in about 1490. According to Foster, the name "Flemish Islands" is derived from their supposed discovery by van den Berg in 1432 (*Herbert*, 336). However, Santos gives the name as Willem van der Hagen and the date as 1450, which makes Herbert's account accurate; the Flemish settlers were sent by Prince Henry the Navigator; his sister Isabel was Duchess of Burgundy, in whose territories Flanders then lay. By 1490 there were 2000 Flemish people on the Azores. For details, see Robert L. Santos, *Azoreans to California: A History of Migration and Settlement.* (Denair: Alley-Cass Publications, 1995), 3–33.

[398] Now known as Ponta Delgada.

[399] Dom Antonio de Bragança (1531–1595), Prior of Crato, was the grandson of Manoel I and son of Prince Luis de Beja. During the reign of King Sebastian he served as governor of Tangier (1571) and was taken prisoner by the Moroccans when Sebastian was defeated and killed at the battle of Alcazquivir (1578). He was set free and claimed the Portuguese throne when Sebastian's uncle and successor Henry died, reigning very briefly (1580–1581) and then setting up his government-in-exile in the Azores (1581–1583), although he was defeated by the Duke of Alva. He continued to oppose Spanish

be read at large in Conestaggio's[400] treatise concerning the union of those two crowns. Pico is extraordinary high land and surges in a peak or spire like Tenerife, so far above the clouds as those that sail by find it oft enveloped with fogs, insomuch as the top is seldom to be discerned. One of the highest islands in the world it is reputed, some supposing that it mounts full five miles into the Middle Region, but of more certainty it is the circuit of the isle is disproportionate to its height, for it exceeds not ten miles compass. The higher earth is for the most part sulphur and shows many concave places whereout evaporates smoke and flame, which now and again belch forth brimstone. Notwithstanding, in the valleys below there are delightful shades and chill-cold rivulets, into which when the fire is vomited those contrary elements echo their discontent not a little to the terror and amazement of such as are unacquainted with those encounters; from this contrareity it is, I suppose, these isles are more subject to dreadful earthquakes then other places. Most memorable was that about the year 1591 in Sao Miguel's island, which endured shaking from the 26 day of July unto the 12 of August, to the extreme fright of the inhabitants, especially when they by force perceived the earth remove from place to place and Villafranca,[401] the best town they had, turn topsy-turvy. The ships also that rode at anchor in the bay trembled and quaked, insomuch as the people verily thought Doomsday was at hand and that the fabric of the universe was disjointing. Earthquakes, says Aristotle *l. 2, c. 7 Meteor.* proceed from watery vapours included within the bowels of the earth, which in seeking a passage to its proper element, by making a tumulutary motion shakes the earth, and 'tis observed that these concussions happen oftenest in places within the temperate zone, in regard that in cold places exhalations are not so much increased as they be in hot, where the vapours are spent through excess of heat chiefly where the land is sandy, out of which the exhalations evaporate with ease. Contrarily, as here, where the soil is rocky and mountainous, many hollow caves are found, which, being filled with vapours, troubles the superficies and gives not over till it make an irruption.

Another miracle the Spaniards report for truth how that the isle Corvo rose out of the sea, till then being far underwater. That and Flores were discovered by

---

occupation of Portugal, and lived first in France and then in England, where he lost his fortune and had to return to France and a pension from Henry IV.

[400] Girolamo Franchi di Conestaggio [*Cunestagius*] (d. 1635) was a diplomat, historian, and Archbishop of Capua. The work mentioned here is *Dell' unione del regno di Portogallo alla corona di Castiglia* (1592), translated by Edward Blount as *History of the uniting the Kingdom of Portugal to the Crown of Castile; containing the last wars of the Portugals against the Moors of Africa, the end of the House of Portugal and change of that government* (1600). Some scholars believe that Conestaggio did not write the work and that the real author was Juan de Silva, Count of Portalegre. I am indebted to Professor Sanjay Subrahmanyan of the Department of History, UCLA for information on this author.

[401] Now Vila Franca do Campo.

the Spaniard, but more certain it is that in the year 1588 they had them in subjection, such time as the Earl of Essex,[402] commanding Her Majesty's sea-force, to retaliate the Spaniard landed in despite of the inhabitants and exercised what hostile acts he thought needful. Flores and Corvo were sacked to purpose; Sao Miguel also was given the soldier as free plunder after the Admiral had for public use first sent thence aboard his ship four hundred thousand ducats and upwards in plate, besides merchandise of great value, so well-recruited was that place notwithstanding the noble Earl of Cumberland had examined it eight years before, when most of the Western Isles submitted themselves likewise to his mercy. Faial the year following felt the English no less smart upon the Spanish account, which made the inhabitants execrate the Catholic ambition. In the year 1597 Pico was in like sort sharer in that quarrel, when Sir Walter Ralegh made the isle a prey unto the incensed English, the Spaniard then not so able as afterwards to requite what provocation was added further at Orinoco in the West Indies.

I shall but give this further remembrance, that at St. Michael's the true meridian is only found, for there the needle shows no variation either easterly or westerly. The reason is *inter occulta natura*,[403] guessed at by many but by some certainly discovered, albeit some conjecture it is occasioned by the magnetic virtue of the Earth, which makes the variations more or less according to the different situation of place or distance from either continent. For where there is an equidistancy, as in the mid-way between Asia and America, the needle is ofttimes found to vary least, but undoubtedly it is a fallacious conclusion, seeing the variation is so small at the Cape of Good Hope and other places contiguous to the African continent. Howbeit, the ancient accounts of the first meridian, whence cosmographers assume their longitude in former ages, by Ptolemy and others were placed at the Fortunate Islands, those now called Canaria and Cape Verde, where is very little variation. The rest of the meridional lines are 180, and albeit drawn from N. to S., yet by the same poles are terminated.

---

[402] Robert Devereux, second earl of Essex (1566–1601), Queen Elizabeth I's great favourite and Master of the Horse from 1588. Essex wanted a military career, and in 1589 he joined Drake in an unsuccessful attack by the English fleet on Lisbon. He did distinguish himself at the attack on Cadiz (1591) in which the city was taken, and he embarked for the Azores (1597) with a fleet under Sir Walter Ralegh. In direct defiance of the queen's orders Essex took off in pursuit of the Spanish treasure-fleet and failed to render the Spanish navy incapable of action first. Herbert refers to this engagement here as if it were a significant victory.

[403] Amongst natural secrets.

[England, at last].

Leaving the Azores, the wind being fair and moderate we quickly entered the Cantabrian Seas, where after a little time we were churlishly entertained by loud winds that soon converted to a storm of thrice four and twenty hours continuance, during which we took in our sail and lay a hull, tossed sufficiently, but so good were our ships that the greatest fear we had was being driven nearer the French coast then we desired, for in spite of helm and mizzen the tide or current, if not both, drew us so nigh to Ushant, a small isle upon the most western point or promontary of Brittany (Armorica of old, but now Britain-Britanant) as we were not a little endangered. In that distress we likewise sought the Lord, who as He is the hope of all the ends of the Earth, was pleased to appease the noise of the sea and waves thereof (Psalm 65),[404] and in few hours more gave us the comfortable sight of our own country, not unlike that long-looked-for Ithaca, And well remembering the caution of the poet, "*Turpe mihi abire domo vacuumque redire*,"[405] I have as the greatest adventure thought fit to expose to public view these observations, albeit the issue of youth and haste, which indeed were intended for the private satisfaction of that noble lord, William Earl of Pembroke and the Lord Powys, who gave me the first encouragement to travel.

To conclude: we came to an anchor at Plymouth and returned God hearty thanks for our preservation.

Redituque suo singula gaudent.[406]
FINIS.

---

[404] "O God of our salvation . . . Which stilleth the noise of the seas, the noise of their waves . . ." (5, 7).

[405] "It would be a crime for me to leave home and return empty" (Erasmus, *Adages* 2. 8. 87).

[406] "Each rejoiced at its return" (Boethius, *De consolatione philosophiae* 3m 2. 35).

Bibliography

Primary Sources

Abu'l Fazl. *The Akbarnama*, trans. H. Beveridge. Delhi: Low Price Publications, 1993.

Alighieri, Dante. *The Divine Comedy*, trans. C. H. Sisson. London: Pan Books, 1981.

Apocrypha: Authorized (King James) Version. Cambridge: Cambridge University Press, 2009.

Apuleius. *The Golden Ass*, trans. Robert Graves. Harmondsworth: Penguin, 1950, repr. 1980.

Aristotle, Horace, Longinus. *Classical Literary Criticism*, trans. T.S. Dorsch. Harmondsworth: Penguin, 1965.

Arrian. *Life of Alexander the Great*, trans. A. de Sélincourt. Harmondsworth: Penguin, 1958.

Ascham, Roger. *The Schoolmaster,* ed. Laurence V. Ryan. Ithaca: Cornell University Press, 1967.

Babur. *The Baburnama*, trans. Wheeler M. Thackston. New York: Modern Library, 2002.

Bacon, Francis. *The Major Works, including New Atlantis and the Essays*, ed. Brian Vickers. Oxford: Oxford University Press, 1996.

Balbi, Gasparo. "Voyage to Pegu and Observations There, Circa 1583." *SOAS Bulletin of Burma Research* 1 (2003): 26–35.

Baldaeus, Philip. *A True and Exact Description of the Most Celebrated East-India Coasts of Malabar and Coromandel, as also of the Isle of Ceylon* (1672). London, 1703.

Barbosa, Duarte. *An Account of the Countries Bordering on the Indian Ocean and their Inhabitants* (1518), trans. M.L. Danes. London: Hakluyt Society, 1812; repr. New Delhi: Vedams, 2002.

Baron, Robert. *Mirza: A Tragedie*; Denham, Sir John. *The Sophy*, ed. Parvin Loloi. Salzburg: Poetry Salzburg, 1998.

Berossos and Manetho: Native Traditions in Ancient Mesopotamia and Egypt, trans. G.B. Verbrugghe and J.M. Wickersham. Ann Arbor: University of Michigan Press, 2001.

Best, Thomas. *The Voyage of Thomas Best to the East Indies*, ed. W. Foster. London: Hakluyt Society, 1934.

Bowrey, Thomas. *A Geographical Account of Countries Round the Bay of Bengal 1669–1679*. London, 1682.

Brerewood, Edward. *Inquiries Touching the Diversity of Languages and Religions, through the Chief Parts of the World* (1674). New York: Kessinger Reprints, n.d.

Broecke, Pieter van den. *A Contemporary Dutch Chronicle of Mughal India*, ed. and trans. Brij Narain and Sri Ram Sharma. Calcutta: Susail Gupta, 1957.

Bruton, William. *News from the East Indies*. London, 1638.

Calendar of State Papers Colonial, East India, China and Japan, ed. W. Noel Sainsbury. Vols. 3–4. London: Longman, Green, 1860–1939; repr. Vaduz: Kraus Reprints, 1965–1980.

Camoens, Luiz Vaz de. *The Lusiads*, trans. Landeg White. Oxford: Oxford University Press, 1997.

Carew, George, Lord. *Letters of George, Lord Carew to Sir Thomas Roe, Ambassador to the Court of the Great Mogul, 1615–1617*, ed. John Maclean. London: Camden Society, 1860.

Cartwright, John. *The Preacher's Travels*. London, 1611.

Catullus. *The Complete Poems*, trans. Guy Lee. Oxford: Oxford University Press, 1998.

Chardin, Sir John. *Travels in Persia 1673–1677* (1724), pref. N.M. Penzer, intro. P. Sykes. New York: Dover, 1987. [See also Mavor, William.]

Cicero. *Academica*, ed. James Reid. London: Macmillan, 1874.

———. *The Republic / The Laws*, trans. Niall Rudd. Oxford: Oxford University Press, 1998.

Clifford, Lady Anne. *The Memoirs of 1603 and The Diary of 1618–1619*, ed. Katherine O. Atcheson. Peterborough, Ont.: Broadview, 2007.

Contarini, Ambrosio. *Travels to Tana and Persia*, trans. W. Thomas and S.A. Roy, ed. Lord Stanley of Alderley. 2 vols. London: Hakluyt Society, 1873.

Culpeper, Nicholas. *The Complete Herbal* (1653). Ware: Omega Books, 1985.

De Laet, Joannes. *The Empire of the Great Mogol* (1631), trans. J.S. Hoyland, annot. S.N. Banerjee (1928). Delhi: Oriental Books Reprint Corporation, 1974.

Della Valle, Pietro. *The Travels of Pietro della Valle in India*, trans. G. Havers (1664), ed. Edward Grey. 2 vols. London: Hakluyt Society, 1892.

Denham, Sir John. *The Sophy*. See Baron, Robert.

Diodorus Siculus. *The Historical Library of Diodorus the Sicilian, to which are added the Fragments of Diodorus*, trans. G. Booth. London: Military Chronicle Office, 1814.

Doniger, Wendy, and Brian K. Smith, trans. *The Laws of Manu*. Harmondsworth: Penguin, 1991.

Ferdowsi. *Shahnameh: The Persian Book of Kings,* trans. Dick Davis. Harmondsworth: Penguin, 2007.

———. *Shah-Nama, The Book of Kings,* trans. Reuben Levy. Chicago: University of Chicago Press, 1967.

Finch, William. *India as Seen by William Finch 1608–11,* ed. B. Nath. New York: Vedic Books, 2005.

Fowler, Alastair, ed. *The Oxford Book of Seventeenth-Century Verse.* Oxford: Oxford University Press, 2001.

Frederici, Cesare. *The Voyage and Travaile of M. Caesar Frederick, Merchant of Venice, into the East India, the Indies and Beyond . . .*(1588), trans. Thomas Hickok. *SOAS Bulletin of Burma Research* 2 (2004): 130–63.

Fryer, John. *A New Account of East India and Persia in Nine Years' Travels, 1672– 81.* London, 1698.

Fuller, Thomas. *The Worthies of England.* London: P. A. Nuttall, 1840.

Gerald of Wales (Giraldus Cambrensis). *The Journey through Wales / The Description of Wales,* trans. Lewis Thorpe. Harmondsworth: Penguin, 1978.

Gibbs, Laura, ed. and trans. *Latin Via Proverbs.* 2006. www.latinviaproverbs.com

Gooch, Henry. *A Relation of Sir D. Cotton's Embassy into Persia.* See Stodart, Robert.

Gulbadan. *The History of Humayun,* trans. Annette Beveridge (1901). Delhi: Idarah-i Adabayat-i Delhi, 1972.

Hakluyt, Richard. *Voyages and Discoveries,* ed. Jack Beeching. Harmondsworth: Penguin, 1972.

———, ed. Edmund Goldsmid. 13 vols. Edinburgh: E. and G. Goldsmid, 1888.

Hafiz. *The Gift: Poems by Hafiz, the Great Sufi Master,* trans. Daniel Ladinsky. Harmondsworth: Penguin Compass, 1999.

Hamel, Hendrik. *Journal and A Description of the Kingdom of Korea* (1669), trans. Jean-Paul Buys. Seoul: Royal Asiatic Society, 1998.

Hawkins, William. *Voyages,* ed. Clements Markham. London: Hakluyt Society, 1878.

Head, Richard. *The English Rogue Described in the Life of Meriton Latroon, a Witty Extravagant, Being a Complete History of the Most Eminent Cheats of Both Sexes.* London, 1665.

Hedges, William. *The Diary of Sir William Hedges, Esq.,* ed. Henry Yule. 2 vols. London: Hakluyt Society, 1888.

Hemacandra. *The Lives of the Jain Elders,* trans. R.C.C. Fynes. Oxford: Oxford University Press, 1998.

Herbert, Sir Thomas. *Travels in Persia 1627–1629,* ed. William Foster. London: Routledge, 1928.

Herbert of Chirbury, Edward, Lord. *Pagan Religion (De religione gentilium)* (1645), ed. and trans. John A. Butler. MRTS 152. Ottawa: Dovehouse Editions; Binghamton, NY: MRTS, 1995.

Herodotus. *The Histories*, trans. Robin Waterfield. Oxford: Oxford University Press, 1998.

Horace. *The Complete Odes and Epodes*, trans. W.G. Shepherd. Harmondsworth: Penguin, 1983.

———. *Satires*, trans. Niall Rudd. Harmondsworth: Penguin, 1973.

Howell, James. *Instructions for Foreign Travel*. London, 1642.

Husaini, Khwaja Kamgar. *Ma'asir-i-Jahangiri*, ed. Azra Alavi. Aligarh: Asia Publishing House, 1978.

Ibn Battuta. *The Travels of Ibn Battuta in the Near East, Asia and Africa*, trans. P. Chiesa. New York: Dover Books, 1998.

Jahangir. *The Tuzuk-i Jahangiri, or Memoirs of Jahangir*, trans. A. Rogers (1914). Delhi: Munshiram Manoharlal, 1968.

James I. *Daemonologie* (1597). La Vergne: Nabu Books Reprints, 2009.

———. *Letters of King James I and VI*, ed. J.P. Akrigg. Berkeley: University of California Press, 1984.

Jordanes. *De summa temporum vel origine actibusque gentis Romanorum*, ed. Theodor Mommsen. Berlin: Weidmann, 1882.

Josephus. *The Complete Works*, trans. William Whiston (1737). Grand Rapids: Kegel Publications, 1981.

Jourdain, John. *The Travels of John Jourdain, 1608–1617, Describing his Experiences in Arabia, India and the Malay Archipelago*, ed. W. Foster. Cambridge: Hakluyt Society, 1905.

Julian, Emperor [Flavius Claudius Julianus], *Juliani Imperatoris quae feruntur Epistolae, accedunt ejusdem fragmenta breviora, cum poematiis nec non Galli Caesaris ad Julianum fratrem epistola: Graeco et Latine*. Ed. Ludwig Heinrich Heyler. Mainz: Librariae Kupferbergianae, 1828.

Justin. *Epitome historiarum Philippicarum*, trans. J.S. Watson. London: Bohn, 1853.

Juvenal. *The Sixteen Satires*, trans. Peter Green. Harmondsworth: Penguin, 1967.

Khan, Inayat. *Shah Jahan Nama*, ed. and trans. A.R. Fuller, W.E. Begley, and Z.A. Desai. Delhi: Oxford University Press, 1990.

Lancaster, James. *The Voyages of Sir James Lancaster*, ed. C. Markham and W. Foster. Boston: Adamant Media, 2001.

Le Strange, Guy, ed. and trans. *Don Juan of Persia, a Shi'ah Catholic: Relaciones* (1604). New York: Harper & Brothers, 1926.

Linschoten, Jan Huyghen van. *The Voyage to the East Indies, from the English Translation of 1598*, ed. A.C. Burnell and P.A. Tiele. 2 vols. London: Hakluyt Society, 1885.

Livy. *The Rise of Rome (Books 1–5)*, trans. T.J. Luce. Oxford: Oxford University Press, 1998.

————. *The War with Hannibal*, trans. Aubrey de Sélincourt. Harmondsworth: Penguin, 1965, repr. 1986.

Lord, Henry. *Display of two foreign sects in the East Indies.* London, 1631.

Lucan. *Civil War*, trans. Susan H. Braund. Oxford: Oxford University Press, 1992.

Lucretius. *On the Nature of the Universe*, trans. Ronald Latham. Harmondsworth: Penguin, 1951.

Mander, Sir Geoffrey. "A Civil War Diary by Thomas Daunt of Owlpen, 1645–1650." *Owlpen Papers*: 59–69, www.owlpen.com/archives.shtml

Master, Sir Streynsham. *Diaries 1675–80*, ed. Richard Carnac Temple. 2 vols. London: John Murray, 1911.

Methold, William. *Relations of the Kingdom of Golconda.* See Purchas, Samuel.

Milton, John. *The Riverside Milton*, ed. Roy Flanagan. New York: Houghton Mifflin, 1998.

Molesworth, G., and W. Foster, eds. *The Register of Letters etc. of the Governour and Company of Merchants of London Trading in the East Indies, 1601–1619.* London: B. Quaritch, 1893.

Monserrate, Anthony. *Mongolicae legationis commentarius*, ed. Fr. J. Hosten (1914), trans. J.S. Hoyland, annot. S. Banerjee. Delhi: Oxford University Press, 1931.

Monshi, Iskandar Beg. *History of Shah Abbas the Great*, trans. R.M. Savory. Boulder: Westview Press, 1978.

Monte Croce, Riccoldo di. *Libellus ad nationes orientales,* ed. Kurt Villads Jensen. Odense: University of Southern Denmark Press, 1998.

Mountain, J.H. *A Summary of the Writings of Lactantius.* London: Rivington, 1839.

Mun, Thomas. *A Discourse of Trade to the East Indies.* London, 1621.

Mundy, Peter. *The Travels of Peter Mundy in Europe and Asia 1608–1667*, ed. R.C. Temple. 7 vols. London: Hakluyt Society, 1907–1936.

New English Bible with the Apocrypha. Harmondsworth: Penguin, 1970.

Newton, Thomas. *A History of the Saracens . . . drawn out of Augustine Curio and other sundry good authors.* London, 1575.

Nikitin, Afanasy. *Voyage to India*, ed. and trans. Count M. Wielhorsky [Vyelgorsky] (1858). Cambridge, Ont.: In Parentheses, 2000.

Nixon, Anthony. *The Three English Brothers. Sir Thomas Sherley his Travels . . . Sir Anthony Sherley his Embassage to the Christian Princes. Master Robert Sherley his wars against the Turks with his marriage to the Emperour of Persia his Neece.* London, 1607.

Odoric of Pordenone. *The Travels of Friar Odoric: Cathay and the Way Thither*, trans. Henry Yule (1886). Grand Rapids: W.B. Eerdmans, 2002.

Olearius, Adam. *The Voyages and Travels of the Ambassadors sent by Frederick, Duke of Holstein, to the Great Duke of Muscovy and the King of Persia,* trans. John Davies of Kidwelly (1669). Leiden: IDC Publishers, 1969.

Omar Khayyam. *The Rubaiyat of Omar Khayyam and Other Persian Poems,* ed. and trans. A.J. Arberry. London: Dent, 1972.

Ovid. *Fasti,* trans. James Frazer (1931), rev. G.P. Goold. Cambridge, MA: Harvard University Press, 1989.

———. *Heroides,* trans. Harold Isbell. Harmondsworth: Penguin, 1990.

———. *Love Poems,* trans. A.D. Melville. Oxford: Oxford University Press, 1999.

———. *Metamorphoses,* trans. David Raeburn. Harmondsworth: Penguin, 2004.

———. *Tristia,* trans. A. S. Kline. tkline.pgcc.net/PITBR/Latin/Ovidexile-home.htm

Ovington, John. *A Voyage to Surat in the Year 1689,* ed. H.G. Rawlinson. Oxford: Oxford University Press, 1929.

Palmer, Sir Thomas. *An Essay of the Means how to Make Our Travels into Foreign Countries More Profitable and Honourable.* London, 1606.

Patrologia Latina Database. pld.chadwyck.co.uk

Pelsaert, Francisco. *Jahangir's India: The* Remonstrantie *of Francisco Pelsaert,* trans. W.H. Moreland and P. Geyl. Cambridge: Heffer, 1925.

Philostratus. *Life of Apollonius,* trans. C.P. Jones. Harmondsworth: Penguin, 1970.

Pinto, Fernão Mendes. *The Voyages and Adventures of Fernao Mendes Pinto a Portugal: during his Travels for the space of one-and-twenty years in the Kingdoms of Ethiopia, China, Tartaria, Cochin-China, Calaminham, Siam, Pegu, Japan and a great part of the East Indies,* trans H.C., Gent. London, 1653.

Plato. *The Essential Plato,* trans. B. Jowett, ed. Alain de Botton. New York: QPB, 1999.

Pliny the Elder. *Natural History: A Selection,* trans. John Healy. Harmondsworth: Penguin, 1991.

———, ed. K.E.T. Mayhoff. Leipzig: Teubner, 1906.

Plutarch. *The Rise and Fall of Athens: Nine Greek Lives,* trans. Ian Scott-Kilvert. Harmondsworth: Penguin, 1960.

———. *The Life of Alexander,* trans. Bernadotte Perrin. Cambridge, MA: Harvard University Press, 1919.

———. *Fall of the Roman Republic: Six Lives,* trans. Rex Warner. Harmondsworth: Penguin, 1958.

Propertius. *The Poems of Propertius,* trans. A.E. Watts. Harmondsworth: Penguin, 1961.

Ptolemy. *Geography,* trans. E.L. Stevenson (1932). New York: Dover, 1991.

Purchas, Samuel. *Hakluytus posthumus, or Purchas his pilgrims.* London, 1625.

Quran, trans. Ustadh Abdullah Yusuf Ali. Medina: King Fahd Holy Quran Printing Complex, 1987.

Ralegh, Sir Walter. *History of the World*, ed. Thomas Birch. Oxford: Oxford University Press, 1829.

Ramusio, Giovanni Battista. *Navigatione et viaggi*, ed. R.A. Skelton and G.B. Parkes. Amsterdam: Theatrum Orbis Terrarum, 1967–1970.

The Rig Veda, trans. Wendy O'Flaherty. Harmondsworth: Penguin, 1981.

Roe, Sir Thomas. *The Embassy of Sir Thomas Roe to the Court of the Great Mogul, 1615–1619 as Narrated in his Journal and Correspondences*, ed. William Foster. New York: Kessinger Reprints, n.d.

Rufus, Quintus Curtius. *The History of Alexander*, trans. W. Heckel. Harmondsworth: Penguin, 1984.

Rycaut, Sir Paul. *The History of the Present State of the Ottoman Empire*. London, 1686.

Saadi. *The Rose Garden (Gulistan)*, trans. Omar Ali-Shah. New York: Tractus Books, 1997.

Sandys, George. *Sandys Travels: Containing an History of the Original and Present State of the Turkish Empire, The Mahometan Religion and Ceremonies . . . Lastly, Italy* (London, 1670). La Vergne: Nabu Books Reprints, 2010.

Shirley, Sir Anthony. *Sir Anthony Shirley His Relation of his Travels into Persia*. London, 1613.

Statius. *Silvae*, trans. D.R. Shackleton Bailey. Cambridge, MA: Harvard University Press, 2003.

———. *Thebaid*, trans. A.D. Melville. Oxford: Oxford University Press, 1995.

Stodart, Robert. *The Journal of Robert Stodart, being an account of his experiences as a member of Sir D. Cotton's mission in Persia 1628–29*, ed. E. Denison Ross. London: Luzac, 1935.

Strabo. *The Geography*, trans. H.L. Jones. 8 vols. London: Heinemann, 1917–1933.

Tacitus. *The Agricola and the Germania*, trans. H. Mattingly (1948), rev. S.A. Handford. Harmondsworth: Penguin, 1977.

———. *The Annals of Imperial Rome*, trans. Michael Grant. Harmondsworth: Penguin, 1989.

———. *The Histories*, trans. A. J. Church and W. J. Brodribb. London: Macmillan, 1879.

Tavernier, Jean-Baptiste. *Travels in India by Jean-Baptiste Tavernier, Baron of Aubonne* (1631–1634), trans. V. Ball. 2 vols. London: Macmillan, 1889.

Teixeira, Pedro. *Travels and the History of the Kings of Hormuz*, trans. W.F. Sinclair. London: Hakluyt Society, 1902.

Terry, Edward. *A Voyage to East India* (1622). London, 1655.

Theophanes. *Chronicle*, trans. Harry Turtledove. Philadelphia: University of Pennsylvania Press, 1982.

Tibullus. *The Poems of Tibullus with the Tibullan Collection*, trans. Philip Dunlop. Harmondsworth: Penguin, 1972.

Upanisads, trans. Patrick Olivelle. Oxford: Oxford University Press, 1998.

Valerius Flaccus. *Argonautica*, trans. J.H. Mozely. Cambridge, MA: Harvard University Press, 1934.

Valerius Maximus. *Factorum et dictorum memorabilium libri*, trans. D.R. Shackleton Bailey. Cambridge, MA: Harvard University Press, 2000.

Valmiki. *The Ramayana*, trans. Makhan Lal Sen. Delhi: Munshiram Manoharlal, 1976.

Varthema, Ludovico. *The Travels of Ludovico Varthema in Egypt, Syria, Arabia Deserta and Arabia Felix, to Persia, India and Ethiopia 1503 to 1506*, trans. G.P. Jones. London: Hakluyt Society, 1863.

Virgil. *The Aeneid*, trans. Robert Fitzgerald. New York: Vintage, 1990.

———. *The Eclogues*, trans. Guy Lee. Harmondsworth: Penguin, 1984.

———. *The Georgics of Virgil*, trans. David Ferry. New York: Farrar, Straus & Giroux, 2005.

Wood, Anthony a. *Athenae Oxonienses*, ed. Philip Bliss. London: Rivington et al., 1815.

Xenophon. *The Persian Expedition*, trans. Rex Warner. Harmondsworth: Penguin, 1949.

Ysbrantz [Bontekoe], Willem. *A Memorable Description of the East Indian Voyage of William Ysbrantz Bontekoe, 1618–25*. London, 1646.

The Zend-Avesta or Persian Holy Scripture, ed. and trans. Charles F. Horne. New York: Kessinger Reprints, 2001.

Secondary Works

Abouei, Reza. "Isfahan, the Second Heaven." *Iran Chamber Society* 2006. www.iranchamber.com/geography/articles/isfahan_the_second_heaven.php

Alam, Muzaffar, and Sanjay Subrahmanyan. *Indo-Persian Travels in the Age of Discoveries, 1400–1800*. Cambridge: Cambridge University Press, 2007.

Allen, Charles. *The Search for the Buddha: The Men who Discovered India's Lost Religion*. New York: Carroll and Graf, 2002.

Almond, Philip. *The British Discovery of Buddhism*. Cambridge: Cambridge University Press. 1988.

Alonso, Carlo. "Clemente VIII y la fundación de las misiones católicas en Persia." *Ciudad de Dios* 71 (1958): 196–240.

Amar, V.B. "Shah Jahan's Rebellion and Abdur Rahim Khan Khanan." *Journal of Indian History* 50 (1973): 437–55.

Anderson, Philip. *The English in West India*. Bombay: Smith, Taylor & Co., 1854.

Andrea, Bernadette. "Lady Sherley: The First Persian in England?" *The Muslim World* 95 (2005): 279–95.

Andrews, Kenneth R. *Trade, Plunder and Settlement: Maritime Enterprise and the Genesis of the British Empire, 1480–1630.* Cambridge: Cambridge University Press, 1984.

Archer, Edward. *Tours in Upper India and Parts of the Himalayan Mountains.* 2 vols. London: Richard Bentley, 1833.

Atherton, Ian, and Sanders, Julie, eds. *Interdisciplinary Essays on Culture and Politics in the Caroline Era.* Manchester: University of Manchester Press, 2006.

Attwater, Donald. *The Penguin Dictionary of Saints.* Harmondsworth: Penguin, 1965.

Aune, M.G. "Elephants, Englishmen and India: Early Modern Travel and the Pre-Colonial Movement." *Early Modern Literary Studies* 11 (2005): 1–35.

Awad, Abdul Aziz. "The Gulf in the Seventeenth Century." *British Journal of Middle Eastern Studies* 12 (1985): 123–34.

Backshall, Stephen, et al. *Indonesia: The Rough Guide.* London: Rough Guides, 1999.

Bagnall, Roger S., and Dominic W. Rathbone. *Egypt from Alexander to the Copts: An Archaeological and Historical Guide.* London: British Museum Press, 2004.

Bajan, Lech Alex. "Polish-Persian Diplomatic Relations during the Safavid Period." *Poland-Iran* 2008. http://polandiran.blogspot.com/2008/05/polish-persian-diplomatic-relations.html

Ballaster, Ros. *Fabulous Orients: Fictions of the East in England 1662–1785.* Oxford: Oxford University Press, 2007.

Barbour, Richmond. "Power and Distant Display: Early English 'Ambassadors' in Moghul India." *Harvard Library Quarterly* 61 (2000): 342–68.

———. *Before Orientalism: London's Theatre of the East, 1576–1626.* Cambridge: Cambridge University Press, 2003.

Barraclough, Geoffrey, ed. *The Times Atlas of World History*, rev. ed. (1979). Maplewood, NJ: Hammond, 1984.

Baynes, Norman H. "The First Campaign of Heraclius Against Persia." *English Historical Review* 19 (1904): 694–702.

Beinorius, Audrius. "Buddhism in the Early European Imagination: A Historical Perspective." *Acta Orientalia Vilnensia* 6 (2005): 7–22.

Berinstain, Valérie. *India and the Mughal Dynasty*, trans. Paul G. Bahn. New York: Abrams, 1998.

Bhakkani, Farid. *Nobility under the Great Mughals*, trans. Z.A. Desai. Delhi: Sundeep Prakashan, 2003.

Birchwood, Matthew. *Staging Islam in England: Drama and Culture, 1640–1685.* Woodbridge: D.S. Brewer, 2007.

———, and Matthew Dimmock. *Cultural Encounters between East and West, 1453–1699.* Cambridge: Cambridge Scholars Press, 2005.

Bitterli, Urs. *Cultures in Conflict: Encounters between European and Non-European Cultures, 1492–1800*, trans. R. Robertson. Cambridge: Cambridge University Press, 2003.

Blow, David. *Shah Abbas: The Ruthless King who Became an Iranian Legend.* London: I. B. Tauris, 2009.

Blunt, Wilfrid. *Isfahan: Pearl of Persia.* London: Elek Books, 1966.

Borromeo, Elisabetta. *Voyageurs occidentaux dans l'Empire Ottoman 1600–1644.* 2 vols. Paris: Maisonneuve et Larose, 2007.

Bose, N.K. *Culture and Society in India.* New York: Asia Publishing House, 1967.

Bouquet, Sibylle, ed. *The Green Guide: Thailand.* London: Michelin, 2002.

Boxer, C. R., ed. *South China in the Sixteenth Century. Being the Narratives of Galeote Pereira, Fr. Gaspar de la Cruz, O. P. and Fr. Martín de Rade, O. E. S. A.* London: Hakluyt Society, 1958.

Boyce, Mary. "Gahanbar." In *Encyclopaedia Iranica*, 10:254–56. New York: Bibliotheca Persica Press, 2001.

———. *Zoroastrians: Their Religious Beliefs and Practices.* London: Routledge, 2001.

Boyle, J.A., ed. *The Cambridge History of Iran*, vol. 5, *The Saljuq and Mongol Periods.* Cambridge: Cambridge University Press, 1968.

Brancaforte, Elio. *Visions of Persia: Mapping the Travels of Adam Olearius.* Cambridge, MA: Harvard University Press, 2003.

Braudel, Fernand. *The Mediterranean and the Mediterranean World in the Age of Philip II*, trans. S. Reynolds. 2 vols. New York: Harper, 1966.

Bredsdorff, Asta. *The Trials and Travels of Willem Leyel: An Account of the Danish East India Company in Tranquebar, 1639–1648.* Copenhagen: Museum Tusculanum Press, 2009.

Brockney, Liam M. *Journey to the East: The Jesuit Mission to China, 1579–1724.* Cambridge, MA: Harvard University Press, 2007.

Brown, Michael J. *Itinerant Ambassador: The Life of Sir Thomas Roe.* Lexington: University Press of Kentucky, 1970.

Burke, S.M. *Akbar, the Greatest Mogul.* Delhi: Munshiram Manoharlal, 1989.

Burland, Cottie H. *The Travels of Marco Polo.* New York: McGraw-Hill, 1970.

Buyers, Christopher. *The Royal Ark: Royal and Ruling Houses of Africa, Asia, Oceania and the Americas.* www.4dw.net/royalark/

Byron, Robert. *The Road to Oxiana* (1937). Harmondsworth: Penguin, 1992.

Campbell, Joseph. *The Masks of God.* New York: Viking Press, 1962.

Carey, Daniel. "The Political Economy of Poison: The Kingdom of Makassar and the Early Royal Society." *Renaissance Studies* 17 (2003): 517–44.

Carter, T., and L. Dunstan. *Syria and Lebanon.* Victoria: Lonely Planet Publications, 2004.

Castel, François. *The History of Israel and Judah*, trans. M.J. O'Connell. New York: Paulist Press, 1973.

Chahin, M. *The Kingdom of Armenia*. New York: Dorset Press, 1987.

Chard, Chloe. *Pleasure and Guilt on the Gran Tour: Travel Writing and Imaginative Geography, 1600-1830*. Manchester: Manchester University Press, 1999.

Charpentier, Jarl. Review of *The Embassy of Sir Thomas Roe to India 1615–1619*, ed. W. Foster. *Bulletin of the School of Oriental Studies* 4 (1928): 862–64.

Cheam, Jeremy and Jessamyn. *Malaysia*. Boston: APA Publications, 1999.

Chew, Samuel. *The Crescent and the Rose: Islam and England during the Renaissance*. New York: Oxford University Press, 1937.

Chugg, A.M. *The Lost Tomb of Alexander the Great*. London: Periplus, 2005.

Clarke, Peter. *Zoroastrianism: An Introduction to an Ancient Faith*. Brighton: Sussex Academic Press, 1998.

Clayton, Peter, and Martin Price, eds. *The Seven Wonders of the Ancient World*. London: Routledge, 1989.

Colledge, Malcolm A.R. *The Parthians*. New York: Praeger, 1967.

Commissariat, M.S. *Mandelslo's Travels in Western India 1638–39*. Oxford: Oxford University Press, 1931.

Cotterell, Arthur. *East Asia from Chinese Predominance to the Rise of the Pacific Rim*. London: Pimlico Books, 2002.

Cottrell, Leonard. *The Land of Shinar*. London: Souvenir Press, 1965.

Crawfurd, J. *A Descriptive Dictionary of the Indian Islands and Adjacent Countries*. London: Bradbury & Evans, 1856.

Crowther, Geoffrey, and Raj Prakash. *India: A Travel Survival Kit*. South Yarra: Lonely Planet, 1981.

Cummings, J. *Thailand*. Hawthorn: Lonely Planet Publications, 1990.

Dalrymple, William. *The Last Mughal: The Fall of a Dynasty, Delhi, 1857*. London: Bloomsbury, 2006.

Danvers, Frederik C. *The Portuguese in India*. New Delhi: Asian Educational Services Reprints, 1988.

Das Gupta, Ashin. "Indian Merchants and the Western Indian Ocean: The Early Seventeenth Century." *Modern Asian Studies* 19 (1985): 481–99.

Davies, Robert. "Sir Thomas Herbert." *Yorkshire Archaeological and Topographical Journal* (1870): 182–214.

Davis, Malcolm B., ed. *Japan*. Boston: APA Publications, 1995.

Davis, Sir J. F. *China: A General Description of that Empire and its Inhabitants, with the History of Foreign Intercourse Down to the Events which Produced the Dissolution of 1857*. La Vergne: Nabu Press Reprints, 2010.

Debenham, Frank, ed. *The Reader's Digest Great World Atlas*. London: Reader's Digest Association, 1962.

Der Nersessian, Sirarpie. *The Armenians*. London: Thames & Hudson, 1972.

Dhalla, Maneckji Nusservan. *History of Zoroastrianism*. New York: Oxford University Press, 1938.

Directory of Cities, Towns and Regions in Iran. www. fallingrain.com/world/R/

Dorai, Francis, ed. *Indonesia*. Boston: APA Publications, 2001.

Douglas, J.D., et al, eds. *Illustrated Bible Dictionary.* 3 vols. Leicester: Intervarsity Press, 1980.

D'Silva, John. "The Rebellion of Prince Khusrau according to Jesuit Sources." *Journal of Indian History* 5 (1926): 267–81.

Duff, C. Mabel. *The Chronicle of Indian History.* Delhi: Cosmo Press, 1972.

Edwards, Clara. "Relations of Shah Abbas the Great of Persia with the Mogul Emperors Akbar and Jahangir." *Journal of the American Oriental Society* 35 (1915): 631–60.

Elliott, Mark. *Azerbaijan, with Georgia.* Hindhead: Trailblazer / Arc, 1999.

Elton, Daniel. *The History of Iran.* Westport, CT: Greenwood Press, 2001.

Eraly, Abraham. *The Mughal Throne: The Saga of India's Great Emperors.* London: Weidenfeld & Nicolson, 2003.

Eslami, Farhad, ed. *Iran and Iranian Studies.* Princeton: Princeton University Press, 1998.

Fairbank, John K., Edwin O. Reischauer, and A. Craig. *East Asia: Tradition and Transformation.* New York: Houghton Mifflin, 1989.

Falsafi, Nasrollah. *The Life of Shah Abbas I.* London: Ibex, 1990.

Faruqi, Munis D. "The Forgotten Prince: Mirza Hakim and the Formation of the Mughal Empire in India." *Journal of the Economic and Social History of the Orient* 48 (2005): 487–523.

Ferrier, R.W. "The Armenians and the East India Company in Persia in the Seventeenth and Early Eighteenth Centuries." *Economic History Review* n.s. 26 (1973): 38–62.

———. "An English View of Persian Trade in 1619: Reports from the Merchants Edward Pettus and Thomas Barker." *Journal of the Economic and Social History of the Orient* 19 (1976): 182–214.

———. "The Terms and Conditions under which English Trade was Transacted in Safavid Persia." *Bulletin of the School of Oriental and African Studies* 49 (1981): 48–66.

Findly, Ellison Banks. *Nur Jahan: Empress of Mughal India.* Delhi: Oxford University Press, 1993.

Flood, Gavin. *An Introduction to Hinduism.* Cambridge: Cambridge University Press, 1996.

Floor, Willem. "Dutch Painters in Iran during the First Half of the Seventeenth Century." *Persica* 8 (1979): 145–61.

———, and Edmund Herzig, eds. *Iran and the World in the Safavid Age.* London: I.B. Tauris, 2000.

Flores, Jorge. "'I will do as my father did': On Portuguese and Other European Views of Mughal Succession Crises." *Journal of Portuguese History* 3 (2005): 1–23.

Foster, William, ed. *Early Travels in India, 1583–1619.* Oxford: Oxford University Press, 1921.

———. *England's Quest of Eastern Trade* (1933). London: A.C. Black, 1966.

Fraser, P.M. *Cities of Alexander the Great.* Oxford: Oxford University Press, 1996.

Fritze, Ronald H. "Herbert, Sir Thomas (1606–1682)." In *Oxford Dictionary of National Biography*, 26: 725–27. Oxford: Oxford University Press, 2004.

Frye, R.N. *The Golden Age of Persia.* London: Phoenix Books, 2000.

———, ed. *The Cambridge History of Iran*, vol. 4, *The Period from the Arab Invasion to the Saljuqs.* Cambridge: Cambridge University Press, 1975.

Gascoigne, Bamber. *The Great Moghuls.* London: Jonathan Cape, 1971.

Georges, Ursula. "Personal Names in *The history of the warres betweene the Turkes and the Persians.*" www.s-gabriel.org/names/ursula/warres.html

Ghasemi, Shapour. *The Safavid Empire 1502–1736.* Tehran: Iran Chamber Society, 2006.

Goswamy, B.N. "Malik Ambar: A Remarkable Life." *The Tribune*, 13 August 2006.

Governadores da India. www.genealogia.netopia.pt/pessoas/pes_show

Grant, Michael. *A Guide to the Ancient World: A Dictionary of Classical Place-Names.* New York: Barnes & Noble, 1986.

———. *From Alexander to Cleopatra: The Hellenistic World.* New York: Scribners, 1982.

Greenway, Paul, and David St. Vincent. *Iran.* Hawthorn: Lonely Planet Publications, 1998.

Grove, A.T. *Africa South of the Sahara.* Oxford: Oxford University Press, 1970.

Habib, Irfan. *An Atlas of the Mughal Empire.* Delhi: Oxford University Press, 1982.

———, ed. *Akbar and His India.* Delhi: Oxford University Press, 1997.

Hadfield, Andrew. *Literature, Travel and Colonial Writing in the English Renaissance 1545–1625.* Oxford: Oxford University Press, 2002.

Haig, W., and R. Burn, eds. *The Cambridge History of India*, vol. 4, *The Mughul Period.* Cambridge: Cambridge University Press, 1937.

Hale, John R. *Renaissance Exploration.* New York: W.W. Norton, 1968.

Hall, D.G.E. *Burma* (1950). London: Hutchinson, 1960.

Hamilton, Walter. *The East-India Gazetteer.* London: Parbury, Allen & Co., 1828.

Hane, Mikiso. *Japan: A Historical Survey.* New York: Scribners, 1972.

Harper, Damien. *China.* Victoria: Lonely Planet, 2009.

Haynes, Jonathan. "Two Seventeenth-Century Perspectives on the Middle East: George Sandys and Sir Henry Blount." *Alif: A Journal of Comparative Poetics* 3 (1983): 4–22.

———. *The Humanist as Traveller: George Sandy's Relation of a Journey begun an. Dom. 1610.* Rutherford, NJ: Fairleigh Dickinson University Press, 1986.

Hazlitt, William. *A Dictionary of Ancient Geography.* London: Whittaker, 1851.

Hiriyanna, M. *Outlines of Indian Philosophy.* London: Allen & Unwin, 1958.

Holme, P., and T. Young, eds. *The Cambridge Companion to Travel Writing.* Cambridge: Cambridge University Press, 2002.

Hopkins, Edward C.D. "Parthian City Index." www.parthia.com/parthia_cities.htm

Hourani, Albert. *A History of the Arab Peoples.* Cambridge, MA: Harvard University Press, 1991.

Hughes, T.P. *Dictionary of Islam* (1886). Chicago: Kazi Publications, 1994.

Inden, R. *Imagining India.* London: Hurst, 2000.

Iran: Official Standard Names Approved by the U.S. Board on Geographic Names. Washington, DC: Office of Geography, Department of the Interior, 1956.

Irwin, Robert. *For Lust of Knowing: The Orientalists and their Enemies.* London: Allen Lane, 2006; repr. Harmondsworth: Penguin, 2007.

Jackson, P., and L. Lockhart, eds. *The Cambridge History of Iran,* vol. 6, *The Timurid and Safavid Periods.* Cambridge: Cambridge University Press, 1986.

Jaffar, S.M. *The Mughal Empire from Babur to Aurangzeb.* Delhi: Ess Ess Publications, 1974.

Javadi, Hasan. *Persian Literary Influence on English Literature.* Costa Mesa, CA: Mazda Publishers, 2006.

Jenkins, Romilly J.H. *Byzantium: The Imperial Centuries A.D. 610–1071.* 2nd ed. Toronto: University of Toronto Press, 1987.

Jewish Encyclopedia. www.jewishencyclopedia.com

Jones, A.H.M., and J.R. Martindale. *Prosopography of the Later Roman Empire,* vol. 3A-3B, *A.D., 527–641.* Cambridge: Cambridge University Press, 1992.

Jones, Jack D. *The Royal Prisoner: Charles I at Carisbrooke.* London: Trustees of Carisbrooke Castle Museum, 1978.

Jousiffe, Ann. *Lebanon.* Hawthorn: Lonely Planet Publications, 1998.

Kabbani, R. *Europe's Myth of the Orient.* Bloomington: Indiana University Press, 1986.

Kaegi, Walter E. *Heraclius, Emperor of Byzantium.* Cambridge: Cambridge University Press, 2003.

Kelly, J.N.D. *The Oxford Dictionary of Popes.* Oxford: Oxford University Press, 1988.

Knappert, Jan. *Indian Mythology.* London: Diamond Books, 1995.

Klostermaier, Klaus K. *Hinduism: A Short History.* Oxford: One World, 2000.

Knowles, James. "The Faction of the Flesh: Orientalism and the Caroline Masque." In *The 1630s: Interdisciplinary Essays on Culture and Politics in the Caroline Era,* ed. J. Atherton and J. Sanders, 111–37. Manchester: Manchester University Press, 2006.

Krishnamachariar, M. *History of Classical Sanskrit Literature.* Delhi: Motilal Banarsidass, 1937, repr. 1989.

Kumar, Anil. *Asaf Khan and His Times.* Patna: Kashi Prasad Jayaswal Research Institute, 1986.

Lach, Donald. *Asia in the Making of Europe*. Chicago: University of Chicago Press, 1994.

Lane Fox, Robin. *Alexander the Great*. London: Futura Books, 1978.

Lane-Poole, Stanley. *The Mohammedan Dynasties: Chronological and Genealogical Tables with Historical Introductions* (1893). New York: Frederick Ungar, 1965.

Lang, David Marshall. *The Georgians*. London: Thames & Hudson, 1966.

Lewis, Bernard. *The Muslim Discovery of Europe*. New York: Norton, 2001.

Lewis, Bernard. *What Went Wrong? Western Impact and Middle Eastern Response*. New York: Oxford University Press, 2002.

Logan, William. *Malabar Manual*. 2 vols. Madras: Government Press, 1887.

Lorenzen, David N. "Who Invented Hinduism?" *Comparative Studies in Society and History* 41 (1999): 630–59.

Mackenzie, Norman H. "Sir Thomas Herbert of Tintern, a Parliamentary Royalist." *Historical Research 29* (1956): 32–86.

Madan, T.N. *Non-Renunciation: Themes and Interpretations of Hindu Culture*. Delhi: Oxford University Press, 1987.

Majumdar, R.C., ed. *The Delhi Sultanate*. Bombay: Bharatiya Vidya Baran, 1960.

Malcolm, John. *History of Persia*. 2 vols. London: John Murray, 1815.

Marcus, Amy. *The View from Nebo: How Archaeology is Rewriting the Bible and Reshaping the Middle East*. Boston: Little, Brown, 2000.

Marshall, Peter. *Spectrum Guide to the Maldives*. New York: Interlink Books, 1999.

Marsot, Afaf Lutfi al-Sayyid. *A History of Egypt from the Arab Conquest to the Present*. Cambridge: Cambridge University Press, 2007.

Mason, Philip. *The Men Who Ruled India*. New York: Norton, 1985.

Matar, Nabil. *Islam in Britain, 1558–1685*. New York: Cambridge University Press, 1998.

———. *In the Lands of the Christians: Arabic Travel Writing in the Seventeenth Century*. London: Routledge, 2002.

———. *Britain and Barbary, 1589–1689*. Gainesville: University Press of Florida, 2005.

———. *Turks, Moors and Englishmen in the Age of Discovery*. Cambridge: Cambridge Scholars Press, 2007.

Mather, James. *Pashas: Traders and Travellers in the Islamic World*. New Haven: Yale University Press, 2009.

Matthee, Rudolph P. *The Politics of Trade in Safavid Iran: Silk for Silver, 1600–1730*. Cambridge: Cambridge University Press, 1999.

———. "Between Aloofness and Fascination: Safavid Views of the West." *Iranian Studies* 31 (1998): 219–46.

Maund, Kari. *The Welsh Kings: Warriors, Warlords and Princes*. Stroud: Tempus Books, 2006.

Mavor, William. *Voyages, Travels and Discoveries from the Time of Columbus to the Present.* London: E. Newbury, 1797.

McGregor, W.L. *The History of the Sikhs.* 2 vols. London: J. Madden, 1846.

McJannet, Linda. "Bringing In a Persian." In *Medieval and Renaissance Drama in English*, vol. 12, ed. J. Pitcher, 236–74. Madison, NJ: Fairleigh Dickinson University Press, 1999.

Meherjirana, Dastur Erachji S. *A Guide to the Zoroastrian Religion*, trans. Firoze Kotwal and James W. Boyd. Chico, CA: Scholars Press, 1982.

Meisami, Julie, and Paul Starkey, eds. *Encyclopedia of Arabic Literature.* London: Routledge, 1988.

Melville, Charles. *Safavid Persia.* London: I.B. Tauris, 1996.

Meserve, Margaret. *Empires of Islam in Renaissance Historical Thought.* Cambridge, MA: Harvard University Press, 2008.

Meyer, Karl E., and Shareen Blair Brysac. *Tournament of Shadows: The Great Game and the Race for Empire in Central Asia.* Washington, DC: Counterpoint, 1999.

Mikaberidze, Alexander. *History of Georgian-Iranian Relations.* [Website no longer exists.]

———, ed. *Dictionary of Georgian National Biography.* www.georgianbiography. com

Milton, Giles. *Samurai William: The Adventurer Who Unlocked Japan.* London: Hodder & Stoughton, 2002.

Mitter, Partha. *Much Maligned Monsters: History of European Reaction to Indian Art.* Oxford: Clarendon Press, 1977.

Modi, J.J. "The Marriage Ceremony of the Parsis." Bombay: privately printed, 1921.

Moore, Wendy, ed. *West Malaysia and Singapore.* Lincolnwood: Passport Books, 1993.

Morgan, David. *Medieval Persia 1040–1797.* London: Longman, 1988.

Moseley, H. "Robert Baron, Author of *Mirza.*" *Notes & Queries,* 2nd ser., 9 (1914): 1.

Muir, William. *The Caliphate: Its Rise, Decline and Fall* (1898). Beirut: Khayats Reprints, 1963.

Mukhia, Harbans. *The Mughals of India.* Oxford: Blackwell, 2008.

Munter, Robert, and C.L. Cross, eds. *Englishmen Abroad.* Lewiston: Edwin Mellen Press, 1986.

Narain, A.K. "Alexander and India." *Greece and Rome,* 2nd ser. 12 (1965): 155–56.

Nayar, Pramod K. "Marvellous Excesses: English Travel Writing and India, 1608–1727." *Journal of British Studies* 44 (2005): 213–38.

Newman, Andrew T. *Safavid Iran: Rebirth of a Persian Empire.* London: I.B. Tauris, 2006.

Nezan-Mafi, Mohammed Taghi. *Persian Recreations: Theatricality in Anglo-Persian Diplomatic History.* Boston: Boston University Press, 1999.

Nicholl, Charles. "Field of Bones." *London Review of Books* 21.17 (2 September 1999): 3–7.

Nielsen, N.C., et al., eds. *Religions of the World.* New York: St Martin's Press, 1983.

Nofziger, George, and M. Walton. *Islam at War: A History.* London: Praeger-Greenwood, 2003.

Oaten, R. F. *Early Travellers in India During the Fifteenth, Sixteenth and Seventeenth Centuries.* Madras: Asian Educational Society Reprints, 1991.

Obeidat, Merwan, and Ibrahim Mumayiz. "Anglo-American Literary Sources on the Muslim Orient." *Journal of American Studies of Turkey* 13 (2001): 47–72.

Olivelle, Patrick. *Dharmasutras: The Law Codes of Ancient India.* Oxford: Oxford University Press, 1999.

Olmstead, A.T. *History of the Persian Empire.* Chicago: University of Chicago Press, 1959.

Oxford Dictionary of National Biography. Oxford: Oxford University Press, 2004.

Packard, Jerrold M. *Sons of Heaven: A Portrait of the Japanese Monarchy.* New York: Collier Books, 1989.

Parker, K., ed. *Early Modern Tales of Orient: A Critical Anthology.* London: Routledge, 1999.

Parker, R., and W Dubberstein. *Babylonian Chronology 623 B.C.–A.D. 45.* Providence: Brown University Press, 1956.

Pathak, Arunahandra, ed. *Maharashtra State Gazetteers.* Bombay: Directorate of Government Printing, 1962.

Pearson, N.M. *The Portuguese in India.* Cambridge: Cambridge University Press, 1987.

Peirce, Leslie P. *The Imperial Harem: Women and Sovereignty in the Ottoman Empire.* Oxford: Oxford University Press, 1997.

Plunkett, Richard, and Brigitte Ellemor. *Sri Lanka.* Melbourne: Lonely Planet Publications, 2003.

———, and T. Masters. *Georgia, Armenia and Azerbaijan.* Hawthorn: Lonely Planet Publications, 2004.

Prasad, Beni. *History of Jahangir.* Allahabad: The Indian Press, 1962.

Prasad, Ishwari. *The Life and Times of Humayun.* Bombay: Orient Longmans, 1955.

———. *The Mughal Empire.* Allahabad: Chugh Publishing, 1974.

Prasad, Ram Chandra. *Early English Travellers in India.* Delhi: Motilal Banarsidass, 1980.

Pretzler, Maria. "Travel and Travel Writing." In *The Oxford Handbook of Hellenic Studies*, ed. G. Boys-Stones et al., 352–63. Oxford: Oxford University Press, 2009.

Puhvel, Jaan. *Comparative Mythology*. Baltimore: Johns Hopkins University Press, 1988.

Quinn, Sholeh A. *Historical Writing During the Reign of Shah Abbas*. Salt Lake City: University of Utah Press, 2000.

Rabino, H.L. "A Journey in Mazenderan (from Resht to Sari)." *Geographical Journal* 42 (1913): 435–54.

Radhakrishnan, Sarvepalli. *The Hindu View of Life* (1927). London: Unwin, 1971.

———— and Charles A. Moore. *A Sourcebook in Indian Philosophy*. Princeton: Princeton University Press, 1957.

Raman, Shankar. *Framing "India": The Colonial Imaginary in Early Modern Culture*. Stanford: Stanford University Press, 2002.

Raychaudhury, Tapan. *Bengal under Akbar and Jahangir*. Delhi: Munshiram Manoharlal, 1953.

Richards, John F. *The Mughal Empire*. Cambridge: Cambridge University Press, 1995.

Roden, Claudia. *A New Book of Middle Eastern Food*. Harmondsworth: Penguin, 1985.

Rogers, R.W. *A History of Babylonia and Assyria*. New York: Abingdon Press, 1915.

Rogerson, Barnaby. *The Prophet Muhammad: A Biography*. London: Abacus Books, 2003.

Rubiés, Joan-Pau. *Travel and Ethnology in the Renaissance: South India Through European Eyes 1250–1625*. Cambridge: Cambridge University Press, 2000.

Russell, G.A. *The 'Arabick' Interest of the Natural Philosophers in Seventeenth-Century England*. Leiden: Brill, 1994.

Sahab, A., ed. *Atlas of Geographical Maps and Historical Documents on the Persian Gulf*. Tehran: Geographic and Drafting Institute, 1979.

Said, Edward W. *Orientalism*. New York: Vintage Books, 1979.

Saksena, B.P. *History of Shah Jahan of Delhi*. Allahabad: Central Book Depot, 1968.

Salahi, M.A. *Muhammad, Man and Prophet*. Shaftesbury: Element Books, 1995.

Sami, G.R., and Gorgan Roodi. "Sophy and the Persian Prince: Shakespeare and Persia." *The Iranian*, 22 October 2002.

Sansom, George. *A History of Japan 1615–1867*. Stanford: Stanford University Press, 1963.

Savory, Roger M. *Studies on the History of Safavid Iran*. London: Variorum Reprints, 1987.

————. *Iran Under the Safavids.* Cambridge: Cambridge University Press, 1990.

Scammell, G.V. "England, Portugal and the *Estado da India*, c. 1500–1635." *Modern Asian Studies* 16 (1982): 177–92.

Serjeant, R.B. *The Portuguese Off the South Arabian Coast: Hadrami Chronicles with Yemeni and European Accounts of Dutch Pirates Off Mocha in the Seventeenth Century.* Oxford: Oxford University Press, 1963.

Severin, Tim. *Tracking Marco Polo.* London: Zenith Books, 1984.

Shah, Tahir, and Anne O'Neill. *Spectrum Guide to Jordan.* New York: Interlink Books, 1999.

Shaw, Stanford J. *A History of the Ottoman Empire and Modern Turkey*, vol. 1: *Empire of the Gazis.* Cambridge: Cambridge University Press, 1976.

Silverberg, Robert. *The Realm of Prester John.* Cleveland: Ohio University Press, 1996.

Simkin, C.G.F. *The Traditional Trade of Asia.* New York: Oxford University Press, 1968.

Simpson, D.P. *Cassell's Latin-English/English-Latin Dictionary.* London; Cassell, 1968.

Singh, Jyotsna G. *Colonial Narratives / Cultural Dialogues: "Discoveries" of India in the Language of Colonialism.* London: Routledge, 1996.

Singh, Sarina, et al. *India.* Victoria: Lonely Planet Publications, 2003.

Smith, C. Ross. *In Search of India.* Philadelphia: Chilton, 1960.

Smith, W. *Dictionary of Christian Antiquities.* London: John Murray, 1875–1880.

————. *Dictionary of Christian Biography, Literature, Sects and Doctrine.* London: John Murray, 1887.

————. *Sacred Annals, or Researches into the History and Religion of Mankind.* London: John Murray, 1882.

———— and S. Cheetham. *Dictionary of Greek and Roman Biography and Mythology.* 2 vols. London: John Murray, 1875.

Socorras Cayetano, J. "The Portuguese in Lower Burma: Filipe de Brito de Nicote." *Luso-Brazilian Review* 3 (1966): 3–24.

Sohrabi, Bahram. "Early Swedish Travellers to Persia." *Iranian Studies* 38 (2005): 631–60.

Soren, D., A. Ben Khader, and H. Slim. *Carthage: Uncovering the Mysteries and Splendors of Ancient Tunisia.* New York: Simon & Schuster, 1990.

Southwood, James. "Thomas Stephens, S.J., the First Englishman in India." *Bulletin of the School of Oriental Studies* 3 (1924): 231–38.

Spence, Jonathan D. *The Memory Palace of Matteo Ricci.* Harmondsworth: Penguin, 1985.

Srivastava, Ashirabdi Lal. *Akbar the Great*, vol. 1, *Political History 1542–1605.* Agra: Shiva Lal Agarwala, 1962.

Srivastava, Brij Bushan Lal. "The Fate of Khusrau." *Journal of Indian History* 42 (1964): 479–92.

Stevens, Henry. *The Dawn of British Trade to the East Indies: as recorded in the Court Minutes of the East India Company, 1599–1603.* London: F. Cass Reprints, 1967.

Stiffe, Arthur W. "Ancient Trading Centres of the Persian Gulf." *Geographical Journal* 25 (1896): 644–49.

Strachan, Michael. *The Life and Adventures of Thomas Coryate.* Oxford: Oxford University Press, 1962.

Sweetman, Will. "Unity and Plurality: Hinduism and the Religions of India in Early European Scholarship." *Religion* 31 (2001): 209–24.

Sykes, Percy. "A Sixth Journey in Persia." *Geographical Journal* 37 (1911): 1–19.

Teles a Cunha, João. "The Royal Family and the Struggle for Power in Hormuz (1565–1622)." *Anais de historia de Além-mar* 3 (2000): 177–98.

Teltscher, Kate. *India Inscribed: European and British Writing on India 1600–1800.* New Delhi: Oxford University Press, 1995.

The Times Atlas of the World, 10th ed. New York: Crown Publishers, 1999.

Tod, James. *Annals and Antiquities of Rajasthan* (1839). 2 vols. London: Routledge & Kegan Paul, 1962.

Treadgold, Warren T. *A History of the Byzantine State and Society.* Stanford: Stanford University Press, 1997.

Van Erde, Katherine S. *Wenceslaus Hollar, Delineator of his Time.* Charlottesville: University of Virginia Press, 1970.

Van Garbe, Richard. *Akbar, Emperor of India.* New York: Kessinger Reprints, n.d.

Van Itallie, Nancy, ed. *China.* New York: Fodor, 2000.

Vitkus, Daniel. *Piracy, Slavery and Redemption: Barbary Captivity Narratives from Early Modern England.* New York: Columbia University Press, 2001.

Von Stahl, A.F. "Notes on the March of Alexander the Great from Ecbatana to Hyrcania." *Geographical Journal* 64 (1924): 312–29.

Warnke, Sarah. *Images of the Educational Traveller in Early Modern England.* Leiden: Brill, 1994.

Weekes, Richard V. *Pakistan: Birth and Growth of a Muslim Nation.* New York: Van Nostrand, 1964.

Welch, Stuart Cary. *Persian Painting: Five Royal Safavid Manuscripts of the Seventeenth Century.* New York: George Braziller, 1976.

Wessels, C. *Early Jesuit Travellers in Central Asia 1603–1721.* The Hague: Nijhoff, 1924.

White, Robert C. "Early Geographical Dictionaries." *Geographical Review* 58 (1968): 652–59.

Whitelock, Lt. Frederick. "A Descriptive Sketch of the Islands and Coasts Situated at the Entrance of the Persian Gulf." *Journal of the Royal Geographical Society of London* 8 (1838): 170–84.

Wilmot, A. *History of the Colony of the Cape of Good Hope from its Discovery to the Year 1819.* Cape Town: J.C. Juta, 1869.

Wolfe, Michael, ed. *One Thousand Roads to Mecca: Ten Centuries of Travelers Writing about the Muslim Pilgrimage.* New York: Grove Press, 1977.

Wolpert, Stanley. *A New History of India.* New York: Oxford University Press, 1989.

Wood, Alfred C. *A History of the Levant Company.* Oxford: Oxford University Press, 1935.

Yarshater, Ehsan, ed. *Encyclopaedia Iranica.* 14 vols. to date. London: Routledge; New York: Bibliotheca Persica Press, 1986–.

———. *The Cambridge History of Iran*, vol. 3.1–2, *The Seleucian, Parthian and Sasanian Periods.* Cambridge: Cambridge University Press, 1986.

Yule, Henry, and A.C. Burnell. *Hobson-Jobson: The Anglo-Indian Dictionary* (1886). Ware: Wordsworth Reference, 1996.

Zinsser, William, ed. *They Went: The Art and Craft of Travel Writing.* Boston: Houghton Mifflin, 1991.

Appendix I

This appendix contains some passages from the 1634 edition which the editor felt were of interest either because they actually expanded on what Herbert wrote in 1677, or they were passages which he had expunged.

1. Sir Dodmore Cotton and Emam Qoli Khan play diplomatic games

At our entrance into his metropolis, he [Emam Qoli Khan] was two days' journey thence, at his house of pleasure. Sir Robert Sherley rode to acquaint him with our ambassador being there; he knew it well enough, and thought we should attend his leisure, so after we had reposed six days in the city, our ambassador acquainted Sheykh Ali Beg with his desire to part. "What?" replies he, "would you go ere you see the Duke's face?" He answered, his business swayed him to another end; he came to see his master. So next day the Duke came to Shiraz, followed by two thousand horses, and rested two days without sending or taking notice of us. At length he sent a gentleman to our ambassador with a compliment of welcome and bade him to visit him; our ambassador sent him word he had come so great a journey as excused him. If the Duke would please to ride thither, he was his servant.

The Duke stormed greatly to see his greatness slighted, and after a pause, fearing to affront him because the King of Persia had beforehand writ to him and others through his kingdom as we travelled to respect us, sernt word he would come the next day and see him, but he did not. His son, a gentleman of eighteen years old, came to excuse his father and without any stay departed. Next day our ambassador sent the Duke's son word by Sheykh Ali Beg he would trouble him. The Duke was not well pleased his son should have the visit, so that at our ambassador's alighting, we were conveyed into the Duke's gallery, which was very long and richly-furnished with plate, rich carpets, dancing-wenches and Ganymedes.

The Duke was set at the very end, cross-legged like a tailor, but his fierce aspect and bravery denied that title. He stirred not one foot till our ambassador was at him, and then, standing up, embraced him. We had wine, women and a banquet to accompany us, and after two hours' stay departed.

(62–63)

2. Queen Ketevan disposes of Kustandil Khan

. . . this army of the Persians, so soon as they arrived near to Georgia, was affronted by the Queen, wife of the murdered Alexander, eldest brother unto Kustandil, and being a lady of faithful memory to her destroyed husband, a very good Christian of great wit and courage and much-beloved of her people, she rather chose to sacrifice herself, if that would be sufficient, then see the downfall of her countrymen the Georgians. So, courageously entering the Persian army, discloses who she is, and as an ambassador required the sacred law of nations, to speak freely and return to the King her son without disturbance, which granted her, she desires a parley with her brother Kustandil, that, hearing of her being there, issued forth is bravery and show of insolence, demanding her business.

This poor lady, after some signs of sorrow and respect unto his person, begins to reprehend him mildly, sets before him his late murders, how odious they were to all the Christians, and, as she believed, unto infidels. What could he expect, when he had ruined his countrymen, burned all their trees and cities, he might easily know the Persians used him for their own advantageous attempts, and that he should never be without the brand of traitor and parricide, that as yet the means was open to redeem the good opinion of his subjects, which he must look to do if ever he would be famous to fight against them or secure to defend his own. Say they had offended him, yet no virtue more deified a Prince then clemency, and in some measure they deserved mercy, the destruction of their beloved Princes slain by him and undeservingly moving their choler, and that it might be his own case, which fidelity (no doubt) would please his soul, though in other joys and with the immortal, he knew the Georgians could never be vanquished without infinite murder, the valour of one Georgian equal to contend with five Persians, the very Mamelukes, Janissaries and chief commanders of Persia and India now being Georgians, who doubtless would bear revenge in their hearts should he be so cruel to their kindred. She beseeched him, if he could not be dissuaded, to condescend thus far, that they two might next day meet conveniently between both armies, where after discourse they would refer peace or war unto his judgment.

This parley ended, proud Kustandil, after some notions of pride and haughtiness, bids her rest confident of his resolutions, that as Nature had graced him with the dignity of being eldest (his brothers being murdered) and the safety of Georgia depended upon the care and fame of such a person as he reputed himself, he would, after some chastisement of his rebels, take upon him the defence and government of that kingdom, and for Teimuraz their supposed king, her son, he should not want preferment, either the inheritance of Mingrelia, a forced right, Kartli or some such dukedom should give him satisfaction, in the extreme of his desires or merits his infancy and doubt of legitimation secluding him awhile from enjoying any sovereignty, and that his deserts and rights might appear perfect in view of all men, he accepted of her motion and would with twenty horsemen meet her in an appointed place 'twixt both the armies, where his title and plea of right and entrance should defend itself as well in conference as battle.

This granted, after two days respite, according to the articles, Kustandil Khan and the Queen of Georgia met at the place appointed, where she began her premeditated oratory, persuading him to look with pity on his country, the widows, aged men, orphans, innocent children and such motives, begging mercy. Then she represented the weakness of his designs, withstood both by the enraged armies of the Georgians, resolved to maintain their liberty to the last man, the favour Teimuraz had with the Persians, in whose court he was educated and lived much-honoured and affected by the people and king, who, when Kustandil had discharged the utmost of his rage was sure of small thanks from Abbas, King of Persia, in that there was no conquest, the Georgian and Persian being friends, but a provocation against their loyalty and alliance. This under fraud she spoke that he might be reconciled, and by fair doings lay a better ground of his advancement and retreat from Persia, whereby he might become commander, and have means to recover his faith, which he ought to look after repentantly and with more zeal then the conquest of the universe besides. The Georgians, passing by his irreligion and his Mahometanism, had a very good opinion of his valour and knowledge in arms, so that they were desirous to entertaine him as their governor, by his expertness encouraging them to a defence against the Turks and Persians, both whom in all occasions were insulting over them, because indefensive and without government, and that she had faithfully spoke what she desired, though it was in great part against the dignity and security of Teimuraz her son, as then in Persia.

Whereto, Kustandil Khan, beyond measure efflated with pride and high opinions of his worth and conquests (judging his being there, no less), replied in few words that he was fearless of his establishment in his father's royalties, that amongst such haughty and perfidious people he had rather come in as a conqueror then by right of succession, that himself and his good friends the Persians had suffered in their honour so exceedingly, that without battle and blood they could not part well satisfied, that he had his army *in battalia*, and resolved to execute, that, notwithstanding he perceived the Georgians ready to receive them in serries, he doubted not to massacre the best of them. For as he had incorporated himself unto another people in religion, speech, order and action, and such as loved him, he would never trust his own countrymen, who had with such peaceable faces so lately betrayed him, and whom he knew irreconcilable. And so he assured her, in a word, he sought revenge and murder, not excepting the innocents, at which the heroic Queen sighed and shook her javelin, saying "If it will be no better, then God destroy the homicide!" Immediately upon that sign he was shot to the heart and sunk down dead with a wrathful countenance, as only grieving he perished in this base sort, without recompense, at the sight of which the Queen and the ambushed musketeers, hid of purpose to destroy him, forthwith retired to their army, who expected the event and received her joyfully.

(78–79)

Appendix II

Rulers of Persia, India (Mughal Empire) and the Ottoman Empire. *Mentioned by Herbert.

1. Persia

Ismail I 1502–1524*
Tahmasp 1524–1576*
Ismail II 1576–1578*
Mohammed Khodabanda 1578–1587*
Abbas I 1587–1629*
Safi 1629–42*
Abbas II 1642–1667*
Soleyman 1667–1694

2. Mughal Empire

Babur 1526–1530*
Humayun 1530–1540 (1st reign)*

Afghan Rulers in Delhi
Sher Shah Suri 1540–1545*
Islam Shah 1545–1553
Firuz Shah 1553
Mohammed Shah Adil 1553–1555
Ibrahim Shah 1555
Sikander Shah 1555
Adil Shah 1555–1556

Mughals (restored)
Humayun 1556 (2nd reign)
Akbar I 1556–1605*
Jahangir 1605–1627*
Dawar Bakhsh (Bulaqi) 1627–1628*
Shah Jahan 1628–1657*

Murad Bakhsh 1658 (in Gujarat)
Shah Shuja 1657–1660 (in Bengal)
Aurangzeb 1658–1707

3. Ottoman Empire

Selim I 1512–1520*
Suleiman I 1520–1566*
Selim II 1566–1574*
Murad III 1574–1595*
Mehmet III 1595–1603*
Ahmet I 1603–1617*
Mustafa I 1617–1618 (1st reign)*
Osman II 1618–1622*
Mustafa I 1622–1623 (2nd reign)
Murad IV 1623–1640*
Ibrahim 1640–1648
Mehmet IV 1648–1687